ORACLE8*i*
The Complete Reference

ANNIVERSARY
10th
Edition

**Best-Selling Oracle
Book of All Time!**

Oracle Press™

Oracle8*i*: The Complete Reference

Kevin Loney
George Koch

Osborne/**McGraw-Hill**

Berkeley New York St. Louis San Francisco
Auckland Bogotá Hamburg London Madrid
Mexico City Milan Montreal New Delhi Panama City
Paris São Paulo Singapore Sydney Tokyo Toronto

Osborne/**McGraw-Hill**
2600 Tenth Street
Berkeley, California 94710
U.S.A.

For information on translations or book distributors outside the U.S.A., or to arrange bulk purchase discounts for sales promotions, premiums, or fund-raisers, please contact Osborne/**McGraw-Hill** at the above address.

Oracle8*i*: The Complete Reference

1234567890 DOC DOC 019876543210

Book P/N 0-07-212362-1   and   CD P/N 0-07-212363-X
parts of
ISBN 0-07-212364-8

Publisher
    Brandon A. Nordin

**Associate Publisher and
Editor-in-Chief**
    Scott Rogers

Acquisitions Editor
    Jeremy Judson

Project Editor
    Janet Walden

Acquisitions Coordinator
    Monika Faltiss

Technical Editor
    Leslie Tierstein

Copy Editor
    William McManus

Proofreader
    Mike McGee

Indexer
    David Heiret

Computer Designer
    Jani Beckwith
    Michelle Galicia
    Roberta Steele

Illustrator
    Michael Mueller
    Beth Young

Series Design
    Jani Beckwith

This book was composed with Corel VENTURA™ Publisher.

To my parents, and to Sue, Emily, and Rachel
—K.L.

To Elwood Brant, Jr. (Woody), 1949-1990
—G.K.

About the Authors

Kevin Loney, a veteran Oracle developer and DBA, is the author of the best-selling *Oracle8i DBA Handbook* and coauthor of *Oracle8 Advanced Tuning and Administration* and *Oracle SQL & PL/SQL Annotated Archives.* An independent consultant, he frequently makes presentations at Oracle conferences and contributes to *ORACLE Magazine.* He can be found online at http://www.kevinloney.com, and is the editor for the database-related search engine at http://www.lonyx.com.

George Koch is a leading authority on relational database applications. A popular speaker and widely published author, he is also the creator of THESIS, the securities trading, accounting, and portfolio management system that was the first major commercial applications product in the world to employ a relational database (Oracle) and provide English language querying to its users. He is a former senior vice president of Oracle Corporation.

Contents at a Glance

v

Contents

PART I
Critical Database Concepts

PART II
SQL and SQL*PLUS

PART III
PL/SQL

PART IV

Object-Relational Databases

PART V
Java in Oracle

PART VI
Hitchhiker's Guides

PART VII

Designing for Performance

PART VIII

Alphabetical Reference

PART IX

Appendix

Preface

The Intriguing History of This Book

 first encountered Oracle in 1982, in the process of evaluating database management systems for a major commercial application that my company was preparing to design and build. At its conclusion, our evaluation was characterized in *ComputerWorld* as the single-most "grueling" study of DBMSs that had ever been conducted. The study was so tough on the vendors whose products we examined that word of it made the press as far away as New Zealand, and publications as far afield as the *Christian Science Monitor*.

We began the study with 108 candidate companies, then narrowed the field to sixteen finalists, including most of the major database vendors of the time, and all types of databases: network, hierarchical, relational, and others. After the rigorous final round of questions, two of the major vendors participating asked that the results of the study of their products never be published. A salesman from a third vendor quit his job at the end of one of the sessions. We knew how to ask tough questions.

Oracle, known then as Relational Software, Inc., had fewer than 25 employees at the time, and only a few major accounts. Nevertheless, when the study was completed, we announced Oracle as the winner. We declared that Oracle was technically the best product on the market, and that the management team at RSI looked capable enough to carry the company forward successfully. Our radical proclamation was made at a time when few people even knew what the term "relational" meant, and those who did had very few positive things to say about it. Many IS exectives loudly criticized our conclusions and predicted that Oracle and the relational database would go nowhere.

Oracle today is the largest database company, and the second largest software company in the world. The relational database is now the world standard.

Koch Systems Corporation, the company I owned and ran at the time, became Oracle's first Valued Added Reseller. We developed the world's first major commercial relational application, a securities trading and accounting system called THESIS. This product was used by major banks and corporations to manage their investment portfolios. Even IBM bought THESIS, and it allowed Oracle to be installed at IBM headquarters in spite of vigorous internal opposition. After all, IBM was the leading database company at the time, with IMS and DB2 as their flagship products.

Oracle was continuing to refine its young product, to understand the kinds of features and functionality that would make it productive and useful in the business world, and our development efforts at Koch Systems contributed to that refinement. Some of Oracle's features were the direct results of requests that we made of Oracle's developers, and our outspoken advocacy of an end-user bias in application design and naming conventions has influenced a generation of programmers who learned Oracle in our shop or read articles which we published.

All of this intimate involvement with the development and use of Oracle led us to an early and unmatched expertise with the product and its capabilities. Since I have always loved sharing discoveries and knowledge—to help shorten the learning time necessary with new technologies and ideas, and save others the cost of making the same mistakes I did—I decided to turn what we'd learned into a book.

Oracle: The Complete Reference was conceived in 1988 to pull together all of the fundamental commands and techniques used across the Oracle product line, as well as give solid guidance in how to develop applications using Oracle and SQL. Part I of the book was aimed both at developers and end-users, so that they could share a common language and understanding during the application development process: developers and end users working side by side—a wild concept when the book was first conceived.

Linda Allen, a respected literary agent in San Francisco, introduced me to Liz Fisher, then the editor at Osborne/McGraw-Hill. Liz liked the idea very much. Contracts were drawn, and the first edition was scheduled to be released in 1989. But a now-departed senior executive at McGraw-Hill heard of the project and instantly canceled its development, pronouncing that "Oracle is a flash in the pan. It is going nowhere." A year later, when Oracle Corporation had again doubled in size and the senior executive was gone, the effort was restarted, and the first edition finally arrived in 1990.

Almost immediately, it became the No. 1 book in its category, a position it has maintained for a decade.

In July of 1990, I was hired by Oracle to run its Applications Division. I became senior vice president of the company and guided the division (with a lot of talented help) to worldwide success. While at Oracle, I also introduced Osborne/McGraw-Hill to Oracle senior management, and after opposition from an Oracle vice president who didn't see any value in the idea (he's no longer with Oracle), Oracle Press was born.

Oracle Press is now the leading publisher of Oracle-based reference manuals in the world.

In 1992, Bob Muller, a former developer at both Koch Systems and Oracle, took over responsibilities for technical updates to the book, as my duties at Oracle precluded any more than editorial review of changes. This produced *Oracle7: The Complete Reference*. This was Bob's first published book, and he has since gone on to write several other popular books on development and database design.

In 1994 I left Oracle to fulfill a long-held desire—full-time ministry—and today I'm the pastor of Church of the Resurrection (http://www.resurrection.org) in West Chicago, Illinois. I continue to write in publications as diverse as the *Wall Street Journal* and *Christianity Today*, and I've recently published a book in England, *The Country Parson's Advice to His Parishioner*, from Monarch Books. I also sit on the board of directors of Apropos, a leading call center applications company, but I no longer work in Oracle application development.

Also in 1994, Kevin Loney, a highly respected independent Oracle consultant and author (http://www.kevinloney.com), took over the updating and rewriting responsibilities for the third edition of the book, and has continued ever since. He has contributed major new sections (such as the "Hitchhiker's Guide"), and fully integrated new Oracle product features into all sections of the book. He has also integrated many readers' comments into the structure and content of the book, making its current form the product of both its readers and its authors. Those efforts have allowed *Oracle: The Complete Reference* to stay at the top of its field and continue to be the single-most comprehensive guide to Oracle—still unmatched in range, content, and authority. I am a real fan of Kevin's and am most impressed by his knowledge and thoroughness.

Oracle: The Complete Reference is now available in eight languages, and is found on the desks of developers and Oracle product users all over the world. Not only has it been No. 1 in its category (with two editions out, it once was both No. 1 and No. 4), it has also been regularly in the top 100 of *all* books sold through Amazon.com. At one point it was the No. 7 best-selling book of all books sold in Brazil! Its reputation and enduring success are unparalleled in its marketplace.

Like Oracle itself, the book has survived and prospered in spite of the recurring predictions of failure from many quarters. Perhaps this brief history can be an encouragement to others who face opposition but have a clear vision of what is needed in the years ahead.

As Winston Churchill said, "Never give in, never give in, never give in—in nothing great or small, large or petty—never give in except to convictions of honor and good sense."

George Byron Koch
GeorgeKoch@GeorgeKoch.com
Wheaton, Illinois
April, 2000

Acknowledgments

This book is the product of many hands, and countless hours from many people. My thanks go out to all those who helped, whether through their comments, feedback, edits, or suggestions. For additional information about the book, see the publisher's site (http://www.osborne.com) and my site (http://www.kevinloney.com). For a database of links related to Oracle topics across the Web, see http://www.lonyx.com.

Special thanks to Leslie Tierstein, who served as technical editor for this edition. Her thoroughness and advice is greatly appreciated. If there is an error in here somewhere, it must have happened after Leslie read it.

Thanks to my colleagues and friends, including Eyal Aronoff, John Beresniewicz, Steve Bobrowski, Rachel Carmichael, Steven Feuerstein, Mike McDonnell, Marlene Theriault, and Craig Warman. This book has benefited from the knowledge they have shared, so be sure and thank them when you see them at conferences.

Thanks to the folks at Osborne/McGraw-Hill who guided this product through its stages: Scott Rogers, Janet Walden, Monika Faltiss, and Jeremy Judson, and the others at Osborne with whom I never directly worked. Thanks also to the "Oracle" component of Oracle Press, including Julie Gibbs and Marsha Bazley. This book would not have been possible without the earlier excellent work of George Koch and Robert Muller.

Thanks to the writers and friends along the way: Jerry Gross; Jan Riess; Robert Meissner; Marie Paretti; Br. Declan Kane, CFX; Br. William Griffin, CFX; Chris O'Neill; Cheryl Bittner; Bill Fleming; and the PSCI team.

Special thanks to Sue, Emily, and Rachel and the rest of the home team. As always, this has been a joint effort.

—Kevin Loney

Introduction

racle is the most widely used database in the world. It runs on virtually every kind of computer. It functions virtually identically on all these machines, so when you learn it on one, you can use it on any other. This fact makes knowledgeable Oracle users and developers very much in demand, and makes your Oracle knowledge and skills very portable.

Oracle documentation is thoroughgoing and voluminous, currently spanning multiple CDs. *Oracle8i: The Complete Reference* is the first entity that has gathered all of the major Oracle definitions, commands, functions, features, and products together in a single, massive core reference—one volume that every Oracle user and developer can keep handy on his or her desk.

The audience for this book will usually fall into one of three categories:

- *An Oracle end user*   Oracle can easily be used for simple operations such as entering data and running standard reports. But such an approach would ignore its great power; it would be like buying a high-performance racing car, and then pulling it around with a horse. With the introduction provided in the first two sections of this book, even an end user with little or no data processing background can become a proficient Oracle user—generating ad hoc, English-language reports, guiding developers in the creation of new features and functions, and improving the speed and accuracy of the real work done in a business. The language of the book is simple, clear English without data processing jargon, and with few assumptions about previous knowledge of computers or databases. It will help beginners to become experts with an easy-to-follow format and numerous real examples.

- *A developer who is new to Oracle*   With as many volumes of documentation as Oracle provides, finding a key command or concept can be a time-consuming effort. This book attempts to provide a more organized and efficient manner of learning the essentials of the product. The format coaches a developer new to Oracle quickly through the basic concepts, covers areas of common difficulty, examines misunderstanding of the product and relational development, and sets clear guidelines for effective application building.

- *An experienced Oracle developer*   As with any product of great breadth and sophistication, there are important issues about which little, if anything, has been published. Knowledge comes through long experience, but is often not transferred to others. This book delves deeply into many such subject areas (such as precedence in UNION, INTERSECTION, and MINUS operators; inheritance and CONNECT BY; eliminating NOT IN with an outer join; using interMedia; implementing the object-relational and Java options; and many others). The text also reveals many common misconceptions and suggests rigorous guidelines for naming conventions, application development techniques, and design and performance issues.

For every user and developer, the final section of this book is devoted to a comprehensive Alphabetical Reference containing all major Oracle concepts, commands, functions, and features including proper syntax, cross-references, and examples. This is the largest single reference published on the subject and could be a book unto itself.

How This Book Is Organized

There are nine major parts to this book, and a CD-ROM.

Part I is an introduction to "Critical Database Concepts." These chapters are essential reading for any Oracle user, new or veteran, from key-entry clerk to database administrator. They establish the common vocabulary that both end users and developers can use to coherently and intelligently share concepts and assure the success of any development effort. This introductory section is intended for both developers and end users of Oracle. It explores the basic ideas and vocabulary of relational databases and points out the dangers, classical errors, and profound opportunities in relational database applications.

Part II, "SQL and SQL*Plus," teaches the theory and techniques of relational database systems and applications, including SQL (Structured Query Language) and SQLPLUS. The section begins with relatively few assumptions about data processing knowledge on the part of the reader, and then advances step-by-step, through some very deep issues and complex techniques. The method very consciously uses clear, conversational English, with unique and interesting examples, and strictly avoids the use of undefined terms or jargon. This section is aimed primarily at developers and end users who are new to Oracle, or need a quick review of certain Oracle features. It moves step-by-step through the basic capabilities of SQL and Oracle's interactive query facility, SQLPLUS. When you've completed this section you should have a thorough understanding of all SQL key words, functions, and operators. You should be able to produce complex reports, create tables, and insert, update, and delete data from an Oracle database.

The later chapters of Part II provide some very advanced methods in SQLPLUS, Oracle's simple, command-line interface, and in-depth descriptions of the new and very powerful features of Oracle. This is intended for developers who are already familiar with Oracle, and especially those familiar with previous versions of Oracle, but who have discovered needs they couldn't readily fill. Some of these techniques are previously unpublished and, in some cases, have been thought impossible. The tips and advanced techniques covered here demonstrate how to use Oracle in powerful and creative ways. These include taking advantage of distributed database capabilities, loading data files, and performing advanced text-based searches.

Part III, "PL/SQL," provides coverage of PL/SQL. The topics include a review of PL/SQL structures, plus triggers, stored procedures, and packages.

Part IV, "Object-Relational Databases," provides extensive coverage of object-oriented features such as abstract datatypes, methods, object views, object tables, nested tables, varying arrays, and large objects (LOBs).

Part V, "Java in Oracle," provides coverage of the Java features introduced in Oracle8i. This section includes an overview of Java syntax as well as chapters on JDBC and SQLJ and Java stored procedures.

Part VI contains several guides: a developer's guide to the data dictionary, a guide to Oracle's optimizer, an overview of WebDB, and a beginner's guide to database administration.

Part VII, "Designing for Performance," addresses vital issues in the design of useful and well-received applications. Oracle tools provide a great opportunity to create applications that are effective and well-loved by their users, but many developers are unaware of some of the approaches and successes that are possible. This section of the book is aimed specifically at developers—those individuals whose responsibility it is to understand a business (or other) application, and design and program an Oracle application to satisfy it. This section should not be completely incomprehensible to an end user, but the audience is assumed to have a technical data processing background, and experience in developing computer application programs. The purpose here is to discuss the techniques of developing with Oracle that have proven effective and valuable to end users, as well as to propose some new approaches to design in areas that have been largely, and sadly, ignored. This section includes "The Ten Commandments of Humane Design," a list of all of the vital rules of the development process. A user-oriented guide to the Oracle optimizer concludes this section.

Part VIII, the "Alphabetical Reference," is the complete reference for the Oracle server. Reading the introductory pages to this reference will make its use much more effective and understandable. This section contains references for most major Oracle commands, keywords, products, features and functions, with extensive cross-referencing of topics. The reference is intended for use by both developers and users of Oracle but assumes some familiarity with the products. To make the most productive use of any of the entries, it would be worthwhile to read the first six pages of the reference. These explain in greater detail what is and is not included and how to read the entries.

Part IX, "Appendix," contains the table creation statements and row insertions for all of the tables used in this book. For anyone learning Oracle, having these tables available on your own Oracle ID, or on a practice ID, will make trying or expanding on the examples very easy.

The CD that accompanies this book contains a special electronic edition of *Oracle8i: The Complete Reference*. Now, with this electronic version, you can easily store all of the valuable information contained in the book on your PC while the print version of the book remains in your office or home.

NOTE
This special electronic version of Oracle8i: The Complete
Reference, *is copy-protected. However, we have not
copy-protected Appendix A, "Tables Used in This Book,"
so that you have access to all of the tables used in the
print edition without retyping! You can use these tables to
easily work your way through the examples and experiment
with the many techniques that are illustrated in this book.*

Style Conventions Used in This Book

Except when testing for an equality (such as, City = 'CHICAGO'), Oracle ignores upper- and lowercase. In the formal listing of commands, functions, and their format (syntax) in the Alphabetical Reference, this book will follow Oracle's documentation style of putting all SQL in UPPERCASE, and all variables in lowercase italic.

Most users and developers of Oracle, however, never key all their SQL in uppercase. It's too much trouble, and Oracle doesn't care anyway. This book therefore will follow somewhat different style conventions in its examples (as opposed to its formal command and function formats, mentioned earlier), primarily for readability. They are as follows:

- Italic and boldface will not be used in example listings.

- **select**, **from**, **where**, **order by**, **having**, and **group by** will be in lowercase.

- SQLPLUS commands will be in lowercase: **column**, **set**, **save**, **ttitle**, and so on.

- SQL operators and functions will be in uppercase, such as **IN**, **BETWEEN**, **UPPER**, **SOUNDEX**, and so on.

- Columns will use upper- and lowercase, as in Feature, EastWest, Longitude, and so on.

- Tables will be in uppercase, such as in NEWSPAPER, WEATHER, LOCATION, and so on.

Chapter 3 contains an introduction to the style for chapters of the book through 41. Part VIII, the Alphabetical Reference, contains an important introductory section on style conventions that should be read carefully before the alphabetical listings are used.

PART
I

Critical Database
Concepts

CHAPTER
1

Sharing Knowledge and Success

or an Oracle8 application to be built and used rapidly and effectively, users and developers must share a common language and a deep and common understanding of both the business application and the Oracle tools.

This is a new approach to development. Historically, the systems analyst studied the business requirements and built an application to meet those needs. The user was involved only in describing the business and, perhaps, in reviewing the functionality of the application after it was completed.

With the new tools and approaches available, and especially with Oracle, applications can be built that more closely match the needs and work habits of the business—but only if a common understanding exists.

This book is aimed specifically at fostering this understanding, and at providing the means for both user and developer to exploit Oracle's full potential. The end user will know details about the business that the developer will not comprehend. The developer will understand internal functions and features of Oracle and the computer environment that will be too technically complex for the end user. But these areas of exclusive expertise will be minor compared with what both end users and developers can share in using Oracle. There is a remarkable opportunity here.

It is no secret that "business" people and "systems" people have been in conflict for decades. Reasons for this include differences in knowledge, culture, professional interests and goals, and the alienation that simple physical separation between groups can often produce. To be fair, this syndrome is not peculiar to data processing. The same thing occurs between people in accounting, personnel, or senior management, as members of each group gather apart from other groups on a separate floor or in a separate building or city. Relations between the individuals from one group and another become formalized, strained, and abnormal. Artificial barriers and procedures that stem from this isolationism become established, and these also contribute to the syndrome.

This is all very well, you say, and may be interesting to sociologists, but what does it have to do with Oracle?

Because Oracle isn't cloaked in arcane language that only systems professionals can comprehend, it fundamentally changes the nature of the relationship between business and systems people. Anybody can understand it. Anybody can use it. Information that previously was trapped in computer systems until someone in systems created a new report and released it now is accessible, instantly, to a business person, simply by typing an English query. This changes the rules of the game.

Where Oracle is used, it has radically improved the understanding between the two camps, has increased their knowledge of one another, and has even begun to normalize relations between them. This has also produced superior applications and end results.

Since its first release, Oracle has been based on the easily understood relational model (explained shortly), so nonprogrammers can readily understand what Oracle does and how it does it. This makes it approachable and unimposing.

Furthermore, Oracle was created to run identically on virtually any kind of computer. Thus, it doesn't matter which manufacturer sold you your equipment; Oracle works on it. These features all contributed directly to the profound success of the product and the company.

In a marketplace populated by computer companies with "proprietary" hardware, "proprietary" operating systems, "proprietary" databases, and "proprietary" applications, Oracle gives business users and systems departments new control over their lives and futures. They are no longer bound to the database product of a single hardware vendor. Oracle runs on nearly every kind of computer. This is a basic revolution in the workplace and in application development, with consequences that will extend far into the future.

Some individuals neither accept nor understand this yet, nor do they realize just how vital it is that the dated and artificial barriers between "users" and "systems" continue to fall. But the advent of cooperative development will profoundly affect applications and their usefulness.

However, many application developers have fallen into an easy trap with Oracle: carrying forward unhelpful methods from previous-generation system designs. There is a lot to unlearn. Many of the techniques (and limitations) that were indispensable to a previous generation of systems not only are unnecessary in designing with Oracle, they are positively counterproductive. In the process of explaining Oracle, the burden of these old habits and approaches must be lifted. There are refreshing new possibilities available.

Throughout this book, the intent will be to explain Oracle in a way that is clear and simple, in terms that both users and developers can understand and share. Outdated or inappropriate design and management techniques will be exposed and replaced.

The Cooperative Approach

Oracle is an *object-relational database*. A relational database is an extremely simple way of thinking about and managing the data used in a business. It is nothing more than a collection of tables of data. We all encounter tables every day: weather reports, stock charts, sports scores. These are all tables, with column headings and rows of information simply presented. Even so, the relational approach can be sophisticated and powerful enough for even the most complex of businesses. An object-relational database supports all of the features of a relational database while also supporting object-oriented concepts and features.

Unfortunately, the very people who can benefit most from a relational database—the business users—usually understand it the least. Application developers, who must build systems that these users need to do their jobs, often find relational concepts difficult to explain in simple terms. A common language is needed to make this cooperative approach work.

The first two parts of this book explain, in readily understandable terms, just what a relational database is and how to use it effectively in business. It may seem that this discussion is for the benefit of "users" only. An experienced relational application designer may be inclined to skip these early chapters and simply use the book as a primary source Oracle reference. Resist that temptation! Although much of this material may seem like elementary review, it is an opportunity for an application designer to acquire a clear, consistent, and workable terminology with which to talk to users about their needs and how these needs might be quickly met. If you are an application designer, this discussion may also help you unlearn some unnecessary and probably unconscious design habits. Many of these habits will be uncovered in the course of introducing the relational approach. It is important to realize that even Oracle's power can be diminished considerably by design methods appropriate only to nonrelational development.

If you are an end user, understanding the basic ideas behind object-relational databases will help you express your needs cogently to application developers and comprehend how those needs can be met. An average person working in a business role can go from beginner to expert in short order. With Oracle, you'll have the power to get and use information, have hands-on control over reports and data, and possess a clear-eyed understanding of what the application does and how it does it. Oracle gives you, the user, the ability to control an application or query facility expertly and *know* whether you are getting all the available flexibility and power.

You also will be able to unburden programmers of their least favorite task: writing new reports. In large organizations, as much as 95 percent of all programming backlog is composed of new report requests. Because you can write your own reports, in minutes instead of months, you will be delighted to have the responsibility.

Everyone Has "Data"

A library keeps lists of members, books, and fines. The owner of a baseball card collection keeps track of players' names, dates, averages, and card values. In any business, certain pieces of information about customers, products, prices, financial status, and so on must be saved. These pieces of information are called *data*.

Information philosophers like to say that data is just data until it is organized in a meaningful way, at which point it becomes "information." If this is true, then Oracle is also a means of easily turning data into information. Oracle will sort through and manipulate data to reveal pieces of knowledge hidden there—such as totals, buying trends, or other relationships—which are as yet undiscovered. You will learn how to make these discoveries. The main point here is that you have data, and you do three basic things with it: acquire it, store it, and retrieve it.

Once you've achieved the basics, you can make computations with data, move it from one place to another, or modify it. This is called *processing*, and, fundamentally, it involves the same three steps that affect how information is organized.

You could do all of this with a cigar box, pencil, and paper, but as the volume of data increases, your tools tend to change. You may use a file cabinet, calculators, pencils, and paper. While at some point it makes sense to make the leap to computers, your tasks remain the same.

A *relational database management system* (often called an RDBMS for short) such as Oracle gives you a way of doing these tasks in an understandable and reasonably uncomplicated way. Oracle basically does three things:

■ Lets you put data into it

■ Keeps the data

■ Lets you get the data out and work with it

Figure 1-1 shows how simple this process is.

Oracle supports this in-keep-out approach and provides clever tools that allow you considerable sophistication in how the data is captured, edited, modified, and put in; how you keep it securely; and how you get it out to manipulate and report on it.

FIGURE 1-1. *What Oracle does with data*

An *object-relational database management system (ORDBMS)* extends the capabilities of the RDBMS to support object-oriented concepts. You can use Oracle as an RDBMS or take advantage of its object-oriented features.

The Familiar Language of Oracle

The information stored in Oracle is kept in tables—much like the weather table from a daily newspaper shown in Figure 1-2.

This table has four columns: City, Temperature, Humidity, and Condition. It also has a row for each city from Athens to Sydney. Last, it has a table name: WEATHER.

These are the three major characteristics of most tables you'll see in print: *columns, rows,* and a *name.* The same is true in a relational database. Anyone can understand the words and the ideas they represent, because the words used to describe the parts of a table in an Oracle database are the same words used in everyday conversation. The words have no special, unusual, or esoteric meanings. What you see is what you get.

Tables of Information

Oracle stores information in tables, an example of which is shown in Figure 1-3. Each of these tables has one or more columns. The column headings, such as City, Temperature, Humidity, and Condition shown in the example, describe the kind of information kept in the column. The information is stored row after row (city after city). Each unique set of data, such as the temperature, humidity, and condition for the city of Manchester, gets its own row.

	WEATHER		
City	Temperature	Humidity	Condition
Athens.......	97	89	Sunny
Chicago......	66	88	Rain
Lima.........	45	79	Rain
Manchester...	66	98	Fog
Paris........	81	62	Cloudy
Sparta.......	74	63	Cloudy
Sydney.......	29	12	Snow

FIGURE 1-2.   *A weather table from a newspaper*

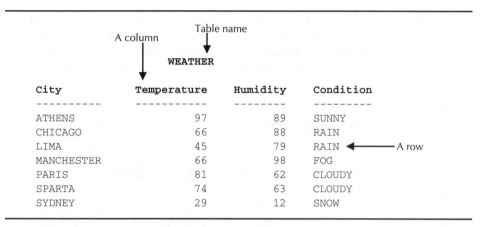

FIGURE 1-3.   *A WEATHER table from Oracle*

Oracle avoids specialized, academic terminology in order to make the
product more approachable. In research papers on relational theory, a column
may be called an "attribute," a row may be called a "tuple" (rhymes with "couple"),
and a table may be called an "entity." For an end user, however, these terms are
confusing. More than anything, they are an unnecessary renaming of things for
which there are already commonly understood names in our shared everyday
language. Oracle takes advantage of this shared language, and developers can
too. It is imperative to recognize the wall of mistrust and misunderstanding that
the use of unnecessary technical jargon produces. Like Oracle, this book will stick
with "tables," "columns," and "rows."

Structured Query Language

Oracle was the first company to release a product that used the English-based
Structured Query Language, or *SQL.* This language allowed end users to extract
information themselves, without using a systems group for every little report.

Oracle's query language has structure, just as English or any other language has
structure. It has rules of grammar and syntax, but they are basically the normal rules
of careful English speech and can be readily understood.

SQL, pronounced either "sequel" or "S.Q.L.," is an astonishingly capable tool,
as you will see. Using it does not require any programming experience.

Here's an example of how you might use SQL. If someone asked you to select
from the preceding WEATHER table the city where the humidity is 89, you would
quickly respond "Athens." If you were asked to select cities where the temperature
is 66, you would respond "Chicago and Manchester."

Oracle is able to answer these same questions, nearly as easily as you are, and in response to simple queries very much like the ones you were just asked. The key words used in a query to Oracle are **select**, **from**, **where**, and **order by**. They are clues to Oracle to help it understand your request and respond with the correct answer.

A Simple Oracle Query

If Oracle had the example WEATHER table in its database, your first query to it would be simply this:

```
select City from WEATHER where Humidity = 89
```

Oracle would respond:

```
City
----------
ATHENS
```

Your second query would be this:

```
select City from WEATHER where Temperature = 66
```

For this query, Oracle would respond:

```
City
----------
MANCHESTER
CHICAGO
```

As you can see, each of these queries uses the key words **select**, **from**, and **where**. What about **order by**? Suppose you wanted to see all the cities listed in order by their temperature. You'd simply type this:

```
select City, Temperature from WEATHER
    order by Temperature
```

and Oracle would instantly respond with this:

```
City          Temperature
----------    -----------
SYDNEY                 29
LIMA                   45
MANCHESTER             66
CHICAGO                66
SPARTA                 74
PARIS                  81
ATHENS                 97
```

Oracle has quickly reordered your table by temperature. (This table lists lowest temperatures first; in a later chapter, you'll learn how to specify whether you want low numbers or high numbers first.)

There are many other questions you can ask with Oracle's query facility, but these examples show how easy it is to obtain the information you need from an Oracle database in the form that will be most useful to you. You can build complicated requests from simple pieces of information, but the method used to do this will always be understandable. For instance, you can combine the **where** and **order by** key words, both simple by themselves, and tell Oracle to select those cities where the temperature is greater than 80, and show them in order by increasing temperature. You would type this:

```
select City, Temperature from WEATHER
  where Temperature > 80
  order by Temperature
```

and Oracle would instantly respond with this:

```
City          Temperature
-----------   -----------
PARIS                  81
ATHENS                 97
```

Or, to be even more specific, request cities where the temperature is greater than 80 and the humidity is less than 70:

```
select City, Temperature, Humidity from WEATHER
  where Temperature > 80
    and Humidity < 70
  order by Temperature
```

and Oracle would respond with this:

```
City          Temperature Humidity
-----------   ----------- --------
PARIS                  81       62
```

Why It Is Called "Relational"

Notice that the WEATHER table lists cities from several countries, and some countries have more than one city listed. Suppose you need to know in which country a particular city is located. You could create a separate LOCATION table of cities and their countries, as shown in Figure 1-4.

LOCATION

City	Country
ATHENS	GREECE
CHICAGO	UNITED STATES
CONAKRY	GUINEA
LIMA	PERU
MADRAS	INDIA
MADRID	SPAIN
MANCHESTER	ENGLAND
MOSCOW	RUSSIA
PARIS	FRANCE
ROME	ITALY
SHENYANG	CHINA
SPARTA	GREECE
SYDNEY	AUSTRALIA
TOKYO	JAPAN

WEATHER

City	Temperature	Humidity	Condition
ATHENS	97	89	SUNNY
CHICAGO	66	88	RAIN
LIMA	45	79	RAIN
MANCHESTER	66	98	FOG
PARIS	81	62	CLOUDY
SPARTA	74	63	CLOUDY
SYDNEY	29	12	SNOW

FIGURE 1-4. *WEATHER and LOCATION tables*

For any city in the WEATHER table, you can simply look at the LOCATION table, find the name in the City column, look over to the Country column in the same row, and see the country's name.

These are two completely separate and independent tables. Each contains its own information in columns and rows. They have one significant thing in common: the City column. For each city name in the WEATHER table, there is an identical city name in the LOCATION table.

For instance, what is the current temperature, humidity, and condition in an Australian city? Look at the two tables, figure it out, and then resume reading this.

How did you solve it? You found just one AUSTRALIA entry, under the Country column, in the LOCATION table. Next to it, in the City column of the same row, was the name of the city, SYDNEY. You took this name, SYDNEY, and then looked for it in the City column of the WEATHER table. When you found it, you moved across the row and found the Temperature, Humidity, and Condition: 29, 12, and SNOW.

Even though the tables are independent, you can easily see that they are related. The city name in one table is *related* to the city name in the other (see Figure 1-5). This relationship is the basis for the name *relational* database.

This is the basic idea of a relational database (sometimes called a *relational model*). Data is stored in tables. Tables have columns, rows, and names. Tables can be related to each other if each has a column with a common type of information.

That's it. It's as simple as it seems.

```
                                                         LOCATION

                                                 City          Country
                           WEATHER               ----------    -------
                                                 ATHENS        GREECE
                                                 CHICAGO       UNITED STATES
     City        Temperature    Humidity  Condition  CONAKRY       GUINEA
     ----------   -----------    --------  ---------  LIMA          PERU
     ATHENS            97            89    SUNNY   MADRAS        INDIA
     CHICAGO           66            88    RAIN    MADRID        SPAIN
     LIMA              45            79    RAIN    MANCHESTER    ENGLAND
     MANCHESTER        66            98    FOG     MOSCOW        RUSSIA
     PARIS             81            62    CLOUDY  PARIS         FRANCE
     SPARTA            74            63    CLOUDY  ROME          ITALY
     SYDNEY            29            12    SNOW    SHENYANG      CHINA
                                                 SPARTA        GREECE
                                                 SYDNEY        AUSTRALIA
                         Relationship            TOKYO         JAPAN
```

FIGURE 1-5.   *The relationship between the WEATHER and LOCATION tables*

Some Common, Everyday Examples

Once you understand the basic idea of relational databases, you'll begin to see tables, rows, and columns everywhere. Not that you didn't see them before, but you probably didn't think about them in quite the same way. Many of the tables that you are accustomed to seeing could be stored in Oracle. They could be used to quickly answer questions that would take you quite some time to answer using nearly any other method.

A typical stock market report in the paper might look like the one in Figure 1-6. This is a small portion of a dense, alphabetical listing that fills several narrow columns on several pages in a newspaper. Which stock traded the most shares? Which had the biggest percentage change in its price, either positively or negatively? The answers to these questions can be obtained through simple English queries in Oracle, which can find the answers much faster than you could by searching the columns on the newspaper page.

Figure 1-7 is an index to a newspaper. What's in section F? If you read the paper from front to back, in what order would you read the articles? The answers to these questions are obtainable via simple English queries in Oracle. You will learn how to do all of these queries, and even build the tables to store the information, in the course of using this reference.

Company	Close Yesterday	Close Today	Shares Traded
Ad Specialty	31.75	31.75	18,333,876
Apple Cannery	33.75	36.50	25,787,229
AT Space	46.75	48.00	11,398,323
August Enterprises	15.00	15.00	12,221,711
Brandon Ellipsis	32.75	33.50	25,789,769
General Entropy	64.25	66.00	7,598,562
Geneva Rocketry	22.75	27.25	22,533,944
Hayward Antiseptic	104.25	106.00	3,358,561
IDK	95.00	95.25	9,443,523
India Cosmetics	30.75	30.75	8,134,878
Isaiah James Storage	13.25	13.75	22,112,171
KDK Airlines	80.00	85.25	7,481,566
Kentgen Biophysics	18.25	19.50	6,636,863
LaVay Cosmetics	21.50	22.00	3,341,542
Local Development	26.75	27.25	2,596,934
Maxtide	8.25	8.00	2,836,893
MBK Communications	43.25	41.00	10,022,980
Memory Graphics	15.50	14.25	4,557,992
Micro Token	77.00	76.50	25,205,667
Nancy Lee Features	13.50	14.25	14,222,692
Northern Boreal	26.75	28.00	1,348,323
Ockham Systems	21.50	22.00	7,052,990
Oscar Coal Drayage	87.00	88.50	25,798,992
Robert James Apparel	23.25	24.00	19,032,481
Soup Sensations	16.25	16.75	22,574,879
Wonder Labs	5.00	5.00	2,553,712

FIGURE 1-6.   *A stock market table*

A 100-Year-Old Example

An old, decaying ledger book, first dated in 1896 and belonging to G. B. Talbot, contains the entries shown in Figure 1-8.

Entries like these go on for pages, day after day, through 1905. Dora Talbot paid her workers a dollar a day for their efforts, and George B. Talbot (perhaps her son) kept the books. A few of the workers appear in the book many times, others only once or twice.

George also had a few pages with the names and addresses of the workers, as shown in Figure 1-9. The relationship that links these two tables is the workers' names. If George wanted to send a boy around, with cash in pay envelopes, to each of the workers at the end of the month, what would he have to do? He'd first have to sum up the wages paid for each worker, put those total amounts in each

Feature	Sections	Page
Births	F	7
Bridge	B	2
Business	E	1
Classified	F	8
Comics	C	4
Doctor's In	F	6
Editorials	A	12
Modern Life	B	1
Movies	B	4
National News	A	1
Obituaries	F	6
Sports	D	1
Television	B	7
Weather	C	2

FIGURE 1-7. *A table based on sections of a newspaper*

FIGURE 1-8. *G. B. Talbot's ledger book*

FIGURE 1-9. *Addresses of workers in Talbot's ledger book*

envelope, and write each worker's name on the front. Then, he'd look up each address in the second section of his ledger book, write it on the front of the envelope, and send the boy off.

G. B. Talbot has a genuine relational database. It uses paper and ink to store its information, rather than a computer disk drive. Even though the joining of the tables is done by his fingers, eyes, and mind rather than a CPU, it is a real, legitimate relational database. It is even fairly close to what a relational application designer would call *normalized,* a word that simply means the data is collected into natural groupings: daily pay and addresses are not mixed together in a single section (table) of the ledger.

The entries in this ledger, both for wages and addresses, could easily be Oracle tables. The questions or tasks G. B. Talbot must have faced could be made much simpler. You will learn how to enter and retrieve data in the pages ahead, using both current examples and Talbot's old ledger entries to discover Oracle's power.

CHAPTER
2

The Dangers in a Relational Database

s with any new technology or new venture, it's sensible to think through not only the benefits and opportunities that are presented, but also the costs and risks. In a relatively new technology such as a relational database, not enough time has elapsed for most companies to have "old hands" around who know what to avoid and how to avoid it.

Combine a relational database with a series of powerful and easy-to-use tools, as Oracle does, and the possibility of being seduced into disaster by its simplicity becomes real. Add in object-oriented and web capabilities, and the dangers increase.

This chapter discusses some of the dangers that both developers and users need to consider. Part IV will cover these and additional issues in more depth, especially those of interest to developers in their task of building an accommodating and productive application.

Is It Really as Easy as They Say?

According to the database vendors—the industry evangelists—developing an application using a relational database and the associated "fourth-generation" tools will be as much as 20 times faster than traditional system development. And it will be very easy: ultimately, programmers and systems analysts will be used less, and end users will control their own destinies.

Critics of the relational approach warn that relational systems are inherently slower than others, that users who are given control of query and report writing will overwhelm computers, and that a company will lose face and fortune if a more traditional approach is not taken. The press cites stories of huge applications that simply failed to run when they were put into production.

So, what's the truth? The truth is that the rules of the game have changed. Fourth-generation development efforts make very different demands upon companies and management than do more traditional methods. There are issues and risks that are brand new and not obvious. Once these are identified and understood, the risk is no greater, and probably much smaller, than in traditional development.

What Are the Risks?

The primary risk is that developing relational database applications *is* as easy as they say. Understanding tables, columns, and rows isn't difficult. The relationship between two tables is conceptually simple. Even *normalization,* the process of analyzing the inherent or "normal" relationships between the various elements of a company's data, is fairly easy to learn.

Unfortunately, this often produces instant "experts," full of confidence and naiveté, but with little experience in building real, production-quality applications. For a tiny marketing database, or a home inventory application, this doesn't matter very much. The mistakes made will reveal themselves in time, the lessons will be learned, and the errors will be avoided the next time around. In an important application, however, this is a sure formula for disaster. This lack of experience is usually behind the press's stories of major project failures.

Older development methods are generally slower, primarily because the tasks of the older methods—coding, submitting a job for compilation, linking, and testing—result in a slower pace. The cycle, particularly on a mainframe, is often so tedious that programmers spend a good deal of time "desk-checking" in order to avoid going through the delay of another full cycle because of an error in the code.

Fourth-generation tools seduce developers into rushing into production. Changes can be made and implemented so quickly that testing is given short shrift. The elimination of virtually all desk-checking compounds the problem. When the negative incentive (the long cycle) that encouraged desk-checking disappeared, desk-checking went with it. The attitude of many seems to be, "If the application isn't quite right, we can fix it quickly. If the data gets corrupted, we can patch it with a quick update. If it's not fast enough, we can tune it on the fly. Let's get it in ahead of schedule and show the stuff we're made of."

This problem is made worse by an interesting sociological phenomenon: many of the developers of relational applications are recent college graduates. They've learned relational or object-oriented theory and design in school and are ready to make their mark. More-seasoned developers, as a class, haven't learned the new technology: they're busy supporting and enhancing the technologies they know, which support their companies' current information systems. The result is that inexperienced developers tend to end up on the relational projects, are sometimes less inclined to test, and are less sensitive to the consequences of failure than those who have already lived through several complete application development cycles.

The testing cycle in an important Oracle project should be longer and more thorough than in a traditional project. This is true even if proper project controls are in place, and even if seasoned project managers are guiding the project, because there will be less desk-checking and an inherent overconfidence. This testing must check the correctness of data entry screens and reports, of data loads and updates, of data integrity and concurrence, and particularly of transaction and storage volumes during peak loads.

Because it really is as easy as they say, application development with Oracle's tools can be breathtakingly rapid. But this automatically reduces the amount of testing done as a normal part of development, and the planned testing and quality assurance must be consciously lengthened to compensate. This is not usually foreseen by those new to either Oracle or fourth-generation tools, but you must budget for it in your project plan.

The Importance of the New Vision

Many of us look forward to the day when we can simply say, like Captain Kirk, "Computer..."; make our query in English; and have our answer readily at hand. Perhaps, closer to home, we look to the day when we can type a "natural" language query in English, and have the answer back, on our screen, in seconds.

We are closer to these goals than most of us realize. The limiting factor is no longer technology, but rather the rigor of thought in our application designs. Oracle can straightforwardly build English-based systems that are easily understood and exploited by unsophisticated users. The potential is there, already available in Oracle's database and tools, but only a few have understood and used it.

Clarity and understandability should be the hallmarks of any Oracle application. Applications can operate in English, be understood readily by end users who have no programming background, and provide information based on a simple English query.

How? First of all, a major goal of the design effort must be to make the application easy to understand and simple to use. If you err, it must always be in this direction, even if it means consuming more CPU or disk space. The limitation of this approach is that you could make an application exceptionally easy to use by creating overly complex programs that are nearly impossible to maintain or enhance. This would be an equally bad mistake. However, all things being equal, an end-user orientation should never be sacrificed for clever coding.

Changing Environments

Consider that in 1969, the cost to run a computer with a processing speed of four million instructions per second (MIPS) was about $1,000 per hour. By 1989, that cost was about $45 per hour, and continues to plummet to this day. Labor costs, on the other hand, have risen steadily, not just because of the general trend, but also because salaries of individual employees increase the longer they stay with a company and the better they become at their jobs. This means that any work that can be shifted from human laborers to machines is a good investment.

Have we factored this incredible shift into our application designs? The answer is "somewhat," but terribly unevenly. The real progress has been in *environments,* such as the visionary work first done at Xerox Palo Alto Research Center (PARC), and then on the Macintosh, and now in MS-Windows, web-based browsers, and other graphical, icon-based systems. These environments are much easier to learn and understand than the older, character-based environments, and people who use them can produce in minutes what previously took days. The improvement in some cases has been so huge we've entirely lost sight of how hard some tasks used to be.

Unfortunately, this concept of an accommodating and friendly environment hasn't been grasped by many application developers. Even when they work in these environments, they continue old habits that are just no longer appropriate.

Codes, Abbreviations, and Naming Standards

The problem of old programming habits is most pronounced in codes, abbreviations, and naming standards, which are almost completely ignored when the needs of end users are considered. When these three issues are thought about at all, usually only the needs and conventions of the systems groups are considered. This may seem like a dry and uninteresting problem to be forced to think through, but it can make the difference between great success and grudging acceptance, between an order-of-magnitude leap in productivity and a marginal gain, between interested, effective users and bored, harried users who make continual demands on the developers.

Here's what happened. Business records used to be kept in ledgers and journals. Each event or transaction was written down, line by line, in English. Take a look at Talbot's ledger in Figure 2-1. Any codes? Nope. Any abbreviations? Yes, a few everyday abbreviations that any English-speaking reader would understand immediately. When Talbot sold a cord of wood on January 28, he wrote "Jan 28 (1 Crd) Wood Methest Church 2.00."

15

FIGURE 2-1. *A page from Talbot's ledger*

In many applications today, this same transaction would be represented in the computer files with something like "028 04 1 4 60227 3137"—that is, the Julian date for the 28th day of the year, transaction code 04 (a sell) of quantity 1 of quantity type 4 (cord) of item 60227 (60=wood, 22=unfinished, 7=cut) to customer 3137 (Methodist Church). Key entry clerks would actually have to know or look up most of these codes and type them in at the appropriately labeled fields on their screens. This is an extreme example, but literally thousands of applications take exactly this approach and are every bit as difficult to learn or understand.

This problem has been most pronounced in large, conventional mainframe systems development. As relational databases are introduced into these groups, they are used simply as replacements for older input/output methods such as VSAM and IMS. The power and features of the relational database are virtually wasted when used in such a fashion.

Why Are Codes Used Instead of English?

Why use codes at all? Two primary justifications are usually offered:

- A category has so many items in it that all of them can't reasonably be represented or remembered in English.

- To save space in the computer.

The second point is an anachronism. Memory (at one time, doughnut-shaped ferrite mounted on wire grids) and permanent storage (tapes or big magnetic drums) were once so expensive and CPUs so slow (with less power than a hand-held calculator) that programmers had to cram every piece of information into the smallest possible space. Numbers, character for character, take half of the computer storage space of letters, and codes (such as 3137 for Kentgen, Gerhardt) reduce the demands on the machine even more.

Because machines were expensive, developers had to use codes for *everything* to make *anything* work at all. It was a technical solution to an economic problem. For users, who had to learn all sorts of meaningless codes, the demands were terrible. Machines were too slow and too expensive to accommodate the humans, so the humans were trained to accommodate the machines. It was a necessary evil.

This economic justification for codes vanished years ago. Computers are now fast enough and cheap enough to accommodate the way people work, and use words that people understand. It's high time that they did so. Yet, without really thinking through the justifications, developers and designers continue to use codes willy-nilly, as if it were still 1969.

The first point—that of too many items per category—is more substantive, but much less so than it first appears. One idea is that it takes less effort (and is therefore less expensive) for someone to key in the numbers "3137" than "Kentgen,

Gerhardt." This justification is untrue in Oracle. Not only is it more costly to train people to know the correct customer, product, transaction, and other codes, and more expensive because of the cost of mistakes (which are high with code-based systems), but using codes also means not using Oracle fully; Oracle is able to take the first few characters of "Kentgen, Gerhardt" and fill in the rest of the name itself. It can do the same thing with product names, transactions (a "b" will automatically fill in with "buy," an "s" with "sell"), and so on, throughout an application. It does this with very robust pattern-matching abilities.

The Benefit of User Feedback

There is an immediate additional benefit: key entry errors drop almost to zero because the users get immediate feedback, in English, of the business information they're entering. Digits don't get transposed; codes don't get remembered incorrectly; and, in financial applications, money rarely is lost in accounts due to entry errors, with significant savings.

Applications also become much more comprehensible. Screens and reports are transformed from arcane arrays of numbers and codes into a readable and understandable format. The change of application design from code-oriented to English-oriented has a profound and invigorating effect on a company and its employees. For users who have been burdened by code manuals, an English-based application produces a tremendous psychological release.

How to Reduce the Confusion

Another version of the "too many items per category" justification is that the number of products, customers, or transaction types is just too great to differentiate each by name, or there are too many items in a category that are identical or very similar (customers named "John Smith," for instance). A category can contain too many entries to make the options easy to remember or differentiate, but more often this is evidence of an incomplete job of categorizing information: too many dissimilar things are crammed into too broad a category. Developing an application with a strong English-based (or French, German, Spanish, and so on) orientation, as opposed to code-based, requires time spent with users and developers—taking apart the information of the business, understanding its natural relationships and categories, and then carefully constructing a database and naming scheme that simply and accurately reflects these discoveries.

There are three basic steps to doing this:

1. Normalize the data.

2. Choose English names for the tables and columns.

3. Choose English words for the data.

Each of these steps will be explained in order. The goal is to design an application in which the data is sensibly organized, is stored in tables and columns whose names are familiar to the user, and is described in familiar terms, not codes.

Normalization

Relations between countries, or between departments in a company, or between users and developers, are usually the product of particular historical circumstances, which may define current relations even though the circumstances have long since passed. The result of this can be abnormal relations, or, in current parlance, dysfunctional relations. History and circumstance often have the same effect on data—on how it is collected, organized, and reported. And data, too, can become abnormal and dysfunctional.

Normalization is the process of putting things right, making them normal. The origin of the term is the Latin word *norma,* which was a carpenter's square that was used for assuring a right angle. In geometry, when a line is at a right angle to another line, it is said to be "normal" to it. In a relational database, the term also has a specific mathematical meaning having to do with separating elements of data (such as names, addresses, or skills) into *affinity groups,* and defining the normal, or "right," relationships between them.

The basic concepts of normalization are being introduced here so that users can contribute to the design of an application they will be using, or better understand one that's already been built. It would be a mistake, however, to think that this process is really only applicable to designing a database or a computer application. Normalization results in deep insights into the information used in a business and how the various elements of that information are related to each other. This will prove educational in areas apart from databases and computers.

The Logical Model

An early step in the analysis process is the building of a *logical model,* which is simply a normalized diagram of the data used by the business. Knowing why and how the data gets broken apart and segregated is essential to understanding the model, and the model is essential to building an application that will support the business for a long time, without requiring extraordinary support. Part VII of this book covers this more completely, particularly as it applies to developers.

Normalization is usually discussed in terms of *form*: First, Second, and Third Normal Form are the most common, with Third representing the most highly normalized state. G. B. Talbot keeps track of the various people who work for him. Most of these people do pick-up work and stay at one of the many lodging houses in town. He's developed a simple form to collect this information, which looks like Figure 2-2.

Name: John Pearson Age 27
Lodging: Rose Hill for Men
Mgr: John Peletier
Rte 9, N. Compston
Skills:
1. combine driver, can harness, drive, groom horses, adjust blades.
2. average smithy, can stack for fire, run bellows, cut, shoe horses.
3. good woodcutter, can mark and fell trees, split, stack, haul.
??

FIGURE 2-2. *Worker information*

If Talbot were to follow older techniques, he may well design a database that matches the basic layout of this form. It seems like a straightforward enough approach, basically following the "pieces of paper in the cigar box" model. Many applications have been designed in this way. The application designers took copies of existing forms—invoices, sales receipts, employment applications, statements, worker information sheets—and built systems based on their content and layout.

Thinking this through, however, reveals some lurking problems. Assume that Talbot's form became the table design in Oracle. The table might be called WORKER, and the columns might be Name, Age, Lodging, Manager, Address, Skill1, Skill2, and Skill3 (see Figure 2-3). The users of this table already have a problem: on Talbot's piece of paper, he can list as many skills as he likes, while in the WORKER table, users are limited to listing just three skills.

Suppose that in addition to pieces of paper in the cigar box, Talbot enters the same elements of information in Oracle to test his database WORKER table. Every piece of paper becomes a row of information. But, what happens when Peletier (the manager on Talbot's form) moves to New Hampshire, and a new manager takes over? Someone has to go through every worker form in the cigar box (and every row, in the WORKER table) and correct all of those that say "Peletier." And what if Rose Hill (where Pearson lives) is bought by Major Resorts International, which changes the address to "One Major Resorts Way"? Again, all of the workers' records must be changed. What will Talbot do when John Pearson adds a fourth skill? And

```
                    WORKER Table
                    -------------
                    Name
                    Age
                    Lodging
                    Manager
                    Address
                    Skill1
                    Skill2
                    Skill3

                       .

                       .

                       .

                       ?
```

FIGURE 2-3.   *Talbot's WORKER table with lurking problems*

is "good" or "average" really a legitimate part of a skill, or is it a level of ability that perhaps should be a separate column?

These are not really computer or technical issues, even though they became apparent because you were designing a database. They are much more basic issues of how to sensibly and logically organize the information of a business. They are the issues that normalization addresses. This is done with a step-by-step reorganization of the elements of the data into affinity groups, by eliminating dysfunctional relationships, and by assuring normal relationships.

FIRST NORMAL FORM   Step one of the reorganization is to put the data into First Normal Form. This is done by moving data into separate tables, where the data in each table is of a similar type, and giving each table a *primary key*—a unique label or identifier. This eliminates repeating groups of data, such as the skills in Talbot's paper form (which became just three skills in the first attempt at a WORKER table).

Instead of having only three skills allowed per worker, each worker's skills are placed in a separate table, with a row per name, skill, and skill description. This eliminates the need for a variable number of skills in the WORKER table and is a better design than limiting the WORKER table to just three skills.

Next, you define the primary key to each table: what will uniquely identify and allow you to extract one row of information? For simplicity's sake, assume the workers' names are unique, so Name is the primary key to the WORKER table. Since each worker may have several rows in the SKILL table, Name plus Skill is the whole primary key to the SKILL table (two parts are combined to make a whole). Figure 2-4 shows Talbot's worker data put into First Normal Form.

FIGURE 2-4   *Talbot's workers in First Normal Form*

To find out what John Pearson's ability is as a woodcutter, as well as get a description of what skills a woodcutter has, you would simply type this query:

```
select Ability, Description
  from SKILL
 where Name = 'John Pearson' and Skill = 'Woodcutter';
```

Oracle would respond with this:

```
Ability Description
------- -------------------------------------
Good    Mark And Fell Trees, Split, Stack, Haul
```

What will lead you to a unique row in the SKILL table? It's both Name and Skill. But Skill Description is only dependent on Skill, regardless of whose name is there. This leads to the next step.

SECOND NORMAL FORM   Step two, Second Normal Form, entails taking out data that's only dependent on a part of the key. To put things in Second Normal Form, you take Skill and Description off to a third table. The primary key to the third table is just Skill, and its long-winded description appears only once. If left in the First Normal Form SKILL table, the long descriptions would be repeated for every worker that had the skill. Further, if the last worker with smithy skills left town, when he was eliminated from the database, the description of smithy skills would vanish. With Second Normal Form, the skill and description can be in the database even if no one currently has the skill. Skills can even be added, like "job descriptions," before locating anyone who has them. Figure 2-5 shows Talbot's worker data put into Second Normal Form.

THIRD NORMAL FORM   Step three, Third Normal Form, means getting rid of anything in the tables that doesn't depend solely on the primary key. The lodging

```
WORKER Table     WORKER SKILL Table     SKILL Table
-------------    --------------------   -----------
Name             Name                   Skill
Age              Skill                  Description
Lodging          Ability
Manager
Address
```

FIGURE 2-5. *Talbot's workers in Second Normal Form*

information for the worker is *dependent* on his living there (if he moves, you update his row with the name of the new lodging he lives in), but the lodging manager's name and the lodging address are *independent* of whether this worker lives there or not. Lodging information is therefore moved out to a separate table, and for the sake of convenience, a shorthand version of the lodging house name is used as the primary key, and the full name is kept as LongName. Figure 2-6 shows the tables in Third Normal Form, and Figure 2-7 graphically shows the relationships of the tables.

Any time the data is in Third Normal Form, it is already automatically in Second and First Normal Form. The whole process can therefore actually be accomplished less tediously than by going from form to form. Simply arrange the data so that the columns in each table, other than the primary key, are dependent only on the *whole primary key.*

Third Normal Form is sometimes described as "the key, the whole key, and nothing but the key."

Navigating Through the Data

Talbot's database is now in Third Normal Form. Figure 2-8 shows a sample of what these tables might contain. It's easy to see how these four tables are related. You navigate from one to the other to pull out information on a particular worker, based

```
WORKER Table     WORKER SKILL Table     SKILL Table     LODGING Table
-------------    --------------------   -----------     --------------
Name             Name                   Skill           Lodging
Age              Skill                  Description     LongName
Lodging          Ability                                Manager
                                                         Address
```

FIGURE 2-6. *Talbot's workers in Third Normal Form*

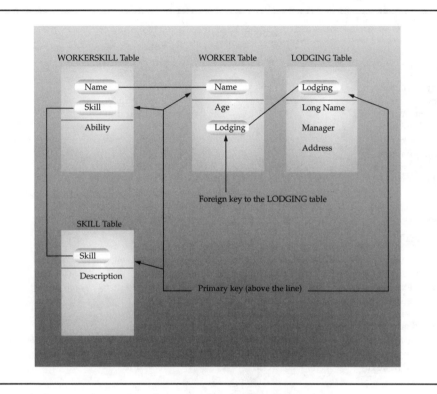

FIGURE 2-7. *Relationships between the worker tables*

on the keys to each table. The primary key in each table is able to uniquely identify a single row. Choose John Pearson, for instance, and you can readily discover his age in the WORKER table, because Name is the primary key.

Look up John Pearson in the Name column and Woodcutter in the Skill column in the WORKER SKILL table, and you'll find his Ability as a woodcutter, which is Good. The Name and Skill columns taken together form the primary key for this table, meaning that they will pick out only one row. Look up Woodcutter in the SKILL table and you will see a description of what a woodcutter needs to be able to do.

When you looked up John Pearson in the WORKER table, you also saw that his Lodging was Rose Hill. This is the primary key to the LODGING table. When you look up Rose Hill there, you find its LongName, Rose Hill For Men; the Manager, John Peletier; and the Address, Rfd 3, N. Edmeston. When the primary key of the LODGING table appears in another table, as it does in the WORKER table, it is called a *foreign key*—sort of like an embassy or consulate that is a local "key" to a foreign country.

```
                    The WORKER Table
NAME                    AGE               LODGING
----------------------  ----              -----------
Adah Talbot             23                Papa King
Bart Sarjeant           22                Cranmer
Dick Jones              18                Rose Hill
Elbert Talbot           43                Weitbrocht
Helen Brandt            15
Jed Hopkins             33                Matts
John Pearson            27                Rose Hill
Victoria Lynn           32                Mullers
Wilfred Lowell          67


                  The WORKER SKILL Table
NAME                    SKILL             ABILITY
----------------------  -----------       ----------
Adah Talbot             Work              Good
Dick Jones              Smithy            Excellent
Elbert Talbot           Discus            Slow
Helen Brandt            Combine Driver    Very Fast
John Pearson            Combine Driver
John Pearson            Woodcutter        Good
John Pearson            Smithy            Average
Victoria Lynn           Smithy            Precise
Wilfred Lowell          Work              Average
Wilfred Lowell          Discus            Average


                    The SKILL Table
SKILL               DESCRIPTION
---------------     -------------------------------------------
Combine Driver      Harness, Drive, Groom Horses, Adjust Blades
Discus              Harness, Drive, Groom Horses, Blade Depth
Grave Digger        Mark and Cut Sod, Dig, Shore, Fill, Resod
Smithy              Stack for Fire, Run Bellows, Cut, Shoe Horses
Woodcutter          Mark and Fell Trees, Split, Stack, Haul
Work                General Unskilled Labor


                   The LODGING Table
LODGING         LONGNAME                MANAGER          ADDRESS
-----------     --------------------    --------------   --------------
Cranmer         Cranmer Retreat House   Thom Cranmer     Hill St, Berkeley
Matts           Matts Long Bunk House   Roland Brandt    3 Mile Rd, Keene
Mullers         Mullers Coed Lodging    Ken Muller       120 Main, Edmeston
Papa King       Papa King Rooming       William King     127 Main, Edmeston
Rose Hill       Rose Hill For Men       John Peletier    Rfd 3, N. Edmeston
Weitbrockt      Weitbrocht Rooming      Eunice Benson    320 Geneva, Keene
```

FIGURE 2-8. *Information in Talbot's tables*

These tables also show real-world characteristics: Talbot doesn't know where Brandt or Lowell live, doesn't have a skill listed for Sarjeant or Hopkins, and doesn't assess Pearson's ability as a combine driver. Because the data is organized logically, Talbot is also able to keep a record of a gravedigger's expected skills, even though none of the current workers has those skills.

This is a sensible and logical way to organize information, even if the "tables" are written in a ledger book or on scraps of paper in cigar boxes. Of course, there is still some work to do to turn this into a real database. For instance, you probably ought to break Address up into component parts, such as Street, City, State, and so on. Name probably ought to be broken into First Name and Last Name, and you might want to find a way to restrict the options for the Ability column in the WORKER SKILL table.

This whole process is called normalization. It really isn't any trickier than this. There are some other issues involved in a good design, but the basics of analyzing the "normal" relationships among the various elements of data are just as simple and straightforward as they've just been explained. It makes sense regardless of whether or not a relational database or a computer is involved at all.

One caution needs to be raised, however. Normalization is a part of the process of analysis. It is not design. Design of a database application includes many other considerations, and it is a fundamental mistake to believe that the normalized tables of the logical model are the "design" for the actual database. This fundamental confusion of analysis and design contributes to the stories in the press about the failure of major relational applications. These issues are addressed for developers more fully in Part VII.

English Names for Tables and Columns

Once the relationships between the various elements of the data in an application are understood and the data elements are segregated appropriately, considerable thought must be devoted to choosing names for the tables and columns into which the data will be placed. This is an area given too little attention, even by those who should know better. Table and column names are often developed without consulting end users and without rigorous review. Both of these failings have serious consequences when it comes to actually using an application.

For example, consider Talbot's tables from the last section. They contain these columns:

```
WORKER Table     WORKER SKILL Table     SKILL Table      LODGING Table
-------------    ------------------     ------------     -------------
Name             Name                   Skill            Lodging
Age              Skill                  Description      LongName
Lodging          Ability                                 Manager
                                                         Address
```

These table and column names are virtually all self-evident. An end user, even one new to relational ideas and SQL, would have little difficulty understanding or even replicating a query such as this:

```
select Name, Age, Lodging
   from WORKER
 order by Age;
```

Users understand this because the words are all familiar. There are no obscure or ill-defined terms. When tables with many more columns in them must be defined, naming the columns can be more difficult, but a few consistently enforced rules will help immensely. Consider some of the difficulties commonly caused by lack of naming conventions. What if Talbot had chosen these names instead?

```
WORKERS Table   WS                  SKILL         ACCOMMODATIONS
-------------   -----------------   -----------   --------------
wkrname         wswkrname           skil          alocnam
wage            wskil               des           alngname
locnam          ablty                             mgr
                                                  addr
```

The naming techniques in this table, as bizarre as they look, are unfortunately very common. They represent tables and columns named by following the conventions (and lack of conventions) used by several well-known vendors and developers. Table 2-1 shows some real examples of column and table names from these same sources.

Tables	Columns		
DEPT	ADD1	EMPNO	NOTES
EMP	AU_LNAME	ENAME	ORD_NUM
EMPS	AU_ORD	ENUMBER	PNAME
MYEMPS	BLOC	ESAL	PROJNO
PE	CDLEXP	HIGHQTY	PUBDATE
PERSONNEL	DEPTNO	HIRANGE	QTYOH
PROJ	DISCOUNTTYPE	LORANGE	SLSTAXPCT
TITLES	DNAME	LOWQTY	WORKHRS

TABLE 2-1. *Table and Column Names from Various Sources*

Here are a few of the more obvious difficulties in the list of names:

■ *Abbreviations are used without good reason.* This makes remembering the "spelling" of a table or column name virtually impossible. The names may as well be codes, because the users will have to look them up.

■ *Abbreviations are inconsistent.* In one instance it's LOW, in another it's LO. Which is it, NUMBER, NUM, or NO? Is it EMPNO or ENO? Is it EMPNAME or ENAME?

■ *The purpose or meaning of a column or table is not apparent from the name.* In addition to abbreviations making the spelling of names difficult to remember, they obscure the nature of the data the column or table contains. What is PE? SLSTAXPCT? CDLEXP?

■ *Underlines are used inconsistently.* Sometimes they are used to separate words in a name, other times they are not. How will anyone remember which name does or doesn't have an underline?

■ *Use of plurals is inconsistent.* Is it EMP or EMPS? Is it NOTE or NOTES?

■ *Rules apparently used have immediate limitations.* If the first letter of the table name is to be used for a name column, as in DNAME, what happens when a DIVISION table becomes necessary? Does the name column in that table also get called DNAME? If so, why isn't the column in both simply called NAME?

These are only a few of the most obvious difficulties. Users subjected to poor naming of tables and columns will not be able to simply type English queries. The queries won't have the intuitive and familiar "feel" that the WORKER table query has, and this will harm the acceptance and usefulness of the application significantly.

Programmers used to be required to create names that were a maximum of six to eight characters in length. As a result, names unavoidably were confused mixes of letters, numbers, and cryptic abbreviations. Like so many other restrictions forced on users by older technology, this one is just no longer applicable. Oracle allows table and column names up to 30 characters long. This gives designers plenty of room to create full, unambiguous, and descriptive names.

The difficulties outlined here imply solutions, such as avoiding abbreviations and plurals, and either eliminating underlines or using them consistently. These quick rules of thumb will go a long way in solving the naming confusion so prevalent today. At the same time, naming conventions need to be simple, easily understood, and easily remembered. Part VII will develop naming conventions more completely. In a sense, what is called for is a normalization of names. In much the same way that data is analyzed logically, segregated by purpose, and thereby normalized, the same sort of logical attention needs to be given to naming standards. The job of building an application is improperly done without it.

English Terms for the Data

Having raised the important issue of naming conventions for tables and columns, the next step is to look at the data itself. After all, when the data from the tables is printed on a report, how self-evident the data is will determine how understandable the report is. In Talbot's example, Skill might have been a two-number code, with 01 meaning "smithy," 02 meaning "combine driver," and so on, and 99 meaning "general unskilled labor." Ability could have been a rating scale from 1 to 10. Is this an improvement? If you asked another person about Dick Jones, would you want to hear that he was a 9 at 01? Why should a machine be permitted to be less clear, particularly when it is simple to design applications that can say "excellent smithy"?

Additionally, keeping the information in English makes writing and understanding queries much simpler. Which of these two SQL requests and answers is more obvious? This one:

```
select wswkrname, ablty, wskil
    from ws;

WSWKRNAME                AB WS
------------------------ -- --
Adah Talbot              07 99
Dick Jones               10 01
Elbert Talbot            03 03
Helen Brandt             08 02
John Pearson                02
John Pearson             07 04
John Pearson             05 01
Victoria Lynn            09 01
Wilfred Lowell           05 99
Wilfred Lowell           05 03
```

or this one:

```
select Name, Ability, Skill
    from WORKERSKILL;
NAME                     ABILITY    SKILL
------------------------ ---------- --------------
Adah Talbot              Good       Work
Dick Jones               Excellent  Smithy
Elbert Talbot            Slow       Discus
Helen Brandt             Very Fast  Combine Driver
John Pearson                        Combine Driver
John Pearson             Good       Woodcutter
John Pearson             Average    Smithy
Victoria Lynn            Precise    Smithy
Wilfred Lowell           Average    Work
Wilfred Lowell           Average    Discus
```

Capitalization in Names and Data

Oracle makes it slightly easier to remember table and column names by ignoring whether you type in capital letters, small letters, or a mixture of the two. It stores table and column names in its internal data dictionary in capitals (uppercase). When you type a query, it instantly converts the table and column names to uppercase, and then checks for them in the dictionary. Some other relational systems are case-sensitive. If users type a column name as "Ability," but the database thinks it is "ability" or "ABILITY" (depending on what it was told when the table was created), it will not understand the query.

The ability to create case-sensitive table names is promoted as a benefit because it allows programmers to create many tables with, for instance, similar names. They can make a worker table, a Worker table, a wORker table, and so on, ad infinitum. These will all be separate tables. How is anyone, including the programmer, supposed to remember the differences? This is a drawback, not a benefit, and Oracle was wise not to fall into this trap.

A similar case can be made for data stored in a database. There are ways to find information from the database regardless of whether the data is in uppercase or lowercase, but these methods impose an unnecessary burden. With few exceptions, such as legal text or form letter paragraphs, it is much easier to store data in the database in uppercase. It makes queries easier and provides a more consistent appearance on reports. When and if some of this data needs to be put into lowercase, or mixed uppercase and lowercase (such as the name and address on a letter), then the Oracle functions that perform the conversion can be invoked. It will be less trouble overall, and less confusing, to store and report data in uppercase.

Looking back over this chapter, you'll see that this practice was not followed. Rather, it was delayed until the subject could be introduced and put in its proper context. From here on, with the exception of one or two tables and a few isolated instances, data in the database will be in uppercase.

Normalizing Names

There are several query tools that have come on the market whose purpose is to let you make queries using common English words instead of odd conglomerations, such as those found in Table 2-1. These products work by building a logical map between the common English words and the hard-to-remember, non-English column names, table names, and codes. The mapping takes careful thought, but once completed, it makes the user's interaction with the application easy. Why not put the care in at the beginning? Why create a need for yet another layer, another product, and more work, when much of the confusion can be avoided simply by naming things better the first time around?

For performance reasons, it may be that some of an application's data must still be stored in a coded fashion within the computer's database. These codes should *not* be exposed to users, either during data entry or retrieval, and Oracle allows them to be easily hidden.

The instant that data entry requires codes, key entry errors increase. When reports contain codes instead of English, errors of interpretation begin. And when users need to create new or ad hoc reports, their ability to do so quickly and accurately is severely impaired both by codes and by not being able to remember strange column and table names.

Seizing the Opportunity

Oracle gives users the power to see and work with English throughout the entire application. It is a waste of Oracle's power to ignore this opportunity, and it will without question produce a less understandable and less productive application. Developers should seize the opportunity. Users should demand it. Both will benefit immeasurably.

CHAPTER
3

The Basic Parts of
Speech in SQL

ith the Structured Query Language, or SQL, you tell Oracle which information you want it to **select**, **insert**, **update**, or **delete**. In fact, these four verbs are the primary words you will use to give Oracle instructions.

In Chapter 1, you saw what is meant by "relational," how tables are organized into columns and rows, and how to instruct Oracle to select certain columns from a table and show you the information in them row by row.

In this and the following chapters, you will learn how to do this more completely. In later sections of this book, you will see how to use Web-based tools to access Oracle. In this section, you will learn how to interact with SQL*PLUS, a powerful Oracle product that can take your instructions for Oracle, check them for correctness, submit them to Oracle, and then modify or reformat the response Oracle gives, based on orders or directions that you've set in place. It *interacts* with you, which means you can "talk" to it, and it will "talk" back. You can give it directions, and it will follow them precisely. It will tell you if it doesn't understand something you've told it to do.

It may be a little confusing at first to understand the difference between what SQL*PLUS is doing and what Oracle is doing, especially since the error messages that Oracle produces are simply passed on to you by SQL*PLUS, but you will see as you work through this book where the differences lie.

As you get started, just think of SQL*PLUS as a coworker—an assistant who follows your instructions and helps you do your work more quickly. You interact with this coworker by typing on your keyboard.

You may follow the examples in this and subsequent chapters by typing the commands shown. Your Oracle and SQL*PLUS programs should respond just as they do in these examples. You do need to make certain that the tables used in this book have been loaded into your copy of Oracle.

You can understand what is described in this book without actually typing it in yourself; for example, you can use the commands shown with your own tables. It will probably be clearer and easier, though, if you have the same tables loaded into Oracle that are used here, and practice using the same queries.

Appendix A contains instructions on loading the tables. Assuming that you have done this, connect to SQL*PLUS and begin working by typing this:

```
sqlplus
```

(If you want to run SQL*PLUS from your desktop client machine, select the SQL Plus program in your Oracle program group.) This starts SQL*PLUS. (Note that you don't type the * that is in the middle of the official product name, and the asterisk doesn't appear in the program name, either. From here on, SQLPLUS will be referred to without the asterisk.) Since Oracle is careful to guard who can access the data it stores, it always requires that you enter an ID and password to connect to it. Oracle will display a copyright message, and then ask for your username and password. To gain access to the tables described in this book, enter the word **practice** for both username and password. SQLPLUS will announce that you're connected to Oracle, and then will display this prompt:

```
SQL>
```

You are now in SQLPLUS, and it awaits your instructions. If the command fails, it means one of four things: you are not on the proper subdirectory to use Oracle, Oracle is not in your path, you are not authorized to use SQLPLUS, or Oracle hasn't been installed properly on your computer. If you get this message:

```
ERROR: ORA-1017: invalid username/password; logon denied
```

it means either that you've entered the username or password incorrectly, or that the practice username has not yet been set up on your copy of Oracle. After three unsuccessful attempts to enter a username and password that Oracle recognizes, SQLPLUS will terminate the attempt to log on, with this message:

```
unable to CONNECT to ORACLE after 3 attempts, exiting SQL*Plus
```

If you get this message, either contact your company's database administrator or follow the installation guidelines in Appendix A. Assuming everything is in order, and the SQL> prompt has appeared, you may now begin working with SQLPLUS.

When you want to quit working and leave SQLPLUS, type this:

```
quit
```

Style

First, some comments on style. SQLPLUS doesn't care whether the SQL commands you type are in uppercase or lowercase. This command:

```
SeLeCt feaTURE, section, PAGE FROM newsPaPeR;
```

will produce exactly the same result as this one:

```
select Feature, Section, Page from NEWSPAPER;
```

Case matters only when SQLPLUS or Oracle is checking an alphanumeric value for equality. If you tell Oracle to find a row where Section = 'f' and Section is really equal to 'F', Oracle won't find it (since f and F are not identical). Aside from this use, case is completely irrelevant. (Incidentally, the letter 'F', as used here, is called a *literal,* meaning that you want Section to be tested literally against the letter 'F', not a column *named* F. The single quote marks enclosing the letter tell Oracle that this is a literal, and not a column name.)

As a matter of style, this book follows certain conventions about case to make text and listings easier to read:

- **select**, **from**, **where**, **order by**, **having**, and **group by** will always be lowercase and boldface.

- SQLPLUS commands also will be lowercase and boldface: **column**, **set**, **save**, **ttitle**, and so on.

- **IN**, **BETWEEN**, **UPPER**, **SOUNDEX**, and other SQL operators and functions will be uppercase and boldface.

- Column names will be mixed uppercase and lowercase without boldface: Feature, EastWest, Longitude, and so on.

- Table names will be uppercase without boldface: NEWSPAPER, WEATHER, LOCATION, and so on.

You may wish to follow similar conventions in creating your own queries, or your company already may have standards it would like you to use, or you may choose to invent your own. The goal of any such standards should always be to make your work simple to read and understand.

Creating the **NEWSPAPER** Table

The examples in this book are based on the tables created by the scripts shown in Appendix A. Each table is created via the **create table** command, which specifies the names of the columns in the table, as well as the characteristics of those columns. Here is the **create table** command for the NEWSPAPER table, which is used in many of the examples in this chapter:

```
create table NEWSPAPER (
Feature        VARCHAR2(15) not null,
Section        CHAR(1),
Page           NUMBER
);
```

In later chapters in this book, you'll see how to interpret all the clauses of this command. For now, you can read it as: "Create a table called NEWSPAPER. It will have three columns, named Feature (a varying-length character column), Section (a fixed-length character column), and Page (a numeric column). The values in the Feature column can be up to 15 characters long, and every row must have a value for Feature. Section values will all be 1 character long."

In later chapters, you'll see how to extend this simple command to add constraints, indexes, and storage clauses. For now, the NEWSPAPER table will be kept simple so that the examples can focus on SQL.

Using SQL to select Data from Tables

Figure 3-1 shows a table of features from a local newspaper. If this were an Oracle table, rather than just paper and ink on the front of the local paper, SQLPLUS would display it for you if you typed this:

```
select Feature, Section, Page from NEWSPAPER;

FEATURE          S      PAGE
--------------- - ----------
National News    A         1
Sports           D         1
Editorials       A        12
Business         E         1
Weather          C         2
Television       B         7
Births           F         7
Classified       F         8
Doctor Is In     F         6
Modern Life      B         1
Comics           C         4
Movies           B         4
Bridge           B         2
Obituaries       F         6

14 rows selected.
```

What's different between the table in the listing and the one from the newspaper in Figure 3-1? Both tables have the same information, but the format differs. For example, the column headings differ slightly. In fact, they even differ slightly from the columns you just asked for in the **select** statement.

The column named Section shows up as just the letter 'S,' and although you used uppercase and lowercase letters to type this:

```
select Feature, Section, Page from NEWSPAPER;
```

Feature	Section	Page
Births	F	7
Bridge	B	2
Business	E	1
Classified	F	8
Comics	C	4
Doctor Is In	F	6
Editorials	A	12
Modern Life	B	1
Movies	B	4
National News	A	1
Obituaries	F	6
Sports	D	1
Television	B	7
Weather	C	2

FIGURE 3-1. *A table of newspaper sections*

the column headings came back with all of the letters in uppercase.

These changes are the result of the assumptions SQLPLUS makes about how information should be presented. You can change these assumptions, and you likely will, but until you give it different orders, this is how SQLPLUS changes what you input:

- It changes all the column headings to uppercase.

- It allows columns to be only as wide as the column is defined to be in Oracle.

- It squeezes out any spaces if the column heading is a function. (This will be demonstrated in Chapter 7.)

The first point is obvious. The column names you used were shifted to uppercase. The second point is not obvious. How *are* the columns defined? To find out, ask Oracle. Simply tell SQLPLUS to describe the table, as shown here:

```
describe NEWSPAPER

Name                              Null?     Type
-------------------------------   --------  -------
FEATURE                           NOT NULL  VARCHAR2(15)
SECTION                                     CHAR(1)
PAGE                                        NUMBER
```

This display is a descriptive table that lists the columns and their definitions for the NEWSPAPER table; **describe** works for any table. Note that the details in this description match the **create table** command given earlier in this chapter.

The first column tells the names of the columns in the table being described.

The second column, Null?, is really a rule about the column named to its left. When the NEWSPAPER table was created, the **NOT NULL** rule instructed Oracle not to allow any user to add a new row to the table if he or she left the Feature column empty (**NULL** means empty).

Of course, in a table such as NEWSPAPER, it probably would have been worthwhile to use the same rule for all three columns. What good is it to know the title of a Feature without also knowing what Section it's in and what Page it's on? But, for the sake of this example, only Feature was created with the rule that it could not be **NULL**.

Because Section and Page have nothing in the Null? column, they are allowed to be empty in any row of the NEWSPAPER table.

The third column, Type, tells the basic nature of the individual columns. Feature is a VARCHAR2 (variable-length character) column that can be up to 15 characters (letters, numbers, symbols, or spaces) long.

Section is a character column as well, but it is only one character long! The creator of the table knew that newspaper sections in the local paper are only a single letter, so the column was defined to be only as wide as it needed to be. It was defined using the CHAR datatype, which is used for fixed-length character strings. When SQLPLUS went to display the results of your query:

```
select Feature, Section, Page from NEWSPAPER;
```

it knew from Oracle that Section was a maximum of only one character. It assumed that you did not want to use up more space than this, so it displayed a column just one character wide, and used as much of the column name as it could: 'S'.

The third column in the NEWSPAPER table is Page, which is simply a number. Notice that the Page column shows up as ten spaces wide, even though no pages use more than two digits—numbers usually are not defined as having a maximum width, so SQLPLUS assumes a maximum just to get started.

You also may have noticed that the heading for the only column composed solely of numbers, Page, was *right-justified*—that is, it sits over on the right side of the column, whereas the headings for columns that contain characters sit over on the left. This is standard alignment for column headings in SQLPLUS. Like other column features, you'll later learn how to change alignment as needed.

Finally, SQLPLUS tells you how many rows it found in Oracle's NEWSPAPER table. (Notice the "14 rows selected" notation at the bottom of the display.) This is called *feedback*. You can make SQLPLUS stop giving feedback by setting the **feedback** option, as shown here:

```
set feedback off
```

or you can set a minimum number of rows for **feedback** to work:

```
set feedback 25
```

This last example tells Oracle that you don't want to know how many rows have been displayed until there have been at least 25. Unless you tell SQLPLUS differently, **feedback** is set to 6.

The **set** command is a SQLPLUS command, which means that it is an instruction telling SQLPLUS how to act. There are many SQLPLUS options, such as **feedback**, that you can set. Several of these will be shown and used in this chapter and in the chapters to follow. For a complete list, look up **set** in the Alphabetical Reference section of this book.

The **set** command has a counterpart named **show** that allows you to see what instructions you've given to SQLPLUS. For instance, you can check the setting of **feedback** by typing

```
show feedback
```

SQLPLUS will respond with

```
FEEDBACK ON for 25 or more rows
```

The width used to display numbers also is changed by the **set** command. You check it by typing

```
show numwidth
```

SQLPLUS will reply as shown here:

```
numwidth 9
```

Since 9 is a wide width for displaying page numbers that never contain more than two digits, shrink the display by typing

```
set numwidth 5
```

However, this means that all number columns will be five digits wide. If you anticipate having numbers with more than five digits, you must use a number higher than 5. Individual columns in the display also can be set independently. This will be covered in Chapter 6.

select, from, where, and order by

You will use four primary keywords in SQL when selecting information from an Oracle table: **select**, **from**, **where**, and **order by**. You will use **select** and **from** in every Oracle query you do.

The **select** keyword tells Oracle which columns you want, and **from** tells Oracle the names of the table or tables those columns are in. The NEWSPAPER table example showed how these are used. In the first line that you entered, a comma follows each column name except the last. You'll notice that a correctly typed SQL query reads pretty much like an English sentence. A query in SQLPLUS usually ends with a semicolon (sometimes called the *SQL terminator*). The **where** keyword tells Oracle what qualifiers you'd like to put on the information it is selecting. For example, if you input this:

```
select Feature, Section, Page from NEWSPAPER
 where Section = 'F';


FEATURE          S  PAGE
---------------- -  -----
Births           F     7
Classified       F     8
Obituaries       F     6
Doctor Is In     F     6
```

Oracle checks each row in the NEWSPAPER table before sending the row back to you. It skips over those without the single letter 'F' in their Section column. It returns those where the Section entry is 'F', and SQLPLUS displays them to you.

To tell Oracle that you want the information it returns sorted in the order you specify, use **order by**. You can be as elaborate as you like about the order you request. Consider these examples:

```
select Feature, Section, Page from NEWSPAPER
 where Section = 'F'
 order by Feature;
```

```
FEATURE          S   PAGE
--------------   -   -----
Births           F      7
Classified       F      8
Doctor Is In     F      6
Obituaries       F      6
```

They are nearly reversed when ordered by page, as shown here:

```
select Feature, Section, Page from NEWSPAPER
 where Section = 'F'
 order by Page;
```

```
FEATURE          S   PAGE
--------------   -   -----
Obituaries       F      6
Doctor Is In     F      6
Births           F      7
Classified       F      8
```

In the next example, Oracle first puts the Features in order by Page (see the previous listing to observe the order they are in when they are ordered only by Page). It then puts them in further order by Feature, listing Doctor Is In ahead of Obituaries.

```
select Feature, Section, Page from NEWSPAPER
 where Section = 'F'
 order by Page, Feature;
```

```
FEATURE          S   PAGE
--------------   -   -----
Doctor Is In     F      6
Obituaries       F      6
Births           F      7
Classified       F      8
```

Using **order by** also can reverse the normal order, like this:

```
select Feature, Section, Page from NEWSPAPER
 where Section = 'F'
 order by Page desc, Feature;
```

```
FEATURE          S   PAGE
--------------   -   -----
Classified       F      8
Births           F      7
```

```
Doctor Is In    F     6
Obituaries      F     6
```

The **desc** keyword stands for *descending*. Because it followed the word "Page" in the **order by** line, it put the page numbers in descending order. It would have the same effect on the Feature column if it followed the word "Feature" in the **order by** line.

Notice that **select**, **from**, **where**, and **order by** each has its own way of structuring the words that follow it. The groups of words including these keywords are often called *clauses*. See examples of each clause in Figure 3-2.

Logic and Value

Just as the **order by** clause can have several parts, so can the **where** clause, but with a significantly greater degree of sophistication. You control the extent to which you use **where** through the careful use of logical instructions to Oracle on what you expect it to return to you. These instructions are expressed using mathematical symbols called *logical operators*. These are explained shortly, and also are listed in the Alphabetical Reference section of this book, both individually by name, and grouped under the heading "Logical Operators."

The following is a simple example where the values in the Page column are tested to see if any equals 6. Every row where this is true is returned to you. Any row in which Page is not equal to 6 is skipped (in other words, those rows for which Page = 6 is false).

```
select Feature, Section, Page
  from NEWSPAPER
 where Page = 6;


FEATURE          S  PAGE
---------------  -  -----
Obituaries       F     6
Doctor Is In     F     6
```

Select Feature, Section, Page   <--**select clause**
  from NEWSPAPER   <--**from clause**
 where Section = 'F'   <--**where clause**

FIGURE 3-2. *Relational clauses*

The equal sign is called a *logical operator,* because it operates by making a logical test that compares the values on either side of it—in this case, the value of Page and the value 6—to see if they are equal.

In this example, no quotes are placed around the value being checked, because the column the value is compared to (the Page column) is defined as a NUMBER datatype. Number values do not require quotes around them during comparisons.

Single-Value Tests

You can use one of several logical operators to test against a single value, as shown in the upcoming sidebar "Logical Tests Against a Single Value." Take a few examples from any of the expressions listed in this sidebar. They all work similarly and can be combined at will, although they must follow certain rules about how they'll act together.

Equal, Greater Than, Less Than, Not Equal

Logical tests can compare values, both for equality and for relative value. Here, a simple test is made for all sections equal to B:

```
select Feature, Section, Page
  from NEWSPAPER
 where Section = 'B';
FEATURE           S  PAGE
--------------    -  -----
Television        B     7
Modern Life       B     1
Movies            B     4
Bridge            B     2
```

The following is the test for all pages greater than 4:

```
select Feature, Section, Page
  from NEWSPAPER
 where Page > 4;

FEATURE           S  PAGE
--------------    -  -----
Editorials        A    12
Television        B     7
Births            F     7
Classified        F     8
Obituaries        F     6
Doctor Is In      F     6
```

The following is the test for sections greater than B (this means later in the alphabet than B):

```
select Feature, Section, Page
   from NEWSPAPER
 where Section > 'B';
```

```
FEATURE          S   PAGE
---------------  -   -----
Sports           D     1
Business         E     1
Weather          C     2
Births           F     7
Classified       F     8
Comics           C     4
Obituaries       F     6
Doctor Is In     F     6
```

Just as a test can be made for greater than, so can a test be made for less than, as shown here (all page numbers less than 8):

```
select Feature, Section, Page
   from NEWSPAPER
 where Page < 8;
```

```
FEATURE          S      PAGE
---------------  -   ----------
National News    A        1
Sports           D        1
Business         E        1
Weather          C        2
Television       B        7
Births           F        7
Modern Life      B        1
Comics           C        4
Movies           B        4
Bridge           B        2
Obituaries       F        6
Doctor Is In     F        6
```

The opposite of the test for equality is the *not equal* test, as given here:

```
select Feature, Section, Page
   from NEWSPAPER
 where Page != 1;
```

```
FEATURE           S       PAGE
--------------    -     ----------
Editorials        A         12
Weather           C          2
Television        B          7
Births            F          7
Classified        F          8
Comics            C          4
Movies            B          4
Bridge            B          2
Obituaries        F          6
Doctor Is In      F          6
```

Be careful when using the *greater than* and *less than* operators against numbers that are stored in character datatype columns. All values in VARCHAR2 and CHAR columns will be treated as characters during comparisons. Therefore, numbers that are stored in those types of columns will be compared as if they were character strings, not numbers. If the column's datatype is NUMBER, then 12 is greater than 9. If it is a character column, then 9 is greater than 12, because the character '9' is greater than the character '1'.

LIKE

One of the most powerful features of SQL is a marvelous pattern-matching operator called **LIKE**, which is able to search through the rows of a database column for values that look like a pattern you describe. It uses two special characters to denote which kind of matching to do: a percent sign, called a *wildcard,* and an underline, called a *position marker.* To look for all of the Features that begin with the letters 'Mo,' use the following:

```
select Feature, Section, Page from NEWSPAPER
 where Feature LIKE 'Mo%';

FEATURE           S       PAGE
--------------    -     ----------
Modern Life       B          1
Movies            B          4
```

The percent sign (%) means anything is acceptable here: one character, a hundred characters, or no characters. If the first letters are 'Mo', **LIKE** will find the Feature. If the query had used 'MO%' as its search condition instead, then no rows would have been returned, due to Oracle's case-sensitivity in data values. If you

Logical Tests Against a Single Value

All of these operators work with letters or numbers, and with columns or literals.

EQUAL, GREATER THAN, LESS THAN, NOT EQUAL

Page=	6	Page is equal to 6
Page>	6	Page is greater than 6
Page>=	6	Page is greater than or equal to 6
Page<	6	Page is less than 6
Page<=	6	Page is less than or equal to 6
Page!=	6	Page is not equal to 6
Page^=	6	Page is not equal to 6
Page<>	6	Page is not equal to 6

Because some keyboards lack an exclamation mark (!) or a caret (^), Oracle allows three ways of typing the not equal operator. The final alternative, <>, qualifies as a not equal operator because it permits only numbers less than 6 (in this example) or greater than 6, but not 6 itself.

LIKE

Feature LIKE 'Mo%'	Feature begins with the letters Mo
Feature LIKE '_ _ l%'	Feature has an l in the third position
Feature LIKE '%o%o%'	Feature has two o's in it

LIKE performs pattern matching. An underline character (_) represents one space. A percent sign (%) represents any number of spaces or characters.

IS NULL, IS NOT NULL

Precipitation IS NULL	Precipitation is unknown
Precipitation IS NOT NULL	Precipitation is known

> **NULL** tests to see if data exists in a column for a row. If the column is completely empty, it is said to be **NULL**. The word **IS** must be used with **NULL** and **NOT NULL**; equal, greater than, or less than signs do not work with **NULL** and **NOT NULL.**

wish to find those Features that have the letter 'i' in the third position of their titles, and you don't care which two characters precede the 'i' or what set of characters follows, using two underlines (_ _) specifies that any character in those two positions is acceptable. Position three must have a lowercase 'i'; the percent sign after that says anything is okay.

```
select Feature, Section, Page from NEWSPAPER
  where Feature LIKE '__i%';


FEATURE          S     PAGE
--------------- - ----------
Editorials       A        12
Bridge           B         2
Obituaries       F         6
```

Multiple percent signs also can be used. To find those words with two lowercase 'o's anywhere in the Feature title, three percent signs are used, as shown here:

```
select Feature, Section, Page from NEWSPAPER
  where Feature LIKE '%o%o%';


FEATURE          S     PAGE
--------------- - ----------
Doctor Is In     F         6
```

For the sake of comparison, the following is the same query, but it is looking for two 'i's:

```
select Feature, Section, Page from NEWSPAPER
  where Feature LIKE '%i%i%';


FEATURE          S     PAGE
--------------- - ----------
```

```
Editorials      A        12
Television      B         7
Classified      F         8
Obituaries      F         6
```

This pattern-matching feature can play an important role in making an application friendlier by simplifying searches for names, products, addresses, and other partially remembered items.

NULL and NOT NULL

The NEWSPAPER table has no columns in it that are **NULL**, even though the **describe** you did on it showed that they were allowed. The COMFORT table following contains, among other data, the precipitation for San Francisco, California and Keene, New Hampshire, for four sample dates during 1999:

```
select City, SampleDate, Precipitation
   from COMFORT;


CITY           SAMPLEDAT PRECIPITATION
-------------- --------- -------------
SAN FRANCISCO  21-MAR-99            .5
SAN FRANCISCO  22-JUN-99            .1
SAN FRANCISCO  23-SEP-99            .1
SAN FRANCISCO  22-DEC-99           2.3
KEENE          21-MAR-99           4.4
KEENE          22-JUN-99           1.3
KEENE          23-SEP-99
KEENE          22-DEC-99           3.9
```

You can find out the city and dates on which precipitation was not measured with this query:

```
select City, SampleDate, Precipitation
   from COMFORT
 where Precipitation IS NULL;


CITY           SAMPLEDAT PRECIPITATION
-------------- --------- -------------
KEENE          23-SEP-99
```

IS NULL essentially instructs Oracle to identify columns in which the data is missing. You don't know for that day whether the value should be 0, 1, or 5 inches. Because it is unknown, the value in the column is not set to 0; it stays empty. By using **NOT**, you also can find those cities and dates for which data exists, with this query:

```
select City, SampleDate, Precipitation
   from COMFORT
 where Precipitation IS NOT NULL;


CITY           SAMPLEDAT PRECIPITATION
------------- --------- -------------
SAN FRANCISCO 21-MAR-99            .5
SAN FRANCISCO 22-JUN-99            .1
SAN FRANCISCO 23-SEP-99            .1
SAN FRANCISCO 22-DEC-99           2.3
KEENE         21-MAR-99           4.4
KEENE         22-JUN-99           1.3
KEENE         22-DEC-99           3.9
```

Oracle lets you use the relational operators (=, !=, and so on) with **NULL**, but this kind of comparison will not return meaningful results. Use **IS** or **IS NOT** for comparing values to **NULL**.

Simple Tests Against a List of Values

If there are logical operators that test against a single value, are there others that will test against many values, such as a list? The sidebar "Logical Tests Against a List of Values" shows just such a group of operators.

Here are a few examples of how these logical operators are used:

```
select Feature, Section, Page
   from NEWSPAPER
 where Section IN ('A','B','F');


FEATURE         S      PAGE
-------------- - ----------
National News   A         1
Editorials      A        12
Television       B        7
Births          F         7
Classified      F         8
Modern Life     B         1
Movies          B         4
Bridge          B         2
Obituaries      F         6
Doctor Is In    F         6
```

Logical Tests Against a List of Values
Logical tests with numbers:

Page IN (1,2,3)	Page is in the list (1,2,3)
Page NOT IN (1,2,3)	Page is not in the list (1,2,3)
Page BETWEEN 6 AND 10	Page is equal to 6, 10, or anything in between
Page NOT BETWEEN 6 AND 10	Page is below 6 or above 10

With letters (or characters):

Section IN ('A','C','F')	Section is in the list ('A', 'C', 'F')
Section NOT IN ('A', 'C', 'F')	Section is not in the list ('A', 'C', 'F')
Section BETWEEN 'B' AND 'D'	Section is equal to 'B', 'D', or anything in between (alphabetically)
Section NOT BETWEEN 'B' AND 'D'	Section is below 'B' or above 'D' (alphabetically)

```
select Feature, Section, Page
   from NEWSPAPER
 where Section NOT IN ('A','B','F');


FEATURE           S      PAGE
--------------- - ----------
Sports            D         1
Business          E         1
Weather           C         2
Comics            C         4
```

```
select Feature, Section, Page
   from NEWSPAPER
 where Page BETWEEN 7 and 10;
```

```
FEATURE         S      PAGE
--------------- - ----------
Television      B         7
Births          F         7
Classified      F         8
```

These logical tests also can be combined, as in this case:

```
select Feature, Section, Page
   from NEWSPAPER
 where Section = 'F'
   AND Page > 7;
```

```
FEATURE         S      PAGE
--------------- - ----------
Classified      F         8
```

The **AND** command has been used to combine two logical expressions and requires any row Oracle examines to pass *both* tests; both Section = 'F' and Page > 7 must be true for a row to be returned to you. Alternatively, **OR** can be used, and will return rows to you if *either* logical expression turns out to be true:

```
select Feature, Section, Page
   from NEWSPAPER
 where Section = 'F'
    OR Page > 7;
```

```
FEATURE         S  PAGE
--------------- - -----
Editorials      A    12
Births          F     7
Classified      F     8
Obituaries      F     6
Doctor Is In    F     6
```

There are some Sections here that qualify even though they are not equal to 'F', because their Page is greater than 7, and there are other Sections whose Page is less than or equal to 7, but whose Section is equal to 'F'.

Finally, choose those features in Section F between pages 7 and 10 with this query:

```
select Feature, Section, Page
   from NEWSPAPER
 where Section = 'F'
    and Page BETWEEN 7 AND 10;
```

```
FEATURE         S  PAGE
--------------- - -----
```

```
Births          F     7
Classified      F     8
```

There are a few additional *many-value operators* whose use is more complex; they will be covered in Chapter 8. They also can be found, along with those just discussed, in the Alphabetical Reference section of this book, under "Logical Operators."

Combining Logic

Both **AND** and **OR** follow the commonsense meaning of the words. They can be combined in a virtually unlimited number of ways, but you must use care, because **AND**s and **OR**s get convoluted very easily.

Suppose you want to find the Features in the paper that the editors tend to bury, those that are placed somewhere past page 2 of section A or B. You might try this:

```
select Feature, Section, Page
   from NEWSPAPER
 where Section = 'A'
    or Section = 'B'
   and Page > 2;


FEATURE          S  PAGE
--------------   -  -----
National News    A     1
Editorials       A    12
Television       B     7
Movies           B     4
```

Note that the result you got back from Oracle is not what you wanted. Somehow, page 1 of section A was included. Apparently, the "and Page > 2" only affected the rows for section B. If you now move the "and Page > 2" up to the middle of the **where** clause, the result is different, but still wrong:

```
select Feature, Section, Page
   from NEWSPAPER
 where Section = 'A'
   and Page > 2
    or Section = 'B';

FEATURE          S  PAGE
--------------   -  -----
Editorials       A    12
Television       B     7
```

```
Modern Life      B     1
Movies           B     4
Bridge           B     2
```

What happens if you put the "Page > 2" first? Still wrong:

```
select Feature, Section, Page
  from NEWSPAPER
 where Page > 2
   and Section = 'A'
    or Section = 'B';


FEATURE          S  PAGE
---------------  -  -----
Editorials       A    12
Television       B     7
Modern Life      B     1
Movies           B     4
Bridge           B     2
```

Why is this happening? Is there a way to get Oracle to answer the question correctly? Although both **AND** and **OR** are logical connectors, **AND** is stronger. It binds the logical expressions on either side of it more strongly than **OR** does (technically, **AND** is said to have *higher precedence*), which means this **where** clause:

```
where Section = 'A'
   or Section = 'B'
  and Page > 2;
```

is interpreted to read, "where Section = 'A', or where Section = 'B' *and* Page > 2." If you look at each of the failed examples just given, you'll see how this interpretation affected the result. The **AND** is always acted on first.

You can break this bonding by using parentheses that enclose those expressions you want to be interpreted together. Parentheses override the normal precedence:

```
select Feature, Section, Page
  from NEWSPAPER
 where Page > 2   and ( Section = 'A'
       or Section = 'B' );


FEATURE          S PAGE
-----------------  - ----
Editorials       A   12
Television       B    7
Movies           B    4
```

The result is exactly what you wanted in the first place. Note that while you can type this with the sections listed first, the result is identical because the parentheses tell Oracle what to interpret together. Compare this to the different results caused by changing the order in the first three examples, where parentheses were not used.

Another Use for where: Subqueries

What if the logical operators in the previous sidebars, "Logical Tests Against a Single Value" and "Logical Tests Against a List of Values," could be used not just with a single literal value (such as 'F') or a typed list of values (such as 4,2,7 or 'A','C','F'), but with values brought back by an Oracle query? In fact, this is a powerful feature of SQL.

Imagine that you are the author of the "Doctor Is In" feature, and each newspaper that publishes your column sends along a copy of the table of contents that includes your piece. Of course, each editor rates your importance a little differently, and places you in a section he or she deems suited to your feature. Without knowing ahead of time where your feature is, or with what other features you are placed, how could you write a query to find out where a particular local paper places you? You might do this:

```
select Section from NEWSPAPER
  where Feature = 'Doctor Is In';

S
-
F
```

The result is 'F'. Knowing this, you could do this query:

```
select FEATURE from NEWSPAPER
  where Section = 'F';

FEATURE
---------------
Births
Classified
Obituaries
Doctor Is In
```

You're in there with births, deaths, and classified ads. Could the two separate queries have been combined into one? Yes, as shown here:

```
select FEATURE from NEWSPAPER
  where Section = (select Section from NEWSPAPER
                    where Feature = 'Doctor Is In');
```

```
FEATURE
---------------
Births
Classified
Obituaries
Doctor Is In
```

Single Values from a Subquery

In effect, the **select** in parentheses (called a *subquery*) brought back a single value, F. The main query then treated this F as if it were a literal 'F', as was used in the previous query. Remember that the equal sign is a single-value test (refer to Figure 3-2). It can't work with lists, so if your subquery returned more than one row, you'd get an error message like this:

```
select * from NEWSPAPER
  where Section = (select Section from NEWSPAPER
                     where Page = 1);

ERROR: ORA-1427:  single-row subquery returns more than one row
```

All of the logical operators that test single values can work with subqueries, as long as the subquery returns a single row. For instance, you can ask for all of the features in the paper where the section is *less than* (earlier in the alphabet) the section that carries your column. The asterisk in this **select** shows a shorthand way to request all the columns in a table without listing them individually. They will be displayed in the order in which they were created in the table.

```
select * from NEWSPAPER
  where Section < (select Section from NEWSPAPER
                     where Feature = 'Doctor Is In');

FEATURE           S  PAGE
---------------   -  -----
National News     A     1
Sports            D     1
Editorials        A    12
Business          E     1
Weather           C     2
Television        B     7
Modern Life       B     1
Comics            C     4
Movies            B     4
```

```
Bridge          B     2
```

```
10 rows selected.
```

Ten other features rank ahead of your medical advice in this local paper.

Lists of Values from a Subquery

Just as the single-value logical operators can be used on a subquery, so can the many-value operators. If a subquery returns one or more rows, the value in the column for each row will be stacked up in a list. For example, suppose you want to know the cities and countries where it is cloudy. You could have a table of complete weather information for all cities, and a LOCATION table for all cities and their countries, as shown here:

```
select City, Country from LOCATION;

CITY                          COUNTRY
----------------------------  ---------------------------
ATHENS                        GREECE
CHICAGO                       UNITED STATES
CONAKRY                       GUINEA
LIMA                          PERU
MADRAS                        INDIA
MANCHESTER                    ENGLAND
MOSCOW                        RUSSIA
PARIS                         FRANCE
SHENYANG                      CHINA
ROME                          ITALY
TOKYO                         JAPAN
SYDNEY                        AUSTRALIA
SPARTA                        GREECE
MADRID                        SPAIN
```

```
select City, Condition from WEATHER;

CITY        CONDITION
----------- -----------
LIMA        RAIN
PARIS       CLOUDY
MANCHESTER  FOG
ATHENS      SUNNY
CHICAGO     RAIN
SYDNEY      SNOW
SPARTA      CLOUDY
```

First, you'd discover which cities were cloudy:

```
select City from WEATHER
  where Condition = 'CLOUDY';

CITY
-----------

PARIS
SPARTA
```

Then, you would build a list including those cities and use it to query the LOCATION table:

```
select City, Country from LOCATION
  where City IN ('PARIS', 'SPARTA');

CITY                        COUNTRY
------------------------    -------------------------

PARIS                       FRANCE
SPARTA                      GREECE
```

The same task can be accomplished by a subquery, where the **select** in parentheses builds a list of cities that are tested by the **IN** operator, as shown here:

```
select City, Country from LOCATION
  where City IN (select City from WEATHER
                   where Condition = 'CLOUDY');

CITY                        COUNTRY
------------------------    -------------------------

PARIS                       FRANCE
SPARTA                      GREECE
```

The other many-value operators work similarly. The fundamental task is to build a subquery that produces a list that can be logically tested. The following are some relevant points:

- The subquery must either have only one column, or compare its selected columns to multiple columns in parentheses in the main query (covered in Chapter 12).

- The subquery must be enclosed in parentheses.

- Subqueries that produce only one row can be used with *either* single- or many-value operators.

- Subqueries that produce more than one row can be used *only* with many-value operators.

- **BETWEEN** *cannot* be used with a subquery; that is,

```
select * from WEATHER
 where Temperature BETWEEN 60
                   AND (select Temperature
                          from WEATHER
                         where City = 'PARIS');
```

will not work. All other many-value operators will work with subqueries.

Combining Tables

If you've normalized your data, you'll probably need to combine two or more tables to get all the information you want.

Suppose you are the Oracle at Delphi. The Athenians come to ask about the forces of nature that might affect the expected attack by the Spartans, as well as the direction from which they are likely to appear:

```
select City, Condition, Temperature from WEATHER;
```

CITY	CONDITION	TEMPERATURE
LIMA	RAIN	45
PARIS	CLOUDY	81
MANCHESTER	FOG	66
ATHENS	SUNNY	97
CHICAGO	RAIN	66
SYDNEY	SNOW	29
SPARTA	CLOUDY	74

You realize your geography is rusty, so you query the LOCATION table:

```
select City, Longitude, EastWest, Latitude, NorthSouth
   from LOCATION;
```

CITY	LONGITUDE	E	LATITUDE	N
ATHENS	23.43	E	37.58	N
CHICAGO	87.38	W	41.53	N
CONAKRY	13.43	W	9.31	N
LIMA	77.03	W	12.03	S

```
MADRAS                          80.17 E    13.05 N
MANCHESTER                       2.15 W    53.3  N
MOSCOW                          37.35 E    55.45 N
PARIS                            2.2  E    48.52 N
SHENYANG                       123.3  E    41.48 N
ROME                            12.29 E    41.54 N
TOKYO                          139.5  E    35.42 N
SYDNEY                         151.1  E    33.52 S
SPARTA                          22.27 E    37.05 N
MADRID                           3.14 W    40.24 N
```

This is much more than you need, and it doesn't have any weather information. Yet these two tables, WEATHER and LOCATION, have a column in common: City. You can therefore put the information from the two tables together by joining them. You merely use the **where** clause to tell Oracle what the two tables have in common (this is similar to the example given in Chapter 1):

```
select WEATHER.City, Condition, Temperature, Latitude,
       NorthSouth, Longitude, EastWest
  from WEATHER, LOCATION
 where WEATHER.City = LOCATION.City;
```

```
CITY          CONDITION     TEMPERATURE LATITUDE N LONGITUDE E
-----------   -----------   ----------- -------- - --------- -
ATHENS        SUNNY                  97    37.58 N     23.43 E
CHICAGO       RAIN                   66    41.53 N     87.38 W
LIMA          RAIN                   45    12.03 S     77.03 W
MANCHESTER    FOG                    66    53.3  N      2.15 W
PARIS         CLOUDY                 81    48.52 N      2.2  E
SPARTA        CLOUDY                 74    37.05 N     22.27 E
SYDNEY        SNOW                   29    33.52 S    151.1  E
```

Notice that the only rows in this combined table are those where the same city is in *both* tables. The **where** clause is still executing your logic, as it did earlier in the case of the NEWSPAPER table. The logic you gave described the relationship between the two tables. It says, "select those rows in the WEATHER table and the LOCATION table where the cities are equal." If a city was only in one table, it would have nothing to be equal to in the other table. The notation used in the **select** statement is TABLE.ColumnName—in this case, WEATHER.City.

The **select** clause has chosen those columns from the two tables that you'd like to see displayed; any columns in either table that you did not ask for are simply ignored. If the first line had simply said this:

```
select City, Condition, Temperature, Latitude
```

then Oracle would not have known to which City you were referring. Oracle would tell you that the column name City was ambiguous. The correct wording in the **select** clause is WEATHER.City or LOCATION.City. In this example, it won't make a bit of difference which of these alternatives is used, but you will encounter cases where the choice of identically named columns from two or more tables will contain very different data.

The **where** clause also requires the names of the tables to accompany the identical column name by which the tables are combined: "where weather dot city equals location dot city"—that is, where the City column in the WEATHER table equals the City column in the LOCATION table.

Consider that the combination of the two tables looks like a single table with seven columns and seven rows. Everything that you excluded is gone. There is no Humidity column here, even though it is a part of the WEATHER table. There is no Country column here, even though it is a part of the LOCATION table. And of the 14 cities in the LOCATION table, only those that are in the WEATHER table are here in this table. Your **where** clause didn't allow the others to be selected.

A table that is built from columns in one or more tables is sometimes called a *projection,* or a *result table.*

Creating a View

There is even more here than meets the eye. Not only does this look like a new table, you can give it a name and treat it like one. This is called *creating a view.* A *view* is a way of hiding the logic that created the joined table just displayed. It works this way:

```
create view INVASION AS
select WEATHER.City, Condition, Temperature, Latitude,
       NorthSouth, Longitude, EastWest
  from WEATHER, LOCATION
 where WEATHER.City = LOCATION.City;

View created.
```

Now you can act as if INVASION were a real table with its own rows and columns. You can even ask Oracle to describe it to you:

```
describe INVASION

Name                                     Null?    Type
-------------------------------------    --------  ----
CITY                                               VARCHAR2(11)
```

```
CONDITION                        VARCHAR2(9)
TEMPERATURE                      NUMBER
LATITUDE                         NUMBER
NORTHSOUTH                       CHAR(1)
LONGITUDE                        NUMBER
EASTWEST                         CHAR(1)
```

You can query it, too (note that you will not have to specify which table the City columns were from, because that logic is hidden inside the view):

```
select City, Condition, Temperature, Latitude, NorthSouth,
       Longitude, EastWest
  from INVASION;

CITY        CONDITION   TEMPERATURE LATITUDE N LONGITUDE E
----------  ----------  ----------- -------- - --------- -
ATHENS      SUNNY               97    37.58 N     23.43 E
CHICAGO     RAIN                66    41.53 N     87.38 W
LIMA        RAIN                45    12.03 S     77.03 W
MANCHESTER  FOG                 66     53.3 N      2.15 W
PARIS       CLOUDY              81    48.52 N       2.2 E
SPARTA      CLOUDY              74    37.05 N     22.27 E
SYDNEY      SNOW                29    33.52 S     151.1 E
```

There will be some Oracle functions you won't be able to use on a view that you can use on a plain table, but they are few, and mostly involve modifying rows and indexing tables, which will be discussed in later chapters. For the most part, a view behaves and can be manipulated just like any other table.

NOTE
Views do not contain any data. Tables contain data.
As of Oracle8i, you can create "materialized views"
that contain data, but they are truly tables, not views.

Suppose now you realize that you don't really need information about Chicago or other cities outside of Greece, so you change the query. Will the following work?

```
select City, Condition, Temperature, Latitude, NorthSouth,
       Longitude, EastWest
  from INVASION
 where Country = 'GREECE';
```

SQLPLUS passes back this message from Oracle:

```
 where Country = 'GREECE'
         *
ERROR at line 4: ORA-0704:  invalid column name
```

Why? Because even though Country is a real column in one of the tables behind the view called INVASION, it was not in the **select** clause when the view was created. It is as if it does not exist. So, you must go back to the **create view** statement and include only the country of Greece there:

```
create or replace view INVASION as
select WEATHER.City, Condition, Temperature, Latitude,
       NorthSouth, Longitude, EastWest
  from WEATHER, LOCATION
 where WEATHER.City = LOCATION.City
   and Country = 'GREECE';

View created.
```

Using the **create or replace view** command allows you to create a new version of a view without first dropping the old one. This command will make it easier to administer users' privileges to access the view, as will be described in Chapter 19.

The logic of the **where** clause has now been expanded to include both joining two tables and a single-value test on a column in one of those tables. Now, query Oracle. You'll get this response:

```
select City, Condition, Temperature, Latitude, NorthSouth,
       Longitude, EastWest
  from INVASION;


CITY           CONDITION    TEMPERATURE LATITUDE N LONGITUDE E
-------------- ------------ ----------- -------- - --------- -
ATHENS         SUNNY                 97    37.58 N     23.43 E
SPARTA         CLOUDY                74    37.05 N     22.27 E
```

This allows you to warn the Athenians that the Spartans are likely to appear from the southwest but will be overheated and tired from their march. With a little trigonometry, you could even make Oracle calculate how far they will have marched. The old Oracle at Delphi was always ambiguous in her predictions. She would have said, "The Spartans the Athenians will conquer." You can at least offer some facts.

Expanding the View of View

This power of views to hide or even modify data can be used for a variety of useful purposes. Very complex reports can be built up by the creation of a series of simple views, and specific individuals or groups can be restricted to seeing only certain pieces of the whole table.

In fact, any qualifications you can put into a query can become part of a view. You could, for instance, let supervisors looking at a payroll table see only their own salaries and those of the people working for them, or restrict operating divisions in a company to seeing only their own financial results, even though the table actually contains results for all divisions. Most importantly, views are *not* snapshots of the data at a certain point in the past. They are dynamic, and always reflect the data in the underlying tables. The instant data in a table is changed, any views created with that table change as well.

For example, you may create a view that restricts values based on column values. As shown here, a query that restricts the LOCATION table on the Country column could be used to limit the rows that are visible via the view:

```
create or replace view PERU_LOCATIONS as
select * from LOCATION
 where Country = 'PERU';
```

A user querying PERU_LOCATIONS would not be able to see any rows from any country other than Peru.

The queries used to define views may also reference *pseudo-columns.* A pseudo-column is a "column" that returns a value when it is selected, but is not an actual column in a table. The User pseudo-column, when selected, will always return the Oracle username that executed the query. So, if a column in the table contains usernames, those values can be compared against the User pseudo-column to restrict its rows, as shown in the following listing. In this example, the NAME table is queried. If the value of its Name column is the same as the name of the user entering the query, then rows will be returned.

```
create or replace view RESTRICTED_NAMES
select * from NAME
 where Name = User;
```

This type of view is very useful when users require access to selected rows in a table. It prevents them from seeing any rows that do not match their Oracle username.

Views are powerful tools. There will be more to come on the subject in Chapter 18.

The **where** clause can be used to join two tables based on a common column. The resulting set of data can be turned into a view (with its own name), which can be treated as if it were a regular table itself. The power of a view is in its ability to limit or change the way data is seen by a user, even though the underlying tables themselves are not affected.

CHAPTER
4

The Basics of Object-Relational Databases

s of Oracle8, you can extend your relational database to include object-oriented concepts and structures. In this chapter, you will see an overview of the major object-oriented features available in Oracle8 and the impact they have on SQL. You will see detailed descriptions of more-advanced object-oriented features in later chapters; this chapter introduces the concepts and provides a general overview.

Do I Have to Use Objects?

Just because you use Oracle8 does not mean you have to use object-oriented programming (OOP) concepts when implementing your database. In fact, the database is referred to as an object-relational database management system (ORDBMS). The implication for developers is that three different "flavors" of Oracle are available:

Relational	The traditional Oracle relational database management system (RDBMS)
Object-relational	The traditional Oracle relational database, extended to include object-oriented concepts and structures such as abstract datatypes, nested tables, and varying arrays
Object-oriented	An object-oriented database whose design is based solely on object-oriented analysis and design

Oracle provides full support for all three implementations. If you have previously used Oracle as a relational database, you can use Oracle8 in the same manner. Since the OOP capabilities are extensions to the relational database, you can select which OOP features you wish to use when enhancing existing relational applications. If you want to redesign and implement your application using only OOP features, you can also do that. Regardless of the method you choose, you should first be familiar with the functions and features of the core Oracle relational database. Even if you plan to use only OOP capabilities, you still need to know the functions and datatypes available in Oracle, as well as its programming languages (SQL and PL/SQL).

In this chapter, you will see the basic parts of speech for SQL extended to include object-relational structures. In the following chapters, you will find detailed descriptions of Oracle's functions, followed by sections on PL/SQL, Oracle's procedural programming language, triggers, and procedures. Following the chapters on PL/SQL and procedures, you will explore several chapters on the implementation of OOP features. You should understand Oracle's functions, structures, and programming languages before implementing the more advanced OOP and object-relational structures.

Why Should I Use Objects?

Since you don't *have* to use objects, should you use them at all? At first, using OOP features may seem to complicate the design and implementation of your database systems—just as adding new features to any system may automatically increase its complexity. OOP adherents claim that objects reduce complexity by giving you an intuitive way of representing complex data and its relations. For example, if you want to move a car, you can either move the car (an object) or you can break it into its components (tires, steering column, and so on), move the components individually, and then perform a join in the new location. Treating the car as an object is a more natural way of relating to it and simplifies your interaction with it.

Besides simplifying your interactions with data, objects may help you in other ways. In this chapter, you will see examples of three benefits that come from using OOP features:

- **Object reuse** If you write OOP code, you increase the chances of reusing previously written code modules. Similarly, if you create OOP database objects, you increase the chances that the database objects can be reused.

- **Standards adherence** If you create standard objects, you increase the chance that they will be reused. If multiple applications or tables use the same set of database objects, you have created a de facto standard for the database objects. For example, if you create standard datatypes to use for all addresses, then all the addresses in your database will use the same internal format.

- **Defined access paths** For each object, you can define the procedures and functions that act upon it—you can unite the data and the methods that access it. Having the access paths defined in this manner allows you to standardize the data access methods and enhance the reusability of the objects.

The costs of using objects are chiefly the added complexity of the system and the time it takes to learn how to implement the features. But, as you'll see in this chapter, the basics of extending the Oracle RDBMS to include OOP capabilities build easily upon the relational model presented in the earlier chapters. The short time required to develop and use abstract datatypes, as shown later in this chapter, should help you gauge the time required for learning OOP features.

Everybody Has Objects

Everybody has data, and everybody has methods of interacting with data. Since the combination of data and methods makes up an object, everybody has objects. Consider Talbot's list of employees again, as shown in Figure 4-1. He has a standard

FIGURE 4-1.   *Addresses for Talbot's workers*

for the structure of an address—it starts with a person's name, followed by a lodging name, street name, and city name. When he adds a new person to his list of Dora's help, he follows the same procedure. Methods for the employees' address data could include the following:

Add_Person	For adding a person to the list
Update_Person	For updating a person's entry
Remove_Person	For deleting a person from the list
Count_Lodging	For counting the number of workers per lodging

As shown by the Count_Lodging method, methods do not have to manipulate the data; they can report on the data. They can perform functions on the data and return the result of the function to the user. For example, if Talbot stored his workers' birth dates, then an Age method could be used to calculate and report the workers' ages.

Oracle supports many different types of objects. In the following sections, you will see descriptions of the major object types available.

Abstract Datatypes

Abstract datatypes are datatypes that consist of one or more subtypes. Rather than being constrained to the standard Oracle datatypes of NUMBER, DATE, and VARCHAR2, abstract datatypes can more accurately describe your data. For example, an abstract datatype for addresses may consist of the following columns:

```
Street   VARCHAR2(50)
City     VARCHAR2(25)
State    CHAR(2)
Zip      NUMBER
```

When you create a table that uses address information, you could create a column that uses the abstract datatype for addresses—and thus contains the Street, City, State, and Zip columns that are part of that datatype. Abstract datatypes can be nested; they can contain references to other abstract datatypes. You will see a detailed example of nested abstract datatypes in the next section of this chapter.

Two of the benefits listed earlier for objects—reuse and standards adherence—are realized from using abstract datatypes. When you create an abstract datatype, you create a standard for the representation of abstract data elements (such as addresses, people, or companies). If you use the same abstract datatype in multiple places, then you can be sure that the same logical data is represented in the same manner in those places. The reuse of the abstract datatype leads to the enforcement of standard representation for the data.

You can use abstract datatypes to create *object tables.* In an object table, the columns of the table map to the columns of the abstract datatype.

Nested Tables

A *nested table* is a table within a table. A nested table is a collection of rows, represented as a column within the main table. For each record within the main table, the nested table may contain multiple rows. In one sense, it's a way of storing a one-to-many relationship within one table. Consider a table that contains information about departments, each of which may have many projects in progress at any one time. In a strictly relational model, you would create two separate tables—DEPARTMENT and PROJECT.

Nested tables allow you to store the information about projects within the DEPARTMENT table. The PROJECT table records can be accessed directly via the DEPARTMENT table, without the need to perform a join. The ability to select the data without traversing joins may make the data easier to access for users.

Even if you do not define methods for accessing the nested data, you have clearly associated the department and project data. In a strictly relational model, the association between the DEPARTMENT and PROJECT tables would be accomplished via foreign key relationships. For examples of nested tables and other collection types, see Chapter 29.

Varying Arrays

A *varying array* is, like a nested table, a collection. A varying array is a set of objects, each with the same datatype. The size of the array is limited when it is created. When you create a varying array in a table, the array is treated as a column in the main table. Conceptually, a varying array is a nested table with a limited set of rows.

Varying arrays, also known as VARRAYS, allow you to store repeating values in tables. For example, suppose you have a PROJECT table, and projects have workers assigned to them. In the example system, a project can have many workers, and a worker can work on multiple projects. In a strictly relational implementation, you can create a PROJECT table, a WORKER table, and an intersection table PROJECT_WORKER that stores the relationships between them.

You can use varying arrays to store the worker names in the PROJECT table. If projects are limited to ten workers or fewer, you can create a varying array with a limit of ten entries. The datatype for the varying arrays will be whatever datatype is appropriate for the worker name values. The varying array can then be populated, so that for each project, you can select the names of all of the project's workers—without querying the WORKER table. For each project record in the PROJECT table, there would be multiple entries in the varying array holding the worker names. For examples of varying arrays and other collection types, see Chapter 29.

Large Objects

A *large object,* or *LOB,* is capable of storing large volumes of data. The LOB datatypes available are BLOB, CLOB, NCLOB, and BFILE. The BLOB datatype is used for binary data, and can extend to 4GB in length. The CLOB datatype stores character data and can also store up to 4GB. The NCLOB datatype is used to store CLOB data for multibyte character sets. The data for BLOB, CLOB, and NCLOB datatypes is stored inside the database. Thus, you could have a single row in the database that is over 4GB in length.

The fourth LOB datatype, BFILE, is a pointer to an external file. The files referenced by BFILEs exist on the operating system; the database only maintains a pointer to the file. The size of the external file is limited only by the operating system. Since the data is stored outside the database, Oracle does not maintain the concurrency or integrity of the data.

You can use multiple LOBs per table. For example, you could have a table with a CLOB column and two BLOB columns. This is an improvement over the LONG datatype, since you can only have one LONG per table. Oracle provides a number of functions and procedures to manipulate and select LOB data. Chapter 30 is dedicated to LOBs; see that chapter for a detailed description of LOB creation and use.

References

Nested tables and varying arrays are *embedded objects*—they are physically embedded within another object. Another type of object, called a *referenced object,* is physically separate from the objects that refer to it. References, also known as REFs, are essentially pointers to row objects. A "row object" is different from a "column object." An example of a "column object" is a varying array—it is an object that is treated as a column in a table. A "row object," on the other hand, always represents a row.

The implementation of references is described in Chapter 31. As noted earlier in this chapter, you do not have to use all the available OOP capabilities within Oracle. References are typically among the last OOP features implemented when migrating a relational application to an object-relational or OOP approach.

Object Views

Object views allow you to add OOP concepts on top of your existing relational tables. For example, you can create an abstract datatype based on an existing table's definition. Object views give you the benefits of relational table storage and OOP structures. Object views allow you to begin to develop OOP features within your relational database—a bridge between the relational and OOP worlds.

Before using object views, you should be familiar with abstract datatypes and triggers. See Chapter 28 for a full description of object views.

Naming Conventions for Objects

Chapter 2 ended with a brief discussion of the naming standards for tables and columns. In general, you should use common, descriptive words for table and column names. Part VII develops the rules for naming conventions more completely, but for the OOP examples in this book, the following rules will be enforced:

- Table and column names are singular (such as EMPLOYEE, Name, and State)

- Abstract datatype names are singular nouns with an _TY suffix (such as PERSON_TY or ADDRESS_TY)

- Table and datatype names are always uppercase (such as EMPLOYEE or PERSON_TY)

- Column names are always capitalized (such as State and Start_Date)

■ Object view names are singular nouns with an _OV suffix (such as PERSON_OV or ADDRESS_OV)

■ Nested table names are plural nouns with an _NT suffix (such as WORKERS_NT)

■ Varying array names are plural nouns with an _VA suffix (such as WORKERS_VA)

The name of an object should consist of two parts: the core object name and the suffix. The core object name should follow your naming standards; the suffixes help to identify special types of objects.

Features of Objects

An object has a name, a standard representation, and a standard collection of operations that affect it. The operations that affect the object are called *methods*. Thus, an abstract datatype has a name, a standard representation, and defined methods for accessing the data. All objects that use the abstract datatype will share the same structure, methods, and representation. Abstract datatypes model *classes* of data within the database.

Abstract datatypes are part of an OOP concept called *abstraction*—the conceptual existence of classes within the database. As noted earlier in this chapter, abstract datatypes may be nested. It is not necessary to create physical tables at each level of abstraction; instead, the structural existence of the abstract types is sufficient. The methods attached to each level of abstraction may be called from the higher levels of abstraction. If the PERSON datatype uses the ADDRESS datatype, for example, you could access the ADDRESS datatype's methods during a call to a PERSON datatype.

During the creation of objects, they *inherit* the structures of the data elements they are descended from. For example, consider the earlier example of a car; if "car" is a class of data, then "sedan," a type of car, would inherit the structural definitions of "car." From a data perspective, nested abstract datatypes inherit the representations of their "parents."

In addition to inheriting data structures, classes can inherit the behavior of their "parent" classes—a concept called *implementation inheritance*. That is, you can execute a method against an object even if the object does not use that method—provided the method is defined for one of the classes that are the "parents" of the current object.

If a data structure can only be accessed via a defined set of methods, then the structure is said to be *encapsulated* by the methods. In an encapsulated system, the methods define all the access paths to the data.

However, Oracle's OOP implementation is based on a relational system; and in a relational system, the means of accessing data is never fully limited. Thus, data within Oracle usually can't be completely encapsulated. You can approximate encapsulation by limiting access to tables and forcing all access to be accomplished via procedures and functions, but this prevents you from realizing the true power of a relational database.

Consider the LOCATION and WEATHER queries performed in Chapter 1. If the WEATHER data had been fully encapsulated, you never would have been able to write the simple query that told you about the weather in different cities. As noted earlier in this chapter, Oracle supports the relational, object-relational, and OOP models. Since Oracle supports all three models via a relational engine, and since encapsulation violates the driving ideals of relational databases, encapsulation is the most difficult OOP concept to enforce in Oracle.

Oracle8 does not presently support an OOP concept called *polymorphism*, which is the ability of the same instruction to be interpreted different ways by different objects.

A Common Object Example

Let's consider an object found in most systems: addresses. Even in a system as simple as Talbot's, addresses are maintained and selected. In the case of Talbot's ledger, the addresses for workers were maintained (refer to Figure 4-1). These addresses follow a standard format—the name of the lodging, followed by the street address and city for the lodging. You can use this as the basis for an abstract datatype for addresses. First, expand it to include additional address information, such as the state and Zip code. Next, use the **create type** command to create an abstract datatype:

```
create type ADDRESS_TY as object
(Street  VARCHAR2(50),
 City    VARCHAR2(25),
 State   CHAR(2),
 Zip     NUMBER);
/
```

The **create type** command is the most important command in object-relational databases. What the command in this example says is "create an abstract datatype named ADDRESS_TY. It will be represented as having four attributes, named Street, City, State, and Zip, using the defined datatypes and lengths for each column." So far, no methods have been created by the user—but the database has internally created methods that will be used whenever the ADDRESS_TY object is accessed. For information on creating your own methods, see Chapter 28 and the **create type body** command entry in the Alphabetical Reference.

Within the **create type** command, the **as object** clause explicitly identifies ADDRESS_TY as an OOP implementation.

Now that the ADDRESS_TY datatype exists, you can use it within other datatypes. For example, Talbot may decide to create a standard datatype for people. People have names and addresses. Therefore, Talbot can create the following type:

```
create type PERSON_TY as object
(Name        VARCHAR2(25),
 Address     ADDRESS_TY);
/
```

What did Talbot do here? First, the datatype was given a name—PERSON_TY— and identified as an object via the **as object** clause. Then, two columns were defined. This line,

```
(Name        VARCHAR2(25),
```

defines the first column of PERSON_TY's representation. The second line,

```
Address     ADDRESS_TY);
```

defines the second column of PERSON_TY's representation. The second column, Address, uses the ADDRESS_TY abstract datatype previously created. What are the columns within ADDRESS_TY? According to the ADDRESS_TY definition, they are

```
create type ADDRESS_TY as object
(Street   VARCHAR2(50),
 City     VARCHAR2(25),
 State    CHAR(2),
 Zip      NUMBER);
/
```

Based on these definitions, a PERSON_TY entry will have Name, Street, City, State, and Zip columns—even though only one of those columns is explicitly defined within the PERSON_TY type definition.

You can imagine how this capability to define and reuse abstract datatypes can simplify data representation within your database. For example, a Street column is seldom used by itself; it is almost always used as part of an address. Abstract datatypes allow you to join elements together and deal with the whole—the address—instead of the parts—the Street and other columns that constitute the address.

Talbot can now use the PERSON_TY datatype in the process of table creation.

The Structure of a Simple Object

Try as you might, you can't insert data into PERSON_TY. The reason is straightforward: a datatype describes data, it does not store data. You cannot store data in a NUMBER datatype, and you cannot store data in a datatype that you define, either. To store data, you have to create a table that uses your datatype.

The following command creates a table named CUSTOMER. A customer has a Customer_ID and all the attributes of a person (via the PERSON_TY datatype).

```
create table CUSTOMER
(Customer_ID    NUMBER,
 Person         PERSON_TY);
```

What happens if you **describe** the CUSTOMER table? The output will show the following column definitions:

```
describe CUSTOMER
```

Name	Null?	Type
CUSTOMER_ID		NUMBER
PERSON		PERSON_TY

The **describe** command shows that the Person column of the CUSTOMER table has been defined using the PERSON_TY datatype. You can further explore the data dictionary to see the construction of the PERSON_TY datatype. The columns of an abstract datatype are referred to as its *attributes*. Within the data dictionary, the USER_TYPE_ATTRS view displays information about the attributes of a user's abstract datatypes.

NOTE
The data dictionary *is a series of tables and views that contains information about the structures and users in the database. You can query the data dictionary for useful information about the database objects that you own or have been granted access to. See Chapter 35 for a user-oriented guide to the data dictionary views available to you.*

In the following query, the name, length, and datatype are selected for each of the attributes within the PERSON_TY datatype:

```
select Attr_Name,
       Length,
```

```
        Attr_Type_Name
  from USER_TYPE_ATTRS
 where Type_Name = 'PERSON_TY';


ATTR_NAME                          LENGTH ATTR_TYPE_NAME
----------------------------- ---------- ------------------
NAME                                   25 VARCHAR2
ADDRESS                                   ADDRESS_TY
```

The query output shows that the PERSON_TY type consists of a Name column (defined as a VARCHAR2 column with a length of 25) and an Address column (defined using the ADDRESS_TY type). You can query USER_TYPE_ATTRS again to see the attributes of the ADDRESS_TY datatype:

```
select Attr_Name,
       Length,
       Attr_Type_Name
  from USER_TYPE_ATTRS
 where Type_Name = 'ADDRESS_TY';


ATTR_NAME                          LENGTH ATTR_TYPE_NAME
----------------------------- ---------- ------------------
STREET                                 50 VARCHAR2
CITY                                   25 VARCHAR2
STATE                                   2 CHAR
ZIP                                      NUMBER
```

You will not often be called upon to completely decompose the types that constitute a table; but if you need to, you can use the queries shown in this section to "drill down" through the layers of abstraction. Once you know the structures of each of the abstract datatypes used by the table, you can insert records into it.

NOTE
If you do not own the tables and types you are trying to find information about, you can query ALL_TAB_COLUMNS and ALL_TYPE_ATTRS in place of USER_TAB_COLUMNS and USER_TYPE_ATTRS. The ALL_TAB_COLUMNS and ALL_TYPE_ATTRS views show all the columns and attributes for the tables and types that you either own or have been granted access to. Both ALL_TAB_COLUMNS and ALL_TYPE_ATTRS contain an Owner column that identifies the table's or type's owner. See Chapter 35 for a description of the data dictionary views.

Inserting Records into **CUSTOMER**

Oracle creates methods, called *constructor methods,* for data management when you create an abstract datatype. A constructor method is a program that is named after the datatype; its parameters are the names of the attributes defined for the datatype. When you need to insert records into a table based on abstract datatypes, you use the constructor methods. For example, the CUSTOMER table uses the PERSON_TY datatype, and the PERSON_TY datatype uses the ADDRESS_TY datatype. To insert a record into the CUSTOMER table, you need to insert a record using the PERSON_TY and ADDRESS_TY datatypes' constructor methods.

In the following example, a record is inserted into CUSTOMER using the constructor methods for the PERSON_TY and ADDRESS_TY datatypes. The constructor methods for these datatypes are shown in bold in the example; they have the same names as the datatypes:

```
insert into CUSTOMER values
(1,
 PERSON_TY('NEIL MULLANE',
           ADDRESS_TY('57 MT PLEASANT ST',
                      'FINN', 'NH', 11111)));

1 row created.
```

The **insert** command provides the values to be inserted as a row in the CUSTOMER table. The values provided must match the columns in the table.

In this example, a Customer_ID value of 1 is specified. Next, the values for the Person column are inserted, using the PERSON_TY constructor method (shown in bold). Within the PERSON_TY datatype, a Name is specified, and then the ADDRESS_TY constructor method is used to insert the Address values. So, for the record inserted in the example, the Name value is 'NEIL MULLANE', and the Street value is '57 MT PLEASANT ST'. Note that the parameters for the constructor method are in the same order as the attributes of the datatype.

A second record can be inserted into CUSTOMER, using the exact same format for the calls to the constructor methods (again shown in bold):

```
insert into CUSTOMER
(2,
 PERSON_TY('SEYMOUR HESTER',
           ADDRESS_TY('1 STEPAHEAD RD',
                      'BRIANT', 'NH', 11111)));
```

The second record has now been inserted into the CUSTOMER table. You only need to use constructor methods when you are manipulating records in tables that use abstract datatypes.

Selecting from Abstract Datatypes

If you want to select the Customer_ID values from CUSTOMER, you simply query that column's values from the table:

```
select Customer_ID
   from CUSTOMER;

CUSTOMER_ID
-----------
          1
          2
```

Querying the Customer_ID values is straightforward, since that column is a normal datatype within the CUSTOMER table.

What if you want to select the persons' names from CUSTOMER? You couldn't query it as shown here:

```
select Name    /* this will not work */
   from CUSTOMER
```

because Name is not a column in CUSTOMER. You'll get the following error:

```
select Name
       *
ERROR at line 1:
ORA-00904: invalid column name
```

Oracle reports this error because Name is not a column within the CUSTOMER table. Name is an attribute within the PERSON_TY abstract datatype. To see the Name values, you therefore need to query the Name attribute within the Person column. You can't query PERSON_TY directly; it's just a datatype, not a table. The query structure is shown in the following example:

```
select Customer_ID, C.Person.Name
   from CUSTOMER C;
```

Notice the syntax for the Name column:

```
            C.Person.Name
```

First, note that the access of the datatype's attribute requires the use of a table alias. A *table alias,* also known as a *correlation variable,* allows Oracle to resolve any ambiguity regarding the name of the object being selected.

As a column name, Person.Name points to the Name attribute within the PERSON_TY datatype. The format for the column name is

```
Correlation.Column.Attribute
```

This may be a little confusing. During **insert**s, you use the name of the *datatype* (actually, you use the name of the constructor method, which is the same as the name of the datatype). During **select**s, you use the name of the *column*.

What if you want to **select** the Street values from the CUSTOMER table? The Street column is part of the ADDRESS_TY datatype, which in turn is part of the PERSON_TY datatype. To select this data, extend the Column.Attribute format to include the nested type. The format will be as follows:

```
Correlation.Column.Column.Attribute
```

Thus, to select the Street attribute of the Address attribute within the Person column, your query will be

```
select C.Person.Address.Street
  from CUSTOMER C;

PERSON.ADDRESS.STREET
--------------------------------------------------
57 MT PLEASANT ST
1 STEPAHEAD RD
```

The syntax

```
select C.Person.Address.Street
```

tells Oracle exactly how to find the Street attribute. The correlation variable can be any name you choose (following Oracle's naming standards for tables) as long as it does not conflict with the name of any other table in the query.

If you use abstract datatypes, you can neither **insert** nor **select** values for the abstract datatypes' attributes without knowing the exact structure of the attributes. For example, you cannot **select** the CUSTOMER table's City values unless you know that City is part of the Address attribute, and that Address is part of the Person column. You cannot **insert** or **update** a column's values unless you know the datatype that it is a part of and the nesting of datatypes needed to reach it.

What if you need to reference the City column as part of a **where** clause? As in the prior examples, you can refer to City as part of the Address attribute, nested within the Person column, as shown next.

```
select C.Person.Name,
       C.Person.Address.City
  from CUSTOMER C
 where C.Person.Address.City like 'F%';

PERSON.NAME                 PERSON.ADDRESS.CITY
------------------------    ------------------------
NEIL MULLANE                FINN
```

When updating data within abstract datatypes, refer to its attributes via the Column.Attribute syntax shown in the preceding examples. For example, to change the City value for the customers who live in Briant, NH, execute the following **update**:

```
update CUSTOMER C
   set C.Person.Address.City = 'HART'
 where C.Person.Address.City = 'BRIANT';
```

Oracle will use the **where** clause to find the right records to update, and the **set** clause to set the new values for the rows' City columns.

As shown in these examples, using abstract datatypes simplifies the representation of the data but may complicate the way in which you query and work with the data. You need to weigh the benefits of abstract datatypes—more intuitive representation of the data—against the potential increase in complexity of data access.

In later chapters, you will see descriptions of the use and implementation of additional OOP features, such as nested tables and varying arrays. Abstract datatypes provide a common starting point for implementing OOP features within an Oracle database. In Chapter 28, you will see further uses of abstract datatypes; nested tables and varying arrays are described in Chapter 29.

Object-Oriented Analysis and Design

In Chapter 2, you saw the basics of normalization—designing a relational database application. When you consider adding in OOP features, such as abstract datatypes, you need to approach database design from a slightly different perspective. For example, in traditional normalization, you try to relate each attribute to its primary key. In OOP design, you go beyond normalization and seek groups of columns that define a common object representation.

For example, in relational design, a CUSTOMER table may be created as follows:

```
create table CUSTOMER
(Customer_ID  NUMBER primary key,
 Name         VARCHAR2(25),
 Street       VARCHAR2(50),
 City         VARCHAR2(25),
 State        CHAR(2),
 Zip          NUMBER);
```

From a Third Normal Form perspective, this is a proper representation of the CUSTOMER table. Each of the attributes is related solely to the Customer_ID (the primary key of the table). But looking at the table, you can see that there are columns that, when grouped together, represent an object. The examples earlier in this chapter grouped the Street, City, State, and Zip columns into a single datatype called ADDRESS_TY. Creating the ADDRESS_TY abstract datatype allows you to use that datatype in multiple tables. If the abstract datatype is used in multiple relational tables, then you benefit from object reuse and from adherence to the standard definition of attribute structures.

Once you define abstract datatypes, you should look for relationships between them to see if they should be nested (as PERSON_TY and ADDRESS_TY are). When analyzing your database design for types, you should focus on those types that most likely will be reused or that will always behave in the same manner. Once you have defined the types, you can apply them in the creation of new database objects. If your tables already exist, you can use object views to overlay OOP designs on relational tables. See Chapter 28 for information on object views.

Once your types are defined, you can create methods for each type. The methods define the behavior of data access involving the types. Usually, methods are created based on "use cases"—how is the data used? There should be methods to account for each manner in which the data is used. You will see examples of user-defined methods in Chapter 28.

Going Forward

Oracle enables you to use the database as a strictly relational database, as an object-relational database, or as an OOP database. At its core, Oracle is a relational database; the OOP features are implemented as extensions on the relational engine. Therefore, you should be very familiar with Oracle's relational features before starting to use its OOP features. This part of this book mirrors that approach. In Part II, you will see detailed descriptions of Oracle's implementation of the SQL language. That part of the book focuses on the implementation of SQL for relational tables; the same functions will work against tables that use OOP features such as abstract datatypes. Following the chapters on SQL usage, you will see sections on PL/SQL (Oracle's procedural extension to SQL) and Java. Once you know PL/SQL, you will be able to create your own methods for your datatypes, as explained in the OOP-related chapters. When planning to use the advanced features, remember that they are extensions to SQL; a firm grounding in SQL is essential to their effective use.

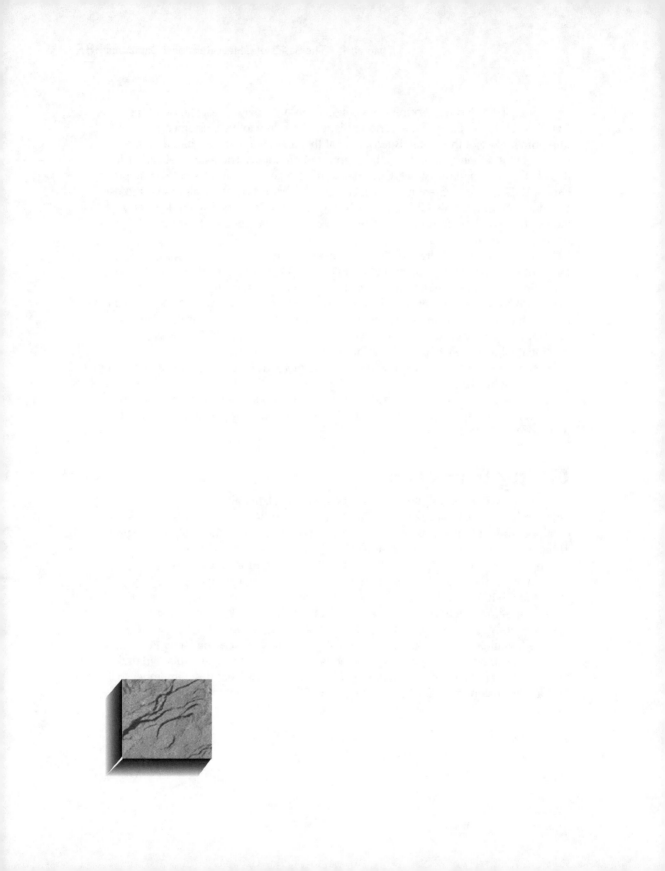

CHAPTER
5

Introduction to
Web-Enabled Databases

any of the examples in this book focus on the use of SQL within the database. The examples assume that you can log in directly to an Oracle database, or that you are using a client-based tool that allows you to enter commands into a database. With the introduction of Web-based technologies, your ability to interact with the database has been augmented by new options. You still need to know SQL, but to take advantage of these options, you may need to understand Web listeners, new toolsets, languages such as Java, and application programming interfaces (APIs) such as JDBC and SQLJ.

The complexity of the environment may be daunting at first. Consider a simple architecture, shown in Figure 5-1, in which two computers are involved in the application—a client and a server. The database resides on the server, and the user interacts with the server via the client. The client and the server rely on the underlying network for their communications, and each runs a version of Oracle's Net8 tool. The server listens for Net8 requests issued by the client.

Now consider a three-tier architecture, shown in Figure 5-2. A three-tier architecture has three separate components: a client, an application server, and a database server. In implementing a three-tier architecture, you have many more choices available than you have in the traditional client-server architecture. The communications protocol used to communicate between the client and the application server can be different from that used to communicate between the application server and the database server. The workload distribution among the three components can vary widely across applications. The performance and reliability of the components in both stand-alone and networked mode can influence the success or failure of the application.

NOTE
In some three-tier implementations, the application server and the database server reside on the same physical server.

Client   Network   Server

FIGURE 5-1.   *Client-server architecture*

FIGURE 5-2.   *Three-tier architecture*

The three-tier architecture significantly increases your opportunities for distributing an application's workload over multiple servers. However, it also increases the number of points of failure in the architecture, and complicates the configuration of a preproduction test environment. Oracle supports many different ways of implementing a three-tier architecture, and you will need to select the architecture that best suits the needs of your application. You should reevaluate your environment needs for each new application rather than assume that a single architecture will seamlessly support every desired outcome.

Most Web-enabled databases rely on a three-tier model. Typically, an existing database server is made available for Web-based access. To make the database available, the server must be accessible via an external network. To provide this network access, a second server is commonly used as a firewall, restricting the kinds of commands that can be passed to the database server. The application server can act as a firewall.

Consider the architecture shown in Figure 5-3. Based on Figure 5-2, it shows one possible configuration for a Web-enabled database. In Figure 5-3, the client is a computer with access to the Internet, running a browser. That client communicates with the application server via the Hypertext Transfer Protocol (HTTP). The application

FIGURE 5-3.   *Common Web-based implementation*

server, in turn, executes commands against the database, formats the results in Hypertext Markup Language (HTML), and returns the results to the client.

In this configuration, the application server provides authentication services (to make sure the client is allowed to initiate the request), database connection services, and application processing services. The client's role is to initiate the request and display the results returned, while the database serves as the repository for the data. Clearly, you should restrict the privileges available to the application server to make sure only authorized commands can be performed on behalf of clients.

Where Does SQL Fit in?

SQL is the standard language for accessing Oracle data, so where in a Web-based architecture does it fit? SQL and Oracle's procedural language, PL/SQL, is commonly used in the following places:

- Within the database server, in the form of stored procedures and packages (see Chapter 27)

- In commands executed to create and maintain the database structures

- In direct queries of the database

- In scripts and batch processes executed on the database server

- In commands issued by the application server

You may have additional places within your architecture where SQL is used, but the preceding are the most common. Since the client and the application server may not be communicating via SQL, you need to have a Web listener running on the application server in order to receive HTTP requests. The application server will then be able to receive requests from clients (via HTTP) and begin to act on them. If the application server communicates with the database server via SQL, then the application server will require Net8 as well.

Instead of using standard SQL to communicate with the database server, the application server can use Java Database Connectivity (JDBC) and SQLJ (a precompiler that generates JDBC code). See Chapter 33 for details on the creation and use of JDBC and SQLJ programs. If you use JDBC or SQLJ, you still need to provide Net8 on the application server to support database connectivity. You also need to know SQL and the ways in which JDBC and SQLJ provide support for different result sets.

Where Does Java Fit in?

With the ubiquity of Java on the Web, you may be tempted to create a fully Java-based database application. In that architecture, the client communicates with the application server via either HTTP or the Internet Inter-ORB Protocol (IIOP). Within the database, you can create Java classes, and the application server would interact with those Java classes via IIOP. Thus, you can create a Web-enabled database that does not rely on Net8 for any of its connectivity.

Within the database, you can write your stored procedures in either PL/SQL (see Chapter 27) or Java (see Chapter 34). In general, you should use these languages for the functions they perform best: PL/SQL for database interaction and Java for non-database-related functions. If you use Java exclusively throughout your application, you should expect to encounter performance or functionality limitations during its production usage.

Java is well suited for use on the client and application server. In your application development process, you should test the implications of using Java in place of PL/SQL or SQL for your database access. PL/SQL has been part of the Oracle kernel for over a decade and is well suited for quick data retrieval and manipulation. Although Java technically fits into all the servers shown in Figure 5-3, you need to evaluate how well it performs for your purposes.

Where Does WebDB Fit in?

WebDB is an Oracle product that is used to create Web sites and applications (WebDB is described in Chapter 37). The core data for the sites and applications is stored in Oracle tables. When a client accesses the site, the client's request is handled by a Web listener, such as the Oracle Application Server (OAS). The Web listener executes PL/SQL functions stored within the database. Those functions return the requested data embedded within HTML tags. The listener then returns that data to the client, and the site is displayed within the client's browser.

The table concept introduced in Chapter 1 may help to illustrate this process. To display the WEATHER table in a client browser, you could create a WebDB application. The WEATHER table will reside within the database on the database server. To display the data in tabular format, the query by the application server will embed HTML table formatting tags in the output. The result is an HTML file that contains the embedded HTML table formatting tags along with the data from the WEATHER table's rows.

In Chapter 37, you will see the basic configuration of WebDB and its usage. WebDB is rapidly changing as new versions are introduced. You can presently use WebDB for a variety of purposes:

- Web site development

- Web application development

- Ad hoc querying of the data dictionary

- Ad hoc querying of application tables

- Database administration

You can use WebDB for many purposes, but you should consider your desired outcomes before implementing it. As WebDB requires a three-tier architecture, you need to make sure this architecture fits your environment and your processing capabilities.

Where Does iFS Fit in?

You can store large objects (LOBs) within the database by using the LOB datatypes—Chapter 30 is devoted to this topic. Since you can access the database via the Web, why not store all of your files inside the database? You could then access them via the Web in the same way you access tabular data via WebDB. That is the basic thrust behind Oracle's Internet File System (iFS) product.

NOTE
At the time of this writing, the iFS product has not yet been released in production, so its features and capabilities may change from its current set. As features are made available in a production-released product, supplemental articles will be posted on http://www.osborne.com, the publisher's web site.

The iFS architecture greatly expands the basic capabilities previously illustrated in Figure 5-3. Instead of retrieving only structured data from relational tables on the database server, iFS enables you to retrieve unstructured data (such as a word processing document or a presentation) from that server. You can create and manage relationships between the unstructured documents and the structured data within your tables.

Consider Talbot's list of workers. Each worker has a record in the WORKER table. Each worker may have a résumé. To store that résumé in the database for later retrieval, you have several options that do not require iFS:

■ Insert the résumé text into a VARCHAR2 or LONG column in the database (see Chapter 7)

■ Insert the résumé text into a CLOB or BLOB datatype column (see Chapter 30)

■ Store the file at the operating system level and use a BFILE datatype column to point to it (see Chapter 30)

Each of these options has limitations. If you insert the text of the résumé into the database, then you lose all the formatting commands—page breaks, bold, and so forth. If you insert the file into a BLOB datatype, then your ability to manipulate the file is limited. If you store the file at the operating system level and use a BFILE datatype, then there is no true connection between the database and the file—you can delete the file at the operating system level, leaving the database with an invalid pointer to a file that no longer exists.

Managing the connections between structured entries in tables and unstructured files becomes even more difficult when you consider some of the basic features of any mature file management system: access control and versioning. In a file system, you should be able to limit the access to specific files within a directory, based on the users issuing the request. At the database level, files are stored as separate rows—so you would need the ability to issue row-level grants to your users.

In terms of versioning, file systems offer the ability to maintain multiple versions of a file, or to revert to an earlier version of the file. Versioning considerations are common to unstructured data management, but are not commonly part of structured data management. Consider the WORKER table entries. If one of the workers changes his or her name, Talbot would go into the WORKER table and update the row to reflect the new name. As soon as the change is committed, the old value is gone; no older version is automatically maintained by Oracle. Each row exists once. You could build an application to track such changes (via triggers, as described in Chapter 26), but that is not a standard feature of Oracle-based applications. By contrast, you expect that a file system will give you the opportunity to store multiple versions of a file, with the ability to rename or alter that file as you wish. You would also expect that the file system would give you the ability to set different privilege levels on different versions of the same document.

Via a three-tier architecture, iFS lets users manage their files over a network. The files may be stored directly in the database. As a result, database administrators (DBAs) will need to perform some of the functions currently performed by the system administrators for your servers. Unstructured data typically requires more space per row than structured data—the workers' résumé files may be larger than their WORKER table entries. As a result, the size of the database may increase dramatically. The increase in database size will increase the amount of time required to create, back up, restore, tune, and administer the database. The amount of disk space or tape space required to back up the database will likewise increase unless you specifically exclude the unstructured portions of the data from your backups.

Enabling unstructured files to be accessed via a three-tier Oracle-based architecture requires that the files be transported from the database to the application server, and from the application server to the client. You need to weigh the network and server performance implications of that architecture against its benefits: the ability to integrate the structured data in your tables with the unstructured data in your files. Being able to integrate these two types of data allows you to integrate your requests for data, potentially streamlining your application architecture and supporting more sophisticated queries.

Within a Web-enabled database, there is room for all technologies—PL/SQL in packages, SQL in scripts, Java in classes, WebDB as a user interface, and iFS as an integrating technology. As new development tools and integration components become available, look to complement your current architecture. Integrating your data access methods and data presentation technologies should simplify your application maintenance and design, giving you an extendable platform for your future application requirements.

PART
II

SQL and SQL*PLUS

CHAPTER
6

Basic SQLPLUS Reports
and Commands

QLPLUS is usually thought of as a kind of interactive report writer. It uses SQL to get information from the Oracle database, and lets you create polished, well-formatted reports by giving you easy control over titles, column headings, subtotals and totals, reformatting of numbers and text, and much more. It also can be used to change the database by using **insert**, **update**, and **delete** commands in SQL. SQLPLUS can even be used as a code generator, where a series of commands in SQLPLUS can dynamically build a program and then execute it.

SQLPLUS is most commonly used for simple queries and printed reports. Getting SQLPLUS to format information in reports according to your taste and needs requires only a handful of *commands,* or keywords that instruct SQLPLUS how to behave. They are listed in Table 6-1. Detailed explanations, examples, and additional features of each of these commands are given in the Alphabetical Reference section of this book.

In this chapter, you will see a basic report that was written using SQLPLUS, along with an explanation of the features used to create it. If building a report seems a bit daunting at first, don't worry. Once you try the steps, you'll find them simple to understand, and they will soon become familiar.

You can write SQLPLUS reports while working interactively with SQLPLUS—that is, you can type commands about page headings, column titles, formatting, breaks, totals, and so on, and then execute a SQL query, and SQLPLUS will immediately produce the report formatted to your specifications. For quick answers to simple questions that aren't likely to recur, this is a fine approach. More common, however, are complex reports that need to be produced periodically, and that you'll want to print rather than just view on the screen. Unfortunately, when you quit SQLPLUS, it promptly forgets every instruction you've given it. If you were restricted to using SQLPLUS only in this interactive way, then running the same report at a later time would require typing everything all over again.

The alternative is very straightforward. You simply type the commands, line by line, into a file. SQLPLUS can then read this file as if it were a script, and execute your commands just as if you were typing them. In effect, you create a report program, but you do it without a programmer or a compiler. You create this file using any of the popular editor programs available or even (given certain restrictions) a word processor.

The editor is not a part of Oracle. Editors come in hundreds of varieties, and every company or person seems to have a favorite. Oracle realized this, and decided to let you choose which editor program to use, rather than packaging a program with Oracle and forcing you to use it. When you're ready to use your editor program, you suspend SQLPLUS, jump over to the editor program, create or change your SQLPLUS report program (also called a *start file*), and then jump back to SQLPLUS right at the spot you left and run that report (see Figure 6-1).

SQLPLUS also has a tiny, built-in editor of its own, sometimes called the *command line editor,* which allows you to quickly modify a SQL query without leaving SQLPLUS. Its use will be covered later in this chapter.

Command	Definition
remark	Tells SQLPLUS that the words to follow are to be treated as comments, not instructions.
set headsep	The heading separator identifies the single character that tells SQLPLUS to split a title onto two or more lines.
ttitle	Sets the top title for each page of a report.
btitle	Sets the bottom title for each page of a report.
column	Gives SQLPLUS a variety of instructions on the heading, format, and treatment of a column.
break on	Tells SQLPLUS where to put spaces between sections of a report, or where to break for subtotals and totals.
compute sum	Makes SQLPLUS calculate subtotals.
set linesize	Sets the maximum number of characters allowed on any line of the report.
set pagesize	Sets the maximum number of lines per page.
set newpage	Sets the number of blank lines between pages.
spool	Moves a report you would normally see displayed on the screen into a file, so you can print it.
/*/**	Marks the beginning and ending of a comment within a SQL entry. Similar to **remark**.
--	Marks the beginning of an inline comment within a SQL entry. Treats everything from the mark to the end of the line as a comment. Similar to **remark**.
set pause	Makes the screen display stop between pages of display.
save	Saves the SQL query you're creating into the file of your choice.
host	Sends any command to the host operating system.
start	Tells SQLPLUS to follow (execute) the instructions you've saved in a file.
edit	Pops you out of SQLPLUS and into an editor of your choice.
define _editor	Tells SQLPLUS the name of the editor of your choice.

TABLE 6-1. *Basic SQLPLUS Commands*

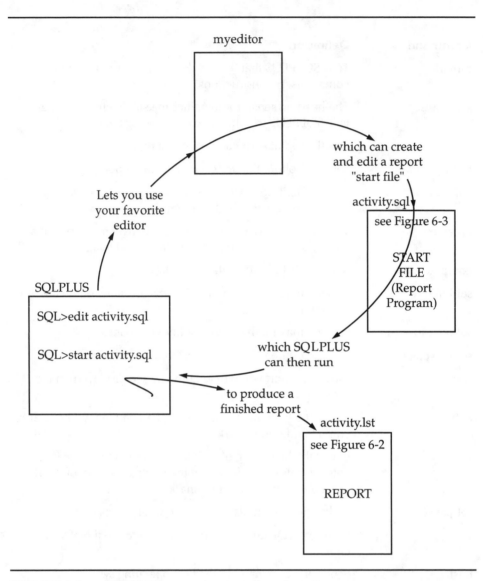

FIGURE 6-1.   *SQLPLUS lets you use your favorite editor to create report programs*

Building a Simple Report

Figure 6-2 shows a quick and easy report produced for G. B. Talbot, detailing items he sold during the second half of 1901 and his income for that period.

```
Sat Feb 03                                                    page    1
                            Sales by Product During 1901
                            Second Six Months (Jul-Dec)


                          What Was
Date        To Whom Sold  Sold                Quan  Type    RATE     Ext
---------   ------------------  ------------------  ----  ------  -----  -----
15-OCT-01 GENERAL STORE   BEEF                 935  LB      0.03   28.05
15-NOV-01 FRED FULLER                           37  LB      0.04    1.48
21-NOV-01 ROLAND BRANDT                        116  LB      0.06    6.96
22-NOV-01 GERHARDT KENTGEN                      118  LB      0.06    7.08
                          *****************                    -----
                          sum                                  43.57


03-OCT-01 GARY KENTGEN    BOOT BETWEEN HORSE     1  EACH   12.50   12.50
11-NOV-01 PAT LAVAY                              1  EACH    6.00    6.00
                          *****************                    -----
                          sum                                  18.50


29-AUG-01 GERHARDT KENTGEN BUTTER                5  LB      0.23    1.15
11-NOV-01 PAT LAVAY                              1  LB      0.15    0.15
16-NOV-01 VICTORIA LYNN                          5  LB      0.16    0.80
18-NOV-01 JOHN PEARSON                           6  LB      0.16    0.96
                          *****************                    -----
                          sum                                   3.06


                          What Was
Date        To Whom Sold  Sold                Quan  Type    RATE     Ext
---------   ------------------  ------------------  ----  ------  -----  -----
25-JUL-01 SAM DYE         CALF                   1  EACH    1.00    1.00
                          *****************                    -----
                          sum                                   1.00


03-JUL-01 SAM DYE         HEFER                  1  EACH   35.00   35.00
12-OCT-01 GEORGE B.                              1  EACH   35.00   35.00
          MCCORMICK
10-NOV-01 PAT LAVAY                              1  EACH   28.00   28.00
14-NOV-01 MORRIS ARNOLD                          1  EACH   35.00   35.00
20-NOV-01 PALMER WALBOM                          1  EACH   30.00   30.00
                          *****************                    ------
                          sum                                 163.00

                    from G. B. Talbot's Ledger
```

FIGURE 6-2. *SQLPLUS report for G. B. Talbot*

Figure 6-3 shows the SQLPLUS start file that produced this report, in this case named activity.sql. To run this report program in SQLPLUS, type this:

```
start activity.sql
```

```
rem         Name: activity.sql   Type: start file report
rem  Written by: G. Koch
rem
rem Description: Report of G. B. Talbot sales by product
rem             during second half of 1901.


set headsep !

ttitle 'Sales by Product During 1901!Second Six Months (Jul-Dec)'
btitle 'from G. B. Talbot''s Ledger'

column Item heading 'What Was!Sold'
column Item format a18
column Item truncated

column Person heading 'To Whom Sold' format a18 word_wrapped
column Rate format 90.99
column ActionDate heading 'Date'
column QuantityType heading 'Type' format a8 truncated
column Quantity heading 'Quan' format 9990
column Ext format 990.99
break on Item skip 2
compute sum of Ext on Item

set linesize 79
set pagesize 50
set newpage 0

spool activity.1st

select ActionDate, Person, Item, Quantity, QuantityType,
       Rate, Quantity * Rate "Ext"
  from Ledger
 where Action = 'SOLD'                /* last 6 months only */
       and ActionDate BETWEEN TO-DATE('01-JUL-1901','DD-MON-YYYY')
                 and TO-DATE('31-DEC-1901','DD-MON-YYYY')
order by Item, ActionDate;

spool off
```

FIGURE 6-3. *Start file activity.sql used to produce report*

How to Distinguish Between SQLPLUS and SQL

The **select** statement toward the bottom of Figure 6-3, beginning with the word "select" and ending with the semicolon (;), is Structured Query Language—the language you use to talk to the Oracle database. Every other command on the page is a SQLPLUS command, used to format the results of a SQL query into a report.

The SQLPLUS **start** command causes SQLPLUS to read the file activity.sql and execute the instructions you've placed in it. Reviewing this start file will show you the basic SQLPLUS instructions you can use to produce reports or change the way SQLPLUS interacts with you. Depending on your experience, this may seem formidable or elementary. It is made up of a series of simple instructions to SQLPLUS.

① remark

The first five lines of Figure 6-3, at Circle 1, are documentation about the start file itself. These lines begin with

```
rem
```

which stands for **remark**. SQLPLUS ignores anything on a line that begins with **rem**, thus allowing you to add comments, documentation, and explanations to any start file you create. It is always a good idea to place remarks at the top of a start file, giving the filename, its creator and date of creation, the name of anyone who has modified it, the date of modification, what was modified, and an explanation of the purpose of the file. This will prove invaluable later on, as dozens of reports begin to accumulate.

② set headsep

The punctuation that follows **set headsep** (for **head**ing **sep**arator) at Circle 2 in Figure 6-3 tells SQLPLUS how you will indicate where you wish to break a page title or a column heading that runs longer than one line. When you first activate SQLPLUS, the default **headsep** character is the vertical bar (|), but some keyboards do not have this character. If your keyboard doesn't, or if you prefer a different character (such as the exclamation point, as shown in the example), you may choose any character on the keyboard.

 `set headsep !`

 CAUTION
Choosing a character that may otherwise appear in a title or column heading will cause unexpected splitting.

③ ttitle and btitle

The line at Circle 3 in Figure 6-3 indicates immediately how **headsep** is used. This line:

`ttitle 'Sales by Product During 1901!Second Six Months (Jul-Dec)'`

instructs SQLPLUS to put this **top title** at the top of each page of the report. The exclamation mark between "1901" and "Second" produces the split title you see in Figure 6-2. The title you choose must be enclosed in single quotation marks. This line:

`btitle 'from G. B. Talbot''s Ledger'`

works similarly to **ttitle**, except that it goes on the **b**ottom of each page (as the **b** indicates), and also must be in single quotation marks. Note the pair of single quotation marks at the end of "Talbot," and look at the effect in Figure 6-2. Because single quotes are used to enclose the entire title, an apostrophe (the same character on your keyboard) would trick SQLPLUS into believing the title had ended. To avoid this, put two single quotation marks right next to each other when you want to print a single quotation mark. Because both SQL and SQLPLUS rely on single quotation marks to enclose strings of characters, this technique is used throughout SQL and SQLPLUS whenever an apostrophe needs to be printed or displayed. This can confuse even veteran SQL users, however, so whenever possible, avoid possessives and contractions that call for an apostrophe.

When using **ttitle** this way, SQLPLUS will always center the title you choose based on the **linesize** you set (**linesize** will be discussed later in the chapter), and will always place the day, month, and date the report was run in the upper-left corner, and the page number in the upper-right corner.

There is another, more sophisticated method of using both **ttitle** and **btitle** that allows you to control placement of title information yourself, and even include variable information from your query in the title. These techniques will be covered in Chapter 14. You can use the **repheader** and **repfooter** commands to create headers and footers for reports. See the Alphabetical Reference section of this book for descriptions of **repheader** and **repfooter**.

④ column

column allows you to change the heading and format of any column in a **select** statement. Look at the report in Figure 6-2. The third column is actually called Item in the database and in the first line of the **select** statement at the bottom of Figure 6-3. However, look at Circle 4. The line:

```
column Item heading 'What Was!Sold'
```

relabels the column and gives it a new heading. This heading, like the report title, breaks onto two lines because it has the **headsep** character (**!**) embedded in it. The line:

```
column Item format a18
```

sets the width for display at 18. The *a* in a18 tells SQLPLUS that this is an alphabetic column, as opposed to a numeric column. The width can be set to virtually any value, irrespective of how the column is defined in the database. If you look at the LEDGER table from which this report is produced, you see this:

```
describe LEDGER
```

Name	Null?	Type
ACTIONDATE		DATE
ACTION		VARCHAR2(8)
ITEM		VARCHAR2(30)
QUANTITY		NUMBER
QUANTITYTYPE		VARCHAR2(10)
RATE		NUMBER
AMOUNT		NUMBER(9,2)
PERSON		VARCHAR2(25)

The Item column is defined as 30 characters wide, so it's possible that some items will have more than 18 characters. If you did nothing else in defining this column on the report, any item more than 18 characters long (such as BOOT BETWEEN HORSES) would wrap onto the next line, as in the following:

```
What Was
Sold
------------------
```

```
BOOT BETWEEN HORSE
S
```

The results look peculiar. To solve this, another **column** instruction is given:

```
column Item truncated
```

This instruction tells SQL to chop off any extra characters that go beyond the width specified in the line "column Item format a18." In Figure 6-2, look at the What Was Sold column for October 3, 1901, and you'll see that the *S* on HORSES was simply trimmed away. (BOOT BETWEEN HORSES, incidentally, refers to plowing a field.)

(5)   Although the three **column** instructions given here for the Item column were placed on three separate lines, it is possible to combine them on a single line, as Circle 5 points out:

```
column Person heading 'To Whom Sold' format a18 word_wrapped
```

This instruction is very similar to that used for the Item column, except that here, **word_wrapped** takes the place of **truncated**. Notice GEORGE B. MCCORMICK in Figure 6-2 (on October 12). This item was too long to fit in the 18 spaces allotted by this **column** command, so it was wrapped onto a second line, but the division was between the words or names. This is what **word_wrapped** does.

(6)   Circle 6 in Figure 6-3 shows an example of formatting a number:

```
column Rate format 90.99
```

This defines a column with room for four digits and a decimal point. If you count the spaces in the report for the Rate column, you'll see six spaces. Just looking at the **column** command might lead you to believe the column would be five spaces wide, but this would leave no room for a minus sign if the number were negative, so an extra space on the left is always provided for numbers. The 0 in 90.99 tells SQLPLUS that for a number below 1.00, such as .99, a 0 rather than a blank will be put in the dollar position: 0.99. If you look at the report in Figure 6-2, you'll see it does just that.

(7)   Circle 7 in Figure 6-3 refers to a column that didn't appear in the table when we had SQLPLUS describe it:

```
column Ext format 990.99
```

What is Ext? Look at the **select** statement at the bottom of Figure 6-3. Ext appears in the line:

```
Quantity * Rate AS Ext
```

which tells SQL to multiply the Quantity column times the Rate column and treat the result as if it were a new column named Ext. In bookkeeping, a quantity times a rate is often called the *extension*. SQL is able to do a computation on the fly and give the computation with a simpler column name (Ext as an abbreviation of Extension, for example). As a consequence, SQLPLUS sees a column named Ext, and all of its formatting and other commands will act as if it were a real column in the table. The **column** command for **Ext** is an example. "Ext" is referred to as a *column alias*—another name to use when referring to a column.

⑧ **break on**

Look at Circle 8 in Figure 6-3. Note on the report in Figure 6-2 how the transactions for each kind of Item are grouped together under What Was Sold. This effect was produced by the line:

```
break on Item skip 2
```

as well as by the line:

```
order by Item
```

in the **select** statement near the end of the start file.

SQLPLUS looks at each row as it is brought back from Oracle, and keeps track of the value in Item. For the first four rows, this value is BEEF, so SQLPLUS displays the rows it has gotten. On the fifth row, Item changes from BEEF to BOOT BETWEEN HORSES. SQLPLUS remembers your break instructions, which tell it that when Item changes, it should break away from the normal display of row after row, and skip two lines. You'll notice two lines between the Item sections on the report. Unless the items were collected together because of the **order by** clause, it wouldn't make sense for **break on** to skip two lines every time the Item changed. This is why the **break on** command and the **order by** clause must be coordinated.

You also may notice that BEEF is only printed on the first line of its section, as are BOOT BETWEEN HORSE, BUTTER, CALF, and HEFER (this is the spelling in the original ledger). This is done to eliminate the duplicate printing of each of these items for every row in each section, which is visually unattractive. If you wish, you can force it to duplicate the item on each row of its section, by altering the **break on** command to read

```
break on Item duplicate skip 2
```

The report output in Figure 6-2 shows no grand total for the report. To be able to get a grand total for a report, add an additional break using the **break on report** command. Be careful when adding breaks, since they all need to be created by a single command; entering two consecutive **break on** commands will cause the first command's instructions to be replaced by the second command.

To add a grand total for this report, modify the **break on** command to read

```
break on Item duplicate skip 2 on report
```

⑨ compute sum

The totals calculated for each section on the report were produced by the **compute sum** command at Circle 9. This command always works in conjunction with the **break on** command, and the totals it computes will always be for the section specified by the **break on**. It is probably wise to consider these two related commands as a single unit:

```
break on Item skip 2
compute sum of Ext on Item
```

In other words, this tells Oracle to compute the sum of the extensions for each item. Oracle will do this first for BEEF, and then for BOOT BETWEEN HORSES, BUTTER, CALF, and HEFER. Every time SQLPLUS sees a new Item, it calculates and prints a total for the previous Item. **compute sum** also puts a row of asterisks below the column that **break on** is using, and prints the word "sum" underneath. For reports with many columns that need to be added, a separate **compute sum** statement is used for each total. It also is possible to have several different kinds of breaks on a large report (for Item, Person, and Date, for example) along with coordinated **compute sum** commands. See Chapter 14 for details.

You can use a **break on** command without a **compute sum** command, such as for organizing your report into sections where no totals are needed (addresses with a **break on** City would be an example), but the reverse is not true.

NOTE
*Every **compute sum** command must have a **break on** command to guide it, and the **on** portion of both commands must match (such as **on Item** in the preceeding example, **break on Item skip 2** and **compute sum of Ext on Item**).*

The following are the basic rules:

 Every **break on** must have a related **order by**.

■ Every **compute sum** must have a related **break on**.

This makes sense, of course, but it's easy to forget one of the pieces. In addition to **compute sum**, you can also **compute avg**, **compute count**, **compute max**, or compute any other of Oracle's grouping functions on the set of records.

⑩ set linesize

The three commands at Circle 10 in Figure 6-3 control the gross dimensions of your report. The command **set linesize** governs the maximum number of characters that will appear on a single line. For letter-size paper, this number is usually around 70 or 80, unless your printer uses a very compressed (narrow) character font.

If you put more columns of information in your SQL query than will fit into the **linesize** you've allotted, SQLPLUS will wrap the additional columns down onto the next line and stack columns under each other. You actually can use this to very good effect when a lot of data needs to be presented. Chapter 14 gives an example of this.

SQLPLUS also uses **linesize** to determine where to center the **ttitle**, and where to place the date and page number. Both date and page number appear on the top line, and the distance between the first letter of the date and the last number of the page number will always equal the **linesize** you set.

set pagesize

The **set pagesize** command sets the total number of lines SQLPLUS will place on each page, including the **ttitle**, **btitle**, **column** headings, and any blank lines it prints. On letter- and computer-size paper, this is usually 66 (6 lines per inch times 11 inches). **set pagesize** is coordinated with **set newpage**.

set newpage

A better name for **set newpage** might have been "set blank lines" because what it really does is print blank lines before the top line (date, page number) of each page in your report. This is useful both for adjusting the position of reports coming out on single pages on a laser printer, and for skipping over the perforations between the pages of computer paper.

NOTE

*set pagesize does not set the size of the body of the report (the number of printed lines from the date down to the **btitle**); it sets the total length of the page, measured in lines.*

Thus, if you type this:

```
set pagesize 66
set newpage 9
```

SQLPLUS produces a report starting with 9 blank lines, followed by 57 lines of information (counting from the date down to the **btitle**). If you increase the size of **newpage**, SQLPLUS puts fewer rows of information on each page, but produces more pages altogether.

That's understandable, you say, but what's been done at Circle 10 on Figure 6-3? It says

```
set pagesize 50
set newpage 0
```

This is a strange size for a report page—is SQLPLUS to put zero blank lines between pages? No. Instead, the 0 after **newpage** switches on a special property it has: **set newpage 0** produces a *top-of-form character* (usually a hex 13) just before the date on each page. Most modern printers respond to this by moving immediately to the top of the next page, where the printing of the report will begin. The combination of **set pagesize 50** and **set newpage 0** produces a report whose body of information is exactly 50 lines long, and which has a top-of-form character at the beginning of each page. This is a cleaner and simpler way to control page printing than jockeying around with blank lines and lines per page. As of Oracle8, you can use the **set newpage none** command, which will result in no blank lines and no form feeds between report pages.

⑪ **spool**

In the early days of computers, most file storage was done on spools of either magnetic wire or tape. Writing information into a file and spooling a file were virtually synonymous. The term has survived, and *spooling* now generally refers to any process of moving information from one place to another. In SQLPLUS,

```
spool activity.lst
```

tells SQL to take all of the output from SQLPLUS and write it to the file named activity.lst. Once you've told SQLPLUS to spool, it continues to do so until you tell it to stop, which you do by inputting

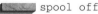
```
spool off
```

This means, for instance, that you could type

```
spool work.fil
```

and then type a SQL query, such as

```
select Feature, Section, Page from NEWSPAPER
where Section = 'F';

FEATURE         S  PAGE
--------------- -  ----
Births          F    7
Classified      F    8
Obituaries      F    6
Doctor Is In    F    6
```

or a series of SQLPLUS commands, such as:

```
set pagesize 60
column Section heading 'My Favorites'
```

or anything else. Whatever prompts SQLPLUS produces, whatever error messages you get, whatever appears on the computer screen while spooling—it all ends up in the file work.fil. Spooling doesn't discriminate. It records everything that happens from the instant you use the **spool** command until you use **spool off**, which brings us back to G. B. Talbot's report at Circle 11 of Figure 6-3:

```
spool activity.lst
```

This phrase is carefully placed as the command just before the **select** statement, and **spool off** immediately follows. Had **spool activity.lst** appeared any earlier, the SQLPLUS commands you were issuing would have ended up on the first page of your report file. Instead, it goes into the file activity.lst, which is what you see in Figure 6-2: the results of the SQL query, formatted according to your instructions, and nothing more. You are now free to print the file, confident that a clean report will show up on your printer.

⑫ **/* */**

Circle 12 of Figure 6-3 shows how a comment can be embedded in a SQL statement. This is different in method and use from the **remark** statement discussed earlier. **remark** (or **rem**) must appear at the beginning of a line, and works only for the single line on which it appears. Furthermore, a multiple-line SQL statement is not permitted to have a **remark** within it. That is,

```
select Feature, Section, Page
rem this is just a comment
```

```
 from NEWSPAPER
where Section = 'F';
```

is wrong. It will not work, and you'll get an error message. However, you can embed remarks in SQL following the method shown at Circle 12, or like this:

```
select Feature, Section, Page
 /* this is just a comment */
  from NEWSPAPER
 where Section = 'F';
```

The secret lies in knowing that **/*** tells SQLPLUS a comment has begun. Everything it sees from that point forward, even if it continues for many words and lines, is regarded as a comment until SQLPLUS sees ***/**, which tells it that the comment has ended. You can also use the characters "−−" to begin a comment. The end of the line ends the comment. This kind of comment works just like **remark** except that you use − − (two dashes) instead of **rem**.

Within the query, the **TO_DATE** function is used to make sure that the dates are compared to dates in the 20th century (the 1900s). If the full century value had not been specified, Oracle would have assumed a century value—and since the dates are so far in the past, it may have chosen the wrong century value for our data. You'll see how century values are handled and the formatting possibilities for the **TO_DATE** function in Chapter 9.

Some Clarification on Column Headings

It's possible that the difference between the renaming that occurs in this:

```
Quantity * Rate AS Ext
```

and the new heading given the column Item in this:

```
column Item heading 'What Was!Sold'
```

is not quite clear, particularly if you look at this command:

```
compute sum of Ext on Item
```

Why isn't it **compute sum of Ext on 'What Was!Sold'**? The reason is that SQLPLUS commands are aware only of columns that actually appear in the **select** statement. Every **column** command refers to a column in the **select** statement. Both **break on** and **compute** refer only to columns in the **select** statement. The only

reason a **column** command or a **compute** command is aware of the column Ext is
that it got its name in the **select** statement itself. The renaming of "Quantity * Rate"
to "Ext" is something done by SQL, *not* by SQLPLUS.

Other Features

It's not terribly difficult to look at a start file and the report it produces and see how
all of the formatting and computation was accomplished. It's possible to begin by
creating the start file, typing into it each of the commands you expect to need, and
then running it in SQLPLUS to see if it was correct. But when creating reports for
the first time, it is often much simpler to experiment interactively with SQLPLUS,
adjusting column formats, the SQL query, the titles, and the totals, until what you
really want begins to take shape.

Command Line Editor

When you type a SQL statement, SQLPLUS remembers each line as you enter it,
storing it in what is called the *SQL buffer* (a fancy name for a computer scratchpad
where your SQL statements are kept). Suppose you'd entered this query:

```
select Featuer, Section, Page
   from NEWSPAPER
 where Section = 'F';
```

SQLPLUS responds with the following:

```
select Featuer, Section, Page
       *
ERROR at line 1: ORA-0704:  invalid column name
```

You realize you've misspelled "Feature." You do not have to retype the entire
query. The command line editor is already present and waiting for instructions. First,
ask it to list your query:

```
list
```

SQLPLUS immediately responds with this:

```
1    select Featuer, Section, Page
2    from NEWSPAPER
3*   where Section = 'F'
```

Notice that SQLPLUS shows all three lines and numbers them. It also places an asterisk next to line 3, which means it is the line your editing commands are able to affect. But you want to change line 1, so you type, and SQLPLUS lists, this:

```
list 1

   1* select Featuer, Section, Page
```

Line 1 is displayed and is now the current line. You can change it by typing this:

```
change /Featuer/Feature

   1* select Feature, Section, Page
```

You can check the whole query again with this:

```
list

   1  select Feature, Section, Page
   2     from NEWSPAPER
   3*  where Section = 'F'
```

If you believe this is correct, enter a single slash after the prompt. This slash has nothing to do with the **change** command or the editor. Instead, it tells SQLPLUS to execute the SQL in the buffer.

```
/

FEATURE          S   PAGE
---------------  -   ----
Births           F     7
Classified       F     8
Obituaries       F     6
Doctor Is In     F     6
```

The **change** command requires that you mark the start and end of the text to be changed with a slash (/) or some other character. The line:

```
change $Featuer$Feature
```

would have worked just as well. SQLPLUS looks at the first character after the word "change" and assumes that is the character you've chosen to use to mark the start and end of the incorrect text (these markers are usually called *delimiters*). You can also delete the current line, as shown here:

```
list
```

```
    1   select Feature, Section, Page
    2      from NEWSPAPER
    3*   where Section = 'F'
```

```
del
```

```
list
```

```
    1   select Feature, Section, Page
    2      from NEWSPAPER
```

del will delete just what is on the current line. You can pass the **del** command a range of line numbers, to delete multiple lines at once, by specifying the first and last line numbers for the range of lines to delete. To delete lines 3 through 7, use **del 3 7**. Note this has a space before the number of the first line to delete (3) and another space before the number of the last line to delete (7). If you leave out the space between the 3 and the 7, SQLPLUS will try to delete line 37. To delete from line 2 to the end of the buffer, use **del 2 LAST**.

The word "delete" (spelled out) will erase all of the lines and put the word "delete" as line 1. This will only cause problems, so avoid typing the whole word "delete." If your goal is to clear out the **select** statement completely, type this:

```
clear buffer
```

If you'd like to append something to the current line, you can use the **append** command:

```
list 1
```

```
    1*  select Feature, Section, Page
```

```
append   "Where It Is"
```

```
    1*  select Feature, Section, Page "Where It Is"
```

append places its text right up against the end of the current line, with no spaces in between. To put a space in, as was done here, type *two* spaces between the word **append** and the text.

You may also **input** a whole new line after the current line, as shown here:

```
list
```

```
    1   select Feature, Section, Page "Where It Is"
```

```
  2*    from NEWSPAPER

input where Section = 'A'

list

  1  select Feature, Section, Page "Where It Is"
  2      from NEWSPAPER
  3* where Section = 'A'
```

and then set the column heading for the WhereItIs column:

```
column WhereItIs heading "WhereItIs"
```

and then run the query:

```
/

FEATURE         S Where It Is
--------------- - -----------
National News   A           1
Editorials      A          12
```

To review, the command line editor can **list** the SQL statement you've typed, **change** or **del**ete the current line (marked by the asterisk), **append** something onto the end of the current line, or **input** an entire line after the current line. Once your corrections are made, the SQL statement will execute if you type a slash at the SQL> prompt. Each of these commands can be abbreviated to its own first letter, except **del**, which must be exactly the three letters **del**.

The command line editor can edit only your SQL statement. It cannot edit SQLPLUS commands. If you've typed **column Item format a18**, for instance, and want to change it to **column Item format a20**, you must retype the whole thing (this is in the SQLPLUS interactive mode—if you've got the commands in a file, you obviously can change them with your own editor). You also can use the command line editor to change SQLPLUS commands. This will be discussed in Chapter 14.

Also note that in interactive mode, once you've started to type a SQL statement, you must complete it before you can enter any additional SQLPLUS commands, such as **column** formats or **ttitle**. As soon as SQLPLUS sees the word **select**, it assumes everything to follow is part of the **select** statement until it sees *either* a semicolon (;) at the end of the last SQL statement line *or* a slash (/) at the beginning of the line after the last SQL statement line.

This is correct:

```
select * from LEDGER;
```

```
select * from LEDGER
/
```

This is not:

```
select * from LEDGER/
```

set pause

During the development of a new report or when using SQLPLUS for quick queries of the database, it's usually helpful to set the **linesize** at 79 or 80, the **pagesize** at 24, and **newpage** at 1. You accompany this with two related commands, as shown here:

```
set pause 'More. . .'
set pause on
```

The effect of this combination is to produce exactly one full screen of information for each page of the report that is produced, and to pause at each page for viewing ("More. . ." will appear in the lower-left corner) until the ENTER key is hit. After the various column headings and titles are worked out, the **pagesize** can be readjusted for a page of paper, and the pause eliminated with this:

```
set pause off
```

save

If the changes you wish to make to your SQL statement are extensive, or you simply wish to work in your own editor, save the SQL you've created so far, in interactive mode, by writing the SQL to a file, like this:

```
save fred.sql
```

SQLPLUS responds with

```
Created file fred.sql
```

Your SQL (but not any **column**, **ttitle**, or other SQLPLUS commands) is now in a file named fred.sql (or a name of your choice), which you can edit using your own editor.

If the file already exists, then you must use the **replace** option (abbreviated **repl**) of the **save** command to save the new query in a file with that name. For this example, the syntax would be

```
save fred.sql repl
```

store

You can use the **store** command to save your current SQLPLUS environment settings to a file. The following will create a file called my_settings.sql and will store the settings in that file:

```
store set my_settings.sql create
```

If the my_settings.sql file already existed, you could use the **replace** option instead of **create**, and replace the old file with the new settings. You could also use the **append** option to append the new settings to an existing file.

editing

Everyone has a favorite editor. Word processing programs can be used with SQLPLUS, but only if you save the files created in them in ASCII format (see your word processor manual for details on how to do this). Editors are just programs themselves. They are normally invoked simply by typing their name at the operating system prompt. On UNIX, it usually looks something like this:

```
> vi fred.sql
```

In this example, vi is your editor's name, and fred.sql represents the file you want to edit (the start file described previously was used here only as an example—you would enter the real name of whatever file you want to edit). Other kinds of computers won't necessarily have the **>** prompt, but they will have something equivalent. If you can invoke an editor this way on your computer, it is nearly certain you can do it from within SQLPLUS, *except* that you don't type the name of your editor, but rather the word **edit**:

```
SQL> edit fred.sql
```

You should first tell SQLPLUS your editor's name. You do this while in SQLPLUS by *defining* the editor, like this:

```
define _editor = "vi"
```

(That's an underline before the *e* in editor.) SQLPLUS will then remember the name of your editor (until you **quit** SQLPLUS) and allow you to use it any time you wish. See the sidebar "Using Login.sql to Define the Editor" later in this chapter for directions on making this happen automatically.

host

In the unlikely event that none of the editing commands described in the previous section work, but you do have an editor you'd like to use, you can invoke it by typing this:

```
host vi fred.sql
```

Using login.sql to Define the Editor

If you'd like SQLPLUS to define your editor automatically, put the **define _editor** command in a file named login.sql. This is a special filename that SQLPLUS always looks for whenever it starts up. If it finds login.sql, it executes any commands in it as if you had entered them by hand. It looks first at the directory you are in when you type **SQLPLUS**. If it doesn't find login.sql there, it then looks in the home directory for Oracle. If it doesn't find login.sql there, it stops looking.

You can put virtually any command in login.sql that you can use in SQLPLUS, including both SQLPLUS commands and SQL statements; all of them will be executed before SQLPLUS gives you the **SQL>** prompt. This can be a convenient way to set up your own individual SQLPLUS environment, with all the basic layouts the way you prefer them. Advanced use of login.sql is covered in Chapter 14. Here's an example of a typical login.sql file:

```
prompt Login.sql loaded.
set feedback off
set sqlprompt 'What now, boss? '
set sqlnumber off
set numwidth 5
set pagesize 24
set linesize 79
define _editor="kedit"
```

Another file, named glogin.sql, is used to establish default SQLPLUS settings for all users of a database. This file, usually stored in the administrative directory for SQLPLUS, is useful in enforcing column and environment settings for multiple users.

The meaning of each of these commands can be found in the Alphabetical Reference section of this book.

host tells SQLPLUS that this is a command to simply hand back to the operating system for execution (a **$** will work in place of **host**), and is the equivalent of typing **vi fred.sql** at the > prompt. Incidentally, this same **host** command can be used to execute almost any operating system command from within SQLPLUS, including **dir**, **copy**, **move**, **erase**, **cls**, and others.

Adding SQLPLUS Commands

Once you've saved a SQL statement into a file, such as fred.sql, you can add to the file any SQLPLUS commands you wish. Essentially, you can build it in a similar fashion to activity.sql in Figure 6-3. When you've finished working on it, you can exit your editor and be returned to SQLPLUS.

start

Once you are back in SQLPLUS, test your editing work by executing the file you've just edited:

```
start fred.sql
```

All of the SQLPLUS and SQL commands in that file will execute, line by line, just as if you'd entered each one of them by hand. If you've included a **spool** and a **spool off** command in the file, you can use your editor to view the results of your work. This is just what was shown in Figure 6-2—the product of starting activity.sql and spooling its results into activity.lst.

To develop a report, use steps like these, in cycles:

1. Use SQLPLUS to build a SQL query interactively. When it appears close to being satisfactory, save it under a name such as **test.sql**. (The extension .sql is usually reserved for start files, scripts that will execute to produce a report.)

2. Edit the file test.sql using a favorite editor. Add **column**, **break**, **compute**, **set**, and **spool** commands to the file. You usually spool to a file with the extension .lst, such as test.lst. Exit the editor.

3. Back in SQLPLUS, the file test.sql is **start**ed. Its results fly past on the screen, but also go into the file test.lst. The editor examines this file.

4. Incorporate any necessary changes into test.sql and run it again.

5. Continue this process until the report is correct and polished.

Checking the **SQLPLUS** Environment

You saw earlier that the command line editor couldn't change SQLPLUS commands, because it could affect only SQL statements—those lines stored in the SQL buffer. You also saw that you could **save** SQL statements and **store** environment settings into files, where they could be modified using your own editor.

If you'd like to check how a particular column was defined, type

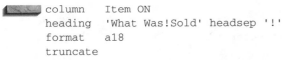

```
column Item
```

without anything following the column name. SQLPLUS will then list all of the instructions you've given about that column, as shown here:

```
column    Item ON
heading   'What Was!Sold' headsep '!'
format    a18
truncate
```

If you type just the word **column**, without any column name following it, then *all* of the columns will be listed:

```
column    Ext ON
format    990.99

column    Quantity ON
heading   'Quan'
format    9990

column    QuantityType ON
heading   'Type'
format    a8
truncate

column    ActionDate ON
heading   'Date'

column    Rate ON
format    90.99

column    Person ON
heading   'To Whom Sold'
format    a18
```

```
word_wrap
column    Item ON
heading   'What Was!Sold' headsep '!'
format    a18
truncate
```

ttitle, **btitle**, **break**, and **compute** are displayed simply by typing their names, with nothing following. SQLPLUS answers back immediately with the current definitions. The first line in each of the next examples is what you type; the following lines show SQLPLUS's replies:

```
ttitle
ttitle ON and is the following 56 characters:
Sales by Product During 1901!Second Six Months (Jul-Dec)

btitle
btitle ON and is the following 26 characters:
from G. B. Talbot's Ledger

break
break on Item skip 2 nodup

compute
COMPUTE sum OF Ext ON Item
```

Looking at those settings (also called *parameters*) that follow the **set** command requires using the word **show**:

```
show headsep
headsep "!" (hex 21)

show linesize
linesize 79

show pagesize
pagesize 50

show newpage
newpage 0
```

See the Alphabetical Reference section of this book under **set** and **show** for a complete list of parameters.

The **ttitle** and **btitle** settings can be disabled by using the **btitle off** and **ttitle off** commands. The following listing shows these commands. SQLPLUS does not reply to the commands.

```
ttitle off

btitle off
```

The settings for columns, breaks, and computes can be disabled via the **clear columns**, **clear breaks**, and **clear computes** commands. The first line in each example in the following listings is what you type; the following lines show what SQLPLUS replies:

```
clear columns
columns cleared

clear breaks
breaks cleared

clear computes
computes cleared
```

Building Blocks

This has been a fairly dense chapter, particularly if SQLPLUS is new to you, yet on reflection, you'll probably agree that what was introduced here is not really difficult. If Figure 6-3 looked daunting when you began the chapter, look at it again now. Is there any line on it that you don't understand, or don't have a sense of what is being done and why? You could, if you wished, simply copy this file (activity.sql) into another file with a different name, and begin to modify it to suit your own tastes, and to query against your own tables. The structure of any reports you produce will, after all, be very similar.

There is a lot going on in activity.sql, but it is made up of simple building blocks. This will be the approach used throughout the book. Oracle provides building blocks, and lots of them, but each separate block is understandable and useful.

In the previous chapters, you learned how to select data out of the database, choosing certain columns and ignoring others, choosing certain rows based on logical restrictions you set up, and combining two tables to give you information not available from either one on its own.

In this chapter, you learned how to give orders that SQLPLUS can follow in formatting and producing the pages and headings of polished reports.

In the next several chapters, you'll change and format your data row by row. Your expertise and confidence should grow chapter by chapter; by the end of Part II of this book, you should be able to produce very sophisticated reports in short order, to the considerable benefit of your company and you.

CHAPTER
7

Getting Text Information and Changing It

his chapter introduces *string functions,* which are software tools that allow you to manipulate a string of letters or other characters. To quickly reference individual functions, look them up by name in the Alphabetical Reference section of this book. This chapter focuses on the manipulation of text strings; to perform word searches (including word stem expansions and fuzzy matches), you should use Oracle's ConText Option (now called interMedia), which is described in Chapter 24.

Functions in Oracle work in one of two ways. Some functions create new objects from old ones; they produce a result that is a modification of the original information, such as turning lowercase characters into uppercase. Other functions produce a result that tells you something about the information, such as how many characters are in a word or sentence.

NOTE
*If you are using PL/SQL, you can create your own functions with the **create function** statement. See Chapter 27 for details.*

Datatypes

Just as people can be classified into different types based on certain characteristics (shy, ornery, outgoing, smart, silly, and so forth), different kinds of data can be classified into *datatypes* based on certain characteristics.

Datatypes in Oracle include NUMBER, CHAR (short for CHARACTER), DATE, VARCHAR2, LONG, RAW, LONG RAW, BLOB, CLOB, and BFILE. The first three are probably obvious. The rest are special datatypes that you'll encounter later. A full explanation of each of these can be found by name or under "Datatypes" in the Alphabetical Reference section of this book. Each datatype is covered in detail in the chapters ahead. As with people, some of the "types" overlap and some are fairly rare.

If the information is the character (VARCHAR2 or CHAR) type of information— a mixture of letters, punctuation marks, numbers, and spaces (also called *alphanumeric*)—you'll need string functions to modify or inform you about it. Oracle's SQL provides quite a few such tools.

What Is a String?

A *string* is a simple concept: a bunch of things in a line, like houses, popcorn or pearls, numbers, or characters in a sentence.

Strings are frequently encountered in managing information. Names are strings of characters, as in Juan L'Heureaux. Phone numbers are strings of numbers, dashes, and sometimes parentheses, as in (415) 555-2676. Even a pure number, such as 5443702, can be considered as either a number or a string of characters.

NOTE
Datatypes that are restricted to pure numbers (plus a decimal point and minus sign, if needed) are called NUMBER, and are not usually referred to as strings. A number can be used in certain ways that a string cannot, and vice versa.

Strings that can include any mixture of letters, numbers, spaces, and other symbols (such as punctuation marks and special characters) are called *character strings,* or just *character* for short.

In Oracle, CHARACTER is abbreviated CHAR. This is pronounced "care," like the first part of the word "character." It is not pronounced "char" as in "charcoal," nor is it pronounced "car."

There are two string datatypes in Oracle. CHAR strings are always a fixed length. If you set a value to a string with a length less than that of a CHAR column, Oracle automatically pads the string with blanks. When you compare CHAR strings, Oracle compares the strings by padding them out to equal lengths with blanks. This means that if you compare "character " with "character" in CHAR columns, Oracle considers the strings to be the same. The VARCHAR2 datatype is a varying-length string. The VARCHAR datatype is synonymous with VARCHAR2, but this may change in future versions of Oracle, so you should avoid using VARCHAR. Use CHAR for fixed-length character string fields and VARCHAR2 for all other character string fields.

The simple Oracle string functions, explained in this chapter, are shown in Table 7-1. You will learn more-advanced string functions and how to use them in Chapter 16.

Notation

Functions are shown with this kind of notation:

```
FUNCTION(string [,option])
```

The function itself will be in uppercase. The thing it affects (usually a string) will be shown in lowercase italics. Any time the word *string* appears, it represents either a literal string of characters or the name of a character column in a table. When you actually use a string function, any literal must be in single quotes; any column name must appear without quotes.

Function Name	Use
| |	Glues or concatenates two strings together. The | symbol is called a vertical bar or pipe.
CONCAT	CONCATenates two strings together (same as | |).
INITCAP	INITial CAPital. Capitalizes the first letter of a word or series of words.
INSTR	Finds the location of a character IN a STRing.
LENGTH	Tells the LENGTH of a string.
LOWER	Converts every letter in a string to LOWERcase.
LPAD	Left PAD. Makes a string a certain length by adding a certain set of characters to the left.
RPAD	Right PAD. Makes a string a certain length by adding a certain set of characters to the right.
RTRIM	Right TRIM. Trims all the occurrences of any one of a set of characters off of the right side of a string.
SOUNDEX	Finds words that SOUND like the EXample specified.
SUBSTR	SUBSTRing. Clips out a piece of a string.
UPPER	Converts every letter in a string into UPPERcase.

TABLE 7-1. *Simple Oracle String Functions*

Every function has only one pair of parentheses. The value that function works on, as well as additional information you can pass to the function, go between the parentheses.

Some functions have *options,* parts that are not always required to make the function work as you wish. Options are always shown in square brackets: [ ]. See the discussion on **LPAD** and **RPAD** in the following section for an example of how this is used.

A simple example of how the **LOWER** function is printed follows:

```
LOWER(string)
```

The word "LOWER" with the two parentheses is the function itself, so it is shown here in uppercase. *string* stands for the actual string of characters to be converted to lowercase, and is shown in lowercase italics. Therefore,

```
LOWER('CAMP DOUGLAS')
```

would produce

```
camp douglas
```

The string 'CAMP DOUGLAS' is a literal (which you learned about in Chapter 3), meaning that it is literally the string of characters that the function **LOWER** is to work on. Oracle uses single quotation marks to denote the beginning and end of any literal string. The string in **LOWER** also could have been the name of a column from a table, in which case the function would have operated on the contents of the column for every row brought back by a **select** statement. For example,

```
select City, LOWER(City), LOWER('City') from WEATHER;
```

would produce this result:

```
CITY         LOWER(CITY)  LOWER('CITY')
-----------  -----------  -------------
LIMA         lima         city
PARIS        paris        city
MANCHESTER   manchester   city
ATHENS       athens       city
CHICAGO      chicago      city
SYDNEY       sydney       city
SPARTA       sparta       city
```

At the top of the second column, in the **LOWER** function, CITY is not inside single quotation marks. This tells Oracle that it is a column name, not a literal.

In the third column's **LOWER** function, 'CITY' is inside single quotation marks. This means you literally want the function **LOWER** to work on the word "CITY" (that is, the string of letters C-I-T-Y), not the column by the same name.

Concatenation (||)

This notation:

```
string || string
```

tells Oracle to concatenate, or stick together, two strings. The strings, of course, can be either column names or literals. For example,

```
select City||Country from LOCATION;
```

```
CITY || COUNTRY
--------------------------------------------------
ATHENSGREECE
CHICAGOUNITED STATES
CONAKRYGUINEA
```

```
LIMAPERU
MADRASINDIA
MANCHESTERENGLAND
MOSCOWRUSSIA
PARISFRANCE
SHENYANGCHINA
ROMEITALY
TOKYOJAPAN
SYDNEYAUSTRALIA
SPARTAGREECE
MADRIDSPAIN
```

Here, the cities vary in width from 4 to 12 characters. The countries push right up against them. This is just how the concatenate function is supposed to work: it glues columns or strings together with no spaces in between.

This isn't very easy to read, of course. To make this a little more readable, you could list cities and countries with a comma and a space between them. You'd simply concatenate the City and Country columns with a literal string of a comma and a space, like this:

```
select City ||', '||Country from LOCATION;

CITY ||','||COUNTRY
-----------------------------------------------------
ATHENS, GREECE
CHICAGO, UNITED STATES
CONAKRY, GUINEA
LIMA, PERU
MADRAS, INDIA
MANCHESTER, ENGLAND
MOSCOW, RUSSIA
PARIS, FRANCE
SHENYANG, CHINA
ROME, ITALY
TOKYO, JAPAN
SYDNEY, AUSTRALIA
SPARTA, GREECE
MADRID, SPAIN
```

Notice the column title. See Chapter 6 for a review of column titles.

You could also use the **CONCAT** function to concatenate strings. The query

```
select CONCAT(City, Country) from LOCATION;
```

is equivalent to

```
select City||Country from LOCATION;
```

How to Cut and Paste Strings

In this section, you learn about a series of functions that often confuse users: **LPAD**, **RPAD**, **LTRIM**, **RTRIM**, **LENGTH**, **SUBSTR**, and **INSTR**. These all serve a common purpose: they allow you to *cut* and *paste.*

Each of these functions does some part of cutting and pasting. For example, **LENGTH** tells you how many characters are in a string. **SUBSTR** lets you clip out and use a *substring*—a portion of a string—starting at one position in the string and continuing for a given length. **INSTR** lets you find the location of a group of characters within another string. **LPAD** and **RPAD** allow you to easily concatenate spaces or other characters on the left or right side of a string. And, finally, **LTRIM** and **RTRIM** clip characters off of the ends of strings. Most interesting is that all of these functions can be used in combination with each other, as you'll soon see.

RPAD and LPAD

RPAD and **LPAD** are very similar functions. **RPAD** allows you to "pad" the right side of a column with any set of characters. The character set can be almost anything: spaces, periods, commas, letters or numbers, pound signs (#), or even exclamation marks (!). **LPAD** does the same thing as **RPAD**, but to the left side.

Here are the formats for **RPAD** and **LPAD**:

```
RPAD(string,length [,'set'])

LPAD(string,length [,'set'])
```

string is the name of a CHAR or VARCHAR2 column from the database (or a literal string), *length* is the total number of characters long that the result should be (in other words, its width), and *set* is the set of characters that do the padding. The set must be enclosed in single quotation marks. The square brackets mean that the set (and the comma that precedes it) are optional. If you leave this off, the function will automatically pad with spaces. This is sometimes called the *default*; that is, if you don't tell the function which set of characters to use, it will use spaces by default.

Many users produce tables with dots to help guide the eye from one side of the page to the other. Here's how **RPAD** does this:

```
select RPAD(City,35,'.'), Temperature from WEATHER;

RPAD(CITY,35,'.')                   TEMPERATURE
----------------------------------- -----------
LIMA...............................          45
PARIS..............................          81
MANCHESTER.........................          66
ATHENS.............................          97
```

```
CHICAGO........................... 66
SYDNEY............................ 29
SPARTA............................ 74
```

Notice what happened here. **RPAD** took each city, from Lima through Sparta, and concatenated dots on the right of it, adding just enough for each city so that the result (City plus dots) is exactly 35 characters long. The concatenate function (||) could not have done this. It would have added the same number of dots to every city, leaving a ragged edge on the right.

LPAD does the same sort of thing, but on the left. Suppose you want to reformat cities and temperatures so that the cities are right-justified (that is, they all align at the right):

```
select LPAD(City,11), Temperature from WEATHER;

LPAD(CITY,1 TEMPERATURE
----------- -----------
       LIMA          45
      PARIS          81
 MANCHESTER          66
     ATHENS          97
    CHICAGO          66
     SYDNEY          29
     SPARTA          74
```

LTRIM and RTRIM

LTRIM and **RTRIM** are like hedge trimmers. They trim off unwanted characters from the left and right ends of strings. For example, suppose you have a MAGAZINE table with a column in it that contains the titles of magazine articles, but the titles were entered by different people. Some people always put the titles in quotes, while others simply entered the words; some used periods, others didn't; some started titles with "The," while others did not. How do you trim these?

```
select Title from MAGAZINE;

TITLE
------------------------------------
THE BARBERS WHO SHAVE THEMSELVES.
"HUNTING THOREAU IN NEW HAMPSHIRE"
THE ETHNIC NEIGHBORHOOD
RELATIONAL DESIGN AND ENTHALPY
"INTERCONTINENTAL RELATIONS."
```

Here are the formats for **RTRIM** and **LTRIM**:

```
RTRIM(string [,'set'])

LTRIM(string [,'set'])
```

string is the name of the column from the database (or a literal string), and *set* is the collection of characters you want to trim off. If no set of characters is specified, the functions trim off spaces.

You can trim off more than one character at a time; to do so, simply make a list (a string) of the characters you want removed. First, let's get rid of the quotes and periods on the right, as shown here:

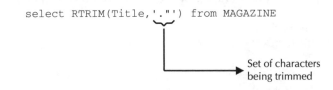

```
select RTRIM(Title,'."') from MAGAZINE
```

Set of characters
being trimmed

The preceding produces this:

```
RTRIM(TITLE,'."')
-----------------------------------
THE BARBERS WHO SHAVE THEMSELVES
"HUNTING THOREAU IN NEW HAMPSHIRE
THE ETHNIC NEIGHBORHOOD
RELATIONAL DESIGN AND ENTHALPY
"INTERCONTINENTAL RELATIONS
```

RTRIM removed both the double quotation marks and the periods from the right side of each of these titles. The *set* of characters you want to remove can be as long as you wish. Oracle will check and recheck the right side of each title until every character in your string has been removed—that is, until it runs into the first character in the string that is *not* in your *set*.

Combining Two Functions

Now what? How do you get rid of the quotes on the left? Title is buried in the middle of the **RTRIM** function. In this section, you learn how to combine functions.

You know that when you ran the **select** statement:

```
select Title from MAGAZINE;
```

the result you got back was the content of the Title column, as shown next.

```
THE BARBERS WHO SHAVE THEMSELVES.
"HUNTING THOREAU IN NEW HAMPSHIRE"
THE ETHNIC NEIGHBORHOOD
RELATIONAL DESIGN AND ENTHALPY
"INTERCONTINENTAL RELATIONS."
```

Remember that the purpose of this:

```
RTRIM(Title,'."')
```

is to take each of these strings and remove the quotes on the right side, effectively producing a result that is a *new* column whose contents are shown here:

```
THE BARBERS WHO SHAVE THEMSELVES
"HUNTING THOREAU IN NEW HAMPSHIRE
THE ETHNIC NEIGHBORHOOD
RELATIONAL DESIGN AND ENTHALPY
"INTERCONTINENTAL RELATIONS
```

Therefore, if you pretend **RTRIM(Title,'."')** is simply a column name itself, you can substitute it for the *string* in this:

```
LTRIM(string,'set')
```

So you simply type your **select** statement to look like this:

```
select LTRIM(RTRIM(Title,'."'),'"') from MAGAZINE;
```

Taking this apart for clarity, you see

Is this how you want it? And what is the result of this combined function?

```
LTRIM(RTRIM(TITLE,'."'),'"')
-----------------------------------
THE BARBERS WHO SHAVE THEMSELVES
HUNTING THOREAU IN NEW HAMPSHIRE
THE ETHNIC NEIGHBORHOOD
```

```
RELATIONAL DESIGN AND ENTHALPY
INTERCONTINENTAL RELATIONS
```

Your titles are cleaned up.

Looking at a combination of functions the first (or the thousandth) time can be confusing, even for an experienced query user. It's difficult to assess which commas and parentheses go with which functions, particularly when a query you've written isn't working correctly; discovering where a comma is missing, or which parenthesis isn't properly matched with another, can be a real adventure.

One simple solution to this is to break functions onto separate lines, at least until they're all working the way you wish. SQLPLUS doesn't care at all where you break a SQL statement, as long as it's not in the middle of a word or a literal string. To better visualize how this **RTRIM** and **LTRIM** combination works, you could type it like this:

```
select LTRIM(
             RTRIM(Title,'."')
                                ,'"')
   from MAGAZINE;
```

This makes what you are trying to do obvious, and it will work even if it is typed on four separate lines with lots of spaces. SQLPLUS simply ignores extra spaces.

Suppose now you decide to trim off THE from the front of two of the titles, as well as the space that follows it (and, of course, the double quote you removed before). You might do this:

```
select LTRIM(RTRIM(Title,'."'),'"THE ')
   from MAGAZINE;
```

which produces the following:

```
LTRIM(RTRIM(TITLE,'."'),'"THE')
---------------------------------
BARBERS WHO SHAVE THEMSELVES
UNTING THOREAU IN NEW HAMPSHIRE
NIC NEIGHBORHOOD
RELATIONAL DESIGN AND ENTHALPY
INTERCONTINENTAL RELATIONS
```

What happened? The second and third row got trimmed more than expected. Why? Because **LTRIM** was busy looking for and trimming off anything that was a double quote, a *T*, an *H*, an *E*, or a space. It was not looking for the word THE. It was looking for the letters in it, and it didn't quit the first time it saw any of the letters it was looking for. It quit when it saw a character that wasn't in its *set*.

What it trimmed: What is left behind:

```
THE                BARBERS WHO SHAVE THEMSELVES
"H                 UNTING THOREAU IN NEW HAMPSHIRE
THE ETH            NIC NEIGHBORHHOOD
                   RELATIONAL DESIGN AND ENTHALPY
"                  INTERCONTINENTAL RELATIONS
```

NOT in the set '"THE'

In the set '"THE'

In other words, all of these:

```
'"THE'
'HET"'
'E"TH'
'H"TE'
'ET"H'
```

and many other combinations of the letters will have the same effect when used as the *set* of an **LTRIM** or **RTRIM**. The order of the letters of the *set* has no effect on how the function works. Note, however, that the *case* of the letters is important. Oracle will check the case of both the letters in the *set* and in the string. It will remove only those with an exact match.

LTRIM and **RTRIM** are designed to remove any characters in a *set* from the left or right of a string. They're not intended to remove words. To do that requires clever use of **INSTR**, **SUBSTR**, and even **DECODE**, which you will learn about in later chapters.

The previous example makes one point clear: it's better to make certain that data gets cleaned up or edited before it is stored in the database. It would have been a lot less trouble if the individuals typing these magazine article titles had simply avoided the use of quotes, periods, and the word THE.

Adding One More Function

Suppose that you decide to **RPAD** your trimmed up Title with dashes and carets, perhaps also asking for a magazine Name and Page number. Your query would look like this:

```
select Name, RPAD(RTRIM(LTRIM(Title,'"'),'."'),47,'-^'), Page
  from MAGAZINE;


NAME            RPAD(RTRIM(LTRIM(TITLE,'"'),'."'),47,'-^')   PAGE
--------------- ----------------------------------------- -----
BERTRAND MONTHLY THE BARBERS WHO SHAVE THEMSELVES-^-^-^-^-^   70
```

```
LIVE FREE OR DIE HUNTING THOREAU IN NEW HAMPSHIRE-^-^-^-^-^    320
PSYCHOLOGICA     THE ETHNIC NEIGHBORHOOD-^-^-^-^-^-^-^-^-^-    246
FADED ISSUES     RELATIONAL DESIGN AND ENTHALPY-^-^-^-^-^-^    279
ENTROPY WIT      INTERCONTINENTAL RELATIONS-^-^-^-^-^-^-^-^     20
```

Each function has parentheses that enclose the column it is going to affect, so the real trick in understanding combined functions in **select** statements is to read from the outside to the inside on both left and right, watching (and even counting) the pairs of parentheses.

LOWER, UPPER, and INITCAP

These three related and very simple functions often are used together. **LOWER** takes any string or column and converts any letters in it to lowercase. **UPPER** does the opposite, converting any letters to uppercase. **INITCAP** takes the initial letter of every word in a string or column and converts just those letters to uppercase.

Here are the formats for these functions:

```
LOWER(string)
UPPER(string)
INITCAP(string)
```

Returning to the WEATHER table, recall that each city is stored in uppercase letters, like this:

```
LIMA
PARIS
ATHENS
CHICAGO
MANCHESTER
SYDNEY
SPARTA
```

Therefore,

```
select City, UPPER(City), LOWER(City), INITCAP(LOWER(City))
   from WEATHER;
```

produces this:

```
City         UPPER(CITY) LOWER(CITY) INITCAP(LOW
-----------  ----------- ----------- -----------
LIMA         LIMA        lima        Lima
PARIS        PARIS       paris       Paris
MANCHESTER   MANCHESTER  manchester  Manchester
ATHENS       ATHENS      athens      Athens
CHICAGO      CHICAGO     chicago     Chicago
```

```
SYDNEY        SYDNEY        sydney        Sydney
SPARTA        SPARTA        sparta        Sparta
```

Look carefully at what is produced in each column, and at the functions that produced it in the SQL statement. The fourth column shows how you can apply **INITCAP** to **LOWER(City)** and have it appear with normal capitalization, even though it is stored as uppercase.

Another example is the Name column as stored in a MAGAZINE table:

```
NAME
----------------
BERTRAND MONTHLY
LIVE FREE OR DIE
PSYCHOLOGICA
FADED ISSUES
ENTROPY WIT
```

and then retrieved with the combined **INITCAP** and **LOWER** functions, as shown here:

```
select INITCAP(LOWER(Name)) from MAGAZINE;

INITCAP(LOWER(NA
----------------
Bertrand Monthly
Live Free Or Die
Psychologica
Faded Issues
Entropy Wit
```

and as applied to the Name, cleaned up Title, and Page (note that you'll also rename the columns):

```
select INITCAP(LOWER(Name)) AS Name,
       INITCAP(LOWER(RTRIM(LTRIM(Title,'"'),'."'))) AS Title,
       Page
  from Magazine;

NAME             TITLE                                  PAGE
---------------- -------------------------------------- -----
Bertrand Monthly The Barbers Who Shave Themselves         70
Live Free Or Die Hunting Thoreau In New Hampshire        320
Psychologica     The Ethnic Neighborhood                 246
Faded Issues     Relational Design And Enthalpy          279
Entropy Wit      Intercontinental Relations               20
```

LENGTH

This one is easy. **LENGTH** tells you how long a string is—how many characters it has in it, including letters, spaces, and anything else.

This is the format for **LENGTH**:

```
LENGTH(string)
```

For example,

```
select Name, LENGTH(Name) from MAGAZINE;
```

```
NAME             LENGTH(NAME)
---------------- ------------
BERTRAND MONTHLY           16
LIVE FREE OR DIE           16
PSYCHOLOGICA               12
FADED ISSUES               12
ENTROPY WIT                11
```

This isn't normally useful by itself, but it can be used as part of another function, for calculating how much space you'll need on a report, or as part of a **where** or an **order by** clause.

SUBSTR

You can use the **SUBSTR** function to clip out a piece of a string.

This is the format for **SUBSTR**:

```
SUBSTR(string,start [,count])
```

This tells SQL to clip out a subsection of the *string*, beginning at position *start* and continuing for *count* characters. If you don't specify the *count*, **SUBSTR** will clip beginning at *start* and continuing to the end of the string. For example,

```
select SUBSTR(Name,6,4) from MAGAZINE;
```

gives you this:

```
SUBS
----
AND
FREE
OLOG
 ISS
PY W
```

You can see how the function works. It clipped out the piece of the magazine name starting in position 6 (counting from the left) and including a total of four characters.

A more practical use might be in separating out phone numbers from a personal address book. For example, assume that you have an ADDRESS table that contains, among other things, last names, first names, and phone numbers, as shown here:

```
select LastName, FirstName, Phone from ADDRESS;
```

LASTNAME	FIRSTNAME	PHONE
BAILEY	WILLIAM	213-293-0223
ADAMS	JACK	415-453-7530
SEP	FELICIA	214-522-8383
DE MEDICI	LEFTY	312-736-1166
DEMIURGE	FRANK	707-767-8900
CASEY	WILLIS	312-684-1414
ZACK	JACK	415-620-6842
YARROW	MARY	415-787-2178
WERSCHKY	ARNY	415-235-7387
BRANT	GLEN	415-526-7512
EDGAR	THEODORE	415-525-6252
HARDIN	HUGGY	617-566-0125
HILD	PHIL	603-934-2242
LOEBEL	FRANK	202-456-1414
MOORE	MARY	718-857-1638
SZEP	FELICIA	214-522-8383
ZIMMERMAN	FRED	503-234-7491

Suppose you want just those phone numbers in the 415 area code. One solution would be to have a separate column called AreaCode. Thoughtful planning about tables and columns will eliminate a good deal of fooling around later with reformatting. However, in this instance, area codes and phone numbers are combined in a single column, so a way must be found to separate out the numbers in the 415 area code.

```
select LastName, FirstName, Phone from ADDRESS
  where Phone like '415-%';
```

LASTNAME	FIRSTNAME	PHONE
ADAMS	JACK	415-453-7530
ZACK	JACK	415-620-6842
YARROW	MARY	415-787-2178
WERSCHKY	ARNY	415-235-7387
BRANT	GLEN	415-526-7512
EDGAR	THEODORE	415-525-6252

Next, since you do not want to dial your own area code when calling friends, you can eliminate this from the result by using another **SUBSTR**:

```
select LastName, FirstName, SUBSTR(Phone,5) from ADDRESS
 where Phone like '415-%';
```

```
LASTNAME                   FIRSTNAME                  SUBSTR(P
------------------------   ------------------------   --------
ADAMS                      JACK                       453-7530
ZACK                       JACK                       620-6842
YARROW                     MARY                       787-2178
WERSCHKY                   ARNY                       235-7387
BRANT                      GLEN                       526-7512
EDGAR                      THEODORE                   525-6252
```

Notice that the default version of **SUBSTR** was used here. **SUBSTR(Phone,5)** tells SQL to clip out the substring of the phone number, starting at position 5 and going to the end of the string. Doing this eliminates the area code.

Of course, this:

```
SUBSTR(Phone,5)
```

has exactly the same effect as the following:

```
SUBSTR(Phone,5,8)
```

You can combine this with the concatenation and column renaming techniques discussed in Chapter 6 to produce a quick listing of local friends' phone numbers, as shown here:

```
select LastName ||', '||FirstName AS Name,
       SUBSTR(Phone,5) AS Phone
  from ADDRESS
 where Phone like '415-%';
```

```
NAME                                                   PHONE
-----------------------------------------------------  --------
ADAMS, JACK                                            453-7530
ZACK, JACK                                             620-6842
YARROW, MARY                                           787-2178
WERSCHKY, ARNY                                         235-7387
BRANT, GLEN                                            526-7512
EDGAR, THEODORE                                        525-6252
```

To produce a dotted line following the name, add the **RPAD** function:

```
select RPAD(LastName ||', '||FirstName,25,'.') AS Name,
       SUBSTR(Phone,5) AS Phone
```

```
    from ADDRESS
   where Phone like '415-%';


NAME                         PHONE
------------------------     --------
ADAMS, JACK..............    453-7530
ZACK, JACK...............    620-6842
YARROW, MARY............     787-2178
WERSCHKY, ARNY..........     235-7387
BRANT, GLEN.............     526-7512
EDGAR, THEODORE.........     525-6252
```

The use of negative numbers in the **SUBSTR** function is undocumented, but it works. Normally, the position value you specify for the starting position is relative to the start of the string. When using a negative number for the position value, it is relative to the *end* of the string. For example,

```
SUBSTR(Phone,-4)
```

would use the fourth position from the end of the Phone column's value as its starting point. Since no length parameter is specified in this example, the remainder of the string will be returned.

> **NOTE**
> *Use this feature only for VARCHAR2 datatype columns. Do not use this feature with columns that use the CHAR datatype. CHAR columns are fixed-length columns, so their values are padded with spaces to extend them to the full length of the column. Using a negative number for the **SUBSTR** position value in a CHAR column will determine the starting position relative to the end of the column, not the end of the string.*

The following example shows the result of this feature when it is used on a VARCHAR2 column:

```
select SUBSTR(Phone,-4)
   from ADDRESS
 where Phone like '415-5%';


SUBS
----
7512
6252
```

The *count* value of the **SUBSTR** function must always be positive or unspecified. Using a negative *count* will return a **NULL** result.

INSTR

The **INSTR** function allows for simple or sophisticated searching through a string for a set of characters, not unlike **LTRIM** and **RTRIM**, except that **INSTR** doesn't clip anything off. It simply tells you where in the string it found what you were searching for. This is similar to the **LIKE** logical operator described in Chapter 3, except that **LIKE** can only be used in a **where** or **having** clause, and **INSTR** can be used anywhere except in the **from** clause. Of course, **LIKE** can be used for complex pattern searches that would be quite difficult, if even possible, using **INSTR**.

This is the format for **INSTR**:

```
INSTR(string,set [,start [,occurrence ] ])
```

INSTR searches in the *string* for a certain *set* of characters. It has two options, one within the other. The first option is the default; it will look for the set starting at position 1. If you specify the location to *start*, it will skip over all the characters up to that point and begin its search there.

The second option is *occurrence*. A *set* of characters may occur more than once in a string, and you may really be interested only in whether something occurs more than once. By default, **INSTR** will look for the first occurrence of the set. By adding the option *occurrence* and making it equal to 3, for example, you can force **INSTR** to skip over the first two occurrences of the set and give the location of the third.

Some examples will make all of this simpler to grasp. Recall the table of magazine articles. Here is a list of their authors:

```
select Author from MAGAZINE;

AUTHOR
------------------------
BONHOEFFER, DIETRICH
CHESTERTON, G. K.
RUTH, GEORGE HERMAN
WHITEHEAD, ALFRED
CROOKES, WILLIAM
```

To find the location of the first occurrence of the letter *O*, **INSTR** is used without its options, and with *set* as 'O' (note the single quotation marks, since this is a literal), as shown in the following listing.

```
select Author, INSTR(Author,'O') from MAGAZINE;

AUTHOR                    INSTR(AUTHOR,'O')
------------------------ -----------------
BONHOEFFER, DIETRICH                     2
CHESTERTON, G. K.                        9
RUTH, GEORGE HERMAN                      9
WHITEHEAD, ALFRED                        0
CROOKES, WILLIAM                         3
```

This is, of course, the same as this:

```
select Author, INSTR(Author,'O',1,1) from MAGAZINE;
```

If it had looked for the second occurrence of the letter *O*, it would have found

```
select Author, INSTR(Author,'O',1,2) from MAGAZINE;

AUTHOR                    INSTR(AUTHOR,'O',1,2)
------------------------ ---------------------
BONHOEFFER, DIETRICH                         5
CHESTERTON, G. K.                            0
RUTH, GEORGE HERMAN                          0
WHITEHEAD, ALFRED                            0
CROOKES, WILLIAM                             4
```

INSTR found the second *O* in Bonhoeffer's name, at position 5, and in Crookes' name, at position 4. Chesterton has only one *O*, so for him, Ruth, and Whitehead, the result is zero, meaning no success—no second *O* was found.

To tell **INSTR** to look for the second occurrence, you also must tell it where to start looking (in this case, position 1). The default value of *start* is 1, which means that's what it uses if you don't specify anything, but the *occurrence* option requires a *start*, so you have to specify both.

If *set* is not just one character but several, **INSTR** gives the location of the first letter of the set, as shown here:

```
select Author, INSTR(Author,'WILLIAM') from MAGAZINE;

AUTHOR                    INSTR(AUTHOR,'WILLIAM')
------------------------ -----------------------
BONHOEFFER, DIETRICH                           0
CHESTERTON, G. K.                              0
RUTH, GEORGE HERMAN                            0
WHITEHEAD, ALFRED                              0
CROOKES, WILLIAM                              10
```

This has many useful applications. In the MAGAZINE table, for instance:

```
select Author, INSTR(Author,',') from MAGAZINE;
```

```
AUTHOR                        INSTR(AUTHOR,',')
------------------------       -----------------
BONHOEFFER, DIETRICH                         11
CHESTERTON, G. K.                            11
RUTH, GEORGE HERMAN                           5
WHITEHEAD, ALFRED                            10
CROOKES, WILLIAM                              8
```

Here, **INSTR** searched the strings of author names for a comma, and then reported back the position in the string where it found it.

Suppose you wish to reformat the names of the authors from the formal "last name/comma/first name" approach, and present them as they are normally spoken, as shown here:

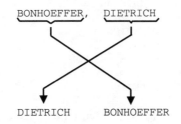

To do this using **INSTR** and **SUBSTR**, find the location of the comma, and use this location to tell **SUBSTR** where to clip. Taking this step by step, first find the comma:

```
select Author, INSTR(Author,',')    from MAGAZINE;
```

```
AUTHOR                        INSTR(AUTHOR,',')
------------------------       -----------------
BONHOEFFER, DIETRICH                         11
CHESTERTON, G. K.                            11
RUTH, GEORGE HERMAN                           5
WHITEHEAD, ALFRED                            10
CROOKES, WILLIAM                              8
```

Two **SUBSTR**s will be needed, one that clips out the author's last name up to the position before the comma, and one that clips out the author's first name from two positions after the comma through to the end.

First, look at the one that clips from position 1 to just before the comma:

```
select Author, SUBSTR(Author,1,INSTR(Author,',')-1)
    from MAGAZINE;

AUTHOR                    SUBSTR(AUTHOR,1,INSTR(AUT
------------------------  -------------------------
BONHOEFFER, DIETRICH      BONHOEFFER
CHESTERTON, G. K.         CHESTERTON
RUTH, GEORGE HERMAN       RUTH
WHITEHEAD, ALFRED         WHITEHEAD
CROOKES, WILLIAM          CROOKES
```

Next, look at the one that clips from two positions past the comma to the end of the string:

```
select Author, SUBSTR(Author,INSTR(Author,',')+2) from MAGAZINE;

AUTHOR                    SUBSTR(AUTHOR,INSTR(AUTHO
------------------------  -------------------------
BONHOEFFER, DIETRICH      DIETRICH
CHESTERTON, G. K.         G. K.
RUTH, GEORGE HERMAN       GEORGE HERMAN
WHITEHEAD, ALFRED         ALFRED
CROOKES, WILLIAM          WILLIAM
```

Look at the combination of these two with the concatenation function putting a space between them, and a quick renaming of the column to ByFirstName:

```
column ByFirstName heading "By First Name"

select Author, SUBSTR(Author,INSTR(Author,',')+2)
               ||' '||
               SUBSTR(Author,1,INSTR(Author,',')-1)
             AS ByFirstName
    from MAGAZINE;

AUTHOR                    By First Name
------------------------  -------------------------
BONHOEFFER, DIETRICH      DIETRICH BONHOEFFER
CHESTERTON, G. K.         G. K. CHESTERTON
RUTH, GEORGE HERMAN       GEORGE HERMAN RUTH
WHITEHEAD, ALFRED         ALFRED WHITEHEAD
CROOKES, WILLIAM          WILLIAM CROOKES
```

It is daunting to look at a SQL statement like this one, but it was built using simple logic, and it can be broken down the same way. Bonhoeffer can provide the example.

The first part looks like this:

```
SUBSTR(Author,INSTR(Author,',')+2)
```

This tells SQL to get the **SUBSTR** of Author starting two positions to the right of the comma and going to the end. This will clip out DIETRICH—the author's first name.

The beginning of the author's first name is found by locating the comma at the end of his last name (**INSTR** does this), and then sliding over two steps to the right (where his first name begins).

The following illustration shows how the **INSTR** function (plus 2) serves as the *start* for the **SUBSTR** function:

This is the second part of the combined statement:

```
||' '||
```

which, of course, simply tells SQL to concatenate a space in the middle.

This is the third part of the combined statement:

```
SUBSTR(Author,1,INSTR(Author,',')-1)
```

This tells SQL to clip out the portion of the author's name starting at position 1 and ending one position before the comma, which results in the author's last name:

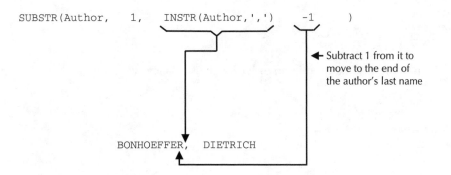

The fourth part simply assigns a column alias:

```
AS ByFirstName
```

It was only possible to accomplish this transposition because each Author record in the MAGAZINE table followed the same formatting conventions. In each record, the last name was always the first word in the string and was immediately followed by a comma. This allowed you to use the **INSTR** function to search for the comma. Once the comma's position was known, you could determine which part of the string was the last name, and the rest of the string was treated as the first name.

This is not often the case. Names are difficult to force into standard formats. Last names may include prefixes (such as von in von Hagel) or suffixes (such as Jr., Sr., and III). Using the previous example's SQL, the name Richards, Jr., Bob would have been transformed into Jr., Bob Richards.

Because of the lack of a standard formatting for names, many applications store the first and last names separately. Titles (such as MD) are usually stored in yet another column. A second option when storing such data is to force it into a single format and use **SUBSTR** and **INSTR** to manipulate that data when needed.

order by and where with String Functions

String functions can be used in a **where** clause, as shown here:

```
select City
  from WEATHER
 where LENGTH(City) < 7;


CITY
-----------
LIMA
PARIS
ATHENS
SPARTA
SYDNEY
```

They can also be used in an **order by** clause, as shown here:

```
select City
  from WEATHER
 order by LENGTH(City);
```

```
CITY
-----------
LIMA
PARIS
ATHENS
SPARTA
SYDNEY
CHICAGO
MANCHESTER
```

These are simple examples; much more complex clauses could be used. For example, you could find all the authors with more than one *O* in their names by using **INSTR** in the **where** clause:

```
select Author from MAGAZINE
  where INSTR(Author,'O',1,2) > 0;

AUTHOR
-------------------------
BONHOEFFER, DIETRICH
CROOKES, WILLIAM
```

This works by finding a second occurrence of the letter *O* in the author names. The **> 0** is a logical technique: recall that functions generally produce two different kinds of results, one that creates new objects, and the other that tells you something about them.

The **INSTR** function tells something about a string, specifically the position of the set it has been asked to find. Here, it is asked to locate the second *O* in the Author string. Its result will be a number that will be greater than zero for those names with at least two *O*'s, and zero for those with one or less (when **INSTR** doesn't find something, its result is a zero). So, a simple test for a result greater than zero checks for the success of the **INSTR** search for a second *O*.

The **where** clause using **INSTR** produces the same result as this:

```
where Author LIKE '%O%O%'
```

Remember that the percent sign (%) is a wildcard, meaning it takes the place of anything, so the **like** clause here tells SQL to look for two *O*'s with anything before, between, or after them. This is probably easier to understand than the previous example of **INSTR**.

There are often several ways to produce the same result in Oracle. Some will be easier to understand, some will work more quickly, some will be more appropriate in certain situations, and some simply will be a matter of personal style.

SOUNDEX

There is one string function that is used almost exclusively in a **where** clause: **SOUNDEX**. It has the unusual ability to find words that sound like other words, virtually regardless of how either is spelled. This is especially useful when you're not certain how a word or name is really spelled.

This is the format for **SOUNDEX**:

```
SOUNDEX(string)
```

Here are a few of examples of its use:

```
select City, Temperature, Condition
   from WEATHER
 where SOUNDEX(City) = SOUNDEX('Sidney');

CITY         TEMPERATURE CONDITION
-----------  ----------- ---------
SYDNEY               29 SNOW

select City, Temperature, Condition from WEATHER
 where SOUNDEX(City) = SOUNDEX('menncestr');

CITY         TEMPERATURE CONDITION
-----------  ----------- ---------
MANCHESTER           66 SUNNY

select Author from MAGAZINE;
 where SOUNDEX(Author) = SOUNDEX('Banheffer');

AUTHOR
------------------------
BONHOEFFER, DIETRICH
```

SOUNDEX compares the sound of the entry in the selected column with the sound of the word in single quotation marks, and looks for a close match. **SOUNDEX** makes certain assumptions about how letters and combinations of letters are usually pronounced in English, and the two words being compared must begin with the same letter. It will not always find the word you're searching for or have misspelled, but it can help.

It is not necessary that one of the two **SOUNDEX**s in the **where** clause have a literal in it. **SOUNDEX** could be used to compare two columns to find those that sound alike.

One useful purpose for this function is cleaning up mailing lists. Many lists have duplicate entries with slight differences in spelling or format of the customers' names. By using **SOUNDEX** to list all the names that sound alike, many of these duplicates can be discovered and eliminated.

Let's apply this to the ADDRESS table:

```
select LastName, FirstName, Phone
   from ADDRESS;
```

```
LASTNAME                 FIRSTNAME                PHONE
------------------------ ------------------------ ------------
BAILEY                   WILLIAM                  213-293-0223
ADAMS                    JACK                     415-453-7530
SEP                      FELICIA                  214-522-8383
DE MEDICI                LEFTY                    312-736-1166
DEMIURGE                 FRANK                    707-767-8900
CASEY                    WILLIS                   312-684-1414
ZACK                     JACK                     415-620-6842
YARROW                   MARY                     415-787-2178
WERSCHKY                 ARNY                     415-235-7387
BRANT                    GLEN                     415-526-7512
EDGAR                    THEODORE                 415-525-6252
HARDIN                   HUGGY                    617-566-0125
HILD                     PHIL                     603-934-2242
LOEBEL                   FRANK                    202-456-1414
MOORE                    MARY                     718-857-1638
SZEP                     FELICIA                  214-522-8383
ZIMMERMAN                FRED                     503-234-7491
```

To find duplicates, you must force Oracle to compare each LastName in the table to all the others in the same table.

Join the ADDRESS table to itself by creating an alias for the table, calling it first **a** and then **b**. Now it is as if there are two tables, a and b, with the common column LastName.

In the **where** clause, any column where the LastName in one table is identical to the LastName in the other table is eliminated. This prevents a LastName from matching to itself.

Those that sound alike are then selected:

```
select a.LastName, a.FirstName, a.Phone
   from ADDRESS a, ADDRESS b
 where a.LastName != b.LastName
   and SOUNDEX(a.LastName) = SOUNDEX(b.LastName);
```

```
LASTNAME                 FIRSTNAME                PHONE
------------------------ ------------------------ ------------
SZEP                     FELICIA                  214-522-8383
SEP                      FELICIA                  214-522-8383
```

You can also perform SOUNDEX searches on individual words within a text entry. For examples of this and other complex text searches, see Chapter 24.

National Language Support

Oracle doesn't have to use English characters; it can represent data in any language through its implementation of *National Language Support.* By using characters made up of longer pieces of information than ordinary characters, Oracle can represent Japanese and other such strings. See **NLSSORT**, **NLS_INITCAP**, **NLS_LOWER**, and **NLS_UPPER** in the Alphabetical Reference section of this book.

Review

Data comes in several types, primarily DATE, NUMBER, and CHARACTER. Character data is basically a string of letters, numbers, and other symbols, and is often called a *character string*, or just a *string*. These strings can be changed or described by string functions. Oracle features two types of character datatypes: variable-length strings (the VARCHAR2 datatype) and fixed-length strings (the CHAR datatype). Values in CHAR columns are padded with spaces to the full column length if they are shorter than the defined length of the column.

Functions such as **RPAD**, **LPAD**, **LTRIM**, **RTRIM**, **LOWER**, **UPPER**, **INITCAP**, and **SUBSTR** actually change the contents of a string or column before displaying them to you.

Functions such as **LENGTH**, **INSTR**, and **SOUNDEX** describe the characteristics of a string, such as how long it is, where in it a certain character is located, or what it sounds like.

All of these functions can be used alone or in combination to select and present information from an Oracle database. This is a straightforward process, built up from simple logical steps that can be combined to accomplish very sophisticated tasks.

CHAPTER

8

Playing the Numbers

irtually everything we do, particularly in business, is measured, explained, and often guided by numbers. While Oracle cannot correct our obsession with numbers and the illusion of control they often give us, it will facilitate capable and thorough analysis of the information in a database. Good mathematical analysis of familiar numbers will often show trends and facts that were initially not apparent.

The Three Classes of Number Functions

Oracle functions deal with three classes of numbers: single values, groups of values, and lists of values. As with string functions (discussed in Chapter 7), some of these functions change the values they are applied to, while others merely report information about the values. The classes are distinguished in this way:

A *single value* is one number, such as these:

- A literal number, such as 544.3702

- A variable in SQLPLUS or PL/SQL

- One number from one column and one row of the database

Oracle single-value functions usually change these values through a calculation.

A *group of values* is all the numbers in one column from a series of rows, such as the closing stock price for all the rows of stocks in the STOCK table. Oracle group-value functions tell you something about the whole group, such as average stock price, but not about the individual members of the group.

A *list of values* is a series of numbers that can include:

- Literal numbers, such as 1, 7.3, 22, 86

- Variables in SQLPLUS or PL/SQL

- Columns, such as OpeningPrice, ClosingPrice, Bid, Ask

Oracle list functions choose one member of a list of values.

Table 8-1 shows these functions by class. Some functions fit into more than one class. Other functions fall somewhere between string and number functions, or are used to convert data from one to the other. These are covered in Chapter 10.

Single-Value Functions

Function	Definition
value1 + value2	Addition
value1 - value2	Subtraction
*value1 * value2*	Multiplication
value1 / value2	Division
ABS(*value*)	ABSolute *value*
ACOS(*value*)	Arc COSine of *value*, in radians
ASIN(*value*)	Arc SINe of *value*, in radians
ATAN(*value*)	Arc TANgent of *value*, in radians
CEIL(*value*)	Numeric CEILing: the smallest integer larger than or equal to *value*
COS(*value*)	COSine of *value*
COSH(*value*)	Hyperbolic COSine of *value*
EXP(*value*)	e raised to *value* EXPonent
FLOOR(*value*)	Largest integer smaller than or equal to *value*
LN(*value*)	Natural Logarithm of *value*
LOG(*value*)	Base 10 LOGarithm of *value*
MOD(*value, divisor*)	MODulus
NVL(*value, substitute*)	*substitute* for *value* if *value* is NULL
POWER(*value, exponent*)	*value* raised to an *exponent* POWER
ROUND(*value, precision*)	ROUNDing of *value* to *precision*
SIGN(*value*)	1 if *value* is positive, −1 if negative, 0 if zero
SIN(*value*)	SINe of *value*
SINH(*value*)	Hyperbolic SINe of *value*

TABLE 8-1.   *Oracle Number Functions by Class*

Single-Value Functions

Function	Definition
SQRT(*value*)	SQuare RooT of *value*
TAN(*value*)	TANgent of *value*
TANH(*value*)	Hyperbolic TANgent of *value*
TRUNC(*value, precision*)	*value* TRUNCated to *precision*
VSIZE(*value*)	Storage SIZE of *value* in Oracle

Group-Value Functions

Function	Definition
AVG(*value*)	AVeraGe of *value* for group of rows
COUNT(*value*)	COUNT of rows for column
GROUPING(*expression*)	Used in conjunction with ROLLUP and CUBE functions to detect NULLs (see Chapter 13)
MAX(*value*)	MAXimum of all *values* for group of rows
MIN(*value*)	MINimum of all *values* for group of rows
STDDEV(*value*)	STanDard DEViation of all *values* for group of rows
SUM(*value*)	SUM of all *values* for group of rows
VARIANCE(*value*)	VARIANCE of all *values* for group of rows

List Functions

Function	Definition
GREATEST(*value1, value2, ...*)	GREATEST *value* of a list
LEAST(*value1, value2, ...*)	LEAST *value* of a list

TABLE 8-1. *Oracle Number Functions by Class* (continued)

Notation

Functions will be shown with this kind of notation:

```
FUNCTION(value [,option])
```

The function itself will be uppercase. Values and options will be shown in lowercase italics. Anytime the word *value* appears this way, it represents one of the following: a literal number, the name of a number column in a table, the result of a calculation, or a variable. Because Oracle does not allow numbers to be used as column names, a literal number should not be in single quotation marks (as a literal string would be in a string function). Column names also must not have quotation marks.

Every function has only one pair of parentheses. The value that function works on, as well as additional information you can pass to the function, goes between the parentheses.

Some functions have *options,* or parts that are not required to make the function work but that can give you more control if you choose to use them. Options are always shown in square brackets: [ ]. The necessary parts of a function always come before the optional parts.

Single-Value Functions

Most single-value functions are pretty straightforward. This section gives short examples, and shows both the results of the functions and how they correspond to columns, rows, and lists. After the examples, you'll see how to combine these functions.

A table named MATH was created to show the calculation effects of the many math functions. It has only four rows and four columns, as shown here:

```
select Name, Above, Below, Empty from MATH;

NAME            ABOVE   BELOW EMPTY
------------ ------- ------- -----
WHOLE NUMBER      11     -22
LOW DECIMAL    33.33  -44.44
MID DECIMAL     55.5   -55.5
HIGH DECIMAL  66.666 -77.777
```

This table is useful because it has values with a variety of characteristics, which are spelled out by the names of the rows. WHOLE NUMBER contains no decimal parts. LOW DECIMAL has decimals that are less than .5, MID DECIMAL has decimals equal to .5, and HIGH DECIMAL has decimals greater than .5. This range is particularly important when using **ROUND** and **TRUNC**ate functions, and in understanding how they affect the value of a number.

To the right of the Name column are three other columns: Above, which contains only numbers above zero (positive numbers); Below, which contains only numbers below zero; and Empty, which is **NULL**.

NOTE
*In Oracle, a number column may have no value in it at all: when it is **NULL**, it is not zero; it is simply empty. This has important implications in making computations, as you will see.*

Not all of the rows in this MATH table are needed to demonstrate how most math functions work, so the examples primarily use the last row, HIGH DECIMAL. In addition, the SQLPLUS **column** command has been used to explicitly show the precision of the calculation, so that the results of functions that affect a number's precision can be clearly seen. To review the SQL and SQLPLUS commands that produced the results that follow, look at the file math.sql (in Appendix A). Chapter 14 discusses numeric formatting issues.

Addition, Subtraction, Multiplication, and Division (+, -, *, and /)

This query shows each of the four basic arithmetic functions, using Above and Below:

```
select Name, Above, Below, Empty,
       Above + Below  AS Plus,
       Above - Below  AS Minus,
       Above * Below  AS Times,
       Above / Below  AS Divided
  from MATH
 where Name = 'HIGH DECIMAL';
```

NAME	ABOVE	BELOW	EMPTY	PLUS	MINUS	TIMES	DIVIDED
HIGH DECIMAL	66.666	-77.777		-11.111	144.443	-5185.081482	.857143

NULL

The same four arithmetic operations are now done again, except instead of using Above and Below, Above and Empty are used. Note that any arithmetic operation that includes a **NULL** value has **NULL** as a result. The calculated columns (columns whose values are the result of a calculation) Plus, Minus, Times, and Divided are all empty.

```
select Name, Above, Below, Empty,
       Above + Empty  AS Plus,
       Above - Empty  AS Minus,
       Above * Empty  AS Times,
```

```
      Above / Empty  AS Divided
   from MATH
 where Name = 'HIGH DECIMAL';

NAME            ABOVE    BELOW  EMPTY    PLUS    MINUS    TIMES    DIVIDED
------------- ------- -------- ------ ------- -------- ------- ---------
HIGH DECIMAL  66.666  -77.777
```

What you see here is evidence that a **NULL** value cannot be used in a calculation. **NULL** isn't the same as zero; think of **NULL** as a value that is unknown. For example, suppose you have a table with the names of your friends and their ages, but the Age column for PAT SMITH is empty, because you don't know it. What's the difference in your ages? It's clearly not your age minus zero. Your age minus an unknown age is also unknown, or **NULL**. You can't fill in an answer because you don't have an answer. Because you can't make the computation, the answer is **NULL**.

This is also the reason you cannot use **NULL** with an equal sign in a **where** clause (see Chapter 3). It makes no sense to say x is unknown and y is unknown, therefore x and y are equal. If Mrs. Wilkins's and Mr. Adams's ages are unknown, it doesn't mean they're the same age.

There also will be instances where **NULL** means a value is irrelevant, such as an apartment number for a house. In some cases, the apartment number might be **NULL** because it is unknown (even though it really exists), while in other cases it is **NULL** because there simply isn't one. **NULL**s will be explored in more detail later in this chapter, under "NULLs in Group-Value Functions."

NVL: NULL-Value Substitution

The previous section states the general case about **NULL**s—that **NULL** represents an unknown or irrelevant value. In particular cases, however, although a value is unknown, you may be able to make a reasonable guess. If you're a package carrier, for instance, and 30 percent of the shippers that call you for pickups can't tell you the weight or volume of their packages, will you declare it completely impossible to estimate how many cargo planes you'll need tonight? Of course not. You know from experience the average weight and volume of your packages, so you'd plug in these numbers for those customers who didn't supply you with the information. Here's the information as supplied by your clients:

```
select Client, Weight from SHIPPING;

CLIENT         WEIGHT
------------- ------
JOHNSON TOOL      59
DAGG SOFTWARE     27
TULLY ANDOVER
```

This is what the **NULL**-value substitution (**NVL**) function does:

```
select Client, NVL(Weight,43) from SHIPPING;

CLIENT          NVL(WEIGHT,43)
------------- --------------
JOHNSON TOOL               59
DAGG SOFTWARE             27
TULLY ANDOVER             43
```

Here you know that the average package weight is 43 pounds, so you use the **NVL** function to plug in 43 any time a client's package has an unknown weight—that is, where the value in the column is **NULL**. In this case, TULLY ANDOVER didn't know the weight of their package when they called it in, but you can still total these and have a fair estimate.

This is the format for **NVL**:

```
NVL(value,substitute)
```

If *value* is **NULL**, this function is equal to *substitute*. If *value* is not **NULL**, this function is equal to *value*. *substitute* can be a literal number, another column, or a computation. If you really were a package carrier with this problem, you could even have a table join in your **select** statement where *substitute* was from a view that actually averaged the weight of all non-**NULL** packages.

NVL is not restricted to numbers. It can be used with CHAR, VARCHAR2, DATE, and other datatypes as well, but the *value* and *substitute* must be the same datatype, and it is really useful only in cases where the data is unknown, not where it's irrelevant.

In the following sections, you'll see descriptions of the usage of the most commonly used arithmetic functions. The syntax for all of the functions is found in the Alphabetical Reference of this book.

ABS: Absolute Value

Absolute value is the measure of the magnitude of something. For instance, in a temperature change or a stock index change, the magnitude of the change has meaning in itself, regardless of the direction of the change (which is important in its own right). Absolute value is always a positive number.

This is the format for **ABS**:

```
ABS(value)
```

Note these examples:

```
ABS(146) = 146
ABS(-30) =  30
```

CEIL

CEIL (for ceiling) simply produces the smallest *integer* (or whole number) that is greater than or equal to a specific value. Pay special attention to its effect on negative numbers.

The following is the format for **CEIL** and some examples:

```
CEIL(value)
```

```
CEIL(2)    =  2
CEIL(1.3)  =  2
CEIL(-2)   = -2
CEIL(-2.3) = -2
```

FLOOR

FLOOR is the intuitive opposite of **CEIL**. This is the format for **FLOOR**, and some examples:

```
FLOOR(value)
```

```
FLOOR(2)    =  2
FLOOR(1.3)  =  1
FLOOR(-2)   = -2
FLOOR(-2.3) = -3
```

MOD

MODulus is an odd little function primarily used in data processing for esoteric tasks, such as "check digits," which helps assure the accurate transmission of a string of numbers. An example of this is given in "Using MOD in DECODE" in Chapter 17. **MOD** divides a value by a divisor and tells you the remainder. For example, **MOD**(23,6) = 5 means divide 23 by 6. The answer is 3 with 5 left over, so 5 is the result of the modulus.

This is the format for **MOD**:

```
MOD(value,divisor)
```

Both *value* and *divisor* can be any real number. The value of **MOD** is zero if *divisor* is zero or negative. Note the following examples:

```
MOD(100,10)  =  0
MOD(22,23)   = 22
MOD(10,3)    =  1
```

```
MOD(-30.23,7)   = -2.23
MOD(4.1,.3)     =    .2
```

The second example shows what **MOD** does whenever the divisor is larger than the dividend (the number being divided). It produces the dividend as a result. Also note this important case where *value* is an integer:

```
MOD(value,1)    = 0
```

The preceding is a good test to see if a number is an integer.

POWER

POWER is simply the ability to raise a value to a given positive exponent, as shown here:

```
POWER(value,exponent)
```

```
POWER(3,2)         =      9
POWER(3,3)         =     27
POWER(-77.777,2)   = 6049.261729
POWER(3,1.086)     =      3.297264
POWER(64,.5)       =      8
```

The exponent can be any real number.

SQRT: Square Root

Oracle has a separate square root function that gives results equivalent to **POWER**(*value*,.5):

```
SQRT(value)
```

```
SQRT(64)     = 8
SQRT(66.666) = 8.16492
SQRT(4)      = 2
```

The square root of a negative number is an imaginary number. Oracle doesn't support imaginary numbers, so it returns an error if you attempt to find the square root of a negative number.

EXP, LN, and LOG

The **EXP**, **LN**, and **LOG** functions are rarely used in business calculations but are quite common in scientific and technical work. **EXP** is *e* (2.71828183...) raised to the specified power; **LN** is the "natural," or base *e*, logarithm of a value. The first two functions are reciprocals of one another; **LN**(**EXP**(*i*)) = *value*. The **LOG** function takes a base and a positive value. **LN**(*value*) is the same as **LOG**(2.71828183,*value*).

EXP(*value*)

```
EXP(3)       =  20.085537
EXP(5)       = 148.413159
```

LN(*value*)

```
LN(3)        = 1.098612
LN(20.085536) = 3
```

LOG(*value*)

```
LOG(EXP(1),3) = 1.098612
LOG(10,100)   = 2
```

ROUND and TRUNC

ROUND and **TRUNC** are two related single-value functions. **TRUNC** truncates, or chops off, digits of precision from a number; **ROUND** rounds numbers to a given number of digits of precision.

Here are the formats for **ROUND** and **TRUNC**:

```
ROUND(value,precision)
TRUNC(value,precision)
```

There are some properties worth paying close attention to here. First, look at this simple example of a **select** from the MATH table. Two digits of precision are called for (counting toward the right from the decimal point).

```
select Name, Above, Below,
       ROUND(Above,2),
       ROUND(Below,2),
       TRUNC(Above,2),
       TRUNC(Below,2)
  from MATH;
```

NAME	ABOVE	BELOW	ROUND (ABOVE,2)	ROUND (BELOW,2)	TRUNC (ABOVE,2)	TRUNC (BELOW,2)
WHOLE NUMBER	11	-22	11	-22	11	-22
LOW DECIMAL	33.33	-44.44	33.33	-44.44	33.33	-44.44
MID DECIMAL	55.5	-55.5	55.5	-55.5	55.5	-55.5
HIGH DECIMAL	66.666	-77.777	66.67	-77.78	66.66	-77.77

Only the bottom row is affected, because only it has three digits beyond the decimal point. Both the positive and negative numbers in the bottom row were rounded or truncated: the 66.666 was rounded to a higher number, 66.67, but the -77.777 was rounded to a lower (more negative) number, -77.78. When rounding is done to zero digits, this is the result:

```
select Name, Above, Below,
       ROUND(Above,0),
       ROUND(Below,0),
       TRUNC(Above,0),
       TRUNC(Below,0)
  from MATH;
```

NAME	ABOVE	BELOW	ROUND (ABOVE,0)	ROUND (BELOW,0)	TRUNC (ABOVE,0)	TRUNC (BELOW,0)
WHOLE NUMBER	11	-22	11	-22	11	-22
LOW DECIMAL	33.33	-44.44	33	-44	33	-44
MID DECIMAL	55.5	-55.5	56	-56	55	-55
HIGH DECIMAL	66.666	-77.777	67	-78	66	-77

Note that the decimal value of .5 was rounded up when 55.5 went to 56. This follows the most common American rounding convention (some rounding conventions round up only if a number is larger than .5). Compare these results with **CEIL** and **FLOOR**. They have significant differences:

```
ROUND(55.5) = 56    ROUND(-55.5) = -56
TRUNC(55.5) = 55    TRUNC(-55.5) = -55
CEIL(55.5)  = 56    CEIL(-55.5)  = -55
FLOOR(55.5) = 55    FLOOR(-55.5) = -56
```

Finally, note that both **ROUND** and **TRUNC** can work with negative precision, moving to the left of the decimal point:

```
select Name, Above, Below,
       ROUND(Above,-1),
       ROUND(Below,-1),
       TRUNC(Above,-1),
       TRUNC(Below,-1)
  from MATH;
```

NAME	ABOVE	BELOW	ROUND (ABOVE,-1)	ROUND (BELOW,-1)	TRUNC (ABOVE,-1)	TRUNC (BELOW,-1)
WHOLE NUMBER	11	-22	10	-20	10	-20
LOW DECIMAL	33.33	-44.44	30	-40	30	-40
MID DECIMAL	55.5	-55.5	60	-60	50	-50
HIGH DECIMAL	66.666	-77.777	70	-80	60	-70

Rounding with a negative number can be useful when producing such things as economic reports, where populations or dollar sums need to be rounded up to the millions, billions, or trillions.

SIGN

SIGN is the flip side of absolute value. Whereas **ABS** tells you the magnitude of a value but not its sign, **SIGN** tells you the sign of a value but not its magnitude.

This is the format for **SIGN**:

```
SIGN(value)
```

```
Examples: SIGN(146) =  1  Compare to: ABS(146) = 146
          SIGN(-30) = -1              ABS(-30) =  30
```

The **SIGN** of 0 is 0:

```
SIGN(0)=0
```

The **SIGN** function is often used in conjunction with the **DECODE** function. **DECODE** will be described in Chapter 17.

SIN, SINH, COS, COSH, TAN, TANH, ACOS, ATAN, ATAN2, and ASIN

The trigonometric functions sine, cosine, and tangent are scientific and technical functions not used much in business. **SIN**, **COS**, and **TAN** give you the standard trigonometric function values for an angle expressed in radians (degrees multiplied by *pi* divided by 180). **SINH**, **COSH**, and **TANH** give you the hyperbolic functions for an angle.

```
SIN(value)
```

```
SIN(30*3.141593/180) = .5
```

```
COSH(value)
```

```
COSH(0)            = 1
```

The **ASIN**, **ACOS**, and **ATAN** functions return the arc sine, arc cosine, and arc tangent values (in radians) of the values provided.

Group-Value Functions

Group-value functions are those statistical functions such as **SUM**, **AVG**, **COUNT**, and the like that tell you something about a group of values taken as a whole: the average age of all of the friends in the table mentioned earlier, for instance, or the oldest member of the group, or the youngest, or the number of members in the group, and more. Even when one of these functions is supplying information about a single row—such as the oldest person—it is still information that is defined by the row's relation to the group.

NULLs in Group-Value Functions

Group-value functions treat **NULL** values differently than single-value functions do. Group functions ignore **NULL** values and calculate a result in spite of them.

Take **AVG** as an example. Suppose you have a list of 100 friends and their ages. If you picked 20 of them at random, and averaged their ages, how different would the result be than if you picked a different list of 20, also at random, and averaged it, or if you averaged all 100? In fact, the averages of these three groups would be very close. What this means is that **AVG** is somewhat insensitive to missing records, even when the missing data represents a high percentage of the total number of records available.

NOTE
Average is not immune to missing data, and there can be cases where it will be significantly off (such as when missing data is not randomly distributed), but these will be less common.

The relative insensitivity to missing data of **AVG** needs to be contrasted with, for instance, **SUM**. How close to correct is the **SUM** of the ages of only 20 friends to the **SUM** of all 100 friends? Not close at all. So if you had a table of friends, but only 20 out of 100 supplied their ages, and 80 out of 100 had **NULL** for their age, which would be a more reliable statistic about the whole group and less sensitive to the absence of data—the **AVG** age of those 20 names, or the **SUM** of them? Note that this is an entirely different issue than whether it is possible to estimate the sum of all 100 based on only 20 (in fact, it is precisely the **AVG** of the 20, times 100). The point is, if you don't know how many rows are **NULL**, you can use the following to provide a fairly reasonable result:

```
select AVG(Age) from LIST;
```

You cannot get a reasonable result from this, however:

```
select SUM(Age) from LIST;
```

This same test of whether or not results are reasonable defines how the other group functions respond to **NULL**s. **STDDEV** and **VARIANCE** are measures of central tendency; they, too, are relatively insensitive to missing data. (These will be covered in "STDDEV and VARIANCE," later in this chapter.)

MAX and **MIN** measure the extremes of your data. They can fluctuate wildly while **AVG** stays relatively constant: if you add a 100-year-old man to a group of 99 people who are 50 years old, the average age only goes up to 50.5—but the maximum age has doubled. Add a newborn baby, and the average goes back to 50, but the minimum age is now 0. It's clear that missing unknown **NULL** values can profoundly affect **MAX**, **MIN**, and **SUM**, so be cautious when using them, particularly if a significant percentage of the data is **NULL**.

Is it possible to create functions that also take into account how sparse the data is and how many values are **NULL** compared to how many have real values, and make good guesses about **MAX**, **MIN**, and **SUM**? Yes, but such functions would be statistical projections, which must make explicit their assumptions about a particular set of data. It is not an appropriate task for a general-purpose group function. Some statisticians would argue that these functions should return **NULL** if they encounter any **NULL**s, since returning any value can be misleading. Oracle returns something rather than nothing, but leaves it up to you to decide whether the result is reasonable.

COUNT is a special case. It can go either way with **NULL** values, but it always returns a number; it will never evaluate to **NULL**. Format and usage for **COUNT** will be shown shortly, but to simply contrast it with the other group functions, it will count all of the non-**NULL** rows of a column, or it will count all of the rows. In other words, if asked to count the ages of 100 friends, **COUNT** will return a value of 20 (since only 20 of the 100 gave their age). If asked to count the rows in a table of friends without specifying a column, it will return 100. An example of these differences is given in "DISTINCT in Group Functions," later in this chapter.

Examples of Single- and Group-Value Functions

Neither the group-value functions nor the single-value functions are particularly difficult to understand, but a practical overview of how each function works is helpful in fleshing out some of the options and consequences of their use.

The COMFORT table in these examples contains basic temperature data by city at noon and midnight on each of four sample days each year: the equinoxes (about March 21 and September 23) and the solstices (about June 22 and December 22). You ought to be able to characterize cities based on their temperatures on these days each year.

For the sake of these examples, this table has only eight rows: the data from the four dates in 1999 for San Francisco, California and Keene, New Hampshire.

You can use Oracle's number functions to analyze these cities, their average temperature, the volatility of the temperature, and so on, for 1999. With more years and data on more cities, an analysis of temperature patterns and variability throughout the century could be made.

The table looks like this:

```
describe COMFORT

Name                            Null?   Type
------------------------------- ------  ----
CITY                                    VARCHAR2(13)
SAMPLEDATE                              DATE
NOON                                    NUMBER
MIDNIGHT                                NUMBER
```

It contains this data:

```
select * from COMFORT;

CITY          SAMPLEDAT NOON MIDNIGHT
------------- --------- ---- --------
SAN FRANCISCO 21-MAR-99 62.5     42.3
SAN FRANCISCO 22-JUN-99 51.1     71.9
SAN FRANCISCO 23-SEP-99          61.5
SAN FRANCISCO 22-DEC-99 52.6     39.8
KEENE         21-MAR-99 39.9     -1.2
KEENE         22-JUN-99 85.1     66.7
KEENE         23-SEP-99 99.8     82.6
KEENE         22-DEC-99 -7.2     -1.2
```

AVG, COUNT, MAX, MIN, and SUM

Due to a power failure, the noon temperature in San Francisco on September 23 did not get recorded. The consequences of this can be seen in the following query:

```
select AVG(Noon), COUNT(Noon), MAX(Noon), MIN(Noon), SUM(Noon)
  from COMFORT
 where City = 'SAN FRANCISCO';

AVG(NOON) COUNT(NOON) MAX(NOON) MIN(NOON) SUM(NOON)
--------- ----------- --------- --------- ---------
     55.4           3      62.5      51.1     166.2
```

AVG(Noon) is the average of the three temperatures that are known. **COUNT**(Noon) is the average of those that are not **NULL**. **MAX** and **MIN** are self-evident. **SUM**(Noon) is the sum of only three dates because of the **NULL** for September 23. Note that

```
SUM(NOON)
---------
    166.2
```

is by no coincidence exactly three times the **AVG**(Noon).

Combining Group-Value and Single-Value Functions

Suppose you would like to know how much the temperature changes in the course of a day. This is a measure of *volatility*. Your first attempt to answer the question might be to subtract the temperature at midnight from the temperature at noon:

```
select City, SampleDate, Noon-Midnight
   from COMFORT
 where City = 'KEENE';

CITY            SAMPLEDAT NOON-MIDNIGHT
--------------- --------- -------------
KEENE           21-MAR-99          41.1
KEENE           22-JUN-99          18.4
KEENE           23-SEP-99          17.2
KEENE           22-DEC-99            -6
```

With only four rows to consider in this table, you can quickly convert (or ignore) the pesky minus sign. Volatility in temperature is really a magnitude—which means it asks by how much the temperature changed. It doesn't include a sign, so the -6 isn't really correct. If it goes uncorrected, and is included in a further calculation, such as the average change in a year, the answer you get will be absolutely wrong, as shown here:

```
select AVG(Noon-Midnight)
   from COMFORT
 where City = 'KEENE';

AVG(NOON-MIDNIGHT)
------------------
             17.68
```

The correct answer requires an absolute value, as shown next.

```
select AVG(ABS(Noon-Midnight))
  from COMFORT
 where City = 'KEENE';

AVG(ABS(NOON-MIDNIGHT))
-----------------------
                  20.68
```

Combining functions this way follows the same technique given in Chapter 7 in the section on string functions. An entire function such as

```
ABS(Noon-Midnight)
```

is simply plugged into another function as its value, like this:

```
AVG(value)
```

which produces

```
AVG(ABS(Noon-Midnight))
```

This shows both single-value and group-value functions at work. You see that you can place single-value functions inside group-value functions. The single-value functions will calculate a result for every row, and the group-value functions will view that result as if it were the actual value for the row. Single-value functions can be combined (*nested* inside each other) almost without limit. Group-value functions can contain single-value functions in place of their value. They can, in fact, contain many single-value functions in place of their value.

What about combining group functions? First of all, it doesn't make any sense to nest them this way:

```
select SUM(AVG(Noon)) from COMFORT;
```

The preceding will produce this error:

```
ERROR at line 1:
ORA-00978: nested group function without GROUP BY
```

Besides, if it actually worked, it would produce exactly the same result as this:

```
AVG(Noon)
```

because the result of **AVG**(Noon) is just a single value. The **SUM** of a single value is just the single value, so it is not meaningful to nest group functions. The exception to this rule is in the use of **group by** in the **select** statement, the absence of which is why Oracle produced the error message here. This is covered in Chapter 11.

It *can* be meaningful to add, subtract, multiply, or divide the results of two or more group functions. For example,

```
select MAX(Noon) - MIN(Noon)
  from COMFORT
 where City = 'SAN FRANCISCO';


MAX(NOON)-MIN(NOON)
-------------------
              11.4
```

gives the range of the temperatures in a year. In fact, a quick comparison of San Francisco and Keene could be done with just a bit more effort:

```
select City, AVG(Noon), MAX(Noon), MIN(Noon),
       MAX(Noon) - MIN(Noon) AS Swing
  from COMFORT
 group by City;


CITY           AVG(NOON) MAX(NOON) MIN(NOON) SWING
------------- --------- --------- --------- -----
KEENE              54.4      99.8      -7.2   107
SAN FRANCISCO      55.4      62.5      51.1  11.4
```

This query is a good example of discovering information in your data: the average temperature in the two cities is nearly identical, but the huge temperature swing in Keene, compared to San Francisco, says a lot about the yearly temperature volatility of the two cities, and the relative effort required to dress (or heat and cool a home) in one city compared to the other. The **group by** clause will be explained in detail in Chapter 11. Briefly, in this example it forced the group functions to work not on the total table, but on the subgroups of temperatures by city.

STDDEV and VARIANCE

Standard deviation and variance have their common statistical meanings, and use the same format as all group functions:

```
select MAX(Noon), AVG(Noon), MIN(Noon), STDDEV(Noon),
       VARIANCE(Noon)
  from COMFORT
 where City = 'KEENE';
```

```
MAX(NOON)  AVG(NOON)  MIN(NOON)  STDDEV(NOON)  VARIANCE(NOON)
---------  ---------  ---------  ------------  --------------
     99.8       54.4       -7.2         48.33            2336
```

DISTINCT in Group Functions

All group-value functions have a **DISTINCT** versus **ALL** option. **COUNT** provides a good example of how this works.

This is the format for **COUNT** (I means "or"):

```
COUNT([DISTINCT | ALL] value)
```

Here is an example:

```
select COUNT(DISTINCT City), COUNT(City), COUNT(*)
   from COMFORT;

COUNT(DISTINCTCITY) COUNT(CITY) COUNT(*)
------------------- ----------- --------
                  2           8        8
```

This query shows a couple of interesting results. First, **DISTINCT** forces **COUNT** to count only the number of unique city names. If asked to count the **DISTINCT** midnight temperatures, it would return 7, because two of the eight temperatures were the same. When **COUNT** is used on City but not forced to look at **DISTINCT** cities, it finds 8.

This also shows that **COUNT** can work on a character column. It's not making a computation on the values in the column, as **SUM** or **AVG** must; it is merely counting how many rows have a value in the specified column.

COUNT has another unique property: *value* can be an asterisk, meaning that **COUNT** tells you how many rows are in the table, regardless of whether any specific columns are **NULL**. It will count a row even if all of its fields are **NULL**.

The other group functions do not share **COUNT**'s ability to use an asterisk, nor its ability to use a character column for *value* (although **MAX** and **MIN** can). They do all share its use of **DISTINCT**, which forces each of them to operate only on unique values. A table with values such as this:

```
select FirstName, Age from BIRTHDAY;

FIRSTNAME         AGE
---------------   ----
GEORGE             42
ROBERT             52
NANCY              42
VICTORIA           42
FRANK              42
```

would produce this result:

```
select AVG(DISTINCT Age) AS Average,
       SUM(DISTINCT Age) AS Total
  from BIRTHDAY;


AVERAGE  TOTAL
-------  ------
     47      94
```

which, if you wanted to know the average age of your friends, is not the right answer. The use of **DISTINCT** other than in **COUNT** is likely to be extremely rare, except perhaps in some statistical calculations. **MAX** and **MIN** produce the same result with or without **DISTINCT**.

The alternative option to **DISTINCT** is **ALL**, which is the default. **ALL** tells SQL to check every row, even if the value is a duplicate of the value in another row. You do not need to type **ALL**; if you don't type in **DISTINCT**, **ALL** is used automatically.

List Functions

Unlike the group-value functions, which work on a group of rows, the list functions work on a group of columns, either actual or calculated values, within a single row. In other words, list functions compare the values of each of several columns and pick either the greatest or least of the list. Consider the COMFORT table, shown here:

```
select * from COMFORT;

CITY           SAMPLEDAT NOON  MIDNIGHT
-------------  --------- ----  --------
SAN FRANCISCO  21-MAR-99 62.5      42.3
SAN FRANCISCO  22-JUN-99 51.1      71.9
SAN FRANCISCO  23-SEP-99           61.5
SAN FRANCISCO  22-DEC-99 52.6      39.8
KEENE          21-MAR-99 39.9      -1.2
KEENE          22-JUN-99 85.1      66.7
KEENE          23-SEP-99 99.8      82.6
KEENE          22-DEC-99 -7.2      -1.2
```

Now compare this query result with the following one. Note especially June and September in San Francisco, and December in Keene:

```
select City, SampleDate, GREATEST(Midnight,Noon) AS High,
       LEAST(Midnight,Noon) AS Low
  from COMFORT;
```

```
CITY          SAMPLEDAT High  Low
------------- --------- ----  ----
SAN FRANCISCO 21-MAR-99 62.5  42.3
SAN FRANCISCO 22-JUN-99 71.9  51.1
SAN FRANCISCO 23-SEP-99
SAN FRANCISCO 22-DEC-99 52.6  39.8
KEENE         21-MAR-99 39.9  -1.2
KEENE         22-JUN-99 85.1  66.7
KEENE         23-SEP-99 99.8  82.6
KEENE         22-DEC-99 -1.2  -7.2
```

September in San Francisco has a **NULL** result because **GREATEST** and **LEAST** couldn't legitimately compare an actual midnight temperature with an unknown noon temperature. In the other two instances, the midnight temperature was actually higher than the noon temperature.

These are the formats for **GREATEST** and **LEAST**:

```
GREATEST(value1,value2,value3. . .)
LEAST(value1,value2,value3. . .)
```

Both **GREATEST** and **LEAST** can be used with many values, and the values can be columns, literal numbers, calculations, or combinations of other columns. **GREATEST** and **LEAST** can also be used with character columns. For example, they can choose the names that fall last (**GREATEST**) or first (**LEAST**) in alphabetical order:

```
GREATEST('Bob','George','Andrew','Isaiah') = Isaiah
   LEAST('Bob','George','Andrew','Isaiah') = Andrew
```

Finding Rows with MAX or MIN

Which city had the highest temperature ever recorded, and on what date? The answer is easy with just eight rows to look at, but what if you have data from every city in the country and for every day of every year for the last 50 years? Assume for now that the highest temperature for the year occurred closer to noon than midnight. The following won't work:

```
select City, SampleDate, MAX(Noon)
   from COMFORT;
```

Oracle flags the City column and gives this error message:

```
select City, SampleDate, MAX(Noon)
       *
ERROR at line 1:
ORA-00937: not a single-group group function
```

This error message is a bit opaque. It means that Oracle has detected a flaw in the logic of the question. Asking for columns means you want individual rows to appear; asking for **MAX**, a group function, means you want a group result for all rows. These are two different kinds of requests. The first asks for a set of rows, the second requests just one computed row, so there is a conflict. Here is how to construct the query:

```
select City, SampleDate, Noon
   from COMFORT
 where Noon = (select MAX(Noon) from COMFORT);

CITY          SAMPLEDAT  NOON
------------  ---------- -----
KEENE         23-SEP-99  99.8
```

This only produces one row. You might think, therefore, that the combination of a request for the City and SampleDate columns along with the **MAX** of noon is not so contradictory as was just implied. But what if you'd asked for minimum temperature instead?

```
select City, SampleDate, Midnight
   from COMFORT
 where Midnight = (select MIN(Midnight) from COMFORT);

CITY          SAMPLEDAT MIDNIGHT
------------  --------- --------
KEENE         21-MAR-99     -1.2
KEENE         22-DEC-99     -1.2
```

Two rows! More than one satisfied the **MIN** request, so there is a conflict in trying to combine a regular column request with a group function.

It is also possible to use two subqueries, each with a group-value function in it (or two subqueries, where one does and the other doesn't have a group function). Suppose you want to know the highest and lowest noon temperatures for the year:

```
select City, SampleDate, Noon
   from COMFORT
 where Noon = (select MAX(Noon) from COMFORT)
    or Noon = (select MIN(Noon) from COMFORT);

CITY          SAMPLEDAT  NOON
------------  --------- -----
KEENE         23-SEP-99  99.8
KEENE         22-DEC-99  -7.2
```

Precedence and Parentheses

When more than one arithmetic or logical operator is used in a single calculation, which one is executed first, and does it matter what order they are in? Consider the following query of the DUAL table (a one-column, one-row table provided by Oracle):

```
select 2/2/4 from DUAL;

2/2/4
-----
  .25
```

When parentheses are introduced, although the numbers and the operation (division) stay the same, the answer changes considerably:

```
select 2/(2/4) from DUAL;

2/(2/4)
-------
      4
```

The reason for this is *precedence.* Precedence defines the order in which mathematical computations are made, not just in Oracle but in mathematics in general. The rules are simple: parentheses have the highest precedence, then multiplication and division, then addition and subtraction. When an equation is computed, any calculations inside of parentheses are made first. Multiplication and division are next. Finally, any addition and subtraction are completed. When operations of equal precedence are to be performed, they are executed from left to right. Here are a few examples:

```
2*4/2*3 = 12            (the same as ( (2*4)/2 )*3)
(2*4)/(2*3) = 1.333
4-2*5 = -6             (the same as 4 - (2*5))
(4-2)*5 = 10
```

AND or **OR** also obey precedence rules, with **AND** having the higher precedence. Observe the effect of the **AND**, and also the left-to-right order, in these two queries:

```
select * from NEWSPAPER
  where Section = 'B' AND Page = 1 OR Page = 2;
```

```
FEATURE          S  PAGE
--------------   -  -----
Weather          C    2
Modern Life      B    1
Bridge           B    2

3 rows selected.

select * from NEWSPAPER
 where Page = 1 OR Page = 2 AND Section = 'B';

FEATURE          S  PAGE
--------------   -  -----
National News    A    1
Sports           D    1
Business         E    1
Modern Life      B    1
Bridge           B    2

5 rows selected.
```

If what you really desire is page 1 or 2 in Section B, then parentheses are needed to overcome the precedence of the **AND**. Parentheses override any other operations.

```
select * from NEWSPAPER
 where Section = 'B' AND (Page = 1 OR Page = 2);

FEATURE          S  PAGE
--------------   -  -----
Modern Life      B    1
Bridge           B    2

2 rows selected.
```

The truth is, even experienced programmers and mathematicians have trouble remembering what will execute first when they write a query or an equation. It is always wise to make explicit the order you want Oracle to follow. Use parentheses whenever there could be the slightest risk of confusion.

Review

Single-value functions work on values in a row-by-row fashion. List functions compare columns and choose just one, again in a row-by-row fashion. Single-value functions almost always change the value of the column they are applied to. This doesn't mean, of course, that they have modified the database from which the value was drawn, but they do make a calculation with that value, and the result is different than the original value. For example:

```
ROUND(99.308,-1) = 90
```

The result of the **ROUND** function is to *change* the 99.308 value to 90. List functions don't change values in this way, but rather they simply choose (or report) the **GREATEST** or **LEAST** of a series of values in a row. Both single-value and list functions will not produce a result if they encounter a value that is **NULL**.

Both single-value and list functions can be used anywhere an expression can be used, such as in the **select** and **where** clauses.

The group-value functions tell something about a whole group of numbers— all of the rows in a set. The group-value functions tell you the average of those numbers, or the largest of them, or how many there are, or the standard deviation of the values, and so on. Group functions ignore **NULL** values, and this fact must be kept firmly in mind when reporting about groups of values; otherwise, there is considerable risk of misunderstanding the data.

Group-value functions also can report information on subgroups within a table, or be used to create a summary view of information from one or more tables. Chapter 11 gives details on these additional features.

Finally, mathematical and logical precedence affect the order in which queries are evaluated, and this can have a dramatic effect on query results. Get into the habit of using parentheses to make the order you desire both explicit and easy to understand.

CHAPTER
9

Dates: Then, Now, and the Difference

ne of Oracle's more unusual strengths is its ability to store and calculate dates, and the number of seconds, minutes, hours, days, months, and years between dates. It also has the remarkable ability to format dates in virtually any manner you can conceive of, from a simple 01-MAY-00, to May 1st in the 774th Year of the Reign of Louis IX. You probably won't use many of these date-formatting and computing functions, but the most basic ones will prove to be very important.

Date Arithmetic

DATE is an Oracle datatype, just as CHAR and NUMBER are, and it has its own unique properties. The DATE datatype is stored in a special internal Oracle format that includes not just the month, day, and year, but also the hour, minute, and second. The benefit of all this detail should be obvious. If you have, for instance, a customer help desk, for each call that is logged in, Oracle can automatically store the date and time of the call in a single Date column. You can format the Date column on a report to show just the date, or the date and the hour, or the date, hour, and minute, or the date, hour, minute, and second.

SQLPLUS and SQL recognize columns that are of the DATE datatype, and understand that instructions to do arithmetic with them call for *date arithmetic*, not regular math. Adding one to a date, for instance, will give you another *date:* the next day. Subtracting one date from another will give you a *number:* count of days between the two dates.

However, since Oracle dates can include hours, minutes, and seconds, doing date arithmetic can prove to be tricky, since Oracle could tell you the difference between today and tomorrow is .516 days! (This will be explained later in this chapter.)

NOTE
The examples from Talbot's ledger reflect the actual transaction dates found there—thus, many of the example dates are from the year 1901. In the scripts provided in Appendix A, the inserted date values for Talbot's ledger explicitly include the century. Depending on your database parameters (and the current date), a year value of 01 may be interpreted as either 1901 or 2001. To avoid century ambiguity, the examples in this chapter that are potentially affected by century ambiguity will use all four digits of the year.

SysDate

Oracle taps into the computer's operating system for the current date and time. It makes these available to you through a special column called SysDate. Think of SysDate as a function whose result is always the current date and time, and that can be used anywhere any other Oracle function can be used. You also can regard it as a hidden column or pseudo-column that is in every table. Here, SysDate shows today's date:

```
select SysDate from DUAL;

SYSDATE
---------
01-MAR-00
```

> **NOTE**
> *DUAL is a small but useful Oracle table created for testing functions or doing quick calculations. Later in this chapter, the sidebar "The DUAL Table for Quick Tests and Calculations" describes DUAL.*

The Difference Between Two Dates

HOLIDAY is a table of some secular holidays in the United States during 2000:

```
select Holiday, ActualDate, CelebratedDate from HOLIDAY;

HOLIDAY                     ACTUALDAT CELEBRATE
------------------------ --------- ---------
NEW YEAR DAY                01-JAN-00 01-JAN-00
MARTIN LUTHER KING, JR.     15-JAN-00 17-JAN-00
LINCOLNS BIRTHDAY           12-FEB-00 21-FEB-00
WASHINGTONS BIRTHDAY        22-FEB-00 21-FEB-00
FAST DAY, NEW HAMPSHIRE     22-FEB-00 22-FEB-00
MEMORIAL DAY                30-MAY-00 29-MAY-00
INDEPENDENCE DAY            04-JUL-00 04-JUL-00
LABOR DAY                   04-SEP-00 04-SEP-00
COLUMBUS DAY                08-OCT-00 09-OCT-00
THANKSGIVING                23-NOV-00 23-NOV-00
```

Which holidays are not celebrated on the actual date of their anniversary during 2000? This can be easily answered by subtracting the CelebratedDate from the ActualDate. If the answer is not zero, then there is a difference between the two dates:

```
select Holiday, ActualDate, CelebratedDate
  from Holiday
 where CelebratedDate - ActualDate != 0;
```

```
HOLIDAY                       ACTUALDAT CELEBRATE
----------------------------  --------- ---------
MARTIN LUTHER KING, JR.       15-JAN-00 17-JAN-00
LINCOLNS BIRTHDAY             12-FEB-00 21-FEB-00
WASHINGTONS BIRTHDAY          22-FEB-00 21-FEB-00
MEMORIAL DAY                  30-MAY-00 29-MAY-00
COLUMBUS DAY                  08-OCT-00 09-OCT-00
```

The DUAL Table for Quick Tests and Calculations

DUAL is a tiny table Oracle provides with only one row and one column in it:

```
describe DUAL
```

Name	Null?	Type
DUMMY		CHAR(1)

Since Oracle's many functions work on both columns and literals, using DUAL lets you see some functioning using just literals. In these examples, the **select** statement doesn't care which columns are in the table, and a single row is sufficient to demonstrate a point. For example, suppose you want to quickly calculate **POWER**(4,3)—four "cubed":

```
select POWER(4,3) from DUAL;
```

```
POWER(4,3)
----------
        64
```

The actual column in DUAL is irrelevant. This means that you can experiment with date formatting and arithmetic using the DUAL table and the date functions in order to understand how they work. Then, those functions can be applied to actual dates in real tables.

Date Functions

The major functions performed on DATE datatype columns are:

- **ADD_MONTHS**(*date,count*)   **Add**s *count* **months** to *date*.

- **GREATEST**(*date1,date2,date3,...*)   Picks latest date from list of dates.

- **LEAST**(*date1,date2,date3,...*)   Picks earliest date from list of dates.

- **LAST_DAY**(*date*)   Gives date of **last day** of month that *date* is in.

- **MONTHS_BETWEEN**(*date2,date1*)   Gives *date2–date1* in **months** (can be fractional months).

- **NEXT_DAY**(*date,'day'*)   Gives date of **next day** after *date*, where '*day*' is 'Monday', 'Tuesday', and so on.

- **NEW_TIME**(*date,'this','other'*)   Gives the *date* (and time) in *this* time zone. *this* will be replaced by a three-letter abbreviation for the current time zone. *other* will be replaced by a three-letter abbreviation for the other time zone for which you'd like to know the time and date.

Time zones are as follows:

AST/ADT	Atlantic standard/daylight time
BST/BDT	Bering standard/daylight time
CST/CDT	Central standard/daylight time
EST/EDT	Eastern standard/daylight time
GMT	Greenwich mean time
HST/HDT	Alaska-Hawaii standard/daylight time
MST/MDT	Mountain standard/daylight time
NST	Newfoundland standard time
PST/PDT	Pacific standard/daylight time
YST/YDT	Yukon standard/daylight time

- **ROUND**(*date,'format'*) Without *format* specified, **round**s a *date* to 12 A.M. (midnight, the beginning of that day) if time of *date* is before noon; otherwise, **round**s up to next day. For use of *format* for rounding, see ROUND in the Alphabetical Reference.

- **TRUNC**(*date,'format'*) Without *format* specified, sets a *date* to 12 A.M. (midnight, the beginning of that day). For use of *format* for truncating, see TRUNC in the Alphabetical Reference.

- **TO_CHAR**(*date,'format'*) Reformats *date* according to *format*.*

- **TO_DATE**(*string,'format'*) Converts a *string* in a given `format` into an Oracle date. Will also accept a *number* instead of a *string*, with certain limits. *'format'* is restricted.

*See the sidebar "Date Formats" later in this chapter.

Adding Months

If February 22 is "Fast Day" in New Hampshire, perhaps six months later could be celebrated as "Feast Day." If so, what would the date be? Simply use the **ADD_MONTHS** function, adding a **count** of six months, as shown here:

```
column FeastDay heading "Feast Day"

select ADD_MONTHS(CelebratedDate,6) AS FeastDay
  from HOLIDAY
 where Holiday like 'FAST%';

Feast Day
---------
22-AUG-00
```

Subtracting Months

If picnic area reservations have to be made at least six months before Columbus Day, what's the last day you can make them? Take the CelebratedDate for Columbus Day, and use **ADD_MONTHS**, adding a *negative* **count** of six months (this is the same as subtracting months). This will tell you the date six months before Columbus Day. Then subtract one day.

```
column LastDay heading "Last Day"

select ADD_MONTHS(CelebratedDate,-6) - 1 AS LastDay
  from HOLIDAY
 where Holiday = 'COLUMBUS DAY';


Last Day
---------
08-APR-00
```

GREATEST and LEAST

Which comes first for each of the holidays that were moved to fall on Mondays, the actual or the celebrated date? The **LEAST** function chooses the earliest date from a list of dates, whether columns or literals; **GREATEST** chooses the latest date. These **GREATEST** and **LEAST** functions are exactly the same ones that are used with numbers and character strings:

```
select Holiday, LEAST(ActualDate, CelebratedDate) AS First,
       ActualDate, CelebratedDate
  from HOLIDAY
 where ActualDate - CelebratedDate != 0;

HOLIDAY                    FIRST     ACTUALDAT CELEBRATE
------------------------  --------- --------- ---------
MARTIN LUTHER KING, JR.   15-JAN-00 15-JAN-00 17-JAN-00
LINCOLNS BIRTHDAY         12-FEB-00 12-FEB-00 21-FEB-00
WASHINGTONS BIRTHDAY      21-FEB-00 22-FEB-00 21-FEB-00
MEMORIAL DAY              29-MAY-00 30-MAY-00 29-MAY-00
COLUMBUS DAY              08-OCT-00 08-OCT-00 09-OCT-00
```

Here, **LEAST** worked just fine, because it operated on DATE columns from a table. What about literals?

```
select LEAST('20-JAN-00','20-DEC-00') from DUAL;

LEAST('20
---------
20-DEC-00
```

This is quite wrong, almost as if you'd said **GREATEST** instead of **LEAST**. December 20, 2000, is not earlier than January 20, 2000. Why did this happen? Because **LEAST** treated these literals as *strings*.

A Warning About GREATEST and LEAST

Unlike many other Oracle functions and logical operators, the **GREATEST** and **LEAST** functions will not evaluate literal strings that are in date format as dates. The dates are treated as strings:

```
select Holiday, CelebratedDate
  from HOLIDAY
 where CelebratedDate =  LEAST('17-JAN-00', '04-SEP-00');


HOLIDAY                 CELEBRATE
---------------------   ---------
LABOR DAY               04-SEP-00
```

In order for **LEAST** and **GREATEST** to work properly, the function **TO_DATE** must be applied to the literal strings:

```
select Holiday, CelebratedDate
  from HOLIDAY
 where CelebratedDate = LEAST( TO_DATE('17-JAN-00'),
                               TO_DATE('04-SEP-00') );


HOLIDAY                         CELEBRATE
------------------------------  ---------
MARTIN LUTHER KING, JR.         17-JAN-00
```

It did not know to treat them as dates. The **TO_DATE** function converts these literals into an internal DATE format that Oracle can use for its date-oriented functions:

```
select LEAST( TO_DATE('20-JAN-00'), TO_DATE('20-DEC-00') )
  from DUAL;

LEAST(TO_
---------
20-JAN-00
```

NEXT_DAY

NEXT_DAY computes the date of the next named day of the week (that is, Sunday, Monday, Tuesday, Wednesday, Thursday, Friday, or Saturday) after the given date.

For example, suppose payday is always the first Friday after the 15th of the month. The table PAYDAY contains only the pay cycle dates, each one being the 15th of the month, with one row for each month of the year:

```
select CycleDate from PAYDAY;

CYCLEDATE
---------
15-JAN-00
15-FEB-00
15-MAR-00
15-APR-00
15-MAY-00
15-JUN-00
15-JUL-00
15-AUG-00
15-SEP-00
15-OCT-00
15-NOV-00
15-DEC-00
```

What will be the actual payment dates?

```
column Payday heading "Pay Day"

select NEXT_DAY(CycleDate,'FRIDAY') AS Payday
  from PAYDAY;

Pay Day!
---------
21-JAN-00
18-FEB-00
17-MAR-00
21-APR-00
19-MAY-00
16-JUN-00
21-JUL-00
18-AUG-00
22-SEP-00
20-OCT-00
17-NOV-00
22-DEC-00
```

This is nearly correct, except for September and December, because **NEXT_DAY** is the date of the *next* Friday after the cycle date. Since September 15 and

December 15 are Fridays, this (wrongly) gives the following Friday instead. The correct version is as follows:

```
column Payday heading "Pay Day"

select NEXT_DAY(CycleDate-1,'FRIDAY') AS PayDay
  from PAYDAY;
```

NEXT_DAY is really a "greater than" kind of function. It asks for the next date *greater than* the given date that falls on a specific day of the week. To catch those cycle dates that are already on Friday, subtract one from the cycle date. This makes every cycle date appear one day earlier to **NEXT_DAY**. The paydays are then always the correct Friday.

LAST_DAY

LAST_DAY produces the date of the last day of the month. Suppose that commissions and bonuses are always paid on the last day of the month. What are those dates in 2000?

```
column EndMonth heading "End Month"

select LAST_DAY(CycleDate) AS EndMonth
  from PAYDAY;

End Month
---------
31-JAN-00
29-FEB-00
31-MAR-00
30-APR-00
31-MAY-00
30-JUN-00
31-JUL-00
31-AUG-00
30-SEP-00
31-OCT-00
30-NOV-00
31-DEC-00
```

MONTHS_BETWEEN Two Dates

You recently came across a file containing the birthdates of a group of friends. You load the information into a table called BIRTHDAY and display it:

```
select FirstName, LastName, BirthDate from BIRTHDAY;
```

```
FIRSTNAME        LASTNAME         BIRTHDATE
---------------  ---------------  ---------
GEORGE           SAND             12-MAY-46
ROBERT           JAMES            23-AUG-37
NANCY            LEE              02-FEB-47
VICTORIA         LYNN             20-MAY-49
FRANK            PILOT            11-NOV-42
```

To calculate each person's age, compute the months between today's date and their birthdates, and divide by 12 to get the years:

```
select FirstName, LastName, Birthdate ,
       MONTHS_BETWEEN(SysDate,Birthdate)/12 AS Age
  from BIRTHDAY;
```

The division will print the Age with a decimal component. Since most people over the age of seven don't report their age using portions of years, you may want to apply a **FLOOR** function to the computation.

Combining Date Functions

You are hired on March 16, 2000 at a great new job, with a starting salary that is lower than you had hoped, but with a promise of a review the first of the month after six months have passed. If the current date is March 16, 2000, when is your review date?

```
select SysDate AS Today,
       LAST_DAY(ADD_MONTHS(SysDate,6)) + 1 Review
  from DUAL;
```

```
TODAY      REVIEW
---------  ---------
16-MAR-00  01-OCT-00
```

ADD_MONTHS takes the SysDate and adds six months to it. **LAST_DAY** takes this result and figures the last day of that month. You then add 1 to the date to get the first day of the next month. How many days until that review? You simply subtract today's date from it. Note the use of parentheses to assure the proper order of the calculation:

```
select (LAST_DAY(ADD_MONTHS(SysDate,6))+ 1)-SysDate  Wait
  from DUAL;
```

```
 WAIT
-----
  199
```

ROUND and TRUNC in Date Calculations

Here is today's SysDate:

```
SYSDATE
---------
16-MAR-00
```

In the beginning of the chapter, it was noted that Oracle could subtract one date from another, such as tomorrow minus today, and come up with an answer other than a whole number. Let's look at it:

```
select TO_DATE('17-MAR-00') - SysDate from DUAL;

TO_DATE('17-MAR-00')-SYSDATE
----------------------------
                        .516
```

The reason for the fractional number of days between today and tomorrow is that Oracle keeps hours, minutes, and seconds with its dates, and SysDate is always current, up to the second. It is obviously less than a full day until tomorrow.

To simplify some of the difficulties you might encounter using fractions of days, Oracle makes a couple of assumptions about dates:

- A date entered as a literal, such as '17-MAR-00', is given a default time of 12 A.M. (midnight) at the beginning of that day.

- A date entered through SQLPLUS, unless a time is specifically assigned to it, is set to 12 A.M. (midnight) at the beginning of that day.

- SysDate always includes both the date and the time, unless you intentionally round it off. The **ROUND** function on any date sets it to 12 A.M. of that day if the time is before exactly noon, and to 12 A.M. the next day if it is after noon. The **TRUNC** function acts similarly, except that it sets the time to 12 A.M. for any time up to and including one second before midnight.

To get the rounded number of days between today and tomorrow, use this:

```
select TO_DATE('17-MAR-00') - ROUND(SysDate) from DUAL;

TO_DATE('17-MAR-00')-ROUND(SYSDATE)
-----------------------------------
                                  1
```

ROUND, without a 'format' (see the earlier sidebar, "Date Functions"), always rounds a date to 12 A.M. of the closest day. If dates that you will be working with contain times other than noon, either use **ROUND** or accept possible fractional results in your calculations. **TRUNC** works similarly, but sets the time to 12 A.M. of the current day.

TO_DATE and TO_CHAR Formatting

TO_DATE and **TO_CHAR** are alike insofar as they both have powerful formatting capabilities. They are opposite insofar as **TO_DATE** converts a character string or a number into an Oracle date, whereas **TO_CHAR** converts an Oracle date into a character string. The formats for these two functions are as follows:

```
TO_CHAR(date[,'format'[,'NLSparameters']])
```

```
TO_DATE(string[,'format'[,'NLSparameters']])
```

date must be a column defined as a DATE datatype in Oracle. It cannot be a string even if it is in the default date format of DD-MON-YY. The only way to use a string where *date* appears in the **TO_CHAR** function is to enclose it within a **TO_DATE** function.

string is a literal string, a literal number, or a database column containing a string or a number. In every case but one, the format of *string* must correspond to that described by the *format*. Only if a *string* is in the default format can the *format* be left out. The default starts out as 'DD-MON-YY', but you can change this with

```
alter session set NLS_DATE_FORMAT
```

for a given SQL session or with the NLS_DATE_FORMAT init.ora parameter.

format is a collection of more than 40 options, which can be combined in virtually an infinite number of ways. The sidebar "Date Formats" lists these options with explanations. Once you understand the basic method of using the options, putting them into practice is simple.

NLSparameters is a string that sets the NLS_DATE_LANGUAGE option to a specific language, as opposed to using the language for the current SQL session. You shouldn't need to use this option often. Oracle will return day and month names in the language set for the session with **alter session**.

TO_CHAR will be used as an example of how the options work. Defining a column format for the **TO_CHAR** function results is the first task, because without it,

Date Formats

These date formats are used with both **TO_CHAR** and **TO_DATE**:

MM	Number of month: 12
RM	Roman numeral month: XII
MON	Three-letter abbreviation of Month: AUG
MONTH	Month fully spelled out: AUGUST
DDD	Number of days in year, since Jan 1: 354
DD	Number of days in month: 23
D	Number of days in week: 6
DY	Three-letter abbreviation of day: FRI
DAY	Day fully spelled out: FRIDAY
YYYY	Full four-digit year: 1946
Y,YYY	Year, with comma
SYYYY	Signed year: 1000 B.C.=-1000
YYY	Last three digits of year: 946
YY	Last two digits of year: 46
Y	Last one digit of year: 6
IYYY	Four-digit year from ISO standard*
IYY	Three-digit year from ISO standard
IY	Two-digit year from ISO standard
I	One-digit year from ISO standard
RR	Last two digits of year relative to current date
RRRR	Rounded year, accepting either two- or four-digit input
CC	Century: 20 for 1999)
SCC	Century, with BC dates prefixed with -
YEAR	Year spelled out: NINETEEN-FORTY-SIX
SYEAR	Year, with - before BC dates
Q	Number of quarter: 3
WW	Number of weeks in year: 46

IW	Weeks in year from ISO standard
W	Number of weeks in month: 3
J	"Julian"—days since December 31, 4713 B.C.: 2422220
HH	Hours of day, always 1-12: 11
HH12	Same as HH
HH24	Hours of day, 24-hour clock: 17
MI	Minutes of hour: 58
SS	Seconds of minute: 43
SSSSS	Seconds since midnight, always 0-86399: 43000
/,-:.	Punctuation to be incorporated in display for **TO_CHAR** or ignored in format for **TO_DATE**
A.M.	Displays A.M. or P.M., depending upon time of day
P.M.	Same effect as A.M.
AM or PM	Same as A.M. but without periods
B.C.	Displays B.C. or A.D., depending upon date
A.D.	Same as B.C.
BC or AD	Same as B.C. but without periods
E	Abbreviated era name, for Asian calendars
EE	Full era name, for Asian calendars

*ISO is the International Standards Organization, which has a different set of standards for dates than the U.S. formats.

These date formats work only with **TO_CHAR**. They do not work with **TO_DATE**:

| "string" | string is incorporated in display for **TO_CHAR**. |
| Fm | Prefix to Month or Day: fmMONTH or fmday. Suppresses padding of Month or Day (defined earlier) in format. Without fm, all months are displayed at same width. Similarly true for days. With fm, padding is eliminated. Months and days are only as long as their count of characters. |

Fx	Format Exact—specifies exact format matching for the character argument and the date format model.
TH	Suffix to a number: ddTH or DDTH produces 24th or 24TH. Capitalization comes from the case of the number—DD—not from the case of the TH. Works with any number in a date: YYYY, DD, MM, HH, MI, SS, and so on.
SP	Suffix to a number that forces number to be spelled out: DDSP, DdSP, or ddSP produces THREE, Three, or three. Capitalization comes from case of number—DD—not from the case of SP. Works with any number in a date: YYYY, DD, MM, HH, MI, SS, and so on.
SPTH	Suffix combination of TH and SP that forces number to be both spelled out and given an ordinal suffix: Ddspth produces Third. Capitalization comes from case of number—DD—not from the case of SP. Works with any number in a date: YYYY, DD, MM, HH, MI, SS, and so on.
THSP	Same as SPTH.

TO_CHAR will produce a column in SQLPLUS nearly 100 characters wide. By renaming the column (so its heading is intelligible) and setting its format to 30 characters, a practical display is produced:

```
column Formatted format a30 word_wrapped
select BirthDate,
       TO_CHAR(BirthDate,'MM/DD/YY') AS Formatted
  from BIRTHDAY
 where FirstName = 'VICTORIA';

BIRTHDATE FORMATTED
--------- ------------------------------
20-MAY-49 05/20/49
```

BirthDate shows the default Oracle date format: DD-MON-YY, or day of month, dash, three-letter abbreviation for month, dash, last two digits of year. The **TO_CHAR** function in the **select** statement is nearly self-evident. MM, DD, and YY in the

TO_CHAR statement are key symbols to Oracle in formatting the date. The slashes (/) are just punctuation, and Oracle will accept a wide variety of punctuation. It doesn't even need to be sensible. For example, here you see > used as punctuation:

```
select BirthDate, TO_CHAR(BirthDate,'YYMM>DD') Formatted
   from BIRTHDAY
 where FirstName = 'VICTORIA';


BIRTHDATE FORMATTED
--------- ------------------------------
20-MAY-49 4905>20
```

In addition to standard punctuation, Oracle allows you to insert text into the **format**. This is done by enclosing the desired text in *double* quotation marks:

```
select BirthDate,
       TO_CHAR(BirthDate,'Month, DDth "in, um,"
              YyyY') AS Formatted
   from BIRTHDAY ;

BIRTHDATE FORMATTED
--------- ------------------------------
12-MAY-46 May      , 12TH   in, um,
          1946
23-AUG-37 August   , 23RD   in, um,
          1937
02-FEB-47 February , 02ND   in, um,
          1947
20-MAY-49 May      , 20TH   in, um,
          1949
11-NOV-42 November , 11TH   in, um,
          1942
```

Several consequences of the **format** are worth observing here. The full word Month told Oracle to use the full name of the month in the display. Because it was typed with the first letter in uppercase and the remainder in lowercase, each month in the result was formatted the same way. The options for month are as follows:

Format	Result
Month	August
month	august
Mon	Aug
mon	aug

The day of the month is produced by the DD in the **format**. A suffix of **th** on DD tells Oracle to use *ordinal* suffixes, such as "TH", "RD", and "ND" with the number. In this instance, the suffixes are also case-sensitive, but their case is set by the DD, not the **th**:

Format	Result
DDth or DDTH	11TH
Ddth or DdTH	11Th
ddth or ddTH	11th

This same approach holds true for all numbers in the **format**, including century, year, quarter, month, week, day of the month (DD), Julian day, hours, minutes, and seconds.

The words between double quotation marks are simply inserted where they are found. Spaces between any of these format requests are reproduced in the result (look at the three spaces before the word "in" in the preceding example). YyyY is included simply to show that case is irrelevant unless a suffix such as Th is being used (Oracle would regard yyyy, Yyyy, yyyY, yYYy, and yYYY as equivalent).

For simplicity's sake, consider this format request:

```
select BirthDate, TO_CHAR(BirthDate,'Month, ddth, YyyY')
       AS Formatted
  from BIRTHDAY;

BIRTHDATE FORMATTED
--------- -----------------------------
12-MAY-46 May       , 12th, 1946
23-AUG-37 August    , 23rd, 1937
02-FEB-47 February  , 02nd, 1947
20-MAY-49 May       , 20th, 1949
11-NOV-42 November  , 11th, 1942
```

This is a reasonably normal format. The days are all aligned, which makes comparing the rows easy. This is the default alignment, and Oracle accomplishes it by padding the month names on the right with spaces up to a width of nine spaces. There will be circumstances when it is more important for a date to be formatted normally, such as at the top of a letter. The spaces between the month and the comma would look odd. To eliminate the spaces, **fm** is used as a prefix for the words "month" or "day":

Format	Result
Month, ddth	August , 20th
fmMonth, ddth	August, 20th

Format	Result
Day, ddth	Monday , 20th
fmDay, ddth	Monday, 20th

This is illustrated in the following:

```
select BirthDate, TO_CHAR(BirthDate,'fmMonth, ddth, YyyY')
       AS Formatted
   from BIRTHDAY;


BIRTHDATE FORMATTED
--------- ------------------------------
12-MAY-46 May, 12th, 1946
23-AUG-37 August, 23rd, 1937
02-FEB-47 February, 2nd, 1947
20-MAY-49 May, 20th, 1949
11-NOV-42 November, 11th, 1942
```

By combining all of these format controls and adding hours and minutes, you can produce a birth announcement:

```
select FirstName, Birthdate, TO_CHAR(BirthDate,
'"Baby Girl on" fmMonth ddth, YYYY, "at" HH:MI "in the Morning"')
       AS Formatted
   from BIRTHDAY
 where FirstName = 'VICTORIA';


FIRSTNAME       BIRTHDATE FORMATTED
--------------- --------- ------------------------------
VICTORIA        20-MAY-49 Baby Girl on May 20th, 1949,
                          at 3:27 in the Morning
```

Suppose that after looking at this, you decide you'd rather spell out the date. Do this with the **sp** control:

```
select FirstName, Birthdate, TO_CHAR(BirthDate,
'"Baby Girl on the" Ddsp "of" fmMonth, YYYY, "at" HH:MI')
       AS Formatted
   from BIRTHDAY
 where FirstName = 'VICTORIA';

FIRSTNAME       BIRTHDATE FORMATTED
--------------- --------- ------------------------------
VICTORIA        20-MAY-49 Baby Girl on the Twenty of
                          May, 1949, at 3:27
```

Well, 20 was spelled out, but it still doesn't look right. Add the **th** suffix to the **sp**:

```
select FirstName, Birthdate, TO_CHAR(BirthDate,
'"Baby Girl on the" Ddspth "of" fmMonth, YYYY, "at" HH:MI')
     AS Formatted
  from BIRTHDAY
 where FirstName = 'VICTORIA';

FIRSTNAME       BIRTHDATE FORMATTED
--------------- --------- ------------------------------
VICTORIA        20-MAY-49 Baby Girl on the Twentieth of
                          May, 1949, at 3:27
```

But was it 3:27 A.M. or 3:27 P.M.? These could be added inside of double quotation marks, but then the result would always say "A.M." or "P.M.", regardless of the actual time of the day (since double quotation marks enclose a literal). Instead, Oracle lets you add *either* "A.M." or "P.M." after the time, but not in double quotation marks. Oracle then interprets this as a request to display whether it is A.M. or P.M. Note how the **select** has this formatting control entered as P.M., but the result shows A.M., because the birth occurred in the morning:

```
select FirstName, Birthdate, TO_CHAR(BirthDate,
'"Baby Girl on the" Ddspth "of" fmMonth, YYYY, "at" HH:MI P.M.')
     AS Formatted
  from BIRTHDAY
 where FirstName = 'VICTORIA';

FIRSTNAME       BIRTHDATE FORMATTED
--------------- --------- ------------------------------
VICTORIA        20-MAY-49 Baby Girl on the Twentieth of
                          May, 1949, at 3:27 A.M.
```

Consult the sidebar "Date Formats," earlier in the chapter, for a list of all the possible date options. How would you construct a date format for the 774th Year of the Reign of Louis IX? Use date arithmetic to alter the year from A.D. to A.L. (Louis's reign began in 1226, so subtract 1,226 years from the current year) and then simply format the result using **TO_CHAR**.

The Most Common TO_CHAR Error

Always check the date formats when using the **TO_CHAR** function. The most common error is to interchange the 'MM' (Month) format with the 'MI' (Minutes) format when formatting the time portion of a date.

For example, to view the current time, use the **TO_CHAR** function to query the time portion of SysDate:

```
select TO_CHAR(SysDate,'HH:MI:SS') Now
   from DUAL;

NOW
--------
10:01:30
```

This example is correct, since it uses 'MI' to show the minutes. However, users often select 'MM' instead—partly because they are also selecting two other pairs of double letters, 'HH' and 'SS'. Selecting 'MM' will return the month, not the minutes:

```
select TO_CHAR(SysDate,'HH:MM:SS') NowWrong
   from DUAL;

NOWWRONG
--------
10:11:30
```

This time is incorrect, because the month was selected in the minutes place. Since Oracle is so flexible and has so many different supported date formats, it does not prevent you from making this error.

NEW_TIME: Switching Time Zones

The **NEW_TIME** function tells you the time and date of a date column or literal date in other time zones. This is the format for **NEW_TIME**:

```
NEW_TIME(date,'this','other')
```

date is the date (and time) in *this* time zone. *this* will be replaced by a three-letter abbreviation for the current time zone. *other* will be replaced by a three-letter abbreviation of the other time zone for which you'd like to know the time and date. The time zone options are given in the sidebar "Date Functions," earlier in this chapter. To compare just the date, without showing the time, of Victoria's birth between Eastern standard time and Hawaiian standard time, use this:

```
select Birthdate, NEW_TIME(Birthdate,'EST','HST')
   from BIRTHDAY
 where FirstName = 'VICTORIA';

BIRTHDATE NEW_TIME(
--------- ---------
20-MAY-49 19-MAY-49
```

But how could Victoria have been born on two different days? Since every date stored in Oracle also contains a time, it is simple enough using **TO_CHAR** and

NEW_TIME to discover both the date and the time differences between the two zones. This will answer the question:

```
select TO_CHAR(Birthdate,'fmMonth Ddth, YYYY "at" HH:MI AM') AS Birth,
       TO_CHAR(NEW_TIME(Birthdate,'EST','HST'),
       'fmMonth ddth, YYYY "at" HH:MI AM') AS Birth
  from BIRTHDAY
 where FirstName = 'VICTORIA';

BIRTH                           BIRTH
------------------------------  ------------------------------
May 20th, 1949 at 3:27 AM       May 19th, 1949 at 10:27 PM
```

TO_DATE Calculations

TO_DATE follows the same formatting conventions as **TO_CHAR**, with some restrictions. The purpose of **TO_DATE** is to turn a literal string, such as MAY 20, 1949, into an Oracle date format. This allows the date to be used in date calculations.

This is the format for **TO_DATE**:

```
TO_DATE(string[,'format'])
```

To put the string 22-FEB-00 into Oracle date format, use this:

```
select TO_DATE('22-FEB-00,'DD-MON-YY') from DUAL;

TO_DATE('
---------
22-FEB-00
```

Note, however, that the 22-FEB-00 format is already in the default format in which Oracle displays and accepts dates. When a literal string has a date in this format, the *format* in the **TO_DATE** can be left out, with exactly the same result:

```
select TO_DATE('22-FEB-00') from DUAL;

TO_DATE('
---------
22-FEB-00
```

But what century is the date in? Is it 1900 or 2000? If you do not specify the full four-year value for the year, then you are relying on the database to default to the proper century value.

If the string is in a familiar format, but not the default Oracle format of DD-MON-YY, **TO_DATE** fails:

```
select TO_DATE('02/22/00') from DUAL;

ERROR: ORA-01843: not a valid month
```

When the format matches the literal string, the string is successfully converted to a date and is then displayed in default date format:

```
select TO_DATE('02/22/00','MM/DD/YY') from DUAL;

TO_DATE('
---------
22-FEB-00
```

Suppose you need to know the day of the week of February 22. The **TO_CHAR** function will not work, even with the literal string in the proper format, because **TO_CHAR** requires a date (see its format at the very beginning of the "TO_DATE and TO_CHAR Formatting" section):

```
select TO_CHAR('22-FEB-00','Day') from DUAL
ORA-01722: invalid number
```

The message is somewhat misleading, but the point is that the query fails. It will work if you first convert the string to a date. Do this by combining the two functions **TO_CHAR** and **TO_DATE**:

```
select TO_CHAR( TO_DATE('22-FEB-00'), 'Day') from DUAL;

TO_CHAR(TO_DATE('22-FEB-99'),'DAY')
-----------------------------------
Tuesday
```

TO_DATE can also accept numbers, without single quotation marks, instead of strings, as long as they are formatted consistently. Here is an example:

```
select TO_DATE(11051946,'MM DD YYYY') from DUAL;

TO_DATE(1
---------
05-NOV-46
```

The punctuation in the **format** is ignored, but the number must follow the order of the format controls. The number itself must not have punctuation.

How complex can the format control be in **TO_DATE**? Suppose you simply reversed the **TO_CHAR select** statement shown earlier, put its result into the **string** portion of **TO_DATE**, and kept its format the same as **TO_CHAR**:

```
select TO_DATE('Baby Girl on the Twentieth of May, 1949,
       at 3:27 A.M.',
       '"Baby Girl on the" Ddspth "of" fmMonth, YYYY,
       "at" HH:MI P.M.')
       AS Formatted
  from BIRTHDAY
 where FirstName = 'VICTORIA';

ERROR: ORA-01858: a non-numeric character was found
 where a numeric was expected
```

This clearly failed. As it turns out, only a limited number of the **format** controls can be used.

These are the restrictions on **format** that govern **TO_DATE**:

■ No literal strings are allowed, such as "Baby Girl on the".

■ Days cannot be spelled out. They must be numbers.

■ Punctuation is permitted.

■ fm is not necessary. If used, it is ignored.

■ If Month is used, the month in the string must be spelled out. If Mon is used, the month must be a three-letter abbreviation. Uppercase and lowercase are ignored.

This **select** does work:

```
select TO_DATE('August 20, 1949, 3:27 A.M. ', 'Month Dd,
       YYYY, HH:MI P.M.')
       AS Formatted
  from BIRTHDAY
 where FirstName = 'VICTORIA';

FORMATTED
---------
20-AUG-49
```

Dates in where Clauses

Early in this chapter, you saw an example of date arithmetic used in a **where** clause:

```
select Holiday, ActualDate, CelebratedDate
   from Holiday
 where CelebratedDate - ActualDate != 0;


HOLIDAY                  ACTUALDAT CELEBRATE
------------------------ --------- ---------
MARTIN LUTHER KING, JR.  15-JAN-00 17-JAN-00
LINCOLNS BIRTHDAY        12-FEB-00 21-FEB-00
WASHINGTONS BIRTHDAY     22-FEB-00 21-FEB-00
MEMORIAL DAY             30-MAY-00 29-MAY-00
COLUMBUS DAY             08-OCT-00 09-OCT-00
```

Dates can be used with other Oracle logical operators as well, with some warnings and restrictions. The **BETWEEN** operator will do date arithmetic if the column preceding it is a date, even if the test dates are literal strings:

```
select Holiday, CelebratedDate
   from HOLIDAY
 where CelebratedDate BETWEEN
           TO_DATE('01-JAN-2000','DD-MON-YYYY') and
           TO_DATE('22-FEB-2000','DD-MON-YYYY');


HOLIDAY                  CELEBRATE
------------------------ ---------
NEW YEAR DAY             01-JAN-00
MARTIN LUTHER KING, JR.  17-JAN-00
LINCOLNS BIRTHDAY        21-FEB-00
WASHINGTONS BIRTHDAY     21-FEB-00
FAST DAY, NEW HAMPSHIRE  22-FEB-00
```

The logical operator **IN** works as well with literal strings:

```
select Holiday, CelebratedDate
   from HOLIDAY
 where CelebratedDate IN ('01-JAN-00', '22-FEB-00');


HOLIDAY                  CELEBRATE
------------------------ ---------
NEW YEAR DAY             01-JAN-00
FAST DAY, NEW HAMPSHIRE  22-FEB-00
```

If you cannot rely on 2000 being the default century value, then you can use the **TO_DATE** function to specify the century values for the dates within the **IN** operator:

```
select Holiday, CelebratedDate
   from HOLIDAY
 where CelebratedDate IN
       (TO_DATE('01-JAN-2000','DD-MON-YYYY'),
        TO_DATE('22-FEB-2000','DD-MON-YYYY'));


HOLIDAY                      CELEBRATE
------------------------- ---------
NEW YEAR DAY                 01-JAN-00
FAST DAY, NEW HAMPSHIRE    22-FEB-00
```

LEAST and **GREATEST** do not work, because they assume the literal strings are *strings,* not *dates.* Refer to the sidebar "A Warning About GREATEST and LEAST," earlier in this chapter, for an explanation of **LEAST** and **GREATEST**.

Dealing with Multiple Centuries

If your applications use only two-digit values for years, then you may encounter problems related to the year 2000. If you only specify two digits of a year (such as '98' for '1998'), then you are relying on the database to specify the century value (the '19') when the record is inserted. If you are putting in dates prior to the year 2000 (for example, birthdates), then you may encounter problems with the century values assigned to your data.

In Oracle, all date values have century values. If you only specify the last two digits of the year value, then Oracle will, by default, use the current century as the century value when it inserts a record. For example, the following listing shows an **insert** into the BIRTHDAY table.

```
insert into BIRTHDAY
(FirstName, LastName, BirthDate)
values
('ALICIA', 'ANN', '21-NOV-39');
```

In the preceding example, no century value is specified for the BirthDate column, and no age is specified. If you use the **TO_CHAR** function on the BirthDate column, you can see the full BirthDate that Oracle inserted—it defaulted to the current century:

```
select TO_CHAR(BirthDate,'DD-MON-YYYY') AS Bday
   from BIRTHDAY
 where FirstName = 'ALICIA'
   and LastName = 'ANN';

BDAY
-----------
21-NOV-2039
```

For dates that can properly default to the current century, using the default does not present a problem. Alicia's BirthDate value is 21-NOV-2039—wrong by 100 years! Wherever you use dates, you should specify the full four-digit year value.

CHAPTER
10

Conversion and Transformation Functions

his chapter looks at functions that convert, or transform, one datatype into another. Four datatypes and their associated functions have been covered thus far:

- CHAR (fixed-length character strings) and VARCHAR2 (variable-length character strings) include any letter of the alphabet, any number, and any of the symbols on the keyboard. Character literals must be enclosed in single quotation marks: 'Sault Ste. Marie!'

- NUMBER includes just the digits 0 through 9, a decimal point, and a minus sign, if necessary. NUMBER literals are not enclosed in quotation marks: -246.320

- DATE is a special type that includes information about the date, time, and time zone. It has a default format of DD-MON-YY, but can be displayed in many ways using the **TO_CHAR** function as you saw in Chapter 9. DATE literals must be enclosed in single quotation marks: '26-AUG-81'

Each of these datatypes has a group of functions designed especially to manipulate data of its own type, as shown in Table 10-1. String functions are used with character columns or literals, arithmetic functions are used with NUMBER columns or literals, and date functions are used with DATE columns or literals. Most group and miscellaneous functions work with any of these types. Some of these functions change the object they affect (whether CHAR, VARCHAR2, NUMBER, or DATE), while others report information about the object.

String Functions for CHAR & VARCHAR2 Datatypes	Arithmetic Functions for NUMBER Datatype	Date Functions for DATE Datatype
II (concatenation)	+ (addition)	ADD_MONTHS
ASCII	– (subtraction)	LAST_DAY
CHR	* (multiplication)	MONTHS_BETWEEN
CONCAT	/ (division)	NEW_TIME
CONVERT	ABS	NEXT_DAY
INITCAP	ACOS	ROUND
INSTR	ASIN	TRUNC

TABLE 10-1. *Functions by Datatype*

String Functions for CHAR & VARCHAR2 Datatypes	Arithmetic Functions for NUMBER Datatype	Date Functions for DATE Datatype
INSTRB	ATAB	
LENGTH	ATAN2	
LENGTHB	CEIL	
LOWER	COS	
LPAD	COSH	
LTRIM	EXP	
NLS_INITCAP	FLOOR	
NLS_LOWER	LN	
NLS_UPPER	LOG	
NLSSORT	MOD	
REPLACE	POWER	
RPAD	ROUND	
RTRIM	SIGN	
SOUNDEX	SIN	
SUBSTR	SINH	
SUBSTRB	SQRT	
TRANSLATE	TAN	
UID	TANH	
UPPER	TRUNC	
USER		
USERENV		

Group Functions	Conversion Functions	Miscellaneous Functions
AVG	CHARTOROWID	DECODE
COUNT	CONVERT	DUMP
CUBE	HEXTORAW	GREATEST
GLB	RAWTOHEX	GREATEST_LB

TABLE 10-1. *Functions by Datatype* (continued)

Group Functions	Conversion Functions	Miscellaneous Functions
LUB	ROWIDTOCHAR	LEAST
MAX	TO_CHAR	LEAST_UB
MIN	TO_DATE	NVL
ROLLUP	TO_LOB	VSIZE
STDDEV	TO_MULTI_BYTE	
SUM	TO_NUMBER	

TABLE 10-1.   *Functions by Datatype* (continued)

In one sense, most of the functions studied so far have been *transformation functions,* meaning they changed their objects. However, the functions covered in this chapter change their objects in an unusual way: they transform them from one datatype into another, or they make a profound transformation of the data in them. Table 10-2 describes these functions.

The use of two of these functions, **TO_CHAR** and **TO_DATE**, has already been demonstrated in Chapter 9. **TO_CHAR** transforms a date into a character string (in the format you request). **TO_CHAR** can convert not just DATEs but also NUMBERs into character strings. **TO_DATE** is also a transformation function. It takes either a character string or a number and converts it into the DATE datatype. It then can be used in date arithmetic to calculate **MONTHS_BETWEEN**, **NEXT_DAY**, and other date functions.

Elementary Conversion Functions

There are three elementary Oracle functions whose purpose is to convert one datatype into another:

- ■ **TO_CHAR** transforms a DATE or NUMBER into a character string.
- ■ **TO_DATE** transforms a NUMBER, CHAR, or VARCHAR2 into a DATE.
- ■ **TO_NUMBER** transforms a CHAR or VARCHAR2 into a NUMBER.

Why are these transformations important? **TO_DATE** is obviously necessary to accomplish date arithmetic. **TO_CHAR** allows you to manipulate a number as if it were a string, using string functions. **TO_NUMBER** allows you to use a string that

Function Name	Definition
CHARTOROWID	CHARacter TO ROW IDentifier. Changes a character string to act like an internal Oracle row identifier, or RowID.
CONVERT	CONVERTs a character string from one national language character set to another.
DECODE	DECODEs a CHAR, VARCHAR2, or NUMBER into any of several different character strings or NUMBERs, based on value. This is a very powerful *if, then, else* function. Chapter 16 is devoted to DECODE.
HEXTORAW	HEXadecimal TO RAW. Changes a character string of hex numbers into binary.
RAWTOHEX	RAW TO HEXadecimal. Changes a string of binary numbers to a character string of hex numbers.
ROWIDTOCHAR	ROW IDentifier TO CHARacter. Changes an internal Oracle row identifier, or RowID, to act like a character string.
TO_CHAR	TO CHARacter. Converts a NUMBER or DATE so that it acts like a character string.
TO_DATE	TO DATE. Converts a NUMBER, CHAR, or VARCHAR2 to act like a DATE (a special Oracle datatype).
TO_LOB	TO LOB. Converts a LONG to a LOB as part of an **insert as select**.
TO_MULTI_BYTE	TO MULTI_BYTE. Converts the single-byte characters in a character string to multibyte characters.
TO_NUMBER	TO NUMBER. Converts a CHAR or VARCHAR2 to act like a number.
TO_SINGLE_BYTE	TO SINGLE BYTE. Converts the multibyte characters in a CHAR or VARCHAR2 to single bytes.
TRANSLATE	TRANSLATEs characters in a string into different characters.

TABLE 10-2.   *Conversion and Transformation Functions*

happens to contain only numbers as if it were a number; by using it, you can add, subtract, multiply, divide, and so on.

This means that if you stored a nine-digit ZIP code as a number, you could transform it into a string, and then use **SUBSTR** and concatenation to add a dash (such as when printing addresses on envelopes):

```
select SUBSTR(TO_CHAR(948033515),1,5)||'-'||
       SUBSTR(TO_CHAR(948033515),6)  AS Zip
  from DUAL;

ZIP
-----------------------------------------
94803-3515
```

Here, the **TO_CHAR** function transforms the pure number 948033515 (notice that it has no single quotation marks around it, as a CHAR or VARCHAR2 string must) into a character string. **SUBSTR** then clips out positions 1 to 5 of this "string," producing 94803. A dash is concatenated on the right end of this string, and then another **TO_CHAR** creates another "string," which another **SUBSTR** clips out from position 6 to the end. The second string, 3515, is concatenated after the dash. The whole rebuilt string is relabeled Zip, and Oracle displays it: 94803-3515. This **TO_CHAR** function lets you use string manipulation functions on numbers (and dates) as if they were actually strings. Handy? Yes. But watch this:

```
select SUBSTR(948033515,1,5)||'-'||
       SUBSTR(948033515,6) AS Zip
  from DUAL;

ZIP
-----------------------------------------
94803-3515
```

But this shouldn't work, because 948033515 is a NUMBER, not a character string. Yet the string function **SUBSTR** clearly worked anyway. Would it work with an actual NUMBER database column? Here's a table with Zip as a NUMBER:

```
describe ADDRESS

Name                             Null?    Type
-------------------------------- -------- ----
LASTNAME                                  VARCHAR2(25)
FIRSTNAME                                 VARCHAR2(25)
STREET                                    VARCHAR2(50)
CITY                                      VARCHAR2(25)
STATE                                     CHAR(2)
ZIP                                       NUMBER
```

```
PHONE                                    VARCHAR2(12)
EXT                                      VARCHAR2(5)
```

Select just the ZIP code for all the Marys in the table:

```
select SUBSTR(Zip,1,5)||'-'||
       SUBSTR(Zip,6)  AS Zip
  from ADDRESS
 where FirstName = 'MARY';


ZIP
-----------------------------------------
94941-4302
60126-2460
```

SUBSTR works here just as well as it does with strings, even though Zip is a NUMBER column from the ADDRESS table. Will other string functions also work?

```
select Zip, RTRIM(Zip,20)
  from ADDRESS
 where FirstName = 'MARY';

       ZIP RTRIM(ZIP,20)
---------- -------------------------------------
 949414302 9494143
 601262460 60126246
```

The column on the left demonstrates that Zip is a NUMBER; it is even right-justified, as numbers are by default. But the **RTRIM** column is left-justified, just as strings are, and it has removed zeros and twos from the right side of the ZIP codes. Something else is peculiar here. Recall from Chapter 7 the format for **RTRIM**, shown here:

```
RTRIM(string [,'set'])
```

The *set* to be removed from the string is enclosed within single quotation marks, yet in this example,

```
RTRIM(Zip,20)
```

there are no quotation marks. So what is going on?

Automatic Conversion of Datatypes

Oracle is automatically converting these numbers, both the Zip and the 20, into strings, almost as if they both had **TO_CHAR** functions in front of them. In fact, with a few clear exceptions, Oracle will automatically transform any datatype into any other datatype, based on the function that is going to affect it. If it's a string function, Oracle will convert a NUMBER or a DATE instantly into a string, and the string function will work. If it's a DATE function and the column or literal is a string in the format DD-MON-YY, Oracle will convert it into a DATE. If the function is arithmetic and the column or literal is a character string, Oracle will convert it into a NUMBER and do the calculation.

Will this always work? No. To have Oracle automatically convert one datatype into another, the first datatype must already "look" like the datatype it is being converted to. The basic guidelines are given in the upcoming sidebar "Guidelines for Automatic Conversion of Datatypes." These guidelines may be confusing, so a few examples should help to clarify them. The following are the effects of several randomly chosen string functions on NUMBERs and DATEs:

```
select INITCAP(LOWER(SysDate)) from DUAL;

INITCAP(LOWER(SYSDATE))
-----------------------
01-Nov-99
```

Note that the **INITCAP** function put the first letter of "nov" into uppercase even though "nov" was buried in the middle of the string "01-nov-99." This is a feature of **INITCAP** that is not confined to dates, although it is illustrated here for the first time. It works because the following works:

```
select INITCAP('this-is_a.test,of:punctuation;for+initcap')
   from DUAL;

INITCAP('THIS-IS_A.TEST,OF:PUNCTUATION;FO
-----------------------------------------
This-Is_A.Test,Of:Punctuation;For+Initcap
```

INITCAP puts the first letter of every word into uppercase. It determines the beginning of a word based on its being preceded by any character other than a letter. You can also cut and paste dates using string functions, just as if they were strings:

```
select SUBSTR(SysDate,4,3) from DUAL;

SUB
---
NOV
```

Here, a DATE is left-padded with 9's for a total length of 20:

```
select LPAD(SysDate,20,'9') from DUAL;

LPAD(SYSDATE,20,'9')
--------------------
9999999999901-NOV-99
```

LPAD, or any other string function, also can be used on NUMBERs, whether literal (as shown here) or columns:

```
select LPAD(9,20,0) from DUAL;

LPAD(9,20,0)
--------------------
00000000000000000009
```

These examples show how string functions treat both NUMBERs and DATEs as if they were character strings. The result of the function (what you see displayed) is

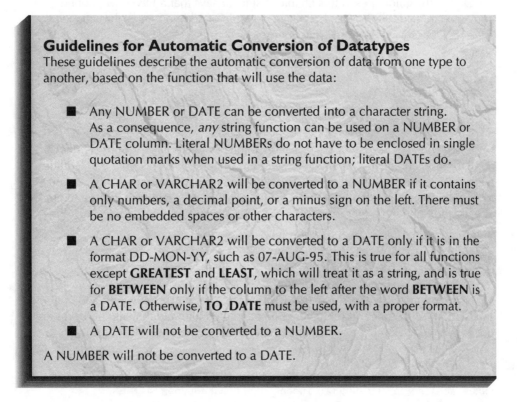

Guidelines for Automatic Conversion of Datatypes
These guidelines describe the automatic conversion of data from one type to another, based on the function that will use the data:

- Any NUMBER or DATE can be converted into a character string. As a consequence, *any* string function can be used on a NUMBER or DATE column. Literal NUMBERs do not have to be enclosed in single quotation marks when used in a string function; literal DATEs do.

- A CHAR or VARCHAR2 will be converted to a NUMBER if it contains only numbers, a decimal point, or a minus sign on the left. There must be no embedded spaces or other characters.

- A CHAR or VARCHAR2 will be converted to a DATE only if it is in the format DD-MON-YY, such as 07-AUG-95. This is true for all functions except **GREATEST** and **LEAST**, which will treat it as a string, and is true for **BETWEEN** only if the column to the left after the word **BETWEEN** is a DATE. Otherwise, **TO_DATE** must be used, with a proper format.

- A DATE will not be converted to a NUMBER.

A NUMBER will not be converted to a DATE.

itself a character string. In this next example, a string (note the single quotation marks) is treated as a NUMBER by the number function **FLOOR**:

```
select FLOOR('-323.78') from DUAL;

FLOOR('-323.78')
----------------
            -324
```

Here, two literal character strings are converted to DATEs for the DATE function **MONTHS_BETWEEN**. This works only because the literal strings are in the default date format DD-MON-YY:

```
select MONTHS_BETWEEN('16-MAY-99','01-NOV-99') from DUAL;

MONTHS_BETWEEN('16-MAY-99','01-NOV-99')
---------------------------------------
                              -5.516129
```

One of the guidelines in this chapter's sidebar says that a DATE will not be converted to a NUMBER. Yet, here is an example of addition and subtraction with a DATE. Does this violate the guideline?

```
select SysDate, SysDate + 1, SysDate - 1 from DUAL;

SYSDATE   SYSDATE+1 SYSDATE-1
--------- --------- ---------
01-NOV-99 02-NOV-99 31-OCT-99
```

It does not, because the addition and subtraction were date arithmetic, not regular arithmetic. Date arithmetic (covered in Chapter 9) works only with addition and subtraction, and only with DATEs. Most functions will automatically convert a character string in default date format into a DATE. An exception is this attempt at date addition with a literal:

```
select '01-NOV-99' + 1 from DUAL;

ERROR: ORA-01722: invalid number
```

Date arithmetic, even with actual DATE datatypes, works only with addition and subtraction. Any other arithmetic function attempted with a date will fail. Dates are not converted to numbers, as this attempt to divide a date by 2 illustrates:

```
select SysDate / 2 from DUAL;
              *
ERROR at line 1: ORA-00932: inconsistent data types
```

Finally, a NUMBER will never be automatically converted to a DATE, because a pure number cannot be in the default format for a DATE, which is DD-MON-YY:

```
select NEXT_DAY(110199,'FRIDAY') from DUAL;
               *
ERROR at line 1: ORA-00932: inconsistent data types
```

To use a NUMBER in a date function, **TO_DATE** is required.

A Warning About Automatic Conversion

The issue of whether it is a good practice to allow SQL to do automatic conversion of datatypes has arguments on either side. On one hand, this practice considerably simplifies and reduces the functions necessary to make a **select** statement work. On the other hand, if your assumption about what will be in the column is wrong (for example, you assume a particular character column will always have a number in it, meaning you can use it in a calculation), then, at some point, a query will stop working, Oracle will produce an error, and time will have to be spent trying to find the problem. Further, another person reading your **select** statement may be confused by what appear to be inappropriate functions at work on characters or numbers.

A simple rule of thumb might be that it is best to use functions where the risk is low, such as string manipulation functions on numbers, rather than arithmetic functions on strings. For your benefit and that of others using your work, always put a note near the **select** statement signaling the use of automatic type conversion.

Specialized Conversion Functions

Oracle includes several specialized conversion functions. Their names and formats are as follows:

CHARTOROWID*(string)*	Converts a CHARacter string TO a ROW ID
ROWIDTOCHAR*(rowid)*	Converts a ROW ID TO a CHARacter string
HEXTORAW*(hexnumber)*	Converts a HEXadecimal number TO a binary number (RAW)
RAWTOHEX*(raw)*	Converts a binary number (RAW) TO a HEXadecimal
TO_LOB*(long)*	Converts a LONG datatype value TO a LOB value
TO_MULTI_BYTE	Converts single-byte characters TO MULTIBYTE characters
TO_SINGLE_BYTE	Converts multibyte characters TO SINGLE-BYTE characters

If you expect to use SQLPLUS and Oracle simply to produce reports, you probably won't ever need any of these functions. On the other hand, if you will use SQLPLUS to **update** the database, expect to build Oracle applications, or are using National Language Support, this information will eventually prove valuable. The functions can be found, by name, in the Alphabetical Reference section of this book.

Transformation Functions

Although in one sense any function that changes its object could be called a transformation function, there are two unusual functions that you can use in many interesting ways to control your output based on your input, instead of simply transforming it. These functions are **TRANSLATE** and **DECODE**.

TRANSLATE

TRANSLATE is a simple function that does an orderly character-by-character substitution in a string. This is the format for **TRANSLATE**:

```
TRANSLATE(string,if,then)
```

TRANSLATE looks at each character in *string*, and then checks *if* to see whether that character is there. If it is, it notes the position in *if* where it found the character, and then looks at the same position in *then*. **TRANSLATE** substitutes whichever character it finds there for the character in *string*. Normally, the function is written on a single line, like this:

```
select TRANSLATE(7671234,234567890,'BCDEFGHIJ')
   from DUAL;

TRANSLATE(7671234,234567890,'BCDEFGHIJ
------------------------------------
GFG1BCD
```

But it might be easier to understand if simply broken onto two lines (SQLPLUS doesn't care, of course):

```
select TRANSLATE(7671234,234567890,
                        'BCDEFGHIJ')
   from DUAL;

TRANSLATE(7671234,234567890,'BCDEFGHIJ
------------------------------------
GFG1BCD
```

When **TRANSLATE** sees a 7 in the *string*, it looks for a 7 in the *if*, and translates it to the character in the same position in the *then* (an uppercase *G*). If the character is not in the *if*, it is not translated (observe what **TRANSLATE** did with the 1).

TRANSLATE is technically a string function, but, as you can see, it will do automatic data conversion and work with a mix of strings and numbers. The following is an example of a very simple code cipher, where every letter in the alphabet is shifted one position. Many years ago, spies used such character-substitution methods to encode messages before sending them. The recipient simply reversed the process. Do you remember the smooth-talking computer, HAL, in the movie *2001: A Space Odyssey*? If you **TRANSLATE** HAL's name with a one-character shift in the alphabet, you get this:

```
select TRANSLATE('HAL','ABCDEFGHIJKLMNOPQRSTUVWXYZ',
                       'BCDEFGHIJKLMNOPQRSTUVWXYZA') AS Who
    from DUAL;

WHO
----
IBM
```

DECODE

If **TRANSLATE** is a character-by-character substitution, **DECODE** can be considered a value-by-value substitution. For every value it sees in a field, **DECODE** checks for a match in a series of *if/then* tests. **DECODE** is an incredibly powerful function, with a broad range of areas where it can be useful. Chapter 17 is devoted entirely to advanced use of **DECODE**.

This is the format for **DECODE**:

```
DECODE(value,if1,then1,if2,then2,if3,then3,. . . ,else)
```

Only three *if/then* combinations are illustrated here, but there is no practical limit. To see how this function works, recall the NEWSPAPER table you saw earlier:

```
select * from NEWSPAPER;

FEATURE          S  PAGE
--------------- - -----
National News    A     1
Sports           D     1
Editorials       A    12
Business         E     1
Weather          C     2
```

```
Television        B     7
Births            F     7
Classified        F     8
Modern Life       B     1
Comics            C     4
Movies            B     4
Bridge            B     2
Obituaries        F     6
Doctor Is In      F     6
```

Suppose you want to change the name of a couple of the regular features. **DECODE** will check each Feature *value*, row by row. If the *value* it finds is 'Sports', then it will substitute 'Games People Play'; if it finds 'Movies', then it will substitute 'Entertainment'; if it finds anything else in the value, then it will use the value of Feature.

In the next example, the page number is decoded. If the page number is 1, then the words 'Front Page' are substituted. If the page number is anything else, the words 'Turn to' are concatenated with the page number. This illustrates that *else* can be a function, a literal, or another column.

```
select Feature, Section,
       DECODE(Page,'1','Front Page','Turn to '||Page)
  from NEWSPAPER;

FEATURE           S DECODE(PAGE,'1','FRONTPAGE','TURNTO'PAGE
---------------   - ---------------------------------------
National News     A Front Page
Sports            D Front Page
Editorials        A Turn to 12
Business          E Front Page
Weather           C Turn to 2
Television        B Turn to 7
Births            F Turn to 7
Classified        F Turn to 8
Modern Life       B Front Page
Comics            C Turn to 4
Movies            B Turn to 4
Bridge            B Turn to 2
Obituaries        F Turn to 6
Doctor Is In      F Turn to 6
```

There are some restrictions on datatypes in the list of *if*s and *then*s, which will be covered in Chapter 17.

Review

Most functions in Oracle, although they are intended for a specific datatype, such as CHAR, VARCHAR2, NUMBER, and DATE, will actually work with other datatypes as well. They do this by performing an automatic type conversion. With a few logical exceptions, and the hope of future compatibility, they will do this as long as the data to be converted "looks" like the datatype required by the function.

Character functions will convert any NUMBER or DATE. NUMBER functions will convert a CHAR or VARCHAR2 if it contains only the digits 0 through 9, a decimal point, or a minus sign on the left. NUMBER functions will not convert DATEs. DATE functions will convert character strings if they are in the format DD-MON-YY. They will not convert NUMBERs.

Two functions, **TRANSLATE** and **DECODE**, will fundamentally change the data they affect. **TRANSLATE** will do a character substitution according to any pattern you specify, and **DECODE** will do a value substitution for any pattern you specify.

CHAPTER
11

Grouping Things Together

p to this point, you've seen how SQL can **select** rows of information from database tables, how the **where** clause can limit the number of rows being returned to only those that meet certain rules that you define, and how the rows returned can be sorted in ascending or descending sequence using **order by**. You've also seen how the values in columns can be modified by character, NUMBER, and DATE functions, and how group functions can tell you something about the whole set of rows.

Beyond the group functions you've seen, there are also two group clauses: **having** and **group by**. These are parallel to the **where** and **order by** clauses except that they act on groups, not on individual rows. These clauses can provide very powerful insights into your data.

To make the display of information consistent and readable in this chapter, the following column definitions have been given to SQLPLUS:

```
column Amount format 999.90
column Average format 999.90
column Item format a16
column Month format a9
column Percent format 99.90
column Person format a25
column Total format 999.90
column YearTotal format 999.90
```

Figure 11-1 is a listing of the ActionDate, Item, Person, and Amount paid to each worker by G. B. Talbot during 1901. The SQL statement that created Figure 11-1 is as follows:

```
select ActionDate, Item, Person, Amount
  from LEDGER
 where Action = 'PAID'
 order by ActionDate;
```

A careful inspection of this table reveals that many of the items are repeated.

```
ACTIONDAT ITEM             PERSON                    AMOUNT
--------- ---------------- ------------------------- -------
04-JAN-01 WORK             GERHARDT KENTGEN             1.00
12-JAN-01 WORK             GEORGE OSCAR                 1.00
19-JAN-01 WORK             GERHARDT KENTGEN             1.00
30-JAN-01 WORK             ELBERT TALBOT                 .50
04-FEB-01 WORK             ELBERT TALBOT                 .50
28-FEB-01 WORK             ELBERT TALBOT                1.00
14-MAR-01 DIGGING OF GRAVE JED HOPKINS                  3.00
20-MAR-01 WORK             DICK JONES                   1.00
01-APR-01 PLOWING          RICHARD KOCH AND BROTHERS    3.00
05-APR-01 WORK             DICK JONES                   1.00
16-APR-01 PLOWING          RICHARD KOCH AND BROTHERS    3.00
27-APR-01 PLOWING          RICHARD KOCH AND BROTHERS    3.00
02-MAY-01 WORK             DICK JONES                   1.00
11-MAY-01 WORK             WILFRED LOWELL               1.20
24-MAY-01 WORK             WILFRED LOWELL               1.20
03-JUN-01 WORK             ELBERT TALBOT                1.00
13-JUN-01 WORK             PETER LAWSON                 1.00
18-JUN-01 THRESHING        WILLIAM SWING                 .50
26-JUN-01 PAINTING         KAY AND PALMER WALLBOM       1.75
14-JUL-01 WORK             WILFRED LOWELL               1.20
15-JUL-01 WORK             KAY AND PALMER WALLBOM       2.25
21-JUL-01 WORK             VICTORIA LYNN                1.00
28-JUL-01 SAWING           DICK JONES                    .75
06-AUG-01 PLOWING          VICTORIA LYNN                1.80
06-AUG-01 PLOWING          ANDREW DYE                   4.00
10-AUG-01 WORK             HELEN BRANDT                 1.00
11-AUG-01 WORK             HELEN BRANDT                 2.00
18-AUG-01 WEEDING          ELBERT TALBOT                 .90
22-AUG-01 SAWING           PETER LAWSON                 1.00
23-AUG-01 SAWING           PETER LAWSON                 1.00
09-SEP-01 WORK             ADAH TALBOT                  1.00
11-SEP-01 WORK             ROLAND BRANDT                 .75
```

FIGURE 11-1. *Dates and amounts paid by G.B. Talbot during 1901*

```
23-SEP-01 DISCUS          RICHARD KOCH AND BROTHERS    1.50
29-SEP-01 WORK            GERHARDT KENTGEN             1.00
07-OCT-01 PLOWING         RICHARD KOCH AND BROTHERS    1.50
07-OCT-01 WORK            JED HOPKINS                  1.00
09-OCT-01 WORK            DONALD ROLLO                  .63
22-OCT-01 PLOWING         DICK JONES                   1.80
07-NOV-01 SAWED WOOD      ANDREW DYE                    .50
10-NOV-01 WORK            JOHN PEARSON                 1.25
12-NOV-01 WORK            PAT LAVAY                    1.50
13-NOV-01 CUT LOGS        PAT LAVAY                     .25
13-NOV-01 DRAWED LOGS     PAT LAVAY                     .75
12-DEC-01 WORK            BART SARJEANT                1.00
13-DEC-01 SAWED WOOD      PAT LAVAY                     .50
17-DEC-01 SAWING          DICK JONES                    .75

46 rows selected.
```

FIGURE 11-1.   *Dates and amounts paid by G.B. Talbot during 1901* (continued)

The Use of group by and having

If Talbot wanted to get a total of the amount he had paid out, grouped by item, he'd write a query like this one:

```
select Item, SUM(Amount) Total, COUNT(Item)
  from LEDGER
 where Action = 'PAID'
 group by Item;
```

```
ITEM               TOTAL COUNT(ITEM)
---------------- ------- -----------
CUT LOGS             .25           1
DIGGING OF GRAVE    3.00           1
DISCUS              1.50           1
DRAWED LOGS          .75           1
PAINTING            1.75           1
PLOWING            18.10           7
SAWED WOOD          1.00           2
SAWING              3.50           4
THRESHING            .50           1
WEEDING              .90           1
WORK               27.98          26

11 rows selected.
```

Notice the mix of a column name, Item, and two group functions, **SUM** and **COUNT**, in the **select** clause. This mix is possible only because Item is referenced in the **group by** clause. If it were not there, the opaque message first encountered in Chapter 8 would have resulted in this:

```
select Item, SUM(Amount) Total, COUNT(Item)
       *
ERROR at line 1: ORA-00937: not a single-group group function
```

This result occurs because the group functions, such as **SUM** and **COUNT**, are designed to tell you something about a group of rows, not the individual rows of the table. The error is avoided by using Item in the **group by** clause, which forces the **SUM** to sum up all the rows grouped within each Item. **COUNT** tells how many rows each of the Items actually has within its group.

The **having** clause works very much like a **where** clause except that its logic is only related to the results of group functions, as opposed to columns or expressions for individual rows, which can still be selected by a **where** clause. Here, the rows in the previous example are further restricted to just those where the **SUM** of the Amount, by Item group, is greater than three dollars:

```
select Item, SUM(Amount) AS Total
   from LEDGER
  where Action = 'PAID'
  group by Item
 having SUM(Amount) > 3;

ITEM               TOTAL
---------------- -------
PLOWING            18.10
SAWING              3.50
WORK               27.98
```

You also could find the items where the average Amount spent per item in the course of the year was greater than the average of all the items. First, let's check to see what the **AVG** of all the items was for the year:

```
select AVG(Amount) AS Average
   from LEDGER
  where ACTION = 'PAID';
AVERAGE
-------
   1.29
```

Next, incorporate this average as a subquery (similar to those you did with a **where** clause in Chapter 3), to test each group of items against the average:

```
select Item, SUM(Amount) AS Total, AVG(Amount) AS Average
   from LEDGER
 where Action = 'PAID'
 group by Item
having AVG(Amount) > (select AVG(Amount)
                        from LEDGER
                       where ACTION = 'PAID');


ITEM               TOTAL AVERAGE
---------------- ------- -------
DIGGING OF GRAVE    3.00    3.00
DISCUS              1.50    1.50
PAINTING            1.75    1.75
PLOWING            18.10    2.59
```

The **having** clause tests the average amount by Item (because the items are **group**ed **by** Item) against the average amount for all the Items paid during the year. Note the differences and similarities between the Total column and the Average column. Grouping the data from the LEDGER table by Item tells you how much money was paid out, by Item, as well as the average amount paid, by Item. Talbot's LEDGER table can also yield similar information by Person:

```
select Person, SUM(Amount) Total
   from LEDGER
 where Action = 'PAID'
 group by Person;


PERSON                    TOTAL
------------------------ -------
ADAH TALBOT                1.00
ANDREW DYE                 4.50
BART SARJEANT              1.00
DICK JONES                 6.30
DONALD ROLLO                .63
ELBERT TALBOT              3.90
GEORGE OSCAR               1.00
GERHARDT KENTGEN           3.00
HELEN BRANDT               3.00
JED HOPKINS                4.00
JOHN PEARSON               1.25
KAY AND PALMER WALBOM      4.00
PAT LAVAY                  3.00
PETER LAWSON               3.00
RICHARD KOCH AND BROTHERS 12.00
ROLAND BRANDT               .75
VICTORIA LYNN              2.80
WILFRED LOWELL             3.60
```

```
WILLIAM SWING                  .50

19 rows selected.
```

This is a useful summary alphabetized by Person, but what about an alternative order for display? You can't use this:

```
group by SUM(Amount)
```

because then the rows for each person would no longer be collected (grouped) together. Besides, the purpose of **group by** is not to produce a desired sequence, but rather to collect "like" things together. The order they appear in is a by-product of how **group by** works; **group by** is not meant to be used to change the sorting order.

Adding an order by

The solution for creating an alternative order for display is the addition of an **order by** clause following the **having** clause. You could add this:

```
order by Person desc
```

which would reverse the order of the list, or you could add this:

```
order by Total desc
```

For example, 19 people worked for Talbot in 1901, doing some 46 tasks over the course of the year (refer to Figure 11-1). Of those workers who Talbot paid more than a dollar during 1901, who did Talbot pay the most, and what is the relative rank of the workers by income?

```
select Person, SUM(Amount) AS Total
   from LEDGER
 where Action = 'PAID'
 group by Person
having SUM(Amount) > 1.00
 order by Total desc;

PERSON                      TOTAL
------------------------    -------
RICHARD KOCH AND BROTHERS   12.00
DICK JONES                   6.30
ANDREW DYE                   4.50
JED HOPKINS                  4.00
KAY AND PALMER WALBOM        4.00
ELBERT TALBOT                3.90
WILFRED LOWELL               3.60
```

```
GERHARDT KENTGEN            3.00
PETER LAWSON               3.00
PAT LAVAY                  3.00
HELEN BRANDT               3.00
VICTORIA LYNN              2.80
JOHN PEARSON               1.25

12 rows selected.
```

Although you can use the column alias as part of the **order by** clause, you can't use it as part of the **having** clause. Attempting to use **having Total > 1.00** as a clause in this query will result in an "invalid column name" error.

Order of Execution

The previous query has quite a collection of competing clauses! Here are the rules Oracle uses to execute each of them, and the order in which execution takes place:

1. Choose rows based on the **where** clause.

2. Group those rows together based on the **group by** clause.

3. Calculate the results of the group functions for each group.

4. Choose and eliminate groups based on the **having** clause.

5. Order the groups based on the results of the group functions in the **order by** clause. The **order by** clause must use either a group function or a column specified in the **group by** clause.

The order of execution is important because it has a direct impact on the performance of your queries. In general, the more records that can be eliminated via **where** clauses, the faster the query will execute. This performance benefit is due to the reduction in the number of rows that must be processed during the **group by** operation.

If a query is written to use a **having** clause to eliminate groups, then you should check to see if the **having** condition can be rewritten as a **where** clause. In many cases, this rewrite won't be possible. It is usually only available when the **having** clause is used to eliminate groups based on the grouping columns.

For example, if you have this query:

```
select Person, SUM(Amount) AS Total
  from LEDGER
 where Action = 'PAID'
 group by Person
having Person like 'P%'
 order by SUM(Amount) desc;
```

then the order of execution would be, in order:

1. Eliminate rows based on

   ```
   where Action = 'PAID'
   ```

2. Group the remaining rows based on

   ```
   group by Person
   ```

3. For each Person, calculate the

   ```
   SUM(Amount)
   ```

4. Eliminate groups based on

   ```
   having Person like 'P%'
   ```

5. Order the remaining groups.

This query will run faster if the *groups* eliminated in Step 4 can be eliminated as *rows* in Step 1. If they are eliminated at Step 1, fewer rows will be grouped (Step 2), fewer calculations will be performed (Step 3), and no groups will be eliminated (Step 4). Each of these steps in the execution will run faster.

Since the **having** condition in this example is not based on a calculated column, it is easily changed into a **where** condition:

```
select Person, SUM(Amount) AS Total
  from LEDGER
 where Action = 'PAID'
   and Person like 'P%'
 group by Person
 order by Total desc;
```

Views of Groups

In Chapter 3, a view called INVASION was created for the Oracle at Delphi, which joined together the WEATHER and LOCATION tables. This view appeared to be a table in its own right, with columns and rows, but each of its rows contained columns that actually came from two separate tables.

The same process of creating a view can be used with groups. The difference is that each row will contain information about a group of rows—a kind of subtotal table. For example, consider this group query:

```
select LAST_DAY(ActionDate) MONTH,
       SUM(Amount) Total
  from LEDGER
 where Action = 'PAID'
 group by LAST_DAY(ActionDate);
```

```
MONTH       TOTAL
---------   -------
31-JAN-01    3.50
28-FEB-01    1.50
31-MAR-01    4.00
30-APR-01   10.00
31-MAY-01    3.40
30-JUN-01    4.25
31-JUL-01    5.20
31-AUG-01   11.70
30-SEP-01    4.25
31-OCT-01    4.93
30-NOV-01    4.25
31-DEC-01    2.25

12 rows selected.
```

What's being done here is really rather simple. This is a table (technically, a view) of the monthly amounts Talbot paid out for all items combined. This expression:

 LAST_DAY(ActionDate)

forces every real ActionDate encountered to be the last day of the month. If ActionDate were the column in the **select** clause, you'd get subtotals by day, instead of by month. The same sort of thing could have been accomplished with this:

 TO_CHAR(ActionDate,'MON')

except that the result would have ended up in alphabetical order by month, instead of in normal month order. You now can give this result a name and create a view:

```
create or replace view MONTHTOTAL as
select LAST_DAY(ActionDate) AS MONTH,
       SUM(Amount) AS Total
  from LEDGER
 where Action = 'PAID'
 group by LAST_DAY(ActionDate);

View created.
```

Renaming Columns with Aliases

Notice the names MONTH and Total in the **select** clause. These *rename* the columns they follow. The new names are called *aliases,* because they are used to disguise the real names of the underlying columns (which are complicated because they have functions). This is similar to what you saw in the SQLPLUS report in Chapter 6 in Figure 6-3, when Quantity times Rate was renamed Ext:

```
Quantity * Rate Ext
```

In fact, now that this view is created, you can describe it like this:

```
describe MONTHTOTAL
```

```
Name                            Null?    Type
------------------------------- -------- ----
MONTH                                    DATE
TOTAL                                    NUMBER
```

When you query the table, you can (and must) now use the new column names:

```
select Month, Total
   from MONTHTOTAL;
```

```
MONTH         TOTAL
---------  -------
31-JAN-01     3.50
28-FEB-01     1.50
31-MAR-01     4.00
30-APR-01    10.00
31-MAY-01     3.40
30-JUN-01     4.25
31-JUL-01     5.20
31-AUG-01    11.70
30-SEP-01     4.25
31-OCT-01     4.93
30-NOV-01     4.25
31-DEC-01     2.25
```

```
12 rows selected.
```

"Total" is referred to as a *column alias*—another name to use when referring to a column.

In the description of the view, and in the query, there is no evidence of the **LAST_DAY**(ActionDate) or **SUM**(Amount)—just their new names, MONTH and TOTAL. It is as if the view MONTHTOTAL was a real table with rows of monthly sums. Why?

Oracle automatically takes a single word, without quotes, and uses it to rename the column it follows. When it does this, Oracle forces the word—the alias—into uppercase, regardless of how it was typed. You can see evidence of this by comparing the column names in the **create view** and the **describe** commands. Even though MONTH was typed in uppercase and Total was typed in mixed upper- and lowercase in the **create view**, they are both in uppercase in the table description that Oracle keeps internally. When creating a view, *never put double quotes around your column aliases*. Always leave aliases in **create view** statements without quotes. This will cause them to be stored in uppercase, which is required for Oracle to find them. See the sidebar "Aliases in View Creation" for a warning on aliases.

You now have monthly totals collected in a view. A total for the entire year could also be created, using YEARTOTAL as both the view name and the column alias for **SUM**(Amount):

```
create or replace view YEARTOTAL as
select SUM(Amount) YEARTOTAL
   from LEDGER
 where Action = 'PAID';

View created.
```

If you query the view, you'll discover it has only one record:

```
select YEARTOTAL
   from YEARTOTAL;

YEARTOTAL
---------
    59.23
```

Aliases in View Creation
Internally, Oracle works with all column and table names in uppercase. This is how they are stored in its data dictionary, and this is how it always expects them to be. When aliases are typed to create a view, they should always be naked—without quotation marks around them. Putting double quotation marks around an alias can force the column name stored internally by Oracle to be in mixed case. If you do this, Oracle will not be able to find the column when you execute a **select** unless you enclose the column name within quotes during all of your queries.

Never use double quotation marks in creating aliases for a view.

The Power of Views of Groups

Now you'll see the real power of a relational database. You've created views of Talbot's underlying ledger that contain totals by groups: by Item, by Person, by Month, and by Year. These views can now be *joined* together, just like the tables were in Chapter 3, to reveal information never before apparent. For instance, what percentage of the year's payments were made each month?

```
select Month, Total, (Total/YearTotal)*100 AS Percent
   from MONTHTOTAL, YEARTOTAL
 order by Month;


MONTH         TOTAL PERCENT
---------   ------- -------
31-JAN-01     3.50    5.91
28-FEB-01     1.50    2.53
31-MAR-01     4.00    6.75
30-APR-01    10.00   16.88
31-MAY-01     3.40    5.74
30-JUN-01     4.25    7.18
31-JUL-01     5.20    8.78
31-AUG-01    11.70   19.75
30-SEP-01     4.25    7.18
31-OCT-01     4.93    8.32
30-NOV-01     4.25    7.18
31-DEC-01     2.25    3.80


12 rows selected.
```

In this query, two views are listed in the **from** clause, but they are not joined in a **where** clause. Why not?

In this particular case, no **where** clause is necessary, because one of the views, YEARTOTAL, will only return one row (as shown in the previous listing). Both the MONTHTOTAL and the YEARTOTAL views were created with the assumption that only one year's data would be stored in the LEDGER table. If data for multiple years is to be stored in the LEDGER table, both of these views need to be re-created to **group by** a Year column as well. That column would then be used to join them (since the YEARTOTAL view might then return more than one row).

The same results could have been obtained by directly joining the LEDGER *table* with the YEARTOTAL *view,* but as you can see, the query is immensely more complicated and difficult to understand:

```
select LAST_DAY(ActionDate) MONTH,
       SUM(Amount) Total,
```

```
        (SUM(Amount)/YearTotal)*100   Percent
  from LEDGER, YEARTOTAL
where Action = 'PAID'
group by LAST_DAY(ActionDate), YearTotal;
```

Would it be possible to go one step further and simply join the LEDGER table to itself, once for monthly totals and once for the yearly total, without creating any views at all? The answer is no, because the **group by** for monthly totals is in conflict with the **group by** for a yearly total. To create queries that compare one grouping of rows (such as by month) with another grouping of rows (such as by year), at least one of the groupings must be a view. Beyond this technical restriction, however, it is just simpler and easier to understand doing the queries with views. Compare the last two examples, and the difference in clarity is apparent. Views hide complexity.

The views also give you more power to use the many character, NUMBER, and DATE datatypes at will, without worrying about things like months appearing in alphabetical order. Now that the MONTHTOTAL view exists, you can modify the display of the month with a simple **SUBSTR** (**TO_CHAR** could also be used):

```
select SUBSTR(Month,4,3), Total,
        (Total/YearTotal)*100 AS Percent
  from MONTHTOTAL, YEARTOTAL
 order by Month;

SUB   TOTAL PERCENT
---   ----- -------
JAN   3.50   5.91
FEB   1.50   2.53
MAR   4.00   6.75
APR  10.00  16.88
MAY   3.40   5.74
JUN   4.25   7.18
JUL   5.20   8.78
AUG  11.70  19.75
SEP   4.25   7.18
OCT   4.93   8.32
NOV   4.25   7.18
DEC   2.25   3.80

12 rows selected.
```

Logic in the having Clause

In the **having** clause, the choice of the group function, and the column on which it operates, might bear no relation to the columns or group functions in the **select** clause:

```
select Person, SUM(Amount) AS Total
   from LEDGER
  where Action = 'PAID'
  group by Person
having COUNT(Item) > 1
  order by Total desc;


PERSON                          TOTAL
------------------------        -------
RICHARD KOCH AND BROTHERS       12.00
DICK JONES                       6.30
ANDREW DYE                       4.50
JED HOPKINS                      4.00
KAY AND PALMER WALBOM            4.00
ELBERT TALBOT                    3.90
WILFRED LOWELL                   3.60
GERHARDT KENTGEN                 3.00
PETER LAWSON                     3.00
PAT LAVAY                        3.00
HELEN BRANDT                     3.00
VICTORIA LYNN                    2.80

12 rows selected.
```

Here, the **having** clause selected only those persons (the **group by** collected all the rows into groups by Person) who had more than one Item. Anyone who only did a task once for Talbot is eliminated. Those who did any task more than once are included.

The sort of query shown in the last listing is very effective for determining which rows in a table have duplicate values in specific columns. For example, if you are trying to establish a new unique index on a column (or set of columns) in a table, and the index creation fails due to uniqueness problems with the data, then you can easily determine which rows caused the problem.

First, select the columns that you want to be unique, followed by a **COUNT**(*) column. **Group by** the columns you want to be unique, and use the **having** clause to return only those groups having **COUNT**(*)>1. The only records returned will be duplicates. The following query shows this check being performed for the Person column of the LEDGER table:

```
select Person, COUNT(*)
   from LEDGER
  group by Person
having COUNT(*)>1
  order by Person;
```

order by with Columns and Group Functions

The **order by** clause is executed after the **where**, **group by**, and **having** clauses. It can employ group functions, or columns from the **group by**, or a combination. If it uses a group function, that function operates on the groups, and then the **order by** sorts the *results* of the function in order. If the **order by** uses a column from the **group by**, it sorts the rows that are returned based on that column. Group functions and single columns (so long as the column is in the **group by**) can be combined in the **order by**.

In the **order by** clause, you can specify a group function and the column it affects even though they have nothing at all to do with the group functions or columns in the **select**, **group by**, or **having** clause. On the other hand, if you specify a column in the **order by** clause that is not part of a group function, it must be in the **group by** clause. This query shows the count of Items and the total amount paid per Person, but it puts them in order by the average Amount they were paid per item:

```
select Person, COUNT(Item), SUM(Amount) AS Total
   from LEDGER
 where Action = 'PAID'
 group by Person
having COUNT(Item) > 1
 order by AVG(Amount);
```

PERSON	COUNT(ITEM)	TOTAL
PAT LAVAY	4	3.00
ELBERT TALBOT	5	3.90
GERHARDT KENTGEN	3	3.00
PETER LAWSON	3	3.00
DICK JONES	6	6.30
WILFRED LOWELL	3	3.60
VICTORIA LYNN	2	2.80
HELEN BRANDT	2	3.00
JED HOPKINS	2	4.00
KAY AND PALMER WALBOM	2	4.00
ANDREW DYE	2	4.50
RICHARD KOCH AND BROTHERS	5	12.00

```
12 rows selected.
```

If this is a little hard to believe, look at the same query with the **AVG**(Amount) added to the **select** clause:

```
select Person, COUNT(Item), SUM(Amount) AS Total,
       AVG(Amount)
  from LEDGER
 where Action = 'PAID'
 group by Person
having COUNT(Item) > 1
 order by AVG(Amount);
```

PERSON	COUNT(ITEM)	TOTAL	AVG(AMOUNT)
PAT LAVAY	4	3.00	.75
ELBERT TALBOT	5	3.90	.78
GERHARDT KENTGEN	3	3.00	1
PETER LAWSON	3	3.00	1
DICK JONES	6	6.30	1.05
WILFRED LOWELL	3	3.60	1.2
VICTORIA LYNN	2	2.80	1.4
HELEN BRANDT	2	3.00	1.5
JED HOPKINS	2	4.00	2
KAY AND PALMER WALBOM	2	4.00	2
ANDREW DYE	2	4.50	2.25
RICHARD KOCH AND BROTHERS	5	12.00	2.4

```
12 rows selected.
```

You can check any of these results by hand with the full ledger listings given previously in Figure 11-1.

Join Columns

As explained in Chapters 1 and 3, joining two tables together requires that they have a relationship defined by a common column. This is also true in joining views, or tables and views. The only exception is when one of the tables or views has just a single row, as the YEARTOTAL table does. In this case, SQL joins the single row to every row in the other table or view, and no reference to the joining columns needs to be made in the **where** clause of the query.

Any attempt to join two tables that each has more than one row without specifying the joined columns in the **where** clause will produce what's known as a *Cartesian* *product,* usually a giant result where every row in one table is joined with every row in the other table. A small 80-row table joined to a small 100-row table in this way would produce 8,000 rows in your display, and few of them would be at all meaningful.

where, having, group by, and order by

Tables in Oracle can be grouped into collections of related rows, such as by Item, Date, or Person. This is done using the **group by** clause, which collects only those rows in the table that pass the logical test of the **where** clause:

```
where Action = 'PAID'
group by person
```

The **having** clause looks at these groups and eliminates any based on whether they pass the logical test of the group function used in the **having** clause, such as:

```
having SUM(Amount) > 5
```

Those groups whose **SUM**(Amount) is greater than five are returned to you. Each group has just one row in the resulting table that is displayed. The **having** clause need not (and often will not) correspond to the group functions in the **select** clause. After these rows have been chosen by the **having** clause, they can be placed in the desired sequence by an **order by**:

```
order by AVG(Amount)
```

The **order by** must use either a column named in the **group by** or any appropriate group function that can reference any column without regard to the **select** or the **having** clause. Its group function will make its computation row by row for each group created by the **group by** clause.

All of these powerful grouping features can be combined to create complex summary views of the underlying table, which appear very simple. Once created, their columns can be manipulated, and their rows selected, just as with any other table. These views also can be joined to each other, and to tables, to produce deep insights into the data.

CHAPTER
12

When One Query
Depends upon Another

his chapter and Chapter 13 introduce more difficult concepts than we've previously seen. While many of these concepts are rarely used in the normal course of running queries or producing reports, there will be occasions that call for the techniques taught in these chapters. If they seem too challenging as you study them, read on anyway. The odds are good that by the time you need these methods, you'll be able to use them.

Advanced Subqueries

You've encountered *subqueries*—those **select** statements that are part of a **where** clause in a preceding **select** statement—in earlier chapters. Subqueries also can be used in **insert**, **update**, and **delete** statements. This use will be covered in Chapter 15.

Often, a subquery will provide an alternative approach to a query. For example, suppose George Talbot needs a combine driver quickly (a combine is a machine that moves through a field to harvest, head, thresh, and clean grains such as wheat and oats). He can't afford to send someone off to another town to search for a driver, so he has to find someone in Edmeston or North Edmeston. One way to locate such a person is with a three-way table join, using the tables that were normalized back in Chapter 2. These are shown in Figure 12-1.

```
select WORKER.Name, WORKER.Lodging
   from WORKER, WORKERSKILL, LODGING
 where WORKER.Name = WORKERSKILL.Name
   and WORKER.Lodging = LODGING.Lodging
   and Skill = 'COMBINE DRIVER'
   and Address LIKE '%EDMESTON%';


NAME                         LODGING
------------------------     ---------------
JOHN PEARSON                 ROSE HILL
```

Three tables are joined in the same way that two tables are. The common columns are set equal to each other in the **where** clause, as shown in Figure 12-2. To join three tables together, two of them must each be joined to a third.

> **NOTE**
> *Not every table is joined to every other table. In fact, the number of links between the tables (such as WORKER.Name = WORKERSKILL.Name) is usually one less than the number of tables being joined.*

The WORKER Table

NAME	AGE	LODGING
ADAH TALBOT	23	PAPA KING
ANDREW DYE	29	ROSE HILL
BART SARJEANT	22	CRANMER
DICK JONES	18	ROSE HILL
DONALD ROLLO	16	MATTS
ELBERT TALBOT	43	WEITBROCHT
GEORGE OSCAR	41	ROSE HILL
GERHARDT KENTGEN	55	PAPA KING
HELEN BRANDT	15	
JED HOPKINS	33	MATTS
JOHN PEARSON	27	ROSE HILL
KAY AND PALMER WALLBOM		ROSE HILL
PAT LAVAY	21	ROSE HILL
PETER LAWSON	25	CRANMER
RICHARD KOCH AND BROTHERS		WEITBROCHT
ROLAND BRANDT	35	MATTS
VICTORIA LYNN	32	MULLERS
WILFRED LOWELL	67	
WILLIAM SWING	15	CRANMER

The WORKERSKILL Table

NAME	SKILL	ABILITY
ADAH TALBOT	WORK	GOOD
DICK JONES	SMITHY	EXCELLENT
ELBERT TALBOT	DISCUS	SLOW
HELEN BRANDT	COMBINE DRIVER	VERY FAST
JOHN PEARSON	COMBINE DRIVER	
JOHN PEARSON	WOODCUTTER	GOOD
JOHN PEARSON	SMITHY	AVERAGE
VICTORIA LYNN	SMITHY	PRECISE
WILFRED LOWELL	WORK	AVERAGE
WILFRED LOWELL	DISCUS	AVERAGE

FIGURE 12-1. *Information in Talbot's tables*

The SKILL Table

SKILL	DESCRIPTION
COMBINE DRIVER	HARNESS, DRIVE, GROOM HORSES, ADJUST BLADES
DISCUS	HARNESS, DRIVE, GROOM HORSES, BLADE DEPTH
GRAVE DIGGER	MARK AND CUT SOD, DIG, SHORE, FILL, RESOD
SMITHY	STACK FOR HIRE, RUN BELLOWS, CUT, SHOE HORSES
WOODCUTTER	MARK AND FELL TREES, SPLIT, STACK, HAUL
WORK	GENERAL UNSKILLED LABOR

The LODGING Table

LODGING	LONGNAME	MANAGER	ADDRESS
CRANMER	CRANMER RETREAT HOUSE	THOM CRANMER	HILL ST, BERKELEY
MATTS	MATTS LONG BUNK HOUSE	ROLAND BRANDT	3 MILE RD, KEENE
MULLERS	MULLERS COED LODGING	KEN MULLER	120 MAIN, EDMESTON
PAPA KING	PAPA KING ROOMING	WILLIAM KING	127 MAIN, EDMESTON
ROSE HILL	ROSE HILL FOR MEN	JOHN PELETIER	RFD 3, N. EDMESTON
WEITBROCHT	WEITBROCHT ROOMING	EUNICE BENSON	320 GENEVA, KEENE

FIGURE 12-1. *Information in Talbot's tables* (continued)

Once the tables are joined, as shown in the first two lines of the **where** clause, then Skill and Address can be used to find a nearby combine driver.

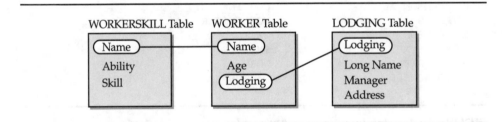

FIGURE 12-2. *A three-way table join*

Correlated Subqueries

Is there another way to accomplish this same result? Recall that a **where** clause can contain a subquery **select**. Subquery **select**s can be nested—that is, a **where** clause in a subquery also can contain a **where** clause with a subquery, which can contain a **where** clause with a subquery—on down for more levels than you are ever likely to need. It's common wisdom, widely published, that you can do this down to 16 levels. The number is actually higher, but you'll never even need 16, and performance may become very poor with more than a few levels. The following shows three **select**s, each connected to another through a **where** clause:

```
select Name, Lodging
   from WORKER
 where Name IN
       (select Name
          from WORKERSKILL
         where Skill = 'COMBINE DRIVER'
           and Lodging IN
               (select Lodging
                  from LODGING
                 where Address LIKE '%EDMESTON%'));


NAME                         LODGING
------------------------     ---------------
JOHN PEARSON                 ROSE HILL
```

This query selects any workers who drive a combine and live in lodging located in Edmeston. It does this simply by requesting a worker whose Name is in the WORKERSKILL table with a Skill of 'COMBINE DRIVER' and whose Lodging is in the LODGING table with an Address LIKE '%EDMESTON%'. This is an example of a subquery that contains subqueries, but it has an additional feature. Look at the **where** clause of the second **select** statement:

```
(select Name
   from WORKERSKILL
  where Skill = 'COMBINE DRIVER'
    and Lodging IN
```

At first glance, this looks reasonable, but it contains the Lodging column. Is the Lodging column in the WORKERSKILL table? It is not. So why does this query work? The reason is that, because this is a subquery, Oracle assumes the column Lodging to be from the first **select** statement, the one that contains the subquery in its **where** clause. This is called a *correlated* subquery, because for every Name in the main (outer) query that has a Skill of 'COMBINE DRIVER', the Lodging is correlated in the second **where** clause.

Said differently, a subquery may refer to a column in a table used in its main query (the query that has the subquery in its **where** clause).

```
select Name, Lodging
   from WORKER
 where Name IN
         (select Name
             from WORKSKILL                        Correlated,
          where skill = 'COMBINE DRIVER            same column
            and Lodging IN
                 (select Lodging
                     from LODGING
                  where Address LIKE ('%EDMESTON%')));
```

This correlated subquery in effect joins information from three tables to answer the question of whether any combine drivers live nearby.

You've also seen how this same query can be performed with a three-way table join. Can any correlated subquery be replaced by a table join? No. Suppose Talbot wanted to know which of his workers were the oldest in each lodging house. Here are the maximum ages by house:

```
select Lodging, MAX(Age)
   from WORKER
 group by Lodging;
LODGING     MAX(AGE)
---------- --------
                 67
CRANMER          25
MATTS            35
MULLERS          32
PAPA KING        55
ROSE HILL        41
WEITBROCHT       43
```

How would you incorporate this into a query? The Lodging column in the upper **select** is correlated with the Lodging column in the subquery **select**:

```
select Name, Age, Lodging
   from WORKER W
 where Age =
         (select MAX(Age) from WORKER
```

```
      where W.Lodging = Lodging);
```

```
NAME                        AGE LODGING
----------------------- ----- ----------
ELBERT TALBOT                43 WEITBROCHT
GEORGE OSCAR                 41 ROSE HILL
GERHARDT KENTGEN             55 PAPA KING
PETER LAWSON                 25 CRANMER
ROLAND BRANDT                35 MATTS
VICTORIA LYNN               32 MULLERS
```

You'll observe the use of correlation names here. WORKER has been given a correlation name (alias) of W, and one of the Lodging columns in the lower **where** clause has been designated W.Lodging. This is done because both the top **select** and the subquery use the same table, and each has a column named Lodging. Without this ability to rename (give an alias to) one of the tables, there would be no way for the lower **where** clause to distinguish one Lodging from the other. Would it work to give the second WORKER table the alias instead?

```
select Name, Age, Lodging
   from WORKER
 where Age =
       (select MAX(Age)
           from WORKER W
         where W.Lodging = Lodging);
NAME                        AGE LODGING
----------------------- ----- ----------
GERHARDT KENTGEN             55 PAPA KING
```

Clearly, it does not work. The second **where** clause does not detect that Lodging should belong to the main query's WORKER table, and therefore believes that W.Lodging and Lodging each is its own Lodging column. Since these are always equal (except for **NULL**s), the subquery does not produce the maximum age for each lodging; instead, it produces the maximum age from all the lodgings.

This brings up one of the effects of equality tests with **NULL**s, as discussed in Chapter 3: The oldest person overall is Wilfred Lowell, but this last query produced Gerhardt Kentgen, and the query just before produced only those workers who had real values in their Lodging column (the column was not **NULL**). Both of these effects are due to this **where** clause:

```
where W.Lodging = Lodging);
```

The mere existence of this test, with the equal sign, excludes any Lodging whose value is **NULL**. To include those workers for whom you do not have a Lodging value, use the **NVL** function, as shown next.

```
select Name, Age, Lodging
   from WORKER W
 where Age =
        (select MAX(Age)
           from WORKER
          where NVL(W.Lodging,'X') = NVL(Lodging,'X'));


NAME                        AGE LODGING
------------------------- ----- ----------
ELBERT TALBOT                43 WEITBROCHT
GEORGE OSCAR                 41 ROSE HILL
GERHARDT KENTGEN             55 PAPA KING
PETER LAWSON                 25 CRANMER
ROLAND BRANDT                35 MATTS
VICTORIA LYNN               32 MULLERS
WILFRED LOWELL              67
```

The substitute of X could have been anything as long as the same substitute was used in both **NVL** functions. If the **NVL** function were to be added to the query that produced only GERHARDT KENTGEN, the result would have been WILFRED LOWELL instead. Another way to write the same query (oldest person per lodging house) is shown here:

```
select Name, Age, Lodging
   from WORKER
 where (Lodging, Age) IN
        (select Lodging, MAX(Age)
           from WORKER
          group by Lodging);


NAME                        AGE LODGING
------------------------- ----- ----------
PETER LAWSON                 25 CRANMER
ROLAND BRANDT                35 MATTS
VICTORIA LYNN               32 MULLERS
GERHARDT KENTGEN             55 PAPA KING
GEORGE OSCAR                 41 ROSE HILL
ELBERT TALBOT                43 WEITBROCHT
```

These two columns are being tested simultaneously against a subquery. The **IN** is necessary because the subquery produces more than one row; otherwise, an equal sign could have been used. When two or more columns are tested at the same time against the results of a subquery, they must be enclosed in parentheses, as shown with (Lodging, Age). Note that this query did not find WILFRED LOWELL, because the **IN** ignores **NULL** values.

Coordinating Logical Tests

John Pearson falls ill. He's been a stalwart of the Talbot crew for many months. Who else has his skills, and where do they live? A list of the workers who have skills that Talbot knows about is easily retrieved from the WORKER and WORKERSKILL tables:

```
select WORKER.Name, Lodging, Skill
    from WORKER, WORKERSKILL
 where WORKER.Name = WORKERSKILL.Name;
```

```
NAME                     LODGING     SKILL
------------------------ ----------- --------------
ADAH TALBOT              PAPA KING   WORK
DICK JONES               ROSE HILL   SMITHY
ELBERT TALBOT            WEITBROCHT  DISCUS
HELEN BRANDT                         COMBINE DRIVER
JOHN PEARSON             ROSE HILL   COMBINE DRIVER
JOHN PEARSON             ROSE HILL   WOODCUTTER
JOHN PEARSON             ROSE HILL   SMITHY
VICTORIA LYNN            MULLERS     SMITHY
WILFRED LOWELL                       WORK
WILFRED LOWELL                       DISCUS
```

Rather than search by hand through this list (or the much longer list a business is likely to have of its workers' skills), let Oracle do it for you. This query simply asks which workers have Pearson's skills, and where each lives:

```
select WORKER.Name, Lodging, Skill
    from WORKER, WORKERSKILL
 where WORKER.Name = WORKERSKILL.Name
    and Skill IN
         (select Skill
            from WORKERSKILL
          where Name = 'JOHN PEARSON')
  order by WORKER.Name;
```

```
NAME                     LODGING     SKILL
------------------------ ----------- --------------
DICK JONES               ROSE HILL   SMITHY
HELEN BRANDT                         COMBINE DRIVER
JOHN PEARSON             ROSE HILL   COMBINE DRIVER
JOHN PEARSON             ROSE HILL   WOODCUTTER
JOHN PEARSON             ROSE HILL   SMITHY
VICTORIA LYNN            MULLERS     SMITHY
```

Not surprisingly, it turns out that Pearson has Pearson's skills. To exclude him from the query, another **and** is added to the **where** clause:

```
select WORKER.Name, Lodging, Skill
   from WORKER, WORKERSKILL
 where WORKER.Name = WORKERSKILL.Name
   and Skill IN
        (select Skill
           from WORKERSKILL
          where Name = 'JOHN PEARSON')
   and WORKER.Name != 'JOHN PEARSON'
 order by WORKER.Name;
NAME                         LODGING     SKILL
------------------------     ----------  --------------
DICK JONES                   ROSE HILL   SMITHY
HELEN BRANDT                             COMBINE DRIVER
VICTORIA LYNN                MULLERS     SMITHY
```

This **and** is a part of the main query, even though it follows the subquery.

EXISTS and Its Correlated Subquery

EXISTS is a test for existence. It is placed the way **IN** might be placed with a subquery, but differs in two ways:

- It does not match a column or columns.

- It is typically used only with a correlated subquery.

Suppose Talbot wanted the names and skills of workers possessing more than one skill. Finding just the *names* of those with more than one skill is simple:

```
select Name
   from WORKERSKILL
  group by Name
having COUNT(Skill) > 1;

NAME
------------------------
JOHN PEARSON
WILFRED LOWELL
```

Attempting to find both Name and Skill fails, however, because the **group by** made necessary by the **COUNT**(Skill) is on the primary key of the WORKERSKILL table (Name, Skill). Since each primary key, by definition, uniquely identifies only one row, the count of skills for that one row can never be greater than one, so the **having** clause always tests false—it doesn't find any rows:

```
select Name, Skill
   from WORKERSKILL
 group by Name, Skill
having COUNT(Skill) > 1;


no rows selected.
```

EXISTS provides a solution. The following subquery asks, for each Name selected in the outer query, whether a Name exists in the WORKERSKILL table with a count of skills greater than one. If the answer for a given name is yes, the **EXISTS** test is true, and the outer query **select**s a Name and Skill. The worker names are correlated by the WS alias given to the first WORKERSKILL table.

```
select Name, Skill
   from WORKERSKILL WS
 where EXISTS
        (select *
           from WORKERSKILL
          where WS.Name = Name
          group by Name
          having COUNT(Skill) > 1);


NAME                          SKILL
--------------------------    --------------
JOHN PEARSON                  COMBINE DRIVER
JOHN PEARSON                  SMITHY
JOHN PEARSON                  WOODCUTTER
WILFRED LOWELL                WORK
WILFRED LOWELL                DISCUS
```

This same query could have been built using **IN** and a test on the column Name. No correlated subquery is necessary here:

```
select Name, Skill
   from WORKERSKILL WS
 where Name IN
        (select Name
           from WORKERSKILL
          group by Name
          having COUNT(Skill) > 1);
```

Outer Joins

The WORKER table contains all of Talbot's employees and ages, but doesn't list skills. The WORKERSKILL table contains only those employees who have skills. How would you go about producing a report of all employees, with their ages and skills, regardless of whether they have skills or not? Your first attempt might be to join the two tables. Notice the extensive use of aliases in this query. For convenience, each table is renamed, one A and the other B, and A and B appear anywhere the table names normally would appear.

```
select A.Name, Age, Skill
   from WORKER A, WORKERSKILL B
  where A.Name = B.Name
  order by A.Name;
```

```
NAME                        AGE SKILL
------------------------- ----- --------------
ADAH TALBOT                  23 WORK
DICK JONES                   18 SMITHY
ELBERT TALBOT                43 DISCUS
HELEN BRANDT                 15 COMBINE DRIVER
JOHN PEARSON                 27 COMBINE DRIVER
JOHN PEARSON                 27 SMITHY
JOHN PEARSON                 27 WOODCUTTER
VICTORIA LYNN                32 SMITHY
WILFRED LOWELL               67 WORK
WILFRED LOWELL               67 DISCUS
```

Unfortunately, this result only includes those employees who have skills. The solution to producing a complete list is an *outer join*. This is a technique in which Oracle adds extra matching rows with nothing in them to one table (in this case, the WORKERSKILL table) so that the result is as long as the other table (the WORKER table). Basically, every row in the WORKER table that couldn't find a match in WORKERSKILL gets listed anyway:

```
select A.Name, Age, Skill
   from WORKER A, WORKERSKILL B
  where A.Name = B.Name(+)
  order by A.Name;
```

```
NAME                        AGE SKILL
------------------------- ----- --------------
ADAH TALBOT                  23 WORK
ANDREW DYE                   29
BART SARJEANT                22
DICK JONES                   18 SMITHY
```

```
DONALD ROLLO                   16
ELBERT TALBOT                  43 DISCUS
GEORGE OSCAR                   41
GERHARDT KENTGEN               55
HELEN BRANDT                   15 COMBINE DRIVER
JED HOPKINS                    33
JOHN PEARSON                   27 COMBINE DRIVER
JOHN PEARSON                   27 WOODCUTTER
JOHN PEARSON                   27 SMITHY
KAY AND PALMER WALLBOM
PAT LAVAY                      21
PETER LAWSON                   25
RICHARD KOCH AND BROTHERS
ROLAND BRANDT                  35
VICTORIA LYNN                  32 SMITHY
WILFRED LOWELL                 67 WORK
WILFRED LOWELL                 67 DISCUS
WILLIAM SWING                  15
```

Think of the (+), which must immediately follow the join column of the shorter table, as saying "add an extra (**NULL**) row of B.Name any time there's no match for A.Name." As you can see, all workers are listed, along with age and skill. Those for whom there was no match simply got an empty Skill column.

Replacing NOT IN with an Outer Join

The various logical tests that can be done in a **where** clause all have their separate performance measures. A **NOT IN** test may force a full read of the table in the subquery **select**. Suppose Talbot needed workers for a particular project, but wanted to be sure not to call anyone who had smithy skills, because he knew he'd need them for another project. To select workers without smithy skills, and their lodging, he could construct a query like this one:

```
select A.Name, Lodging
   from WORKER A
 where A.Name NOT IN
       (select Name
          from WORKERSKILL
         where Skill = 'SMITHY')
order by A.Name;

NAME                         LODGING
------------------------     ----------
ADAH TALBOT                  PAPA KING
ANDREW DYE                   ROSE HILL
BART SARJEANT                CRANMER
DONALD ROLLO                 MATTS
ELBERT TALBOT                WEITBROCHT
```

```
GEORGE OSCAR              ROSE HILL
GERHARDT KENTGEN          PAPA KING
HELEN BRANDT
JED HOPKINS               MATTS
KAY AND PALMER WALLBOM    ROSE HILL
PAT LAVAY                 ROSE HILL
PETER LAWSON              CRANMER
RICHARD KOCH AND BROTHERS WEITBROCHT
ROLAND BRANDT             MATTS
WILFRED LOWELL
WILLIAM SWING             CRANMER
```

This is typically the way such a query would be written, even though experienced Oracle users know it may be slow. The following query uses an outer join and produces the same result. The difference is that this one is much more efficient:

```
select A.Name, Lodging
  from WORKER A, WORKERSKILL B
 where A.Name = B.Name(+)
   and B.Name is NULL
   and B.Skill(+) = 'SMITHY' order by A.Name;
```

Why does it work and give the same results as the **NOT IN**? The outer join between the two tables assures that all rows are available for the test, including those workers for whom no skills are listed in the WORKERSKILL table. The line

```
B.Name is NULL
```

produces only those workers who don't appear in the WORKERSKILL table (no skills listed), and the line

```
B.Skill(+) = 'SMITHY'
```

adds those who are in the WORKERSKILL table but who don't have a skill of 'SMITHY' (therefore, the B.Skill(+) invented one).

The logic here is obscure, but it works. The best way to use this technique is simply to follow the model. Save this method for use where a **NOT IN** will be searching a big table, and put plenty of explanatory comments nearby.

Replacing NOT IN with NOT EXISTS

A faster and more straightforward way of performing this type of query requires using the **NOT EXISTS** clause. **NOT EXISTS** is typically used to determine which values in one table do not have matching values in another table. In usage, it is identical to the **EXISTS** clause; in the following examples, you'll see the difference in the query logic and the records returned.

Retrieving data from two tables such as these typically requires that they be joined. However, joining two tables—such as SKILL and WORKERSKILL—will by definition exclude the records that exist only in one of those tables. But what if *those* are the records you care about?

For example, what if you want to know which Skills in the SKILL table are not covered by the skills of the current staff of workers? The workers' skills are listed in the WORKERSKILL table, so a query that joins SKILL and WORKERSKILL on the Skill column will exclude the Skills that are not covered:

```
select SKILL.Skill
   from SKILL, WORKERSKILL
 where SKILL.Skill = WORKERSKILL.Skill;
```

NOT EXISTS allows you to use a correlated subquery to eliminate from a table all records that may successfully be joined to another table. For this example, that means you can eliminate from the SKILL table all Skills that are present in the Skill column of the WORKERSKILL table. The following query shows how this is done:

```
select SKILL.Skill
   from SKILL
 where NOT EXISTS
     (select 'x' from WORKERSKILL
       where WORKERSKILL.Skill = SKILL.Skill);

SKILL
-------------
GRAVE DIGGER
```

As this query shows, there are no workers in the WORKERSKILL table who have 'GRAVE DIGGER' as a Skill. How does this query work?

For each record in the SKILL table, the **NOT EXISTS** subquery is checked. If the join of that record to the WORKERSKILL table returns a row, then the subquery succeeds. **NOT EXISTS** tells the query to reverse that return code; therefore, any row in SKILL that can be successfully joined to WORKERSKILL will not be returned by the outer query. The only row left is the one skill that does not have a record in WORKERSKILL.

NOT EXISTS is a very efficient way to perform this type of query, especially when multiple columns are used for the join. Because it uses a join, **NOT EXISTS** is frequently able to use available indexes, whereas **NOT IN** may not be able to use those indexes. The ability to use indexes for this type of query can have a dramatic impact on the query's performance.

UNION, INTERSECT, and MINUS

Sometimes, you need to combine information of a similar type from more than one table. A classic example of this is merging two or more mailing lists prior to a mailing campaign. Depending upon the purpose of a particular mailing, you might want to send letters to any of these combinations of people:

- Everyone in both lists (while avoiding sending two letters to someone who happens to be in both lists)
- Only those people who are in both lists
- Those people in only one of the lists

These three combinations of lists are known in Oracle as **UNION**, **INTERSECT**, and **MINUS**. Suppose Talbot has two lists, one of his longtime employees and the other of prospective workers that he has acquired from another employer. The longtime employee list includes these eight names:

```
select Name from LONGTIME;

NAME
--------------
ADAH TALBOT
DICK JONES
DONALD ROLLO
ELBERT TALBOT
GEORGE OSCAR
PAT LAVAY
PETER LAWSON
WILFRED LOWELL
```

The prospective worker list includes these eight employees:

```
select Name from PROSPECT;

NAME
--------------
ADAH TALBOT
DORY KENSON
ELBERT TALBOT
GEORGE PHEPPS
JED HOPKINS
PAT LAVAY
TED BUTCHER
WILFRED LOWELL
```

The most straightforward use of **UNION** is this combination of the two tables. Note that it contains 12, not 16, names. Those in both lists appear only once:

```
select Name from LONGTIME
  UNION
select Name from PROSPECT;

NAME
--------------
ADAH TALBOT
DICK JONES
DONALD ROLLO
DORY KENSON
ELBERT TALBOT
GEORGE OSCAR
GEORGE PHEPPS
JED HOPKINS
PAT LAVAY
PETER LAWSON
TED BUTCHER
WILFRED LOWELL
```

To show the duplicates, you can use the **UNION ALL** operator. When you use **UNION ALL**, any duplicates from the two lists are given twice in the result. For example, the preceding query would have 16 names rather than 12 if you used **UNION ALL**.

In the following, the two lists of eight are intersected. This list contains only those names that are in *both* underlying tables:

```
select Name from LONGTIME
  INTERSECT
select Name from PROSPECT;

NAME
--------------
ADAH TALBOT
ELBERT TALBOT
PAT LAVAY
WILFRED LOWELL
```

Next, the names in the second table are subtracted from those in the first table. Here, PROSPECT is subtracted from LONGTIME. The only names remaining are those that are in the LONGTIME table and not in the PROSPECT table:

```
select Name from LONGTIME
  MINUS
select Name from PROSPECT;
```

```
NAME
--------------
DICK JONES
DONALD ROLLO
GEORGE OSCAR
PETER LAWSON
```

This is not the same, of course, as subtracting LONGTIME from PROSPECT. Here, the only names remaining are those listed in PROSPECT but not in LONGTIME:

```
select Name from PROSPECT
  MINUS
select Name from LONGTIME;

NAME
--------------
DORY KENSON
GEORGE PHEPPS
JED HOPKINS
TED BUTCHER
```

You've just learned the basics of **UNION**, **INTERSECT**, and **MINUS**. Now let's go into details. In combining two tables, Oracle does not concern itself with column names on either side of the combination operator—that is, Oracle will require that each **select** statement be valid and have valid columns for its own table(s), but the column names in the first **select** statement do not have to be the same as those in the second. Oracle does have these stipulations:

- The **select** statements must have the same number of columns.

- The corresponding columns in the **select** statements must be the same datatype (they needn't be the same length).

The following query is nonsensical, getting lodging from one table and names from the other, but because both Lodging and Name are the same datatype, the query will run:

```
select Lodging from LONGTIME
  UNION
select Name from PROSPECT;

LODGING
------------------------
ADAH TALBOT
```

```
CRANMER
DORY KENSON
ELBERT TALBOT
GEORGE PHEPPS
JED HOPKINS
MATTS
PAPA KING
PAT LAVAY
ROSE HILL
TED BUTCHER
WEITBROCHT
WILFRED LOWELL
```

Next, three columns are selected. Since the LONGTIME table is similar in structure to the WORKER table, it has Name, Lodging, and Age columns. The PROSPECT table, however, has only Name and Address columns. The following **select** matches Lodging and Address (since they contain similar information) and adds a literal 0 to the PROSPECT table **select** statement to match the numeric Age column in the LONGTIME **select** statement:

```
select Name, Lodging, Age from LONGTIME
 UNION
select Name, Address, 0 from PROSPECT;


NAME            LODGING                   AGE
--------------  ------------------------  -----
ADAH TALBOT     23 ZWING, EDMESTON            0
ADAH TALBOT     PAPA KING                    23
DICK JONES      ROSE HILL                    18
DONALD ROLLO    MATTS                        16
DORY KENSON     GEN. DEL., BAYBAC             0
ELBERT TALBOT   3 MILE ROAD, WALPOLE          0
ELBERT TALBOT   WEITBROCHT                   43
GEORGE OSCAR    ROSE HILL                    41
GEORGE PHEPPS   206 POLE, KINGSLEY            0
JED HOPKINS     GEN. DEL., TURBOW             0
PAT LAVAY       1 EASY ST, JACKSON            0
PAT LAVAY       ROSE HILL                    21
PETER LAWSON    CRANMER                      25
TED BUTCHER     RFD 1, BRIGHTON               0
WILFRED LOWELL                                0
WILFRED LOWELL                               67
```

You'll quickly see that many names appear twice, because the checking for duplicates that **UNION** always does operates over *all* of the columns being selected.

NOTE
*The duplicate checking that **UNION** does ignores **NULL** columns. If this previous query had not included Age, WILFRED LOWELL would only have appeared once. This may not seem entirely logical, since a **NULL** in one table isn't equal to a **NULL** in the other one, but that's how **UNION** works.*

The **INTERSECT** of these same columns produces no records, because no rows in both tables (that include these columns) are identical. If this next query had excluded Age, only WILFRED LOWELL would have shown up. **INTERSECT** also *ignores* **NULL** columns.

```
select Name, Lodging, Age from LONGTIME
  INTERSECT
select Name, Address, 0 from PROSPECT;

no rows selected
```

How about **order by**? If these operators normally sort the results according to the columns that appear, how can that sorting be changed? Oracle uses the column names from the first **select** statement in giving the query results. Consequently, only column names from the first **select** statement can be used in the **order by**:

```
select Name, Lodging, Age from LONGTIME
  UNION
select Name, Address, 0 from PROSPECT
  order by Address;
         *
ERROR at line 4: ORA-00904: invalid column name
```

An attempt to **order by** a column from the second **select** clause results in an error.
You can use combination operators with two or more tables, but when you do, precedence becomes an issue, especially if **INTERSECT** and **MINUS** appear. Use parentheses to force the order you desire.

IN Subqueries

Combination operators can be used in subqueries, but, with one exception, they have equivalent constructions using the operators **IN**, **AND**, and **OR**.

UNION

Here, the WORKER list is checked for those names that are in either the PROSPECT or the LONGTIME table. Of course, the names also must be in the WORKER table.

Unlike the combinations of two tables *not* in a subquery, this **select** is restricted to the names in only one of the three tables, those already in the WORKER table:

```
select Name
  from WORKER
 where Name IN
        (select Name from PROSPECT)
         UNION
        (select Name from LONGTIME);

NAME
--------------
ADAH TALBOT
DICK JONES
DONALD ROLLO
ELBERT TALBOT
GEORGE OSCAR
JED HOPKINS
PAT LAVAY
PETER LAWSON
WILFRED LOWELL
```

The preceding seems to be the logical equivalent to this:

```
select Name
  from WORKER
 where Name IN
        (select Name from PROSPECT)
    OR Name IN
        (select Name from LONGTIME);

NAME
--------------
ADAH TALBOT
DICK JONES
DONALD ROLLO
ELBERT TALBOT
GEORGE OSCAR
JED HOPKINS
PAT LAVAY
PETER LAWSON
WILFRED LOWELL
```

It appears that an **OR** construction can be built that is equivalent to the **UNION**.

A Warning About UNION

Reverse the order of the tables that are **UNION**ed and see what happened in the following listing (the asterisks were added after the fact to highlight the differences).

```
select Name from WORKER
  where Name IN
        (select Name from LONGTIME)
          UNION
        (select Name from PROSPECT);
NAME
-----------------------
ADAH TALBOT
DICK JONES
DONALD ROLLO
DORY KENSON          *
ELBERT TALBOT
GEORGE OSCAR
GEORGE PHEPPS        *
JED HOPKINS
PAT LAVAY
PETER LAWSON
TED BUTCHER          *
WILFRED LOWELL
```

Three names appear in the result that are not in the previous two versions of the query, and they are not even in the WORKER table! Why? Because the **IN** has higher precedence than the **UNION**. This means the test of this:

```
Name IN
(select Name from LONGTIME)
```

is first evaluated, and its result is then **UNION**ed with this:

```
(select Name from PROSPECT)
```

This result is not at all intuitive. If this is the kind of result you want, put plenty of comments near your SQL statement, because no one will ever guess this is what you intended. Otherwise, always enclose a **UNION**ed set of **select**s in parentheses, to force precedence:

```
select Name from WORKER
  where Name IN (
        (select Name from LONGTIME)
          UNION
        (select Name from PROSPECT) );

NAME
-----------------------
ADAH TALBOT
DICK JONES
DONALD ROLLO
ELBERT TALBOT
```

```
GEORGE OSCAR
JED HOPKINS
PAT LAVAY
PETER LAWSON
WILFRED LOWELL
```

INTERSECT

Here, the WORKER table is checked for those names that are in both the PROSPECT table and the LONGTIME table. Reversing the order of the **INTERSECT**ed tables will not affect the result.

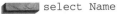

```
select Name
   from WORKER
 where Name IN
       (select Name from PROSPECT)
        INTERSECT
       (select Name from LONGTIME);


NAME
--------------
ADAH TALBOT
ELBERT TALBOT
PAT LAVAY
WILFRED LOWELL
```

The following gives you the same result:

```
select Name
   from WORKER
 where Name IN
       (select Name from PROSPECT)
    AND Name IN
       (select Name from LONGTIME);


NAME
--------------
ADAH TALBOT
ELBERT TALBOT
PAT LAVAY
WILFRED LOWELL
```

MINUS

The PROSPECT table **MINUS** the LONGTIME table produces only one name that is in the WORKER table, as shown in the following listing. Reversing the order of the **MINUS**ed tables *will* change the results of this query, as will be shown shortly.

```
select Name
   from WORKER
  where Name IN
        (select Name from PROSPECT)
          MINUS
        (select Name from LONGTIME);

NAME
--------------
JED HOPKINS
```

Here is the equivalent query without **MINUS**:

```
select Name
   from WORKER
  where Name IN
        (select Name from PROSPECT)
    and Name NOT IN
        (select Name from LONGTIME);

NAME
--------------
JED HOPKINS
```

Reversing the order of the tables produces these results:

```
select Name from WORKER
  where Name IN
        (select Name from LONGTIME)
          MINUS
        (select Name from PROSPECT);

NAME
------------------------
DICK JONES
DONALD ROLLO
GEORGE OSCAR
PETER LAWSON
```

This is a much more intuitive result than the reversal of tables in **UNION**, because here, which table is subtracted from the other has obvious consequences (refer to the earlier section, "UNION, INTERSECT, and MINUS," for details of **MINUS**ed tables), and the precedence of the **IN** will not change the result.

A Warning About MINUS

It is not uncommon to use **MINUS** when one of the tables in the subquery is the same as the outer query table. The danger here is that if that table is the table after the **MINUS**, it is subtracted *from itself.* Without other qualifiers (such as in the **where** clause of the **select** following the **MINUS**), no records will be selected.

```
select Name
   from PROSPECT
 where Name IN
         (select Name from LONGTIME)
           MINUS
         (select Name from PROSPECT);
```

```
no rows selected
```

Restrictions on
UNION, INTERSECT, and MINUS

Queries that use a **UNION**, **INTERSECT**, or **MINUS** in their **where** clause must have the same number and type of columns in their **select** list:

```
select Name from WORKER
  where (Name, Lodging) IN
         (select Name, Lodging from LONGTIME)
           MINUS
         (select Name, Address from PROSPECT);
```

```
ERROR at line 1: ORA-01789:  query block has incorrect number of
result columns
```

But an equivalent **IN** construction does not have this limitation:

```
select Name from WORKER
  where (Name, Lodging) IN
         (select Name, Lodging from LONGTIME)
    AND (Name, Lodging) NOT IN
         (select Name, Address from PROSPECT);
```

```
NAME
-----------------------
ADAH TALBOT
DICK JONES
DONALD ROLLO
ELBERT TALBOT
GEORGE OSCAR
PAT LAVAY
PETER LAWSON
```

To make the **MINUS** version work, all the columns in the **where** clause must be in the **select** clause. They must also, of course, be in the **select** clause of the **MINUS**ed **select** statements:

```
select Name, Lodging from WORKER
  where (Name, Lodging) IN
        (select Name, Lodging from LONGTIME)
         MINUS
        (select Name, Address from PROSPECT);
```

```
NAME                     LODGING
------------------------ -----------------------------------
ADAH TALBOT              PAPA KING
DICK JONES               ROSE HILL
DONALD ROLLO             MATTS
ELBERT TALBOT            WEITBROCHT
GEORGE OSCAR             ROSE HILL
PAT LAVAY                ROSE HILL
PETER LAWSON             CRANMER
```

Some books and other published materials suggest that combination operators cannot be used in subqueries. This is untrue. Here is an example of how to use them:

```
select Name from WORKER
  where (Name, Lodging) IN
        (select Name, Lodging from WORKER
          where (Name, Lodging) IN
                (select Name, Address from PROSPECT)
                 UNION
                (select Name, Lodging from LONGTIME) );
```

```
NAME
------------------------
ADAH TALBOT
DICK JONES
DONALD ROLLO
ELBERT TALBOT
GEORGE OSCAR
PAT LAVAY
PETER LAWSON
```

The use of combination operators in place of **IN**, **AND**, and **OR** is a matter of personal style. Most SQL users regard **IN**, **AND**, and **OR** as being clearer and easier to understand than combination operators.

CHAPTER
13

Some Complex
Possibilities

his chapter continues the study of the more complex Oracle functions and features. Of particular interest here is the creation of simple and group queries that can be turned into views, the use of totals in calculations, and the creation of reports showing tree structure. Like the techniques covered in Chapter 12, these techniques are not essential for most reporting needs, and if they look overly difficult, don't be frightened off. If you are new to Oracle and the use of its query facilities, it is enough to know that these capabilities exist and can be turned to if needed.

Creating a Complex View

Views can build upon each other. In Chapter 11, you saw the concept of creating a view of a grouping of rows from a table. Here, the concept is extended to show how views can be joined to other views and tables to produce yet another view. Although this technique sounds a bit complicated, it actually simplifies the task of querying and reporting. The following is a list of expenses G. B. Talbot incurred during March of 1901. It was a difficult month. These items, spellings (such as MEDISON instead of MEDICINE), and prices are directly from the ledger.

```
column Amount format 999.90
column Item format a23
column Person format a16

select ActionDate, Item, Person, Amount
  from LEDGER
 where ActionDate BETWEEN
          TO_DATE('01-MAR-1901','DD-MON-YYYY') and
          TO_DATE('31-MAR-1901','DD-MON-YYYY')
   and Action IN ('BOUGHT','PAID')
 order by ActionDate;


ACTIONDAT ITEM                    PERSON             AMOUNT
--------- ----------------------- ---------------- ------
05-MAR-01 TELEPHONE CALL          PHONE COMPANY        .20
06-MAR-01 MEDISON FOR INDIGESTION DR. CARLSTROM        .40
06-MAR-01 PANTS                   GENERAL STORE        .75
07-MAR-01 SHOEING                 BLACKSMITH           .35
07-MAR-01 MAIL BOX                POST OFFICE         1.00
08-MAR-01 TOBACCO FOR LICE        MILL                 .25
10-MAR-01 STOVE PIPE THIMBLES     VERNA HARDWARE      1.00
13-MAR-01 THERMOMETER             GENERAL STORE        .15
14-MAR-01 LOT IN CEMETERY NO. 80  METHODIST CHURCH   25.00
14-MAR-01 DIGGING OF GRAVE        JED HOPKINS         3.00
16-MAR-01 GRINDING                MILL                 .16
20-MAR-01 WORK                    DICK JONES          1.00
```

```
22-MAR-01 MILK CANS                 VERNA HARDWARE   5.00
23-MAR-01 CLOTH FOR DRESS LINING    GENERAL STORE     .54
25-MAR-01 BOOTS FOR SHIRLEY         GENERAL STORE    2.50
27-MAR-01 HOMINY                    MILL              .77
30-MAR-01 FIXING SHIRLEYS WATCH     MANNER JEWELERS   .25
```

When reordered by Person, you can see how Talbot's expenditures were concentrated:

```
select ActionDate, Item, Person, Amount
   from LEDGER
 where ActionDate BETWEEN
          TO_DATE('01-MAR-1901','DD-MON-YYYY') and
          TO_DATE('31-MAR-1901','DD-MON-YYYY')
   and Action IN ('BOUGHT','PAID')
 order by Person, ActionDate;


ACTIONDAT ITEM                     PERSON             AMOUNT
--------- ------------------------ ------------------ ------
07-MAR-01 SHOEING                  BLACKSMITH            .35
20-MAR-01 WORK                     DICK JONES           1.00
06-MAR-01 MEDISON FOR INDIGESTION  DR. CARLSTROM         .40
06-MAR-01 PANTS                    GENERAL STORE         .75
13-MAR-01 THERMOMETER              GENERAL STORE         .15
23-MAR-01 CLOTH FOR DRESS LINING   GENERAL STORE         .54
25-MAR-01 BOOTS FOR SHIRLEY        GENERAL STORE        2.50
14-MAR-01 DIGGING OF GRAVE         JED HOPKINS          3.00
30-MAR-01 FIXING SHIRLEYS WATCH    MANNER JEWELERS       .25
14-MAR-01 LOT IN CEMETERY NO. 80   METHODIST CHURCH    25.00
08-MAR-01 TOBACCO FOR LICE         MILL                  .25
16-MAR-01 GRINDING                 MILL                  .16
27-MAR-01 HOMINY                   MILL                  .77
05-MAR-01 TELEPHONE CALL           PHONE COMPANY         .20
07-MAR-01 MAIL BOX                 POST OFFICE          1.00
10-MAR-01 STOVE PIPE THIMBLES      VERNA HARDWARE       1.00
22-MAR-01 MILK CANS                VERNA HARDWARE       5.00
```

A View of a Group

A view is created of this table, grouped by Person (using the **group by** clause), so that you can see how much Talbot spent with each supplier. Note the use of aliases for the computed column.

```
create or replace view ITEMTOTAL as
select Person, SUM(Amount) AS ItemTotal
   from LEDGER
 where ActionDate BETWEEN
          TO_DATE('01-MAR-1901','DD-MON-YYYY') and
```

```
            TO_DATE('31-MAR-1901','DD-MON-YYYY')
     and Action IN ('BOUGHT','PAID')
  group by Person;

View created.
```

Here is what the view contains:

```
column ItemTotal format 99,999.90

select * from ITEMTOTAL;

PERSON            ITEMTOTAL
---------------- ---------
BLACKSMITH             .35
DICK JONES            1.00
DR. CARLSTROM          .40
GENERAL STORE         3.94
JED HOPKINS           3.00
MANNER JEWELERS        .25
METHODIST CHURCH     25.00
MILL                 1.18
PHONE COMPANY          .20
POST OFFICE          1.00
VERNA HARDWARE        6.00
```

A View of the Total

Next, another view is created of exactly the same information, but without a **group by** clause. This creates a total for all of the records.

```
create or replace view TOTAL as
select SUM(Amount) AS TOTAL
  from LEDGER
 where ActionDate BETWEEN
          TO_DATE('01-MAR-1901','DD-MON-YYYY') and
          TO_DATE('31-MAR-1901','DD-MON-YYYY')
    and Action IN ('BOUGHT','PAID');

View created.
```

This view contains just one record:

```
select * from TOTAL;

  TOTAL
-------
  42.32
```

The Combined View

Finally, yet another view is created. This one contains the base table, LEDGER; the view of totals by item, ITEMTOTAL; and the view of the total expense for all items, TOTAL. Note again the use of aliases both for computed columns and for the underlying table and view names. This view is in effect a three-way join of a table to itself, using views that summarize the table in two different ways.

```
create or replace view ByItem as
select L.Person AS Person, L.Item, L.Amount,
       100*L.Amount/I.ItemTotal AS ByPerson,
       100*L.Amount/T.Total AS ByTotal
  from LEDGER L, ITEMTOTAL I, TOTAL T
 where L.PERSON = I.PERSON
   and L.ActionDate BETWEEN
          TO_DATE('01-MAR-1901','DD-MON-YYYY') and
          TO_DATE('31-MAR-1901','DD-MON-YYYY')
   and L.Action IN ('BOUGHT','PAID');

View created.
```

NOTE
As a matter of good coding technique, any queries that refer to multiple tables should use table aliases, and the selected columns should be prefixed by the table aliases. By following this syntax guideline, you will quickly know the base table for any selected column in any query. If you use the object-relational database management system (ORDBMS) features of Oracle, you have to use table aliases to access the attributes of abstract datatypes.

Now, three **compute sum**s are put into place, along with a **break on** to force the summing (addition) to occur. Look at how simple the **select** statement is here:

```
column ByPerson format 9,999.99
column ByTotal format 9,999.99

break on Person skip 1
compute sum of ByPerson on Person
compute sum of ByTotal  on Person
compute sum of Amount   on Person

select Person, Item, Amount, ByPerson, ByTotal
  from ByItem
 order by Person;
```

Yet, look at the tremendous wealth of information it produces! The output shows not only each item and its price on one line, but also its percentage of all the expenses to that person and its percentage of overall expenses:

```
PERSON             ITEM                      AMOUNT BYPERSON BYTOTAL
----------------   ------------------------  ------ -------- -------
BLACKSMITH         SHOEING                      .35   100.00     .83
****************                              ------ -------- -------
sum                                             .35   100.00     .83


DICK JONES         WORK                        1.00   100.00    2.36
****************                              ------ -------- -------
sum                                            1.00   100.00    2.36


DR. CARLSTROM      MEDISON FOR INDIGESTION      .40   100.00     .95
****************                              ------ -------- -------
sum                                             .40   100.00     .95


GENERAL STORE      PANTS                        .75    19.04    1.77
                   BOOTS FOR SHIRLEY           2.50    63.45    5.91
                   CLOTH FOR DRESS LINING       .54    13.71    1.28
                   THERMOMETER                  .15     3.81     .35
****************                              ------ -------- -------
sum                                            3.94   100.00    9.31


JED HOPKINS        DIGGING OF GRAVE            3.00   100.00    7.09
****************                              ------ -------- -------
sum                                            3.00   100.00    7.09


MANNER JEWELERS    FIXING SHIRLEYS WATCH        .25   100.00     .59
****************                              ------ -------- -------
sum                                             .25   100.00     .59


METHODIST CHURCH LOT IN CEMETERY NO. 80      25.00   100.00   59.07
****************                              ------ -------- -------
sum                                           25.00   100.00   59.07


MILL               TOBACCO FOR LICE             .25    21.19     .59
                   HOMINY                       .77    65.25    1.82
                   GRINDING                     .16    13.56     .38
****************                              ------ -------- -------
sum                                            1.18   100.00    2.79
```

```
PHONE COMPANY      TELEPHONE CALL              .20    100.00      .47
* * * * * * * * * * * * * * * *                ------ --------  -------
sum                                            .20    100.00      .47


POST OFFICE        MAIL BOX                   1.00    100.00     2.36
* * * * * * * * * * * * * * * *                ------ --------  -------
sum                                          1.00    100.00     2.36


VERNA HARDWARE     STOVE PIPE THIMBLES        1.00     16.67     2.36
                   MILK CANS                  5.00     83.33    11.81
* * * * * * * * * * * * * * * *                ------ --------  -------
sum                                          6.00    100.00    14.18
```

With this technique of using both summary views of a table joined to itself and views of several tables joined together, you can create views and reports that include weighted averages, effective yield, percentage of total, percentage of subtotal, and many similar calculations. There is no effective limit to how many views can be built on top of each other, although even the most complex calculations seldom require more than three or four levels of views built upon views. The **break on report** command, which is used for grand totals, is discussed in Chapter 14.

Using Subqueries Within the from Clause

When you write a query that joins a table to a view, the view must already exist. If the view would only be used for that one query, though, you may be able to embed within the query the **select** statement that you would normally use to create the view.

In the previous section of this chapter, the view TOTAL was created to compute the sum of LEDGER.Amount for specific ActionDate values. The following listing shows the syntax for the TOTAL view:

```
create or replace view TOTAL as
select SUM(Amount) AS TOTAL
   from LEDGER
  where ActionDate BETWEEN
           TO_DATE('01-MAR-1901','DD-MON-YYYY') and
           TO_DATE('31-MAR-1901','DD-MON-YYYY')
    and Action IN ('BOUGHT','PAID');
```

The TOTAL view can be joined to LEDGER to show the percentage that each Amount value contributed to the sum of all the Amount values. The following query joins LEDGER to TOTAL and applies the same **where** clause conditions to the LEDGER table as were applied to the TOTAL view:

```
select L.Person, L.Amount, 100*L.Amount/T.Total
   from LEDGER L, TOTAL T
  where L.ActionDate BETWEEN
           TO_DATE('01-MAR-1901','DD-MON-YYYY') AND
           TO_DATE('31-MAR-1901','DD-MON-YYYY')
    and L.Action IN ('BOUGHT','PAID');
```

When the preceding query is executed, Oracle will determine the output of the view (the single row summary of the Amount column) and use that value while resolving the rest of the query.

You can place the view's syntax directly into the **from** clause of the query; you don't need to create the TOTAL view. The following listing shows the combined query. In the combined query, the TOTAL view's SQL is entered as a subquery in the query's **from** clause. The Total column from the subquery is used in the column list of the main query. The combined query is functionally identical to the query that used the TOTAL view.

```
select L1.Person, L1.Amount, 100*L1.Amount/Total
   from LEDGER L1,
      (select SUM(Amount) TOTAL
         from LEDGER
        where ActionDate BETWEEN
                 TO_DATE('01-MAR-1901','DD-MON-YYYY') and
                 TO_DATE('31-MAR-1901','DD-MON-YYYY')
          and Action IN ('BOUGHT','PAID') )
  where ActionDate BETWEEN
           TO_DATE('01-MAR-1901','DD-MON-YYYY') and
           TO_DATE('31-MAR-1901','DD-MON-YYYY')
    and Action IN ('BOUGHT','PAID');
```

The benefit of the integrated approach is that you no longer need to create and maintain the TOTAL view. The query that required the view now contains a *subquery* that replaces the view definition.

Subqueries can be complex. If you need to join columns from the subquery with columns from another table, simply give each column a unique alias, and reference the aliases in joins in the query's **where** clause.

Using Temporary Tables

As of Oracle8i, you can create a table that exists solely for your session, or whose data persists for the duration of your transaction. You can use temporary tables to support specialized rollups or specific application processing requirements.

To create a temporary table, use the **create global temporary table** command. When you create a temporary table, you can specify whether it should last for the duration of your session (via the **on commit preserve rows** clause) or whether its rows should be deleted when the transaction completes (via the **on commit delete rows** clause).

Unlike a permanent table, a temporary table does not automatically allocate space when it is created. Space will be dynamically allocated for the table as rows are inserted:

```
create global temporary table YEAR_ROLLUP (
    Year   NUMBER(4),
    Month  VARCHAR2(9),
    Amount NUMBER)
on commit preserve rows;
```

If you query the Duration column of USER_TABLES for this table, it will have a value of SYS$TRANSACTION.

Now that the YEAR_ROLLUP table exists, you can populate it, such as via an **insert as select** command with a complex query. You can then query the YEAR_ROLLUP table as part of a join with other tables. You may find this method simpler to implement than the methods shown in the prior sections.

Using ROLLUP, GROUPING, and CUBE

How can you perform grouping operations, such as totals, within a single SQL statement rather than via SQL*Plus commands? As of Oracle8i, you can use the **ROLLUP** and **CUBE** functions to enhance the grouping actions performed within your queries. The following listing shows a LEDGER query for items bought in March:

```
select Person, Action, SUM(Amount)
   from LEDGER
 where ActionDate between
```

```
        TO_DATE('01-MAR-1901','DD-MON-YYYY') and
        TO_DATE('31-MAR-1901','DD-MON-YYYY')
   and Action in ('BOUGHT')
 group by Person, Action;


PERSON                    ACTION   SUM(AMOUNT)
------------------------- -------- -----------
BLACKSMITH                BOUGHT           .35
DR. CARLSTROM             BOUGHT            .4
GENERAL STORE             BOUGHT          3.94
MANNER JEWELERS           BOUGHT           .25
METHODIST CHURCH          BOUGHT            25
MILL                      BOUGHT          1.18
PHONE COMPANY             BOUGHT            .2
POST OFFICE               BOUGHT             1
VERNA HARDWARE            BOUGHT             6
```

Instead of simply grouping by Person and Action, you can use the **ROLLUP** function to generate subtotals and totals. In the following example, the **group by** clause is modified to include a **ROLLUP** function call. Notice the additional rows generated at the end of the result set.

```
select Person, Action, SUM(Amount)
   from LEDGER
 where ActionDate between
        TO_DATE('01-MAR-1901','DD-MON-YYYY') and
        TO_DATE('31-MAR-1901','DD-MON-YYYY')
   and Action in ('BOUGHT')
 group by ROLLUP(Action, Person);


PERSON                    ACTION   SUM(AMOUNT)
------------------------- -------- -----------
BLACKSMITH                BOUGHT           .35
DR. CARLSTROM             BOUGHT            .4
GENERAL STORE             BOUGHT          3.94
MANNER JEWELERS           BOUGHT           .25
METHODIST CHURCH          BOUGHT            25
MILL                      BOUGHT          1.18
PHONE COMPANY             BOUGHT            .2
POST OFFICE               BOUGHT             1
VERNA HARDWARE            BOUGHT             6
                          BOUGHT         38.32
                                         38.32
```

The two lines at the end of the listing are the rollup: first by Action (the sum of all BOUGHT amounts) and then for all Actions. Rather than using a **break on action**

on report command, the **ROLLUP** function within the **group by** clause generated the subtotals and totals within one query.

Let's refine the appearance of the report. The subtotal and total rows have a blank value listed under the columns by which the rollup is being performed: the subtotal line for the Action 'BOUGHT' has a blank entry for the Person; the total line for all Actions and Persons is blank for both of those columns. You can use the **GROUPING** function to determine whether the row is a total or subtotal (generated by the **ROLLUP**) or corresponds to a **NULL** value in the database. In the **select** clause, the Person column will be selected as follows:

```
select DECODE(GROUPING(Person),1, 'All persons',Person),
```

The **GROUPING** function will return a value of 1 if the column's value is generated by a **ROLLUP** action. This query uses **DECODE** (discussed at length in Chapter 17) to evaluate the result of the **GROUPING** function. If the **GROUPING** output is 1, the value was generated by the **ROLLUP** function, and Oracle will print all persons; otherwise, it will print the value of the Person column. You can apply similar logic to the Action column. The full query is shown in the following listing, along with its output:

```
select DECODE(GROUPING(Person),1,'All persons',Person),
       DECODE(GROUPING(Action),1,'All actions',Action),
       SUM(Amount)
  from LEDGER
 where ActionDate between
       TO_DATE('01-MAR-1901','DD-MON-YYYY') and
       TO_DATE('31-MAR-1901','DD-MON-YYYY')
   and Action in ('BOUGHT')
 group by ROLLUP(Action, Person);
```

PERSON	ACTION	SUM(AMOUNT)
BLACKSMITH	BOUGHT	.35
DR. CARLSTROM	BOUGHT	.4
GENERAL STORE	BOUGHT	3.94
MANNER JEWELERS	BOUGHT	.25
METHODIST CHURCH	BOUGHT	25
MILL	BOUGHT	1.18
PHONE COMPANY	BOUGHT	.2
POST OFFICE	BOUGHT	1
VERNA HARDWARE	BOUGHT	6
All persons	BOUGHT	38.32
All persons	All actions	38.32

You can use the **CUBE** function to generate subtotals for all combinations of the values in the **group by** clause. For two values in the **ROLLUP** clause (as in the last example), two levels of subtotals will be generated. For two values in a **CUBE** clause, four values will be generated. Let's expand the query of LODGING and WORKER to incorporate the WORKERSKILL table, and then determine which skills are to be found among the workers in each lodging. The following query uses the **CUBE** function to generate this information; a **break** command is added for readability:

```
break on Lodging dup skip 1

select DECODE(GROUPING(LODGING.Lodging), 1, 'All Lodgings',
       LODGING.Lodging) AS Lodging,
       DECODE(GROUPING(WORKERSKILL.Skill), 1, 'All Skills', Skill)
         AS Skill,
       COUNT(*) AS Total_Workers
  from WORKER, LODGING, WORKERSKILL
 where WORKER.Lodging = LODGING.Lodging
   and WORKER.Name = WORKERSKILL.Name
 group by CUBE (LODGING.Lodging, WORKERSKILL.Skill);
```

This query's output is shown in the following listing:

```
LODGING              SKILL                       TOTAL_WORKERS
----------------     -------------------------   -------------
MULLERS              SMITHY                                  1
MULLERS              All Skills                              1

PAPA KING            WORK                                    1
PAPA KING            All Skills                              1

ROSE HILL            COMBINE DRIVER                          1
ROSE HILL            SMITHY                                  2
ROSE HILL            WOODCUTTER                              1
ROSE HILL            All Skills                              4

WEITBROCHT           DISCUS                                  1
WEITBROCHT           All Skills                              1

All Lodgings         COMBINE DRIVER                          1
All Lodgings         DISCUS                                  1
All Lodgings         SMITHY                                  3
All Lodgings         WOODCUTTER                              1
All Lodgings         WORK                                    1
All Lodgings         All Skills                              7
```

Since there are only ten rows in WORKERSKILL, there aren't matches for all of the workers. However, this output shows Talbot where to find a combine driver and a woodcutter—and the cube results also show the skills for which he may need to add more workers. If you had used **ROLLUP** in place of **CUBE**, Oracle would have displayed the All Lodgings – All Skills row shown in the preceding listing, but not the five All Lodgings rows that precede it.

Family Trees and connect by

One of Oracle's more interesting but little used or understood facilities is its **connect by** clause. Put simply, it is a method to report in order the branches of a *family tree.* Such trees are encountered often: the genealogy of human families, livestock, horses, corporate management, company divisions, manufacturing, literature, ideas, evolution, scientific research, and theory—even views built upon views.

The **connect by** clause provides a means to report on all of the family members in any of these many trees. It lets you exclude branches or individual members of a family tree, and allows you to travel through the tree either up or down, reporting on the family members encountered during the trip.

The earliest ancestor in the tree is technically called the *root node.* In everyday English, this would be called the trunk. Extending from the trunk are branches, which have other branches, which have still other branches. The forks where one or more branches split away from a larger branch are called *nodes,* and the very end of a branch is called a *leaf,* or a *leaf node.* Figure 13-1 shows a picture of such a tree.

The following is a table of cows and bulls born between January 1900 and October 1908. Each offspring, as born, is entered as a row in the table, along with its sex, parents (the cow and bull), and its birthdate. If you compare the Cows and Offspring in this table with Figure 13-1, you'll find they correspond. EVE has no cow or bull parent, because she was the first generation, and ADAM and BANDIT are bulls brought in for breeding, again with no parents in the table.

```
column Cow format a6
column Bull format a6
column Offspring format a10
column Sex format a3

select * from BREEDING
 order by Birthdate;

OFFSPRING  SEX COW    BULL   BIRTHDATE
---------- --- ------ ------ ---------
EVE        F
ADAM       M
BANDIT     M
BETSY      F   EVE    ADAM   02-JAN-00
POCO       M   EVE    ADAM   15-JUL-00
GRETA      F   EVE    BANDIT 12-MAR-01
```

```
MANDY     F    EVE      POCO     22-AUG-02
CINDY     F    EVE      POCO     09-FEB-03
NOVI      F    BETSY    ADAM     30-MAR-03
GINNY     F    BETSY    BANDIT   04-DEC-03
DUKE      M    MANDY    BANDIT   24-JUL-04
TEDDI     F    BETSY    BANDIT   12-AUG-05
SUZY      F    GINNY    DUKE     03-APR-06
PAULA     F    MANDY    POCO     21-DEC-06
RUTH      F    GINNY    DUKE     25-DEC-06
DELLA     F    SUZY     BANDIT   11-OCT-08
```

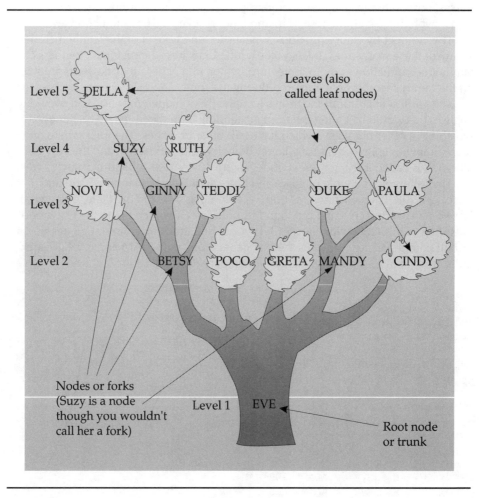

FIGURE 13-1. *Talbot's cows and bulls, starting with Eve*

Next, a query is written to illustrate the family relationships visually. This is done using **LPAD** and a special column, Level, that comes along with **connect by**. Level is a number, from 1 for EVE to 5 for DELLA, that is really the *generation*. If EVE is the first generation of cattle Talbot keeps, then DELLA is the fifth generation. Whenever the **connect by** clause is used, the Level column can be used in the **select** statement to discover the generation of each row. Level is a *pseudo-column,* like SysDate and User. It's not really a part of the table, but it is available under specific circumstances. The next listing shows an example of using Level.

The results of this query are apparent in the following table, but why did the **select** statement produce this? How does it work?

```
select Cow, Bull, LPAD(' ',6*(Level-1))||Offspring AS Offspring,
       Sex, Birthdate
  from BREEDING
 start with Offspring = 'EVE'
 connect by Cow = PRIOR Offspring;
```

```
COW     BULL    OFFSPRING                           SEX BIRTHDATE
------  ------  ----------------------------------  --- ---------
                EVE                                 F
EVE     ADAM        BETSY                           F   02-JAN-00
BETSY   ADAM            NOVI                        F   30-MAR-03
BETSY   BANDIT          GINNY                       F   04-DEC-03
GINNY   DUKE                SUZY                    F   03-APR-06
SUZY    BANDIT                  DELLA               F   11-OCT-08
GINNY   DUKE                RUTH                    F   25-DEC-06
BETSY   BANDIT          TEDDI                       F   12-AUG-05
EVE     ADAM        POCO                            M   15-JUL-00
EVE     BANDIT      GRETA                           F   12-MAR-01
EVE     POCO        MANDY                           F   22-AUG-02
MANDY   BANDIT          DUKE                        M   24-JUL-04
MANDY   POCO            PAULA                       F   21-DEC-06
EVE     POCO        CINDY                           F   09-FEB-03
```

Note that this is really Figure 13-1 turned clockwise onto its side. EVE isn't centered, but she is the root node (trunk) of this tree. Her children are BETSY, POCO, GRETA, MANDY, and CINDY. BETSY's children are NOVI, GINNY, and TEDDI. GINNY's children are SUZY and RUTH. And SUZY's child is DELLA. MANDY also has two children, DUKE and PAULA.

This tree started with EVE as the first "offspring." If the SQL statement had said **start with** MANDY, only MANDY, DUKE, and PAULA would have been selected. **start with** defines the beginning of that portion of the tree that will be displayed, and it includes only branches stretching out from the individual that **start with** specifies. **start with** acts just as its name implies.

The **LPAD** in the **select** statement is probably somewhat confusing. Recall from Chapter 7 the format for **LPAD**:

```
LPAD(string,length [,'set'])
```

That is, take the specified *string* and left-pad it for the specified *length* with the specified *set* of characters. If no set is specified, left-pad the string with blanks. Compare this syntax to the **LPAD** in the **select** statement shown earlier:

```
LPAD(' ',6*(Level-1))
```

In this case, the *string* is a single character, a space (indicated by the literal space enclosed in single quotation marks). The 6*(Level-1) is the *length,* and since the **set** is not specified, spaces will be used. In other words, this tells SQL to take this string of one space and left-pad it to the number of spaces determined by 6*(Level-1), a calculation made by first subtracting 1 from the Level and then multiplying this result by 6. For EVE the Level is 1, so 6*(1-1), or 0 spaces, is used. For BETSY, the Level (her generation) is 2, so an **LPAD** of 6 is used. Thus, for each generation after the first, six additional spaces will be concatenated to the left of the Offspring column. The effect is obvious in the result just shown. The name of each Offspring is indented by left-padding with the number of spaces corresponding to its Level or generation.

Why is this done, instead of simply applying the **LPAD** directly to Offspring? For two reasons. First, a direct **LPAD** on Offspring would cause the names of the Offspring to be right-justified. The names at each level would end up having their last letters lined up vertically. Second, if Level-1 is equal to 0, as it is for EVE, the resulting **LPAD** of EVE will be 0 characters wide. EVE will vanish:

```
select Cow, Bull, LPAD(Offspring,6*(Level-1),' ') AS Offspring,
       Sex, Birthdate   from BREEDING
 start with Offspring = 'EVE'
connect by Cow = PRIOR Offspring;
```

COW	BULL	OFFSPRING	SEX	BIRTHDATE
			F	
EVE	ADAM	BETSY	F	02-JAN-00
BETSY	ADAM	NOVI	F	30-MAR-03
BETSY	BANDIT	GINNY	F	04-DEC-03
GINNY	DUKE	SUZY	F	03-APR-06
SUZY	BANDIT	DELLA	F	11-OCT-08
GINNY	DUKE	RUTH	F	25-DEC-06
BETSY	BANDIT	TEDDI	F	12-AUG-05
EVE	ADAM	POCO	M	15-JUL-00
EVE	BANDIT	GRETA	F	12-MAR-01

```
EVE     POCO      MANDY                     F    22-AUG-02
MANDY   BANDIT            DUKE              M    24-JUL-04
MANDY   POCO                 PAULA         F    21-DEC-06
EVE     POCO      CINDY                     F    09-FEB-03
```

Thus, to get the proper spacing for each level, to ensure that EVE appears, and to make the names line up vertically on the left, the **LPAD** should be used with the concatenated function, and not directly on the Offspring column.

Now, how does **connect by** work? Look again at Figure 13-1. Starting with NOVI and traveling downward, which cows are the offspring prior to NOVI? The first is BETSY, and the offspring just prior to BETSY is EVE. Even though it is not instantly readable, this clause:

```
connect by Cow = PRIOR Offspring
```

tells SQL to find the next row in which the value in the Cow column is equal to the value in the Offspring column in the prior row. Look at the table and you'll see that this is true.

Excluding Individuals and Branches

There are two methods of excluding cows from a report. One uses the normal **where** clause technique, and the other uses the **connect by** clause itself. The difference is that the exclusion using the **connect by** clause will exclude not just the cow mentioned, but all of its children as well. If you use **connect by** to exclude BETSY, then NOVI, GINNY, TEDDI, SUZY, RUTH, and DELLA all vanish. The **connect by** really tracks the tree structure. If BETSY had never been born, none of her offspring would have been either. In this example, the **and** clause modifies the **connect by** clause:

```
select Cow, Bull, LPAD(' ',6*(Level-1))||Offspring AS Offspring,
       Sex, Birthdate
  from BREEDING
 start with Offspring = 'EVE'
connect by Cow = PRIOR Offspring
   and Offspring != 'BETSY';
```

```
COW     BULL    OFFSPRING                        SEX BIRTHDATE
------  ------  -------------------------------  --- ---------
                EVE                              F
EVE     ADAM        POCO                         M    15-JUL-00
EVE     BANDIT      GRETA                        F    12-MAR-01
EVE     POCO        MANDY                        F    22-AUG-02
MANDY   BANDIT          DUKE                     M    24-JUL-04
MANDY   POCO                PAULA                F    21-DEC-06
EVE     POCO        CINDY                        F    09-FEB-03
```

The **where** clause removes only the cow or cows it mentions. If BETSY dies, she is removed from the chart, but her offspring are not. In fact, notice that BETSY is still there under the Cow column as mother of her children, NOVI, GINNY, and TEDDI:

```
select Cow, Bull, LPAD(' ',6*(Level-1))||Offspring AS Offspring,
       Sex, Birthdate
  from BREEDING
 where Offspring != 'BETSY'
 start with Offspring = 'EVE'
connect by Cow = PRIOR Offspring;
```

COW	BULL	OFFSPRING			SEX	BIRTHDATE
		EVE			F	
BETSY	ADAM	NOVI			F	30-MAR-03
BETSY	BANDIT	GINNY			F	04-DEC-03
GINNY	DUKE	SUZY			F	03-APR-06
SUZY	BANDIT		DELLA		F	11-OCT-08
GINNY	DUKE	RUTH			F	25-DEC-06
BETSY	BANDIT	TEDDI			F	12-AUG-05
EVE	ADAM	POCO			M	15-JUL-00
EVE	BANDIT	GRETA			F	12-MAR-01
EVE	POCO	MANDY			F	22-AUG-02
MANDY	BANDIT	DUKE			M	24-JUL-04
MANDY	POCO	PAULA			F	21-DEC-06
EVE	POCO	CINDY			F	09-FEB-03

The order in which the family tree is displayed when using **connect by** is basically level by level, left to right, as shown in Figure 13-1, starting with the lowest level, Level 1. For example, you may wish to alter this order to collect the cows and their offspring by birthdate:

```
select Cow, Bull, LPAD(' ',6*(Level-1))||Offspring AS Offspring,
       Sex, Birthdate   from BREEDING
 start with Offspring = 'EVE'
connect by Cow = PRIOR Offspring
 order by Cow, Birthdate;
```

COW	BULL	OFFSPRING		SEX	BIRTHDATE
		EVE		F	
BETSY	ADAM	NOVI		F	30-MAR-03
BETSY	BANDIT	GINNY		F	04-DEC-03
BETSY	BANDIT	TEDDI		F	12-AUG-05
EVE	ADAM	BETSY		F	02-JAN-00

```
EVE       ADAM      POCO                        M   15-JUL-00
EVE       BANDIT    GRETA                       F   12-MAR-01
EVE       POCO      MANDY                       F   22-AUG-02
EVE       POCO      CINDY                       F   09-FEB-03
GINNY     DUKE                  SUZY            F   03-APR-06
GINNY     DUKE                  RUTH            F   25-DEC-06
MANDY     BANDIT         DUKE                   M   24-JUL-04
MANDY     POCO           PAULA                  F   21-DEC-06
SUZY      BANDIT                       DELLA    F   11-OCT-08
```

The generations are still obvious in the display, but Offspring are more closely grouped with their mother. Another way to look at the same family tree is by Birthdate, as follows:

```
select Cow, Bull, LPAD(' ',6*(Level-1))||Offspring AS Offspring,
       Sex, Birthdate
  from BREEDING
 start with Offspring = 'EVE'
connect by Cow = PRIOR Offspring
 order by Birthdate;


COW       BULL    OFFSPRING                         SEX BIRTHDATE
------    ------  --------------------------------  --- ---------
                  EVE                               F
EVE       ADAM      BETSY                           F   02-JAN-00
EVE       ADAM      POCO                            M   15-JUL-00
EVE       BANDIT    GRETA                           F   12-MAR-01
EVE       POCO      MANDY                           F   22-AUG-02
EVE       POCO      CINDY                           F   09-FEB-03
BETSY     ADAM          NOVI                        F   30-MAR-03
BETSY     BANDIT        GINNY                       F   04-DEC-03
MANDY     BANDIT        DUKE                        M   24-JUL-04
BETSY     BANDIT        TEDDI                       F   12-AUG-05
GINNY     DUKE              SUZY                    F   03-APR-06
MANDY     POCO          PAULA                       F   21-DEC-06
GINNY     DUKE              RUTH                    F   25-DEC-06
SUZY      BANDIT                  DELLA             F   11-OCT-08
```

Now, the order of the rows no longer shows generations, as in a tree, but the indenting still preserves this information. You can't tell what offspring belong to which parents without looking at the Cow and Bull columns, though.

Traveling Toward the Roots

Thus far, the direction of travel in reporting on the family tree has been from parents toward children. Is it possible to start with a child, and move backward to parent, grandparent, great-grandparent, and so on? To do so, the word **prior** is simply moved to the other side of the equal sign. The following traces DELLA's ancestry:

```
select Cow, Bull, LPAD(' ',6*(Level-1))||Offspring AS Offspring,
       Sex, Birthdate
  from BREEDING
 start with Offspring = 'DELLA'
connect by Offspring = PRIOR Cow;


COW     BULL    OFFSPRING                       SEX BIRTHDATE
------  ------  ------------------------------  --- ---------
SUZY    BANDIT  DELLA                           F   11-OCT-08
GINNY   DUKE          SUZY                      F   03-APR-06
BETSY   BANDIT              GINNY               F   04-DEC-03
EVE     ADAM                      BETSY         F   02-JAN-00
                                        EVE     F
```

This shows DELLA's own roots, but is a bit confusing if compared to the previous displays. It looks like DELLA is the ancestor, and EVE the great-great-granddaughter. Adding an **order by** for Birthdate helps, but EVE is still further to the right:

```
select Cow, Bull, LPAD(' ',6*(Level-1))||Offspring AS Offspring,
       Sex, Birthdate
  from BREEDING
 start with Offspring = 'DELLA'
connect by Offspring = PRIOR Cow
 order by Birthdate;


COW     BULL    OFFSPRING                       SEX BIRTHDATE

------  ------  ------------------------------  --- ---------
                                        EVE     F
EVE     ADAM                      BETSY         F   02-JAN-00
BETSY   BANDIT              GINNY               F   04-DEC-03
GINNY   DUKE          SUZY                      F   03-APR-06
SUZY    BANDIT  DELLA                           F   11-OCT-08
```

The solution is simply to change the calculation in the **LPAD**:

```
select Cow, Bull, LPAD(' ',6*(5-Level))||Offspring Offspring,
       Sex, Birthdate
  from BREEDING
 start with Offspring = 'DELLA'
connect by Offspring = PRIOR Cow
 order by Birthdate;
```

```
COW     BULL    OFFSPRING                       SEX BIRTHDATE
------  ------  ------------------------------  --- ---------
                EVE                             F
EVE     ADAM          BETSY                     F   02-JAN-00
BETSY   BANDIT              GINNY               F   04-DEC-03
GINNY   DUKE                      SUZY          F   03-APR-06
SUZY    BANDIT                          DELLA   F   11-OCT-08
```

Finally, look how different this report is when the **connect by** tracks the parentage of the Bull. Here are Adam's offspring:

```
select Cow, Bull, LPAD(' ',6*(Level-1))||Offspring AS Offspring,
       Sex, Birthdate
  from BREEDING
 start with Offspring = 'ADAM'
connect by PRIOR Offspring = Bull;
```

```
COW     BULL    OFFSPRING                       SEX BIRTHDATE
------  ------  ------------------------------  --- ---------
                ADAM                            M
EVE     ADAM          BETSY                     F   02-JAN-00
EVE     ADAM          POCO                      M   15-JUL-00
EVE     POCO                MANDY               F   22-AUG-02
EVE     POCO                CINDY               F   09-FEB-03
MANDY   POCO                      PAULA         F   21-DEC-06
BETSY   ADAM          NOVI                      F   30-MAR-03
```

ADAM and BANDIT were the original bulls at the initiation of the herd. To create a single tree that reports both ADAM's and BANDIT's offspring, you would have to invent a "father" for the two of them, which would be the root of the tree. One of the advantages that these alternative trees have over the type of tree shown earlier is that many inheritance groups, from families to projects to divisions within companies, can be accurately portrayed in more than one way:

```
select Cow, Bull, LPAD(' ',6*(Level-1))||Offspring AS Offspring,
       Sex, Birthdate
  from BREEDING
 start with Offspring = 'BANDIT'
connect by PRIOR Offspring = Bull;
```

```
COW     BULL    OFFSPRING                       SEX BIRTHDATE
------  ------  ------------------------------  --- ---------
                BANDIT                          M
EVE     BANDIT        GRETA                     F   12-MAR-01
BETSY   BANDIT        GINNY                     F   04-DEC-03
MANDY   BANDIT        DUKE                      M   24-JUL-04
GINNY   DUKE                SUZY                F   03-APR-06
```

```
GINNY   DUKE                RUTH            F    25-DEC-06
BETSY   BANDIT      TEDDI                   F    12-AUG-05
SUZY    BANDIT      DELLA                   F    11-OCT-08
```

The Basic Rules

Using **connect by** and **start with** to create tree-like reports is not difficult, but certain basic rules must be followed:

- The order of the clauses when using **connect by** is as follows:

    select
    from
    where
    start with
    connect by
    order by

- **prior** forces reporting to be from the root out toward the leaves (if the **prior** column is the parent) or from a leaf toward the root (if the **prior** column is the child)

- A **where** clause eliminates individuals from the tree, but not their descendants (or ancestors, if **prior** is on the right side of the equal sign)

- A qualification in the **connect by** (particularly a not equal) eliminates both an individual and all of its descendants (or ancestors, depending on how you trace the tree)

- **connect by** cannot be used with a table join in the **where** clause

This particular set of commands is one that few people are likely to remember correctly. However, with a basic understanding of the tree and inheritance, constructing a proper **select** statement to report on a tree should just be a matter of referring to this chapter for correct syntax.

CHAPTER
14

Building a Report
in SQLPLUS

hapter 6 showed basic formatting of reports, and Chapters 3 and 11 gave methods for using groups and views. This chapter looks at more advanced formatting methods as well as more complex computations of weighted averages. A number of interrelationships among various SQLPLUS commands are not documented in any of the manuals or books on Oracle. This chapter will review these interrelationships as well.

Advanced Formatting

Chapter 1 showed an example of a stock table from the newspaper. Here, you will actually manipulate that table to draw nonobvious information from it. For the sake of brevity, the stocks examined will be limited to a small number in three industries: electronics, space, and medical. These are the column commands in effect:

```
column Net format 99.90
column Industry format a11
column Company format a18
column CloseToday heading 'Close|Today' format 999.90
column CloseYesterday heading 'Close|Yest.' format 999.90
column Volume format 999,999,999
```

The first **select** simply retrieves the stocks in the three industries, calculates the difference in closing prices between today and yesterday, and sorts the stocks in order by Industry and Company, as shown in Figure 14-1.

This is a good beginning, but to make it more meaningful, some additional features must be added. A new column is calculated to show the percentage of change between one day's trading and the next day's trading:

```
(CloseToday/CloseYesterday)*100 - 100 AS Percent,
```

The calculation is given the alias Percent, and column formatting is put in place for it. Additionally, both Company and Industry columns are cut back considerably to make room for additional columns, which will be added shortly. Of course, on a wide report, such as one with 132 columns, this may not be necessary. It is done here for space considerations.

```
column Percent heading 'Percent|Change' format 9999.90
column Company format a8 trunc
column Industry heading 'Ind' format a5 trunc
```

```
select Industry, Company,
       CloseYesterday, CloseToday,
       (CloseToday - CloseYesterday) AS Net,
       Volume    from STOCK
 where Industry in ('ELECTRONICS', 'SPACE', 'MEDICAL')
 order by Industry, Company
/
```

```
                            Close   Close
INDUSTRY     COMPANY        Yest.   Today    NET      VOLUME
-----------  ------------------  -------  -------  ------  ------------
ELECTRONICS  IDK             95.00   95.25    .25   9,443,523
ELECTRONICS  MEMORY GRAPHICS 15.50   14.25  -1.25   4,557,992
ELECTRONICS  MICRO TOKEN     77.00   76.50   -.50  25,205,667
MEDICAL      AT SPACE        46.75   48.00   1.25  11,398,323
MEDICAL      AUGUST ENTERPRISES 15.00 15.00   .00  12,221,711
MEDICAL      HAYWARD ANTISEPTIC 104.25 106.00 1.75  3,358,561
MEDICAL      KENTGEN BIOPHYSICS 18.25 19.50  1.25   6,636,863
SPACE        BRANDON ELLIPSIS 32.75  33.50    .75  25,789,769
SPACE        GENERAL ENTROPY  64.25  66.00   1.75   7,598,562
SPACE        GENEVA ROCKETRY  22.75  27.25   4.25  22,533,944
SPACE        NORTHERN BOREAL  26.75  28.00   1.25   1,348,323
SPACE        OCKHAM SYSTEMS   21.50  22.00    .50   7,052,990
SPACE        WONDER LABS       5.00   5.00    .00   2,553,712
```

FIGURE 14-1. *Closing stock prices and volumes*

break on

Next, a **break on** command is set up to put a blank line between the end of an Industry group and the beginning of the next Industry; the sum of the daily Volume, by Industry, is then computed. Note the coordination between **break on** and **compute sum** in Figure 14-2.

The **break on** and **compute sum** are now expanded, as shown in Figure 14-3. The order of the columns in the **break on** is critical, as will be explained shortly. The **compute sum** has been instructed to calculate the Volume on breaks of both the Industry and Report columns.

```
break on Industry skip 1

compute sum of Volume on Industry

select Industry,
       Company,
       CloseYesterday, CloseToday,
       (CloseToday - CloseYesterday) AS Net,
       (CloseToday/CloseYesterday)*100 - 100 AS Percent,
       Volume
  from STOCK
 where Industry in ('ELECTRONICS', 'SPACE', 'MEDICAL')
 order by Industry, Company
/
```

Ind	COMPANY	Close Yest.	Close Today	NET	Percent Change	VOLUME
ELECT	IDK	95.00	95.25	.25	.26	9,443,523
	MEMORY G	15.50	14.25	-1.25	-8.06	4,557,992
	MICRO TO	77.00	76.50	-.50	-.65	25,205,667
*****						------------
sum						39,207,182
MEDIC	AT SPACE	46.75	48.00	1.25	2.67	11,398,323
	AUGUST E	15.00	15.00	.00	.00	12,221,711
	HAYWARD	104.25	106.00	1.75	1.68	3,358,561
	KENTGEN	18.25	19.50	1.25	6.85	6,636,863
*****						------------
sum						33,615,458
SPACE	BRANDON	32.75	33.50	.75	2.29	25,789,769
	GENERAL	64.25	66.00	1.75	2.72	7,598,562
	GENEVA R	22.75	27.25	4.50	19.78	22,533,944
	NORTHERN	26.75	28.00	1.25	4.67	1,348,323
	OCKHAM S	21.50	22.00	.50	2.33	7,052,990
	WONDER L	5.00	5.00	.00	.00	2,553,712
*****						------------
sum						66,877,300

FIGURE 14-2.   *Stock report with a **break on** Industry and **compute sum** of Volume*

The Volume is shown for each industry, as before, but now a total volume for all industries has been added. The **compute** command has been expanded to allow you to **compute** the sum on **Report**. This must be coordinated with the **break on:**

```
break on Report on Industry skip 1
compute sum of Volume on Industry Report
```

```
break on Report on Industry skip 1

compute sum of Volume on Industry Report

select Industry,
       Company,
       CloseYesterday,
       CloseToday,
       (CloseToday - CloseYesterday) AS Net,
       (CloseToday/CloseYesterday)*100 - 100 AS Percent,
       Volume
  from STOCK
 where Industry in ('ELECTRONICS', 'SPACE', 'MEDICAL')
 order by Industry, Company
/
```

```
Current Portfolio                               March 1st, 2000
                          Industry Listings
                   Close   Close         Percent
Ind   COMPANY      Yest.   Today   NET   Change        VOLUME
----- --------     -----   -----   ----- -------   ------------
ELECT IDK          95.00   95.25    .25     .26       9,443,523
      MEMORY G     15.50   14.25  -1.25   -8.06       4,557,992
      MICRO TO     77.00   76.50   -.50    -.65      25,205,667
*****                                              ------------
sum                                                  39,207,182


MEDIC AT SPACE     46.75   48.00   1.25    2.67      11,398,323
      AUGUST E     15.00   15.00    .00     .00      12,221,711
      HAYWARD     104.25  106.00   1.75    1.68       3,358,561
      KENTGEN      18.25   19.50   1.25    6.85       6,636,863
*****                                              ------------
sum                                                  33,615,458


SPACE BRANDON      32.75   33.50    .75    2.29      25,789,769
      GENERAL      64.25   66.00   1.75    2.72       7,598,562
      GENEVA R     22.75   27.25   4.50   19.78      22,533,944
      NORTHERN     26.75   28.00   1.25    4.67       1,348,323
      OCKHAM S     21.50   22.00    .50    2.33       7,052,990
      WONDER L      5.00    5.00    .00     .00       2,553,712
*****                                              ------------
sum                                                  66,877,300


                                                   ------------
                                                   139,699,940
portfoli.sql
```

FIGURE 14-3. *Stock report with **break on** and **compute sum** on Report for grand totals*

This will produce a sum of Volume for the entire report. This is the **break on** and **compute** that appear in Figure 14-3. The placement of **on Report** in the **break on** command is unimportant: **on Report** will always be the final break.

Next, the report is given a top title and a bottom title, using the extensive formatting capabilities of **ttitle** and **btitle**. See the sidebar "ttitle and btitle Formatting Commands" for an explanation of this.

```
ttitle left 'Current Portfolio' -
       right 'March 1st, 2000'        skip 1 -
       center 'Industry Listings   '  skip 2;

btitle left 'portfoli.sql';
```

Order of Columns in break on

You can get into trouble if the order of the columns in **break on** is incorrect. Suppose that you wish to report on revenues by company, division, department, and project (where a division has departments, and departments have projects). If you input this:

```
break on Project on Department on Division on Company
```

then the totals for each of these entities would be calculated every time the project changed, and they wouldn't be accumulated totals, only those for the project. This would be worthless. Instead, the **break on** must be in order from the largest grouping to the smallest, like this:

```
break on Company on Division on Department on Project
```

ttitle and btitle Formatting Commands
The results of these **ttitle** and **btitle** commands can be seen later in this chapter in Figure 14-5:

```
ttitle left 'Current Portfolio' -
       right xINDUSTRY                skip 1 -
       center 'Industry Listings   '  skip 4;
```

left, **right**, and **center** define where the string that follows is to be placed on the page. A dash at the end of a line means another line of title commands follows. **skip** tells how many blank lines to print after printing this line. Text in single quotation marks is printed as is. Words not inside of single quotation marks are usually variables. If they've been defined by **accept**, **NEW_VALUE**, or **define**, their values will print in the title. If they have not been defined, the name of the variable will print instead.

```
btitle left 'portfoli.sql on ' xTODAY -
       right 'Page ' format 999 sql.pno;
```

sql.pno is a variable that contains the current page number. Formatting commands can be placed anywhere in a title, and they will control formatting for any variables from there forward in the **ttitle** or **btitle** unless another formatting command is encountered.

For additional options for these commands, look in the Alphabetical Reference at the end of this book under **ttitle**.

break on Row

SQLPLUS also allows **compute**s and **break**s to be made **on Row**. Like **on Report**, the **break on** and **compute** must be coordinated.

Adding Views

In order for the report to be useful, computations of each stock in relation to its industry segment and to the whole are important. Two views are therefore created, shown next. The first summarizes stock Volume, grouped by Industry. The second summarizes total stock volume.

```
create or replace view INDUSTRY as
select Industry, SUM(Volume) AS Volume
  from STOCK
 where Industry in ('ELECTRONICS', 'SPACE', 'MEDICAL')
 group by Industry
/

create or replace view MARKET as
select SUM(Volume) AS Volume
```

```
  from STOCK
 where Industry in ('ELECTRONICS', 'SPACE', 'MEDICAL')
/
```

This practice of creating views in a SQLPLUS report is intended only for temporary views that have no particular use outside of the report. More widely used views that are shared by others and used as if they were regular tables in the database would be neither dropped nor created in a SQLPLUS start file that was used just for a report. They would simply be a part of the **from** clause in the **select** statement.

Columns Used with ttitle and btitle

Some additional column definitions are now added, along with a new column, PartOfInd (explained later in the chapter). See Circle A in Figure 14-4.

Two columns that will appear in **ttitle** and **btitle** are put in with the **NEW_VALUE** command. Look at Circle B in Figure 14-4, and its effect in Circle 1 in Figure 14-5. The column Today was used to produce today's date in the **btitle**. How did this work? First of all, Today is an alias for a formatted SysDate in the **select** statement:

```
TO_CHAR(SysDate,'fmMonth ddth, yyyy') AS Today
```

NEW_VALUE placed the contents of the Today column (November 1st, 1999 in this example) into a variable named xToday, which is then used in **btitle**:

```
btitle left 'portfoli.sql on ' xToday -
       right 'Page ' format 999 sql.pno;
```

The variable could have had any name. xToday was chosen to make it easy to spot in the listing, but it could even have the same name as the column Today, or something else, such as DateVar or XYZ. **portfoli.sql** is simply the name of the start file used to produce this report. It's a useful practice to print somewhere on the report the name of the start file used to create the report, so that if it needs to be rerun, it can be found quickly.

The last part of **format 999 sql.pno**, **sql.pno**, is a variable that always contains the current page number. You can use it anywhere in either **ttitle** or **btitle**. By placing it in the **btitle** after the word "right," it shows up on the bottom-right corner of each page.

The **format 999** that precedes it designates the format for the page number. Any time a formatting command like this appears in **ttitle** or **btitle**, it defines the format of any number or characters in the variables that follow it, all the way to the end of the **ttitle** or **btitle** command, unless another format command is encountered.

```
column User noprint

column PartOfInd heading 'Part|of Ind' format 999.90    ◄──────(A)

column Today    NEW_VALUE xTODAY noprint format a1 trunc
column Industry NEW_VALUE xINDUSTRY                      ◄──────(B)

ttitle left 'Current Portfolio' -
       right xINDUSTRY                    skip 1 -
       center 'Industry Listings  '   skip 4
btitle left 'portfoli.sql on ' xTODAY -
       right 'Page ' format 999 sql.pno

clear breaks    ◄────(C)
clear computes  ◄

break on Report page on Industry page   ◄──────(D)

compute sum of Volume on Report Industry
compute sum of PartOfInd on Industry    ◄──────(E)
compute avg of Net Percent on Industry
compute avg of Net Percent PartOfInd on Report

select S.Industry,
       Company,
       CloseYesterday, CloseToday,
       (CloseToday - CloseYesterday) AS Net,
       (CloseToday - CloseYesterday)*(S. Volume/I.Volume) AS PartOfInd,
       (CloseToday/CloseYesterday)*100 - 100 AS Percent,
       S.Volume,
       TO_CHAR(SysDate,'fmMonth ddth, yyyy') AS Today
  from STOCK S, INDUSTRY I
 where S.Industry = I.Industry
   AND I.Industry in ('ELECTRONICS', 'SPACE', 'MEDICAL')
 order by I.Industry, Company
/
```

FIGURE 14-4. *SQLPLUS commands for report by industry*

A Warning About Variables

There are two other items of importance in the **column** command:

```
column Today NEW_VALUE xToday noprint format a1 trunc
```

```
Current Portfolio                        ②――――▶ ELECTRONICS
                        Industry Listings

            Close    Close            Part Percent
  Ind  COMPANY  Yest.    Today    NET  of Ind  Change        VOLUME
  ---- --------- ------- ------- ------ ------- ------- ------------
  ELECT IDK       95.00    95.25    .25     .06     .26    9,443,523
        MEMORY G  15.50    14.25  -1.25    -.15   -8.06    4,557,992
        MICRO TO  77.00    76.50   -.50    -.32    -.65   25,205,667
  *****                          ------ ------- ------- ------------
  avg                              -.50           -2.82
  sum                                     -.41          39,207,182

  portfoli.sql on March 1st, 2000    ◀――――①            Page      1
```

```
Current Portfolio                        ③――――▶ MEDICAL
                        Industry Listings

            Close    Close            Part Percent
  Ind  COMPANY  Yest.    Today    NET  of Ind  Change        VOLUME
  ----- -------- ------- ------- ------ ------- ------- ------------
  MEDIC AT SPACE  46.75    48.00   1.25     .42    2.67   11,398,323
        AUGUST E  15.00    15.00    .00     .00     .00   12,221,711
        HAYWARD  104.25   106.00   1.75     .17    1.68    3,358,561
        KENTGEN   18.25    19.50   1.25     .25    6.85    6,636,863
  *****                          ------ ------- ------- ------------
  avg                              1.06            2.80
  sum                                      .85          33,615,458

  portfoli.sql on March 1st, 2000                      Page      2
```

FIGURE 14-5. *Report by industry, one industry per page*

noprint tells SQLPLUS not to display this column when it prints the results of the SQL statement. Without it, the date would appear on every row of the report. **format a1 trunc** is a bit more esoteric. Dates that have been reformatted by **TO_CHAR** get a default width of about 100 characters (this was discussed in Chapter 9). Even though the **noprint** option is in effect, SQLPLUS gets confused and counts the width of the Today column when deciding whether **linesize** has been exceeded. The effect is to completely foul up the formatting of the rows as they are displayed or printed. By changing the format to **a1 trunc**, this effect is minimized.

```
Current Portfolio                                    4          SPACE

                        Industry Listings

              Close   Close            Part Percent
   Ind   COMPANY  Yest.   Today    NET  of Ind  Change       VOLUME
   ----- -------- ------- ------- ------ ------- ------- ------------

   SPACE BRANDON    32.75   33.50    .75     .29    2.29   25,789,769
         GENERAL    64.25   66.00   1.75     .20    2.72    7,598,562
         GENEVA R   22.75   27.25   4.50    1.52   19.78   22,533,944
         NORTHERN   26.75   28.00   1.25     .03    4.67    1,348,323
         OCKHAM S   21.50   22.00    .50     .05    2.33    7,052,990
         WONDER L    5.00    5.00    .00     .00     .00    2,553,712
   *****                          ------ ------- ------- ------------
   avg              5         1.46            5.30
   sum                                2.08           66,877,300

   portfoli.sql on March 1st, 2000                     Page      3
```

```
Current Portfolio                                             SPACE

                        Industry Listings

              Close   Close            Part Percent
   Ind   COMPANY  Yest.   Today    NET  of Ind  Change       VOLUME
   ----- -------- ------- ------- ------ ------- ------- ------------
                                 ------ ------- ------- ------------
                           6       .88     .19    2.66
                                                  139,699,940

   portfoli.sql on March 1st, 2000                     Page      4
```

FIGURE 14-5.   *Report by industry, one industry per page* (continued)

The other column with **NEW_VALUE** is Industry. This column already has some column definitions in effect:

```
column Industry heading 'Ind' format a5 trunc
```

and now a new one is added as shown in the following listing (remember that different instructions for a column may be given on several lines).

```
column Industry NEW_VALUE xIndustry
```

Like Today, this **column** command inserts the contents of the column from
the **select** statement into a variable called xIndustry. The value in this variable is
coordinated with the **break on**. It gets the value of Industry when the *first* row
is read, and keeps it until a new value is encountered and the **break on** forces
a new page, as shown at Circles 2, 3, and 4 in Figure 14-5.

Here's what SQLPLUS does:

1. Delays printing anything on a page until the **break on** detects a change in
   the value of Industry or enough rows are retrieved to fill the page.

2. Prints the **ttitle** with the value xIndustry had before the value changed
   (or the page got full).

3. Moves the value of xIndustry into an OLD_VALUE variable and saves it.

4. Prints the rows on the page.

5. Loads the new value into xIndustry.

6. Prints the **btitle**.

7. Begins collecting rows for the next page, and goes back to the first step.

What this means is that if xIndustry had been placed in the **btitle** instead of the
ttitle, it would contain the Industry for the following page, instead of the one being
printed. MEDICAL (Circle 3) would be at the bottom of page 1, SPACE (Circle 4)
would be at the bottom of page 2, and so on. To use the **btitle** properly for column
values retrieved in the query, you would use this:

```
column Industry OLD_VALUE xIndustry;
```

More on break on and compute

Circle C in Figure 14-4 immediately precedes the **break on** and **compute**
commands. Once a **compute** command is in place, it continues to be active until
you either clear it or leave SQLPLUS. This means you can have **compute** commands
from previous reports that will execute on a current report, producing all sorts of
unwanted effects.

The **break on** command also persists, although any new **break on** command will
completely replace it. It is good practice to **clear breaks** and **clear computes** just
before setting up new ones.

Here are the options available for **break on**:

- **break on** *column*
- **break on row**
- **break on page**
- **break on report**

column can be a column name, an alias, or an expression such as **SUBSTR**(Industry,1,4). Each of these options can be followed by one of these actions:

- **skip** *n*
- **skip page**

or by nothing. **break on** *column* produces the action any time the value in the selected column changes. **break on row** forces a break with every row. **break on page** forces a break every time a page is filled (in the current example, xIndustry will always contain the value in the Industry column for the first row of the page with this option). **break on report** takes the specified action every time a report ends.

The **skip** actions are to skip one or more lines (that is, print them blank) or to go to the top of a new page. Recall from Chapter 3 that **break on** is used only once, with all of the columns and actions you wish. See Circle D in Figure 14-4.

The command **compute**, on the other hand, can be reused for each type of computation and for one or more columns at once. Circle E shows a variety of ways in which it can be used. Note how columns appear on either side of the **on** in the **compute** commands. No commas are used anywhere in either **break on** or **compute** commands.

Here are possible computations:

compute avg	**compute num**
compute count	**compute sum**
compute max	**compute std**
compute min	**compute var**

These have the same meanings for a column in a SQLPLUS report that **AVG( )**, **COUNT( )**, **MAX( )**, **MIN( )**, **STDDEV( )**, **SUM( )**, and **VARIANCE( )** have in SQL.

All of them except **num** ignore **NULL**s, and none of them is able to use the **DISTINCT** keyword. **compute num** is similar to **compute count**, except that **compute count** produces the count of non-**NULL** rows, and **compute num** produces the count of *all* rows.

Displaying Current breaks and computes

Entering just the word **break** or **compute** in SQLPLUS will cause it to display the **break**s and **compute**s it has in effect at the moment.

Running Several computes at Once

Figure 14-4 contains the following **compute** statements:

```
compute sum of Volume on Report Industry
compute sum of PartOfInd on Industry
compute avg of Net Percent on Industry
compute avg of Net Percent PartOfInd on Report
```

Look at Circles 5 and 6 in Figure 14-5 and you'll see the effects of all of these. Observe that the **avg** calculation for each column appears on one line, and the **sum** (where there is one) appears on the following line. Further, the words **sum** and **avg** appear *under the column* that follows the word **on** in the **compute** statement. They're missing at Circle 6 for the grand totals because these are made on Report, and Report is not a column, so **sum** and **avg** can't appear under a column.

The Volume **sum** at Circle 5 is just for the Space industry stocks. The Volume **sum** at Circle 6 is for all industries (page 4 of this report contains only the grand totals and averages). Note that the first **compute** here is for the **sum** of one column, Volume, on both Report and Industry. (Incidentally, the order of the columns in a **compute** is irrelevant, unlike in a **break on**.)

The next **compute**, for PartOfInd on Industry, requires some explanation. (PartOfInd refers to its part of the industry point shift or a change in stock price over all the stocks in the industry.) PartOfInd comes from a portion of the **select** statement:

```
(CloseToday - CloseYesterday)*(S.Volume/I.Volume) AS PartOfInd,
```

This calculation weights the net change in a stock versus the other stocks in its Industry, based on the volume traded. Compare the actual Net change between BRANDON and NORTHERN in the SPACE industry. BRANDON changed only .75 but traded over 25 million shares. NORTHERN changed 1.25 but traded only about 1 million shares. The contribution of BRANDON to the upward shift in the SPACE industry is thus considerably greater than that of NORTHERN; this is reflected in the relative values for the two under the PartOfInd column.

Now compare the **sum** of the PartOfInd column, 2.08, with the **avg** of the Net column, 1.46 (from the very next **compute**). Which is more representative of the change in stock price in this industry? It is the **sum** of PartOfInd, because its values are weighted by stock volume. This example is given to show the difference between a simple average in a column and a weighted average, and to show how summary information is calculated. In one case, it is done by averaging, in another it's done by summing.

This is not the place to launch a detailed discussion of weighted averages, percentages, or statistical calculations, but it is appropriate to point out that significant differences will result from various methods of calculation. This will often affect decisions that are being made, so care and caution are in order.

The final **compute** calls for the average of Net, Percent, and PartOfInd on Report. These values are shown at Circle 6 as .88, .19, and 2.66, respectively. Look at the last line of Figure 14-6. This is the same report as that in Figure 14-5, with a few exceptions. It is on one page instead of four; its upper-right title is the date, not the industry segment; and its bottom line has an additional and different result for averages and totals:

```
Market Averages and Totals      1.09       2.66  139,699,940
```

These are the correct results, and they differ from those that are or can be calculated from the columns displayed using *any* **compute** statement, because the **compute** statements lack the weighting of the total industry volume. So, how was this result produced? The answer is in Figure 14-7. At Circle F, the **btitle** was turned off, and at Circle G (just following the **select** that produced the main body of the report) is an additional **select** that includes the label Market Averages and Totals, and a proper calculation of them.

This **select** statement is preceded by **set heading off** and **ttitle off**. These are necessary because a new **select** will normally force a new top title to print. The **set heading off** command is used to turn off the *column* titles that normally would appear above this line. The **btitle** at Circle F had to be turned off before the first **select** executed, because the completion of the first **select** would cause the **btitle** to print before the second **select** could even execute.

As shown in the sample report outputs in this chapter (Figures 14-2, 14-3, 14-5, and 14-6), when a **compute** command is used, the computed value is labeled with the function that was executed. For example, in Figure 14-6, both an **AVG** and a **SUM** function are computed; the output shows a label of "avg" for the **AVG** calculation, and "sum" for the **SUM** calculation. You can override the default labels and specify your own labels for computed functions in the **compute** command. See the **label** clause of COMPUTE in the Alphabetical Reference for details. To avoid having the **compute** commands apply to the Volume column of the second query, the **clear computes** command is executed after the first query.

```
Current Portfolio                              March 1st, 2000
                        Industry Listings

           Close   Close          Part Percent
 Ind  COMPANY  Yest.   Today   NET  of Ind  Change       VOLUME
----- -------  ------- ------- ------ ------- ------- ------------
ELECT IDK       95.00   95.25   .25     .06     .26    9,443,523
      MEMORY G  15.50   14.25 -1.25    -.15   -8.06    4,557,992
      MICRO TO  77.00   76.50  -.50    -.32    -.65   25,205,667
*****                          ------ ------- ------- ------------
avg                             -.50          -2.82
sum                                    -.41          39,207,182

MEDIC AT SPACE  46.75   48.00  1.25     .42    2.67   11,398,323
      AUGUST E  15.00   15.00   .00     .00     .00   12,221,711
      HAYWARD  104.25  106.00  1.75     .17    1.68    3,358,561
      KENTGEN   18.25   19.50  1.25     .25    6.85    6,636,863
*****                          ------ ------- ------- ------------
avg                             1.06           2.80
sum                                     .85          33,615,458

SPACE BRANDON   32.75   33.50   .75     .29    2.29   25,789,769
      GENERAL   64.25   66.00  1.75     .20    2.72    7,598,562
      GENEVA R  22.75   27.25  4.50    1.52   19.78   22,533,944
      NORTHERN  26.75   28.00  1.25     .03    4.67    1,348,323
      OCKHAM S  21.50   22.00   .50     .05    2.33    7,052,990
      WONDER L   5.00    5.00   .00     .00     .00    2,553,712
*****                          ------ ------- ------- ------------
avg                             1.46           5.30
sum                                    2.08          66,877,300

                               ------ ------- ------- ------------
                                .88     .19    2.66
                                                     139,699,940


Market Averages and Totals     1.09           2.66  139,699,940
```

FIGURE 14-6. *Revised report with correct market averages and totals*

set termout off and set termout on

Another useful pair of commands is **set termout off** and **set termout on**. The former is often used in a start file just before the **spool** command, and the latter is often

```
ttitle left 'Current Portfolio'    right xTODAY skip 1 -
       center 'Industry Listings'      skip 2;

btitle off ◄───────────(F)

clear breaks
clear computes


break on Report on Industry skip 1


compute sum of Volume on Report Industry
compute sum of PartOfInd on Industry
compute avg of Net Percent on Industry
compute avg of Net Percent PartOfInd on Report

select S.Industry,
       Company,
       CloseYesterday, CloseToday,
       (CloseToday - CloseYesterday) AS Net,
       (CloseToday - CloseYesterday)*(S.Volume/I.Volume) AS PartOfInd,
       (CloseToday/CloseYesterday)*100 - 100 AS Percent,
       S.Volume, User,
       To_CHAR(SysDate,'fmMonth ddth, yyyy') AS Today
  from STOCK S, INDUSTRY I
 where S.Industry = I.Industry
   AND I.Industry in ('ELECTRONICS', 'SPACE', 'MEDICAL')
 order by I.Industry, Company
/
set heading off
ttitle off
clear computes
select 'Market Averages and Totals    ',                    ◄───────(G)
       SUM(((CloseToday-CloseYesterday)*S.Volume)/M.Volume) AS Net,
       '        ',
       AVG((CloseToday/CloseYesterday))*100 - 100 AS Percent,
       SUM(S.Volume) AS Volume
  from STOCK S, MARKET M
 where Industry in ('ELECTRONICS', 'SPACE', 'MEDICAL')
/
```

FIGURE 14-7. *How the correct market averages and totals were produced*

used just after it. The effect is to suppress the display of the report to the screen. For reports that are going to be printed, this saves time (they'll run faster) and avoids the annoying rolling of data across the screen. The spooling to a file continues to work properly.

Variables in SQLPLUS

If you're using SQLPLUS interactively, you can check on the current **ttitle** and **btitle** at any time by typing their names alone on a line. SQLPLUS immediately shows you their contents:

```
ttitle
ttitle ON and is the following 113 characters:
left 'Current Portfolio'          right xTODAY
skip 1            center 'Industry Listings   '  skip 2
```

Note the presence of xTODAY, which is a variable, rather than its current contents. SQLPLUS is capable of storing and using many variables—those used in **ttitle** and **btitle** are only some of them. The current variables and their values can be discovered by typing **define**:

```
define
DEFINE _SQLPLUS_RELEASE = "801050000" (CHAR)
DEFINE _EDITOR        = "vi" (CHAR)
DEFINE _O_VERSION     = "Oracle8i Enterprise Edition Release 8.1.5.0.0
With the Partitioning and Java options
PL/SQL Release 8.1.5.0.0 - Production" (CHAR)
DEFINE _O_RELEASE     = "801050000" (CHAR)
DEFINE XINDUSTRY    = "SPACE" (CHAR)
DEFINE XTODAY       = "March 1st, 2000" (CHAR)
```

The EDITOR variable is the editor you use when you type the word **edit**. You saw how to set this up in your login.sql file back in Chapter 6. The other variables identify which version and release of Oracle you are using.

The last variables are defined in the stock market queries, and their contents are just those displayed in the reports. SQLPLUS stores variables for **ttitle** and **btitle** by defining them as equal to some value, and then allows you to use them whenever a query is being executed. In fact, variables can be used many places in a report other than in titles.

Suppose your stock database were updated automatically by a pricing service, and you wished to check regularly the closing prices and volumes on a stock-by-stock basis. This could be easily accomplished with variables in the **where** clause. Normally, you would type this query:

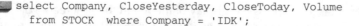

```
select Company, CloseYesterday, CloseToday, Volume
  from STOCK  where Company = 'IDK';
```

```
                     Close   Close
COMPANY              Yest.   Today       VOLUME
------------------   -----   -----   ------------
IDK                  95.00   95.25    9,443,523
```

Alternatively, you could type this into a start file named, for example, closing.sql:

```
column CloseToday heading 'Close|Today' format 999.90
column CloseYesterday heading 'Close|Yest.' format 999.90
column Volume format 999,999,999

accept xCompany prompt 'Enter Company name: '

select Company, CloseYesterday, CloseToday, Volume
  from STOCK
 where Company = '&xCompany';
```

In this file, xCompany is a variable you have invented, such as xIndustry or xToday. **accept** tells SQLPLUS to accept input from the keyboard, and **prompt** tells it to display a message. Note that the variable name must be preceded by the ampersand (&) when it appears in the SQL **select** statement, but not when it appears in the **accept** or in a title. Then, when you type this:

```
start closing.sql
```

the screen displays this:

```
Enter Company name:
```

You then type **MEMORY GRAPHICS**. SQLPLUS will display the following:

```
select Company, CloseYesterday, CloseToday, Volume
  from STOCK
 where Company = '&xCompany';

old   3:   where Company = '&xCompany'
new   3:   where Company = 'MEMORY GRAPHICS'

                     Close   Close
COMPANY              Yest.   Today       VOLUME
------------------   -----   -----   ------------
MEMORY GRAPHICS      15.50   14.25    4,557,992
```

First, it shows you the query you have set up. Next, it shows you the **where** clause—first with the variable in it, and then with the value you typed. Finally, it shows you the results of the query.

If you then typed **start closing.sql** again, but typed **IDK** for Company name, the **old** and **new** would show this:

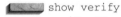
```
old   3:  where Company = 'MEMORY GRAPHICS'
new   3:  where Company = 'IDK'
```

and the result would be for IDK. It is unnecessary for the **select** and the **old** and **new** to be displayed each time. Both of these can be controlled, the first by the **set echo** command and the second by **set verify**. To see what these are set at currently, type the **show** command followed by the keyword **verify** or **echo**:

```
show verify
verify ON

show echo
echo ON
```

The revised version of the start file looks like this:

```
column CloseToday heading 'Close|Today' format 999.90
column CloseYesterday heading 'Close|Yest.' format 999.90
column Volume format 999,999,999

set echo off
set verify off
set sqlcase upper
accept xCompany prompt 'Enter Company name: '

select Company, CloseYesterday, CloseToday, Volume
  from STOCK
 where Company = '&xCompany';
```

set sqlcase upper tells SQLPLUS to convert anything keyed into the variable (using the **accept**) to uppercase before executing the query. This can be helpful if you've stored your data in uppercase (which is a good practice) but don't want to force people to type in uppercase any time they run a query. Now when the start file is executed, this is what happens:

```
start closing.sql

Enter Company name: memory graphics

                      Close   Close
COMPANY               Yest.   Today        VOLUME
------------------    -------  -------  ------------
MEMORY GRAPHICS       15.50   14.25     4,557,992
```

The use of variables in start files can be very helpful, particularly for reports in which the basic format of the report stays the same but certain parameters change, such as date, company division, stock name, project, client, and so on. When the report starts, it asks the person using it for these details and then it runs. As just shown, typing only the word **define** will result in a list of all the variables currently defined. Typing **define** with just one name will show only that variable's contents:

```
define xCompany

DEFINE XCOMPANY     = "memory graphics" (CHAR)
```

After a start file has completed, any variables are held by SQLPLUS until you exit or intentionally **undefine** them:

```
undefine xCompany
```

An attempt now to see the variable's value produces the following:

```
define xCompany

symbol xcompany is UNDEFINED
```

You also can define a variable within the start file without using the **accept** command. Simply assign a value directly, as shown here:

```
define xCompany = 'IDK'
```

Any place that &xCompany appears in the start file will have IDK substituted.

Other Places to Use Variables

Any variable that you define using either **accept** or **define** can be used directly in a **btitle** or **ttitle** command without using the **NEW_VALUE** column command. **NEW_VALUE** simply takes the contents of a column and issues its own **define** command for the variable name following **NEW_VALUE**. The single difference in using the variable in titles, as opposed to the SQL statement, is that in titles the variable is not preceded by an ampersand.

Variables also can be used in a setup start file, as explained later in this chapter in "Using mask.sql."

Numeric Formatting

The default method SQLPLUS uses for formatting numbers is to right-justify them in a column, without commas, using decimal points only if the number is not an integer. The table NUMBERTEST contains columns named Value1 and Value2, which have identical numbers in each column. These will be used to show how numeric formatting works. The first query shows the default formatting:

```
select Value1, Value2 from NUMBERTEST;

    VALUE1       VALUE2
------------ ------------
           0            0
       .0001        .0001
        1234         1234
      1234.5       1234.5

     1234.56      1234.56
    1234.567     1234.567
    98761235     98761235
```

Row five is **NULL**. Notice how the decimal point moves from row to row. Just as columns can be formatted individually in queries, the default format can be changed:

```
set numformat 9,999,999

select Value1, Value2 from NUMBERTEST;

    VALUE1      VALUE2
---------- ----------
         0          0
         0          0
     1,234      1,234
     1,235      1,235

     1,235      1,235
     1,235      1,235
  ########   ########
```

Now, row eight is filled with pound signs. The problem with row eight is that the format defined is too narrow. You can fix this by adding another digit on the left, as shown here:

```
set numformat 99,999,999

select Value1, Value2 from NUMBERTEST;

    VALUE1      VALUE2
----------- -----------
          0           0
          0           0
      1,234       1,234
      1,235       1,235

      1,235       1,235
      1,235       1,235
 98,761,235  98,761,235
```

Using mask.sql

Columns used in one report may also need to be used regularly in several reports. Instead of retyping the formatting commands for these columns in every start file, it can be useful to keep all the basic column commands in a single file. This file might be called mask.sql, because it contains formatting (also called *masking*) information for columns. For example, the file might look like the following:

```
REM     File mask.sql
set numwidth 12
set numformat 999,999,999.90

column Net format 99.90
column Industry format a11
column Company format a18
column CloseToday heading 'Close|Today' format 999.90
column CloseYesterday heading 'Close|Yest.' format 999.90
column Volume format 999,999,999

define xDepartment = 'Systems Planning Dept. 3404'
```

This is then effectively embedded in a start file (usually near the top) simply by including this line:

```
start mask.sql
```

Numeric Formatting Options

These options work with both **set numformat** and the **column format** command:

9999990	The count of nines and zeros determines the maximum digits that can be displayed.
999,999,999.99	Commas and decimals will be placed in the pattern shown.
999990	Displays a zero if the value is zero.
099999	Displays numbers with leading zeros.
$99999	A dollar sign is placed in front of every number.
B99999	The display will be blank if the value is zero. This is the default.
99999MI	If the number is negative, a minus sign follows the number. The default is for the negative sign to be on left.
99999PR	Negative numbers are displayed within < and >.
9.999EEEE	The display will be in scientific notation.
999V99	Multiplies number by 10^n, where n is the number of digits to the right of V. 999V99 turns 1234 into 123400.

show all and spooling

You've seen several commands that use the **set** command, and whose current status can be determined using the **show** command, such as **feedback**, **echo**, **verify**, **heading**, and so on. There are actually about 50 such commands that can be **set**. These can all be displayed at once using this:

```
show all
```

Unfortunately, these fly by so quickly on the screen that it's impossible to read most of them. You can solve this problem by spooling. Simply **spool** to a file, as in the previous example, execute **show all**, and then **spool off**. You can now look at the current status of all the **set** commands using your editor on the file. You can look up these commands in the Alphabetical Reference at the end of this book under **set**. The rows returned by the **show all** command will be ordered alphabetically.

As an alternative, you can use the **store** command described in Chapter 6 to save your current SQLPLUS environment settings to a file (like mask.sql). You can then execute this file at a later date to reset your environment settings.

Folding onto New Lines

Information retrieved from a database is often just fine with only one line of column titles, and columns of data stacked below them. Occasionally, however, a different kind of layout is preferable. Sometimes, this can be accomplished using literal columns of nothing but blank spaces, to properly position real data on more than one line and have it line up properly. These literal columns are given an alias in the SQL and then a blank heading in the **column** command. The technique parallels what was done for the total line in Figure 14-6. For example, look at this:

```
column Industry format a14 trunc
column B format a21 heading ' '
column Company format a20
column Volume format 999,999,999 justify left

select Industry, ' ' AS B,
       Company,
       CloseYesterday, CloseToday,
       (CloseToday - CloseYesterday) AS Net,
       Volume
  from STOCK
 where Industry in ('ADVERTISING','GARMENT')
 order by Industry, Company;


INDUSTRY                                        COMPANY
-------------- --------------------- ---------------------
CLOSEYESTERDAY CLOSETODAY     NET VOLUME
-------------- ---------- ---------- ------------
ADVERTISING                          AD SPECIALTY
        31.75      31.75         0   18,333,876
ADVERTISING                          MBK COMMUNICATIONS
        43.25         41     -2.25   10,022,980
ADVERTISING                          NANCY LEE FEATURES
         13.5      14.25       .75   14,222,692
GARMENT                              ROBERT JAMES APPAREL
        23.25         24       .75   19,032,481
```

A literal column of one space, given an alias of *B*, is defined by the **column** command as 21 characters wide with a blank heading. This is used specifically to move the company names over so that the columns line up as desired, with stock Volume directly below the Company name, and column B for CloseToday and Net lining up with the blank.

fold_after and fold_before

Next, look at how the column command **fold_after** affects every column in the **select**:

```
clear columns
column Net format 99.90
column A format a15 fold_after 1
column Company format a20 fold_after 1
column CloseToday heading 'Close|Today' format 999.90 -
   fold_after
column CloseYesterday heading 'Close|Yest.' format 999.90 -
   fold_after 1
column Net fold_after 1
column Volume format 999,999,999 fold_after 1
set heading off

select Industry||',' AS A,
       Company,
       CloseYesterday,
       CloseToday, (CloseToday - CloseYesterday) AS Net,
       Volume
  from STOCK
 where Industry in ('ADVERTISING','GARMENT')
 order by Industry, Company;
```

The previous query produces the following output. Note that even though CloseToday had no number following its **fold_after** clause, SQLPLUS used a default of 1.

```
ADVERTISING,
AD SPECIALTY
  31.75
  31.75
   .00
  18,333,876

ADVERTISING,
MBK COMMUNICATIONS
  43.25
```

```
   41.00
   -2.25
   10,022,980

ADVERTISING,
NANCY LEE FEATURES
   13.50
   14.25
   .75
   14,222,692

GARMENT,
ROBERT JAMES APPAREL
   23.25
   24.00
   .75
   19,032,481
```

Additional Reporting Controls

Many of the commands illustrated here, as well as in other chapters, have options considerably beyond those used in these examples. All of the options for each of these commands can be found in the Alphabetical Reference, under the individual command names.

CHAPTER
15

Changing Data: insert, update, and delete

ntil now, virtually everything you've learned about Oracle, SQL, and SQLPLUS has related to selecting data from tables in the database. This chapter shows how to *change* the data in a table: how to insert new rows, update the values of columns in rows, and delete rows entirely. Although these topics have not been covered explicitly, nearly everything you already know about SQL, including datatypes, calculations, string formatting, **where** clauses, and the like, can be used here, so there really isn't much new to learn. Oracle gives you a transparent, distributed database capability that inserts, updates, and deletes data in remote databases as well (see Chapter 22).

insert

The SQL command **insert** lets you place a row of information directly into a table (or indirectly, through a view). The COMFORT table tracks temperatures at noon and midnight and daily precipitation, city by city, for four sample dates through the year:

 describe COMFORT

Name	Null?	Type
CITY		VARCHAR2 (13)
SAMPLEDATE		DATE
NOON		NUMBER
MIDNIGHT		NUMBER
PRECIPITATION		NUMBER

To add a new row to this table, use this:

```
insert into COMFORT
values ('WALPOLE', TO_DATE('21-MAR-1999','DD-MON-YYYY'),
        56.7, 43.8, 0);
```

1 row created.

The word **values** must precede the list of data to be inserted. A character string must be in single quotation marks. Numbers can stand by themselves. Each field is separated by commas, and the fields must be in the same order as the columns are when the table is described.

A date must be in single quotation marks and in the default Oracle date format. To insert a date not in default format, use the **TO_DATE** function, with a formatting mask, as shown in the following:

```
insert into COMFORT
values ('WALPOLE', TO_DATE('06/22/1999','MM/DD/YYYY'),
        56.7, 43.8, 0);
```

```
1 row created.
```

Inserting a Time

Inserting dates without time values will produce a default time of midnight, the very beginning of the day. If you wish to insert a date with a time other than midnight, simply use the **TO_DATE** function and include a time:

```
insert into COMFORT
values ('WALPOLE', TO_DATE('06/22/1999 1:35',
        'MM/DD/YYYY HH24:MI'), 56.7, 43.8, 0);
```

```
1 row created.
```

Columns also can be inserted out of the order they appear when described, if you first (before the word **values**) list the order the data is in. This doesn't change the fundamental order of the columns in the table. It simply allows you to list the data fields in a different order. (See Chapters 28 and 29 for information on inserting data into objects in Oracle8.)

NOTE
*You also can "insert" a **NULL**. This simply means
the column will be left empty for this row, as shown
in the following:*

```
insert into COMFORT
        (SampleDate,  Precipitation, City, Noon, Midnight)
values (TO_DATE('23-SEP-1999','DD-MON-YYYY'), NULL,
        'WALPOLE', 86.3, 72.1);
```

```
1 row created.
```

insert with select

You also can insert information that has been selected from a table. Here, a mix of columns selected from the COMFORT table, together with literal values for SampleDate (22-DEC-99) and City (WALPOLE), are inserted. Note the **where** clause in the **select** statement, which will retrieve only one row. Had the **select** retrieved five rows, five new ones would have been inserted; if ten rows had been retrieved, then ten new rows would have been inserted; and so on.

```
insert into COMFORT
       (SampleDate, Precipitation, City, Noon, Midnight)
select TO_DATE('22-DEC-1999','DD-MON-YYYY'), Precipitation,
       'WALPOLE', Noon, Midnight
  from COMFORT
 where City = 'KEENE'
   and SampleDate = TO_DATE('22-DEC-1999','DD-MON-YYYY');
```

```
1 row created.
```

NOTE
*You cannot use the **insert into...select from** syntax with LONG datatypes unless you are using the **TO_LOB** function to insert the LONG data into a LOB column.*

Of course, you don't need to simply insert the value in a selected column. You can modify the column using any of the appropriate string, date, or number functions within the **select** statement. The results of those functions are what will be inserted. You can attempt to **insert** a value in a column that exceeds its width (for character datatypes) or its magnitude (for number datatypes). You have to fit within the constraints you defined on your columns. These attempts will produce a "value too large for column" or "mismatched datatype" error message. If you now query the COMFORT table for the city of Walpole, the results will be the records you inserted:

```
select * from COMFORT
 where City = 'WALPOLE';
```

CITY	SAMPLEDAT	NOON	MIDNIGHT	PRECIPITATION
WALPOLE	21-MAR-99	56.7	43.8	0
WALPOLE	22-JUN-99	56.7	43.8	0
WALPOLE	23-SEP-99	86.3	72.1	
WALPOLE	22-DEC-99	-7.2	-1.2	3.9

```
4 rows selected.
```

An Aside About Performance
As you will learn in Chapter 36, Oracle uses an optimizer to determine the most efficient way to perform each SQL command. For **insert** statements, Oracle tries to insert each new record into an existing block of data already allocated to the table. This execution plan optimizes the use of space required to store the data. However,

it may not provide adequate performance for an **insert** with a **select** command that inserts multiple rows. You can override the execution plan by using the APPEND hint to improve the performance of large inserts. The APPEND hint will tell the database to find the last block into which the table's data has ever been inserted. The new records will be inserted starting in the next block following the last previously used block. Since the data is being written into new blocks of the table, there is much less space management work for the database to do during the **insert**. Therefore, the **insert** may complete faster when the APPEND hint is used.

You specify the APPEND hint within the **insert** command. A hint looks like a comment—it starts with /* and ends with */. The only difference is that the starting set of characters includes a + before the name of the hint. The following example shows an **insert** command whose data is appended to the table:

```
insert /*+ APPEND */ into WORKER (Name)
select Name from PROSPECT;
```

The records from the PROSPECT table will be inserted into the WORKER table. Instead of attempting to reuse previously used space within the WORKER table, the new records will be placed at the end of the table's physical storage space.

Since the new records will not attempt to reuse available space that the table has already used, the space requirements for the WORKER table may increase. In general, you should use the APPEND hint only when inserting large volumes of data into tables with little reusable space. The point at which appended records will be inserted is called the table's *high-water mark*—and the only way to reset the high-water mark is to **truncate** the table. Since **truncate** will delete all records and cannot be rolled back, you should make sure you have a backup of the table's data prior to performing the **truncate**. See **truncate** in the Alphabetical Reference for further details.

rollback, commit, and autocommit

When you insert, update, or delete data from the database, you can reverse, or *roll back,* the work you've done. This can be very important when an error is discovered. The process of committing or rolling back work is controlled by two SQLPLUS commands, **commit** and **rollback**. Additionally, SQLPLUS has the facility to automatically commit your work without your explicitly telling it to do so. This is controlled by the **autocommit** feature of **set**. Like other **set** features, you can **show** it, like this:

```
show autocommit

autocommit OFF
```

OFF is the default. You can also specify a number for the **autocommit** value; this value will determine the number of commands after which Oracle will issue a **commit**. This means **insert**s, **update**s, and **delete**s are not made final until you **commit** them:

```
commit;
```

```
commit complete
```

Until you **commit**, only you can see how your work affects the tables. Anyone else with access to these tables will continue to get the old information. You will see *new* information whenever you **select** from the table. Your work is, in effect, in a "staging" area, which you interact with until you **commit**. You can do quite a large number of **insert**s, **update**s, and **delete**s, and still undo the work (return the tables to the way they used to be) by issuing this command:

```
rollback;
```

```
rollback complete
```

However, the message "rollback complete" can be misleading. It means only that Oracle has rolled back any work that hasn't been committed. If you **commit** a series of transactions, either explicitly with the word **commit** or implicitly by another action (an example of which is shown next), the "rollback complete" message won't really mean anything. The two sidebars "How commit and rollback Work" and "How commit and rollback Work in SQL," later in the chapter, give a picture of how **commit** and **rollback** affect a table of dogs' names.

Implicit commit

The actions that will force a **commit** to occur, even without your instructing it to, are **quit**, **exit** (the equivalent of **quit**), and any DDL command. Using any of these commands is just like using **commit**.

Auto rollback

If you've completed a series of **insert**s, **update**s, or **delete**s, but have not yet explicitly or implicitly committed them, and you experience serious difficulties, such as a computer failure, Oracle will automatically roll back any uncommitted work. If the machine or database goes down, it does this as cleanup work the next time the database is brought back up.

How commit and rollback Work

A database table has only one column and row in it. The table is CANINE and the column is Name. It already has one dog in it, TROUBLE, which is incorrectly spelled as "TRAUBLE," and the diagrams show the attempts of TROUBLE's keeper to add other dogs to the table and correct the spelling of his name. This assumes the **autocommit** feature of SQLPLUS is off. See the next sidebar to view the SQL equivalent of the actions in this diagram:

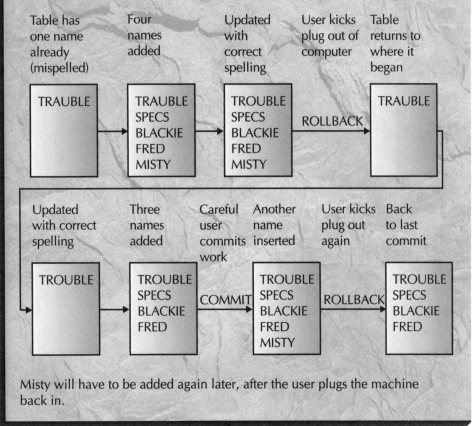

Misty will have to be added again later, after the user plugs the machine back in.

How commit and rollback Work in SQL

In SQL, the sequence shown in the illustration in the previous boxed section, "How commit and rollback Work" would look like this:

```
select * from CANINE:

NAME
-------
TRAUBLE

insert into CANINE values ('SPECS');
insert into CANINE values ('BLACKIE');
insert into CANINE values ('FRED');
insert into CANINE values ('MISTY');

update CANINE set Name = 'TROUBLE' where Name = 'TRAUBLE';

rollback;

select * from CANINE:

NAME
--------
TRAUBLE

update CANINE set Name = 'TROUBLE' where Name = 'TRAUBLE';

insert into CANINE values ('SPECS');
insert into CANINE values ('BLACKIE');
insert into CANINE values ('FRED');

commit;

insert into CANINE values ('MISTY');

rollback;

select * from CANINE:

NAME
-------
TROUBLE
SPECS
BLACKIE
FRED
```

delete

Removing a row or rows from a table requires the **delete** command. The **where** clause is essential to removing only the rows you intend. **delete** without a **where** clause will empty the table completely. The following command deletes the Walpole entries from the COMFORT table.

```
delete from COMFORT where City = 'WALPOLE';

4 rows deleted.
```

Of course, a **where** clause in a **delete**, just as in an **update** or a **select** that is part of an **insert**, can contain as much logic as any **select** statement, and may include subqueries, unions, intersects, and so on. You can always **rollback** a bad **insert**, **update**, or **delete**, but you really should experiment with the **select** before actually making the change to the database, to make sure you are doing the right thing.

Now that you've just deleted the rows where City = 'WALPOLE', you can test the effect of that **delete** with a simple query:

```
select * from COMFORT
  where City = 'WALPOLE';

no rows selected
```

Now **rollback** the **delete** and run the same query:

```
rollback;
rollback complete

select * from COMFORT
  where City = 'WALPOLE';

CITY          SAMPLEDAT     NOON   MIDNIGHT PRECIPITATION
------------- --------- ---------- ---------- -------------
WALPOLE       21-MAR-99     56.7      43.8              0
WALPOLE       22-JUN-99     56.7      43.8              0
WALPOLE       23-SEP-99     86.3      72.1
WALPOLE       22-DEC-99     -7.2      -1.2            3.9

4 rows selected.
```

This illustrates that recovery is possible, so long as a **commit** hasn't occurred.

An additional command for deleting records, **truncate**, does not behave the same as **delete**. Whereas **delete** allows you to **commit** or **rollback** the deletion,

truncate automatically deletes all records from the table. The action of the **truncate** command cannot be rolled back or committed; the truncated records are unrecoverable. See the **truncate** command in the Alphabetical Reference for further details.

update

update requires setting specific values for each column you wish to change, and specifying which row or rows you wish to affect by using a carefully constructed **where** clause:

```
update COMFORT set Precipitation = .5, Midnight = 73.1
  where City = 'WALPOLE'
    and SampleDate = TO_DATE('22-DEC-1999','DD-MON-YYYY');

1 row updated.
```

Here is the effect:

```
select * from COMFORT
  where City = 'WALPOLE';
```

CITY	SAMPLEDAT	NOON	MIDNIGHT	PRECIPITATION
WALPOLE	21-MAR-99	56.7	43.8	0
WALPOLE	22-JUN-99	56.7	43.8	0
WALPOLE	23-SEP-99	86.3	72.1	
WALPOLE	22-DEC-99	-7.2	73.1	.5

```
4 rows selected.
```

What if you later discover that the thermometer used in Walpole consistently reports its temperatures too low by one degree? You also can do calculations, string functions, and almost any other legitimate function in setting a value for the **update** (just as you can for an **insert**, or in the **where** clause of a **delete**). Here, each temperature in WALPOLE is increased by one degree:

```
update COMFORT set Midnight = Midnight + 1, Noon = Noon + 1
  where City = 'WALPOLE';

4 rows updated.
```

Here is the effect of the **update**:

```
select * from COMFORT
  where City = 'WALPOLE';
```

```
CITY            SAMPLEDAT      NOON   MIDNIGHT PRECIPITATION
------------    ---------   ---------- ---------- -------------
WALPOLE         21-MAR-99      57.7       44.8               0
WALPOLE         22-JUN-99      57.7       44.8               0
WALPOLE         23-SEP-99      87.3       73.1
WALPOLE         22-DEC-99      -6.2       74.1              .5
```

4 rows selected.

As with **delete**, the **where** clause is critical. Without one, every row in the database will be updated. With an improperly constructed **where** clause, the wrong rows will be updated, often in ways that are hard to discover or fix, especially if your work has been committed. Always **set feedback on** when doing **update**s, and look at the feedback to be sure the number of rows updated is what you expected it to be. Query the rows after you **update** to see if the expected change took place.

update with Embedded select

It is possible to set values in an **update** by embedding a **select** statement right in the middle of it. Note that this **select** has its own **where** clause, picking out the temperature from the City of MANCHESTER from the WEATHER table, and the **update** has its own **where** clause to affect just the City of WALPOLE on a certain day:

```
update COMFORT set Midnight =
       (select Temperature
          from WEATHER
         where City = 'MANCHESTER')
 where City = 'WALPOLE'
   AND SampleDate = TO_DATE('22-DEC-1999','DD-MON-YYYY');
```

1 row updated.

Here is the effect of the **update**:

```
select * from COMFORT
  where City = 'WALPOLE';
```

CITY	SAMPLEDAT	NOON	MIDNIGHT	PRECIPITATION
WALPOLE	21-MAR-99	57.7	44.8	0
WALPOLE	22-JUN-99	57.7	44.8	0
WALPOLE	23-SEP-99	87.3	73.1	
WALPOLE	22-DEC-99	-6.2	66	.5

4 rows selected.

When using subqueries with **update**s, you must be certain that the subquery will
return no more than one record for each of the records to be updated; otherwise,
the **update** will fail. See Chapter 12 for details on correlated queries.

You also can use an embedded **select** to **update** multiple columns at once. The
columns must be in parentheses and separated by a comma, as shown here:

```
update COMFORT set (Noon, Midnight) =
       (select Humidity, Temperature
          from WEATHER
         where City = 'MANCHESTER')
 where City = 'WALPOLE'
   AND SampleDate = TO_DATE('22-DEC-1999','DD-MON-YYYY');
```

1 row updated.

Here is the effect:

```
select * from COMFORT
 where City = 'WALPOLE';
```

CITY	SAMPLEDAT	NOON	MIDNIGHT	PRECIPITATION
WALPOLE	21-MAR-99	57.7	44.8	0
WALPOLE	22-JUN-99	57.7	44.8	0
WALPOLE	23-SEP-99	87.3	73.1	
WALPOLE	22-DEC-99	98	66	.5

4 rows selected.

update with NULL

You also can update a table and set a column equal to **NULL**. This is the sole
instance of using the equal sign with **NULL**, instead of the word "is." For example,

```
update COMFORT set Noon = NULL
 where City = 'WALPOLE'
   AND SampleDate = TO_DATE('22-DEC-1999','DD-MON-YYYY');
```

1 row updated.

will set the noon temperature to **NULL** for Walpole on December 22, 1999.

NOTE
*The primary issues with **insert**, **update**, and **delete**
are careful construction of **where** clauses to affect
(or **insert**) only the rows you really wish, and the
normal use of SQL functions within these **insert**s,
updates, and **delete**s. It is extremely important that
you exercise caution about committing work before
you are certain it is correct. These three commands
extend the power of Oracle well beyond simple
query, and allow direct manipulation of data.*

CHAPTER
16

Advanced Use of Functions and Variables

n previous chapters, you've seen definitions and examples for character, number, and date functions, as well as for the use of variables. The examples ranged from simple to fairly complex, and enough explanation was provided so that you could construct rather sophisticated combined functions on your own.

This chapter expands on some of the earlier uses and shows examples of how functions can be combined to solve more difficult problems. Oracle has made solving some of these problems easier using SQL itself, but the examples in this chapter can expand your thinking about how to apply functions to solve real problems.

Functions in order by

Functions can be used in an **order by** to change the sorting sequence. Here, these **SUBSTR** functions cause the list of authors to be put in alphabetical order by first name:

```
select Author
  from MAGAZINE
 order by SUBSTR(Author,INSTR(Author,',')+2);


AUTHOR
------------------------

WHITEHEAD, ALFRED
BONHOEFFER, DIETRICH
CHESTERTON, G.K.
RUTH, GEORGE HERMAN
CROOKES, WILLIAM
```

Bar Charts and Graphs

You also can produce simple bar charts and graphs in SQLPLUS, using a mix of **LPAD** and a numeric calculation. First, look at the column formatting commands that will be used:

```
column Name format a16
column Age Format 999
column Graph Heading 'Age|    1    2    3    4    5    6    7-
|....0....0....0....0....0....0....0' justify c
column Graph format a35
```

The first two of these commands (lines) are straightforward. The third requires some explanation. The dash at the end of the third line tells SQLPLUS the **column** command is wrapped onto the next line. If the dash appears at the end of a line, SQLPLUS assumes that it means another line of this command follows. Here is the SQL statement that produced the horizontal bar chart in Figure 16-1. Workers whose age is unknown are not included.

```
                                            Age
                                  1     2     3     4     5     6     7
          NAME                AGE ....0....0....0....0....0....0....0
          ---------------     ---- -----------------------------------
          HELEN BRANDT         15 oooooooo
          WILLIAM SWING        15 oooooooo
          DONALD ROLLO         16 oooooooo
          DICK JONES           18 ooooooooo
          PAT LAVAY            21 oooooooooo
          BART SARJEANT        22 oooooooooo
          ADAH TALBOT          23 oooooooooooo
          PETER LAWSON         25 ooooooooooooo
          JOHN PEARSON         27 oooooooooooooo
          ANDREW DYE           29 ooooooooooooooo
          VICTORIA LYNN        32 oooooooooooooooo
          JED HOPKINS          33 ooooooooooooooooo
          ROLAND BRANDT        35 oooooooooooooooooo
          GEORGE OSCAR         41 ooooooooooooooooooooo
          ELBERT TALBOT        43 oooooooooooooooooooooo
          GERHARDT KENTGEN     55 ooooooooooooooooooooooooooooo
          WILFRED LOWELL       67 ooooooooooooooooooooooooooooooooooo
```

FIGURE 16-1. *Horizontal bar chart of age by person*

```
select Name, Age, LPAD('o',ROUND(Age/2,0),'o') AS Graph
   from WORKER
where Age is NOT NULL
 order by Age;
```

This use of **LPAD** is similar to what was done in Chapter 13, where Talbot's cows and bulls were shown in their family tree. Basically, a lowercase *o* is the column here, and it is padded on the left with a number of additional lowercase *o*'s, to the maximum width determined by **ROUND**(Age/2,0).

Notice that the scale of the column heading is in increments of two. A simple change to the SQL will produce a classic graph rather than a bar chart. The literal column is changed from an *o* to a lowercase *x*, and the padding on the left is done by spaces. The results of this SQL statement are shown in Figure 16-2.

```
select Name, Age, LPAD('x',ROUND(Age/2,0),' ') AS Graph
   from WORKER
where Age is NOT NULL
 order by Age;
```

```
                                    Age
                           1    2    3    4    5    6    7
          NAME        AGE  ....0....0....0....0....0....0....0
          ---------------- ----  ------------------------------------
          HELEN BRANDT      15       x
          WILLIAM SWING     15       x
          DONALD ROLLO      16       x
          DICK JONES        18         x
          PAT LAVAY         21           x
          BART SARJEANT     22           x
          ADAH TALBOT       23            x
          PETER LAWSON      25             x
          JOHN PEARSON      27              x
          ANDREW DYE        29               x
          VICTORIA LYNN     32                x
          JED HOPKINS       33                 x
          ROLAND BRANDT     35                  x
          GEORGE OSCAR      41                      x
          ELBERT TALBOT     43                       x
          GERHARDT KENTGEN  55                            x
          WILFRED LOWELL    67                                 x
```

FIGURE 16-2.   *Graph of age by person*

Another way to graph age is by its distribution rather than by person. First, a
view is created that puts each age into its decade. Thus 15, 16, and 18 become 10;
20 through 29 become 20; 30 through 39 become 30; and so on:

```
create view AGERANGE as
select TRUNC(Age,-1) AS Decade
   from WORKER;

View created.
```

Next, a column heading is set up, similar to the previous heading although
shorter and in increments of one:

```
column Graph Heading 'Count|         1    1|....5....0....5'-
justify c
```

```
column Graph format a15
column People Heading 'Head|Count' format 9999
```

The next SQL determines the count of workers that are represented in each decade. Since those with an unknown age were not excluded either here or in the view, a blank line appears at the bottom of the bar chart for those with a **NULL** age (see Figure 16-3).

```
select Decade, COUNT(Decade) AS People,
       LPAD('o',COUNT(Decade),'o') AS Graph
  from AGERANGE
 group by Decade;
```

Because **COUNT** ignores **NULL**s, it could not include the number of workers for whom the age is unknown in Figure 16-3. If, instead of counting the non-**NULL** rows in the Decade column, you use **COUNT**(*), a graph will be drawn for every row, and the bar chart will appear as shown in Figure 16-4. The following is the SQL that produced this result:

```
select Decade, COUNT(*) AS People,
       LPAD('o',COUNT(*),'o') AS Graph
  from AGERANGE
 group by Decade;
```

```
                                  Count
                        Head        1    1
             DECADE Count  ....5....0....5
             -------------- ----- ---------------
                 10      4 oooo
                 20      6 oooooo
                 30      3 ooo
                 40      2 oo
                 50      1 o
                 60      1 o
                        0
```

FIGURE 16-3.   *Distribution of age by decade*

```
                         Count
                 Head        1    1
         DECADE  Count  ....5....0....5
        --------------  -----  ---------------
                 10     4  oooo
                 20     6  oooooo
                 30     3  ooo
                 40     2  oo
                 50     1  o
                 60     1  o
                        1  o
```

FIGURE 16-4. *Distribution of age, counting all workers*

Using TRANSLATE

TRANSLATE converts characters in a string into different characters, based on a substitution plan you give it, from *if* to *then*:

TRANSLATE(`string`,`if`,`then`)

In the following SQL, the letters in a sentence are replaced. Any time an uppercase *T* is detected, it is replaced by an uppercase *T*. In effect, nothing changes. Any time an uppercase vowel is detected, however, it is replaced by a lowercase version of the same vowel. Any letter not in the TAEIOU string is left alone. When a letter is found in TAEIOU, its position is checked in the TAEIOU string, and the letter there is substituted. Thus, the letter *E*, at position 3 in TAEIOU, is replaced by *e*, in position 3 of Taeiou:

```
select TRANSLATE('NOW VOWELS ARE UNDER ATTACK','TAEIOU','Taeiou')
   from DUAL;

TRANSLATE('NOWVOWELSAREUNDE
--------------------------
NoW VoWeLS aRe uNDeR aTTaCK
```

Eliminating Characters

Extending this logic, what happens if the *if* string is TAEIOU and the *then* string is only *T*? Checking for the letter *E* (as in the word VOWELS) finds it in position 3 of TAEIOU. There is no position 3 in the *then* string (which is just the letter *T*), so the value in position 3 is nothing. So *E* is replaced by nothing. This same process is applied to all of the vowels. They appear in the *if* string, but not in the *then* string. As a result, they disappear, as shown here:

```
select TRANSLATE('NOW VOWELS ARE UNDER ATTACK','TAEIOU','T')
   from DUAL;

TRANSLATE('NOWVOWELSAREUNDE
---------------------------
NW VWLS R NDR TTCK
```

This feature of **TRANSLATE**, the ability to eliminate characters from a string, can prove very useful in cleaning up data. Recall the magazine titles in Chapter 7:

```
select Title from MAGAZINE;

TITLE
-------------------------------------
THE BARBERS WHO SHAVE THEMSELVES.
"HUNTING THOREAU IN NEW HAMPSHIRE"
THE ETHNIC NEIGHBORHOOD
RELATIONAL DESIGN AND ENTHALPY
"INTERCONTINENTAL RELATIONS."
```

The method used in Chapter 7 to clean out the periods and double quotes was a nested combination of **LTRIM** and **RTRIM**:

```
select LTRIM( RTRIM(Title,'."') ,'"') from MAGAZINE;
```

The same goal can be accomplished with a single use of **TRANSLATE**:

```
select TRANSLATE(Title,'T"'.','T') AS TITLE
   from MAGAZINE;

TITLE
-------------------------------------
THE BARBERS WHO SHAVE THEMSELVES
HUNTING THOREAU IN NEW HAMPSHIRE
THE ETHNIC NEIGHBORHOOD
RELATIONAL DESIGN AND ENTHALPY
INTERCONTINENTAL RELATIONS
```

Cleaning Up Dollar Signs and Commas

Suppose you have a file of data from an old accounting system and you've stored it in the format in which you received it, including commas, decimal points, and even dollar signs. How would you clean up the data in the column to move it into a *pure number column* that doesn't allow commas or dollar signs?

You could use the **TO_CHAR** function to clean up the numeric formats, or you could use the **TRANSLATE** function.

The COMMA table simply lists 11 rows of comma-formatted numbers. Here it is, along with the translation that erases the commas and dollar signs:

```
select AmountChar, TRANSLATE(AmountChar,'1,$','1')
  from COMMA;

AMOUNTCHAR              TRANSLATE(AMOUNTCHAR
--------------------   --------------------
$0                     0
$0.25                  0.25
$1.25                  1.25
$12.25                 12.25
$123.25                123.25
$1,234.25              1234.25
$12,345.25             12345.25
$123,456.25            123456.25
$1,234,567.25          1234567.25
$12,345,678.25         12345678.25
$123,456,789.25        123456789.25
```

The SQL says, "Look for either a 1, a comma, or a dollar sign. If you find a 1, replace it with a 1. If you find a comma or a dollar sign, replace it with nothing." Why is there always at least one letter or number translated, a 1 here, and a *T* in the previous example? Because, without at least one real character in the *then* string, **TRANSLATE** produces nothing:

```
select AmountChar, TRANSLATE(AmountChar,',$','') from COMMA;

AMOUNTCHAR              TRANSLATE(AMOUNTCHAR
--------------------   --------------------
$0
$0.25
$1.25
$12.25
$123.25
$1,234.25
$12,345.25
$123,456.25
$1,234,567.25
$12,345,678.25
$123,456,789.25
```

The *then* string was blank, and the *if* string held only those characters to be eliminated. But this approach does not work. At least one character must be in both the *if* and *then* strings. If this approach can be used to get commas and other characters out of a string, is there a way to get them in, such as comma-editing a number to display it?

The way to put commas into a number is to use the **TO_CHAR** function. As its name implies, this function changes the number to a character string, which allows the introduction of dollar signs and commas, among other symbols. See the "Number Formats" entry in the Alphabetical Reference of the book for a complete listing of the format options for numbers. The following example shows how to format a number with commas. A format mask tells Oracle how to format the character string that will be created by this command:

```
select TO_CHAR(123456789,'999,999,999') AS CommaTest
   from DUAL;
COMMATEST
-----------
123,456,789
```

Complex Cut and Paste

The NAME table contains a list of names as you might receive them from a mailing list company or another application. First name, last name, and initials are all in one column:

```
select Name from NAME;

NAME
------------------------
HORATIO NELSON
VALDO
MARIE DE MEDICIS
FLAVIUS JOSEPHUS
EDYTHE P. M. GAMMIERE
```

Suppose you want to cut and paste these names and put them into a table with FirstName and LastName columns. How would you go about it? The technique learned in Chapter 7 involved using **INSTR** to locate a space, and using the number it returns in a **SUBSTR** to clip out the portion up to that space. Here's an attempt to do just that for the first name:

```
select SUBSTR(Name,1,INSTR(Name,' '))
   from NAME;
```

```
SUBSTR(NAME,1,INSTR(NAME,
------------------------
HORATIO

MARIE
FLAVIUS
EDYTHE
```

VALDO has vanished! The problem is that these names are not as consistent as the authors' names were in Chapter 7. One of these names (probably a magician) is only one name long, so there is no space for the **INSTR** to find. When **INSTR** has an unsuccessful search, it returns a 0. The **SUBSTR** of the name VALDO, starting at position 1 and going for 0 positions, is nothing, so he disappears. This is solved with **DECODE**. In place of this:

```
INSTR(Name,' ')
```

you put the entire expression, like this:

```
DECODE(INSTR(Name,' '),0,99,INSTR(Name,' '))
```

DECODE's format is this:

```
DECODE(value,if1,then1[,if2,then2,if3,then3]...,else)
```

In the preceding example, **DECODE** tests the value of **INSTR**(Name,' '). If it is equal to 0, **DECODE** substitutes 99; otherwise, it returns the default value, which is also **INSTR**(Name, ' '). The choice of 99 as a substitute is arbitrary. It will create an effective **SUBSTR** function for VALDO that looks like this:

```
SUBSTR('VALDO',1,99)
```

This works because **SUBSTR** will clip out text from the starting number, 1, to the ending number or the end of the string, whichever comes first. With the **DECODE** function in place, the first names are retrieved correctly:

```
select SUBSTR(Name,1,
       DECODE(INSTR(Name,' '),0,99,INSTR(Name,' ')))
  from NAME;

SUBSTR(NAME,1,DECODE(INST
------------------------
HORATIO
VALDO
MARIE
```

```
FLAVIUS
EDYTHE
```

How about the last names? You could use **INSTR** again to search for a space, and use the location of the space in the string, plus one (+1), as the starting point for **SUBSTR**. No ending point is required for **SUBSTR**, because you want it to go to the end of the name. This is what happens:

```
select SUBSTR(Name,INSTR(Name,' ')+1)
   from NAME;

SUBSTR(NAME,INSTR(NAME,''
-------------------------
NELSON
VALDO
DE MEDICIS
JOSEPHUS
P. M. GAMMIERE
```

This didn't quite work. One solution is to use three **INSTR** functions, looking successively for the first, second, or third occurrence of a space in the name. Each of these **INSTR**s will return either the location where it found a space or a 0 if it didn't find any. In a name with only one space, the second and third **INSTR**s will both return 0. The **GREATEST** function, therefore, will pick the number returned by the **INSTR** that found the space furthest into the name:

```
select SUBSTR(Name,
GREATEST(INSTR(Name,' '),INSTR(Name,' ',1,2),INSTR(Name,' ',1
,3)) +1)
   from NAME;

SUBSTR(NAME,GREATEST(INST
-------------------------
NELSON
VALDO
MEDICIS
JOSEPHUS
GAMMIERE
```

Except for the fact that you also got VALDO again, this worked. (**GREATEST** also could have been used similarly in place of **DECODE** in the previous example.) There is a second and simpler method:

```
select SUBSTR(Name,INSTR(Name,' ',-1)+1)
   from NAME;
```

```
SUBSTR(NAME,INSTR(NAME,''
------------------------
NELSON
VALDO
MEDICIS
JOSEPHUS
GAMMIERE
```

The -1 in the **INSTR** tells it to start its search in the final position and go *backward,* or right to left, in the Name column. When it finds the space, **INSTR** returns its position, counting from the left as usual. The -1 simply makes **INSTR** start searching from the end rather than from the beginning. A -2 would make it start searching from the second position from the end, and so on.

The +1 in the **SUBSTR** command has the same purpose as in the previous example: once the space is found, **SUBSTR** has to move one position to the right to begin clipping out the Name. If no space is found, the **INSTR** returns 0, and **SUBSTR** therefore starts with position 1. That's why VALDO made the list.

How do you get rid of VALDO? Add an ending position to the **SUBSTR** instead of its default (which goes automatically all the way to the end). The ending position is found by using this:

```
DECODE(INSTR(Name,' '),0,0,LENGTH(Name))
```

which says, "Find the position of a space in the Name. If the position is 0, return 0; otherwise, return the **LENGTH** of the Name." For VALDO, the **DECODE** produces 0 as the ending position for **SUBSTR**, so nothing is displayed. For any other name, because there is a space somewhere, the **LENGTH** of the Name becomes the ending position for the **SUBSTR**, so the whole last name is displayed.

This is similar to the **DECODE** used to extract the first name, except that the value 99 used there has been replaced by **LENGTH**(Name), which will always work, whereas 99 would fail for a name longer than 99 characters. This won't matter here, but in other uses of **DECODE** and **SUBSTR**, it could be important:

```
select SUBSTR(Name,
       INSTR(Name,' ',-1)+1,
       DECODE(INSTR(Name,' '), 0, 0, LENGTH(Name)))
  from NAME;

SUBSTR(NAME,INSTR(NAME,''
------------------------
NELSON
```

```
MEDICIS
JOSEPHUS
GAMMIERE
```

This **DECODE** also could have been replaced by a **GREATEST**:

```
select SUBSTR(Name,
       INSTR(Name,' ',-1)+1,
       GREATEST(INSTR(Name,' '),0))
  from NAME;
```

A third method to accomplish the same end uses **RTRIM**. Remember that **RTRIM** eliminates everything specified in its *set* from the right side of a string until it encounters any character not in its *set*. The **RTRIM** here effectively erases all the letters on the right until it hits the first space (just before the last name) or reaches the beginning of the string:

```
select
SUBSTR(Name,LENGTH(RTRIM(NAME,'ABCDEFGHIJKLMNOPQRSTUVWXYZ'))
     +1)
  from NAME;

SUBSTR(NAME,LENGTH(RTRIM(
-------------------------
NELSON

MEDICIS
JOSEPHUS
GAMMIERE
```

LENGTH then measures the resulting string (with the last name erased). This tells you the position of the space before the last name. Add 1 to this number, do a **SUBSTR** starting there, and you'll get just the last name. Let's create a table with FirstName and LastName columns (you'll see complete details on creating tables in Chapter 18):

```
create table TWONAME(
FirstName     VARCHAR2(25),
LastName      VARCHAR2(25)
);

Table created.
```

Now, use an **insert** with a subquery to load the table data with the first and last names from the NAME table:

```
insert into TWONAME (FirstName, LastName)
select
    SUBSTR(Name,1,DECODE(INSTR(Name,' '),0,99,INSTR(Name,' '))),
    SUBSTR(Name,LENGTH(RTRIM(NAME,'ABCDEFGHIJKLMNOPQRSTUVWXYZ'))+1)
    from NAME;
```

Check the contents of the TWONAME table:

```
select * from TWONAME;

FIRSTNAME                LASTNAME
------------------------ -------------------------
HORATIO                  NELSON
VALDO
MARIE                    MEDICIS
FLAVIUS                  JOSEPHUS
EDYTHE                   GAMMIERE
```

You can use similar techniques to extract the middle initial or initials, and apply these methods elsewhere as well, such as to addresses, product descriptions, company names, and so on.

When moving data from an old system to a new one, reformatting is frequently necessary and often difficult. The facilities exist in SQL, but they require some knowledge of how the functions work and some thoughtfulness to avoid the kinds of difficulties shown in the examples so far in this chapter.

Counting String Occurrences Within Larger Strings

You can use a combination of the **LENGTH** and **REPLACE** functions to determine how many times a string (such as ABC) occurs within a larger string (such as ABCDEFABC). The **REPLACE** function replaces a character or characters in a string with zero or more characters. Thus,

```
REPLACE('ADAH', 'A', 'BLAH')
```

will evaluate the string ADAH. Everywhere an *A* is found, it will be replaced with the string BLAH. Thus, the function shown in this example will return the string BLAHDBLAHH.

You can use the **REPLACE** function to eliminate characters from strings. For example, you can replace the character string you're searching for with **NULL** values. Thus,

```
REPLACE('GEORGE', 'GE', NULL)
```

returns a value of OR. The two separate occurrences of GE in GEORGE were each set to **NULL**.

You can use the **REPLACE** function to determine how many times a string (like GE) is found in a larger string (like GEORGE). First, replace the string with **NULL** values:

```
select REPLACE('GEORGE', 'GE', NULL)
   from DUAL;
```

The result of that query will be OR. More importantly, the **LENGTH** of the result of that query will provide information about how many times the string was found. The following query will tell you how long the resulting string is:

```
select LENGTH(REPLACE('GEORGE', 'GE', NULL))
   from DUAL;
```

Now you can tell how many times the string was found. If you subtract the length of the shortened string from the original string and divide that difference by the length of the search string, the result will be the number of times the search string was found:

```
select (LENGTH('GEORGE')
        - LENGTH(REPLACE('GEORGE', 'GE', NULL)) )
        / LENGTH('GE')
   from DUAL;
```

This example uses strings instead of character columns in order to be simpler to understand; in real applications, you would replace the original string (GEORGE) with your column name. The length of the string GEORGE is six characters. The length of GEORGE after GE is replaced with **NULL** is two characters. Therefore, the difference in the lengths of the original and shortened strings is four characters. Dividing four characters by the length of the search string (two characters) tells you that the string was found twice.

The only problem with this method occurs when the search string is zero characters in length (since you cannot divide by zero). Searching for a zero-length string may indicate a problem with the application logic that initiated the search.

Additional Facts About Variables

The command **accept** forces SQLPLUS to **define** the variable as equal to the entered value, and it can do this with a text message, with control over the datatype entered, and even with the response blanked out from viewing (such as for passwords; see the entry for accept in the Alphabetical Reference).

You can pass arguments to a start file when it is started by embedding numbered variables in the **select** statements (rather than variables with names).

To select all of Talbot's transactions between one date and another, the **select** statement might look like this:

```
select * from LEDGER
  where ActionDate BETWEEN '&1' AND '&2';
```

The query would then be started like this:

```
start ledger.sql 01-JAN-01 31-DEC-01
```

The start file ledger.sql would begin, with 01-JAN-01 substituted for &1, and 31-DEC-01 substituted for &2. As with other variables, character and DATE datatypes must be enclosed in single quotation marks in the SQL statement. One limitation of this is that each argument following the word **start** must be a single word without spaces.

Variable substitutions are not restricted to the SQL statement. The start file also may use variables for such things as SQLPLUS commands.

Variables can be concatenated simply by pushing them together. You can concatenate a variable with a constant by using a period:

```
select SUM(Amount)
  from LEDGER
 where ActionDate BETWEEN '01-&&Month.-01'
                     AND LAST_DAY(TO_DATE('01-&&Month.-01'));
```

This **select** statement will query once for a month and then build the two dates using a period as a concatenation operator.

NOTE
No period is necessary before the variable—only after it. The ampersand (&) tells SQLPLUS that a variable is beginning.

Related set Commands

Normally, the ampersand denotes a variable. This can be changed with **set define** followed by the single symbol that you'd prefer to use to denote a variable.

    set escape defines a character you can place just in front of the ampersand (or other defined symbol) so that SQLPLUS will treat the symbol as a literal, not as denoting a variable.

    set concat can change the default concatenation operator for variables, which is the period, to another single symbol. This variable concatenation is used in addition to, and separately from, the SQL concatenation operator, which is usually two broken vertical bars (||).

    set scan turns variable substitution **off** or **on** for the SQL statement. If **scan** is **off**, any variable in a **select** statement is treated as a literal—for example, **&Test** is treated as the literal word **&Test**, not as the value it is defined as. Variables used in SQLPLUS commands, however, are still substituted as before.

CHAPTER
17

DECODE: Amazing Power in a Single Word

he **DECODE** function is without doubt one of the most powerful in Oracle's SQL. It is one of several extensions Oracle added to the standard SQL language. This chapter will explore a number of ways that **DECODE** can be used, including the generation of "cross-tab" reports.

This is an advanced and often difficult chapter. Most of what is illustrated here is unnecessary for the vast majority of reporting; don't be concerned if it seems beyond your needs. Its real value is more for sophisticated reporting and programming.

if, then, else

In programming and logic, a common construction of a problem is in the pattern *if, then, else.* For example, *if* this day is a Saturday, *then* Adah will play at home; *if* this day is a Sunday, *then* Adah will go to her grandparent's home; *if* this day is a holiday, *then* Adah will go over to Aunt Dora's; *else* Adah will go to school. In each case, "this day" was tested, and if it was one of a list of certain days, then a certain result followed, or else (if it was none of those days) another result followed. **DECODE** follows this kind of logic. Chapter 10 provided an introduction that demonstrated the basic structure and usage of **DECODE**.

This is **DECODE**'s format:

```
DECODE(value,if1,then1,if2,then2,if3,then3,. . . ,else)
```

value represents any column in a table (regardless of datatype) or any result of a computation, such as one date minus another, a **SUBSTR** of a character column, one number times another, and so on. *value* is tested for each row. If *value* equals *if1*, then the result of the **DECODE** is *then1*; if *value* equals *if2*, then the result of the **DECODE** is *then2*; and so on, for virtually as many *if/then* pairs as you can construct. If *value* equals none of the *if*s, then the result of the **DECODE** is *else*. Each of the *if*s, *then*s, and the *else* also can be a column or the result of a function or computation.

Example: Aging Invoices

Suppose George Talbot had a table or a view called INVOICE that contained outstanding invoices, their dates, and the related client names. If he were to look at this on December 15, 1901, it might contain the results shown in Figure 17-1.

```
column ClientName format a14
column InvoiceDate heading 'Date of|Invoice'

select ClientName, InvoiceDate, Amount
  from INVOICE;
```

```
                  Date of
CLIENTNAME        Invoice   AMOUNT
---------------   --------- ------
ELBERT TALBOT     23-OCT-01   5.03
JOHN PEARSON      09-NOV-01   2.02
DICK JONES        12-SEP-01  11.12
GENERAL STORE     09-NOV-01  22.10
ADAH TALBOT       17-NOV-01   8.29
GENERAL STORE     01-SEP-01  21.32
ADAH TALBOT       15-NOV-01   7.33
GENERAL STORE     04-OCT-01   8.42
KAY WALLBOM       04-OCT-01   1.43
JOHN PEARSON      13-OCT-01  12.41
DICK JONES        23-OCT-01   4.49
GENERAL STORE     23-NOV-01  40.36
GENERAL STORE     30-OCT-01   7.47
MORRIS ARNOLD     03-OCT-01   3.55
ROLAND BRANDT     22-OCT-01  13.65
MORRIS ARNOLD     21-SEP-01   9.87
VICTORIA LYNN     09-OCT-01   8.98
GENERAL STORE     22-OCT-01  17.58
```

FIGURE 17-1.   *Clients and invoice amounts due*

As he looks through this list, he realizes some of these invoices have been outstanding for a rather long time. He asks you to try to analyze how serious a problem he has. Your first attempt is to put the clients in order by date, as shown in Figure 17-2.

This is more useful, but it still doesn't produce any real insights into the magnitude of Talbot's problem. Therefore, you create a **DECODE** expression to show how these invoices and amounts are spread through time. This is shown in

```
select ClientName, InvoiceDate, Amount
  from INVOICE
  order by InvoiceDate;

                       Date of
CLIENTNAME             Invoice    AMOUNT
----------------       ---------  ------
GENERAL STORE          01-SEP-01   21.32
DICK JONES             12-SEP-01   11.12
MORRIS ARNOLD          21-SEP-01    9.87
MORRIS ARNOLD          03-OCT-01    3.55
GENERAL STORE          04-OCT-01    8.42
KAY WALLBOM            04-OCT-01    1.43
VICTORIA LYNN          09-OCT-01    8.98
JOHN PEARSON           13-OCT-01   12.41
ROLAND BRANDT          22-OCT-01   13.65
GENERAL STORE          22-OCT-01   17.58
ELBERT TALBOT          23-OCT-01    5.03
DICK JONES             23-OCT-01    4.49
GENERAL STORE          30-OCT-01    7.47
JOHN PEARSON           09-NOV-01    2.02
GENERAL STORE          09-NOV-01   22.10
ADAH TALBOT            15-NOV-01    7.33
ADAH TALBOT            17-NOV-01    8.29
GENERAL STORE          23-NOV-01   40.36
```

FIGURE 17-2. *Clients in order by invoice date*

Figure 17-3. Consider just the **DECODE** expression for NINETY days, which will show the logic used in each of the **DECODE** expressions:

```
DECODE(TRUNC((AsOf-InvoiceDate)/30),3,Amount,NULL) AS NINETY
```

AsOf is a date: December 15, 1901. The date here is from a small table, ASOF, created just for "as of " reporting and with only one date in it. SysDate also might be used if a query like this were always current, but AsOf is more useful when the report will be "as of" a certain day, rather than today. (A variable also could be used in a start file, with the **TO_DATE** function.)

The value that is being decoded is a computation. It extends from the *T* after the opening parenthesis to the first comma. In this **DECODE**, the InvoiceDate of each row is subtracted from the AsOf date. The result is the number of days that have elapsed since the invoice date. This interval is now divided by 30, giving the number of 30-day periods since the invoice date.

```
select ClientName,
       TRUNC((AsOf-InvoiceDate)/30) AS DAYS,
       DECODE(TRUNC((AsOf-InvoiceDate)/30),0,Amount, NULL) AS THIS,
       DECODE(TRUNC((AsOf-InvoiceDate)/30),1,Amount, NULL) AS THIRTY,
       DECODE(TRUNC((AsOf-InvoiceDate)/30),2,Amount, NULL) AS SIXTY,
       DECODE(TRUNC((AsOf-InvoiceDate)/30),3,Amount, NULL) AS NINETY
   from INVOICE, ASOF
 order by InvoiceDate;


CLIENTNAME        DAYS   THIS    THIRTY   SIXTY   NINETY
------------      -----  -----   -------  ------  -------
GENERAL STORE       3                             21.32
DICK JONES          3                             11.12
MORRIS ARNOLD       2                     9.87
MORRIS ARNOLD       2                     3.55
GENERAL STORE       2                     8.42
KAY WALLBOM         2                     1.43
VICTORIA LYNN       2                     8.98
JOHN PEARSON        2                     12.41
ROLAND BRANDT       1           13.65
GENERAL STORE       1           17.58
ELBERT TALBOT       1           5.03
DICK JONES          1           4.49
GENERAL STORE       1           7.47
JOHN PEARSON        1           2.02
GENERAL STORE       1           22.1
ADAH TALBOT         1           7.33
ADAH TALBOT         0    8.29
GENERAL STORE       0    40.36
```

FIGURE 17-3.   *DECODE used to spread amounts due over time*

For intervals other than exact multiples of 30, this will not be a whole number, so it's truncated, thereby assuring a whole number as a result. Any date less than 30 days before December 15 will produce a 0. A date 30 to 59 days before will produce a 1. A date 60 to 89 days before will produce a 2. A date 90 to 119 days before will produce a 3. The number 0, 1, 2, or 3 is the *value* in the **DECODE** statement.

Look again at the last **DECODE**. Following the first comma is a 3. This is the *if* test. If the *value* is 3, *then* the whole **DECODE** statement will be the Amount in this row. If the *value* is anything other than 3 (meaning less than 90 days or more than 119), the **DECODE** will be equal to **NULL**. Compare the invoice dates in Figure 17-2 with the amounts in the NINETY column of Figure 17-3, and you'll see how this logic works.

Collecting Clients Together

As the next step in your analysis, you may want to collect all the clients together, along with the amounts they owe by period. A simple **order by** added to the last SQL statement accomplishes this, as shown in Figure 17-4.

```
select ClientName,
       TRUNC((AsOf-InvoiceDate)/30) AS DAYS,
       DECODE(TRUNC((AsOf-InvoiceDate)/30),0,Amount, NULL) AS THIS,
       DECODE(TRUNC((AsOf-InvoiceDate)/30),1,Amount, NULL) AS THIRTY,
       DECODE(TRUNC((AsOf-InvoiceDate)/30),2,Amount, NULL) AS SIXTY,
       DECODE(TRUNC((AsOf-InvoiceDate)/30),3,Amount, NULL) AS NINETY
  from INVOICE, ASOF
 order by ClientName, InvoiceDate;
```

CLIENTNAME	DAYS	THIS	THIRTY	SIXTY	NINETY
ADAH TALBOT	1		7.33		
ADAH TALBOT	0	8.29			
DICK JONES	3				11.12
DICK JONES	1		4.49		
ELBERT TALBOT	1		5.03		
GENERAL STORE	3				21.32
GENERAL STORE	2			8.42	
GENERAL STORE	1		17.58		
GENERAL STORE	1		7.47		
GENERAL STORE	1		22.1		
GENERAL STORE	0	40.36			
JOHN PEARSON	2			12.41	
JOHN PEARSON	1		2.02		
KAY WALLBOM	2			1.43	
MORRIS ARNOLD	2			9.87	
MORRIS ARNOLD	2			3.55	
ROLAND BRANDT	1		13.65		
VICTORIA LYNN	2			8.98	

FIGURE 17-4. *Client invoices grouped together*

Unfortunately, each invoice produces its own row in this display. It would be more useful to total up the amounts owed if each client took up a single row, with the amount owed spread out by period. This is done with a view:

```
create or replace view AGING as
select ClientName,
       SUM(DECODE(TRUNC((AsOf-InvoiceDate)/30),0,Amount,NULL))
          AS THIS,
       SUM(DECODE(TRUNC((AsOf-InvoiceDate)/30),1,Amount,NULL))
          AS THIRTY,
       SUM(DECODE(TRUNC((AsOf-InvoiceDate)/30),2,Amount,NULL))
          AS SIXTY,
       SUM(DECODE(TRUNC((AsOf-InvoiceDate)/30),3,Amount,NULL))
          AS NINETY,
       SUM(Amount) AS TOTAL
  from INVOICE, ASOF
 group by ClientName;
```

The view is followed by a simple query, with column headings, and **compute** and **break on** used to show totals by column. Each client is consolidated to a single row, showing the amount owed per period, as well as in total. The query is shown in Figure 17-5.

Flipping a Table onto Its Side

A table, as we have seen again and again, is made up of columns and rows. The columns are *predefined*: each has a specific name and datatype, and there are a limited number of them per table. Rows are different: in any table, they will vary in number from zero to millions, and the value in a column can change from row to row, and is not predefined. It can be virtually anything, so long as it fits the datatype.

This states the general case—that is, it is true of tables in general. However, tables are often much more restricted, stable, and defined than this. A table of holiday names, for instance, won't require new rows of holidays very often.

Other tables are somewhat more volatile, but may remain stable for an extended period of time, or the values in certain columns, such as the names of major clients, may remain unchanged. Circumstances like these provide the opportunity to use **DECODE** in a most unusual way: to flip a table on its side, to turn some of the values in rows into columns. Here, the INVOICE table is turned sideways in a view

```
column User noprint
column This heading 'CURRENT'
compute sum of This Thirty Sixty Ninety Total on User
break on Report skip 1

select *
  from AGING;
```

CLIENTNAME	CURRENT	THIRTY	SIXTY	NINETY	TOTAL
ADAH TALBOT	8.29	7.33			15.62
DICK JONES		4.49		11.12	15.61
ELBERT TALBOT		5.03			5.03
GENERAL STORE	40.36	47.15	8.42	21.32	117.25
JOHN PEARSON		2.02	12.41		14.43
KAY WALLBOM			1.43		1.43
MORRIS ARNOLD			13.42		13.42
ROLAND BRANDT		13.65			13.65
VICTORIA LYNN			8.98		8.98
	48.65	79.67	44.66	32.44	205.42

FIGURE 17-5. *Clients consolidated to a single row each*

called ClientByDate. For each InvoiceDate, each ClientName becomes a number column containing the amount of the invoice on that date:

```
create or replace view ClientByDate as
select InvoiceDate,
       SUM(DECODE(ClientName,'ADAH TALBOT', Amount, 0))
          AS AdahTalbot,
       SUM(DECODE(ClientName,'ELBERT TALBOT', Amount, 0))
          AS ElbertTalbot,
       SUM(DECODE(ClientName,'VICTORIA LYNN', Amount, 0))
          AS VictoriaLynn,
       SUM(DECODE(ClientName,'JOHN PEARSON', Amount, 0))
          AS JohnPearson,
       SUM(DECODE(ClientName,'DICK JONES', Amount, 0))
          AS DickJones,
       SUM(DECODE(ClientName,'GENERAL STORE', Amount, 0))
          AS GeneralStore,
       SUM(DECODE(ClientName,'KAY WALLBOM', Amount, 0))
          AS KayWallbom,
       SUM(DECODE(ClientName,'MORRIS ARNOLD', Amount, 0))
```

```
        AS MorrisArnold,
    SUM(DECODE(ClientName,'ROLAND BRANDT', Amount, 0))
        AS RolandBrandt
  from INVOICE
group by InvoiceDate;
```

When this view is described, it reveals this:

```
describe CLIENTBYDATE

Name                                   Null?    Type
-----------------------------------    -------  ----
INVOICEDATE                                     DATE
ADAHTALBOT                                      NUMBER
ELBERTTALBOT                                    NUMBER
VICTORIALYNN                                    NUMBER
JOHNPEARSON                                     NUMBER
DICKJONES                                       NUMBER
GENERALSTORE                                    NUMBER
KAYWALLBOM                                      NUMBER
MORRISARNOLD                                    NUMBER
ROLANDBRANDT                                    NUMBER
```

Querying this view reveals a row for every date, with either 0 or an amount owed under each column (see Figure 17-6). Note that only five of the clients were included in this query, simply to make it easier to read.

This view could have a further view built upon it, perhaps summing the totals by client for all dates and consolidating horizontally all amounts for all clients. This method turns vertical calculations into horizontal ones, and horizontal calculations into vertical ones. It is especially powerful in complex array and matrix-like computations. In effect, this flipping is also what was done in the invoice-aging example, where the InvoiceDate, broken into 30-day periods, was converted into four columns.

Using MOD in DECODE

The modulus function, **MOD**, can be used in conjunction with **DECODE** and RowNum to produce useful effects. RowNum is a pseudo-column (a column that isn't really in the table, such as SysDate). It is the number of each row counted as it is retrieved from the database; that is, when you execute a **select** statement, the first row returned is given the RowNum of 1, the second is assigned 2, and so on. RowNum is not a part of the row's location in the table or database, and has nothing to do with RowID. It is a number tacked onto the row as it is being pulled from the database.

```
column InvoiceDate heading 'Date of|Invoice'

select InvoiceDate, ElbertTalbot, GeneralStore, DickJones, KayWallbom,
       RolandBrandt
  from CLIENTBYDATE;
```

Date of Invoice	ELBERTTALBOT	GENERALSTORE	DICKJONES	KAYWALLBOM	ROLANDBRANDT
01-SEP-01	0	21.32	0	0	0
12-SEP-01	0	0	11.12	0	0
21-SEP-01	0	0	0	0	0
03-OCT-01	0	0	0	0	0
04-OCT-01	0	8.42	0	1.43	0
09-OCT-01	0	0	0	0	0
13-OCT-01	0	0	0	0	0
22-OCT-01	0	17.58	0	0	13.65
23-OCT-01	5.03	0	4.49	0	0
30-OCT-01	0	7.47	0	0	0
09-NOV-01	0	22.1	0	0	0
15-NOV-01	0	0	0	0	0
17-NOV-01	0	0	0	0	0
23-NOV-01	0	40.36	0	0	0

FIGURE 17-6. *A table flipped on its side*

In Figure 17-7, a **select** statement retrieves the InvoiceDate and Amount from the INVOICE table. The RowNum also is displayed in the far-left column. The second column is a combination of **DECODE** and **MOD**. Each RowNum is divided by 5 in the modulus function. The result is the value in the **DECODE**. If RowNum is evenly divisible by 5, the result of **MOD** is 0, and then the result of the **DECODE** is RowNum. If RowNum is not a multiple of 5, the result of **MOD** will not be 0, so **DECODE** will produce a **NULL** result.

Since **DECODE** acts by comparing a value to another value, you can use **MOD** within **DECODE** to facilitate comparisons. For example, for any integer value, **MOD**(*value*,1) will always be 0. If you need to perform different operations based for integer values, then your **DECODE** clause may be of the form:

```
DECODE(MOD(value,1),0,if_integer_clause,if_not_integer_clause)
```

order by and RowNum

Because RowNum can be used to such great benefit in **DECODE**, it's important to understand that this number is attached to a row when it is first pulled from the database, *before* Oracle executes any **order by** you've given it. As a result, if you

```
column Line Format 9999
select RowNum,DECODE(MOD(RowNum,5),0,RowNum, NULL) Line,
       InvoiceDate,Amount
  from INVOICE;
```

| | | Date of | |
ROWNUM	LINE	Invoice	AMOUNT
1		23-OCT-01	5.03
2		09-NOV-01	2.02
3		12-SEP-01	11.12
4		09-NOV-01	22.1
5	5	17-NOV-01	8.29
6		01-SEP-01	21.32
7		15-NOV-01	7.33
8		04-OCT-01	8.42
9		04-OCT-01	1.43
10	10	13-OCT-01	12.41
11		23-OCT-01	4.49
12		23-NOV-01	40.36
13		30-OCT-01	7.47
14		03-OCT-01	3.55
15	15	22-OCT-01	13.65
16		21-SEP-01	9.87
17		22-OCT-01	17.58
18		09-OCT-01	8.98

FIGURE 17-7. *Numbering lines using **DECODE** and **MOD***

attempt to add an **order by** to the first query that used **DECODE** and **MOD**, you get the results shown in Figure 17-8.

You can see that the **order by** has rearranged the order of the row numbers, which destroys the usefulness of the **DECODE**.

NOTE
*If it is important to put the rows in a certain order, such as by InvoiceDate, and also to use the features of the **DECODE**, **MOD**, and RowNum combination, this can be accomplished by creating a view where a **group by** does the ordering, as shown here:*

```
create or replace view DATEANDAMOUNT as
select InvoiceDate, Amount
  from INVOICE
 group by InvoiceDate, Amount;
```

See "order by in Views" in Chapter 18 for warnings about this practice.

```
select RowNum,DECODE(MOD(RowNum,5),0,RowNum,NULL) Line,
       InvoiceDate,Amount
  from INVOICE
 order by InvoiceDate;

                     Date of
    ROWNUM  LINE   Invoice     AMOUNT
    --------  ----   ---------   -------
         6            01-SEP-01    21.32
         3            12-SEP-01    11.12
        16            21-SEP-01     9.87
        14            03-OCT-01     3.55
         8            04-OCT-01     8.42
         9            04-OCT-01     1.43
        18            09-OCT-01     8.98
        10     10    13-OCT-01    12.41
        15     15    22-OCT-01    13.65
        17            22-OCT-01    17.58
         1            23-OCT-01     5.03
        11            23-OCT-01     4.49
        13            30-OCT-01     7.47
         2            09-NOV-01     2.02
         4            09-NOV-01     22.1
         7            15-NOV-01     7.33
         5      5    17-NOV-01     8.29
        12            23-NOV-01    40.36
```

FIGURE 17-8.   *The effect of **order by** on RowNum*

The **select** statement then attaches row numbers to each row as it is retrieved from this view, and the goal of date order, and the use of **DECODE**, **MOD**, and RowNum, is accomplished, as shown in Figure 17-9.

Columns and Computations in then and else

Thus far, the *value* portion of **DECODE** has been the only real location of column names or computations. These can easily occur in the *then* and *else* portions of **DECODE**, as well. Suppose Talbot has a PAY table that lists workers and their daily rates of pay, as shown in Figure 17-10. He also constructs an AVERAGEPAY view, which calculates the average pay of all his workers:

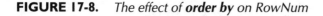

```
create or replace view AVERAGEPAY as
select AVG(DailyRate) AveragePay
  from PAY;
```

```
select RowNum,DECODE(MOD(RowNum,5),0,RowNum,NULL) Line,
       InvoiceDate,Amount
  from DATEANDAMOUNT;
```

```
                 Date of
ROWNUM   LINE   Invoice      AMOUNT
-------- ----   ---------    -------
       1         01-SEP-01    21.32
       2         12-SEP-01    11.12
       3         21-SEP-01     9.87
       4         03-OCT-01     3.55
       5      5  04-OCT-01     1.43
       6         04-OCT-01     8.42
       7         09-OCT-01     8.98
       8         13-OCT-01    12.41
       9         22-OCT-01    13.65
      10     10  22-OCT-01    17.58
      11         23-OCT-01     4.49
      12         23-OCT-01     5.03
      13         30-OCT-01     7.47
      14         09-NOV-01     2.02
      15     15  09-NOV-01    22.1
      16         15-NOV-01     7.33
      17         17-NOV-01     8.29
      18         23-NOV-01    40.36
```

FIGURE 17-9.   *Using **group by** in place of **order by** for RowNum*

```
column DailyRate format 9999999.99
select Name, DailyRate from PAY;
```

```
NAME                     DAILYRATE
------------------------ ----------
ADAH TALBOT                   1.00
ANDREW DYE                     .75
BART SARJEANT                  .75
DICK JONES                    1.00
GEORGE OSCAR                  1.25
PAT LAVAY                     1.25
```

FIGURE 17-10.   *Talbot's workers and daily rates of pay*

Talbot then decides to give his workers a raise. Those workers earning exactly the average wage continue to earn the (existing) average wage. The rest will get a 15-percent pay hike. In this **select** statement, the *value* in the **DECODE** is DailyRate. The *if* is AveragePay. The *then* is DailyRate. The *else* is DailyRate times 1.15. This illustrates the use of columns and computations in the *if, then,* and *else* portions of **DECODE**, as demonstrated in Figure 17-11.

Greater Than, Less Than, and Equal To in DECODE

The format of the **DECODE** statement would seem to imply that it really can only do a series of equality tests, since the *value* is successively tested for equality against a list of *if*s. However, clever use of functions and computations in the place of *value* can allow **DECODE** to have the effective ability to act based on a value being greater than, less than, or equal to another value.

In Figure 17-12, for example, DailyRate is compared to AveragePay for each worker. Those who make more than the AveragePay are given a 5-percent raise. Those who make less than average are given a 15-percent raise. Those who make exactly average wages get no raise at all. How is this accomplished?

```
column NewRate    format 9999999.99

select Name, DailyRate,
       DECODE( DailyRate, AveragePay, DailyRate,
       DailyRate*1.15) AS NewRate
  from PAY, AVERAGEPAY;

NAME                          DAILYRATE    NEWRATE
---------------------------   ----------   ----------
ADAH TALBOT                           1       1.00
ANDREW DYE                          .75        .86
BART SARJEANT                       .75        .86
DICK JONES                            1       1.00
GEORGE OSCAR                       1.25       1.44
PAT LAVAY                          1.25       1.44
```

FIGURE 17-11.   *A 15-percent pay hike for workers not earning the average pay*

```
select Name, DailyRate,
       DECODE( SIGN( (DailyRate/AveragePay)-1 ),
         1, DailyRate*1.05, -1, DailyRate*1.15, DailyRate) AS NewRate
  from PAY, AVERAGEPAY;


NAME                      DAILYRATE    NEWRATE
----------------------    ----------   ----------
ADAH TALBOT                    1.00        1.00
ANDREW DYE                      .75         .86
BART SARJEANT                   .75         .86
DICK JONES                     1.00        1.00
GEORGE OSCAR                   1.25        1.31
PAT LAVAY                      1.25        1.31
```

FIGURE 17-12.   *Pay hikes based on ratio of worker's pay to average*

The DailyRate is divided by the AveragePay. For someone earning more than average, this ratio will be a number greater than 1. For someone earning exactly the average wage, this ratio will be exactly the number 1. And for those earning less than average wages, this ratio will be a number less than 1 but greater than 0.

Now subtract 1 from each of these numbers. Big earners will get a number above 0. Average earners will get a 0. Small earners will get a number below 0.

The **SIGN** of each of these is 1, 0, and --1 (see Chapter 8 for a review of **SIGN**). Thus, the *value* in the **DECODE** is 1, 0, or --1, depending upon wages. If it is 1, DailyRate is multiplied by 1.05. If it is --1, DailyRate is multiplied by 1.15. If it is 0 (the *else*), the worker continues to get DailyRate.

This approach can be used to accomplish complex, single-pass updates, whereas the alternative would be a series of **update** statements with different **set** statements and **where** clauses.

This same approach can be used with other functions, as well. **GREATEST**, with a list of columns, could be the *value* in **DECODE**, or the *if, then*, or *else*. Extremely complex procedural logic can be used when it is needed.

To summarize this chapter, **DECODE** is a powerful function that uses *if, then, else* logic, and that can be combined with other Oracle functions to produce spreads of values (such as aging of invoices), effectively flip tables onto their sides, control display and page movement, make calculations, and force row-by-row changes based on the *value* in a column (or computation) being tested.

CHAPTER
18

Creating, Dropping,
and Altering Tables
and Views

ntil now, the emphasis of this book has been on using tables. This chapter looks at creating, dropping, and changing tables, creating views, and creating a table from a table.

Creating a Table

Consider the TROUBLE table. This is similar to the COMFORT table discussed earlier in the book, but is used to track cities with unusual weather patterns.

 `describe TROUBLE`

```
Name                             Null?    Type
-------------------------------- -------- ----
CITY                             NOT NULL VARCHAR2(13)
SAMPLEDATE                       NOT NULL DATE
NOON                                      NUMBER(3,1)
MIDNIGHT                                  NUMBER(3,1)
PRECIPITATION                             NUMBER
```

The columns in the TROUBLE table represent the three major datatypes in Oracle—VARCHAR2, DATE, and NUMBER. Here is the SQL that created this Oracle table:

```
create table TROUBLE (
City          VARCHAR2(13) NOT NULL,
SampleDate    DATE NOT NULL,
Noon          NUMBER(3,1),
Midnight      NUMBER(3,1),
Precipitation NUMBER
);
```

These are the basic elements of this command:

- The words **create table**
- The name of the table
- An opening parenthesis
- Column definitions
- A closing parenthesis
- A SQL terminator

The individual column definitions are separated by commas. There is no comma after the last column definition. The table and column names must start with a letter of the alphabet, but may include letters, numbers, and underscores. Names may be 1 to 30 characters in length, must be unique within the table, and cannot be an Oracle reserved word (see "Object Names" in the Alphabetical Reference of this book).

Case does not matter in creating a table. There are no options for DATE datatypes. Character datatypes must have their maximum length specified. NUMBERs may be either high-precision (up to 38 digits) or specified-precision, based on the maximum number of digits and the number of places allowed to the right of the decimal (an Amount field for U.S. currency, for instance, would have only two decimal places).

NOTE
Do not enclose table and column names within double quotes, or case will matter. This can be disastrous for your users or developers.

See Part IV of this book for additional **create table** options for the object-relational features.

Character Width and NUMBER Precision

Specifying the maximum length for character (CHAR and VARCHAR2) columns and the precision for NUMBER columns has consequences that must be considered during the design of the table. Improper decisions can be corrected later, using the **alter table** command, but the process can be difficult.

Deciding on a Proper Width

A character column that is not wide enough for the data you want to put in it will cause an **insert** to fail and result in this error message:

```
ERROR at line 1: ORA-01401: inserted value too large for column
```

The maximum width for CHAR (fixed-length) columns is 2,000 characters. VARCHAR2 (varying-length character) columns can have up to 4,000 characters. In assigning width to a column, allot enough space to allow for all future possibilities. A CHAR(15) for a city name, for instance, is just going to get you in trouble later on. You'll have to either alter the table or truncate or distort the names of some cities.

NOTE
*There is no penalty in Oracle for defining a wide VARCHAR2 column. Oracle is clever enough not to store blank spaces at the end of VARCHAR2 columns. The city name SAN FRANCISCO, for example, will be stored in 13 spaces even if you've defined the column as VARCHAR2(50). And if a column has nothing in it (**NULL**), Oracle will store nothing in the column, not even a blank space (it does store a couple of bytes of internal database control information, but this is unaffected by the size you specify for the column). The only effect that choosing a higher number will have is in the default SQLPLUS column formatting. SQLPLUS will create a default heading the same width as the VARCHAR2 definition.*

Choosing NUMBER Precision

A NUMBER column with incorrect precision will have one of two consequences. Oracle will either reject the attempt to **insert** the row of data, or drop some of the data's precision. Here are four rows of data about to be entered into Oracle:

```
insert into TROUBLE values
    ('PLEASANT LAKE', TO_DATE('21-MAR-1999','DD-MON-YYYY'),
     39.99,  -1.31, 3.6);

insert into TROUBLE values
    ('PLEASANT LAKE', TO_DATE('22-JUN-1999','DD-MON-YYYY'),
     101.44,  86.2, 1.63);

insert into TROUBLE values
    ('PLEASANT LAKE', TO_DATE('23-SEP-1999','DD-MON-YYYY'),
     92.85,  79.6, 1.00003);

insert into TROUBLE values
    ('PLEASANT LAKE', TO_DATE('22-DEC-1999','DD-MON-YYYY'),
     -17.445, -10.4, 2.4);
```

These are the results of this attempt:

```
1 row created.

insert into TROUBLE values ('PLEASANT LAKE',
```

```
    TO_DATE('22-JUN-1999','DD-MON-YYYY'), 101.44, 86.2, 1.63)
```

```
ERROR at line 1: ORA-01438: value larger than specified
precision allowed for this column
1 row created.
```

```
1 row created.
```

The first, third, and fourth rows were inserted, but the second **insert** failed because 101.44 exceeded the precision set in the **create table** statement, where Noon was defined as NUMBER(3,1). The 3 here indicates the maximum number of digits Oracle will store. The 1 means that one of those three digits is reserved for a position to the right of the decimal point. Thus, 12.3 would be a legitimate number, but 123.4 would not be.

Note that the error here is caused by the 101, not the .44, because NUMBER(3,1) leaves only two positions available to the left of the decimal point. The .44 will not cause the "value larger than specified precision" error. It would simply be rounded to one decimal place. This will be demonstrated shortly, but first, look at the results of a query of the four rows we've attempted to **insert**:

```
select * from TROUBLE;
```

```
CITY            SAMPLEDAT     NOON MIDNIGHT PRECIPITATION
-------------  ---------  -------- -------- -------------
PLEASANT LAKE  21-MAR-99     39.9    -1.31           3.6
PLEASANT LAKE  23-SEP-99     92.9    79.6        1.00003
PLEASANT LAKE  22-DEC-99    -17.4   -10.4           2.4
```

The three rows were successfully inserted; only the problematic row is missing. Oracle automatically backed out the single **insert** statement that failed.

Rounding During Insertion

If you correct the **create table** statement and increase the number of digits available for Noon and Midnight, as shown here:

```
create table TROUBLE (
City           VARCHAR2(13) NOT NULL,
SampleDate     DATE NOT NULL,
Noon           NUMBER(4,1),
Midnight       NUMBER(4,1),
Precipitation  NUMBER
);
```

then the four **insert** statements will all be successful. A query now will reveal this:

```
select * from TROUBLE;

CITY           SAMPLEDAT   NOON MIDNIGHT PRECIPITATION
-------------- --------- -------- -------- -------------
PLEASANT LAKE 21-MAR-99       40     -1.3           3.6
PLEASANT LAKE 22-JUN-99    101.4     86.2          1.63
PLEASANT LAKE 23-SEP-99     92.9     79.6       1.00003
PLEASANT LAKE 22-DEC-99    -17.4    -10.4           2.4
```

Look at the first **insert** statement. The value for Noon is 39.99. In the query, it is rounded to 40. Midnight in the **insert** is -1.31. In the query it is -1.3. Oracle rounds the number based on the digit just to the right of the allowed precision. Table 18-1 shows the effects of precision in several examples.

In insert Statement	Actual Value in Table
For precision of NUMBER(4,1)	
123.4	123.4
123.44	123.4
123.45	123.5
123.445	123.4
1234.5	**insert** fails
For precision of NUMBER(4)	
123.4	123
123.44	123
123.45	123
123.445	123
1234.5	1235
12345	**insert** fails

TABLE 18-1. *Examples of the Effect of Precision on Inserted Values*

In insert Statement	Actual Value in Table
For precision of NUMBER(4,-1)	
123.4	120
123.44	120
123.45	120
123.445	120
125	130
1234.5	1230
12345	**insert** fails
For precision of NUMBER	
123.4	123.4
123.44	123.44
123.45	123.45
123.445	123.445
125	125
1234.5	1234.5
12345.6789012345678	12345.6789012345678

TABLE 18-1. *Examples of the Effect of Precision on Inserted Values* (continued)

Constraints in create table

The **create table** statement lets you enforce several different kinds of constraints on a table: candidate keys, primary keys, foreign keys, and check conditions. A **constraint** clause can constrain a single column or group of columns in a table. The point of these constraints is to get Oracle to do most of the work in maintaining the integrity of your database. The more constraints you add to a table definition, the less work you have to do in applications to maintain the data. On the other hand, the more constraints there are in a table, the longer it takes to update the data.

There are two ways to specify constraints: as part of the column definition (a *column* constraint) or at the end of the **create table** statement (a *table* constraint). Clauses that constrain several columns must be table constraints.

The Candidate Key

A *candidate key* is a combination of one or more columns, the values of which uniquely identify each row of a table. The following listing shows the creation of a UNIQUE constraint for the TROUBLE table:

```
create table TROUBLE (
City            VARCHAR2(13) NOT NULL,
SampleDate      DATE NOT NULL,
Noon            NUMBER(4,1),
Midnight        NUMBER(4,1),
Precipitation NUMBER,
constraint TROUBLE_UQ UNIQUE (City, SampleDate)
);
```

The key of this table is the combination of City and SampleDate. Notice that both columns are also declared to be **NOT NULL**. This feature allows you to prevent data from being entered into the table without certain columns having data in them. Clearly, temperature and precipitation information is not useful without knowing where or when it was collected. This technique is common for columns that are the primary key of a table, but is also useful if certain columns are critical for the row of data to be meaningful. If **NOT NULL** isn't specified, the column can have **NULL** values.

The Primary Key

The *primary key* of a table is one of the candidate keys that you give some special characteristics. You can have only one primary key, and a primary key column cannot contain **NULL**s:

```
create table TROUBLE (
City            VARCHAR2(13),
SampleDate      DATE,
Noon            NUMBER(4,1),
Midnight        NUMBER(4,1),
Precipitation NUMBER,
constraint TROUBLE_PK PRIMARY KEY (City, SampleDate)
);
```

This **create table** statement has the same effect as the previous one, except that you can have several UNIQUE constraints but only one PRIMARY KEY constraint.

For single-column primary or candidate keys, you can define the key on the column with a column constraint instead of a table constraint:

```
create table WORKER (
Name            VARCHAR2(25) PRIMARY KEY,
Age             NUMBER,
Lodging         VARCHAR2(15)
);
```

In this case, the Name column is the primary key, and Oracle will generate a name for the PRIMARY KEY constraint. This is not recommended if you want to enforce a common naming standard for keys, as discussed later in "Naming Constraints."

The Foreign Key

A *foreign key* is a combination of columns with values based on the primary key values from another table. A foreign key constraint, also known as a *referential integrity constraint,* specifies that the values of the foreign key correspond to actual values of the primary key in the other table. In the WORKER table, for example, the Lodging column refers to values for the Lodging column in the LODGING table:

```
create table WORKER (
Name            VARCHAR2(25),
Age             NUMBER,
Lodging         VARCHAR2(15),
constraint      WORKER_PK PRIMARY KEY(Name),
foreign key (Lodging) REFERENCES LODGING(Lodging)
);
```

You can refer to a primary or unique key, even in the same table. However, you can't refer to a table in a remote database in the **references** clause. You can use the table form (which is used here to create a PRIMARY KEY on the TROUBLE table) instead of the column form to specify foreign keys with multiple columns.

Sometimes you may want to delete these dependent rows when you delete the row they depend on. In the case of WORKER and LODGING, if you delete LODGING, you'll want to make the Lodging column **NULL**. In another case, you might want to delete the whole row. The clause **on delete cascade** added to the **references** clause tells Oracle to delete the dependent row when you delete the corresponding row in the parent table. This action automatically maintains referential integrity. For more information on the clauses **on delete cascade** and **references**, consult "Integrity Constraint" in the Alphabetical Reference of this book.

The Check Constraint

Many columns must have values that are within a certain range or that satisfy certain conditions. With a *CHECK constraint,* you can specify an expression that must always be true for every row in the table. For example, if Talbot employs only workers between the ages of 18 and 65, the constraint would look like this:

```
create table WORKER (
Name           VARCHAR2(25),
Age            NUMBER CHECK (Age BETWEEN 18 AND 65),
Lodging        VARCHAR2(15),
constraint     WORKER_PK PRIMARY KEY(Name),
foreign key (Lodging) REFERENCES LODGING(Lodging)
);
```

A column-level CHECK constraint can't refer to values in other rows; it can't use the pseudo-columns SysDate, UID, User, UserEnv, CurrVal, NextVal, Level, or RowNum. You can use the table constraint form (as opposed to the column constraint form) to refer to multiple columns in a CHECK constraint.

Naming Constraints

You can name your constraints. If you use an effective naming scheme for your constraint names, you will be better able to identify and manage the constraints. The name of a constraint should identify the table it acts upon and the type of constraint it represents. For example, the primary key on the TROUBLE table could be named TROUBLE_PK.

You can specify a name for a constraint when you create the constraint. If you do not specify a name for the constraint, then Oracle will generate a name. Most of Oracle's generated constraint names are of the form SYS_C######; for example, SYS_C000145. Since the system-generated constraint name does not tell you anything about the table or the constraint, you should name your constraints.

In the following example, the PRIMARY KEY constraint is created, and named, as part of the **create table** command for the TROUBLE table. Notice the **constraint** clause:

```
create table TROUBLE (
City           VARCHAR2(13),
SampleDate     DATE,
Noon           NUMBER(4,1),
Midnight       NUMBER(4,1),
Precipitation NUMBER,
constraint TROUBLE_PK PRIMARY KEY (City, SampleDate)
);
```

The **constraint** clause of the **create table** command names the constraint (in this case, TROUBLE_PK). You may use this constraint name later when enabling or disabling constraints.

Dropping Tables

Dropping tables is very simple. You use the words **drop table** and the table name, as shown here:

```
drop table TROUBLE;

Table dropped.
```

You drop a table only when you no longer need it. In Oracle, the **truncate** command lets you remove all the rows in the table and reclaim the space for other uses without removing the table definition from the database.

Truncating is also very simple:

```
truncate table TROUBLE;

Table truncated.
```

Truncating can't be rolled back. If there are triggers that delete rows that depend on rows in the table, truncating does not execute those triggers. You should be *sure* you really want to **truncate** before doing it.

Altering Tables

Tables can be altered in one of three ways: by adding a column to an existing table; by changing a column's definition; or by dropping a column. Adding a column is straightforward, and similar to creating a table. Suppose you decide to add two new columns to the TROUBLE table: Condition, which you believe should be **NOT NULL**, and Wind, for the wind speed. The first attempt looks like this:

```
alter table TROUBLE add (
Condition    VARCHAR2(9) NOT NULL,
Wind         NUMBER(3)
);

alter table TROUBLE add (
            *
ERROR at line 1: ORA-01758: table must be empty to add
mandatory (NOT NULL) column
```

You get an error message because you cannot add a column defined as **NOT NULL**—when you try to add it, the column won't have anything in it. Each row in the table would have a new empty column defined as **NOT NULL**.

There are two alternatives. The **alter table** command's **add** clause will work with a **NOT NULL** column if the table is empty, but usually, it is impractical to empty a table of all its rows just to add a **NOT NULL** column. And you can't use Export and Import if you add a column after Exporting but before Importing.

The alternative is to first alter the table by adding the column without the **NOT NULL** restriction:

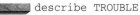
```
alter table TROUBLE add (
Condition     VARCHAR2(9),
Wind          NUMBER(3)
);

Table altered.
```

Then, fill the column with data for every row (either with legitimate data or a placeholder until legitimate data can be obtained):

```
update TROUBLE set Condition = 'SUNNY';
```

Finally, alter the table again, and modify the column definition to **NOT NULL**:

```
alter table TROUBLE modify (
Condition     VARCHAR2(9) NOT NULL,
City          VARCHAR2(17)
);

Table altered.
```

Note that the City column was also modified to enlarge it to 17 characters (just to show how this is done). When the table is described, it shows this:

```
describe TROUBLE
```

```
Name                                Null?     Type
----------------------------------- --------  ----
CITY                                NOT NULL  VARCHAR2(17)
SAMPLEDATE                          NOT NULL  DATE
NOON                                          NUMBER(4,1)
MIDNIGHT                                      NUMBER(4,1)
PRECIPITATION                                 NUMBER
CONDITION                           NOT NULL  VARCHAR2(9)
WIND                                          NUMBER(3)
```

The table contains the following:

```
select * from TROUBLE;

CITY              SAMPLEDAT   NOON MIDNIGHT PRECIPITATION CONDITION WIND
---------------   --------- ------ -------- ------------- --------- ----
PLEASANT LAKE     21-MAR-99     40     -1.3           3.6 SUNNY
PLEASANT LAKE     22-JUN-99  101.4     86.2          1.63 SUNNY
PLEASANT LAKE     23-SEP-99   92.9     79.6       1.00003 SUNNY
PLEASANT LAKE     22-DEC-99  -17.4    -10.4           2.4 SUNNY
```

Here you see the effect of the changes. City is now 17 characters wide instead of 13. Condition has been added to the table as **NOT NULL** and is SUNNY (temporarily). WIND has been added, and is **NULL**.

To make a **NOT NULL** column nullable, use the **alter table** command with the **NULL** clause, as follows:

```
alter table TROUBLE modify
(Condition NULL);
```

The Rules for Adding or Modifying a Column

These are the rules for adding a column to a table:

- You may add a column at any time if **NOT NULL** isn't specified.

- You may add a **NOT NULL** column in three steps:

   1. Add the column without **NOT NULL** specified.

   2. Fill every row in that column with data.

   3. Modify the column to be **NOT NULL**.

These are the rules for modifying a column:

- You can increase a character column's width at any time.

- You can increase the number of digits in a NUMBER column at any time.

- You can increase or decrease the number of decimal places in a NUMBER column at any time.

In addition, if a column is **NULL** for every row of the table, you can make any of these changes:

- You can change the column's datatype.

- You can decrease a character column's width.

- You can decrease the number of digits in a NUMBER column.

You can only change the datatype of a column if the column is empty (**NULL**) in all rows of the table.

Dropping a Column

As of Oracle8i, you can drop a column from a table. Dropping a column is more complicated than adding or modifying a column, because of the additional work that Oracle has to do. Just removing the column from the list of columns in the table—so it doesn't show up when you **select** * from the table—is easy. It's recovering the space that was actually taken up by the column values that is more complex, and potentially very time-consuming for the database. For this reason, you can drop a column immediately or you can mark it as "unused," to be dropped at a later time. If the column is dropped immediately, the action may impact performance. If the column is marked as unused, there will be no impact on performance. The column can actually be dropped at a later time when the database is less heavily used.

To drop a column, use either the **set unused** clause or the **drop** clause of the **alter table** command. You cannot drop a pseudo-column, a column of a nested table, or a partition key column.

In the following example, column Wind is dropped from the TROUBLE table:

```
alter table TROUBLE drop column Wind;
```

Alternatively, you can mark the Wind column as unused:

```
alter table TROUBLE set unused column Wind;
```

Marking a column as "unused" does not release the space previously used by the column, until you drop the unused columns:

```
alter table TROUBLE drop unused columns;
```

You can query USER_UNUSED_COL_TABS, DBA_UNUSED_COL_TABS, and ALL_UNUSED_COL_TABS to see all tables with columns marked as unused.

NOTE
Once you have marked a column as "unused," you cannot access that column.

You can drop multiple columns in a single command, as shown in the following listing:

```
alter table TROUBLE drop (Condition, Wind);
```

NOTE
*When dropping multiple columns, the **column** keyword of the **alter table** command should not be used; it causes a syntax error. The multiple column names must be enclosed in parentheses, as shown in the preceding listing.*

If the dropped columns are part of primary keys or unique constraints, then you will need to also use the **cascade constraints** clause as part of your **alter table** command. If you drop a column that belongs to a primary key, Oracle will drop both the column and the primary key index.

Creating a View

Since you've already seen the techniques for creating a view in prior chapters, they will not be reviewed here. However, this section gives several additional points about views that will prove useful.

If a view is based on a single underlying table, you can **insert**, **update**, or **delete** rows in the view. This will actually insert, update, or delete rows in the underlying table. There are restrictions on your ability to do this, although the restrictions are quite sensible:

■ You cannot **insert** if the underlying table has any **NOT NULL** columns that don't appear in the view.

■ You cannot **insert** or **update** if any one of the view's columns referenced in the **insert** or **update** contains functions or calculations.

■ You cannot **insert**, **update**, or **delete** if the view contains **group by**, **distinct**, or a reference to the pseudo-column RowNum.

You can **insert** into a view based on multiple tables if Oracle can determine the proper rows to insert. In a multitable view, Oracle determines which of the tables are *key-preserved.* If a view contains enough columns from a table to identify the primary key for that table, then the key is preserved and Oracle may be able to insert rows into the table via the view.

Stability of a View

Remember that the results of querying a view are built instantly from a table (or tables) when you execute the query. Until that moment, the view has no data of its own, as a table does. It is merely a description (a SQL statement) of what information to pull out of other tables and how to organize it. As a consequence, if a table is dropped, the validity of a view is destroyed. Attempting to query a view where the underlying table has been dropped will produce an error message about the view.

NOTE
The sole exception to this rule is the use of materialized views, introduced in Oracle8i. In fact, a materialized view is actually a table that stores data one would normally query via a view. Materialized views are very similar in structure to snapshots, and they are described in detail in Chapter 23.

In the following sequence, a view is created on an existing table, the table is dropped, and the view then is queried.
First the view is created:

```
create view RAIN as
select City, Precipitation
   from TROUBLE;

View created.
```

The underlying table is dropped:

```
drop table TROUBLE;

Table dropped.
```

The view is queried:

```
select * from RAIN
              *
ERROR at line 1: ORA-00942: table or view does not exist
```

Similarly, a view is created using the asterisk in the view creation:

```
create view RAIN as
select * from TROUBLE;

View created.
```

But then the underlying table is altered:

```
alter table TROUBLE add (
Warning      VARCHAR2(20)
);

Table altered.
```

Despite the change to the view's base table, the view is still valid and will access the new columns in the TROUBLE table.

To re-create a view while keeping in place all the privileges that have been granted for it, use the **create or replace view** command, as shown in the following listing. This command will replace the view text of an existing view with the new view text, while the old grants on the view will not be affected.

```
create or replace view RAIN as
select * from TROUBLE;
```

order by in Views

You cannot use an **order by** in a **create view** statement. Occasionally, a **group by**, which can be used, may accomplish the purpose for which an **order by** might be used, as was demonstrated in Chapter 17, in the "order by and RowNum" section. However, even if there are no group functions in the **select** clause, the **group by** can still consolidate rows. Consider this query from the COMFORT table with an **order by**:

```
select City, Precipitation
  from COMFORT
 order by Precipitation;
```

```
CITY          PRECIPITATION
------------- -------------
KEENE
SAN FRANCISCO           .1
SAN FRANCISCO           .1
SAN FRANCISCO           .5
KEENE                  1.3
SAN FRANCISCO          2.3
KEENE                  3.9
KEENE                  4.4

8 rows selected.
```

The same query in a view, using a **group by** instead of an **order by**, causes the two identical SAN FRANCISCO rows (with Precipitation of .1) to be compressed into one:

```
create view DISCOMFORT as
select City, Precipitation
  from COMFORT
 group by Precipitation, City;

View created.
```

When queried, only seven rows remain:

```
select * from DISCOMFORT;

CITY          PRECIPITATION
------------- -------------
KEENE
SAN FRANCISCO           .1
SAN FRANCISCO           .5
KEENE                  1.3
SAN FRANCISCO          2.3
KEENE                  3.9
KEENE                  4.4

7 rows selected.
```

This probably isn't what you intended to occur. Although a **group by** will put a view in order, using it for this purpose can cause problems. It is generally better to simply use an **order by** in the **select** statement that queries the view. If you use the preceding method, then you should add the RowNum pseudo-column to the **group by** clause, as shown in the following listing. Since each row will have a unique RowNum value, no rows will be eliminated.

```
create view DISCOMFORT as
select City, Precipitation
  from COMFORT
 group by Precipitation, City, RowNum;
```

Note that the groups are not guaranteed to be presented in order.

Creating a Read-Only View

You can use the **with read only** clause of the **create view** command to prevent users from manipulating records via the view. Consider the RAIN view created in the previous section:

```
create or replace view RAIN as
select * from TROUBLE;
```

If a user has the ability to **delete** records from the TROUBLE table, then the user could **delete** the TROUBLE records via the RAIN view:

```
delete from RAIN;
```

The user could also **insert** or **update** the records in the TROUBLE table by performing those operations against the RAIN view. If the view is based on a join of multiple tables, then the user's ability to **update** the view's records is limited; a view's base tables cannot be updated unless only one table is involved in the **update** and the updated table's full primary key is included in the view's columns.

To prevent modifications to the base tables via a view, you can use the **with read only** clause of the **create view** command. If you use the **with read only** clause when creating a view, users will *only* be able to **select** records from the view. Users will be unable to manipulate the records obtained from the view even if the view is based on a single table:

```
create or replace view RAIN as
select * from TROUBLE
  with read only;
```

You can also use INSTEAD OF triggers to manage the data manipulation commands executed against views. See Chapter 28 for details on INSTEAD OF triggers.

Creating a Table from a Table

The RAIN view that was previously created from the TROUBLE table could alternatively have been a table. Oracle lets you create a new table on the fly, based on a **select** statement on an existing table:

```
create table RAIN as
select City, Precipitation
   from TROUBLE;

Table created.
```

NOTE
*The **create table ... as select ...** command will not work if one of the selected columns uses the LONG datatype.*

When the new table is described, it reveals that it has "inherited" its column definitions from the TROUBLE table. A table created in this fashion can include all columns, using an asterisk if you like, or a subset of columns from another table. It also can include "invented" columns, which are the product of functions or the combination of other columns, just as in a view. The character column definitions will adjust to the size necessary to contain the data in the invented columns. NUMBER columns that had specified precision in the source table, but undergo computation in inventing a new column, will simply be NUMBER columns, with no specified precision, in the new table. When the table RAIN is described, it shows its column definitions:

```
describe RAIN

Name                            Null?    Type
------------------------------- -------- ----
CITY                            NOT NULL VARCHAR2(13)
PRECIPITATION                            NUMBER
```

When RAIN is queried, it contains just the columns and data selected from the TROUBLE table as follows:

```
select * from RAIN;

CITY          PRECIPITATION
------------- -------------
PLEASANT LAKE           3.6
```

```
PLEASANT LAKE          1.63
PLEASANT LAKE        1.00003
PLEASANT LAKE          2.4
```

You also can use this technique to create a table with column definitions like that of the source table, but with no rows in it, by building a **where** clause that will select no rows from the old table:

```
create table RAIN as
select City, Precipitation
  from TROUBLE
 where 1=2;

Table created.
```

Querying this table will show there is nothing in it:

```
select * from RAIN;

no rows selected.
```

You can create a table based on a query without generating *redo log entries* (chronological records of database actions used during database recoveries). Avoiding the generation of these entries is accomplished by using the **nologging** keyword in the **create table** command. When the redo log entries are circumvented in this way, the performance of the **create table** command will improve, since less work is being done; the larger the table, the greater the impact. However, since the new table's creation is not being written to the *redo log files* (which record the redo log entries), the table will not be re-created if, following a database failure, those redo log files are used to recover the database. Therefore, you should consider performing a backup of the database soon after using the **nologging** option if you want to be able to recover the new table.

The following example shows how to use the **nologging** keyword during table creations based on queries. By default, table creations based on queries generate redo log entries.

```
create table RAIN
nologging
as
select * from TROUBLE;

Table created.
```

Note that you can specify **nologging** at the partition level and at the LOB level. The use of **nologging** will improve the performance of the operations that create the initial data in the table. See Chapter 21 for details on the use of **unrecoverable** to improve the performance of bulk data loads.

Creating an Index-Organized Table

An *index-organized table* keeps its data sorted according to the primary key column values for the table. Index-organized tables store their data as if the entire table was stored in an index. Indexes are described more fully in Chapter 20; in Oracle, they serve two main purposes:

- **To enforce uniqueness**   When a PRIMARY KEY or UNIQUE constraint is created, Oracle creates an index to enforce the uniqueness of the indexed columns.

- **To improve performance**   When a query can use an index, the performance of the query may dramatically improve. See Chapter 36 for details on the conditions under which a query may use an index.

An index-organized table allows you to store the entire table's data in an index. A normal index only stores the indexed columns in the index; an index-organized table stores all of the table's columns in the index.

Because the table's data is stored as an index, the rows of the table do not have RowIDs. Therefore, you cannot select the RowID pseudo-column values from an index-only table. In Oracle8, you could not create additional indexes on the table, but this restriction has been removed as of Oracle8i.

To create an index-organized table, use the **organization index** clause of the **create table** command, as shown in the following example:

```
create table TROUBLE (
City          VARCHAR2(13),
SampleDate    DATE,
Noon          NUMBER(4,1),
Midnight      NUMBER(4,1),
Precipitation NUMBER,
constraint TROUBLE_PK PRIMARY KEY (City, SampleDate))
organization index;
```

To create TROUBLE as an index-organized table, you must create a PRIMARY KEY constraint on it.

An index-organized table is appropriate if you will always be accessing the TROUBLE data by the City and SampleDate columns (in the **where** clauses of your queries). To minimize the amount of active management of the index required, you should use index-organized tables only if the table's data is very static. If the table's data changes frequently, or if you need to index additional columns of the table, then you should use a regular table, with indexes as appropriate.

In general, index-organized tables are most effective when the primary key constitutes a large part of the table's columns. If the table contains many frequently accessed columns that are not part of the primary key, then the index-organized table will need to repeatedly access its overflow area. Despite this drawback, you may choose to use index-organized tables to take advantage of a key feature that is not available with standard tables: the ability to use the **move online** option of the **alter table** command. You can use that option to move a table from one tablespace to another while it is being accessed by **insert**s, **update**s, and **delete**s. You cannot use the **move online** option for partitioned index-organized tables. Partitioning is described in the next section.

Using Partitioned Tables

As of Oracle8, you can divide the rows of a single table into multiple parts. Dividing a table's data in this manner is called *partitioning* the table; the table that is partitioned is called a *partitioned table,* and the parts are called *partitions.*

Partitioning is useful for very large tables. By splitting a large table's rows across multiple smaller partitions, you accomplish several important goals:

■ The performance of queries against the tables may improve, since Oracle may have to only search one partition (one part of the table) instead of the entire table to resolve a query.

■ The table may be easier to manage. Since the partitioned table's data is stored in multiple parts, it may be easier to load and delete data in the partitions than in the large table.

■ Backup and recovery operations may perform better. Since the partitions are smaller than the partitioned table, you may have more options for backing up and recovering the partitions than you would have for a single large table.

The Oracle optimizer will know that the table has been partitioned; as shown later in this section, you can also specify the partition to use as part of the **from** clause of your queries.

Creating a Partitioned Table

To create a partitioned table, you specify how to set up the partitions of the table's data as part of the **create table** command. Typically, tables are partitioned by ranges of values.

Consider the WORKER table:

```
create table WORKER (
Name            VARCHAR2(25),
Age             NUMBER,
Lodging         VARCHAR2(15),
constraint      WORKER_PK PRIMARY KEY(Name)
);
```

If you will be storing a large number of records in the WORKER table, then you may wish to separate the WORKER rows across multiple partitions. To partition the table's records, use the **partition by range** clause of the **create table** command, as shown next. The ranges will determine the values stored in each partition.

```
create table WORKER (
Name            VARCHAR2(25),
Age             NUMBER,
Lodging         VARCHAR2(15),
constraint      WORKER_PK PRIMARY KEY(Name)
)
partition by range (Lodging)
  (partition PART1   values less than ('F')
    tablespace PART1_TS,
   partition PART2   values less than ('N')
    tablespace PART2_TS,
   partition PART3   values less than ('T')
    tablespace PART3_TS,
   partition PART4   values less than (MAXVALUE)
    tablespace PART4_TS)
;
```

The WORKER table will be partitioned based on the values in the Lodging column:

```
partition by range (Lodging)
```

For any Lodging values less than *F*, the record will be stored in the partition named PART1. The PART1 partition will be stored in the PART1_TS tablespace (see Chapter 20 for details on tablespaces). Any Lodging in the range between *F* and *N* will be stored in the PART2 partition; values between *N* and *T* will be stored in the PART3 partition. Any value greater than *T* will be stored in the PART4 partition. Note that in the PART4 partition definition, the range clause is

```
partition PART4   values less than (MAXVALUE)
```

You do not need to specify a maximum value for the last partition; the **maxvalue** keyword tells Oracle to use the partition to store any data that could not be stored in the earlier partitions.

Notice that for each partition, you only specify the maximum value for the range. The minimum value for the range is implicitly determined by Oracle.

Range partitions were the only type of partition available in Oracle8. Oracle8i also includes *hash partitions.* A hash partition determines the physical placement of data by performing a hash function on the values of the partition key. In *range partitioning,* consecutive values of the partition key are usually stored in the same partition. In *hash partitioning,* consecutive values of the partition key are not necessarily stored in the same partition. Hash partitioning distributes a set of records over a greater set of partitions than range partitioning does, potentially decreasing the likelihood for I/O contention.

To create a hash partition, use the **partition by hash** clause in place of the **partition by range** clause, as shown in the following listing:

```
create table WORKER (
Name            VARCHAR2(25) primary key,
Age             NUMBER,
Lodging         VARCHAR2(15),
constraint      WORKER_PK PRIMARY KEY(Name)
)
partition by hash (Lodging)
partitions 10;
```

You can name each partition and specify its tablespace, just as you would for range partitioning, as shown here:

```
create table WORKER (
Name            VARCHAR2(25) primary key,
Age             NUMBER,
Lodging         VARCHAR2(15),
constraint      WORKER_PK PRIMARY KEY(Name)
)
partition by hash (Lodging)
partitions 2
store in (PART1_TS, PART2_TS);
```

Following the **partition by hash (Lodging)** line, you have two choices for format:

■ As shown in the preceding listing, you can specify the number of partitions and the tablespaces to use:

```
partitions 2
store in (PART1_TS, PART2_TS);
```

This method will create partitions with system-generated names of the format SYS_P*nnn*. The number of tablespaces specified in the **store in** clause does not have to equal the number of partitions. If more partitions than tablespaces are specified, the partitions will be assigned to the tablespaces in a round-robin fashion.

■ You can specify named partitions:

```
partition by hash (Lodging)
(partition P1 tablespace P1_TS,
 partition P2 tablespace P2_TS);
```

In this method, each partition is given a name and a tablespace, with the option of using an additional **lob** or **varray** storage clause (see Chapters 29 and 30). This method gives you more control over the location of the partitions, with the added benefit of letting you specify meaningful names for the partitions.

Creating Subpartitions

As of Oracle8i, you can create *subpartitions*—partitions of partitions. You can use subpartitions to combine the two types of partitions: range partitions and hash partitions. You can use hash partitions in combination with range partitions, creating hash partitions of the range partitions. For very large tables, this composite partitioning may be an effective way of separating the data into manageable and tunable divisions.

The following example range-partitions the WORKER table by the Lodging column, and hash-partitions the Lodging partitions by Name values:

```
create table WORKER (
Name           VARCHAR2(25) primary key,
Age            NUMBER,
Lodging        VARCHAR2(15),
constraint     WORKER_PK PRIMARY KEY(Name)
)
partition by range (Lodging)
subpartition by hash (Name)
subpartitions 10
  (partition PART1   values less than ('F')
    tablespace PART1_TS,
```

```
partition PART2   values less than ('L')
 tablespace PART2_TS,
partition PART3   values less than ('T')
 tablespace PART3_TS,
partition PART4   values less than (MAXVALUE)
 tablespace PART4_TS);
```

The WORKER table will be range-partitioned into four partitions, using the ranges specified for the four named partitions. Each of those partitions will be hash-partitioned on the Name column.

Indexing Partitions

When you create a partitioned table, you should create an index on the table. The index may be partitioned according to the same range values that were used to partition the table. In the following listing, the **create index** command for the WORKER table is shown:

```
create index WORKER_LODGING
   on WORKER(Lodging)
    local
    (partition PART1
      tablespace PART1_NDX_TS,
     partition PART2
      tablespace PART2_NDX_TS,
     partition PART3
      tablespace PART3_NDX_TS,
     partition PART4
      tablespace PART4_NDX_TS)
```

Notice the **local** keyword. In this **create index** command, no ranges are specified. Instead, the **local** keyword tells Oracle to create a separate index for each partition of the WORKER table. There were four partitions created on WORKER. This index will create four separate indexes—one for each partition. Since there is one index per partition, the indexes are "local" to the partitions.

You can also create "global" indexes. A global index may contain values from multiple partitions. The index itself may be partitioned, as shown in this example:

```
create index WORKER_LODGING
on WORKER(Lodging)
 global partition by range (Lodging)
 (partition PART1   values less than ('F')
   tablespace PART1_NDX_TS,
  partition PART2   values less than ('N')
   tablespace PART2_NDX_TS,
  partition PART3   values less than ('T')
```

```
    tablespace PART3_NDX_TS,
  partition PART4   values less than (MAXVALUE)
   tablespace PART4_NDX_TS)
;
```

The **global** clause in this **create index** command allows you to specify ranges for the index values that are different from the ranges for the table partitions. Local indexes may be easier to manage than global indexes; however, global indexes may perform uniqueness checks faster than local (partitioned) indexes perform them.

NOTE
You cannot create global indexes for hash partitions or subpartitions.

Managing Partitioned Tables

You can use the **alter table** command to **add**, **drop**, **exchange**, **move**, **modify**, **rename**, **split**, and **truncate** partitions. These **alter table** command options allow you to alter the existing partition structure, as may be required after a partitioned table has been used heavily. For example, the distribution of the Lodging values within the partitioned table may have changed, or the maximum value may have increased. See the "ALTER TABLE" entry in the Alphabetical Reference for information on these options.

Querying Directly from Partitions

If you know the partition from which you will be retrieving your data, you can specify the name of the partition as part of the **from** clause of your query. For example, suppose you want to query the records for the workers whose Lodgings begin with the letter *R*. The optimizer should be able to use the partition definitions to determine that only the PART3 partition could contain data that can resolve this query. If you wish, you can tell Oracle to use PART3 as part of your query:

```
select *
  from WORKER partition (PART3)
 where Name like 'R%';
```

This example explicitly names the partition in which Oracle is to search for the *R* lodging records. If the partition is modified (for example, if its range of values is altered), then PART3 may no longer be the partition that contains the *R* records. Thus, you should use great care when using this syntax.

In general, this syntax is not necessary, because Oracle places CHECK constraints on each of the partitions. When you query from the partitioned table, Oracle uses the CHECK constraints to determine which partitions should be involved in resolving the query. This process may result in a small number of rows being searched for the query, thus improving query performance. Additionally, the partitions may be stored in different tablespaces (and thus on separate disk devices), helping to reduce the potential for disk I/O contention during the processing of the query.

During an **insert** into the partitioned table, Oracle uses the partitions' CHECK constraints to determine which partition the record should be inserted into. Thus, you can use a partitioned table as if it were a single table, and rely on Oracle to manage the internal separation of the data.

CHAPTER
19

By What Authority?

nformation is vital to success, but when damaged or in the wrong hands, it can threaten success. Oracle provides extensive security features to safeguard your information from both unauthorized viewing and intentional or inadvertent damage. This security is provided by granting or revoking privileges on a person-by-person and privilege-by-privilege basis, and is in addition to (and independent of) any security your computer system already has. Oracle uses the **create user**, **create role**, and **grant** commands to control data access.

Users, Roles, and Privileges

Every Oracle user has a name and password, and owns any tables, views, and other resources that he or she creates. An Oracle *role* is a set of *privileges* (or the type of access that each user needs, depending on his or her status and responsibilities). You can grant or bestow specific privileges to roles and then assign roles to the appropriate users. A user can also grant privileges directly to other users.

   Database system privileges let you execute specific sets of commands. The CREATE TABLE privilege, for example, lets you create tables. The GRANT ANY PRIVILEGE privilege allows you to grant any system privilege.

   Database object privileges give you the ability to perform some operation on various objects. The DELETE privilege, for example, lets you delete rows from tables and views. The SELECT privilege allows you to query with a **select** from tables, views, sequences, and snapshots.

   See "Privilege" in the Alphabetical Reference at the end of this book for a complete list of system and object privileges.

Creating a User

The Oracle system comes with two users already created, SYSTEM and SYS. You log on to the SYSTEM user to create other users, since SYSTEM has that privilege.

   When installing Oracle, you (or a system administrator) first create a user for yourself.

   This is the format for the **create user** command:

```
create user user identified {by password | externally};
```

   Other privileges can be set via this command; see the **create user** command in the Alphabetical Reference for details.

   To connect your computer system's userid and password into Oracle's security so that only one logon is required, use **externally** instead of giving a password. A system administrator (who has a great many privileges) may want the extra security of having a separate password. Let's call the system administrator Dora in the following examples:

```
create user Dora identified by avocado;
```

Dora's account now exists and is secured by a password.

You also can set up the user with specific *tablespaces* (space on disk for the user's tables—discussed in the following chapter) and *quotas* (limits) for space and resource usage. See **create user** in the Alphabetical Reference and Chapter 20 for a discussion of tablespaces and resources.

To change a password, use the **alter user** command:

```
alter user Dora identified by psyche;
```

Now Dora has the password "psyche" instead of "avocado."

Password Management

As of Oracle8, passwords can expire, and accounts may be locked due to repeated failed attempts to connect. When you change your password, a password history may be maintained to prevent reuse of previous passwords.

The expiration characteristics of your account's password are determined by the profile assigned to your account. Profiles, which are created by the **create profile** command, are managed by the DBA (database administrator, discussed later in the chapter). See the "CREATE PROFILE" entry in the Alphabetical Reference for full details on the **create profile** command. Relative to passwords and account access, profiles can enforce the following:

- The "lifetime" of your password, which determines how frequently you must change it

- The grace period following your password's "expiration date" during which you can change the password

- The number of consecutive failed connect attempts allowed before the account is automatically "locked"

- The number of days the account will remain locked

- The number of days that must pass before you can reuse a password

- The number of password changes that must pass before you can reuse a password

Additional password management features allow the minimum length of passwords to be enforced.

In addition to the **alter user** command, you can use the **password** command in SQLPLUS to change your password. If you use the **password** command, your new password will not be displayed on the screen as you type. Users with dba authority can change any user's password via the **password** command; other users can change only their own password.

When you enter the **password** command, you will be prompted for the old and new passwords, as shown in the following listing:

```
password
Changing password for dora
Old password:
New password:
Retype new password:
```

When the password has been successfully changed, you will receive the feedback:

```
Password changed
```

Three Standard Roles

Now that Dora has an account, what can she do in Oracle? At this point, nothing—Dora has no system privileges.

Oracle provides three standard roles for compatibility with previous versions: CONNECT, RESOURCE, and DBA.

The CONNECT Role

Occasional users, particularly those who do not need to create tables, will usually be given only the CONNECT role. CONNECT is simply the privilege to use Oracle at all. This right becomes meaningful with the addition of access to specific tables belonging to other users, and the privilege to select, insert, update, and delete rows in these tables, as each of these rights is granted. Users who have the CONNECT role may also create tables, views, sequences, clusters, synonyms (discussed in this chapter), sessions (see the Alphabetical Reference), and links to other databases (see Chapter 22).

The RESOURCE Role

More sophisticated and regular users of the database may be granted the RESOURCE role. RESOURCE gives users the additional rights to create their own tables, sequences, procedures, triggers, indexes, and clusters (see Part III of this book for a discussion of stored procedures and triggers).

The DBA Role

The DBA (*database administrator*) role has all system privileges—including unlimited space quotas—and the ability to grant all privileges to other users. In this chapter, *dba* refers to the person who is the database administrator and has the DBA role, while *DBA* refers just to those privileges encompassed by the DBA role. SYSTEM is for use by a DBA user. Some of the rights that are reserved for the dba are never given to, or needed by, normal users. Little time will be spent here on those rights. Other rights typically used by dbas are also regularly used by and important to users. This subset of DBA privileges will be explained shortly. In Oracle, the DBA is granted the EXP_FULL_DATABASE and IMP_FULL_DATABASE roles, which in turn have privileges necessary for exporting and importing the full Oracle database.

Format for the grant Command

Here is the format for the **grant** command for system privileges:

```
grant {system privilege | role}
      [, {system privilege | role},. . .]
      to {user | role} [, {user | role}]. . .
      [with admin option]
```

By using the **grant** command, you can grant any system privilege or role to another user, to another role, or to **public**. The **with admin option** clause permits the grantee to bestow the privilege or role on other users or roles. The grantor can revoke a role from a user as well.

Revoking Privileges

Privileges granted can be taken away. The **revoke** command is similar to the **grant** command:

```
revoke {system privilege | role}
       [, {system privilege | role},. . .]
       from {user | role} [, {user | role}]. . .
```

An individual with the DBA role can revoke CONNECT, RESOURCE, DBA, or any other privilege or role from anyone, including another dba. This, of course, is dangerous, and is why DBA privileges should be given neither lightly nor to more than a tiny minority who really need them.

NOTE
Revoking everything from a given user does not eliminate that user from Oracle, nor does it destroy any tables that user had created; it simply prohibits that user's access to them. Other users with access to the tables will still have exactly the same access they've always had.

To remove a user and all the resources owned by that user, use the **drop user** command like this:

```
drop user user [cascade];
```

The **cascade** option drops the user along with all the objects owned by the user, including referential integrity constraints. The **cascade** option invalidates views, synonyms, stored procedures, functions, or packages that refer to objects in the dropped user's schema. If you don't use the **cascade** option and there are still objects owned by the user, Oracle does not drop the user and instead returns an error message.

What Users Can Grant

A user can grant privileges on any object he or she owns. The dba can grant any system privilege (because the DBA role has the GRANT ANY and the GRANT ANY ROLE privileges).

Suppose that user Dora owns the COMFORT table and is a dba. She creates two new users, Bob and Judy, with these privileges:

```
create user Judy identified by sarah;

User created.

grant CONNECT to Judy;

Role granted.

create user Bob identified by carolyn;

User created.

grant CONNECT, RESOURCE to bob;

Role granted.
```

This sequence of commands gives both Judy and Bob the ability to connect to Oracle, and gives Bob some extra capabilities. But can either do anything with Dora's tables? Not without explicit access.

To give others access to your tables, use a second form of the **grant** command:

```
grant object privilege [(column [, column])]
    on object to {user | role}
    [with grant option];
```

The privileges a user can grant include these:

■ On the user's tables, views, and snapshots (materialized views):
INSERT
UPDATE (all or specific columns)
DELETE
SELECT
The INSERT, UPDATE, and DELETE privileges can only be granted on snapshots (materialized views) if they are updateable. See Chapter 23 for details on the creation of snapshots and materialized views.

■ On tables, you can also grant:
ALTER (table—all or specific columns—or sequence)
REFERENCES
INDEX (columns in a table)
ALL (of the items previously listed)

■ On procedures, functions, packages, abstract datatypes, libraries, indextypes, and operators:
EXECUTE

■ On sequences:
SELECT
ALTER

■ On directories (for BFILE LOB datatypes):
READ

The privilege granted must be one of the object privileges (ALL, ALTER, DELETE, EXECUTE, INDEX, INSERT, READ, REFERENCES, SELECT, or UPDATE). These privileges give the grantee the ability to take some action on the object. The object can be one of the objects listed here or a synonym for any of these objects.

When you execute another user's procedure or function, it is executed using the privileges of its owner. This means that you don't need explicit access to the data the procedure or function uses; you see only the result of the execution, not the underlying data.

Dora gives Bob SELECT access to the COMFORT table:

```
grant select on COMFORT to Bob;

Grant succeeded.
```

The **with grant option** clause of the **grant** command allows the recipient of that grant to pass along the privileges he or she has received to other users. If the user

Dora grants privileges on her tables to the user Bob **with grant option**, then Bob can make grants on Dora's tables to other users (Bob can only pass along those privileges—such as SELECT—that he has been granted). If you intend to create views based on another user's tables and grant access to those views to other users, you first must be granted access **with grant option** to the base tables.

Moving to Another User with connect

To test the success of her grant, Dora connects to Bob's username with the **connect** command. This may be used via one of the following methods:

- By entering both the username and password on the same line as the command

- By entering the command alone and then responding to prompts

- By entering the command and username and responding to the prompt for the password

The latter two methods suppress display of the password and are therefore inherently more secure. The following listing shows a sample connection to the database.

```
connect Bob/carolyn

Connected.
```

Once connected, Dora selects from the table to which Bob has been given SELECT access.

NOTE
Unless a synonym is used, the table name must be preceded by the username of the table's owner. Without this, Oracle will say the table does not exist.

```
select * from Dora.COMFORT;

CITY          SAMPLEDAT NOON  MIDNIGHT PRECIPITATION
------------- --------- ----- -------- -------------
SAN FRANCISCO 21-MAR-99 62.5     42.3             .5
SAN FRANCISCO 22-JUN-99 51.1     71.9             .1
SAN FRANCISCO 23-SEP-99          61.5             .1
SAN FRANCISCO 22-DEC-99 52.6     39.8            2.3
KEENE         21-MAR-99 39.9     -1.2            4.4
KEENE         22-JUN-99 85.1     66.7            1.3
```

```
KEENE          23-SEP-99  99.8     82.6
KEENE          22-DEC-99  -7.2     -1.2              3.9
```

For convenience, a view named COMFORT is created, which is simply a straight **select** from the table Dora.COMFORT:

```
create view COMFORT as select * from Dora.COMFORT;
```

```
View created.
```

Selecting from this view will produce exactly the same results as selecting from Dora.COMFORT:

```
select * from COMFORT;
```

```
CITY          SAMPLEDAT NOON MIDNIGHT PRECIPITATION
------------- --------- ---- -------- -------------
SAN FRANCISCO 21-MAR-99 62.5     42.3            .5
SAN FRANCISCO 22-JUN-99 51.1     71.9            .1
SAN FRANCISCO 23-SEP-99          61.5            .1
SAN FRANCISCO 22-DEC-99 52.6     39.8           2.3
KEENE         21-MAR-99 39.9     -1.2           4.4
KEENE         22-JUN-99 85.1     66.7           1.3
KEENE         23-SEP-99 99.8     82.6
KEENE         22-DEC-99 -7.2     -1.2           3.9
```

Now Dora returns to her own username and creates a view that selects only a part of the COMFORT table:

```
connect Dora/psyche
Connected.
```

```
create view SOMECOMFORT as
select * from COMFORT
 where City = 'KEENE';
```

```
View created.
```

She then grants both SELECT and UPDATE privileges to Bob *on this view,* and revokes all privileges from Bob (via the **revoke** command) for the whole COMFORT table:

```
grant select, update on SOMECOMFORT to Bob;
```

```
Grant succeeded.
```

```
revoke all on COMFORT from Bob;
```

```
Revoke succeeded.
```

Dora then reconnects to Bob's username to test the effects of this change:

```
connect Bob/carolyn
Connected.

select * from COMFORT;
                *
ERROR at line 1: ORA-00942: table or view does not exist
```

Attempting to select from his COMFORT view fails because the underlying table named in Bob's view was the Dora.COMFORT table. Not surprisingly, attempting to select from Dora.COMFORT would produce exactly the same message. Next, an attempt to select from Dora.SOMECOMFORT is made:

```
select * from Dora.SOMECOMFORT;

CITY          SAMPLEDAT  NOON MIDNIGHT PRECIPITATION
------------- ---------- ----- -------- -------------
KEENE         21-MAR-99  39.9     -1.2           4.4
KEENE         22-JUN-99  85.1     66.7           1.3
KEENE         23-SEP-99  99.8     82.6
KEENE         22-DEC-99  -7.2     -1.2           3.9
```

This works perfectly well, even though direct access to the COMFORT table had been revoked, because Dora gave Bob access to a portion of COMFORT through the SOMECOMFORT view. It is just that portion of the table related to KEENE.

This shows a powerful security feature of Oracle: you can create a view using virtually any restrictions you like or any computations in the columns, and then give access to the view, rather than to the underlying tables, to other users. They will see only the information the view presents. This can even be extended to be user-specific. The "Security by User" section later in this chapter gives complete details on this feature.

Now, the view LITTLECOMFORT is created under Bob's username, on top of the view SOMECOMFORT:

```
create view LITTLECOMFORT as select * from Dora.SOMECOMFORT;

View created.
```

and the row for September 23, 1999, is updated:

```
update LITTLECOMFORT set Noon = 88
  where SampleDate = TO_DATE('23-SEP-1999','DD-MON-YYYY');

1 row updated.
```

When the view LITTLECOMFORT is queried, it shows the effect of the update:

```
select * from LITTLECOMFORT;

CITY          SAMPLEDAT NOON MIDNIGHT PRECIPITATION
------------- --------- ---- -------- -------------
KEENE         21-MAR-99 39.9     -1.2           4.4
KEENE         22-JUN-99 85.1     66.7           1.3
KEENE         23-SEP-99   88     82.6
KEENE         22-DEC-99 -7.2     -1.2           3.9
```

A query of Dora.SOMECOMFORT would show the same results, as would a query of COMFORT itself if Dora made it on her own username. The update was successful against the underlying table even though it went through two views (LITTLECOMFORT and SOMECOMFORT) to reach it.

NOTE
You need to grant users SELECT access to any table in which they can update or delete records. This is in keeping with the evolving ANSI standard and reflects the fact that a user who only had UPDATE or DELETE privilege on a table could use the database's feedback comments to discover information about the underlying data.

create synonym

An alternative method to creating a view that includes an entire table or view from another user is to create a synonym:

```
create synonym LITTLECOMFORT for Dora.SOMECOMFORT;
```

This synonym can be treated exactly like a view. See the **create synonym** command in the Alphabetical Reference.

Using Ungranted Privileges

Let's say an attempt is made to delete the row you just updated:

```
delete from LITTLECOMFORT where SampleDate = '23-SEP-99';
                                 *
ERROR at line 1: ORA-01031: insufficient privileges
```

Bob has not been given DELETE privileges by Dora, so the attempt fails.

Passing on Privileges

Bob can grant authority for other users to access his tables, but cannot bestow on other users access to tables that don't belong to him. Here, he attempts to give INSERT authority to Judy:

```
grant insert on Dora.SOMECOMFORT to Judy;
              *
ERROR at line 1: ORA-01031: insufficient privileges
```

Because Bob does not have this authority, he fails to give it to Judy. Next, Bob tries to pass on the privilege he does have, SELECT:

```
grant select on Dora.SOMECOMFORT to Judy;
              *
ERROR at line 1: ORA-01031: insufficient privileges
```

He cannot grant this privilege, either, because the view SOMECOMFORT does not belong to him. If he had been granted access to SOMECOMFORT **with grant option**, then the preceding **grant** command would have succeeded. The view LITTLECOMFORT does belong to him, though, so he can try to pass authority to that on to Judy:

```
grant select on LITTLECOMFORT to Judy;

ERROR at line 1:
ORA-01720: grant option does not exist for 'DORA.SOMECOMFORT'
```

Since the LITTLECOMFORT view relies on one of Dora's views, and Bob was not granted SELECT **with grant option** on that view, Bob's grant fails.

In addition, a new table, owned by Bob, is created and loaded with the current information from his view LITTLECOMFORT:

```
create table NOCOMFORT as
select * from LITTLECOMFORT;

Table created.
```

SELECT privileges on it are granted to Judy as well:

```
grant select on NOCOMFORT to Judy;

Grant succeeded.
```

To test this grant, Judy's username is connected, like this:

```
connect Judy/sarah
Connected.
```

Queries are made against the table for which Bob granted the SELECT privilege to Judy:

```
select * from Bob.NOCOMFORT;

CITY          SAMPLEDAT  NOON  MIDNIGHT  PRECIPITATION
------------- ---------  ----- --------  -------------
KEENE         21-MAR-99  39.9    -1.2         4.4
KEENE         22-JUN-99  85.1    66.7         1.3
KEENE         23-SEP-99  99.8    82.6
KEENE         22-DEC-99  -7.2    -1.2         3.9
```

This grant was successful. A NOCOMFORT table was created, and owned, by Bob's username. He was able to successfully give access to this table.

If Dora wishes Bob to be able to pass on his privileges to others, she can add another clause to the **grant** statement:

```
grant select, update on SOMECOMFORT to Bob with grant option;

Grant succeeded.
```

The **with grant option** clause enables Bob to pass on access to SOMECOMFORT to Judy through his LITTLECOMFORT view. Note that attempts to access a table to which a user does not have the SELECT privilege always result in this message:

```
ERROR at line 1: ORA-00942: table or view does not exist
```

This message appears rather than a message about not having access privilege so that a person without permission to query a table doesn't know that it even exists.

Creating a Role

In addition to the three system roles shown earlier in this chapter—CONNECT, RESOURCE, and DBA—you can create your own roles within Oracle. The roles you create can comprise table or system privileges or a combination of both. In the following sections, you will see how to create and administer roles.

To create a role, you need to have the CREATE ROLE system privilege. The syntax for role creation is shown in the following listing:

```
create role role_name
[not identified|identified [by password|externally]];
```

When a role is first created, it has no privileges associated with it. Password options for roles are discussed in "Adding a Password to a Role," later in this chapter.

Two sample **create role** commands are shown in the following example:

```
create role CLERK;
create role MANAGER;
```

The first command creates a role called CLERK, which will be used in the examples in the following sections of this chapter. The second command creates a role called MANAGER, which will also be featured in those examples.

Granting Privileges to a Role

Once a role has been created, you may grant privileges to it. The syntax for the **grant** command is the same for roles as it was for users. When granting privileges to roles, you use the role name in the **to** clause of the **grant** command, as shown in the following listing:

```
grant select on COMFORT to CLERK;
```

As shown in this example, the role name takes the place of the username in the **grant** command. The privilege to select from the COMFORT table will now be available to any user of the CLERK role.

If you are a dba, or have been granted the GRANT ANY PRIVILEGE system role, then you may grant system privileges—such as CREATE SESSION, CREATE SYNONYM, and CREATE VIEW—to roles. These privileges will then be available to any user of your role.

The ability to log in to the database is given via the CREATE SESSION system privilege. In the following example, this privilege is granted to the CLERK role. This privilege is also granted to the MANAGER role, along with the CREATE DATABASE LINK system privilege.

```
grant CREATE SESSION to CLERK;
grant CREATE SESSION, CREATE DATABASE LINK to MANAGER;
```

Granting a Role to Another Role

Roles can be granted to other roles. You can do this via the **grant** command, as shown in the following example:

```
grant CLERK to MANAGER;
```

In this example, the CLERK role is granted to the MANAGER role. Even though you have not directly granted any table privileges to the MANAGER role, it will now inherit any privileges that have been granted to the CLERK role. Organizing roles in this way is a common design for hierarchical organizations.

When granting a role to another role (or to a user, as in the following section), you may grant the role using the **with admin option** clause, as shown in the following listing:

```
grant CLERK to MANAGER with admin option;
```

If the **with admin option** clause is used, then the grantee has the authority to grant the role to other users or roles. The grantee can also alter or drop the role.

Granting a Role to Users

Roles can be granted to users. When granted to users, roles can be thought of as named sets of privileges. Instead of granting each privilege to each user, you grant the privileges to the role and then grant the role to each user. This greatly simplifies the administrative tasks involved in the management of privileges.

NOTE
Privileges that are granted to users via roles cannot be used as the basis for views, procedures, functions, packages, or foreign keys. When creating these types of database objects, you must rely on direct grants of the necessary privileges.

You can grant a role to a user via the **grant** command, as shown in the following example:

```
grant CLERK to Bob;
```

The user Bob in this example will have all of the privileges that were granted to the CLERK role (CREATE SESSION and SELECT privileges on COMFORT).

When granting a role to a user, you may grant the role using the **with admin option** clause, as shown in the following listing:

```
grant MANAGER to Dora with admin option;
```

Dora now has the authority to grant the MANAGER role to other users or roles, or to alter or drop the role.

Adding a Password to a Role

You can use the **alter role** command for only one purpose: to change the authority needed to enable it. By default, roles do not have passwords associated with them. To enable security for a role, use the **identified** keyword in the **alter role** command. There are two ways to implement this security.

First, you can use the **identified by** clause of the **alter role** command to specify a password, as shown in the following listing:

```
alter role MANAGER identified by cygnusxi;
```

Any time a user tries to activate that role, the password will be required. If, however, that role is set up as a default role for the user, then no password will be required for that role when the user logs in. See the upcoming "Enabling and Disabling Roles" section of this chapter for more details on these topics.

Roles can be tied to operating system privileges as well. If this capability is available on your operating system, then you use the **identified externally** clause of the **alter role** command. When the role is enabled, Oracle will check the operating system to verify your access. Altering a role to use this security feature is shown in the following example:

```
alter role MANAGER identified externally;
```

In most UNIX systems, the verification process uses the /etc/group file. To use this file for any operating system, the OS_ROLES database startup parameter in the init.ora file must be set to TRUE.

The following example of this verification process is for a database instance called "Local" on a UNIX system. The server's /etc/group file may contain the following entry:

```
ora_local_manager_d:NONE:1:dora
```

This entry grants the MANAGER role to the account named Dora. The **_d** suffix indicates that this role is to be granted by default when Dora logs in. An **_a** suffix would indicate that this role is to be enabled **with admin option**. If this role were also the user's default role, then the suffix would be **_ad**. If more than one user were granted this role, then the additional usernames would be appended to the /etc/group entry, as shown in the following listing:

```
ora_local_manager_d:NONE:1:dora,judy
```

If you use this option, all roles in the database will be enabled via the operating system.

Removing a Password from a Role

To remove a password from a role, use the **not identified** clause of the **alter role** command, as shown in the following listing. By default, roles do not have passwords.

```
alter role MANAGER not identified;
```

Enabling and Disabling Roles

When a user's account is altered, a list of default roles for that user can be created. This is done via the **default role** clause of the **alter user** command. The default action of this command sets all of a user's roles as default roles, enabling all of them every time the user logs in.

The syntax for this portion of the **alter user** command is as follows:

```
alter user username
default role {[role1, role2]
[all|all except role1, role2][NONE]};
```

As shown by this syntax, a user can be altered to have, by default, specific roles enabled, all roles enabled, all except specific roles enabled, or no roles enabled. For example, the following **alter user** command will enable the CLERK role whenever Bob logs in:

```
alter user Bob
default role CLERK;
```

To enable a nondefault role, use the **set role** command, as shown in this example:

```
set role CLERK;
```

You may also use the **all** and **all except** clauses that were available in the **alter user** command:

```
set role all;
set role all except CLERK;
```

If a role has a password associated with it, that password must be specified via an **identified by** clause:

```
set role MANAGER identified by cygnusxi;
```

To disable a role in your session, use the **set role none** command, as shown in the following listing. This will disable all roles in your current session. Once all of the roles have been disabled, reenable the ones you want.

```
set role none;
```

Since you may find it necessary to execute a **set role none** command from time to time, you may wish to grant the CREATE SESSION privilege to users directly rather than via roles.

Revoking Privileges from a Role

To revoke a privilege from a role, use the **revoke** command, described earlier in this chapter. Specify the privilege, object name (if it is an object privilege), and role name, as shown in the following example:

```
revoke SELECT on COMFORT from CLERK;
```

Users of the CLERK role will then be unable to query the COMFORT table.

Dropping a Role

To drop a role, use the **drop role** command, as shown in the following example:

```
drop role MANAGER;
drop role CLERK;
```

The roles you specify, and their associated privileges, will be removed from the database entirely.

Granting update to Specific Columns

You may wish to grant users the SELECT privilege to more columns than you wish to grant them the UPDATE privilege. Since SELECT columns can be restricted through a view, to further restrict the columns that can be updated requires a special form of the user's **grant** command. Here is an example for two COMFORT columns:

```
grant update (Noon, Midnight) on COMFORT to Judy;
```

Revoking Privileges

If object privileges can be granted, they can also be taken away. This is similar to the **grant** command:

```
revoke object privilege [, object privilege . . .]
on object
from {user | role} [,{user | role}]
[cascade constraints];
```

revoke all removes any of the privileges listed previously, from SELECT through INDEX; revoking individual privileges will leave intact others that had also been granted. The **with grant option** is revoked along with the privilege to which it was attached.

If a user defines referential integrity constraints on the object, Oracle drops these constraints if you revoke privileges on the object using the **cascade constraints** option.

Security by User

Access to tables can be granted specifically, table by table, and view by view, to each user. There is, however, an additional technique that will simplify this process in some cases. Recall Talbot's WORKER table:

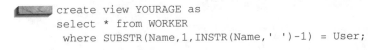

```
select * from WORKER;

NAME                            AGE LODGING
------------------------------- ----- ---------------
ADAH TALBOT                      23 PAPA KING
ANDREW DYE                       29 ROSE HILL
BART SARJEANT                    22 CRANMER
DICK JONES                       18 ROSE HILL
DONALD ROLLO                     16 MATTS
ELBERT TALBOT                    43 WEITBROCHT
GEORGE OSCAR                     41 ROSE HILL
GERHARDT KENTGEN                 55 PAPA KING
HELEN BRANDT                     15
JED HOPKINS                      33 MATTS
JOHN PEARSON                     27 ROSE HILL
KAY AND PALMER WALLBOM              ROSE HILL
PAT LAVAY                        21 ROSE HILL
PETER LAWSON                     25 CRANMER
RICHARD KOCH AND BROTHERS           WEITBROCHT
ROLAND BRANDT                    35 MATTS
VICTORIA LYNN                    32 MULLERS
WILFRED LOWELL                   67
WILLIAM SWING                    15 CRANMER
```

To enable each worker to access this table, but restrict the access given to a view of only each worker's own single row, you could create 19 separate views, each with a different name in the **where** clause, and you could make separate grants to each of these views for each worker. Alternatively, you could create a view whose **where** clause contained User, the pseudo-column, like this:

```
create view YOURAGE as
select * from WORKER
  where SUBSTR(Name,1,INSTR(Name,' ')-1) = User;

View created.
```

When a user named George creates this view and queries the WORKER table through the YOURAGE view, the **where** clause finds his username, GEORGE, in the Name column (see the **where** clause), and produces the following:

```
select * from YOURAGE;

NAME                            AGE LODGING
------------------------        ----- ---------------
GEORGE OSCAR                     41 ROSE HILL
```

Now George grants **select** on this view to Bart Sarjeant:

```
grant SELECT on YOURAGE to Bart;
```

He then connects to Bart to check the effect:

```
connect Bart/stjohn
Connected.

select * from George.YOURAGE;

NAME                            AGE LODGING
------------------------        ----- ---------------
BART SARJEANT                    22 CRANMER
```

Amazingly, the result for Bart is his own row, not George's, because the pseudo-column User, in George's view, is always equal to the user of SQLPLUS at the moment the view is queried.

Granting Access to the Public

Rather than grant access to every worker, the **grant** command can be generalized to the public:

```
grant select on YOURAGE to public;
```

This gives everyone access, including users created after this grant was made. However, each user will still have to access the table using George's username as a prefix. To avoid this, a dba may create a *public synonym* (which creates a name accessible to all users that stands for George.YOURAGE):

```
create public synonym YOURAGE for George.YOURAGE;
```

From this point forward, anyone can access YOURAGE without prefixing it with George. This approach gives tremendous flexibility for security. Workers could see only their own salaries, for instance, in a table that contains salaries for everyone. If, however, a user creates a table or view with the same name as a public synonym, any future SQL statements by this user will act on this new table or view, and not on the one by the same name to which the public has access.

Granting Limited Resources

When granting resource quotas in an Oracle database, the **quota** parameter of the **create user** or **alter user** command is used, as shown in the following listing. In this example, Bob is granted a quota of 100MB in the USERS tablespace.

```
alter user Bob
quota 100M on USERS;
```

A user's space quota may be set when the user is created, via the **create user** command. If there is no limit on the user's space quota, then you can grant that user the UNLIMITED TABLESPACE system privilege. See the **create user** and **alter user** commands in the Alphabetical Reference for further details on these commands.

Profiles can also be used to enforce other resource limits, such as the amount of CPU time or idle time a user's requests to Oracle can take. A profile detailing these resource limits is created and then assigned to one or more users. See the **create profile** and **alter user** command entries in the Alphabetical Reference for full details.

CHAPTER
20

Changing the
Oracle Surroundings

ike Chapter 19, this chapter looks at that subset of database administrator (DBA) functions used by most Oracle users—functions not restricted to DBAs. These include indexes on tables, clusters, sequence generators, and allocations of space for tables and indexes. This chapter shows how Oracle's databases are structured internally, which helps in understanding how Oracle's many features actually work and how they interrelate. Only limited options of the **create index**, **create tablespace**, and **create cluster** commands will be shown in this chapter. Full options are shown in the Alphabetical Reference, later in this book.

Indexes

An *index* is a simple concept. It is typically a listing of *keywords* accompanied by the *location* of information on a subject. To find information on indexes, for instance, you look up the word "indexes" in the index at the back of this book. It will give the number of the page you are reading now. The word "indexes" is the key, and the page numbers given point you to the location of discussions about indexes in this book. This is related to the idea of primary keys in Oracle, which was described in Chapter 2.

While indexes are not strictly necessary to running Oracle, they do speed the process. For example, while you could find the information on indexes simply by reading through this book until you encountered the page with the information on it, this would be slow and time-consuming. Because the index at the back of the book is in alphabetical order, you can quickly go to the appropriate spot in the index (without reading every entry) where "index" is found. This is quicker than reading through the book from front to back, obviously. These same principles apply to Oracle indexes. Consider the WORKERSKILL table:

```
select * from WORKERSKILL;
```

NAME	SKILL	ABILITY
DICK JONES	SMITHY	EXCELLENT
JOHN PEARSON	COMBINE DRIVER	
JOHN PEARSON	SMITHY	AVERAGE
HELEN BRANDT	COMBINE DRIVER	VERY FAST
JOHN PEARSON	WOODCUTTER	GOOD
VICTORIA LYNN	SMITHY	PRECISE
ADAH TALBOT	WORK	GOOD
WILFRED LOWELL	WORK	AVERAGE
ELBERT TALBOT	DISCUS	SLOW
WILFRED LOWELL	DISCUS	AVERAGE

Few tables that you will use in actual practice are as short as the WORKERSKILL table, and they will seldom be in alphabetical order. The following query asks Oracle to find a specific worker's skill level:

```
select *
   from WORKERSKILL
 where Name = 'HELEN BRANDT';
```

If WORKERSKILL does not have an index on the Name column, Oracle has to read every row in the table until it finds all Names that match the **where** clause of your query.

To speed this process, you can create an index on the Name column. Then, when you execute the same query, Oracle first looks in the index, which is sorted, thus finding the worker named Helen Brandt very quickly (Oracle doesn't read every entry, but jumps directly to the close vicinity of the name, much as you would in looking through the index of a book). The index entry then gives Oracle the exact location in the table (and on disk) of the row(s) for Helen Brandt.

Knowing this, it is clear how indexing an important column (one that's likely to appear in a **where** clause) will speed up Oracle's response to a query. Indexing will likewise speed up queries where two tables are joined, if the columns that are related (by the **where** clause) are indexed. These are the basics of indexing; the rest of this chapter shows a number of additional features and issues related to indexing that will affect how quickly it works. For the impact of indexes on the optimization of your queries, see Chapter 36.

Creating an Index

You create an index via the **create index** command. The full command syntax is shown in the Alphabetical Reference. Its most commonly used format is as follows:

```
create [bitmap] [unique] index index on table(column [,column]. . .);
```

index must be a unique name and follow the naming conventions of Oracle columns. *table* is simply the name of the table on which the index will be established, and *column* is the name of the column.

Bitmap indexes allow you to create useful indexes on columns with very few distinct values; see "Creating a Bitmap Index," later in this chapter. You can establish a single index on multiple columns by listing the columns one after the other, separated by commas. Recall the WORKERSKILL table. The primary key to this table is the combination of the worker Name and Skill. The following query produces the table shown at the top of Figure 20-1:

```
select RowID, Name, Skill, Ability
   from WORKERSKILL;
```

```
The WORKERSKILL Table with the RowID for Each Row:

ROWID                 NAME            SKILL           ABILITY
------------------    --------------  --------------  ---------
AAAAsYABQAAAAGzAAA    DICK JONES      SMITHY          EXCELLENT
AAAAsYABQAAAAGzAAB    JOHN PEARSON    COMBINE DRIVER
AAAAsYABQAAAAGzAAC    JOHN PEARSON    SMITHY          AVERAGE
AAAAsYABQAAAAGzAAD    HELEN BRANDT    COMBINE DRIVER  VERY FAST
AAAAsYABQAAAAGzAAE    JOHN PEARSON    WOODCUTTER      GOOD
AAAAsYABQAAAAGzAAF    VICTORIA LYNN   SMITHY          PRECISE
AAAAsYABQAAAAGzAAG    ADAH TALBOT     WORK            GOOD
AAAAsYABQAAAAGzAAH    WILFRED LOWELL  WORK            AVERAGE
AAAAsYABQAAAAGzAAI    ELBERT TALBOT   DISCUS          SLOW
AAAAsYABQAAAAGzAAJ    WILFRED LOWELL  DISCUS          AVERAGE

The Index to the WORKERSKILL Table with the RowID of the Table:

ADAH TALBOT     WORK                    AAAAsYABQAAAAGzAAG
DICK JONES      SMITHY                  AAAAsYABQAAAAGzAAA
ELBERT TALBOT   DISCUS                  AAAAsYABQAAAAGzAAI
HELEN BRANDT    COMBINE DRIVER          AAAAsYABQAAAAGzAAD
JOHN PEARSON    COMBINE DRIVER          AAAAsYABQAAAAGzAAB
JOHN PEARSON    SMITHY                  AAAAsYABQAAAAGzAAC
JOHN PEARSON    WOODCUTTER              AAAAsYABQAAAAGzAAE
VICTORIA LYNN   SMITHY                  AAAAsYABQAAAAGzAAF
WILFRED LOWELL  DISCUS                  AAAAsYABQAAAAGzAAJ
WILFRED LOWELL  WORK                    AAAAsYABQAAAAGzAAH
```

FIGURE 20-1.   *The WORKERSKILL table and its index*

For the sake of this example, the RowID was also selected. This is the internal location of the row (like a page number in a book) that Oracle uses when it stores rows of data in a table.

NOTE
The RowIDs in your database most likely will be different from those shown in Figure 20-1.

Now an index is created on the primary key:

```
create index WORKERSKILL_NAME_SKILL on WORKER(Name, Skill);
```

This is a practical and helpful technique to use to name the index, by combining the table and column names, up to 30 characters. You will not need to know the name of the index for a query; Oracle will use it automatically whenever it can. But, when listing (or dropping) the indexes that you've created (their names are stored in the data dictionary view USER_INDEXES, which you can query), their names will tell you immediately what they do. The index in Oracle looks like the second table in Figure 20-1.

When you execute a query such as this:

```
select Name, Skill, Ability
   from WORKERSKILL
 where Name = 'JOHN PEARSON'
   and Skill = 'WOODCUTTER';
```

Oracle finds the Name and Skill in the index, takes the RowID (AAAAsYABQAAAAGzAAE), and then reads the information at that RowID in the WORKERSKILL table. The index is in a format described as a *B-tree,* which means that it is organized in a structure like a tree, with nodes and leaves (similar to the cows in Chapter 13), and it *restructures* itself automatically whenever a new row is inserted in the table. A discussion of the mechanisms of B-trees is beyond the scope of this book, but can be found in many good computer science texts.

The next few sections cover a number of issues related to the use of indexes.

Enforcing Uniqueness

Recall from Chapter 2 that a set of tables is said to be in Third Normal Form if all of the columns in each table's rows are dependent only the primary key. In the WORKERSKILL table, the primary key is the combination of the Name and Skill. In other tables, a primary key might be an employee ID, a client ID, an account number, or, in a bank, a combination of branch number and account number.

In each of these cases, the uniqueness of the primary key is critical. A bank with duplicate account numbers, or a billing system with duplicate client IDs, would wreak havoc as transactions were posted to accounts belonging to different people but having the same primary key (this is why names usually are not used as primary keys—there are too many duplicates). To avoid this danger, have your database help prevent the creation of duplicate primary keys. Oracle offers two facilities that help:

- You can guarantee the uniqueness of a key through either indexing or constraints.

- You can use the sequence generators (discussed later in this chapter).

Creating a Unique Index

To create an index that will guarantee the uniqueness of the primary key (whether a single- or multiple-column primary key), such as on the WORKERSKILL table, use the primary key constraint on the key columns in the **create table** statement. You also can use a **create unique index** statement, but this statement will fail if any duplicates already exist. If you use the primary key constraint, you will never have duplicates. If the **create unique index** statement succeeds, then any future attempt to **insert** (or **update**) a row that would create a duplicate key will fail and result in this error message:

```
ERROR at line 1: ORA-00001: unique constraint
(WORKERSKILL.WORKERSKILL_NAME_SKILL) violated
```

There could be circumstances in which you would want to enforce uniqueness on something other than a primary key, and the unique constraint lets you do this. For example, if you included a social security number for each person, but the primary key was a sequence, you would want to ensure the uniqueness of the Social Security column as well with a unique constraint.

Consider the STOCK table, for example. Its primary key is the Company column. However, the Symbol column should be unique as well. To enforce the uniqueness of both of these columns, create two separate constraints when creating the table, as shown in the following listing:

```
create table STOCK (
Company          VARCHAR2(20) constraint PK_STOCK primary key,
Symbol           VARCHAR2(6) constraint UK_STOCK unique,
Industry         VARCHAR2(15),
CloseYesterday   NUMBER(6,2),
CloseToday       NUMBER(6,2),
Volume           NUMBER);
```

When creating the primary key and unique constraints specified for the STOCK table, Oracle will automatically create unique indexes to enforce those constraints. See "Placing an Index in the Database," later in this chapter, for details concerning the location of the created indexes.

Creating a Bitmap Index

To help tune queries that use nonselective columns in their limiting conditions, you can use bitmap indexes. Bitmap indexes should only be used if the data is infrequently updated, because they add to the cost of all data manipulation transactions against the tables they index.

Bitmap indexes are appropriate when nonselective columns are used as limiting conditions in a query. For example, if there are very few distinct Lodging values in a very large WORKER table, then you would not usually create a B-tree index on Lodging, even if it is commonly used in **where** clauses. However, Lodging may be able to take advantage of a bitmap index.

Internally, a bitmap index maps the distinct values for the columns to each record. For this example, assume there are only two Lodging values (WEITBROCHT and MATTS) in a very large WORKER table. Since there are two Lodging values, there are two separate bitmap entries for the Lodging bitmap index. If the first five rows in the table have a Lodging value of MATTS, and the next five have a Lodging value of WEITBROCHT, then the Lodging bitmap entries would resemble those shown in the following listing:

```
Lodging bitmaps:
    MATTS:       < 1 1 1 1 1 0 0 0 0 0 >
    WEITBROCHT: < 0 0 0 0 0 1 1 1 1 1 >
```

In the preceding listing, each number represents a row in the WORKER table. Since ten rows are considered, ten bitmap values are shown. Reading the bitmap for Lodging, the first five records have a value of MATTS (the '1' values), and the next five do not (the 0 values). You could have more than two possible values for the column, in which case there would be a separate bitmap entry for each possible value.

The Oracle optimizer can dynamically convert bitmap index entries to RowIDs during query processing. This conversion capability allows the optimizer to use indexes on columns that have many distinct values (via B-tree indexes) and on those that have few distinct values (via bitmap indexes).

To create a bitmap index, use the **bitmap** clause of the **create index** command, as shown in the following listing. You should indicate its nature as a bitmap index within the index name so that it will be easy to detect during tuning operations.

```
create bitmap index WORKER$BITMAP_LODGING
    on WORKER(Lodging);
```

If you choose to use bitmap indexes, you will need to weigh the performance benefit during queries against the performance cost during data manipulation commands. The more bitmap indexes there are on a table, the greater the cost will be during each transaction. You should not use bitmap indexes on a column that frequently has new values added to it. Each addition of a new value to the Lodging column will require that a corresponding new bitmap be created.

When to Create an Index

Indexes are most useful on larger tables, on columns that are likely to appear in **where** clauses either as a simple equality, such as this shown next.

```
where Name = 'JOHN PEARSON'
   and Skill = 'WOODCUTTER'
```

or in joins, such as this:

```
where WORKER.Lodging = LODGING.Lodging
```

Indexes also produce quicker retrievals for indexed columns in **where** clauses, except those **where** clauses using **IS NOT NULL** and **IS NULL** on the indexed column (see Chapter 36). If there is no **where** clause, no index is used.

Variety in Indexed Columns

Traditional (B-tree) indexes are most useful on columns with a significant amount of variety in their data. For instance, a column that indicates whether a company is a current client with a *Y* or *N* would be a poor choice for a traditional index, and could actually slow down a query. A telephone number column would be a good candidate. An area code column would be marginal, depending on the distribution of unique area code values in the table.

When a primary key involves more than one column, it is better to put the column with the most variety first in the primary key constraint. If the columns have relatively equal variety, put the column likely to be accessed most often first.

Small tables may be better left unindexed, except to enforce uniqueness in the primary key. A small table is one with fewer than 30 rows; in a given application, a table with up to 100 or more rows may still be considered small. Beyond that, indexing will nearly always be productive.

On the other hand, bitmap indexes present a viable indexing alternative for columns that have very few distinct values. Bitmap indexes are commonly used for "flag" columns that are restricted to values such as Y and N. Bitmap indexes are particularly effective when multiple bitmap indexes are used in a query; the optimizer can quickly evaluate the bitmaps and determine which rows meet all of the criteria for which bitmap indexes are available.

How Many Indexes to Use on a Table

You can create many indexes on a single table, with many columns in a single index. The tradeoff for indexing too many columns is the speed of inserting new rows: every index also must have a new entry made in it when an **insert** is done. If your table will be used primarily for queries, the only cost of indexing as many columns as you can (that have variety, and will be used in **where** clauses, of course) is using some extra disk space.

Except in cluster indexes (discussed later in this chapter), columns that are **NULL** will not appear in an index. If, for instance, you indexed the Noon column in the COMFORT table, as shown here:

```
select * from COMFORT;

CITY          SAMPLEDAT NOON MIDNIGHT PRECIPITATION
------------- --------- ---- -------- -------------
SAN FRANCISCO 21-MAR-99 62.5     42.3            .5
SAN FRANCISCO 22-JUN-99 51.1     71.9            .1
SAN FRANCISCO 23-SEP-99          61.5            .1
SAN FRANCISCO 22-DEC-99 52.6     39.8           2.3
KEENE         21-MAR-99 39.9     -1.2           4.4
KEENE         22-JUN-99 85.1     66.7           1.3
KEENE         23-SEP-99 99.8     82.6
KEENE         22-DEC-99 -7.2     -1.2           3.9
```

there would be an entry in the index for every row except the San Francisco 23-SEP-99 record, because the value for Noon on that date is **NULL**.

Indexes based on more than one column will have an entry if any of the columns are not **NULL**. If all columns are **NULL** for a given row, no entry will appear for it in the index.

Since indexes are typically used by **where** clauses that contain an equality, the row with a **NULL** column will not be returned to you by the **select** statement (remember that nothing is equal to **NULL**). This may be the desired effect. You might, for instance, keep a column of commissions for salespeople, but leave the column **NULL**, rather than 0, if a salesperson has no commission. A query that says

```
select Name, Commission
   from COMMISSION
 where Commission > 0;
```

may run faster, because salespeople who have no commission will not even appear in the index on the Commission column.

Placing an Index in the Database

You can specify where the index to a table is placed by assigning it to a specific tablespace. As was briefly mentioned in Chapter 19, a *tablespace* is a section of disk where tables and indexes are stored, and one database may have several, each with its own name. An index for a table should be placed in a tablespace that is on a physically separate disk drive than the data tablespace. This will reduce the potential for disk contention between the tablespaces' files.

To specify the tablespace in which to locate an index, the normal **create index** statement is simply followed by the word **tablespace** and the tablespace name, as shown here:

```
create index workerskill_name_skill on WORKER(Name, Skill)
      tablespace GBTALBOT;
```

GBTALBOT is the name given to a tablespace previously created by the database administrator. The use of the **tablespace** option in a **create index** statement lets you physically separate your tables from their associated indexes.

When you create a primary key or unique constraint, Oracle will automatically create an index to enforce uniqueness. Unless you specify otherwise, that index will be created in the same tablespace as the table that the constraint modifies, and will use the default storage parameters for that tablespace. Since that storage location is typically undesirable, you should take advantage of the **using index** clause when creating primary key and unique constraints.

The **using index** clause allows you to specify the storage parameters and tablespace location for an index created by a constraint. In the following example, a primary key is created on the Company column of the STOCK table. The primary key constraint is given the name PK_STOCK. The index associated with that primary key is directed to the INDEXES tablespace, with certain storage parameters. A unique constraint is created on the Symbol column, and its index is also placed in the INDEXES tablespace. Both constraints are specified at the table level (rather than at the column level) to better illustrate the **using index** syntax.

```
create table STOCK (
Company          VARCHAR2(20),
Symbol           VARCHAR2(6),
Industry         VARCHAR2(15),
CloseYesterday   NUMBER(6,2),
CloseToday       NUMBER(6,2),
Volume           NUMBER,
  constraint PK_STOCK  primary key (Company)
      using index tablespace INDEXES
    storage (initial 1M next 1M),
  constraint UQ_STOCK  unique (Symbol)
      using index tablespace INDEXES
    storage (initial 1M next 1M))
;
```

See "Integrity Constraint" in the Alphabetical Reference for further options for the **using index** clause, and see **create index** in the Alphabetical Reference for performance-related index creation options.

Rebuilding an Index

Oracle provides a *fast index rebuild* capability that allows you to re-create an index without having to drop the existing index. The currently available index is used as the data source for the index, instead of using the table as the data source. During the index rebuild, you can change its **storage** parameters and **tablespace** assignment.

In the following example, the WORKER_PK index is rebuilt (via the **rebuild** clause). Its storage parameters are changed to use an initial extent size of 8MB and a next extent size of 4MB, in the INDX_2 tablespace.

```
alter index WORKER_PK rebuild
storage (initial 8M next 4M pctincrease 0)
tablespace INDX_2;
```

> **NOTE**
> *When the WORKER_PK index is rebuilt, there must be enough space for both the old index and the new index to exist simultaneously. After the new index has been created, the old index will be dropped and its space will be freed.*

When you create an index that is based on previously indexed columns, Oracle may be able to use the existing indexes as data sources for the new index. For example, if you create a two-column index on the Name and Lodging columns, and later decide to create an index on just the Name column, Oracle will use the existing index as the data source for the new index. As a result, the performance of your **create index** commands will improve—if you create the indexes in an order that can take advantage of this feature.

Function-based Indexes

As of Oracle8i, you can create *function-based indexes*. Prior to Oracle8i, any query that performed a function on a column could not use that column's index. Thus, this query could not use an index on the Name column:

```
select * from WORKER
  where UPPER(Name) = 'WILFRED LOWELL';
```

but this query could:

```
select * from WORKER
  where Name = 'WILFRED LOWELL';
```

since the second query does not perform the **UPPER** function on the Name column. As of Oracle8i, you can create indexes that allow function-based accesses to be supported by index accesses. Instead of creating an index on the column Name, you can create an index on the column expression UPPER(Name), as shown in the following listing:

```
create index WORKER$UPPER_NAME on
WORKER(UPPER(Name));
```

Although function-based indexes can be useful, be sure to consider the following questions when creating them:

- Can you restrict the functions that will be used on the column? If so, can you restrict all functions from being performed on the column?

- Do you have adequate storage space for the additional indexes?

- When you drop the table, you will be dropping more indexes (and therefore more extents) than before; how will that impact the time required to drop the table?

Function-based indexes are useful, but you should implement them sparingly. The more indexes you create on a table, the longer all **insert**s, **update**s, and **delete**s will take.

Tablespace and the Structure of the Database

People who have worked with computers for any period of time are familiar with the concept of a file; it's a place on disk where information is stored, and it has a name. Its size is usually not fixed: if you add information to the file, it can grow larger and take up more disk space, up to the maximum available. This process is managed by the operating system, and often involves distributing the information in the file over several smaller sections of the disk that are not physically near each other. The operating system handles the logical connection of these smaller sections without your being aware of it at all. To you, the file looks like a single whole.

Oracle uses files as a part of its organizational scheme, but its logical structure goes beyond the concept of a file. A tablespace is an area of disk consisting of one or more disk files. A tablespace can contain many tables, indexes, or clusters. Because a tablespace has a fixed size, it can get full as rows are added to its tables. When this happens, the tablespace can be expanded by someone who has DBA authority. The expansion is accomplished either by creating a new disk file and adding it to the tablespace or by extending the existing datafiles. New rows can then be added to existing tables, and those tables will therefore have rows in both files. One or more tablespaces, together, makes up a database.

NOTE
DBAs can also set up files to extend automatically. Files that can dynamically extend eliminate potential problems in the database activity but decrease your control over the application's space usage.

Each table has a single area of disk space, called a *segment,* set aside for it in the tablespace. Each segment, in turn, has an initial area of disk space, called the *initial extent,* set aside for it in the tablespace. Once the segment has used up this space, the *next extent,* another single area of disk space, is set aside for it. When it has used this up as well, yet another next extent is set aside. This process continues with every table until the whole tablespace is full. At that point, someone has to add a new file to the tablespace or extend the tablespace's files before any more growth in the tables can take place.

If this is confusing, an old parallel (see Figure 20-2) might help clarify it. Think of a database as a town block, and each tablespace as a fenced-in lot. At first, the block is fairly sparse: there are only a few fenced-in lots and plenty of open, unclaimed space. Lot one (tablespace one) is owned by G. B. Talbot, and he calls it "Homestead One." He plants several garden plots: rows of corn, rows of beans, and rows of carrots. Each of these plots corresponds to a table with its rows, and each is planted in its own area, or "initial extent." After the carrots, he decides to plant more corn, but he's used up that section of the lot, so he plants more corn over on the other side of the yard. His corn is now in its next extent (its second extent). He continues similarly with additional rows of beans and carrots, until the yard is a patchwork of sections of each.

Eventually, he fills the lot entirely. His tablespace is full. He then purchases some empty land down at the other end of the block, fences in the lot, and dubs it "Homestead Two." His tablespace is now larger. Even though the lots (files) are not physically connected, Talbot still owns both of them. The tablespace is still "G. B. Talbot," and contains two lots, Homestead One and Homestead Two. He can now plant more rows of corn, beans, and carrots in his second lot. They continue to consume additional "extents."

Every database also contains a *system* tablespace. This is the town hall for the block, where the ownership records and addresses are kept. It contains the data dictionary, and the names and locations of all the tablespaces, tables, indexes, and clusters for this database.

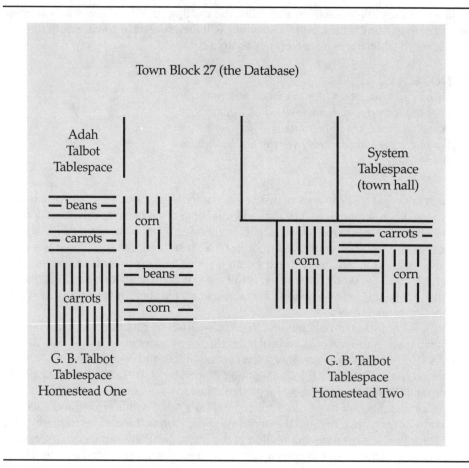

FIGURE 20-2. *Oracle database structure as a town block*

Figure 20-3 shows how a database looks with a typical collection of tablespaces, tables, indexes, clusters, and extents. The database is created and named by the system database administrator, who usually also sets up tablespaces and grants use of them to individual users. In this database, named TALBOT, tablespaces have been set up named ADAH, JONES, SYSTEM, and GEORGE.

Within a tablespace are tables, indexes, and clusters. Each table starts out with an initial extent allocated to it, and a next extent size that governs the amount of space allocated each time it grows beyond its current extent. In this figure, the COMFORT, WEATHER, and WORKER tables have all grown beyond their initial

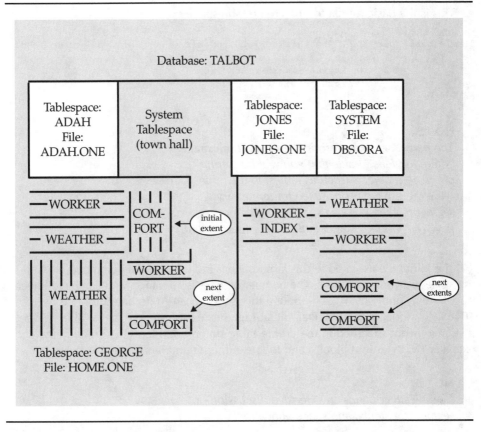

FIGURE 20-3.   *Oracle database structure*

extent, and have completely consumed the initial file, HOME.ONE, of the tablespace. COMFORT has grown into two additional extents in the second file, HOME.TWO. Both WEATHER and WORKER also have an additional extent in the second file. An index on the WORKER table was created after the second file became necessary.

create tablespace

The **create tablespace** command allows one or more files to be assigned immediately to the tablespace. It also specifies a default space for any tables created without an explicit storage clause mentioned in the **create table** statement.

This is the basic format for the **create tablespace** command:

```
create tablespace TALBOT datafile '/db01/oracle/GBT/talbot.dbf' size 1000K
default storage (initial 1M next 1M
                 minextents 1 maxextents 100
                 pctincrease 0)
permanent;
```

NOTE
*The **permanent** keyword in the **create tablespace** command tells Oracle that you will be storing permanent objects (such as tables) in the tablespace. If the tablespace is only used for temporary segments, then you can specify the **temporary** keyword instead. The default value is **permanent**.*

The initial file assigned to this tablespace is included in the command, as well as its size in *bytes,* not blocks. The number of bytes is an integer and can be followed by a *K* (to multiply by 1024—about a thousand) or an *M* (to be multiplied by 1048576—about a million). **Default storage** sets up the storage that a table will get if storage is not specified in the **create table** statement. Here, the initial default extent is 1M bytes (not blocks) and the next (incremental) extent is 1M bytes.

NOTE
Chapter 38 contains an extensive discussion of segments, extents, and space allocation.

minextents allows you to set aside additional extents beyond the first at the time a table is created. These additional extents will not necessarily be contiguous (physically adjacent) with the initial extent, or with each other, but the space will at least be reserved.

maxextents is the limit of additional extents allowed. You can specify **maxextents unlimited**, in which case there is no limit to the number of extents allowed for the table or index.

pctincrease is a growth factor for extents. When set to a non-zero value, each incremental extent will be the specified percentage larger than the one before it. This has the effect of reducing the number of extents, and noncontiguous space, used by a table that grows large. However, it causes the space allocated to the table to grow exponentially. If the data volume in the table grows at a constant rate, you should set **pctincrease** to 0.

The default values for storage are operating-system-specific. The minimum and maximum values for each of these options are available in the Alphabetical Reference under **create table** and "Storage." These options may be changed with the **alter tablespace** command. The **create table** command for the LEDGER table looks like this:

```
create table LEDGER (
ActionDate       DATE,
Action           VARCHAR2(8),
Item             VARCHAR2(30),
Quantity         NUMBER,
QuantityType     VARCHAR2(10),
Rate             NUMBER,
Amount           NUMBER(9,2),
Person           VARCHAR2(25)
)
tablespace TALBOT
;
```

In this form, the LEDGER table will inherit the default storage definitions of the TALBOT tablespace. To override these defaults, the **storage** clause is used in the **create table** command:

```
create table LEDGER (
ActionDate       DATE,
Action           VARCHAR2(8),
Item             VARCHAR2(30),
Quantity         NUMBER,
QuantityType     VARCHAR2(10),
Rate             NUMBER,
Amount           NUMBER(9,2),
Person           VARCHAR2(25)
)
tablespace TALBOT
storage (initial 512K next 512K
                minextents 2 maxextents 50
                pctincrease 0)
;
```

If you use temporary tables (see Chapter 13), you can create a tablespace dedicated to their storage needs. Use the **create temporary tablespace** command (fully described in the Alphabetical Reference) to support this special type of table.

Clusters

Clustering is a method of storing tables that are intimately related and often joined together into the same area on disk. For example, instead of the WORKER table being in one section of the disk and the WORKERSKILL table being somewhere else, their rows could be interleaved together in a single area, called a *cluster*. The *cluster key* is the column or columns by which the tables are usually joined in a query (for example, Name for the WORKER and WORKERSKILL tables). To cluster tables, you must own the tables you are going to cluster together.

The following is the basic format of the **create cluster** command:

```
create cluster cluster (column datatype [,column
     datatype]. . .) [other options];
```

The *cluster* name follows the table-naming conventions, and *column datatype* is the name and datatype you will use as the cluster key. The *column* name may be the same as one of the columns of a table you will put in this cluster, or it may be any other valid name. Here's an example:

```
create cluster WORKERandSKILL (Judy VARCHAR2(25));

Cluster created.
```

This creates a cluster (a space is set aside, as it would be for a table) with nothing in it. The use of Judy for the cluster key is irrelevant; you'll never use it again. Next, tables are created to be included in this cluster:

```
create table WORKER (
Name            VARCHAR2(25) not null,
Age             NUMBER,
Lodging         VARCHAR2(15)
)
cluster WORKERandSKILL (Name)
;
```

Prior to inserting rows into WORKER, you must create a cluster index:

```
create index WORKERANDSKILL_NDX
on cluster WORKERandSKILL;
```

Recall that the presence of a **cluster** clause here precludes the use of a **tablespace** or **storage** clause. Note how this structure differs from a standard **create table** statement:

```
create table WORKER (
Name           VARCHAR2(25) not null,
Age            NUMBER,
Lodging        VARCHAR2(15)
);
```

In the first **create table** statement, the cluster **WORKERandSKILL (Name)** clause *follows* the closing parenthesis of the list of columns being created in the table. **WORKERandSKILL** is the name of the cluster previously created. Name is the column in this table that will be stored in the cluster key Judy. It is possible to have multiple cluster keys in the **create cluster** statement, and to have multiple columns stored in those keys in the **create table** statement. Notice that nowhere does either statement say explicitly that the Name column goes into the Judy cluster key. The matchup is done by position only: Name and Judy were both the first objects mentioned in their respective cluster statements. Multiple columns and cluster keys are matched first to first, second to second, third to third, and so on. Now a second table is added to the cluster:

```
create table WORKERSKILL (
Name           VARCHAR2(25) not null,
Skill          VARCHAR2(25) not null,
Ability        VARCHAR2(15)
)
cluster WORKERandSKILL (Name)
;
```

How the Tables Are Stored

Figure 20-4 illustrates how the data is stored in a cluster. Recall that the WORKER table has three columns: Name, Age, and Lodging. The WORKERSKILL table also has three columns: Name, Skill, and Ability. When these two tables are clustered, each unique Name is actually stored only once, in the cluster key. To each Name are attached the columns from both of these tables.

The data from both of these tables is actually stored in a single location, almost as if the cluster were a big table containing data drawn from both of the tables that make it up.

An additional cluster option, a *hash cluster,* uses the cluster column values to determine the physical location in which the row is stored. See the entry for the **create cluster** command in the Alphabetical Reference.

Sequences

You can assign unique numbers, such as customer IDs, to columns in your database by using a sequence; you don't need to create a special table and code to keep

```
AGE  LODGING     NAME                            SKILL          ABILITY
----  ----------  ------------------------      --------------  ---------
  23  PAPA KING   ADAH TALBOT                     WORK           GOOD
  29  ROSE HILL   ANDREW DYE
  22  CRANMER     BART SARJEANT
  18  ROSE HILL   DICK JONES                      SMITHY         EXCELLENT
  16  MATTS       DONALD ROLLO
  43  WEITBROCHT  ELBERT TALBOT                   DISCUS         SLOW
  41  ROSE HILL   GEORGE OSCAR
  55  PAPA KING   GERHARDT KENTGEN
  15              HELEN BRANDT                    COMBINE DRIVER VERY FAST
  33  MATTS       JED HOPKINS
  27  ROSE HILL   JOHN PEARSON                    COMBINE DRIVER
                                                  WOODCUTTER     GOOD
                                                  SMITHY         AVERAGE
      ROSE HILL   KAY AND PALMER WALLBOM
  21  ROSE HILL   PAT LAVAY
  25  CRANMER     PETER LAWSON
      WEITBROCHT  RICHARD KOCH AND BROTHERS
  35  MATTS       ROLAND BRANDT
  32  MULLERS     VICTORIA LYNN                   SMITHY         PRECISE
  67              WILFRED LOWELL                  WORK           AVERAGE
                                                  DISCUS         AVERAGE
  15  CRANMER     WILLIAM SWING
```

from the WORKER table

from the WORKERSKILL table

cluster key

FIGURE 20-4. *How data is stored in clusters*

track of the unique numbers in use. This is done by using the **create sequence** command, as shown here:

```
create sequence CustomerID increment by 1 start with 1000;
```

This will create a sequence that can be accessed by **insert** and **update** statements (also **select**, although this is rare). Typically, the unique sequence value is created with a statement like the following:

```
insert into CUSTOMER
            (Name, Contact, ID)
values
            ('COLE CONSTRUCTION', 'VERONICA',CustomerID.NextVal);
```

The NextVal attached to CustomerID tells Oracle you want the next available sequence number from the CustomerID sequence. This is guaranteed to be unique; Oracle will not give it to anyone else. To use the same number more than once (such as in a series of **insert**s into related tables), CurrVal is used instead of NextVal, *after the first use.* That is, using NextVal assures that the sequence table gets incremented and that you get a unique number, so you have to use NextVal first. Once you've used NextVal, that number is stored in CurrVal for your use anywhere, until you use NextVal again, at which point both NextVal and CurrVal change to the new sequence number.

If you use both NextVal and CurrVal in a single SQL statement, both will contain the value retrieved by NextVal. Neither of these can be used in subqueries, as columns in the **select** clause of a view, with **DISTINCT**, **UNION**, **INTERSECT**, or **MINUS**, or in the **order by**, **group by**, or **having** clause of a **select** statement.

You can also cache sequence values in memory for faster access, and you can make the sequence cycle back to its starting value once a maximum value is reached. See **create sequence** in the Alphabetical Reference.

CHAPTER
21

Using SQL*Loader
to Load Data

n the scripts provided in Appendix A, a large number of **insert** commands are executed. In place of those **insert**s, you could create a file containing the data to be loaded, and then use Oracle's SQL*Loader utility to load the data. This chapter provides you with an overview of the use of SQL*Loader and its major capabilities. Two additional data-movement utilities, Export and Import, are covered in Chapter 38. SQL*Loader, Export, and Import are described in great detail in the *Oracle8i Utilities* provided with the standard Oracle documentation set.

SQL*Loader loads data from external files into tables in the Oracle database. SQL*Loader requires two primary files: the data file, which contains the information to be loaded, and the control file, which contains information on the format of the data, the records and fields within the file, the order in which they are to be loaded, and even, when needed, the names of the multiple files that will be used for data. You can also combine the control file information into the data file itself, although the two are usually separated to make it easier to reuse the control file.

When executed, SQL*Loader will automatically create a log file and a "bad" file. The log file records the status of the load, such as the number of rows processed and the number of rows committed. The "bad" file will contain all the rows that were rejected during the load due to data errors, such as nonunique values in primary key columns.

Within the control file, you can specify additional commands to govern the load criteria. If these criteria are not met by a row, the row will be written to a "discard" file. The log, bad, and discard files will have the extensions .log, .bad, and .dsc, respectively. Control files are typically given the extension .ctl.

SQL*Loader is a powerful utility for loading data, for several reasons:

- It is highly flexible, allowing you to manipulate the data as it is being loaded.

- You can use SQL*Loader to break a single large data set into multiple sets of data during commit processing, significantly reducing the size of the transactions processed by the load.

- You can use its Direct Path loading option to perform loads very quickly.

To start using SQL*Loader, you should first become familiar with the control file, as described in the next section.

The Control File

The control file tells Oracle how to read and load the data. The control file tells SQL*Loader where to find the source data for the load and the tables into which to load the data, along with any other rules that must be applied during the load processing. These rules can include restrictions for discards (similar to **where** clauses for queries) and instructions for combining multiple physical rows in an input file into a single row during an **insert**. SQL*Loader will use the control file to create the **insert** commands executed for the data load.

The control file is created at the operating system level, using any text editor that enables you to save plain text files. Within the control file, commands do not have to obey any rigid formatting requirements, but standardizing your command syntax will make later maintenance of the control file simpler.

The following listing shows a sample control file for loading data into the LODGING table:

```
LOAD DATA
INFILE 'lodging.dat'
INTO TABLE LODGING
(Lodging          POSITION(01:15)    CHAR,
 Longname         POSITION(16:55)    CHAR,
 Manager          POSITION(56:80)    CHAR,
 Address          POSITION(81:110)   CHAR)
```

In this example, data is loaded from the file lodging.dat into the LODGING table. The lodging.dat file contains the data for all four of the LODGING columns, with white space padding out the unused characters in those fields. Thus, the LongName column value always begins at space 16 in the file, even if the Lodging value is less than 15 characters. Although this formatting makes the input file larger, it simplifies the loading process. No length needs to be given for the fields, since the starting and ending positions within the input data stream effectively give the field length.

The **infile** clause names the input file, and the **into table** clause specifies the table into which the data will be loaded. Each of the columns is listed, along with the position where its data resides in each physical record in the file. This format allows you to load data even if the source data's column order does not match the order of columns in your table.

To perform this load, the user executing the load must have INSERT privilege on the LODGING table.

Loading Variable-Length Data

If the columns in your input file have variable lengths, you can use SQL*Loader commands to tell Oracle how to determine when a value ends. In the following example, a comma separates the input values:

```
LOAD DATA
INFILE 'lodging.dat'
BADFILE '/user/load/lodging.bad'
```

```
TRUNCATE
INTO TABLE LODGING
FIELDS TERMINATED BY ","
(Lodging, Longname, Manager, Address)
```

The **fields terminated by ","** clause tells SQL*Loader that during the load, each column value will be terminated by a comma. Thus, the input file does not have to be 110 characters wide for each row, as was the case in the first load example. The lengths of the columns are not specified in the control file, since they will be determined during the load.

In this example, the name of the bad file is specified by the **badfile** clause. In general, the name of the bad file is only given when you wish to redirect the file to a different directory.

This example also shows the use of the **truncate** clause within a control file. When this control file is executed by SQL*Loader, the LODGING table will be **truncate**d before the start of the load. Since **truncate** commands cannot be rolled back, you should use care when using this option. In addition to **truncate**, you can use the following options:

- **append**   Use to add rows to the table.

- **insert**   Use to add rows to an empty table. If the table is not empty, the load will abort with an error.

- **replace**   Use to empty the table and then add the new rows. The user must have DELETE privilege on the table.

Starting the Load

To execute the commands in the control file, you need to run SQL*Loader with the appropriate parameters. SQL*Loader is started via the **SQLLDR** command at the operating system prompt.

NOTE
*The SQL*Loader executable may consist of the name SQLLDR followed by a version number. Consult your platform-specific Oracle documentation for the exact name.*

When you execute **SQLLDR**, you need to specify the control file, username/password, and other critical load information, as shown in Table 21-1.

SQLLDR Keyword	Description
Userid	Username and password for the load, separated by a slash.
Control	Name of the control file.
Log	Name of the log file.
Bad	Name of the bad file.
Discard	Name of the discard file.
Discardmax	Maximum number of rows to discard before stopping the load. The default is to allow all discards.
Skip	Number of logical rows in the input file to skip before starting to load data. Usually used during reloads from the same input file following a partial load. The default is 0.
Load	Number of logical rows to load. The default is all.
Errors	Number of errors to allow. The default is 50.
Rows	Number of rows to commit at a time. Use this parameter to break up the transaction size during the load. The default for conventional path loads is 64; the default for Direct Path loads is all rows.
Bindsize	Size of conventional path bind array, in bytes. The default is operating-system-dependent.
Silent	Suppress messages during the load.
Direct	Use Direct Path loading. The default is FALSE.
Parfile	Name of the parameter file that contains additional load parameter specifications.
Parallel	Perform parallel loading. The default is FALSE.
File	File to allocate extents from (for parallel loading).
Skip_Unusable_Indexes	Allows loads into tables that have indexes in unusable states. The default is FALSE.
Skip_Index_Maintenance	Stops index maintenance for Direct Path loads, leaving them in unusable states. The default is FALSE.

TABLE 21-1. *SQLLDR Parameters*

Each load must have a control file, since none of the input parameters specifies critical information for the load—the input file and the table being loaded.

If you wish, you can separate the arguments to **SQLLDR** with commas. Enter them with the keywords (such as **userid** or **log**), followed by the parameter value. Keywords are always followed by an equal sign (=) and the appropriate argument.

If the **userid** keyword is omitted, you will be asked for it. If a slash is given after the equal sign, an OPS$ login default ID and password will be used. You also can use a Net8 database specification string to log on to a remote database and load the data into it. For example, your command may start

```
sqlldr userid=usernm/mypass@dev
```

The **direct** keyword, which invokes the Direct Path load option, is described in "Direct Path Loading" later in this chapter.

The SILENT parameter tells **SQLLDR** to suppress certain informative data:

- HEADER suppresses the SQL*LOADER header.

- FEEDBACK suppresses the feedback at each commit point.

- ERRORS suppresses the logging (in the log file) of each record that caused an Oracle error, although the count is still logged.

- DISCARDS suppresses the logging (in the log file) of each record that was discarded, although the count is still logged.

- PARTITIONS disables the writing of the per-partition statistics to the log file.

- ALL suppresses all of the preceding.

If more than one of these is entered, separate each with a comma and enclose the list in parentheses. For example, you can suppress the **header** and **errors** information via the following keyword setting:

```
silent=(HEADER,ERRORS)
```

NOTE
Commands in the control file override any in the calling command line.

Let's load a sample set of data into the LODGING table, which has four columns (Lodging, LongName, Manager, and Address). The data to be loaded is in a file called lodging.dat, and consists of two records:

```
GoodLodging,Good Lodging Record,John Goodman,123 Okeedokee Drive
BadLodgingRecord,Bad Lodging Record,John Badman, 321 OkeedokeeDrive
```

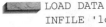

NOTE
Each line is ended by a carriage return. Even though the first line's last value is not as long as the column it is being loaded into, the row will stop at the carriage return.

The data is separated by commas, and we don't wish to delete the data previously loaded into LODGING, so the control file will look like this:

```
LOAD DATA
INFILE 'lodging.dat'
APPEND
INTO TABLE LODGING
FIELDS TERMINATED BY ","
(Lodging, Longname, Manager, Address)
```

Next, run **SQLLDR** and tell it to use the control file:

```
sqlldr practice/practice control=lodging.ctl log=lodging.log
```

When the load completes, you should have one successfully loaded record and one failure. The successfully loaded record will be in the LODGING table:

```
select * from LODGING
where Lodging like 'Good%';

LODGING           LONGNAME
---------------   ----------------------------------------
GoodLodging       Good Lodging Record
```

A file named lodging.bad will be created, and will contain one record:

```
BadLodgingRecord,Bad Lodging Record,John Badman, 321 OkeedokeeDrive
```

Why was that record rejected? Check the log file, lodging.log, which will say, in part:

```
Record 2: Rejected - Error on table LODGING.
ORA-01401: inserted value too large for column

Table LODGING:
  1 Row successfully loaded.
  1 Rows not loaded due to data errors.
```

Row 2, the "BadLodgingRecord" row, was rejected because the value for the Lodging column is 16 characters long, while the column is defined as a VARCHAR2(15).

Logical and Physical Records

In Table 21-1, several of the keywords refer to "logical" rows. A *logical* row is a row that is inserted into the database. Depending on the structure of the input file, multiple physical rows may be combined to make a single logical row.

For example, the input file may look like this:

```
CRANMER,CRANMER RETREAT HOUSE,THOM CRANMER,HILL ST BERKELEY
```

in which case there would be a one-to-one relationship between that physical record and the logical record it creates. But the data file may look like this instead:

```
CRANMER,
CRANMER RETREAT HOUSE,
THOM CRANMER,
HILL ST BERKELEY
```

To combine the data, you need to use continuation rules. In this case, the column values are split one to a line, so there is a set number of physical records for each logical record. To combine them, use the **concatenate** clause within the control file. In this case, you would specify **concatenate 4** to create a single logical row from the four physical rows.

The logic for creating a single logical record from multiple physical records can be much more complex than a simple concatenation. You can use the **continueif** clause to specify the conditions that cause logical records to be continued. You can further manipulate the input data to create multiple logical records from a single physical record (via the use of multiple **into table** clauses). See the control file syntax in the "SQLLDR" entry of the Alphabetical Reference in this book and the notes in the following section.

Control File Syntax Notes

The full syntax for SQL*Loader control files is shown in the "SQLLDR" entry in the Alphabetical Reference, so it is not repeated here.

Within the **load** clause, you can specify that the load is **recoverable** or **unrecoverable**. The **unrecoverable** clause only applies to Direct Path loading, and is described in "Tuning Data Loads" later in this chapter.

In addition to using the **concatenate** clause, you can use the **continueif** clause to control the manner in which physical records are assembled into logical records. The **this** clause refers to the current physical record, while the **next** clause refers to the next physical record. For example, you could create a two-character continuation character at the start of each physical record. If that record should be concatenated to the preceding record, set that value equal to '**'. You could then use the **continueif next (1:2)='**'** clause to create a single logical record from the multiple physical records. The '**' continuation character will not be part of the merged record.

The syntax for the **into table** clause includes a **when** clause. The **when** clause, shown in the preceding listing, serves as a filter applied to rows prior to their insertion into the table. For example, you can specify

```
when manager='THOM CRANMER'
```

to load only Thom Cranmer's records into the table. Any row that does not pass the **when** condition will be written to the discard file. Thus, the discard file contains rows that can be used for later loads, but that did not pass the current set of **when** conditions. You can use multiple **when** conditions, connected with **and** clauses.

Use the **trailing nullcols** clause if you are loading variable-length records for which the last column does not always have a value. With this clause in effect, SQL*Loader will generate **NULL** values for those columns.

As shown in an example earlier in this chapter, you can use the **fields terminated by** clause to load variable-length data. Rather than being terminated by a character, the fields can be **terminated by whitespace** or **enclosed by** characters or **optionally enclosed by** other characters.

When you load DATE datatype values, you can specify a date mask. For example, if you had a column named HireDate and the incoming data is in the format Mon-DD-YYYY in the first 11 places of the record, you could specify the HireDate portion of the load as follows:

```
HireDate POSITION (1:11) DATE "Mon-DD-YYYY"
```

Within the **into table** clause, you can use the **recnum** keyword to assign a record number to each logical record as it is read from the data file, and that value will be inserted into the assigned column of the table. The **constant** keyword allows you to assign a constant value to a column during the load. For character columns, enclose the constant value within single quotes. If you use the **sysdate** keyword, the selected column will be populated with the current system date and time.

If you use the **sequence** option, SQL*Loader will maintain a sequence of values during the load. As records are processed, the sequence value will be increased by the increment you specify. If the rows fail during **insert** (and are sent to the bad file), those sequence values will not be reused. If you use the **max** keyword within the sequence option, the sequence values will use the current maximum value of the column as the starting point for the sequence.

If you store numbers in VARCHAR2 columns, avoid using the **sequence** option for those columns. For example, if your table already contains the values 1 through

10 in a VARCHAR2 column, then the maximum value within that column is 9—the greatest character string. Using that as the basis for a **sequence** option will cause SQL*Loader to attempt to **insert** a record using 10 as the newly created value—and that may conflict with the existing record.

Managing Data Loads

Loading large data volumes is a batch operation. Batch operations should not be performed concurrently with the small transactions prevalent in many database applications. If you have many concurrent users executing small transactions against a table, you should schedule your batch operations against that table to occur at a time when no users are accessing the table.

Oracle maintains *read consistency* for users' queries. If you execute the SQL*Loader job against the table at the same time that other users are querying the table, Oracle will internally maintain rollback segment entries to enable those users to see their data as it existed when they first queried the data. To minimize the amount of work Oracle must perform to maintain read consistency (and to minimize the associated performance degradation caused by this overhead), schedule your long-running data load jobs to be performed when few other actions are occurring in the database. In particular, avoid contention with other accesses of the same table.

Design your data load processing to be easy to maintain and reuse. Establish guidelines for the structure and format of the input data files. The more standardized the input data formats are, the simpler it will be to reuse old control files for the data loads. For repeated scheduled loads into the same table, your goal should be to reuse the same control file each time. Following each load, you will need to review and move the log, bad, data, and discard files so they do not accidentally get overwritten.

Within the control file, use comments to indicate any special processing functions being performed. To create a comment within the control file, begin the line with two dashes, as shown in the following example:

```
-- Limit the load to LA employees:
when Location='LA'
```

If you have properly commented your control file, you will increase the chance that it can be reused during future loads. You will also simplify the maintenance of the data load process itself, as described in the next section.

Repeating Data Loads

Data loads do not always work exactly as planned. Many variables are involved in a data load, and not all of them will always be under your control. For example, the owner of the source data may change its data formatting, invalidating part of your control file. Business rules may change, forcing additional changes. Database structures and space availability may change, further affecting your ability to load the data.

In an ideal case, a data load will either fully succeed or fully fail. However, in many cases, a data load will partially succeed, making the recovery process more difficult. If some of the records have been inserted into the table, then attempting to reinsert those records should result in a primary key violation. If you are generating the primary key value during the insert (via the **sequence** option), then those rows may not fail the second time—and will be inserted twice.

To determine where a load failed, use the log file. The log file will record the commit points as well as the errors encountered. All of the rejected records should be in either the bad file or the discard file. You can minimize the recovery effort by forcing the load to fail if many errors are encountered. To force the load to abort before a large number of errors is encountered, use the **errors** keyword of the **SQLLDR** command. You can also use the **discardmax** keyword to limit the number of discarded records permitted before the load aborts.

If you set **errors** to 0, the first error will cause the load to fail. What if that load fails after 100 records have been inserted? You will have two options: identify and delete the inserted records and reapply the whole load, or skip the successfully inserted records. You can use the **skip** keyword of **SQLLDR** to skip the first 100 records during its load processing. The load will then continue with record 101 (which has hopefully been fixed prior to the reload attempt). If you cannot identify the rows that have just been loaded into the table, you will need to use the **skip** option during the restart process.

The proper settings for **errors** and **discardmax** depend on the load. If you have full control over the data load process, and the data is properly "cleaned" before being extracted to a load file, you may have very little tolerance for errors and discards. On the other hand, if you do not have control over the source for the input data file, you need to set **errors** and **discardmax** high enough to allow the load to complete. After the load has completed, you need to review the log file, correct the data in the bad file, and reload the data using the original bad file as the new input file. If rows have been incorrectly discarded, you need to do an additional load using the original discard file as the new input file.

After modifying the errant Lodging value, you can rerun the LODGING table load example using the original lodging.dat file. During the reload, you have two options when using the original input data file:

■ Skip the first row by specifying **skip=1** in the **SQLLDR** command line.

■ Attempt to load both rows, whereby the first row fails because it has already been loaded (and thus causes a primary key violation).

Alternatively, you can use the bad file as the new input data file and not worry about errors and skipped rows.

Tuning Data Loads

In addition to running the data load processes at off-peak hours, you can take other steps to improve the load performance. The following steps all impact your overall database environment, and must be coordinated with the database administrator. The tuning of a data load should not be allowed to have a negative impact on the database or on the business processes it supports.

First, the data loads may be timed to occur while the database is in NOARCHIVELOG mode. While in NOARCHIVELOG mode, the database does not keep an archive of its online redo log files prior to overwriting them. Eliminating the archiving process improves the performance of transactions. Since the data is being loaded from a file, you can re-create the loaded data at a later time by reloading the data file rather than recovering it from an archived redo log file.

However, there are significant potential issues with disabling NOARCHIVELOG mode. You will not be able to perform a point-in-time recovery of the database unless archiving is enabled. If there are nonbatch transactions performed in the database, you will likely need to run the database in ARCHIVELOG mode all the time, including during your loads. Furthermore, switching between ARCHIVELOG and NOARCHIVELOG modes requires you to shut down the instance. If you switch the instance to NOARCHIVELOG mode, perform your data load, and then switch the instance back to ARCHIVELOG mode, you should perform a backup of the database (see Chapter 38) immediately following the restart.

Instead of running the entire database in NOARCHIVELOG mode, you can disable archiving for your data load process by using the **unrecoverable** keyword within SQL*Loader. The **unrecoverable** option disables the writing of redo log entries for the transactions within the data load. You should only use this option if you will be able to re-create the transactions from the input files during a recovery. If you follow this strategy, you must have adequate space to store old input files in case they are needed for future recoveries. The **unrecoverable** option is only available for Direct Path loads, as described in the next section.

If your operating environment has multiple processors, you can take advantage of the CPUs by parallelizing the data load. The **parallel** option of **SQLLDR**, as described in the next section, uses multiple concurrent data load processes to reduce the overall time required to load the data.

In addition to these approaches, you should work with your database administrator to make sure the database environment and structures are properly tuned for data loads. Tuning efforts should include the following:

- Preallocate space for the table, to minimize dynamic extensions during the loads.

- Allocate sufficient memory resources to the shared memory areas, including the log buffer area.

- Streamline the data writing process by creating multiple database writer (DBWR) processes for the database.

- Remove any unnecessary triggers during the data loads. If possible, disable or remove the triggers prior to the load, and perform the triggers' operations on the loaded data manually after it has been loaded.

- Remove or disable any unnecessary constraints on the table. You can use SQL*Loader to dynamically disable and reenable constraints.

- Remove any indexes on the tables. If the data has been properly cleaned prior to the data load, then uniqueness checks and foreign key validations will not be necessary during the loads. Dropping indexes prior to data loads significantly improves performance.

If you leave indexes on during a data load, Oracle must manage and rebalance the index with each inserted record. The larger your data load is, the more work Oracle will have to do to manage the associated indexes. If you can, you should consider dropping the indexes prior to the load and then re-creating them after the load completes. The only time indexes do not cause a penalty for data load performance is during a Direct Path load, as described in the next section.

Direct Path Loading

SQL*Loader, when inserting records, generates a large number of **insert** statements. To avoid the overhead associated with using large number of **insert**s, you may use the Direct Path option in SQL*Loader. The Direct Path option creates preformatted data blocks and inserts those blocks into the table. As a result, the performance of your load can dramatically improve. To use the Direct Path option, you must not be performing any functions on the values being read from the input file.

Any indexes on the table being loaded will be placed into a temporary DIRECT LOAD state (you can query the index status from USER_INDEXES). Oracle will move the old index values to a temporary index it creates and manages. Once the load has completed, the old index values will be merged with the new values to create the new index, and Oracle will drop the temporary index it created. When the index is once again valid, its status will change to VALID. To minimize the amount of space necessary for the temporary index, presort the data by the indexed columns. The name of the index for which the data is presorted should be specified via a **sorted indexes** clause in the control file.

To use the direct path option, specify

```
DIRECT=TRUE
```

as a keyword on the **SQLLDR** command line or include this option in the control file.

If you use the Direct Path option, you can use the **unrecoverable** keyword to improve your data load performance. This instructs Oracle not to generate redo log entries for the load. If you need to recover the database at a later point, you will need to reexecute the data load in order to recover the table's data. All conventional path loads are recoverable, and all Direct Path loads are recoverable by default.

Direct Path loads are faster than conventional loads, and **unrecoverable** Direct Path loads are faster still. Since performing **unrecoverable** loads impacts your recovery operations, you need to weigh the costs of that impact against the performance benefit you will realize. If your hardware environment has additional resources available during the load, you can use the **parallel** Direct Path load option to divide the data load work among multiple processes. The parallel Direct Path operations may complete the load job faster than a single Direct Path load.

Instead of using the **parallel** option, you could partition the table being loaded (see Chapter 18). Since SQL*Loader allows you to load a single partition, you could execute multiple concurrent SQL*Loader jobs to populate the separate partitions of a partitioned table. This method requires more database administration work (to configure and manage the partitions), but it gives you more flexibility in the parallelization and scheduling of the load jobs.

Direct Path loading may impact the space required for the table's data. Since Direct Path loading inserts blocks of data, it does not follow the usual methods for allocating space within a table. The blocks are inserted at the end of the table, after its *high-water mark,* which is the highest block into which the table's data has ever been written. If you **insert** 100 blocks worth of data into a table and then **delete** all of the rows, the high-water mark for the table will still be set at 100. If you then perform a conventional SQL*Loader data load, the rows will be inserted into the already allocated blocks. If you instead perform a Direct Path load, Oracle will insert new blocks of data following block 100, potentially increasing the space allocation for the table. The only way to lower the high-water mark for a table is to **truncate** it (which deletes all rows and cannot be rolled back) or to drop and re-create it. You should work with your database administrator to identify space issues prior to starting your load.

CHAPTER
22

Accessing Remote Data

s your databases grow in size and number, you will very likely need to share data among them. Sharing data requires a method of locating and accessing the data. In Oracle, remote data accesses such as queries and updates are enabled through the use of database links. As described in this chapter, database links allow users to treat a group of distributed databases as if they were a single, integrated database. In this chapter, you will also find information about direct connections to remote databases, such as those used in client-server applications.

Database Links

Database links tell Oracle how to get from one database to another. You may also specify the access path in an ad hoc fashion (see "Dynamic Links: Using the SQLPLUS copy Command," later in this chapter). If you will frequently use the same connection to a remote database, then a database link is appropriate.

How a Database Link Works

A database link requires that Net8 (the current version of the SQL*Net product) be running on each of the machines (*hosts*) involved in the remote database access. Net8 is usually started by the database administrator (DBA) or the system manager. A sample architecture for a remote access using a database link is shown in Figure 22-1. This figure shows two hosts, each running Net8. There is a database on each of the hosts. A database link establishes a connection from the first database (named LOCAL, on the Branch host) to the second database (named REMOTE, on the Headquarters host). The database link shown in Figure 22-1 is software that is located in the Local database.

Database links specify the following connection information:

- The communications protocol (such as TCP/IP) to use during the connection

- The host on which the remote database resides

- The name of the database on the remote host

- The name of a valid account in the remote database

- The password for that account

When used, a database link actually logs in as a user in the remote database, and then logs out when the remote data access is complete. A database link can be *private,* owned by a single user, or *public,* in which case all users in the Local database can use the link.

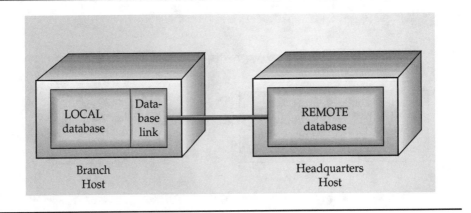

FIGURE 22-1. *Sample architecture for a database link*

The syntax for creating a database link is shown in "Syntax for Database Links," later in this chapter.

Using a Database Link for Remote Queries

If you are a user in the Local database shown in Figure 22-1, you can access objects in the Remote database via a database link. To do this, simply append the database link name to the name of any table or view that is accessible to the remote account. When appending the database link name to a table or view name, you must precede the database link name with an @ sign (pronounced "at").

For local tables, you reference the table name in the **from** clause:

```
select *
  from WORKER;
```

For remote tables, use a database link named REMOTE_CONNECT. In the **from** clause, reference the table name followed by @REMOTE_CONNECT:

```
select *
  from WORKER@REMOTE_CONNECT;
```

When the database link in the preceding query is used, Oracle will log in to the database specified by the database link, using the username and password provided by the link. It will then query the WORKER table in that account and return the data to the user who initiated the query. This is shown graphically in Figure 22-2. The REMOTE_CONNECT database link shown in Figure 22-2 is located in the Local database.

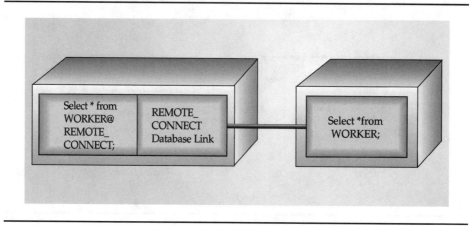

FIGURE 22-2. *Using a database link for a remote query*

As shown in Figure 22-2, logging in to the Local database and using the REMOTE_CONNECT database link in your **from** clause returns the same results as logging in directly to the remote database and executing the query without the database link. It makes the remote database seem local.

> **NOTE**
> *The maximum number of database links that can be used in a single query is set via the OPEN_LINKS parameter in the database's init.ora initialization file. This parameter usually defaults to four.*

There are restrictions to the queries that are executed using database links. You should avoid using database links in queries that use the **connect by**, **start with**, and **prior** keywords. Some queries using these keywords will work (for example, if **prior** is not used outside of the **connect by** clause, and **start with** does not use a subquery), but most uses of tree-structured queries will fail when using database links.

Using a Database Link for Synonyms and Views

You may create local synonyms and views that reference remote objects. To do this, reference the database link name, preceded by an @ sign, wherever you refer to a remote table. The following example shows how to do this for synonyms. The

create synonym command in this example is executed from an account in the Local database.

```
create synonym WORKER_SYN
    for WORKER@REMOTE_CONNECT;
```

In this example, a synonym called WORKER_SYN is created for the WORKER table accessed via the REMOTE_CONNECT database link. Every time this synonym is used in a **from** clause of a query, the remote database will be queried. This is very similar to the remote queries shown earlier; the only real change is that the database link is now defined as part of a local object (in this case, a synonym).

What if the remote account that is accessed by the database link does not own the table being referenced? In that event, any synonyms that are available to the remote account (either private or public) can be used. If no such synonyms exist for a table that the remote account has been granted access to, then you must specify the table owner's name in the query, as shown in the following example:

```
create synonym WORKERSKILL_SYN
    for Talbot.WORKERSKILL@REMOTE_CONNECT;
```

In this example, the remote account used by the database link does not own the WORKERSKILL table, nor does the remote account have a synonym called WORKERSKILL. It does, however, have privileges on the WORKERSKILL table owned by the remote user Talbot in the Remote database. Therefore, the owner and table name are specified; both are interpreted in the remote database. The syntax for these queries and synonyms is almost the same as if everything were in the local database; the only addition is the database link name.

To use a database link in a view, simply add it as a suffix to table names in the **create view** command. The following example creates a view in the local database of a remote table using the REMOTE_CONNECT database link:

```
create view LOCAL_EMPLOYEE_VIEW
as
select * from WORKER@REMOTE_CONNECT
 where Lodging = 'ROSE HILL';
```

The **from** clause in this example refers to WORKER@REMOTE_CONNECT. Therefore, the base table for this view is not in the same database as the view. Also note that a **where** clause is placed on the query, to limit the number of records returned by it for the view.

This view may now be treated the same as any other view in the local database. Access to this view can be granted to other users, provided those users also have access to the REMOTE_CONNECT database link.

Using a Database Link for Remote Updates

The database link syntax for remote **update**s is the same as that for remote queries. Append the name of the database link to the name of the table being updated. For example, to change the Lodging values for workers in a remote WORKER table, you would execute the **update** command shown in the following listing:

```
update WORKER@REMOTE_CONNECT
    set Lodging = 'CRANMER'
 where Lodging = 'ROSE HILL';
```

This **update** command will use the REMOTE_CONNECT database link to log in to the remote database. It will then **update** the WORKER table in that database, based on the **set** and **where** conditions specified.

You can use subqueries in the **set** portion of the **update** command (refer to Chapter 15). The **from** clause of such subqueries can reference either the local database or a remote database. To refer to the remote database in a subquery, append the database link name to the table names in the **from** clause of the subquery. An example of this is shown in the following listing:

```
update WORKER@REMOTE_CONNECT        /*in remote database*/
    set Lodging =
        (select Lodging
         from LODGING@REMOTE_CONNECT  /*in remote database*/
         where Manager = 'KEN MULLER')
 where Lodging = 'ROSE HILL';
```

NOTE
*If you do not append the database link name to the table names in the **from** clause of **update** subqueries, tables in the local database will be used. This is true even if the table being updated is in a remote database.*

In this example, the remote WORKER table is updated based on the LODGING value on the remote LODGING table. If the database link is not used in the subquery, as in the following example, then the LODGING table in the local database will be used instead. If this is unintended, it will cause local data to be mixed into the remote database table. If you're doing it on purpose, be *very* careful.

```
update WORKER@REMOTE_CONNECT          /*in remote database*/
    set Lodging =
        (select Lodging
           from LODGING                /*in local database*/
           where Manager = 'KEN MULLER')
where Lodging = 'ROSE HILL';
```

Syntax for Database Links

You can create a database link with the following command:

```
create [public] database link REMOTE_CONNECT
connect to [current_user | username identified by password]
using 'connect string';
```

The specific syntax to use when creating a database link depends upon two criteria:

■ The "public" or "private" status of the database link

■ The use of default or explicit logins for the remote database

These criteria and their associated syntax are described in turn in the following sections.

NOTE
To create a database link, you must have CREATE DATABASE LINK system privilege. The account to which you will be connecting in the remote database must have CREATE SESSION privilege. Both of these system privileges are included as part of the CONNECT role in Oracle.

Public vs. Private Database Links

A *public* database link is available to all users in a database. By contrast, a *private* database link is only available to the user who created it. It is not possible for one user to grant access on a private database link to another user. The database link must either be public (available to all users) or private.

To specify a database link as public, use the **public** keyword in the **create database link** command, as shown in the following example.

```
create public database link REMOTE_CONNECT
connect to username identified by password
   using 'connect string';
```

NOTE
To create a public database link, you must have
CREATE PUBLIC DATABASE LINK system privilege.
This privilege is included in the DBA role in Oracle.

Default vs. Explicit Logins

In place of the **connect to ... identified by ...** clause, you can use **connect to current_user** when creating a database link. If you use the **current_user** option, then when that link is used, it will attempt to open a session in the remote database that has the same username and password as the local database account. This is called a *default login,* since the username/password combination will default to the combination in use in the local database.

The following listing shows an example of a public database link created with a default login (the use of default logins is described further in "Using the User Pseudo-column in Views," later in this chapter):

```
create public database link REMOTE_CONNECT
connect to current_user
 using 'connect_string';
```

When this database link is used, it will attempt to log in to the remote database using the current user's username and password. If the current username is not valid in the remote database, or if the password is different, then the login attempt will fail. This failure will cause the SQL statement using the link to fail.

An *explicit* login specifies a username and password that the database link will use while connecting to the remote database. No matter which local account uses the link, the same remote account will be used. The following listing shows the creation of a database link with an explicit login:

```
create public database link REMOTE_CONNECT
connect to WAREHOUSE identified by ACCESS339
   using 'connect_string';
```

This example shows a common usage of explicit logins in database links. In the remote database, a user named Warehouse was created, and was given the password ACCESS339. The Warehouse account can then be granted SELECT access to specific tables, solely for use by database links. The REMOTE_CONNECT database link then provides access to the remote Warehouse account for all local users.

Connect String Syntax

Net8 uses *service names* to identify remote connections. The connection details for these service names are contained in files that are distributed to each host in the network. When a service name is encountered, Oracle checks the local Net8 configuration file (called tnsnames.ora) to determine which protocol, host name, and database name to use during the connection. All of the connection information is found in external files.

When using Net8, you must know the name of the service that points to the remote database. For example, if the service name HQ specifies the connection parameters for the database you need, then HQ should be used as the connect string in the **create database link** command. The following example shows a private database link, using a default login and a Net8 service name:

```
create database link REMOTE_CONNECT
connect to current_user
 using 'HQ';
```

When this link is used, Oracle checks the tnsnames.ora file on the local host to determine which database to connect to. When it attempts to log in to that database, it uses the current user's username and password.

The tnsnames.ora files for a network of databases should be coordinated by the DBAs for those databases. A typical entry in the tnsnames.ora file (for a network using the TCP/IP protocol) is shown in the following listing:

```
HQ =(DESCRIPTION=
        (ADDRESS_LIST =
                (ADDRESS = (PROTOCOL=TCP)
                (HOST=host1)
                (PORT=1521))
         )
        (CONNECT DATA=
                (SERVICE_NAME = HQ.host1)
         )
      )
```

In this listing, the HQ service name is mapped to a connect descriptor that tells the database which protocol to use (TCP/IP), and which host (host1) and database (HQ) to connect to. The "port" information refers to the port on the host that will be used for the connection; that data is environment-specific. Different protocols will have different keywords, but they all must convey the same content.

Using Synonyms for Location Transparency

Over the lifespan of an application, its data very likely will move from one database to another, or from one host to another. Therefore, it will simplify application maintenance if the exact physical location of a database object is shielded from the user (and the application).

The best way to implement such location transparency is through the use of synonyms. Instead of writing applications (or SQLPLUS reports) that contain queries that specify a table's owner, such as

```
select *
  from Talbot.WORKER;
```

you should create a synonym for that table, and then reference the synonym in the query:

```
create synonym WORKER
   for Talbot.WORKER;

select *
  from WORKER;
```

The logic required to find the data has thus been moved out of your application and into the database. Moving the table location logic to the database will be a benefit any time you move the table (for example, when moving from a development database to a test database).

In addition to hiding the ownership of tables from an application, you can hide the data's physical location through the use of database links and synonyms. By using local synonyms for remote tables, you move another layer of logic out of the application and into the database. For example, the local synonym WORKERSKILL, as defined in the following listing, refers to a table that is located in a different database, on a different host. If that table ever moves, only the link has to be changed; the application code, which uses the synonym, will not change.

```
create synonym WORKERSKILL
   for WORKERSKILL@REMOTE_CONNECT;
```

If the remote account used by the database link is not the owner of the object being referenced, then you have two options. First, you can reference an available synonym in the remote database:

```
create synonym WORKERSKILL
    for WORKERSKILL@REMOTE_CONNECT;
```

where WORKERSKILL, in the remote account used by the database link, is a synonym for another user's WORKERSKILL table.

The second option is to include the remote owner's name when creating the local synonym, as shown in the following listing.

```
create synonym WORKERSKILL
    for Talbot.WORKERSKILL@REMOTE_CONNECT;
```

These two examples will result in the same functionality for your queries, but there are differences between them. The second example, which includes the owner name, is potentially more difficult to maintain, because you are not using a synonym in the remote database. The two examples also have slightly different functionality when the **describe** command is used. If the remote account accesses a synonym (instead of a table), you will not be able to **describe** that table, even though you can **select** from it. For **describe** to work correctly, you need to use the format shown in the last example and specify the owner.

Using the User Pseudo-column in Views

The User pseudo-column is very useful when you are using remote data access methods. For example, you may not want all remote users to see all records in a table. To solve this problem, you must think of remote users as special users within your database. To enforce the data restriction, you need to create a view that the remote accounts will access. But what can you use in the **where** clause to properly restrict the records? The User pseudo-column, combined with properly selected usernames, allows you to enforce this restriction.

As you may recall from Chapter 3, queries used to define views may also reference *pseudo-columns*. A pseudo-column is a "column" that returns a value when it is selected, but it is not an actual column in a table. The User pseudo-column, when selected, always returns the Oracle username that executed the query. So, if a column in the table contains usernames, those values can be compared against the User pseudo-column to restrict its records, as shown in the following example. In this example, the NAME table is queried. If the value of its Name column is the same as the name of the user entering the query, then records will be returned.

```
create or replace view RESTRICTED_NAMES
     as select * from NAME
  where Name = User;
```

NOTE
We need to shift our point of view for this discussion. Since the discussion concerns operations on the database that owns the table being queried, that database will be referred to as the "local" database, and the users from other databases will be referred to as "remote" users.

When restricting remote access to the rows of your table, you should first consider which columns would be the best to use for the restriction. There are usually logical divisions to the data within a table, such as Department or State. For each distinct division, create a separate user account in your local database. For this example, let's add a Department column to the WORKER table:

```
alter table WORKER
add
(Department VARCHAR2(10));
```

Suppose you have four major departments represented in your WORKER table, and you have created an account for each department. You could then set up each remote user's database link to use his or her specific user account in your local database. For this example, assume the departments are called NORTH, EAST, SOUTH, and WEST. For each of the departments, a specific database link would be created. For example, the members of the SOUTH department would use the database link shown in the following listing:

```
create database link SOUTH_LINK
connect to SOUTH identified by PAW
  using 'HQ';
```

The database link shown in this example is a private database link with an explicit login to the SOUTH account in the remote database.

When remote users query via their database links (such as SOUTH_LINK from the previous example), they will be logged in to the HQ database, with their Department name (such as SOUTH) as their username. Thus, the value of the User column for any table that the user queries will be SOUTH.

Now create a view of your base table, comparing the User pseudo-column to the value of the Department column in the view's **where** clause (this use of the User pseudo-column was first demonstrated in Chapter 19):

```
create or replace view RESTRICTED_WORKER
     as select *
   from WORKER
 where Department = User;
```

A user who connects via the SOUTH_LINK database link—and thus is logged in as the SOUTH user—would only be able to see the WORKER records that have a Department value equal to 'SOUTH'. If users are accessing your table from a remote database, then their logins are occurring via database links—and you know the local accounts they are using because you set them up.

This type of restriction can also be performed in the remote database rather than in the database where the table resides. Users in the remote database may create views within their databases of the following form:

```
create or replace view SOUTH_WORKERS
     as select *
   from WORKER@REMOTE_CONNECT
 where Department = 'SOUTH';
```

In this case, the Department restriction is still in force, but it is administered locally, and the Department restriction is coded into the view's query. Choosing between the two restriction options (local or remote) is based on the number of accounts required for the desired restriction to be enforced.

To secure your production database, you should limit the privileges granted to the accounts used by database links. Grant those privileges via roles, and use views (with the **with read only** or **with check option** clause) to further limit the ability of those accounts to be used to make unauthorized changes to the data.

Dynamic Links: Using the SQLPLUS copy Command

The SQLPLUS **copy** command is an underutilized, underappreciated command. It allows data to be copied between databases (or within the same database) via SQLPLUS. Although it allows you to select which columns to copy, it works best when all the columns of a table are being chosen. The greatest benefit from using this command is its ability to **commit** after each array of data has been processed (explained shortly). This in turn generates transactions that are of a manageable size.

Consider the case of a large table, such as WORKER. What if the WORKER table has 100,000 rows that use a total of 100MB of space, and you need to make a copy of that table into a different database? The easiest option involves creating a database link and then using that link in a **create table ... as select** command, as shown next.

```
create database link REMOTE_CONNECT
connect to TALBOT identified by LEDGER
  using 'HQ';

create table WORKER
as
select * from WORKER@REMOTE_CONNECT;
```

The first command creates the database link, and the second creates a new table based on all the data in the remote table.

Unfortunately, this option creates a very large transaction (all 100,000 rows would be **insert**ed into the new table as a single transaction) that places a large burden on internal Oracle structures called *rollback segments.* Rollback segments (see Chapter 38) store the prior image of data until that data is committed to the database. Since this table is being populated by a single **insert**, a single, large transaction is generated, which will very likely exceed the space in the currently available rollback segments. This failure will in turn cause the table creation to fail.

To break the transaction into smaller entries, use the SQLPLUS **copy** command, which has the following syntax:

```
copy from
[remote username/remote password@connect string]
[to username/password@connect string]
{append|create|insert|replace}
table name
using subquery;
```

If the current account is to be the destination of the copied data, then the word **to** plus the local username, password, and connect string are not necessary. If the current account is to be the source of the copied data, then the remote connection information for the data source is not necessary.

To set the transaction entry size, use the SQLPLUS **set** command to set a value for the **arraysize** parameter. This determines the number of records that will be retrieved in each batch. The **copycommit** parameter tells SQLPLUS how many batches should be committed at one time. The following SQLPLUS script accomplishes the same data-copying goal that the **create table as** command met; however, it breaks up the single transaction into multiple transactions. In this example, the data is committed after every 1,000 records. This reduces the transaction's rollback segment entry size needed from 100MB to 1MB.

```
set copycommit 1
set arraysize 1000

copy from TALBOT/LEDGER@HQ -
```

```
create WORKER -
using -
select * from WORKER
```

NOTE
Except for the last line, each line in the **copy**
command must be terminated with a dash (-), since
this is a SQLPLUS command.

The different data options within the **copy** command are described in Table 22-1.
The feedback provided by the **copy** command may be confusing at first. After
the final commit is complete, the database reports to the user the number of records
that were committed in the *last* batch. It does not report the total number of records
committed (unless they are all committed in a single batch).

Connecting to a Remote Database

In addition to the interdatabase connections described earlier in this chapter, you may
connect directly to a remote database via an Oracle tool. Thus, instead of typing

```
sqlplus username/password
```

and accessing your local database, you can go directly to a remote database. To do
this, enter your username and password along with the Net8 connect string for the
remote database:

```
sqlplus username/password@HQ
```

This command will log you in directly to the HQ database. The host
configuration for this type of login is shown in Figure 22-3; the Branch host has the
Oracle tools (such as SQLPLUS) on it and is running Net8, and the Remote host is
running Net8 and has an Oracle database. There may or may not be a database on
the Branch host; specifying the Net8 connect string to the remote database forces
Oracle to ignore any local databases.

As Figure 22-3 shows, there are very few hardware requirements for the Branch
host. All it has to support is the front-end tool and Net8—a typical configuration
for client-server applications. A client machine, such as the Branch host, is used
primarily for presentation of the data via the database access tools. The server side,
such as the Headquarters host, is used to maintain the data and process the data
access requests from users.

Option	Description
APPEND	Inserts the rows into the destination table. Automatically creates the table if it does not exist.
CREATE	Creates the table and then inserts the rows.
INSERT	Inserts the rows into the destination table if it exists; otherwise, returns an error. When using INSERT, all columns must be specified in the **using** subquery.
REPLACE	Drops the existing destination table and replaces it with a new table containing the copied data.

TABLE 22-1. *Data Options for the **copy** Command*

Regardless of the configuration you use and the configuration tools available, you need to tell Net8 how to find the remote database. Work with your DBA to make sure the remote server is properly configured to listen for new connection requests, and to make sure the client machines are properly configured to issue those requests.

FIGURE 22-3. *Sample architecture for a remote connection*

CHAPTER
23

Snapshots and
Materialized Views

o improve the performance of an application, you can make local copies of remote tables that use distributed data, or create summary tables based on **group by** operations. Oracle provides *snapshots* as a means of creating local copies of remote tables. As of Oracle8i, you can use *materialized views* to create summary tables based on aggregations of a table's data. Snapshots are considered to be synonymous with materialized views, and the terms are used interchangeably in this chapter and in Oracle. For example, when you execute the **create snapshot** command, Oracle responds with the message "Materialized view created." Materialized views based on remote data are sometimes still referred to as snapshots.

Materialized views offer optimization improvements that were not previously available. In this chapter, you will see the general usage of snapshots and materialized views, including their refresh strategies, followed by a description of the optimization strategies implemented via materialized views.

Materialized views can be used to replicate all or part of a single table, or to replicate the result of a query against multiple tables; refreshes of the replicated data can be done automatically by the database at time intervals that you specify.

Functionality

Materialized views are copies (also known as *replicas*) of data, based upon queries. In its simplest form, a materialized view can be thought of as a table created by a command such as the following:

```
create table LOCAL_LEDGER
as
select * from LEDGER@REMOTE_CONNECT;
```

In this example, a table named LOCAL_LEDGER is created in the local database and is populated with data from a remote database (defined by the database link named REMOTE_CONNECT). Once the LOCAL_LEDGER table is created, though, its data may immediately become out of sync with the master table (LEDGER@REMOTE_CONNECT). Also, LOCAL_LEDGER may be updated by local users, further complicating its synchronization with the master table.

Despite these synchronization problems, there are benefits to replicating data in this way. Creating local copies of remote data may improve the performance of distributed queries, particularly if the tables' data does not change frequently. Materialized views are also useful for decision-support environments, in which complex queries are used to periodically "roll up" data into summary tables for use during analyses.

Oracle lets you manage the synchronization of master tables with their materialized views. When materialized views are created, a *refresh interval* is established to schedule refreshes of replicated data. Local updates can be prevented, and transaction-based refreshes can be used. Transaction-based refreshes, available for some types of snapshots, send from the master database only those rows that have changed for the snapshot. This capability, described in "Simple vs. Complex" and "create materialized view log/snapshot log Syntax," later in this chapter, may significantly improve the performance of your refreshes.

Required System Privileges

To create a snapshot or materialized view, you must have the privileges needed to create the underlying objects it will use. You must have the CREATE SNAPSHOT or CREATE MATERIALIZED VIEW privilege, as well as the CREATE TABLE, CREATE VIEW, and CREATE INDEX system privileges. In addition, you must have either the UNLIMITED TABLESPACE system privilege or a sufficient specified space quota in a local tablespace.

The underlying objects that the materialized view will use are stored in your user account (also called a *schema*). If the materialized view is to be created in a schema other than your own, then you must have the CREATE ANY SNAPSHOT or CREATE ANY MATERIALIZED VIEW system privilege, as well as the CREATE ANY TABLE, CREATE ANY VIEW, and CREATE ANY INDEX system privileges. In addition, you must have either the UNLIMITED TABLESPACE system privilege or a sufficient specified space quota in a local tablespace.

Materialized views of remote tables require queries of remote tables; therefore, you must have privileges to use a database link that accesses the remote database. The link you use can be either public or private. If the database link is private, you need to have the CREATE DATABASE LINK system privilege. See Chapter 22 for further information on database links.

If you are creating materialized views to take advantage of the *query rewrite* feature (in which the optimizer dynamically chooses to select data from the materialized view instead of the underlying table), you must have QUERY REWRITE privilege. If the tables are in another user's schema, you must have the GLOBAL QUERY REWRITE privilege.

Required Table Privileges

When creating a materialized view, you can reference tables in a remote database via a database link. The account that the database link uses in the remote database must have access to the tables and views used by the database link. You cannot create a materialized view based on objects owned by the user SYS.

Within the local database, you can grant SELECT privilege on a materialized view to other local users. Since most materialized views are read-only (although they can be updatable), no additional grants are necessary. If you create an updatable materialized view, you must grant users UPDATE privilege on both the snapshot and the underlying local table it accesses. For information on the local objects created by materialized views, see "Local and Remote Objects Created," later in this chapter.

Simple vs. Complex

The queries that form the bases of materialized views are grouped into two categories: *simple* and *complex*. If a materialized view uses a simple query, it is a simple materialized view. A simple query:

- Selects rows from only one table (not a view)

- Does not perform any set operations, joins, **group by**s, or **connect by**s

If the materialized view uses a complex query (that is, a query that does not qualify as a simple query), then it is a complex materialized view. The distinction between simple and complex materialized views affects the options that are available for refreshes. Those options are described in "Refreshing Snapshots and Materialized Views," later in this chapter, but it is important to keep these distinctions in mind while you are first considering how to use materialized views.

Each of the records contained in the result set of a simple query maps to a single record in the master table. A simple materialized view does not need to contain all the records from the master table; a **where** clause can be used to restrict the rows returned. If a materialized view uses a simple query, then it is a simple materialized view.

A complex materialized view is one whose query violates either of the rules previously specified for a simple materialized view. Therefore, any materialized view whose query contains a **group by** clause is, by definition, a complex materialized view.

You do not specify the type (simple or complex) of materialized view to use when you create a materialized view. Oracle will examine the view's query and determine the view type and the default refresh options available. You may override these options, as explained later in the "create materialized view/snapshot Syntax" section.

Read-Only vs. Updatable

A read-only materialized view cannot pass data changes from itself back to its master table. An updatable materialized view can send changes to its master table.

Although that may seem to be a simple distinction, the underlying differences between these two types of materialized views are not simple. A read-only materialized view is implemented as a **create table as select** command. When transactions occur, they occur only within the master table; the transactions are later sent to the read-only materialized view. Thus, the method by which the rows in the materialized view change is controlled—the materialized view's rows only change following a change to the materialized view's master table.

In an updatable materialized view, there is less control over the method by which rows in the materialized view are changed. Rows may be changed based on changes in the master table, or rows may be changed directly by users of the materialized view. As a result, you need to send records from the master table to the materialized view, *and* vice versa. Since multiple sources of changes exist, multiple masters exist (referred to in Oracle documentation as a *multimaster configuration*).

If you use updatable materialized views, you need to treat the materialized view as a master, complete with all of the underlying replication structures and facilities normally found at master sites. You also need to decide how the records will be propagated from the materialized view back to the master. During the transfer of records from snapshot to master, you need to decide how you will reconcile conflicts. For example, what if the record with ID=1 is deleted at the materialized view site, while at the master site, a record is created in a separate table that references (via a foreign key) the ID=1 record? You cannot delete the ID=1 record from the master site, since that record has a "child" record that relates to it. You cannot insert the child record at the materialized view site, since the parent (ID=1) record has been deleted. How do you plan to resolve such conflicts?

Read-only materialized views let you avoid the need for conflict resolution by forcing all transactions to occur in the controlled master table. This may limit your functionality, but it is an appropriate solution for the vast majority of replication needs. If you need multimaster replication, see the *Oracle8i Replication* guide for guidelines and detailed implementation instructions.

create materialized view/snapshot Syntax

The basic syntax for creating a snapshot or materialized view is shown in the following listing. See the Alphabetical Reference for the full command syntax. Following the command description, examples are given that illustrate the creation of local replicas of remote data.

```
create [materialized view | snapshot] [user.]name
   { { pctfree integer
     | pctused integer
     | initrans integer
     | maxtrans integer
```

```
            | tablespace tablespace
            | storage storage}
     | cluster cluster (column [, column] ...) } ...
       [using {index [ pctfree integer
                      | pctused integer
                      | initrans integer
                      | maxtrans integer ]
                    | [ default] [ master | local] rollback segment
                        [rollback_segment] } ]
       [refresh [fast | complete | force]
                [on demand | commit]
                [start with date] [next date]
                [with {primary key | rowid}] ]
       [for update]
       [enable query rewrite | disable query rewrite]  as query
```

The **create materialized view/snapshot** command has four sections. The first
section is the header, in which the materialized view is named (the first line in
the listing):

```
create [materialized view | snapshot] [user.]name
```

The materialized view will be created in your user account (schema) unless a
different username is specified in the header. In the second section, the storage
parameters are set:

```
     { { pctfree integer
       | pctused integer
       | initrans integer
       | maxtrans integer
       | tablespace tablespace
       | storage storage}
     | cluster cluster (column [, column] ...) } ...
       [using {index [ pctfree integer
                      | pctused integer
                      | initrans integer
                      | maxtrans integer ]
                    | [ default] [ master | local] rollback segment
                        [rollback_segment] } ]
```

The storage parameters will be applied to a table that will be created in the local
database. For information about the available storage parameters, see the "Storage"
entry in the Alphabetical Reference.

NOTE
You can specify the storage parameters to be used for the index that is automatically created on the materialized view. You can also specify the rollback segment to be used during the materialized view creation and refresh operations. Being able to specify a rollback segment allows you to better support large transactions that may occur during materialized view operations.

In the third section, the refresh options are set, and you specify whether the materialized view is RowID-based or primary key–based:

```
[refresh [fast | complete | force]
     [on demand | commit]
     [start with date] [next date]
     [with {primary key | rowid}] ]
```

The **refresh** option specifies the mechanism Oracle should use when refreshing the materialized view. The three options available are **fast**, **complete**, and **force**. Fast refreshes are only available for simple materialized views; they use tables called *materialized view logs* to send specific rows from the master table to the materialized view (in previous versions of Oracle, these were called *snapshot logs*). Complete refreshes completely re-create the materialized view. The **force** option for refreshes tells Oracle to use a fast refresh if it is available; otherwise, a complete refresh will be used. If you have created a simple materialized view but want to use complete refreshes, specify refresh **complete** in your **create snapshot/materialized view** command. The refresh options are further described in "Refreshing Snapshots and Materialized Views," later in this chapter. Within this section of the **create snapshot/materialized view** command, you also specify the mechanism used to relate values in the materialized view to the master table—whether RowIDs or primary key values should be used. By default, primary keys are used.

If the master query for the materialized view references a join or a single-table aggregate, you can use the **on commit** option to control the replication of changes. If you use **on commit**, changes will be sent from the master to the replica when the changes are committed on the master table. If you specify **on demand**, the refresh will occur when you manually execute a refresh command.

The fourth section of the **create snapshot/materialized view** command is the query that the materialized view will use:

```
[for update]
[enable query rewrite | disable query rewrite]    as query
```

If you specify **for update**, the materialized view will be updatable; otherwise, it will be read-only. Most materialized views are read-only replicas of the master data. If you use updatable materialized views, you need to be concerned with issues such as two-way replication of changes and the reconciliation of conflicting data changes. Updatable materialized views are an example of multimaster replication; for full details on implementing a multimaster replication environment, see the *Oracle8i Replication* guide.

NOTE
The query that forms the basis of the snapshot should not use the User or SysDate pseudo-columns.

The following example creates a read-only materialized view called LOCAL_LEDGER in a local database, based on a remote table named LEDGER that is accessible via the REMOTE_CONNECT database link:

```
create materialized view LOCAL_LEDGER
storage (initial 100K next 100K pctincrease 0)
tablespace SNAPS
refresh fast
start with SysDate next SysDate+7
with ROWID
as
select * from LEDGER@REMOTE_CONNECT;
```

The command shown in the preceding example will create a read-only simple materialized view called LOCAL_LEDGER. Its underlying table will be created with the specified storage parameters in a tablespace named SNAPS. Since the data in the materialized view's local base table will be changing over time, it is usually worthwhile to store materialized views in their own tablespace (SNAPS, in this example). Because the example creates a simple materialized view, the **fast** refresh option is specified. The materialized view's query specifies that the entire LEDGER table, with no modifications, is to be copied to the local database. As soon as the LOCAL_LEDGER materialized view is created, its underlying table will be populated with the LEDGER data. Thereafter, the materialized view will be refreshed every seven days. The storage parameters that are not specified will use the default values for those parameters for the SNAPS tablespace.

The following example creates a complex materialized view named LOCAL_LEDGER_TOTALS in a local database, based on a remote table named LEDGER in a database accessed via the REMOTE_CONNECT database link. The major differences between this materialized view and the LOCAL_LEDGER materialized view are shown in bold.

```
create materialized view LOCAL_LEDGER_TOTALS
storage (initial 50K next 50K pctincrease 0)
tablespace SNAPS
refresh complete
start with SysDate next SysDate+7
as
select Person, Action, SUM(Amount) Sum_Amount
   from LEDGER@REMOTE_CONNECT
group by Person, Action;
```

The query in the LOCAL_LEDGER_TOTALS example groups the Amount values by Person and Action (in the LEDGER table, the Action values are BOUGHT, SOLD, PAID, and RECEIVED).

There are a few important points to note about the two examples shown in this section:

■ The **group by** query used in the LOCAL_LEDGER_TOTALS materialized view could be performed in SQLPLUS against the LOCAL_LEDGER materialized view. That is, the **group by** operation can be performed outside of the materialized view.

■ Since LOCAL_LEDGER_TOTALS uses a **group by** clause, it is a complex materialized view. Therefore, only complete refreshes may be used. LOCAL_LEDGER, as a simple materialized view, can use fast refreshes.

The two materialized views shown in the preceding examples reference the same table. Since one of the materialized views is a simple materialized view that replicates all columns and all rows of the master table, the second materialized view may at first appear to be redundant. However, sometimes the second, complex materialized view is the more useful of the two.

How can this be? First, remember that these materialized views are being used to service the query needs of *local* users. If those users always perform **group by** operations in their queries, and their grouping columns are fixed, then LOCAL_LEDGER_TOTALS may be more useful to them. Second, if the transaction volume on the master LEDGER table is very high, or the master LEDGER table is very small, then there may not be a significant difference in the refresh times of the fast and complete refreshes. The most appropriate materialized view is the one that is most productive for your users.

RowID vs. Primary Key–Based Snapshots and Materialized Views

You can base materialized views on primary key values of the master table instead of basing them on the master table's RowIDs. You should decide between these options based on several factors:

- **System stability**   If the master site is not stable, then you may need to perform database recoveries involving the master table. When you use Oracle's Export and Import utilities to perform recoveries, the RowID values of rows are likely to change. If the system requires frequent Exports and Imports, you should use primary key–based materialized views.

- **Amount of data replicated**   If you normally don't replicate the primary key columns, you can reduce the amount of data replicated by replicating the RowID values instead.

- **Amount of data sent during refreshes**   During refreshes, RowID-based materialized views usually require less data to be sent to the materialized view than primary key–based materialized views require (unless the primary key is a very short column).

- **Size of materialized view log table**   Oracle allows you to store the changes to master tables in separate tables called *materialized view logs* (described later in this chapter). If the primary key consists of many columns, then the materialized view log table for a primary key–based materialized view may be considerably larger than the materialized view log for a comparable RowID-based materialized view.

- **Referential integrity**   To use primary key–based materialized views, you must have defined a primary key on the master table. If you cannot define a primary key on the master table, then you must use RowID-based materialized views.

Underlying Objects Created

When you create a materialized view, a number of objects are created in the local and remote databases. The supporting objects created within a database are the same for both simple and complex materialized views. With simple materialized views, you have the ability to create additional objects called *materialized view logs,* which are discussed in "create materialized view log/snapshot log Syntax," later in this chapter.

Consider the simple materialized view shown in the last section:

```
create materialized view LOCAL_LEDGER
storage (initial 100K next 100K pctincrease 0)
tablespace SNAPS
refresh complete
start with SysDate next SysDate+7
with ROWID
as
select * from LEDGER@REMOTE_CONNECT;
```

Within the local database, this command will create the following objects in the materialized view owner's schema:

■   A table named LOCAL_LEDGER that is the *local base table* for the materialized view of the remote table. This table contains the replicated data. Prior to Oracle8.1.5, Oracle would create a view named LOCAL_LEDGER to be accessed by users of the local materialized view.

■   If the materialized view is a simple materialized view, then Oracle will create an index on the materialized view's local base table (LOCAL_LEDGER). See "Indexing Materialized View Tables."

There is only one permissible change that should be made to these underlying objects: the LOCAL_LEDGER table should be indexed to reflect the query paths that are normally used by local users. If you do index the materialized view's local base table, then you need to factor in your indexes' storage requirements when you estimate the materialized view's space needs. See the following section, "Indexing Materialized View Tables," for further details.

No supporting objects are created in the remote database unless you use materialized view logs to record changes to rows in the master table. Materialized view logs are described in "create materialized view log/snapshot log Syntax," earlier in this chapter.

Indexing Materialized View Tables

As noted in the preceding discussion, the *local base table* contains the data that has been replicated. Because that data has been replicated with a goal in mind (usually to improve performance in the database or the network), it is important to follow through to that goal after the materialized view has been created. Performance improvements for queries are usually gained through the use of indexes. Columns that are frequently used in the **where** clauses of queries should be indexed; if a set of columns is frequently accessed in queries, then a concatenated index on that set of columns can be created. (See Chapter 36 for more information on the Oracle optimizer.)

Oracle does not automatically create indexes for complex materialized views. You need to create these indexes manually. To create indexes on your local base table, use the **create index** command (see the Alphabetical Reference). Do *not* create any constraints on the materialized view's local base table.

Since no indexes are created on the columns that users are likely to query from the materialized view, you should create indexes on the materialized view's local base table.

Using Materialized Views to Alter Query Execution Paths

For a large database, a materialized view may offer several performance benefits. You can use materialized views to influence the optimizer to change the execution paths for queries. This feature, called *query rewrite,* enables the optimizer to use a materialized view in place of the table queried by the materialized view, even if the materialized view is not named in the query. For example, if you have a large SALES table, you may create a materialized view that sums the SALES data by region. If a user queries the SALES table for the sum of the SALES data for a region, Oracle can redirect that query to use your materialized view in place of the SALES table. As a result, you can reduce the number of accesses against your largest tables, improving the system performance. Further, since the data in the materialized view is already grouped by region, summarization does not have to be performed at the time the query is issued.

To effectively use the query rewrite capability, you should create a dimension that defines the hierarchies within the table's data. For example, countries are part of continents, and you can create tables to support this hierarchy:

```
create dimension GEOGRAPHY
    level COUNTRY_ID      is COUNTRY.Country
    level CONTINENT_id    is CONTINENT.Continent
    hierarchy COUNTRY_ROLLUP (
        COUNTRY_ID            child of
        CONTINENT_ID
    join key COUNTRY.Continent references CONTINENT_id);
```

If you summarize your SALES data in a materialized view at the country level, then the optimizer will be able to redirect queries for country-level SALES data to the materialized view. Since the materialized view should contain less data than the SALES table, the query of the materialized view should yield a performance improvement over a similar query of the SALES table.

To enable a materialized view for query rewrite, all of the master tables for the materialized view must be in the materialized view's schema, and you must have the QUERY REWRITE system privilege. If the view and the tables are in separate schemas, you must have the GLOBAL QUERY REWRITE system privilege. In general, you should create materialized views in the same schema as the tables on which they are based; otherwise, you will need to manage the permissions and grants required to create and maintain the materialized view.

Refreshing Snapshots and Materialized Views

The data in a materialized view may be replicated either once (when the view is created) or at intervals. The **create materialized view/snapshot** command allows you to set the refresh interval, delegating the responsibility for scheduling and performing the refreshes to the database. In the following sections, you will see how to perform both manual and automatic refreshes.

Automatic Refreshes

Consider the LOCAL_LEDGER materialized view described earlier. Its refresh schedule settings, defined by its **create materialized view** command, are shown in bold in the following listing:

```
create materialized view LOCAL_LEDGER
storage (initial 100K next 100K pctincrease 0)
tablespace SNAPS
refresh fast
start with SysDate next SysDate+7
with ROWID
as
select * from LEDGER@REMOTE_CONNECT;
```

The refresh schedule has three components. First, the type of refresh (**fast**, **complete**, or **force**) is specified. Fast refreshes use *materialized view logs* (described later in this chapter) to send changed rows from the master table to the materialized view. Fast refreshes are only available for simple materialized views. Complete refreshes completely re-create the materialized view. The **force** option for refreshes tells Oracle to use a fast refresh if it is available; otherwise, a complete refresh will be used.

The **start with** clause tells the database when to perform the first replication from the master table to the local base table. It must evaluate to a future point in time. If you do not specify a **start with** time but specify a **next** value, Oracle will use the **next** clause to determine the start time. To maintain control over your replication schedule, you should specify a value for the **start with** clause.

The **next** clause tells Oracle how long to wait between refreshes. Since it will be applied to a different base time each time the materialized view is refreshed, the **next** clause specifies a date expression instead of a fixed date. In the previous example, the expression is

```
next SysDate+7
```

Every time the materialized view is refreshed, the next refresh will be scheduled for seven days later. Although the refresh schedule in this example is fairly simple, you can use many of Oracle's date functions to customize a refresh schedule. For example, if you want to refresh every Monday at noon, regardless of the current date, you can set the **next** clause to

```
NEXT_DAY(TRUNC(SysDate, 'MONDAY'))+12/24
```

This example will find the next Monday after the current system date; the time portion of that date will be truncated, and 12 hours will be added to the date. (For information on date functions in Oracle, see Chapter 9.)

For automatic materialized view refreshes to occur, you must have at least one background snapshot refresh process running in your database. The refresh process, called SNP*n* (where *n* is a number from 0 to 9), periodically "wakes up" and checks whether any materialized views in the database need to be refreshed. The number of SNP*n* processes running in your database is determined by an initialization parameter called JOB_QUEUE_PROCESSES. That parameter must be set (in your init.ora file) to a value greater than 0; for most cases, a value of 1 should be sufficient.

The interval, in seconds, between wake-up calls to the SNP*n* processes is set by the JOB_QUEUE_INTERVAL parameter in the init.ora parameter file. The default interval is 60 seconds.

If the database is not running the SNP*n* processes, you need to use manual refresh methods, described in the next section.

Manual Refreshes

In addition to the database's automatic refreshes, you can perform manual refreshes of materialized views. These override the normally scheduled refreshes; the new **start with** value will be based on the time of your manual refresh.

The LOCAL_LEDGER_TOTALS materialized view defined earlier contained the following specifications about its refresh interval:

```
refresh complete
start with SysDate next SysDate+7
```

As noted in the previous section, the **start with** and **next** clauses provide input to Oracle's scheduling for refreshes of materialized views. However, you may wish to override these settings if significant changes have occurred in the master table. For example, after a major data load in the master table, the materialized view should be refreshed in order to limit the amount of inconsistency between the materialized view and the master table.

You can manually refresh the snapshot via the DBMS_SNAPSHOT package provided in Oracle. This is a public package owned by the user SYS (for more information on packages and procedures, see Chapter 27). A procedure named REFRESH within this package can be used to refresh a materialized view. An example of the command's usage is shown in the following listing. In this example, the user **execute**s the procedure, passing it two parameters. The parameters passed to the procedure are described following the example.

```
execute DBMS_SNAPSHOT.REFRESH('LOCAL_LEDGER_TOTALS','?');
```

The REFRESH procedure of the DBMS_SNAPSHOT package takes two parameters. The first is the name of the snapshot, which should be prefixed by the name of the snapshot's owner (if other than the user executing this procedure). The second parameter is the manual refresh option. The available values for the manual refresh option are listed in Table 23-1.

Another procedure in the DBMS_SNAPSHOT package can be used to refresh all the materialized views that are scheduled to be automatically refreshed. This procedure, named REFRESH_ALL, will refresh each snapshot separately. It does not accept any parameters. The following listing shows an example of its execution:

```
execute DBMS_SNAPSHOT.REFRESH_ALL;
```

Manual Refresh Option	Description
F, f	Fast refresh
C, c	Complete refresh
?	The default refresh option for the snapshot should be used
A	Always perform a complete refresh

TABLE 23-1.   *Refresh Options*

When this command is run, every materialized view that is due to be automatically refreshed is refreshed, one by one. Since the materialized views are not all refreshed at the same time, a database or server failure during the execution of this procedure may cause the local materialized views to be out of sync with each other. If that happens, simply rerun this procedure after the database has been recovered.

A separate package, DBMS_MVIEW, contains an expanded set of refresh procedures. These include DBMS_MVIEW.REFRESH_DEPENDENT, which will refresh all table-based materialized views that depend on a given list of tables. See the *Oracle8i Tuning* guide for details on this package.

Using Refresh Groups

Related materialized views can be collected into *refresh groups*. The purpose of a refresh group is to coordinate the refresh schedules of its members. Materialized views whose master tables have relationships with other materialized view master tables are good candidates for membership in refresh groups. Coordinating the refresh schedules of the materialized views will maintain the master tables' referential integrity in the materialized views. If refresh groups are not used, then the data in the materialized views may be inconsistent with regard to the master tables' referential integrity.

All manipulation of refresh groups is achieved via the DBMS_REFRESH package. The procedures within that package are MAKE, ADD, SUBTRACT, CHANGE, DESTROY, and REFRESH. In the following sections, you will see how to use these procedures to manage refresh groups. Information about existing refresh groups can be queried from the USER_REFRESH and USER_REFRESH_CHILDREN data dictionary views.

NOTE
Snapshots that belong to a refresh group do not have to belong to the same schema, but they all have to be stored within the same database.

Creating a Refresh Group

Create a refresh group by executing the MAKE procedure in the DBMS_REFRESH package, whose structure is shown in the following listing:

```
DBMS_REFRESH.MAKE (
    name      IN VARCHAR2,
    { list      IN VARCHAR2,
```

```
  | tab      IN DBMS_UTILITY.UNCL_ARRAY,}
next_date IN DATE,
interval  IN VARCHAR2,
implicit_destroy      IN BOOLEAN DEFAULT FALSE,
lax                   IN BOOLEAN DEFAULT FALSE,
job                   IN BINARY_INTEGER DEFAULT 0,
rollback_seg          IN VARCHAR2 DEFAULT NULL,
push_deferred_rpc     IN BOOLEAN DEFAULT TRUE,
refresh_after_errors  IN BOOLEAN DEFAULT FALSE,
purge_option          IN BINARY_INTEGER := NULL,
parallelism           IN BINARY_INTEGER := NULL,
heap_size             IN BINARY_INTEGER := NULL);
```

The *list* and *tab* parameters are mutually exclusive. The *tab* parameter would be used to pass a PL/SQL table of materialized view names to the procedure. The last nine parameters for this procedure have default values that are usually acceptable. You can use the following command to create a refresh group for the LEDGER snapshots created earlier in this chapter:

```
execute DBMS_REFRESH.MAKE
(name => 'ledger_group',
 list => 'local_ledger, local_ledger_totals',
 next_date => SysDate,
 interval => 'SysDate+7');
```

NOTE
The list *parameter, which is the second parameter in the listing, has a single quote at its beginning and at its end, with none between. In this example, two materialized views, LOCAL_LEDGER and LOCAL_LEDGER_TOTALS, are passed to the procedure via a single parameter.*

The preceding command will create a refresh group named LEDGER_GROUP, with the two LEDGER-based materialized views as its members. Note that the refresh group name is enclosed in single quotes, as is the *list* of members (but not each member).

If the refresh group is going to contain a materialized view that is already a member of another refresh group (for example, during a move of a materialized view from an old refresh group to a newly created refresh group), then you must set the *lax* parameter to TRUE. A materialized view can only belong to one refresh group at a time.

Adding Members to a Refresh Group

To add snapshots to an existing refresh group, use the ADD procedure of the DBMS_REFRESH package, whose structure is as follows:

```
DBMS_REFRESH.ADD
( name       IN VARCHAR2,
 { list      IN VARCHAR2
   | tab      IN DBMS_UTILITY.UNCL_ARRAY, }
   lax       IN BOOLEAN  DEFAULT FALSE );
```

As with the MAKE procedure, the ADD procedure's *lax* parameter does not have to be specified unless a materialized view is being moved between two refresh groups. When this procedure is executed with the *lax* parameter set to TRUE, the materialized view is moved to the new refresh group and is automatically deleted from the old refresh group.

Removing Members from a Refresh Group

To remove materialized views from an existing refresh group, use the SUBTRACT procedure of the DBMS_REFRESH package, whose structure is as follows:

```
DBMS_REFRESH.SUBTRACT
( name       IN VARCHAR2,
  {list      IN VARCHAR2
  | tab      IN DBMS_UTILITY.UNCL_ARRAY, }
  lax       IN BOOLEAN  DEFAULT FALSE );
```

As with the MAKE and ADD procedures, a single materialized view, a list (separated by commas), or a PL/SQL table containing one or more materialized view names may serve as input to this procedure.

Changing a Refresh Group's Refresh Schedule

The refresh schedule for a refresh group may be altered via the CHANGE procedure of the DBMS_REFRESH package, whose structure is shown in the following listing:

```
DBMS_REFRESH.CHANGE
 ( name                IN VARCHAR2,
   next_date           IN DATE := NULL,
   interval            IN VARCHAR2 := NULL,
   implicit_destroy    IN BOOLEAN  := NULL,
   rollback_seg        IN VARCHAR2 := NULL,
   push_deferred_rpc   IN BOOLEAN := NULL,
   refresh_after_errors IN BOOLEAN := NULL,
   purge_option        IN BINARY_INTEGER := NULL,
   parallelism         IN BINARY_INTEGER := NULL,
   heap_size           IN BINARY_INTEGER := NULL);
```

The *next_date* parameter is analogous to the **start with** clause in the **create snapshot** command. The *interval* parameter is analogous to the **next** clause in the **create snapshot** command.

For example, to change the LEDGER_GROUP's schedule so that it will be replicated every three days, you can execute the following command (which specifies a **NULL** value for the *next_date* parameter, leaving that value unchanged):

```
execute DBMS_REFRESH.CHANGE
(name => 'ledger_group',
 next_date => null,
 interval => 'SysDate+3');
```

After this command is executed, the refresh cycle for the LEDGER_GROUP refresh group will be changed to every three days.

Deleting a Refresh Group

To delete a refresh group, use the DESTROY procedure of the DBMS_REFRESH package, as shown in the following example. Its only parameter is the name of the refresh group.

```
execute DBMS_REFRESH.DESTROY(name => 'ledger_group');
```

You may also implicitly destroy the refresh group. If you set the *implicit_destroy* parameter to TRUE when you created the group with the MAKE procedure, then the refresh group will be deleted (destroyed) when its last member is removed from the group (usually via the SUBTRACT procedure).

Manually Refreshing a Refresh Group

A refresh group may be manually refreshed via the REFRESH procedure of the DBMS_REFRESH package. The REFRESH procedure accepts the name of the refresh group as its only parameter. The following command will refresh the refresh group named LEDGER_GROUP:

```
execute DBMS_REFRESH.REFRESH(name => 'ledger_group');
```

create materialized view log/snapshot log Syntax

In simple materialized views, each record in the materialized view is based on a single row in a single master table. When simple materialized views are used, a *materialized view log* can be created on the master table. The materialized view log is a table that records the date on which every changed row within the master table last replicated. The record of changed rows can then be used during refreshes to send out to the snapshots only those rows that have changed in the master table. Multiple simple materialized views based on the same table can use the same materialized view log.

The full syntax for the **create materialized view log/snapshot log** command is shown in the Alphabetical Reference. The following listing shows part of the syntax; as you may note from its syntax, it has all of the parameters normally associated with tables:

```
create { materialized view | snapshot} log on [schema.]table
  [ with {[primary key] [,rowid] [,(filter column)
      | ,(filter column) ...]}
  [ pctfree integer
  | pctused integer
  | initrans integer
  | maxtrans integer
  | tablespace tablespace
  | storage storage];
```

The **create materialized view log/snapshot log** command is executed in the master table's database, usually by the owner of the master table. Materialized view logs should not be created for tables that are only involved in complex materialized views (since they wouldn't be used). No name is specified for the materialized view log.

A materialized view log for the LEDGER table can be created via the following command, executed from within the account that owns the table:

```
create materialized view log on LEDGER
with ROWID
tablespace SNAP_LOGS
storage (initial 40K next 40K pctincrease 0);
```

The command shown in this example creates a materialized view log in a tablespace named SNAP_LOGS. Because materialized view logs may grow unpredictably over time, you may wish to store their associated objects in tablespaces that are dedicated to materialized view logs. The LOCAL_LEDGER materialized view was created using the **with ROWID** clause, so the materialized view log for the LEDGER table should also be created using the **with ROWID** clause.

Required System Privileges

To create the materialized view log, you must have CREATE TABLE and CREATE TRIGGER system privileges. If you are creating the materialized view log from a user account that does not own the master table, you need to have CREATE ANY TABLE and CREATE ANY TRIGGER system privileges.

Local and Remote Objects Created

When a materialized view log is created, two objects are created in the master table's schema. From the perspective of the materialized view owner, the **create snapshot log** command occurs in the remote database, and the objects it creates are all in the remote database. The materialized view log creates a table and a trigger:

- A table is created to store the RowIDs of the rows that change in the master table (if a RowID-based materialized view is created), along with a separate timestamp column to record the time the changed rows were last replicated.

- An AFTER ROW trigger is created to insert the key values—either RowIDs or primary key values—and refresh timestamps of updated, inserted, or deleted rows into the materialized view log table.

The "filter" columns shown in the **create materialized view log/snapshot log** command are related to the use of subqueries within materialized view queries. You can use a subquery within a materialized view query only if the subquery completely preserves the key values of the replicated data. Subqueries can be used only with primary key–based materialized views.

Altering Materialized Views and Logs

You may alter the storage parameters, refresh option, and refresh schedule for existing snapshots. If you are unsure of the current settings for a snapshot, check the USER_SNAPSHOTS data dictionary view.

The syntax for the **alter snapshot/materialized view** command is shown in the Alphabetical Reference. The command in the following listing alters the refresh option used by the LOCAL_LEDGER materialized view:

```
alter materialized view LOCAL_LEDGER
refresh complete;
```

All future refreshes of LOCAL_LEDGER will refresh the entire local base table.

To alter a materialized view, you must either own the materialized view or have ALTER ANY SNAPSHOT or ALTER ANY MATERIALIZED VIEW system privilege.

The storage parameters for materialized view logs may be modified via the **alter snapshot log/materialized view log** command. The syntax for this command is shown in the Alphabetical Reference.

Changing the storage-related parameters for a materialized view log will change the storage parameters on the materialized view log's table. For example, the following command will change the **next** parameter within the **storage** clause for the materialized view log:

```
alter materialized view log on LEDGER
storage (next 100K);
```

To alter a materialized view log, you must own the table, have ALTER privilege for the table, or have ALTER ANY TABLE system privilege.

Dropping Materialized Views and Logs

To drop a materialized view, you must have the system privileges required to drop both the materialized view and all of its related objects. You need to have DROP SNAPSHOT or DROP MATERIALIZED VIEW if the object is in your schema, or either DROP ANY SNAPSHOT or DROP ANY MATERIALIZED VIEW system privilege if the snapshot is not in your schema.

The following command drops the LOCAL_LEDGER_TOTALS materialized view created earlier in this chapter:

```
drop materialized view LOCAL_LEDGER_TOTALS;
```

Materialized view logs can be dropped via the **drop snapshot log/materialized view log** command. Once the materialized view log is dropped from a master table, no fast refreshes can be performed for simple materialized views based on that table. A materialized view log should be dropped when no simple materialized views are based on the master table. The following command drops the materialized view log that was created on the LEDGER table earlier in this chapter:

```
drop materialized view log on LEDGER;
```

To drop a materialized view log, you must have the ability to drop both the materialized view log and its related objects. If you own the materialized view log, you must have the DROP TABLE and DROP TRIGGER system privileges. If you do not own the materialized view log, you need the DROP ANY TABLE and DROP ANY TRIGGER system privileges to execute this command.

CHAPTER
24

Using interMedia Text
for Text Searches

fter using his database for a while, Talbot notices a trend that is common to many database applications: the amount of text stored in the database increases. New prospects send in résumés, and their résumés are added to the PROSPECT table. Employees are evaluated, and their evaluations are added to the database. As the amount of text increases in the database, so does the complexity of the text queries performed against the database. Instead of just performing string matches, Talbot needs new text-search features—such as weighting the terms in a search of multiple terms or ranking the results of a text search.

You can use Oracle's interMedia Text (IMT) option to perform text-based searches. In prior versions, this feature was known as the ConText Cartridge. If you have previously used ConText, you may find the configuration for IMT to be simpler and better integrated with the Oracle kernel.

You can use IMT to perform wildcard searching, "fuzzy matches," relevance ranking, proximity searching, term weighting, and word expansions. In this chapter, you'll see how to use IMT as part of a query that involves text searching.

Adding Text to the Database

Text can be added to the database either by physically storing the text in a table or by storing pointers to external files in the database. That is, for Talbot's prospects, you can store the résumés either in the database or in external files. If you store the résumés in external files, then you store the filenames in the database.

To store the résumés in the database, Talbot expands the PROSPECT table. Originally, the PROSPECT table included only two columns:

```
create table PROSPECT (
Name          VARCHAR2(25) not null,
Address       VARCHAR2(35))
/
```

To support the text data, a third column is added to the PROSPECT table, as shown in the following listing:

```
alter table PROSPECT add
(Resume       LONG)
/
```

The Resume column of the PROSPECT table is defined as having a LONG datatype. In the following listing, a single Resume value is added to the PROSPECT table. The PROSPECT entry for Wilfred Lowell is updated; in the listing, a carriage return is entered after every line.

```
update PROSPECT
   set Resume = 'Past experience with hoes, pitchforks, and various
garden implements. Highly recommended by previous employer. Excellent
safety record.  Previously worked with Jed Hopkins at Plumstead Farm.
Education includes a degree in engineering.'
 where Name = 'WILFRED LOWELL';
```

Now that you have updated Wilfred Lowell's entry to include a Resume value, you can select that value from the database:

```
select Resume
   from PROSPECT
 where Name = 'WILFRED LOWELL';
```

The output from the preceding query is shown in the following listing:

```
RESUME
-----------------------------------------------------------
Past experience with hoes, pitchforks, and various
garden implements. Highly rec
```

What happened to the output? By default, only the first 80 characters of LONG datatypes are displayed. To change this setting, use the **set long** command within SQLPLUS, as shown in the following listing:

```
set long 1000
select Resume
  from PROSPECT
 where Name = 'WILFRED LOWELL';

RESUME
-----------------------------------------------------------------
Past experience with hoes, pitchforks, and various
garden implements. Highly recommended by previous employer. Excellent
safety record.  Previously worked with Jed Hopkins at Plumstead Farm.
Education includes a degree in engineering.
```

The text stored in the LONG column includes the carriage returns that were entered when the Resume value was specified.

Querying Text from the Database

Suppose Talbot wants to see the names of all the prospects who have experience or degrees in engineering. He could enter

```
select Name
   from PROSPECT
 where Resume like '%engineer%';
```

However, that query will fail, since Resume is defined as a LONG datatype. The error message is displayed in the following listing:

```
 where Resume like '%engineer%'
       *
ERROR at line 3:
ORA-00932: inconsistent datatypes
```

What if Talbot wants to determine how long the longest Resume entry is (for use in a subsequent **set long** command)? The following won't work:

```
select LENGTH(Resume)
   from PROSPECT
 where Name = 'WILFRED LOWELL';

select LENGTH(Resume)
               *
ERROR at line 1:
ORA-00932: inconsistent datatypes
```

The "inconsistent datatypes" error is raised because Talbot is attempting to perform text-string-manipulation functions on a column (Resume) that has a LONG datatype. If Talbot had used a VARCHAR2 datatype instead, the preceding queries would have succeeded—but the text storage would have been limited by the VARCHAR2 datatype (4,000 characters).

Thus, if you want to store more than 4,000 characters of text per column, you can't use a VARCHAR2 for your text searches. If you were to use VARCHAR2 datatypes for your text fields, you would have to decide how to store the data— should you store the text in all uppercase, or force users to use text string functions such as **UPPER** when executing their queries?

Furthermore, if the text is already formatted—such as a document created using MS Word—then you could use the LONG RAW datatype of a LOB datatype (see Chapter 30) to store the MS Word file inside the database. How could you query such a document using the text-search capabilities available in Oracle?

Text Indexes

You can use the IMT option to perform text searches as part of database queries. To create and use text-searching capabilities, you need to have the CTXAPP role enabled for your account.

NOTE
Before using IMT, you may need to configure your database environment to support text searches. See the documentation for the ctxsrv utility for your operating system to get details concerning the environment configuration.

To use IMT, you need to create a *text index* on the column in which the text is stored. "Text index" is a slightly confusing term—it is actually a collection of tables and indexes that store information about the text stored in the column.

NOTE
Unlike prior versions of Oracle and ConText, you no longer need to create policies before creating text indexes. You can alter the preferences for the text indexes; see the interMedia Text documentation to learn the procedures for changing index preferences.

Before creating a text index on a table, you must create a primary key for the table (if one does not already exist):

```
alter table PROSPECT add
(constraint PROSPECT_PK primary key (Name));
```

You can create a text index via a special version of the **create index** command, as shown in the following listing:

```
create index Resume_Index on PROSPECT(Resume)
indextype is ctxsys.context;
```

When the text index is created, Oracle creates a number of indexes and tables in your schema to support your text queries. You can rebuild your text index via the **alter index** command, just as you would for any other index.

Text Queries

If a text index is created on the Resume column of the PROSPECT table, then text-searching capabilities increase dramatically. Talbot can now look for any Resume that contains the word engineering:

```
select Name
  from PROSPECT
 where CONTAINS(Resume, 'engineering')>0;
```

The **CONTAINS** function checks the text index for the Resume column. If the word "engineering" is found in the Resume column's text index, then a *score* greater than 0 is returned by the database, and the matching Name value is returned. The score is an evaluation of how well the record being returned matches the criteria specified in the **CONTAINS** function.

How a Text Query Works

When a function such as **CONTAINS** is used in a query, the text portion of the query is processed by Oracle. The remainder of the query is processed just like a regular query within the database. The results of the text query processing and the regular query processing are merged to return a single set of records to the user.

Available Text Query Expressions

IMT would be rather limited if it allowed you to search only for exact matches of words. IMT offers a broad array of text-searching capabilities you can use to customize your queries. Most of the text-searching capabilities are enabled via the **CONTAINS** function, which can appear only in the **where** clause of a **select** statement; never in the **where** clauses of **insert**s, **update**s, or **delete**s.

The operators within the **CONTAINS** function allow you to perform the following text searches:

- Exact matches of a word or phrase

- Exact matches of multiple words, using Boolean logic to combine searches

- Searches based on how close words are to each other in the text

- Searches for words that share the same word "stem"

- "Fuzzy" matches of words

- Searches for words that sound like other words

In the following sections, you will see examples of these types of text searches, along with information about the operators you can use to customize text searches.

Searching for an Exact Match of a Word

In the PROSPECT table, a single Resume value has been updated to include Wilfred Lowell's background information. As Talbot's database of prospects grows, the number of résumés grows as well. The following listing shows the first résumé that was entered in the PROSPECT table; the queries in the rest of this chapter will involve using different text-search methods to retrieve this data.

```
set long 1000
select Resume
  from PROSPECT
 where Name = 'WILFRED LOWELL';

RESUME
--------------------------------------------------------------------
Past experience with hoes, pitchforks, and various
garden implements. Highly recommended by previous employer. Excellent
safety record.  Previously worked with Jed Hopkins at Plumstead Farm.
Education includes a degree in engineering.
```

In the following listing, Talbot queries his PROSPECT table for all prospects whose Resume includes the word "engineering:"

```
select Name
  from PROSPECT
 where CONTAINS(Resume, 'engineering')>0;
```

Within the **CONTAINS** function, the > sign is called a *threshold* operator. The preceding text search can be translated to the following:

```
select all the Name column values
from the PROSPECT table
where the score for the text search of the Resume column
for an exact match of the word 'engineering'
exceeds a threshold value of 0.
```

The threshold analysis compares the score—the internal score Oracle calculated when the text search was performed—to the specified threshold value. Score values for individual searches range from 0 to 10 for each occurrence of the search string within the text. You can even display the score as part of your query.

To show the text-search score, use the **SCORE** function, which has a single parameter—a label you assign to the score within the text search:

```
select Name, SCORE(10)
  from PROSPECT
 where CONTAINS(Resume, 'engineering', 10)>0;

NAME                         SCORE(10)
------------------------ ---------
WILFRED LOWELL                    6
```

In this listing, the **CONTAINS** function's parameters are modified to include a label (10) for the text-search operation performed. The **SCORE** function will display the score of the text search associated with that label.

You can use the **SCORE** function in the **select** list (as shown in the preceding query) or in a **group by** clause or an **order by** clause.

Searching for an Exact Match of Multiple Words

What if you want to search the text for multiple words? You can use Boolean logic (ANDs and ORs) to combine the results of multiple text searches in a single query. You can also search for multiple terms within the same **CONTAINS** function and let Oracle resolve the search results.

For example, if Talbot wanted to search for prospects who had the words "engineering" and "safety" in the résumé text, he could enter the following query:

```
select Name
  from PROSPECT
 where CONTAINS(Resume, 'engineering AND safety')>0;
```

Instead of using AND, Talbot could have used an ampersand, &:

```
select Name
  from PROSPECT
 where CONTAINS(Resume, 'engineering & safety')>0;
```

Unfortunately, using an ampersand has unexpected results within SQL*Plus: you are prompted for a value for *safety*,

```
Enter value for safety:
```

because SQL*Plus treats the & character as the start of a variable name. You can respond by entering the following value:

```
& safety
```

Alternatively, you can tell SQL*Plus not to scan for variables, in which case the & character will not be treated as the start of a variable name:

```
set scan off
```

Using either the & character or the word AND denotes an AND operation—so the **CONTAINS** function will return a row only if the Resume includes *both* the words "engineering" and "safety." Each search must pass the threshold criteria defined for the search scores. Since the ampersand is also a special character in SQL*Plus, you can replace the & symbol with the word AND, as shown in the following listing:

```
select Name
   from PROSPECT
  where CONTAINS(Resume, 'engineering AND safety')>0;
```

The query in this listing does *not* search for the phrase "engineering and safety," because the word AND is used to join the two search conditions. In the next section of this chapter, you will see how to search for phrases.

If you want to search for more than two terms, just add them to the **CONTAINS** clause, as shown in the following listing:

```
select Name
   from PROSPECT
  where CONTAINS(Resume, 'engineering AND safety AND turbine')
            >0;
```

The query in this listing returns a row only if its search scores for "engineering," "safety," and "turbine" are each greater than 0.

In addition to AND, you can use the OR operator—in which case a record is returned if either of the search conditions meets the defined threshold. The symbol for OR in IMT is a vertical line (|), so the following two queries are processed identically:

```
select Name
   from PROSPECT
  where CONTAINS(Resume, 'engineering OR safety')>0;

select Name
   from PROSPECT
  where CONTAINS(Resume, 'engineering | safety')>0;
```

When these queries are executed, a record is returned if either of the two separate searches (for "engineering" and "safety") returns a score greater than 0.

The ACCUM (accumulate) operator provides another method for combining searches. ACCUM adds together the scores of the individual searches and compares the accumulated score to the threshold value. The symbol for ACCUM is a comma (,), so the two queries shown in the following listing are equivalent:

```
select Name
   from PROSPECT
  where CONTAINS(Resume, 'engineering ACCUM safety')>0;

select Name
   from PROSPECT
  where CONTAINS(Resume, 'engineering, safety')>0;
```

You can also use IMT to subtract the scores from multiple searches before comparing the result to the threshold score. The MINUS operator subtracts the score of the second term's search from the score of the first term's search. The query in the following listing will determine the search score for "engineering" and subtract from it the search score for "mechanic;" the difference is compared to the threshold score.

```
select Name
   from PROSPECT
  where CONTAINS(Resume, 'engineering MINUS safety')>0;
```

You can use the symbol - in place of the MINUS operator, as shown in the following listing:

```
select Name
   from PROSPECT
  where CONTAINS(Resume, 'engineering - safety')>0;
```

You can use parentheses to clarify the logic within your search criteria. For example, if your search uses both ANDs and ORs, then you should use parentheses to clarify the way in which the rows are processed. For example, the following query returns a row if the searched text contains either the word "digging" or both the words "hoeing" and "planting:"

```
select Name
   from PROSPECT
  where CONTAINS(Resume,'digging OR (hoeing AND planting)')
        >0;
```

If you change the location of the parentheses, you change the logic of the **CONTAINS** function processing. The following query returns a row if the searched text contains either "digging" or "hoeing" and also contains the word "planting:"

```
select Name
   from PROSPECT
  where CONTAINS(Resume,'(digging OR hoeing) AND planting')
         >0;
```

When evaluating the scores of multiple searches, you can tell IMT to weigh the scores of some searches more heavily than others. For example, if you want the search score for "engineering" to be doubled when compared to the threshold score, you can use the asterisk symbol (*) to indicate the factor by which the search score should be multiplied.

The following query will double the search score for "engineering," because it is evaluated in an OR condition:

```
select Name
   from PROSPECT
 where CONTAINS(Resume, 'engineering*2 OR mechanic*1')>5;
```

You can weight the search scores to indicate the relevance of the terms in the search. If one term is the most important term in the search, then give that term the highest weighting. Through the use of the AND, OR, ACCUM, and MINUS operators, you should be able to search for any combination of word matches. In the next section, you will see how to search for phrases.

Searching for an Exact Match of a Phrase

When searching for an exact match for a phrase, you specify the whole phrase as part of the **CONTAINS** function. If your phrase includes reserved words (such as "and," "or," or "minus"), then you need to use the grouping operators shown in this section so that the search is executed properly.

In the following query, Talbot searches for anyone whose Resume entry includes the phrase "highly recommended." Wilfred Lowell's entry will be returned even though the case of his entry is different from the case of the search text; for his entry, the word "highly" is capitalized ("Highly").

```
select Name
   from PROSPECT
 where CONTAINS(Resume, 'highly recommended')>0;
```

If the search phrase includes a reserved word within IMT, then you must use curly braces ({}) to enclose the text. The following query searches for the phrase "day and night." The word "and" is enclosed in braces.

```
select Name
   from PROSPECT
 where CONTAINS(Resume, 'day {and} night')>0;
```

The query of 'day {and} night' is different from a query of 'day and night'. The query of 'day {and} night' returns a record only if the *phrase* "day and night" exists in the searched text. The query of 'day and night' returns a record if the search score for the *word* "day" and the search score for the *word* "night" are both above the threshold score.

You can enclose the entire phrase within curly braces, in which case any reserved words within the phrase will be treated as part of the search criteria. The following query searches for the phrase "day and night" by placing braces around the entire phrase:

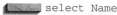

```
select Name
  from PROSPECT
 where CONTAINS(Resume, '{day and night}')>0;
```

Searches for Words that Are Near Each Other

You can use IMT's *proximity search* capability to perform a text search based on how close terms are to each other within the searched document. A proximity search returns a high score for words that are next to each other, and returns a low score for words that are far apart. If the words are next to each other, the proximity search returns a score of 100.

To use proximity searching, use the keyword NEAR, as shown in the following example:

```
select Name
  from PROSPECT
 where CONTAINS(Resume, 'education NEAR engineering')>0;
```

You can replace the NEAR operator with its equivalent symbol, the semicolon (;). The revised query is shown in the following listing:

```
select Name
  from PROSPECT
 where CONTAINS(Resume, 'education ; engineering')>0;
```

You can use the phrase- and word-searching methods shown in this chapter to search for exact matches of words and phrases, as well as to perform proximity searches of exact words and phrases. Thus far, all the searches have used exact matches of the search terms as the basis for the search. In the next sections, you will see how to expand the search terms via four methods: wildcards, word stems, fuzzy matches, and SOUNDEX searches.

Using Wildcards During Searches

In the previous examples in this chapter, Talbot searched the PROSPECT résumés for text values that exactly match the criteria he specified. For example, he searched for "engineering" but not "engineer." You can use wildcards to expand the list of valid search terms used during your query.

Just as in regular text-string wildcard processing, two wildcards are available:

Character	Description
%	Percent sign; multiple-character wildcard
_	Underscore; single-character wildcard

The following query will search for all text matches for all words that start with the characters "engineer:"

```
select Name
  from PROSPECT
 where CONTAINS(Resume, 'engineer%')>0;
```

The following query limits the expansion of the text string to two characters. In place of the % sign in the preceding query, two underscores (_ _) are used. Since the underscore is a single-character wildcard, the text string cannot expand beyond two characters during the search. For example, the word "engineers" could be returned by the text search, but the word "engineering" is too long to be returned.

```
select Name
  from PROSPECT
 where CONTAINS(Resume, 'engineer__')>0;
```

You should use wildcards when you are certain of some of the characters within the search string. If you are uncertain of the search string, you should use one of the methods described in the following sections—word stems, fuzzy matches, and SOUNDEX matches.

Searching for Words that Share the Same Stem

Rather than using wildcards, you can use *stem-expansion* capabilities to expand the list of text strings. Given the "stem" of a word, Oracle will expand the list of words to search for to include all words having the same stem. Sample expansions are shown here:

Stem	Sample Expansions
Play	plays played playing playful
Works	working work worked workman workhorse
Have	had has haven't hasn't

Since "works" and "work" have the same stem, a stem-expansion search using the word "works" will return text containing the word "work."

To use stem expansion within a query, you need to use the dollar sign ($) symbol. Within the search string, the '$' should immediately precede the word to be expanded, with no space between the '$' and the word.

In the following query, Talbot queries the PROSPECT table for all résumés that include the word "safety" and any word that shares the stem of the word "recommend:"

```
select Name
  from PROSPECT
 where CONTAINS(Resume, 'safety AND $recommend')>0;
```

When this query is executed, Oracle expands the word "recommend" to include all words with the same stem, and then performs the search. If a résumé contains one of the words with a stem of "recommend" and also contains the word "safety," then the record will be returned to the user.

The expansion of terms via word stems simplifies the querying process for the user. You no longer need to know what form of a verb was used when the text was entered—all forms are used as the basis for the search. You do not need to specify specific text strings, as you do when querying for exact matches or using wildcards. Instead, you specify a word, and IMT dynamically determines all the words that should be searched for, based on the word you specified.

Searching for Fuzzy Matches

A *fuzzy match* expands the specified search term to include words that are spelled similarly but that do not necessarily have the same word stem. Fuzzy matches are most helpful when the text contains misspellings. The misspellings can be either in the searched text or in the search string specified by the user during the query.

For example, if Talbot enters the following query, Wilfred Lowell's Resume entry will not be displayed, because its text does not contain the word "hose:"

```
select Name
  from PROSPECT
 where CONTAINS(Resume, 'hose')>0;
```

It does, however, contain the word "hoes." A fuzzy match will return résumés containing the word "hoes," even though "hoes" has a different word stem than the word used as the search term.

To use a fuzzy match, precede the search term with a question mark, with no space between the question mark and the beginning of the search term. In the following example, Talbot modifies the query to use a fuzzy match and return words that are similar to the word "hose:"

```
select Name
   from PROSPECT
 where CONTAINS(Resume, '?hose')>0;
```

Searches for Words that Sound Like Other Words

Stem-expansion searches expand a search term to multiple terms based on the stem of the word. Fuzzy matches expand a search term based on similar words in the text index. A third kind of search-term expansion, SOUNDEX, expands search terms based on how the word sounds. The SOUNDEX expansion method uses the same text-matching logic available via the **SOUNDEX** function in SQL.

To use the SOUNDEX option, you must precede the search term with an exclamation mark (!), with no space between the exclamation mark and the search term. During the search, Oracle evaluates the SOUNDEX values of the terms in the text index and searches for all words that have the same SOUNDEX value.

In the following query, Talbot searches for all résumés that include the word "safely," using a SOUNDEX match technique:

```
select Name
   from PROSPECT
 where CONTAINS(Resume, '!safely')>0;
```

Wilfred Lowell's résumé does not include the word "safely." When the query is executed, however, his résumé is returned, because the words "safely" and "safety" sound similar:

```
set long 1000
select Resume
   from PROSPECT
 where CONTAINS(Resume, '!safely')>0;

RESUME
--------------------------------------------------------------------
Past experience with hoes, pitchforks, and various
garden implements. Highly recommended by previous employer. Excellent
safety record.  Previously worked with Jed Hopkins at Plumstead Farm.
Education includes a degree in engineering.
```

Since "safely" and "safety" sound similar in English but do not have the same meaning, you should use care when implementing SOUNDEX searches.

SOUNDEX searches are commonly used when performing searches on peoples' names, to allow for minor changes in spellings of similar names. For example, you could use a SOUNDEX search to search for résumés that include names sounding like "Hoppkinz:"

```
select Name
   from PROSPECT
 where CONTAINS(Resume, '!Hoppkinz')>0;
```

Because Wilfred Lowell's résumé contains the name "Jed Hopkins," it will be returned by this query.

Combining Search Methods

You can combine the available text-search methods, and you can nest search methods. For example, you can combine two search criteria via an AND operator:

```
select Name
   from PROSPECT
 where CONTAINS(Resume, 'engineering AND safely')>0;
```

You can modify the query to use a stem-expansion search on the word "engineering," as shown in the following listing. To use a stem-expansion search, you add a '$' to the beginning of the search term to be expanded:

```
select Name
   from PROSPECT
 where CONTAINS(Resume, '$engineering AND safely')>0;
```

Next, you can change the "safely" search to be a SOUNDEX search instead:

```
select Name
   from PROSPECT
 where CONTAINS(Resume, '$engineering AND !safely')>0;
```

When you execute this query, you find that the term "safety" is returned as one of the SOUNDEX search terms. If you decide to eliminate "safety" as a search term via the MINUS operator, simply add the MINUS operator within the **CONTAINS** function, as shown in the following listing:

```
select Name
   from PROSPECT
 where CONTAINS(Resume, '$engineering AND
                   (!safely MINUS safety)')>0;
```

You can also *nest* operators, allowing you to perform stem expansions on the terms returned by a fuzzy match. In the following example, a fuzzy match is performed on the word "safely," and the terms returned from the fuzzy match are expanded using stem expansion:

```
select Name
   from PROSPECT
 where CONTAINS(Resume, '$?safely')>0;
```

The available search operations are summarized in Table 24-1.

Using the ABOUT Operator

In interMedia Text, you can search on themes of documents. Thematic searching is integrated with text-term searching. You can use the ABOUT operator to search for terms that have to do with the theme of the document rather than the specific terms within the document. For example:

```
select Name
   from PROSPECT
 where CONTAINS(Resume, 'ABOUT(engineer)')>0;
```

For further details on advanced uses of interMedia Text, such as the use of thesauri for searching through related terms, see the *Oracle8i interMedia Text Reference* provided as part of the Oracle documentation.

Operator	Description
OR	Returns a record if either search term has a score that exceeds the threshold
|	Same as OR
AND	Returns a record if both search terms have a score that exceeds the threshold
&	Same as AND
ACCUM	Returns a record if the sum of the search terms' scores exceeds the threshold
,	Same as ACCUM

TABLE 24-1. *Available Search Operations*

Operator	Description
MINUS	Returns a record if the score of the first search minus the score of the second search exceeds the threshold
-	Same as MINUS
*	Assigns different weights to the score of the searches
NEAR	The score will be based on how near the search terms are to each other in the searched text
;	Same as NEAR
{}	Encloses reserved words such as AND if they are part of the search term
%	Multiple-character wildcard
_	Single-character wildcard
$	Performs stem expansion of the search term prior to performing the search
?	Performs a fuzzy match of the search term prior to performing the search
!	Performs a SOUNDEX search
()	Specifies the order in which search criteria are evaluated

TABLE 24-1. *Available Search Operations* (continued)

PART
III

PL/SQL

CHAPTER
25

An Introduction
to PL/SQL

L/SQL is Oracle's procedural language (PL) superset of the Structured Query Language (SQL). You can use PL/SQL to do such things as codify your business rules through the creation of stored procedures and packages, trigger database events to occur, or add programming logic to the execution of SQL commands.

The steps involved in the creation of triggers, stored procedures, and packages are described in the following chapters in this section of this book. In this chapter, you will see the basic structures and syntax used in PL/SQL.

PL/SQL Overview

PL/SQL code is grouped into structures called *blocks*. If you create a stored procedure or package, you give the block of PL/SQL code a name; if the block of PL/SQL code is not given a name, then it is called an *anonymous* block. The examples in this chapter will feature anonymous blocks of PL/SQL code; the following chapters illustrate the creation of named blocks.

A block of PL/SQL code contains three sections, as listed in Table 25-1.

Within a PL/SQL block, the first section is the Declarations section. Within the Declarations section, you define the variables and cursors that the block will use. The Declarations section starts with the keyword **declare** and ends when the Executable Commands section starts (as indicated by the keyword **begin**). The Executable Commands section is followed by the Exception Handling section; the **exception** keyword signals the start of the Exception Handling section. The PL/SQL block is terminated by the **end** keyword.

The structure of a typical PL/SQL block is shown in the following listing:

```
declare
  <declarations section>
begin
  <executable commands>
 exception
  <exception handling>
end;
```

In the following sections of this chapter, you will see descriptions of each section of the PL/SQL block.

Declarations Section

The Declarations section begins a PL/SQL block. The Declarations section starts with the **declare** keyword, followed by a list of variable and cursor definitions. You

Section	Description
Declarations	Defines and initializes the variables and cursors used in the block
Executable Commands	Uses flow-control commands (such as **if** commands and loops) to execute the commands and assign values to the declared variables
Exception Handling	Provides customized handling of error conditions

TABLE 25-1. *Sections of an Anonymous PL/SQL Block*

can define variables to have constant values, and variables can inherit datatypes from existing columns and query results, as shown in the following examples.

In the following listing, the area of a circle is calculated. The result is stored in a table named AREAS. The AREAS table has two columns, to store radius and area values. The area of the circle is calculated by squaring the value for the circle's radius and multiplying that value times the constant *pi*:

```
declare
    pi      constant NUMBER(9,7) := 3.1415926;
    radius  INTEGER(5);
    area    NUMBER(14,2);
begin
    radius := 3;
    area := pi*power(radius,2);
    insert into AREAS values (radius, area);
end;
/
```

The **end;** signals the end of the PL/SQL block, and the **/** executes the PL/SQL block. When the PL/SQL block is executed, you will receive the following response from Oracle:

```
PL/SQL procedure successfully completed.
```

To verify that that PL/SQL block completed correctly, you can select from the database the rows that were inserted by the PL/SQL code. The query and results in the following listing show the row the PL/SQL block created in the AREAS table.

```
select *
  from AREAS;

    RADIUS       AREA
---------- ----------
         3     28.27
```

The output shows that a single row was inserted into the AREAS table by the PL/SQL block. Only one row was created, because only one radius value was specified.

In the first section of the PL/SQL block, shown in the following listing, three variables are declared. You must declare the variables that will be used in the Executable Commands section of the PL/SQL block.

```
declare
  pi      constant NUMBER(9,7) := 3.1415926;
  radius  INTEGER(5);
  area    NUMBER(14,2);
```

The first variable declared is *pi*, which is set to a constant value via the **constant** keyword. The value is assigned via the **:=** operator:

```
pi      constant NUMBER(9,7) := 3.1415926;
```

The next two variables are defined, but are not given default values:

```
radius INTEGER(5);
area    NUMBER(14,2);
```

You can assign an initial value to a variable in the Declarations section. To set an initial value for a variable, simply follow its datatype specification with the value assignment, as shown in the following listing:

```
radius INTEGER(5)   := 3;
```

In the example, the datatypes include NUMBER and INTEGER. PL/SQL datatypes include all of the valid SQL datatypes as well as complex datatypes based on query structures.

In the following example, a cursor is declared to retrieve a record from the RADIUS_VALS table. RADIUS_VALS is a table with one column, named Radius, that holds radius values to be used in these examples. The cursor is declared in the Declarations section, and a variable named rad_val is declared with a datatype based on the cursor's results.

```
declare
    pi      constant NUMBER(9,7) := 3.1415926;
    area    NUMBER(14,2);
    cursor rad_cursor is
        select * from RADIUS_VALS;
    rad_val rad_cursor%ROWTYPE;
begin
    open rad_cursor;
    fetch rad_cursor into rad_val;
        area := pi*power(rad_val.radius,2);
        insert into AREAS values (rad_val.radius, area);
    close rad_cursor;
end;
/
```

For this example, the table RADIUS_VALS contains a single row with a Radius value of 3.

In the first part of the Declarations section, the *pi* and *area* variables are defined, as they were in the examples earlier in this chapter. The radius variable is not defined; instead, a cursor named rad_cursor is defined. The cursor definition consists of a cursor name (rad_cursor) and a query (**select * from RADIUS_VALS;**). A cursor holds the results of a query for processing by other commands within the PL/SQL block:

```
declare
    pi      constant NUMBER(9,7) := 3.1415926;
    area    NUMBER(14,2);
    cursor rad_cursor is
        select * from RADIUS_VALS;
```

A final declaration creates a variable whose structure is anchored by the cursor's result set:

```
    rad_val rad_cursor%ROWTYPE;
```

The rad_val variable will be able to reference each column of the query's result set. In this example, the query only returns a single column, but if the table contained multiple columns, you would be able to reference all of them via the rad_val variable.

In addition to the %ROWTYPE declaration, you can use the %TYPE declaration to inherit datatype information. If you use the %ROWTYPE declaration, the variable inherits the column and datatype information for all the columns in the cursor's result set. If you use the %TYPE declaration, then the variable only inherits the definition of the column used to define it. You can even base %TYPE definitions on cursors, as shown in the following example.

```
cursor rad_cursor is
      select * from RADIUS_VALS;
rad_val rad_cursor%ROWTYPE;
rad_val_radius  rad_val.Radius%TYPE;
```

In the preceding listing, the rad_val variable inherits the datatypes of the result set of the rad_cursor cursor. The rad_val_radius variable inherits the datatype of the Radius column within the rad_val variable.

The advantage of datatype anchoring using %ROWTYPE and %TYPE definitions is that it makes the datatype definitions in your PL/SQL code independent of the underlying data structures. If the RADIUS_VALS Radius column is changed from a NUMBER(5) datatype to a NUMBER(4,2) datatype, you do not need to modify your PL/SQL code; the datatype assigned to the associated variables will be determined dynamically at runtime.

Executable Commands Section

In the Executable Commands section, you manipulate the variables and cursors declared in the Declarations section of your PL/SQL block. The Executable Commands section always starts with the keyword **begin**. In the following listing, the first PL/SQL block example from the Declarations section is repeated: the area of a circle is calculated, and the results are inserted into the AREAS table:

```
declare
   pi      constant NUMBER(9,7) := 3.1415926;
   radius INTEGER(5);
   area   NUMBER(14,2);
begin
   radius := 3;
   area := pi*power(radius,2);
   insert into AREAS values (radius, area);
end;
/
```

In the preceding listing, the Executable Commands section is

```
begin
   radius := 3;
   area := pi*power(radius,2);
   insert into AREAS values (radius, area);
end;
```

Following the **begin** keyword, the PL/SQL block's work begins. First, a value is assigned to the radius variable, and the radius variable and the *pi* constant value are used to determine the value of the area variable. The radius and area values are then inserted into the AREAS table.

The Executable Commands section of the PL/SQL block may contain commands that execute the cursors declared in the Declarations section. In the following example (from the "Declarations Section" section of this chapter), the Executable Commands section features several commands concerning the rad_cursor cursor:

```
declare
    pi      constant NUMBER(9,7) := 3.1415926;
    area    NUMBER(14,2);
    cursor rad_cursor is
        select * from RADIUS_VALS;
    rad_val rad_cursor%ROWTYPE;
begin
    open rad_cursor;
    fetch rad_cursor into rad_val;
      area := pi*power(rad_val.radius,2);
      insert into AREAS values (rad_val.radius, area);
    close rad_cursor;
end;
/
```

In the first command involving the cursor, the **open** command is used:

```
open rad_cursor;
```

When the rad_cursor cursor is **open**ed, the query declared for that cursor is executed and the records to be returned are identified. Next, records are **fetch**ed from the cursor:

```
fetch rad_cursor into rad_val;
```

In the Declarations section, the *rad_val* variable was declared to anchor its datatypes to the rad_cursor cursor:

```
cursor rad_cursor is
    select * from RADIUS_VALS;
rad_val rad_cursor%ROWTYPE;
```

When you **fetch** a record from the cursor into the *rad_val* variable, you can still address each column value selected via the cursor's query. When the cursor's data is no longer needed, you can **close** the cursor, as shown in the following listing:

```
close rad_cursor;
```

The Executable Commands section may contain conditional logic, such as **if** commands and loops. In the following sections, you will see examples of each of the major types of flow-control operations permitted in PL/SQL. You can use the flow-control operations to alter the manner in which the fetched records and executable commands are managed.

Conditional Logic

Within PL/SQL, you can use **if**, **else**, and **elsif** commands to control the flow of commands within the Executable Commands section. The formats of the available conditional-logic commands (excluding loops, which are covered in the next section) are shown in the following listing:

```
if   <some condition>
   then  <some command>
elsif  <some condition>
   then  <some command>
else  <some command>
end if;
```

You can nest **if** conditions within each other, as shown in the following listing:

```
if   <some condition>
   then
     if  <some condition>
     then  <some command>
     end if;
else  <some command>
end if;
```

By nesting **if** conditions, you can quickly develop complex logic flows within your Executable Commands section. When nesting **if** conditions, make sure you are not making the flow control more complex than it needs to be; always check to see whether logical conditions can be combined into simpler orders.

The area of a circle example used in the previous section will now be modified to include conditional logic. In the following listing, the Executable Commands section of the PL/SQL block has been modified to include **if** and **then** commands:

```
declare
   pi      constant NUMBER(9,7) := 3.1415926;
   area    NUMBER(14,2);
   cursor rad_cursor is
       select * from RADIUS_VALS;
   rad_val rad_cursor%ROWTYPE;
begin
```

```
open rad_cursor;
fetch rad_cursor into rad_val;
  area := pi*power(rad_val.radius,2);
  if  area >30
  then
    insert into AREAS values (rad_val.radius, area);
  end if;
close rad_cursor;
end;
/
```

In the preceding listing, an **if** condition is used to control the flow of commands within the Executable Commands section of the PL/SQL block. The flow-control commands are shown in the following listing:

```
if  area >30
  then
    insert into AREAS values (rad_val.radius, area);
  end if;
```

The flow-control commands in this example begin after the area variable's value has been determined. If the value is greater than 30, then a record will be inserted into the AREAS table; if the value is less than 30, then no record will be inserted into the table. You can use this sort of flow control to direct which of several SQL statements are to be executed, based on the conditions in your **if** conditions.

The following listing shows syntax for flow control involving SQL commands:

```
if  area>30
  then    <some command>
elsif  area<10
  then    <some command>
else  <some command>
end if;
```

Loops

You can use loops to process multiple records within a single PL/SQL block. PL/SQL supports three types of loops:

Simple loops	A loop that keeps repeating until an **exit** or **exit when** statement is reached within the loop
FOR loops	A loop that repeats a specified number of times
WHILE loops	A loop that repeats until a condition is met

In the following sections, you will see examples of each type of loop. The loop examples will use as their starting point the PL/SQL blocks used previously in this chapter. You can use loops to process multiple records from a cursor.

Simple Loops

In the following listing, a simple loop is used to generate multiple rows in the AREAS table. The loop is started by the **loop** keyword, and the **exit when** clause determines when the loop should be exited. An **end loop** clause signals the end of the loop.

```
declare
   pi      constant NUMBER(9,7) := 3.1415926;
   radius  INTEGER(5);
   area    NUMBER(14,2);
begin
   radius := 3;
   loop
      area := pi*power(radius,2);
         insert into AREAS values (radius, area);
      radius := radius+1;
      exit when area >100;
   end loop;
end;
/
```

The loop section of the example establishes the flow control for the commands in the Executable Commands section of the PL/SQL block. The steps within the loop are described in the following commented version of the **loop** commands:

```
loop
      /* Calculate the area, based on the radius value.   */
   area := pi*power(radius,2);
      /* Insert the current values into the AREAS table.  */
      insert into AREAS values (radius, area);
      /* Increment the radius value by 1.                 */
   radius := radius+1;
      /* Evaluate the last calculated area.  If the value */
      /* exceeds 100, then exit.  Otherwise, repeat the   */
      /* loop using the new radius value.                 */
   exit when area >100;
      /* Signal the end of the loop.                      */
   end loop;
```

The loop should generate multiple entries in the AREAS table. The first record will be the record generated by a Radius value of 3. Once an *area* value exceeds 100, no more records will be inserted into the AREAS table.

Sample output following the execution of the PL/SQL block is shown in the following listing:

```
select *
  from AREAS
 order by Radius;

    RADIUS        AREA
---------- ----------
         3       28.27
         4       50.27
         5       78.54
         6       113.1
```

Since the *area* value for a Radius value of 6 exceeds 100, no further Radius values are processed and the PL/SQL block completes.

Simple Cursor Loops

You can use the attributes of a cursor—such as whether or not any rows are left to be fetched—as the exit criteria for a loop. In the following example, a cursor is executed until no more rows are returned by the query. To determine the status of the cursor, the cursor's attributes are checked. Cursors have four attributes you can use in your program:

%FOUND	A record can be fetched from the cursor
%NOTFOUND	No more records can be fetched from the cursor
%ISOPEN	The cursor has been opened
%ROWCOUNT	The number of rows fetched from the cursor so far

The %FOUND, %NOTFOUND, and %ISOPEN cursor attributes are Booleans; they are set to either TRUE or FALSE. Because they are Boolean attributes, you can evaluate their settings without explicitly matching them to values of TRUE or FALSE. For example, the following command will cause an exit to occur when rad_cursor%NOTFOUND is TRUE:

```
exit when rad_cursor%NOTFOUND;
```

In the following listing, a simple loop is used to process multiple rows from a cursor:

```
declare
    pi      constant NUMBER(9,7) := 3.1415926;
    area    NUMBER(14,2);
    cursor rad_cursor is
        select * from RADIUS_VALS;
    rad_val rad_cursor%ROWTYPE;
begin
    open rad_cursor;
    loop
      fetch rad_cursor into rad_val;
      exit when rad_cursor%NOTFOUND;
        area := pi*power(rad_val.radius,2);
        insert into AREAS values (rad_val.radius, area);
    end loop;
    close rad_cursor;
end;
/
```

The loop section of the PL/SQL block performs the same processing as the simple loop shown in the previous section, with one exception—instead of basing the exit criteria on the Area value, the cursor's %NOTFOUND attribute is checked. If no more rows are found in the cursor, then %NOTFOUND will be TRUE—and thus, the loop will be exited. The commented version of the loop is shown in the following listing:

```
loop
        /*  Within the loop, fetch a record.       */
      fetch rad_cursor into rad_val;
        /*  If the fetch attempt reveals no more    */
        /*  records in the cursor, then exit the loop. */
      exit when rad_cursor%NOTFOUND;
        /*  If the fetch attempt returned a record,  */
        /*  then process the Radius value and insert */
        /*  a record into the AREAS table.           */
        area := pi*power(rad_val.radius,2);
        insert into AREAS values (rad_val.radius, area);
        /*  Signal the end of the loop.              */
      end loop;
```

When the preceding PL/SQL block is executed, every record in the RADIUS_VALS table will be processed by the loop. So far, the RADIUS_VALS table only contains one record—a Radius value of 3. Prior to executing the PL/SQL block for this section, add two new Radius values to the RADIUS_VALS table: 4 and 10.

The following listing shows the addition of the new records to the
RADIUS_VALS table:

```
insert into RADIUS_VALS values (4);
insert into RADIUS_VALS values (10);
commit;

select *
  from RADIUS_VALS
 order by Radius;

    RADIUS
----------
         3
         4
        10
```

Once the new records have been added to the RADIUS_VALS table, execute the
PL/SQL block shown earlier in this section. The output of the PL/SQL block is shown
in the following listing:

```
select *
  from AREAS
 order by Radius;

    RADIUS        AREA
---------- ----------
         3       28.27
         4       50.27
        10      314.16
```

The query of the AREAS table shows that every record in the RADIUS_VALS
table was fetched from the cursor and processed. Once there were no more records
to process in the cursor, the loop was exited and the PL/SQL block completed.

FOR Loops

In simple loops, the loop executes until an **exit** condition is met. In a FOR loop, the
loop executes a specified number of times. An example of a FOR loop is shown in
the following listing. The FOR loop's start is indicated by the keyword **for**, followed
by the criteria used to determine when the processing should exit the loop. Since
the number of times the loop is executed is set when the loop is begun, an **exit**
command isn't needed within the loop.

In the following example, the areas of circles are calculated based on Radius
values ranging from 1 through 7, inclusive.

```
declare
    pi      constant NUMBER(9,7) := 3.1415926;
    radius INTEGER(5);
    area   NUMBER(14,2);
begin
    for radius in 1..7 loop
      area := pi*power(radius,2);
      insert into AREAS values (radius, area);
    end loop;
end;
/
```

The steps involved in processing the loop are shown in the following commented listing:

```
    /*  Specify the criteria for the number of loop      */
    /*  executions.                                       */
  for radius in 1..7 loop
    /*  Calculate the area using the current Radius       */
    /*  value.                                            */
    area := pi*power(radius,2);
    /*  Insert the area and radius values into the AREAS */
    /*  table.                                            */
    insert into AREAS values (radius, area);
    /*  Signal the end of the loop.                       */
  end loop;
```

Note that there is no line that says

```
radius := radius+1;
```

in the FOR loop. Since the specification of the loop specifies

```
for radius in 1..7 loop
```

the Radius values are already specified. For each value, all of the commands within the loop are executed (these commands can include other conditional logic, such as **if** conditions). Once the loop has completed processing a Radius value, the limits on the **for** clause are checked, and either the next Radius value is used or the loop execution is complete.

Sample output from the FOR loop execution is shown in the following listing:

```
select *
  from AREAS
 order by Radius;
```

```
    RADIUS        AREA
---------- ----------
         1        3.14
         2       12.57
         3       28.27
         4       50.27
         5       78.54
         6       113.1
         7      153.94
```

7 rows selected.

Cursor FOR Loops

In FOR loops, the loop executes a specified number of times. In a Cursor FOR loop, the results of a query are used to dynamically determine the number of times the loop is executed. In a Cursor FOR loop, the opening, fetching, and closing of cursors is performed implicitly; you do not need to explicitly command these actions.

The following listing shows a Cursor FOR loop that queries the RADIUS_VALS table and inserts records into the AREAS table:

```
declare
  pi      constant NUMBER(9,7) := 3.1415926;
  area    NUMBER(14,2);
  cursor rad_cursor is
      select * from RADIUS_VALS;
begin
  for rad_val in rad_cursor
    loop
      area := pi*power(rad_val.radius,2);
      insert into AREAS values (rad_val.radius, area);
    end loop;
end;
/
```

In a Cursor FOR loop, there is no **open** or **fetch** command. The command

```
for rad_val in rad_cursor
```

implicitly opens the *rad_cursor* cursor and fetches a value into the *rad_val* variable. When no more records are in the cursor, the loop is exited and the cursor is closed. In a Cursor FOR loop, there is no need for a **close** command. Note that *rad_val* is not explicitly declared in the block.

The loop portion of the PL/SQL block is shown in the following listing, with comments to indicate the flow of control. The loop is controlled by the existence of a fetchable record in the *rad_cursor* cursor. There is no need to check the cursor's %NOTFOUND attribute—that is automated via the Cursor FOR loop.

```
    /*  If a record can be fetched from the cursor,     */
    /*  then fetch it into the rad_val variable.  If    */
    /*  no rows can be fetched, then skip the loop.      */
  for rad_val in rad_cursor
    /*  Begin the loop commands.                         */
    loop
       /*  Calculate the area based on the Radius value */
       /*  and insert a record into the AREAS table.    */
      area := pi*power(rad_val.radius,2);
      insert into AREAS values (rad_val.radius, area);
    /*  Signal the end of the loop commands.            */
    end loop;
```

Sample output is shown in the following listing; for this example, the RADIUS_VALS table has three records, with Radius values of 3, 4, and 10:

```
select *
   from RADIUS_VALS
 order by Radius;

     RADIUS
 ----------
          3
          4
         10
```

The execution of the PL/SQL block with the Cursor FOR loop will generate the following records in the AREAS table:

```
select *
   from AREAS
 order by Radius;

     RADIUS        AREA
 ---------- ----------
          3       28.27
          4       50.27
         10      314.16
```

WHILE Loops

In a WHILE loop, the loop is processed until an exit condition is met. Instead of specifying the exit condition via an **exit** command within the loop, the exit condition is specified in the **while** command that initiates the loop.

In the following listing, a WHILE loop is created so that multiple Radius values will be processed. If the current value of the Radius variable meets the **while** condition in the loop's specification, then the loop's commands are processed. Once a Radius value fails the **while** condition in the loop's specification, the loop's execution is terminated:

```
declare
  pi      constant NUMBER(9,7) := 3.1415926;
  radius INTEGER(5);
  area    NUMBER(14,2);
begin
  radius := 3;
  while radius<=7
    loop
      area := pi*power(radius,2);
      insert into AREAS values (radius, area);
    radius := radius+1;
  end loop;
end;
/
```

The WHILE loop is similar in structure to the simple loop, since it terminates the loop based on a variable's value. The following listing shows the steps involved in the loop, with embedded comments:

```
    /*  Set an initial value for the Radius variable.  */
  radius := 3;
    /*  Establish the criteria for the termination of  */
    /*  the loop.  If the condition is met, execute the  */
    /*  commands within the loop.  If the condition is  */
    /*  not met, then terminate the loop.  */
  while radius<=7
    /*  Begin the commands to be executed.  */
    loop
      /*  Calculate the area based on the current  */
      /*  Radius value and insert a record in the  */
      /*  AREAS table.  */
      area := pi*power(radius,2);
      insert into AREAS values (radius, area);
    /*  Set a new value for the Radius variable.  The  */
    /*  new value of Radius will be evaluated against  */
    /*  the termination criteria and the loop commands  */
    /*  will be executed for the new Radius value or  */
    /*  the loop will terminate.  */
    radius := radius+1;
    /*  Signal the end of the commands within the loop. */
  end loop;
```

When executed, the PL/SQL block in the previous listing will generate records in the AREAS table. The output of the PL/SQL block is shown in the following listing:

```
select *
  from AREAS
 order by Radius;

    RADIUS       AREA
---------- ----------
         3      28.27
         4      50.27
         5      78.54
         6      113.1
         7     153.94
```

Because of the value assigned to the Radius variable prior to the loop, the loop is forced to execute at least once. You should verify that your variable assignments meet the conditions used to limit the loop executions.

Exception Handling Section

When user-defined or system-related exceptions (errors) are encountered, the control of the PL/SQL block shifts to the Exception Handling section. Within the Exception Handling section, the **when** clause is used to evaluate which exception is to be "raised"—that is, executed.

If an exception is raised within the Executable Commands section of your PL/SQL block, the flow of commands immediately leaves the Executable Commands section and searches the Exception Handling section for an exception matching the error encountered. PL/SQL provides a set of system-defined exceptions and allows you to add your own exceptions. Examples of user-defined exceptions are shown in Chapters 26 and 27.

The Exception Handling section always begins with the keyword **exception**, and it precedes the **end** command that terminates the Executable Commands section of the PL/SQL block. The placement of the Exception Handling section within the PL/SQL block is shown in the following listing:

```
declare
   <declarations section>
begin
   <executable commands>
 exception
   <exception handling>
end;
```

The Exception Handling section of a PL/SQL block is optional—none of the PL/SQL blocks shown previously in this chapter included an Exception Handling section. However, the examples shown in this chapter have been based on a very small set of known input values with very limited processing performed.

In the following listing, the simple loop for calculating the area of a circle is shown, with two modifications (shown in bold). A new variable named *some_variable* is declared in the Declarations section, and a calculation to determine the variable's value is created in the Executable Commands section.

```
declare
    pi       constant NUMBER(9,7) := 3.1415926;
    radius INTEGER(5);
    area    NUMBER(14,2);
    some_variable    NUMBER(14,2);
begin
   radius := 3;
   loop
     some_variable := 1/(radius-4);
     area := pi*power(radius,2);
       insert into AREAS values (radius, area);
     radius := radius+1;
     exit when area >100;
   end loop;
end;
/
```

Because the calculation for *some_variable* involves division, you may encounter a situation in which the calculation attempts to divide by zero—an error condition. The first time through the loop, the Radius variable (with an initial value of 3) is processed and a record is inserted into the AREAS table. The second time through the loop, the Radius variable has a value of 4—and the calculation for *some_variable* encounters an error:

```
declare
*
ERROR at line 1:
ORA-01476: divisor is equal to zero
ORA-06512: at line 9
```

Since an error was encountered, the first row inserted into AREAS is rolled back, and the PL/SQL block terminates.

You can modify the processing of the error condition by adding an Exception Handling section to the PL/SQL block, as shown in the following listing.

```
declare
    pi      constant NUMBER(9,7) := 3.1415926;
    radius INTEGER(5);
    area    NUMBER(14,2);
    some_variable    NUMBER(14,2);
begin
  radius := 3;
  loop
    some_variable := 1/(radius-4);
    area := pi*power(radius,2);
      insert into AREAS values (radius, area);
    radius := radius+1;
    exit when area >100;
  end loop;
exception
  when ZERO_DIVIDE
    then insert into AREAS values (0,0);
end;
/
```

The Exception Handling section of the PL/SQL block is repeated in the following listing:

```
exception
  when ZERO_DIVIDE
    then insert into AREAS values (0,0);
```

When the PL/SQL block encounters an error, it scans the Exception Handling section for the defined exceptions. In this case, it finds the ZERO_DIVIDE exception, which is one of the system-defined exceptions available in PL/SQL. In addition to the system-defined exceptions and user-defined exceptions, you can use the **when others** clause to address all exceptions not defined within your Exception Handling section. The command within the Exception Handling section for the matching exception is executed and a row is inserted into the AREAS table. The output of the PL/SQL block is shown in the following listing:

```
select *
  from AREAS;

    RADIUS        AREA
---------- ----------
         3       28.27
         0           0
```

The output shows that the first *radius* value (3) was processed, and the exception was encountered on the second pass through the loop.

NOTE
*Once an exception is encountered, you cannot return to your normal flow of command processing within the Executable Commands section. If you need to maintain control within the Executable Commands section, you should use **if** conditions to test for possible exceptions before they are encountered by the program.*

The available system-defined exceptions are listed in the "Exceptions" entry in the Alphabetical Reference. Examples of user-defined exceptions are shown in Chapters 26 and 27.

CHAPTER
26

Triggers

trigger defines an action the database should take when some database-related event occurs. Triggers may be used to supplement declarative referential integrity, to enforce complex business rules, or to audit changes to data. The code within a trigger, called the *trigger body,* is made up of PL/SQL blocks (refer to Chapter 25).

The execution of triggers is transparent to the user. Triggers are executed by the database when specific types of data manipulation commands are performed on specific tables. Such commands may include **insert**s, **update**s, and **delete**s. Updates of specific columns may also be used as triggering events. As of Oracle8i, triggering events may also include DDL commands and database events (such as shutdowns and logins).

Because of their flexibility, triggers may supplement referential integrity; they should not be used to replace it. When enforcing the business rules in an application, you should first rely on the declarative referential integrity available with Oracle; use triggers to enforce rules that cannot be coded through referential integrity.

Required System Privileges

To *create* a trigger on a table, you must be able to alter that table. Therefore, you must either own the table, have the ALTER privilege for the table, or have the ALTER ANY TABLE system privilege. In addition, you must have the CREATE TRIGGER system privilege; to create triggers in another user's account (also called a *schema*), you must have the CREATE ANY TRIGGER system privilege. The CREATE TRIGGER system privilege is part of the RESOURCE role provided with Oracle.

To *alter* a trigger, you must either own the trigger or have the ALTER ANY TRIGGER system privilege. You may also alter triggers by altering the tables they are based on, which requires that you have either the ALTER privilege for that table or the ALTER ANY TABLE system privilege. For information on altering triggers, see "Enabling and Disabling Triggers," later in this chapter.

To create a trigger on a database-level event, you must have the ADMINISTER DATABASE TRIGGER system privilege.

Required Table Privileges

Triggers may reference tables other than the one that initiated the triggering event. For example, if you use triggers to audit changes to data in the LEDGER table, then you may insert a record into a different table (say, LEDGER_AUDIT) every time a record is changed in LEDGER. To do this, you need to have privileges to insert into LEDGER_AUDIT (to perform the triggered transaction).

NOTE
The privileges needed for triggered transactions cannot come from roles; they must be granted directly to the creator of the trigger.

Types of Triggers

A trigger's type is defined by the type of triggering transaction and by the level at which the trigger is executed. In the following sections, you will see descriptions of these classifications, along with relevant restrictions.

Row-Level Triggers

Row-level triggers execute once for each row in a transaction. For the LEDGER table auditing example described earlier, each row that is changed in the LEDGER table may be processed by the trigger. Row-level triggers are the most common type of trigger; they are often used in data auditing applications. Row-level triggers are also useful for keeping distributed data in sync. Snapshots, which use row-level triggers for this purpose, are described in Chapter 23.

Row-level triggers are created using the **for each row** clause in the **create trigger** command. The syntax for triggers is shown in "Trigger Syntax," later in this chapter.

Statement-Level Triggers

Statement-level triggers execute once for each transaction. For example, if a single transaction inserted 500 rows into the LEDGER table, then a statement-level trigger on that table would only be executed once. Statement-level triggers therefore are not often used for data-related activities; they are normally used to enforce additional security measures on the types of transactions that may be performed on a table.

Statement-level triggers are the default type of trigger created via the **create trigger** command. The syntax for triggers is shown in "Trigger Syntax," later in this chapter.

BEFORE and AFTER Triggers

Because triggers are executed by events, they may be set to occur immediately before or after those events. Since the events that execute triggers include database transactions, triggers can be executed immediately before or after **insert**s, **update**s, and **delete**s. For database-level events, additional restrictions apply; you cannot trigger an event to occur before a logon or startup takes place.

Within the trigger, you can reference the old and new values involved in the transaction. The access required for the old and new data may determine which type of trigger you need. "Old" refers to the data as it existed prior to the transaction; **update**s and **delete**s usually reference old values. "New" values are the data values that the transaction creates (such as the columns in an inserted record).

If you need to set a column value in an inserted row via your trigger, then you need to use a BEFORE INSERT trigger to access the "new" values. Using an AFTER INSERT trigger would not allow you to set the inserted value, since the row will already have been inserted into the table.

AFTER row-level triggers are frequently used in auditing applications, since they do not fire until the row has been modified. The row's successful modification implies that it has passed the referential integrity constraints defined for that table.

INSTEAD OF Triggers

You can use INSTEAD OF triggers to tell Oracle what to do *instead of* performing the actions that invoked the trigger. For example, you could use an INSTEAD OF trigger on a view to redirect **insert**s into a table or to **update** multiple tables that are part of a view. You can use INSTEAD OF triggers on either object views (see Chapter 28) or relational views.

For example, if a view involves a join of two tables, your ability to use the **update** command on records in the view is limited. However, if you use an INSTEAD OF trigger, you can tell Oracle how to **update**, **delete**, or **insert** records in the view's underlying tables when a user attempts to change values via the view. The code in the INSTEAD OF trigger is executed *in place of* the **insert**, **update**, or **delete** command you enter.

In this chapter, you will see how to implement basic triggers. INSTEAD OF triggers, which were initially introduced to support object views, are described in Chapter 28.

Schema Triggers

As of Oracle8i, you can create triggers on schema operations. The allowable triggering events include **create table**, **alter table**, and **drop table**. You can even create triggers to prevent users from dropping their own tables! For the most part, schema-level triggers provide two capabilities: preventing DDL operations and providing additional security monitoring when DDL operations occur.

Database-Level Triggers

You can create triggers to be fired on database events, including errors, logons, logoffs, shutdowns, and startups. You can use this type of trigger to automate database maintenance or auditing actions.

Trigger Syntax

The full syntax for the **create trigger** command is shown in the Alphabetical Reference section of this book. The following listing contains an abbreviated version of the command syntax:

```
create [or replace] trigger [user.]trigger
    {before | after | instead of}
    { DML event [on table]
    | DDL event on [SCHEMA | DATABASE]
    | database event on [SCHEMA | DATABASE]}
    for each {row | statement} [when (condition)] ] pl/sql_block
```

The syntax options available depend on the type of trigger in use. For example, a trigger on a DML event will follow this syntax:

```
create [or replace] trigger [user.]trigger
    {before | after | instead of}
    { delete
    | insert
    | update [of column [, column] ...] }
        [or { delete
            | insert
            | update [of column [, column] ... ] } ] ...
    on [user.]{TABLE | VIEW}
    [ [referencing { old [as] old
                  | new [as] new} ...]
    for each {row | statement} [when (condition)] ] pl/sql_block
```

Clearly, there is a great deal of flexibility in the design of a trigger. The **before** and **after** keywords indicate whether the trigger should be executed before or after the triggering transaction. If the **instead of** clause is used, the trigger's code will be executed instead of the event that caused the trigger to be invoked. The **delete**, **insert**, and **update** keywords (the last of which may include a column list) indicate the type of data manipulation that will constitute a triggering event. When referring to the old and new values of columns, you can use the defaults ("old" and "new") or you can use the **referencing** clause to specify other names.

When the **for each row** clause is used, the trigger will be a row-level trigger; otherwise, it will be a statement-level trigger. The **when** clause is used to further restrict when the trigger is executed. The restrictions enforced in the **when** clause may include checks of old and new data values.

For example, suppose we want to monitor any adjustments to an Amount column value that are greater than 10 percent. The following row-level BEFORE UPDATE trigger will be executed only if the new value of the Amount column is more than 10 percent greater than its old value. This example also illustrates the use of the **new** keyword, which refers to the new value of the column, and the **old** keyword, which refers to the old value of the column.

```
create trigger ledger_bef_upd_row
before update on LEDGER
for each row
when (new.Amount/old.Amount>1.1)
begin
insert into LEDGER_AUDIT
 values (:old.ActionDate, :old.Action, :old.Item,
 :old.Quantity, :old.QuantityType, :old.Rate,
 :old.Amount, :old.Person);
end;
```

Breaking this **create trigger** command into its components makes it easier to understand. First, the trigger is named:

```
create trigger ledger_bef_upd_row
```

The name of the trigger contains the name of the table it acts upon and the type of trigger it is. (See "Naming Triggers," later in this chapter, for information on naming conventions.)

This trigger applies to the LEDGER table; it will be executed **before update** transactions have been committed to the database:

```
before update on LEDGER
```

Because the **for each row** clause is used, the trigger will apply to each row in the transaction. If this clause is not used, then the trigger will execute at the statement level.

```
for each row
```

The **when** clause adds further criteria to the triggering condition. The triggering event not only must be an **update** of the LEDGER table, but also must reflect an increase of over 10 percent in the value of the Amount column.

```
when (new.Amount/old.Amount>1.1)
```

The PL/SQL code shown in the following listing is the trigger body. The commands shown here are to be executed for every **update** of the LEDGER table that passes the **when** condition. For this to succeed, the LEDGER_AUDIT table must exist, and the owner of the trigger must have been granted privileges (directly, not via roles) on that table. This example **insert**s the old values from the LEDGER record into the LEDGER_AUDIT table before the LEDGER record is updated.

```
begin
insert into LEDGER_AUDIT
 values (:old.Action_Date, :old.Action, :old.Item,
 :old.Quantity, :old.QuantityType, :old.Rate,
 :old.Amount, :old.Person);
end;
```

NOTE
*When referencing the **new** and **old** keywords in the PL/SQL block, they are preceded by colons (:).*

This example is typical of auditing triggers. The auditing activity is completely transparent to the user who performs the **update** of the LEDGER table.

Combining DML Trigger Types

Triggers for multiple **insert**, **update**, and **delete** commands on a table can be combined into a single trigger, provided they are all at the same level (row level or statement level). The following example shows a trigger that is executed whenever an **insert** or an **update** occurs. Two points (shown in bold) should stand out in this example: the **update** portion of the trigger occurs only when the Amount column is updated, and an **if** clause is used within the PL/SQL block to determine which of the two commands invoked the trigger.

```
create trigger ledger_bef_upd_ins_row
before insert or update of Amount on LEDGER
for each row
begin
 IF INSERTING THEN
  insert into LEDGER_AUDIT
   values (:new.Action_Date, :new.Action, :new.Item,
   :new.Quantity, :new.QuantityType, :new.Rate,
   :new.Amount, :new.Person);
 ELSE  -- if not inserting, then we are updating Amount
  insert into LEDGER_AUDIT
   values (:old.Action_Date, :old.Action, :old.Item,
   :old.Quantity, :old.QuantityType, :old.Rate,
   :old.Amount, :old.Person);
 end if;
end;
```

Again, look at the trigger's component parts. First, it is named and identified as a **before insert** and **before update** (of Amount) trigger, executing **for each row**:

```
create trigger ledger_bef_upd_ins_row
before insert or update of Amount on LEDGER
for each row
```

The trigger body then follows. In the first part of the trigger body, shown in the following listing, the type of transaction is checked via an **if** clause. Valid transaction types are INSERTING, DELETING, and UPDATING. In this case, the trigger checks to see if the record is being inserted into the LEDGER table. If it is, then the first part of the trigger body is executed. The INSERTING portion of the trigger body inserts the new values of the record into the LEDGER_AUDIT table.

```
begin
   IF INSERTING THEN
     insert into LEDGER_AUDIT
       values (:new.Action_Date, :new.Action, :new.Item,
       :new.Quantity, :new.QuantityType, :new.Rate,
       :new.Amount, :new.Person);
```

Other transaction types can then be checked. In this example, because the trigger executed, the transaction must be either an **insert** or an **update** of the Amount column. Since the **if** clause in the first half of the trigger body checks for **insert**s, and the trigger is only executed for **insert**s and **update**s, the only conditions that should execute the second half of the trigger body are **update**s of Amount. Therefore, no additional **if** clauses are necessary to determine the transaction type. This portion of the trigger body is the same as in the previous example: prior to being updated, the old values in the row are written to the LEDGER_AUDIT table.

```
ELSE   -- if not inserting, then we are updating Amount
   insert into LEDGER_AUDIT
     values (:old.Action_Date, :old.Action, :old.Item,
     :old.Quantity, :old.QuantityType, :old.Rate,
     :old.Amount, :old.Person);
end;
```

Combining trigger types in this manner may help you to coordinate trigger development among multiple developers, since it consolidates all the database events that depend on a single table.

Setting Inserted Values

You may use triggers to set column values during **insert**s and **update**s. For example, you may have partially denormalized your LEDGER table to include derived data, such as **UPPER**(Person). Storing this data in an uppercase format (for this example, in the column UpperPerson) allows you to display data to the users in its natural format while using the uppercase column during queries.

Since UpperPerson is derived data, it may be out of sync with the Person column. That is, there may be times immediately after transactions during which UpperPerson does not equal **UPPER**(Person). Consider an insert into the LEDGER table; unless your application supplies a value for UpperPerson during **insert**s, that column's value will be **NULL**.

To avoid this synchronization problem, you can use a database trigger. Put a BEFORE INSERT and a BEFORE UPDATE trigger on the table. They will act at the row level. As shown in the following listing, they will set a new value for UpperPerson every time Person is changed:

```
create trigger ledger_bef_upd_ins_row
before insert or update of Person on LEDGER
for each row
begin
  :new.UpperPerson := UPPER(:new.Person);
end;
```

In this example, the trigger body determines the value for UpperPerson by using the **UPPER** function on the Person column. This trigger will be executed every time a row is inserted into LEDGER and every time the Person column is updated. The Person and UpperPerson columns will thus be kept in sync.

Maintaining Duplicated Data

The method of setting values via triggers, shown in the previous section, can be combined with the remote data access methods described in Chapter 22. As with snapshots, you may replicate all or part of the rows in a table.

For example, you may wish to create and maintain a second copy of your application's audit log. By doing so, you safeguard against a single application wiping out the audit log records created by multiple applications. Duplicate audit logs are frequently used in security monitoring.

Consider the LEDGER_AUDIT table used in the examples in this chapter. A second table, LEDGER_AUDIT_DUP, could be created, possibly in a remote database. For this example, assume that a database link called AUDIT_LINK can be used to connect the user to the database in which LEDGER_AUDIT_DUP resides (refer to Chapter 21 for details on database links).

To automate populating the LEDGER_AUDIT_DUP table, the following trigger could be placed on the LEDGER_AUDIT table:

```
create trigger ledger_after_ins_row
before insert on LEDGER_AUDIT
for each row
begin
 insert into LEDGER_AUDIT_DUP@AUDIT_LINK
    values (:new.Action_Date, :new.Action, :new.Item,
    :new.Quantity, :new.QuantityType, :new.Rate,
    :new.Amount, :new.Person);
end;
```

As the trigger header shows, this trigger executes for each row that is inserted into the LEDGER_AUDIT table. It inserts a single record into the LEDGER_AUDIT_DUP table in the database defined by the AUDIT_LINK database link. AUDIT_LINK may point to a database located on a remote server, although you'd be better off using a snapshot in that case (refer to Chapter 23).

Customizing Error Conditions

Within a single trigger, you may establish different error conditions. For each of the error conditions you define, you may select an error message that appears when the error occurs. The error numbers and messages that are displayed to the user are set via the RAISE_APPLICATION_ERROR procedure, which may be called from within any trigger.

The following example shows a statement-level BEFORE DELETE trigger on the LEDGER table. When a user attempts to **delete** a record from the LEDGER table, this trigger is executed and checks two system conditions: that the day of the week is neither Saturday nor Sunday, and that the Oracle username of the account performing the **delete** begins with the letters "FIN." The trigger's components will be described following the listing.

```
create trigger ledger_bef_del
before delete on LEDGER
declare
  weekend_error EXCEPTION;
  not_finance_user EXCEPTION;
begin
  IF TO_CHAR(SysDate,'DY') = 'SAT' or
     TO_CHAR(SysDate,'DY') = 'SUN' THEN
   RAISE weekend_error;
  END IF;
  IF SUBSTR(User,1,3) <> 'FIN' THEN
```

```
     RAISE not_finance_user;
EXCEPTION
  WHEN weekend_error THEN
     RAISE_APPLICATION_ERROR (-20001,
       'Deletions not allowed on weekends');
  WHEN not_finance_user THEN
     RAISE_APPLICATION_ERROR (-20002,
       'Deletions only allowed by Finance users');
end;
```

The header of the trigger defines it as a statement-level BEFORE DELETE trigger:

```
create trigger ledger_bef_del
before delete on LEDGER
```

There are no **when** clauses in this trigger, so the trigger body is executed for all **delete**s.

The next portion of the trigger declares the names of the two exceptions that are defined within this trigger:

```
declare
   weekend_error EXCEPTION;
   not_finance_user EXCEPTION;
```

The first part of the trigger body contains an **if** clause that uses the **TO_CHAR** function on the SysDate pseudo-column. If the current day is either Saturday or Sunday, then the WEEKEND_ERROR error condition is executed. This error condition, called an *exception,* must be defined within the trigger body.

```
begin
   IF TO_CHAR(SysDate,'DY') = 'SAT' or
      TO_CHAR(SysDate,'DY') = 'SUN' THEN
    RAISE weekend_error;
   END IF;
```

A second **if** clause checks the User pseudo-column to see if its first three letters are "FIN." If the username does not begin with "FIN," then the NOT_FINANCE_USER exception is executed. In this example, the operator <> is used; this is equivalent to != (meaning "not equals").

```
IF SUBSTR(User,1,3) <> 'FIN' THEN
     RAISE not_finance_user;
```

The final portion of the trigger body tells the trigger how to handle the exceptions. It begins with the keyword EXCEPTION, followed by a **when** clause for each of the exceptions. Each of the exceptions in this trigger calls the RAISE_APPLICATION_ERROR procedure, which takes two input parameters: the error number (which must be between -20001 and -20999), and the error message to be displayed. In this example, two different error messages are defined, one for each of the defined exceptions:

```
EXCEPTION
   WHEN weekend_error THEN
     RAISE_APPLICATION_ERROR (-20001,
      'Deletions not allowed on weekends');
   WHEN not_finance_user THEN
     RAISE_APPLICATION_ERROR (-20002,
      'Deletions only allowed by Finance users');
end;
```

The use of the RAISE_APPLICATION_ERROR procedure gives you great flexibility in managing the error conditions that may be encountered within your trigger. For a further description of procedures, see Chapter 27.

Calling Procedures Within Triggers

Rather than creating a large block of code within a trigger body, you can save the code as a stored procedure and call the procedure from within the trigger, by using the **call** command, as shown in the following listing:

```
create trigger ledger_after_ins_row
before insert on LEDGER_AUDIT
for each row
begin
 call INSERT_LEDGER_DUP(:new.Action_Date, :new.Action, :new.Item,
    :new.Quantity, :new.QuantityType, :new.Rate,
    :new.Amount, :new.Person);
end;
```

Naming Triggers

The name of a trigger should clearly indicate the table it applies to, the DML commands that trigger it, its before/after status, and whether it is a row-level or statement-level trigger. Since a trigger name cannot exceed 30 characters in length, you need to use a standard set of abbreviations when naming. In general, the trigger name should include as much of the table name as possible. Thus, when creating a BEFORE UPDATE, row-level trigger on a table named BALANCE_SHEET, you should not name the trigger BEFORE_UPDATE_ROW_LEVEL_BAL_SH. A better name would be BALANCE_SHEET_BU_ROW.

Creating DDL Event Triggers

As of Oracle8i, you can create triggers that are executed when a DDL event occurs. If you are planning to use this feature solely for security purposes, you should investigate using the **audit** command instead. You can use a DDL event trigger to execute the trigger code for **create**, **alter**, and **drop** commands performed on a cluster, function, index, package, procedure, role, sequence, synonym, table, tablespace, trigger, type, user, or view. If you use the **on schema** clause, the trigger will execute for any new data dictionary objects created in your schema. The following example will execute a procedure named INSERT_AUDIT_RECORD whenever objects are created within your schema:

```
create trigger CREATE_DB_OBJECT_AUDIT
after create on schema
begin
  call INSERT_AUDIT_RECORD (sys.dictionary_obj_name);
end;
/
```

As shown in this example, you can reference system attributes such as the object name. The available attributes are listed in Table 26-1.

Attribute	Description
Sysevent	Name of the event firing the trigger, such as create table
Instance_Num	Number of the instance
Database_Name	Name of the database
Server_Error	The error number on the error stack at the specified position (1 for top of stack)
Is_Servererror	Boolean; TRUE if the error is on the error stack
Login_User	Name of the user
Dictionary_Obj_Type	Type of object
Dictionary_Obj_Name	Name of the object
Dictionary_Obj_Owner	Owner of the object
Des_Encrypted_Password	Encrypted password of the user being created or altered

TABLE 26-1.   *System Event Attributes*

To protect the objects within a schema, you may wish to create a trigger that is executed for each attempted **drop table** command. That trigger will have to be a BEFORE DROP trigger:

```
create or replace trigger PREVENT_DROP
   before drop on Talbot.schema
begin
   if Dictionary_Obj_Owner = 'TALBOT'
      and Dictionary_Obj_Name like 'LED%'
      and Dictionary_Obj_Type = 'TABLE'
   then
      RAISE_APPLICATION_ERROR (
         -20002, 'Operation not permitted.');
   end if;
end;
/
```

Note that the trigger references the event attributes within its **if** clauses. Attempting to drop a table in the Talbot schema whose name starts with LED results in the following:

```
drop table ledger;
*
ERROR at line 1:
ORA-00604: error occurred at recursive SQL level 1
ORA-20002: Operation not permitted.
ORA-06512: at line 6
```

You can use the RAISE_APPLICATION_ERROR procedure to further customize the error message displayed to the user.

Creating Database Event Triggers

Like DML events, database events can execute triggers. When a database event occurs (a shutdown, startup, or error), you can execute a trigger that references the attributes of the event (as with DDL events). You could use a database event to perform system maintenance functions immediately after each database startup.

For example, the following trigger pins packages on each database startup. Pinning packages is an effective way of keeping large PL/SQL objects in the shared pool of memory, improving performance and enhancing database stability. This trigger, PIN_ON_STARTUP, will run each time the database is started.

```
create or replace trigger PIN_ON_STARTUP
after startup on database
begin
```

```
    DBMS_SHARED_POOL.KEEP (
        'SYS.STANDARD', 'P');
end;
/
```

This example shows a simple trigger that will be executed immediately after a database startup. You can modify the list of packages in the trigger body to include those most used by your applications.

Startup and shutdown triggers can access the Instance_Num, Database_Name, Login_User, and Sysevent attributes listed in Table 26-1. See the Alphabetical Reference for the full **create trigger** command syntax.

Enabling and Disabling Triggers

Unlike declarative integrity constraints (such as NOT NULL and PRIMARY KEY), triggers do not affect all rows in a table. They only affect transactions of the specified type, and then only while the trigger is enabled. Any data created prior to a trigger's creation will not be affected by the trigger.

By default, a trigger is enabled when it is created. However, there are situations in which you may wish to disable a trigger. The two most common reasons involve data loads. During large data loads, you may wish to disable triggers that would execute during the load. Disabling the triggers during data loads may dramatically improve the performance of the load. After the data has been loaded, you need to manually perform the data manipulation that the trigger would have performed had it been enabled during the data load.

The second data load–related reason for disabling a trigger occurs when a data load fails and has to be performed a second time. In such a case, it is likely that the data load partially succeeded—and thus the trigger was executed for a portion of the records loaded. During a subsequent load, the same records would be inserted. Thus, it is possible that the same trigger will be executed twice for the same transaction (when that transaction occurs during both loads). Depending on the nature of the transactions and the triggers, this may not be desirable. If the trigger was enabled during the failed load, then it may need to be disabled prior to the start of a second data load process. After the data has been loaded, you need to manually perform the data manipulation that the trigger would have performed had it been enabled during the data load.

To enable a trigger, use the **alter trigger** command with the **enable** keyword. To use this command, you must either own the table or have the ALTER ANY TRIGGER system privilege. A sample **alter trigger** command is shown in the following listing:

```
alter trigger ledger_bef_upd_row enable;
```

A second method of enabling triggers uses the **alter table** command, with the **enable all triggers** clause. You may not enable specific triggers with this command; you must use the **alter trigger** command to do that. The following example shows the usage of the **alter table** command:

```
alter table LEDGER enable all triggers;
```

To use the **alter table** command, you must either own the table or have the ALTER ANY TABLE system privilege.

You can disable triggers using the same basic commands (requiring the same privileges) with modifications to their clauses. For the **alter trigger** command, use the **disable** clause:

```
alter trigger ledger_bef_upd_row disable;
```

For the **alter table** command, use the **disable all triggers** clause:

```
alter table LEDGER disable all triggers;
```

You can manually compile triggers. Use the **alter trigger compile** command to manually compile existing triggers that have become invalid. Since triggers have dependencies, they can become invalid if an object the trigger depends on changes. The **alter trigger debug** command allows PL/SQL information to be generated during trigger recompilation.

Replacing Triggers

The status of a trigger is the only portion that can be altered. To alter a trigger's body, the trigger must be re-created or replaced. When replacing a trigger, use the **create or replace trigger** command (refer to "Trigger Syntax," earlier in the chapter).

Dropping Triggers

Triggers may be dropped via the **drop trigger** command. To drop a trigger, you must either own the trigger or have the DROP ANY TRIGGER system privilege. An example of this command is shown in the following listing:

```
drop trigger ledger_bef_upd_row;
```

CHAPTER
27

Procedures, Functions,
and Packages

ophisticated business rules and application logic can be stored as *procedures* within Oracle. Stored procedures—groups of SQL, PL/SQL, and Java statements—enable you to move code that enforces business rules from your application to the database. As a result, the code will be stored once for use by multiple applications. Because Oracle supports stored procedures, the code within your applications should become more consistent and easier to maintain.

NOTE
For details on Java and its use in stored procedures, see Chapters 32, 33, and 34. This chapter will focus on PL/SQL procedures.

You may group procedures and other PL/SQL commands into *packages*. In the following sections, you will see implementation details and recommendations for packages, procedures, and *functions* (procedures that can return values to the user). You may experience performance gains when using procedures, for two reasons:

- The processing of complex business rules may be performed within the database—and therefore by the server. In client-server or three-tier applications, shifting complex processing from the application (on the client) to the database (on the server) may dramatically improve performance.

- Because the procedural code is stored within the database and is fairly static, you may also benefit from the reuse of the same queries within the database. The Shared SQL Area in the System Global Area (SGA) will store the parsed versions of the executed commands. Thus, the second time a procedure is executed, it may be able to take advantage of the parsing that was previously performed, improving the performance of the procedure's execution.

In addition to these advantages, your application development efforts may also benefit. Business rules that are consolidated within the database no longer need to be written into each application, thus saving you time during application creation and simplifying the maintenance process.

Required System Privileges

To create a procedural object, you must have the CREATE PROCEDURE system privilege (which is part of the RESOURCE role). If the procedural object will be in another user's schema, then you must have the CREATE ANY PROCEDURE system privilege.

Executing Procedures

Once a procedural object has been created, it may be executed. When a procedural object is executed, it may rely on the table privileges of its owner, but may *not* rely on the privileges of the user who is executing it. In that case, a user executing a procedure does not need to be granted access to the tables that the procedure accesses.

In prior versions of Oracle, the only option was for the procedural objects to be executed under the privileges of the procedure owner (called *definer rights*). As of Oracle8i, you can use *invoker rights,* in which case the procedures execute under the privileges of the user executing the privilege. If a procedure uses invoker rights, the user must have access to all of the database objects accessed by the procedure. Unless stated otherwise, the examples in this chapter assume users are executing procedures under the owner's privileges.

To allow other users to execute your procedural object, **grant** them the EXECUTE privilege on that object, as shown in the following example:

```
grant execute on MY_PROCEDURE to Dora;
```

The user Dora will now be able to execute the procedure named MY_PROCEDURE—even if she does not have privileges on any of the tables that MY_PROCEDURE uses. If you do not **grant** the EXECUTE privilege to users, then they must have the EXECUTE ANY PROCEDURE system privilege in order to execute the procedure.

When executed, procedures usually have variables passed to them. For example, a procedure that interacts with the LEDGER table may accept a value for the Person column as its input. In this example, we will assume that the procedure creates a new record in the WORKER table when a new employee is first paid (causing a LEDGER entry). This procedure can be called from any application within the database (provided the user calling the procedure has been granted the EXECUTE privilege for it).

The syntax used to execute a procedure depends on the environment from which the procedure is called. From within SQLPLUS, a procedure can be executed by using the **execute** command, followed by the procedure name. Any arguments to be passed to the procedure must be enclosed in parentheses following the procedure name, as shown in the following example (which uses a procedure called NEW_WORKER):

```
execute NEW_WORKER('ADAH TALBOT');
```

The command will execute the NEW_WORKER procedure, passing to it the value ADAH TALBOT.

From within another procedure, function, package, or trigger, the procedure can be called without the **execute** command. If the NEW_WORKER procedure was called from a trigger on the LEDGER table, the body of that trigger may include the following command:

```
NEW_WORKER(:new.Person);
```

The NEW_WORKER procedure will be executed using the new value of the Person column as its input. (See Chapter 26 for further information on the use of old and new values within triggers.)

To execute a procedure owned by another user, you must either create a synonym for that procedure or reference the owner's name during the execution, as shown in the following listing:

```
execute Dora.NEW_WORKER('ADAH TALBOT');
```

The command will execute the NEW_WORKER procedure owned by Dora.

Alternatively, a synonym for the procedure could be created by using the following command:

```
create synonym NEW_WORKER for Dora.NEW_WORKER;
```

The owner of that synonym would then no longer need to refer to the procedure's owner to execute the procedure. You could simply enter the command:

```
execute NEW_WORKER('ADAH TALBOT');
```

and the synonym would point to the proper procedure.

When executing remote procedures, the name of a database link must be specified (see Chapter 22 for information on database links). The name of the database link must immediately follow the procedure's name and precede the variables, as shown in the following example:

```
execute NEW_WORKER@REMOTE_CONNECT('ADAH TALBOT');
```

The command uses the REMOTE_CONNECT database link to access a procedure called NEW_WORKER in a remote database.

To make the location of the procedure transparent to the user, a synonym may be created for the remote procedure, as shown in the following example:

```
create synonym NEW_WORKER
    for NEW_WORKER@REMOTE_CONNECT;
```

Once this synonym has been created, the user may refer to the remote procedure by using the name of the synonym. Oracle assumes that all remote procedure calls involve updates in the remote database.

Required Table Privileges

Procedural objects may reference tables. For the objects to execute properly, the owner of the procedure, package, or function being executed must have privileges on the tables it uses. Unless you are using invoker rights, the user who is executing the procedural object does not need privileges on its underlying tables.

NOTE
The privileges needed for procedures, packages, and functions cannot come from roles; they must be granted directly to the owner of the procedure, package, or function.

Procedures vs. Functions

Unlike procedures, functions can return a value to the caller (procedures cannot return values). This value is returned through the use of the **return** keyword within the function. Examples of functions are shown in "create function Syntax," later in this chapter.

Procedures vs. Packages

Packages are groups of procedures, functions, variables, and SQL statements grouped together into a single unit. To execute a procedure within a package, you must first list the package name, and then list the procedure name, as shown in the following example:

```
execute LEDGER_PACKAGE.NEW_WORKER('ADAH TALBOT');
```

Here, the NEW_WORKER procedure within the LEDGER_PACKAGE package was executed.

Packages allow multiple procedures to use the same variables and cursors. Procedures within packages may be either available to the public (as is the NEW_WORKER procedure in the prior example) or private, in which case they are only accessible via commands from within the package (such as calls from other procedures). Examples of packages are shown in "create package Syntax," later in this chapter.

Packages may also include commands that are to be executed each time the package is called, regardless of the procedure or function called within the package. Thus, packages not only group procedures but also give you the ability to execute commands that are not procedure-specific. See "Initializing Packages," later in this chapter, for an example of code that is executed each time a package is called.

create procedure Syntax

The syntax for the **create procedure** command is shown in the Alphabetical Reference. At a high level, the syntax is

```
create [or replace] procedure [user.] procedure
[(argument [IN|OUT|IN OUT] datatype
[,argument [IN|OUT|IN OUT] datatype]...)]
[AUTHID  {DEFINER | CURRENT_USER}  ]
{IS|AS} {PL/SQL block |
           LANGUAGE {C_declaration | JAVA Java_declaration} }  ;
```

Both the header and the body of the procedure are created by this command.

The NEW_WORKER procedure is created by the command shown in the following listing:

```
create procedure NEW_WORKER (Person_Name IN varchar2)
AS
  BEGIN
    insert into WORKER
      (Name, Age, Lodging)
    values
      (Person_Name, null, null);
  END;
/
```

Here, the NEW_WORKER procedure will accept a person's name as its input. It can be called from any application. It inserts a record into the WORKER table, with **NULL** values for the Age and Lodging columns.

If a procedure already exists, you may replace it via the **create or replace procedure** command. The benefit of using this command (instead of dropping and re-creating the old procedure) is that the EXECUTE privilege grants previously made on the procedure will remain in place.

The IN qualifier is used for arguments for which values must be specified when calling the procedure. In the NEW_WORKER examples earlier in this chapter, the Person argument would be declared as IN. The OUT qualifier signifies that the procedure passes a value back to the caller through this argument. The IN OUT qualifier signifies that the argument is both an IN and an OUT: a value must be specified for this argument when the procedure is called, and the procedure will return a value to the caller via this argument. If no qualifier type is specified, then the default value is IN.

AUTHID refers to the type of authentication: definer rights (the default) or invoker rights (the CURRENT_USER).

By default, a procedure consists of a block of code written in PL/SQL (*block* refers to the code that the procedure will execute when called). In the NEW_WORKER example, the block is as follows:

```
BEGIN
    insert into WORKER
      (Name, Age, Lodging)
    values
      (Person_Name, null, null);
END;
```

The PL/SQL block shown is fairly simple, consisting of a single SQL statement. PL/SQL blocks within procedures can include any DML statement; they cannot be used for DDL statements (such as **create view**).

Alternatively, LANGUAGE refers to the language in which the code is written. For Java examples, see Chapter 34.

create function Syntax

The syntax for the **create function** command is very similar to the syntax for the **create procedure** command:

```
create [or replace] function [user.] function
[(argument [IN|OUT|IN OUT] datatype
[,argument [IN|OUT|IN OUT] datatype]...)]
RETURN datatype
[AUTHID  {DEFINER | CURRENT_USER}]
{ {IS|AS} {PL/SQL block |
          LANGUAGE [C specification | JAVA specification] } };
```

Both the header and the body of the function are created by this command.

The **return** keyword specifies the datatype of the function's return value. This can be any valid PL/SQL datatype. Every function must have a **return** clause, since the function must, by definition, return a value to the calling environment.

The following example shows a function named BALANCE_CHECK, which returns the status of the BOUGHT and SOLD transactions for a Person in the

LEDGER table. The input is the Person's name, while the output is the balance for that Person.

```
create function BALANCE_CHECK (Person_Name IN varchar2)
   RETURN NUMBER
   IS
     balance NUMBER(10,2);
   BEGIN
       select SUM(DECODE(Action,'BOUGHT',Amount,0))
         - SUM(DECODE(Action,'SOLD',Amount,0))
         INTO balance
         from LEDGER
       where Person = Person_Name;
    RETURN(balance);
    END;
   /
```

To show the differences between procedures and functions, we'll look at this function piece by piece. First, the function is named and the input is specified:

```
create function BALANCE_CHECK (Person_Name IN varchar2)
```

Next, we define the characteristics of the value to be returned. The definition of the variable whose value will be returned has three parts: its datatype, its name, and its length. The datatype in this example is set via the **return number** clause. The variable is then named *balance,* and is defined as a NUMBER(10,2). Thus, all three parts of the variable—its datatype, its name, and its length—have been defined.

```
RETURN NUMBER
   IS
     balance NUMBER(10,2);
```

The PL/SQL block follows. In the SQL statement, the sum of all SOLD amounts is subtracted from the sum of all BOUGHT amounts for that Person. The difference between those sums is selected into a variable called *balance* (which we previously defined). The **RETURN**(balance) command line then returns the value in the *balance* variable to the calling program.

```
BEGIN
       select SUM(DECODE(Action,'BOUGHT',Amount,0))
         - SUM(DECODE(Action,'SOLD',Amount,0))
         INTO balance
         from LEDGER
       where Person = Person_Name;
    RETURN(balance);
    END;
   /
```

If a function already exists, you may replace it via the **create or replace function** command. If you use the **or replace** clause, any EXECUTE grants previously made on the function will remain in place.

If the function is to be created in a different account (also known as a *schema*), then you must have the CREATE ANY PROCEDURE system privilege. If no schema is specified, then the function will be created in your schema. To create a function in your schema, you must have been granted the CREATE PROCEDURE system privilege (which is part of the RESOURCE role). Having the privilege to create procedures gives you the privilege to create functions and packages as well.

Referencing Remote Tables in Procedures

Remote tables can be accessed by the SQL statements in procedures. A remote table can be queried via a database link in the procedure, as shown in the following example. In this example, the NEW_WORKER procedure inserts a record into the WORKER table in the database defined by the REMOTE_CONNECT database link.

```
create or replace procedure NEW_WORKER
  (Person_Name IN varchar2)
AS
  BEGIN
    insert into WORKER@REMOTE_CONNECT
      (Name, Age, Lodging)
    values
      (Person_Name, null, null);
  END;
/
```

Procedures may also use local synonyms. For example, you may create a local synonym for a remote table, as follows:

```
create synonym WORKER for WORKER@REMOTE_CONNECT;
```

You can then rewrite your procedure to remove the database link specifications:

```
create or replace procedure NEW_WORKER
  (Person_Name IN varchar2)
AS
  BEGIN
    insert into WORKER
      (Name, Age, Lodging)
    values
      (Person_Name, null, null);
  END;
/
```

Removing database link names from procedures allows you to remove the details of the table's physical location from the procedure. If the table changes location, only the synonym will change, while the procedure will still be valid.

Debugging Procedures

The SQLPLUS **show errors** command displays all the errors associated with the most recently created procedural object. This command checks the USER_ERRORS data dictionary view for the errors associated with the most recent compilation attempt for that object. **show errors** displays the line and column number for each error, as well as the text of the error message.

To view errors associated with previously created procedural objects, you may query USER_ERRORS directly, as shown in the following listing. This example queries USER_ERRORS for error messages encountered during the creation of the BALANCE_CHECK function shown earlier in this chapter.

```
select Line,       /*Line number of the error./*
       Position,   /*Column number of the error.*/
       Text        /*Text of the error message.*/
  from USER_ERRORS
 where Name = 'BALANCE_CHECK'
   and Type = 'FUNCTION'
 order by Sequence;
```

Valid values for the Type column are PROCEDURE, PACKAGE, FUNCTION, and PACKAGE BODY.

Two other data dictionary view levels—ALL and DBA—may also be used to retrieve information about errors involving procedural objects. For information on these views, see Chapter 35.

Using the DBMS_OUTPUT Package

In addition to the debugging information provided by the **show errors** command, you may use the DBMS_OUTPUT package, one of a set of packages that is automatically installed when you create an Oracle database.

To use DBMS_OUTPUT, you must issue the **set serveroutput on** command before executing the procedural object you will be debugging.

DBMS_OUTPUT allows you to use three debugging functions within your package:

PUT	Puts multiple outputs on the same line
PUT_LINE	Puts each output on a separate line
NEW_LINE	Used with PUT; signals the end of the current output line

PUT and PUT_LINE are used to generate the debugging information you wish to display. For example, if you are debugging a procedure that includes a loop (refer to Chapter 25), you may wish to track the changes in a variable with each pass through the loop. To track the variable's value, you may use a command similar to the one shown in the following listing. In this example, the value of the Amount column is printed, prefixed by the literal string 'Amount:'.

```
PUT_LINE('Amount:'||Amount);
```

You may also use PUT and PUT_LINE outside of loops, but such uses may be better accomplished via the use of the **RETURN** command in functions (refer to "create function Syntax," earlier in this chapter).

Creating Your Own Functions

Rather than just calling custom functions via **execute** commands, you may use them within SQL expressions. This enables you to extend the functionality of SQL, customizing it to your needs. Such functions can be used in the same manner as Oracle-provided functions, such as **SUBSTR** and **TO_CHAR**. Custom functions cannot be used in CHECK or DEFAULT constraints and cannot manipulate any database values.

You can call either stand-alone functions (created via the **create function** command shown in the previous sections) or functions declared in package specifications (to be covered in "create package Syntax" later in this chapter). Procedures are not directly callable from SQL, but may be called by the functions you create.

For example, consider the BALANCE_CHECK function shown earlier in this chapter, which calculated the difference between the BOUGHT and SOLD balances for people. It had a single input variable—the person's name. However, to see the BALANCE_CHECK results for all of the workers, you would normally need to execute this procedure once for each record in the WORKER table.

You can improve the BALANCE_CHECK calculation process. Consider the following query:

```
select Name,
       BALANCE_CHECK(Name)
  from WORKER;
```

This single query uses the custom BALANCE_CHECK function to calculate the difference between the BOUGHT and SOLD balances for all workers.

The query output is as follows:

```
NAME                          BALANCE_CHECK(NAME)
---------------------------   -------------------
BART SARJEANT                                   0
ELBERT TALBOT                                   0
```

```
DONALD ROLLO                          0
JED HOPKINS                           0
WILLIAM SWING                         0
JOHN PEARSON                       -.96
GEORGE OSCAR                        4.5
KAY AND PALMER WALLBOM                0
PAT LAVAY                        -35.15
RICHARD KOCH AND BROTHERS             0
DICK JONES                            0
ADAH TALBOT                          -2
ROLAND BRANDT                     -6.96
PETER LAWSON                        6.5
VICTORIA LYNN                       6.1
WILFRED LOWELL                        0
HELEN BRANDT                       6.75
GERHARDT KENTGEN                  -9.23
ANDREW DYE                        46.75

19 rows selected.
```

The query selected each name from WORKER; for each name, it executed the BALANCE_CHECK function, which selected data from LEDGER.

To take advantage of this feature, your functions must follow the same guidelines as Oracle's functions. Most notably, they must not update the database, and must contain only IN parameters.

NOTE
Although this technique works, it has performance costs. The more data there is in the table, the bigger the performance penalty will be when comparing this method to a traditional join.

Customizing Error Conditions

You may establish different error conditions within procedural objects (refer to Chapter 26 for examples of customized error conditions within triggers). For each of the error conditions you define, you may select an error message that will appear when the error occurs. The error numbers and messages that are displayed to the user are set by you via the RAISE_APPLICATION_ERROR procedure, which may be called from within any procedural object.

You can call RAISE_APPLICATION_ERROR from within procedures, packages, and functions. It requires two inputs: the message number and the message text. You get to assign both the message number and the text that will be displayed to the user. This is a very powerful addition to the standard exceptions that are available in PL/SQL (see "Exception" in the Alphabetical Reference).

The following example shows the BALANCE_CHECK function defined earlier in this chapter. Now, however, it has an additional section (shown in bold). Titled EXCEPTION, this section tells Oracle how to handle nonstandard processing. In this example, the NO_DATA_FOUND exception's standard message is overridden via the RAISE_APPLICATION_ERROR procedure.

```
create or replace function BALANCE_CHECK (Person_Name IN varchar2)
   RETURN NUMBER
   IS
      balance NUMBER(10,2);
   BEGIN
      select SUM(DECODE(Action,'BOUGHT',Amount,0))
         - SUM(DECODE(Action,'SOLD',Amount,0))
         INTO balance
         from LEDGER
       where Person = Person_Name;
    RETURN(balance);
    EXCEPTION
      WHEN NO_DATA_FOUND THEN
         RAISE_APPLICATION_ERROR (-20100,
            'No BOUGHT or SOLD entries for that Person.');
    END;
/
```

In the preceding example, the NO_DATA_FOUND exception was used. If you wish to define custom exceptions, you need to name the exception in a Declarations section of the procedure, which immediately precedes the **begin** command. As shown in the following listing, this section should include entries for each of the custom exceptions you have defined, listed as type EXCEPTION:

```
declare
some_custom_error EXCEPTION;
```

> **NOTE**
> *If you are using the exceptions already defined within PL/SQL, you do not need to list them in the Declarations section of the procedural object. See "Exception" in the Alphabetical Reference for a list of the predefined exceptions.*

In the **exception** portion of the procedural object's code, you tell the database how to handle the exceptions. It begins with the keyword **exception**, followed by a **WHEN** clause for each exception. Each exception may call the RAISE_APPLICATION_ERROR procedure, which takes two input parameters: the error number (which must be between -20001 and -20999) and the error message to be displayed. In the preceding example, only one exception was defined. Multiple exceptions can be defined, as shown in the following listing; you may use the **when others** clause to handle all nonspecified exceptions:

```
EXCEPTION
    WHEN NO_DATA_FOUND THEN
        RAISE_APPLICATION_ERROR (-20100,
            'No BOUGHT or SOLD entries for that Person.');
    WHEN some_custom_error THEN
        RAISE_APPLICATION_ERROR (-20101,
            'Some custom error message.');
```

The use of the RAISE_APPLICATION_ERROR procedure gives you great flexibility in managing the error conditions that may be encountered within procedural objects.

Naming Procedures and Functions

Procedures and functions should be named according to the business function they perform or business rule they enforce. There should be no ambiguity about their purpose.

The NEW_WORKER procedure shown earlier should be renamed. NEW_WORKER performs a business function—inserting records into WORKER—so its name should reflect that function. A better choice for the name would be ADD_NEW_WORKER. Since it performs a function, a verb (in this case, "add") must describe what it does. The name of the procedure should also include the name of the major table(s) it impacts. If the tables are properly named, then the name of the table should be the direct object upon which the verb acts (in this case, WORKER). See Chapter 39 for further information on object names.

For the sake of consistency, we will continue to refer to the procedure as NEW_WORKER for the remainder of this chapter.

create package Syntax

When creating packages, the package specification and the package body are created separately. Thus, there are two commands to use: **create package** for the package specification, and **create package body** for the package body. Both of these commands require that you have the CREATE PROCEDURE system privilege. If the package is to be created in a schema other than your own, then you must have the CREATE ANY PROCEDURE system privilege.

The following is the syntax for creating package specifications:

```
create [or replace] package [user.] package
{IS | AS}
[AUTHID  {DEFINER | CURRENT_USER} ]
 package specification;
```

A *package specification* consists of the list of functions, procedures, variables, constants, cursors, and exceptions that will be available to users of the package.

A sample **create package** command is shown in the following listing. In this example, the LEDGER_PACKAGE package is created. The BALANCE_CHECK function and NEW_WORKER procedure seen earlier in this chapter are included in the package.

```
create or replace package LEDGER_PACKAGE
AS
   function BALANCE_CHECK(Person_Name VARCHAR2) return NUMBER;
   procedure NEW_WORKER(Person_Name IN VARCHAR2);
end LEDGER_PACKAGE;
/
```

NOTE
*You may append the name of the procedural object to the **end** clause, as shown in the preceding example. This may make it easier to coordinate the logic within your code.*

A *package body* contains the blocks and specifications for all of the public objects listed in the package specification. The package body may include objects that are not listed in the package specification; such objects are said to be *private* and are not available to users of the package. Private objects may only be called by other objects within the same package body. A package body may also include code that is run every time the package is invoked, regardless of the part of the package that is executed—see "Initializing Packages," later in this chapter, for an example.

The syntax for creating package bodies is as follows:

```
create [or replace] package body [user.] package body
{IS | AS}
 package body;
```

The name of the package body should be the same as the name of the package specification.

Continuing the LEDGER_PACKAGE example, its package body can be created via the **create package body** command shown in the following example:

```
create package body LEDGER_PACKAGE
AS
function BALANCE_CHECK (Person_Name IN varchar2)
   RETURN NUMBER
   IS
     balance NUMBER(10,2);
   BEGIN
      select SUM(DECODE(Action,'BOUGHT',Amount,0))
       - SUM(DECODE(Action,'SOLD',Amount,0))
       INTO balance
       from LEDGER
       where Person = Person_Name;
   RETURN(balance);
   EXCEPTION
      WHEN NO_DATA_FOUND THEN
         RAISE_APPLICATION_ERROR (-20100,
            'No BOUGHT or SOLD entries for that Person.');
   END BALANCE_CHECK;
procedure NEW_WORKER
  (Person_Name IN varchar2)
AS
   BEGIN
      insert into WORKER
         (Name, Age, Lodging)
      values
         (Person_Name, null, null);
   END NEW_WORKER;
END LEDGER_PACKAGE;
/
```

The **create package body** command shown in the preceding example combines the **create function** command for the BALANCE_CHECK function with the **create procedure** command for the NEW_WORKER procedure. The **end** clauses all have the names of their associated objects appended to them (shown in bold in the prior listing). Modifying the **end** clauses in this manner helps to clarify the ending points of the object code.

Additional functions, procedures, exceptions, variables, cursors, and constants may be defined within the package body, but they will not be available to the public unless they have been declared within the package specification (via the **create package** command). If a user has been granted the EXECUTE privilege on a package, then that user can access any of the public objects that are declared in the package specification.

Initializing Packages

Packages may include code that is to be run the first time a user executes the package. In the following example, the LEDGER_PACKAGE package body is modified to include a SQL statement that records the current user's username and the timestamp for the start of the package execution. Two new variables must also be declared in the package body to record these values.

Since the two new variables are declared within the package body, they are not available to the public. Within the package body, they are separated from the procedures and functions. The package initialization code is shown in bold in the following listing:

```
create or replace package body LEDGER_PACKAGE
AS
User_Name VARCHAR2(30);
Entry_Date DATE;
function BALANCE_CHECK (Person_Name IN varchar2)
  RETURN NUMBER
  IS
    balance NUMBER(10,2);
  BEGIN
    select SUM(DECODE(Action,'BOUGHT',Amount,0))
      - SUM(DECODE(Action,'SOLD',Amount,0))
      INTO balance
      from LEDGER
    where Person = Person_Name;
  RETURN(balance);
  EXCEPTION
    WHEN NO_DATA_FOUND THEN
        RAISE_APPLICATION_ERROR (-20100,
          'No BOUGHT or SOLD entries for that Person.');
  END BALANCE_CHECK;
procedure NEW_WORKER
  (Person_Name IN varchar2)
AS
  BEGIN
    insert into WORKER
      (Name, Age, Lodging)
    values
      (Person_Name, null, null);
  END NEW_WORKER;
BEGIN
  select User, SysDate
    into User_Name, Entry_Date
    from DUAL;
END LEDGER_PACKAGE;
/
```

NOTE
The code that is to be run every time the package is executed is stored in its own PL/SQL block at the bottom of the package body. It does not have its own **end** *clause; it uses the package body's* **end** *clause.*

Every time the LEDGER_PACKAGE package is executed, the User_Name and Entry_Date variables will be populated by the query shown in the previous listing. These two variables can then be used by the functions and procedures within the package.

To **execute** a procedure or function that is within a package, specify both the package name and the name of the procedure or function in the **execute** command, as follows:

```
execute LEDGER_PACKAGE.BALANCE_CHECK('ADAH TALBOT');
```

Viewing Source Code for Procedural Objects

The source code for existing procedures, functions, packages, and package bodies can be queried from the following data dictionary views:

USER_SOURCE	For procedural objects owned by the user
ALL_SOURCE	For procedural objects owned by the user or to which the user has been granted access
DBA_SOURCE	For all procedural objects in the database

Select information from the USER_SOURCE view via a query similar to the one shown in the following listing. In this example, the Text column is selected, ordered by the Line number. The Name of the object and the object Type are used to define which object's source code is to be displayed. The following example uses the NEW_WORKER procedure shown earlier in this chapter:

```
select Text
  from USER_SOURCE
 where Name = 'NEW_WORKER'
   and Type = 'PROCEDURE'
 order by Line;
```

```
TEXT
-------------------------------------------------
procedure NEW_WORKER
 (Person_Name IN varchar2)
AS
  BEGIN
     insert into WORKER
       (Name, Age, Lodging)
     values
       (Person_Name, null, null);
  END;
```

As shown in the preceding example, the USER_SOURCE view contains one record for each line of the NEW_WORKER procedure. The sequence of the lines is maintained by the Line column; therefore, the Line column should be used in the **order by** clause.

Valid values for the Type column are PROCEDURE, FUNCTION, PACKAGE, and PACKAGE BODY.

Compiling Procedures, Functions, and Packages

Oracle compiles procedural objects when they are created. However, these may become invalid if the database objects they reference change. The next time the procedural objects are executed, they will be recompiled by the database.

You can avoid this runtime compiling—and the performance degradation it may cause—by explicitly recompiling the procedures, functions, and packages. To recompile a procedure, use the **alter procedure** command, as shown in the following listing. The **compile** clause is the only valid option for this command.

```
alter procedure NEW_WORKER compile;
```

To recompile a procedure, you must either own the procedure or have the ALTER ANY PROCEDURE system privilege.

To recompile a function, use the **alter function** command, with the **compile** clause:

```
alter function NEW_WORKER compile;
```

To recompile a function, you must either own the function or have the ALTER ANY PROCEDURE system privilege.

When recompiling packages, you may either recompile both the package specification and the body or just recompile the package body. By default, both the package specification and the package body are recompiled. You cannot use the **alter function** or **alter procedure** command to recompile functions and procedures stored within a package.

If the source code for the procedures or functions within the package body has changed but the package specification has not, you may wish to recompile only the package body. In most cases, it is appropriate to recompile both the specification and the package body.

The following is the syntax for the **alter package** command:

```
alter package [user.] package_name
compile [PACKAGE | BODY];
```

To recompile a package, use the preceding **alter package** command with the **compile** clause, as follows:

```
alter package LEDGER_PACKAGE compile;
```

To recompile a package, you must either own the package or have the ALTER ANY PROCEDURE system privilege. Since neither PACKAGE nor BODY was specified in the preceding example, the default of PACKAGE was used, resulting in the recompilation of both the package specification and the package body.

Replacing Procedures, Functions, and Packages

Procedures, functions, and packages may be replaced via their respective **create or replace** command. Using the **or replace** clause keeps in place any existing grants that have been made for those objects. If you choose to drop and re-create procedural objects, you have to regrant any EXECUTE privileges that had previously been granted.

Dropping Procedures, Functions, and Packages

To drop a procedure, use the **drop procedure** command, as follows:

```
drop procedure NEW_WORKER;
```

To drop a procedure, you must either own the procedure or have the DROP ANY PROCEDURE system privilege.

To drop a function, use the **drop function** command, as follows:

```
drop function BALANCE_CHECK;
```

To drop a function, you must either own the function or have the DROP ANY PROCEDURE system privilege.

To drop a package, use the **drop package** command, as follows:

```
drop package LEDGER_PACKAGE;
```

To drop a package, you must either own the package or have the DROP ANY PROCEDURE system privilege.

To drop a package body, use the **drop package** command with the **body** clause, as follows:

```
drop package body LEDGER_PACKAGE;
```

To drop a package body, you must either own the package or have the DROP ANY PROCEDURE system privilege.

PART
IV

Object-Relational Databases

CHAPTER
28

Implementing Types, Object Views, and Methods

n this chapter, you will see further details on the use of abstract datatypes, first introduced in Chapter 4. This chapter covers topics such as security administration for abstract datatypes and the indexing of abstract datatype attributes. The creation of methods for abstract datatypes is also shown, along with the use of object views and INSTEAD OF triggers.

To use the information provided in this chapter, you should be familiar with abstract datatypes (see Chapter 4), views (see Chapter 18), the **grant** command (see Chapter 19), indexes (see Chapter 20), and PL/SQL procedures and triggers (Chapters 25, 26, and 27). Elements of each of these topics play a part in the implementation of an object-relational database. The first section of this chapter provides a high-level review of the abstract datatypes shown in Chapter 4.

Revisiting Abstract Datatypes

As described in Chapter 4, you can use abstract datatypes to group related columns into objects. For example, columns that are part of address information can be grouped into an ADDRESS_TY datatype via the **create type** command:

```
create type ADDRESS_TY as object
(Street   VARCHAR2(50),
 City     VARCHAR2(25),
 State    CHAR(2),
 Zip      NUMBER);
/
```

The **create type** command in the preceding listing creates an ADDRESS_TY abstract datatype. You can use ADDRESS_TY when creating additional database objects. For example, the following **create type** command creates the PERSON_TY datatype, using the ADDRESS_TY datatype as the datatype for its Address column:

```
create type PERSON_TY as object
(Name       VARCHAR2(25),
 Address    ADDRESS_TY);
/
```

Because the Address column of the PERSON_TY datatype uses the ADDRESS_TY datatype, it holds not one value but four—the four columns that constitute the ADDRESS_TY datatype.

Security for Abstract Datatypes

The previous example assumed that the same user owned both the ADDRESS_TY datatype and the PERSON_TY datatype. What if the owner of the PERSON_TY datatype were different from the ADDRESS_TY datatype's owner?

For example, what if the account named Dora owns the ADDRESS_TY datatype, and the user of the account named George tries to create the PERSON_TY datatype? George executes the following command:

```
create type PERSON_TY as object
(Name      VARCHAR2(25),
 Address   ADDRESS_TY);
/
```

If George does not own the ADDRESS_TY abstract datatype, then Oracle will respond to this **create type** command with the following message:

```
Warning: Type created with compilation errors.
```

The compilation errors are caused by problems creating the *constructor method*—a special method created by Oracle when the datatype is created. Oracle cannot resolve the reference to the ADDRESS_TY datatype, since George does not own a datatype with that name. George could issue the **create type** command again (using the **or replace** clause) to specifically reference Dora's ADDRESS_TY datatype:

```
create or replace type PERSON_TY as object
(Name      VARCHAR2(25),
 Address   Dora.ADDRESS_TY);

Warning: Type created with compilation errors.
```

To see the errors associated with the datatype creation, use the **show errors** command:

```
show errors
Errors for TYPE PERSON_TY:

LINE/COL ERROR
-------- --------------------------------------------------------
0/0      PL/SQL: Compilation unit analysis terminated
3/11     PLS-00201: identifier 'DORA.ADDRESS_TY' must be declared
```

George will not be able to create the PERSON_TY datatype (which includes the ADDRESS_TY datatype) unless Dora first **grant**s him EXECUTE privilege on her type. The following listing shows this grant:

```
grant EXECUTE on ADDRESS_TY to George;
```

Now that the proper grants are in place, George can create a datatype that is based on Dora's ADDRESS_TY datatype, as shown in the following listing.

```
create or replace type PERSON_TY as object
(Name      VARCHAR2(25),
 Address   Dora.ADDRESS_TY);
```

Using another user's datatypes is not trivial. For example, during **insert** operations, you must specify the owner of each type. George can create a table based on his PERSON_TY datatype (which includes Dora's ADDRESS_TY datatype), as shown in the following listing:

```
create table CUSTOMER
(Customer_ID  NUMBER,
 Person       PERSON_TY);
```

If George owned the PERSON_TY and ADDRESS_TY datatypes, an **insert** into CUSTOMER would use the format:

```
insert into CUSTOMER values
(1,PERSON_TY('SomeName',
    ADDRESS_TY('StreetValue','CityValue','ST',11111)))
```

Since George does not own the ADDRESS_TY datatype, this command will fail. During the **insert**, the ADDRESS_TY constructor method is used—and Dora owns it. Therefore, the **insert** command must be modified to specify Dora as the owner of ADDRESS_TY. The following example shows the corrected **insert** statement, with the reference to Dora shown in bold:

```
insert into CUSTOMER values
(1,PERSON_TY('SomeName',
    Dora.ADDRESS_TY('StreetValue','CityValue','ST',11111)))
```

Can George use a synonym for Dora's datatype? No. Although George *can* create a synonym named ADDRESS_TY:

```
create synonym ADDRESS_TY for Dora.ADDRESS_TY;
```

this synonym cannot be used:

```
create type PERSON2_TY
(Name      VARCHAR2(25),
 Address   ADDRESS_TY);

create type PERSON2_TY
*
ERROR at line 1:
ORA-22863: synonym for datatype DORA.ADDRESS_TY not allowed
```

As shown by the error message, you cannot use a synonym for another user's datatype. Therefore, you will need to refer to the datatype's owner during each **insert** command.

NOTE
*When you create a synonym, Oracle does not check the validity of the object for which you are creating a synonym. When you **create synonym x for y**, Oracle does not check to make sure that y is a valid object name or valid object type. The validity of that object is only checked when the object is accessed via the synonym.*

In a relational-only implementation of Oracle, you grant the EXECUTE privilege on procedural objects, such as procedures and packages. Within the object-relational implementation of Oracle, the EXECUTE privilege is extended to cover abstract datatypes as well. The EXECUTE privilege is appropriate because abstract datatypes can include *methods*—PL/SQL functions and procedures that operate on the datatype. If you grant someone the privilege to use your datatype, you are granting the user the privilege to execute the methods you have defined on the datatype. Although Dora did not yet define any methods on the ADDRESS_TY datatype, Oracle automatically creates constructor methods to access the data. Any object (such as PERSON_TY) that uses the ADDRESS_TY datatype uses the constructor method associated with ADDRESS_TY. Even if you haven't created any methods for your abstract datatype, there are still procedures associated with it.

Indexing Abstract Datatype Attributes

In the example from Chapter 4, the CUSTOMER table was created. As shown in the following listing, the CUSTOMER table contains a normal column (Customer_ID) and a Person column that is defined by the PERSON_TY abstract datatype:

```
create table CUSTOMER
(Customer_ID    NUMBER,
 Person         PERSON_TY);
```

From the datatype definitions shown in the previous section of this chapter, you can see that PERSON_TY has one column (Name) followed by an Address column defined by the ADDRESS_TY datatype.

As shown in Chapter 4, you fully qualify the datatype attributes when referencing columns within the abstract datatypes, by prefacing the attribute name with the column name, and by prefacing the column name with a correlation variable. For example, the following query returns the Customer_ID column along with the Name column. The Name column is an attribute of the datatype that defines the Person column, so you refer to the attribute as Person.Name:

```
select Customer_ID, C.Person.Name
   from CUSTOMER C;
```

NOTE
When querying the attributes of an abstract datatype, you must use a correlation variable for the table, as shown in this example.

You can refer to attributes within the ADDRESS_TY datatype by specifying the full path through the related columns. For example, the Street column is referred to as Person.Address.Street, fully describing its location within the structure of the table. In the following example, the City column is referenced twice: once in the list of columns to select, and once within the **where** clause. In each reference, a correlation variable (in this example, *C*) is required.

```
select C.Person.Name,
       C.Person.Address.City
  from CUSTOMER C
 where C.Person.Address.City like 'F%';
```

Because the City column is used with a range search in the **where** clause, the Oracle optimizer may be able to use an index when resolving the query. If an index is available on the City column, then Oracle can quickly find all the rows that have City values starting with the letter *F*, as requested by the query.

NOTE
The inner workings of the Oracle optimizer—and the conditions under which indexes are used—are described in Chapter 36. See that chapter for guidelines regarding the columns to index.

To create an index on a column that is part of an abstract datatype, you need to specify the full path to the column as part of the **create index** command. To create an index on the City column (which is part of the Address column), you can execute the following command:

```
create index I_CUSTOMER$CITY
on CUSTOMER(Person.Address.City);
```

This command will create an index named I_CUSTOMER$CITY on the Person.Address.City column. Whenever the City column is accessed, the Oracle optimizer will evaluate the SQL used to access the data and determine if the new index can be useful to improve the performance of the access.

> **NOTE**
> In the **create index** command, you do not use correlation variables when referencing the attributes of abstract datatypes.

When creating tables based on abstract datatypes, you should consider how the columns within the abstract datatypes will be accessed. If, like the City column in the previous example, certain columns will commonly be used as part of limiting conditions in queries, then they should be indexed. In this regard, the representation of multiple columns in a single abstract datatype may hinder your application performance, since it may obscure the need to index specific columns within the datatype. When using abstract datatypes, you become accustomed to treating a group of columns as a single entity, such as the Address columns or the Person columns. It is important to remember that the optimizer, when evaluating query access paths, will consider the columns individually. In addition, remember that indexing the City column in one table that uses the ADDRESS_TY datatype does not affect the City column in a second table that uses the ADDRESS_TY datatype. For example, if there is a second table named BRANCH that uses the ADDRESS_TY datatype, then *its* City column will not be indexed unless you create an index for it. The fact that there is an index on the City column in the CUSTOMER table will have no impact on the City column in the BRANCH table.

Thus, one of the advantages of abstract datatypes—the ability to improve adherence to standards for logical data representation—does not extend to the physical data representation. You need to address each physical implementation separately.

Implementing Object Views

The CUSTOMER table created in the previous section of this chapter assumed that a PERSON_TY datatype already existed. When implementing object-relational database applications, you should first use the relational database design methods described in the first part of this book. After the database design is properly normalized, you should look for groups of columns (or individual columns) that constitute the representation of an abstract datatype. You can then create your tables based on the abstract datatypes, as shown earlier in this chapter.

But what if your tables already exist? What if you had previously created a relational database application and now want to implement object-relational concepts in your application without rebuilding and re-creating the entire application? To do this, you need the ability to overlay object-oriented (OO) structures, such as abstract datatypes, on existing relational tables. Oracle provides *object views* as a means for defining objects used by existing relational tables.

NOTE
Throughout the examples in this book, the names of object views will always end with the suffix OV.

In the examples earlier in this chapter, the order of operations was as follows:

1. Create the ADDRESS_TY datatype.

2. Create the PERSON_TY datatype, using the ADDRESS_TY datatype.

3. Create the CUSTOMER table, using the PERSON_TY datatype.

If the CUSTOMER table already existed, you could create the ADDRESS_TY and PERSON_TY datatypes, and use object views to relate them to the CUSTOMER table. In the following listing, the CUSTOMER table is created as a relational table, using only the normally provided datatypes:

```
create table CUSTOMER
(Customer_ID NUMBER    primary key,
 Name        VARCHAR2(25),
 Street      VARCHAR2(50),
 City        VARCHAR2(25),
 State       CHAR(2),
 Zip         NUMBER);
```

If you want to create another table or application that stores information about people and addresses, you may choose to create the ADDRESS_TY and PERSON_TY datatypes. However, for consistency, they should be applied to the CUSTOMER table as well.

With the CUSTOMER table already created (and possibly containing data), you should create the abstract datatypes. First, create ADDRESS_TY:

NOTE
The following listings assume that the ADDRESS_TY and PERSON_TY datatypes do not already exist in your schema.

```
create or replace type ADDRESS_TY as object
(Street   VARCHAR2(50),
 City     VARCHAR2(25),
 State    CHAR(2),
 Zip      NUMBER);
/
```

Next, create PERSON_TY, which uses ADDRESS_TY:

```
create or replace type PERSON_TY as object
(Name        VARCHAR2(25),
 Address     ADDRESS_TY);
/
```

Now, create an object view based on the CUSTOMER table using the datatypes you have defined. An object view starts with the **create view** command. Within the **create view** command, you specify the query that will form the basis of the view. You'll use the datatypes you just created. The code for creating the CUSTOMER_OV object view is shown in the following listing:

```
create view CUSTOMER_OV (Customer_ID, Person) as
select Customer_ID,
       PERSON_TY(Name,
       ADDRESS_TY(Street, City, State, Zip))
  from CUSTOMER;
```

Let's look at this command closely. In the first line, the object view is named:

```
create view CUSTOMER_OV (Customer_ID, Person) as
```

The CUSTOMER_OV view will have two columns: the Customer_ID column and the Person column (the latter is defined by the PERSON_TY datatype). Note that you cannot specify "object" as an option within the **create view** command.

In the next section, you create the query that will form the basis for the view:

```
select Customer_ID,
       PERSON_TY(Name,
       ADDRESS_TY(Street, City, State, Zip))
  from CUSTOMER;
```

This example presents several important syntax issues. When a table is built on existing abstract datatypes, you select column values from the table by referring to the names of the columns (such as Person and Address) instead of their constructor methods. When creating the object view, however, you refer to the names of the constructor methods (PERSON_TY and ADDRESS_TY) instead.

NOTE
See Chapter 4 for examples of queries that refer to columns defined by abstract datatypes.

You can use a **where** clause in the query that forms the basis of the object view. In the following example, the CUSTOMER_OV is modified to include a **where** clause that limits it to showing the CUSTOMER values for which the State column has a value of 'DE':

```
create or replace view CUSTOMER_OV (Customer_ID, Person) as
select Customer_ID,
       PERSON_TY(Name,
       ADDRESS_TY(Street, City, State, Zip))
  from CUSTOMER
 where State = 'DE';
```

Note that when you create the object view CUSTOMER_OV, the **where** clause of the view's base query does not refer to the abstract datatype. Instead, it refers directly to the CUSTOMER table. The **where** clause refers directly to the State column because the query refers directly to the CUSTOMER table—a relational table that is not based on any abstract datatypes.

To create object views based on existing relational tables, the order of operations is as follows:

   1. Create the CUSTOMER table.

   2. Create the ADDRESS_TY datatype.

   3. Create the PERSON_TY datatype, using the ADDRESS_TY datatype.

   4. Create the CUSTOMER_OV object view, using the defined datatypes.

There are two main benefits to using object views. First, they allow you to create abstract datatypes within tables that already exist. Since you can use the same abstract datatypes in multiple tables within your application, you can improve your application's adherence to standard representation of data and your ability to reuse existing objects. Since you can define methods for the abstract datatypes, the methods will apply to the data within any new tables you create as well as to your existing tables.

Second, object views provide two different ways to enter data into the base table, as you will see in the next section. The flexibility of data manipulation for object views—being able to treat the base table as either a relational table or an object table—is a significant benefit for application developers. In the next section, you will see the data-manipulation options available for object views.

Manipulating Data via Object Views

You can update the data in the CUSTOMER table via the CUSTOMER_OV object view, or you can update the CUSTOMER table directly. By treating CUSTOMER as just a table, you can insert data into it via a normal SQL **insert** command, as shown in the following example:

```
insert into CUSTOMER values
(123,'SIGMUND','47 HAFFNER RD','LEWISTON','NJ',22222);
```

This **insert** command inserts a single record into the CUSTOMER table. Even though you have created an object view on the table, you can still treat the CUSTOMER table as a regular relational table.

Since the object view has been created on the CUSTOMER table, you can **insert** into CUSTOMER via the constructor methods used by the view. As previously described in Chapter 4, when you insert data into an object that uses abstract datatypes, you specify the names of the constructor methods within the **insert** command. The example shown in the following listing inserts a single record into the CUSTOMER_OV object view using the CUSTOMER_TY, PERSON_TY, and ADDRESS_TY constructor methods:

```
insert into CUSTOMER_OV values
   (234,
   PERSON_TY('EVELYN',
   ADDRESS_TY('555 HIGH ST','LOWLANDS PARK','NE',33333))));
```

Since you can use either method to insert values into the CUSTOMER_OV object view, you can standardize the manner in which your application performs data manipulation. If your **insert**s are all based on abstract datatypes, then you can use the same kind of code for **insert**s regardless of whether the abstract datatypes were created before or after the table.

Using INSTEAD OF Triggers

If you create an object view, you can use an INSTEAD OF trigger. Views cannot use the standard table-based triggers described in Chapter 26. You can use INSTEAD OF triggers to tell Oracle how to update the underlying tables that are part of the view. You can use INSTEAD OF triggers on either object views or standard relational views.

For example, if a view involves a join of two tables, your ability to **update** records in the view is limited. However, if you use an INSTEAD OF trigger, you can tell Oracle how to **update**, **delete**, or **insert** records in tables when a user attempts to change values via the view. The code in the INSTEAD OF trigger is executed *in place of* the **insert**, **update**, or **delete** command you enter.

Let's consider two of Talbot's most-used tables: WORKER and LODGING. The WORKER table has three columns: Name, Age, and Lodging. The LODGING table has four columns: Lodging, LongName, Manager, and Address. You could select all of the columns from both tables by joining them on the Lodging column, as shown here:

```
select WORKER.Name,
       WORKER.Age,
       WORKER.Lodging,
       LODGING.Lodging,
       LODGING.LongName,
       LODGING.Manager,
       LODGING.Address
  from WORKER, LODGING
 where WORKER.Lodging = LODGING.Lodging;
```

Now you can select which columns you want from each table and use this query as the basis for a view. For example, you can select the worker name, lodging, and lodging manager name from the two tables:

```
create view WORKER_LODGING_MANAGER as
select WORKER.Name,
       LODGING.Lodging,
       LODGING.Manager
  from WORKER, LODGING
 where WORKER.Lodging = LODGING.Lodging;
```

You can select values from this view—and if you use INSTEAD OF triggers, you can also perform data manipulation via this view.

Consider this record:

```
select *
  from WORKER_LODGING_MANAGER
 where Name = 'BART SARJEANT';


NAME                     LODGING          MANAGER
------------------------ ---------------- ------------------
BART SARJEANT            CRANMER          THOM CRANMER
```

Bart Sarjeant resides in the lodging named CRANMER, managed by Thom Cranmer. However, he has decided to move to the WEITBROCHT lodging instead. You can indicate this in one of two ways. You can perform the update directly against the WORKER table:

```
update WORKER
    set Lodging = 'WEITBROCHT'
 where Name = 'BART SARJEANT';
```

or you can use an INSTEAD OF trigger and update via the WORKER_LODGING_ MANAGER view.

In the following listing, an INSTEAD OF trigger for the WORKER_LODGING_ MANAGER view is shown:

```
create trigger WORKER_LODGING_MANAGER_update
instead of UPDATE on WORKER_LODGING_MANAGER
for each row
begin
  if :old.Name <> :new.Name
  then
    update WORKER
       set Name = :new.Name
     where Name = :old.Name;
  end if;
  if :old.Lodging <> :new.Lodging
  then
    update WORKER
       set Lodging = :new.Lodging
     where Name = :old.Name;
  end if;
  if :old.Manager <> :new.Manager
  then
    update LODGING
       set Manager = :new.Manager
     where Lodging = :old.Lodging;
  end if;
end;
/
```

In the first part of this trigger, the trigger is named and its purpose is described via the **instead of** clause. The trigger has been named to make its function clear: it is used to support **update** commands executed against the WORKER_LODGING_ MANAGER view. It is a row-level trigger; each changed row will be processed, as shown next.

```
create trigger WORKER_LODGING_MANAGER_update
instead of UPDATE on WORKER_LODGING_MANAGER
for each row
```

The next section of the trigger tells Oracle how to process the **update**. In the first check within the trigger body, the Name value is checked. If the old Name value is equal to the new Name value, then no changes are made. If the values are not the same, then the WORKER table is updated with the new Name value:

```
begin
  if :old.Name <> :new.Name
  then
    update WORKER
      set Name = :new.Name
    where Name = :old.Name;
  end if;
```

In the next section of the trigger, the Lodging value is evaluated. If the Lodging value has changed, then the WORKER table is updated to reflect the new Lodging value for the WORKER:

```
  if :old.Lodging <> :new.Lodging
  then
    update WORKER
      set Lodging = :new.Lodging
    where Name = :old.Name;
  end if;
```

In the final section of the trigger, the Manager column is evaluated; if it has been changed, then the LODGING table is updated with the new value:

```
  if :old.Manager <> :new.Manager
  then
    update LODGING
      set Manager = :new.Manager
    where Lodging = :old.Lodging;
  end if;
end;
/
```

Thus, the view relies on two tables—WORKER and LODGING—and an **update** of the view can update *either* or *both* of the tables. The INSTEAD OF trigger, introduced to support object views, is a powerful tool for application development.

You can now **update** the WORKER_LODGING_MANAGER view directly and have the trigger **update** the proper underlying table. For example, the following command will update the WORKER table:

```
update WORKER_LODGING_MANAGER
    set Lodging = 'WEITBROCHT'
 where Name = 'BART SARJEANT';

1 row updated.
```

Verify the **update** by querying the WORKER table:

```
select Name, Lodging
  from WORKER
 where Name = 'BART SARJEANT';

NAME                          LODGING
------------------------      ---------------
BART SARJEANT                 WEITBROCHT
```

You can also update the LODGING table via the WORKER_LODGING_ MANAGER view, making John Peletier the new manager of Bart Sarjeant's lodging:

```
update WORKER_LODGING_MANAGER
    set Manager = 'JOHN PELETIER'
 where Name = 'BART SARJEANT';

1 row updated.
```

Verify the change by selecting John Peletier's rows from the LODGING table:

```
select *
  from LODGING
 where Manager = 'JOHN PELETIER';

LODGING          LONGNAME
---------------  ----------------------------------------
MANAGER                       ADDRESS
------------------------      ----------------------------
ROSE HILL        ROSE HILL FOR MEN
JOHN PELETIER                 RFD 3, N. EDMESTON

WEITBROCHT       WEITBROCHT ROOMING
JOHN PELETIER                 320 GENEVA, KEENE
```

INSTEAD OF triggers are very powerful. As shown in this example, you can use them to perform operations against different database tables, using the flow-control logic available within PL/SQL.

Methods

When you created an object view on the CUSTOMER table, you defined abstract datatypes that the table used. Those datatypes help to standardize the representation of data, but they serve another purpose as well. You can define methods that apply to datatypes, and by applying those datatypes to existing tables, you can apply those methods to the data in those tables.

Consider the CUSTOMER_OV object view:

```
create or replace view CUSTOMER_OV (Customer_ID, Person) as
select Customer_ID,
       PERSON_TY(Name,
       ADDRESS_TY(Street, City, State, Zip))
  from CUSTOMER;
```

This view applies the PERSON_TY and ADDRESS_TY abstract datatypes to the data in the CUSTOMER table. If any methods are associated with those datatypes, they will apply to the data in the table. When you create an abstract datatype, you use the **create type** command. When you create a method, you use the **create type body** command.

Syntax for Creating Methods

Before creating the body for a method, you must name the method within the datatype declaration. For example, let's create a new datatype, ANIMAL_TY. The datatype definition for ANIMAL_TY is shown in the following listing:

```
create or replace type ANIMAL_TY as object
(Breed      VARCHAR2(25),
 Name       VARCHAR2(25),
 BirthDate  DATE,
member function AGE (BirthDate IN DATE) return NUMBER);
 /
```

The ANIMAL_TY datatype could be used as part of an object view on the BREEDING table used in Chapter 13. In the BREEDING table, the name of an offspring, its sex, its parents, and its birthdate are recorded.

Within the **create type** command, this line:

```
member function AGE (BirthDate IN DATE) return NUMBER)
```

names the function that is a "member" of the ANIMAL_TY datatype. Since AGE will return a value, it is a function; if no values were returned, it would be a procedure (see Chapter 27). To define the AGE function, use the **create type body** command, whose full syntax is shown in the Alphabetical Reference.

Let's create the AGE function as a member function within the ANIMAL_TY datatype. The AGE function will return the age, in days, of the animals:

```
create or replace type body ANIMAL_TY as
member function Age (BirthDate DATE) return NUMBER is
begin
  RETURN ROUND(SysDate - BirthDate);
end;
end;
/
```

If you had additional functions or procedures to code, you would specify them within the same **create type body** command, before the final **end** clause.

Now that the AGE function has been created, it is associated with the ANIMAL_TY datatype. If a table uses this datatype, then it can use the AGE function. However, there is a problem with the way in which the function is specified. The AGE function, as previously defined in the **create type body** command, does not explicitly restrict **update**s. The AGE function does not update any data, but there is no guarantee that the type body will not later be changed to cause AGE to update data. To call a member function within a SQL statement, you need to make sure that the function cannot update the database. Therefore, you need to modify the function specification in the **create type** command. The modification is shown in bold in the following listing:

```
create or replace type ANIMAL_TY as object
(Breed      VARCHAR2(25),
 Name       VARCHAR2(25),
 BirthDate  DATE,
member function AGE (BirthDate IN DATE) return NUMBER,
PRAGMA RESTRICT_REFERENCES(AGE, WNDS)));
/
```

> **NOTE**
> *You cannot drop or re-create a type that is in use by a table. Therefore, it is critical that you make this modification before creating a table that uses the ANIMAL_TY datatype.*

The following line

```
PRAGMA RESTRICT_REFERENCES(AGE, WNDS));
```

tells Oracle that the AGE function operates in the Write No Database State—it cannot modify the database. Other available restrictions are Read No Database

State (RNDS—no queries performed), Write No Package State (WNPS—no values of packaged variables are changed), and Read No Package State (RNPS—no values of packaged variables are referenced).

You can now use the AGE function within a query. If ANIMAL_TY is used as the datatype for a column named Animal in the table named ANIMAL, then the table structure could be as follows:

```
create table ANIMAL
(ID      NUMBER,
 Animal  ANIMAL_TY);

insert into ANIMAL values
(11,ANIMAL_TY('COW','MIMI',TO_DATE('01-JAN-1997','DD-MON-YYYY')));
```

You can now invoke the AGE function, which is part of the ANIMAL_TY datatype. Like the attributes of an abstract datatype, the member methods are referenced via the column names that use the datatypes (in this case, Animal.AGE):

```
select A.Animal.AGE(A.Animal.BirthDate)
   from ANIMAL A;

A.ANIMAL.AGE(A.ANIMAL.BIRTHDATE)
--------------------------------
                            1034
```

The A.Animal.AGE(A.Animal.BirthDate) call executes the AGE method within the ANIMAL_TY datatype. Therefore, you do not have to store variable data such as age within your database. Instead, you can store static data—such as birthdate—in your database and use function and procedure calls to derive the variable data.

NOTE
In this example, you need to use correlation variables in two places—when calling the AGE method and when passing the name of the Birthdate column to that method.

Managing Methods

You can add new methods to a datatype by altering the datatype (via the **alter type** command). When altering a datatype, list all of its methods, both the old and the new. After altering the datatype, alter the datatype's body, listing all of the datatype's methods in a single command.

You do not need to grant EXECUTE privilege on the member functions and procedures of abstract datatypes. If you grant another user EXECUTE privilege on the ANIMAL_TY datatype, that user automatically has EXECUTE privilege on the methods that are part of the datatype. Thus, the grant of access to the datatype includes both the data representation and its data access methods, in accordance with OO concepts.

When creating member functions, you can specify them as being map methods or order methods (or neither, as in the case of the ANIMAL_TY.Age member function). A *map method* returns the relative position of a given record in the ordering of all records within the object. A type body can contain only one map method, which must be a function.

An *order method* is a member function that takes a record in the object as an explicit argument and returns an integer value. If the returned value is negative, zero, or positive, the implicit "self" argument of the function is less than, equal to, or greater than, respectively, that of the explicitly specified record. When multiple rows within an object are compared in an **order by** clause, the order method is automatically executed to order the rows returned. A datatype specification can contain only one order method, which must be a function with the return type INTEGER.

The notion of ordering within the rows of an abstract datatype may have more relevance when you consider the implementation of *collectors*—datatypes that hold multiple values per row. Oracle offers two types of collectors, called *nested tables* and *varying arrays.* In the next chapter, you will see how to implement these collector types.

CHAPTER
29

Collectors
(Nested Tables and
Varying Arrays)

s described in Chapter 28, you can implement object-relational features such as abstract datatypes and object views in your applications. In this chapter, you will see how to use *collectors*—sets of elements that are treated as part of a single row. The two types of collectors available are *nested tables* and *varying arrays*. This chapter explains the differences between these two types of collectors, as well as how to implement and manage them.

Collectors make use of abstract datatypes. You should be familiar with the creation and implementation of abstract datatypes (see Chapters 4 and 28) before attempting to use varying arrays and nested tables.

Varying Arrays

A varying array allows you to store repeating attributes of a record in a single row. For example, suppose Dora Talbot wants to track which of her tools were borrowed by which of her workers. You could model this in a relational database by creating a BORROWER table:

```
create table BORROWER
(Name              VARCHAR2(25),
 Tool              VARCHAR2(25),
constraint BORROWER_PK primary key (Name, Tool));
```

The primary key of the BORROWER table is the combination of the Name column and the Tool column. Thus, if a single worker borrowed three tools, the worker's name would be repeated in each of the three records.

Even though the worker's Name value does not change, it is repeated in each record because it is part of the primary key. Collectors such as varying arrays allow you to repeat *only* those column values that change, potentially saving storage space. You can use collectors to accurately represent relationships between datatypes in your database objects. In the following sections, you will see how to create and use collectors.

Creating a Varying Array

You can create a varying array based on either an abstract datatype or one of Oracle's standard datatypes (such as NUMBER). For example, you could create a new datatype, TOOL_TY, as shown in the following listing, which has only one column; you should limit varying arrays to one column. If you need to use multiple columns in an array, consider using nested tables (described later in this chapter).

```
create type TOOL_TY as object
(ToolName  VARCHAR2(25));
/
```

The TOOL_TY abstract datatype has one attribute: ToolName. To use this datatype as part of a varying array in a BORROWER table, you need to decide what will be the maximum number of tools per borrower. For this example, assume that you will loan out no more than five tools per borrower.

You do not have to create the base type—in this case, TOOL_TY—before you can create a varying array (to be named TOOLS_VA). Since the varying array is based on only one column, you can create the TOOLS_VA type in a single step. To create the varying array, use the **as varray()** clause of the **create type** command:

```
create or replace type TOOLS_VA as varray(5) of VARCHAR2(25);
/
```

When this **create type** command is executed, a type named TOOLS_VA is created. The **as varray(5)** clause tells Oracle that a varying array is being created, and it will hold a maximum of five entries per record. The name of the varying array is pluralized—TOOLS instead of TOOL—to show that this type will be used to hold multiple records. The suffix VA makes it clear that the type is a varying array.

Now that you have created the varying array TOOLS_VA, you can use that as part of the creation of either a table or an abstract datatype. In the following listing, the BORROWER table is created using the TOOLS_VA varying array as a datatype for its Tool column:

```
create table BORROWER
(Name            VARCHAR2(25),
 Tools           TOOLS_VA,
constraint BORROWER_PK primary key (Name));
```

In the BORROWER table, the column name that uses the varying array, Tools, is pluralized to indicate that it may contain multiple values per BORROWER record. The Name column is the primary key of the BORROWER table, so it will not be repeated for each new tool borrowed.

Describing the Varying Array

The BORROWER table will contain one record for each borrower, even if that borrower has multiple tools. The multiple tools will be stored in the Tools column, using the TOOLS_VA varying array. You can describe the BORROWER table as follows:

```
desc BORROWER
```

Name	Null?	Type
NAME	NOT NULL	VARCHAR2(25)
TOOLS		TOOLS_VA

You can also use the USER_TAB_COLUMNS data dictionary view to see information about the structure of the Tools column:

```
select Column_Name,
       Data_Type
  from USER_TAB_COLUMNS
 where Table_Name = 'BORROWER';
```

```
COLUMN_NAME                              DATA_TYPE
------------------------------           ------------------------------
NAME                                     VARCHAR2
TOOLS                                    TOOLS_VA
```

From the USER_TAB_COLUMNS output, you can see that the Tools column uses the TOOLS_VA varying array as its datatype. What kind of datatype is TOOLS_VA? You can query the USER_TYPES data dictionary view to see the datatypes:

```
select TypeCode,
       Attributes
  from USER_TYPES
 where Type_Name = 'TOOLS_VA';
```

```
TYPECODE                                 ATTRIBUTES
------------------------------           ----------
COLLECTION                                        0
```

The USER_TYPE output shows that TOOLS_VA is a collector, with no attributes.

Since TOOLS_VA is a collector, there may be an upper limit to the number of entries it can contain per record. You can query the USER_COLL_TYPES data dictionary view to see the characteristics of the varying array, including the abstract datatype on which it is based:

```
select Coll_Type,
       Elem_Type_Owner,
       Elem_Type_Name,
       Upper_Bound,
       Length
  from USER_COLL_TYPES
 where Type_Name = 'TOOLS_VA';
```

```
COLL_TYPE                                ELEM_TYPE_OWNER
------------------------------           ------------------------------
ELEM_TYPE_NAME                           UPPER_BOUND    LENGTH
------------------------------           -----------    ----------
VARYING ARRAY
VARCHAR2                                            5            25
```

NOTE
If you base a varying array on an existing abstract datatype, then the datatype's owner will be displayed in the Elem_Type_Owner column, and the datatype's name will be displayed in the Elem_Type_Name column. Since TOOLS_VA uses VARCHAR2 instead of an abstract datatype, the Elem_Type_Owner column's value is **NULL**.

From the queries of the data dictionary, you can see that the BORROWER.Tools column uses the TOOLS_VA varying array, and that the array contains a maximum of five values whose structure is defined as VARCHAR2(25). You need to know this information to be able to **insert** records into the BORROWER table. If the varying array were based on an abstract datatype, you could query the USER_TYPE_ATTRS data dictionary view to determine which attributes are part of the abstract datatype. The structure of the datatypes within the varying array determines the syntax that is required when inserting data into the BORROWER table.

Inserting Records into the Varying Array

When a datatype is created, the database automatically creates a method called a *constructor method* for the datatype. As shown in Chapter 28, you need to use the constructor method when inserting records into columns that use an abstract datatype. Since a varying array is an abstract datatype, you need to use constructor methods to **insert** records into tables that use varying arrays. Furthermore, since the varying array is itself an abstract datatype, you may need to nest calls to multiple constructor methods to **insert** a record into a table that uses a varying array.

The columns of the BORROWER table are Name and Tools, the last of which is a varying array using the TOOLS_VA datatype. The following command will **insert** a single record into the BORROWER table. In this example, the record will have a single Name column value and three Tools values.

```
insert into BORROWER values
('JED HOPKINS',
   TOOLS_VA('HAMMER','SLEDGE','AX'));
```

This **insert** command first specifies the value for the Name column. Because the Name column is not part of any abstract datatype, it is populated in the same way as you would **insert** values into any relational table:

```
insert into BORROWER values
('JED HOPKINS',
```

The next part of the **insert** command inserts records into the Tools column. Because the Tools column uses the TOOLS_VA varying array, you need to use the TOOLS_VA constructor method:

```
TOOLS_VA('HAMMER','SLEDGE','AX'));
```

Since this is a varying array, you can pass multiple values to the TOOLS_VA constructor method. That is what is shown in the preceding example; for the single worker name, three tools are listed in the single **insert**. If the varying array had been based on the TOOL_TY datatype, then you would have instead nested calls to the TOOL_TY datatype within the TOOLS_VA execution:

```
insert into BORROWER values
('JED HOPKINS',
   TOOLS_VA(
      TOOL_TY('HAMMER'),
      TOOL_TY('SLEDGE'),
      TOOL_TY('AX')));
```

Basing the varying array on a standard datatype (such as VARCHAR2 or NUMBER) instead of an abstract datatype thus simplifies the **insert** command by eliminating the nesting of calls to additional constructor methods.

The TOOLS_VA varying array was defined to have up to five values. In this **insert** command, only three values were entered for the row; the other two are uninitialized. If you wish to set the uninitialized values to **NULL**, then you can specify that in the **insert** command:

```
insert into BORROWER values
('JED HOPKINS',
   TOOLS_VA('HAMMER','SLEDGE','AX',NULL,NULL));
```

If you specify too many values to insert into the varying array, you will get this error:

```
ORA-22909: exceeded maximum VARRAY limit
```

You cannot insert records into a table that contains a varying array unless you know the structure of the datatypes within the array. This example assumed that all the datatypes used by the BORROWER table are within the schema that is used to create the BORROWER table. If the datatypes are owned by a separate schema, the creator of the BORROWER table will need EXECUTE privilege on those datatypes. During inserts, the creator of the BORROWER table needs to explicitly specify the owners of the datatypes. See Chapter 28 for examples of using datatypes owned by other schemas.

Selecting Data from Varying Arrays

When you insert records into a varying array, you need to make sure that the number of entries you insert does not exceed the varying array's maximum. The maximum number of entries is specified when the varying array is created, and can be queried from USER_COLL_TYPES, as shown in the previous section of this chapter.

You can query the varying array to determine its maximum number of entries per row, called its LIMIT, and the current number of entries per row, called its COUNT. However, this query cannot be performed directly, via a SQL **select** command. To retrieve the COUNT and LIMIT from a varying array, you need to use PL/SQL. You can use a set of nested loops, as shown in the next listing.

NOTE
For an overview of PL/SQL and Cursor
FOR loops, see Chapter 25.

```
set serveroutput on
declare
    cursor borrower_cursor is
      select * from BORROWER;
begin
    for borrower_rec in borrower_cursor
    loop
      dbms_output.put_line('Contact Name: '||borrower_rec.Name);
      for i in 1..borrower_rec.Tools.Count
      loop
        dbms_output.put_line(borrower_rec.Tools(i));
      end loop;
    end loop;
end;
/
```

The following is the output of this PL/SQL script:

```
Contact Name: JED HOPKINS
HAMMER
SLEDGE
AX

PL/SQL procedure successfully completed.
```

The script uses several PL/SQL features to retrieve the data from the varying array. The data will be displayed via the PUT_LINE procedure of the DBMS_OUTPUT package (see Chapter 27), so you must first enable PL/SQL output to be displayed, as shown next.

```
set serveroutput on
```

In the Declarations section of the PL/SQL block, a cursor is declared; the cursor's query selects all the values from the BORROWER table:

```
declare
    cursor borrower_cursor is
      select * from BORROWER;
```

The Executable Commands section of the PL/SQL block contains two nested FOR loops. In the first loop, each record from the cursor is evaluated, and the Name value is printed via the PUT_LINE procedure:

```
begin
    for borrower_rec in borrower_cursor
    loop
      dbms_output.put_line('Contact Name: '||borrower_rec.Name);
```

NOTE
*You can only print character data via PUT_LINE. Therefore, you may need to use the **TO_CHAR** function on numeric data before printing it via PUT_LINE.*

In the next section of the PL/SQL block, the rows are evaluated further to retrieve the data stored in the varying array. A second FOR loop, nested within the earlier loop, is executed. The FOR loop is limited by the number of values in the array, as defined by the **COUNT** method (the maximum number of values in the array is available via a method named **LIMIT**).

The values in the Tools array will be printed, one by one, by this loop:

```
    for i in 1..borrower_rec.Tools.Count
     loop
       dbms_output.put_line(borrower_rec.Tools(i));
```

The notation

```
Tools(i)
```

tells Oracle to print the array value that corresponds to the value of *i*. Thus, the first time through the loop, the first value in the array is printed; then the value of *i* is incremented, and the second value in the array is printed.

The last part of the PL/SQL block closes the two nested loops and ends the block:

```
   end loop;
   end loop;
end;
/
```

Because it involves nested loops within PL/SQL, this method of selecting data from varying arrays is not trivial.

You can use the **table** function in the **from** clause to simplify the process of selecting data from varying arrays. Consider the following query and its output:

```
select B.Name, N.*
   from BORROWER B, Table(B.Tools) N;

NAME                       COLUMN_VALUE
-----------------------    -------------------------
JED HOPKINS                HAMMER
JED HOPKINS                SLEDGE
JED HOPKINS                AX
```

How did that work? The **table** clause took as its input the name of the varying array, and its output is given the alias *N*. The values within *N* are selected, which generates the second column of the output. This method is simpler than the PL/SQL method, but it has the potential to be much more confusing.

For greater flexibility in selecting data from collectors, you should consider the use of nested tables, as described in the next section.

Nested Tables

Whereas varying arrays have a limited number of entries, a second type of collector, *nested tables,* has no limit on the number of entries per row. A nested table is, as its name implies, a table within a table. In this case, it is a table that is represented as a column within another table. You can have multiple rows in the nested table for each row in the main table.

For example, if you have a table of animal breeders, you may also have data about their animals. Using a nested table, you could store the information about breeders and all of their animals within the same table. Consider the ANIMAL_TY datatype introduced in Chapter 28:

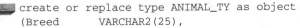

```
create or replace type ANIMAL_TY as object
(Breed        VARCHAR2(25),
```

```
Name         VARCHAR2(25),
BirthDate    DATE);
```

NOTE
*To keep this example simple, this version
of the ANIMAL_TY datatype does not include
any methods.*

The ANIMAL_TY datatype contains a record for each animal—its breed, name, and birthdate. To use this datatype as the basis for a nested table, you need to create a new abstract datatype:

```
create type ANIMALS_NT as table of ANIMAL_TY;
/
```

The **as table of** clause of this **create type** command tells Oracle that you will be using this type as the basis for a nested table. The name of the type, ANIMALS_NT, has a pluralized root to indicate that it stores multiple rows, and has the suffix NT to indicate that it will be a nested table.

You can now create a table of breeders, using the ANIMALS_NT datatype:

```
create table BREEDER
(BreederName      VARCHAR2(25),
 Animals          ANIMALS_NT)
 nested table ANIMALS store as ANIMALS_NT_TAB;
```

In this **create table** command, the BREEDER table is created. The first column of the BREEDER table is a Breeder Name column. The second column is a column named Animals, whose definition is the nested table ANIMALS_NT:

```
create table BREEDER
(Breeder Name     VARCHAR2(25),
 Animals          ANIMALS_NT);
```

When creating a table that includes a nested table, you must specify the name of the table that will be used to store the nested table's data. That is, the data for the nested table is not stored "inline" with the rest of the table's data. Instead, it is stored apart from the main table. Thus, the data in the Animals column will be stored in one table, and the data in the Name column will be stored in a separate table. Oracle will maintain pointers between the tables. In this example, the "out-of-line" data for the nested table is stored in a table named ANIMALS_NT_TAB:

```
nested table ANIMALS store as ANIMALS_NT_TAB;
```

This example highlights the importance of naming standards for collectors. If you pluralize the column names ("Animals" instead of "Animal") and consistently use suffixes (TY, NT, and so forth), you can tell what an object is just by looking at its name. Furthermore, since nested tables and varying arrays may be based directly on previously defined datatypes, their names may mirror the names of the datatypes on which they are based. Thus, a datatype named ANIMAL_TY could be used as the basis for a varying array named ANIMALS_VA or a nested table named ANIMALS_NT. The nested table would have an associated out-of-line table named ANIMALS_NT_TAB. If you know that a table named ANIMALS_NT_TAB exists, you automatically know that it stores data based on a datatype named ANIMAL_TY.

Inserting Records into a Nested Table

You can **insert** records into a nested table by using the constructor methods for its datatype. For the Animals column, the datatype is ANIMALS_NT; thus, you will use the ANIMALS_NT constructor method. The ANIMALS_NT type, in turn, uses the ANIMAL_TY datatype. As shown in the following example, inserting a record into the BREEDER table requires you to use both the ANIMALS_NT and ANIMAL_TY constructor methods. In the example, three animals are listed for the breeder named Jane James.

```
insert into BREEDER values
('JANE JAMES',
  ANIMALS_NT(
          ANIMAL_TY('DOG', 'BUTCH', '31-MAR-97'),
          ANIMAL_TY('DOG', 'ROVER', '05-JUN-97'),
          ANIMAL_TY('DOG', 'JULIO', '10-JUN-97')
));
```

This **insert** command first specifies the name of the breeder:

```
insert into BREEDER values
('JANE JAMES',
```

Next, the value for the Animals column must be entered. Since the Animals column uses the ANIMALS_NT nested table, the ANIMALS_NT constructor method is invoked in this line:

```
  ANIMALS_NT(
```

The ANIMALS_NT nested table uses the ANIMAL_TY datatype, so the ANIMAL_TY constructor method is invoked for each record inserted:

```
        ANIMAL_TY('DOG', 'BUTCH', '31-MAR-97'),
        ANIMAL_TY('DOG', 'ROVER', '05-JUN-97'),
        ANIMAL_TY('DOG', 'JULIO', '10-JUN-97')
```

The final two parentheses complete the command, closing the call to the ANIMALS_NT constructor method and closing the list of **insert**ed values:

```
));
```

If you do not already know the datatype structure of the table, you need to query the data dictionary before you can query the table. First, describe BREEDER or query USER_TAB_COLUMNS to see the definitions of the columns:

```
select Column_Name,
       Data_Type
  from USER_TAB_COLUMNS
 where Table_Name = 'BREEDER';

COLUMN_NAME                           DATA_TYPE
-----------------------------------   -------------------------
BREEDERNAME                           VARCHAR2
ANIMALS                               ANIMALS_NT
```

The USER_TAB_COLUMNS output shows that the Animals column uses the ANIMALS_NT datatype. To verify that the ANIMALS_NT datatype is a collector, check USER_TYPES:

```
select TypeCode,
       Attributes
  from USER_TYPES
 where Type_Name = 'ANIMALS_NT';

TYPECODE                        ATTRIBUTES
------------------------------  ----------
COLLECTION                               0
```

To see the datatype used as the basis for the nested table, query USER_COLL_TYPES:

```
select Coll_Type,
       Elem_Type_Owner,
       Elem_Type_Name,
       Upper_Bound,
```

```
        Length
  from USER_COLL_TYPES
 where Type_Name = 'ANIMALS_NT';


COLL_TYPE                         ELEM_TYPE_OWNER
-----------------------------     -------------------------
ELEM_TYPE_NAME                    UPPER_BOUND     LENGTH
-----------------------------     -----------  ----------
TABLE                             TALBOT
ANIMAL_TY
```

The output from USER_COLL_TYPES shows that the ANIMALS_NT nested table is based on the ANIMAL_TY abstract datatype. You can query USER_TYPE_ATTRS to see the attributes of ANIMAL_TY:

```
select Attr_Name,
       Length,
       Attr_Type_Name
  from USER_TYPE_ATTRS
 where Type_Name = 'ANIMAL_TY';


ATTR_NAME                         LENGTH ATTR_TYPE_NAME
-----------------------------     ---------- ----------------
BREED                                 25 VARCHAR2
NAME                                  25 VARCHAR2
BIRTHDATE                                DATE
```

Thus, you can use the data dictionary views to determine the datatype structure of nested tables. You need to know the datatype structures and the nested table structures to effectively use the BREEDER table. In the next section, you will see how to query data from a nested table. Unlike varying arrays, queries of nested tables are not limited to PL/SQL; however, to query nested tables, you need to be familiar with several extensions to SQL.

Querying Nested Tables

Nested tables support a great variety of queries. A nested table is a column within a table. To support queries of the columns and rows of a nested table, Oracle provides a special keyword, **THE**. To see how the **THE** keyword is used, first consider the nested table by itself. If it were a normal column of a relational table, you would be able to query it via a normal **select** command:

```
select BirthDate   /* This won't work.*/
  from ANIMALS_NT
 where Name = 'JULIO';
```

ANIMALS_NT is not a normal table; it's a datatype. To select columns (such as BirthDate) from the nested table, you first have to "flatten" the table so that it can be queried. That's where the **THE** function is used. First, select the nested table column from the main table:

```
select Animals
   from BREEDER
  where BreederName = 'JANE JAMES'
```

Next, enclose this query within the **THE** function:

```
THE(select Animals
       from BREEDER
      where BreederName = 'JANE JAMES')
```

Now, you can query the nested table's columns, using the clause in the preceding listing as the *table name* in the query's **from** clause:

```
select NT.BirthDate
   from THE(select Animals
               from BREEDER
              where BreederName = 'JANE JAMES') NT
  where NT.Name = 'JULIO';

BIRTHDATE
---------
10-JUN-97
```

The **THE** function flattens the query of the nested table and allows you to query the entire BREEDER table. The **from** clause contains the query of the nested table column, and the resulting "table" is given the alias NT:

```
  from THE(select Animals
              from BREEDER
             where Breeder_Name = 'JANE JAMES') NT
```

The **where** clause of the query specifies limiting conditions for the query:

```
where NT.Name = 'JULIO';
```

The column list in the query specifies the nested table columns to display:

```
select NT.BirthDate
```

Thus, you can apply limiting criteria both to values within the nested table (the animal's name) and to values within the main table (the breeder's name).

You can also use the **table** function to query a nested table:

```
select NT.Birthdate
   from BREEDER B, table(B.Animals) NT
 where BreederName = 'JANE JAMES'
   and NT.Name = 'JULIO'


BIRTHDATE
---------
10-JUN-97
```

What's going on in this query? As shown in the varying array example earlier in this chapter, the **table** clause in the **from** clause takes the name of the collector—in this case, the Animals column of the BREEDER table—as its input. It flattens the nested table, allowing you to select columns from it (such as NT.Birthdate) and apply **where** clauses. You can use the **table** clause as shown in this example, but be sure to document your use of it, for the benefit of others who may be maintaining the code at a later date.

Further Uses of the THE Function and table Clause

You can use the **THE** function whenever you need to perform **insert**s or **update**s directly against the nested table. For example, a breeder likely will have more animals as time goes by, so you need the ability to add new records to the ANIMALS_NT nested table within the BREEDER table. You will have to **insert** records into the nested table without adding new records into the BREEDER table, and you will need to relate the new Animal records to breeders who are already in the BREEDER table.

Consider the following **insert** statement:

```
insert into
  THE(select Animals
           from BREEDER
          where BreederName = 'JANE JAMES')
values
(ANIMAL_TY('DOG', 'MARCUS', '01-AUG-97'));
```

The **THE** function in this example is used in place of the table name. The clause

```
THE(select Animals
           from BREEDER
          where BreederName = 'JANE JAMES')
```

selects the nested table from within the main BREEDER table for the row in which the BreederName column has the value JANE JAMES. You **insert** directly into the nested table using the constructor method for the nested table's datatype (ANIMAL_TY):

```
values
(ANIMAL_TY('DOG', 'MARCUS', '01-AUG-97'));
```

Rewriting this to use the **table** clause, you can use the **table** clause in place of the **THE** function, as shown here:

```
insert into table(select Animals
                      from BREEDER
                     where BreederName = 'JANE JAMES')
values
(ANIMAL_TY('DOG','MARCUS','01-AUG-97'))
```

Performing Inserts Based on Queries

In the examples of using the **THE** function, the purpose of the queries and data manipulation language (DML) operations was to manipulate the data within the nested table. If you are trying to deal with the main table, then you need to take a slightly different approach in your queries.

For example, what if you need to perform an **insert as select** involving only the nested table portion of the BREEDER table? That is, you will be inserting a new record into BREEDER, but the nested table values will be based on values already entered for another record. The breeder named Jane James has decided to bring another person (Joan Thomas) into her business, and you want to enter the new breeder's information into your BREEDER table.

You could try just inserting values into the table:

```
insert into BREEDER values
('JOAN THOMAS'...
```

but you cannot directly embed **select** (for the nested table values) within this **insert**. You could try to embed the new breeder name value within a query of the nested table (using the **THE** function to query the nested table):

```
insert into BREEDER
select 'JOAN THOMAS', NT.Breed, NT.Name, NT.BirthDate
  from THE(select Animals
             from BREEDER
            where BreederName = 'JANE JAMES') NT;
```

but this will fail, too, because too many values are supplied; the BREEDER table only has two columns. Even though one of the columns is a nested table, you cannot directly **insert** into its columns in this manner.

To solve this problem, Oracle introduces two keywords: **cast** and **multiset**. The **cast** keyword allows you to "cast" the result of a query as a nested table. The **multiset** keyword allows the cast query to contain multiple records. You use **cast** and **multiset** together, as shown in the following example, in which the inserted BREEDER record is corrected to use the **cast** and **multiset** keywords:

```
insert into BREEDER values
('JOAN THOMAS',
   cast(multiset(
          select *
            from THE(select Animals from BREEDER
                      where BreederName = 'JANE JAMES'))
        as ANIMALS_NT));
```

Did the **insert** work properly? You can query the BREEDER table to see the animals in the nested table of the JOAN THOMAS record:

```
select NT.Name
   from THE(select Animals
              from BREEDER
              where BreederName = 'JOAN THOMAS') NT;

NAME
-------------------------
BUTCH
ROVER
JULIO
MARCUS
```

The record for Joan Thomas has been successfully inserted, and all of the nested table (Animals column) entries for Jane James have been created as values for Joan Thomas, as well. How did this **insert** command work? First, it listed the new value for the BreederName column—the value that was part of the main table and was not being selected from an existing nested table:

```
insert into BREEDER values
('JOAN THOMAS',
```

Next, the subquery had to be executed against the nested table. The rows we wanted were the Animals column values for which the breeder was Jane James. If the nested table were a relational (flat) table, the query would be as follows:

```
select Animals from BREEDER
  where BreederName = 'JANE JAMES';
```

Since Animals is a nested table, we had to use the **THE** function and **select** from the nested table as part of the **from** clause of a query:

```
select *
    from THE(select Animals from BREEDER
             where BreederName = 'JANE JAMES')
```

Since we used the nested table values as part of an **insert** into a main table, we needed to use the **cast** and **multiset** keywords to cast the results of this query as a nested table:

```
cast(multiset(
            select *
              from THE(select Animals from BREEDER
                       where BreederName = 'JANE JAMES'))
        as ANIMALS_NT));
```

Note that the result of the nested table query of the Animals column is cast as ANIMALS_NT—the nested table datatype that was used to define the Animals column. The combined **insert** command, shown next, is an example of the power of nested tables. You can query and perform data manipulation commands directly against the nested table values, or you can use them as part of commands that operate on the main tables. To effectively use nested tables in your SQL, you should be familiar with the use of **THE**, **cast**, and **multiset**. In the next section, you will see additional management issues related to the use of nested tables and varying arrays.

```
insert into BREEDER values
('JOAN THOMAS',
  cast(multiset(
            select *
              from THE(select Animals from BREEDER
                       where BreederName = 'JANE JAMES'))
        as ANIMALS_NT));
```

Management Issues for Nested Tables and Varying Arrays

The administrative tasks required for nested tables and varying arrays have several differences, which are demonstrated in the following sections, along with advice on which collector type may best meet your criteria.

Managing Large Collections

When storing data that is related to a table, you can choose one of three methods: a varying array, a nested table, or a separate table. If you have a limited number of rows, a varying array may be appropriate. As the number of rows increases, however, you may begin to encounter performance problems while accessing the varying array. These problems may be caused by a characteristic of varying arrays: they cannot be indexed. Relational tables, however, can be indexed. As a result, the performance of a collector may worsen as it grows in size. Also, when new Oracle features are first introduced, they may not support collectors—transportable tablespaces, for example, cannot include varying arrays.

Varying arrays are further burdened by the difficulty in querying data from them. If varying arrays are not a good solution for a large set of related records, which alternative should you use: a nested table or a separate relational table? It depends. Nested tables and relational tables serve different purposes, so your answer depends on what you are trying to do with the data. The key differences are as follows:

■ Nested tables are abstract datatypes, created via the **create type** command. Therefore, they can have methods associated with them. If you plan to attach methods to the data, then you should use nested tables instead of relational tables. Alternatively, you could consider using object views with methods, as described in Chapter 28.

■ Relational tables are easily related to other relational tables. If the data may be related to many other tables, then it may be best not to nest the data within one table. Storing it in its own table will give you the greatest flexibility in managing the data relationships.

Although the name of the nested table (such as ANIMALS_NT_TAB) is specified during creation, you cannot perform all normal table-related functions on it. When you use a collector to store data, it is not stored in a table that you can manipulate the way you treat a relational table. If you want to treat the table as a relational table, you must create it as a relational table via the **create table** command, not as a nested table within another table.

Variability in Collectors

As noted in Chapter 4, abstract datatypes can help you to enforce standards within your database. However, you may not be able to realize the same standardization benefits when you are using collectors. Consider the TOOLS_VA varying array shown earlier in this chapter. If another application or table wants to use a TOOLS_VA varying array, that application must use the same definition for the array—including the same maximum number of values. However, the new application may have a different value for the maximum number of tools. Thus, the array must be altered to support the greatest possible number of values it may contain in any of its implementations. As a result, the usefulness of the array's limiting powers may diminish. To support multiple array limits, you would need to create multiple arrays—eliminating any object reuse benefits you may have received from creating the varying arrays. You would then need to manage the different array limits and know what the limit is in each array.

You may also find that multiple nested tables are similar, with a difference in only one or two columns. You may be tempted to create a single, all-inclusive nested table type that is used in multiple tables, but that table would also encounter management problems. You would need to know which columns of the nested table were valid for which implementations. If you cannot use the same column structure, with the same meaning and relevance of the columns in each instance, then you should not use a shared nested table datatype. If you want to use nested tables in that environment, you should create a separate nested table datatype for each instance in which you will use the nested table, and manage them all separately. Having multiple nested table datatypes will complicate the management of the database.

Location of the Data

In a varying array, the data in the array is stored with the rest of the data in the table. In nested tables, however, the data may be stored out-of-line. As a result, the amount of data scanned during queries that do not involve the collector data may be less for a nested table than for a varying array. That is, during a query, the database will not need to read through the data in the nested table; if a varying array is used, then the database may need to read through the varying array's data to find the data it needs. Out-of-line data, as used by nested tables, can improve the performance of queries.

Out-of-line collector data mimics the way the data would be stored in a normal relational database application. For example, in a relational application, you would store related data (such as workers and skills) in separate tables, and the tables would be physically stored apart. Out-of-line nested tables store their data apart from the main table but maintain a relationship with the main table. Out-of-line data may improve the performance of queries by distributing across multiple tables the I/O performed against the table.

Out-of-line data is also used to store the large objects (LOBs) that are stored internally. In the next chapter, you will see how to create and manipulate LOB values up to 4GB in length. The combination of abstract datatypes, object views, collectors, and LOBs provides a strong foundation for the implementation of an object-relational database application. In Chapter 31, you will see how to extend these objects further toward the creation of an object-oriented database.

CHAPTER
30

Using Large Objects

ou can use a LONG datatype to store character data up to 2GB in length per row; the LONG RAW datatype provides storage for long binary data. You can use the LOB datatypes (BLOB, CLOB, NCLOB, and BFILE) for storage of long data. If you use one of these datatypes to store large objects (LOBs), you can take advantage of new capabilities for viewing and manipulating the data. In this chapter, you will see how to use the LOB datatypes and how to manipulate the long data—which does not even have to be stored within the database!

Available Datatypes

Four types of LOBs are supported. The datatypes and their descriptions are shown in Table 30-1.

You can create multiple LOBs per table. For example, suppose Dora Talbot wants to create a PROPOSAL table to track formal proposals she submits. Dora's proposal records consist of a series of word processing files and spreadsheets used to document and price the proposed work. The PROPOSAL table will contain VARCHAR2 datatypes (for columns such as the name of the proposal recipient)

LOB Datatype	Description
BLOB	Binary LOB; binary data, up to 4GB in length, stored in the database
CLOB	Character LOB; character data, up to 4GB in length, stored in the database
BFILE	Binary File; read-only binary data stored outside the database, the length of which is limited by the operating system
NCLOB	A CLOB column that supports a multibyte character set

TABLE 30-1. *LOB Datatypes*

plus LOB datatypes (containing the word processing and spreadsheet files). The **create table** command in the following listing creates the PROPOSAL table:

```
create table PROPOSAL
(Proposal_ID        NUMBER(10),
 Recipient_Name     VARCHAR2(25),
 Proposal_Name      VARCHAR2(25),
 Short_Description  VARCHAR2(1000),
 Proposal_Text      CLOB,
 Budget             BLOB,
 Cover_Letter       BFILE,
constraint PROPOSAL_PK primary key (Proposal_ID));
```

Since Dora may submit multiple proposals to the same recipient, she assigns each proposal a Proposal_ID number. For each proposal, she stores the recipient of the proposal, the name of the proposal, and a short description. Then, taking advantage of the LOB datatypes available in Oracle, she adds three additional columns:

Proposal_Text	A CLOB containing the text of the proposal
Budget	A BLOB containing a spreadsheet showing Dora's calculations of the cost and profit for the proposed work
Cover_Letter	A binary file stored outside the database that contains Dora's cover letter that accompanies the proposal

Thus, each row in the PROPOSAL table will have up to three LOB values stored. Oracle will use the normal database capabilities to support data integrity and concurrency for the Proposal and Budget entries, but not for the Cover_Letter values. Since the Cover_Letter column uses the BFILE datatype, its data is stored outside the database. Internally, the database stores only a locator value that allows it to find the external file. Oracle does not guarantee the data integrity of BFILE files stored outside the database. Also, Oracle does not validate that the file exists when you insert a record using a BFILE datatype. Data concurrency and integrity are maintained only for internally stored LOBs.

The data for the LOB columns, whether stored inside or outside the database, is not physically stored with the PROPOSAL table. Within the PROPOSAL table,

Oracle stores locator values that point to data locations. For BFILE datatypes, the locator points to an external file; for BLOB and CLOB datatypes, the locator points to a separate data location that the database creates to hold the LOB data. Thus, the LOB data is not necessarily stored directly with the rest of the data in the PROPOSAL table.

Storing the data *out-of-line* like this allows the database to avoid having to scan the LOB data each time it reads multiple rows from the database. The LOB data will only be read when it is required; otherwise, only its locator values will be read. You can specify the storage parameters (tablespace and sizing) for the area used to hold the LOB data, as described in the next section.

Specifying Storage for LOB Data

When you create a table that includes a LOB column, you can specify the storage parameters for the area used for the LOB data. Thus, for a table that has no LOB columns, you would have a **storage** clause in the **create table** command (see Chapter 20). If the table has at least one LOB column, then you also need an additional **lob** clause within your **create table** command.

Consider Dora's PROPOSAL table, this time with **storage** and **tablespace** clauses:

```
create table PROPOSAL
(Proposal_ID          NUMBER(10),
 Recipient_Name       VARCHAR2(25),
 Proposal_Name        VARCHAR2(25),
 Short_Description     VARCHAR2(1000),
 Proposal_Text         CLOB,
 Budget                BLOB,
 Cover_Letter          BFILE,
constraint PROPOSAL_PK primary key (Proposal_ID))
storage (initial 50K next 50K pctincrease 0)
tablespace PROPOSALS;
```

Since there are three LOB columns, the **create table** command should be modified to include the storage specifications for the out-of-line LOB data. Two of the LOB columns—Proposal_Text and Budget—will store data within the database. The revised version of the **create table** command is shown in the following listing:

```
create table PROPOSAL
(Proposal_ID          NUMBER(10),
 Recipient_Name       VARCHAR2(25),
 Proposal_Name        VARCHAR2(25),
 Short_Description     VARCHAR2(1000),
```

```
Proposal_Text        CLOB,
Budget               BLOB,
Cover_Letter         BFILE,
constraint PROPOSAL_PK primary key (Proposal_ID))
storage (initial 50K next 50K pctincrease 0)
tablespace PROPOSALS
lob (Proposal_Text, Budget) store as
(tablespace Proposal_Lobs
     storage (initial 100K next 100K pctincrease 0)
            chunk 16K pctversion 10 nocache logging);
```

The last four lines of the **create table** command tell Oracle how to store the out-of-line LOB data. The instructions are as follows:

```
lob (Proposal_Text, Budget) store as
(tablespace Proposal_Lobs
     storage (initial 100K next 100K pctincrease 0)
            chunk 16K pctversion 10 nocache logging);
```

The **lob** clause tells Oracle that the next set of commands deals with the out-of-line storage specifications for the table's LOB columns. The two LOB columns (Proposal_Text and Budget) are explicitly listed. When the two columns' values are stored out-of-line, they are stored in a segment as specified via the **lob** clause:

```
lob (Proposal_Text, Budget) store as
```

> **NOTE**
> *If there were only one LOB column, you could
> specify a name for the LOB segment. You would
> name the segment immediately after the **store as**
> clause in the preceding command.*

The next two lines specify the tablespace and storage parameters for the out-of-line LOB storage. The **tablespace** clause assigns the out-of-line data to the PROPOSAL_LOBS tablespace, and the **storage** clause is used to specify the **initial**, **next**, and **pctincrease** values the out-of-line data storage will use. See the entry for the **storage** clause in the Alphabetical Reference for an explanation of the available storage parameters for segments.

```
(tablespace Proposal_Lobs
     storage (initial 100K next 100K pctincrease 0)
```

Since the segments are for storing LOB data, several additional parameters are available, and they are specified within the **lob** clause:

```
chunk 16K pctversion 10
```

The **chunk** LOB storage parameter tells Oracle how much space to allocate during each LOB value manipulation. The default **chunk** size is 1K, going up to a maximum value of 32K.

The **pctversion** parameter is the maximum percentage of overall LOB storage space used for creating new versions of the LOB. By default, older versions of the LOB data will not be overwritten until 10 percent of the available LOB storage space is used.

The last two parameters of the LOB storage space tell Oracle how to handle the LOB data during reads and writes:

```
nocache logging);
```

The **nocache** parameter in the **lob** storage clause specifies that the LOB values are not stored in memory for faster access during queries. The default **lob** storage default is **nocache**; its opposite is **cache**.

The **logging** parameter specifies that all operations against the LOB data will be recorded in the database's redo log files. The opposite of **logging**, **nologging**, keeps operations from being recorded in the redo log files, thereby improving the performance of table-creation operations. You can also specify the **tablespace** and **storage** parameters for a LOB index. See the **create table** command entry in the Alphabetical Reference for the full syntax related to LOB indexes.

Now that the table has been created, Dora can begin to enter records into it. In the next section, you will see how to insert LOB values into the PROPOSAL table and how to use the DBMS_LOB package to manipulate the values.

Manipulating and Selecting LOB Values

LOB data can be selected or manipulated in several ways; the usual way of manipulating LOB data is via the DBMS_LOB package. Other methods for manipulating LOB data include using application programming interface (API) and Oracle Call Interface (OCI) programs. In this section, you will see the use of the DBMS_LOB package used for LOB data manipulation. As these examples demonstrate, LOBs are much more flexible than LONG datatypes in terms of data manipulation possibilities. However, they are not as simple to select and manipulate as VARCHAR2 columns are.

Initializing Values

Consider Dora's PROPOSAL table again, as shown in Table 30-2. The Proposal_ID column is the primary key column for the PROPOSAL table. The PROPOSAL table contains three LOB columns—one BLOB column, one CLOB, and one BFILE. For each of the LOB columns, Oracle will store a *locator value* that tells it where to find any out-of-line data stored for the record.

When you insert a record into a table that contains LOBs, you use the DBMS_LOB package to tell Oracle to create an empty locator value for the internally stored LOB columns. An empty locator value is different from a **NULL** value. If an internally stored LOB column's value is **NULL**, then you have to set it to an empty locator value before updating it to a non-**NULL** value.

Suppose that Dora begins to work on a proposal and enters a record in the PROPOSAL table. At this point, she has neither a budget spreadsheet nor a cover letter. The **insert** command she could use is shown in the following listing:

```
insert into PROPOSAL
(Proposal_ID, Recipient_Name, Proposal_Name, Short_Description,
 Proposal_Text,
 Budget, Cover_Letter)
values
(1, 'DOT PHILLIPS', 'CLEAR PHILLIPS FIELD', NULL,
 'This is the text of a proposal to clear Phillips field.',
  EMPTY_BLOB(),NULL);
```

Column Name	Datatype
Proposal_ID	NUMBER(10)
Recipient_Name	VARCHAR2(25)
Proposal_Name	VARCHAR2(25)
Short_Description	VARCHAR2(1000)
Proposal_Text	CLOB
Budget	BLOB
Cover_Letter	BFILE

TABLE 30-2. *Columns Within the PROPOSAL Table*

The inserted record has a Proposal_ID of 1 and a Recipient_Name of DOT PHILLIPS. The Proposal_Name value is CLEAR PHILLIPS FIELD and the Short_Description column is left **NULL** for now. The Proposal_Text column is set equal to a short character string for now—'This is the text of a proposal to clear Phillips field.' To set the Budget column to an empty locator value, the EMPTY_BLOB function is used. If you had wanted to set a CLOB datatype column equal to an empty locator value, then you would have used the EMPTY_CLOB function. The Cover_Letter column, since it is an externally stored BFILE value, is set to **NULL**.

To set an internally stored LOB column to an empty locator value, you have to know its datatype:

BLOB	Use EMPTY_BLOB()
CLOB	Use EMPTY_CLOB()
NCLOB	Use EMPTY_CLOB()

You use the BFILENAME procedure to point to directories and files. Before entering a value for the directory, a user with the DBA role or CREATE ANY DIRECTORY system privilege must create the directory. To create a directory, use the **create directory** command, as shown in the following example:

```
create directory proposal_dir as '/U01/PROPOSAL/LETTERS';
```

When inserting BFILE entries, you refer to the logical directory name—such as proposal_dir—instead of the physical directory name on the operating system. Users with DBA authority can grant READ access to the directory names to users. See the entry for the **create directory** command in the Alphabetical Reference for further details.

You can now enter a second PROPOSAL record; this record will have a Cover_Letter value:

```
insert into PROPOSAL
(Proposal_ID, Recipient_Name, Proposal_Name, Short_Description,
 Proposal_Text, Budget,
Cover_Letter)
values
(2, 'BRAD OHMONT', 'REBUILD FENCE', NULL,
 EMPTY_CLOB(), EMPTY_BLOB(),
 BFILENAME('proposal_dir','P2.DOC'));
```

In this listing, a second proposal—rebuilding a fence—is inserted into the PROPOSAL table. The EMPTY_CLOB() and EMPTY_BLOB() functions are used to insert empty locator values in the table. The BFILENAME function tells Oracle exactly where to find the cover letter—it's in the proposal_dir directory and its name is P2.DOC. Within the BFILENAME function, the first parameter is always the directory name, and the second parameter is the name of the file within that directory.

When you select the value from a LOB column, Oracle uses the locator value to find the data that is associated with the LOB data. You never need to know or specify the locator values. And, as you'll see in the following sections, you can do things with LOB values that are impossible to do with LONG datatypes.

insert with Subqueries

What if you want to duplicate a proposal record? For example, suppose Dora Talbot begins to work on a third proposal, and it is very similar to her first proposal:

```
insert into PROPOSAL
(Proposal_ID, Recipient_Name, Proposal_Name, Short_Description,
 Proposal_Text, Budget, Cover_Letter)
select 3, 'SKIP GATES', 'CLEAR GATES FIELD', NULL,
          Proposal_Text, Budget, Cover_Letter
  from PROPOSAL
 where Proposal_ID = 1;
```

This **insert** command tells Oracle to find the PROPOSAL record with a Proposal_ID value of 1. Take the Proposal_Text, Budget, and Cover_Letter column values and the literal values specified (3, SKIP GATES, and so forth) and insert a new record into the PROPOSAL table. Note that the selected columns include LOB columns! If the LOB columns contain empty locator values, the inserted columns will be set to empty locator values. The ability to perform **insert**s based on queries is a significant advantage of using LOB datatypes—you cannot perform this type of **insert** if a LONG column is part of the query.

NOTE
*If you use **insert as select** to populate LOB values, you may have multiple BFILE values pointing to the same external file. You may need to **update** the new values to point to the correct external files. Oracle does not maintain data integrity for the external files.*

Updating LOB Values

In the third record that was created, the Proposal_Text value was copied from the first record. If Dora wants to update the Proposal_Text value of the record that has a Proposal_ID of 3, she can execute the following command:

```
update PROPOSAL
   set Proposal_Text = 'This is the new proposal text.'
 where Proposal_ID = 3;
```

She can also **update** the Cover_Letter column to point to the correct cover letter. She can use the BFILENAME function to point to the correct file:

```
update PROPOSAL
   set Cover_Letter = BFILENAME('proposal_dir', 'P3.DOC')
 where Proposal_ID = 3;
```

You can update **NULL** values of BFILE columns without first setting them to empty locator values. If you had inserted a record with a **NULL** value for Budget (a BLOB column), you could not update the Budget column's value unless you first set its value to EMPTY_BLOB() via an **update** command. After setting the value to EMPTY_BLOB() and establishing an empty locator value, you could then **update** the Budget column value.

Using DBMS_LOB to Manipulate LOB Values

You can use the DBMS_LOB package to change or select LOB values. In the following sections, you will see how to perform SQL functions such as **SUBSTR** and **INSTR** on LOB values, as well as how to append to LOB values, compare LOB values, and read LOB values.

The string comparison and manipulation procedures and functions available within the DBMS_LOB package are listed in Table 30-3. The procedures and functions that select data are listed first, followed by those that manipulate data.

The procedures and functions available within the DBMS_LOB package are described in the following sections in the order. Additional functions that are specific to BFILE datatypes are listed in Table 30-4. When using BFILEs, the maximum number of files you can concurrently have open is limited by the setting of the SESSION_MAX_OPEN_FILES parameter in the database's init.ora file. The default maximum number of concurrently open BFILE files is ten.

Procedure or Function	Description
APPEND	Procedure used to append the contents of one LOB value to another LOB value
COMPARE	Function used to compare two LOB values
COPY	Procedure used to copy all or part of a LOB value from one LOB column to another
CREATETEMPORARY	Procedure used to create a temporary BLOB or CLOB and index in the user's default tablespace
ERASE	Procedure used to erase all or part of a LOB value
FREETEMPORARY	Procedure to free the temporary LOB created via CREATETEMPORARY
GETCHUNKSIZE	Function used to determine the space used in a LOB chunk
GETLENGTH	Function used to perform the SQL LENGTH function on a LOB value
INSTR	Function used to perform the SQL INSTR function on a LOB value
ISOPEN	Function used to determine whether a LOB is already open
ISTEMPORARY	Function used to determine whether a LOB was created via CREATETEMPORARY
OPEN	Procedure used to open a LOB in read-only or read-write mode
READ	Procedure used to read a piece of a LOB value
SUBSTR	Function used to perform the SQL SUBSTR function on a LOB value
TRIM	Procedure used to perform the SQL RTRIM function on a LOB value

TABLE 30-3.   *Procedures and Functions Within the DBMS_LOB Package*

Procedure or Function	Description
WRITE	Procedure used to write data into the LOB value at a specified point within the LOB value
WRITEAPPEND	Procedure used to write data into the LOB value starting at the end of the current value

TABLE 30-3. *Procedures and Functions Within the DBMS_LOB Package (continued)*

Procedure or Function	Description
FILEOPEN	Procedure used to open files for reading
FILECLOSE	Procedure used to close specific files; for every FILEOPEN call, there must be a matching FILECLOSE call
FILECLOSEALL	Procedure used to close all open files
FILEEXISTS	Function used to determine whether the external file referenced by a BFILE locator value exists
FILEGETNAME	Procedure used to get the name of the external file referenced by a BFILE locator value
FILEISOPEN	Function used to determine whether the external file is open
LOADFROMFILE	Procedure used to load data from a BFILE into a BLOB or CLOB datatype

TABLE 30-4. *BFILE-Specific Procedures and Functions Within the DBMS_LOB Package*

In the following examples, the Proposal_Text CLOB column is used to show the impact of the major procedures and functions.

READ

The READ procedure reads a piece of a LOB value. In the PROPOSAL table example, the Proposal_Text for the first row is

```
select Proposal_Text
  from PROPOSAL
 where Proposal_ID = 1;

PROPOSAL_TEXT
----------------------------------------------------------------
This is the text of a proposal to clear Phillips field.
```

This is a fairly short description, so it could have been stored in a VARCHAR2 datatype column. Since it is stored in a CLOB column, though, its maximum length is much greater than it would have been if it had been stored in a VARCHAR2 column—it can expand to 4GB in length. For these examples, we'll use this short string for purposes of demonstration; you can use the same functions and operations against longer CLOB strings, as well.

The READ procedure has four parameters, which must be specified in this order:

1. The LOB locator

2. The number of bytes or characters to be read

3. The offset (starting point of the read) from the beginning of the LOB value

4. The output data from the READ procedure

If the end of the LOB value is reached before the specified number of bytes is read, the READ procedure will return an error.

Because the READ procedure requires the LOB locator as input, the READ procedure is executed within PL/SQL blocks. You will need to select the LOB locator value, provide that as input to the READ procedure, and then display the text read via the DBMS_OUTPUT package.

A WORD ABOUT THE DBMS_OUTPUT PACKAGE   As noted in Chapter 27, you can use the DBMS_OUTPUT package to display the values of variables within a PL/SQL block. The PUT_LINE procedure within DBMS_OUTPUT displays the specified output on a line. Before using the DBMS_OUTPUT package, you should first execute the **set serveroutput on** command. In the next section, you'll see how to create the PL/SQL block that will read the data from a LOB.

A READ EXAMPLE   To use the READ procedure, you need to know the locator value of the LOB you want to read. The locator value must be selected from the table that contains the LOB. Since the locator value must be supplied as input to the READ procedure, you should use PL/SQL variables to hold the locator value. The READ procedure, in turn, will place its output in a PL/SQL variable. You can use the DBMS_OUTPUT package to display the output value. The structure of the PL/SQL block for this example is as follows:

```
declare
    variable to hold locator value
    variable to hold the amount (the number of characters/bytes to read)
    variable to hold the offset
    variable to hold the output
begin
  set value for amount_var;
  set value for offset_var;
  select locator value into locator var from table;
  DBMS_LOB.READ(locator var, amount var, offset var, output var);
  DBMS_OUTPUT.PUT_LINE('Output:' || output var);
end;
/
```

NOTE
See Chapter 25 for an overview of PL/SQL blocks and their components.

For the PROPOSAL table, selecting the first ten characters from the Proposal_Text column would look like this:

```
declare
    locator_var    CLOB;
    amount_var     INTEGER;
    offset_var     INTEGER;
    output_var     VARCHAR2(10);
```

```
begin
  amount_var := 10;
  offset_var := 1;
  select Proposal_Text into locator_var
    from PROPOSAL
   where Proposal_ID = 1;
  DBMS_LOB.READ(locator_var, amount_var, offset_var, output_var);
  DBMS_OUTPUT.PUT_LINE('Start of proposal text: ' || output_var);
end;
/
```

When the preceding PL/SQL block is executed, the output will be

```
Start of proposal text: This is th

PL/SQL procedure successfully completed.
```

The output shows the first ten characters of the Proposal_Text value, starting at the first character of the LOB value.

The PL/SQL block in the preceding example first declared the variables to use:

```
declare
    locator_var    CLOB;
    amount_var     INTEGER;
    offset_var     INTEGER;
    output_var     VARCHAR2(10);
```

Next, values were assigned to the variables:

```
begin
  amount_var := 10;
  offset_var := 1;
```

The locator value was selected from the table and stored in a variable named *locator_var*:

```
select Proposal_Text into locator_var
    from PROPOSAL
   where Proposal_ID = 1;
```

Next, the READ procedure was called, using the values that had been assigned so far:

```
DBMS_LOB.READ(locator_var, amount_var, offset_var, output_var);
```

As a result of the execution of the READ procedure, the *output_var* variable will be populated with the data that was read. The PUT_LINE procedure displays that data:

```
DBMS_OUTPUT.PUT_LINE('Start of proposal text: ' || output_var);
```

This format for PL/SQL blocks will be used throughout the rest of this chapter.

If you want to select a different portion of the Proposal_Text CLOB, just change the amount and offset variables. If you change the number of characters read, you need to change the size of the output variable, too. In the following example, 12 characters are read from the Proposal_Text, starting from the 10th character:

```
declare
    locator_var    CLOB;
    amount_var     INTEGER;
    offset_var     INTEGER;
    output_var     VARCHAR2(12);
begin
  amount_var := 12;
  offset_var := 10;
  select Proposal_Text into locator_var
    from PROPOSAL
  where Proposal_ID = 1;
  DBMS_LOB.READ(locator_var, amount_var, offset_var, output_var);
  DBMS_OUTPUT.PUT_LINE('Part of proposal text: ' || output_var);
end;
/
```

Output from this PL/SQL block is shown in the following listing:

```
Part of proposal text: he text of a

PL/SQL procedure successfully completed.
```

If Proposal_Text had been created as a VARCHAR2 column, you could have selected this data using the **SUBSTR** function. However, you would have been limited to a maximum length of 4,000 characters. Also, note that the LOB column can contain binary data (BLOB datatypes), and you can use the READ procedure to select data from BLOBs in the same way you select from CLOBs. For BLOBs, you should **declare** the output buffer to use the RAW datatype. In PL/SQL, RAW and

VARCHAR2 datatypes (used for the output variables for CLOB and BLOB reads) have a maximum length of 32,767 characters.

SUBSTR

The SUBSTR function within the DBMS_LOB package performs the SQL **SUBSTR** function on a LOB value. This function has three input parameters, which must be specified in this order:

1. The LOB locator

2. The number of bytes or characters to be read

3. The offset (starting point of the read) from the beginning of the LOB value

Because SUBSTR is a function, there is no output variable value returned directly from SUBSTR, as there was with READ. For the READ procedure, you declared an output variable and then populated it within the READ procedure call. The PL/SQL block used for the READ procedure is shown in the following listing, with the lines related to the output variable shown in bold:

```
declare
    locator_var     CLOB;
    amount_var      INTEGER;
    offset_var      INTEGER;
    output_var      VARCHAR2(12);
begin
    amount_var := 12;
    offset_var := 10;
    select Proposal_Text into locator_var
      from PROPOSAL
    where Proposal_ID = 1;
    DBMS_LOB.READ(locator_var, amount_var, offset_var, output_var);
    DBMS_OUTPUT.PUT_LINE('Section of proposal text: ' || output_var);
end;
/
```

Since SUBSTR is a function, you will populate the output variable differently. The format will be

```
output_var := DBMS_LOB.SUBSTR(locator_var, amount_var, offset_var);
```

The following PL/SQL block uses the SUBSTR function of the DBMS_LOB package to select 12 characters from the Proposal_Text LOB column, starting at the 10th character:

```
declare
    locator_var    CLOB;
    amount_var     INTEGER;
    offset_var     INTEGER;
    output_var     VARCHAR2(12);
begin
  amount_var := 12;
  offset_var := 10;
  select Proposal_Text into locator_var
    from PROPOSAL
   where Proposal_ID = 1;
  output_var := DBMS_LOB.SUBSTR(locator_var, amount_var, offset_var);
  DBMS_OUTPUT.PUT_LINE('Substring of proposal text: ' || output_var);
end;
/
```

Sample output is shown in the following listing:

```
Substring of proposal text: he text of a

PL/SQL procedure successfully completed.
```

The SUBSTR example differs from the READ example in only two ways: the name of the function call, and the manner of assigning a value to the output variable. As with the READ procedure example, the PUT_LINE procedure of the DBMS_OUTPUT package is used to display the results.

In general, you should use the SUBSTR function whenever you are interested in selecting only a specific section of the LOB value. The READ function can be used to select only a portion of a text string (as in the previous examples), but it is more often used within a loop. For example, suppose the LOB value is larger than the largest allowed RAW or VARCHAR2 variable in PL/SQL (32,767 characters). In that case, you can use the READ procedure within a loop to read all the data from the LOB value. (Refer to Chapter 25 for details on the different loop options available in PL/SQL.)

INSTR

The INSTR function within the DBMS_LOB package performs the SQL **INSTR** function on a LOB value.

The INSTR function has four input parameters, which must be specified in this order:

1. The LOB locator

2. The pattern to be tested for (RAW bytes for BLOBs, character strings for CLOBs)

3. The offset (starting point of the read) from the beginning of the LOB value

4. The occurrence of the pattern within the LOB value

The INSTR function within DBMS_LOB searches the LOB for a specific pattern of bytes or characters. The occurrence variable allows you to specify which occurrence of the pattern within the searched value should be returned. The output of the INSTR function is the position of the start of the pattern within the searched string. For example, in SQL,

```
INSTR('ABCABC', 'A', 1, 1) = 1
```

means that within the string ABCABC, the pattern A is searched for, starting at the first position of the string, and looking for the first occurrence. The A is found in the first position of the searched string. If you start the search at the second position of the string, the answer will be different:

```
INSTR('ABCABC', 'A', 2, 1) = 4
```

Since this **INSTR** starts at the second position, the first A is not part of the value that is searched. Instead, the first A found is the one in the fourth position.

If you change the last parameter in the SQL **INSTR** to look for the second occurrence of the string A, starting at the second position, then the pattern is not found:

```
INSTR('ABCABC', 'A', 2, 2) = 0
```

If the SQL **INSTR** function cannot find the matching occurrence of the pattern, then a 0 is returned. The INSTR function of the DBMS_LOB package operates in the same manner.

Because INSTR is a function, you need to assign its output variable in the same manner as the SUBSTR function's output variable was assigned. In the following listing, the Proposal_Text CLOB value is searched for the string 'pr'. A *position_var* variable is declared to hold the output of the INSTR function.

```
declare
    locator_var    CLOB;
    pattern_var    VARCHAR2(2);
    offset_var     INTEGER;
    occur_var      INTEGER;
    position_var   INTEGER;
begin
  pattern_var := 'pr';
  offset_var := 1;
  occur_var := 1;
  select Proposal_Text into locator_var
    from PROPOSAL
   where Proposal_ID = 1;
  position_var := DBMS_LOB.INSTR(locator_var, pattern_var,
offset_var, occur_var);
  DBMS_OUTPUT.PUT_LINE('Found string at position: ' || position_var);
end;
/
```

The output would be

```
Found string at position: 23

PL/SQL procedure successfully completed.
```

The output shows that the search string 'pr' is found within the Proposal_Text, starting at the 23rd character of the LOB value.

GETLENGTH

The GETLENGTH function of the DBMS_LOB package returns the length of the LOB value. The DBMS_LOB.GETLENGTH function is similar in function to the SQL **LENGTH** function, but is used only for LOB values. You cannot use the SQL **LENGTH** function on LOB values.

The GETLENGTH function of the DBMS_LOB package has only one input parameter: the locator value for the LOB. In the following listing, variables are declared to hold the locator value and the output value. The GETLENGTH function is then executed, and the result is reported via the PUT_LINE procedure:

```
declare
    locator_var    CLOB;
    length_var     INTEGER;
begin
  select Proposal_Text into locator_var
    from PROPOSAL
   where Proposal_ID = 1;
  length_var := DBMS_LOB.GETLENGTH(locator_var);
```

```
    DBMS_OUTPUT.PUT_LINE('Length of LOB: ' || length_var);
end;
/
```

The following is the GETLENGTH output:

```
Length of LOB: 55
```

```
PL/SQL procedure successfully completed.
```

If the LOB value is **NULL**, then the GETLENGTH function will return a value of **NULL**.

COMPARE

The COMPARE function of the DBMS_LOB package compares two LOB values. If the two LOB values are the same, then the COMPARE function returns a 0; otherwise, it returns a non-zero integer value (usually 1 or -1). To execute the COMPARE function, the DBMS_LOB package essentially performs two READ functions and compares the results. Thus, for each of the LOB values to be compared, you need to supply a locator value and an offset value; the number of characters or bytes to be compared will be the same for both LOB values. You can only compare LOBs of the same datatype.

The COMPARE function has five input parameters, which must be specified in this order:

 1. The LOB locator for the first LOB

 2. The LOB locator for the second LOB

 3. The amount variable (the number of bytes or characters to compare)

 4. The offset (starting point of the read) from the beginning of the first LOB value

 5. The offset (starting point of the read) from the beginning of the second LOB value

Since the two LOBs being compared can have different offset values, you can compare the first part of one LOB value with the second part of a different LOB value. In the example in the following listing, Dora compares the first 25 characters of the Proposal_Text values from two entries: the Proposal_ID 1 record, and the Proposal_ID 3 record:

```
declare
    first_locator_var      CLOB;
    second_locator_var     CLOB;
    amount_var             INTEGER;
    first_offset_var       INTEGER;
```

```
        second_offset_var    INTEGER;
        output_var           INTEGER;
begin
  amount_var        := 25;
  first_offset_var  := 1;
  second_offset_var := 1;
  select Proposal_Text into first_locator_var
    from PROPOSAL
   where Proposal_ID = 1;
  select Proposal_Text into second_locator_var
    from PROPOSAL
   where Proposal_ID = 3;
  output_var :=DBMS_LOB.COMPARE(first_locator_var, second_locator_var,
         amount_var, first_offset_var, second_offset_var);
  DBMS_OUTPUT.PUT_LINE('Comparison value (0 if the same): '||
    output_var);
end;
/
```

The following is the output:

```
Comparison value (0 if the same): 1

PL/SQL procedure successfully completed.
```

If the two strings are the same, then the COMPARE function will return a 0.

In the following listing, the same two LOBs are compared, but this time only their first five characters are used for the comparison. Since both start with the characters "This ", the COMPARE will return a 0.

```
declare
    first_locator_var    CLOB;
    second_locator_var   CLOB;
    amount_var           INTEGER;
    first_offset_var     INTEGER;
    second_offset_var    INTEGER;
    output_var           INTEGER;
begin
  amount_var        := 5;
  first_offset_var  := 1;
  second_offset_var := 1;
  select Proposal_Text into first_locator_var
    from PROPOSAL
   where Proposal_ID = 1;
  select Proposal_Text into second_locator_var
    from PROPOSAL
   where Proposal_ID = 3;
```

```
output_var :=DBMS_LOB.COMPARE(first_locator_var, second_locator_var,
        amount_var, first_offset_var, second_offset_var);
DBMS_OUTPUT.PUT_LINE('Comparison value (0 if the same): ' ||
  output_var);
end;
/
```

The output for the revised COMPARE is

```
Comparison value (0 if the same): 0

PL/SQL procedure successfully completed.
```

The COMPARE function allows you to compare character strings to character strings and compare binary data to binary data. If you are using the COMPARE function on BLOB columns, you should define the locator variables as RAW datatypes.

WRITE

The WRITE procedure of the DBMS_LOB package allows you to write data in specific locations of the LOB. For example, you can write binary data into a section of a BLOB, overwriting the existing data there. You can write character data into CLOB fields using the WRITE procedure. This procedure has four input parameters, which must be specified in this order:

1. The LOB locator for the LOB

2. The amount variable (the number of bytes or characters to write)

3. The offset (starting point of the write) from the beginning of the LOB value

4. The buffer variable assigned to the character string or binary data being added

Because the WRITE procedure updates the LOB value, you should first lock the row via a **select for update**, as shown in bold in the following listing. In this example, a record is selected and locked. The text ADD NEW TEXT is then written to the LOB value, overwriting the data starting in position 10 (as defined by the offset variable).

```
declare
    locator_var    CLOB;
    amount_var     INTEGER;
    offset_var     INTEGER;
    buffer_var     VARCHAR2(12);
begin
  amount_var := 12;
  offset_var := 10;
  buffer_var := 'ADD NEW TEXT';
```

```
select Proposal_Text into locator_var
  from PROPOSAL
 where Proposal_ID = 3
   for update;
 DBMS_LOB.WRITE(locator_var, amount_var, offset_var, buffer_var);
commit;
end;
/
```

Since the WRITE procedure changes the data, a **commit** command is added before the **end** clause of the PL/SQL block.

For the WRITE procedure, no output is provided. To see the changed data, you need to select the LOB value from the table again:

```
select Proposal_Text
  from PROPOSAL
 where Proposal_ID = 3;
```

```
PROPOSAL_TEXT
-----------------------------------------------------------
This is tADD NEW TEXTsal text.
```

The WRITE procedure overwrote 12 characters, starting at the 10th character of the Proposal_Text. You can use the WRITEAPPEND procedure to append new data to the end of an existing LOB value.

APPEND

The APPEND procedure of the DBMS_LOB package appends data from one LOB to a second LOB. Since this amounts to an update of a LOB value, the record being updated should be locked prior to executing the APPEND procedure.

The APPEND procedure takes only two parameters: the locator value for the destination LOB, and the locator value for the source LOB. If either parameter is **NULL**, the APPEND procedure will return an error.

In the following example, two locator variables are defined. The first locator variable is named *dest_locator_var*; this is the locator value for the LOB into which the data is to be appended. The second locator variable, *source_locator_var*, is the locator value for the source data that is to be appended to the destination LOB. The destination LOB, since it is being updated, is locked via a **select for update** command. In this example, the Proposal_Text value for the Proposal_ID 1 record is appended to the Proposal_Text value for the Proposal_ID 3 record:

```
declare
    dest_locator_var      CLOB;
    source_locator_var    CLOB;
```

```
begin
  select Proposal_Text into dest_locator_var
    from PROPOSAL
   where Proposal_ID = 3
     for update;
  select Proposal_Text into source_locator_var
    from PROPOSAL
   where Proposal_ID = 1;
  DBMS_LOB.APPEND(dest_locator_var, source_locator_var);
commit;
end;
/
```

To see the changed data, you can select the record from the PROPOSAL table:

```
select Proposal_Text
  from PROPOSAL
 where Proposal_ID = 3;

PROPOSAL_TEXT
------------------------------------------------------------------
This is tADD NEW TEXTsal text. This is the text of a proposal to clear
Phillips f
```

What happened to the rest of the text? By default, only 80 characters of LONG and LOB values are displayed during queries. To see the rest of the text, use the **set long** command:

```
set long 1000

select Proposal_Text
  from PROPOSAL
 where Proposal_ID = 3;

PROPOSAL_TEXT
------------------------------------------------------------------
This is tADD NEW TEXTsal text. This is the text of a proposal to clear
Phillips field.
```

In this example, the first 1,000 characters of the LOB value were displayed. If you need to know how long the LOB is, use the GETLENGTH function as described earlier in this chapter.

In addition to allowing you to append CLOB values, the APPEND procedure allows you to append BLOB values. When appending BLOB data, you need to be aware of the format of the BLOB data and the impact of appending new data on the end of the BLOB value. For BLOB values, the APPEND function may be most useful for applications in which the BLOB contains only raw data (such as digital data transmissions) rather than formatted binary data (such as spreadsheet files formatted by a program).

ERASE

You can use the ERASE procedure of the DBMS_LOB package to erase the characters or bytes in any part of a LOB. You can use ERASE to erase the entire LOB value, or you can specify which section of the LOB to erase. ERASE is similar in function to WRITE. If you ERASE data in a BLOB value, the data is replaced with zero-byte filler. If you ERASE data in a CLOB value, spaces are inserted into the CLOB.

Since you are updating a LOB value, you should follow the standard procedures for LOB updates: lock the row and commit when the procedure has completed.

In the following PL/SQL block, a portion of the Proposal_Text for the record with Proposal_ID 3 is erased. The erased characters will start at an offset of 10 and continue for 17 characters. The parameters for the ERASE procedure, in order, are

1. The LOB locator for the LOB

2. The amount variable (the number of bytes or characters to erase)

3. The offset (starting point of the erasure) from the beginning of the LOB value

```
declare
    locator_var    CLOB;
    amount_var     INTEGER;
    offset_var     INTEGER;
begin
  amount_var := 17;
  offset_var := 10;
  select Proposal_Text into locator_var
    from PROPOSAL
   where Proposal_ID = 3
     for update;
  DBMS_LOB.ERASE(locator_var, amount_var, offset_var);
commit;
end;
/
```

The change to the record can be seen by querying the Proposal_Text value:

```
select Proposal_Text
   from PROPOSAL
  where Proposal_ID = 3;
```

```
PROPOSAL_TEXT
-----------------------------------------------------------------
This is t                   is the text of a proposal to clear
Phillips field.
```

NOTE
The space previously held by the erased data is replaced by blanks; the rest of the data in the LOB does not change its position.

TRIM

You can use the TRIM procedure of the DBMS_LOB package to reduce the size of a LOB value by trimming characters or bytes from the end of the value (such as the SQL **RTRIM** function). When the TRIM procedure is executed, you specify the locator value for the LOB and the LOB's new length.

In the following listing, the Proposal_Text for the Proposal_ID 3 record is trimmed to its first ten characters. Since the TRIM procedure changes the data, a **commit** command is added before the **end** clause of the PL/SQL block.

```
declare
    locator_var      CLOB;
    new_length_var   INTEGER;
begin
  new_length_var   := 10;
  select Proposal_Text into locator_var
    from PROPOSAL
   where Proposal_ID = 3
     for update;
  DBMS_LOB.TRIM(locator_var, new_length_var);
commit;
end;
/
```

For the TRIM procedure, no output is provided. To see the changed data, you need to select the LOB value from the table again:

```
select Proposal_Text
    from PROPOSAL
   where Proposal_ID = 3;
```

```
PROPOSAL_TEXT
-----------------------------------------------------------------
This is t
```

The sample output shows the results of the TRIM procedure following the ERASE procedure executed in the preceding section.

COPY

You can use the COPY procedure of the DBMS_LOB package to copy data from a part of one LOB into a second LOB. Unlike the APPEND procedure, you do not have to copy the full text of one LOB value into another. During the COPY procedure, you can specify the offset to read from and the offset to write to. The five parameters of the COPY procedure are, in order:

1. The destination LOB locator

2. The source LOB locator

3. The amount (the number of characters or bytes to copy)

4. The offset to start writing to within the destination LOB value

5. The offset to start reading from within the destination LOB value

COPY is a combination of the READ and WRITE capabilities. Like the WRITE operation, the COPY procedure modifies the LOB value. Therefore, the record should first be locked, and the PL/SQL block must contain a **commit** command. In the following example, the first 55 characters of the Proposal_ID 1 record are copied to the Proposal_ID 3 record. Since the destination LOB uses an offset of 1, the copied data will *overwrite* data within the destination LOB.

```
declare
    dest_locator_var     CLOB;
    source_locator_var   CLOB;
    amount_var           INTEGER;
    dest_offset_var      INTEGER;
    source_offset_var    INTEGER;
begin
  amount_var         := 55;
  dest_offset_var    := 1;
  source_offset_var  := 1;
  select Proposal_Text into dest_locator_var
    from PROPOSAL
   where Proposal_ID = 3
     for update;
  select Proposal_Text into source_locator_var
    from PROPOSAL
   where Proposal_ID = 1;
```

```
    DBMS_LOB.COPY(dest_locator_var, source_locator_var,
        amount_var, dest_offset_var, source_offset_var);
commit;
end;
/
```

The COPY procedure displays no output. To see the changed data, you need to select the LOB value from the table again:

```
select Proposal_Text
    from PROPOSAL
    where Proposal_ID = 3;


PROPOSAL_TEXT
--------------------------------------------------------
This is the text of a proposal to clear Phillips field.
```

Using the BFILE Functions and Procedures

Since BFILE values are stored externally, several functions and procedures are used to manipulate the files prior to executing READ, SUBSTR, INSTR, GETLENGTH, or COMPARE operations on BFILE LOBs. The BFILE-related procedures and functions within DBMS_LOB, shown earlier in Table 30-4, allow you to open files, close files, get the filename, check whether a file exists, and check whether a file is open. The existence-check function is necessary because Oracle does not maintain the data stored in the external file; Oracle only maintains the pointer created via the BFILENAME procedure when the record is inserted or updated. Table 30-5 shows the BFILE-related procedures and functions with their input and output parameters.

You should use the procedures and functions in Table 30-5 to control the files used by your PL/SQL code. For example, to read the first 10 bytes from the Cover_Letter BFILE for the Proposal_ID 2 record, you would open the file and then execute the READ procedure. The PUT_LINE procedure of the DBMS_OUTPUT package can then be called to show the data that was read.

If you use an Exception Handling section in your PL/SQL block, then you need to be sure to include FILECLOSE procedure calls within the declared exceptions. (Refer to Chapter 25 for further details on exception handling within PL/SQL blocks.)

To move data from an external file into a BLOB datatype, you can create a BFILE datatype in a table and use the BFILENAME function to create a LOB locator that points to the external file. You can then open the file and use the LOADFROMFILE procedure to load the BLOB datatype with the data from the external file.

If the data is presently in a LONG datatype, you can use the **TO_LOB** SQL function to move the data from the LONG column to a BLOB column as part of an **insert as select** command.

Procedure or Function	Input Parameters	Output Parameters
FILECLOSE	File locator	None
FILECLOSEALL	None	None
FILEEXISTS	File locator	Integer value
FILEGETNAME	File locator	Directory alias, filename
FILEISOPEN	File locator	Integer value
FILEOPEN	File locator, open mode	None
LOADFROMFILE	Destination LOB, source file, amount to copy, destination offset, source offset	None

TABLE 30-5. *Input and Output Parameters for BFILE-Related Procedures and Functions*

Deleting LOBS

When you delete LOB values, the locator value is deleted. If the deleted value is an internal LOB (BLOB, CLOB, or NCLOB), then both the locator and the LOB value are deleted. If the deleted value is an external LOB (BFILE), then only the locator value is deleted; you will need to manually delete the file to which the locator points.

CHAPTER
31

Advanced
Object-Oriented
Concepts

o this point, all of the object-oriented programming (OOP) features of Oracle shown in this book have shared two characteristics: they are embedded objects, and they are column objects. An *embedded object* is one that is completely contained within another. For example, a nested table is contained within a table, so it is an embedded object. Although a nested table's data is stored apart from the main table, its data can only be accessed via the main table. A *column object* is one that is represented as a column in a table. For example, a varying array is represented as a column in a table, so it is a column object.

To take advantage of OOP capabilities, a database must also support *row objects*—objects that are represented as rows instead of columns. The row objects are not embedded objects; instead, they are *referenced objects,* accessible via references from other objects. In this chapter, you will see how row objects are created and referenced.

As you will see in this chapter, row objects can be extended for use within some of the objects discussed in prior chapters (such as object views). In addition to row objects, this chapter covers the application of objects to PL/SQL—creating Object PL/SQL.

Row Objects vs. Column Objects

The distinction between row objects and column objects is critical. First, consider column objects. Column objects are based on extensions of features already in the database. An abstract datatype or a varying array can be embedded as a column within a table, just like a column can be. A nested table or a large object (LOB) can be stored in a single column of a table. In each case, the object is represented as a column within a table.

Nested tables and LOBs, however, involve data that is stored out-of-line from the main table. When you use a LOB (refer to Chapter 30), you specify the storage values for the table that will store the LOB data, and Oracle creates LOB locators that point from the main table to the rows in the LOB table. When you create a nested table, you specify the name of the table in which the nested table's records will be stored—and Oracle creates pointers from the main table to the records in the nested tables. Thus, the main table and its embedded nested table are related.

In row objects, the objects are represented as rows, not columns. The data is not embedded within the main table; instead, the main table contains a reference to another table. Nested tables, since they are stored apart from the main table, provide a useful tool for understanding row objects. What if the nested table's data is not embedded within the main table, and each of its rows is a row object? The main table will define references to the related data.

The object-relational features of Oracle described in the earlier chapters relied on column objects. In this chapter, the focus is on the advanced OOP capabilities, which are based on row objects. You use row objects to create references between the rows of different tables.

Object Tables and OIDs

In an *object table,* each row is a row object. An object table differs from a normal relational table in several ways. First, each row within the object table has an *OID*—an object identifier value—assigned by Oracle when the row is created. Second, the rows of an object table can be referenced by other objects within the database.

You can create an object table via the **create table** command. Consider the ANIMAL_TY datatype shown in previous chapters:

```
create or replace type ANIMAL_TY as object
(Breed       VARCHAR2(25),
 Name        VARCHAR2(25),
 BirthDate   DATE);
/
```

NOTE
To keep this example simple, the ANIMAL_TY datatype is created without any member functions.

To create an object table of the ANIMAL_TY datatype, issue the following **create table** command:

```
create table ANIMAL of ANIMAL_TY;

Table created.
```

Note that the command has an unusual syntax—creating the table **of** an abstract datatype. The resulting table may first appear to be a normal relational table:

```
describe ANIMAL

Name                              Null?     Type
------------------------------- --------  ----
BREED                                     VARCHAR2(25)
NAME                                      VARCHAR2(25)
BIRTHDATE                                 DATE
```

The ANIMAL table's columns map to the attributes of the ANIMAL_TY datatype. However, there are significant differences in how you can use the table, since it is an object table. As noted earlier in this section, each row within the object table will have an OID value, and the rows can be referenced as objects.

Inserting Rows into Object Tables

Because ANIMAL is an object table, you can use its datatype's constructor method when **insert**ing data into the table. Since the ANIMAL table is based on the ANIMAL_TY abstract datatype, the ANIMAL_TY constructor method can be used when **insert**ing values into ANIMAL.

NOTE
Refer to Chapters 4 and 28 for detailed discussions of constructor methods.

In the following listing, three rows are **insert**ed into the ANIMAL object table. In each command, the ANIMAL_TY constructor method is called.

```
insert into ANIMAL values
        (ANIMAL_TY('MULE','FRANCES',
                 TO_DATE('01-APR-1997','DD-MON-YYYY')));
insert into ANIMAL values
        (ANIMAL_TY('DOG','BENJI',
                 TO_DATE('03-SEP-1996','DD-MON-YYYY')));
insert into ANIMAL values
        (ANIMAL_TY('CROCODILE','LYLE',
                 TO_DATE('14-MAY-1997','DD-MON-YYYY')));
```

If the abstract datatype on which the object table is based is itself based on a second abstract datatype, you may need to nest calls to multiple constructor methods within your **insert** command. (Refer to Chapter 4 for examples of nested abstract datatypes.)

NOTE
If an object table is based on a datatype that does not contain any nested datatypes, you can also **insert** *records into the object table using the normal* **insert** *command syntax for relational tables.*

When you **insert** a row into an object table, Oracle assigns an OID to the row. Having an OID allows you to use the row as a referenceable object. OID values are not reused.

Selecting Values from Object Tables

When the ANIMAL table was created, it was based entirely on the ANIMAL_TY datatype:

```
create table ANIMAL of ANIMAL_TY;
```

When you select from a table that contains an abstract datatype, you refer to the abstract datatype's columns as part of the table's columns. That is, if you used the ANIMAL_TY datatype as the basis for a *column* named Animal, then you would select the animal names by selecting Animal.Name from the table.

An object table, though, is based on a datatype—it has no other columns. Therefore, you do not need to reference the datatype when accessing the columns. To select the names from the ANIMAL table, just query the datatype's attributes directly:

```
select Name
   from ANIMAL;

NAME
------------------------
FRANCES
BENJI
LYLE
```

You can refer to the columns within the **where** clause just as if ANIMAL were a relational table:

```
select Name
   from ANIMAL
 where Breed = 'CROCODILE';

NAME
------------------------
LYLE
```

If the ANIMAL_TY datatype used another abstract datatype for one of its columns, that datatype's column would be referenced during all **select**s, **update**s, and **delete**s. (Refer to Chapter 4 for examples of queries from nested abstract datatypes.)

Updates and Deletes from Object Tables

If the object table is based on an abstract datatype that uses no other abstract datatypes, then an **update** or **delete** of an object table uses the same format as you would use for relational tables. In this example, the ANIMAL_TY datatype does not use any other abstract datatype for one of its columns, so your **update**s and **delete**s from the ANIMAL object table behave the same as if ANIMAL were a relational table.

In the following command, one of the rows of ANIMAL is **update**d:

```
update ANIMAL
   set BirthDate = TO_DATE('01-MAY-1997','DD-MON-YYYY')
 where Name = 'LYLE';

1 row updated.
```

Note that during the **update**, the columns of the object table are referred to as if ANIMAL were a relational table. During a **delete**, you use the same means to reference the object table's columns in the **where** clause:

```
delete from ANIMAL
 where Name = 'LYLE';

1 row deleted.
```

Keeping a crocodile alongside mules and dogs probably wasn't such a good idea anyway.

The REF Function

The **REF** function allows you to reference existing row objects. For example, the ANIMAL table has (after the deletion of one row, shown in the previous section) two row objects, each of which has an OID value assigned to it. You can see the OID assigned by using the **REF** function, as shown here:

```
select REF(A)
   from ANIMAL  A
 where Name = 'FRANCES';

REF(A)
--------------------------------------------------
000028020915A58C5FAEC1502EE034080009D0DADE15538856
F10606EEE034080009D0DADE100001250000
```

NOTE
Your REF values should be different than the ones shown here, but should have the same format.

In this example, the ANIMAL table was given the alias *A*, and that alias was used as input to the **REF** function. The output shows the OID for the row object that met the limiting condition of the query.

NOTE
*The **REF** function takes as its input the alias given to the object table. The other functions shown later in this chapter also take aliases as inputs, so you should be familiar with this syntax.*

Since the **REF** function can only reference row objects, you cannot reference column objects. Column objects include abstract datatypes, LOBs, and collectors.

As you can see, the **REF** function by itself does not give you any useful information. You need to use another function—**DEREF**—that translates the **REF** output into values. You can then use **REF** and **DEREF** to reference row object values, as described in the next section.

Using the DEREF Function

The **REF** function takes a row object as its argument and returns a reference value. The **DEREF** function does the opposite—it takes a reference value (the OID generated for a reference) and returns the value of the row object.

Earlier in this chapter, the ANIMAL object table was created using the ANIMAL_TY abstract datatype:

```
create table ANIMAL of ANIMAL_TY;
```

To see how **DEREF** and **REF** work together, consider a table that is related to the ANIMAL table. The KEEPER table will track the people who take care of the animals. It will have a column for the name of the keeper (KeeperName) and a reference to the ANIMAL object table (AnimalKept), as shown in the following listing:

```
create table KEEPER
 (KeeperName        VARCHAR2(25),
  AnimalKept        REF  ANIMAL_TY);
```

The first part of the **create table** command looks normal:

```
create table KEEPER
 (KeeperName        VARCHAR2(25),
```

but the last line shows a new feature:

 `AnimalKept     REF  ANIMAL_TY);`

The AnimalKept column references data that is stored elsewhere. The **REF** function points the AnimalKept column to the ANIMAL_TY datatype. Since ANIMAL is the object table for the ANIMAL_TY datatype, the AnimalKept column points to the row objects within the ANIMAL object table.

When you **describe** the KEEPER table, you can see that its AnimalKept column relies on a **REF**:

```
describe KEEPER

Name                            Null?    Type
------------------------------- -------- ----
KEEPERNAME                               VARCHAR2(25)
ANIMALKEPT                               REF OF ANIMAL_TY
```

Now, **insert** a record into KEEPER. You need to use the **REF** function to store the ANIMAL references in the AnimalKept column.

```
insert into KEEPER
select 'CATHERINE WEILZ',
       REF(A)
  from ANIMAL A
 where Name = 'BENJI';
```

Let's look at this **insert** command closely. First, the KeeperName value is selected as a literal value from the ANIMAL table:

```
insert into KEEPER
select 'CATHERINE WEILZ',
```

Next, the value for the AnimalKept column must be specified. But the datatype of AnimalKept is REF OF ANIMAL_TY, so you must select the reference from the ANIMAL object table to populate the AnimalKept column:

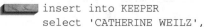
```
       REF(A)
  from ANIMAL A
 where Name = 'BENJI';
```

What's going on here? First, the ANIMAL object table is queried, and the **REF** function returns the OID for the row object selected. The OID is then stored in the KEEPER table as a pointer to that row object in the ANIMAL object table.

Does the KEEPER table contain the animal information? No. KEEPER contains the name of the keeper and a reference to a row object in the ANIMAL table. You can see the reference OID by querying KEEPER:

```
select * from KEEPER;

KEEPERNAME          ANIMALKEPT
------------------- ------------------------------------------------
CATHERINE WEILZ     000022020815A58C5FAEC2502EE034080009D0DADE15538856
                    F10606EEE034080009D0DADE
```

The AnimalKept column, as shown in this listing, contains the reference to the row object, not the value of the data stored in the row object.

You can't see the referenced value unless you use the **DEREF** function. When you select from KEEPER, Oracle will use the OID to evaluate the reference (**REF**). The **DEREF** function will take the reference and return a value.

In the following query, the value of the AnimalKept column in KEEPER is the parameter passed to the **DEREF** function. **DEREF** will take the OID from AnimalKept and find the referenced object; the function will evaluate the reference and return the values to the user.

```
select DEREF(K.AnimalKept)
  from KEEPER K
 where KeeperName = 'CATHERINE WEILZ';

DEREF(K.ANIMALKEPT)(BREED, NAME, BIRTHDATE)
----------------------------------------------------
ANIMAL_TY('DOG', 'BENJI', '03-SEP-96')
```

NOTE
*The parameter for the **DEREF** function is the column name of the REF column, not the table name.*

The result shows that the CATHERINE WEILZ record in KEEPER references an ANIMAL record for the animal named BENJI. A few aspects of this query are noteworthy:

- The query used a reference to a row object to travel from one table (KEEPER) to a second (the ANIMAL object table). Thus, a join is performed in the background, without you specifying the join criteria.

- The object table itself is not mentioned in the query. The only table listed in the query is KEEPER. You do not need to know the name of the object table to **DEREF** its values.

- The entire referenced row object was returned, not just part of the row.

These are significant differences that separate object queries from relational queries. Thus, when querying your tables, you need to know the way in which their relationships are established. Are the relationships based on foreign keys and primary keys, or on object tables and **REF** datatypes? To help smooth the transition between relational and object-oriented approaches, Oracle allows you to create object views that contain **REF**s superimposed on existing relational tables. See "Object Views with REFs," later in this chapter.

The VALUE Function

The **DEREF** function was applied to the relational table—the KEEPER table, in this case. The **DEREF** function returns the value of the reference that goes from the relational table to the object table.

What about querying from the object table? Can you select from ANIMAL?

```
select * from ANIMAL;

BREED                     NAME                      BIRTHDATE
------------------------- ------------------------- ---------
MULE                      FRANCES                   01-APR-97
DOG                       BENJI                     03-SEP-96
```

Even though ANIMAL is an object table, you can select from it as if it were a relational table. This is consistent with the examples of inserts and selects shown earlier in this chapter. However, that is not what was shown via the **DEREF**. The **DEREF** showed the full structure of the abstract datatype used by the ANIMAL object table:

```
select DEREF(K.AnimalKept)
  from KEEPER K
 where KeeperName = 'CATHERINE WEILZ';

DEREF(K.ANIMALKEPT)(BREED, NAME, BIRTHDATE)
---------------------------------------------------
ANIMAL_TY('DOG', 'BENJI', '03-SEP-96')
```

To see the same structures from a query of the ANIMAL object table, use the **VALUE** function. As shown in the following listing, **VALUE** shows you the data in the same format that **DEREF** will use. The parameter for the **VALUE** function is the table alias.

```
select VALUE(A)
  from ANIMAL A
 where Name = 'BENJI';

A(BREED, NAME, BIRTHDATE)
-----------------------------------------------
ANIMAL_TY('DOG', 'BENJI', '03-SEP-96')
```

The **VALUE** function is useful when debugging references and within PL/SQL, as shown in "Object PL/SQL," later in this chapter. Since it allows you to query the formatted values directly from the object table, you can select those values without using the **DEREF** query of KEEPER's AnimalKept column.

Invalid References

You can **delete** the object to which a reference points. For example, you can **delete** a row from the ANIMAL object table to which a KEEPER record points:

```
delete from ANIMAL
 where Name = 'BENJI';
```

The record in KEEPER that references this ANIMAL record will now have what is called a *dangling REF*. If you **insert** a new ANIMAL row for the animal named BENJI, it won't be recognized as being part of the same reference established earlier. The reason is that the first time you **insert**ed a BENJI row, Oracle generated an OID for the row object, and that is what the KEEPER column referenced. When you **delete**d the row object, the OID went away—and Oracle does not reuse OID numbers. Therefore, when the new BENJI record is entered, it is given a *new* OID value—and the KEEPER record still points to the old value.

This is a critical difference between relational and OOP systems. In a relational system, the join between two tables is dependent only on the current data. In an OOP system, the join is between objects—and just because two objects have the same data, that doesn't mean they are the same.

Object Views with REFs

You can use object views to superimpose OOP structures on existing relational tables (refer to Chapter 28). For example, you can create abstract datatypes and use them within the object view of an existing table. Using object views allows you to access the table via either relational command syntax or abstract datatype syntax. As a result, object views provide an important technological bridge from existing relational applications to object-relational applications.

A Quick Review of Object Views

The example from Chapter 28 will serve as part of the basis for the advanced object views in this chapter. First, a CUSTOMER table is created, with the Customer_ID column as its primary key:

```
create table CUSTOMER
(Customer_ID NUMBER constraint CUSTOMER_PK primary key,
 Name        VARCHAR2(25),
 Street      VARCHAR2(50),
 City        VARCHAR2(25),
 State       CHAR(2),
 Zip         NUMBER);
```

Next, two abstract datatypes are created. The first, ADDRESS_TY, contains attributes for addresses: Street, City, State, and Zip. The second, PERSON_TY, contains a Name attribute plus an Address attribute that uses the ADDRESS_TY datatype, as shown in the following listing:

```
create or replace type ADDRESS_TY as object
(Street   VARCHAR2(50),
 City     VARCHAR2(25),
 State    CHAR(2),
 Zip      NUMBER);
/

create or replace type PERSON_TY as object
(Name       VARCHAR2(25),
 Address    ADDRESS_TY);
/
```

Since the CUSTOMER table was created without using the ADDRESS_TY and PERSON_TY datatypes, you need to use object views in order to access CUSTOMER data via object-based accesses (such as methods). You can create an object view that specifies the abstract datatypes that apply to the CUSTOMER table. In the following listing, the CUSTOMER_OV object view is created:

```
create view CUSTOMER_OV (Customer_ID, Person) as
select Customer_ID,
       PERSON_TY(Name,
       ADDRESS_TY(Street, City, State, Zip))
  from CUSTOMER;
```

In the creation of the CUSTOMER_OV object view, the constructor methods for the two abstract datatypes (ADDRESS_TY and PERSON_TY) are specified. You can now access the CUSTOMER table directly (as a relational table) or via the constructor methods for the abstract datatypes.

The CUSTOMER table will be used in the next set of examples in this chapter.

Object Views Involving References

If the CUSTOMER table shown in the previous section is related to another table, you can use object views to create a reference between the tables. That is, Oracle will use the existing primary key/foreign key relationships to simulate OIDs for use by **REF**s between the tables. You will thus be able to access the tables either as relational tables or as objects. When you treat the tables as objects, you will be able to use the **REF**s to automatically perform joins of the tables (refer to "Using the **DEREF** Function," earlier in this chapter, for examples).

The CUSTOMER table has a primary key of Customer_ID. Let's create a small table that will contain a foreign key reference to the Customer_ID column. In the following listing, the CUSTOMER_CALL table is created. The primary key of the CUSTOMER_CALL table is the combination of Customer_ID and Call_Number. The Customer_ID column of CUSTOMER_CALL is a foreign key back to CUSTOMER—you cannot record a call for a customer who does not already have a record in CUSTOMER. A single nonkey attribute, Call_Date, is created within the CUSTOMER_CALL table.

```
create table CUSTOMER_CALL
(Customer_ID    NUMBER,
 Call_Number    NUMBER,
 Call_Date      DATE,
 constraint CUSTOMER_CALL_PK
     primary key (Customer_ID, Call_Number),
 constraint CUSTOMER_CALL_FK foreign key (Customer_ID)
    references CUSTOMER(Customer_ID));
```

For example, you could have the following CUSTOMER and CUSTOMER_CALL entries:

```
insert into CUSTOMER values
(123,'SIGMUND','47 HAFFNER RD','LEWISTON','NJ',22222);

insert into CUSTOMER values
(234,'EVELYN','555 HIGH ST','LOWLANDS PARK','NE',33333);

insert into CUSTOMER_CALL values
(123,1,TRUNC(SysDate)-1);
insert into CUSTOMER_CALL values
(123,2,TRUNC(SysDate));
```

The foreign key from CUSTOMER_CALL to CUSTOMER defines the relationship between the tables. From an OOP point of view, the records in CUSTOMER_CALL reference the records in CUSTOMER. Therefore, we must find a way to assign OID values to the records in CUSTOMER and generate references in CUSTOMER_CALL.

How to Generate OIDs

First, use an object view to assign OIDs to the records in CUSTOMER. Remember that OIDs are assigned to records in an object table—and an object table, in turn, is based on an abstract datatype. Therefore, we first need to create an abstract datatype that has the same structure as the CUSTOMER table:

```
create or replace type CUSTOMER_TY as object
(Customer_ID NUMBER,
 Name        VARCHAR2(25),
 Street      VARCHAR2(50),
 City        VARCHAR2(25),
 State       CHAR(2),
 Zip         NUMBER);
/
```

Now, create an object view based on the CUSTOMER_TY type, while assigning OID values to the records in CUSTOMER:

```
create or replace view CUSTOMER_OV of CUSTOMER_TY
with object OID (Customer_ID) as
select Customer_ID, Name, Street, City, State, Zip
  from CUSTOMER;
```

The first part of this **create view** command gives the view its name (CUSTOMER_OV) and tells Oracle that the view's structure is based on the CUSTOMER_TY datatype:

```
create view CUSTOMER_OV of CUSTOMER_TY
```

The next part of the **create view** command tells the database how to construct OID values for the rows in CUSTOMER. The **with object OID** clause is followed by the column to use for the OID—in this case, the Customer_ID value. This will allow you to address the rows within the CUSTOMER table as if they were referenceable row objects within an object table.

```
with object OID (Customer_ID) as
```

The final part of the **create view** command gives the query on which the view's data access will be based. The columns in the query must match the columns in the view's base datatype.

```
select Customer_ID, Name, Street, City, State, Zip
   from CUSTOMER;
```

The rows of CUSTOMER are now accessible as row objects via the CUSTOMER_OV view. The OID values generated for the CUSTOMER_OV rows are called pkOIDs, because they are based on the primary key values. Any relational tables can be accessed as row objects if you create object views for them.

How to Generate References

The rows of CUSTOMER_CALL reference rows in CUSTOMER. From a relational perspective, the relationship is determined by the foreign key pointing from the CUSTOMER_CALL.Customer_ID column to the CUSTOMER.Customer_ID column. Now that the CUSTOMER_OV object view has been created, and the rows in CUSTOMER can be accessed via OIDs, you need to create reference values in CUSTOMER_CALL that reference CUSTOMER. Once the **REF**s are in place, you will be able to use the **DEREF** function (shown earlier in this chapter) to access the CUSTOMER data from within CUSTOMER_CALL.

The **create view** command for the object view of CUSTOMER_CALL is shown in the following listing. It uses a new function, **MAKE_REF**, which is described following the listing.

```
create view CUSTOMER_CALL_OV as
select MAKE_REF(CUSTOMER_OV, Customer_ID) Customer_ID,
       Call_Number,
       Call_Date
  from CUSTOMER_CALL;
```

With the exception of the **MAKE_REF** operation, this **create view** command looks like a normal **create view** command. The **MAKE_REF** operation is shown in this line:

```
select MAKE_REF(CUSTOMER_OV, Customer_ID) Customer_ID,
```

The **MAKE_REF** function takes as arguments the name of the object view being referenced and the name of the column (or columns) that form the foreign key in the local table. In this case, the Customer_ID column of the CUSTOMER_CALL table references the column that is used as the basis of OID generation in the

CUSTOMER_OV object view. Therefore, two parameters are passed to **MAKE_REF**: CUSTOMER_OV and Customer_ID. The result of the **MAKE_REF** operation is given the column alias Customer_ID. Since this command creates a view, the result of an operation must be given a column alias.

What does **MAKE_REF** do? It creates references (called pkREFs, since they are based on primary keys) from the CUSTOMER_CALL_OV view to the CUSTOMER_OV view. You can now query the two views as if CUSTOMER_OV were an object table and CUSTOMER_CALL_OV were a table that contains a REF datatype that references CUSTOMER_OV.

Querying the Object Views

The queries of the object views with REFs mirror the structure of the queries of table REFs. You use the **DEREF** function to select the value of the referenced data, as shown earlier in this chapter. Applied to the object views, the query will be

```
select DEREF(CCOV.Customer_ID)
  from CUSTOMER_CALL_OV CCOV
 where Call_Date = TRUNC(SysDate);

DEREF(CCOV.CUSTOMER_ID)(CUSTOMER_ID, NAME, STREET, CITY, STATE, ZIP)
-----------------------------------------------------------------
CUSTOMER_TY(123, 'SIGMUND', '47 HAFFNER RD', 'LEWISTON', 'NJ', 22222)
```

The query found the record in CUSTOMER_CALL for which the Call_Date value was the current system date. It then took the Customer_ID value from that record and evaluated its reference. That Customer_ID value, from the **MAKE_REF** function, pointed to a pkOID value in the CUSTOMER_OV object view. The CUSTOMER_OV object view returned the record whose pkOID matched the referenced value. The **DEREF** function then returned the value of the referenced row. The query thus returned rows from CUSTOMER even though the user only queried CUSTOMER_CALL.

Object views of column objects enable you to work with tables as if they were both relational tables and object-relational tables. When extended to row objects, object views enable you to generate OID values based on established foreign key/primary key relationships. Object views allow you to continue to use the existing constraints and standard **insert**, **update**, **delete**, and **select** commands. They also allow you to use OOP features such as references against the same tables. Object views thus provide an important technological bridge for migrating to an OOP database architecture.

As described earlier in this chapter, Oracle performs joins that resolve the references defined in the database. When the referenced data is retrieved, it brings back the entire row object that was referenced. To reference the data, you need to establish pkOIDs in the table that is the "primary key" table in the relationship, and use **MAKE_REF** to generate references in the table that is the "foreign key" table in the relationship. You can then work with the data as if it were stored in object tables.

Object PL/SQL

PL/SQL programs can use the abstract datatypes you have created. Whereas earlier versions of PL/SQL could only use the Oracle-provided datatypes (such as DATE, NUMBER, and VARCHAR2), you can now use your own user-defined datatypes as well. The result is the merging of SQL, procedural logic, and OOP extensions—a combination referred to as *object PL/SQL*.

The following anonymous PL/SQL block uses object PL/SQL concepts. The CUSTOMER_TY abstract datatype is used as the datatype for the *Cust1* variable, and its value is populated by a query of the CUSTOMER_OV object view.

```
set serveroutput on
declare
     Cust1         CUSTOMER_TY;
begin
     select VALUE(COV)   into Cust1
       from CUSTOMER_OV COV
      where Customer_ID = 123;
     DBMS_OUTPUT.PUT_LINE(Cust1.Name,Cust1.Street);
end;
/
```

The output of this PL/SQL block is

```
SIGMUND
47 HAFFNER RD
```

In the first part of the PL/SQL block, a variable is declared using the CUSTOMER_TY datatype:

```
declare
     Cust1         CUSTOMER_TY;
```

The *Cust1* variable value is selected from the CUSTOMER_OV object view (created in the previous section of this chapter). The **VALUE** function is used to retrieve the data in the structure of the abstract datatype. Since the data will be selected in the structure of the abstract datatype, you need to use the CUSTOMER_OV object view created on the CUSTOMER table.

```
begin
    select VALUE(COV)   into Cust1
      from CUSTOMER_OV COV
     where Customer_ID = 123;
```

The Cust1.Name and Cust1.Street values are then retrieved from the attributes of the Cust1 variable and displayed. You cannot pass the entire *Cust1* variable to the PUT_LINE procedure.

```
    DBMS_OUTPUT.PUT_LINE(Cust1.Name,Cust1.Street);
end;
/
```

This is a deliberately simple example, but it shows the power of object PL/SQL. You can use object PL/SQL anywhere you use abstract datatypes. Your PL/SQL is thus no longer bound to the Oracle-provided datatypes, and may more accurately reflect the objects in your database. In this example, an object view was queried to illustrate that the queries can access either column objects or row objects. You can then select the attributes of the abstract datatype and manipulate or display them. If you have defined methods for the abstract datatype, you can apply them as well.

For example, you can call the datatype's constructor methods within your PL/SQL blocks. In the following example, a variable named NewCust is defined using the CUSTOMER_TY datatype. The NewCust variable is then set equal to a set of values called by the CUSTOMER_TY constructor method. The NewCust variable's set of values is then **insert**ed via the CUSTOMER_OV object view.

```
declare
    NewCust      CUSTOMER_TY;
begin
    NewCust :=
      CUSTOMER_TY(345,'NewCust','StreetVal', 'City','ST',00000);
    insert into CUSTOMER_OV
    values (NewCust);
end;
/
```

You can see the result of the **insert** by querying CUSTOMER_OV:

```
select Customer_ID, Name from CUSTOMER_OV;

CUSTOMER_ID NAME
----------- ------------------------
        123 SIGMUND
        234 EVELYN
        345 NewCust
```

In addition to calling constructor methods, you can call the methods you have created on your abstract datatypes. If you will be comparing the values of variables that use the abstract datatypes, you will need to define map or order methods for the datatypes. This capability allows you to further extend object PL/SQL—you define the datatypes and the functions at the database level, and they are callable within any of your PL/SQL programs. Object PL/SQL represents a significant enhancement over traditional PL/SQL.

Objects in the Database

The features available in Oracle—column objects, row objects, and object extensions to PL/SQL—enable you to implement objects in your database without sacrificing the investment you have already made in analysis and design. You can continue to create systems based on relational design techniques and tune them based on relational access methods. The tools that Oracle provides allow you to create an OOP layer above your relational tables. Once you have that layer in place, you can access the relational data as if it were stored in a fully OOP database.

Having an OOP layer allows you to realize some of the benefits of an OOP system, such as abstraction and encapsulation. You can apply the methods for each abstract datatype across a set of consistently implemented objects, and benefit from object reuse and standards enforcement. At the same time, you can benefit from Oracle's relational features. The ability to use both relational and object technology within an application lets you use the proper tool for the proper job within the database.

When implementing the object portion of an object-relational database, start by defining the abstract datatypes that are the core components of your business. Every object-relational feature, whether it relates to column objects or row objects, is based on an abstract datatype. The better you have defined your datatypes and their methods, the better you will be able to implement objects. If necessary, nest objects so that you can have multiple variations of the same core datatype. The result will be a database that is properly designed to take advantage of the relational and OOP features Oracle provides now, and will provide in versions to come.

PART

V

Java in Oracle

CHAPTER
32

An Introduction to Java

n this chapter, you will see an overview of Java as it relates to Oracle database applications. There are numerous uses of Java beyond Oracle applications, and there are many features of the language that will not be used by most Oracle developers. The goal of this chapter is to provide developers who have a background in SQL and PL/SQL with an understanding of the Java language structures. This is not an exhaustive review of Java (there are numerous books that accomplish that goal) but rather a short overview of the Java language components most commonly used by Oracle developers.

Although there are many cases in which PL/SQL and Java correlate well to each other, there are significant differences in terminology and usage. That shouldn't be surprising, since the two programming languages were developed independently. Furthermore, PL/SQL's object-oriented capabilities were not part of its initial implementation, whereas Java has been object-oriented since its inception. To use Java effectively, you need to take a different approach than the one you may have taken in the past with PL/SQL.

Chapter 25 presented an introduction to the PL/SQL language structures and flow control. This chapter mirrors that approach: you will see the structures used by Java and the basic flow-control methods provided. Where applicable, you will also see the matching PL/SQL structures. You should be familiar with PL/SQL (Chapter 25), packages, functions, and procedures (Chapter 27), and abstract datatypes and methods (Chapter 28) before reading this chapter.

Java vs. PL/SQL: An Overview

In comparing PL/SQL to Java, you get no further than the basic PL/SQL structure—a block—before you encounter a significant difference in terminology between the two languages. In PL/SQL, a *block* is a structured piece of code that has a Declarations section, an Executable Commands section, and an Exception Handling section. For a PL/SQL block, the structure may be represented as follows:

```
declare
   <declarations section>
begin
  <executable commands>
 exception
  <exception handling>
end;
```

In Java, the term *block* refers to a much smaller subset of code. In Java, a block is a collection of statements enclosed by curly braces, { and }. For example, the following pseudocode contains two Java blocks:

```
if (some condition) {
  block of code to process if condition is met
}
else {
  block of code to process if condition is not met
}
```

Within PL/SQL, that entire code section would be merely one part of a larger block; within Java, it contains two separate blocks. Throughout this chapter, all references to "blocks" refer to Java blocks unless otherwise specified.

A second major difference between PL/SQL and Java is in the declaration of variables. In a PL/SQL block, you define your variables before you begin the Executable Commands section. In a Java program, you can define variables where they are needed within the program. A Java program has no Declarations section comparable to the one used in PL/SQL blocks.

Throughout this chapter, you will see a number of other differences between PL/SQL and Java. It's important to remember that Java does not replace PL/SQL within your applications—you can continue to use PL/SQL for Oracle applications. For data-retrieval operations, you should test the performance of PL/SQL and Java before deciding on a technical direction to follow.

Getting Started

To use the examples in this section, you need a copy of the Java Development Kit (JDK), which is available for free download from http://java.sun.com. You need to install the JDK on the server on which you will be running the Java programs.

Declarations

Within Java, you can declare variables as needed. A variable has a name and a datatype, and is used to store a data value during the program's execution. A variable also has a scope, allowing it to be publicly accessible or private—similar to the manner in which procedures within packages can have private variables.

Examples of Java variable declarations include:

```
char    aCharVariable = 'J';
boolean aBooleanVariable = false;
```

By convention, Java variables always start with a lowercase letter, as shown in this example. In the example, the datatypes are CHAR and BOOLEAN, and each variable is assigned a value. Note that the assignment character in Java is =, as opposed to := or => in PL/SQL. Each declaration is terminated with a semicolon.

The available primitive datatypes in Java are listed in Table 32-1.

Datatype	Description
byte	Byte-length integer
short	Short integer
int	Integer
long	Long integer
float	Single-precision floating-point real number
double	Double-precision floating-point real number
char	A single character
boolean	A Boolean value, true or false

TABLE 32-1. *Primitive Datatypes in Java*

In addition to the primitive datatypes listed in Table 32-1, you can use reference datatypes, which are based on the contents of variables. You may note that there is no primitive datatype for variable-length character strings—Java provides a String class for that purpose. Classes are discussed later in this chapter.

Executable Commands

You can assign values to variables via the use of expressions and statements. The arithmetic operators supported by Java include:

Operator	Description
*	Multiplication
/	Division
+	Addition
-	Subtraction
%	Modulus

In addition to these operators, you can use Java's unary operators to simplify your coding. For example, you can increment variables via the ++ operator:

```
aLoopCounter = aLoopCounter++;
```

NOTE
The ++ operator is called a unary operator because it has only one operand. If an operator requires two operands (such as =), it is called a binary operator.

In PL/SQL, that would have been written:

```
aLoopCounter := aLoopCounter +1;
```

If the ++ operator is placed in front of the variable name, then it is a *preincrement* operator rather than a *postincrement* operator:

```
int anotherCounter = ++aLoopCounter;
```

In this example, the variable *anotherCounter* is set to the incremented value of *aLoopCounter*. By contrast,

```
int anotherCounter = aLoopCounter++;
```

sets *anotherCounter* to the value of *aLoopCounter* before it is incremented. You can decrement a variable's value, via the – unary operator:

```
aLoopCounter = aLoopCounter--;
```

You can also combine the assignment of values with an operation. For example, instead of writing

```
aNumberVariable = aNumberVariable * 2;
```

you can write

```
aNumberVariable *= 2;
```

You can perform similar combinations using /=, %=, +=, and -=.
If you perform multiple arithmetic operations, you should use parentheses to clearly indicate the order in which the operations should be evaluated, as shown in the following example.

```
aNumberVariable = (aNumberVariable*2) +2;
```

Terminating these operations with semicolons makes them *statements—* complete units of execution.

Conditional Logic

You can evaluate variables by using expressions and statements. To do so, you may use one or more of the fundamental classes provided as part of Java. A full listing of those methods is beyond the scope of this book; see Sun's Java documentation site or one of the many Java books available for the functionality currently provided.

NOTE
The number of supplied classes has changed dramatically with each release of Java. Java 1.1 has 504 classes; Java 1.2 has 1520 classes.

In the following listing, the Character.isUpperCase method is used to evaluate the *aCharVariable* declared earlier:

```
if (Character.isUpperCase(aCharVariable)) {
  some commands to execute
}
```

If the *aCharVariable* value is uppercase, the commands in the following block will be executed; otherwise, flow will continue to the next part of the program.

The following is the general syntax for **if** clauses:

```
if (expression) {
  statement
}
```

Notice the lack of a **then** clause. If the expression being evaluated is true, the following block is automatically executed.

You can also have **else** clauses to evaluate different conditions, as shown in the following listing:

```
if (expression) {
  statement
}
else {
  statement
}
```

If you have multiple conditions to check, you can use the **else if** clause to evaluate each in turn, ending with an **else** clause. The following listing illustrates the use of **else if** clauses.

```
if (aCharVariable == 'V') {
   statement
}
else if (aCharVariable == 'J') {
   statement
}
else {
   statement
}
```

In addition to supporting **if** clauses for conditional logic, Java features a **switch** clause. Used in conjunction with its **break** clause and statement labels, the **switch** clause can approximate the functionality of **goto** clauses (which Java does not support). First, let's look at a simple **switch** example. Using the **case** statement, multiple values of the *aMonth* variable are evaluated. Depending on the *aMonth* value, the text name for the month is displayed, and the processing leaves the **switch** block by means of a **break**.

```
int aMonth;
switch (aMonth) {
   case 1:  System.out.println("January"); break;
   case 2:  System.out.println("February"); break;
   case 3:  System.out.println("March"); break;
   default: System.out.println("Out of range"); break;
}
```

This kind of code is much more complex to write than a simple **TO_CHAR**, but it illustrates the **switch** usage. The **switch** operator takes the *aMonth* variable as its input, and evaluates its value. If the value matches a **case** value, then the System.out.println method is called to print the month's name, and processing control leaves the **switch** block by means of a **break**. If the value does not match one of the **case** clauses, then the **default** option is executed.

Where does control go? By default, it goes to the next section of the program. However, you have the option of creating labels for sections of your code, and passing the name of those labels to the **break** clause. The following listing shows an example of a label and a **break** clause:

```
somelabel:
if (aCharVariable == 'V') {
   statement
} else
{
   statement
```

```
}
int aMonth=2;
switch (aMonth) {
  case 1:  System.out.println("January"); break somelabel;
  case 2:  System.out.println("February"); break someotherlabel;
  case 3:  System.out.println("March"); break somethirdlabel;
  default: System.out.println("Out of range"); break;
}
```

In this example, the **if** clause is evaluated, followed by the **switch** clause. Note that the *aMonth* variable is not declared until just before it is needed. For this example, the *aMonth* variable is assigned a value of 2, so the program will display the word "February" and will then branch over to the section of code identified by the someotherlabel label. If the *aMonth* value had been 1, then the **if** clause at the beginning of the code listing would have been reexecuted.

Java also supports a *ternary* operator—an operator that takes three operands and whose function is similar to that of **DECODE**. Acting as an inline if-else combination, the ternary operator evaluates an expression. If the expression evaluates to true, then the second operand is returned, else the third is returned. The syntax is as follows:

```
expression ? operand1 : operand2
```

The following listing shows a sample ternary operation:

```
aStatusVariable = (aCharVariable == 'V') ? 'OK' : 'Invalid';
```

In this example, the expression

```
(aCharVariable == 'V')
```

is evaluated. If it is true, "OK" is returned; otherwise, "Invalid" is returned.

You can use the ternary operator to simulate the use of a **GREATEST** function:

```
double greatest = (a > b) ? a : b;
```

In this example, the expression (a>b) is evaluated, where *a* and *b* are the names of variables. If that expression is true, *a*'s value is returned; otherwise *b*'s value is returned.

You can combine multiple logic checks via the use of AND and OR operations. In Java, an AND operation is represented by the && operator:

```
if (aCharVariable == 'V' && aMonth == 3) {
  statement
}
```

The OR operation is represented by ||, as shown in the following listing:

```
if (aCharVariable == 'V' || aMonth == 3) {
   statement
}
```

For performance reasons, the && and || operations are carried out only if required; the second expression is not evaluated if the first expression is false.

Loops

Java supports two main types of loops: WHILE loops and FOR loops. In this section, you will see examples of each type. Since Java is not written as an extension of SQL, it does not support cursor FOR loops as PL/SQL does.

WHILE Loops

A **while** clause evaluates a condition; if the condition is true, then the associated block of statements is executed. The syntax for a WHILE loop is of the form:

```
while (expression) {
   statement
}
```

The WHILE loop executes the block of statements (the section within the { and } braces) repeatedly until the *expression* is no longer true:

```
int aNumberVariable = 3;
while (aNumberVariable < 7)  {
   some_processing_statement
   aNumberVariable++;
}
```

In this example, a counter variable (*aNumberVariable*) is created and initialized. The variable's value is then evaluated via the **while** clause. If the value is less than 7, the associated statement block is executed. As part of that block, the variable is incremented. When the block completes, the variable is again evaluated and the loop continues.

NOTE
For examples of WHILE loop processing, see "Classes" later in this chapter.

You could also write this as a **do-while** block:

```
int aNumberVariable = 3;
do {
  some_processing_statement
  aNumberVariable++;
} while (aNumberVariable < 7);
```

In a **do-while** block, the variable's value is not evaluated until the block has been processed at least one time.

FOR Loops

You can use a FOR loop to repeatedly execute a block of code. In a FOR loop, you must specify an initial value, a termination value, and an increment for the loop counter. The loop counter will be incremented each time through the loop by the increment you specify until the termination value is reached. The following is the syntax for a FOR loop:

```
for (initialization; termination; increment) {
  statement;
}
```

The prior section's **while** example can be rewritten with a **for** clause, as shown in the following listing:

```
for (int aNumberVariable=3; aNumberVariable<7; aNumberVariable++)  {
  some_processing_statement
}
```

The **for** clause version for this example is much shorter than the **while** version. In this example, the *aNumberVariable* variable is declared and initialized within the FOR loop. As long as the variable's value does not exceed 7, the block will be executed. For each pass through the loop, the variable's value is incremented by 1 via the ++ unary operator.

Within a loop, you can use the **continue** clause to jump to another statement within the loop. If you just use the **continue** clause by itself, the process flow will jump to the end of the loop body and evaluate the loop's termination test. If you use **continue** with a label (as shown previously in the section on the **switch** clause), processing will continue at the next iteration of the labeled loop.

Cursors and Loops

Within PL/SQL, you can use cursor FOR loops to iterate through the results of a query. You can use Java's WHILE and FOR loops to simulate the functionality of a

PL/SQL cursor FOR loop. The examples provided with Oracle8i show how this can be accomplished. Java examples are found in the /jdbc/demo directory under the Oracle software home directory. The Employee.java file found there creates the Employee class within Java. As part of that class, the example issues the following commands:

```
Statement stmt  conn.createStatement();
ResultSet rset = stmt.executeQuery ("select ENAME from EMP");
//iterate through the result set and print the employee names
while (rset.next ())
  System.out.println (rset.getString (1));
```

This example assumes that a connection to the database has already been established. The first line of the example creates a variable called *stmt*, based on a connection variable called *conn* (not shown in this partial listing). The second line of the example creates a variable called *rset*, based on the result set that the query *stmt* will return. Following a comment (prefixed by //), a **while** clause fetches each row in the result set. If the fetch retrieves a row from the result set, the ENAME from that EMP row is printed; otherwise, the loop will end.

The JDBC (Java Database Connectivity; see also Chapter 33) demos provided by Oracle show samples of queries involving procedure calls, LOBs, and DML. In most cases, your Java code will be performing in a similar manner to the previous example: write the process flow-control language in Java and pass it a statement to execute. Based on the outcome of that statement, you can direct different actions to occur via the use of **while**, **for**, **if**, **break**, **continue**, and **switch** clauses, as shown earlier in this chapter.

Exception Handling

Java provides a robust set of error-handling routines and enables you to create complex error-handling procedures. In PL/SQL, you **raise** an exception; in Java, you **throw** exceptions. If an exception is thrown, you need to use the Java **catch** clause to capture and properly process the exception. When you first begin writing in Java, you will likely encounter exceptions, due to the case sensitivity of the language.

Java's exception-handling syntax is based on three blocks: **try**, **catch**, and **finally**. The **try** block includes the statements that might throw an exception. The **catch** block immediately following the **try** block associates exception handlers with the exceptions that may be thrown by the **try** block. The **finally** block cleans up any system resources not properly cleaned up during the **catch** block processing. The general structure is as follows:

```
try {
  statements
} catch ( ) {
```

```
    statements
} catch ( ) {
    statements
} finally {
    statements
}
```

For example, the following code comes from the PLSQL.java example file provided as part of Oracle8i:

```
Statement stmt = conn.createStatement ();
try { stmt.execute ("drop table plsqltest");
} catch (SQLException e) { }
```

In this example, a variable named *stmt* is created to execute a **drop table** command. If the execution fails—for example, if the table does not exist—how will that error be processed? The **catch** clause tells Java to handle it via a method called SQLException, a standard part of Oracle's Java implementation. As shown in the example, the **catch** clause takes two parameters (an object name and a variable name) and is optionally followed by a block of statements to execute.

The **try** block can contain multiple statements, or you can create separate **try** blocks for each statement. In general, it is easier to manage exception handling if you consolidate your **catch** blocks, so consolidating your **try** blocks will help you manage your code as it changes and grows.

The **finally** block cleans up the state of the current code section before passing control to any subsequent parts of the program. At runtime, the contents of the **finally** block are always executed, regardless of the outcome of the **try** block. For example, you could use the **finally** block to close a database connection.

Reserved Words

The reserved words in Java are listed in Table 32-2. You cannot use these words as the names of classes, methods, or variables.

Classes

In the prior sections of this chapter, you saw the basic syntax structures for Java. In this section, you will see how to use that syntax to create and use objects. A simple program for printing the word "Oracle" is shown in the following listing:

```
public class HelloOracle {
  public static void main (String[] args) {
    System.out.println("Oracle");
  }
}
```

abstract	else	interface	super
boolean	extends	long	switch
break	false	native	synchronized
byte	final	new	this
case	finally	null	throw
catch	float	package	throws
char	for	private	transient
class	goto	protected	true
const	if	public	try
continue	implements	return	void
default	import	short	volatile
do	instanceof	static	while
double	int	strictfp	

TABLE 32-2.   *Reserved Words in Java*

This example creates a *class* called HelloOracle. Within the HelloOracle class, a public method called main is created. The main method prints the word "Oracle." This is significantly more complex than

```
select 'Oracle' from dual;
```

but the Java version has features lacking from the SQL version. HelloOracle is a class, and as such its methods can be called from within other classes. HelloOracle could have multiple methods; in this example, it has only the main method.

The main method's declaration (**public static void main**) has a number of keywords that you should become familiar with:

Public   Defining the class as **public** allows all classes to call this method.

Static   Declares that this is a class variable; you use **static** to declare class methods. Other options include **final** for variables whose values cannot change (similar to PL/SQL's **constant** option).

Void   Specifies the type of procedure. Since this procedure does not return values, its type is **void**.

In this example, the method is given the name main because that will simplify running the class's method. Now that the class has been created, you can compile and load it.

NOTE
To compile and execute a Java class, you must have the JDK on your server. The following examples assume that the binaries that are part of that kit are located in a directory that is automatically searched via the PATH environment variable. The programs referenced here (javac and java) are located in the /bin subdirectory of the JDK software directory.

First, save the program as a plain text file called HelloOracle.java. Next, compile it:

```
javac HelloOracle.java
```

A new file, called HelloOracle.class, will be created on your server. You can then run the class:

```
java HelloOracle
```

And the output will be displayed:

```
Oracle
```

As shown in this example, a class has two parts. The first is a Declaration section, in which the class is given a name, along with other optional attributes related to its inheritance of other classes' attributes. The second part of the class is the class body, in which all of the class variables and methods are defined. As with abstract datatypes in Oracle, Java classes have methods associated with them for the manipulation of their related data.

Let's consider a more complex example. The following listing is a Java program that computes the area of a circle, given a radius value as input (see Chapter 25 for the PL/SQL version):

```
// AreaOfCircle.java
//
public class AreaOfCircle {
 public static void main(String[] args) {
   int input=Integer.parseInt(args[0]);
   double result=area(input);
```

```
    System.out.println(result);
    }
public static double area (int rad) {
    double pi=3.1415926;
    double areacircle=pi*rad*rad;
    return areacircle;
    }
}
```

NOTE
*Be sure to include a closing brace, }, for each block.
In the examples shown in this chapter, the closing
braces are always on a line by themselves to
simplify debugging and processing flow-control
errors that may arise.*

First, note that the class and the name of the file must be the same. In this
case, the class is named AreaOfCircle, so this text is stored in a file called
AreaOfCircle.java. The class has two methods, called main and area. When you
execute the class, the main method is automatically executed. The main method
takes the string provided as input and parses it as an integer into the *input* variable:

```
int input=Integer.parseInt(args[0]);
```

Next, a variable named *result* is declared, and set equal to the expression
area(input):

```
double result=area(input);
```

To process that directive, the area method is executed, using the *input* variable's
value as its input. That method is as follows:

```
public static double area (int rad) {
    double pi=3.1415926;
    double areacircle=pi*rad*rad;
    return areacircle;
```

In its definition, the area method specifies that it will accept one variable, an
integer type named *rad*. That variable's value (passed from the *input* variable in the
main method) is then processed, and a variable named *areacircle* is calculated and
returned to main. In main, that value is then printed:

```
    double result=area(input);
    System.out.println(result);
```

Testing the program is straightforward:

```
javac AreaOfCircle.java
java AreaOfCircle 10
```

The following is the output:

```
314.15926
```

Let's extend this example to include WHILE loop processing. In this example, the area method will be called repeatedly until the resulting input value exceeds a given value:

```
//  AreaOfCircleWhile.java
//
public class AreaOfCircleWhile {
 public static void main(String[] args) {
   int input=Integer.parseInt(args[0]);
   while (input < 7) {
      double result=area(input);
      System.out.println(result);
      input++;
      }
   }
 public static double area (int rad) {
   double pi=3.1415926;
   double areacircle=pi*rad*rad;
   return areacircle;
   }
}
```

In this listing, the area method is unchanged from the prior example. The change is in the main method:

```
   int input=Integer.parseInt(args[0]);
   while (input < 7) {
      double result=area(input);
      System.out.println(result);
      input++;
      }
```

While the input value is less than 7, the input value will be processed. After the area for that radius value has been calculated and printed, the input value is incremented:

```
input++;
```

and the loop is evaluated again. Sample output is shown in the following listing.

```
java AreaOfCircleWhile 4

50.2654816
78.539815
113.0973360000001
```

The output shows the area calculations for input radius values of 4, 5, and 6.

This example is not as complete as a finished program—there is no exception handling, for example—but the structure is the important lesson to learn from this example. In addition to the methods shown in this example, you could create a constructor for the AreaOfCircleWhile class. All Java classes can have constructors to initialize new objects based on the class. The constructor's name is the same as the name of the class. If you create a class with no constructor, then Java will create a default constructor at runtime. Like a method, the constructor body can contain local variable declarations, loops, and statement blocks. The constructor initializes these variables for the class.

In the following chapters, you will see how to implement Java within Oracle: within stored procedures and via SQLJ/JDBC. Those chapters assume that you have the basic knowledge of Java that is provided in this chapter. For additional information about the Java language, please see the Sun Microsystems web site and the variety of books devoted to Java.

CHAPTER
33

JDBC and SQLJ
Programming

ava Database Connectivity (JDBC) and SQLJ build on the Java and programming basics described earlier in this book. The discussions and examples in this chapter assume you are familiar with the Java syntax and structures described in Chapter 32. This chapter does not cover every aspect of JDBC and SQLJ; readers looking for detailed coverage of SQLJ should see *Oracle8i SQLJ Programming* (Oracle Press, 1999).

You can use JDBC to execute dynamic SQL statements in Java programs. For example, the Employee.java demo, found in the /jdbc/demo directory under the Oracle software home directory, issues the following commands after establishing a database connection:

```
Statement stmt  conn.createStatement();
ResultSet rset = stmt.executeQuery ("select ENAME from EMP");
//iterate through the result set and print the employee names
while (rset.next ())
  System.out.println (rset.getString (1));
```

When you execute a SQL statement via JDBC—in this case, **select Ename from EMP**—the SQL statement is not checked for errors until it is run. The JDBC program that contains the SQL command will compile even if the SQL statement is invalid. JDBC is thus suited for use by dynamic SQL.

By contrast, SQLJ performs a precompilation step that includes syntax checks for the SQL embedded within the program. SQLJ also performs type checking and schema checking to make sure the data can be properly retrieved and processed. When the SQLJ precompilation is complete, the result is a Java program that runs via JDBC calls. Thus, SQLJ and JDBC, though distinct, are interrelated.

Getting Started

To use the examples in this section, you need a copy of the Java Development Kit (JDK), which is available for free download from http://java.sun.com. You need to install the JDK on the server on which you will be developing and running the Java programs.

Additional Steps for NT Users

If you will be accessing Oracle8i on NT, you must set the CLASSPATH and PATH system variables to find the classes111.zip file (for JDK 1.1.8) provided by Oracle. The file is located in the /jdbc/lib directory beneath your Oracle home directory. For JDK 1.0.2, use the classes102.zip file found in the /jdbc/lib directory.

NOTE
This step is not performed by the standard Oracle8i for NT installation, so you need to do it manually. If the system variables are not properly set, you will not be able to compile Java classes that use Oracle's JDBC classes.

To set your system variables, click the System icon within the Control Panel. Choose the Environment tab to list the environment variables and their definitions. The PATH variable should already be set, so select it and edit its value. Add the new entry to the end of the list, as shown in the following listing. This value should be separated from the other values in the list by a semicolon.

```
E:\Oracle\Ora81\jdbc\lib\classes111.zip
```

Replace "E:\Oracle\Ora81" with your Oracle software home directory. You should also add the JDK binaries directory to the PATH setting. The next listing shows the PATH setting expanded to include a JDK 1.1.8 binaries directory (replace "E:\jdk118" with the directory in which you downloaded the JDK):

```
E:\Oracle\Ora81\jdbc\lib\classes111.zip;E:\jdk118\bin
```

Next, create an environment variable named CLASSPATH. This variable must have two entries, separated by a semicolon. The first entry must be a period, which denotes the current directory. The second entry must be the directory for the classes111.zip file, using the same form and value as you used for the PATH value:

```
.;E:\Oracle\Ora81\jdbc\lib\classes111.zip
```

If CLASSPATH is not set correctly, you get a NoClassDefFoundError error when you run a compiled class.

NOTE
Be sure to use a version of the JDK that is compatible with the Oracle release you are using. If you use a new release of the JDK with an older release of Oracle's drivers, you may encounter "access violation" errors when executing your programs.

Testing Your Connection

Oracle provides a sample program called JdbcCheckup.java that you can use to verify your JDBC configuration. This file may be in a Zip file (demo.zip on the /jdbc/demo directory), in which case you need to extract it before running the program. Compile and execute the JdbcCheckup.java class:

```
javac JdbcCheckup.java
java JdbcCheckup
```

When you execute JdbcCheckup, you are prompted for a username, password, and connect string for a database. That connection information will be used to attempt a connection; if successful, that attempt will return the following output:

```
Connecting to the database...Connecting...
connected.
Hello World.
Your JDBC installation is correct.
```

If you don't receive feedback telling you that your installation is correct, you need to check your configuration. Common problems include incorrectly set environment variables (PATH and CLASSPATH) and mismatched versions of database connection drivers. If you change the environment variable values via the Control Panel, you need to shut down and restart the command windows for the changes to take effect.

Using the JDBC Classes

JDBC is implemented in Oracle via a set of Oracle-provided classes whose names begin with java.sql. The JdbcCheckup.java class, shown in the following listing, provides a good roadmap for beginning JDBC programmers:

```
/*
 * This sample can be used to check the JDBC installation.
 * Just run it and provide the connect information. It will select
 * "Hello World" from the database.
 */

// You need to import the java.sql package to use JDBC
import java.sql.*;

// We import java.io to be able to read from the command line
import java.io.*;
```

```
class JdbcCheckup
{
  public static void main (String args [])
       throws SQLException, IOException
  {
    // Load the Oracle JDBC driver
    DriverManager.registerDriver(new oracle.jdbc.driver.OracleDriver());

    // Prompt the user for connect information
    System.out.println ("Please enter information to test connection
to the database");
    String user;
    String password;
    String database;

    user = readEntry ("user: ");
    int slash_index = user.indexOf ('/');
    if (slash_index != -1)
    {
      password = user.substring (slash_index + 1);
      user = user.substring (0, slash_index);
    }
    else
      password = readEntry ("password: ");
    database = readEntry ("database (a TNSNAME entry): ");

    System.out.print ("Connecting to the database...");
    System.out.flush ();

    System.out.println ("Connecting...");
    Connection conn =
      DriverManager.getConnection ("jdbc:oracle:oci8:@" + database,
           user, password);

    System.out.println ("connected.");

    // Create a statement
    Statement stmt = conn.createStatement ();

    // Do the SQL "Hello World" thing
  ResultSet rset=stmt.executeQuery("select 'Hello World' from dual");

    while (rset.next ())
      System.out.println (rset.getString (1));

    System.out.println ("Your JDBC installation is correct.");
```

```
      // close the resultSet
      rset.close();

      // Close the statement
      stmt.close();

      // Close the connection
      conn.close();
   }

   // Utility function to read a line from standard input
   static String readEntry (String prompt)
   {
      try
      {
         StringBuffer buffer = new StringBuffer ();
         System.out.print (prompt);
         System.out.flush ();
         int c = System.in.read ();
         while (c != '\n' && c != -1)
         {
            buffer.append ((char)c);
            c = System.in.read ();
         }
         return buffer.toString ().trim ();
      }
      catch (IOException e)
      {
         return "";
      }
   }
}
```

Starting at the top, this script first imports the java.sql classes provided by Oracle:

```
import java.sql.*;
```

and the driver is then registered:

```
DriverManager.registerDriver(new oracle.jdbc.driver.OracleDriver());
```

When you are prompted for information, the *user* variable is populated via a call to the readEntry function:

```
user = readEntry ("user: ");
```

The readEntry function is defined later in the class, in the section beginning

```
// Utility function to read a line from standard input
   static String readEntry (String prompt)
```

Once the connection data has been input, a *connection object* is created to maintain the state of the database session. The getConnection call in the following listing starts the connection:

```
Connection conn =
        DriverManager.getConnection ("jdbc:oracle:oci8:@" + database,
            user, password);
```

If you receive an error during the connection, this step is usually the cause. An incorrect username/password combination or a mismatched set of drivers will cause this step to fail.

By default, a connection object is created with **autocommit** turned on—every transaction is automatically committed. To change that setting, you can use the following command (assuming you name the connection object conn, as shown in the example):

```
conn.setAutoCommit(false);
```

The class then creates a statement, executes a hard-coded query, and prints the output:

```
// Create a statement
    Statement stmt = conn.createStatement ();
// Do the SQL "Hello World" thing
  ResultSet rset =stmt.executeQuery("select 'Hello World' from dual");
 while (rset.next ())
    System.out.println (rset.getString (1));
```

The result set, statement, and connection are then closed and the program completes. Note that there are two steps in executing the statement: first, it's created via the call to the createStatement method, and then it's executed via the executeQuery method. In place of executeQuery, you can use execute or executeUpdate depending on the command to be executed.

Using JDBC for Data Manipulation

Let's combine the pieces that have been described so far: the basic connection syntax from this chapter with the Java classes from Chapter 32. The example in this section will query the RADIUS_VALS table, calculate an area for each value, and insert those values into the AREAS table. Thus, it requires the use of the Java equivalent of a cursor FOR loop, along with support for executable commands and **insert**s.

The following listing, JdbcCircle.java, contains the connection components from JdbcCheckup.java. The executable commands for the circle area start in the section called RetrieveRadius, shown in bold in the listing.

```java
// You need to import the java.sql package to use JDBC
import java.sql.*;
// We import java.io to be able to read from the command line
import java.io.*;

class JdbcCircle
{
  public static void main (String args [])
      throws SQLException, IOException
  {
    // Load the Oracle JDBC driver
  DriverManager.registerDriver(new oracle.jdbc.driver.OracleDriver());
    // Prompt the user for connect information
   System.out.println ("Please enter information to test connection");
    String user;
    String password;
    String database;

    user = readEntry ("user: ");
    int slash_index = user.indexOf ('/');
    if (slash_index != -1)
    {
      password = user.substring (slash_index + 1);
      user = user.substring (0, slash_index);
    }
    else
      password = readEntry ("password: ");
    database = readEntry ("database (a TNSNAME entry): ");
    System.out.print ("Connecting to the database...");
    System.out.flush ();
    System.out.println ("Connecting...");
    Connection conn =
      DriverManager.getConnection ("jdbc:oracle:oci8:@" + database,
          user, password);
    System.out.println ("connected.");

    // Create a statement
    Statement stmt = conn.createStatement ();
```

```
// RetrieveRadius
ResultSet rset =stmt.executeQuery("select Radius from RADIUS_VALS");

  while (rset.next ())  {
  // if you wish to print the values:
  // System.out.println (rset.getInt ("RADIUS"));
  int radInput =  rset.getInt ("RADIUS");

  // Retrieve Radius value, calculate area:
  double result = area(radInput);

  // insert the value into AREAS
 String sql = "insert into AREAS values ("+radInput+","+result+ ")";
  // If you want to print the SQL statement:
  // System.out.println(sql);

  // Create a statement for the insert:
  Statement insArea = conn.createStatement();
  // Execute the insert:
  boolean insertResult = insArea.execute(sql);
}
  // close the resultSet
  rset.close();
  // Close the statement
  stmt.close();
  // Close the connection
  conn.close();
}
// Utility function to calculate the area
public static double area (int rad) {
  double pi=3.1415926;
  double areacircle=pi*rad*rad;
  return areacircle;
  }

// Utility function to read a line from standard input
static String readEntry (String prompt)
{
  try
  {
    StringBuffer buffer = new StringBuffer ();
    System.out.print (prompt);
    System.out.flush ();
    int c = System.in.read ();
    while (c != '\n' && c != -1)
    {
```

```
        buffer.append ((char)c);
        c = System.in.read ();
      }
      return buffer.toString ().trim ();
    }
    catch (IOException e)
    {
      return "";
    }
  }
}
```

In the RetrieveRadius section, the query to be executed is passed to the executeQuery method. The result of the query is stored in a variable named *rset*.

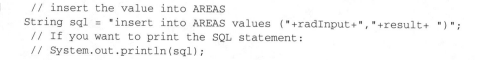

```
// RetrieveRadius
   ResultSet rset =stmt.executeQuery("select Radius from RADIUS_VALS");
```

As noted in Chapter 32, you can use a **while** loop in Java to approximate the functionality of a PL/SQL cursor FOR loop. The following section of the RetrieveRadius section uses the getInt method to retrieve the integer Radius value from the result set. If the value had been a string, then the getString method would have been used instead.

```
   while (rset.next ())  {
   // if you wish to print the values:
   // System.out.println (rset.getInt ("RADIUS"));
   int radInput =  rset.getInt ("RADIUS");
```

The *radInput* variable, assigned in the preceding listing, can now be used as input to the area calculation. The area calculation is performed via a utility function (see the full JdbcCircle listing) based on the code examples presented in Chapter 32.

```
// Retrieve Radius value, calculate area:
   double result = area(radInput);
```

We now have the radius value (the *radInput* variable) and the area value (the *result* variable) to use when populating the AREAS table. Let's build the **insert** statement to perform the insert. First, use the string concatenation functions in Java to concatenate text with the variable values. Make sure not to include a semicolon at the end of the generated command string.

```
   // insert the value into AREAS
   String sql = "insert into AREAS values ("+radInput+","+result+ ")";
   // If you want to print the SQL statement:
   // System.out.println(sql);
```

Next, create a statement and execute the **insert** command (via a call to the *sql* variable that contains the command text):

```
// Create a statement for the insert:
Statement insArea = conn.createStatement();
// Execute the insert:
boolean insertResult = insArea.execute(sql);
```

Did it work? Compile and execute the JdbcCircle.java file, and then check the AREAS table:

```
select * from AREAS
  order by Radius;

  RADIUS      AREA
--------- ---------
        3 28.274333
        4 50.265482
       10 314.15926
```

This example is based on a simple calculation—the area of a circle—but illustrates the key concepts in JDBC development: connecting to the database, retrieving data, implementing a cursor FOR loop, assigning variables, generating a dynamic SQL statement, and executing DML. In the next section, you will see this example written in SQLJ to illustrate the functionality and coding differences between the two languages.

SQLJ

SQLJ is a preprocessor that embeds SQL commands as JDBC calls within a Java program. Unlike JDBC, SQLJ performs syntax checking on SQL statements during the compilation process. In the next section, you will see how to configure SQLJ. SQLJ requires the use of an additional set of classes, in the translator.zip file, to generate the Java classes.

Additional Setup Steps for SQLJ

If you will be accessing Oracle8i on NT, you must set the CLASSPATH and PATH system variables to include the translator.zip file (for JDK 1.1.8) provided by Oracle. The file is located in the /sqlj/lib directory beneath the Oracle home directory.

NOTE
This step is not performed by the standard Oracle8i for NT installation, so you need to do it manually. If the system variables are not properly set, you will not be able to compile Java classes that use Oracle's SQLJ classes.

To set your system variables, click the System icon within your Control Panel. Choose the Environment tab to list the environment variables and their definitions. The PATH variable should already be set, so select it and edit its value. If you did not add the JDBC class libraries and JDK binaries to your PATH setting (as shown earlier in this chapter), then you must add them before using SQLJ. Add the new entries to the end of the list, as shown in the following listing. These values should be separated from each other and from the other values in the list by a semicolon. In the following listing, the one-line PATH setting is shown on two lines.

```
E:\Oracle\Ora81\jdbc\lib\classes111.zip;E:\jdk118\bin;
E:\Oracle\Ora81\sqlj\lib\translator.zip
```

Replace "E:\Oracle\Ora81" with your Oracle software home directory, and replace "E:\jdk118" with the directory in which you downloaded the JDK. The CLASSPATH environment variable for SQLJ developers is different from that used by JDBC developers. For JDBC development, you only need the classes111.zip file to be in the path.

For SQLJ, you need to add the SQLJ translator.zip file directory, usually the /sqlj/lib directory under the Oracle software home directory. In the following listing, the one-line CLASSPATH setting is shown on two lines.

```
.;E:\Oracle\Ora81\jdbc\lib\classes111.zip;
E\Oracle\Ora81\sqlj\lib\translator.zip
```

NOTE
Replace "E:\Oracle\Ora81" with your Oracle software home directory.

If you encounter errors when compiling the SQLJ examples in this chapter, check your CLASSPATH environment variable. You may need to shut down and restart your command window for changes to your CLASSPATH settings to take effect.

NOTE
Be sure to use a version of the JDK that is compatible with the Oracle release you are using. If you use a new release of the JDK with an older release of Oracle's drivers, you may encounter "access violation" errors when executing your programs.

Testing Your SQLJ Configuration

Oracle provides a test script called TestInstallSQLJ.sqlj in the /sqlj/demo directory below the Oracle software home directory. TestInstallSQLJ.sqlj, in turn, reads a file named connect.properties in the same directory. The connect.properties file identifies the database, username, and password to be used for the demonstration connection. For example, the connect.properties file may contain the following entries:

```
sqlj.url=jdbc:oracle:oci8:@
sqlj.user=scott
sqlj.password=tiger
```

NOTE
Add the name of your database directly after the @ in the sqlj.url entry, and use your test username and password in place of the preceding listing's example values.

The TestInstallSQLJ.sqlj demo file inserts a row into a table named SALES, which has a column named Item_Name. For the purposes of this demo, you can create the SALES table with the following command:

```
create table SALES
 (Item_Number      NUMBER,
  Item_Name        CHAR(30),
  Sales_Date       DATE,
  Cost             NUMBER,
  Sales_Rep_Number NUMBER,
  Sales_Rep_Name   CHAR(20));
```

If you already have a SCOTT/TIGER account in your database, you can use that account and its SALES table for the connection test (although doing so will delete the rows presently in that table). If you prefer using JDBC for your table creation, you can run the TestInstallCreateTable.java class provided in the /sqlj/demo directory to create the SALES table. The TestInstallCreateTable.java file relies on the connection information specified in the connect.properties file.

With the SALES table in place and the connect.properties file properly configured, translate the TestInstallSQLJ.sqlj file:

```
sqlj TestInstallSQLJ.sqlj
```

This step should complete with no reported errors. As part of the SQLJ translation, the Java class will be compiled, so you can execute the program:

```
java TestInstallSQLJ
```

If your configuration is correct, you should see the following output:

```
Hello, SQLJ!
```

NOTE
*The longest part of the translation step is the Java compilation. If the translation process generates a JAVA file, you can manually compile that file (via **javac**). Depending on the errors encountered during compilation, manually compiling the file may provide you with more relevant debugging information than the translator provides.*

Using the SQLJ Classes

When you translated the TestInstallSQLJ.sqlj file, several new files were created, including a TestInstallSQL.java file and a compiled TestInstallSQLJ.class file. Having seen a JDBC file earlier in this chapter, you should skim through the TestInstallSQLJ.java file to see what the translator did. You will see that it creates a class called MyIter:

```
class MyIter
extends sqlj.runtime.ref.ResultSetIterImpl
implements sqlj.runtime.NamedIterator
{
```

```
public MyIter(sqlj.runtime.profile.RTResultSet resultSet)
  throws java.sql.SQLException
{
  super(resultSet);
  ITEM_NAMENdx = findColumn("ITEM_NAME");
}
public String ITEM_NAME()
  throws java.sql.SQLException
{
  return resultSet.getString(ITEM_NAMENdx);
}
private int ITEM_NAMENdx;
}
```

The MyIter class is a SQLJ iterator—a structure used to iterate through the results of queries returning multiple rows. Later in the file, the iterator is used as the basis for the query:

```
    MyIter iter;

//  #sql iter = { SELECT ITEM_NAME FROM SALES  };
```

And the query is executed:

```
    sqlj.runtime.profile.RTResultSet __sJT_result =
__sJT_execCtx.executeQuery();
    iter = new MyIter(__sJT_result);
```

SQLJ screens the JDBC details from you; you do not need to manually enter all the query-management code yourself. For each SQL statement, SQLJ creates the code needed to execute it via JDBC and Java. First, it creates a *connection context* object. The connection context maintains the JDBC connection. Each statement that is executed uses a different connection context object. For example, the TestInstallSQLJ.java file contains the following command to create a connection context:

```
  sqlj.runtime.ConnectionContext __sJT_connCtx =
sqlj.runtime.ref.DefaultContext.getDefaultContext();
```

In the preceding command, a connection context object is created based on the default context options. A default context supports a connection that your classes can use to access the database without having to specify a connection context object.

Within the connection context, all the commands are executed via *execution context* objects. Within TestInstallSQLJ.java, you should see commands similar to the following to create an execution context:

```
    sqlj.runtime.ExecutionContext __sJT_execCtx =
__sJT_connCtx.getExecutionContext();
    if (__sJT_execCtx == null)
sqlj.runtime.error.RuntimeRefErrors.raise_NULL_EXEC_CTX();
    synchronized (__sJT_execCtx) {
      sqlj.runtime.profile.RTStatement __sJT_stmt =
__sJT_execCtx.registerStatement(__sJT_connCtx,
TestInstallSQLJ_SJProfileKeys.getKey(0), 0);
```

The last line of the preceding listing refers to *profile keys*. When you translated the TestInstallSQLJ.sqlj file, Oracle automatically created several files in addition to the TestInstallSQLJ.java file. The translator retrieves the SQL statements from the SQLJ file you created and creates two files: a file with a .ser extension that stores the statement profiles, and a file with a .class extension that stores the profile keys. Thus, when you read the TestInstallSQLJ.java file, you will see that the SQL commands are commented out, as shown in the following listing:

```
//  #sql iter = { SELECT ITEM_NAME FROM SALES  };
```

The actual SQL commands executed by the program are not visible unless you have the source code (either the .sqlj file or the .java file created by the translator).

Using SQLJ for Data Manipulation

Using TestInstallSQLJ.sqlj as a basis, you can develop a program that retrieves data from the RADIUS_VALS table, performs the circle area calculation, and inserts the results into the AREAS table. Because SQLJ handles the JDBC connection management, the logic flow of the SQLJ program should be simpler to follow than the JDBC program, for people with a background in PL/SQL.

The following listing is the SqljCircle.sqlj file. As in the JdbcCircle.java example earlier in this chapter, the area calculation is performed via a utility function. The most relevant part for this example—the commands needed to extract and manipulate the data—is shown in bold.

```
/* Import SQLExceptions class.  The SQLException comes from
   JDBC. Executable #sql clauses result in calls to JDBC, so methods
   containing executable #sql clauses must either catch or throw
   SQLException.
 */
import java.sql.SQLException ;
import oracle.sqlj.runtime.Oracle;

// iterator for the select
#sql iterator MyIter (int Radius);
```

```
class SqljCircle
{
  //Main method
  public static void main (String args[])
  {
    try {
      /* if you're using a non-Oracle JDBC Driver, add a call here to
         DriverManager.registerDriver() to register your Driver
      */
      // set the default connection to the URL, user, and password
      // specified in your connect.properties file
      Oracle.connect(SqljCircle.class, "connect.properties");
      SqljCircle ti = new SqljCircle();
      ti.runExample();
    } catch (SQLException e) {
      System.err.println("Error running the example: " + e);
    }
  } //End of method main

  //Method that runs the example
  void runExample() throws SQLException
  {

MyIter iter;

#sql iter = { select Radius from RADIUS_VALS};
    while (iter.next())      {
    // To see the radius values:
    //System.out.println(iter.Radius());

    int radInput =  iter.Radius();
    double result=area(radInput);
    // To see the result values:
    //System.out.println(result);

#sql { insert into AREAS values(:radInput,:result)};
#sql {commit};
    }
    iter.close();
  }

  // Utility function to calculate the area
  public static double area (int rad) {
    double pi=3.1415926;
    double areacircle=pi*rad*rad;
    return areacircle;
    }
}
```

Since the query of RADIUS_VALS will return multiple rows, an iterator is specified within the SQLJ file. If you prefer, you can create and use JDBC result sets instead (see the JDBC examples earlier in this chapter). When you execute the query for the program, the result is passed as the value for the iterator:

```
#sql iter = { select Radius from RADIUS_VALS};
```

Next, use a **while** loop to evaluate the rows:

```
while (iter.next())      {
// To see the radius values:
//System.out.println(iter.Radius());
```

For each row passed to the iterator, capture the Radius value and use that as the *radInput* value. Then, create the *result* variable to hold the calculated area value based on the Radius value.

```
int radInput =  iter.Radius();
double result=area(radInput);
// To see the result values:
//System.out.println(result);
```

Now that the values have been calculated, you can insert them into the AREAS table. This example assumes that the AREAS table is empty prior to executing the SqljCircle class. Within the **insert** command, the *radInput* and *result* variables are prefixed by a colon. Note that the entire command is enclosed within curly braces, {}, and that no semicolon appears within the braces. Each row is committed following each insert.

```
#sql { insert into AREAS values(:radInput,:result)};
#sql {commit};
```

This example contains an explicit **commit** command so that you can add additional criteria to control the commit frequency within the application.

Now, close the iterator:

```
iter.close();
```

and you're done. You can check the AREAS table for the result:

```
select * from AREAS
 order by Radius;

   RADIUS      AREA
 --------- ---------
       3 28.274333
       4 50.265482
      10 314.15926
```

Because it supports SQL calls so easily, SQLJ is attractive to first-time JDBC programmers. By comparison, the SqljCircle.java file generated by the translator is three times longer than the SqljCircle.sqlj file. See the Oracle documentation for further information on the options available for implementing and managing iterators.

This chapter provides an overview of SQL's capabilities—queries, data manipulation, multirow result set management, variable assignments, and DML operations. For additional information regarding SQLJ's capabilities, please see Oracle's SQLJ documentation and *Oracle8i SQLJ Programming* (Oracle Press, 1999).

CHAPTER
34

Java Stored Procedures

s of Oracle8i, you can write stored procedures, triggers, object type methods, and functions that call Java classes. In this chapter, you will see a sample set of Java procedures, along with the commands required to execute a procedure. To get the most from this chapter, you should already be familiar with Java structures (refer to Chapter 32) and the uses of Java classes, JDBC, and SQLJ (refer to Chapter 33). You should also be familiar with the basic syntax and usage of stored procedures (refer to Chapter 27).

To focus on the database access operations of the Java classes, the example in this chapter is brief. The following class, called AreasDML, contains methods to insert and delete records from the AREAS table. In this example, the calculation of the area is not performed; rather, all required values are supplied during the **insert**. The following listing shows the AreasDML.sqlj file:

```
import sqlj.runtime.*;
import sqlj.runtime.ref.*;
import java.sql.SQLException ;
import oracle.sqlj.runtime.Oracle;
import java.sql.*;

class AreasDML
{
  //Insert method
  public static void insert (
    oracle.sql.NUMBER   radius,
    oracle.sql.NUMBER   area ) throws SQLException {
    try {
        #sql {insert into AREAS values
                (:radius, :area)   };
        } catch (SQLException e) {System.err.println(e.getMessage());}
    }
    //End of method insert

  //Delete method
  public static void delete (
    oracle.sql.NUMBER   radius,
    oracle.sql.NUMBER   area ) throws SQLException {
    try {
        #sql {delete from AREAS
              where Radius = :radius};
        } catch (SQLException e) {System.err.println(e.getMessage());}
    }
    //End of method delete
}
```

The AreasDML.sqlj file defines the AreasDML class. Within the AreasDML class, there are separate methods for processing **insert**s and **delete**s. In each of the method specifications, the datatypes for the AREAS table's columns are listed:

```
public static void insert (
    oracle.sql.NUMBER   radius,
    oracle.sql.NUMBER   area )
```

These parameters use the datatypes provided as part of Oracle's class libraries. If you use the standard Java datatypes, you may encounter datatype-related problems during the class execution. The next part of the insert method inserts the values into the AREAS table:

```
#sql {insert into AREAS values
        (:radius, :area)  };
```

Note that the variable names are case-sensitive—they must exactly match the names declared earlier.

The delete method is very similar in structure. Its SQL statement is

```
#sql {delete from AREAS
        where Radius = :radius};
```

Note that no part of the class creates a connection to the database, in contrast with the examples in Chapter 33. The connection used to invoke this class will provide the connection context for the class's methods.

Verify that the class compiles properly by processing it via the SQLJ preprocessor:

```
sqlj AreasDML.sqlj
```

This step should complete successfully. If you encounter errors during this compilation step, check your SQLJ environment configuration (see Chapter 33).

Loading the Class into the Database

Before loading a class into the database, confirm that it compiles properly via SQLJ. You can then use the loadjava utility to load the class into the database. The syntax for the loadjava utility is as follows:

```
loadjava {-user | -u} username/password[@database]
    [-option_name -option_name ...] filename filename ...
```

The options available for the loadjava utility are shown in Table 34-1.

Option	Description
andresolve	Compiles source files and resolves each class file as it is loaded.
debug	Generates debugging information.
definer	Specifies that the methods of uploaded classes will execute with the privileges of their definer, not their invoker. By default, methods execute with the privileges of their invoker.
encoding	Sets (or resets) the option -encoding in the database table JAVA$OPTIONS to the specified value.
force	Forces the loading of Java class files regardless of whether they have been loaded before. By default, previously loaded class files are rejected.
grant	Grants EXECUTE privilege on uploaded classes to the listed users and roles.
oci8	Directs loadjava to communicate with the database using the OCI JDBC driver. This option (the default) and -thin are mutually exclusive.
oracleresolver	Binds newly created class schema objects to a specific resolver spec.
resolve	Resolves all external references in the loaded and compiled classes. If this option is not specified, files are loaded but not compiled or resolved until runtime.
resolver	Binds newly created class schema objects to a user-defined resolver spec.
schema	Specifies the schema for newly created objects.
synonym	Automatically creates a public synonym for the uploaded classes.
thin	Directs loadjava to communicate with the database using the thin JDBC driver. This option and –oci8 are mutually exclusive.
verbose	Enables the display of progress messages during loadjava execution.

TABLE 34-1. *loadjava Utility Options*

For example, to load the AreasDML.sqlj file into the Talbot schema, you can use the following command:

```
loadjava -u Talbot/ledger@orcl.world -verbose AreasDML.sqlj
```

You should see the following output:

```
initialization complete
loading   : AreasDML
creating  : AreasDML
```

NOTE
*The name of the class should not match the name of
any of the existing objects in your schema.*

The AreasDML class is now loaded into the database. Here's what it created
(as queried from USER_OBJECTS):

OBJECT_NAME	OBJECT_TYPE
AreasDML	JAVA CLASS
AreasDML	JAVA SOURCE
AreasDML_SJProfileKeys	JAVA CLASS
CREATE$JAVA$LOB$TABLE	TABLE
JAVA$CLASS$MD5$TABLE	TABLE
LOADLOBS	PACKAGE
LOADLOBS	PACKAGE BODY
SYS_C001282	INDEX
SYS_C001283	INDEX
SYS_LOB0000012333C00002$$	LOB

(The names of the indexes and LOB, which start with SYS_, will be different in your
database, since each name includes a sequence number that is database-specific.)
Although CREATE$JAVA$LOB$TABLE is listed as a table, you can't select data from
it. The AreasDML source, class, and profile keys should be familiar from the SQLJ
examples in Chapter 33.

How to Access the Class
Now that the AreasDML class has been loaded into the database, you must create
a procedure to call each of the methods. The **create procedure** command in the
following listing creates a procedure called InsertAreaViaJava:

```
create or replace procedure InsertAreaViaJava
  (Radius   NUMBER,
   Area     NUMBER)
  as
```

```
language JAVA
name 'AreasDML.insert(
  oracle.sql.NUMBER, oracle.sql.NUMBER)';
/
```

This brief procedure has two parameters—Radius and Area. Its **language JAVA** clause tells Oracle that the procedure is calling a Java method. The name of the method is specified in the **name** clause (be sure to be consistent with your use of capital letters). The formats for the Java method call are then specified.

A separate procedure will delete the AREA table's records via a method call:

```
create or replace procedure DeleteAreaViaJava
(Radius   NUMBER,
 Area     NUMBER)
as
language JAVA
name 'AreasDML.delete(
  oracle.sql.NUMBER, oracle.sql.NUMBER)';
/
```

Now, go into SQL*Plus and use the **call** command to execute the Java classes. For this example, start with the AREAS table empty:

```
delete from AREAS;
commit;

call InsertAreaViaJava(10,314.15);
```

You will see this response:

```
Call completed.
```

The **call** command will pass the values 10 and 314.15 as parameters to the InsertAreaViaJava stored procedure. It will format them according to the specifications in the **name** clause and will pass them to the AreasDML.insert method. That method will use your current connection to execute its SQLJ commands, and the row will be inserted. Most of these libraries and classes will not have been loaded yet within the database. That's a lot of steps to go through, so the performance will be affected. You can verify its success by querying the AREAS table:

```
select * from AREAS;

   RADIUS      AREA
--------- ---------
       10    314.15
```

And you can delete that record via a call to DeleteAreaViaJava:

```
call DeleteAreaViaJava(10,314.15);
```

Oracle will reply

```
Call completed.
```

The call to DeleteAreaViaJava will complete much faster than the call to InsertAreaViaJava, because your Java libraries will have been loaded the first time you executed InsertAreaViaJava.

Check out the error handling by passing a character string to be inserted:

```
call InsertAreaViaJava('J',314.15)
                         *
ERROR at line 1:
ORA-01722: invalid number
```

As expected, the datatype mismatch was handled as an exception by the procedure definition.

Where to Perform Commands

The AreasDML example is intended to provide an overview of the implementation of Java stored procedures. Suppose you now want to make the procedures more complex. Since area and radius are directly related to each other, you only need to accept the radius value as input to the procedure. You could then calculate the area and insert the calculated value. As shown in Chapters 25, 32, and 33, you can perform those calculations either in Java or in PL/SQL.

Your choice of a platform and language for your data processing will impact your performance. Consider the following performance results of insertions into the AREAS table. These tests were conducted on a Windows NT platform using Oracle 8.1.5.0. The first test uses standard SQL:

```
set timing on
insert into areas values (1,3.1415);

1 row created.

real: 70
```

As expected, that task completes quickly—70 milliseconds. For the second test, call the InsertAreaViaJava procedure that calls the AreasDML class:

```
call InsertAreaViaJava(10,314.15);

Call completed.

 real: 54979
```

The first invocation of the InsertAreaViaJava procedure required an unacceptably long time to complete—almost 55 seconds. What happens if you run it a second time?

```
call InsertAreaViaJava(3,28.274);

Call completed.

 real: 80
```

The second time you run the procedure, all the classes have already been loaded. As a result, the procedure completes in 80 milliseconds—longer than the standard SQL method but acceptable for online usage.

If you now log out and log back in, what is the performance?

```
call InsertAreaViaJava(0,0);

Call completed.

 real: 391
```

Logging out and logging back in impacts your performance, but not nearly as much as the first execution of the procedure. When you use Java stored procedures, you must therefore be aware of the way in which the application interacts with Oracle. If your users frequently log out and log back in, then they will pay a performance penalty the first time they execute the procedure following each login. Furthermore, the first execution of the procedure following a database startup will pay the most severe performance penalty. The performance impact of these actions must be taken into account during the design stage of your application development.

To reduce the performance penalties associated with the Java stored procedure calls:

■ Execute each Java stored procedure following database startup. In the case of the AreasDML example, this may involve inserting and deleting a test record following each startup.

■ Reduce the number of short-term database connections; for example, by "connection pooling."

■ Perform most of your direct database manipulation via standard SQL and PL/SQL.

Java is an appropriate technology to use for many computational processes and for display manipulation. In general, SQL and PL/SQL are more efficient than Java for database connections and data manipulation. When designing applications that integrate Java, SQL, and PL/SQL, focus on using each language for the functions that it performs best.

The calculation of a circle's area is simple arithmetic, handled easily by both PL/SQL and Java. Thus, you could put the area calculation in either part of the application—in a PL/SQL procedure that calculates the area prior to passing it to SQLJ to be inserted, or as part of the SQLJ class. In general, actions that involve selecting data from the database and manipulating it are best handled by PL/SQL and SQL. Computations on the selected data may be processed faster by Java. In your application design, be sure to use the proper tool for the proper function, and avoid unnecessary performance penalties.

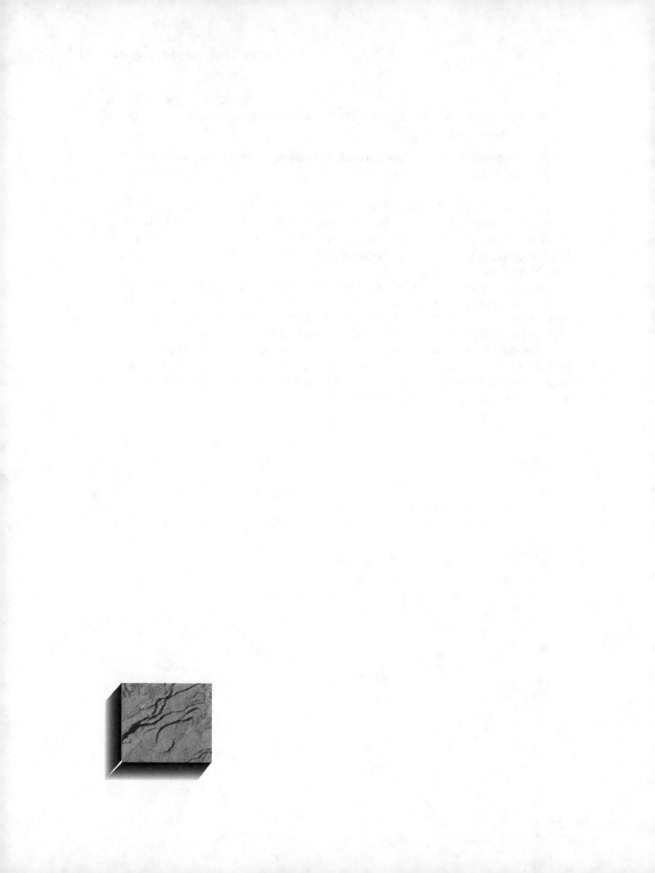

PART VI

Hitchhiker's Guides

CHAPTER
35

The Hitchhiker's Guide
to the Oracle8i
Data Dictionary

racle's data dictionary stores all the information that is used to manage the objects in the database. Although the data dictionary is usually the domain of database administrators (DBAs), it also is a source of valuable information for developers and end users.

In this chapter, you will see the data dictionary—Oracle's "Yellow Pages"—from the perspective of an end user; thus, the data dictionary tables and views are not listed alphabetically, but rather are grouped by function (tables, security, and so on). This organization is designed to let you quickly find your way to the information you need. The most-used data dictionary views are all shown here, along with examples of their usage.

Depending on which Oracle configuration options you are using, some of the groups will not apply to your database. The most commonly used views are listed first. The groupings used in this chapter are, in order:

- The Road Maps: DICTIONARY (DICT) and DICT_COLUMNS

- Things You Select from: Tables (and Columns), Views, Synonyms, and Sequences

- Constraints and Comments

- Indexes and Clusters

- Abstract Datatypes, ORDBMS-Related Structures, and LOBs

- Database Links, Snapshots, and Materialized Views

- Triggers, Procedures, Functions, and Packages

- Dimensions

- Space Allocation and Usage, Including Partitions and Subpartitions

- Users and Privileges

- Roles

- Auditing

- Miscellaneous

A Note About Nomenclature

With some exceptions, the names of the objects in the Oracle data dictionary begin with one of three prefixes: "USER," "ALL," or "DBA." Records in the "USER" views usually show information about objects owned by the account performing the query. Records in the "ALL" views include the "USER" records plus information about objects on which privileges have been granted to PUBLIC or to the user. "DBA" views encompass all of the database objects, regardless of owner. For most database objects, "USER," "ALL," and "DBA" views are available.

In keeping with the user focus of this guide, the emphasis will be on the "USER" views or those that are accessible to all users. The "ALL" and "DBA" views will be described when they are applicable.

The Road Maps: DICTIONARY (DICT) and DICT_COLUMNS

Descriptions for the objects that make up the Oracle data dictionary are accessible via a view named DICTIONARY. This view, also accessible via the public synonym DICT, queries the database to determine which data dictionary views you can see. It also searches for public synonyms for those views.

The following example queries DICT for the names of all data dictionary views whose names include the string VIEWS. Selecting from DICT via a non-DBA account, as shown in the following listing, returns the object name and comments for each data dictionary object that matches your search criteria. There are only two columns in this view: Table_Name and the table's associated Comments.

```
column Comments format a50

select Table_Name, Comments
  from DICT
 where Table_Name like '%VIEWS%';


TABLE_NAME               COMMENTS
---------------------    --------------------------------------------------
ALL_VIEWS                Description of views accessible to the user
USER_VIEWS               Description of the user's own views
```

You can query the columns of the dictionary views via the DICT_COLUMNS view. Like the DICTIONARY view, DICT_COLUMNS displays the comments that have been entered into the database for the data dictionary views. DICT_COLUMNS has three columns: Table_Name, Column_Name, and

Comments. Querying DICT_COLUMNS lets you determine which data dictionary views would be most useful for your needs.

For example, if you want to view space allocation and usage information for your database objects but are not sure which data dictionary views store that information, you can query DICT_COLUMNS, as shown in the following example, which looks for all the dictionary tables that have a column named Blocks:

```
select Table_Name
   from DICT_COLUMNS
 where Column_Name = 'BLOCKS'
   and Table_Name like 'USER%';


TABLE_NAME
-------------------
USER_ALL_TABLES
USER_EXTENTS
USER_FREE_SPACE
USER_OBJECT_TABLES
USER_SEGMENTS
USER_TABLES
USER_TAB_PARTITIONS
USER_TAB_SUBPARTITIONS
USER_TS_QUOTAS
```

To list all of the available column names that you could have used in the last example, query DICT_COLUMNS:

```
select distinct Column_Name
   from DICT_COLUMNS
 order by Column_Name;
```

Whenever you're unsure about where to find the data you want, just check DICTIONARY and DICT_COLUMNS. If it appears that a large number of views could be useful, query DICTIONARY (as in the first example) to see the Comments on each view.

Things You Select from: Tables (and Columns), Views, Synonyms, and Sequences

The set of objects owned by a user is referred to as the user's *catalog*. There is one catalog per user. The catalog lists all of those objects that the user can **select** records from; that is, any object that can be listed in the **from** clause of a query. Although sequences are not referenced directly in **from** clauses, Oracle includes them in the catalog. In this section, you will see how to retrieve information about tables, columns, views, synonyms, sequences, and the user catalog.

Catalog: USER_CATALOG (CAT)

Querying USER_CATALOG will display all tables, views, synonyms, and sequences the user owns. The Table_Name column shows the name of the object (even if it is not a table), and the Table_Type column shows the type of object.

```
select Table_Name, Table_Type
  from USER_CATALOG
 where Table_Name like 'T%';


TABLE_NAME              TABLE_TYPE
-------------------- ----------
TROUBLE                 TABLE
TWONAME                 TABLE
```

USER_CATALOG may also be referred to by the public synonym CAT.

Two additional catalogs are available. ALL_CATALOG lists everything in your USER_CATALOG view plus any objects that you or PUBLIC have been granted access to. DBA_CATALOG is a DBA-level version of the catalog showing all tables, views, sequences, and synonyms in the database. In addition to the Table_Name and Table_Type columns shown in the USER_CATALOG query, ALL_CATALOG and DBA_CATALOG include an Owner column.

Objects: USER_OBJECTS (OBJ)

USER_CATALOG only displays information for tables, views, sequences, and synonyms. To retrieve information on all types of objects, query USER_OBJECTS. You can use this view to find out about many types of objects, including clusters, database links, functions, indexes, packages, package bodies, Java classes, abstract datatypes, resource plans, sequences, synonyms, tables, triggers, and views. USER_OBJECTS' columns are listed in Table 35-1.

USER_OBJECTS (also known by its public synonym OBJ) contains several vital pieces of information that are not found in other data dictionary views. It records the creation date of objects (the Created column) and the last time an object was altered (the Last_DDL_Time column). These columns are very useful when trying to reconcile different sets of objects in the same application.

Column Name	Description
Object_Name	The name of the object
SubObject_Name	The name of the subobject, such as a partition name
Object_ID	A unique, Oracle-assigned ID for the object
Data_Object_ID	The object number of the segment that contains the object's data
Object_Type	The object type ('TABLE', 'INDEX', 'TABLE PARTITION', and so on)
Created	The timestamp for the object's creation (a DATE column)
Last_DDL_Time	The timestamp for the last DDL command used on the object, including **alter**, **grant**, and **revoke**
Timestamp	The timestamp for the object's creation (same as Created, but stored as a character column)
Status	The status of the object ('VALID' or 'INVALID')
Temporary	A flag to indicate whether the object is a temporary table
Generated	A flag to indicate whether the object's name was system-generated
Secondary	A flag to indicate whether the object is a secondary index created by a domain index

TABLE 35-1. *Columns in USER_OBJECTS*

The following example selects the creation date and last alteration date for several objects. Note that the Object_Name column is a VARCHAR2(128), so it must be formatted.

```
column Object_Name format a19

select Object_Name, Created, Last_DDL_Time
  from USER_OBJECTS
 where Object_Name like 'T%';

OBJECT_NAME          CREATED   LAST_DDL_TIME
-------------------- --------- -------------
TROUBLE              07-AUG-01 14-AUG-01
TWONAME              07-AUG-01 07-AUG-01
```

This example shows the date on which these objects were last created, and the date on which they were last altered. The data in this listing shows that the two objects were created on the same day, but that the TROUBLE table was later altered.

NOTE
If you re-create objects in any way, such as via the Import utility (see Chapter 38), their Created values will change to the last time they were created.

Two additional object listings are available. ALL_OBJECTS lists everything in your USER_OBJECTS view plus any objects for which access has been granted to you or PUBLIC. DBA_OBJECTS is a DBA-level version of the object listing, showing all of the objects in the database. In addition to the columns shown in the USER_OBJECTS view, ALL_OBJECTS and DBA_OBJECTS include an Owner column.

Tables: USER_TABLES (TABS)

Although all of a user's objects are shown in USER_OBJECTS, few attributes of those objects are shown there. To get more information about an object, you need to look at the view that is specific to that type of object. For tables, that view is USER_TABLES. It can also be referenced via the public synonym TABS.

NOTE
Earlier versions of Oracle included a view called TAB. That view, which is similar in function to TABS, is still supported because of Oracle products that reference it. However, TAB does not contain the columns that TABS contains. Use TABS in your data dictionary queries.

The columns in USER_TABLES can be divided into four major categories (Identification, Space-Related, Statistics-Related, and Other), as shown in Table 35-2.

The table's name is shown in the Table_Name column. The Backed_Up column shows whether or not the table has been backed up since its last modification. The Partitioned column will have a value of 'Y' if the table has been partitioned (data dictionary views related to partitions are described in the "Space Allocation and Usage" section of this chapter). If the table is an object table, then the Table_Type_Owner column will show the owner of the type.

Identification	Space-Related	Statistics-Related	Other
Table_Name	Tablespace_Name	Num_Rows	Degree
Backed_Up	Cluster_Name	Blocks	Instances
Partitioned	Pct_Free	Empty_Blocks	Cache
Table_Type	Pct_Used	Avg_Space	Table_Lock
Table_Type_Owner	Ini_Trans	Chain_Cnt	Buffer_Pool
Packed	Max_Trans	Avg_Row_Len	Row_Movement
IOT_Name	Initial_Extent	Sample_Size	Duration
Logging	Next_Extent	Last_Analyzed	Skip_Corrupt
IOT_Type	Min_Extents	Avg_Space_Freelist_Blocks	Monitoring
Temporary	Max_Extents	Num_Freelist_Blocks	
Nested	Pct_Increase	Global_Stats	
Secondary	Freelists	User_Stats	
	Freelist_Groups		

TABLE 35-2.   *Columns in USER_TABLES*

The "Space-Related" columns are described in the "Storage" entry of the Alphabetical Reference. The "Statistics-Related" columns are populated when the table is analyzed (see the **analyze** command in the Alphabetical Reference).

Querying the Table_Name column from USER_TABLES will display the names of all of the tables in the current account. The following example lists all of the tables whose names begin with the letter *L*:

```
select Table_Name from USER_TABLES
 where Table_Name like 'L%';

TABLE_NAME
------------------------------
LEDGER
LOCATION
LODGING
LONGTIME
```

The ALL_TABLES view shows all of the tables owned by the user as well as any to which the user has been granted access. Most third-party reporting tools that list available tables for queries obtain that list by querying ALL_TABLES. Since ALL_TABLES can contain entries for multiple users, it contains an Owner column in addition to the columns shown in Table 35-2. DBA_TABLES, which lists all tables in the database, has the same column definitions as ALL_TABLES.

The Degree and Instances columns in the "Other" category of Table 35-2 relate to how the table is queried during parallel queries. For information on Degree, Instances, and the other table parameters, see CREATE TABLE in the Alphabetical Reference.

Columns: USER_TAB_COLUMNS (COLS)

Although users do not query from columns, the data dictionary view that shows columns is closely tied to the data dictionary view of tables. This view, called USER_TAB_COLUMNS, lists information specific to columns. USER_TAB_COLUMNS can also be queried via the public synonym COLS.

The columns you can query from USER_TAB_COLUMNS can be separated into three major categories, as shown in Table 35-3.

Identification	Definition-Related	Statistics-Related
Table_Name	Data_Type	Num_Distinct
Column_Name	Data_Length	Low_Value
Column_ID	Data_Precision	High_Value
Character_Set_Name	Data_Scale	Density
Char_Col_Decl_Length	Nullable	Num_Nulls
	Default_Length	Num_Buckets
	Data_Default	Last_Analyzed
	Data_Type_Mod	Sample_Size
	Data_Type_Owner	Global_Stats
		User_Stats
		Avg_Col_Len

TABLE 35-3. *Columns in USER_TAB_COLUMNS*

The Table_Name and Column_Name columns contain the names of your tables and columns. The usage of the "Definition-Related" columns is described in the "Datatypes" entry in the Alphabetical Reference. The "Statistics-Related" columns are populated when the table is analyzed (see the **analyze** command in the Alphabetical Reference). Statistics for columns are also provided in the USER_TAB_COL_STATISTICS view (described shortly).

To see the column definitions for a table, query USER_TAB_COLUMNS, specifying the Table_Name in the **where** clause:

```
select Column_Name, Data_Type
  from USER_TAB_COLUMNS
 where Table_Name = 'NEWSPAPER';

COLUMN_NAME     DATA_TYPE
-------------   ---------
FEATURE         VARCHAR2
SECTION         CHAR
PAGE            NUMBER
```

The information in this example is also obtainable via the SQLPLUS **describe** command; however, **describe** does not give you the option of seeing the column defaults and statistics. The ALL_TAB_COLUMNS view shows the columns for all of the tables and views owned by the user as well as any to which the user has been granted access. Since ALL_TAB_COLUMNS can contain entries for multiple users, it contains an Owner column in addition to the columns shown in Table 35-3. DBA_TAB_COLUMNS, which lists the column definitions for all tables and views in the database, has the same column definitions as ALL_TAB_COLUMNS.

Column Statistics

As of Oracle8, most of the column statistics have been moved from USER_TAB_COLUMNS to USER_TAB_COL_STATISTICS. The columns available in USER_TAB_COL_STATISTICS are the "Statistics-Related" columns of USER_TAB_COLUMNS shown in Table 35-3 plus the Table_Name and Column_Name columns.

USER_TAB_COL_STATISTICS contains statistics columns that are also provided via USER_TAB_COLUMNS for backward-compatibility. You should access them via USER_TAB_COL_STATISTICS.

Column Value Histograms

You can use histograms to improve the analysis used by the cost-based optimizer. The USER_TAB_HISTOGRAMS view contains information about each column's histogram, including the Table_Name, Column_Name, Endpoint_Number, and Endpoint_Value. The values in USER_TAB_HISTOGRAMS are used by the optimizer to determine the distribution of the column values within the table. "ALL" and "DBA" versions of USER_TAB_HISTOGRAMS are available.

Updatable Columns

You can update records in views that contain joins in their view queries, provided the join meets certain criteria. The USER_UPDATABLE_COLUMNS view lists all columns you can update. You can query the Owner, Table_Name, and Column_Name for the column; the Updatable column will have a value of YES if the column can be updated, and a value of NO if the column cannot be updated. You can also query to determine if you can insert or delete records from the view via the Insertable and Deletable columns.

Views: USER_VIEWS

The base query of a view is accessible via the USER_VIEWS data dictionary view, which contains nine columns; the three main columns are as follows:

View_Name	The name of the view
Text_Length	The length of the view's base query, in characters
Text	The query that the view uses

The other six columns, described later in this section, are related to object views.

NOTE
This section only applies to traditional views. For materialized views, see "Database Links, Snapshots, and Materialized Views," later in the chapter.

The Text column is a LONG datatype. This may cause a problem when querying USER_VIEWS via SQLPLUS, because SQLPLUS truncates LONGs. The point at which truncation occurs, however, can be changed via the **set long** command. USER_VIEWS provides a mechanism for determining the proper setting for the LONG truncation point, as you'll see in the following example.

The Text_Length column shows the length of the view's query. Therefore, the SQLPLUS LONG truncation point must be set to a value equal to or greater than the view's Text_Length value. For example, the following listing shows a view whose View_Name is AGING and whose Text_Length is 500:

```
select View_Name, Text_Length
  from USER_VIEWS
 where View_Name = 'AGING';

View_Name          Text_Length
----------------   -------------
AGING                  500
```

Since the length of the view's text is 500 characters, use the **set long** command to increase the LONG truncation point to at least 500 (the default is 80) to see the full text of the view's query:

```
set long 500
```

You can then query USER_VIEWS for the view's Text, using the query shown in the following listing:

```
select Text
  from USER_VIEWS
 where View_Name = 'AGING';
```

If you had not used the **set long** command, then the output would have been truncated at 80 characters, with no message telling you why the truncation occurred. Before querying other views, you will need to recheck their Text_Length values.

You can query the column definitions for views from USER_TAB_COLUMNS, the same view you query for tables.

If you use column aliases in your views, and your column aliases are part of the view's query, then your data dictionary queries for information about views will be simplified. Since the entire text of the view's query is displayed in USER_VIEWS, the column aliases will be displayed as well.

You can create views using this format:

```
create view NEWSPAPER_VIEW (SomeFeature, SomeSection)
     as select Feature, Section
  from NEWSPAPER;
```

Listing the column names in the header of the **create view** command removes the column aliases from the query and thus prevents you from seeing them via USER_VIEWS. The only way to see the view's column names would be by querying USER_TAB_COLUMNS. If the column names are in the query, then you only need to query one data dictionary view (USER_VIEWS) for both the query and the column names.

For example, given the NEWSPAPER_VIEW view created in the last example, if you were to query USER_VIEWS, you would see

```
select Text
  from USER_VIEWS
 where View_Name ='NEWSPAPER_VIEW';

TEXT
----------------------------------------
select Feature, Section from NEWSPAPER
```

This query does *not* show you the new column names you assigned, since you did not make those column names part of the view's query. To make those column names show up in USER_VIEWS, add them as column aliases in the view's query:

```
create view NEWSPAPER_VIEW
    as select Feature SomeFeature, Section SomeSection
  from NEWSPAPER;
```

Now when you query USER_VIEWS, the column aliases will be displayed as part of the view's query text:

```
select Text
   from USER_VIEWS
 where View_Name ='NEWSPAPER_VIEW';


TEXT
-------------------------------------------------
select Feature SomeFeature, Section SomeSection
  from NEWSPAPER
```

To support object views, Oracle8 added six new columns to USER_VIEWS:

Type_Text	Type clause of the typed view
Text_Type_Length	Length of the type clause of the typed view
OID_Text	WITH OID clause of the typed view
OID_Text_Length	Length of the WITH OID clause of the typed view
View_Type_Owner	Owner of the view's type for typed views
View_Type	Type of the view

See Chapters 28 and 31 for information on object views and types.

The ALL_VIEWS view lists all of the views owned by the user as well as any views to which the user has been granted access. Since ALL_VIEWS can contain entries for multiple users, it contains an Owner column in addition to the columns listed earlier in this section. DBA_VIEWS, which lists all views in the database, has the same column definitions as ALL_VIEWS.

Synonyms: USER_SYNONYMS (SYN)

USER_SYNONYMS lists all of the synonyms that a user owns. The columns are as follows:

Synonym_Name	The name of the synonym
Table_Owner	The owner of the table that the synonym refers to

Table_Name	The name of the table that the synonym refers to
DB_Link	The name of the database link used in the synonym

USER_SYNONYMS is useful when debugging programs or resolving problems with users' access to objects within applications. USER_SYNONYMS is also known by the public synonym SYN.

The DB_Link column will be **NULL** if the synonym does not use a database link. Therefore, if you want to see a list of the database links currently in use by the synonyms owned by your account, execute this query:

```
select distinct DB_Link
  from USER_SYNONYMS
 where DB_Link is not null;
```

The ALL_SYNONYMS view lists all of the synonyms owned by the user, public synonyms, and all synonyms to which the user has been granted access. Since ALL_SYNONYMS can contain entries for multiple users, it contains an Owner column in addition to the columns listed earlier in this section. DBA_SYNONYMS, which lists all synonyms in the database, has the same column definitions as ALL_SYNONYMS.

Sequences: USER_SEQUENCES (SEQ)

To display the attributes of sequences, you can query the USER_SEQUENCES data dictionary view. This view can also be queried using the public synonym SEQ. The columns of USER_SEQUENCES are listed in Table 35-4.

The Last_Number column is not updated during normal database operation; it is used during database restart/recovery operations.

ALL_SEQUENCES lists all of the sequences owned by the user or to which the user has been granted access. Since ALL_SEQUENCES can contain entries for multiple users, it contains a Sequence_Owner column in addition to the columns listed in Table 35-4. DBA_SEQUENCES, which lists all sequences in the database, has the same column definitions as ALL_SEQUENCES.

Constraints and Comments

Constraints and comments help you to understand how tables and columns relate to each other. Comments are strictly informational; they do not enforce any conditions on the data stored in the objects they describe. Constraints, on the other hand, define the conditions under which that data is valid. Typical constraints include NOT NULL, UNIQUE, PRIMARY KEY, and FOREIGN KEY. In the next sections, you will see how to retrieve data about constraints and comments from the data dictionary.

Column Name	Description
Sequence_Name	Name of the sequence
Min_Value	Minimum value of the sequence
Max_Value	Maximum value of the sequence
Increment_By	Increment between sequence values
Cycle_Flag	A flag to indicate whether the values should cycle back to the Min_Value once the Max_Value is reached
Order_Flag	A flag to indicate whether sequence numbers are generated in order
Cache_Size	The number of sequence entries cached in memory
Last_Number	The last sequence number written to disk or cached

TABLE 35-4. *Columns in USER_SEQUENCES*

Constraints: USER_CONSTRAINTS

Constraint information is accessible via the USER_CONSTRAINTS view. This information is very useful when trying to alter data constraints or resolve problems with an application's data. The columns of this view are listed in Table 35-5.

Although this is a "USER" view, it contains an Owner column. In this view, Owner refers to the owner of the constraint, not the owner of the table (which is the user).

Valid values for the Constraint_Type column are shown in Table 35-5. Understanding the constraint types is crucial when you are trying to get useful information about your constraints.

FOREIGN KEY constraints will always have values for the R_Owner and R_Constraint_Name columns. These two columns will tell you which constraint the FOREIGN KEY references. A FOREIGN KEY references another *constraint,* not another column. NOT NULL constraints on columns are stored as CHECK constraints, so they have a Constraint_Type of 'C'.

Querying USER_CONSTRAINTS will give you the names of all the constraints on a table. This is important when trying to interpret error messages that only provide the name of the constraint that was violated.

Once you know the name and type of a constraint, you can check the columns associated with it via the USER_CONS_COLUMNS view, described in the next section.

Column Name	Description
Owner	The owner of the constraint
Constraint_Name	The name of the constraint
Constraint_Type	The type of constraint: 'C' CHECK constraint; includes NOT NULLs 'P' PRIMARY KEY constraint 'R' FOREIGN KEY (reference) constraint 'U' UNIQUE constraint 'V' WITH CHECK OPTION constraint (for views) 'O' WITH READ ONLY constraint (for views)
Table_Name	The name of the table associated with the constraint
Search_Condition	The search condition used (for CHECK constraints)
R_Owner	The owner of the table referenced by a FOREIGN KEY constraint
R_Constraint_Name	The name of the constraint referenced by a FOREIGN KEY constraint
Delete_Rule	The action to take on the FOREIGN KEY tables when a PRIMARY KEY record is deleted (CASCADE or NO ACTION)
Status	The status of the constraint (ENABLED or DISABLED)
Deferrable	A flag to indicate whether the constraint can be deferred
Deferred	A flag to indicate whether the constraint was initially deferred
Validated	A flag (VALIDATED or NOT VALIDATED) to indicate whether all data obeys the constraint
Generated	A flag to indicate whether the constraint name has been generated by the database

TABLE 35-5. *Columns in USER_CONSTRAINTS*

Column Name	Description
Bad	A flag to indicate whether a date was used in the constraint creation without specifying a century value for CHECK constraints; applies only to constraints in databases upgraded from prior versions of Oracle. Such constraints may result in ORA-02436 errors if not dropped and re-created properly
Rely	If set, the optimizer will use this flag
Last_Change	The date the constraint was last enabled or disabled

TABLE 35-5.   *Columns in USER_CONSTRAINTS* (continued)

For example, you may want to know which columns are part of the PRIMARY KEY of a certain table. To do this, you first need to identify the name of the PRIMARY KEY constraint on that table. This query will return that information:

```
select Owner, Constraint_Name
  from USER_CONSTRAINTS
 where Table_Name = 'BIRTHDAY'
   and Constraint_Type = 'P';

OWNER        CONSTRAINT_NAME
----------   -------------------
TALBOT       SYS_C0008791
```

The Constraint_Name shown here is system-generated; you should give constraints names at the time you create them. See "Integrity Constraint" in the Alphabetical Reference for further details. If a constraint name has been system-generated, that fact will be indicated via the Generated column.

If you defer a constraint (as indicated by the Deferred column), the constraint will not be enforced for the duration of a transaction. For example, if you were performing bulk **update**s on related tables and could not guarantee the order of transactions, you may decide to defer constraint checking on the tables until all of the **update**s have completed.

ALL_CONSTRAINTS lists the constraints on all of the tables that the user can access. DBA_CONSTRAINTS lists all of the constraints in the database. Each of these views has the same set of columns as USER_CONSTRAINTS (since they all include the Owner column).

Constraint Columns: USER_CONS_COLUMNS

You can view the columns associated with constraints via the USER_CONS_COLUMNS data dictionary view. If you have already queried USER_CONSTRAINTS to obtain the types and names of the constraints involved, you can use USER_CONS_COLUMNS to determine which columns are involved in the constraint. The columns in this view are the following:

Owner	The owner of the constraint
Constraint_Name	The name of the constraint
Table_Name	The name of the table associated with the constraint
Column_Name	The name of the column associated with the constraint
Position	The order of the column within the constraint definition

There are only two columns in USER_CONS_COLUMNS that are not in USER_CONSTRAINTS: Column_Name and Position. A sample query of this table, using the Constraint_Name from the USER_CONSTRAINTS example, is shown in the following listing:

```
select Column_Name, Position
  from USER_CONS_COLUMNS
 where Constraint_Name = 'SYS_C0008791';

COLUMN_NAME   POSITION
------------ --------
FIRSTNAME           1
LASTNAME            2
```

As shown in the preceding listing, the combination of FirstName and LastName forms the primary key for the BIRTHDAY table.

The Position column is significant. When you create a UNIQUE or PRIMARY KEY constraint, Oracle automatically creates a unique index on the set of columns you specify. The index is created based on the column order you specify. The column order, in turn, affects the performance of the index. An index comprising multiple columns will not be used by the optimizer unless the leading column of that index (Position='1') is used in the query's **where** clause. See Chapter 36 for further details on optimizers.

The ALL_CONS_COLUMNS and DBA_CONS_COLUMNS views have the same column definitions as USER_CONS_COLUMNS. ALL_CONS_COLUMNS can be used to display column information about constraints on all tables that the user can access regardless of owner. DBA_CONS_COLUMNS lists the column-level constraint information for the entire database.

Constraint Exceptions: EXCEPTIONS

When enabling constraints on tables that already contain data, you may encounter constraint violations within the data. For example, you may attempt to create a PRIMARY KEY constraint on a column that contains the same value for multiple records. Attempting to create a PRIMARY KEY constraint on such a column would fail.

Oracle allows you to capture information about the rows that cause constraint creation to fail. First, create a table called EXCEPTIONS in your schema; the SQL script that should be used to create this table is named utlexcpt.sql, and is usually located in the /rdbms/admin directory under the Oracle home directory.

The EXCEPTIONS table contains four columns: Row_ID (the RowID of each row that violated the constraint), Owner (the owner of the violated constraint), Table_Name (the table on which the violated constraint was created), and Constraint (the constraint violated by the row). After creating the EXCEPTIONS table, attempt to enable a PRIMARY KEY constraint:

```
alter table NEWSPAPER enable PRIMARY KEY
exceptions into EXCEPTIONS;

ORA-02437: cannot enable (NEWSPAPER.SYS_C00516) - primary key violated
```

The constraint creation fails, and a reference to all rows that violate the constraint is placed in the EXCEPTIONS table. For example, if the PRIMARY KEY constraint in the last example generated exceptions, then you could query the EXCEPTIONS table as shown in the following listing:

```
select Owner, Table_Name, Constraint from EXCEPTIONS;

OWNER      TABLE_NAME CONSTRAINT
---------- ---------- ----------
TALBOT     NEWSPAPER  SYS_C00516
TALBOT     NEWSPAPER  SYS_C00516
```

Two rows violated the constraint named SYS_C00516 (which, in this example, is the constraint name given to the PRIMARY KEY constraint for the NEWSPAPER table). You can determine which rows of the NEWSPAPER table correspond to these exceptions by joining the Row_ID column of the EXCEPTIONS table to the RowID pseudo-column of the table on which the constraint was being placed (in this example, the NEWSPAPER table):

```
select *
  from NEWSPAPER
 where RowID in
       (select Row_ID from EXCEPTIONS);
```

The rows that caused the constraint violations will then be displayed.

> **NOTE**
> *Row_ID is an actual column in the EXCEPTIONS table, with a datatype of ROWID. It is joined to the RowID pseudo-column in the table from which the exceptions were generated.*

Table Comments: USER_TAB_COMMENTS

You can add a comment to a table, view, or column after it has been created. Comments on the data dictionary views are the basis for the records displayed via the DICTIONARY and DICT_COLUMNS views. To display comments about your own tables, use the USER_TAB_COMMENTS view.

USER_TAB_COMMENTS contains three columns:

Table_Name	The name of the table or view
Table_Type	The object type (table, object table, or view)
Comments	Comments that have been entered for the object

Query USER_TAB_COMMENTS by specifying the Table_Name you wish to see the Comments for, as shown in the following listing:

```
select Comments
  from USER_TAB_COMMENTS
 where Table_Name = 'BIRTHDAY';
```

To add a comment to a table, use the **comment** command, as shown in the following listing:

```
comment on table BIRTHDAY is 'Birthday list for Blacksburg
       employees';
```

To remove a comment, set the comment to two single quotes with no space between them:

```
comment on table BIRTHDAY is '';
```

You can view the comments on all of the tables you can access via the ALL_TAB_COMMENTS view. ALL_TAB_COMMENTS has an additional column, Owner, which specifies the owner of the table. DBA_TAB_COMMENTS lists all of the tables in the database, and it has an Owner column as well.

Column Comments: **USER_COL_COMMENTS**

USER_COL_COMMENTS displays the comments that have been entered for columns within your tables. These comments are added to the database via the **comment** command. USER_COL_COMMENTS contains three columns:

Table_Name	The name of the table or view
Column_Name	The name of the column
Comments	Comments that have been entered for the column

Query USER_COL_COMMENTS by specifying the Table_Name and Column_Name you wish to see the Comments for:

```
select Comments
  from USER_COL_COMMENTS
 where Table_Name = 'BIRTHDAY'
   and Column_Name = 'AGE';
```

To add a comment to a column, use the **comment** command, as shown in the following listing:

```
comment on column BIRTHDAY.AGE is 'Age in years';
```

To remove a comment, set the comment to two single quotes with no space between them:

```
comment on column BIRTHDAY.AGE is '';
```

You can view the column comments on all of the tables you can access via the ALL_COL_COMMENTS view. ALL_COL_COMMENTS has an additional column, Owner, which specifies the owner of the table. DBA_COL_COMMENTS lists all of the columns in all of the tables in the database, and it has an Owner column as well.

Indexes and Clusters

Indexes and clusters do not change the data that is stored in tables; however, they do change the way that data is stored and accessed. In the following sections, you will see data dictionary views that describe indexes and clusters. You will see descriptions of the data dictionary views related to partitioned indexes in "Space Allocation and Usage" in this chapter.

Indexes: USER_INDEXES (IND)

In Oracle, indexes are very closely related to constraints. The PRIMARY KEY and UNIQUE constraints always have associated unique indexes. Like constraints, two data dictionary views are used to query information about indexes: USER_INDEXES and USER_IND_COLUMNS. USER_INDEXES is also known by its public synonym, IND.

The columns in USER_INDEXES can be grouped into four categories, as shown in Table 35-6.

The name of the index is shown in the Index_Name column. The owner and name for the table being indexed are in the Table_Owner and Table_Name columns. The Uniqueness column will be set to UNIQUE for unique indexes and set to NONUNIQUE for nonunique indexes. Table_Type records whether the index is on a 'TABLE' or a 'CLUSTER'.

The "Space-Related" columns are described in the "Storage" entry in the Alphabetical Reference. The "Statistics-Related" columns are populated when the table is analyzed (see the **analyze** command in the Alphabetical Reference). The Degree and Instances columns refer to the degree of parallelism used when the index is created.

To see all of the indexes on a table, query USER_INDEXES using the Table_Owner and Table_Name columns in the **where** clause, as shown in the following listing:

```
select Index_Name, Uniqueness
  from USER_INDEXES
 where Table_Owner = 'TALBOT'
   and Table_Name = 'BIRTHDAY';

INDEX_NAME        UNIQUENESS
----------------  ----------
PK_BIRTHDAY       UNIQUE
```

The query output in the preceding example shows that an index named PK_BIRTHDAY exists on the BIRTHDAY table. By using the same naming standard for all of your indexes, you can make it very easy to identify the purpose and table

Identification	Space-Related	Statistics-Related	Other
Index_Name	Tablespace_Name	Blevel	Degree
Table_Owner	Ini_Trans	Leaf_Blocks	Instances
Table_Name	Max_Trans	Distinct_Keys	Include_Column
Table_Type	Initial_Extent	Avg_Leaf_Blocks_Per_Key	Buffer_Pool
Uniqueness	Next_Extent	Avg_Data_Blocks_Per_Key	Duration
Status	Min_Extents	Clustering_Factor	Pct_Direct_Access
Partitioned	Max_Extents	Num_Rows	Parameters
Index_Type	Pct_Increase	Sample_Size	Domidx_Status
Temporary	Pct_Free	Last_Analyzed	Domidx_Opstatus
Generated	Freelists	User_Stats	Funcidx_Status
Logging	Freelist_Groups	Global_Stats	
Compression	Pct_Threshold		
Prefix_Length			
Secondary			
Ityp_Owner			
Ityp_Name			

TABLE 35-6. *Columns in USER_INDEXES*

for an index just by looking at the Index_Name. In this example, PK signifies PRIMARY KEY; the constraint name can be specified during constraint creation to supersede the system-generated constraint name.

The Clustering_Factor column is not directly related to clusters, but rather represents the degree to which the rows in the table are ordered. The more ordered those rows are, the more efficient range queries will be (*range queries* are those in which a range of values is given for a column, such as **where LastName like 'A%'**).

To discover which columns are part of the index, and their order within the index, you need to query the USER_IND_COLUMNS view, which is described in the next section.

ALL_INDEXES shows all of the indexes owned by the user as well as any created on tables to which the user has been granted access. Since ALL_INDEXES can contain entries for multiple users, it contains an Owner column in addition to the columns shown in Table 35-6. DBA_INDEXES, which lists all indexes in the database, has the same column definitions as ALL_INDEXES.

Indexed Columns: USER_IND_COLUMNS

You can determine which columns are in an index by querying USER_IND_COLUMNS. The columns available via this view are as follows:

Index_Name	The name of the index
Table_Name	The name of the indexed table
Column_Name	The name of a column within the index
Column_Position	The column's position within the index
Column_Length	The indexed length of the column
Descend	A Y/N flag to indicate whether or not the column is sorted in descending order

Four columns in this view are not in USER_INDEXES: Column_Name, Column_Position, Column_Length, and Descend. Column_Length, like the statistics-related columns in USER_INDEXES, is populated when the index's base table is analyzed (see the **analyze** command in the Alphabetical Reference). A sample query of this table, using the Index_Name from the USER_INDEXES example, is shown in the following listing (in this example, the Column_Position column is given the alias Pos):

```
select Column_Name, Column_Position Pos
  from USER_IND_COLUMNS
 where Index_Name = 'PK_BIRTHDAY';


COLUMN_NAME   POS
-----------   ---
FIRSTNAME       1
LASTNAME        2
```

As can be seen from this query, the PK_BIRTHDAY index consists of two columns: FirstName and LastName, in that order. The ordering of the columns will determine whether the index can be used for certain queries. If users frequently use the LastName column in their **where** clauses, and do not use the FirstName column in those queries, then this index may need to be re-created, with the LASTNAME in the first position. An index comprising multiple columns will not be used by the optimizer unless the leading column of that index (Column_Position='1') is used in the **where** clause. See Chapter 36 for further details on the optimizer.

The ALL_IND_COLUMNS and DBA_IND_COLUMNS views have the same column definitions as USER_IND_COLUMNS. ALL_IND_COLUMNS can be used to display column information about indexes on all tables that the user can access regardless of owner. DBA_IND_COLUMNS lists the column-level index information for the entire database.

Clusters: USER_CLUSTERS (CLU)

The storage and statistics parameters associated with clusters are accessible via USER_CLUSTERS (also known by the public synonym CLU). The columns in this data dictionary view are shown in Table 35-7, separated by type.

The Cluster_Name column contains the name of the cluster. Cluster_Type specifies whether the cluster uses a standard B-tree index or a hashing function for the cluster.

The usage of the "Space-Related" columns is described in the "Storage" entry in the Alphabetical Reference. The "Statistics-Related" columns are populated when the table is analyzed (see the **analyze** command in the Alphabetical Reference).

Identification	Space-Related	Statistics-Related	Other
Cluster_Name	Tablespace_Name	Avg_Blocks_Per_Key	Degree
Cluster_Type	Pct_Free	Hashkeys	Instances
Function	Pct_Used		Cache
	Key_Size		Buffer_Pool
	Ini_Trans		Single_Table
	Max_Trans		
	Initial_Extent		
	Next_Extent		
	Min_Extents		
	Max_Extents		
	Pct_Increase		
	Freelists		
	Freelist_Groups		

TABLE 35-7. *Columns in USER_CLUSTERS*

ALL_CLUSTERS and DBA_CLUSTERS have an additional column, Owner, since they list clusters in multiple schemas.

You can specify a hashing function for a cluster. User-specified hashing functions are most useful if the following conditions exist:

■ The cluster key column is numeric

■ The cluster key column values are sequentially assigned

■ You know the maximum number of cluster key column values for the table

If all three conditions are met, you can use the **hash is** clause of the **create cluster** command to specify your own hashing function (see **create cluster** in the Alphabetical Reference).

Cluster Columns: **USER_CLU_COLUMNS**

To see the mapping of table columns to cluster columns, query USER_CLU_COLUMNS, whose columns are the following:

Cluster_Name	The name of the cluster
Clu_Column_Name	The name of the key column in the cluster
Table_Name	The name of a table within the cluster
Tab_Column_Name	The name of the key column in the table

Since a single cluster can store data from multiple tables, USER_CLU_COLUMNS is useful for determining which columns of which tables map to the cluster's columns.

There is no "ALL" version of this view. There is only USER_CLU_COLUMNS for the user's cluster columns, and DBA_CLU_COLUMNS, which shows the column mappings for all clusters in the database.

Abstract Datatypes, ORDBMS-Related Structures, and LOBs

In the following sections, you will see the data dictionary views associated with object-relational structures such as abstract datatypes, methods, and large objects (LOBs). "ALL" and "DBA" versions of all of these data dictionary views are available. Because they contain records for multiple owners, the "ALL" and "DBA" versions of these views contain Owner columns as well as the columns listed in this section.

Abstract Datatypes: USER_TYPES

Abstract datatypes created within your schema are listed in USER_TYPES, which includes columns for the Type_Name, number of attributes (Attributes), and number of methods (Methods) defined for the datatype.

For example, the ANIMAL_TY datatype has three attributes and one method (methods are defined via the **create type body** command), as shown in the following listing:

```
select Type_Name,
       Attributes,
       Methods
  from USER_TYPES;

TYPE_NAME                       ATTRIBUTES    METHODS
-----------------------------   ----------   ----------
ANIMAL_TY                                3            1
```

Datatype Attributes: USER_TYPE_ATTRS

To see the attributes of a datatype, you need to query the USER_TYPE_ATTRS view. The columns in USER_TYPE_ATTRS are shown in Table 35-8.

Column Name	Description
TYPE_NAME	Name of the type
ATTR_NAME	Name of the attribute
ATTR_TYPE_MOD	The type modifier of the attribute
ATTR_TYPE_OWNER	Owner of the attribute's type, if the attribute is based on another datatype
ATTR_TYPE_NAME	Name of the type of the attribute
LENGTH	Length of the attribute
PRECISION	Precision of the attribute
SCALE	Scale of the attribute
CHARACTER_SET_NAME	Character set of the attribute
ATTR_NO	Ordinal position of the attribute within the type definition

TABLE 35-8. *Columns in USER_TYPE_ATTRS*

You can query USER_TYPE_ATTRS to see the relationships between nested abstract datatypes. For example, the PERSON_TY datatype uses the ADDRESS_TY datatype, as shown in the following listing:

```
select Attr_Name,
       Length,
       Attr_Type_Name
  from USER_TYPE_ATTRS
 where Type_Name = 'PERSON_TY';


ATTR_NAME                         LENGTH ATTR_TYPE_NAME
------------------------------ ---------- ------------------
NAME                                  25 VARCHAR2
ADDRESS                                  ADDRESS_TY
```

Datatype Methods: USER_TYPE_METHODS and USER_METHOD_PARAMS

If a type has methods defined for it, then you query USER_TYPE_METHODS to determine the methods' names. USER_TYPE_METHODS contains columns showing the type name (Type_Name), method name (Method_Name), method number (Method_No, used for overloaded methods), and type of method (Method_Type). USER_TYPE_METHODS also includes columns that show the number of parameters (Parameters) and results (Results) returned by the method.

For example, the ANIMAL_TY datatype has one method, a member function named AGE. The AGE method has one input parameter (Birthdate) and one output result (the age, in days). Querying USER_TYPE_METHODS shows that *two* parameters are defined for AGE, not one as expected:

```
select Parameters,
       Results
  from USER_TYPE_METHODS
 where Type_Name = 'ANIMAL_TY'
   and Method_Name = 'AGE';


PARAMETERS    RESULTS
---------- ----------
         2          1
```

Why does AGE have two parameters if it only has one input parameter defined? To find out, you can query USER_METHOD_PARAMS, which describes the parameters for your methods:

```
select Param_Name, Param_No, Param_Type_Name
  from USER_METHOD_PARAMS;
```

```
PARAM_NAME                        PARAM_NO PARAM_TYPE_NAME
------------------------------- ---------- ----------------
SELF                                     1 ANIMAL_TY
BIRTHDATE                                2 DATE
```

USER_METHOD_PARAMS shows that for each method, Oracle creates an implicit SELF parameter. The results of your methods are shown in USER_METHOD_RESULTS:

```
select Method_Name,
       Result_Type_Name
  from USER_METHOD_RESULTS
 where Type_Name = 'ANIMAL_TY';

METHOD_NAME                       RESULT_TYPE_NAME
------------------------------- ----------------------------
AGE                               NUMBER
```

Other Datatypes: USER_REFS, USER_COLL_TYPES, and USER_NESTED_TABLES

If you use REFs (see Chapter 31), then you can query the USER_REFS data dictionary view to display the REFs you have defined. USER_REFS will show the name of the table containing the REF column (Table_Name) and the column name of the object column (Column_Name). The attributes of the REF—such as whether or not it is stored with the RowID—are also accessible via USER_REFS.

Collector types (nested tables and varying arrays) are described via the USER_COLL_TYPES data dictionary view. The columns of USER_COLL_TYPES include Type_Name, Coll_Name (the name of the collector), Upper_Bound (for varying arrays), and the Length and Precision of the elements. You can use USER_COLL_TYPES in conjunction with the abstract datatype data dictionary views shown earlier in this section to determine the type structure of a collector. You can also query USER_NESTED_TABLES and USER_VARRAYS to see details for your collections.

LOBs: USER_LOBS

As described in Chapter 30, you can store large objects inside the database. The USER_LOBS view provides information on the LOBs defined in your tables, as shown in the following listing:

```
column column_name format A30

select Table_Name,
       Column_Name
```

```
from USER_LOBS;

TABLE_NAME                        COLUMN_NAME
------------------------------    ----------------------------
PROPOSAL                          PROPOSAL_TEXT
PROPOSAL                          BUDGET
```

USER_LOBS also shows the names of the segments used to hold the LOB data when it grows large; however, it does not show the datatypes of the LOB columns. To see the LOB datatypes, you can either **describe** the table that includes the LOBs or query USER_TAB_COLUMNS (as shown earlier in this chapter).

To use BFILE datatypes for LOBs, you have to create directories (see the entry for the **create directory** command in the Alphabetical Reference). The ALL_DIRECTORIES data dictionary shows the Owner, Directory_Name, and Directory_Path for each directory to which you have been granted access. A "DBA" version of this view is also available. No "USER" version of this view is available.

Database Links, Snapshots, and Materialized Views

Database links and snapshots are used to manage access to remote data. As of Oracle8i, materialized views and snapshots are synonymous, but the data dictionary information about them is stored in multiple forms. Depending on the type of materialized view you use, you may be able to use materialized view logs. In the following sections, you will see descriptions of the data dictionary views that can be used to display information about database links, snapshots, and materialized views. For further information on database links, see Chapter 22. For further information on snapshots and materialized views, see Chapter 23.

Database Links: USER_DB_LINKS

To see the database links created under your account, query USER_DB_LINKS. The columns of this view, including the link name (DB_Link), username to connect to (Username), and the connection string (Host), show the information about the remote connection that the link will be used to establish. The Username and Password values will be used to log in to the remote database defined by the Host value.

The Host column stores the Net8 connect descriptors. This column stores the exact character string you specify during the **create database link** command, and does not alter its case. Therefore, you should be careful with the case you use when creating database links. Otherwise, your queries against USER_DB_LINKS will have to take into account inconsistencies in the case of the Host column. For example, looking for a database link that uses the 'HQ' service descriptor would require you to enter

```
select * from USER_DB_LINKS
  where UPPER(Host) = 'HQ';
```

since it is possible that there are entries with a Host value of 'hq' instead of 'HQ'.

NOTE
*If you are using default logins to the remote database, then Password will be **NULL**.*

The ALL_DB_LINKS view lists all of the database links that either are owned by the user or are PUBLIC database links. DBA_DB_LINKS lists all database links in the database. ALL_DB_LINKS and DBA_DB_LINKS share most of the same column definitions as USER_DB_LINKS; they have an Owner column in place of the Password column.

See Chapter 22 for further information on the uses of database links.

Snapshots: USER_SNAPSHOTS

You can query USER_SNAPSHOTS to display information about the snapshots owned by your account. This view, whose columns are listed in Table 35-9, shows the structural information about the snapshot as well as its refresh schedule.

When a snapshot is created, several database objects are created. In the local database, Oracle creates a table that is populated with the remote table's data, plus, for simple snapshots, the RowIDs or primary keys for that data. Oracle then creates a view of this table, using the snapshot's name for the view's name. See Chapter 23 for further details on snapshots.

The name of the snapshot view is found in the Name column of USER_SNAPSHOTS. The local base table for that view is the Table_Name column in USER_SNAPSHOTS. The table that the snapshot uses in the remote database is defined by the Master_Owner and Master columns.

To determine which database links are being used by your snapshots, query the Master_Link column, as shown in the following example:

```
select Master_Link
  from USER_SNAPSHOTS;
```

Column Name	Description
Owner	The account that owns the snapshot
Name	The name of the snapshot
Table_Name	The base table (in the local database) for the snapshot
Master_View	The name of the view used during snapshot refreshes
Master_Owner	The account that owns the base table (in the remote database) for the snapshot
Master	The base table (in the remote database) for the snapshot
Master_Link	The database link used to access the master database
Can_Use_Log	A flag to indicate whether the snapshot can use a snapshot log (YES or NO)
Updatable	A flag to indicate whether the snapshot can be updated
Refresh_Method	Values used to drive a fast refresh of the snapshot
Last_Refresh	A timestamp to record the last time the snapshot's data was refreshed
Error	Any error that was encountered during the last refresh attempt
FR_Operations	The status of fast refresh operations (REGENERATE or VALID)
CR_Operations	The status of complete refresh operations (REGENERATE or VALID)
Type	Type of refresh performed (COMPLETE, FAST, or FORCE)
Next	The date function used to determine the next refresh date
Start_With	The date function used to determine the starting and next refresh dates
Refresh_Group	The name of the snapshot refresh group to which the snapshot belongs
Update_Trig	In Oracle8, this column is always null; it is provided for backward-compatibility with earlier versions of Oracle

TABLE 35-9. *Columns in USER_SNAPSHOTS*

Column Name	Description
Update_Log	The name of the table that logs changes made to an updatable snapshot
Query	The query used as a basis for the snapshot
Master_Rollback_Seg	The rollback segment to use during snapshot population and refresh operations
Status	Status of snapshot contents
Refresh_Mode	How and when the snapshot will be refreshed
Prebuilt	A YES/NO flag to indicate whether or not the snapshot was created based on a prebuilt base table

TABLE 35-9. *Columns in USER_SNAPSHOTS* (continued)

The names of the database links returned by this query can be used as input for queries against USER_DB_LINKS. This query will display all of the database link information available for database links used in your snapshots:

```
select *
  from USER_DB_LINKS
 where DB_Link in
    (select Master_Link
       from USER_SNAPSHOTS);
```

Additional queries that are useful in the management of snapshots are provided in Chapter 23.

The ALL_SNAPSHOTS and DBA_SNAPSHOTS views have the same column definitions as USER_SNAPSHOTS. You can use ALL_SNAPSHOTS to display information about all snapshots that the user can access regardless of owner. DBA_SNAPSHOTS lists snapshot information for all users in the database.

Two additional snapshot-related views—USER_REFRESH and USER_REFRESH_CHILDREN—display information about refresh groups. See Chapter 23 for information about refresh groups.

Snapshot Logs: USER_SNAPSHOT_LOGS

Snapshot logs can be used by simple snapshots to determine which records in the master table need to be refreshed in remote snapshots of that table. Information about a user's snapshot logs can be queried from the USER_SNAPSHOT_LOGS data dictionary view, described in Table 35-10. Restrictions on the use of snapshot logs are discussed in Chapter 23.

USER_SNAPSHOT_LOGS is usually queried for maintenance purposes, such as to determine the name of the trigger used to create the snapshot log records.

There is no "ALL" version of this view. DBA_SNAPSHOT_LOGS has the same column definitions as USER_SNAPSHOT_LOGS, but shows all snapshot logs in the database.

Materialized Views

Snapshots and materialized views are synonymous, but some data dictionary views are specific to the features introduced to support materialized views. All of these views include the abbreviation MVIEW in their names.

You can query USER_MVIEW_ANALYSIS to see the materialized views that support query rewrite. If a materialized view had been created as a snapshot prior to Oracle8i, or if it contains references to a remote table, then it will not be listed in

Column Name	Description
Log_Owner	Owner of the snapshot log
Master	The name of the base table for which changes are being logged
Log_Table	The name of the table that holds the log records (which consist of RowIDs or primary keys and timestamps)
Log_Trigger	The name of the AFTER ROW trigger on the base (Master) table that inserts records into the snapshot log table (Log_Table)
RowIDs	A flag to indicate whether the snapshot is ROWID-based
Primary_Key	A flag to indicate whether the snapshot is primary key–based
Filter_Columns	The filter columns, for snapshots that use subqueries
Current_Snapshots	The date the snapshot was last refreshed
Snapshot_ID	A unique identifier for the snapshot

TABLE 35-10. *Columns in USER_SNAPSHOT_LOGS*

this view. You can query the owner of the materialized view, its name (Mview_Name), and the owner of the base table (Mview_Table_Owner). Many of the columns in this view are flags, such as Summary ('Y' if the view contains an aggregation), Known_Stale ('Y' if the view's data is inconsistent with the base table), and Contains_Views ('Y' if the materialized view references a view).

If the materialized view contains aggregations, you can query USER_MVIEW_AGGREGATES for details on the aggregations. Columns in this view are as follows:

Owner	Owner of the materialized view
Mview_Name	Name of the materialized view
Position_in_Select	Position within the query
Container_Column	Name of the column
Agg_Function	Aggregate function
DistinctFlag	'Y' if the aggregation uses the DISTINCT function
Measure	The SQL text of the measure, excluding the aggregate function

You can query details of the detail relations within materialized views from the USER_MVIEW_DETAIL_RELATIONS and USER_MVIEW_KEYS data dictionary views. If the materialized view is based on joins, see USER_MVIEW_JOINS for the join details. In general, USER_MVIEW_ANALYSIS will be the most commonly used data dictionary view related to materialized views.

Triggers, Procedures, Functions, and Packages

You can use procedures, packages, and triggers—blocks of PL/SQL code stored in the database—to enforce business rules or to perform complicated processing. Triggers are described in Chapter 26. Procedures, functions, and packages are described in Chapter 27. In the following sections, you will see how to query the data dictionary for information about triggers, procedures, packages, and functions.

Triggers: USER_TRIGGERS

USER_TRIGGERS contains information about the triggers owned by your account. This view, whose columns are listed in Table 35-11, shows the trigger type and body.

Column Name	Description
Trigger_Name	Name of the trigger
Trigger_Type	The type of trigger (BEFORE STATEMENT, BEFORE EACH ROW, and so on)
Triggering_Event	The command that executes the trigger (INSERT, UPDATE, or DELETE)
Table_Owner	The owner of the table that the trigger is defined for
Base_Object_Type	The type of object on which the trigger is based (TABLE, VIEW, SCHEMA, or DATABASE)
Table_Name	The name of the table that the trigger is defined for
Column_Name	For nested table triggers, the name of the nested table column
Referencing_Names	Names used for referencing OLD and NEW values in the trigger
When_Clause	The **when** clause used for the trigger
Status	Whether the trigger is ENABLED or DISABLED
Description	The description for the trigger
Action_Type	Action type for the trigger body (CALL or PL/SQL)
Trigger_Body	The trigger text

TABLE 35-11. *Columns in USER_TRIGGERS*

The following query will list the name, type, and triggering event for all triggers on Talbot's LEDGER table:

```
select Trigger_Name, Trigger_Type, Triggering_Event
  from USER_TRIGGERS
 where Table_Owner = 'TALBOT'
   and Table_Name = 'LEDGER';
```

The ALL_TRIGGERS view lists the triggers for all tables to which you have access. DBA_TRIGGERS lists all of the triggers in the database. Both of these views contain an additional column, Owner, which records the owner of the trigger.

A second trigger-related data dictionary view, USER_TRIGGER_COLS, shows how columns are used by a trigger. It lists the name of each column affected by a trigger, as well as how the trigger is used. Like USER_TRIGGERS, "ALL" and "DBA" versions of this data dictionary view are available.

Procedures, Functions, and Packages: USER_SOURCE

The source code for existing procedures, functions, packages, and package bodies can be queried from the USER_SOURCE data dictionary view. The Type column in USER_SOURCE identifies the procedural object as a 'PROCEDURE', 'FUNCTION', 'PACKAGE', 'PACKAGE BODY', 'TYPE', or 'TYPE BODY'. Each line of code is stored in a separate record in USER_SOURCE.

You can select information from USER_SOURCE via a query similar to the one shown in the following listing. In this example, the Text column is selected and ordered by Line number. The Name of the object and the object Type are used to specify which object's source code to display.

```
select Text
   from USER_SOURCE
  where Name = 'NEW_WORKER'
    and Type = 'PROCEDURE'
  order by Line;

TEXT
----------------------------------------------------
procedure NEW_WORKER
  (Person_Name IN varchar2)
AS
  BEGIN
     insert into WORKER
       (Name, Age, Lodging)
     values
       (Person_Name, null, null);
  END;
```

As shown in the preceding example, the USER_SOURCE view contains one record for each line of the NEW_WORKER procedure. The sequence of the lines is maintained by the Line column; therefore, the Line column should be used in the **order by** clause.

The ALL_SOURCE and DBA_SOURCE views have all of the columns found in USER_SOURCE plus an additional Owner column (the owner of the object). ALL_SOURCE can be used to display the source code for all procedural objects that the user can access regardless of owner. DBA_SOURCE lists the source code for all users in the database.

Code Errors: USER_ERRORS

The **show errors** command in SQLPLUS checks the USER_ERRORS data dictionary view for the errors associated with the most recent compilation attempt for a procedural object. **show errors** will display the line and column number for each error, as well as the text of the error message.

To view errors associated with previously created procedural objects, you may query USER_ERRORS directly. You may need to do this when viewing errors associated with package bodies, since a package compilation that results in an error may not display the package body's error when you execute the **show error** command. You may also need to query USER_ERRORS when you encounter compilation errors with multiple procedural objects.

The following are the columns available in USER_ERRORS:

Name	The name of the procedural object
Type	The object type ('PROCEDURE', 'FUNCTION', 'PACKAGE', 'PACKAGE BODY', 'TYPE', or 'TYPE BODY')
Sequence	The line sequence number, for use in the query's **order by** clause
Line	The line number within the source code at which the error occurs
Position	The position within the Line at which the error occurs
Text	The text of the error message

A sample query against USER_ERRORS is shown in the following listing. Queries against this view should always include the Sequence column in the **order by** clause. "ALL" and "DBA" versions of this view are also available; they feature an additional column, Owner, which records the owner of the object.

```
select Line, Position, Text
  from USER_ERRORS
 where Name = 'NEW_WORKER'
   and Type = 'PROCEDURE'
 order by Sequence;
```

Code Size: USER_OBJECT_SIZE

You can query the amount of space used in the SYSTEM tablespace for a procedural object from the USER_OBJECT_SIZE data dictionary view. As shown in the following listing, the four separate size areas can be added together to determine the total space used in the SYSTEM data dictionary tables to store the object. The four Size columns, along with the Name and Type columns, constitute all of the columns in this view.

```
select Source_Size+Code_Size+Parsed_Size+Error_Size Total
  from USER_OBJECT_SIZE
 where Name = 'NEW_WORKER'
   and Type = 'PROCEDURE';
```

There is also a "DBA" version of this view available: DBA_OBJECT_SIZE lists the sizes for all objects in the database.

Dimensions

As of Oracle8*i*, you can create and maintain dimensions and hierarchies. For example, you may have a table named COUNTRY, with columns named Country and Continent. A second table, named CONTINENT, may have a column named Continent. You can create a dimension to reflect the relationship between these elements:

```
create dimension GEOGRAPHY
    level COUNTRY_ID      is COUNTRY.Country
    level CONTINENT_ID    is CONTINENT.Continent
    hierarchy COUNTRY_ROLLUP (
       COUNTRY_ID             child of
       CONTINENT_ID
    join key COUNTRY.Continent references CONTINENT_id);
```

You can query the Dimension_Name column of the USER_DIMENSIONS view to see the names of your dimensions. USER_DIMENSIONS also contains columns for the dimension owner (Owner), state (the Invalid column, set to 'Y' or 'N'), and revision level (the Revision column). The attributes of a dimension are accessed via additional data dictionary views.

To see the hierarchies within a dimension, query USER_DIM_HIERARCHIES. This view has only three columns: Owner, Dimension_Name, and Hierarchy_Name. Querying USER_DIM_HIERARCHIES for the GEOGRAPHY dimension returns the name of its hierarchies:

```
select Hierarchy_Name
  from USER_DIM_HIERARCHIES;


HIERARCHY_NAME
------------------------------
COUNTRY_ROLLUP
```

You can see the hierarchy details for COUNTRY_ROLLUP by querying USER_DIM_CHILD_OF, as shown in the following listing:

```
column join_key_id format a4

select Child_Level_Name,
       Parent_Level_Name,
       Position, Join_Key_Id
  from USER_DIM_CHILD_OF
where Hierarchy_Name = 'COUNTRY_ROLLUP'


CHILD_LEVEL_NAME       PARENT_LEVEL_NAME              POSITION JOIN
---------------------  ----------------------------- --------- ----
COUNTRY_ID             CONTINENT_ID                       1 1
```

To see the join key for a hierarchy, query USER_DIM_JOIN_KEY:

```
select Level_name, Child_Join_Column
  from USER_DIM_JOIN_KEY
 where Dimension_Name = 'GEOGRAPHY'
   and Hierarchy_Name = 'COUNTRY_ROLLUP'

LEVEL_NAME                        CHILD_JOIN_COLUMN
-----------------------------     -------------------------------
CONTINENT_ID                      CONTINENT
```

You can see the levels of a dimension by querying the USER_DIM_LEVELS data dictionary view, and see the key columns for the levels via USER_DIM_LEVEL_KEY. Attribute information for dimensions is accessible via USER_DIM_ATTRIBUTES.

There are "ALL" and "DBA" views of all of the data dictionary views related to dimensions. Because the "USER" views for dimensions contain an Owner column, there are no additional columns found in the corresponding "ALL" and "DBA" views.

Space Allocation and Usage, Including Partitions and Subpartitions

You can query the data dictionary to determine the space that is available and allocated for database objects. In the following sections, you will see how to determine the default storage parameters for objects, your space usage quota, available free space, and the way in which objects are physically stored. For information on Oracle's methods of storing data, see Chapters 20 and 38.

Tablespaces: USER_TABLESPACES

You can query the USER_TABLESPACES data dictionary view to determine which tablespaces you have been granted access to and the default storage parameters in each. A tablespace's default storage parameters will be used for each object stored within that tablespace unless the **create** or **alter** command for that object specifies its own storage parameters. The storage-related columns in USER_TABLESPACES, listed in Table 35-12, are very similar to the storage-related columns in USER_TABLES. See the "Storage" entry of the Alphabetical Reference for further details.

Column Name	Description
Tablespace_Name	The name of the tablespace
Initial_Extent	The default INITIAL parameter for objects in the tablespace
Next_Extent	The default NEXT parameter for objects in the tablespace
Min_Extents	The default MINEXTENTS parameter for objects in the tablespace
Max_Extents	The default MAXEXTENTS parameter for objects in the tablespace
Pct_Increase	The default PCTINCREASE parameter for objects in the tablespace
Min_Extlen	The minimum extent size for objects in the tablespace
Status	The tablespace's status ('ONLINE', 'OFFLINE', 'INVALID', 'READ ONLY'). An "invalid" tablespace is one that has been dropped; its record is still visible via this view
Contents	A flag to indicate whether the tablespace is used to store permanent objects ('PERMANENT') or only temporary segments ('TEMPORARY')
Logging	A flag to indicate the default LOGGING/NOLOGGING parameter value for objects in the tablespace
Extent_Management	Where extent management is performed for the tablespace ('DICTIONARY' or 'LOCAL')
Allocation_Type	Type of extent allocation in effect

TABLE 35-12.   *Columns of USER_TABLESPACES*

There is no "ALL" version of this view. DBA_TABLESPACES shows the storage parameters for all tablespaces.

Space Quotas: USER_TS_QUOTAS

USER_TS_QUOTAS is a very useful view for determining the amount of space you have currently allocated and the maximum amount of space available to you by tablespace. A sample query of USER_TS_QUOTAS is shown in the following listing:

```
select * from USER_TS_QUOTAS;

TABLESPACE_NAME       BYTES  MAX_BYTES     BLOCKS MAX_BLOCKS
--------------- ---------- ---------- ---------- ----------
USERS                 67584          0         33          0
```

USER_TS_QUOTAS contains one record for each Tablespace_Name. The Bytes column reflects the number of bytes allocated to objects owned by the user. Max_Bytes is the maximum number of bytes the user can own in that tablespace; if there is no quota for that tablespace, then Max_Bytes will display a value of 0. The Bytes and Max_Bytes columns are translated into Oracle blocks in the Blocks and Max_Blocks columns, respectively.

There is no "ALL" version of this view. DBA_TS_QUOTAS shows the storage quotas for all users for all tablespaces and is a very effective way to list space usage across the entire database.

Segments and Extents: USER_SEGMENTS and USER_EXTENTS

As described in Chapter 20, space is allocated to objects (such as tables, clusters, and indexes) in *segments*, the physical counterparts to the logical objects created in the database. You can query USER_SEGMENTS to see the current storage parameters and space usage in effect for your segments. USER_SEGMENTS is very useful when you are in danger of exceeding one of the storage limits; its columns are listed in Table 35-13.

Segments consist of contiguous sections called *extents*. The extents that constitute segments are described in USER_EXTENTS. In USER_EXTENTS, you will see the actual size of each extent within the segment; this is very useful for tracking the impact of changes to the **next** and **pctincrease** settings. In addition to the Segment_Name, Segment_Type, and Tablespace_Name columns, USER_EXTENTS has four new columns: Extent_ID (to identify the extent within the segment), Bytes (the size of the extent, in bytes), Blocks (the size of the extent, in Oracle blocks), and Partition_Name (if the segment is part of a partitioned object).

Column Name	Description
Segment_Name	The name of the segment
Partition_Name	**NULL** if the object is not partitioned; otherwise, the segment's partition name
Segment_Type	The type of segment ('TABLE', 'CLUSTER', 'INDEX', 'ROLLBACK', 'DEFERRED ROLLBACK', 'TEMPORARY', 'CACHE', 'INDEX PARTITION', 'TABLE PARTITION')
Tablespace_Name	The name of the tablespace in which the segment is stored
Bytes	The number of bytes allocated to the segment
Blocks	The number of Oracle blocks allocated to the segment
Extents	The number of extents in the segment
Initial_Extent	The size of the initial extent in the segment
Next_Extent	The value of the NEXT parameter for the segment
Min_Extents	The minimum number of extents in the segment
Max_Extents	The value of the MAXEXTENTS parameter for the segment
Pct_Increase	The value of the PCTINCREASE parameter for the segment
Freelists	The number of process freelists (lists of data blocks in the segment that can be used during inserts) allocated to the segment; if a segment has multiple freelists, then contention for free blocks during concurrent **inserts** will be lessened
Freelist_Groups	The number of freelist groups (the number of groups of freelists, for use with the Parallel Server option) allocated to the segment
Buffer_Pool	Buffer pool into which the segment will be read ('DEFAULT', 'KEEP', or 'RECYCLE') if you have defined multiple buffer pools

TABLE 35-13. *Columns in USER_SEGMENTS*

Both USER_SEGMENTS and USER_EXTENTS have "DBA" versions, which are useful for listing the space usage of objects across owners. Both DBA_SEGMENTS and DBA_EXTENTS have an additional Owner column. If you want to list all of the owners who own segments in a tablespace, you can query based on the Tablespace_Name column in DBA_SEGMENTS, and list all of the owners of segments in that tablespace.

Partitions and Subpartitions

A single table's data can be stored across multiple partitions. See Chapter 20 for examples of partitions and descriptions of the indexing options available. To see how a table is partitioned, you should query the USER_PART_TABLES data dictionary view, whose columns are listed, by category, in Table 35-14.

Most of the columns of USER_PART_TABLES define the default storage parameters for the table partitions. When a partition is added to the table, it will by default use the storage parameters shown in USER_PART_TABLES. USER_PART_TABLES also shows the number of partitions in the table (Partition_ Count), the number of columns in the partition key (Partitioning_Key_Count), and the type of partitioning (Partitioning_Type). Valid Partitioning_Type values are 'RANGE' and 'HASH'.

USER_PART_TABLES stores a single row for each table that has been partitioned. To see information about each of the individual partitions that belong to the table, you can query USER_TAB_PARTITIONS. In USER_TAB_PARTITIONS, you

Identification	Storage-Related
Table_Name	Def_Tablespace_Name
Partitioning_Type	Def_Pct_Free
Subpartitioning_Type	Def_Pct_Used
Partition_Count	Def_Ini_Trans
Def_Subpartition_Count	Def_Max_Trans
Partitioning_Key_Count	Def_Initial_Extent
Subpartitioning_Key_Count	Def_Next_Extent
Def_Logging	Def_Min_Extents
Def_Buffer_Pool	Def_Max_Extents
	Def_Pct_Increase
	Def_Freelists
	Def_Freelist_Groups

TABLE 35-14. *Columns in USER_PART_TABLES*

will see one row for each of the table's partitions. The columns of USER_TAB_PARTITIONS are shown, by category, in Table 35-15.

USER_TAB_PARTITIONS contains columns that identify the table to which the partition belongs, and shows the partition's storage parameters and the statistics for the partition. The "Statistics-Related" columns are populated when the table is analyzed (see the **analyze** command in the Alphabetical Reference). The "Identification" columns show the high value for the range used to define the partition (High_Value) and the position of the partition within the table (Partition_Position).

The columns used for the partition key are accessible via the USER_PART_KEY_COLUMNS data dictionary view. USER_PART_KEY_COLUMNS contains only four columns:

Name	The name of the partitioned table or index
Object_Type	Object type (TABLE or INDEX)
Column_Name	The name of the column that is part of the partition key
Column_Position	The position of the column within the partition key

Identification	Storage-Related	Statistics-Related
Table_Name	Tablespace_Name	Num_Rows
Composite	Pct_Free	Blocks
Partition_Name	Pct_Used	Empty_Blocks
Subpartition_Count	Ini_Trans	Avg_Space
High_Value	Max_Trans	Chain_Cnt
High_Value_Length	Initial_Extent	Avg_Row_Len
Partition_Position	Next_Extent	Sample_Size
Backed_Up	Min_Extent	Last_Analyzed
Logging	Max_Extent	Global_Stats
Buffer_Pool	Pct_Increase	User_Stats
	Freelists	
	Freelist_Groups	

TABLE 35-15. *Columns in USER_TAB_PARTITIONS*

Statistics for the partition columns are accessible via the USER_PART_
COL_STATISTICS data dictionary view. The columns in USER_PART_COL_
STATISTICS closely mirror those in USER_TAB_COL_STATISTICS.

Data distribution within the partitions is recorded during the processing of
the **analyze** command. The data histogram information for partitions is accessible
via the USER_PART_HISTOGRAMS data dictionary view. The columns of this
view are Table_Name, Partition_Name, Column_Name, Bucket_Number, and
Endpoint_Value.

Since indexes may be partitioned, there is a USER_IND_PARTITIONS data
dictionary view available. The columns in USER_IND_PARTITIONS can be grouped
into three categories, as shown in Table 35-16.

The columns in USER_IND_PARTITIONS parallel those in USER_INDEXES, with
a few modifications to the "Identification" columns. The "Identification" columns
for partitioned indexes show the name of the partition, the high value for the
partition, and the position of the partition within the table. The "Statistics-Related"
columns are populated when the partition is analyzed (see the **analyze** command in
the Alphabetical Reference). The "Space-Related" columns describe the space

Identification	Space-Related	Statistics-Related
Index_Name	Tablespace_Name	Blevel
Composite	Ini_Trans	Leaf_Blocks
Partition_Name	Max_Trans	Distinct_Keys
Subpartition_Count	Initial_Extent	Avg_Leaf_Blocks_Per_Key
High_Value	Next_Extent	Avg_Data_Blocks_Per_Key
High_Value_Length	Min_Extent	Clustering_Factor
Partition_Position	Max_Extent	Num_Rows
Status	Pct_Increase	Sample_Size
Logging	Pct_Free	Last_Analyzed
Buffer_Pool	Freelists	User_Stats
Compression	Freelist_Groups	Pct_Direct_Access
		Global_Stats

TABLE 35-16. *Columns in USER_IND_PARTITIONS*

allocation for the index; see the "Storage" entry in the Alphabetical Reference for information on storage parameters.

If a partition has subpartitions, you can see the details for the subpartitions via data dictionary views. USER_IND_SUBPARTITIONS contains the "Space-Related" and "Statistics-Related" columns of USER_IND_PARTITIONS, along with columns to identify the subpartition (Subpartition_Name and Subpartition_Position). Similarly, USER_TAB_SUBPARTITIONS contains the "Space-Related" and "Statistics-Related" columns of USER_TAB_PARTITIONS along with Subpartition_Name and Subpartition_Position columns. Thus, you can determine the space definitions of each of your partitions and subpartitions.

As shown earlier in this section, you can query the USER_PART_COL_STATISTICS and USER_PART_HISTOGRAMS data dictionary views for statistical information regarding partitions. For subpartitions, you can query USER_SUBPART_COL_STATISTICS and USER_SUBPART_HISTOGRAMS, whose structures mirror that of the partition statistics views. To see the subpartition key columns, you can query USER_SUBPART_KEY_COLUMNS, whose column structure is identical to that of USER_PART_KEY_COLUMNS.

Free Space: USER_FREE_SPACE

In addition to viewing the space you have used, you can also query the data dictionary to see how much space is currently marked as "free" space. USER_FREE_SPACE lists the free extents in all tablespaces accessible to the user. It lists by Tablespace_Name the File_ID, Block_ID, and relative file number of the starting point of the free extent. The size of the free extent is listed in both bytes and blocks. DBA_FREE_SPACE is frequently used by DBAs to monitor the amount of free space available and the degree to which it has become fragmented.

Users and Privileges

Users and their privileges are recorded within the data dictionary. In the following sections, you will see how to query the data dictionary for information about user accounts, resource limits, and user privileges.

Users: USER_USERS

You can query USER_USERS to list information about your account. The USER_USERS view includes your Username, User_ID (a number assigned by the database), Default_Tablespace, Temporary_Tablespace, and Created date (when your account was created). The Account_Status column in USER_USERS displays the status of your account, whether it is locked, unlocked ('OPEN'), or expired. If the account is locked, the Lock_Date column will display the date the account was locked and the Expiry_Date column will display the date of expiration. You can also query information about the resource consumer group (Initial_Rsrc_Consumer_Group) assigned to you by the DBA, and your External_Name value.

ALL_USERS contains only the Username, User_ID, and Created columns from USER_USERS, but it lists that information for all accounts in the database. ALL_USERS is useful when you need to know the usernames that are available (for example, during **grant** commands). DBA_USERS contains all of the columns in USER_USERS, plus two additional columns: Password (the encrypted password for the account) and Profile (the user's resource profile). DBA_USERS lists this information for all users in the database.

Resource Limits: USER_RESOURCE_LIMITS

In Oracle, *profiles* can be used to place limits on the amount of system and database resources available to a user. If no profiles are created in a database, the default profile, which specifies unlimited resources for all users, will be used. The resources that can be limited are described in the **create profile** entry of the Alphabetical Reference. Profiles enforce additional security measures, such as expiration dates on accounts and the minimum length of passwords.

To view the limits that are in place for your current session, you can query USER_RESOURCE_LIMITS. Its columns are the following:

Resource_Name	The name of the resource (e.g., SESSIONS_PER_USER)
Limit	The limit placed on this resource

USER_PASSWORD_LIMITS describes the password profile parameters for the user. It has the same columns as USER_RESOURCE_LIMITS.

There is no "ALL" or "DBA" version of this view; it is limited to the user's current session. To see the cost associated with each available resource, you can query the RESOURCE_COST view. DBAs can access the DBA_PROFILES view to see the resource limits for all profiles. The Resource_Type column of DBA_PROFILES indicates whether the resource profile is a 'PASSWORD' or 'KERNEL' profile.

Table Privileges: USER_TAB_PRIVS

To view grants for which you are the grantee, the grantor, or the object owner, query USER_TAB_PRIVS (user table privileges). In addition to its Grantee, Grantor, and Owner columns, this view contains columns for the Table_Name, Privilege, and a flag (set to 'YES' or 'NO') to indicate whether the privilege was granted **with admin option** (Grantable).

USER_TAB_PRIVS_MADE displays the USER_TAB_PRIVS records for which the user is the owner (it therefore lacks an Owner column). USER_TAB_PRIVS_RECD (user table privileges received) displays the USER_TAB_PRIVS records for which the user is the grantee (it therefore lacks a Grantee column). Since both USER_TAB_PRIVS_ MADE and USER_TAB_PRIVS_RECD are simply subsets of USER_TAB_PRIVS, you can duplicate their functionality simply by querying against USER_TAB_PRIVS with an appropriate **where** clause to view the subset you want.

There are "ALL" versions available for USER_TAB_PRIVS, USER_TAB_PRIVS_MADE, and USER_TAB_PRIVS_RECD. The "ALL" versions list those objects for which either the user or PUBLIC is the grantee or grantor. There is a "DBA" version of USER_TAB_PRIVS named DBA_TAB_PRIVS that lists all object privileges granted to all users in the database. DBA_TAB_PRIVS and ALL_TAB_PRIVS have the same column definitions as USER_TAB_PRIVS.

Column Privileges: USER_COL_PRIVS

In addition to granting privileges on tables, you can also grant privileges at the column level. For example, you can grant users the ability to **update** only certain columns in a table. See Chapter 19 and the **grant** command in the Alphabetical Reference for further details.

The data dictionary views used to display column privileges are almost identical in design to the table privileges views described in the previous section. The only modification is the addition of a Column_Name column to each of the views. USER_COL_PRIVS is analogous to USER_TAB_PRIVS, USER_COL_PRIVS_MADE is analogous to USER_TAB_PRIVS_MADE, and USER_COL_PRIVS_RECD is analogous to USER_TAB_PRIVS_RECD.

"ALL" versions are available for all of the column privileges views. DBA_COL_PRIVS lists all column privileges that have been granted to users in the database (just as DBA_TAB_PRIVS lists all table privileges granted to users).

System Privileges: USER_SYS_PRIVS

USER_SYS_PRIVS lists the system privileges that have been granted to the user. Its columns are Username, Privilege, and Admin_Option (a flag set to 'YES' or 'NO' to indicate whether the privilege was granted **with admin option**). All system privileges directly granted to a user are displayed via this view. System privileges granted to a user via a role are not displayed here. In this example, the Talbot user has been granted CREATE SESSION privilege via a role; therefore, that privilege is not displayed in this listing:

```
select * from USER_SYS_PRIVS;

USERNAME          PRIVILEGE                                 ADM
--------------    ------------------------------------      ---
TALBOT            CREATE PROCEDURE                          NO
TALBOT            CREATE TRIGGER                            NO
```

There is no "ALL" version of this view. To see the system privileges granted to all users in the database, query DBA_SYS_PRIVS, which has the same column definitions as USER_SYS_PRIVS.

Roles

In addition to privileges granted directly to users, sets of privileges may be grouped into roles. Roles may be granted to users or to other roles, and may be comprised of both object and system privileges. For information on the use and management of roles, see Chapter 19.

To see which roles have been granted to you, query the USER_ROLE_PRIVS data dictionary view. Any roles that have been granted to PUBLIC will also be listed here. The available columns for USER_ROLE_PRIVS are as follows:

Username	The username (may be 'PUBLIC')
Granted_Role	The name of the role granted to the user
Admin_Option	A flag to indicate whether the role was granted **with admin option** ('YES' or 'NO')
Default_Role	A flag to indicate whether the role is the user's default role ('YES' or 'NO')
OS_Granted	A flag to indicate whether the operating system is being used to manage roles ('YES' or 'NO')

To list all of the roles available in the database, you need to have DBA authority; you can then query DBA_ROLES to list all roles. DBA_ROLE_PRIVS lists the assignment of those roles to all of the users in the database.

Roles may receive three different types of grants, and each has a corresponding data dictionary view:

Table/column grants	ROLE_TAB_PRIVS. Similar to USER_TAB_PRIVS and USER_COL_PRIVS, except that it has a Role column instead of a Grantee column
System privileges	ROLE_SYS_PRIVS. Similar to USER_SYS_PRIVS, except that it has a Role column instead of a Username column
Role grants	ROLE_ROLE_PRIVS. Lists all roles that have been granted to other roles

NOTE
If you are not a DBA, these data dictionary views list only those roles that have been granted to you.

In addition to these views, there are two views, each with a single column, that list the privileges and roles enabled for the current session:

SESSION_PRIVS   The Privilege column lists all system privileges available to the session, whether granted directly or via roles

SESSION_ROLES   The Role column lists all roles that are currently enabled for the session

SESSION_PRIVS and SESSION_ROLES are available to all users.

NOTE
See Chapter 19 for information on enabling and disabling roles and the setting of default roles.

Auditing

As a non-DBA user within an Oracle database, you cannot enable the database's auditing features. If, however, auditing has been enabled, there are data dictionary views that anyone can use to view the audit trail.

Many different audit trail data dictionary views are available. Most of these views are based on a single audit trail table in the database (SYS.AUD$). The most generic of the audit trail views available is named USER_AUDIT_TRAIL. Its columns are described in Table 35-17. Since this view shows the audit records for many different types of actions, many of the columns may be inapplicable for any given row. The "DBA" version of this view, DBA_AUDIT_TRAIL, lists all entries from the audit trail table; USER_AUDIT_TRAIL lists only those that are relevant to the user.

As shown in Table 35-17, a vast array of auditing capabilities is available (see the **audit** command in the Alphabetical Reference for a complete listing). Each type of audit can be accessed via its own data dictionary view. The following are the available views:

USER_AUDIT_OBJECT   For statements concerning objects

USER_AUDIT_SESSION   For connections and disconnections

USER_AUDIT_STATEMENT   For **grant**, **revoke**, **audit**, **noaudit**, and **alter system** commands issued by the user

There are "DBA" versions available for each of the "USER" views in the previous list; the "DBA" versions show all of the audit trail records that fit into the view's category.

Column Name	Description
OS_Username	The audited user's operating system account
Username	The Oracle username of the audited user
UserHost	A numeric ID for the instance used by the audited user
Terminal	The user's operating system terminal identifier
TimeStamp	The date and time the audit record was created
Owner	The owner of the object affected by an action (for action audits)
Obj_Name	The name of the object affected by an action (for action audits)
Action	The numeric code for the audited action
Action_Name	The name of the audited action
New_Owner	The owner of the object named in the New_Name column
New_Name	The new name of an object that has been **renam**ed
Obj_Privilege	The object privilege that has been **grant**ed or **revoke**d
Sys_Privilege	The system privilege that has been **grant**ed or **revoke**d
Admin_Option	A flag to indicate whether the role or system privilege was **grant**ed **with admin option** ('Y' or 'N')
Grantee	The username specified in a **grant** or **revoke** command
Audit_Option	The auditing options set via an **audit** command
Ses_Actions	A string of characters serving as a session summary, recording success and failure for different actions
Logoff_Time	The date and time the user logged off
Logoff_LRead	The number of logical reads performed during the session
Logoff_PRead	The number of physical reads performed during the session
Logoff_LWrite	The number of logical writes performed during the session
Logoff_DLock	The number of deadlocks detected during the session
Comment_Text	A text comment on the audit trail entry
SessionID	The numeric ID for the session

TABLE 35-17. *Columns in USER_AUDIT_TRAIL*

Column Name	Description
EntryID	A numeric ID for the audit trail entry
StatementID	The numeric ID for each command that was executed
ReturnCode	The return code for each command that was executed; if the command was successful, then the ReturnCode will be 0
Priv_Used	The system privilege used to execute the action
Object_Label	The label associated with the object (for Trusted Oracle)
Session_Label	The label associated with the session (for Trusted Oracle)

TABLE 35-17.   *Columns in USER_AUDIT_TRAIL* (continued)

You can view the auditing options that are currently in effect for your objects by querying USER_OBJ_AUDIT_OPTS. For each object listed in USER_OBJ_AUDIT_OPTS, the audit options for each command that may be performed on that object (identified by the Object_Name and Object_Type columns) are listed in USER_OBJ_AUDIT_OPTS. The column names of USER_OBJ_AUDIT_OPTS correspond to the first three letters of the command (for example, Alt for **alter**, Upd for **update**, and so on). Each column will record whether that command is audited for that object when the command is successful ('S'), unsuccessful ('U'), or both. The default auditing options in effect for any new objects in the database can be displayed via the ALL_DEF_AUDIT_OPTS view, which has the same column naming conventions as USER_OBJ_AUDIT_OPTS.

The commands that can be audited are stored in a reference table named AUDIT_ACTIONS, which has two columns: Action (the numeric code for the action) and Name (the name of the action/command). Action and Name correspond to the Action and Action_Name columns of USER_AUDIT_TRAIL.

DBAs can use several additional auditing views that do not have "USER" counterparts, including DBA_AUDIT_EXISTS, DBA_PRIV_AUDIT_OPTS, DBA_STMT_AUDIT_OPTS, and STMT_AUDIT_OPTION_MAP. See the *Oracle Server Administrator's Guide* for details on these DBA-only views.

Miscellaneous

In addition to the data dictionary views described earlier in this chapter, several miscellaneous views and tables may be available within your data dictionary. These views and tables include DBA-only views and the table used when the **explain plan** command is executed. In the following sections, you will see brief descriptions for each of the miscellaneous view types.

Monitoring: The V$ Dynamic Performance Tables

The views that monitor the database environment performance are called the *system statistics views.* The system statistics tables, also called the dynamic performance tables, are commonly referred to as the *V$* (pronounced "Vee-Dollar") tables, because they all begin with the letter *V* followed by the dollar sign ($).

The definitions and usage of columns within the monitoring views are subject to change with each version of the database that is released. Correctly interpreting the results of ad hoc queries against views usually requires referring to the *Oracle Server Administrator's Guide.* The V$ tables are normally used only by the DBA. Consult the *Oracle Server Reference* and the *Oracle8i DBA Handbook* for details on the use of the V$ views.

CHAINED_ROWS

When a row no longer fits within the data block its row header is stored in, that row may store the remainder of its data in a different block or set of blocks. Such a row is said to be *chained,* and chained rows may cause poor performance due to the increased number of blocks that must be read to read a single row.

The **analyze** command can be used to generate a listing of the chained rows within a table. This listing of chained rows can be stored in a table called CHAINED_ROWS. To create the CHAINED_ROWS table in your schema, run the utlchain.sql script (usually found in the /rdbms/admin subdirectory under the Oracle home directory).

To populate the CHAINED_ROWS table, use the **list chained rows into** clause of the **analyze** command, as shown in the following listing:

```
analyze LEDGER list chained rows into CHAINED_ROWS;
```

The CHAINED_ROWS table lists the Owner_Name, Table_Name, Cluster_Name (if the table is in a cluster), Partition_Name (if the table is partitioned), Subpartition_Name (if the table contains subpartitions), Head_RowID (the RowID for the row), and a TimeStamp column that shows the last time the table or cluster was analyzed. You can query the table based on the Head_RowID values in CHAINED_ROWS, as shown in the following example:

```
select * from LEDGER
 where RowID in
        (select Head_RowID
          from CHAINED_ROWS
          where Table_Name = 'LEDGER');
```

If the chained row is short in length, then it may be possible to eliminate the chaining by deleting and reinserting the row.

PLAN_TABLE

When tuning SQL statements, you may wish to determine the steps that the optimizer will take to execute your query. To view the query path, you must first create a table in your schema named PLAN_TABLE. The script used to create this table is called utlxplan.sql, and is usually stored in the /rdbms/admin subdirectory of the Oracle software home directory.

After you have created the PLAN_TABLE table in your schema, you can use the **explain plan** command, which will generate records in your PLAN_TABLE, tagged with the Statement_ID value you specify for the query you wish to have explained:

```
explain plan
set Statement_ID = 'MYTEST'
for
select * from LEDGER
 where Person like 'S%';
```

The ID and Parent_ID columns in PLAN_TABLE establish the hierarchy of steps (Operations) that the optimizer will follow when executing the query. See Chapter 36 for details on the Oracle optimizer and the interpretation of PLAN_TABLE records.

Interdependencies: USER_DEPENDENCIES and IDEPTREE

Objects within Oracle databases can depend upon each other. For example, a stored procedure may depend upon a table, or a package may depend upon a package body. When an object within the database changes, any procedural object that depends upon it will have to be recompiled. This recompilation can take place either automatically at runtime (with a consequential performance penalty) or manually (see Chapter 27 for details on compiling procedural objects).

Two sets of data dictionary views are available to help you track dependencies. The first is USER_DEPENDENCIES, which lists all *direct* dependencies of objects. However, this only goes one level down the dependency tree. To fully evaluate dependencies, you must create the recursive dependency-tracking objects in your schema. To create these objects, run the utldtree.sql script (usually located in the /rdbms/admin subdirectory of the Oracle home directory). This script creates two objects you can query: DEPTREE and IDEPTREE. They contain identical information, but IDEPTREE is indented based on the pseudo-column Level, and is thus easier to read and interpret.

DBA-Only Views

Since this chapter is intended for use by developers and end users, the data dictionary views available only to DBAs are not covered here. The DBA-only views are used to provide information about distributed transactions, lock contention, rollback segments, and other internal database functions. For information on the use of the DBA-only views, see the *Oracle Server Administrator's Guide*.

Trusted Oracle

Users of Trusted Oracle can view two additional data dictionary views:

| ALL_LABELS | All system labels |
| ALL_MOUNTED_DBS | All mounted databases |

For details on the usage of these views, see the *Trusted Oracle Server Administrator's Guide*.

SQL*Loader Direct Load Views

To manage the direct load option within SQL*Loader, Oracle maintains a number of data dictionary views. These generally are only queried for debugging purposes, upon request from Oracle Customer Support. The SQL*Loader direct load option is described under the "SQLLDR" entry in the Alphabetical Reference; its supporting data dictionary views are listed here. For details on the use of these views, see the catldr.sql script, usually located in the /rdbms/admin subdirectory of the Oracle home directory.

- LOADER_COL_INFO
- LOADER_CONSTRAINT_INFO
- LOADER_FILE_TS
- LOADER_PARAM_INFO
- LOADER_PART_INFO
- LOADER_REF_INFO

■   LOADER_TAB_INFO

■   LOADER_TRIGGER_INFO

For details on the use of these views, see the catldr.sql script, usually located in the /rdbms/admin subdirectory of the Oracle home directory.

National Language Support (NLS) Views

Three data dictionary views are used to display information about the National Language Support parameters currently in effect in the database. Nonstandard values for the NLS parameters (such as NLS_DATE_FORMAT and NLS_SORT) can be set via the database's init.ora file or via the **alter session** command. (See the **alter session** command in the Alphabetical Reference for further information on NLS settings.) To see the current NLS settings for your session, instance, and database, query NLS_SESSION_PARAMETERS, NLS_INSTANCE_PARAMETERS, and NLS_DATABASE_PARAMETERS, respectively.

Libraries

Your PL/SQL routines (see Chapter 25) can call external C programs. To see which external C program libraries are owned by you, you can query USER_LIBRARIES, which displays the name of the library (Library_Name), the associated file (File_Spec), whether or not the library is dynamically loadable (Dynamic), and the library's status (Status). ALL_LIBRARIES and DBA_LIBRARIES are also available; they include an additional Owner column to indicate the owner of the library. For further information on libraries, see the entry for the **create library** command in the Alphabetical Reference.

Heterogeneous Services

To support the management of heterogeneous services, Oracle provides 16 data dictionary views. All of the views in this category begin with the letters HS instead of DBA. In general, these views are used primarily by DBAs. For details on the HS views, see the *Oracle8i Server Reference.*

Indextypes and Operators

Operators and indextypes are closely related. You can use the **create operator** command to create a new operator and define its bindings. You can reference operators in indextypes and in SQL statements. The operators, in turn, reference functions, packages, types, and other user-defined objects.

You can query the USER_OPERATORS view to see each operator's Owner, Operator_Name, and Number_of_Binds values. Ancillary information for operators is accessible via USER_OPANCILLARY, and you can query USER_OPARGUMENTS to see the operator arguments. You can query USER_OPBINDINGS to see the operator bindings.

USER_INDEX_OPERATORS lists the operators supported by indextypes. Indextypes, in turn, are displayed via USER_INDEXTYPES. There are "ALL" and "DBA" views of all the operator and indextype views.

Outlines

When you use stored outlines, you can retrieve the name of, and details for, the outlines via the USER_OUTLINES data dictionary views. To see the hints that make up the outlines, query USER_OUTLINE_HINTS. There are "ALL" and "DBA" versions of USER_OUTLINES and USER_OUTLINE_HINTS.

CHAPTER
36

The Hitchhiker's Guide
to the Oracle Optimizer

ithin the relational model, the physical location of data is unimportant. Within Oracle, the physical location of your data and the operation used to retrieve the data are unimportant—until the database needs to find the data. If you query the database, you should be aware of the operations Oracle performs to retrieve and manipulate the data. The better you understand the execution path Oracle uses to perform your query, the better you will be able to manipulate and tune the query.

In this chapter, you will see the operations Oracle uses to query and process data, presented from a user's perspective. First, the operations that access tables are described, followed by index access operations, data set operations, joins, and miscellaneous operations. For each type of operation, relevant tuning information is provided to help you use the operation in the most efficient and effective manner possible.

Before beginning to tune your queries, you need to decide which optimizer you will be using.

Which Optimizer?

The Oracle optimizer has two primary modes of operation: cost-based or rule-based. To set the optimizer goal, you can specify CHOOSE (for cost-based) or RULE (for rule-based) for the OPTIMIZER_MODE parameter in your database's init.ora file. You can override the optimizer's default operations at the query and session level, as shown later in this chapter.

Setting OPTIMIZER_MODE to RULE invokes the *rule-based optimizer (RBO)*, which evaluates possible execution paths and rates the alternative execution paths based on a series of syntactical rules. In general, the RBO is seldom used by new applications, and is found primarily in applications developed and tuned for earlier versions of Oracle.

Setting OPTIMIZER_MODE to CHOOSE invokes the *cost-based optimizer (CBO)*. You can use the **analyze** command to generate statistics about the objects in your database. The generated statistics include the number of rows in a table and the number of distinct keys in an index. Based on the statistics, the CBO evaluates the cost of the available execution paths and selects the execution path that has the lowest relative cost. If you use the CBO, you need to make sure that you run the **analyze** command frequently enough for the statistics to accurately reflect the data within your database. If a query references tables that have been analyzed and tables that have not been analyzed, the CBO may decide to perform full table scans of the tables that have not been analyzed. To reduce the potential for unplanned full table scans, you should use either the RBO or the CBO consistently throughout your database.

Operations That Access Tables

Two operations directly access the rows of a table: a full table scan and a RowID-based access to the table. For information on operations that access table rows via clusters, see "Queries That Use Clusters," later in this chapter.

TABLE ACCESS FULL

A full table scan sequentially reads each row of a table. The optimizer calls the operation used during a full table scan a TABLE ACCESS FULL. To optimize the performance of a full table scan, Oracle reads multiple blocks during each database read.

A full table scan is used whenever there is no **where** clause on a query. For example, the following query selects all of the rows from the WORKER table:

```
select *
  from WORKER;
```

To resolve the preceding query, Oracle will perform a full table scan of the WORKER table. If the WORKER table is small, a full table scan of WORKER may be fairly quick, incurring little performance cost. However, as WORKER grows in size, the cost of performing a full table scan grows. If you have multiple users performing full table scans of WORKER, then the cost associated with the full table scans grows even faster.

Depending on the data being selected, the optimizer may choose to use a full scan of an index in place of a full table scan.

TABLE ACCESS BY ROWID

To improve the performance of table accesses, you can use Oracle operations that allow you to access rows by their RowID values. The RowID records the physical location where the row is stored. Oracle uses indexes to correlate data values with RowID values—and thus with physical locations of the data. Given the RowID of a row, Oracle can use the TABLE ACCESS BY ROWID operation to retrieve the row.

When you know the RowID, you know exactly where the row is physically located. However, you do not need to memorize the RowIDs for your rows; instead, you can use indexes to access the RowID information, as described in the next major section, "Operations That Use Indexes." Because indexes provide quick access to RowID values, they help to improve the performance of queries that make use of indexed columns.

Related Hints

Within a query, you can specify hints that direct the CBO in its processing of the query. To specify a hint, use the syntax shown in the following example. Immediately after the **select** keyword, enter the following string:

```
/*+
```

Next, add the hint, such as

```
FULL(worker)
```

Close the hint with the following string:

```
*/
```

Hints use Oracle's syntax for comments within queries, with the addition of the "+" sign at the start of the hint. Throughout this chapter, the hints relevant to each operation will be described. For table accesses, there are two relevant hints: FULL and ROWID. The FULL hint tells Oracle to perform a full table scan (the TABLE ACCESS FULL operation) on the listed table, as shown in the following listing:

```
select /*+ FULL(worker) */
  from WORKER
 where Lodging = 'ROSE HILL';
```

The ROWID hint tells the optimizer to use a TABLE ACCESS BY ROWID operation to access the rows in the table. In general, you should use a TABLE ACCESS BY ROWID operation whenever you need to return rows quickly to users and whenever the tables are large. To use the TABLE ACCESS BY ROWID operation, you need to either know the RowID values or use an index.

Operations That Use Indexes

Within Oracle are two major types of indexes: *unique indexes,* in which each row of the indexed table contains a unique value for the indexed column(s), and *nonunique indexes,* in which the rows' indexed values can repeat. The operations used to read data from the indexes depends on the type of index in use and the way in which you write the query that accesses the index.

Consider the LODGING table:

```
create table LODGING (
Lodging       VARCHAR2(15) not null,
LongName      VARCHAR2(40),
```

```
Manager        VARCHAR2(25),
Address        VARCHAR2(30)
);
```

By default, no indexes are created on the LODGING table. However, suppose
the Lodging column is the primary key for the LODGING table—that is, it uniquely
identifies each row, and each attribute is dependent on the Lodging value. You can
create a PRIMARY KEY constraint on the LODGING table to enforce the uniqueness
of the Lodging column and to allow FOREIGN KEY constraints to reference the
Lodging values.

Whenever a PRIMARY KEY or UNIQUE constraint is created, Oracle creates
a unique index to enforce uniqueness of the values in the column. The **alter table**
command shown in the following listing includes a **using index** clause to force the
index to be located in the INDEXES tablespace:

```
alter table LODGING
    add constraint LODGING_PK primary key (Lodging)
using index tablespace INDEXES;
```

As defined by the **alter table** command, a primary key constraint named
LODGING_PK will be created on the LODGING table. The index that supports the
primary key will be named LODGING_PK.

You can create indexes on other columns of the LODGING table manually.
For example, you could create a nonunique index on the Manager column via the
create index command:

```
create index LODGING$MANAGER
    on LODGING(Manager)
tablespace INDEXES;
```

The LODGING table now has two indexes on it: a unique index on the Lodging
column, and a nonunique index on the Manager column. One or more of the
indexes could be used during the resolution of a query, depending on how the
query is written and executed.

INDEX UNIQUE SCAN

To use an index during a query, your query must be written to allow the use of an
index. In most cases, you allow the optimizer to use an index via the **where** clause
of the query. For example, the following query could use the unique index on the
Lodging column:

```
select *
    from LODGING
 where Lodging = 'ROSE HILL';
```

Internally, the execution of the preceding query will be divided into two steps. First, the LODGING_PK index will be accessed via an INDEX UNIQUE SCAN operation. The RowID value that matches the 'Rose Hill' Lodging value will be returned from the index; that RowID value will then be used to query LODGING via a TABLE ACCESS BY ROWID operation.

If the value requested by the query had been contained within the index, then Oracle would not have needed to use the TABLE ACCESS BY ROWID operation; since the data would be in the index, the index would be all that is needed to satisfy the query. Because the query selected all columns from the LODGING table, and the index did not contain all of the columns of the LODGING table, the TABLE ACCESS BY ROWID operation was necessary.

INDEX RANGE SCAN

If you query the database based on a range of values, or if you query using a nonunique index, then an INDEX RANGE SCAN operation is used to query the index.

Consider the LODGING table again, with a unique index on its Lodging column. A query of the form

```
select Lodging
   from LODGING
 where Lodging like 'M%';
```

would return all Lodging values beginning with 'M'. Since the **where** clause uses the Lodging column, the LODGING_PK index on the Lodging column can be used while resolving the query. However, a unique value is not specified in the **where** clause; a range of values is specified. Therefore, the unique LODGING_PK index will be accessed via an INDEX RANGE SCAN operation. Because INDEX RANGE SCAN operations require reading multiple values from the index, they are less efficient than INDEX UNIQUE SCAN operations.

In the preceding example, only the Lodging column was selected by the query. Since the values for the Lodging column are stored in the LODGING_PK index—which is being scanned—there is no need for the database to access the LODGING table directly during the query execution. The INDEX RANGE SCAN of LODGING_PK is the only operation required to resolve the query.

The Manager column of the LODGING table has a nonunique index on its values. If you specify a limiting condition for Manager values in your query's **where** clause, an INDEX RANGE SCAN of the Manager index may be performed. Since the LODGING$MANAGER index is a nonunique index, the database cannot perform an INDEX UNIQUE SCAN on LODGING$MANAGER, even if Manager is equated to a single value in your query. For example, the query

```
select Lodging
   from LODGING
 where Manager = 'THOM CRANMER';
```

could access the LODGING$MANAGER index via an INDEX RANGE SCAN operation, but not via an INDEX UNIQUE SCAN operation. Since the preceding query selects the Lodging column from the table, and the Lodging column is not in the LODGING$MANAGER index, the INDEX RANGE SCAN must be followed by a TABLE ACCESS BY ROWID.

When Indexes Are Used

Since indexes have a great impact on the performance of queries, you should be aware of the conditions under which an index will be used to resolve a query. The following sections describe the conditions that can cause an index to be used while resolving a query.

If You Set an Indexed Column Equal to a Value

In the LODGING table, the Manager column has a nonunique index named LODGING$MANAGER. A query that sets the Manager column equal to a value will be able to use the LODGING$MANAGER index.

The following query sets the Manager column equal to the value 'THOM CRANMER':

```
select Lodging
  from LODGING
 where Manager = 'THOM CRANMER';
```

Since the LODGING$MANAGER index is a nonunique index, this query may return multiple rows, and an INDEX RANGE SCAN operation will always be used when reading data from it. The execution of the preceding query will involve two operations: an INDEX RANGE SCAN of LODGING$MANAGER (to get the RowID values for all of the rows with 'THOM CRANMER' values in the Manager column), followed by a TABLE ACCESS BY ROWID of the LODGING table (to retrieve the Lodging column values).

If a column has a unique index created on it, and the column is equal to a value, then an INDEX UNIQUE SCAN will be used instead of an INDEX RANGE SCAN.

If You Specify a Range of Values for an Indexed Column

You do not need to specify explicit values in order for an index to be used. The INDEX RANGE SCAN operation can scan an index for ranges of values. In the following query, the Manager column of the LODGING table is queried for a range of values (those that start with *R*):

```
select Lodging
  from LODGING
 where Manager like 'R%';
```

When specifying a range of values for a column, an index will not be used to resolve the query if the first character specified is a wildcard. The following query will *not* use the LODGING$MANAGER index:

```
select Lodging
   from LODGING
 where Manager like '%CRANMER';
```

Since the first character of the string used for value comparisons is a wildcard, the index cannot be used to find the associated data quickly. Therefore, a full table scan (TABLE ACCESS FULL operation) will be performed instead.

If No Functions Are Performed on the Column in the where Clause

Consider the following query, which will use the LODGING$MANAGER index:

```
select Lodging
   from LODGING
 where Manager = 'THOM CRANMER';
```

What if you did not know whether the values in the Manager column were stored as uppercase, mixed case, or lowercase values? In that event, you may write the query as follows:

```
select Lodging
   from LODGING
 where UPPER(Manager) = 'THOM CRANMER';
```

The **UPPER** function changes the Manager values to uppercase before comparing them to the value 'THOM CRANMER'. However, using the function on the column may prevent the optimizer from using an index on that column. The preceding query (using the **UPPER** function) will perform a TABLE ACCESS FULL of the LODGING table unless you have created a function-based index on **UPPER**(Manager).

If you concatenate two columns together or a string to a column, then indexes on those columns will not be used. The index stores the real value for the column, and any change to that value will prevent the optimizer from using the index.

If No IS NULL or IS NOT NULL Checks
Are Used for the Indexed Column

NULL values are not stored in indexes. Therefore, the following query will not use an index; there is no way the index could help to resolve the query:

```
select Lodging
   from LODGING
 where Manager is null;
```

Since Manager is the only column with a limiting condition in the query, and the limiting condition is a **NULL** check, the LODGING$MANAGER index will not be used and a TABLE ACCESS FULL operation will be used to resolve the query.

What if an **IS NOT NULL** check is performed on the column? All of the non-**NULL** values for the column are stored in the index; however, the index search would not be efficient. To resolve the query, the optimizer would need to read every value from the index and access the table for each row returned from the index. In most cases, it would be more efficient to perform a full table scan than to perform an index scan (with associated TABLE ACCESS BY ROWID operations) for all of the values returned from the index. Therefore, the following query should not use an index:

```
select Lodging
   from LODGING
 where Manager is not null;
```

If Equivalence Conditions Are Used

In the examples in the prior sections, the Manager value was set equal to a value:

```
select Lodging
   from LODGING
 where Manager = 'THOM CRANMER';
```

What if you wanted to select all of the records that did not have 'THOM CRANMER' as the Manager value? The = would be replaced with !=, and the query would now be

```
select Lodging
   from LODGING
 where Manager != 'THOM CRANMER';
```

When resolving the revised query, the optimizer will not use an index. Indexes are used when values are set equal to another value—when the limiting conditions are equalities, not inequalities.

Another example of an inequality is the **not in** clause, when used with a subquery. The following query selects values from the WORKER table for workers who do not live in lodgings managed by Thom Cranmer:

```
select Name
   from WORKER
 where Lodging not in
(select Lodging
   from LODGING
 where Manager = 'THOM CRANMER');
```

In some cases, the query in the preceding listing would not be able to use an index on the Lodging column of the WORKER table, since it is not set equal to any value. Instead, the WORKER.Lodging value is used with a **not in** clause to eliminate the rows that match those returned by the subquery. To use an index, you must set the indexed column equal to a value. In many cases, Oracle now internally rewrites the **not in** as a **not exists** clause, allowing the query to use an index. The following query, which uses an **in** clause, could use an index on the WORKER.Lodging column:

```
select Name
  from WORKER
 where Lodging in
(select Lodging
   from LODGING
  where Manager = 'THOM CRANMER');
```

If the Leading Column of a Multicolumn Index Is Set Equal to a Value

An index can be created on a single column or on multiple columns. If the index is created on multiple columns, the index will only be used if the leading column of the index is used in a limiting condition of the query. If your query specifies values for only the nonleading columns of the index, the index will not be used to resolve the query.

If the MAX or MIN Function Is Used

If you select the **MAX** or **MIN** value of an indexed column, the optimizer may use the index to quickly find the maximum or minimum value for the column.

If the Index Is Selective

All of the previous rules for determining if an index will be used consider only the syntax of the query being performed and the structure of the index available. If you are using the CBO, the optimizer can use the selectivity of the index to judge whether using the index will lower the cost of executing the query.

In a highly selective index, a small number of records are associated with each distinct column value. For example, if there are 100 records in a table and 80 distinct values for a column in that table, the selectivity of an index on that column is 80/100 = 0.80. The higher the selectivity, the fewer the number of rows returned for each distinct value in the column.

The number of rows returned per distinct value is important during range scans. If an index has a low selectivity, then the many INDEX RANGE SCAN operations and TABLE ACCESS BY ROWID operations used to retrieve the data may involve more work than a TABLE ACCESS FULL of the table.

The selectivity of an index is not considered by the optimizer unless you are using the CBO and have analyzed the index. The optimizer can use histograms to make judgments about the distribution of data within a table. For example, if the data values are heavily skewed so that most of the values are in a very small data range, the optimizer may avoid using the index for values in that range while using the index for values outside the range. Histograms are enabled by default.

Combining Output from Multiple Index Scans

Multiple indexes—or multiple scans of the same index—can be used to resolve a single query. For the LODGING table, two indexes are available: the unique LODGING_PK index on the Lodging column, and the LODGING$MANAGER index on the Manager column. In the following sections, you will see how the optimizer integrates the output of multiple scans via the AND-EQUAL and CONCATENATION operations.

AND-EQUAL of Multiple Indexes

If limiting conditions are specified for multiple indexed columns in a query, the optimizer may be able to use multiple indexes when resolving the query.

The following query specifies values for both the Lodging and Manager columns of the LODGING table:

```
select *
  from LODGING
 where Lodging > 'M'
   and Manager > 'M';
```

The query's **where** clause contains two separate limiting conditions. Each of the limiting conditions corresponds to a different index: the first to LODGING_PK and the second to LODGING$MANAGER. When resolving the query, the optimizer may use both indexes. Each index will be scanned via an INDEX RANGE SCAN operation. The RowIDs returned from the scan of the LODGING_PK index will be compared with those returned from the scan of the LODGING$MANAGER index. The RowIDs that are returned from both indexes will be used during the subsequent TABLE ACCESS BY ROWID operation. Figure 36-1 shows the order in which the operations are executed.

The AND-EQUAL operation, as shown in Figure 36-1, compares the results of the two index scans. In general, accesses of a single multicolumn index (in which the leading column is used in a limiting condition in the query's **where** clause) will perform better than an AND-EQUAL of multiple single-column indexes.

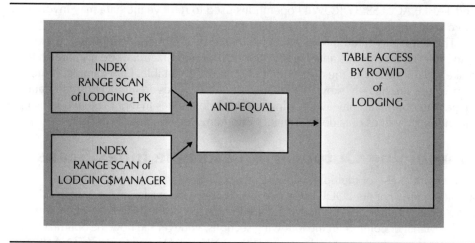

FIGURE 36-1. *Order of operations for the AND-EQUAL example*

CONCATENATION of Multiple Scans

If you specify a list of values for a column's limiting condition, the optimizer may perform multiple scans and concatenate the results of the scans. For example, the query in the following listing specifies two separate values for the LODGING.Manager value:

```
select *
  from LODGING
 where Manager in ('THOM CRANMER', 'KEN MULLER');
```

Since a range of values is not used, a single INDEX RANGE SCAN operation may be inefficient when resolving the query. Therefore, the optimizer may choose to perform two separate scans of the same index and concatenate the results.

When resolving the query, the optimizer may perform an INDEX RANGE SCAN on LODGING$MANAGER for each of the limiting conditions. The RowIDs returned from the index scans are used to access the rows in the LODGING table (via TABLE ACCESS BY ROWID operations). The rows returned from each of the TABLE ACCESS BY ROWID operations are combined into a single set of rows via the CONCATENATION operation.

Related Hints

Several hints are available to direct the optimizer in its use of indexes. The INDEX hint is the most commonly used index-related hint. The INDEX hint tells the optimizer to use an index-based scan on the specified table. You do not need to mention the index name when using the INDEX hint, although you can list specific indexes if you choose.

For example, the following query uses the INDEX hint to suggest the use of an index on the LODGING table during the resolution of the query:

```
select /*+ INDEX(lodging) */      Lodging
   from LODGING
 where Manager = 'THOM CRANMER';
```

According to the rules provided earlier in this section, the preceding query should use the index without the hint being needed. However, if the index is nonselective and you are using the CBO, then the optimizer may choose to ignore the index. If you know that the index is selective for the data values given, you can use the INDEX hint to force an index-based data access path to be used.

In the following example, the LODGING$MANAGER index on the LODGING table is specified in the hint; the LODGING$MANAGER index will be used when resolving the query:

```
select /*+ INDEX(lodging lodging$manager) */      Lodging
   from LODGING
 where Manager = 'THOM CRANMER';
```

If you do not list a specific index in the hint, and multiple indexes are available for the table, then the optimizer evaluates the available indexes and chooses the index whose scan is likely to have the lowest cost. The optimizer could also choose to scan several indexes and merge them via the AND-EQUAL operation described in the previous section.

A second hint, INDEX_ASC, functions the same as the INDEX hint: it suggests an ascending index scan for resolving queries against specific tables. A third index-based hint, INDEX_DESC, tells the optimizer to scan the index in descending order (from its highest value to its lowest).

Additional Tuning Issues for Indexes

When creating indexes on a table, two issues commonly arise: should you use multiple indexes or a single concatenated index, and if you use a concatenated index, which column should be the leading column of the index?

In general, it is faster for the optimizer to scan a single concatenated index than to scan and merge two separate indexes. The more rows returned from the scan, the more likely the concatenated index scan will outperform the merge of the two index scans. As you add more columns to the concatenated index, it becomes less efficient for range scans.

For the concatenated index, which column should be the leading column of the index? The leading column should be very frequently used as a limiting condition against the table, and it should be highly selective. In a concatenated index, the optimizer will base its estimates of the index's selectivity (and thus its likelihood of being used) on the selectivity of the leading column of the index. Of these two criteria—being used in limiting conditions and being the most selective column—the first is more important. If the leading column of the index is not used in a limiting condition (as described earlier in this chapter), the index will not be used.

A highly selective index based on a column that is never used in limiting conditions will never be used. A poorly selective index on a column that is frequently used in limiting conditions will not benefit your performance greatly. If you cannot achieve the goal of creating an index that is both highly selective and frequently used, then you should consider creating separate indexes for the columns to be indexed.

Most applications emphasize online transaction processing over batch processing; there may be many concurrent online users but a small number of concurrent batch users. In general, index-based scans allow online users to access data more quickly than if a full table scan had been performed. Therefore, when creating your application, you should be aware of the kinds of queries executed within the application and the limiting conditions in those queries. If you are familiar with the queries executed against the database, you may be able to index the tables so that the online users can quickly retrieve the data they need.

Operations That Manipulate Data Sets

Once the data has been returned from the table or index, it can be manipulated. You can group the records, sort them, count them, lock them, or merge the results of the query with the results of other queries (via the **UNION**, **MINUS**, and **INTERSECT** operators). In the following sections, you will see how the data manipulation operations are used.

Most of the operations that manipulate sets of records do not return records to the users until the entire operation is completed. For example, sorting records while eliminating duplicates (known as a SORT UNIQUE operation) cannot return records to the user until all of the records have been evaluated for uniqueness. On the other hand, index scan operations and table access operations can return records to the user as soon as a record is found.

When an INDEX RANGE SCAN operation is performed, the first row returned from the query passes the criteria of the limiting conditions set by the query—there is no need to evaluate the next record returned prior to displaying the first record. If a set operation—such as a sorting operation—is performed, then the records will not be immediately displayed. During set operations, the user will have to wait for all rows to be processed by the operation. Therefore, you should limit the number of set operations performed by queries used by online users (to limit the perceived response time of the application). Sorting and grouping operations are most common in large reports and batch transactions.

Ordering Rows

Three of Oracle's internal operations sort rows without grouping the rows. The first is the SORT ORDER BY operation, which is used when an **order by** clause is used in a query. For example, the WORKER table is queried. WORKER has three columns: Name, Age, and Lodging. The Age column of the WORKER table is not indexed. The following query selects all of the records from the WORKER table, sorted by Age:

```
select Name, Age
   from WORKER
 order by Age;
```

When the preceding query is executed, the optimizer will retrieve the data from the WORKER table via a TABLE ACCESS FULL operation (since there are no limiting conditions for the query, all rows will be returned). The retrieved records will not be immediately displayed to the user; a SORT ORDER BY operation will sort the records before the user sees any results.

Occasionally, a sorting operation may be required to eliminate duplicates as it sorts records. For example, what if you only want to see the distinct Age values in the WORKER table? The query would be as follows:

```
select DISTINCT Age
   from WORKER;
```

As with the prior query, this query has no limiting conditions, so a TABLE ACCESS FULL operation will be used to retrieve the records from the WORKER table. However, the **DISTINCT** function tells the optimizer to only return the distinct values for the Age column. To eliminate the duplicate Age values, the optimizer uses a SORT UNIQUE operation.

To resolve the query, the optimizer takes the records returned by the TABLE ACCESS FULL operation and sorts them via a SORT UNIQUE operation. No records will be displayed to the user until all of the records have been processed.

In addition to being used by the **DISTINCT** function, the SORT UNIQUE operation is invoked when the **MINUS, INTERSECT,** and **UNION** (but not **UNION ALL**) functions are used.

A third sorting operation, SORT JOIN, is always used as part of a MERGE JOIN operation and is never used on its own. The implications of SORT JOIN on the performance of joins is described in "Operations That Perform Joins," later in this chapter.

Grouping Rows

Two of Oracle's internal operations sort rows while grouping like records together. The two operations—SORT AGGREGATE and SORT GROUP BY—are used in conjunction with grouping functions (such as **MIN**, **MAX**, and **COUNT**). The syntax of the query determines which operation is used.

In the following query, the maximum Age value is selected from the WORKER table:

```
select MAX(Age)
   from WORKER;
```

To resolve the query, the optimizer will perform two separate operations. First, a TABLE ACCESS FULL operation will select the Age values from the table. Second, the rows will be analyzed via a SORT AGGREGATE operation, which will return the maximum Age value to the user.

If the Age column were indexed, the index could be used to resolve queries of the maximum or minimum value for the index (as described in "Operations That Use Indexes," earlier in this chapter). Since the Age column is not indexed, a sorting operation is required. The maximum Age value will not be returned by this query until all of the records have been read and the SORT AGGREGATE operation has completed.

The SORT AGGREGATE operation was used in the preceding example because there is no **group by** clause in the query. Queries that use the **group by** clause use an internal operation named SORT GROUP BY.

What if you want to know the number of workers in each lodging? The following query selects the count of each Lodging value from the WORKER table using a **group by** clause:

```
select Lodging, COUNT(*)
   from WORKER
 group by Lodging;
```

This query returns one record for each distinct Lodging value. For each Lodging value, the number of its occurrences in the WORKER table will be calculated and displayed in the **COUNT**(*) column.

To resolve this query, Oracle will first perform a full table scan (there are no limiting conditions for the query). Since a **group by** clause is used, the rows returned from the TABLE ACCESS FULL operation will be processed by a SORT GROUP BY operation. Once all the rows have been sorted into groups and the count for each group has been calculated, the records will be returned to the user. As with the other sorting operations, no records are returned to the user until all of the records have been processed.

The operations to this point have involved simple examples—full table scans, index scans, and sorting operations. Most queries that access a single table use the operations described in the previous sections. When tuning a query for an online user, avoid using the sorting and grouping operations that force users to wait for records to be processed. When possible, write queries that allow application users to receive records quickly as the query is resolved. The fewer sorting and grouping operations you perform, the faster the first record will be returned to the user. In a batch transaction, the performance of the query is measured by its overall time to complete, not the time to return the first row. As a result, batch transactions may use sorting and grouping operations without impacting the perceived performance of the application.

Operations Using RowNum

Queries that use the RowNum pseudo-column use either the COUNT or COUNT STOPKEY operation to increment the RowNum counter. If a limiting condition is applied to the RowNum pseudo-column, such as

```
where RowNum < 10
```

then the COUNT STOPKEY operation is used. If no limiting condition is specified for the RowNum pseudo-column, then the COUNT operation is used. The COUNT and COUNT STOPKEY operations are not related to the **COUNT** function.

The following query will use the COUNT operation during its execution, since it refers to the RowNum pseudo-column:

```
select Name,
       RowNum
  from WORKER;
```

To resolve the preceding query, the optimizer will perform a full table scan (a TABLE ACCESS FULL operation against the WORKER table), followed by a COUNT operation to generate the RowNum values for each returned row. The COUNT operation does not need to wait for the entire set of records to be available. As each record is returned from the WORKER table, the RowNum counter is incremented and the RowNum for the record is determined.

In the following example, a limiting condition is placed on the RowNum pseudo-column:

```
select Name,
       RowNum
  from WORKER
 where RowNum < 10;
```

To enforce the limiting condition, the optimizer replaces the COUNT operation with a COUNT STOPKEY operation, which compares the incremented value of the RowNum pseudo-column with the limiting condition supplied. When the RowNum value exceeds the value specified in the limiting condition, no more rows are returned by the query.

UNION, MINUS, and INTERSECT

The **UNION**, **MINUS**, and **INTERSECT** functions allow the results of multiple queries to be processed and compared. Each of the functions has an associated operation—the names of the operations are UNION, MINUS, and INTERSECTION.

The following query selects all of the Name values from the PROSPECT table and from the LONGTIME table:

```
select Name
   from PROSPECT
 UNION
select Name
   from LONGTIME;
```

When the preceding query is executed, the optimizer will execute each of the queries separately, then combine the results. The first query is

```
select Name
   from PROSPECT
```

There are no limiting conditions in the query, so the PROSPECT table will be accessed via a TABLE ACCESS FULL operation.

The second query is

```
select Name
   from LONGTIME;
```

There are no limiting conditions in the query, so the LONGTIME table will be accessed via a TABLE ACCESS FULL operation.

Since the query performs a **UNION** of the results of the two queries, the two result sets will then be merged via a UNION-ALL operation. Using the **UNION** function forces Oracle to eliminate duplicate records, so the result set is processed by a SORT UNIQUE operation before the records are returned to the user. The order of operations for the **UNION** function is shown in Figure 36-2.

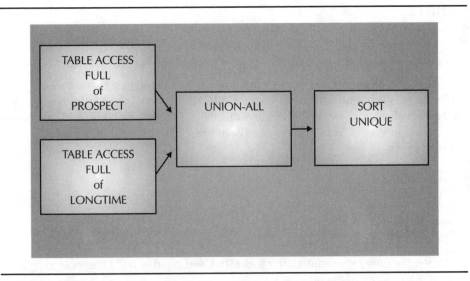

FIGURE 36-2. *Order of operations for the **UNION** function*

If the query had used a **UNION ALL** function in place of **UNION**, the SORT UNIQUE operation (see Figure 36-2) would not have been necessary. The query would be

```
select Name
  from PROSPECT
 UNION ALL
select Name
  from LONGTIME;
```

When processing the revised query, the optimizer would perform the table scans required by the two queries, followed by a UNION-ALL operation. No SORT UNIQUE operation would be required, since a **UNION ALL** function does not eliminate duplicate records.

When processing the **UNION** query, the optimizer addresses each of the **UNION**ed queries separately. Although the examples shown in the preceding listings all involved simple queries with full table scans, the **UNION**ed queries can be very complex, with correspondingly complex execution paths. The results are not returned to the user until all of the records have been processed.

NOTE
*UNION ALL is a row operation. UNION, which
includes a SORT UNIQUE, is a set operation.*

When a **MINUS** function is used, the query is processed in a manner very
similar to the execution path used for the **UNION** example. In the following query,
the Name values from the WORKER and PROSPECT tables are compared. If a Name
value exists in WORKER but does not exist in PROSPECT, then that value will be
returned by the query.

```
select Name
   from WORKER
 MINUS
select Name
   from PROSPECT;
```

When the query is executed, the two **MINUS**ed queries will be executed
separately. The first of the queries,

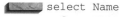
```
select Name
   from WORKER
```

requires a full table scan of the WORKER table. The second query,

```
select Name
   from PROSPECT;
```

requires a full table scan of the PROSPECT table.
To execute the **MINUS** function, each of the sets of records returned by the full
table scans is sorted via a SORT UNIQUE operation (in which rows are sorted and
duplicates are eliminated). The sorted sets of rows are then processed by the MINUS
operation. The order of operations for the **MINUS** function is shown in Figure 36-3.
As shown in Figure 36-3, the MINUS operation is not performed until each set
of records returned by the queries is sorted. Neither of the sorting operations returns
records until the sorting operation completes, so the MINUS operation cannot begin
until both of the SORT UNIQUE operations have completed. Like the UNION query
example, the example query shown for the MINUS operation will perform poorly
for online users who measure performance by the speed with which the first row is
returned by the query.

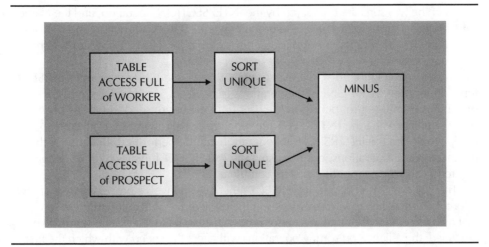

FIGURE 36-3.   *Order of operations for the **MINUS** function*

The **INTERSECT** function compares the results of two queries and determines the rows they have in common. The following query determines the Name values that are found in both the PROSPECT and the LONGTIME tables:

```
select Name from PROSPECT
 INTERSECT
select Name from LONGTIME;
```

To process the **INTERSECT** query, the optimizer starts by evaluating each of the queries separately. The first query,

```
select Name from PROSPECT
```

requires a TABLE ACCESS FULL operation against the PROSPECT table. The second query,

```
select Name from LONGTIME;
```

requires a TABLE ACCESS FULL operation against the LONGTIME table. The results of the two table scans are each processed separately by SORT UNIQUE operations. That is, the rows from PROSPECT are sorted, and the rows from LONGTIME are sorted. The results of the two sorts are compared by the INTERSECTION operation, and the Name values returned from both sorts are returned by the **INTERSECT** function.

Figure 36-4 shows the order of operations for the **INTERSECT** function for the preceding example.

As shown in Figure 36-4, the execution path of a query that uses an **INTERSECT** function requires SORT UNIQUE operations to be used. Since SORT UNIQUE operations do not return records to the user until the entire set of rows has been sorted, queries using the **INTERSECT** function will have to wait for both sorts to complete before the INTERSECTION operation can be performed. Because of the reliance on sort operations, queries using the **INTERSECT** function will not return any records to the user until the sorts complete.

The **UNION**, **MINUS**, and **INTERSECT** functions all involve processing sets of rows prior to returning any rows to the user. Online users of an application may perceive that queries using these functions perform poorly, even if the table accesses involved are tuned; the reliance on sorting operations will affect the speed with which the first row is returned to the user.

Selecting Rows for Update

You can lock rows by using the **select for update** syntax. For example, the following query selects the rows from the WORKER table and locks them to prevent other users from acquiring update locks on the rows. Using **select for update** allows you to use the **where current of** clause in **insert**, **update**, and **delete** commands. A

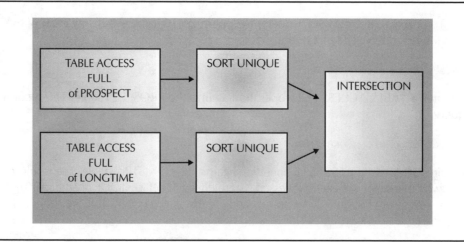

FIGURE 36-4. *Order of operations for the* **INTERSECT** *function*

commit will invalidate the cursor, so you will need to reissue the **select for update** after every **commit**.

```
select *
  from WORKER
    for update of Name;
```

When the preceding query is executed, the optimizer will first perform a TABLE ACCESS FULL operation to retrieve the rows from the WORKER table. The TABLE ACCESS FULL operation returns rows as soon as they are retrieved; it does not wait for the full set to be retrieved. However, a second operation must be performed by this query. The FOR UPDATE operation is called to lock the records. It is a set-based operation (like the sorting operations), so it does not return any rows to the user until the complete set of rows has been locked.

Selecting from Views

When you create a view, Oracle stores the query that the view is based on. For example, the following view is based on the WORKER table:

```
create or replace view OVER_20_WORKER as
select Name, Age
  from WORKER
 where Age >20;
```

When you select from the OVER_20_WORKER view, the optimizer will take the criteria from your query and combine them with the query text of the view. If you specify limiting conditions in your query of the view, those limiting conditions will—if possible—be applied to the view's query text. For example, if you execute the query

```
select Name, Age
  from OVER_20_WORKER
 where Name > 'M';
```

the optimizer will combine your limiting condition

```
where Name > 'M'
```

with the view's query text, and it will execute the query

```
select Name, Age
  from WORKER
 where Age >20
   and Name > 'M';
```

In this example, the view will have no impact on the performance of the query. When the view's text is merged with your query's limiting conditions, the options available to the optimizer increase. For example, if there is an index on the Name column in the WORKER table, the combined query would be able to use that index (since Name is equated to a range of values in the **where** clause).

The way that a view is processed depends on the query on which the view is based. If the view's query text cannot be merged with the query that uses the view, the view will be resolved first before the rest of the conditions are applied. Consider the following view:

```
create or replace view WORKER_AGE_COUNT as
select Age, COUNT(*) Count_Age
  from WORKER
 group by Age;
```

The WORKER_AGE_COUNT view will display one row for each distinct Age value in the WORKER table along with the number of records that have that value. The Count_Age column of the WORKER_AGE_COUNT view records the count per distinct Age value.

How will the optimizer process the following query of the WORKER_AGE_COUNT view?

```
select *
  from WORKER_AGE_COUNT
 where Count_Age > 1;
```

The query refers to the view's Count_Age column. However, the query's **where** clause cannot be combined with the view's query text, since Count_Age is created via a grouping operation. The **where** clause cannot be applied until *after* the result set from the WORKER_AGE_COUNT view has been completely resolved.

Views that contain grouping operations are resolved before the rest of the query's criteria are applied. Like the sorting operations, views with grouping operations do not return any records until the entire result set has been processed. If the view does not contain grouping operations, the query text may be merged with the limiting conditions of the query that selects from the view. As a result, views with grouping operations limit the number of choices available to the optimizer and do not return records until all of the rows are processed—and such views may perform poorly when queried by online users.

When the query is processed, the optimizer will first resolve the view. Since the view's query is

```
select Age, COUNT(*) Count_Age
  from WORKER
 group by Age;
```

the optimizer will read the data from the WORKER table via a TABLE ACCESS FULL operation. Since a **group by** clause is used, the rows from the TABLE ACCESS FULL operation will be processed by a SORT GROUP BY operation. Two new operations—FILTER and VIEW—will then process the data. The FILTER operation is used to eliminate rows based on the criteria in the query:

```
where Count_Age > 10
```

The VIEW operation takes the output of the FILTER operation and returns the output to the user. The flow of operations for the query of the WORKER_AGE_COUNT view is shown in Figure 36-5.

If you use views that have **group by** clauses, rows will not be returned from the views until all of the rows have been processed by the view. As a result, it may take a long time for the first row to be returned by the query, and the perceived performance of the view by online users may be unacceptable. If you can remove the sorting and grouping operations from your views, you increase the likelihood

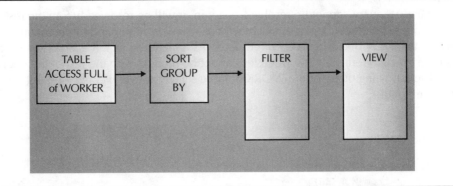

FIGURE 36-5. *Order of operations for the view query*

that the view text can be merged with the text of the query that calls the view—and as a result, the performance may improve (although the query may use other set operations that negatively impact the performance).

Selecting from Subqueries

Whenever possible, the optimizer will combine the text from a subquery with the rest of the query. For example, consider the following query:

```
select *
  from WORKER
 where Lodging =
       (select Lodging
          from LODGING
         where Manager = 'KEN MULLER');
```

The optimizer, in evaluating the preceding query, will determine that the query is functionally equivalent to the following join of the WORKER and LODGING tables:

```
select WORKER.*
  from WORKER, LODGING
 where WORKER.Lodging = LODGING.Lodging
   and Manager = 'KEN MULLER';
```

With the query now written as a join, the optimizer has a number of operations available to process the data (as described in "Operations That Perform Joins," later in this chapter).

If the subquery cannot be resolved as a join, it will be resolved before the rest of the query text is processed against the data—similar in function to the manner in which the VIEW operation is used for views. As a matter of fact, the VIEW operation is used for subqueries if the subqueries cannot be merged with the rest of the query! The following query of the WORKER table selects above-average workers (based on Age, that is):

```
select Name
  from WORKER
 where Age >
       (select AVG(Age)
          from WORKER);
```

In processing this query, the optimizer cannot merge the subquery and the query text that calls it. As a result, the subquery will be processed first—a TABLE ACCESS FULL of the WORKER table, followed by a SORT AGGREGATE operation to determine the average Age value. Once the average Age value is determined, that value will be returned to the main query, supplying the value to which Age values should be compared (in a FILTER operation).

Subqueries that rely on grouping operations have the same tuning issues as views that contain grouping operations. The rows from such subqueries must be fully processed before the rest of the query's limiting conditions can be applied.

When the query text is merged with the view text, the options available to the optimizer increase. For example, the combination of the query's limiting conditions with the view's limiting conditions may allow a previously unusable index to be used during the execution of the query.

The automatic merging of the query text and view text can be disabled via hints, as described in the following section.

Additional Tuning Issues

If you are tuning queries that will be used by online users, you should try to reduce the number of sorting operations. When using the operations that manipulate sets of records, you should try to reduce the number of nested sorting operations.

For example, a **UNION** of queries in which each query contains a **group by** clause will require nested sorts; a sorting operation would be required for each of the queries, followed by the SORT UNIQUE operation required for the **UNION**. The sort operation required for the **UNION** will not be able to *begin* until the sorts for the **group by** clauses have completed. The more deeply nested the sorts are, the greater the performance impact on your queries.

If you are using **UNION** functions, check the structures and data in the tables to see if it is possible for both queries to return the same records. For example, you may be querying data from two separate sources and reporting the results via a single query using the **UNION** function. If it is not possible for the two queries to return the same rows, then you could replace the **UNION** function with **UNION ALL**—and avoid the SORT UNIQUE operation performed by the **UNION** function.

Operations That Perform Joins

Often, a single query will need to select columns from multiple tables. To select the data from multiple tables, the tables are joined in the SQL statement—the tables are listed in the **from** clause, and the join conditions are listed in the **where** clause. In the following example, the WORKER and LODGING tables are joined, based on their common Lodging column values:

```
select WORKER.Name, LODGING.Manager
  from WORKER, LODGING
 where WORKER.Lodging = LODGING.Lodging;
```

The join conditions can function as limiting conditions for the join. Since the WORKER.Lodging column is equated to a value in the **where** clause, the optimizer may be able to use an index on the WORKER.Lodging column during the execution of the query. If an index is available on the LODGING.Lodging column, that index would be considered for use by the optimizer as well.

Oracle has three methods for processing joins: MERGE JOIN operations, NESTED LOOPS operations, and HASH JOIN operations. Based on the conditions in your query, the available indexes, and (for CBO) the available statistics, the optimizer will choose which join operation to use. Depending on the nature of your application and queries, you may want to force the optimizer to use a method different from its first choice of join methods. In the following sections, you will see the characteristics of the different join methods and the conditions under which each is most useful.

How Oracle Handles Joins of More than Two Tables

If a query joins more than two tables, the optimizer treats the query as a set of multiple joins. For example, if your query joined three tables, then the optimizer would execute the joins by joining two of the tables together, and then joining the result set of that join to the third table. The size of the result set from the initial join impacts the performance of the rest of the joins. If the size of the result set from the initial join is large, then many rows will be processed by the second join.

If your query joins three tables of varying size—such as a small table named SMALL, a medium-sized table named MEDIUM, and a large table named LARGE—you need to be aware of the order in which the tables will be joined. If the join of MEDIUM to LARGE will return many rows, then the join of the result set of that join with the SMALL table may perform a great deal of work. Alternatively, if SMALL and MEDIUM were joined first, then the join between the result set of the SMALL-MEDIUM join and the LARGE table may minimize the amount of work performed by the query. Following the rest of the sections on the join operations, "Displaying the Execution Path," which describes the **explain plan** and **set autotrace on** commands, will show how you can interpret the order of joins.

MERGE JOIN

In a MERGE JOIN operation, the two inputs to the join are processed separately, sorted, and joined. MERGE JOIN operations are commonly used when there are no indexes available for the limiting conditions of the query.

In the following query, the WORKER and LODGING tables are joined. If neither table has an index on its Lodging column, then there are no indexes that can be used during the query (since there are no other limiting conditions in the query).

```
select WORKER.Name, LODGING.Manager
  from WORKER, LODGING
 where WORKER.Lodging = LODGING.Lodging;
```

To resolve the query, the optimizer may choose to perform a MERGE JOIN of the tables. To perform the MERGE JOIN, each of the tables is read individually (usually by a TABLE ACCESS FULL operation). The set of rows returned from the table scan of the WORKER table is sorted by a SORT JOIN operation, and the set of rows returned from the table scan of the LODGING table is sorted by a separate SORT JOIN operation. The data from the SORT JOIN operations is then merged via a MERGE JOIN operation. Figure 36-6 shows the order of operations for the MERGE JOIN example.

When a MERGE JOIN operation is used to join two sets of records, each set of records is processed separately before being joined. The MERGE JOIN operation cannot begin until it has received data from both of the SORT JOIN operations that provide input to it. The SORT JOIN operations, in turn, will not provide data to the MERGE JOIN operation until all of the rows have been sorted.

Because the MERGE JOIN operation has to wait for two separate SORT JOIN operations to complete, a join that uses the MERGE JOIN operation will typically perform poorly for online users. The perceived poor performance is due to the delay in returning the first row of the join to the users. As the tables increase in size, the time required for the sorts to be completed increases dramatically. If the tables are of greatly unequal size, then the sorting operation performed on the larger table will negatively impact the performance of the overall query.

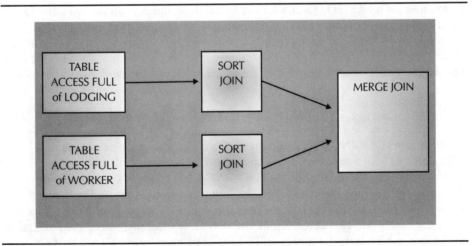

FIGURE 36-6.   *Order of operations for the MERGE JOIN operation*

Since MERGE JOIN operations involve full scanning and sorting of the tables involved, you should only use MERGE JOIN operations if both tables are very small or if both tables are very large. If both tables are very small, then the process of scanning and sorting the tables will complete quickly. If both tables are very large, then the sorting and scanning operations required by MERGE JOIN operations can take advantage of Oracle's parallel options.

Oracle can parallelize operations, allowing multiple processors to participate in the execution of a single command. Among the operations that can be parallelized are the TABLE ACCESS FULL and sorting operations. Since a MERGE JOIN uses the TABLE ACCESS FULL and sorting operations, it can take full advantage of Oracle's parallel options. Parallelizing queries involving MERGE JOIN operations frequently improves the performance of the queries (provided there are adequate system resources available to support the parallel operations).

NESTED LOOPS

NESTED LOOPS operations join two tables via a looping method: the records from one table are retrieved, and for each record retrieved, an access is performed of the second table. The access of the second table is performed via an index-based access.

The query from the preceding MERGE JOIN section is shown in the following listing:

```
select WORKER.Name, LODGING.Manager
  from WORKER, LODGING
 where WORKER.Lodging = LODGING.Lodging;
```

In order for a NESTED LOOPS join to be used, an index must be available for use with the query. In the MERGE JOIN example, it was assumed that the two tables had no indexes. In the following listing, a primary key is created on the LODGING table. Because the PRIMARY KEY constraint will implicitly create a unique index on the Lodging column of the LODGING table, an index will be available to the join.

```
alter table LODGING add
constraint LODGING_PK primary key (Lodging);
```

When the LODGING_PK constraint is created, a unique index named LODGING_PK will automatically be created on the Lodging column.

Since the Lodging column of the LODGING table is used as part of the join condition in the query, the LODGING_PK index can resolve the query. When the query is executed, a NESTED LOOPS operation can be used to execute the join.

To execute a NESTED LOOPS join, the optimizer must first select a *driving table* for the join, which is the table that will be read first (usually via a TABLE ACCESS FULL operation). For each record in the driving table, the second table in the join will be queried. The example query joins WORKER and LODGING, based on values of the Lodging column. Since an index is available on the Lodging column of the LODGING table, and no comparable index is available on the WORKER table, the WORKER table will be used as the driving table for the query.

During the NESTED LOOPS execution, a TABLE ACCESS FULL operation will select all of the records from the WORKER table. The LODGING_PK index of the LODGING table will be probed to determine if it contains an entry for the value in the current record from the WORKER table. If a match is found, then the RowID for the matching LODGING row will be retrieved from the index, and the row will be selected from the LODGING table via a TABLE ACCESS BY ROWID operation. The flow of operations for the NESTED LOOPS join is shown in Figure 36-7.

As shown in Figure 36-7, three data access operations are involved in the NESTED LOOPS join: a TABLE ACCESS FULL, an INDEX UNIQUE SCAN, and a TABLE ACCESS BY ROWID. Each of these data access methods returns records to successive operations as soon as a record is found—they do not wait for the whole set of records to be selected. Because these operations can provide the first matching rows quickly to users, NESTED LOOPS joins are commonly used for joins that are frequently executed by online users.

When implementing NESTED LOOPS joins, you need to consider the size of the driving table. If the driving table is large, then the TABLE ACCESS FULL operation performed on it may negatively affect the performance of the query. If multiple

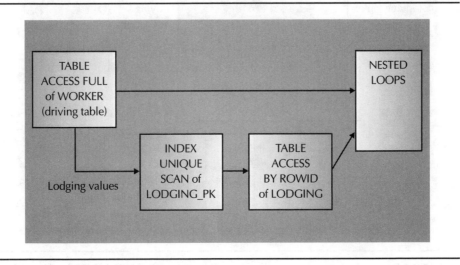

FIGURE 36-7. *Order of operations for the NESTED LOOPS operation*

indexes are available, then Oracle will select a driving table for the query. The method of selection for the driving table depends on the optimizer in use. If you are using the CBO, then the optimizer will check the statistics for the size of the tables and the selectivity of the indexes and will choose the path with the lowest overall cost. If you are using the RBO, and indexes are available for all join conditions, then the driving table will usually be the table that is listed *last* in the **from** clause.

When joining three tables together, Oracle performs two separate joins: a join of two tables to generate a set of records, and then a join between that set of records and the third table. If NESTED LOOPS joins are used, then the order in which the tables are joined is critical. The output from the first join generates a set of records, and that set of records is used as the driving table for the second join. Figure 36-8 shows the flow of operations for a three-table NESTED LOOPS join between WORKER, LODGING, and a third table.

By comparing Figure 36-7 with Figure 36-8, you can see how the two-table join forms the basis for the three-table join in this example. As shown in Figure 36-8,

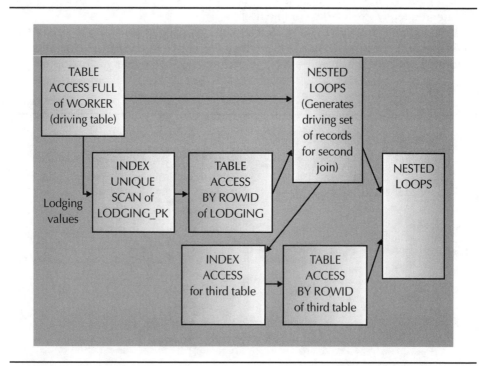

FIGURE 36-8. *Order of operations for a three-table NESTED LOOPS join*

the size of the set of records returned by the first join impacts the performance of the second join—and thus may have a significant impact on the performance of the overall query. You should attempt to join the smallest, most selective tables first, so that the impact of those joins on future joins will be negligible. If large tables are joined in the first join of a multijoin query, then the size of the tables will impact each successive join and will negatively impact the overall performance of the query.

NESTED LOOPS joins are useful when the tables in the join are of unequal size—you can use the smaller table as the driving table and select from the larger table via an index-based access. The more selective the index is, the faster the query will complete.

HASH JOIN

The optimizer may dynamically choose to perform joins using the HASH JOIN operation in place of either MERGE JOIN or NESTED LOOPS. The HASH JOIN operation compares two tables in memory. During a hash join, the first table is scanned and the database applies "hashing" functions to the data to prepare the table for the join. The values from the second table are then read (typically via a TABLE ACCESS FULL operation), and the hashing function compares the second table with the first table. The rows that result in matches are returned to the user.

NOTE
Although they have similar names, hash joins have nothing to do with hash clusters or with the TABLE ACCESS HASH operation discussed later in this chapter.

The optimizer may choose to perform hash joins even if indexes are available. In the sample query shown in the following listing, the WORKER and LODGING tables are joined on the Lodging column:

```
select WORKER.Name, LODGING.Manager
  from WORKER, LODGING
 where WORKER.Lodging = LODGING.Lodging;
```

The LODGING table has a unique index on its Lodging column. Since the index is available and can be used to evaluate the join conditions, the optimizer may choose to perform a NESTED LOOPS join of the two tables. However, the optimizer could also choose to perform a hash join. If a hash join is performed, then each table will be read via a separate TABLE ACCESS FULL operation. The data from the table scans will serve as input to a HASH JOIN operation.

Because hash joins rely on full table scans, they will be most effective when you are using Oracle's parallel options to improve the performance of full table scans. Hash joins use memory (the amount of memory allocated for a hash join is specified via init.ora parameters), so applications that make extensive use of hash joins may need to increase the amount of memory available in the database's System Global Area.

The order of operations for a hash join is shown in Figure 36-9. As shown, the hash join does not rely on operations that process sets of rows. The operations involved in hash joins return records quickly to users. Hash joins are appropriate for queries executed by online users if the tables are small and can be scanned quickly.

Processing Outer Joins

When processing an outer join, the optimizer will use one of the three methods described in the previous sections. For example, if the sample query were performing an outer join between WORKER and LODGING, then a NESTED LOOPS OUTER operation may be used instead of a NESTED LOOPS operation. In a NESTED LOOPS OUTER operation, the table that is the "outer" table for the outer join is typically used as the driving table for the query; as the records of the inner table are scanned for matching records, **NULL** values are returned for rows with no matches.

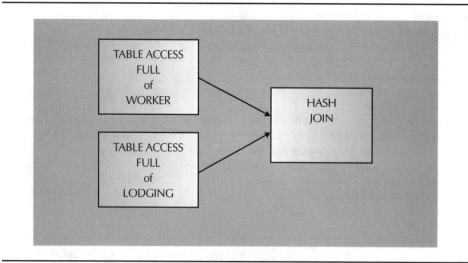

FIGURE 36-9. *Order of operations for the HASH JOIN operation*

Related Hints

You can use hints to override the optimizer's selection of a join method. Hints allow you to specify the type of join method to use or the goal of the join method.

In addition to the hints described in this section, you can use the FULL and INDEX hints, described earlier, to influence the way in which joins are processed. For example, if you use a hint to force a NESTED LOOPS join to be used, then you may also use an INDEX hint to specify which index should be used during the NESTED LOOPS join and which table should be accessed via a full table scan.

Hints About Goals

You can specify a hint that directs the optimizer to execute a query with a specific goal in mind. The available goals related to joins are the following:

- **ALL_ROWS**   Execute the query so that all of the rows are returned as quickly as possible.

- **FIRST_ROWS**   Execute the query so that the first row will be returned as quickly as possible.

By default, the optimizer will execute a query using an execution path that is selected to minimize the total time needed to resolve the query. Thus, the default is to use ALL_ROWS as the goal. If the optimizer is only concerned about the total time needed to return all rows for the query, then set-based operations such as sorts and MERGE JOIN can be used. However, the ALL_ROWS goal may not always be appropriate. For example, online users tend to judge the performance of a system based on the time it takes for a query to return the first row of data. The users thus have FIRST_ROWS as their primary goal, with the time it takes to return all of the rows as a secondary goal.

The available hints mimic the goals: the ALL_ROWS hint allows the optimizer to choose from all available operations to minimize the overall processing time for the query, while the FIRST_ROWS hint tells the optimizer to select an execution path that minimizes the time required to return the first row to the user.

NOTE
You should only use the ALL_ROWS or FIRST_ROWS hint if you have first analyzed the tables.

In the following example, the query from the join examples is modified to include the ALL_ROWS hint:

```
select /*+ ALL_ROWS */ WORKER.Name, LODGING.Manager
   from WORKER, LODGING
 where WORKER.Lodging = LODGING.Lodging;
```

You could modify this query to use the FIRST_ROWS hint instead:

```
select /*+ FIRST_ROWS */ WORKER.Name, LODGING.Manager
   from WORKER, LODGING
 where WORKER.Lodging = LODGING.Lodging;
```

If you use the FIRST_ROWS hint, the optimizer will be less likely to use MERGE JOIN and more likely to use NESTED LOOPS. The join method selected partly depends on the rest of the query. For example, the join query example does not contain an **order by** clause (which is a set operation performed by the SORT ORDER BY operation). If the query is revised to contain an **order by** clause, as shown in the following listing, how does that change the join processing?

```
select /*+ FIRST_ROWS */ WORKER.Name, LODGING.Manager
   from WORKER, LODGING
 where WORKER.Lodging = LODGING.Lodging
 order by WORKER.Name;
```

With an **order by** clause added to the query, the SORT ORDER BY operation will be the last operation performed before the output is shown to the user. The SORT ORDER BY operation will not complete—and will not display any records to the user—until all of the records have been sorted. Therefore, the FIRST_ROWS hint in this example tells the optimizer to perform the join as quickly as possible, providing the data to the SORT ORDER BY operation as quickly as possible. The addition of the sorting operation (the **order by** clause) in the query may negate or change the impact of the FIRST_ROWS hint on the query's execution path (since a SORT ORDER BY operation will be slow to return records to the user regardless of the join method chosen).

Hints About Methods

In addition to specifying the goals the optimizer should use when evaluating join method alternatives, you can list the specific operations to use and the tables to use them on. If a query involves only two tables, you do not need to specify the tables to join when providing a hint for a join method to use.

The USE_NL hint tells the optimizer to use a NESTED LOOPS operation to join tables. In the following example, the USE_NL hint is specified for the join query example. Within the hint, the LODGING table is listed as the inner table for the join.

```
select /*+ USE_NL(LODGING) */
       WORKER.Name, LODGING.Manager
  from WORKER, LODGING
 where WORKER.Lodging = LODGING.Lodging
 order by WORKER.Name;
```

If you want all of the joins in a many-table query to use NESTED LOOPS operations, you could just specify the USE_NL hint with no table references, as shown in the following example:

```
select /*+ USE_NL */
       WORKER.Name, LODGING.Manager
  from WORKER, LODGING
 where WORKER.Lodging = LODGING.Lodging
 order by WORKER.Name;
```

In general, you should specify table names whenever you use a hint to specify a join method, because you do not know how the query may be used in the future. You may not even know how the database objects are currently set up—for example, one of the objects in your **from** clause may be a view that has been tuned to use MERGE JOIN operations.

If you specify a table in a hint, you should refer to the table alias. That is, if your **from** clause refers to a table as

```
from FRED.HIS_TABLE, ME.MY_TABLE
```

then you should *not* specify a hint such as

```
/*+ USE_NL(ME.MY_TABLE) */
```

Instead, you should refer to the table by its name, without the owner:

```
/*+ USE_NL(my_table) */
```

If multiple tables have the same name, then you should assign table aliases to the tables and refer to the aliases in the hint. For example, if you join a table to itself, then the **from** clause may include the text shown in the following listing:

```
from WORKER W1, WORKER W2
```

A hint forcing the WORKER-WORKER join to use NESTED LOOPS would be written to use the table aliases, as shown in the following listing:

```
/*+ USE_NL(w2) */
```

The optimizer will ignore any hint that isn't written with the proper syntax. Any hint with improper syntax will be treated as a comment (since it is enclosed within the **/*** and ***/** characters).

NOTE
USE_NL is a hint, not a rule. The optimizer may recognize the hint and choose to ignore it, based on the statistics available when the query is executed.

If you are using NESTED LOOPS joins, then you need to be concerned about the order in which the tables are joined. The ORDERED hint, when used with NESTED LOOPS joins, influences the order in which tables are joined.

When you use the ORDERED hint, the tables will be joined in the order in which they are listed in the **from** clause of the query. If the **from** clause contains three tables, such as

```
from WORKER, LODGING, WORKERSKILL
```

then the first two tables will be joined by the first join, and the result of that join will be joined to the third table.

Since the order of joins is critical to the performance of NESTED LOOPS joins, the ORDERED hint is often used in conjunction with the USE_NL hint. If you use hints to specify the join order, you need to be certain that the relative distribution of values within the joined tables will not change dramatically over time; otherwise, the specified join order may cause performance problems in the future.

You can use the USE_MERGE hint to tell the optimizer to perform a MERGE JOIN between specified tables. In the following listing, the hint instructs the optimizer to perform a MERGE JOIN operation between the WORKER and LODGING tables:

```
select /*+ USE_MERGE(worker,lodging) */
       WORKER.Name, LODGING.Manager
  from WORKER, LODGING
 where WORKER.Lodging = LODGING.Lodging;
```

You can use the USE_HASH hint to tell the optimizer to consider using a HASH JOIN method. If no tables are specified, then the optimizer will select the first table to be scanned into memory based on the available statistics.

```
select /*+ USE_HASH */
       WORKER.Name, LODGING.Manager
  from WORKER, LODGING
 where WORKER.Lodging = LODGING.Lodging;
```

If you are using the CBO but have previously tuned your queries to use rule-based optimization, you can tell the CBO to use the rule-based method when processing your query. The RULE hint tells the optimizer to use the RBO to optimize the query; all other hints in the query will be ignored. In the following example, the RULE hint is used during a join:

```
select /*+ RULE */
       WORKER.Name, LODGING.Manager
  from WORKER, LODGING
 where WORKER.Lodging = LODGING.Lodging;
```

In general, you should only use the RULE hint if you have tuned your queries specifically for the RBO. Although the RULE hint is still supported, you should investigate using the CBO in its place for your queries.

You can set the optimizer goal at the session level via the **alter session** command. In the following example, the session's optimizer_goal parameter is changed to RULE:

```
alter session set optimizer_goal = RULE;
```

For the remainder of the session, the RBO will be used as the optimizer. Other settings for the session's optimizer_goal parameter include COST, CHOOSE, ALL_ROWS, and FIRST_ROWS.

Additional Tuning Issues

As noted in the discussions of NESTED LOOPS and MERGE JOIN operations, operations differ in the time they take to return the first row from a query. Since MERGE JOIN relies on set-based operations, it will not return records to the user until all of the rows have been processed. NESTED LOOPS, on the other hand, can return rows to the user as soon as rows are available.

Because NESTED LOOPS joins are capable of returning rows to users quickly, they are often used for queries that are frequently executed by online users. Their efficiency at returning the first row, however, is often impacted by set-based operations applied to the rows that have been selected. For example, adding an **order by** clause to a query adds a SORT ORDER BY operation to the end of the query processing—and no rows will be displayed to the user until all of the rows have been sorted.

As described in "Operations That Use Indexes," earlier in this chapter, using functions on a column prevents the database from using an index on that column during data searches unless you have created a function-based index. You can use this information to dynamically disable indexes and influence the join method chosen. For example, the following query does not specify a join hint, but it disables the use of indexes on the Lodging column by concatenating the Lodging values with a null string:

```
select WORKER.Name, LODGING.Manager
  from WORKER, LODGING
 where WORKER.Lodging||'' = LODGING.Lodging||'';
```

The dynamic disabling of indexes allows you to force MERGE JOIN operations to be used even if you are using the RBO (in which no hints are accepted).

As noted during the discussion of the NESTED LOOPS operation, the order of joins is as important as the join method selected. If a large or nonselective join is the first join in a series, the large data set returned will negatively impact the performance of the subsequent joins in the query as well as the performance of the query as a whole.

Depending on the hints, optimizer goal, and statistics, the optimizer may choose to use a variety of join methods within the same query. For example, the optimizer may evaluate a three-table query as a NESTED LOOPS join of two tables, followed by a MERGE JOIN of the NESTED LOOPS output with the third table. Such combinations of join types are usually found when the ALL_ROWS optimizer goal is in effect.

To see the order of operations, you can use the **set autotrace on** command to see the execution path, as described in the next section.

Displaying the Execution Path

You can display the execution path for a query in either of two ways:

- Use the **explain plan** command
- Use the **set autotrace on** command

In the following sections, both commands are explained; for the remainder of the chapter, the **set autotrace on** command will be used to illustrate execution paths as reported by the optimizer.

Using set autotrace on

You can have the **explain plan** automatically displayed for every transaction you execute within SQLPLUS. The **set autotrace on** command will cause each query, after being executed, to display both its execution path and high-level trace information about the processing involved in resolving the query.

To use the **set autotrace on** command, you must have first created a PLAN_TABLE table within your account. The PLAN_TABLE structure may change with each release of Oracle, so you should drop and re-create your copy of PLAN_TABLE with each Oracle upgrade. The commands shown in the following listing will drop any existing PLAN_TABLE and replace it with the current version.

NOTE
*In order for you to use **set autotrace on**, your DBA must have first created the PLUSTRACE role in the database and granted that role to your account. The PLUSTRACE role gives you access to the underlying performance-related views in the Oracle data dictionary.*

The following example refers to $ORACLE_HOME. Replace that symbol with the home directory for Oracle software on your operating system. The file that creates the PLAN_TABLE table is located in the /rdbms/admin subdirectory under the Oracle software home directory.

```
drop table PLAN_TABLE;
@$ORACLE_HOME/rdbms/admin/utlxplan.sql
```

When you use **set autotrace on**, records are inserted into PLAN_TABLE to show the order of operations executed. After the query completes, the data is displayed. After the query's data is displayed, the order of operations is shown, followed by statistical information about the query processing. The following explanation of **set autotrace on** focuses on the section of the output that displays the order of operations.

If you use the **set autotrace on** command, you will not see the explain plan for your queries until *after* they complete. The **explain plan** command (described next) shows the execution paths without running the queries first. Therefore, if the performance of a query is unknown, you may choose to use the **explain plan** command before running it. If you are fairly certain that the performance of a query is acceptable, use **set autotrace on** to verify its execution path.

In the following example, a full table scan of the LODGING table is executed. The rows of output are not displayed in this output, for the sake of brevity. The order of operations is displayed below the query.

```
select *
   from LODGING;

Execution Plan
----------------------------------------------------------
```

```
0       SELECT STATEMENT Optimizer=CHOOSE
1    0    TABLE ACCESS (FULL) OF 'LODGING'
```

The "Execution Plan" shows the steps the optimizer will use to execute the query. Each step is assigned an ID value (starting with 0). The second number shows the "parent" operation of the current operation. Thus, for the preceding example, the second operation—the TABLE ACCESS (FULL) OF 'LODGING'—has a parent operation (the **select** statement itself).

You can generate the order of operations for DML commands, too. In the following example, a **delete** statement's execution path is shown:

```
delete *
  from LODGING;

Execution Plan
----------------------------------------------------------
0       DELETE STATEMENT Optimizer=CHOOSE
1    0    TABLE ACCESS (FULL) OF 'LODGING'
```

The **delete** command, as expected, involves a full table scan. If you have analyzed your tables, the Execution Plan column's output will also show the number of rows from each table, the relative cost of each step, and the overall cost of the operation. You could use that information to pinpoint the operations that are the most costly during the processing of the query.

In the following example, a slightly more complex query is executed. An index-based query is made against the LODGING table, using the LODGING_PK index.

```
select *
  from LODGING
 where Lodging > 'S';

Execution Plan
----------------------------------------------------------
0       SELECT STATEMENT Optimizer=CHOOSE
1    0    TABLE ACCESS (BY ROWID) OF 'LODGING'
2    1      INDEX (RANGE SCAN) OF 'LODGING_PK'
```

This listing includes three operations. Operation #2, the INDEX RANGE SCAN, provides data to operation #1, the TABLE ACCESS BY ROWID operation. The data returned from the TABLE ACCESS BY ROWID is used to satisfy the query (operation #0).

The preceding output also shows that the optimizer is automatically indenting each successive step within the execution plan. In general, you should read the list of operations from the inside out and from top to bottom. Thus, if two operations are listed, the one that is the most indented will usually be executed first. If the two operations are at the same level of indentation, then the one that is listed first (with the lowest operation number) will be executed first.

In the following example, WORKER and LODGING are joined without the benefit of indexes:

```
select WORKER.Name, LODGING.Manager
  from WORKER, LODGING
 where WORKER.Lodging||'' = LODGING.Lodging||'';


Execution Plan
----------------------------------------------------------
    0      SELECT STATEMENT Optimizer=CHOOSE
    1   0    MERGE JOIN
    2   1      SORT (JOIN)
    3   2        TABLE ACCESS (FULL) OF 'LODGING'
    4   1      SORT (JOIN)
    5   4        TABLE ACCESS (FULL) OF 'WORKER'
```

The indentation here may seem confusing at first, but the operational parentage information provided by the operation numbers clarifies the order of operations. The innermost operations are performed first—the two TABLE ACCESS FULL operations. Next, the two SORT JOIN operations are performed (the LODGING sort by operation #2 and the WORKER sort by operation #4), which both have operation #1, the MERGE JOIN, as their parent operations. The MERGE JOIN operation provides data back to the user via the **select** statement.

The flow of operations for the MERGE JOIN example, shown in Figure 36-10, shows the same information as is provided in the **set autotrace on** output.

If the same query were run as a NESTED LOOPS join, a different execution path would be generated. As shown in the following listing, the NESTED LOOPS join would be able to take advantage of the LODGING_PK index on the Lodging column of the LODGING table:

```
select WORKER.Name, LODGING.Manager
  from WORKER, LODGING
 where WORKER.Lodging = LODGING.Lodging;


Execution Plan
----------------------------------------------------------
    0      SELECT STATEMENT Optimizer=CHOOSE
    1   0    NESTED LOOPS
    2   1      TABLE ACCESS (FULL) OF 'WORKER'
    3   1      TABLE ACCESS (BY ROWID) OF 'LODGING'
    4   3        INDEX (UNIQUE SCAN) OF 'LODGING_PK'
```

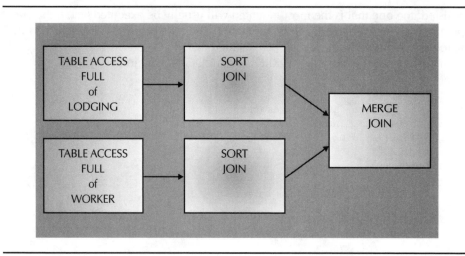

FIGURE 36-10. *Order of operations for the MERGE JOIN example*

NESTED LOOPS joins are among the few execution paths that do not follow the "read from the inside out" rule of indented execution paths. To read the NESTED LOOPS execution path correctly, examine the order of the operations that directly provide data to the NESTED LOOPS operation (in this case, operations #2 and #3). Of those two operations, the operation with the lowest number (#2, in this example) is executed first. Thus, the TABLE ACCESS FULL of the WORKER table is executed first (WORKER is the driving table for the query).

Once you have established the driving table for the query, the rest of the execution path can be read from the inside out and from top to bottom. The second operation performed is the INDEX UNIQUE SCAN of the LODGING_PK index. The data from the LODGING_PK index is used to select rows from the LODGING table, and the NESTED LOOPS operation is then able to return rows to the user.

If a hash join had been selected instead of a NESTED LOOPS join, the execution path would have been

```
Execution Plan
----------------------------------------------------------
   0      SELECT STATEMENT Optimizer=CHOOSE
   1    0   HASH JOIN
   2    1     TABLE ACCESS (FULL) OF 'WORKER'
   3    1     TABLE ACCESS (FULL) OF 'LODGING'
```

The hash join execution path shows that two full table scans are performed. Since the two operations are listed at the same level of indentation, the WORKER table is scanned first (since it has the lower operation number).

> **NOTE**
> *When using the **set autotrace on** command, you do not have to manage the records within the PLAN_TABLE. Oracle will automatically delete the records it inserts into PLAN_TABLE once the execution path has been displayed.*

If you use the parallel query options or query remote databases, an additional section of the **set autotrace on** output will show the text of the queries executed by the parallel query server processes or the query executed within the remote database.

To disable the autotrace feature, use the **set autotrace off** command.

Using explain plan

You can use the **explain plan** command to generate the execution path for a query without first running the query. To use the **explain plan** command, you must first create a PLAN_TABLE table in your schema (see the previous instructions on creating the table). To determine the execution path of a query, prefix the query with the following SQL:

```
explain plan
set Statement_ID = 'TEST'
for
```

To make the tuning process simpler, always use the same Statement_ID value and delete the records for each execution path before using the **explain plan** command a second time.

An example of the execution of the **explain plan** command is shown in the following listing. The query shown in the listing will not be run during the command; only its execution path steps will be generated, and they will be inserted as records in PLAN_TABLE.

```
explain plan
set Statement_ID = 'TEST'
for
select WORKER.Name, LODGING.Manager
```

```
   from WORKER, LODGING
   where WORKER.Lodging = LODGING.Lodging;
```

Statement processed.

When the **explain plan** command is executed, records will be inserted into PLAN_TABLE. You can query PLAN_TABLE using the following query. The results of the query will show the operations performed at each step and the parent-child relationships between the execution path steps, similar to the indented display of the **set autotrace on** command.

```
select
   LPAD(' ',2*Level)||Operation||' '||Options
                 ||' '||Object_Name  Execution_Path
from PLAN_TABLE
where Statement_ID = 'TEST'
connect by prior ID = Parent_ID and Statement_ID = 'TEST'
start with ID=1;
```

The query shown in the preceding listing uses the **connect by** operator to evaluate the hierarchy of steps in the query's execution path. The query in the listing assumes the Statement_ID field has been set to 'TEST'. The execution path steps will be displayed in the column given the Execution_Path alias.

The output from the preceding query is shown in the following listing:

```
Execution Plan
-------------------------------------------------------------
NESTED LOOPS
  TABLE ACCESS (FULL) OF 'WORKER'
  TABLE ACCESS (BY ROWID) OF 'LODGING'
    INDEX (UNIQUE SCAN) OF 'LODGING_PK'
```

If you wish, you can expand the query to include other columns from PLAN_TABLE, such as the ID and Parent_ID columns that provided the operation number and parent operation number, respectively, in the **set autotrace on** examples.

You can also select data from the Cost column, which displays the relative "cost" of each step. The following query displays all the relevant columns from the PLAN_TABLE:

```
select ID ID_plus_exp,
       Parent_ID parent_id_plus_exp,
       LPAD(' ',2*(level-1))|| /* Indent for the level */
       Operation|| /* The operation */
       DECODE(other_tag,null,'','*')|| /* displays '*' if parallel */
       DECODE(options,null,'',' ('||options||')')|| /* display the options */
       DECODE(object_name,null,'',' of '''||object_name||'''')||
       DECODE(object_type,null,'',' '||object_type||')')||
       DECODE(id,0,decode(optimizer,null,'',' optimizer='||optimizer))||
```

```
        DECODE(cost,null,'',' (cost='||cost|| /* display cost info. */
        DECODE(cardinality,null,'',' card='||cardinality)|| /* cardinality */
        DECODE(bytes,null,'',' bytes='||bytes)||')') plan_plus_exp,
        object_node object_node_plus_exp /* parallel and remote info */
   from PLAN_TABLE
 start with ID=0 and Statement_ID='TEST'
connect by prior ID=Parent_ID and Statement_ID='TEST'
 order by ID,Position;
```

Implementing Stored Outlines

As you migrate from one database to another, the execution paths for your queries may change. Your execution paths may change for several reasons:

- You may be using a different optimizer in different databases (cost-based in one, rule-based in another).

- You may have enabled different optimizer features in the different databases.

- The statistics for the queried tables may differ in the databases.

- The frequency with which statistics are gathered may differ among the databases.

- The databases may be running different versions of the Oracle kernel.

The effects of these differences on your execution paths can be dramatic, and can have a significant negative impact on your query performance as you migrate or upgrade your application. To minimize the impact of these differences on your query performance, Oracle introduced a feature called a *stored outline* in Oracle8i.

A stored outline stores a set of hints for a query. Those hints will be used every time the query is executed. Using the stored hints will increase the likelihood that the query will use the same execution path each time. Hints do not mandate an execution path (they're hints, not commands) but do decrease the impact of database moves on your query performance.

To start creating hints for all queries, set the CREATE_STORED_OUTLINES init.ora parameter to TRUE; thereafter, all the outlines will be saved under the DEFAULT category. As an alternative, you can create custom categories of outlines and use the category name as a value in the init.ora file, as shown in the following listing:

```
CREATE_STORED_OUTLINES = development
```

In this example, stored outlines will be stored for queries within the DEVELOPMENT category.

You must have the CREATE ANY OUTLINE system privilege in order to create an outline. Use the **create outline** command to create an outline for a query, as shown in the following listing:

```
create outline PAYMENTS
    for category DEVELOPMENT
      on
select SUM(Amount)
   from LEDGER
 where Action = 'PAID';
```

NOTE
If you do not specify a name for your outline, the outline will be given a system-generated name.

If you have set CREATE_STORED_OUTLINES to TRUE in your init.ora file, the RDBMS will create stored outlines for your queries; using the **create outline** command gives you more control over the outlines that are created.

NOTE
You can create outlines for DML commands and for **create table as select** *commands.*

Once an outline has been created, you can alter it. For example, you may need to alter the outline to reflect significant changes in data volumes and distribution. You can use the **rebuild** clause of the **alter outline** command to regenerate the hints used during query execution:

```
alter outline PAYMENTS rebuild;
```

You can also rename an outline via the **rename** clause of the **alter outline** command:

```
alter outline PAYMENTS rename to LEDGER_PAYMENTS;
```

You can change the category of an outline via the **change category** clause, as shown in the following example:

```
alter outline PAYMENTS change category to DEFAULT;
```

For the stored outlines to be used by the optimizer, set the USE_STORED_OUTLINES init.ora parameter to TRUE or to a category name (such as

DEVELOPMENT in the earlier examples). If stored outline use is enabled, any query with a stored outline will use the hints generated when the outline was created. You can also enable USE_STORED_OUTLINES at the session level via the **alter session** command.

To manage stored outlines, use the OUTLN_PKG package, which gives you three capabilities:

- Drop outlines that have never been used

- Drop outlines within a specific category

- Move outlines from one category to another

Each of these three capabilities has a corresponding procedure within OUTLN_PKG. To drop outlines that have never been used, execute the DROP_UNUSED procedure, as shown in the following listing:

```
execute OUTLN_PKG.DROP_UNUSED;
```

To drop all of the outlines within a category, execute the DROP_BY_CAT procedure, which has the name of the category as its only input parameter. The following example drops all of the outlines within the DEVELOPMENT category:

```
execute OUTLN_PKG.DROP_BY_CAT -
   (category_name => 'DEVELOPMENT');
```

To reassign outlines from an old category to a new category, use the UPDATE_BY_CAT procedure, as shown in the following example:

```
execute OUTLN_PKG.UPDATE_BY_CAT -
   (old_category_name => 'DEVELOPMENT', -
   new_category_name => 'TEST');
```

To drop a specific outline, use the **drop outline** command.

Miscellaneous Operations

In addition to the operations shown previously in this chapter—table access, index access, data set manipulation, and joins—a number of other operations are used by the optimizer when executing a query. The operations described in the following sections can impact your query's performance, but they tend to be less tunable or less frequently used than the operations previously described.

Filtering Rows

When a **where** clause is used to eliminate rows for a query, Oracle may use a FILTER operation to select the rows that meet the **where** clause criteria. The FILTER operation is not always shown in the **set autotrace on** output, even though it may be used. Consider the following query of the WORKER table:

```
select *
  from WORKER
 where Name like 'S%'
   and Age >20;
```

If the WORKER table has an index on its Name column, then the preceding query will be executed in two steps: an INDEX RANGE SCAN on the Name column's index, followed by a TABLE ACCESS BY ROWID operation on the WORKER table (since all columns are selected). The following limiting condition on the Age column

```
and Age >20;
```

will be applied as part of a FILTER operation; however, the FILTER operation will not be explicitly listed as part of the execution path. Instead, the FILTER operation will be performed as part of the TABLE ACCESS BY ROWID operation. When a FILTER operation is listed explicitly in a query's execution path, it usually indicates that no index is available to assist in the processing of a limiting condition. FILTER operations are commonly seen in queries that use the **connect by** clause and occasionally during the processing of VIEW operations.

Queries That Use connect by Clauses

When a query uses a **connect by** clause, Oracle uses a CONNECT BY operation to execute the query. The execution path will show that the CONNECT BY operation usually takes three inputs as it progresses up and down a "tree" of records. For best performance from a **connect by** query, you should create a set of indexes that can be used by the columns in the **connect by** clause.

For example, the **connect by** examples shown throughout this book use the BREEDING table to illustrate the family history of cows and bulls. The following query travels from the root node of the family tree (the cow named 'EVE') to the descendants. A **connect by** query can be written to travel either from the root to its descendants or from a descendant to its ancestors.

```
select Cow,
       Bull,
```

```
      LPAD(' ',6*(Level-1))||Offspring  Offspring,
      Sex,
      Birthdate
  from BREEDING
 start with Offspring = 'EVE'
connect by Cow = PRIOR Offspring;
```

With no indexes on the BREEDING table, the following execution path is generated for this query (as reported via **set autotrace on**):

```
Execution Plan
--------------------------------------------------------
   0       SELECT STATEMENT Optimizer=CHOOSE
   1    0   CONNECT BY
   2    1     TABLE ACCESS (FULL) OF 'BREEDING'
   3    1     TABLE ACCESS (BY ROWID) OF 'BREEDING'
   4    1     TABLE ACCESS (FULL) OF 'BREEDING'
```

The CONNECT BY operation has three inputs: an initial table scan to determine the location of the root node, followed by a pair of table access operations to traverse the data tree. Of the three data access operations that supply data to the CONNECT BY operation, two are TABLE ACCESS FULL operations.

To reduce the number of TABLE ACCESS FULL operations required by the CONNECT BY operation, you should create a pair of concatenated indexes on the columns used in the **connect by** clause. For the query of the BREEDING table, the **connect by** clause is

```
connect by Cow = PRIOR Offspring
```

To properly index the data for the query, you can create two concatenated indexes of the Cow and Offspring columns. In the first index, the Cow column should be the leading column. In the second index, reverse the order of the columns in the index. The pair of indexes created on the Cow and Offspring columns can be used regardless of the direction used when traversing the data tree.

In the following listing, the two concatenated indexes are created:

```
create index Cow$Offspring
on BREEDING(Cow,Offspring);

create index Offspring$Cow
on BREEDING(Offspring, Cow);
```

With those two indexes available, the execution path for the query of the BREEDING table will now use index-based accesses instead of full table scans, as shown in the following listing:

```
Execution Plan
-----------------------------------------------------------
   0        SELECT STATEMENT Optimizer=CHOOSE
   1    0     CONNECT BY
   2    1       INDEX (RANGE SCAN) OF 'OFFSPRING$COW'
   3    1       TABLE ACCESS (BY ROWID) OF 'BREEDING'
   4    1       TABLE ACCESS (BY ROWID) OF 'BREEDING'
   5    4         INDEX (RANGE SCAN) OF 'COW$OFFSPRING'
```

In the preceding listing, the two TABLE ACCESS FULL operations for the BREEDING table have been replaced by index-based accesses. In general, index-based accesses will perform better than full table scans for **connect by** queries, particularly if there are multiple levels in the data tree.

Queries That Use Sequences

When a query selects values from a sequence, a SEQUENCE operation will appear in the execution path for the query. In general, sequence values are selected by querying DUAL (the public synonym for the SYS.DUAL table). If another table is already involved in the query, you do not need to add DUAL to the query in order to select from the sequence.

For example, the following query selects the next value from the CustomerID sequence:

```
select CustomerID.NextVal
   from DUAL;
```

The use of DUAL as a base table for the query is arbitrary; the important criteria are that the table be accessible and that it have one row in it for each sequence number you want returned.

To improve the performance of queries that generate values from sequences, you can "cache" a preallocated set of sequence values in memory. By default, 20 sequence values will be cached. When caching sequence values, Oracle will not replenish the cache until all 20 values have been used. If the database is shut down, any cached sequence values will be lost; on database startup, the next 20 values will be cached.

For example, you can alter the CustomerID sequence to cache 20 values via the command shown in the following listing:

```
alter sequence CustomerID cache 20;
```

If you select 12 values from the CustomerID sequence, 8 will still be left in the cache. If you then shut down the database, those 8 values will be lost. When the database is restarted, another 20 CustomerID sequence values—starting after the last previously cached value—will be cached. Thus, there will be a gap of eight CustomerID sequence values in the values selected from the sequence.

Queries That Use Database Links

If a query uses a database link to access remote data, the optimizer will show that a REMOTE operation is used. When a REMOTE operation is used, the Other column of the PLAN_TABLE table will record the query that is executed in the remote database. When tuning a query that uses remote objects, you should seek to minimize the amount of traffic between the instances. Minimizing the traffic between databases includes limiting both the size of the data sent from the remote database to the local database and the number of times the remote database is accessed during the query.

Queries That Use Clusters

If a table is stored in a cluster, a TABLE ACCESS CLUSTER operation can be used to access the table. In general, data manipulation against clustered tables performs poorly when compared to data manipulation against nonclustered tables. If your tables will be frequently modified by **insert**, **update**, and **delete**, then using clusters may negatively impact the performance of your application. Clusters are most appropriate when the data stored in them is static.

For the NESTED LOOPS join example, the WORKER table was used as the driving table and an index-based access was used to find matching records in the LODGING table. During the access to the LODGING data, the LODGING_PK index was used. If the LODGING table was stored in a cluster, and the Lodging column was the cluster key column, then the operations used to access the data within the NESTED LOOPS join would have changed slightly.

If LODGING were in a cluster, then WORKER could still be the driving table for the join. The access to the LODGING table's data would be a two-step process: an INDEX UNIQUE SCAN of the cluster key's index, followed by a TABLE ACCESS CLUSTER of the LODGING table. A TABLE ACCESS CLUSTER operation is used whenever data is read from a table after selecting index values from the cluster index for the table's cluster.

If LODGING were in a hash cluster, the method of reading the data from the table would change completely. In a hash cluster, the physical location of a row is determined by the values in the row. If LODGING were in a hash cluster, and the Lodging column values were used as the hashing function for the hash cluster, then the query

```
select *
  from LODGING
 where Lodging = 'ROSE HILL';
```

would use a TABLE ACCESS HASH operation to read the data. Since the physical location of the data would already be known by the optimizer, no index-based accesses would be necessary.

Related Hints

You can use the HASH hint to tell the optimizer to use a TABLE ACCESS HASH operation when scanning a table. When you specify the HASH hint, you should provide the name (or alias) of the table to be read via the TABLE ACCESS HASH operation.

NOTE
There is no relation between hash clusters and hash joins. To specify the use of hash joins, use the USE_HASH hint.

If you are using nonhash clusters, then you can specify that a table be read via a TABLE ACCESS CLUSTER operation via the CLUSTER hint. In general, the CLUSTER and HASH hints are mostly used when the queries being modified do not contain joins. If a query contains a join, you should use the join-related hints to have the greatest impact on the query's chosen execution path.

Additional Tuning Issues

In addition to the operations and hints listed in the previous sections, you can use two other sets of hints to influence the query processing. The additional hints allow you to control the parallelism of queries and the caching of data within the System Global Area (SGA).

If your server has multiple processors, and the data being queried is distributed across multiple devices, then you may be able to improve the processing of your queries by parallelizing the data access and sorting operations. When a query is parallelized, multiple processes are run in parallel, each of which accesses or sorts data. A query coordinator process distributes the workload and assembles the query results for the user.

The *degree of parallelism*—the number of scanning or sorting processes started for a query—can be set at the table level (see the **create table** command in the Alphabetical Reference). The optimizer will detect the table-level settings for the degree of parallelism and will determine the number of query server processes to be used during the query. The optimizer will dynamically check the number of processors and devices involved in the query and will base its parallelism decisions on the available resources.

You can influence the parallelism of your queries via the PARALLEL hint. In the following example, a degree of parallelism of four is set for a query of the LODGING table:

```
select /*+ PARALLEL (lodging,4) */
   from LODGING;
```

If you are using the Oracle Parallel Server option, you can specify an "instances" parameter in the PARALLEL hint. In the following query, the full table scan process will be parallelized, with a proposed degree of parallelism of four across two instances:

```
select /*+ PARALLEL(lodging,4,2) */
   from LODGING
 order by Manager;
```

In the preceding query, a second operation—the SORT ORDER BY operation for the **order by Manager** clause—was added. Because the sorting operation can also be parallelized, the query may use eight query server processes instead of four (four for the table scan and four for the sort). The optimizer will dynamically determine the degree of parallelism to use based on the table's settings, the database layout, and the available system resources.

If you wish to disable parallelism for a query, you can use the NOPARALLEL hint. The NOPARALLEL hint may be used if you wish to execute serially a query against a table whose queries are typically executed in a parallelized fashion.

If a small table (less than five database blocks in size) is read via a full table scan, that table's data is marked to be kept in the SGA for as long as possible. Data read via index scans and TABLE ACCESS BY ROWID operations is also kept in the SGA for as long as possible and is removed only when necessary by additional memory requests from the application. If a table is larger than five blocks, and it is read via a full table scan, its blocks will normally be marked for removal from the SGA as early as possible. If the table read by a full table scan is larger than five blocks, and you want its data to be kept in memory for as long as possible, you can mark the table as a "cached" table, using the **cache** clause of the **create table** or **alter table** command.

If a large table has not been marked as a cached table, and you want its data to stay in the SGA after the query completes, you can use the CACHE hint to tell the optimizer to keep the data in the SGA for as long as possible. The CACHE hint is usually used in conjunction with the FULL hint.

In the following listing, the WORKER table is queried; although its data will be read via a TABLE ACCESS FULL operation, the data will not be immediately removed from the SGA:

```
select /*+ FULL(worker) CACHE(worker) */    *
  from WORKER;
```

If a table is commonly used by many queries or users, and there is no appropriate indexing scheme available for the query, then you should use caching to improve the performance of accesses to that table. Caching is most useful for static tables. To dynamically disable the cache settings for a table, use the NOCACHE hint.

Review

The preceding sections have shown the methods used by the optimizer to access and manipulate data. When tuning queries, you need to keep in mind several factors:

- **The goal of the user**   Do you want rows to be quickly returned, or do you care more about the total throughput time for the query?

- **The type of joins used**   Are the tables properly indexed to take advantage of NESTED LOOPS operations?

- **The size of the tables**   How large are the tables that are being queried? If there are multiple joins, how large is the set of data returned from each join?

- **The selectivity of the data**   How selective are the indexes in use?

- **The sorting operations**   How many sorting operations are performed? Are nested sorting operations being performed?

If you can carefully manage the issues related to performance, then the number of "problem" queries within your database should diminish. If a query appears to be taking more resources than it should, then you should use the **set autotrace on** or **explain plan** command to determine the order of operations used for the query. You can use the tips and discussions provided throughout this chapter to then tune the operations or the set of operations. The tuned query will then be able to meet your goals.

CHAPTER
37

A Brief Introduction
to WebDB

ou can Web-enable your Oracle database via Oracle's WebDB tool. WebDB enables you to create an application that users can access via a web browser. The application data, and the application itself, is stored in an Oracle database. This architecture is based on the three-tier application architecture described in Chapter 5.

The generated application may feature the components found on most web sites: static pages, dynamic data display, and data entry forms. When you create a site via WebDB, you control the way in which the application components are displayed to the end user.

Oracle's WebDB product provides users and developers with a wizard-based development environment for Web applications. It is relatively easy to learn and use; you can use it to develop applications, manage databases, or perform ad hoc queries. In this chapter, you will see a brief overview of WebDB's capabilities—covering them all in detail would require another book!

The examples in this chapter are based on WebDB 2.1. Later versions of the WebDB product will likely present information differently, but much of the underlying architecture may stay the same. WebDB is implemented as a set of PL/SQL packages inside your database. When you execute a database command via WebDB, Oracle executes the command via the WebDB PL/SQL packages, wraps the result in the appropriate HTML tags, and displays the result in your browser window.

NOTE
This chapter does not describe the details for installing WebDB in your environment, because the installation requirements change by version and operating system.

Internal Architecture

WebDB's internal architecture relies on a set of PL/SQL packages. In WebDB 2.1, the core set of PL/SQL packages is owned by a user named WEBDB. When you create a new site via WebDB, Oracle will create a new owner within your database (such as WEBDB_NEW). WebDB will create a copy of its packages in the WEBDB_NEW schema, and you will then be able to use WEBDB_NEW for your site development.

The WEBDB_NEW schema will contain tables used both for the site display and for the site statistics gathering. Hits against the site will be written to the WWV_HITS1 and WWV_HITS2 tables, and site searches will be recorded in the WWV_SEARCHES1 and WWV_SEARCHES2 tables. Sections of the site are called *folders* (called *corners* in earlier versions of WebDB), and the table that holds folder information is still called WWV_CORNERS. In each folder, you can create items—the WWV_THINGS table contains these entries.

For the most part, you will not need to modify the table and index structures used by WebDB. Tables that are frequently queried (such as WWV_CORNERS and WWV_THINGS) have up to seven indexes each, while tables that are frequently inserted into (such as the hits and searches logs) have no indexes. If you frequently query the site statistics tables (either via SQL or via WebDB's Administration screens), you may decide to create indexes on the hits and searches logs' table—but you will pay a performance penalty for each insert thereafter.

Creating a Folder

To create a folder within a WebDB site, you need to log on to the site using the WebDB site administrator account (such as WEBDB_NEW). To log on, you need to go to the proper URL for your environment. When prompted, provide your username and password. You should see an Administration icon in the navigation bar on the left portion of the screen. Figure 37-1 shows the top half of the Administration screen with the navigation bar minimized. Figure 37-2 shows the bottom half of the Administration screen.

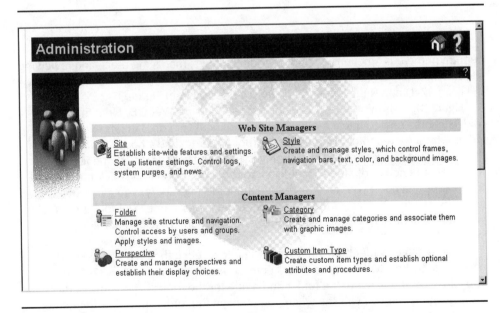

FIGURE 37-1. *Top portion of the Administration screen*

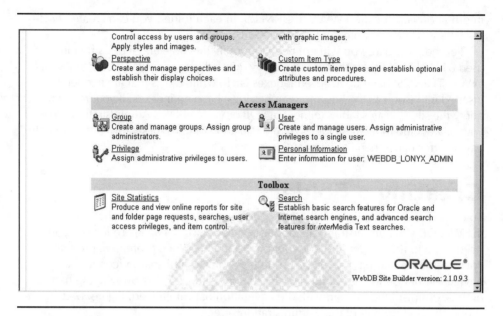

FIGURE 37-2. *Bottom portion of the Administration screen*

As shown in Figures 37-1 and 37-2, you can use the Administration screen to perform numerous functions, including adding folders, managing users, and reviewing site statistics. Clicking the Folder option (shown under the Content Managers section in Figure 37-1) opens the Folder Manager screen, shown in Figure 37-3.

Figure 37-3 shows the folders of a site created using WebDB. Note that folders can be related to each other in a hierarchical fashion—in this example, the Administrative Area folder is beneath the root folder (called Choose a Category in this site). Next to each folder is a set of icons. To edit a folder, click the icon that looks like a pencil and paper. To delete a folder and its contents, click the X next to the folder name. If you need to change the folder hierarchy, you can move the folder by clicking the last of the icons next to the folder name. The folder hierarchy will then be redisplayed, and you will have to select the new parent folder for your folder.

To add a new folder beneath an existing folder, click the plus sign (+) next to the parent folder. You will then see a data entry screen (shown in Figure 37-4) in which you can enter the name of the folder and a title for the folder. The name of the folder is the name you will see when you manage the folder; its title is the name displayed to the users.

FIGURE 37-3.   *Folder Manager screen*

FIGURE 37-4.   *Data entry screen for creating a folder*

Creating Items

When you edit a folder, you have the ability to add items to it. The Item Wizard screen, shown in Figure 37-5, displays the available options. You can insert URLs, files, WebDB components, and PL/SQL calls, among other things, as items within your application. Whatever you insert as an item will be inserted in the database (in the WWV_THINGS table described earlier).

You can use the Item Wizard screen to insert a URL as a record—in that case, you are storing links to other sites, much as a search engine contains links to other sites. You can also store entire files in your WebDB database, such as flat files, presentations, spreadsheets—whatever will fit in your database. Those objects will be stored in tables and will therefore impact the space requirements for your database.

Before storing large volumes of external file data in your database, you should investigate the use of the URL option. That is, you may be able to store the files outside the database and point to those files with a URL. Doing so will make your database smaller and more manageable, while supporting file system operations (such as versioning and access control) for the files. Unless the files are stored on a separate server apart from the database, the performance of the URL option should not be noticeably different from having files stored within the database.

FIGURE 37-5. *Item Wizard screen*

User and Site Administration

Because the WEBDB user has the power to create other users, it has the DBA role. If you are responsible for the database administration for your WebDB site, you can take advantage of WebDB's inherent administration features. Figure 37-6 shows the User Manager screen.

Via the User Manager screen, you can create a new user while specifying the user's default tablespace, temporary tablespace, and profile. Thus, a DBA could give the WebDB site administrator the task of creating all new users in the database, effectively streamlining the user administration process.

In practice, you may not use the User Manager site often. When you create the WEBDB_NEW site, Oracle creates separate accounts for the site administrator and the public users. The site administrator username is generally of the form WEBDB_NEW_ADMIN, while the public username is of the form WEBDB_NEW_PUBLIC. All users of the site will be logged in as WEBDB_NEW_PUBLIC, with read-only privileges on the site objects. The WEBDB_NEW_ADMIN user will not own the site objects, but will have privileges on the objects owned by WEBDB_NEW.

FIGURE 37-6. *User Manager screen*

Site administration is supported via WebDB by the Site Statistics Manager screen, shown in Figure 37-7. You can display the most-accessed folders for any time period, as well as the most commonly executed searches for the site.

Since the Site Statistics Manager screen is based on the site log tables, its performance will degrade as those tables grow larger. As noted previously, those tables are not indexed. To effectively query those tables, you should periodically replicate your site statistics tables to a separate database and truncate the statistics tables in the main database. You can then query the replicated statistics tables without impacting the performance of the main database.

The following script shows a query of WWV_CORNERS and WWV_HITS (a **union** view that combines WWV_HITS1 and WWV_HITS2). This query will display the number of hits for each folder. In general, executing this query has much less of a performance impact on your system than the Site Statistics Manager screen has, since no additional queries are required to generate the special screen formatting.

```
select C.Title, COUNT(*)
  from WWV_CORNERS C, WWV_HITS  H
 where H.CornerID = C.ID
   and H.Time > TO_DATE('&begindate')
 group by C.Title
 order by COUNT(*);
```

FIGURE 37-7. *Site Statistics Manager screen*

Sample output from this query is shown in the following listing:

```
TITLE                             COUNT(*)
--------------------------------- --------
Post resumes and search for jobs      104
Visit Our Sponsors                    122
Backup and Recovery                   124
Tools                                 155
Certification                         221
General References                    261
Tuning                                300
Scripts                               370
```

The output shows the number of hits recorded for eight folders. You could write similar queries to display the statistics by IP address, browser, or search term. As you add items, reports, and screens to your WebDB site, you can create additional queries against WebDB's tables to report your statistics. You can then create screens based on your queries, and add those screens as part of your WebDB application—using WebDB to monitor your WebDB site. The flexibility and ease of learning for the WebDB toolset are great strengths that you should take advantage of in your web site development.

CHAPTER
38

Beginner's Guide to Database Administration

n this chapter, you will see the basic steps involved in administering an Oracle database. There are many components to the database administrator (DBA) job, and there are books written specifically for DBAs. This chapter will provide an overview of the tasks of a DBA, along with guidance on the usage of standard DBA tools.

In earlier chapters, you have already seen many of the functions of a DBA, such as creating tables, indexes, views, users, synonyms, database links, and packages. The DBA topics described in this chapter will therefore focus on the production-control functions of the DBA role:

- Creating a database

- Starting and stopping the database

- Sizing and managing the memory areas for the database

- Allocating and managing space for the objects

- Creating and managing rollback segments

- Performing backups

For each of these topics, many options are available to developers and DBAs. The following sections of this chapter should provide you with enough information to get started, and to learn what questions to ask of your DBAs and system administrators.

Creating a Database

The simplest way to generate a **create database** script is via the Oracle Installer utility. When you install Oracle, the Installer gives you the option to create a database. If you use that option, the Installer will create a small database that is useful for practice, and can be deleted once you are done practicing. The important product of the Oracle Installer's database creation process is the set of database creation scripts it generates. The **create database** scripts generated by the Installer provide a solid template for your standard **create database** scripts.

The Installer will create a set of scripts usually in the /dbs subdirectory of the Oracle software home directory (referred to as ORACLE_HOME) on your server. These scripts are stored as plain text files, and you can use them as the basis for any future **create database** commands you need to execute. See the **create database** entry in the Alphabetical Reference for the full command syntax.

The **create database** command is issued from within Server Manager, a line-mode tool for DBAs. The following listing shows the use of Server Manager. In the first line, the **svrmgrl** command starts Server Manager; the following commands are executed from within Server Manager, as indicated by the SVRMGR prompt.

```
svrmgrl
SVRMGR> connect internal as sysdba
SVRMGR> create database...
```

To issue the **connect internal** command successfully, you must have the proper authorization at the operating system and database levels. See your operating system-specific Oracle documentation for information on the operating system rights needed. Depending on your database setup, you may not need the **as sysdba** clause shown in the preceding example.

Using the Oracle Enterprise Manager

Oracle Enterprise Manager (OEM), a graphical user interface (GUI) tool, is supplied as part of the standard Oracle toolset to enable DBAs to manage databases from a personal computer. With the release of Oracle8i, the OEM toolset, version 2.0.4, provides a robust interface for remote database administration. With version 2 of OEM, all DBAs can use the same central repository (a set of tables created in a database) to perform their work. In addition to those changes, OEM version 2 includes task scheduling and assignment features to enable around-the-clock database coverage.

You must make several key decisions before installing and configuring OEM. You need to decide where the OEM repository is to be created and how and when you are going to perform backups to protect this repository. Since you can use OEM as an interface to Oracle Recovery Manager (RMAN), recovery information can be stored in the OEM repository. You may want to create a small, separate database in which to store the OEM repository. You should ensure that this database is backed up frequently so that recovery of the repository is assured.

If you are the only DBA working with the OEM toolset, you will not have to consider who will handle administration of specific databases in your environment. If there are several DBAs at the site, you will need to determine task definitions, database responsibilities, and schedules. With OEM, you can grant levels of access and privilege to each DBA in the group on a task-by-task basis. You can configure OEM to enable you to send e-mail requests and assignments to other DBAs or take control of a problem to speed resolution.

If you have a previous version of OEM installed, migrate that repository to the newest version to take advantage of the new features. If you have more than one repository on your system, you will need to take precautions to ensure that you migrate each version of the repository without damaging currently stored information.

Oracle supports the Simple Network Messaging Protocol (SNMP). By supporting SNMP, Oracle products can be easily integrated into monitoring tools for systems and networks.

Although you do not have to use OEM, it provides a common GUI for managing your databases. As your enterprise grows in size (and in number of databases and DBAs), the consistency of the DBA interface will support consistent implementation of your change-control and production-control processes.

Starting and Stopping the Database

To start a database, issue the **startup** command from within Server Manager, as shown in the following listing. In the examples in this chapter, the name of the database is MYDB.

```
svrmgrl
SVRMGR> connect internal as sysdba;
SVRMGR> startup open MYDB;
```

Alternatively, you can first mount the database and then open it via an **alter database** command:

```
svrmgrl
SVRMGR> connect internal as sysdba;
SVRMGR> startup mount MYDB;
SVRMGR> alter database open;
```

When the database is mounted but not open, you can manage its files. For example, if you moved some of the database's files while the database was shut down, you need to let Oracle know where to find them before it will restart. To give the new locations of the files, you can mount the database (as shown in the preceding listing) and then use the **alter database** command to rename the old files to their new locations. Once you have finished telling Oracle the new locations for the files, you can open the database via the **alter database open** command.

Three primary options are available for shutting down the database. In a normal shutdown (the default), Oracle waits for all users to log out of the database before shutting down. In an immediate shutdown, Oracle rolls back all existing uncommitted transactions and logs out any users currently logged in. In an abort, the database immediately shuts down, and all uncommitted transactions are lost.

NOTE
While the database is in the process of shutting down or starting up, no new logins are permitted.

To perform a normal shutdown, use the **shutdown** command. An immediate shutdown, as shown in the following listing, uses the **shutdown immediate** version of the **shutdown** command. To abort the database, use **shutdown abort**.

```
SVRMGR> connect internal as sysdba;
SVRMGR> shutdown immediate;
```

NOTE
You must connect internal before shutting down the database.

If you use **shutdown abort**, Oracle will automatically perform recovery operations during the next database startup. In normal and immediate **shutdown**s, your shutdown process may stop if deadlocks exist between multiple users. In those cases, you may need to stop the **shutdown** and issue a **shutdown abort** in its place.

NOTE
*If you are shutting down the database to make a backup, you should use either **shutdown** or **shutdown immediate**. If you have problems during your shutdowns, you may use the following sequence: **shutdown abort**, **startup**, and then **shutdown**.*

You may also use OEM to start up and shut down the instance, via the Database menu options on the Instance Manager screens.

Sizing and Managing Memory Areas

When you start a database, Oracle allocates a memory area (the System Global Area, or SGA) shared by all of the database users. The two largest areas of the SGA are the *data block buffer cache* and the *Shared SQL Pool*; their size will directly impact the memory requirements for the database and the performance of database operations. Their sizes are controlled by parameters in the database's initialization file (called init.ora).

The data block buffer cache is an area in the SGA used to hold the data blocks that are read from the data segments in the database, such as tables, indexes, and clusters. The size of the data block buffer cache is determined by the DB_BLOCK_BUFFERS parameter (expressed in terms of number of database blocks) in the init.ora file for the database. The size for the database blocks is set via the

DB_BLOCK_SIZE parameter specified in the init.ora file during database creation. Managing the size of the data block buffer cache is an important part of managing and tuning the database.

Since the data block buffer cache is fixed in size, and is usually smaller than the space used by your tables, it cannot hold all of the database's data in memory at once. Typically, the data block buffer cache is about 1 to 2 percent of the size of the database. Oracle will manage the space available by using a *least recently used (LRU)* algorithm. When free space is needed in the cache, the least recently used blocks will be written out to disk, and new data blocks will take their place in memory. In this manner, the most frequently used data is kept in memory.

If the SGA is not large enough to hold the most frequently used data, then different objects will contend for space within the data block buffer cache. This is particularly likely when multiple applications use the same database and thus share the same SGA. In that case, the most recently used tables and indexes from each application constantly contend for space in the SGA with the most recently used objects from other applications. As a result, requests for data from the data block buffer cache will result in a lower ratio of "hits" to "misses." Data block buffer cache misses result in physical I/Os for data reads, resulting in performance degradation.

The Shared SQL Pool stores the data dictionary cache (information about the database structures) and the *library cache* (information about statements that are run against the database). While the data block buffer and dictionary cache enable sharing of structural and data information among users in the database, the library cache allows the sharing of commonly used SQL statements.

The Shared SQL Pool contains the execution plan and parse tree for SQL statements run against the database. The second time that an identical SQL statement is run (by any user), Oracle is able to take advantage of the parse information available in the Shared SQL Pool to expedite the statement's execution. Like the data block buffer cache, the Shared SQL Pool is managed via an LRU algorithm. As the Shared SQL Pool fills, less recently used execution paths and parse trees will be removed from the library cache to make room for new entries. If the Shared SQL Pool is too small, statements will be continually reloaded into the library cache, affecting performance.

The size (in bytes) of the Shared SQL Pool is set via the SHARED_POOL_SIZE init.ora parameter.

The init.ora File

The characteristics of the database instance—such as the size of the SGA and the number of background processes—are specified during startup. These parameters are stored in a file called *init.ora*. The init.ora file for a database usually contains the database name in the filename; a database named MYDB will typically have an init.ora file named initmydb.ora.

The init.ora file may, in turn, call a corresponding config.ora file. If a config.ora file is used, it usually only stores the parameter values for unchanging information, such as database block size and database name. The initialization file is read only during startup; modifications to it will not take effect until the next startup that uses this file.

Allocating and Managing Space for the Objects

To understand how space should be allocated within the database, you first have to know how the space is used within the database. In this section, you will see an overview of the Oracle database space usage functions.

When a database is created, it is divided into multiple logical sections called *tablespaces*. The SYSTEM tablespace is the first tablespace created. You can then create additional tablespaces to hold different types of data (such as tables, indexes, and rollback segments).

When a tablespace is created, *datafiles* are created to hold its data. These files immediately allocate the space specified during their creation. Each datafile can support only one tablespace.

A database can have multiple users, each of whom has a *schema*. Each user's schema is a collection of logical database objects, such as tables and indexes, that refer to physical data structures that are stored in tablespaces. Objects from a user's schema may be stored in multiple tablespaces, and a single tablespace can contain objects from multiple schemas.

When a database object (such as a table or index) is created, it is assigned to a tablespace via user defaults or specific instructions. A *segment* is created in that tablespace to hold the data associated with that object. The space that is allocated to the segment is never released until the segment is dropped, manually shrunk, or truncated.

A segment is made up of sections called *extents*—contiguous sets of Oracle blocks. Once the existing extents can no longer hold new data, the segment will obtain another extent. The extension process will continue until no more free space is available in the tablespace's datafiles or until an internal maximum number of extents per segment is reached. If a segment is composed of multiple extents, there is no guarantee that those extents will be contiguous.

To review, databases have tablespaces, and tablespaces have datafiles. Within those datafiles, Oracle stores segments for database objects. Each segment can have multiple extents, as shown in the following illustration.

Segment 1 Extent 1	Segment 1 Extent 2	Segment 2 Extent 1	Segment 1 Extent 3	Segment 2 Extent 2	Free Space

Managing the space used by tablespaces, datafiles, segments, and database objects is one of the basic functions of the DBA. The intent of this overview is to aid you in the planning of their physical storage.

Implications of the storage Clause

The amount of space used by a segment is determined by its storage parameters. These parameters are determined by the database at segment-creation time; if no specific storage parameters are given in the **create table**, **create index**, **create cluster**, or **create rollback segment** command, then the database will use the default storage parameters for the tablespace in which the segment is to be stored.

NOTE
*You can assign default tablespaces to users, and assign space quotas within those tablespaces, via the **create user**, **alter user**, and **grant** commands. See the Alphabetical Reference for the command syntax.*

When you create a table, index, or other segment, you can specify a **storage** clause as part of the **create** command. You can also specify a **tablespace** clause, enabling you to direct Oracle to store the data in a particular tablespace. For example, a **create table** command may include the following clauses:

```
tablespace USERS
storage (initial 1M next 1M pctincrease 0
minextents 1 maxextents 200)
```

The storage parameters specify the **initial** extent size, the **next** extent size, the **pctincrease** (a factor by which each successive extent will geometrically grow), the **maxextents** (maximum number of extents), and the **minextents** (minimum number of extents). After the segment has been created, the **initial** and **minextents** values cannot be altered. The default values for the storage parameters for each tablespace are contained in the DBA_TABLESPACES and USER_TABLESPACES views.

When a segment is created, it will acquire at least one extent. The initial extent will be used to store data until it no longer has any free space available (the **pctfree** clause can be used to reserve a percentage of space within each block in the segment to remain available for updates of existing rows). When additional data is added to the segment, the segment will extend by obtaining a second extent of the size specified by the **next** parameter. There is no guarantee that the second extent will be physically contiguous to the first extent. In the **storage** clause shown in the preceding listing, the **initial** extent is 1MB in size, and the **next** extent is 1MB. Because **pctincrease** is set to 0, every later extent will be 1MB as well, up to a maximum of 200 extents (the **maxextents** setting).

The **pctincrease** parameter is designed to minimize the number of extents in growing tables. A non-zero value for this parameter can be very dangerous—it causes the size of each successive extent to increase geometrically by the **pctincrease** factor specified. For example, consider the case of a data segment with an **initial** extent size of 20 Oracle blocks, a **next** extent size of 20 blocks, and a **pctincrease** of 50. Table 38-1 shows the sizes of the first 10 extents in this segment.

In just ten extents, the segment's size has increased by 7,700 percent! Besides being an indicator of inappropriate space planning, this is also an administrative problem for the DBA. The table is badly fragmented, the extents are most likely not contiguous, and the next time this table extends (for even one row of data), it will need over 750 Oracle blocks. A preferable situation would be to have a single extent of the right size, with a small value for **next**, and set the table's **pctincrease** to 0.

Extent Number	Size (in Oracle Blocks)	Total	Comments on Extent Size
1	20	20	Initial
2	20	40	Next
3	30	70	Next*1.5
4	45	115	Next*1.5*1.5
5	70	185	.
6	105	290	.
7	155	445	.
8	230	675	.
9	345	1020	.
10	520	1,540	Next*1.5*1.5*1.5*1.5*1.5*1.5*1.5*1.5

TABLE 38-1.   *The Effect of Using a Non-Zero* **pctincrease**

NOTE
*Setting **pctincrease** to 0 at the tablespace level affects Oracle's ability to automatically coalesce free space in the tablespace. Set the default **pctincrease** for the tablespace to a very low value, such as 1.*

Table Segments

Table segments, also called *data segments,* store the rows of data associated with tables or clusters. Each data segment contains a header block that serves as a space directory for the segment.

Unless it is very large, a properly sized table will have a very small number of extents. The more extents a data segment has, the more work is involved in managing it. In some cases, you cannot have single-extent data segments; since extents cannot span datafiles, a segment that is larger than the largest datafile available will have multiple extents. You can use multiple extents to stripe a segment across disks; striping data, though, is better handled outside of the database (for example, by using RAID-3 or RAID-5 disk arrays).

Once a data segment acquires an extent, it keeps that extent until the segment is either dropped or **truncate**d. The **delete** command has no impact on the amount of space that has been allocated to that table. The number of extents will increase until one of these situations occurs:

- The **maxextents** value is reached

- The user's quota in the tablespace is reached

- The tablespace runs out of space

You can also force a datafile to extend automatically via the **autoextend** options for datafiles.

To minimize the amount of wasted space in a data segment, tune the **pctfree** parameter, which specifies the amount of space that will be kept free within each data block. The free space can then be used when **NULL**-valued columns are updated to have values, or when updates to other values in the row force the row to lengthen. The proper setting of **pctfree** is application-specific, since it is dependent on the nature of the updates that are being performed.

Index Segments

Like table segments, *index segments* hold the space that has been allocated to them until they are dropped; however, they can also be indirectly dropped if the table or cluster they index is dropped. To minimize contention, indexes should be stored in a tablespace that is separated from their associated tables.

Indexes are subject to the same space problems as tables. Their segments have **storage** clauses that specify their **initial**, **next**, **minextents**, **maxextents**, and **pctincrease** values, and they are as likely to be fragmented as their tables are. They must be sized properly before they are created; otherwise, their fragmentation will drag down the database performance—exactly the opposite of their purpose.

You can use the **rebuild** option of the **alter index** command to alter the **storage** and **tablespace** settings for an index. For example, if you create an index with an overly large **initial** extent, you can reclaim the space from that extent by rebuilding the index and specifying a new value for **initial**, as shown in the following example, in which the WORKER_PK index is rebuilt with an **initial** extent of 10MB:

```
alter index WORKER_PK rebuild
tablespace INDEXES
storage (initial 10M next 10M pctincrease 0);
```

During the index **rebuild** process, both the old and the new indexes will exist in the database. Therefore, you must have enough space available to store both indexes before executing the **alter index rebuild** command.

Rollback Segments

To maintain read consistency among multiple users in the database and to be able to roll back transactions, Oracle must have a mechanism for reconstructing a "before image" of data for uncommitted transactions. Oracle uses *rollback segments* within the database to provide a before image of data.

Transactions use rollback segments to record the prior image of data that is changed. For example, a large **delete** operation requires a large rollback segment to hold the records to be deleted. If the **delete** transaction is rolled back, Oracle will use the rollback segment to reconstruct the data.

Queries also use rollback segments. Oracle performs read-consistent queries, so the database must be able to reconstruct data as it existed when a query started. If a transaction completes after a query starts, Oracle will continue to use that transaction's rollback segment entries to reconstruct changed rows. In general, you should avoid scheduling long-running queries concurrently with transactions. Rollback segments will grow to be as large as the transactions they support. Transactions cannot span rollback segments.

The principles of sound design for data segments apply also to rollback segments. Ideal rollback segments will have multiple evenly sized extents that add up to their optimal total size (they will have a minimum of two extents when created). Each extent should be large enough to handle all of the data from a single transaction. If it is not, or if too many users request the same rollback segment, then the rollback segment may extend.

Rollback segments can dynamically shrink to a specified size, or they can be manually shrunk to a size of your choosing. The **optimal** clause of the **storage** clause, which allows rollback segments to shrink to an **optimal** size after extending, helps to provide interim support to systems that have not been properly implemented for the way they are being used.

Temporary Segments

Temporary segments store temporary data during sorting operations (such as large queries, index creations, and unions). Each user has a temporary tablespace specified when the account is created via **create user** or altered via **alter user**. The user's temporary tablespace should be pointed to some place other than SYSTEM (the default).

When a temporary segment is created, it uses the default storage parameters for that tablespace. While the segment is in existence, its storage parameters cannot be altered by changing the default storage parameters for the tablespace. The temporary segment extends itself as necessary, and drops itself when the operation completes or encounters an error. Since the temporary segment itself can lead to errors (by exceeding the maximum number of extents or running out of space in the tablespace), the size of large sorting queries and operations should be taken into consideration when sizing the temporary tablespace.

The temporary tablespace, usually named TEMP, is fragmented by its nature. Temporary segments are constantly created, extended, and then dropped. You must therefore maximize the reusability of dropped extents. For a temporary tablespace, choose an **initial** and **next** extent size of 1/20 to 1/50 of the size of the tablespace. The default settings for **initial** and **next** should be equal for this tablespace. Choose a **pctincrease** of 0; the result will be segments made up of identically sized extents. When these segments are dropped, the next temporary segment to be formed will be able to reuse the dropped extents.

You can specify a tablespace as a *temporary tablespace*. A temporary tablespace cannot be used to hold any permanent segments; it can hold only temporary segments created during operations. The first sort to use the temporary tablespace allocates a temporary segment within the temporary tablespace; when the query completes, the space used by the temporary segment is not dropped, but rather is available for use by other queries, which allows the sorting operation to avoid the costs of allocating and releasing space for temporary segments. If your application frequently uses temporary segments for sorting operations, the sorting process should perform better if a dedicated temporary tablespace is used.

To dedicate a tablespace for temporary segments, specify the **temporary** clause of the **create tablespace** or **alter tablespace** command, as follows:

```
alter tablespace TEMP temporary;
```

NOTE
If there are any permanent segments (tables or indexes, for example) stored in TEMP, the preceding command will fail.

To enable the TEMP tablespace to store permanent (in other words, nontemporary) objects, use the **permanent** clause of the **create tablespace** or **alter tablespace** command, as follows:

```
alter tablespace TEMP permanent;
```

The Contents column in the DBA_TABLESPACES data dictionary view displays the status of the tablespace as either TEMPORARY or PERMANENT.

Free Space

A *free extent* in a tablespace is a collection of contiguous free blocks in the tablespace. A tablespace may contain multiple data extents and one or more free extents. When a segment is dropped, its extents are deallocated and marked as free. However, these free extents are not always recombined with neighboring free extents; the barriers between these free extents may be maintained. The system monitor (SMON) background process periodically coalesces neighboring free extents—provided the default **pctincrease** for the tablespace is non-zero.

When servicing a space request, the database will not merge contiguous free extents unless there is no alternative; thus, small free extents toward the front of the tablespace may be relatively unused, becoming "speed bumps" in the tablespace because they are not, by themselves, of adequate size to be of use. As this usage pattern progresses, the database thus drifts further and further from its ideal space allocation.

If your tablespace has a default **pctincrease** value of 0, then the space coalesce will not happen automatically. However, you can force the database to recombine the contiguous free extents, thus emulating the SMON functionality. Contiguous free space will increase the likelihood of the free extents near the front of the file being reused, thus preserving the free space near the rear of the tablespace file. As a result, new requests for extents are more likely to meet with success.

To force the tablespace to coalesce its free space, use the **coalesce** clause of the **alter tablespace** clause, as follows:

```
alter tablespace DATA coalesce;
```

The preceding command will force the neighboring free extents in the DATA tablespace to be coalesced into larger free extents.

> **NOTE**
> The **alter tablespace** command will not coalesce
> free extents that are separated by data extents.

In an ideal database, all objects are created at their appropriate size (in one extent, if possible), and all free space is always stored together, a resource pool waiting to be used. In reality, free space and data segments become fragmented. Fragmented data segments do not impact query performance, but they make your database maintenance more difficult. You can use the Export and Import utilities (described in "Performing Backups," later in this chapter) to rebuild your database and compress its extent allocations.

Sizing Database Objects

Choosing the proper space allocation for database objects is critical. Developers should begin estimating space requirements before the first database objects are created. Afterward, the space requirements can be refined based on actual usage statistics. The following sections discuss the space estimation methods for tables, indexes, and clusters.

Why Size Objects?

You should size your database objects for four reasons:

- To preallocate space in the database, thereby minimizing the amount of future work required to manage the objects' space requirements

- To reduce the amount of space wasted due to overallocation of space

- To eliminate potential causes of I/O-related performance problems

- To improve the likelihood of a dropped free extent being reused by another segment

You can accomplish these goals by following the sizing methodology shown in the following sections. This methodology is based on Oracle's internal methods for allocating space to database objects. Rather than rely on detailed calculations, the methodology relies on approximations that will dramatically simplify the sizing process while simplifying the long-term maintainability of the database.

Why Oracle Ignores Most Space Calculations

Unless you have calculated your space requests with Oracle's internal space allocation methods in mind, Oracle will most likely ignore your detailed space request. Oracle follows a set of internal rules when allocating space:

■ Oracle only allocates whole blocks, not parts of blocks.

■ Oracle allocates sets of blocks, usually in multiples of five.

■ Oracle may allocate larger or smaller sets of blocks, depending on the available free space in the tablespace.

You can apply these internal rules to your space allocations. For this example, assume that the database block size is 4K and the **pctincrease** for all tables is 0. The following tables will be created:

Table Name	Initial	Next
SmallTab	7K	7K
MediumTab	103K	103K

Before these tables were created, the DBA diligently estimated the space requirements by using the detailed space calculations available in the Oracle documentation. What happened when the tables were created?

For SmallTab, the DBA specified an initial extent size of 7K. However, the database block size is 4K. To avoid splitting a block, Oracle will round the initial extent size up to 8K. However, 8K represents only two blocks. In most environments, Oracle will round the initial extent size up to five blocks—20K. When the time comes to allocate the next extent, Oracle will use the specified **next** value—7K—and perform a similar calculation.

For MediumTab, the **initial** value is 103K. That value needs to be rounded up to a whole block increment, so Oracle will round the value up to 104K, or 26 blocks. At this point, Oracle will analyze the available space in the tablespace. Ideally, Oracle will round up the block allocation to the next multiple of 5 blocks—30 blocks. If there is a free extent in the tablespace that is between 26 and 30 blocks in size, then Oracle may use that free extent for MediumTab's first extent.

When MediumTab allocates its second extent, Oracle performs the same space allocation analysis and allocates a second extent of 30 blocks (120K).

The specified and actual space allocations for SmallTab and MediumTab are as follows:

Table	Initial	Next	FirstExtent	SecondExt
SmallTab	7K	7K	20K	20K
MediumTab	103K	103K	120K	120K

These results may be disheartening to the DBA who performed the space calculations. The SmallTab table only needed 14K for its first two extents; instead, it allocated 40K. The MediumTab table should have needed 206K for its first two extents; instead, it allocated 240K.

As shown through this exercise, there is no point in going through a sizing calculation exercise unless you first consider how Oracle allocates space. If you factor Oracle's space allocation methods into your space calculation methodology, then you will be able to allocate space effectively, with a minimum of changes made by Oracle. Before choosing your extent sizes, however, you should first consider how the size of extents impacts performance.

The Impact of Extent Size on Performance

No direct performance benefit is gained by reducing the number of extents in a table. In some situations (such as in parallel query environments), having multiple extents in a table can significantly reduce I/O contention and enhance your performance. Regardless of the number of extents in your tables, the extents need to be properly sized.

Oracle reads data from tables in two ways: by RowID (usually immediately following an index access) and via full table scans. If the data is read via RowID, the number of extents in the table is not a factor in the read performance. Oracle will read each row from its physical location (as specified in the RowID) and retrieve the data.

If the data is read via a full table scan, the size of the extents can impact performance, because Oracle will read multiple blocks at a time. The number of blocks read at a time is set via the DB_FILE_MULTIBLOCK_READ_COUNT init.ora parameter, and is limited by the operating system's I/O buffer size. For example, if the database block size is 4K and the operating system's I/O buffer size is 64K, you can read up to 16 blocks per read during a full table scan. In that case, setting DB_FILE_MULTIBLOCK_READ_COUNT to a value higher than 16 will not change the performance of the full table scans.

Extent sizes should take advantage of Oracle's ability to perform multiblock reads during full table scans. Thus, if the operating system's I/O buffer is 64K, then extent sizes should be multiples of 64K.

Consider a table that has ten extents, each of which is 64K in size. For this example, the operating system's I/O buffer size is 64K. To perform a full table scan, Oracle must perform ten reads (since 64K is the operating system I/O buffer size). If the data is stored in a single 640K extent, Oracle still must perform ten reads to scan the table. Reducing the number of extents results in no gain in performance.

If the table's extent size is not a multiple of the I/O buffer size, the number of reads required may increase. For the same 640K table, you could create eight extents that are 80K each. To read the first extent, Oracle will perform two reads: one for the first 64K of the extent, and a second read for the last 16K of the extent (reads cannot span extents). To read the whole table, Oracle must therefore perform 2 reads per extent, or 16 reads. Reducing the number of extents from ten to eight increased the number of reads by 60 percent!

To avoid paying a performance penalty for your extent sizes, you must therefore choose between one of the following two strategies:

- Create extents that are significantly larger than your I/O size. If the extents are very large, very few additional reads will be necessary even if the extent size is not a multiple of the I/O buffer size.

- Create extents that are a multiple of the I/O buffer size for your operating system.

If the I/O buffer size for your operating system is 64K, then the pool of extent sizes to choose from is 64K, 128K, 192K, 256K, and so forth. In the next section, you will see how to further reduce the pool of extent sizes from which to choose.

Maximizing the Reuse of Dropped Extents

When a segment is dropped, its extents are returned to the pool of available free extents. Other segments can then allocate the dropped extents as needed. If you use a consistent set of extent sizes, Oracle will be more likely to reuse a dropped extent, resulting in more efficient use of the space in the tablespace.

If you use custom sizes for extents, you will spend more time managing free space (such as defragmenting tablespaces). For example, if you create a table with an initial extent size of 100K, Oracle will allocate a 100K extent for the table. When you drop the table, the 100K extent is marked as a free extent. As noted earlier in this chapter, Oracle will automatically coalesce neighboring free extents if the default **pctincrease** setting for the tablespace is non-zero. For this example, assume that there is no neighboring free extent—the 100K free extent is surrounded on each side by data extents. When Oracle tries to allocate space for another segment, it will consider using the 100K free extent. For example, suppose a new segment requests two extents that are 60K each. Oracle may choose to consume the first 60K of the

100K free extent for the new segment, leaving a 40K free extent in its place. As a result, 40 percent of the free space is wasted.

To avoid wasting free space, you should use a set of extent sizes such that every extent size will hold an integral multiple of every smaller extent size.

Consider the first six values in the set of extent sizes generated earlier:

64K, 128K, 192K, 256K, 320K, 384K

The following list evaluates whether these values avoid wasting free space:

- 64K is the base value.

- 128K holds an even multiple of 64K extents, so that value is acceptable.

- 192K does not hold an even multiple of 128K extents, so that value is not acceptable.

- If 192K is discarded, then 256K is acceptable.

- 320K and 384K do not hold an even multiple of 256K extents, so they are not acceptable.

To meet the criteria, each extent size must be twice the size of the previous extent size. Thus, the acceptable values for extents are as follows:

64K, 128K, 256K, 512K, 1MB, 2MB, 4MB, 8MB, 16MB, 32MB, and so forth.

Using those values for extent sizes eliminates any potential I/O problems and enhances the likelihood that dropped extents will be reused.

One Last Obstacle

As noted earlier, Oracle will round the number of blocks allocated to an extent, usually to a multiple of five. For a 4K block size, the list of acceptable extent sizes (in blocks) is as follows:

16, 32, 64, 128, 256, 512, 1024, 2048, 4096, 8192

None of those values is evenly divisible by five, so Oracle may round them to the following:

20, 35, 65, 130, 260, 515, 1025, 2050, 4100, 8195

But that negates the impact of using the proper extent sizes! However, Oracle may not round those values after all. During its space allocation process, Oracle searches the tablespace for available free extents to use. If you request a 32-block extent, and Oracle finds an available 32-block free extent, you may allocate a 32-block extent rather than a 35-block extent. Furthermore, the larger the extent size, the smaller the impact the rounding has on your multiblock read performance. If you use the larger extent sizes, you will minimize the impact that Oracle's automatic rounding may have on your sizing efforts.

Estimating Space Requirements for Nonclustered Tables

To estimate the space required by a table, you only need to know four values:

- The database block size

- The **pctfree** value for the table

- The average length of a row

- The expected number of rows in the table

To calculate the exact space requirements for a table, you need additional information (such as the number of columns). To perform a quick estimate, the preceding four pieces of information are all you need.

The database block size is set via the DB_BLOCK_SIZE parameter in the database's init.ora file. You cannot change the block size of a database once it is created. To increase a database's block size, you would need to completely re-create it (via the **create database** command) and import any data exported from the old database.

Each database block has an area used for overhead within the block. Estimate the block overhead for tables to account for 90 bytes. Therefore, the available space in a block is as follows:

Database Block Size (in Bytes)	Available Space (in Bytes)
2,048	1,958
4,096	4,006
8,192	8,102

A portion of that available space will be kept free, available for **update**s of rows previously inserted into the block. The **pctfree** setting for the table sets the size of the free space that is unused during **insert**s. Multiply the available space by the

pctfree value to determine how much space is unused. Subtract that value from the available space in the block to determine how much space is available to rows.

For a 4K block size and a table with a **pctfree** setting of 10, the available space is

```
4006 bytes - (0.1*4006 bytes) = 3605.4 bytes, rounded down to 3605 bytes.
```

In every database block in this example, 3,605 bytes are available for new records.

Next, estimate the average row length. Estimate the length of a DATE value to be 8 bytes, and the length of a NUMBER value to be 4 bytes. For VARCHAR2 columns, estimate the actual length of the values stored in the columns.

NOTE
These estimates incorporate additional column overhead. In reality, a DATE value stores 7 bytes, while a NUMBER value is typically 3 bytes.

For example, you may have a table with ten columns and an estimated average row length of 600 bytes. Since there are 3,605 bytes available per block (from the previous estimate), the number of rows per block is

```
3605 bytes per block / 600 bytes per row = 6 rows per block.
```

Now, you need to estimate the number of rows you expect in the table. If the sample table will have 25,000 rows, the number of blocks you need is

```
25,000 rows / 6 rows per block = 4,166 blocks
```

The table will require approximately 4,166 blocks. However, that does not match any of the extent sizes specified in the previous sections. You have two choices:

- Create an **initial** extent of 16MB (4,096 blocks) and a **next** extent of 512K (128 blocks).

- If space is available and you anticipate further growth in the table, create an **initial** extent of 32MB.

If you use the first option, space allocation (4,224 blocks) will exceed your estimate (4,166 blocks) by just over 1 percent. By allocating that additional 1 percent, you will be creating a table whose extents are properly sized both for performance and for optimal reuse of free extents. Relying on a predetermined set of allowed extent sizes greatly simplifies your space management process.

Estimating Space Requirements for Indexes

The estimation process for indexes parallels the estimation process for tables. The estimation process described in this section does not provide exact space allocation requirements; rather, it enables you to quickly estimate the space requirements and match them to a set of standard extent sizes. To estimate the space required by an index, you only need to know four values:

- The database block size

- The **pctfree** value for the index

- The average length of an index entry

- The expected number of entries in the index

The database block size is set via the DB_BLOCK_SIZE parameter in the database's init.ora file. Each database block has an area used for overhead within the block. Estimate the block overhead for an index to be 161 bytes. Therefore, the available space in a block is as follows:

Database Block Size (in Bytes)	Available Space (in Bytes)
2,048	1,887
4,096	3,935
8,192	8,031

A portion of that available space will be kept free, based on the **pctfree** setting for the index. However, index values should not be frequently **updated**. For indexes, **pctfree** is commonly set to a value below 5. Multiply the available space by the **pctfree** value to determine how much space is unused in each block. Subtract that value from the available space in the block to determine how much space is available to index entries.

For a 4K block size and an index with a **pctfree** setting of 2, the available space is

```
3935 bytes - (0.02*3935 bytes) = 3856.3 bytes,
                         rounded down to 3856 bytes.
```

In every database block in this example, 3,856 bytes are available for new index entries.

Next, estimate the average row length of an index entry. If the index is a concatenated index, estimate the length of each column's values and add them together to arrive at the total entry length. Estimate the length of a DATE value to be 8 bytes, and estimate the length of a NUMBER value to be 4 bytes. For VARCHAR2 columns, estimate the actual length of the values stored in the columns.

NOTE
These estimates incorporate additional column overhead. In reality, a DATE value stores 7 bytes, while a NUMBER value is typically 3 bytes.

For example, you may have an index with three columns and an estimated average row length of 17 bytes. Since there are 3,856 bytes available per block (from the previous estimate), the number of entries per block is

```
3856 bytes per block / 17 bytes per entry = 226 entries per block.
```

Now, you need to estimate the number of entries you expect in the index. If the sample index will have 25,000 entries, the number of blocks you need is

```
25,000 rows / 226 entries per block = 111 blocks
```

Your index will require approximately 111 blocks. However, that size (444K) does not match any of the extent sizes specified in the previous sections. You have two choices:

- Create an **initial** extent of 256K and a **next** extent of 64K, specifying **minextents** 4 and **pctincrease** 0 (112 blocks).

- If space is available and you anticipate further growth in the table, create an **initial** extent of 512K (128 blocks).

If you use the first option, your space allocation (112 blocks) will exceed your estimate (111 blocks) by just 1 block. If you use the second option, you will allocate 13 percent more space than your estimate. By following either of these options, you will be creating an index whose extents are properly sized both for performance and for optimal reuse of free extents. Regardless of the space estimate you use, be sure your extent sizes conform to the standard extent sizes you establish for your database.

Creating and Managing Rollback Segments

As noted in the section on rollback segments in the space management section of this chapter, rollback segments dynamically expand and contract to support your transactions. When a database is created, Oracle automatically creates a SYSTEM rollback segment that supports transactions within the data dictionary. A second rollback segment must be created and brought online prior to the use of any non-SYSTEM tablespaces. See the **create database** command scripts created by the Oracle Installer for examples of the **create rollback segment** command.

In general, you should be aware of the following procedures involving rollback segments:

- How to take them online and offline

- How to determine their maximum size

- How to assign transactions to specific rollback segments

These three steps will allow developers to properly support the transaction sizes required for the batch and online portions of applications.

Activating Rollback Segments

Activating a rollback segment makes it available to the database users. A rollback segment may be deactivated without being dropped. It will maintain the space already allocated to it, and can be reactivated at a later date. The following examples provide the full set of rollback segment activation commands.

To create a rollback segment, use the **create rollback segment** command, as shown in the following listing:

```
create rollback segment SEGMENT_NAME
tablespace RBS;
```

Note that the example **create rollback segment** command creates a private rollback segment (since the **public** keyword was not used) and that it creates it in a non-SYSTEM tablespace called RBS. Since no storage parameters are specified, the rollback segment will use the default storage parameters for that tablespace. See the **create rollback segment** command entry in the Alphabetical Reference for the full syntax. As noted earlier in this chapter, you can specify **optimal** as a storage value for rollback segments.

NOTE
*For rollback segments, **pctincrease** cannot be specified and is always set to 0.*

Although the rollback segment has been created, it is not yet in use by the database. To activate the new rollback segment, bring it online using the following command:

```
alter rollback segment SEGMENT_NAME online;
```

Once a rollback segment has been created, you should list it in the database's init.ora file. The following is a sample init.ora entry for rollback segments:

```
rollback_segments    = (r0,r1,r2)
```

NOTE
The SYSTEM rollback segment should never be listed in the init.ora file. The SYSTEM rollback segment can never be dropped; it is always acquired along with any other rollback segments the instance may acquire.

For this database, the rollback segments named r0, r1, and r2 are online. If you deactivate a rollback segment, remove its entry from the init.ora file. When you deactivate a rollback segment, it will remain online until its current active transactions complete. You can view the PENDING OFFLINE status of a rollback segment via the V$ROLLSTAT view.

An active rollback segment can be deactivated via the **alter rollback segment** command:

```
alter rollback segment SEGMENT_NAME offline;
```

To drop a rollback segment, use the **drop rollback segment** command:

```
drop rollback segment SEGMENT_NAME;
```

How to Determine the Maximum Size of a Rollback Segment

A rollback segment is a segment in the database, so you can query its storage values from the DBA_SEGMENTS data dictionary view. When working with rollback segments, it is important to know how large the rollback segment can grow. Since a transaction cannot span rollback segments, rollback segments must be large enough to support the largest transaction you will be executing. As described in the next section, you can force Oracle to use a specific rollback segment for your transactions.

The maximum size of a rollback segment can be determined by querying DBA_SEGMENTS:

```
select Segment_Name,
       Tablespace_Name,
       Bytes  AS Current_Size,
       Initial_Extent + Next_Extent*(Max_Extents-1)
         AS Max_Size
  from DBA_SEGMENTS
 where Segment_Type = 'ROLLBACK';
```

The result of this query tells you the maximum size for the rollback segments, based on the segment definitions. You should then compare that value to the free space within the datafiles for the rollback segment's tablespace. If the datafiles have **autoextend** enabled, the size of the rollback segment datafiles may be limited by either the available disk space or the **maxsize** setting for the datafiles.

Whenever possible, limit the size of batch transactions. The smaller a transaction, the more manageable it is within the database. If you must have a large transaction, then you should isolate that transaction to a specific tablespace, as described in the next section. If you cannot assign the transaction to a rollback segment, then all of the non-SYSTEM rollback segments must be large enough to support the transaction.

If a rollback segment must frequently extend beyond its **optimal** setting, the performance of your transactions may be impacted by this dynamic space management. Set the **optimal** storage parameter for your rollback segments to reflect the average space usage within the segment.

How to Assign Transactions to Specific Rollback Segments

You can use the **set transaction** command to specify which rollback segment a transaction should use. You should execute the **set transaction** command before large transactions to ensure that they use rollback segments that are created specifically for them.

The settings specified via the **set transaction** command will be used only for the current transaction. The following example shows a series of transactions. The first transaction is directed to use the ROLL_BATCH rollback segment. The second transaction (following the second **commit**) will be randomly assigned to a rollback segment.

```
commit;

set transaction use rollback segment ROLL_BATCH;
insert into TABLE_NAME
select * from DATA_LOAD_TABLE;

commit;

REM*   The commit command clears the rollback segment assignment.
REM*   Implicit commits, like those caused by DDL commands, will
REM*   also clear the rollback segment designation.

insert into TABLE_NAME select * from SOME_OTHER_TABLE;
```

If you do not specify a rollback segment for a transaction, Oracle will randomly assign a rollback segment to it. You should have enough rollback segments available to support multiple transactions per rollback segment. Start with one rollback segment per every four to ten concurrent online users, and watch for internal waits (via the V$WAITSTAT dynamic view).

Performing Backups

Like the rest of the material in this chapter, this section provides an overview. Backup and recovery is a complex topic, and all backup and recovery methods should be thoroughly tested and practiced before being implemented in a production environment. The purpose of this section is to give developers an understanding of Oracle's capabilities, along with the impact of the backup decisions on recovery efforts and availability. Before using backup and recovery methods in a production environment, you should refer to books that are dedicated to that topic, including Oracle's documentation.

The backup methods provided by Oracle can be categorized as follows:

- Logical backups, using Export (and its companion utility, Import)
- Physical file system backups: offline backups and online backups
- Incremental physical file system backups via Recovery Manager (RMAN)

The following sections describe each of these methods and their capabilities.

Export and Import

Oracle's Export utility reads the database, including the data dictionary, and writes the output to a binary file called an *export dump file.* You can export the full database, specific users, or specific tables. During exports, you may choose whether to export the data dictionary information (such as grants, indexes, and constraints) associated with tables. The file written by Export will contain the commands necessary to completely re-create all of the chosen objects.

Once data has been exported, it may be imported via Oracle's Import utility, which reads the binary export dump file created by Export and executes the commands found there. For example, these commands may include a **create table** command, followed by an **insert** command to load data into the table.

Data that has been exported does not have to be imported into the same database, or the same schema, as was used to generate the export dump file. You may use the export dump file to create a duplicate set of the exported objects under a different schema or in a separate database.

You can import either all or part of the exported data. If you import the entire export dump file from a Full export, then all of the database objects—including tablespaces, datafiles, and users—will be created during the import. However, it is often useful to pre-create tablespaces and users, to specify the physical distribution of objects in the database.

> **NOTE**
> *If you are only going to import part of the data from the export dump file, then the tablespaces, datafiles, and users that will own and store that data must be set up before the import.*

You can import exported data into an Oracle database created under a higher version of the Oracle kernel. You can use this data migration strategy between consecutive major releases of Oracle (such as from Oracle7 to Oracle 8.0, or from Oracle 8.0 to Oracle 8i). When migrating data between nonconsecutive major releases (for example, from Oracle6 to Oracle8), you should first import the data into the intermediate release (in this example, Oracle7), and then from that database into the later major release (Oracle8).

The Export utility has three levels of functionality:

- **Full mode** The full database is exported. The entire data dictionary is read, and the DDL needed to re-create the full database is written to the export dump file. This file includes definitions for all tablespaces, all users, and all of the objects, data, and privileges in their schemas.

■ **User mode**   A user's objects are exported, as well as the data within them. All grants and indexes created by the user on the user's objects are also exported. Grants and indexes created by users other than the owner are not exported.

■ **Table mode**   A specified table is exported. The table's structure, indexes, and grants are exported, either with or without its data. Table mode can also export the full set of tables owned by a user (by specifying the schema owner but no table names). You can also specify partitions of a table to export via a modified version of Table mode exports.

You can run Export interactively, through OEM or RMAN, or via command files. You can display the Export parameters online via the following command:

```
exp help=Y
```

In the following example, the COMPRESS=Y parameter is used, as the GEORGE and DORA owners are exported. The COMPRESS=Y setting will result in the segments' space definitions being altered so that the current space allocation is compressed into a single extent when the segment is re-created during Import.

```
exp system/manager file=expdat.dmp compress=Y owner=(GEORGE,DORA)
```

This command will run Export while logged in as the SYSTEM account. The GEORGE and DORA accounts will have their objects exported. To export the full database, use FULL=Y.

Consistent Exports

During the process of writing the database's data to the export dump file, Export reads one table at a time. Thus, although the export started at a specific point in time, each table is read at a different time. The data as it exists in each table at the moment Export starts to read *that table* is what will be exported. Since most tables are related to other tables, this may result in inconsistent data being exported if users are modifying data during the export.

Consider the following scenario:

1. The export begins.

2. Sometime during the export, table A is exported.

3. After table A is exported, table B, which has a foreign key to table A is exported.

What if transactions are occurring at the same time? Consider a transaction that involves both table A and table B, but does not **commit** until after table A has been exported.

1. The export begins.

2. A transaction against table A and table B begins.

3. Table A is exported.

4. The transaction is **commit**ted.

5. Table B is exported.

The transaction's data will be exported with table B, but not with table A (since the **commit** had not yet occurred). The export dump file thus contains inconsistent data—in this case, foreign key records from table B without matching primary key records from table A.

To avoid this problem, you have two options. First, you should schedule exports to occur when no one is making modifications to tables. Second, you can use the CONSISTENT parameter on the Export command line. When CONSISTENT=Y, the database will maintain a rollback segment to track any modifications made since the export began. The rollback segment entries can then be used to re-create the data as it existed when the export began. The result is a consistent set of exported data, with two major costs: the need for a very large rollback segment, and the reduced performance of the export as it searches the rollback segment for changes.

Whenever possible, guarantee the consistency of exported data by running exports while the database is not being used or is mounted in **restricted session** mode. If you are unable to do this, then perform a CONSISTENT=Y export of the tables being modified, and a CONSISTENT=N export of the full database. This will minimize the performance penalties incurred, while ensuring the consistency of the most frequently used tables.

Tablespace Exports

To defragment a tablespace, or to create a copy of its objects elsewhere, you need to do a tablespace-level export. Unfortunately, there really is no way to export a specific tablespace. However, if your users are properly distributed among tablespaces, you can use a series of User exports that, taken together, produce the desired result. If you need to move tablespaces between instances, see the "Transportable Tablespace" entry in the Alphabetical Reference for details on Oracle8i's capabilities in this area.

In general, you should separate your objects among tablespaces based on the object types and their uses. For example, application tables should be stored apart from their indexes, and static tables should be stored apart from volatile tables. If multiple users own tables, then you may further divide tablespace assignments so that each user has his or her own tablespace for volatile tables. Separating the tables in this manner will greatly enhance your ability to manage them via Export/Import.

User exports record those database objects that are created by a user. However, certain types of user objects are not recorded by User exports. Specifically, indexes and grants on tables owned by other accounts are not recorded via User exports.

Consider the case of two accounts, GEORGE and DORA. If GEORGE creates an index on one of DORA's tables, a User export of GEORGE will not record the index (since GEORGE does not own the underlying table). A User export of DORA will also not record the index (since the index is owned by GEORGE). The same thing happens with grants: when a second account is capable of creating grants on objects, the usefulness of User exports rapidly diminishes.

Assuming that such *third-party objects* do not exist, or can be easily re-created via scripts, the next issue involves determining which users own objects in which tablespaces. This information is available via the data dictionary views. The following query maps users to tablespaces to determine the distribution of their objects. It does this by looking at the DBA_TABLES and DBA_INDEXES data dictionary views, and spools the output to a file called user_locs.lst.

```
set pagesize 60
break on Owner on Tablespace_Name
column Objects format A20
select
        Owner,
        Tablespace_Name,
        COUNT(*)||' tables' Objects
  from DBA_TABLES
where Owner <> 'SYS'
group by
        Owner,
        Tablespace_Name
union
select
        Owner,
        Tablespace_Name,
        COUNT(*)||' indexes' Objects
  from DBA_INDEXES
where Owner <> 'SYS'
group by
        Owner,
        Tablespace_Name
```

```
spool user_locs.lst
/
spool off
```

The query output will show, by owner, the distribution of objects across tablespaces. Ideally, an owner's objects are located in a small set of tablespaces, and no other owners have objects in those tablespaces.

Before determining the proper combinations of users to export for a tablespace, the inverse mapping—of tablespaces to users—should be done. The following query accomplishes this task. It queries the DBA_TABLES and DBA_INDEXES data dictionary views, and stores the output in a file called ts_locs.lst.

```
set pagesize 60
break on Tablespace_Name on Owner
column Objects format A20
select
        Tablespace_Name,
        Owner,
        COUNT(*)||' tables' Objects
  from DBA_TABLES
where Owner <> 'SYS'
group by
        Tablespace_Name,
        Owner
union
select
        Tablespace_Name,
        Owner,
        COUNT(*)||' indexes' Objects
  from DBA_INDEXES
where Owner <> 'SYS'
group by
        Tablespace_Name,
        Owner

spool ts_locs.lst
/
spool off
```

The preceding query lists, by tablespace, the owners and objects that have space allocated within the tablespace.

If GEORGE owns tables in only two tablespaces, and those tablespaces are only used by the GEORGE account, a User export of GEORGE will export all of the tables in the tablespaces. The following example of an Export command shows the use of the OWNER (for the schema), INDEXES (to export indexes), and GRANTS (to export grants) options:

```
exp system/manager file=hr.dmp owner=HR indexes=Y grants=Y
```

Rollback Segment Requirements During Import

During an Import, Oracle reads the export dump file and issues the commands found there. These commands may include (among others) tablespace creations, table creations, and data inserts. You can see all of the Import options by entering the following command:

```
imp help=Y
```

By default, Import will issue a **commit** after every table is completely imported. Thus, if you have a table that contains 300MB of data, your rollback segments must accommodate a rollback segment entry that is at least that large. This is an unnecessary burden for the rollback segments. To shorten the sizes of the rollback segment entries, specify COMMIT=Y along with a value for BUFFER during the import. A **commit** will then be executed after every BUFFER worth of data, as shown in the following example. In the first import command shown, a **commit** is executed after every table is loaded. In the second command shown, a **commit** is executed after every 64,000 bytes of data are inserted.

```
imp system/manager file=expdat.dmp
imp system/manager file=expdat.dmp buffer=64000 commit=Y
```

How large should BUFFER be? BUFFER should be large enough to handle the largest single row to be imported. In tables with LONG or LOB datatypes, this may be greater than 64K. If you do not know the length of the longest row that was exported, start with a reasonable value (for example, 50,000) and run the import. If an IMP-00020 error is returned, the BUFFER size is not large enough. Increase it and try the import again.

When using COMMIT=Y, remember that a **commit** is performed for each BUFFER array. This implies that if the import of a table fails, some of the rows in that table may have already been imported and **commit**ted. The partial load may then be either used or **delete**d before running the import again.

Importing into Different Accounts

To move objects from one user to another via Export/Import, perform a User export of the owner of the objects. During the import, specify the owner as the FROMUSER and the account that is to own the objects as the TOUSER.

Offline Backups

Offline backups occur when the database has been shut down normally (that is, not due to instance failure). While the database is "offline," the following files are backed up:

- All datafiles
- All control files
- All online redo logs
- The init.ora file (optional)

Having all of these files backed up *while the database is closed* provides a complete image of the database as it existed at the time it was closed. The full set of these files could be retrieved from the backups at a later date and the database would be able to function. It is *not* valid to perform a file system backup of the database while it is open unless an online backup is being performed (as discussed later in this chapter).

An offline backup is a physical backup of the database files made after the database has been shut down via either a **shutdown normal** or a **shutdown immediate**. While the database is shut down, each of the files that are actively used by the database is backed up. These files thus capture a complete image of the database as it existed at the moment it was shut down.

NOTE
*You should not rely on an offline backup performed following a **shutdown abort**. If you must perform a **shutdown abort**, you should restart the database and perform a normal **shutdown** before beginning your offline backup.*

The following files should be backed up during offline backups:

- All datafiles
- All control files

- All online redo logs

- The init.ora file and config.ora file (optional)

Ideally, all of the datafiles are located in directories at the same level on each device. For example, all database files may be stored in an instance-specific subdirectory under an /oracle directory for each device (such as /db01/oracle/MYDB). Directories such as these should contain all of the datafiles, redo log files, and control files for a database. The only file you may optionally add to the offline backup that will not be in this location is the production init.ora file, which should be in the /app/oracle/admin/*INSTANCE_NAME*/pfile subdirectory under the Oracle software base directory.

If you use the directory structure in the prior example, your backup commands are greatly simplified, since you will be able to use wildcards in the filenames. After shutting down the database, back up the files to the backup destination area (either a tape or a separate disk area).

NOTE
If necessary, you can also back up the init.ora and config.ora files at the same time.

Since offline backups involve changes to the database's availability, they are usually scheduled to occur at night.

Offline backups are very reliable. To reduce their impact on the database's availability, you may use online backups. As described in the following section, online backups use Oracle's ARCHIVELOG mode to allow consistent file system backups during database usage.

Online Backups

You can use online backups for any database that is running in ARCHIVELOG mode. In this mode, the online redo logs are archived, creating a full log of all transactions within the database.

Oracle writes to the online redo log files in a cyclical fashion; after filling the first log file, it begins writing to the second log until that one fills, and then begins writing to the third. Once the last online redo log file is filled, the LGWR (Log Writer) background process begins to overwrite the contents of the first redo log file.

When Oracle is run in ARCHIVELOG mode, the ARCH (Archiver) background process makes a copy of each redo log file before overwriting it. These archived redo log files are usually written to a disk device. The archived redo log files may also be written directly to a tape device, but this tends to be very operator-intensive.

You can perform file system backups of a database while that database is open, provided the database is running in ARCHIVELOG mode. An online backup involves setting each tablespace into a backup state, backing up its datafiles, and then restoring the tablespace to its normal state.

NOTE
When using the Oracle-supplied RMAN utility, you do not have to place each tablespace into a backup state. The utility will put the tablespace into and take it out of the backup state automatically.

The database can be fully recovered from an online backup, and can, via the archived redo logs, be rolled forward to any point in time. When the database is then opened, any committed transactions that were in the database at that time will have been restored and any uncommitted transactions will have been rolled back.

While the database is open, the following files are backed up:

- All datafiles

- All archived redo log files

- One control file, via the **alter database** command

Online backup procedures are very powerful for two reasons. First, they provide full point-in-time recovery. Databases that are not running in ARCHIVELOG mode can only be recovered to the point in time when the backup occurred. Second, they allow the database to remain open during the file system backup. Thus, even databases that cannot be shut down due to user requirements can still have file system backups.

Getting Started

To make use of the ARCHIVELOG capability, the database must first be placed in ARCHIVELOG mode. The following listing shows the steps needed to place a database in ARCHIVELOG mode:

```
svrmgrl
SVRMGR> connect internal as sysdba
SVRMGR> startup mount MYDB;
SVRMGR> alter database archivelog;
SVRMGR> archive log start;
SVRMGR> alter database open;
```

The following command will display the current ARCHIVELOG status of the database from within Server Manager:

```
archive log list
```

To change a database back to NOARCHIVELOG mode, use the following set of commands:

```
svrmgrl
SVRMGR> connect internal as sysdba
SVRMGR> startup mount MYDB;
SVRMGR> alter database noarchivelog;
SVRMGR> alter database open;
```

A database that has been placed in ARCHIVELOG mode will remain in that mode until it is placed in NOARCHIVELOG mode.

The location of the archived redo log files is determined by the settings in the database's init.ora file. The archive log destination parameter may also be set via the config.ora file that is referenced as a parameter file in the init.ora file. The two parameters to note are as follows (with sample values):

```
log_archive_dest_1          = /db01/oracle/arch/MYDB/arch
log_archive_start           = TRUE
```

NOTE
Prior to Oracle8i, LOG_ARCHIVE_DEST_1 was called LOG_ARCHIVE_DEST.

In this example, the archived redo log files are being written to the directory /db01/oracle/arch/MYDB. The archived redo log files will all begin with the letters "arch," followed by a sequence number. For example, the archived redo log file directory may contain the following files:

```
arch_170.dbf
arch_171.dbf
arch_172.dbf
```

Each of these files contains the data from a single online redo log. They are numbered sequentially, in the order in which they were created. The size of the archived redo log files varies, but does not exceed the size of the online redo log files.

If the destination directory of the archived redo log files runs out of space, then ARCH will stop processing the online redo log data and the database will stop itself. This situation can be resolved by adding more space to the archived redo log file destination disk or by backing up the archived redo log files and then removing them from this directory.

NOTE
Never delete archived redo log files until you have backed them up. There is no way to skip a missing archived redo log file during a recovery.

Performing Online Database Backups

Once a database is running in ARCHIVELOG mode, you can back it up while it is open and available to users. This capability allows round-the-clock database availability to be achieved while still guaranteeing the recoverability of the database.

Although online backups can be performed during normal working hours, they should be scheduled for the times of the least user activity, for several reasons. First, the online backups will use operating system commands to back up the physical files, and these commands will use most of the available I/O resources in the system (impacting the system performance for interactive users). Second, while the tablespaces are being backed up, the manner in which transactions are written to the archived redo log files changes. If the physical block size of the operating system is less than the Oracle block size, then changing one record in a block will cause the record's entire database block, not just the transaction data, to be written to the archived redo log file. This will use a great deal more space in the archived redo log file destination directory.

The command file for an online backup has three parts:

I. A tablespace-by-tablespace backup of the datafiles, which in turn consists of

    a. Setting the tablespace into backup state via the **alter tablespace begin backup** command

    b. Backing up the tablespace's datafiles

    c. Restoring the tablespace to its normal state via the **alter tablespace end backup** command

2. Backing up the archived redo log files, which consists of

a. Recording which files are in the archived redo log destination directory

b. Backing up the archived redo log files, and then (optionally) deleting or compressing them

3. Backing up the control file via the **alter database backup controlfile** command.

You should create a script to perform the backups. The script should run at the operating system level, with Server Manager commands executed for Steps 1a, 1c, and 3.

When the datafiles are being backed up, you may back them up directly to tape or to disk. If you have enough disk space available, choose the latter option, since it will greatly reduce the time necessary for the backup procedures to complete.

Recovery Manager

As of Oracle8, the OEM tool set includes a Recovery Manager tool. There are really two forms of interaction you can use—RMAN command line mode, or Backup Manager from within the Storage Manager tool. To use Backup Manager, you must enter the tool using the Management Server console.

Recovery Manager keeps track of backups either through a Recovery Catalog or by placing the required information into the control file for the database being backed up. Recovery Manager adds new backup capabilities that are unavailable in the other Oracle backup utilities. Recovery Manager replaces the Enterprise Backup Utility introduced with later versions of Oracle7.

Recovery Manager does not shield you from the backup steps described in this chapter and does not simplify your recovery strategy. In fact, since it adds new features, it may complicate your recovery strategy.

The most significant new capability provided via Recovery Manager is the ability to perform incremental physical backups of datafiles. During a full (called a *level 0*) datafile backup, all of the blocks ever used in the datafile are backed up. During a cumulative (*level 1*) datafile backup, all of the blocks used since the last full datafile backup are backed up. An incremental (*level 2*) datafile backup backs up only those blocks that have changed since the most recent cumulative or full backup. You can define the levels used for incremental backups.

The ability to perform incremental and cumulative backups of datafiles may greatly improve the performance of backups. The greatest performance improvements will be realized by very large databases in which only a small subset of a large tablespace changes. Using the traditional backup methods, you would need to back up all of the datafiles in the tablespace. Using Recovery Manager, you only back up the blocks that have changed since the last backup.

Using Recovery Manager, however, does not diminish backup planning issues. For example, what type of datafile backup will you use? What are the implications for your recovery procedures? What tapes and backup media will you need to have available to perform a recovery? Will you use a recovery catalog or have the cataloging be placed in your control file? You should only use backup procedures that fit your specific database backup performance and capability requirements.

During database recovery using Recovery Manager, you need to know which files are current, which are restored, and the backup method you plan to use. In its present form, Recovery Manager does not shield you from the commands needed to recover the database. Also, Recovery Manager stores its catalog of information in an Oracle database—and you need to back up *that* database or else you may lose your entire backup and recovery catalog of information.

Recovery Manager is only used by DBAs, who need to make the decisions regarding the Recovery Manager architecture for your environment (for example, deciding on the location of the recovery catalog). You should work with your DBA to understand the recovery options in use and their implications for database availability and recovery time.

Performing a Backup with OEM

To perform any level backup using the OEM tool, connect to the OEM console and right-click the appropriate database to bring up the database options. From the database options, select the Backup option from the Backup Manager menu. The Backup Wizard will activate, and you will be shown an Introduction screen.

The Strategy Choice screen (see Figure 38-1), presented after you click the Next button, gives the option of using a predefined backup strategy or customizing your own strategy. The predefined strategy will be displayed here.

Figure 38-2 displays the Backup Frequency options screen, with three choices:

- A Decision Support System (DSS) with a backup frequency of once a week

- A moderately updated system (OLTP) that is not very large, with a backup frequency of every day

- A frequently updated, medium to large database with a backup frequency of full backups weekly and incremental backups nightly

FIGURE 38-1. *Backup Strategy Choice screen*

The default option is a DSS system backed up once a week on Sunday. Once you have selected a strategy, you will be prompted for the time to execute the backup, and the databases to back up. To perform an immediate backup, you can choose the Customize option shown in Figure 38-1.

Where to Go from Here

In this chapter, you've seen a high-level overview of the topics that production DBAs deal with every day. In addition to the topics discussed here, DBAs monitor databases, tune databases, install software, maintain database connectivity, and many other tasks. If you are interested in learning more about those tasks,

FIGURE 38-2. *Backup Frequency options screen*

see your Oracle documentation set or the *Oracle8i DBA Handbook* (Oracle Press, 1999). The more developers understand about database administration, the more likely they are to build applications that take advantage of the database's inherent capabilities.

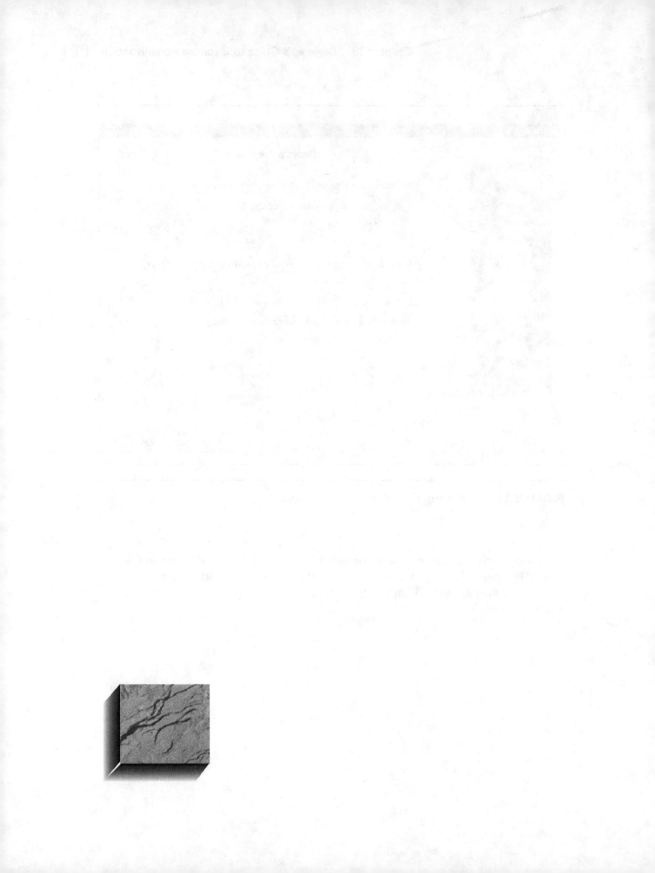

PART
VII

Designing for
Performance

CHAPTER 39

Good Design Has a Human Touch

hapter 2 discussed the need to build applications that are understandable and accommodating to users, and made several recommendations on how to approach this task successfully. If it's been some time since you read Chapter 2, review it now before moving on, because many of the concepts introduced there will be built upon here.

This chapter looks at a method of approaching a development project that takes into account the real business tasks your end users have to accomplish. This distinguishes it from the more common data orientation of many developers and development methodologies. Data normalization and CASE (Computer Aided Software Engineering) technologies have become so much the center of attention with relational application development that a focus on the data and the issues of referential integrity, keys, normalization, and table diagrams has become almost an obsession. They are so often confused with design—and even believed to *be* design—that the reminder that they are analysis is often met with surprise.

Normalization is analysis, not design. And it is only a part of the analysis necessary to understand a business and build a useful application. The goal of application development, after all, is to help the business run more successfully. This is accomplished by improving the speed and efficiency with which business tasks are done, and also by making the environment in which people work as meaningful and supportive as possible. Give people control over their information, and intuitive, straightforward access to it, and they will respond gratefully and productively. Remove the control to a remote group, cloud the information in codes and user-hostile interfaces, and they will be unhappy and unproductive. It doesn't take a genius to figure this out.

The methods outlined in this chapter are not intended to be a rigorous elucidation of the process, and the tools you use and are familiar with for data structures or flows are probably sufficient for the task. The purpose here is to disclose an approach that is effective in creating responsive, appropriate, and accommodating applications.

Understanding the Application Tasks

One of the often-neglected steps in building software is really understanding the end user's job—the tasks that computer automation is intended to support. Occasionally, this is because the application itself is quite specialized; more often, it is because the approach to design tends to be data-oriented. Frequently, these are the major questions asked in the analysis:

- What data should be captured?

- How should the data be processed?

- How should the data be reported?

These questions expand into a series of subquestions, and include issues such as input forms, codes, screen layouts, computations, postings, corrections, audit trails, retention, storage volumes, processing cycles, report formatting, distribution, and maintenance. These are all vitally important areas. One difficulty, however, is that they all focus solely on data.

People *use* data, but they do tasks. One might argue that while this may be true of professional workers, key-entry clerks really only transfer data from an input form to a keyboard; their tasks are very data-oriented. This is a fair portrayal of these jobs today. But is this a consequence of the real job that needs to get done, or is it a symptom of the design of the computer application? Using humans as input devices, particularly for data that is voluminous, consistent in format (as on forms), and in a limited range of variability, is an expensive and antiquated, not to mention dehumanizing, method of capturing data. Like the use of codes to accommodate machine limitations, it's an idea whose time has passed.

This may sound like so much philosophy, but it has practical import in the way application design is done. People *use* data, but they do tasks. And they don't do tasks through to completion one at a time. They do several tasks that are subsets of or in intersection with each other, and they do them all at once, in parallel.

When designers allow this idea to direct the analysis and creation of an application, rather than focusing on the data orientation that has been historically dominant, the very nature of the effort changes significantly. Why have windowing environments been so successful? Because they allow a user to jump quickly between small tasks, keeping them all active without having to shut down and exit one in order to begin another. The windowing environment comes closer to mapping the way people really think and work than the old "one thing at a time" approach ever did. This lesson should not be lost. It should be built upon.

Understanding the application tasks means going far beyond identifying the data elements, normalizing them, and creating screens, processing programs, and reports. It means really understanding what the users do and what their tasks are, and designing the application to be responsive to those tasks, not just to capture the data associated with them. In fact, when the orientation is toward the data, the resulting design will inevitably *distort* the users' tasks rather than support them.

How do you design an application that is responsive to tasks rather than data? The biggest hurdle is simply understanding that focusing on tasks is necessary. This allows you to approach the analysis of the business from a fresh perspective.

The first step in the analysis process is to understand the tasks. For which tasks do the members of this group really need to use computers? What is the real service or product produced? This seems like a fundamental and even simplistic first question, but you'll find that a surprising number of businesspeople are quite unclear about the answer. An amazing number of businesses, from healthcare to banking, from shipping to manufacturing, used to think they were in the data processing business. After all, they input data, process it, and report it, don't they? This delusion is yet another symptom of the data orientation our systems designs have had that has led dozens of companies to attempt to market their imagined "real" product, data processing, with disastrous consequences for most of them.

Hence the importance of learning about a business application: you have to keep an open mind, and may often have to challenge pet notions about what the business is in order to learn what it really is. This is a healthy, if sometimes difficult, process.

And, just as it is essential that businesspeople become literate users of SQL and understand the basics of the relational model, so it is important that application designers really understand the service or product being delivered, and the tasks *necessary* to make that happen. A project team that includes end users who have been introduced to the essentials of SQL and the relational approach, such as by reading this book, and designers who are sensitive to end users' needs and understand the value of a task-oriented, English-based (or native language) application environment, will turn out extraordinarily good systems. The members of such a project team check, support, and enhance each other's efforts.

One approach to this process is to develop two converging documents: a task document and a data document. It is in the process of preparing the task document that the deep understanding of the application comes about. The data document will help implement the vision and assure that the details and rules are all accounted for, but the task document defines the vision of what the business is.

Outline of Tasks

The task document is a joint effort of the business users and the application designers. It lists the tasks associated with the business from the top down. It begins with a basic description of the business. This should be a simple declarative sentence of three to ten words, in the active voice, without commas and with a minimum of adjectives:

> We sell insurance.

It should not be:

> Amalgamated Diversified is a leading international supplier of financial resources, training, information processing, transaction capture and distribution, communications, customer support, and industry direction in the field of shared risk funding for health care maintenance, property preservation, and automobile liability.

There is a tremendous temptation to cram every little detail about a business and its dreams about itself into this first sentence. Don't do it. The effort of trimming the descriptive excesses down to a simple sentence wonderfully focuses the mind. If you can't get the business down to ten words, you haven't understood it yet.

But, as an application designer, creating this sentence isn't your task alone; it is a joint effort with the business user, and it initiates the task documentation process. It provides you with the opportunity to begin serious questioning about what the business does and how it does it. This is a valuable process for the business itself, quite independent of the fact that an application is being built. There will be numerous tasks and subtasks, procedures, and rules that you will encounter that will prove to be meaningless or of marginal use. Typically, these are artifacts of either a previous problem, long since solved, or of information or reporting requests from managers long since departed.

Some wags have suggested that the way to deal with too many reports being created, whether manually or by computer, is to simply stop producing them and see if anyone notices. This is a humorous notion, but the seed of truth it contains needs to be a part of the task documentation process. In fact, it proved quite useful in Y2K remediation efforts—many programs and reports didn't have to be fixed, simply because they were no longer used!

Your approach to the joint effort of documenting tasks allows you to ask skeptical questions and look at (and reevaluate the usefulness of) what may be mere artifacts. Be aware, however, that you need to proceed with the frank acknowledgment that you, as a designer, cannot understand the business as thoroughly as the user does. There is an important line between seizing the opportunity of an application development to rationalize what tasks are done and why, and possibly offending the users by presuming to understand the "real" business better than they do.

Ask the user to describe a task in detail and explain to you the reason for each step. If the reason is a weak one, such as "we've always done it this way," or "I think they use this upstairs for something," red flags should go up. Say that you don't understand, and ask again for an explanation. If the response is still unsatisfactory, put the task and your question on a separate list for resolution. Some of these will be answered simply by someone who knows the subject better, others will require talking to senior management, and many tasks will end up eliminated because they are no longer needed. One of the evidences of a good analysis process is the improvement of existing procedures, independent of, and generally long before, the implementation of a new computer application.

General Format of the Task Document

This is the general format for the task document:

- Summary sentence describing the business (three to ten words)

- Summary sentences describing and numbering the major tasks of the business (short sentences, short words)

- Additional levels of task detail, as needed, within each of the major tasks

By all means, follow the summary sentence for every level with a short, descriptive paragraph, if you wish, but don't use this as an excuse to avoid the effort of making the summary sentence clear and crisp. Major tasks are typically numbered 1.0, 2.0, 3.0, and so on, and are sometimes referred to as zero-level tasks. The levels below each of these are numbered using additional dots, as in 3.1 and 3.1.14. Each major task is taken down to the level where it is a collection of *atomic tasks*—tasks for which no subtask is meaningful in itself and that, once started, is either taken to completion or dropped entirely. Atomic tasks are never left half finished.

Writing a check is an atomic task; filling in the dollar amount is not. Answering the telephone as a customer service representative is not an atomic task; answering the phone and fulfilling the customer's request is atomic. Atomic tasks must be meaningful and must complete an action.

The level at which a task is atomic will vary by task. The task represented by 3.1.14 may be atomic yet still have several additional sublevels. The task 3.2 may be atomic, or 3.1.16.4 may be. What is important is not the numbering scheme (which is nothing more than a method for outlining a hierarchy of tasks) but the decomposition to the atomic level. The atomic tasks are the fundamental building blocks of the business. Two tasks can still be atomic if one occasionally depends upon the other, but only if each can and does get completed independently. If two tasks always depend upon each other, they are not atomic. The real atomic task includes them both.

In most businesses, you will quickly discover that many tasks do not fit neatly into just one of the major (zero-level) tasks, but seem to span two or more, and work in a network or "dotted line" fashion. This is nearly always evidence of improper definition of the major tasks or incomplete atomization of the lower tasks. The goal is to turn each task into a conceptual "object," with a well-defined idea of what it does (its goal in life) and what resources (data, computation, thinking, paper, pencil, and so on) it uses to accomplish its goal.

Insights Resulting from the Task Document

Several insights come out of the task document. First, because the task document is task-oriented rather than data-oriented, it is likely to substantially change the way user screens are designed. It will affect what data is captured, how it is presented, how help is implemented, and how users switch from one task to another. The task orientation will help assure that the most common kinds of jumping between tasks will not require inordinate effort from the user.

Second, the categorization of major tasks will change as conflicts are discovered; this will affect how both the designers and the business users understand the business.

Third, even the summary sentence itself will probably change. Rationalizing a business into atomic task "objects" forces a clearing out of artifacts, misconceptions, and unneeded dependencies that have long weighed down the business unnecessarily.

This is not a painless process, but the benefits in terms of the business's self-understanding, the cleanup of procedures, and the automation of the tasks will usually far exceed the emotional costs and time spent. It helps immensely if there is general understanding going into the project that uncomfortable questions will be asked, incorrect assumptions corrected, and step-by-step adjustments made to the task document until it is completed.

Understanding the Data

In conjunction with the decomposition and description of the tasks, the resources required at each step are described in the task document, especially in terms of the data required. This is done on a task-by-task basis, and the data requirements are then included in the data document. This is a conceptually different approach from the classical view of the data. You will not simply take the forms and screens currently used by each task and record the elements they contain. The flaw in this "piece of paper in a cigar box" approach—first described in Chapter 2—lies in our tendency (even though we don't like to admit it) to accept anything printed on paper as necessary or true.

In looking at each task, you should determine what data is necessary to do the task, rather than what data elements are on the form you use to do the task. By requiring that the definition of the data needed come from the task rather than from any existing forms or screens, you force an examination of the true purpose of the task and the real data requirements. If the person doing the task doesn't know the use to which data is put, the element goes on the list for resolution. An amazing amount of garbage is eliminated by this process.

Once the current data elements have been identified, they must be carefully scrutinized. Numeric and letter codes are always suspect. They disguise real information behind counterintuitive, meaningless symbols. There are times and tasks for which codes are handy, easily remembered, or made necessary by sheer volume. But, in your final design, these cases should be rare and obvious. If they are not, you've lost your way.

In the scrutiny of existing data elements, codes should be set aside for special attention. In each case, ask yourself whether the element should be a code. Its continued use as a code should be viewed suspiciously. There must be good arguments and compelling reasons for perpetuating the disguise. The process for converting codes back into English is fairly simple, but is a joint effort. The codes are first listed, by data element, along with their meanings. These are then examined by users and designers, and short English versions of the meanings are proposed, discussed, and tentatively approved.

In this same discussion, designers and end users should decide on names for the data elements. These will become column names in the database, and will be regularly used in English queries, so the names should be descriptive (avoiding abbreviations, other than those common to the business) and singular (more on this in Chapter 41). Because of the intimate relationship between the column name and the data it contains, the two should be specified simultaneously. A thoughtful choice of a column name will vastly simplify determining its new English contents.

Data elements that are not codes also must be rigorously examined. By this point, you have good reason to believe that all of the data elements you've identified are necessary to the business tasks, but they are not necessarily well-organized. What appears to be one data element in the existing task may in fact be several elements mixed together that require separation. Names, addresses, and phone numbers are very common examples of this, but every application has a wealth of others.

First and last names were mixed together, for example, in Talbot's ledger, and in the table built to store his data. The Name column held both first and last names, even though the tables were in Third Normal Form. This would be an extremely burdensome way to actually implement an application, in spite of the fact that the normalization rules were technically met. To make the application practical and prepare it for English queries, the Name column needs to be decomposed into at least two new columns, LastName and FirstName. This same categorization process is regularly needed in rationalizing other data elements, and is often quite independent of normalization.

The degree of decomposition depends on how the particular data elements are likely to be used. It is possible to go much too far and decompose categories that, though made up of separable pieces, provide no additional value in their new state. Decomposition is application-dependent on an element-by-element basis. Once done, these new elements, which will become columns, need to be thoughtfully named, and the data they will contain needs to be scrutinized. Text data that will fall into a definable number of values should be reviewed for naming. These column names and values, like those of the codes, are tentative.

The Atomic Data Models

Now the process of normalization begins, and with it the drawing of the atomic data models. There are many good texts on the subject and a wide variety of analysis and design tools that can speed the process, so this book doesn't suggest any particular method, since recommending one method may hinder rather than help. The results will look something like Figure 39-1.

A drawing like this should be developed for each atomic transaction, and should be labeled with the task number to which it applies. Included in the drawing are table names, primary and foreign keys, and major columns. Each normalized relationship (the connecting lines) should have a descriptive name, and estimated

FIGURE 39-1. *A data model for the task of adding a new employee*

row counts and transaction rates should appear with each table. Accompanying each drawing is an additional sheet with all of the columns and datatypes, their ranges of value, and the tentative names for the tables, columns, and named values in the columns.

The Atomic Business Model

This data document is now combined with the task document. The combined document is a business model. It's reviewed jointly by the application designers and end users for accuracy and completeness.

The Business Model

At this point, both the application designers and the end users should possess a clear vision of the business, its tasks, and its data. Once corrected and approved, the process of synthesizing the tasks and data models into an overall business model begins. This part of the process sorts common data elements between tasks, completes final, large-scale normalization, and resolves consistent, definitive names for all of the parts.

This can be quite a large drawing for major applications, with supporting documentation that includes the tasks, the data models (with corrected element names, based on the full model), and a list of each of the full-scale tables and their column names, datatypes, and contents. A final check of the effort is made by tracing the data access paths of each transaction in the full business model to determine that all the data the transaction requires is available for selection or insertion, and that no tasks insert data with elements missing that are essential to the model's referential integrity.

With the exception of the effort spent to properly name the various tables, columns, and common values, virtually everything to this point has been analysis, not design. The aim has been to promote understanding of the business and its components.

Data Entry

Screen design does not proceed from the business model. It is not focused on tables, but rather on tasks, so screens are created that support the task orientation and the need to jump between subtasks when necessary. In practical terms, this will often map readily to a primary table used by the task, and to other tables that can be queried for values or updated as the primary table is accessed.

But there will also be occasions where there simply is no main table, but instead a variety of related tables, all of which will supply or receive data to support the task. These screens will look and act quite differently from the typical table-oriented screens developed in many applications, but they will significantly amplify the effectiveness of their users and their contribution to the business. And that's the whole purpose of this approach.

The interaction between the user and the machine is critical; the input and query screens should consistently be task-oriented and descriptive, in English. The use of icons and graphical interfaces play an important role as well. Screens must reflect the way work is actually done, and be built to respond in the language in which business is conducted.

Query and Reporting

If anything sets apart the relational approach, and SQL, from more traditional application environments, it is the ability for end users to easily learn and execute ad hoc queries. These are those reports and one-time queries that are outside of the basic set usually developed and delivered along with the application code.

With SQLPLUS (and other reporting tools), end users are given unprecedented control over their own data. Both the users and developers benefit from this ability: the users, because they can build reports, analyze information, modify their queries, and reexecute them all in a matter of minutes, and the developers, because they are relieved of the undesirable requirement of creating new reports.

Users are granted the power to look into their data, analyze it, and respond with a speed and thoroughness unimaginable just a few years ago. This leap in productivity is greatly extended if the tables, columns, and data values are carefully crafted in English; it is greatly foreshortened if bad naming conventions and meaningless codes and abbreviations are permitted to infect the design. The time spent in the design process to name the objects consistently and descriptively will pay off quickly for the users, and therefore for the business.

Some people, typically those who have not built major relational applications, fear that turning query facilities over to end users will cripple the machine on which the facilities are used. The fear is that users will write inefficient queries that will consume overwhelming numbers of CPU cycles, slowing the machine and every other user. Experience shows that this generally is not true. Users quickly learn which kinds of queries run fast, and which do not. Further, most business intelligence and reporting tools available today can estimate the amount of time a query will take, and restrict access—by user, time of day, or both—to queries that would consume a disproportionate amount of resources. In practice, the demands users make on a machine only occasionally get out of hand, but the benefits they derive far exceed the cost of the processing. Remember the machine cost versus labor cost discussion in Chapter 2. Virtually any time you can move effort from a person to a machine, you save money.

Review

Design includes issues other than naming conventions, data entry, and reporting. Depending upon the size and nature of the application, issues of transaction volume, performance, and ease of querying often force a violation of Third Normal Form. This is not an irredeemable sin, but it does require putting certain controls in place to assure the concurrence and integrity of the data. These issues will be addressed in Chapter 40.

Aside from these concerns, the real goal of design is to clarify and satisfy the needs of the business and business users. If there is a bias, it must always be toward making the application easier to understand and use, particularly at the expense of CPU or disk, but less so if the cost is an internal complexity so great that maintenance and change become difficult and slow.

The purpose of this chapter has not been to direct you to a particular set of tools or diagramming techniques, but rather to explain the need to deeply understand the business, the data, and the needs of users when you are designing and building an effective relational application. Data can be mapped trivially into a relational database. But people do not organize their tasks based on the Third Normal Form of their data. A design that properly supports the way a person works must go beyond a view of the data; significant thought and development are required to implement the design successfully in any environment.

CHAPTER 40

Performance and Design

o major application will run in Third Normal Form.

This is probably as heretical a statement as can be made in the face of modern relational theology, but it needs to be said. Perhaps as CPUs get faster and parallel processing architecture is better exploited, this will no longer be true; more likely, the size of major applications will also increase. Demand for information and analysis will probably continue to outpace the ability of machines to process information in a fully normalized fashion.

Now, before cries for another Inquisition begin, this heresy needs to be explained. The issue of normalization has several components. This chapter does not challenge either the relational model, which is both simple and elegant, or the process of normalization, which is an excellent and rational method of analyzing data and its fundamental relationships. It does challenge these fallacies:

- Normalization completely rationalizes data.

- Normalization accurately maps how humans work with data.

- Normalized data is the best representation of data.

- Data stored nonredundantly will be accessed faster than data stored many times.

- Normalized tables are the best way to store data.

- Referential integrity requires fully normalized tables.

The use of theological language here is intentional. Some people present relational techniques as if they were revealed truth. Normalization, however, is simply a method used to analyze elements of data and their relationships, and the relational model is the theoretical superstructure that supports the process. Together, these provide a way of viewing the world of data.

But they are not the only correct or useful ways to view the data. In fact, in a complex set of relationships, even Third Normal Form becomes insufficient rather quickly. Higher forms have been conceived to cope with these more difficult relations, although they are not often used outside of academia. Theorists readily acknowledge that these forms also fail to completely model reality (according to the number theorist Gödel, any model must remain incomplete).

Oracle is based on a practical approach. It acknowledges the genius of the relational model, but it also provides, unapologetically, tools that permit developers to use their brains and make their own decisions about how to extend the model—by using object-oriented modeling techniques—and where to use normalization, referential integrity, procedural language access, nonset-oriented processing, and other heretical techniques. In the real world, with real data, real users, and real demands for performance and ease of use, this flexibility is fundamental to success. Normalization is analysis, not design. Design encompasses issues, particularly related to performance, ease of use, maintenance, and straightforward completion of business tasks, that are unaccounted for in simple normalization.

Denormalization and Data Integrity

When analyzing the data of a business, normalizing the data to at least Third Normal Form assures that each nonkey column in each table is dependent only on the whole primary key of the table. If the data relationships are complex enough, normalizing to a higher form does a fine, if not complete, job of giving you a deep understanding of the data and of relations between the various elements that must be protected and sustained as the application and database are built.

For a major application, however, or even a simple application where tasks do not readily map to fully normalized tables, once the analysis is complete, the design process may need to denormalize some of the tables in order to build an application that is responsive, maps to the user's tasks, and will actually complete its processing in the time windows available. There are a couple of useful approaches to this task.

However, any recommendations aimed at producing a better response will have to differ from application to application, and will also differ over time as query optimization methods improve and as more and more CPU power becomes available to the computer system and network. Benchmarking your application on your system is the only way to truly optimize your database.

Meaningful Keys

The tables in Chapter 2 were put into Third Normal Form using one of the techniques you'll learn here, although it was not mentioned at the time. Once normalized, the tables and columns looked like this first version:

```
WORKER Table     WORKERSKILL Table    SKILL Table      LODGING Table
------------     ------------------   -----------      -------------
Name             Name                 Skill            Lodging
Age              Skill                Description      LongName
Lodging          Ability                               Manager
                                                       Address
```

In a more typical design, particularly for a large application with many tables, these would have looked more like the following version:

WORKER Table	WORKERSKILL Table	SKILL Table	LODGING Table
WorkerID	WorkerID	SkillID	LodgingID
Name	SkillID	Skill	ShortName
Age	Ability	Description	LongName
LodgingID			Manager
			Address

The shift to WorkerID instead of Name is probably unavoidable. Too many of us have the same names for Name to be a unique primary key. However, the same is not necessarily true of the other keys. In this kind of design, all of the ID columns are usually sequentially assigned, unique, and meaningless numbers. Their sole function is to link one table to another. LodgingID, a number, is a foreign key in the WORKER table that points to just one row of the LODGING table. SkillID is a foreign key in the WORKERSKILL table that points to one row in the SKILL table.

To learn anything at all about a worker's skills and lodging, all four of these tables must be combined in a single join. Yet, the task analysis shows that many of the most common queries seek the name of a worker's Skill and the name of his or her lodging. The additional detailed description of the Skill and the lodging Address and Manager are called for only infrequently. By using the first version of the table design, where the Skill and Lodging are meaningful keys—where they actually contain information, not just an assigned number—only the first two tables need to be joined for the most frequent queries, as in the following:

The WORKER Table

NAME	AGE	LODGING
Adah Talbot	23	Papa King
Bart Sarjeant	22	Cranmer
Dick Jones	18	Rose Hill
Elbert Talbot	43	Weitbrocht
Helen Brandt	15	
Jed Hopkins	33	Matts
John Pearson	27	Rose Hill
Victoria Lynn	32	Mullers
Wilfred Lowell	67	

The WORKER SKILL Table

NAME	SKILL	ABILITY
Adah Talbot	Work	Good
Dick Jones	Smithy	Excellent
Elbert Talbot	Discus	Slow
Helen Brandt	Combine Driver	Very Fast

```
John Pearson           Combine Driver
John Pearson           Woodcutter    Good
John Pearson           Smithy        Average
Victoria Lynn          Smithy        Precise
Wilfred Lowell         Work          Average
Wilfred Lowell         Discus        Average
```

instead of this:

```
            The WORKER Table

NAME                          AGE LODGINGID
------------------------- ----- ---------

Adah Talbot                    23        4
Bart Sarjeant                  22        1
Dick Jones                     18        5
Elbert Talbot                  43        6
Helen Brandt                   15
Jed Hopkins                    33        2
John Pearson                   27        5
Victoria Lynn                  32        3
Wilfred Lowell                 67


            The WORKERSKILL Table

NAME                      SKILLID ABILITY
------------------------- ------- ---------

Adah Talbot                     6 Good
Dick Jones                      4 Excellent
Elbert Talbot                   2 Slow
Helen Brandt                    1 Very Fast
John Pearson                    1
John Pearson                    5 Good
John Pearson                    4 Average
Victoria Lynn                   4 Precise
Wilfred Lowell                  6 Average
Wilfred Lowell                  2 Average
```

Several points need to be made here.

First, meaningful primary keys must, by definition, be unique; they must provide the same relational integrity that a simple number key does.

Second, meaningful values for the primary keys should be chosen with care: they may be more than one word long and may contain spaces, as long as they are short, descriptive, memorable, in English, and avoid codes (other than those that are widely known and common to the business). This will make using them in queries simpler and will reduce errors when they are used in data entry.

Third, the choice of which keys to make meaningful comes from the task analysis; the need for it is virtually indiscernible from the data normalization process, since normalization can proceed with meaningless keys (as in the second example) without any awareness of their impact on tasks. Anyone with practical experience in a major application knows that table joins involving three or more tables, even if only two of them are large, consume a substantial number of CPU cycles. Yet, many of these multitable joins can be avoided if a task analysis has resulted in an understanding of what information will be queried often. This may imply that good performance is the criterion by which good design is measured; rather, it is only one of several criteria, including simplicity, understandability, maintainability, and testability. The use of meaningful keys will contribute to these other goals as well.

Fourth, although the simplicity of a query can be improved with views, by making the four tables appear as one to the user, this method will not solve the performance problem (if there is one). In fact, it will worsen it by forcing, in this case, a four-way join when information from only one or two of the tables may be needed.

Fifth, some purists object to the use of meaningful keys, on the grounds that they might introduce **update** and **delete** anomalies. The question might be that, since primary keys also appear in other tables as foreign keys, what happens if the key value has to change? However, your task analysis will reveal whether this is likely to happen. If so, an artificial key can be used; but if not, the natural key solution is more practical.

Sixth, if your query is just for a column that is indexed, Oracle can retrieve the data from the index alone without ever going to the underlying table, thereby speeding retrieval. With a meaningful key, this data is useful. With a meaningless key, it is not.

In building a major relational application, the use of meaningful keys can simplify relationships between tables and make the application faster and more intuitive. Meaningful keys require additional analysis and design work in creating the application, but quickly pay back the effort expended. However, if the application is small and the computer resources are more than sufficient, the same simplicity and intuitiveness can be delivered through the use of views that hide the table joins from the end user.

Real Denormalization

The use of meaningful keys may not be enough. **select**s, **insert**s, **update**s, **delete**s, and online and batch programs may all still run too slowly on a major application—usually because too many tables have been joined. Again, the task analysis will show the areas where the information requested needs to be retrieved from too many tables at once.

One solution to this is to intentionally violate Third Normal Form in the table design by pushing data redundantly into a table where it is not wholly dependent on the primary key. This should not be done lightly, because the cost of denormalization is increased difficulty in maintaining the code. And the arguments given in Chapter 2 still apply. It is often cheaper to buy more memory and CPU power than to pay for the additional programming and maintenance costs. Assuming, however, that it is clear that performance must be attacked in some other way, denormalization is an effective means.

For example, suppose that whenever Talbot needs a profile of a worker, he always also wants the name of the manager of the worker's lodging. This column is therefore added to the WORKER table itself:

```
WORKER Table      WORKER SKILL Table   SKILL Table     LODGING Table
------------      ------------------   -----------     -------------
Name              Name                 Skill           Lodging
Age               Skill                Description     LongName
Lodging           Ability                              Manager
Manager                                                Address
```

The data in the WORKER table now contains redundancy. For every worker living in Cranmer, for instance, the row now contains this information in addition to Name and Age:

```
LODGING      MANAGER
----------   -------------
Cranmer      Thom Cranmer
```

If 50 of Talbot's workers live at Cranmer, "Thom Cranmer" appears in the WORKER table 50 times. However, if the application is designed carefully, Third Normal Form is still maintained logically, even though it is violated in the physical design of the tables. This is accomplished by continuing to maintain a LODGING table and enforcing two rules:

- Whenever a new worker is added to the WORKER table, the data for the Manager column must come from the LODGING table only. It may not be keyed in independently. If a new worker lives in quarters not yet in the LODGING table, those quarters must be added to the LODGING table first, before the worker can be added to the WORKER table.

- Whenever a change is made to the LODGING table, such as the change of a manager at Cranmer, every row in the WORKER table that contains Cranmer must immediately be updated. To put it in task terminology, the updates of the LODGING table and the updates of the related columns and rows in the WORKER table are together an atomic task. Both must be completed and committed at the same time. This is a tradeoff between performance and transaction complexity.

These rules historically have been implemented in the application. You also can design a data dictionary that supports either *assertion*, where an atomic task such as this is stored and executed automatically when a change is made to the LODGING table, or *procedural logic*, which is executed from the dictionary if certain conditions are met. PL/SQL and triggers implement these rules in Oracle.

Rows, Columns, and Volume

One might sensibly ask what this denormalization will accomplish. Won't queries actually run slower with all that redundant data in the WORKER table? The answer is no. They will almost always run substantially faster. With only one or a few columns of redundant data, odds are excellent that queries will run much faster, since the table join is not required. Queries will run faster because when a row is fetched from a related table (such as LODGING), all the columns are brought back to the CPU's memory, and those columns not named in the **select** are then discarded before the join is made. If only a portion of the LODGING table's data is kept in the WORKER table, a substantially smaller volume of data is fetched and processed by the CPU for a **select**. Further, if the same data is sought by multiple queries, Oracle's buffer caching will make this even faster. Multiple tables and joins are never cached. Updates, however, particularly to the LODGING table, will be slower, because the rows in the WORKER table need to be updated as well.

What about the case when a majority, or even all, of a related table's data is stored in a table—such as putting Lodging, LongName, Manager, and Address all within the WORKER table (still using the LODGING table for data integrity, of course)? What are the competing claims?

A query using a table join where only the foreign key (to the LODGING table) is kept in the WORKER table and the LODGING data is kept in the LODGING table will move less data, overall, to the CPU from the tables stored on disk. The data in the Cranmer LODGING row, for instance, will only be retrieved once and then joined to each related row of the WORKER table in the CPU's memory. This moves less data than having all of the same Cranmer data retrieved over and over again for every worker who lives at Cranmer, if all of the LODGING columns are replicated in the WORKER table.

Substantially less data is being moved from the disk, so will the table join, in this case, be faster? Surprisingly, it may not be.

Memory Binding

Relational database systems are usually CPU-memory-bound—that is, the system resource that most limits their performance is usually CPU memory, not disk access speed or disk I/O rate for the initial retrieval. This may seem counterintuitive, and many a designer (including this author) has spent hours carefully organizing tables on disk, avoiding discontinuity, minimizing head movement, and more, only to gain marginal increases in throughput. A highly tuned database system, where all resources have been balanced, tested, and balanced again, may run into binding other than CPU memory. But CPU memory is usually the first place a relational system becomes bound. This binding is memory size rather than CPU speed.

When memory size is too small, paging occurs, and the operation of storing, sorting, and joining tables together suddenly becomes not a memory task, but is dropped back onto the disk I/O, which is millions of times slower than memory. The effect is like slamming the brakes on the CPU. If additional memory can be added to the machine (and taken advantage of by increasing array sizes or the System Global Area, SGA), it is usually worth the expense. Even so, querying a single table with redundant data will often still be faster than a join.

In any event, Oracle provides monitoring facilities that can be used by a DBA to determine where the real bottlenecks lie. Common queries can be tested readily, perhaps with several alternative physical table designs, using the **set timing on** command in SQLPLUS or other CPU and disk monitoring tools provided with the operating system. Benchmark alternatives when performance becomes an issue. What intuitively seems likely to be faster will often not be.

The Kitchen Junk Drawer

Another practical design technique, one that will often send the same purists mentioned earlier screaming into the woods, is the use of a *common codes table*. This is the design equivalent of that one drawer in every kitchen that collects all of the implements, string, tools, and assorted pieces of junk that don't really fit anywhere else.

Any real application has bits of information and (when unavoidable) codes that occur in extremely small volume, often only a single instance. But there may be dozens of such instances, all unrelated. Theoretically, these do not all belong in the same place. They should each have separate tables all their own. Practically, this would be a pain to manage. The solution is the construction of a relational kitchen junk drawer.

The junk drawer may contain several columns, each of which is a primary key for just one of the rows and **NULL** for all the others. It may contain columns with names so general no one could guess what they mean (code, description), and that contain vastly different kinds of data depending upon the row being fetched.

These tables can be useful and effective, provided you heed a few warnings. First, these tables usually should not be visible to users. They may be used in one or more views, but an end user shouldn't know it. Second, they usually contain information used internally, perhaps to manage a process or to supply a piece of common information (your own company's address, for instance). Third, their integrity must be assured by carefully designed screens and programs, which only a limited, qualified group of systems people can access. If some of the information in them needs to be accessible to users, access should be strictly governed, and should probably be through a view that hides the true form of the table.

Should You Do Any of This?

These techniques, and others like them, are sometimes referred to as "violating normal form," the implication being that you've done something illogical or wrong. You've done nothing of the sort. In fact, in most of the examples here, normal form was maintained logically, if not in the physical table design. The danger is in violating the integrity of the data, in particular its referential integrity: this is the glue that connects related data together and keeps it consistent. Fail to maintain it and you lose information, nearly always irretrievably. This should be of genuine concern. How you design your tables, on the other hand, is a case-by-case issue: What works best for this user and this application?

The Computation Table

A "table lookup"—solving computations that contain well-defined parts by looking up the answer in a table rather than recomputing it each time—is a technique older than data processing. This use is obvious for something like a table of prime numbers, but it can prove valuable in other areas as well.

Many financial computations, for example, use two variables, say x and y, and include fractional exponents and quite extensive multiplication and division; the x variable part of each computation is involved only in one of the four basic arithmetic functions (such as multiplication).

These equations can be calculated once, with the variable x set to 1, for the whole range of possible values of y. The result for a given x and y is then found by looking up the y (which is indexed), retrieving the computed and stored result, and multiplying it by actual x. As with table denormalization, benchmarking is the best way to determine for which calculations this is most productive.

Review

Probably the most disheartening awareness stemming from this discussion of denormalization, referential integrity, memory binding, benchmarking, and the like is that the design process extends well beyond the first vision produced by the task and data analysis efforts. Particularly with major applications, the portion of design time spent in rearranging the tables, benchmarking, and rearranging yet again can exceed that of the initial design work by a considerable amount. This is not mere adjustment or afterthought. You need to expect it, budget for it, and plan to do it rigorously. It is as integral to the design process as determining primary keys. The friendliest application in the world will lose its popularity rapidly if it moves too slowly.

To sensibly build an application, you must strike a balance among three primary factors: ease of use, performance, and maintainability. In a perfect world, these would all be maximized. But in a world where projects have limited development timeframes, machines have limited power, and ease of use usually means additional program complexity, not favoring one factor at the expense of others is a challenge. The real message of this chapter is to convey how serious a process-focused development is and how important it is to be attentive to the competing forces at work.

CHAPTER

41

The Ten Commandments of Humane Design

his chapter reviews some of the issues in database application design a bit more thoroughly, proposes strategies to implement the ideas presented, presents a few new ideas for consideration by the relational community, and ends with "The Ten Commandments of Humane Design," which might more accurately be called the "Ten Suggestions." They are intended to help assure productive and accommodating applications, and avoid the deep chasms some designers (the authors included) have fallen into.

Toward Object Name Normalization

By now, you've read quite a lot of commentary on naming conventions, first in Chapter 2, and then in Chapters 39 and 40. These ideas have been presented rather informally; the basic approach is to choose meaningful, memorable, and descriptive English (or the country's official language, if not English) names, avoiding abbreviations and codes, and using underlines either consistently or not at all. In a large application, table, column, and data names will often be multiword, as in the case of ReversedSuspenseAccount or Last_GL_Close_Date. The goal of thoughtful naming methods is ease of use: the names must be easily remembered and must follow rules that are easily explained and applied. In the pages ahead, a somewhat more rigorous approach to naming is presented, with the ultimate goal of developing a formal process of object name normalization.

Level-Name Integrity

In a relational database system, the hierarchy of objects ranges from the database, to the table owners, to the tables, to the columns, to the data values (see Figure 41-1).

OWNER						
Table1			Table2			
Column 1	Column2		Column 1	Column2		
Value1	Value1		Value1	Value1		
Value2	Value2		Value2	Value2		
Value3	Value3		Value3	Value3		
.	.		.	.		
.	.		.	.		
.	.		.	.		

FIGURE 41-1.   *Database hierarchy*

In very large systems, there may even be multiple databases, and these may be distributed within locations. For the sake of brevity, the higher levels will be ignored for now, but what is said will apply to them as well.

Each level in this hierarchy is defined within the level above it, and each level should be given names appropriate to its own level and should not incorporate names from outside its own level. For example, consider the objects in Figure 41-2.

The full name of a column shows its heritage: George.WORKER.Name. Each level of the hierarchy is separated from those above or below it by a single dot or period. Names must be unique within their own parents: WORKER cannot have two columns called Name. The owner George cannot have two tables named WORKER. If Name is a primary key, it cannot have two data values of Adah Talbot. This is perfectly sensible and logical.

There is no requirement that each of George's tables have a name that is unique throughout the entire database. Other owners may have WORKER tables as well. Even if George is granted access to them, there is no confusion, because he can identify each table uniquely by prefixing its owner's name to the table name, as in Dietrich.WORKER. If George combines a WORKER table of his own with one of Dietrich's, then the Name column in the **select** clause must contain its full identification; that is, Dietrich.WORKER.Name.

It would not be logically consistent to incorporate George's owner name into the name of each of his tables, as in GEOWORKER, GEOWORKERSKILL, and so on. This confuses and complicates the table name by placing part of its parent's name in its own, in effect a violation of *level-name integrity*.

Nevertheless, many designers have adopted the habit of creating column names that attempt to be unique across all tables, and they do this by inserting a part of the table name into each column name, as in WK_Name, WK_Age, WS_Name, and WS_Skill. In some cases, this is simply a bad habit acquired from experience with

FIGURE 41-2. *Database example*

DBMS technologies of the 1970s, where all field names in the entire database had to be unique. In other cases, this is done apparently in an attempt to eliminate the occasional need for table names in **select** and **where** clauses, producing listings like this:

```
select WK_Name, WK_Age, WS_Skill
   from WORKER, WORKERSKILL
 where WK_Name = WS_Name;
```

instead of this:

```
select WORKER.Name, Age, Skill
   from WORKER, WORKERSKILL
 where WORKER.Name = WORKERSKILL.Name;
```

This approach has enormous problems. The first example doesn't accomplish very much. The prefixes require extra keying, confuse the meaning of the columns, and don't readily disclose which tables they refer to. Some designers even use just the first letter of a table as a prefix. For them, the problem of abbreviation gets severe almost immediately, and is worse if several tables all start with the same letter or letters. In the previous example, in a less limited technique, WK and WS were taken as abbreviations for the two tables, but the abbreviation method is not defined anywhere, and the portion of the column name that defines what the column means is pushed off to the right.

One alternative sometimes used is to prefix only those column names that appear in more than one table with a table abbreviation:

```
select WK_Name, Age, Skill
   from WORKER, WORKERSKILL
 where WK_Name = WS_Name;
```

The difficulty here is obvious as well. How does a user remember which columns have prefixes and which don't? What happens to a column without a prefix if a column by the same name is later added to another table? Does it get renamed? If so, what happens to all the reports and views that rely upon it? If its name is left the same, but the new column gets a prefix, how will users remember which is prefixed and which is not?

The claim is sometimes made that this approach allows more brevity in a SQL statement, because table names don't have to be keyed in to the **select** or **where** clauses. Yet the same degree of brevity can be accomplished by using table aliases, as shown in the following:

```
select A.Name, Age, Skill
   from WORKER A, WORKERSKILL B
 where A.Name = B.Name;
```

This method has the added benefit of including the abbreviation chosen for each table right in front of your eyes, in the **from** clause. The use of table aliases has the added benefit of removing any ambiguity regarding the columns being selected. For abstract datatype columns, you must use table aliases (correlation variables) to access the column attributes.

Brevity should never be favored over clarity. Including pieces of table names in column names is a bad technique, because it violates the logical idea of levels, and the level-name integrity that this requires. It is also confusing, requiring users to look up column names virtually every time they want to write a query.

Object names must be unique within their parent, but no incorporation of names from outside an object's own level should be permitted.

The introduction of abstract datatypes in Oracle8 strengthened your ability to create consistent names for attributes. If you create a datatype called ADDRESS_TY, it will have the same attributes each time it is used. Each of the attributes will have a consistent name, datatype, and length, making their implementation more consistent across the enterprise. However, using abstract datatypes in this manner requires that you do both of the following:

- Properly define the datatypes at the start so that you can avoid the need to modify the datatype later

- Support the syntax requirements of abstract datatypes (see Chapter 4 for details)

Foreign Keys

The one area of difficulty with using brief column names is the occasional appearance of a foreign key in a table in which another column has the same name that the foreign key column has in its home table. One possible long-term solution is to allow the use of the full foreign key name, including the table name of its home table, as a column name in the local table, as shown in Figure 41-3.

FIGURE 41-3. *Foreign key with complete name*

If just the EMPLOYEE table were being queried, BRANCH.Badge would identify that column. If the two tables were joined, BRANCH.Badge would unambiguously refer to the Badge column of the BRANCH table. To select it from the EMPLOYEE table would require referencing it as EMPLOYEE.BRANCH.Badge. This method for identifying foreign keys should be sufficiently rigorous, but in reality, it currently is not supported. It's proposed here as an idea to be explored.

The practical need to solve the same-name column problem requires one of the following actions:

- Invent a name that incorporates the source table of the foreign key in its name without using the dot (using an underline, for instance).

- Invent a name that incorporates an abbreviation of the source table of the foreign key in its name.

- Invent a name different from its name in its source table.

- Change the name of the conflicting column.

None of these is particularly attractive, but if you come across the same-name dilemma, you'll need to take one of these actions.

Singular Names

One area of great inconsistency and confusion is the question of whether objects should have singular or plural names. Should it be the WORKER table or the WORKERS table? Should it be the Name column or the Names column?

Some argue that table names should be plural, because they refer to all the rows they contain; hence, WORKERS. Similarly, column names should be plural, because they refer to all the rows they contain; hence, Names.

Others argue that a table is really a set of rows, and it is a row that the column and table names refer to; hence, the names should be singular, WORKER and Name.

One vendor proposes that all table names should be plural, and all column names should be singular; hence, WORKERS and Name. Another vendor proposes that all table names should be singular and each user should decide about the columns. Is it any wonder designers are confused, and with them their long-suffering users?

There are two helpful ways to think about this issue. First, consider some columns common to nearly every database: Name, Address, City, State, and Zip. Other than the first column, does it ever occur to anyone to make these names plural? It is nearly self-evident when considering these names that they describe the contents of a single row, a record. Even though relational databases are "set-oriented," clearly the fundamental unit of a set is a row, and it is the content of that row that is well-described by singular column names. When designing a data entry screen to capture a person's name and address, should it look like this?

```
Names: _____

Addresses: _____

Cities: _____ States __ Zips _____-____
```

Or will you make these column names singular on the screen, since you're capturing *one* name and address at a time, but tell the users that when they write queries they must all be converted to plural? It is simply more intuitive and straightforward to restrict column names to singular.

The argument for table names is less straightforward. They contain the set of rows. Your "photo" album contains a set of many photos. Your "address" book or your "phone" book contains the set of your regular business and personal contacts. You wouldn't expect an "address" book to contain just one address; obviously, it contains a set, each instance of which is characterized as an "address." Likewise, you may have a "car" club, an "investment" portfolio, and a best "restaurant" list.

On the other hand, people sometimes talk about a "receivables" ledger, a "singles" group, or a favorite "foods" list. Groups get named both ways, though the singular form is more common when there is no preposition. You might say "address book," but would always say "book of addresses." It would always be "table of workers," but "worker table" (besides which, "workers table" sounds like something workers own rather than something that contains worker information).

So, although both sides have merit where tables are concerned, the singular usage is more common in everyday speech.

The second way to think about this issue is in terms of consistency and usefulness. If all objects are named consistently, neither you nor a user has to try to remember the rules for what is plural and what isn't. The benefit of this should be obvious. Suppose we decide that all objects will henceforth be plural. We now have an "s" or an "es" on the end of virtually every object, perhaps even on the end of each word in a long multiword object name. Of what possible benefit is it to key all of these extra letters all the time? Is it easier to use? Is it easier to understand? Is it easier to remember? Obviously, it is none of these.

Therefore, the best solution is this: all object names are always singular. The sole exception to this rule is any widely accepted term already commonly used in the business, such as "sales."

Brevity

As mentioned earlier, clarity should never be sacrificed for brevity, but given two equally meaningful, memorable, and descriptive names, always choose the shorter. For example, suppose you are to assign a name to a column that is part of a description of a company's structure. The structure includes division, department, project, and employee columns. The company is acquired by a conglomerate, and your database is to become the reporting mechanism for the new parent. This means a higher level of organization, by company, is going to be required. What will you call it? Here are some alternatives:

Corporation
Enterprise
Business
Company
Firm

Depending upon how the business is organized, any one of these names could be appropriate. Firm, however, is about one-third the size of Corporation, and it is meaningful, memorable, and descriptive. Although Firm is not as commonly used as Company, for instance, it is certainly more common than Enterprise, which has become quite fashionable, and Firm is learned and remembered after one use.

Another example is in the name chosen for the LODGING table and column. It could have been any of these:

Accommodation
Domicile
Dwelling
Lodging
Abode
Home

Because Home is less than one-third the size of Accommodation, and just over half the size of Lodging, it would have been a better choice. Brevity saves keying, and makes object names concise and quickly understood, but it is less important than clarity.

During application development, propose alternative names such as these to a group of users and developers and get their input on choosing the clearest name. How do you build lists of alternatives like these examples? Use a thesaurus and a dictionary. On a project team dedicated to developing superior, productive applications, every team member should be given a thesaurus and a dictionary as basic equipment, and then should be reminded over and over again of the importance of careful object naming.

Object Name Thesaurus

Ultimately, relational databases should include an object name thesaurus, just as they include a data dictionary. This thesaurus should enforce the company's naming standards and assure consistency of name choice and abbreviation (where used).

An object being named must often have multiple words in its name, such as Firm_Home_City. If a new name were proposed, such as Company_Domicile_City, the thesaurus would analyze the component words and rate them. For each of the words, it would approve the choice, declare a violation of standards and suggest an approved alternative, or tell you what word or abbreviation was not recognized. The use of an unapproved name would require either approval from a standards group or person, or production of a report to the DBA that specifies the violation.

Such a thesaurus may require the use of underlines in object naming to make the parsing of the name into component parts a straightforward task. This also helps enforce the consistent use of underlines, rather than the scattered, inconsistent usage within an application that underlines frequently receive now.

If you work directly with a government agency or large firm, that organization may already have object naming standards. The object naming standards of large organizations have over the years radiated into the rest of the commercial marketplace, and may form the basis for the naming standards used at your company. For example, those standards may provide the direction to choose between "Corporation" and "Firm." If they do not, you should develop your naming standards to be consistent both with those base standards and with the guidelines put forth in this chapter.

Intelligent Keys and Column Values

Intelligent keys are so named because they contain nontrivial combinations of information. The term is misleading in the extreme because it implies something positive or worthwhile. A more meaningful term might be "overloaded" keys. General ledger and product codes often fall into this category and contain all the difficulties associated with other codes, and more. Further, the difficulties found in overloaded keys also apply to nonkey columns that are packed with more than one piece of meaningful data.

Typical of an overloaded key or column value is this description: "The first character is the region code. The next four characters are the catalog number. The final digit is the cost center code, unless this is an imported part, in which case an *I* is tagged onto the end of the number, or unless it is a high-volume item, such as screws, in which case only three digits are used for catalog number, and the region code is HD."

Eliminating overloaded key and column values is essential in good relational design. The dependencies built on pieces of these keys (usually foreign keys into other tables) are all at risk if the structure is maintained. Unfortunately, many application areas have overloaded keys that have been used for years and are deeply embedded in the company's tasks. Some of them were created during earlier efforts at automation, using databases that could not support multiple key columns for composite keys. Others came about through historical accretion, by forcing a short code, usually numeric, to mean more and to cover more cases than it was ever intended to at the beginning. Eliminating the existing overloaded keys may have practical ramifications that make it impossible to do immediately. This makes building a new, relational application more difficult.

The solution to this problem is to create a new set of keys, both primary and foreign, that properly normalizes the data; then, make sure that people can access tables only through these new keys. The overloaded key is then kept as an additional, and unique, table column. Access to it is still possible using historical methods (matching the overloaded key in a query, for instance), but the newly structured keys are promoted as the preferred method of access. Over time, with proper training, users will gravitate to the new keys. Eventually, the overloaded keys (and other overloaded column values) can simply be **NULL**ed out or dropped from the table.

Failing to eliminate overloaded keys and values makes extracting information from the database, validating the values, assuring data integrity, and modifying the structure all extremely difficult and costly.

The Commandments

All of the major issues in designing for productivity have now been discussed, primarily in Chapters 2, 39, 40, and this chapter, but also briefly in other chapters. It probably is worthwhile to sum these up in a single place—thus "The Ten Commandments." As noted at the beginning of the chapter, these issues might better be characterized as the "Ten Suggestions." Their presentation does not assume that you need to be told what to do, but rather that you are capable of making rational judgments and can benefit from the experience of others facing the same challenges. The purpose here is not to describe the development cycle, which you probably understand better than you want to, but rather to bias that development with an orientation that will radically change how the application will look, feel, and be used. Careful attention to these ideas can dramatically improve the productivity and happiness of an application's users.

The Ten Commandments of Humane Design

1. Include users. Put them on the project team and teach them the relational model and SQL.

2. Name tables, columns, keys, and data jointly with the users. Develop an application thesaurus to assure name consistency.

3. Use English words that are meaningful, memorable, descriptive, short, and singular. Use underlines consistently or not at all.

4. Don't mix levels in naming.

5. Avoid codes and abbreviations.

6. Use meaningful keys where possible.

7. Decompose overloaded keys.

8. Analyze and design from the tasks, not just the data. Remember that normalization is not design.

9. Move tasks from users to the machine. It is profitable to spend cycles and storage to gain ease of use.

10. Don't be seduced by development speed. Take time and care in analyses, design, testing, and tuning.

PART
VIII

Alphabetical
Reference

his chapter contains references for most major Oracle commands, keywords, products, features, and functions, with extensive cross-referencing of topics. The reference is intended for use by both developers and users of Oracle, but assumes some familiarity with the products. Reading the first four pages of this reference will help you make the most productive use of the entries.

What This Alphabetical Reference Includes

This alphabetical reference contains entries for virtually every Oracle command in SQL, PL/SQL, and SQLPLUS, as well as definitions of all relevant terms used in Oracle and SQL. Each command is listed with its correct format or syntax, an explanation of its purpose and use, the product or products in which it is used, and important details, restrictions, and hints about it, along with examples to illustrate proper usage. Topics are in alphabetical order, and are heavily cross-referenced, both within the alphabetical reference, and to preceding chapters in the book.

What This Alphabetical Reference Does Not Include

This is not a tutorial; it does not explain the screen-oriented development tools, since these are relatively easy to learn and use. Additionally, there are a few areas where usage is likely to be so specialized or infrequent that inclusion here did not seem of much benefit. In these instances, the text refers you to the Oracle manual-or another book-where you can find the needed information.

General Format of Entries

Entries in this reference are typically either definitions of terms or descriptions of functions, commands, and keywords. These are usually structured in seven sections: the keyword, its type, the products in which it is used, a "See also" cross-reference, the format in which the keyword appears, a description of its components, and an example of its use. A typical entry looks like the following:

RPAD
SEE ALSO   CHARACTER FUNCTIONS, **LPAD**, **LTRIM**, **RTRIM**, Chapter 7
FORMAT

```
RPAD(string,length [,'set'])
```

DESCRIPTION   **R**ight **PAD.** RPAD makes a string a certain length by adding a certain set of characters to the right. If set is not specified, the default pad character is a space.
EXAMPLE

```
select RPAD('HELLO ',24,'WORLD') from DUAL;
```

produces this:

```
HELLO WORLDWORLDWORLDWOR
```

The Sections of Each Entry

The **KEYWORD** usually appears on a line by itself. In some cases a brief definition follows. If a keyword has more than one definition, either in different Oracle tools or in different Oracle versions, the keyword will be followed by a brief qualifier, such as (Form 1 - Schema Objects), in order to indicate that more than one listing exists for this keyword.

See also suggests other topics that are closely related to the keyword, or gives the chapter or chapters in the book that give detailed descriptions of how the keyword is used in practice. Occasionally you will be referred to the Oracle manual or other reference book that contains detail beyond the scope of this reference.

Format generally follows the notation of Oracle manuals, with all SQL and other keywords in uppercase. In actual use, these must be entered exactly as they are shown (except that case is irrelevant). Variables and variable parameters are shown in lowercase *italic*. This indicates that some appropriate value should be substituted. When parentheses are shown, they must be entered where they appear, just as are words shown in uppercase.

Standard Usages for Variables

Some standard usages for variables follow:

This Variable	Indicates
column	The name of a column
database	The name of a database
link	The name of a link in Net8
password	A password
segment	The name of a segment
table	The name of a table
tablespace	The name of a tablespace
user	The name of a user or owner
view	The name of a view

Other Formatting Guidelines

Some other guidelines for formatting follow:

- *character* means the value must be a single character.

- *string* typically represents a character column or an expression or column that can be treated like a CHAR or VARCHAR2 column after automatic data conversion.

- *value* usually represents a NUMBER column or an expression or column that can be treated like a NUMBER column after automatic data conversion.

- *date* usually represents a date column or an expression or column that can be treated like a date column after automatic data conversion.

- *integer* must be a whole number, such as -3, 0, or 12.

- *expression* means any form of a column. This could be a literal, a variable, a mathematical computation, a function, or virtually any combination of functions and columns whose final result is a single value, such as a string, a number, or a date.

- Occasionally other notation is used as well, such as *condition* or *query*. This is explained or is apparent in context.

- **Optional** items are enclosed in square brackets, as in **[user.]**, meaning that *user* is not necessarily required.

- **Alternative** items in a list are separated by a single broken vertical bar, as in **OFF | ON**, which should be read "OFF or ON." On some systems this vertical bar is displayed as a solid vertical bar.

- **Required** options, where one item of a list of items is required, are surrounded by curly braces, as in {**OFF | ON**}.

- The **default** item in a list, if there is one, will be listed first.

- Three periods (or ellipses) indicate that the previous expression can be repeated any number of times, as in **column [,*column*]. . .**, which means that **,*column*** may be any number of additional columns separated by commas.

- In rare instances normal notation is either insufficient or inappropriate for what is being shown. In these cases, the **Description** will spell out more fully what is intended in the **Format**.

Other Elements of a Listing

A few commands have a **Return type**, which indicates the datatype of the value returned by a function.

Description is a verbal explanation of the command and its parts. **Boldface** words within the description usually direct references to either commands or variables shown in the **Format** section.

Examples will show either the results of a function, or how a keyword is used in a real query or application. The style of the examples is not the same as that of the **Format** section. Instead, it follows the style of the first part of this book (described in Chapter 3), since this is more typical of real coding practice.

The Order of the Listings

This reference is in alphabetical order, with all entries that begin with symbols coming before the first entry beginning with the letter *A*.

Words that are hyphenated or that have an underscore character in them are alphabetized as if the hyphen or underscore were a space.

Symbols

The symbols are listed in order of appearance with a short definition or name. Those symbols with definitions in **boldface** have full entries dedicated to them, or are prefixes to words that are covered in the pages that follow.

_	**underline (also called underscore, underbar)**
!	**exclamation mark**
"	**double quotation mark**
#	**pound sign**
$	**dollar sign**
?	**question mark**
%	**percent sign**
&	**ampersand**
&&	**double ampersand**

'	single quotation mark or apostrophe
( )	parentheses
*	asterisk or multiplication
**	exponentiation in PL/SQL
+	plus
-	subtraction or hyphen
- -	double hyphen, SQL comment minus or hyphen
.	period or dot, a name or variable separator
..	to
/	division or slash
/*	slash asterisk, SQL comment divided by or slash
:	colon
:=	is set equal to in PL/SQL
;	semicolon
<< >>	label name delimiter in PL/SQL
<	less than
<=	less than or equal to
< >	not equal
!=	not equal
=	equal
>	greater than
>=	greater than or equal to
@	at sign
@@	double at sign
[]	square brackets
^	caret
^=	not equal
{}	curly braces
|	broken vertical bar
||	concatenation

_ (Underscore)

The underscore represents a single position with the **LIKE** operator. *See* **LIKE**.

_EDITOR

See **EDIT**.

! (Exclamation Mark)

SEE ALSO   =, **CONTAINS**, **SOUNDEX**, TEXT SEARCH OPERATORS, Chapter 24

FORMAT   Within SQL, **!** is used as part of the "not equal" expression **!=**. For example, you can select all the city values that are not in the continent of Asia:

```
select City
  from LOCATION
 where Continent != 'ASIA';
```

Within ConText and interMedia Text (IMT), ! signals the text engine to perform a SOUNDEX search. The terms to search for will be expanded to include terms that sound like the search term, using the text's SOUNDEX value to determine possible matches.

```
select Resume
  from PROSPECT
 where CONTAINS(Resume, '!guarding')>0;
```

" (Double Quotation Mark)

SEE ALSO   **ALIAS, TO_CHAR**, Chapters 7 and 9

DESCRIPTION   " surrounds a table or column alias that contains special characters or a space, or surrounds literal text in a date format clause of **TO_CHAR**.

EXAMPLE   Here it is used as an alias:

```
select NEXT_DAY(CycleDate,'FRIDAY') "Pay Day!"
  from PAYDAY;
```

and here it is used as a formatting portion of **TO_CHAR**:

```
select FirstName, Birthdate, TO_CHAR(BirthDate,
       '"Baby Girl on" fmMonth ddth, YYYY, "at" HH:MI "in the Morning"')
       "Formatted"
  from BIRTHDAY
 where FirstName = 'VICTORIA';
```

```
FIRSTNAME       BIRTHDATE Formatted
--------------- --------- ------------------------------
VICTORIA        20-MAY-49 Baby Girl on May 20th, 1949,
                          at 3:27 in the Morning
```

(Pound Sign)

SEE ALSO   **DOCUMENT, REMARK**, /* */, Chapter 6

DESCRIPTION   # completes a block of documentation in a SQLPLUS start file where the block is begun by the word DOCUMENT. SQL*PLUS ignores all lines from the line where it sees the word DOCUMENT until the line after the #.

$ (Dollar Sign)

SEE ALSO   **@@, HOST, START, CONTAINS,** TEXT SEARCH OPERATORS, Chapter 24

FORMAT   For SQL*PLUS:

```
$ host_command
```

For ConText and IMT:

```
select column
  from table
 where CONTAINS(text_column, '$search_term') >0;
```

DESCRIPTION   **$** passes any host command back to the operating system for execution without exiting SQL*PLUS. **$** is shorthand for **HOST**. This doesn't work on all hardware or operating systems. Within ConText and IMT, **$** instructs the search engine to perform a stem expansion on the search term. A stem expansion includes in the search words that have the same word stem. For example, a stem expansion of the word "sing" would include "singing," "sang," and "sung."

? (Question Mark)

SEE ALSO   CONTAINS, TEXT SEARCH OPERATORS, Chapter 24
FORMAT

```
select column
  from table
  where CONTAINS(text_column, '?term')>0;
```

DESCRIPTION   Within ConText and IMT, **?** instructs the text engine to perform a fuzzy match search. The terms to search for will be expanded to include terms that are spelled similar to the search term, using the text index as the source for possible matches.

% (Percent)

% is a wild card used to represent any number of positions and characters with the **LIKE** operator. *See* **LIKE**.

%FOUND

SEE ALSO   %ISOPEN, %NOTFOUND, %ROWCOUNT, **CURSOR, SQL CURSOR**, Chapter 25
FORMAT

```
cursor%FOUND
```

or

```
SQL%FOUND
```

DESCRIPTION   **%FOUND** is a success flag for **select**, **insert**, **update**, and **delete**. *cursor* is the name of an explicit cursor **declared** in a PL/SQL block, or the implicit cursor named **SQL**. **%FOUND** can be attached to a cursor name as a suffix. The two together are a success flag for the execution of **select**, **insert**, **update**, and **delete** statements in PL/SQL blocks.

PL/SQL temporarily sets aside a section of memory as a scratchpad for the execution of SQL statements, and for storing certain kinds of information (or *attributes*) about the state of that execution. If the SQL statement is a **select**, this area will contain one row of data.

%FOUND is one of those attributes. %FOUND is typically tested (via IF/THEN logic) after an explicit **fetch** has been performed from the cursor. It will be TRUE if the **fetch** retrieved a row, and FALSE otherwise. It always evaluates TRUE, FALSE, or NULL. **%NOTFOUND** is the logical opposite. It is FALSE when **%FOUND** is TRUE, TRUE when **%FOUND** is FALSE, and NULL when **%FOUND** is NULL.

Testing **%FOUND** for the condition of an explicit cursor before it is **OPEN**ed raises an EXCEPTION (error code ORA-01001, INVALID CURSOR).

%ISOPEN

SEE ALSO   SQL CURSOR, Chapter 25
FORMAT

```
cursor%ISOPEN
```

DESCRIPTION *cursor* must be either the name of an explicitly declared cursor or the implicit cursor named **SQL**. Evaluates to TRUE if the named cursor is open, FALSE if it is not. **SQL%ISOPEN** will *always* evaluate FALSE, because the SQL cursor is opened and closed automatically when a SQL statement not explicitly declared is executed (*see* **SQL CURSOR**). **%ISOPEN** is used in PL/SQL logic; it cannot be a part of a SQL statement.

%NOTFOUND

See **%FOUND**.

%ROWCOUNT

SEE ALSO   CLOSE, DECLARE, DELETE, FETCH, INSERT, OPEN, SELECT, UPDATE, Chapter 25
FORMAT

```
cursor%ROWCOUNT
```

DESCRIPTION   *cursor* must be either the name of an explicitly declared cursor, or the implicit cursor named SQL. **cursor%ROWCOUNT** contains the cumulative total number of rows that have been **fetch**ed from the active set in this cursor. This can be used to intentionally process only a fixed number of rows, but is more commonly used as an exception handler for **select**s that are intended to return just one row (for example **select. . . into**). In these cases, **%ROWCOUNT** is set to 0 if no rows are returned (**%NOTFOUND** can make this test as well), and to 2 if more than one row is returned, regardless of the actual number.

　　　%ROWCOUNT is used in PL/SQL logic; it cannot be a part of a SQL statement. If **SQL%ROWCOUNT** is used, it can only refer to the most recently opened implicit cursor. If no implicit cursor has been opened, **SQL%ROWCOUNT** returns NULL.

%ROWTYPE

SEE ALSO   FETCH, Chapter 25
FORMAT

```
{[user.]table | cursor}%ROWTYPE
```

DESCRIPTION   **%ROWTYPE** declares a record variable to have the same structure as an entire row in a table (or view), or as a row retrieved by the named cursor. **%ROWTYPE** is used as part of a variable declaration and assures that the variable will contain the appropriate fields and datatypes to handle all of the columns being fetched. If [*user.*]*table* is used, the table (or view) must exist in the database.

　　　For example, recall the WORKER table:

```
Column         Datatype
-------------- ------------------
Name           VARCHAR2(25) not null
Age            NUMBER
Lodging        VARCHAR2(15)
```

　　　To create a variable that will contain corresponding fields, use **declare**, a variable name, and **%ROWTYPE** with the table name, and then select a row into the record. (Note the *, which gets all columns. This is required for the format that uses a table name as a prefix to **%ROWTYPE**.)

```
DECLARE
    WORKER_RECORD    WORKER%rowtype;
BEGIN
    select * into WORKER_RECORD from WORKER
    where Name = 'BART SARJEANT';
    if WORKER_RECORD.Age > 65
        then ...
    end if;
END;
```

Because the WORKER_RECORD has the same structure as the table WORKER, you can reference the Age field as WORKER_RECORD.Age, using notation similar to table.column used in SQL statements. **select. . .into** and **fetch. . .into** are the only methods for loading an entire record variable. Individual fields within the record can be loaded using :=, as shown here:

```
WORKER_RECORD.Age := 44;
```

If a cursor is used as the prefix for **%ROWTYPE**, then it can contain a **select** statement with only as many columns as are needed. However, if a column that is **fetch**ed from a named cursor is an expression, rather than a simple column name, the expression must be given an alias in the **select** statement before it can be referenced using this technique. For instance, suppose the cursor **select** statement was this:

```
DECLARE
cursor employee is select Name, Age + 10 from WORKER;
```

there would be no way to reference the expression Age + 10, so redo it this way:

```
DECLARE
cursor employee is select Name, (Age + 10) New_Age
  from WORKER;
```

The previous example would then look like this:

```
DECLARE
    cursor EMPLOYEE is select Name, (Age + 10) New_Age
  from WORKER
  where Name = 'BART SARJEANT';
    WORKER_RECORD    EMPLOYEE%rowtype;
BEGIN
    open EMPLOYEE;
    fetch EMPLOYEE into WORKER_RECORD;
    if WORKER_RECORD.new_age > 65
        then ...
    end if;
    close EMPLOYEE;
END;
```

New_Age is the alias for Age + 10, and it now can be referenced as a field in WORKER_RECORD. **%ROWTYPE** is used in PL/SQL logic; it cannot be a part of a SQL statement.

%TYPE

SEE ALSO   %ROWTYPE, Chapter 25

FORMAT

```
{[user.]table.column | variable}%TYPE
```

DESCRIPTION   %TYPE is used to declare a variable to be of the same type as a previously declared variable, or as a particular column in a table that exists in the database you're connected to.

EXAMPLE   In this example a new variable, Employee, is made to be the same type as the Name column in the WORKER table. Since Employee now exists, it can be used to declare yet another new variable, New_Worker:

```
Employee    WORKER.Name%TYPE;
New_Worker  Employee%TYPE;
```

& or && (Ampersand or Double Ampersand)

SEE ALSO   :, **ACCEPT**, **DEFINE**, **START**, **CONTAINS**, TEXT SEARCH OPERATORS, Chapters 14 and 24

FORMAT   For SQL*PLUS:

```
&integer
&variable
&&variable
```

For ConText and IMT:

```
select column
  from table
 where CONTAINS(text_column, 'term & term') > 0;
```

DESCRIPTION   **&** and **&&** can be used in several ways (&& applies only to the second definition below):

- Prefix for parameters in a SQL*PLUS start file. Values are substituted for &1, &2, etc. *See* **START**.

- Prefix for a substitution variable in a SQL command in SQL*PLUS. SQL*PLUS will prompt for a value if an undefined **&** or **&&** variable is found. && will define the variable and thereby preserve its value; & will not define or preserve the value, but only substitute what is entered one time. *See* **ACCEPT** and **DEFINE**.

- When using ConText and IMT, **&** is used to signal an AND condition for text searches involving multiple search terms. If any of the search terms is not found, the text will not be returned by the search.

' (Single Quotation Mark)

SEE ALSO   " (Double Quotation Mark), Chapter 7

FORMAT

```
'string'
```

DESCRIPTION   ' surrounds a literal, such as a character string or date constant. To use one quotation mark or an apostrophe in a string constant, use two ' marks (not a double quotation mark). Avoid the use of apostrophes in data (and elsewhere) whenever possible.

EXAMPLE   select 'William' from DUAL;
produces this:

```
William
```

whereas this:

```
select 'William''s brother' from DUAL;
```

produces this:

```
William's brother
```

( ) (Parentheses)
SEE ALSO   PRECEDENCE, SUBQUERY, UPDATE, Chapters 4, 12, and 15
DESCRIPTION   encloses subqueries or lists of columns, or controls precedence.

* (Multiplication)
SEE ALSO   +, -, /, Chapters 8 and 24
FORMAT

```
value1 * value2
```

DESCRIPTION   *value1* * *value2* means *value1* multiplied by *value2*. Within ConText and IMT, * is used to weight the search results for different terms at different strengths.

** (Exponentiation)
SEE ALSO   POWER
FORMAT

```
x ** y
```

DESCRIPTION   *x* is raised to the power *y*. *x* and *y* may be constants, variables, columns, or expressions. Both must be numeric.
EXAMPLE   4**4 = 256

+ (Addition)
SEE ALSO   -, *, /, Chapter 8
FORMAT

```
value1 + value2
```

DESCRIPTION   *value1* + *value2* means *value1* plus *value2*.

- (Subtraction [Form 1])
SEE ALSO   +, *, /, Chapter 8, **CONTAINS, MINUS,** TEXT SEARCH OPERATORS, Chapter 24
FORMAT

```
value1 - value2
```

DESCRIPTION   *value1 - value2* means value1 minus *value2*. Within ConText and IMT, a '-' tells the text search of two terms to subtract the score of the second term's search from the score of the first term's search before comparing the result to the threshold score.

- (Hyphen [Form 2])
SEE ALSO   Chapter 14
FORMAT

```
command text -
        text -
        text
```

DESCRIPTION   SQL*PLUS command continuation. - continues a command on the following line.
EXAMPLE

```
ttitle left 'Current Portfolio' -
right 'November 1st, 1999'        skip 1 -
center 'Industry Listings  '  skip 4;
```

-- (Comment)
SEE ALSO   /* */, **REMARK**, Chapter 6
FORMAT

```
-- any text
```

DESCRIPTION   -- tells Oracle a comment has begun. Everything from that point to the end of the line, is treated as a comment. These delimiters are used only within SQL itself or in PL/SQL and must appear before the SQLTERMINATOR.
EXAMPLE

```
select Feature, Section, Page
-- this is just a comment
  from NEWSPAPER    -- this is another comment
 where Section = 'F'
```

. (Period or Dot [Form 1])
FORMAT

```
&variable.suffix
```

DESCRIPTION   The . is a variable separator, used in SQL*PLUS to separate the variable name from a suffix, so that the suffix is not considered a part of the variable name.
EXAMPLE   Here the suffix "st" is effectively concatenated to the contents of the variable &Avenue.

```
define Avenue = 21
select '100 &Avenue.st Street' from DUAL;
```

produces this:

```
100 21st Street
```

This same technique might also be used in a **where** clause.

. (Period or Dot [Form 2])

SEE ALSO   SYNTAX OPERATORS, Chapters 21, 4, and 40
FORMAT

```
[user.][table.]column
```

DESCRIPTION   The . is a name separator, used to specify the complete name of a column, including (optionally) its table or user. The . is also used to address columns within abstract datatypes during **select**s, **update**s, and **delete**s.

EXAMPLE

```
select Talbot.WORKER.Name
   from Talbot.WORKER, Wallbom.WORKER
 where Talbot.WORKER.Name = Wallbom.WORKER.Name;
```

If the table contains columns based on an abstract datatype, the datatype's attributes may be acccessed via the . notation.

```
select C.Person.Address.City
from Company C
where C.Person.Address.State = 'FL';
```

See Chapter 4 for further examples

.. (To)

See **LOOP**.

/ (Division [Form 1])

SEE ALSO   +, -, *, Chapter 8
FORMAT

```
value1 / value2
```

DESCRIPTION   *value1 / value2* means *value1* divided by *value2*.

/ (Slash [Form 2])

SEE ALSO   ;, **BUFFER, EDIT, GET, RUN, SET**, SQLTERMINATOR, Chapter 14
DESCRIPTION   / executes the SQL in the SQL buffer without displaying it, unlike **RUN**, which displays it first.

/* */ (Comment)

SEE ALSO   REMARK, Chapter 6
FORMAT

```
/* any text */
```

DESCRIPTION   /* tells Oracle a comment has begun. Everything Oracle sees from that point forward, even for many words and lines, it regards as a comment until it sees the ending */, which ends the comment. These delimiters are used only within SQL itself or in a PL/SQL program and must appear before the SQLTERMINATOR. Comments cannot be embedded within comments; that is, a /* is terminated by the first following */, even if there is an intervening /*.

EXAMPLE

```
select Feature, Section, Page
    /* this is a multi-line comment
        used to extensively document the code */
  from NEWSPAPER
 where Section = 'F';
```

: (Colon, Host Variable Prefix)
SEE ALSO   INDICATOR VARIABLE
FORMAT

```
:name
```

DESCRIPTION   *name* is the name of a host variable. When PL/SQL is embedded in a host language through an Oracle precompiler, host variables can be referenced from within the PL/SQL blocks by prefixing their host language names with a colon. In effect, this is the host variable. If PL/SQL changes its value through an assignment (:=), the value of the host variable is changed. Currently these variables must be single value (that is, arrays are not supported). They may be used anywhere a PL/SQL variable can be used. The one exception is in assigning the value NULL to a host variable, which is not supported directly, but requires the use of an indicator variable.

EXAMPLE

```
BEGIN
    select COUNT(*) into :RowCount from LEDGER;
END;
```

:= (Set Equal To)
SEE ALSO   **DECLARE, FETCH, SELECT INTO**, Chapter 25
FORMAT

```
variable := expression
```

DESCRIPTION   The PL/SQL *variable* is set equal to the *expression*, which may be a constant, **NULL**, or a calculation with other variables, literals, and PL/SQL functions.

EXAMPLE

```
Extension := Quantity * Price;
Title := 'BARBERS WHO SHAVE THEMSELVES';
Name := NULL
```

; (Semicolon)
SEE ALSO   / (Slash), **BUFFER, EDIT, GET, RUN, SQLTERMINATOR, CONTAINS, NEAR**, TEXT SEARCH OPERATORS, Chapter 24

DESCRIPTION   ; executes the SQL or the command that precedes it. Within ConText and IMT, ; indicates that a proximity search should be executed for the specified text strings. If the search terms are "summer" and "lease," then a proximity search for the two terms could be

```
select Text
  from SONNET
 where CONTAINS(Text,'summer;lease') >0;
```

When evaluating the text search results, text with the words "summer" and "lease" near to each other in the text will have higher scores than text with the words "summer" and "lease" farther apart.

< < > > (PL/SQL Label Name Delimiter)

See **BEGIN**, BLOCK STRUCTURE, **END**, **GOTO**, **LOOP**, Chapter 25.

@ ("At" Sign [Form 1])

SEE ALSO   @@, START

FORMAT

```
@file
```

DESCRIPTION   @ starts the SQL*PLUS start file named *file*. @ is similar to **START**, but does not allow command line arguments.

@ ("At" Sign [Form 2])

SEE ALSO   **CONNECT**, **COPY**, **DATABASE LINK**, Chapter 21

FORMAT

```
CON[NECT] user[/password] [@database];
COPY [FROM user/password@database]
     [TO user/password@database]
     {APPEND | CREATE | INSERT | REPLACE}
     table [ (column, [column]...) ]
     USING query;
SELECT...   FROM [user.]table[link]  [, [user.]table[@link] ]...
```

DESCRIPTION   @ prefixes a database name in a **CONNECT** or **COPY** command, or a link name in a **from** clause.

@@ (Double "At" Sign)

SEE ALSO   @ (Form 1), START

FORMAT

```
@@file
```

DESCRIPTION   @ starts a nested SQL*PLUS start file named *file*. @@ is similar to @, but differs in that @@, when used in a command file, will search for a start file in the same directory as the command file that called it (rather than in the directory you are in when you execute the command file).

{} (Curly Braces)

SEE ALSO   **CONTAINS**, TEXT SEARCH OPERATORS, Chapter 24

FORMAT   Within ConText and IMT, {} indicate that the enclosed text should be considered part of the search string even if it is a reserved word. For example, if the search term is "in and out," and you want to search for the entire phrase, then you must enclose the word "and" within braces:

```
select Text
  from SONNET
 where CONTAINS(Text,'in {and} out') >0;
```

| (Vertical Bar)

SEE ALSO **BTITLE, HEADSEP, TTITLE,** TEXT SEARCH OPERATORS, Chapter 6, Chapter 24
FORMAT

```
text|text
```

DESCRIPTION When used in a SQL*PLUS **column, ttitle** or **btitle** command, | is the default **headsep** character, and is used to denote the splitting of a line onto a second line. (When used in listings in this Reference, | denotes a break between alternative choices: variable | literal would be read "variable or literal." On some machines this shows as a solid vertical bar.) Within ConText and IMT, | signals an OR condition for searches involving multiple search terms. If either of the search terms is found, and its search score exceeds the specified threshold value, the text will be returned by the search.

EXAMPLE Here's how | is used as a **headsep** character.

```
TTITLE 'This is the First Line|and This is the Second'
```

produces this:

```
This is the First Line
and This is the Second
```

Here's how | is used as an OR clause in a text search query:

```
select column
  from table
 where CONTAINS(text_column, 'term | term') > 0;
```

|| (Concatenation)

SEE ALSO . (Period or Dot [Form 1]), **CONCAT, SUBSTR,** Chapter 7
FORMAT

```
expression1 || expression2
```

DESCRIPTION || concatenates two strings together.

EXAMPLE Use || to display a column of cities, followed by a comma, a space, and the country:

```
select City||', '||Country from LOCATION
```

ABS (Absolute Value)

SEE ALSO NUMBER FUNCTIONS, Chapter 8
FORMAT

```
ABS(value)
```

value must be a number, whether a literal number, the name of a number column, a literal character string containing a valid number, or a character column containing only a valid number.

DESCRIPTION Absolute value is the measure of the magnitude of something, and is always a positive number.

EXAMPLES

```
ABS(146) = 146
ABS(-30) =  30
ABS('-27.88') = 27.88
```

ABSTRACT DATATYPE

Abstract datatypes are datatypes that consist of one or more attributes. Rather than being constrained to the standard Oracle datatypes of NUMBER, DATE, and VARCHAR2, abstract datatypes can consist of multiple attributes and/or other, previously defined abstract datatypes.

EXAMPLE

```
create or replace type PERSON_TY AS
   Name    VARCHAR2 (25),
   Address ADDRESS_TY;
```

Abstract datatypes must have constructor methods associated with them, and may have have additional methods as well. *See* Chapters 4 and 28 for an introduction to abstract datatypes. See CREATE TYPE for format.

ACCEPT

SEE ALSO   **&, &&, DEFINE**, Chapter 14

FORMAT

```
ACC[EPT] variable [NUM[BER]|CHAR|DATE] [FOR[MAT] format]
   [DEF[AULT] default] [PROMPT text | NOPR[OMPT]] [HIDE]
```

DESCRIPTION   **ACCEPT** takes input from a user's keyboard and puts it in the named variable. If the variable has not been previously DEFINED, it is created. NUMBER, CHAR, or DATE determines the datatype of the variable as it is input. CHAR will accept any numbers or characters. DATE accepts character strings in valid date formats (or an error message will be returned). NUMBER will accept only numbers and an optional decimal point and minus sign, otherwise **ACCEPT** will produce an error message. FORMAT specifies the input format for the reply (such as A20). DEFAULT sets the default value if a reply is not given. PROMPT displays the text to the user before accepting the input. NOPROMPT skips a line and waits for input without displaying any prompt. Using neither PROMPT nor NOPROMPT causes ACCEPT to invent a prompt asking for the value of the variable. HIDE suppresses the user's entry, and is valuable for passwords and the like.

EXAMPLE   The following prompts the user with "How hot?" and puts the user's entry in a number variable named Temperature:

```
ACCEPT Temperature NUMBER PROMPT 'How hot? '
```

ACCUMULATE

See TEXT SEARCH OPERATORS.

ACOS

SEE ALSO   **ASIN, ATAN, ATAN2, COS, COSH, EXP, LN, LOG, SIN, SINH, TAN, TANH**

FORMAT

```
ACOS(value)
```

DESCRIPTION   **ACOS** returns the arc cosine of a value. Input values range from -1 to 1; outputs are expressed in radians.

ADD_MONTHS

SEE ALSO   DATE FUNCTIONS, Chapter 9

FORMAT

```
ADD_MONTHS(date,integer)
```

DESCRIPTION   ADD_MONTHS adds a number of months to *date,* and returns the date that is that many months in the future. *date* must be a legitimate Oracle date. *integer* must be an integer; a non-integer value will be truncated to the next smallest integer. A negative value for *integer* will return a date in the past.

EXAMPLE   ADD_MONTHS is executed on November 1, 1999 at 11 P.M.

```
select ADD_MONTHS(SysDate,1), ADD_MONTHS(SysDate,.3) from DUAL;

ADD_MONTH ADD_MONTH
--------- ---------
01-DEC-99 01-NOV-99
```

ADDRESS (ROW)

See ROWID.

ALIAS

Alias is a temporary name assigned to a table or a column within a SQL statement and used to refer to it elsewhere in the same statement (if a table), or in a SQL*PLUS command (if a column). You can use the AS keyword to separate the column definition from its alias. *See* " (Double Quotation Mark), **AS**, and **SELECT**.

ALL

SEE ALSO   ANY, **BETWEEN**, **EXISTS**, **IN**, LOGICAL OPERATORS, Chapter 12

FORMAT

```
operator ALL list
```

DESCRIPTION   != **ALL** is the equivalent of **NOT IN**. *operator* can be any one of =, >, >=, <, <=, != and *list* can be a series of literal strings (such as 'Talbot', 'Jones', 'Hild'), or a series of literal numbers (such as 2, 43, 76, 32.06, 444), or a column from a subquery, where each row of the subquery becomes a member of the list, such as this:

```
LOCATION.City != ALL (select City from WEATHER)
```

It also can be a series of columns in the **where** clause of the main query, as shown here:

```
Prospect != ALL (Vendor, Client)
```

RESTRICTIONS   *list* cannot be a series of columns in a subquery, such as this:

```
Prospect != ALL (select Vendor, Client from . . .)
```

Many people find this operator and the ANY operator very difficult to remember, because the logic for some of their cases is not immediately intuitive. As a result, some form of EXISTS is usually substituted. The combination of an operator with ALL and a list can be illustrated with the following explanations:

Page = ALL (4,2,7)	Page is equal to every item in the list-no number qualifies. A subquery *could* return a list where all the items were identical, and a value of Page could be equal to every one of them, but this would be very rare.
Page > ALL (4,2,7)	Page is greater than the greatest item in the list (4,2,7)-anything larger than 7 qualifies.
Page >= ALL (4,2,7)	Page is greater than or equal to the greatest item in the list (4,2,7)-anything equal to or larger than 7 qualifies.
Page < ALL (4,2,7)	Page is less than the lowest item in the list (4,2,7)-anything below 2 qualifies.
Page <= ALL (4,2,7)	Page is less than or equal to the lowest item in the list (4,2,7)-anything equal to or lower than 2 qualifies.
Page != ALL (4,2,7)	Page is not equal to any item in the list-any number qualifies except 4, 2, and 7

ALLOCATE (Embedded SQL)
SEE ALSO   DECLARE CURSOR
FORMAT

```
EXEC SQL ALLOCATE cursor_variable
```

DESCRIPTION   The **ALLOCATE** clause allocates a cursor variable that will be referenced in a PL/SQL block.

ALTER CLUSTER
SEE ALSO   **CREATE CLUSTER**, **CREATE TABLE**, **STORAGE**, Chapter 20
SYNTAX

physical_attributes_clause::=

allocate_extent_clause::=

deallocate_unused_clause::=

parallel_clause::=

DESCRIPTION   Descriptions of the parameters can be found under **CREATE TABLE** and **STORAGE**. They have the same purpose and effect, except that here they are used to alter a cluster. Size is described under **CREATE CLUSTER**. In order to alter a cluster, you must either own the cluster or have ALTER ANY CLUSTER system privilege.

All tables in a cluster use the values for **PCTFREE, PCTUSED, INITRANS, MAXTRANS, TABLESPACE**, and **STORAGE** set by **CREATE CLUSTER**. **ALTER CLUSTER** changes these values for future cluster blocks, but does not affect those that already exist. **ALTER CLUSTER** does not allow changing the **MINEXTENTS** parameter in **STORAGE**. The **DEALLOCATE UNUSED** clause allows the cluster to shrink in size, freeing unused space.

EXAMPLE

```
alter cluster WORKERandSKILL size 1024 storage (maxextents 30);
```

ALTER DATABASE

SEE ALSO   ALTER ROLLBACK SEGMENT, CREATE DATABASE, RECOVER, START UP, SHUTDOWN, Chapter 39

SYNTAX

recover_clauses::=

general_recovery_clause::=

managed_recovery_clause::=

datafile/tempfile_clauses::=

controlfile_clauses::=

logfile_clauses::=

logfile_descriptor::=

autoextend_clauses::=

maxsize_clause::=

parallel_clause::=

DESCRIPTION To alter a database, you must have the ALTER DATABASE system privilege.
database is the database name, and must be eight or fewer characters long. DB_NAME in init.ora contains the default database name. If database isn't specified, the name DB_NAME is used by default. **ADD LOGFILE** adds a redo file or files to the database. *file_definition* specifies the **LOGFILE** names and sizes:

```
'file' [SIZE integer [K | M] [REUSE]
```

SIZE is the number of bytes set aside for this file. Suffixing this with **K** multiplies the value by 1024; using **M** multiplies it by 1048576. **REUSE** (without **SIZE**) means destroy the contents of any file by this name and give the name to this database. **SIZE** with **REUSE** creates the file if it doesn't exist, and checks its size if it does. **SIZE** alone will create the file if it doesn't exist, but will return an error if it does. The log file is assigned to a thread, either explicitly with the thread clause or to the thread assigned to the current instance of Oracle. A **GROUP** is a collection of log files. You can add a **GROUP** of log files by listing them, and you can name the group with an integer.

ADD LOGFILE MEMBER adds new files to an existing log file group, either by specifying the **GROUP** integer or by listing all the log files in the group.

DROP LOGFILE drops an existing redo log file group. **DROP LOGFILE MEMBER** drops one or more members of a log file group.

RENAME changes the name of an existing database or log file.

ARCHIVELOG and **NOARCHIVELOG** define the way redo log files are used. **NOARCHIVELOG** is the default, and using it means that redo files will be reused without saving their contents elsewhere. This provides instance recovery except from a media failure, such as a disk crash. **ARCHIVELOG** forces redo files to be archived (usually to another disk or a tape), so that you can recover from a media failure. This mode also supports instance recovery.

When a database is first created, it is **MOUNT**ed in **EXCLUSIVE** mode, meaning no one but its creator has access to it. To allow multiple instances to access the database, use **MOUNT PARALLEL** if you have installed the Oracle Parallel Server option.

After mounting a database, you **OPEN** it. **RESETLOGS** resets the redo log, cleaning out any redo entries. You use this option to restore a database after a partial recovery from a media failure. The **NORESETLOGS** option leaves everything the same when you **OPEN** the database.

You can **ENABLE** or **DISABLE** a **THREAD**. **PUBLIC** makes the thread available to any instance not requesting a specific thread.

You can **BACKUP** a **CONTROLFILE** to the specified file.

You can bring a file **ONLINE** or take it **OFFLINE** with the *datafile* clause.

The **AUTOEXTEND** clause can be used to dynamically extend datafiles as needed, in increments of **NEXT** size, to a maximum of **MAXSIZE** (or **UNLIMITED**). You can use the **RESIZE** clause to increase or decrease the size of an existing datafile.

You can **CREATE** a new **DATAFILE** to replace an old one to re-create a data file lost without backup.

You can **RENAME GLOBAL_NAME** to change the name of the database. If you specify a domain, tell Oracle where the database is on the network. You must change references to the database from remote databases as well.

You can **RECOVER** the database with a recover clause. This command performs media recovery for a lost database. You can use multiple recovery processes to apply redo entries to datafiles for each instance. *See* **RECOVER**.

You can use the **RESET COMPATIBILITY** option, in conjunction with the **COMPATIBLE** parameter in the init.ora file, to revert from compatibility with one version of Oracle to a previous version.

You can **SET DBMAC ON** or **OFF** for Trusted Oracle , or **SET DBHIGH** or **DBLOW** to an operating system string.

EXAMPLE

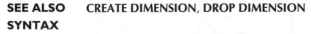

```
alter database add logfile group 1 'biglog.006' size 1m reuse;
```

ALTER DIMENSION

SEE ALSO   CREATE DIMENSION, DROP DIMENSION

SYNTAX

level_clause::=

hierarchy_clause::=

join_clause::=

attribute_clause::=

DESCRIPTION **ALTER DIMENSION** modifies the attributes, hierarchy, and levels of an existing dimension. *See* **CREATE DIMENSION**.

EXAMPLE

```
alter dimension TIME drop hierarchy MONTH_TO_DATE;
```

ALTER FUNCTION

SEE ALSO **CREATE FUNCTION**, **DROP FUNCTION**, Chapter 27

SYNTAX

DESCRIPTION **ALTER FUNCTION** recompiles a PL/SQL function. You can avoid runtime overhead and error messages by explicitly compiling a function in advance. To alter a function, you must either own the function or have the ALTER ANY PROCEDURE system privilege.

ALTER INDEX

SEE ALSO   **CREATE INDEX**, **DROP INDEX**, **STORAGE**, Chapters 18 and 20

SYNTAX

deallocate_unused_clause::=

allocate_extent_clause::=

parallel_clause::=

physical_attributes_clause::=

rebuild_clause::=

compression_clause::=

partitioning_clauses::=

modify_default_attributes_clause::=

modify_partition_clause::=

rename_partition/subpartition_clause::=

drop_partition_clause::=

split_partition_clause::=

partition_description::=

modify_subpartition_clause::=

DESCRIPTION *user* is the user who owns the index you wish to alter (if you are not that user, you must have DBA privileges). *index* is the name of an existing index. *See* **CREATE TABLE** for a description of **INITRANS** and **MAXTRANS**. The default for **INITRANS** for indexes is 2; **MAXTRANS** is 255. **STORAGE** contains subclauses that are described under **STORAGE**. You must have INDEX privilege on the table in order to create an index, and you must also either own the index or have the ALTER ANY INDEX system privilege.

You can use the **REBUILD** clause of the **ALTER INDEX** command to change the storage characteristics of an existing index. **REBUILD** uses the existing index as the basis for the new index. All index storage commands are supported, such as **STORAGE** (for extent allocation), **TABLESPACE** (to move the index to a new tablespace), and **INITRANS** (to change the initial number of entries).

You can modify, rename, drop, split, or rebuild index partitions.

COMPRESS enables key compression, eliminating repeated occurrence of key column values. *integer* specifies the prefix length (number of prefix columns to compress). By default, indexes are not compressed. You cannot compress a bitmapped index.

ALTER JAVA
SEE ALSO   **CREATE JAVA**, **DROP JAVA**, Chapter 34
SYNTAX

invoker_rights_clause::=

DESCRIPTION **ALTER JAVA** recompiles a Java source schema object. You can also use this command to change the authorization enforced (definer or current user). To alter Java source schema objects, you must either own the source or class or have the ALTER ANY PROCEDURE system privilege.

ALTER MATERIALIZED VIEW/SNAPSHOT
SEE ALSO   **CREATE MATERIALIZED VIEW/SNAPSHOT**, **DROP MATERIALIZED VIEW/SNAPSHOT**, Chapter 23

SYNTAX

parallel_clause::=

refresh_clause::=

physical_attributes_clause::=

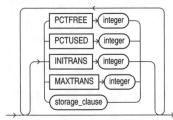

DESCRIPTION   As of ORACLE8i, a snapshot is treated as a materialized view.

ALTER MATERIALIZED VIEW/SNAPSHOT lets you change the storage characteristics or refresh mode and times of a snapshot or materialized view. You can also enable or disable query rewrite for the materialized view. To alter a materialized view, you must own the materialized view or have ALTER ANY SNAPSHOT or ALTER ANY MATERIALIZED VIEW system privilege. *See* **CREATE MATERIALIZED VIEW/SNAPSHOT** and Chapter 23 for details.

EXAMPLE

```
alter materialized view MONTHLY_SALES
    enable query rewrite compile;
```

ALTER MATERIALIZED VIEW LOG/SNAPSHOT LOG

SEE ALSO   CREATE MATERIALIZED VIEW/SNAPSHOT, CREATE MATERIALIZED VIEW LOG/SNAPSHOT LOG, DROP MATERIALIZED VIEW LOG/SNAPSHOT LOG, Chapter 23

SYNTAX

physical_attributes_clause::=

parallel_clause::=

DESCRIPTION   As of Oracle8i, a snapshot is treated as a materialized view.

ALTER MATERIALIZED VIEW LOG/SNAPSHOT LOG lets you change the storage characteristics of a materialized view log/snapshot log. To alter the log, you must either have ALTER privilege on the log table, or you must have the ALTER ANY TABLE system privilege. *See* **CREATE MATERIALIZED VIEW LOG/SNAPSHOT LOG** and Chapter 23.

ALTER OUTLINE

SEE ALSO   **CREATE OUTLINE, DROP OUTLINE**
SYNTAX

DESCRIPTION   You can use **ALTER OUTLINE** to rename a stored outline or to assign it to a different category. Stored outlines maintain sets of hints for previously executed queries. See *Oracle8i Tuning* or *Oracle8i DBA Handbook*.

ALTER PACKAGE

SEE ALSO   **CREATE PACKAGE, DROP PACKAGE**, Chapter 27
SYNTAX

DESCRIPTION   **ALTER PACKAGE** recompiles a package specification and/or body. If you recompile the specification using **PACKAGE**, you recompile both the specification and the body. Recompiling the specification will cause referencing procedures to be recompiled. You can recompile the **BODY** without affecting the specification. To alter a package, you must either be the owner of the package or have the ALTER ANY PROCEDURE system privilege.

ALTER PROCEDURE
SEE ALSO   **CREATE PROCEDURE, DROP PROCEDURE**, Chapter 27
SYNTAX

DESCRIPTION   **ALTER PROCEDURE** recompiles a PL/SQL procedure. You can avoid runtime overhead and error messages by explicitly compiling a procedure in advance. To alter a procedure, you must either own the procedure or have ALTER ANY PROCEDURE system privilege.

ALTER PROFILE
SEE ALSO   **CREATE PROFILE, DROP PROFILE**, Chapter 19
SYNTAX

resource_parameters::=

password_parameters::=

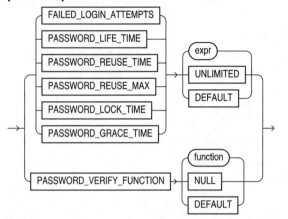

DESCRIPTION   **ALTER PROFILE** lets you modify a particular profile setting. *See* **CREATE PROFILE** for details.

ALTER RESOURCE COST

SEE ALSO   **CREATE PROFILE**
SYNTAX

DESCRIPTION   The resource cost formula calculates the total cost of resources used in an Oracle session. **ALTER RESOURCE COST** lets you assign a weight to several resources. CPU_PER_SESSION is the amount of CPU used in a session in hundredths of a second. CONNECT_TIME is the elapsed time of the session in minutes. LOGICAL_READS_ PER_SESSION is the number of data blocks read from both memory and disk during a session. PRIVATE_SGA is the number of bytes in a private System Global Area (SGA), which is only relevant if you are using the multi-threaded server. By assigning weights, you change the formula used to calculate total resource cost.

ALTER ROLE

SEE ALSO   **CREATE ROLE, DROP ROLE**, Chapter 19
SYNTAX

DESCRIPTION   **ALTER ROLE** lets you modify a role. *See* **CREATE ROLE** and Chapter 19 for details.

ALTER ROLLBACK SEGMENT

SEE ALSO   **CREATE DATABASE, CREATE ROLLBACK SEGMENT, CREATE TABLESPACE, DROP ROLLBACK SEGMENT, STORAGE,** Chapter 38

SYNTAX

DESCRIPTION   *segment* is a name assigned to this rollback segment. **STORAGE** contains subclauses that are described under **STORAGE**. The **INITIAL** and **MINEXTENTS** options are not applicable. A rollback segment can be taken **ONLINE** or **OFFLINE** while the database is open. You can **SHRINK** it to a specified size (the default is its **OPTIMAL** size).

ALTER SEQUENCE

SEE ALSO   **AUDIT, CREATE SEQUENCE, DROP SEQUENCE, GRANT, REVOKE, NEXTVAL** and **CURRVAL** under PSEUDO-COLUMNS, Chapter 20

SYNTAX

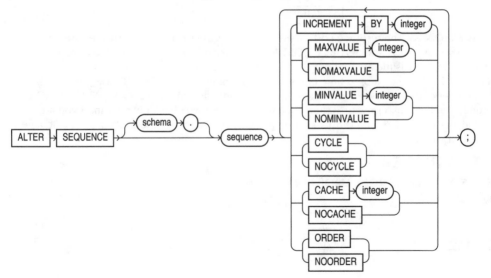

DESCRIPTION   All of these options affect the future use of an existing sequence with the name *sequence*. (Note that **start with** is not available. To change the value with which a sequence starts, you must **DROP** the sequence and **CREATE** it again.)

A new **MAXVALUE** cannot be specified that is lower than the existing **CURRVAL** on an ascending sequence one which has a positive number as its **INCREMENT BY**.) A similar rule applies for **MINVALUE** on a descending sequence (which has a negative **INCREMENT BY**.)

To alter a sequence, you must have ALTER privilege on the sequence or have the ALTER ANY SEQUENCE system privilege.

All other features of **ALTER SEQUENCE** work as they do in **CREATE SEQUENCE**, except that they apply to an existing sequence. *See* **CREATE SEQUENCE** for details.

ALTER SESSION

SEE ALSO   *Oracle8i Tuning, Oracle8i Administrator's Guide*
SYNTAX

set_clause::=

DESCRIPTION   The CREATE SESSION command alters settings in effect for the current user session. To generate performance statistics for SQL statement processing by Oracle, set SQL_TRACE to TRUE. To turn them off, set it to FALSE. The init.ora parameter SQL_TRACE sets the initial value for this trace.

ADVISE allows you to send transaction handling advice to remote databases involved in distributed transactions. You can **CLOSE** a **DATABASE LINK** to eliminate the session's link to a remote database.

The various NLS options (enabled via the *set* clause) let you set up the national language support for a specific session if you have the ALTER SESSION system privilege. NLS_LANGUAGE is the language for errors and other messages and controls the language for month and day names and the sorting mechanism. NLS_TERRITORY sets the date format, decimal character, group separator, local and ISO currency symbols, the first week day for the D date format, and the calculation of ISO week numbers in date functions. NLS_DATE_FORMAT sets the default date format; NLS_DATE_LANGUAGE controls the day and month names; NLS_NUMERIC_ CHARACTERS gives the decimal character and group separator in the format 'dg', where d is the decimal character and g is the group separator; NLS_ISO_CURRENCY gives a territory for a currency symbol; NLS_CURRENCY gives a specific currency symbol; and NLS_SORT changes the linguistic sort sequence. LABEL and MLS_LABEL_FORMAT are part of Trusted ORACLE.

You can specify whether procedures can **COMMIT** or not, and the degree to which DML operations are parallelized. If you enable parallel DML or DDL for your session, you still must specify the PARALLEL hint for the operations to be executed in parallel.

ALTER SNAPSHOT
See **ALTER MATERIALIZED VIEW/SNAPSHOT**

ALTER SNAPSHOT LOG
See **ALTER MATERIALIZED VIEW LOG/SNAPSHOT LOG**

ALTER SYSTEM
SEE ALSO ALTER SESSION, ARCHIVE_LOG, CREATE PROFILE
SYNTAX

archive_log_clause::=

set_clause::=

DESCRIPTION   **ALTER SYSTEM** lets you change your Oracle instance in many ways. Via the **SET** options, you can change many of the init.ora parameter values while the database is running. Not all parameters can be changed, but those that can include **MTS_SERVERS** and **MTS_DISPATCHERS** for multithreaded server and the **LICENSE_MAX_SESSIONS, LICENSE_SESSIONS_WARNING,** and **LICENSE_MAX_ USERS** parameters you can set to establish threshold and maximum limits for the number of sessions and users in your database.

   You can also use the **ALTER SYSTEM** command to **SWITCH LOGFILE**, forcing Oracle to change log file groups.

   CHECKPOINT performs a checkpoint for (**GLOBAL**) all instances or (**LOCAL**) your instance of Oracle. **CHECK DATAFILES** verifies that every instance (**GLOBAL**) or your instance (**LOCAL**) of Oracle can access all online data files.

   ENABLE or **DISABLE RESTRICTED SESSION** turns on or off a restricted session, accessible only to users with that system privilege.

   ENABLE or **DISABLE DISTRIBUTED RECOVERY** turns this option on or off, respectively.

   ARCHIVE LOG manually archives the redo log files or enables automatic archiving.

   FLUSH SHARED_POOL clears all data from the SGA shared pool.

   KILL SESSION ends a session with either the SID column or the SERIAL# column of the V$SESSION table identifying the session. **DISCONNECT SESSION**, unlike **KILL SESSION**, gives you the option of forcing the session's outstanding transactions to be posted prior to the termination of the session.

ALTER TABLE

SEE ALSO   **CREATE TABLE, DISABLE, DROP, ENABLE**, Chapters 18, 20, 29, and 30
SYNTAX

add_column_options::=

LOB_storage_clause::=

LOB_parameters::=

partition_LOB_storage_clause::=

modify_column_options::=

move_table_clause::=

segment_attributes_clause::=

physical_attributes_clause::=

index_organized_table_clause::=

compression_clause::=

index_organized_overflow_clause::=

modify_collection_retrieval_clause::=

storage_clauses::=

modify_LOB_storage_clause::=

modify_LOB_storage_parameters::=

allocate_extent_clause::=

deallocate_unused_clause::=

varray_storage_clause::=

modify_varray_storage_clause::=

nested_table_storage_clause::=

object_properties::=

physical_properties::=

drop_contstraint_clause::=

drop_column_clause::=

records_per_block_clause::=

alter_overflow_clause::=

overflow_clause::=

add_overflow_clause::=

partitioning_clauses::=

modify_default_attributes_clause::=

modify_partitioning_clause::=

partition_attributes::=

add_subpartition_clause::=

subpartition_description::=

modify_subpartition_clause::=

move_partition_clause::=

partition_description::=

partition_level_subpartitioning::=

partitioning_storage_clause::=

move_subpartition_clause::=

add_range_partition_clause::=

add_hash_partition_clause::=

coalesce_partition_clause::=

drop_partition_clause::=

rename_partition/subpartition_clause::=

truncate_partition_clause/truncate_subpartition_clause::=

split_partition_clause::=

merge_partitions_clause::=

exchange_partition_clause/exchange_subpartition_clause::=

row_movement_clause::=

parallel_clause::=

enable_disable_clause::=

using_index_clause::=

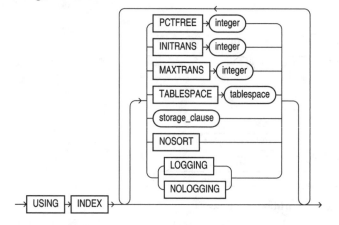

DESCRIPTION   **ALTER TABLE** changes the definition of an existing table. **ADD** allows you to add a new column to the end of an existing table, or add a constraint to the table's definition. These follow the same format used in **CREATE TABLE**.

MODIFY changes an existing column, with some restrictions:

You may change the type of column or decrease its size only if the column is NULL in every row of the table.

A NOT NULL column may be added only to a table with no rows.

An existing column can be modified to NOT NULL only if it has a non-NULL value in every row.

Increasing the length of a NOT NULL column without specifying NULL will leave it NOT NULL.

As of Oracle8i, you can drop columns from tables. You can use the **SET UNUSED** clause to mark columns as unused. When you use the **DROP UNUSED COLUMNS** clause, the table will be reorganized and all unused columns will be dropped.

ALLOCATE EXTENT lets you allocate a new extent explicitly. **ENABLE** and **DISABLE** enable and disable constraints. All other features of **ALTER TABLE** work as they do in **CREATE TABLE**, except that they apply to an existing table. *See* **CREATE TABLE** for details.

In order to alter a table, you must either have the ALTER privilege for that table or the ALTER ANY TABLE system privilege.

When blocks are read from the database, Oracle stores them in the SGA. Oracle maintains a list (the *LRU* list) of the *least recently used* blocks; when extra space is needed in the SGA, the least recently used data blocks are removed from the SGA.

CACHE overrides this behavior by specifying that the blocks for this table , when read, are to be placed at the "most recently used" end of the LRU list. Therefore, the blocks will stay in the SGA longer. This option is useful if the tables are small and fairly static. NOCACHE (the default) reverts the table back to the normal LRU list behavior.

PARALLEL, along with **DEGREE** and **INSTANCES**, specifies the parallel characteristics of the table (for databases using the Parallel Query option). **DEGREE** specifies the number of query servers to use; **INSTANCES** specifies how the table is to be split among instances of a Parallel Server for parallel query processing. An integer *n* specifies that the table is to be split among the specified number of available instances.

You can use **ALTER TABLE** to **ADD, DROP, EXCHANGE, MODIFY, MOVE, SPLIT**, or **TRUNCATE** partitions. *See* Chapter 18 and **CREATE TABLE**.

LOB storage clauses specify the storage area to be used for out-of-line storage of internally-stored LOB data.

The **MOVE ONLINE** option allows you to access a table for DML operations during an online table reorganization. The **MOVE** and **MOVE ONLINE** options are only available for non-partitioned index-organized tables. During a **MOVE ONLINE** operation, parallel DML operations against the table are not supported.

ALTER TABLESPACE

SEE ALSO   **CREATE TABLESPACE, DROP TABLESPACE, STORAGE**, Chapters 20, 38

SYNTAX

datafile/tempfile_clause::=

autoextend_clause::=

maxsize_clause::=

DESCRIPTION   *tablespace* is the name of an existing tablespace. **ADD DATAFILE** adds to the tablespace a file or series of files described according to a *file_definition*, which specifies the database file names and sizes:

```
'file' [SIZE integer [K | M]] [REUSE]
```

The file name format is operating system specific. **SIZE** is the number of bytes set aside for this file. Suffixing this with K multiplies the value by 1024; using M multiplies it by 1048576. **REUSE** (without **SIZE**) means destroy the contents of any file by this name and give the name to this database. **SIZE** and **REUSE** create the file if it doesn't exist, and check its size if it does. **SIZE** alone will create the file if it doesn't exist, but will return an error if it does.

You can use the **AUTOEXTEND** clause to dynamically resize your datafiles as needed, in increments of **NEXT** size, to a maximum of **MAXSIZ** (or UNLIMITED).

NOLOGGING specifies the default action for the writing of redo log entries for certain types of transactions in the tablespace. You can override this setting at the object level. *See* Chapter 21.

RENAME changes the name of an existing tablespace file. The tablespace should be offline while the renaming takes place. Note that **RENAME** does not actually rename the files; it only associates their new names with this tablespace. Actually renaming operating system files must be done with the operating system itself. To properly rename files, first **ALTER TABLESPACE OFFLINE**, rename the files in the operating system, **RENAME** them with **ALTER TABLESPACE**, and then **ALTER TABLESPACE ONLINE**.

DEFAULT STORAGE defines the default storage for all future objects created in this tablespace, unless those defaults are overridden, such as by **CREATE TABLE**. **ONLINE** brings the tablespace back online. **OFFLINE** takes it offline, either without waiting for its users to logoff (**IMMEDIATE**), or after they've all stopped using it (**NORMAL**).

MINIMUM EXTENT sets the minimum size for any extent created in the tablespace. **COALESCE** combines neighboring free extents in the tablespace into fewer, larger free extents.

READ ONLY tablespaces are never updated by Oracle, and can be placed on read-only media. Read-only tablespaces are not backed up. All tablespaces are created read-write. To change a read-only tablespace back to read-write status, use the **READ WRITE** clause.

BEGIN BACKUP can be executed at any time. It assures that all of the database files in this tablespace will be backed up the next time a system backup is done. **END BACKUP** indicates the system backup is finished. If the tablespace is online, any system backup must also back up archive redo logs. If it is offline, this is unnecessary.

TEMPORARY tablespaces cannot contain any permanent objects (such as tables or indexes); they can only hold the temporary segments used by Oracle during the processing of sorting operations and index creations. A **PERMANENT** tablespace can hold every type of Oracle segment.

ALTER TRIGGER

SEE ALSO   **CREATE TRIGGER, DROP TRIGGER, ENABLE, TRIGGER**, Chapter 26

SYNTAX

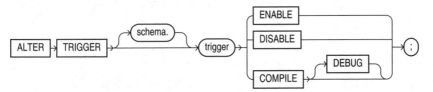

DESCRIPTION   **ALTER TRIGGER** enables, disables, or recompiles a PL/SQL trigger. *See* **CREATE TRIGGER** and Chapter 26 for a discussion of triggers. To use the **ALTER TRIGGER** command, you must either own the trigger or have ALTER ANY TRIGGER system privilege.

You can use the **COMPILE** clause to manually recompile an invalid trigger object. Since triggers have dependencies, they can become invalid if an object the trigger depends on changes. The **DEBUG** clause allows PL/SQL information to be generated during trigger recompilation.

ALTER TYPE

SEE ALSO   **CREATE TYPE**, **CREATE TYPE BODY**, Chapters 4 and 28
SYNTAX

element_list::=

pragma_clause::=

DESCRIPTION   **ALTER TYPE** allows you to modify existing abstract datatypes. When you create a method that acts on the abstract datatype, you use the **CREATE TYPE BODY** command (*see* entry in this chapter). Each method defined in the type body must first be listed in the type. Member functions typically use the PRAGMA RESTRICT_REFERENCES option with the WNDS (Write No Database State) constraint.

ALTER USER

SEE ALSO CREATE TABLESPACE, GRANT, CREATE PROFILE, CREATE USER, Chapter 19

SYNTAX

proxy_clause::=

DESCRIPTION You use **ALTER USER** to change a user's password, or the **DEFAULT** tablespace (for objects the user owns) or **TEMPORARY** tablespace (for temporary segments used by the user). Without **ALTER USER**, the defaults for both of these are set by the defaults of the first tablespace (both for objects and temporary segments) to which the user is **GRANT**ed resource. **ALTER USER** can also change the quota, the resource profile, or the default role (*see* **CREATE USER**). You can use the **PASSWORD EXPIRE** clause to force a user's password to expire, in which case the user must change his or her password during the next login. The **ACCOUNT UNLOCK** clause allows you to unlock an account that has exceeded its maximum number of consecutive failed login attempts. *See* **CREATE PROFILE** for details on password control. To alter a user, you must have the ALTER USER system privilege.

You can use the **PROXY** clause to connect as the specified user and to activate all, some, or none of the user's roles. **PROXY** is typically used in three-tier applications involving application servers.

ALTER VIEW
SEE ALSO **CREATE VIEW, DROP VIEW**, Chapter 18
SYNTAX

ALTER → VIEW → schema. → view → COMPILE → ;

DESCRIPTION ALTER VIEW recompiles a view. Use it to find errors before executing the view. This is particularly useful after changing a base table in some way. To alter a view, you must either own the view or have ALTER ANY TABLE system privilege.

ANALYZE
SEE ALSO Chapter 36
SYNTAX

for_clause::=

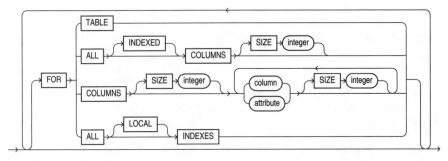

DESCRIPTION   **ANALYZE** lets you collect statistics about a table, cluster, partition, or index for the optimizer, storing them in the data dictionary; it lets you delete these statistics; it validates the structure of an object; and it identifies migrated and chained rows of a table or cluster with a listing in a local table. Estimating is usually faster and pretty much as accurate as **COMPUTE** for optimizer statistics. You use the **VALIDATE STRUCTURE** clause to test an object for possible data corruption. To analyze a table, you must either own the table or have the ANALYZE ANY system privilege.

You can use the **FOR** clause with **COMPUTE STATISTICS** and **ESTIMATE STATISTICS**. The **FOR** clause allows you to alter the default behavior of **ANALYZE**. You can analyze a table without its indexes (**FOR TABLE**), a table and all of its indexed columns (**FOR TABLE FOR INDEXED COLUMNS**), just the indexed columns (**FOR ALL INDEXED COLUMNS**), or just specific columns. The **SIZE** parameter is used to populate data histograms used by the cost-based optimizer during advanced tuning efforts.

The **LIST CHAINED ROWS** clause records information about row chaining in a table you specify.

ANALYZE can only analyze a single object at a time. To analyze an entire schema, you can use the DBMS_UTILITY.ANALYZE_SCHEMA procedure; that procedure takes two parameters-the schema name and the method to use (COMPUTE or ESTIMATE). *See* the *Oracle Server Application Developer's Guide.*

AND

See LOGICAL OPERATORS, PRECEDENCE, TEXT SEARCH OPERATORS.

ANSI

The American National Standards Institute sets standards for the SQL language and its many elements.

ANY

SEE ALSO   ALL, BETWEEN, EXISTS, IN, LOGICAL OPERATORS, Chapter 12
FORMAT

```
operator ANY list
```

DESCRIPTION   = **ANY** is the equivalent of **IN**. *operator* can be any one of =, >, >=, <, <=, != and *list* can be a series of literal strings (such as 'Talbot', 'Jones', or 'Hild'), or series of literal numbers (such as 2, 43, 76, 32.06, or 444), or a column from a subquery, where each row of the subquery becomes a member of the list, as shown here:

```
LOCATION.City = ANY (select City from WEATHER)
```

It also can be a series of columns in the **where** clause of the main query, as shown here:

```
Prospect = ANY (Vendor, Client)
```

RESTRICTIONS   *list* cannot be a series of columns in a subquery, like this:

```
Prospect = ANY (select Vendor, Client from . . .)
```

Many people find this operator and the **ALL** operator very difficult to remember, because the logic for some of their cases is not immediately intuitive. As a result, some form of **EXISTS** is usually substituted.

The combination of an operator with **ANY** and a list can be illustrated with these explanations:

Page = ANY (4,2,7)	Page is in the list (4,2,7)-2, 4, and 7 all qualify.
Page > ANY (4,2,7)	Page is greater than any single item in the list (4,2,7)-even 3 qualifies, because it is greater than 2.
Page >= ANY (4,2,7)	Page is greater than or equal to any single item in the list (4,2,7)-even 2 qualifies, because it is equal to 2.
Page < ANY (4,2,7)	Page is less than any single item in the list (4,2,7)-even 6 qualifies, because it is less than 7.
Page <= ANY (4,2,7)	Page is less than or equal to any single item in the list (4,2,7)-even 7 qualifies.
Page != ANY (4,2,7)	Page is not equal to any single item in the list (4,2,7)-any number qualifies so long as the list has more than one value. With only one value, != ANY is the equivalent of !=.

APPEND

SEE ALSO   **CHANGE, DEL, EDIT, LIST,** Chapter 6

FORMAT

```
A[PPEND] text
```

DESCRIPTION   APPEND is a feature of the SQL*PLUS command line editor. **APPEND** places the text at the end of the current line in the current buffer, with no intervening spaces. If you want a space between the end of the current line and *text*, put two spaces between **APPEND** and *text*. If you want to append a semicolon at the end of a line, put two of them together (one of them will be regarded as a command terminator and discarded).

EXAMPLE

```
APPEND ;;
```

APPLICATION

An application is a set of forms, menus, reports, and other components that satisfies a particular business function. For example, you might build an application to serve as an order entry system.

ARCH PROCESS

One of the background processes used by Oracle, ARCH performs automatic archiving of redo log files when the database is used in **ARCHIVELOG** mode. *See* BACKGROUND PROCESS.

ARCHIVE

In a general sense, archiving means to save data for possible later use. In a specific sense, it means to save the data found in the online redo logs, in the event that the logs are needed to restore media.

ARGUMENT

An argument is an expression within the parentheses of a function, supplying a value for the function to use.

ARRAY PROCESSING

Array processing is processing performed on batches of data rather than one row at a time. In some Oracle utilities such as Export/Import and the precompilers, users can set the size of the array; increasing the array size will generally improve performance.

ARRAYSIZE (SQL*PLUS)

See **SET**.

AS

SEE ALSO   **ALIAS, TO_CHAR**, Chapters 7 and 9

DESCRIPTION   AS is used to separate column formulas from column aliases.

EXAMPLE   Here AS separates the column alias PayDay from its column formula:

```
select NEXT_DAY(CycleDate,'FRIDAY') AS PayDay
from PAYDAY;
```

ASCII

SEE ALSO   CHARACTER FUNCTIONS, **CHR**

FORMAT

```
ASCII(string)
```

DESCRIPTION   ASCII is an acronym for "American Standard Code for Information Interchange." It is a convention for using digital data to represent printable characters.

The **ASCII** function will return the ASCII value of the first (leftmost) character in the string. The ASCII value of a character is an integer between 0 and 254. Those between 0 and 127 are well defined. Those above 127 ("extended ASCII set") tend to differ by country, application, and computer manufacturer. The letter A, for instance, is equal to the ASCII number 65; B is 66; C is 67, and so on. The decimal point is 46. A minus sign is 45. The number 0 is 48; 1 is 49; 2 is 50, and so on.

EXAMPLE

```
select Midnight, ASCII(Midnight) from COMFORT;
```

```
MIDNIGHT ASCII(MIDNIGHT)
-------- ---------------
    42.3              52
    71.9              55
    61.5              54
    39.8              51
    -1.2              45
    66.7              54
    82.6              56
    -1.2              45

select ASCII('.'), ASCII(.5),
```

```
      ASCII('M'), ASCII('MULLER')
  from DUAL;

ASCII('.') ASCII(.5) ASCII('M') ASCII('MULLER')
---------- --------- ---------- ---------------
        46        46         77              77
```

ASIN

SEE ALSO   ACOS, ATAN, ATAN2, COS, COSH, EXP, LN, LOG, SIN, SINH, TAN, TANH
FORMAT

ASIN(*value*)

DESCRIPTION   ASIN returns the arc sine of a value. Input values range from -1 to 1; outputs are expressed in radians.

ASSOCIATE STATISTICS

SEE ALSO   ANALYZE
SYNTAX

column_association::=

function_association::=

using_clause::=

default_cost_clause::=

default_selectivity_clause::=

→ DEFAULT → SELECTIVITY → (default_selectivity) →

DESCRIPTION   **ASSOCIATE STATISTICS** associates a set of statistics functions with one or more columns, standalone functions, packages, types, or indexes. You must have the required privileges to **ALTER** the object being modified.

   You can view associations in USER_USTATS after you analyze the object with which you are associating your statistics functions.

ATAN

SEE ALSO   ACOS, ASIN, ATAN2, COS, COSH, EXP, LN, LOG, SIN, SINH, TAN, TANH

FORMAT

```
ATAN(value)
```

DESCRIPTION   **ATAN** returns the arc tangent of a value. Input values are unbounded; outputs are expressed in radians.

ATAN2

SEE ALSO   ACOS, ASIN, ATAN, COS, COSH, EXP, LN, LOG, SIN, SINH, TAN, TANH

FORMAT

```
ATAN2(value1, value2)
```

DESCRIPTION   **ATAN2** returns the arc tangent of two values. Input values are unbounded; outputs are expressed in radians.

ATTRIBUTE

An attribute can be one of three things:

- A synonym of "characteristic" or "property"
- Another name for column
- A part of an abstract datatype

AUDIT (Form I—SQL Statements)

SEE ALSO   CREATE DATABASE LINK, DATA DICTIONARY, NOAUDIT, PRIVILEGE

SYNTAX

DESCRIPTION The second format of the AUDIT command audits use of a system facility, and requires that you have AUDIT SYSTEM system privilege.

The *statement options* are:

Option	Audits
CLUSTER	Create, alter, drop, or truncate cluster
CONTEXT	Create or drop context
DATABASE LINK	Create or drop database link
DIMENSION	Create, alter, or drop dimensior
DIRECTORY	Create or drop directory
INDEX	Create, alter, or drop index
NOT EXISTS	SQL statements that fail because an object does not exist
PROCEDURE	Create, alter, or drop procedure, function, or package; and create package body
PROFILE	Create, alter, or drop profile
PUBLIC DATABASE LINK	Create or drop public database link
PUBLIC SYNONYM	Create or drop public synonym
ROLE	Create, alter, drop, or set role
ROLLBACK SEGMENT	Create, alter, or drop rollback segment
SEQUENCE	Create, alter, or drop sequence
SESSION	Logon attempts
SYNONYM	Create or drop synonym
SYSTEM AUDIT	Audit or noaudit of SQL statements
SYSTEM GRANT	Audit or noaudit of system privileges and roles
TABLE	Create, alter, drop, or truncate table
TABLESPACE	Create, alter, or drop tablespace
TRIGGER	Create, alter, or drop trigger; alter table with ENABLE|DISABLE ALL TRIGGERS
TYPE	Create, alter, or drop type or type body
USER	Create, alter, or drop user
VIEW	Create or drop view

You may also audit each individual command covered by the statement option. Oracle also provides the following groups of statement options:

- **CONNECT** audits Oracle logons and logoffs.
- **DBA** audits commands that require DBA authority.
- **RESOURCE** audits **CREATE** and **DROP** for tables, clusters, views, indexes, tablespaces, and synonyms.
- **ALL** audits all of these facilities.
- **BY** *user* audits only SQL statements issued by particular users. The default is to audit all users.
- **WHENEVER [NOT] SUCCESSFUL** writes a row to an audit table only when an attempted access to an audited table or system facility is (or is **NOT**) successful. Omitting this optional clause causes a row to be written whether an access is successful or not.

Both **AUDIT** formats commit any pending changes to the database. If remote tables are accessed through a database link, any auditing on the remote system is based on options set there. Auditing information is written to a table named SYS.AUD$ and accessed via views; *see* DATA DICTIONARY VIEWS.

EXAMPLE   This audits all successful logons:

```
audit CONNECT whenever successful;
```

AUDIT (Form 2—Schema Objects)
SEE ALSO   DATA DICTIONARY, NOAUDIT, PRIVILEGE
SYNTAX

DESCRIPTION   The AUDIT command (form 2) audits the specified commands (*options*), when performed on the specified database *object(s)*. *option* specifies which commands should be audited. Options are **ALTER, AUDIT, COMMENT, DELETE, EXECUTE, GRANT, INDEX, INSERT, LOCK, READ, RENAME, SELECT**, and **UPDATE. GRANT** audits both **GRANT** and **REVOKE** commands. **ALL** audits all of these

ON *object* names the object to be audited, which may be owned by *user. object* can be a table, view, synonym of a table or view, sequence, procedure, stored function, package, or materialized view. To audit any of these, you must either own them or have AUDIT ANY system privilege. **ON DEFAULT** means a change to the **DEFAULT** table options, which controls the auditing options assigned to all tables, and requires DBA authority. This default for all tables is set using the word **DEFAULT** instead of a table name:

```
audit grant, insert, update, delete on default;
```

ALTER, EXECUTE, INDEX, and **READ** cannot be used for views. The default options of a view are created by the union of the options of each of the underlying tables plus the **DEFAULT** options. The auditing of tables and views are independent.

For synonyms, the options are the same as tables.

For sequences, the options are **ALTER, AUDIT, GRANT,** and **SELECT.**

EXECUTE can only beused for procedures, functions, abstract datatypes, libraries, or packages, for which you also can audit **AUDIT, GRANT,** and **RENAME** options.

The audit options for materialized views and snapshots are identical to those for tables.

You can audit **AUDIT, GRANT,** and **READ** for directories. For libraries, you can audit **EXECUTE** and **GRANT.**

BY ACCESS or **BY SESSION** writes a row to an audit table for each command or each user session using the table being audited. If this clause is missing, auditing is **BY SESSION** by default. **BY ACCESS** also does **BY SESSION.**

NOAUDIT reverses the effect of **AUDIT.**

If remote tables are accessed through a database link, any auditing on the remote system is based on options set there. Auditing information is written to a table named SYS.AUD$; see DATA DICTIONARY VIEWS.

EXAMPLES   The following audits all attempts to use **update** or **delete** on the WORKER table:

```
audit update, delete on WORKER by access;
```

The following audits all unsuccessful accesses to WORKER:

```
audit all on WORKER whenever not successful;
```

AUDIT TRAIL

An audit trail is a database table written to when auditing is enabled (by the init.ora parameter) and auditing options have been selected by users or the DBA. The table AUD$, owned by SYS, contains all audit trail rows.

AUDITING

Auditing is a set of ORACLE installation and data dictionary features that allow the DBA and users to track usage of the database. The DBA can set default auditing activity. The auditing information is stored in the data dictionary, and SQL statements control which information is stored. For example, you can have all attempts to update a table's data be recorded, or only unsuccessful attempts. Alternatively, you can have all logins to Oracle be recorded, or only unsuccessful attempts to do DBA activities.

AUTHORIZATION

See PRIVILEGE.

AUTOCOMMIT

AUTOCOMMIT is a SQL*PLUS command used to automatically commit changes to the database following any SQL command that **insert**s, **update**s, or **delete**s data in the database. *See* **SET.**

AVG

SEE ALSO   **COMPUTE,** GROUP FUNCTIONS, Chapter 8

FORMAT

```
AVG([DISTINCT] value)
```

DESCRIPTION   **AVG** is the average of value for a group of rows. **DISTINCT** forces only unique values to be averaged. **NULL** rows are ignored by this function, which may affect results.

B-TREE

B-TREE is a high performance indexing structure used by Oracle to create and store indexes.

BACKGROUND PROCESS

A background process is one of the processes used by an instance of multiple-process Oracle to perform and coordinate tasks on behalf of concurrent users of a database. The base processes are named ARCH (archiver), DBWR (database writer), LGWR (log writer), PMON (process monitor), and SMON (system monitor), and exist as long as an instance does.

BEGIN

SEE ALSO   **BLOCK STRUCTURE, DECLARE, END, EXCEPTION, TERMINATOR**, Chapter 25

FORMAT

```
[<<block label>>]
[DECLARE]
BEGIN
    ... block logic ...
END [block];
```

DESCRIPTION   **BEGIN** is the opening statement of a PL/SQL block's executable section. It can be followed with any legal PL/SQL logic, and an exception handler, and is closed with the **END** statement. At least one executable statement is required between **BEGIN** and **END**. *See* **BLOCK STRUCTURE**.

  block is a name given to a PL/SQL block that starts with the word **BEGIN** and finishes with the word **END**. The word **END** is followed by a terminator, usually a semicolon (*see* **TERMINATOR** for exceptions). *block* follows normal naming conventions for objects, and must be bracketed by << and >>. These symbols tell PL/SQL that this is a label. **BEGIN** may optionally be preceded by a section called **DECLARE** (which follows the block label) and may optionally contain a section called **EXCEPTION**.

BETWEEN

See **LOGICAL OPERATORS**.

BFILE

BFILE is a datatype (*see* DATA TYPES) used for binary LOB data stored outside the database. Oracle does not maintain read consistency or data integrity for the externally stored data. Within the database, a LOB locator value is stored to point to the external file. Before creating a BFILE entry, you must first create a directory. *See* **CREATE DIRECTORY**.

BIND PHASE

The bind phase is the phase of SQL statement processing during which all variables are made known to the RDBMS so that actual values can be used during execution of the statement.

BIND VARIABLE

A bind variable is a variable in a SQL statement that must be replaced with a valid value or address of a value in order for the statement to successfully execute.

BITMAP INDEX

A bitmap index is a type of index best suited for columns with few distinct values (and thus, poor selectivity). If there are few distinct values for a column, and it is frequently used as a limiting condition in queries, you should consider using a bitmap index for the column. *See* Chapter 20 for further details on bitmap indexes. For full syntax information, *see* **CREATE INDEX**.

BLOB

A BLOB is a binary large object, stored inside the database. *See* Chapter 30.

BLOCK

A block is the basic unit of storage (physical and logical) for all Oracle data. The number of blocks allocated per Oracle table depends on the tablespace in which the table is created. The Oracle block size varies by operating system and may differ from the block size of the host operating system. Common block sizes are 2048, 4096, and 8192 bytes. For the size of a block on your specific operating system, refer to your *Installation and User's Guide*.

BLOCK STRUCTURE

SEE ALSO   **BEGIN, DECLARE, END, EXCEPTION, GOTO**, Chapter 25

DESCRIPTION   PL/SQL blocks can be embedded in SQL*PLUS and any of several programming languages, through the use of the Oracle precompilers. PL/SQL blocks are structured like this:

```
[<<block>>]
[DECLARE
.. declarations (CURSOR, VARIABLE and EXCEPTION)...]

BEGIN

... block logic (executable code)...

[EXCEPTION

... exception handling logic (for fatal errors)...]

END [block];
```

As the brackets show, both the **DECLARE** and **EXCEPTION** sections are optional. A block may optionally be labeled by a block name, which must be bracketed by << and >>.

The sections of a block must be in this order, although blocks may nest inside of other blocks in either the block logic or exception handling logic sections. *blocks* may be used for branching using a **GOTO**, or as a prefix in referencing a variable in another block (*see* **DECLARE** for details on this). If a variable will be referenced in a cursor declaration, it must be declared before the cursor is declared. *See* Chapter 25 for examples of block structures and loops.

EXAMPLE

```
DECLARE
    pi      constant NUMBER(9,7) := 3.1415926;
    area    NUMBER(14,2);
    cursor rad_cursor is
        select * from RADIUS_VALS;
    rad_val rad_cursor%ROWTYPE;
BEGIN
    open rad_cursor;
    loop
      fetch rad_cursor into rad_val;
        exit when rad_cursor%NOTFOUND;
        area := pi*power(rad_val.radius,2);
        insert into AREAS values (rad_val.radius, area);
    end loop;
    close rad_cursor;
END;
.
/
```

BRANCH

Branches are a series of connected nodes of a logical tree. *See* **CONNECT BY**.

BREAK

SEE ALSO   **CLEAR**, **COMPUTE**, Chapters 6 and 14

FORMAT

```
BRE[AK] ON { REPORT | expression | ROW | PAG[E] } ...
  [ SKI[P] lines | [SKIP] PAGE ]
  [ NODUP[LICATES] | DUP[LICATES] ]


BRE[AK]
```

DESCRIPTION   A break occurs when SQL*PLUS detects a specified change, such as the end of a page or a change in the value of an expression. A break will cause SQL*PLUS to perform some action you've specified in the **BREAK** command, such as **SKIP**, and to print some result from a **COMPUTE** command, such as averages or totals for a column. Only one **BREAK** command may be in effect at a time. A new **BREAK** command may specify changes, and their associated actions, that are to cause a break.

A break **ON REPORT** causes a break at the end of a report or query.

A change in the value of an expression may occur at any time prior to the **REPORT** or **PAGE** break, and there may be several **ON** expression clauses in a single **BREAK** statement; however, their order in the **BREAK** command should be the same as in the **order by** of the **select** statement. That is, each expression that appears in the **BREAK** command also should be placed in the **order by** clause of select, in identical sequence, or the result will be meaningless. In addition, their order should be from the largest grouping to the smallest (for example, ON Corporation, ON Division, ON Project).

ON ROW causes a break for every row selected.

ON PAGE causes a break at the end of each page, and is independent of breaks caused by *expression*, ON ROW, or ON REPORT.

SKIP skips a number of *lines*, and PAGE or SKIP PAGE skips to a new page, before printing the result of the associated **COMPUTE** for the break.

NODUPLICATES suppresses the printing of the values in the expression or column in the **BREAK** for every row except the first one after the **BREAK** occurs.

BREAK by itself will display the current break settings.

CLEAR BREAKS will remove any existing **BREAK**s.

For examples of these in use, *see* Chapter 14.

BTITLE (bottom title)

SEE ALSO   ACCEPT, DEFINE, PARAMETERS, REPFOOTER, REPHEADER, SET HEADSEP, TTITLE, Chapter 14

FORMAT

```
BTI[TLE] [option ['text'|variable]... | OFF | ON]
```

DESCRIPTION   **BTITLE** puts *text* (may be multi-line) at the bottom of each page of a report. OFF and ON suppress and restore the display of the *text* without changing its contents. **BTITLE** by itself displays the current **btitle** options and text or variable. *text* is a bottom title you wish to give this report, and *variable* is a user-defined variable or a system maintained variable, including SQL.LNO, the current line number, SQL.PNO, the current page number, SQL.RELEASE, the current Oracle release number, SQL.SQLCODE, the current error code, and SQL.USER, the user name.

options are described below:

COL[UMN] *n* skips directly to position *n* (from the left margin) of the current line.

S[KIP] *n* prints *n* blank lines. If no *n* is specified, one blank line is printed. If *n* is 0, no blank lines are printed and the current position for printing becomes position 1 of the current line (leftmost on the page).

TAB *n* skips forward *n* positions (backward if *n* is negative).

LE[FT], **CE[NTER]**, and **R[IGHT]** left-justify, center, and right-justify data respectively on the current line. Any text or variables following these commands are justified as a group, up to the end of the command, or a LEFT, CENTER, RIGHT, or COLUMN. CENTER and RIGHT use the value set by the **SET LINESIZE** command to determine where to place the text or variable.

FORMAT string specifies the format model that will control the format of following text or variables, and follows the same syntax as **FORMAT** in a **COLUMN** command, such as **FORMAT** A12 or **FORMAT** $999,999.99. Each time a **FORMAT** appears, it supersedes the previous one that was in effect. If no **FORMAT** model has been specified, the one set by **SET NUMFORMAT** is used. If **NUMFORMAT** has not been set, the default for SQL*PLUS is used.

Data values are printed according to the default format unless a variable has been loaded with a date reformatted by **TO_CHAR**.

Any number of options, text, and variables may be used in a single **btitle**. Each is printed in the order specified, and each is positioned and formatted as specified by the clauses that precede it.

BUFFER

Generally speaking, a buffer is a scratchpad, usually in the computer's memory, where commands are staged for editing and execution.

In SQL*PLUS, a buffer is an area in memory for editing SQL and SQL*PLUS commands. *See* **EDIT** and **SET**.

BUFFERS (DATABASE)

Buffers are temporary storage places for database blocks that are currently being accessed and changed by database users.

BUFFERS (REDO LOG)

Buffers are temporary storage places for redo log entries that are created by transactions within the database.

C LANGUAGE

C is a programming language popular for its portability to many different types of computers. Oracle is itself written primarily in C.

CACHE MANAGER

The cache manager is the process responsible for making sure all changes made by software are propagated to disk in the right order.

CACHES

Caches are temporary holding places for either database data that is currently being accessed or changed by users or data that Oracle requires to support users.

CALL

SEE ALSO   **EXECUTE**

SYNTAX

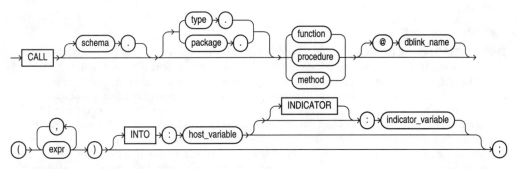

DESCRIPTION   You can use **CALL** to execute a stored procedure or function from within SQL. You must have EXECUTE privilege on the procedure or function, or on the package in which the procedure or function exists.

CALL, RECURSIVE

See RECURSIVE CALL.

CEIL

SEE ALSO   **FLOOR**, NUMBER FUNCTIONS

FORMAT

```
CEIL(value)
```

DESCRIPTION   **CEIL** is the smallest integer higher than or equal to *value*.

EXAMPLE

```
CEIL(2)    =  2
CEIL(1.3)  =  2
CEIL(-2)   = -2
CEIL(-2.3) = -2
```

CHAINED BLOCK

A chained block is a second or subsequent Oracle block designated to store table data, when the originally allocated block is out of space, and rows in that block expand due to **update**s. It is most often used for table data, but index data also can be chained. Chained blocks will have an impact on performance, so if they occur, the **PCTFREE** space definition parameter may be set too low.

CHAINED ROW

A chained row is a row that is stored in more than one database block, and that therefore has several row pieces. Long rows (or LONG data) whose data is greater than the size of a block always have multiple row pieces. The **ANALYZE** command can identify chained rows and can also provide statistics on the number of chained rows. *See* **ANALYZE**.

CHANGE

SEE ALSO   **APPEND**, **DEL**, **EDIT**, **LIST**, Chapter 6

FORMAT

```
C[HANGE] /old text/new text/
```

DESCRIPTION   **CHANGE** is a feature of the SQL*PLUS command line editor. It changes *old text* to *new text* in the current line of the current buffer (the line marked with an * in the LIST).

   CHANGE ignores case in searching for old text. Three dots are a wild card. If *old text* is prefixed with '. . .', everything up to and including the first occurrence of old text is replaced by new text. If old text is suffixed with '. . .', everything including and after the first occurrence of old text is replaced by new text. If old text has . . . embedded in it, everything from the part of old text before the dots, through the part of old text after the dots, is replaced by new text.

   The space between the **CHANGE** and the first / may be omitted; the final delimiter is unnecessary if no trailing spaces need to be inserted. A delimiter other than / may be used. Any character following the word **CHANGE** (other than a space) is assumed to be the delimiter.

EXAMPLES   If this is the current line of the current buffer:

```
where Skill in ('Smithy', 'Grave Digger', 'Combine Driver')
```

then this:

```
C /Smithy/Discus
```

would change the line to this:

```
where Skill in ('Discus', 'Grave Digger', 'Combine Driver')
```

This:

```
C ?Smithy',...?Discus')
```

(note the ? used as delimiter) would change it to this:

```
where Skill in ('Discus')
```

This:

```
C /Grave...Combine/Truck
```

would change it to this:

```
where Skill in ('Smithy', 'Truck Driver')
```

CHAR DATA TYPE

See DATA TYPES.

CHARACTER FUNCTIONS

SEE ALSO   CONVERSION FUNCTIONS, NUMBER FUNCTIONS, OTHER FUNCTIONS, Chapter 7

DESCRIPTION   This is an alphabetical list of all current character functions in Oracle's SQL. Each of these is listed elsewhere in this reference under its own name, with its proper format and use.

FUNCTION NAME AND USE || concatenates two strings. The | symbol is called a broken vertical bar, although on some computers it may be a solid bar.

```
ASCII(string)
```

> **ASCII** gives the ASCII value of the first character of a string.

```
CHR(integer)
```

> **CHR** gives the character with ASCII value equal to a given positive integer.

```
CONCAT(string1,string2)
```

> **CONCAT** concatenates two strings. It is equivalent to ||.

```
INITCAP(string)
```

> This stands for **INIT**ial **CAP**ital. It changes the first letter of a word or series of words into uppercase.

```
INSTR(string, set [, start [ ,occurrence ] ])
```

INSTR finds the location of the beginning of a set of characters **IN** a **STR**ing.

LENGTH(*string*)

This tells the **LENGTH** of a string.

LOWER(*string*)

LOWER converts every letter in a string to lowercase.

LPAD(*string*,*length* [,'*set*'])

LPAD stands for Left **PAD**. It makes a string a specific length by adding a specified set of characters to the left.

LTRIM(*string* [,'*set*'])

LTRIM stands for Left **TRIM**. It trims all the occurrences of any one of a set of characters off of the left side of a string.

NLS_INITCAP(*string*[,'NLS_SORT=*sort*'])

NLS_INITCAP stands for National Language Support Initial Capital. This version of **INITCAP** uses the collating sequence *sort* to do the case conversion.

NLS_LOWER(*string*[,'NLS_SORT=*sort*'])

NLS_LOWER stands for National Language Support **Lower** case. This version of **LOWER** uses the collating sequence *sort* to do the case conversion.

NLS_UPPER(*string*[,'NLS_SORT=*sort*'])

NLS_UPPER stands for National Language Support **Upper** case. This version of **UPPER** uses the collating sequence *sort* to do the case conversion.

NLSSORT(*character*)

Oracle uses National Language Support **SORT.** This gives the collating sequence value of the given character based on the National Language Support option chosen for the site.

REPLACE(*string*, *if* [,*then*])

REPLACE returns *string* with every occurrence of *if* replaced with *then* (zero or more characters). If no *then* string is specified, then all occurrences of *if* are removed. *See* **TRANSLATE.**

RPAD(*string*,*length* [,'*set*'])

RPAD stands for Right **PAD**. It makes a string a specific length by adding a specified set of characters to the right.

RTRIM(*string* [,'*set*'])

RTRIM stands for Right **TRIM**. It trims all the occurrences of any one of a set of characters off of the right side of a string.

SOUNDEX(*string*)

SOUNDEX converts a string to a code value. Names with similar sounds tend to have the same code value. You can use **SOUNDEX** to compare names that might have small spelling differences but are still the same.

SUBSTR(*string*, *start* [,*count*])

SUB STRing clips out a piece of a string beginning at *start* position and counting for *count* characters from *start*.

SUBSTRB(*string*, *start* [,*count*])

SUB STRing **B**yte is the same as **SUBSTR** except that it can deal with multiple-byte strings for National Language Support.

TRANSLATE(*string*,*if*,*then*)

This **TRANSLATE**s a string, character by character, based on a positional matching of characters in the *if* string with characters in the *then* string. *See* **REPLACE**.

UPPER(*string*)

UPPER converts every letter in a string into uppercase.

USERENV(*option*)

USERENV returns information about the **USER ENV**ironment, usually for an audit trail. Options are 'ENTRYID', 'SESSIONID', and 'TERMINAL'.

VSIZE(*string*)

VSIZE gives the storage size of *string* in Oracle.

CHARTOROWID

SEE ALSO   CONVERSION FUNCTIONS, **ROWIDTOCHAR**
FORMAT

CHARTOROWID(*string*)

DESCRIPTION   This stands for **CHAR**acter **TO ROW ID**entifier. It changes a character string to act like an internal Oracle row identifier, or **ROWID**.

CHECKPOINT

A checkpoint is a point in time at which changed blocks of data are written from the SGA to the database.

CHILD

In tree-structured data, a child is a node that is the immediate descendent of another node. The node that the child belongs to is called the parent.

CHR

SEE ALSO   **ASCII**, CHARACTER FUNCTIONS
FORMAT

CHR(*integer*)

DESCRIPTION   **CHR** will return the character with the ASCII value of *integer*. (*integer* means an integer between 0 and 254, since the ASCII value of a character is an integer between 0 and 254.)

Those between 0 and 127 are well defined. Those above 127 (called the extended ASCII set) tend to differ by country, application, and computer manufacturer. The letter A, for instance, is equal to the ASCII number 65, B is 66, C is 67, and so on. The decimal point is 46. A minus sign is 45. The number 0 is 48, 1 is 49, 2 is 50, and so on.

EXAMPLE

```
select CHR(77), CHR(46), CHR(56) from DUAL;

C C C
- - -
M . 8
```

CLAUSE

A clause is a major section of a SQL statement, and is begun by a keyword such as **select**, **insert**, **update**, **delete**, **from**, **where**, **order by**, **group by**, or **having**.

CLEAR

SEE ALSO   BREAK, COLUMN, COMPUTE

FORMAT

```
CL[EAR] option
```

DESCRIPTION   **CLEAR** clears the option.

BRE[AKS] clears breaks set by the **BREAK** command.

BUFF[ER] clears the current buffer.

COL[UMNS] clears options set by the **COLUMN** command.

COMP[UTES] clears options set by the **COMPUTE** command.

SCR[EEN] clears the screen.

SQL clears the SQL buffer.

TIMI[NG] deletes all timing areas created by the **TIMING** command.

EXAMPLES   To clear computes, use this:

```
clear computes
```

To clear column definitions, use this:

```
clear columns
```

CLIENT

Client is a general term for a user, software application, or computer that requires the services, data, or processing of another application or computer.

CLOB

CLOB is a datatype that supports character large objects. *See* Chapter 30.

CLOSE

SEE ALSO   DECLARE, FETCH, FOR, OPEN, Chapter 25

FORMAT

```
CLOSE cursor;
```

DESCRIPTION   **CLOSE** closes the named cursor, and releases its resources to Oracle for use elsewhere. *cursor* must be the name of a currently open cursor.

Even though a cursor has been closed, its definition has not been lost. You can issue **OPEN** *cursor* again, so long as the cursor was explicitly declared. A FOR loop will also implicitly **OPEN** a declared cursor. *See* CURSOR FOR LOOP.

CLOSED DATABASE

A closed database is a database that is associated with an instance (the database is mounted) but not open. Databases must be closed for some database maintenance functions. This can be accomplished via the SQL statement **ALTER DATABASE**.

CLUSTER

A cluster is a means of storing together data from multiple tables, when the data in those tables contains common information and is likely to be accessed concurrently. You can also cluster an individual table. *See* **CREATE CLUSTER** and Chapter 20.

CLUSTER INDEX

A cluster index is one manually created after a cluster has been created and before any DML (that is **select**, **insert**, **update**, or **delete**) statements can operate on the cluster. This index is created on the cluster key columns with the SQL statement **CREATE INDEX**. In Oracle, you can define a hash cluster to index on the primary key. *See* HASH CLUSTER.

CLUSTER KEY

A cluster key is the column or columns that clustered tables have in common, and which is chosen as the storage/access key. For example, two tables, WORKER and WORKERSKILL, might be clustered on the column Name. A cluster key is the same thing as a CLUSTER COLUMN.

CMDSEP

See **SET**.

COALESCE

To coalesce space is to unite adjoining free extents into a single extent. For example, if two 100-block extents are next to each other within a tablespace, then they can be coalesced into a single 200-block extent. The SMON background process will coalesce free space within tablespaces whose default **pctincrease** value is non-zero. You can manually coalesce the free space within a tablespace via the **coalesce** option of the **alter tablespace** command. *See* **ALTER TABLESPACE**.

COLLATION

SEE ALSO   **GROUP BY**, **INDEX**, **ORDER BY**, Chapter 9

DESCRIPTION   The collation or collating sequence is the order in which characters, numbers, and symbols will be sorted because of an **order by** or **group by** clause. These sequences differ based on the collation sequence of the computer's operating system or the national language. EBCDIC (usually IBM and compatible mainframes) and ASCII (most other computers) sequences differ significantly. The Spanish "ll" comes at a certain place in the sequence of characters. In spite of these differences, the following rules always apply:

■ A number with a larger value is considered "greater" than a smaller one. All negative numbers are smaller than all positive numbers. Thus, –10 is smaller than 10; –100 is smaller than –10.

■ A later date is considered greater than an earlier date.

Character strings are compared position by position, starting at the leftmost end of the string, up to the first character that is different. Whichever string has the "greater" character in that position is considered the greater string. One character is considered greater than another if it appears after the other in the computer's collation sequence. Usually this means that a B is greater than an A, but the value of A compared to a, or compared to the number 1, will differ by computer.

The collation comparison varies slightly depending on whether you are using CHAR or VARCHAR2 strings.

If two VARCHAR2 strings are identical up to the end of the shorter one, the longer string is considered greater. If two strings are identical and the same length, they are considered equal.

With CHAR strings, the shorter string is padded with blanks out to the length of the longer string. If the strings are not identical after this padding, the comparison treats the padded blanks as less than any other character, resulting in the same truth value as the VARCHAR comparison. If the strings are identical after, but not before the padding, the CHAR comparison would treat them as equal whereas the VARCHAR2 comparison would not.

In SQL it is important that literal numbers be typed without enclosing single quotes, as '10' would be considered smaller than '6', since the quotes will cause these to be regarded as character strings rather than numbers, and the '6' will be seen as greater than the '1' in the first position of '10'.

COLUMN (Form 1—Definition)

A column is a subdivision of a table with a column name and a specific datatype. For example, in a table of workers, all of the worker's ages would constitute one column. *See* **ROW**.

COLUMN (Form 2—SQL*PLUS)

SEE ALSO   ALIAS, Chapters 6 and 14

FORMAT

```
COL[UMN]    {column | expression}
    [ ALI[AS] alias ]
    [ CLE[AR] | DEF[AULT] ]
    [ FOLD_A[FTER]
    [ FOLD_B[EFORE]
    [ FOR[MAT] format ]
    [ HEA[DING] text
        [ JUS[TIFY] {L[EFT]|C[ENTER]|C[ENTRE]|R[IGHT]} ] ]
    [ LIKE {expression | label} ]
    [ NEWL[INE] ]
    [ NEW_V[ALUE] variable ]
    [ NOPRI[NT]|PRI[NT] ]
    [ NUL[L] text ]
    [ ON | OFF ]
    [ OLD_V[ALUE] variable ]
    [ WRA[PPED]|WOR[D_WRAPPED]|TRU[NCATED] ]...
```

DESCRIPTION   COLUMN controls column and column heading formatting. The options are all cumulative, and may be entered either simultaneously on a single line, or on separate lines at any time; the only requirement is that the word **COLUMN** and the column or expression must appear on each separate line. If one of the options is repeated, the most recent use will be in effect. **COLUMN** by itself displays all the current definitions for all columns. **COLUMN** with only a column or expression will show that column's current definition.

column or *expression* refers to a column or expression used in the **select**. If an expression is used, the expression must be entered exactly the same way that it is in the **select** statement. If the expression in the **select** is **Amount * Rate**, then entering **Rate * Amount** in a COLUMN command will not work. If a column or expression is given an alias in the **select** statement, that alias must be used here.

If you **select** columns with the same name from different tables (in sequential selects), a **COLUMN** command for that column name will apply to both. Avoid this by assigning the columns different aliases in the **select** (not with the **COLUMN** command's **alias** clause), and entering a **COLUMN** command for each column's alias.

ALIAS gives this column a new name, which then may be used to reference the column in **BREAK** and **COLUMN** commands.

CLEAR drops the column definition.

DEFAULT leaves the column defined and ON, but drops any other options.

FOLD_A[FTER] and **FOLD_B[EFORE]** instruct Oracle to fold a single row of output across multiple rows when printed. You can choose to fold the row either before or after the column.

FORMAT specifies the display format of the column. The format must be a literal like A25 or 990.99. Without format specified, the column width is the length as defined in the table.

A LONG column's width defaults to the value of the **SET LONG**. Both regular CHAR and LONG fields can have their width set by a format like **FORMAT A*n***, where *n* is an integer that is the column's new width.

A number column's width defaults to the value of **SET NUMWIDTH**, but is changed by the width in a **format** clause such as FORMAT 999,999.99. These options work with both **set numformat** and the **column format** commands:

Format	Result
9999990	Count of nines or zeros determines maximum digits that can be displayed.
9,999,999.99	Commas and decimals will be placed in the pattern shown. Display will be blank if the value is zero.
999990	Displays a zero if the value is zero.
099999	Displays numbers with leading zeros.
$99999	Dollar sign placed in front of every number.
B99999	Display will be blank if value is zero. This is the default.
99999MI	If number is negative, minus sign follows the number. Default is negative sign on left.
99999PR	Negative numbers bracketed with < and >.
99999EEEE	Display will be in scientific notation. Must be exactly four Es.
999V99	Multiplies number by 10n where *n* is number of digits to right of V. 999V99 turns 1234 into 123400.
DATE	Formats a number column that is a Julian date as MM/DD/YY

HEADING relabels a column heading. The default is the column name or the expression. If text has blanks or punctuation characters, it must be in single quotes. The **HEADSEP** character (usually 'l') in text makes SQL*PLUS begin a new line. The **COLUMN** command will remember the current

HEADSEP character when the column is defined, and continue to use it for this column unless the column is redefined, even if the **HEADSEP** character is changed.

    JUSTIFY aligns the heading over the column. By default this is RIGHT for number columns and LEFT for anything else.

    LIKE replicates the column definitions of a previously defined column for the current one, where either the expression or label was used in the other column definition. Only those features of the other column that have not been explicitly defined for the current column are copied.

    NEWLINE starts a new line before printing the column value.

    NEW_VALUE names a variable to hold the column's value for use in the **ttitle** command. *See* Chapter 14 for usage information.

    NOPRINT and **PRINT** turn the column's display off or on.

    NULL sets text to be displayed if the column has a **NULL** value. The default for this is a string of blanks as wide as the column is defined.

    OFF or **ON** turns all these options for a column off or on without affecting its contents.

    OLD_VALUE names a variable to hold the column's value for use in the **btitle** command. *See* Chapter 13 for usage information.

    WRAPPED, **WORD_WRAPPED**, and **TRUNC** control how SQL*PLUS displays a heading or string value too wide to fit the column. **WRAP** folds the value to the next line. **WORD_WRAP** folds similarly, but breaks on words. **TRUNC** truncates the value to the width of the column definition.

COLUMN CONSTRAINT

A column constraint is an integrity constraint placed on a specific column of a table. *See* INTEGRITY CONSTRAINT.

COMMAND

See **STATEMENT**.

COMMAND LINE

A command line is a line on a computer display where you enter a command.

COMMENT

SEE ALSO   DATA DICTIONARY VIEWS, Chapter 35
SYNTAX

DESCRIPTION   **COMMENT** inserts the comment text about an object or column into the data dictionary.

    You drop a comment from the database only by setting it to a **NULL** value (set *text* to '').

COMMIT

To commit means to make changes to data (**insert**s, **update**s, and **delete**s) permanent. Before changes are stored, both the old and new data exist so that changes can be made, or so that the data can be restored to its prior state ("rolled back"). When a user enters the Oracle SQL command **COMMIT**, all changes from that transaction are made permanent.

COMMIT (Form I—Embedded SQL)

SEE ALSO   ROLLBACK, SAVEPOINT, SET TRANSACTION

FORMAT

```
EXEC SQL [AT database] COMMIT [WORK] [RELEASE]
```

DESCRIPTION   You use **COMMIT** to commit work at various stages within a program. Without the explicit use of **COMMIT**, an entire program's work will be considered one transaction, and will not be committed until the program terminates. Any locks obtained will be held until that time, blocking other users from access. **COMMIT** should be used as often as logically feasible.

   WORK is optional and has no effect on usage; it is provided for ANSI compatibility. **AT** references a remote database accessed by the **DECLARE DATABASE** command. **RELEASE** disconnects you from the database, whether remote or local.

COMMIT (Form 2—PL/SQL Statement)

SEE ALSO   ROLLBACK, SAVEPOINT

SYNTAX

DESCRIPTION   **COMMIT** commits any changes made to the database since the last **COMMIT** was executed implicitly or explicitly. **WORK** is optional and has no effect on usage.

   COMMENT associates a text comment with the transaction. The comment can be viewed via the data dictionary view DBA_2PC_PENDING in the event a distributed transaction fails to complete. FORCE manually commits an in-doubt distributed transaction.

COMMUNICATIONS PROTOCOL

Communications protocol is any one of a number of standard means of connecting two computers together so that they can share information. Protocols consist of several layers of both software and hardware, and may connect homogeneous or heterogeneous computers.

COMPOSITE KEY

A composite key is a primary or foreign key composed of two or more columns.

COMPOSITE PARTITION

A composite partition involves the use of multiple partition methods, such as a range-partitioned table in which the range partitions are then hash partitioned. *See* SUBPARTITION.

COMPRESSED INDEX

A compressed index is an index for which only enough index information is stored to identify unique index entries; information that an index stores with the previous or following key is "compressed" (truncated) and not stored to reduce the storage overhead required by an index. *See also* NONCOMPRESSED INDEX.

COMPUTE

SEE ALSO   **BREAK**, GROUP FUNCTIONS

FORMAT

```
COMP[UTE][AVG|COU[NT]|MAX[IMUM]|MIN[IMUM]|NUM[BER]|STD|SUM|VAR[IANCE]]...
    LABEL label_name
    OF {expression} [, expression]...
    ON [expression | PAGE | REPORT | ROW]...
```

DESCRIPTION   *expression* is a column or expression. **COMPUTE** performs computations on columns or expressions selected from a table. It works only with the **BREAK** command.

By default, Oracle will use the function name (SUM, AVG, etc.) as the label for the result in the query output. **LABEL** allows you to specify a *label_name* that overrides the default value.

OF names the column or expression whose value is to be computed. These columns also must be in the **select** clause, or the **COMPUTE** will be ignored.

ON coordinates the **COMPUTE** with the **BREAK** command. **COMPUTE** prints the computed value and restarts the computation when the ON *expression*'s value changes, or when a specified ROW, PAGE, or REPORT break occurs. *See* **BREAK** for coordination details.

COMPUTE by itself displays the computes in effect.

AVG, MAXIMUM, MINIMUM, STD, SUM, and **VARIANCE** all work on expressions that are numbers. **MAXIMUM** and **MINIMUM** also work on character expressions, but not DATEs. **COUNT** and **NUMBER** work on any expression type.

All of these computes except **NUMBER** ignore rows with **NULL** values:

AVG	Gives average value
COUNT	Gives count of non-**NULL** values
MAXIMUM	Gives maximum value
MINIMUM	Gives minimum value
NUMBER	Gives count of all rows returned
STD	Gives standard deviation
SUM	Gives sum of non-**NULL** values
VARIANCE	Gives variance

Successive computes are simply put in order without commas, such as in this case:

```
compute sum avg max of Amount Rate on report
```

This will compute the sum, average, and maximum of both Amount and Rate for the entire report.

EXAMPLE   To calculate for each Item classification and for the entire report, enter this:

```
break on Item skip 2 on report skip 1
compute sum avg max of Amount Rate on Item report
```

```
select Item, Rate, Amount
  from Ledger
 order by Item;
```

Note the importance of **order by Item** for this to work properly.

CONCAT
See **SET**, ||.

CONCATENATED INDEX (or KEY)

A concatenated index is one that is created on more than one column of a table. It can be used to guarantee that those columns are unique for every row in the table and to speed access to rows via those columns. *See* COMPOSITE KEY.

CONCATENATION

Concatenation is the joining together of strings, represented by the operator "||". For example, concatenation of the strings 'ABC' and 'XYZ' would be denoted 'ABC'||'XYZ', and the resulting value would be 'ABCXYZ'.

CONCURRENCY

Concurrency is a general term meaning the access of the same data by multiple users. In database software, concurrency requires complex software programming to assure that all users see correct data and that all changes are made in the proper order.

CONDITION

A condition is an expression whose value evaluates to either TRUE or FALSE, such as Age > 65.

CONNECT

To connect is to identify yourself to Oracle by your user name and password, in order to access the database.

CONNECT (Form 1)
SEE ALSO   **COMMIT, DISCONNECT**, Chapter 22
FORMAT

```
CON[NECT] user[/password] [@database];
```

DESCRIPTION   You must be in SQL*PLUS to use this command, although you don't need to be logged on to Oracle (*see* **DISCONNECT**). **CONNECT** commits any pending changes, logs you off of Oracle, and logs on as the specified *user*. If the *password* is absent, you are prompted for it. It is not displayed when you type it in response to a prompt.

@database connects to the named database. It may be on your host, or on another computer connected via Net8.

CONNECT (Form 2—Embedded SQL)
SEE ALSO   **COMMIT, DECLARE DATABASE**, Chapter 22

FORMAT

```
EXEC SQL CONNECT :user_password
            [AT database]
            [USING :connect_string]

EXEC SQL CONNECT :user IDENTIFIED BY :password
            [AT database]
            [USING :connect_string]
```

DESCRIPTION   **CONNECT** connects a host program to a local or remote database. It may be used more than once to connect to multiple databases. :*user_password* is a host variable that contains the Oracle user name and password separated by a slash (/). Alternatively, :*user* and :*password* can be entered separately by using the second format.

AT is used to name a database other than the default for this user. It is a required clause to reach any databases other than the user's default database. This name can be used later in other SQL statements with **AT**. This database must be first identified with **DECLARE DATABASE**. **USING** specifies an optional NET8 string (such as a node name) used during the connecting. Without the **USING** string, you will be connected to the user's default database, regardless of the database named in the **AT** line.

CONNECT BY

SEE ALSO   Chapter 13
FORMAT

```
SELECT expression [,expression]...
  FROM [user.]table
 WHERE condition
CONNECT BY [PRIOR] expression = [PRIOR] expression
 START WITH expression = expression
 ORDER BY expression
```

DESCRIPTION   **CONNECT BY** is an operator used in a **select** statement to create reports on inheritance in tree-structured data, such as company organization, family trees, and so on. **START WITH** tells where in the tree to begin. These are the rules:

- The position of **PRIOR** with respect to the **CONNECT BY** expressions determines which expression identifies the root and which identifies the branches of the tree.

- A **where** clause will eliminate individuals from the tree, but not their descendants (or ancestors, depending on the location of **PRIOR**).

- A qualification in the **CONNECT BY** (particularly a not equal instead of the equal sign) will eliminate both an individual and all of its descendants.

- **CONNECT BY** cannot be used with a table join in the **where** clause.

EXAMPLE

```
select Cow, Bull, LPAD(' ',6*(Level-1))||Offspring AS Offspring,
       Sex, Birthdate
  from BREEDING
connect by Offspring = PRIOR Cow
 start with Offspring = 'DELLA'
 order by Birthdate;
```

In this example, the following clause:

```
connect by Offspring = PRIOR Cow
```

means the offspring is the cow **PRIOR** to this one.

CONSISTENCY

Consistency is a general database term and issue requiring that all related data be updated together in the proper order, and that if there is redundant data, all data be consistent.

CONSTRAINT

A rule or restriction concerning a piece of data (such as a **NOT NULL** restriction on a column) that is enforced at the data level, rather than the object or application level. *See* INTEGRITY CONSTRAINT.

constraint_clause

SEE ALSO   **CREATE TABLE**, INTEGRITY CONSTRAINT, Chapter 19.

SYNTAX

table_constraint::=

column_constraint::=

table_ref_constraint::=

table_ref_contraint::=

references_clause::=

constraint_state::=

foreign_key_clause::=

physical_attributes_clause::=

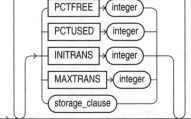

DESCRIPTION   *constraint_clause* is part of the **CREATE TABLE** command. You use the constraint clause to create a constraint or to alter an existing constraint. You can enable and disable constraints. If you disable a constraint and then try to re-enable it, Oracle will check the data. If the constraint cannot be re-enabled, Oracle can write the exceptions out to a separate table for review.

For PRIMARY KEY and UNIQUE constraints, Oracle will create indexes. As part of the constraint clause for those constraints, you can use the **USING INDEX** clause to specify the tablespace and storage for the index.

CONTAINS

CONTAINS is used to evaluate text searches that use the Oracle ConText Option (ConText) or interMedia Text (IMT). *See* TEXT SEARCH OPERATORS and Chapter 24.

CONTEXT

ConText (also referred to as the Oracle ConText Option) is a text search engine available within the Oracle server. Depending on the version of Oracle you use, ConText may also be referred to as interMedia Text, part of the Oracle interMedia product. interMedia Text is abbreviated as IMT. ConText and IMT allow you to perform text searches including fuzzy matches, stem expansions, and phrase searches. *See* Chapter 24.

Context is also the term used for the assignment of a set of security-related packages for an application. *See* **CREATE CONTEXT**.

CONTEXT AREA

A context area is work area in memory where Oracle stores the current SQL statement, and if the statement is a query, one row of the result. The context area holds the state of a cursor.

CONTEXT SERVER

A ConText server is a background server that participates in the resolution of queries involving text searches. You must have ConText servers enabled in order to administer and use ConText. IMT does not have the same requirements. *See* Chapter 24.

CONTROL FILE (DATABASE)

A control file is a small administrative file required by every database, necessary to start and run a database system. A control file is paired with a database, not with an instance. Multiple identical control files are preferred to a single file.

CONTROL FILE (SQL*LOADER)

A SQL*Loader control file tells the SQL*Loader executable where to find the data to be loaded, and how to process the data during the load. Every SQL*Loader session has an associated control file. For control file syntax, see SQLLDR. For details on the use of SQL*Loader, see Chapter 21.

CONVERSION FUNCTIONS

SEE ALSO   CHARACTER FUNCTIONS, NUMBER FUNCTIONS

DESCRIPTION   The following is an alphabetical list of all current conversion and transformation functions in Oracle's SQL. Each of these is listed elsewhere in this reference under its own name, with its format and use.

FUNCTION NAME AND USE

CHARTOROWID(*string*)

> **CHARTOROWID** stands for **CHAR**acter **TO ROW ID**entifier. It changes a character string to act like an internal Oracle row identifier, or **ROWID**.

CONVERT(*string*,[*destination_set*,[*source_set*]])

> **CONVERT**s the characters in string from one standard bit representation to another, such as from US7ASCII to WE8DEC.

DECODE(*value*,*if1*,*then1*,*if2*,*then2*,*if3*,*then3*,. . . ,*else*)

> **DECODE**s a character string, a DATE, or a NUMBER into any of several different strings, DATEs, or NUMBERs, based on value. This is a very powerful IF, THEN, ELSE function. Chapter 17 is devoted to it.

HEXTORAW(*hex_string*)

> **HEXTORAW** stands for **HEX**adecimal **TO RAW**. It changes a character string of hex numbers into binary.

RAWTOHEX(*binary_string*)

> **RAWTOHEX** stands for **RAW TO HEX**adecimal. It changes a string of binary numbers to a character string of hex numbers.

REPLACE(*string*, *if* [,*then*])

> **REPLACE** returns *string* with every occurrence of *if* replaced with *then* (zero or more characters). If no *then* string is specified, then all occurrences of *if* are removed. *See* **TRANSLATE**.

ROWIDTOCHAR(*RowId*)

> **ROWIDTOCHAR** stands for **ROW ID**entifier **TO CHAR**acter. It changes an internal Oracle row identifier, or RowId, to act like a character string.

TO_CHAR(*value*)

TO_CHAR stands for **TO CHAR**acter. It converts a NUMBER so that it acts like a character string.

TO_DATE(*string*, ['*format*'])

TO_DATE converts a NUMBER, CHAR, or VARCHAR2 to act like a DATE (a special Oracle datatype).

TO_LABEL(*string*[,'*format*'])

TO_LABEL converts a character string to a value of RAW MLSLABEL datatype. *See* the *Trusted Oracle Administrator's Guide* for more information.

TO_LOB(*long_column*)

TO_LOB converts LONG values in *long_column* to LOB values. You can apply this function only to a LONG column, and only in the **select** list of a subquery in an **insert** command.

TO_MULTI_BYTE(*string*)

TO_MULTI_BYTE converts a character string containing single-byte characters to the corresponding multi-byte characters. If a particular character has no equivalent, the character appears as a single-byte character. This function lets you mix single- and multi-byte characters in a given string.

TO_NUMBER(*string*)

TO_NUMBER converts a string to act like a number.

TO_SINGLE_BYTE(*string*)

TO_SINGLE_BYTE converts a character string containing multi-byte characters to the corresponding single-byte characters. If a particular character has no equivalent, the character appears as a multi-byte character. This function lets you mix single- and multi-byte characters in a given string.

TRANSLATE(*string*,*if*,*then*)

TRANSLATEs characters in a string into different characters.

CONVERT

SEE ALSO   CONVERSION FUNCTIONS
FORMAT

CONVERT(*string*,[*destination_set*,[*source_set*]])

DESCRIPTION   **CONVERT**s the characters in *string* from one standard bit representation to another, such as from US7ASCII (the default if either set isn't entered) to WE8DEC. This is typically done when data entered into a column on one computer contains characters that can't be properly displayed or printed on another computer. **CONVERT** allows a reasonable translation of one to the other in most cases. The most common sets include:

F7DEX	DEC's 7-bit ASCII set for France
US7ASCII	Standard US 7-bit ASCII set
WE8DEC	DEC's 8-bit ASCII set for Western Europe
WE8HP	HP's 8-bit ASCII set for Western Europe
WE8ISO8859P1	ISO 8859-1 Western Europe 8-bit character set

COPY

SEE ALSO   **CREATE DATABASE LINK**, Chapter 22

FORMAT

```
COPY [FROM user/password@database]
     [TO user/password@database]
     {APPEND | CREATE | INSERT | REPLACE}
     table[  (column [,column]...) ]
     USING query
```

DESCRIPTION   **COPY** copies **FROM** a table **TO** a table in another computer over SQL*NET. **FROM** is the user name, password, and database of the source table, and **TO** is the destination table. Either **FROM** or **TO** may be omitted, in which case the user's default database will be used for the missing clause. The source and destination databases must not be the same, so only one of the **from** and **to** clauses may be absent.

APPEND adds to the destination table; if the table does not exist, it is created. **CREATE** requires that the destination table be created; if it already exists, a 'table already exists' error occurs. **INSERT** adds to the destination table; if the table does not exist, a 'table does not exist' error occurs. **REPLACE** drops the data in the destination table and replaces it with the data from the source table; if the table does not exist, it is created.

table is the name of the destination table. *column*, is the name(s) of the column(s) in the destination table. If named, the number of columns must be the same as in the query. If no columns are named, the copied columns will have the same names in the destination table as they had in the source table. *query* identifies the source table and determines which rows and columns will be copied from it.

SET LONG (*see* **SET**) determines the length of a long field that can be copied. Long columns with data longer than the value of LONG will be truncated. **SET COPYCOMMIT** determines how many sets of rows get copied before a commit. **SET ARRAYSIZE** determines how many rows are in a set.

EXAMPLE   This example copies totaled records from LEDGER in EDMESTON to the database the local SQL*PLUS user is connected to. The table LEDGER_TOTAL is created by the copy. Only two columns are copied, and one of them is a computed column, a sum. These columns are renamed Item and Amount at the destination. Note the use of the dash (-) at the end of each line. This is required. The command does not end with a semicolon (since it is a SQL*Plus command, not a SQL command). *See* the **SET** command for options related to the **COPY** command.

```
copy from GEORGE/TAL@EDMESTON -
create LEDGER_TOTAL (Item, Amount) -
 using select Item, SUM(Amount) -
        from LEDGER -
        group by Item
```

COPYCOMMIT

See **SET**.

COPYTYPECHECK

See **SET**.

CORRELATED QUERY

A correlated query is a subquery that is executed repeatedly, once for each value of a candidate row selected by the main query. The outcome of each execution of the subquery depends on the values of one or more fields in the candidate row; that is, the subquery is correlated with the main query. *See* Chapter 12.

COS

SEE ALSO   ACOS, ASIN, ATAN, ATAN2, COSH, EXP, LN, LOG, SIN, SINH, TAN, TANH

FORMAT

```
COS(value)
```

DESCRIPTION   COS returns the cosine of a value, an angle expressed in radians. You can convert a degree angle into radians by multiplying it by pi/180.

EXAMPLE

```
COL COSINE_180 HEADING "Cosine of 180 degrees"

SELECT COS(180*3.14159/80) COSINE_180 FROM DUAL;

Cosine of 180 degrees
--------------------
                  -1
```

COSH

SEE ALSO   ACOS, ASIN, ATAN, ATAN2, COS, EXP, LN, LOG, SIN, SINH, TAN, TANH

FORMAT

```
COSH(value)
```

DESCRIPTION   COSH returns the hyperbolic cosine of a *value*.

EXAMPLE

```
COL HCOSINE HEADING "Hyperbolic cosine of 0"

SELECT COSH(0) HCOSINE FROM DUAL;

Hyperbolic cosine of 0
---------------------
                    1
```

COUNT

SEE ALSO   GROUP FUNCTIONS, Chapter 8

FORMAT

```
COUNT( [DISTINCT] expression | *)
```

DESCRIPTION   COUNT counts the number of rows where *expression* is non-**NULL**, which are then returned by the query. With **DISTINCT**, COUNT counts only the distinct non-**NULL** rows. With *****, it counts all rows, whether **NULL** or not.

CREATE CLUSTER

SEE ALSO   **CREATE INDEX, CREATE TABLE, STORAGE,** Chapter 20
SYNTAX

physical_attributes_clause::=

parallel_clause::=

DESCRIPTION   **CREATE CLUSTER** creates a cluster for one or more tables. Tables are added to the cluster using **CREATE TABLE** with the **cluster** clause. **CREATE CLUSTER** requires at least one cluster column from each of the tables. These must have the same datatype and size, but are not required to have the same name. For the tables in a cluster, rows with the same cluster column values are kept together on disk in the same area, the same logical block(s). This can improve performance when the cluster columns are the columns by which the tables are usually joined.

Each distinct value in each cluster column is stored only once, regardless of whether it occurs once or many times in the tables and rows. This typically can reduce the amount of disk space needed to store the tables, but each table continues to appear as if it contained all of its own data. The maximum length of all the cluster columns combined (for one **CLUSTER** command) is 239 characters. Tables with LONG columns cannot be clustered.

cluster is the name created for the cluster. *column* and *datatype* follow the method of **CREATE TABLE**, except that **NULL** and **NOT NULL** cannot be specified. However, in the actual **CREATE TABLE** statement, at least one cluster column in a cluster must be **NOT NULL**. **SIZE** sets the size in bytes for a logical block (not a physical block). **SPACE** is the cluster's initial disk allocation, as used in **CREATE TABLE**.

SIZE should be the average amount of space needed to store all the rows from all the clustered tables that are associated with a single cluster key. A small **SIZE** value may increase the time needed to access tables in the cluster, but can reduce disk space usage. **SIZE** should be a proper divisor of the physical block size. If not, Oracle will use the next larger divisor. If **SIZE** exceeds the physical block size, Oracle will use the physical block size instead.

By default, the cluster is indexed, and you must create an index on the cluster key before putting any data in the cluster. If you specify the hash cluster form, however, you don't need to (and can't) create an index on the cluster key. Instead, Oracle uses a hash function to store the rows of the table.

You can create your own hash value as a column of the table and use that for hashing with the **HASH IS** clause to tell Oracle to use that column as the hash value. Otherwise, Oracle uses an internal hash function based on the columns of the cluster key. The **HASHKEYS** clause actually creates the hash cluster and specifies the number of hash values, rounded to the nearest prime number. The minimum value is 2.

See the *storage_clause* entry in the Alphabetical Reference for details on the common storage clause parameters.

CREATE CONTEXT
SEE ALSO   **ALTER CONTEXT**
SYNTAX

DESCRIPTION   A context is a set of attributes used to secure an application. **CREATE CONTEXT** creates a namespace for a **context** and associates the namespace with the externally created package that sets the context. To create a context namespace, you must have CREATE ANY CONTEXT system privilege.

CREATE CONTROLFILE
SEE ALSO   **ALTER DATABASE, CREATE DATABASE**

SYNTAX

DESCRIPTION The **CREATE CONTROLFILE** command re-creates a control file when you have either lost your current control file to media failure, you want to change the name of your database, or you want to change one of the options for the log file for a datafile. In general, this command should only be used by experienced database administrators.

NOTE
Perform a full offline backup all of your database files before using this command.

The **REUSE** option lets existing control files be reused rather than giving an error if any exist. The **SET** option changes the name of the database, specified by the database clause. The **LOGFILE** clause specifies the redo log file groups, all of which must exist. The **RESETLOGS** versus **NORESETLOGS** clause tells Oracle to reset the current logs or not. The **DATAFILE** line specifies the data files for the database, all of which must exist.

The **MAXLOGFILES** option specifies the maximum number of redo log file groups that can be created. The **MAXLOGMEMBERS** option specifies the number of copies for a redo log group. The **MAXLOGHISTORY** option specifies the number of archived redo log file groups for the Parallel Server. The **MAXDATAFILES** option specifies the maximum number of data files that can ever be created for the database. The **MAXINSTANCES** option gives the maximum number of ORACLE instances that can mount and open the database. The **ARCHIVELOG** and **NOARCHIVELOG** options turns archiving of the redo log files on and off, respectively.

The **CREATE CONTROLFILE** command needed for an existing database can be generated via the **ALTER DATABASE BACKUP CONTROLFILE TO TRACE** command.

CREATE DATABASE

SEE ALSO **ALTER DATABASE**, **CREATE CONTROLFILE**, **CREATE ROLLBACK SEGMENT**, **CREATE TABLESPACE**, **SHUTDOWN**, **STARTUP**, Chapter 38

SYNTAX

autoextend_clause::=

maxsize_clause::=

DESCRIPTION *database* is the database name, and must have eight characters or fewer. DB_NAME in init.ora contains the default database name. In general, this command should only be used by experienced database administrators.

NOTE
Using this command in an existing database will erase the specified datafiles.

file_definition specifies the LOGFILE and DATAFILE names and sizes:

```
'file' [SIZE integer [K | M] [REUSE]
```

SIZE is the number of bytes set aside for this file. Suffixing this with K multiplies the value by 1024; M multiplies it by 1048576. **REUSE** (without **SIZE**) means destroy the contents of any file by this name and associate the name with this database. **SIZE** with **REUSE** creates the file if it doesn't exist, and checks its size if it does. **CONTROLFILE REUSE** overwrites the existing control files defined by CONTROL_FILES in init.ora.

LOGFILE names the files to be used as redo log files. If this parameter is not used, Oracle creates two by default. **MAXLOGFILES** overrides the init.ora LOG_FILES parameter, and defines the maximum number of redo log files that can ever be created for this database. This number cannot be increased later except by re-creating the control file.. Minimum is 2. A high number only makes a somewhat larger control file.

DATAFILE names the files to be used for the database itself. These files will automatically be in the SYSTEM tablespace. Omitting this clause causes Oracle to create one file by default. Its name and size differ by operating system. **MAXDATAFILES** sets the absolute upper limit for files that can be created for this database, and overrides the DB_FILES parameter in init.ora. A high number only makes a somewhat larger control file.

When the **AUTOEXTEND** option is turned ON for a datafile, the datafile will dynamically extend as needed in increments of **NEXT** size, to a maximum of **MAXSIZE** (or UNLIMITED).

MAXINSTANCES overrides the INSTANCES parameter in init.ora and sets the maximum number of simultaneous instances that can mount and open this database.

ARCHIVELOG and **NOARCHIVELOG** define the way redo log files are used when the database is first created. **NOARCHIVELOG** is the default, and means that redo files will get reused without saving their contents elsewhere. This provides instance recovery but will not recover from a media failure, such as a disk crash. **ARCHIVELOG** forces redo files to be archived (usually to another disk or a tape), so that you can recover from a media failure. This mode also supports instance recovery. This parameter can be reset by **ALTER DATABASE**.

The **MAXLOGMEMBERS** option specifies the maximum number of copies of a redo log file group. The **MAXLOGHISTORY** option specifies the maximum number of archived redo log files, useful only for the Parallel Server when you are archiving log files. The **CHARACTER SET** option specifies the character set used to store data, which depends on the operating system.

EXCLUSIVE is completely optional, and is used here as a reminder that all databases are created to allow only one instance that has exclusive access to the database. To allow multiple instances (users, processes, and so on) to access the database, you must use the **ALTER DATABASE DISMOUNT** and **ALTER DATABASE MOUNT PARALLEL** commands.

CREATE DATABASE LINK

SEE ALSO   **CREATE SYNONYM**, **SELECT**, Chapter 22
SYNTAX

```
→ CREATE →┬→ SHARED →┬→┬→ PUBLIC →┬→ DATABASE → LINK →( dblink )→
          └──────────┘ └──────────┘
```

authenticated_clause::=

DESCRIPTION   *link* is the name given to the link. *connect_string* is the definition of the remote database that can be accessed through Net8 and defines the link between a local database and a username on a remote database. **PUBLIC** links can only be created by a DBA, but are then available to all users except those who have created a private link with the same name. If **PUBLIC** isn't specified, the link is only available to the user who executed the **CREATE DATABASE LINK** statement. *connect_string* is the Net8 service name for the remote database.

Remote tables can be accessed just like local tables, except that the table name must be suffixed by @*link* in the **from** clause of the **select** statement. Most systems set the maximum number of simultaneous links to four. The DBA can increase this number with the OPEN_LINKS parameter in init.ora.

Tree-structured queries are limited. They may not use the **PRIOR** operator except in the **connect by** clause. **START WITH** cannot contain a subquery. **CONNECT BY** and **START WITH** cannot use the function **USERENV**('ENTRYID'), or the pseudo-column RowNum.

To create a database link, you must have CREATE DATABASE LINK privilege and CREATE SESSION privilege in a remote database. To create a public database link, you must have CREATE PUBLIC DATABASE LINK system privilege.

If you use the **CONNECT TO CURRENT_USER** clause, the link will attempt to open a connection in the remote database using your current username and password. You will therefore need to coordinate any password changes you make between the local database and the remote database or database links may stop working.

If you use the multithreaded server, you can create **SHARED** database links that eliminate the need for many separate dedicated connections via links. When you create a **SHARED** link, you must supply a valid username and password in the remote database to use as an authentication for the connection.

EXAMPLES   The following defines a link named BOSS to George with password TAL on database EDMESTON:

```
create database link BOSS
connect to George identified by TAL
   using 'EDMESTON';
```

You now can query George's tables like this:

```
select ActionDate, Item, Amount
   from LEDGER@BOSS;
```

A synonym could also be created to hide the remoteness of George's tables:

```
create synonym TALBOT_LEDGER for LEDGER@BOSS;
```

CREATE DIMENSION

SEE ALSO ALTER DIMENSION, DROP DIMENSION
SYNTAX

level_clause::=

hierarchy_clause::=

join_clause::=

attribute_clause::=

DESCRIPTION **CREATE DIMENSION** creates hierarchies among related columns in tables, for use by the optimizer. The optimizer will use dimension values when determining whether a materialized view will return the same data as its base table. To create a dimension, you must have CREATE DIMENSION privilege; to create a dimension in another user's schema, you must have the CREATE ANY DIMENSION privilege. The default is to create the dimension NOFORCE, that is, only if the referenced tables and columns already exist and you have object privileges to access them; to create the dimension if the tables and/or columns do not exist or you do not have appropriate privileges, use FORCE.

LEVEL defines the level within the dimension. **HIERARCHY** defines the relationships among the levels. **ATTRIBUTE** assigns specific attributes to levels within the dimension. **JOIN_KEY** defines the join clauses between the levels.

EXAMPLES   For a table named COUNTRY, with columns Country and Continent, and a second table named CONTINENT, with a column named Continent:

```
create dimension GEOGRAPHY
    level COUNTRY_ID       is COUNTRY.Country
    level CONTINENT_id     is CONTINENT.Continent
    hierarchy COUNTRY_ROLLUP (
       COUNTRY_ID          child of
       CONTINENT_ID
    join key COUNTRY.Continent references CONTINENT_id);
```

CREATE DIRECTORY

SEE ALSO   BFILE, Chapter 30

SYNTAX

DESCRIPTION   Within Oracle, a "directory" is an alias for an operating system directory. You must create a directory prior to accessing BFILE datatype values.

CREATE FUNCTION

SEE ALSO   ALTER FUNCTION, BLOCK STRUCTURE, **CREATE LIBRARY**, **CREATE PACKAGE**, **CREATE PROCEDURE**, DATA TYPES, **DROP FUNCTION**, Chapters 25, 27, and 34

SYNTAX

invoker_rights_clause::=

call_spec::=

Java_declaration::=

C_declaration::=

DESCRIPTION *function* is the name of the function being defined. A function may have parameters, named arguments of a certain datatype, and every function returns a value of a certain datatype as specified by the return clause. The PL/SQL block defines the behavior of the function as a series of declarations, PL/SQL program statements, and exceptions.

The IN qualifier means that you have to specify a value for the parameter when you call the function, but since you always have to do this for a function, the syntax is optional. In a procedure, you can have other kinds of parameters. The difference between a function and a procedure is that a function returns a value to the calling environment.

In order to create a function, you must have the CREATE PROCEDURE system privilege. To create a function in another user's account, you must have CREATE ANY PROCEDURE system privilege.

Your function can use C libraries that are stored outside of the database (see **CREATE LIBRARY**). If you use Java within your function, you can provide a Java declaration within the **LANGUAGE** clause. The *invoker_rights* clause lets you specify whether the function executes with the privileges of the function owner (the definer) or the current user (the invoker).

CREATE INDEX
SEE ALSO ANALYZE, **ALTER INDEX**, **DROP INDEX**, INTEGRITY CONSTRAINT, **STORAGE**, Chapters 18 and 20
SYNTAX

cluster_index_clause::=

table_index_clause::=

undex_expr_list::=

index_attributes::=

physical_attributes_clause::=

domain_index_clause::=

global_index_clause::=

local_index_clauses::=

on_range_partitioned_table_clause::=

segment_attributes_clause::=

on_hash_partitioned_table_clause::=

on_composite_partitioned_table_clause::=

index_subpartitioned_clause::=

global_partition_clause::=

parallel_clause::=

DESCRIPTION *index* is a name you assign to this index. It's usually a good idea to make it reflect the table and columns being indexed. *table* and *column*(s) are the table and column(s) for which the index is to be created. A **UNIQUE** index guarantees that each indexed row is unique on the values of the index columns. You can use the unique constraint on the columns to automatically create unique indexes. Specifying multiple columns will create a composite index. **ASC** and **DESC** mean ascending and descending, and are allowed for DB2 compatibility, but have no effect. **CLUSTER** is the name of the cluster key that is indexed for a cluster. Clusters must have their keys indexed for their associated tables to be accessed. (*See* **CREATE TABLE** for a description of **INITRANS** and **MAXTRANS**.) The default for **INITRANS** for indexes is 2; **MAXTRANS** is 255. **PCTFREE** is the percentage of space to leave free in the index for new entries and updates. The minimum is zero.

TABLESPACE is the name of the tablespace to which this index is assigned. **STORAGE** contains subclauses that are described under **STORAGE**. **NOSORT** is an option whose primary value is in reducing the time to create an index if, and only if, the values in the column being indexed are already in ascending order. It doesn't harm anything if they later fall out of ascending order, but **NOSORT** will only work if they are in order when the index is created. If the rows are not in order, **CREATE INDEX** will return an error message, will not damage anything, and will allow you to rerun it without the **NOSORT** option.

PARALLEL, along with **DEGREE** and **INSTANCES**, specifies the parallel characteristics of the index. **DEGREE** specifies the number of query servers to use to create the index; **INSTANCES** specifies how the index is to be split among instances of a Parallel Server for parallel query processing. An integer *n* specifies that the index is to be split among the specified number of available instances.

In order to create an index, you must either own the indexed table, have INDEX privilege on the table, or have CREATE ANY INDEX system privilege. To create a function-based index, you must have the QUERY REWRITE privilege.

BITMAP creates a bitmap index, which can be useful for columns with few distinct values. The **PARTITION** clauses create indexes on partitioned tables.

REVERSE stores the bytes of the indexed value in reverse order. You cannot reverse a bitmap index.

COMPRESS saves storage space by compressing non-unique non-partitioned indexes. During data retrieval, the data will be displayed as if it were uncompressed. You can turn off index compression, use **NOCOMPRESS**.

CREATE INDEXTYPE
SYNTAX

DESCRIPTION   **CREATE INDEXTYPE** specifies the routines used by a domain index. To create an indextype, you must have the CREATE INDEXTYPE system privilege. To create an indextype in another user's schema, you must have CREATE ANY INDEXTYPE.

CREATE JAVA
SEE ALSO   **ALTER JAVA**, **DROP JAVA**, Chapters 32, 33, and 34
SYNTAX

invoker_rights_clause::=

DESCRIPTION   **CREATE JAVA** creates a Java source, class, or resource. You must have the CREATE PROCEDURE system privilege or (to create the object in another user's schema) CREATE ANY PROCEDURE. To replace such a schema object in another user's schema, you must have the ALTER ANY PROCEDURE system privilege.

The **JAVA SOURCE**, **JAVA CLASS**, and **JAVA RESOURCE** clauses load sources, classes, and resources.

The *invoker_rights* clause lets you specify whether the function executes with the privileges of the function owner or the current user.

EXAMPLE   The following command creates a Java source:

```
create java source named "Hello" as
   public class Hello (
      public static String hello() (
         return "Hello World";   ) );
```

CREATE LIBRARY

SEE ALSO   **CREATE FUNCTION, CREATE PACKAGE BODY, CREATE PROCEDURE**, Chapter 27
SYNTAX

DESCRIPTION   **CREATE LIBRARY** creates a library object, allowing you to reference an operating-system shared library, from which SQL and PL/SQL can call external 3GL functions and procedures. To use the procedures and functions stored in the library, you must have been granted EXECUTE privilege on the library.

CREATE MATERIALIZED VIEW/SNAPSHOT

SEE ALSO   **ALTER MATERIALIZED VIEW/SNAPSHOT, CREATE MATERIALIZED VIEW LOG/SNAPSHOT LOG, DROP MATERIALIZED VIEW/SNAPSHOT, STORAGE**, Chapter 23

SYNTAX

refresh_clause::=

parallel_clause::=

DESCRIPTION As of Oracle8i, a snapshot is treated as a materialized view.

CREATE MATERIALIZED VIEW/SNAPSHOT creates a materialized view, a table that holds the results of a query, usually on one or more tables, called master tables. The master tables may be in a local database or in a remote database. You can have the data refreshed at intervals using the **REFRESH** clause.

To enable a materialized view for query rewrite, you must have the QUERY REWRITE system privilege. If the materialized view is based on objects in other schemas, you must have the GLOBAL QUERY REWRITE privilege.

Materialized views cannot contain LONG columns or reference any objects owned by SYS.

A **FAST** refresh uses the materialized view log associated with the master table(s) to refresh the materialized view. A **COMPLETE** refresh reexecutes the query. A **FORCE** refresh lets Oracle make the choice between a **FAST** or a **COMPLETE** refresh. Oracle first refreshes the materialized view on the **START WITH** date. If you give a **NEXT** date, Oracle refreshes the materialized view at intervals specified by the difference between the **START WITH** and **NEXT** dates.

A simple materialized view selects data from a single master table using a simple query. A complex materialized view selects data using a **GROUP BY**, **CONNECT BY**, subquery, join, or set operation in the query. Oracle can do a **FAST** refresh only on simple materialized views that have materialized view logs.

Because of the local objects which materialized views create, the name of a materialized view should not exceed 19 characters in length. In order to create a materialized view in your schema, you must have the CREATE SNAPSHOT or CREATE MATERIALIZED VIEW system privilege. To create a snapshot in another user's schema, you must have the CREATE ANY SNAPSHOT or CREATE ANY MATERIALIZED VIEW system privilege.

EXAMPLE

```
create materialized view EMP_DEPT_COUNT
 tablespace SNAP
storage (initial 100K next 100K pctincrease 0)
refresh complete
     start with to_date('03-JAN-00 02:00', 'dd-mon-yy hh24:mi')
     next to_date('03-JAN-00 02:00', 'dd-mon-yy hh24:mi')+7
as select Deptno, COUNT(*) Dept_Count
    from HR.EMPLOYEE@HR_LINK
    group by Deptno;
```

CREATE MATERIALIZED VIEW LOG/SNAPSHOT LOG

SEE ALSO   ALTER MATERIALIZED VIEW LOG/SNAPSHOT LOG, CREATE MATERIALIZED VIEW/SNAPSHOT, DROP MATERIALIZED VIEW LOG/SNAPSHOT LOG, STORAGE, Chapter 23

SYNTAX

physical_attributes_clause::=

parallel_clause::=

DESCRIPTION   **CREATE MATERIALIZED VIEW LOG/SNAPSHOT LOG** creates a table associated with the master table of a materialized view that tracks changes to the master table's data. Oracle uses the materialized view log to **FAST** refresh the materialized views of a master table. The storage options specify the storage of the table. Oracle logs database changes only if there is a simple materialized view based on the master table.

You can have only one log for a given master table, and the log is stored in the same schema as the master table. In order to create a snapshot log on your own master table, you must have the CREATE TABLE system privilege. If the master table is in another user's schema, you must have the CREATE ANY TABLE and COMMENT ANY TABLE system privileges as well as SELECT privilege on the master table.

CREATE OPERATOR
SYNTAX

binding_clause::=

implementation_clause::=

context_clause::=

using_clause::=

DESCRIPTION **CREATE OPERATOR** creates a new operator and defines its bindings. You can reference operators in indextypes and in SQL statements. The operators, in turn, reference functions, packages, types, and other user-defined objects.

To create an operator, you must have EXECUTE privilege on the functions and operators referenced by the operator, and CREATE OPERATOR system privilege. If the operator is created in another user's schema, you must have CREATE ANY OPERATOR system privilege.

CREATE OUTLINE

SEE ALSO Chapter 36

SYNTAX

DESCRIPTION **CREATE OUTLINE** creates a stored outline, which is a set of hints used to create the execution plan of the associated query. Later executions of the query will use the same set of hints. You can group stored outlines into categories.

To create an operator, you must have CREATE ANY OUTLINE system privilege.

EXAMPLE

```
create outline SALARIES
    for category SPECIAL
      on select Lodging, Manager, Address from LODGING;
```

CREATE PACKAGE

SEE ALSO   ALTER PACKAGE, CREATE FUNCTION, **CREATE PACKAGE BODY**, **CREATE PROCEDURE**, CURSOR, **DROP PACKAGE**, EXCEPTION, RECORD, TABLE, VARIABLE DECLARATION, Chapter 27

SYNTAX

invoker_rights_clause::=

DESCRIPTION   **CREATE PACKAGE** sets up the specification for a PL/SQL package, a group of public procedures, functions, exceptions, variables, constants, and cursors. Adding **OR REPLACE** replaces the package specification if it already exists, which invalidates the package and requires recompilation of the package body and any objects that depend on the package specification.

Packaging your procedures and functions lets them share data through variables, constants, and cursors. It gives you the ability to grant the whole collection at once as part of a role. Oracle accesses all the elements of a package more efficiently than it would if they were separate. If you change the package body, which Oracle stores separately from the package specification, you do not have to recompile anything that uses the package.

In order to create a package, you must have the CREATE PROCEDURE system privilege; to create a package in another user's account, you must have the CREATE ANY PROCEDURE system privilege.

The *invoker_rights* clause lets you specify whether the package code executes with the privileges of the package owner or the current user.

CREATE PACKAGE BODY

SEE ALSO   ALTER PACKAGE, **CREATE FUNCTION**, **CREATE LIBRARY**, **CREATE PACKAGE**, **CREATE PROCEDURE**, CURSOR, **DROP PACKAGE**, EXCEPTION, RECORD, TABLE, VARIABLE DECLARATION, Chapters 25 and 27

SYNTAX

DESCRIPTION **CREATE PACKAGE BODY** builds the body of a previously specified package created with **CREATE PACKAGE**. Adding **OR REPLACE** replaces the package body if it already exists. You must have CREATE PROCEDURE system privilege to create a package body; to create a package body in another user's account, you must have CREATE ANY PROCEDURE system privilege.

CREATE PROCEDURE

SEE ALSO **ALTER PROCEDURE**, BLOCK STRUCTURE, **CREATE LIBRARY**, **CREATE FUNCTION**, **CREATE PACKAGE**, DATA TYPES, **DROP PROCEDURE**, Chapters 25 and 27

SYNTAX

invoker_rights_clause::=

call_spec::=

Java_declaration::=

C_declaration::=

DESCRIPTION **CREATE PROCEDURE** creates the specification and body of a procedure. A procedure may have parameters, named arguments of a certain datatype. The PL/SQL block defines the behavior of the procedure as a series of declarations, PL/SQL program statements, and exceptions.

The IN qualifier means that you have to specify a value for the argument when you call the procedure. The OUT qualifier means that the procedure passes a value back to the caller through this argument. The IN OUT qualifier combines the meaning of both IN and OUT—you specify a value, and the procedure replaces it with a value. If you don't have any qualifier, the argument defaults to IN. The difference between a function and a procedure is that a function returns a value to the calling environment.

The PL/SQL block can refer to programs in an external C library or to a Java call specification. The *invoker_rights* clause lets you specify whether the procedure executes with the privileges of the function owner or the current user.

CREATE PROFILE

SEE ALSO **ALTER PROFILE, ALTER RESOURCE COST, ALTER SYSTEM, ALTER USER, CREATE USER, DROP PROFILE**, Chapter 19

SYNTAX

resource_parameters::=

password_parameters::=

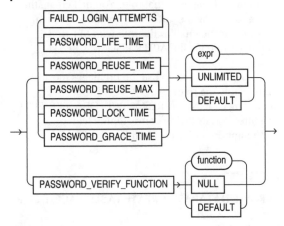

DESCRIPTION   **CREATE PROFILE** creates a set of limits on the use of database resources. When you associate the profile with a user with **CREATE** or **ALTER USER**, you can control what the user does via those limits. To use **CREATE PROFILE**, you must enable resource limits through the initialization parameter RESOURCE_LIMIT or through the **ALTER SYSTEM** command.

SESSIONS_PER_USER limits the user to *integer* concurrent SQL sessions. CPU_PER_ SESSION limits the CPU time in hundredths of seconds. CPU_PER_CALL limits the CPU time for a parse, execute, or fetch call in hundredths of seconds. CONNECT_TIME limits elapsed time of a session in minutes. IDLE_TIME disconnects a user after this number of minutes; this does not apply while a query is running. LOGICAL_READS_PER_SESSION limits the number of blocks read per session; LOGICAL_READS_PER_CALL does the same thing for parse, execute, or fetch calls. PRIVATE_SGA limits the amount of space you can allocate in the SGA as private; the K and M options apply only to this limit. COMPOSITE_LIMIT limits the total resource cost for a session in service units based on a weighted sum of CPU, connect time, logical reads, and private SGA resources.

UNLIMITED means there is no limit on a particular resource. DEFAULT picks up the limit from the DEFAULT profile, which you can change through the **ALTER PROFILE** command.

If a user exceeds a limit, Oracle aborts and rolls back the transaction, then ends the session. You must have CREATE PROFILE system privilege in order to create a profile. You associate a profile to a user with the **ALTER USER** command.

CREATE ROLE
SEE ALSO   **ALTER ROLE, ALTER USER, CREATE USER, DROP ROLE, GRANT, REVOKE, ROLE, SET ROLE**, Chapter 19
SYNTAX

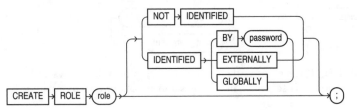

DESCRIPTION   With **CREATE ROLE**, you can create a named role or set of privileges. When you grant the role to a user, you grant him or her all the privileges of that role. You first create the role with **CREATE ROLE**, then grant privileges to the role using the **GRANT** command. When a user wants to access something that the role allows, he or she enables the role with **SET ROLE**. Alternatively, the role can be set as the user's DEFAULT role via the ALTER USER or CREATE USER command.

If you put password protection on the role, the user who wants to use the privileges must supply the password in the **SET ROLE** command to enable the role.

Oracle automatically creates several roles including CONNECT, RESOURCE, DBA, EXP_FULL_DATABASE, and IMP_FULL_DATABASE. The first three roles provide compatibility with prior versions of Oracle. The last two roles let you use the import and export utilities. *See* **ROLE** for a full list.

CREATE ROLLBACK SEGMENT

SEE ALSO   ALTER ROLLBACK SEGMENT, CREATE DATABASE, CREATE TABLESPACE, DROP ROLLBACK SEGMENT, STORAGE, Chapter 38

SYNTAX

DESCRIPTION   *segment* is a name assigned to this rollback segment. *tablespace* is the name of the tablespace to which this rollback segment is assigned. One tablespace may have multiple rollback segments.

STORAGE contains subclauses that are described under **STORAGE**. If **PUBLIC** is used, this rollback segment can be used by any instance that requests it; otherwise it is available only to instances that named it in their init.ora files. *See* Chapter 38 for details concerning the use and management of rollback segments.

CREATE SCHEMA

SEE ALSO   CREATE TABLE, CREATE VIEW, GRANT

SYNTAX

DESCRIPTION   The **CREATE SCHEMA** command creates a collection of tables, views, and privilege grants as a single transaction. The schema name is the same as your Oracle user name.

The **CREATE TABLE**, **CREATE VIEW**, and **GRANT** commands are the standard commands, and the order in which the commands appear is not important, even if there are internal dependencies.

CREATE SEQUENCE

SEE ALSO   ALTER SEQUENCE, AUDIT, DROP SEQUENCE, GRANT, REVOKE, NEXTVAL and CURRVAL under PSEUDO-COLUMNS, Chapter 20

SYNTAX

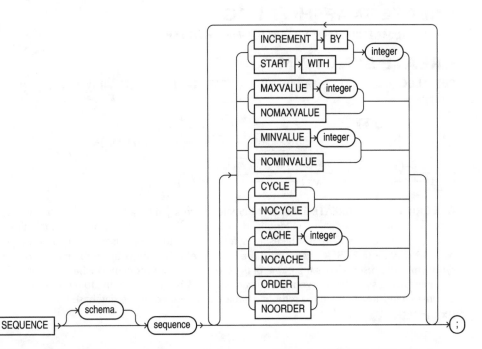

DESCRIPTION   *sequence* is the name given to the sequence. The default **INCREMENT BY** is 1. A positive number will increment the sequence number in an interval equal to the integer. A negative number will cause decrement (decrease the value of) the sequence in the same way. **START WITH** is the number with which the sequence will begin. The default **START WITH** is **MAXVALUE** for descending sequences and **MINVALUE** for ascending; use **START WITH** to override this default.

MINVALUE is the lowest number the sequence will generate. The default is 1 for ascending sequences. **MAXVALUE** is the highest number the sequence will generate. For descending sequence the default is -1. To allow sequences to progress without limitation, specify only **MINVALUE** for ascending and **MAXVALUE** for descending sequences. To stop creating sequence numbers and force an error when an attempt is made to get a new one, specify a **MAXVALUE** on an ascending sequence, or a **MINVALUE** on a descending sequence, plus **NOCYCLE**. To restart either type of sequence where its **MAXVALUE** or **MINVALUE** made it begin, specify **CYCLE**.

CACHE allows a preallocated set of sequence numbers to be kept in memory. The default is 20. The value set must be less than **MAXVALUE** minus **MINVALUE**.

ORDER guarantees that sequence numbers will be assigned to instances requesting them in the order the requests are received. This is useful in applications requiring a history of the sequence in which transactions took place.

To create a sequence in your own schema, you must have the CREATE SEQUENCE system privilege; to create a sequence in another user's schema, you must have the CREATE ANY SEQUENCE system privilege.

CREATE SNAPSHOT

See **CREATE MATERIALIZED VIEW/SNAPSHOT**

CREATE SNAPSHOT LOG

See **CREATE MATERIALIZED VIEW LOG/SNAPSHOT LOG**

CREATE SYNONYM

SEE ALSO   CREATE DATABASE LINK, **CREATE TABLE**, **CREATE VIEW**, Chapters 19 and 22

SYNTAX

DESCRIPTION   **CREATE SYNONYM** creates a synonym for a table, view, sequence, stored procedure, function, package, materialized view, java class object, or synonym, including those on a remote database. **PUBLIC** makes the synonym available to all users, but can only be created by a DBA. Without **PUBLIC**, users must prefix the synonym with your user name. *synonym* is the synonym name. *user.table* is the name of the table, view, or synonym to which the synonym refers. You can have a synonym of synonym. *@database_link* is a database link to a remote database. The synonym refers to a table in the remote database as specified by the database link.

EXAMPLE

```
create synonym TALBOT_LEDGER for LEDGER@BOSS;
```

CREATE TABLE

SEE ALSO   ALTER TABLE, CREATE CLUSTER, CREATE INDEX, CREATE TABLESPACE, CREATE TYPE, DATA TYPES, **DROP TABLE**, INTEGRITY CONSTRAINT, **OBJECT NAMES**, **STORAGE**, Chapters 3, 18, 20, 29, and 30

SYNTAX
relational_table:

object_table:

relational_properties::=

object_properties::=

physical_properties::=

table_properties::=

OID_clause::=

OID_index_clause::=

segment_attributes_clause::=

row_movement_clause::=

physical_attributes_clause::=

index_organized_table_clause::=

compression_clause::=

index_organized_overflow_clause::=

LOB_storage_clause::=

LOB_parameters::=

varray_storage_clause::=

nested_table_storage_clause::=

range_partitioning_clause::=

composite_partitioning_clause::=

partition_definition::=

subpartition_clause::=

partition_level_subpartitioning::=

hash_partitioning_clause::=

partitioning_storage_clause::=

parallel_clause::=

enable_disable_clause::=

using_index_clause::=

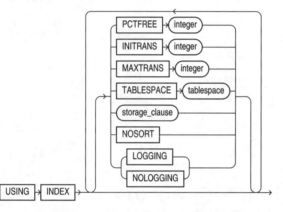

DESCRIPTION   *user* is the table owner. If the table owner is absent, *user* defaults to the user issuing this command. *table* is the table name, and follows Oracle naming conventions.

column is the name of a column, and *datatype* is CHAR, VARCHAR, VARCHAR2, DATE, LONG, NUMBER, ROWID, MLSLABEL, RAW MLSLABEL, RAW, BLOB, CLOB, NCLOB, BFILE, LONG RAW (*see* DATA TYPES). DEFAULT specifies a value to be assigned to the column if a row is inserted without a value for this column. The value can be a simple literal or the result of an expression. The expression, however, cannot include a reference to a column, to Level, or to RowNum.

For an existing abstract data type, you can create an object table. The following example creates an object table called ANIMAL, based on the ANIMAL_TY datatype:

```
create table ANIMAL of ANIMAL_TY;
```

See Chapter 31 for details on the usage of object tables.

See INTEGRITY CONSTRAINT for a full description of the column and table constraints.

CLUSTER includes this table in the named cluster. The table columns listed must correspond in order and datatype to the cluster's cluster columns. The names need not be the same as the corresponding cluster's columns, although matching names can help the user to understand what is being done.

INITRANS tells the initial number of transactions that can update a data block concurrently (**selects** are not counted). **INITRANS** ranges from 1 to 255. 1 is the default. Every transaction takes space (23 bytes in most systems) in the data block itself until the transaction is completed. When more than the **INITRANS** number of transactions are created for the block, space is automatically allocated for them, up to **MAXTRANS**.

MAXTRANS tells the maximum number of transactions that can update a data block concurrently (**select**s are not counted). **MAXTRANS** ranges from 1 to 255. 255 is the default. Every transaction takes space (23 bytes in most systems) in the data block itself until the transaction is completed. Transactions queueing up for execution will occupy more and more free space in the block, although usually there is more free space than is needed for all concurrent transactions.

Whenever Oracle inserts a row into a table, it first looks to see how much space is available in the current block (the size of a block is operating system dependent—see the *Oracle Installation and User's Guide* for your system). If the size of the row will leave less than **PCTFREE** percent in the block, it puts the row in a newly allocated block instead. Default is 10; 0 is the minimum.

PCTUSED defaults to 40. This is the percentage minimum of available space in a block that will make it a candidate for insertion of new rows. Oracle tracks how much space in a block has been made available by deletions. If it falls below **PCTUSED**, Oracle makes the block available for insertions.

STORAGE contains subclauses that are described under STORAGE. **TABLESPACE** is the name of the tablespace to which this table is assigned.

The **ENABLE** and **DISABLE** clauses enable or disable constraints.

PARALLEL, along with **DEGREE** and **INSTANCES**, specifies the parallel characteristics of the table. **DEGREE** specifies the number of query servers to use; **INSTANCES** specifies how the table is to be split among instances of a Parallel Server for parallel query processing. An integer *n* specifies that the table is to be split among the specified number of available instances.

The **PARTITION** clauses control how the table's data is partitioned—by range, by hash, or by a composite of multiple partition methods. *See* Chapter 19 for details on partitioning.

A **TEMPORARY** table contains data that is only visible to the session that creates it. If a temporary table is defined as **GLOBAL**, its definition may be seen by all users. Temporary tables may not be partitioned and cannot support many standard table features (such as varying array data types, LOB datatypes, and index organization). For example, the following command creates a table whose rows will be deleted at the end of the current session

```
create global temporary table WORK_SCHEDULE (
    StartDate DATE,
    EndDate   DATE,
    PayRate   NUMBER)
    on commit preserve rows;
```

The **AS** clause creates the rows of the new table through the returned query rows. The columns and types of the query must match those defined in the **CREATE TABLE**. The query used in the AS clause may not contain any LONG datatype columns. You can turn off logging during the **create table ... as select** operation via the **NOLOGGING** keyword. This option disables the redo log entries that would normally be written during the population of the new table, thus improving performance while impacting your ability to recover that data if an instance failure occurs prior to the next backup.

The **LOB** clause specifies the out-of-line data storage used for internally stored LOB (BLOB, CLOB, and NCLOB) data.

The object table definition section applies to object tables, in which each row has an object ID (OID). *See* Chapter 31.

CREATE TABLESPACE

SEE ALSO **ALTER TABLESPACE**, **DROP TABLESPACE**, **STORAGE**, Chapters 20 and 38

SYNTAX

autoextend_clause::=

maxsize_clause::=

extent_management_clause::=

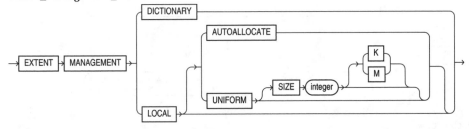

DESCRIPTION   *tablespace* is the name of the tablespace, and follows Oracle naming conventions. The DATAFILE is a file or series of files described according to a *file_definition*, which specifies the file names and sizes:

```
'file' [SIZE integer [K | M] [REUSE]
```

The file format is operating-system specific. **SIZE** is the number of bytes set aside for this file. Suffixing this with K multiplies the value by 1024; M multiplies it by 1048576. **DEFAULT STORAGE** defines the default storage for all objects created in this tablespace, unless those defaults are overridden, such as by **CREATE TABLE. ONLINE**, the default, indicates that this tablespace will become available to users as soon as it is created. **OFFLINE** prevents access to it until **ALTER TABLESPACE** changes it to **ONLINE**. DBA_TABLESPACES gives the status of all the tablespaces.

SIZE and **REUSE** together tell Oracle to reuse the file if it already exists (anything it contains will be wiped out), or create it if it doesn't already exist. **SIZE** without **REUSE** will create a file that does not exist, but return an error if it does. Without **SIZE**, the file must already exist.

The **MINIMUM EXTENT** size parameter specifies the minimum size for extents within the tablespace. The default is operating system and database block size-specific.

When turned ON, the **AUTOEXTEND** option will dynamically extend a datafile as needed in increments of **NEXT** size, to a maximum of **MAXSIZE** (or UNLIMITED). If a tablespace will only be used for temporary segments created during query processing, you can create it as a **TEMPORARY** tablespace. If the tablespace will contain permanent objects (such as tables), then you should use the default setting of **PERMANENT**.

EXTENT MANAGEMENT controls the manner in which the extent management data for a tablespace is recorded. By default, extent usage records are stored in the data dictionary. If you choose the **LOCAL** option, the extent location information is stored in a bitmap within the tablespace's datafiles.

CREATE TEMPORARY TABLESPACE

SEE ALSO   **CREATE TABLE, CREATE TABLESPACE, STORAGE**
SYNTAX

autoextend_clause::=

maxsize_clause::=

DESCRIPTION   **CREATE TEMPORARY TABLESPACE** creates a tablespace that will be used to store temporary tables. The temporary tables stored in this tablespace are not the temporary segments created during sort operations; rather, they are tables created via the **create temporary table** command. *See* **CREATE TABLESPACE** for the tablespace parameters, and **CREATE TABLE** for the syntax for temporary tables.

CREATE TRIGGER
SEE ALSO   **ALTER TABLE**, **ALTER TRIGGER**, BLOCK STRUCTURE, **DROP TRIGGER**, Chapters 26 and 28
SYNTAX

dml_event_clause::=

referencing_clause::=

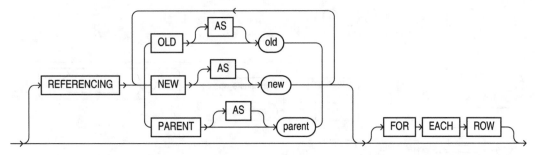

DESCRIPTION **CREATE TRIGGER** creates and enables a database trigger, a stored procedure block associated with a table, specified in the **on** clause, that Oracle automatically executes when the specified SQL statement executes against the table. You can use triggers to enforce complex constraints and to propagate changes throughout the database instead of doing this in your applications. That way you implement the triggered code once instead of having to do it in every application.

The main clause of the **CREATE TRIGGER** command specifies the SQL operation that triggers the block (such as **delete**, **insert**, or **update**) and when the trigger fires (**BEFORE**, **AFTER**, or **INSTEAD OF** executing the triggering operation). If you specify an **OF** clause on an **UPDATE** trigger, the trigger fires only when you update one or more of the specified columns. Note that you can also create triggers that fire when DDL events occur (including **create**, **alter**, and **drop**) and when specific database events occur (logons, logoffs, database startups, shutdowns, and server errors).

The **REFERENCING** clause specifies a correlation name for the table for the OLD and NEW versions of the table. This lets you use the name when referring to columns to avoid confusion, particularly when the table name is OLD or NEW. The default names are OLD and NEW.

The **FOR EACH ROW** clause specifies the trigger to be a row trigger, a trigger fired once for each row affected by the triggering operation. The **WHEN** clause restricts the execution of the trigger to happen only when the *condition* is met. This condition is a SQL condition, not a PL/SQL condition.

You can disable and enable triggers through the **ALTER TRIGGER** and **ALTER TABLE** commands. If a trigger is disabled, ORACLE does not fire the trigger when a potentially triggering operation occurs. The **CREATE TRIGGER** command automatically enables the trigger.

To create a trigger on a table you own, you must have the CREATE TRIGGER system privilege. To create a trigger on another user's table, you must have the CREATE ANY TRIGGER system privilege. The user must have been directly granted all privileges necessary to execute the stored procedure.

CREATE TYPE

SEE ALSO   **CREATE TABLE**, **CREATE TYPE BODY**, Chapters 4, 28, and 29

SYNTAX

create_incomplete_type::=

create_object_type::=

element_list::=

invoker_rights_clause::=

pragma_clause::=

procedure_spec | function_spec::=

call_spec::=

Java_declaration::=

C_declaration::=

create_varray_type::=

create_nested_table_type::=

DESCRIPTION   **CREATE TYPE** creates an abstract datatype, named varying array (VARRAY), nested table type, or an incomplete object type. To create or replace a type, you must have CREATE TYPE privilege. To create a type in another user's schema, you must have CREATE ANY TYPE system privileges.

When creating an abstract datatype, you can base it on Oracle's provided datatypes (such as DATE and NUMBER) and on previously defined abstract datatypes.

An "incomplete" type has a name but no attributes or methods. However, it can be referenced by other object types, and so can be used to define object types that refer to each other. If you have two types that refer to each other, you must create one as an incomplete type, then create the second, then re-create the first with its proper definition.

If you plan to create methods for the type, you need to declare the method names in the type specification. When naming the methods, restrict their ability to modify the database via the **PRAGMA RESTRICT_REFERENCES** clause. The available options are shown in the syntax diagram. At a minimum, your methods should use the WNDS restriction. *See* Chapter 28. For details on VARRAYs and nested tables, see Chapter 29.

EXAMPLES   Creating a type that will have associated methods:

```
create or replace type ANIMAL_TY as object
(Breed        VARCHAR2(25),
 Name         VARCHAR2(25),
 BirthDate  DATE,
member function AGE (BirthDate IN DATE) return NUMBER,
PRAGMA RESTRICT_REFERENCES(AGE, WNDS));
```

Creating a varying array:

```
create or replace type TOOLS_VA as varray(5) of VARCHAR2(25);
```

Creating a type with no methods:

```
create type ADDRESS_TY as object
(Street  VARCHAR2(50),
 City    VARCHAR2(25),
 State   CHAR(2),
 Zip     NUMBER);
```

Creating a type that uses another type:

```
create type PERSON_TY as object
(Name        VARCHAR2(25),
 Address    ADDRESS_TY);
```

CREATE TYPE BODY

SEE ALSO   **CREATE FUNCTION, CREATE PROCEDURE, CREATE TYPE**, Chapters 4, 25, 27, 28, and 29

SYNTAX

procedure_declaration | function_declaration::=

call_spec::=

Java_declaration::=

C_declaration::=

DESCRIPTION   **CREATE TYPE BODY** specifies the methods to be applied to types created via **CREATE TYPE**. You must have the CREATE TYPE privilege in order to create type bodies. To create a type body in another user's schema, you must have the CREATE ANY TYPE privilege.

See Chapter 28 for examples of methods.

EXAMPLE

```
create or replace type body ANIMAL_TY as
member function Age (BirthDate DATE) return NUMBER is
  begin
     RETURN ROUND(SysDate - BirthDate);
  end;
end;
/
```

CREATE USER

SEE ALSO   **ALTER USER, CREATE PROFILE, CREATE ROLE, CREATE TABLESPACE, GRANT,** Chapter 19

SYNTAX

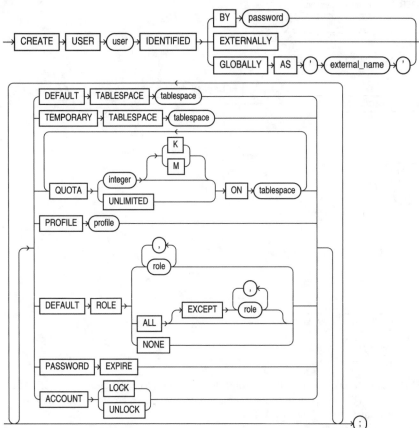

DESCRIPTION **CREATE USER** creates a user account that lets you log onto the database with a certain set of privileges and storage settings. If you specify a password, you must supply that password to logon; if you specify the **EXTERNALLY** option, access is verified through operating system security. External verification uses the OS_AUTHENT_PREFIX initialization parameter to prefix the operating system user id, so the user name you specify in **CREATE USER** should contain that prefix (usually, OPS$).

The **DEFAULT TABLESPACE** is the tablespace in which the user creates objects. The **TEMPORARY TABLESPACE** is the tablespace in which temporary objects are created for the user's operations.

You can put a **QUOTA** on either of these tablespaces that limits the amount of space, in bytes (kilobytes or megabytes for K or M options, respectively), that a user can allocate. The **profile** clause assigns a named profile to the user to limit usage of database resources. Oracle assigns the DEFAULT profile to the user if you don't specify a profile.

When you first create a user, the user has no privileges. You must use the **GRANT** command to grant roles and privileges to the user. You should usually grant **CREATE SESSION** as a minimal privilege.

For information on password expirations and account locking, see **CREATE PROFILE** and Chapter 19.

CREATE VIEW

SEE ALSO   **CREATE SYNONYM, CREATE TABLE, DROP VIEW, RENAME**, INTEGRITY CONSTRAINT,
Chapters 18 and 28

SYNTAX

with_clause::=

DESCRIPTION   **CREATE VIEW** defines a view named *view*. *user* is the name of the user for whom the view is created. The **OR REPLACE** option re-creates the view if it already exists. The **FORCE** option creates the view regardless of whether the tables to which the view refers exist or whether the user has privileges on them. The user still can't execute the view, but he or she can create it. The **NO FORCE** option creates the view only if the base tables exist and the user has privileges on them.

If an alias is specified, the view uses the alias as the name of the corresponding column in the query. If an alias is not specified, the view inherits the column name from the query; in this case each column in a query must have a unique name, one that follows normal Oracle naming conventions. It cannot be an expression. An alias in the query itself also can serve to rename the column.

AS *query* identifies the columns of tables and other views that are to appear in this view. Its **where** clause will determine which rows are to be retrieved.

WITH CHECK OPTION restricts **insert**s and **update**s performed through the view to prevent them from creating rows that the view cannot itself select, based on the **where** clause of the **CREATE VIEW** statement. Thus this:

```
create or replace view WOMEN
   as select Name, Department, Sex
   from EMPLOYEE  where Sex = 'F'
   with check option;
```

prevents you from inserting a row into WOMEN where Sex was either M or NULL, or from changing the value in Sex using an **update**.

WITH CHECK OPTION may be used in a view that is based on another view; however, if the underlying view also has a **WITH CHECK OPTION**, it is ignored.

constraint is a name given to the **CHECK OPTION**. *constraint* is an optional name assigned to this constraint. Without it, Oracle will assign a name in the form **SYS_C***n*, where *n* is an integer. An Oracle-assigned name will usually change during an import, while a user-assigned name will not change.

update and **delete** will work on rows in a view if the view is based on a single table and its query does not contain the **group by** clause, the **distinct** clause, group functions, or references to the pseudo-column RowNum. You may **update** views containing other pseudo-columns or expressions, as long as they are not referenced in the **update**.

You may **insert** rows through a view if the view is based on a single table and if its query does not contain the **group by** clause, the **distinct** clause, group functions, references to any pseudo-columns, or any expressions. If the view is created **WITH READ ONLY**, then only selects are allowed against the view; no data manipulation is allowed.

You can create object views to superimpose abstract datatypes on existing relational tables. *See* Chapter 28.

In order to create a view, you must have the CREATE VIEW system privilege. To create a view in another user's schema, you must have the CREATE ANY VIEW system privilege.

CREATING A DATABASE

Creating a database is the process of making a database ready for initial use. It includes clearing the database files and loading initial database tables required by the RDBMS. This is accomplished via the SQL statement **CREATE DATABASE**.

CTXCTL

The CTXCTL utility simplifies the management of ConText server processes. The utility enables you to quickly start and stop ConText servers, as well as generate a simple status report showing the servers currently in use. The available commands are

help [command]	Shows help information for the specified command
status	Shows running servers
start *n* [ling | query | ddl | dml]	Starts *n* servers
stop pid... | all	Stops server processes
quit	Terminates ctxctl
exit	Terminates ctxctl

See Chapter 24 for information on configuring a database for use by ConText queries.

CUBE

SEE ALSO   **GROUPING, ROLLUP**, Chapter 13

FORMAT

```
GROUP BY CUBE (column1, column2)
```

DESCRIPTION CUBE groups rows based on the values of all possible combinations of expressions for each row, and returns a single row of summary information for each group. You can use the **CUBE** operation to produce **cross-tab reports**. *See* Chapter 13.

CURRENT BUFFER

The current buffer is the one that SQL*PLUS editing commands will affect, and that can be saved to a file with the **SAVE** command. *See* **CHANGE**.

CURRENT LINE

The current line is the one in the current buffer that SQL*PLUS command line editor commands will affect. *See* **CURRENT BUFFER** and **CHANGE**.

CURRVAL

See PSEUDO-COLUMNS.

CURSOR

Cursor has two definitions:

- A cursor is a marker such as a blinking square or line that marks your current position on a CRT screen.
- Cursor is also a synonym for context area-a work area in memory where Orcle stores the current SQL statement. For a query, the area in memory also includes column headings and one row retrieved by the **select** statement.

CURSOR—PL/SQL

SEE ALSO **CREATE PACKAGE**, **CREATE PACKAGE BODY**, Chapter 25
FORMAT

```
CURSOR cursor [(parameter datatype[,parameter datatype]...]
   [IS query]
```

DESCRIPTION You can specify a cursor in a PL/SQL package and declare its body. The specification contains only the list of parameters with their corresponding datatypes, not the **IS** clause, while the body contains both. The parameters may appear anywhere in the query that a constant could appear. You can specify the cursor as a part of the public declarations of the package specification, and then the cursor body as part of the hidden package body.

CURSOR FOR LOOP

In FOR loops, the loop executes a specified number of times. In a cursor FOR loop, the results of a query are used to dynamically determine the number of times the loop is executed. In a cursor FOR loop, the opening, fetching, and closing of cursors is performed implicitly; you do not need to explicitly code these actions.

The following listing shows a cursor FOR loop that queries the RADIUS_VALS table and inserts records into the AREAS table.

```
declare
  pi      constant NUMBER(9,7) := 3.1415926;
  area    NUMBER(14,2);
  cursor rad_cursor is
      select * from RADIUS_VALS;
begin
  for rad_val in rad_cursor
    loop
      area := pi*power(rad_val.radius,2);
      insert into AREAS values (rad_val.radius, area);
    end loop;
end;
.
/
```

In a cursor FOR loop, there is no **open** or **fetch** command. The

```
for rad_val in rad_cursor
```

command implicitly opens the *rad_cursor* cursor and fetches a value into the *rad_val* variable. Note that the *rad_val* variable is not explicitly declared when you use a cursor FOR loop. When there are no more records in the cursor, the loop is exited and the cursor is closed. In a cursor FOR loop, there is no need for a **close** command. *See* Chapter 25 for further information on cursor management within PL/SQL.

DATA CONTROL LANGUAGE (DCL) STATEMENTS

DCL statements are one category of SQL statements. DCL statements, such as **grant connect**, **grant select**, **grant update**, and **revoke dba**, control access to the data and to the database. The other categories are data definition language (DDL) and data manipulation language (DML) statements.

DATA DEFINITION LANGUAGE (DDL) STATEMENTS

DDL statements are one category of SQL statements. DDL statements define (create) or delete (drop) database objects. Examples are **create view**, **create table**, **create index**, **drop table**, **create function**, and **rename table**. Executing any DDL command commits any pending changes to the database. The other categories of SQL statements are data control language (DCL) and data manipulation language (DML) statements.

DATA DEFINITION LOCKS

Data definition locks are locks placed on the data dictionary during changes to the structures (definitions) of database objects (such as tables, indexes, views, and clusters) so that those changes occur with no negative impact on the database data. There are three kinds of locks: dictionary operation locks, dictionary definition locks, and table definition locks.

DATA DICTIONARY

The data dictionary is a comprehensive set of tables and views owned by the DBA users SYS and SYSTEM, which activates when Oracle is initially installed, and is a central source of information for the Oracle RDBMS itself and for all users of Oracle. The tables are automatically maintained by Oracle, and hold a set of views and tables containing information about database objects, users, privileges, events, and use. *See* Chapter 35.

DATA DICTIONARY VIEWS

SEE ALSO   Chapter 35

DESCRIPTION   The Oracle data dictionary views are described in Chapter 35. Most of the following listing, describing the available data dictionary views, was generated by selecting records from the DICTIONARY view in Oracle, via a non-DBA account. The views are listed here in alphabetical order; Chapter 35 groups them by function, and describes them.

TABLE_NAME	Comments
ALL_ALL_TABLES	Description of all object and relational tables accessible to the user
ALL_ARGUMENTS	Arguments in object accessible to the user
ALL_CATALOG	All tables, views, synonyms, sequences accessible to the user
ALL_CLUSTERS	Description of clusters accessible to the user
ALL_CLUSTER_HASH_EXPRESSIONS	Hash functions for all accessible clusters
ALL_COLL_TYPES	Description of named collection types accessible to the user
ALL_COL_COMMENTS	Comments on columns of accessible tables and views
ALL_COL_PRIVS	Grants on columns for which the user is the grantor, grantee, owner, or an enabled role or PUBLIC is the grantee
ALL_COL_PRIVS_MADE	Grants on columns for which the user is owner or grantor
ALL_COL_PRIVS_RECD	Grants on columns for which the user, PUBLIC or enabled role is the grantee
ALL_CONSTRAINTS	Constraint definitions on accessible tables
ALL_CONS_COLUMNS	Information about accessible columns in constraint definitions
ALL_CONTEXT	Description of all active context namespaces under the current session
ALL_DB_LINKS	Database links accessible to the user
ALL_DEF_AUDIT_OPTS	Auditing options for newly created objects
ALL_DEPENDENCIES	Dependencies to and from objects accessible to the user
ALL_DIMENSIONS	Description of the dimension objects accessible to the DBA
ALL_DIM_ATTRIBUTES	Representation of the relationship between a dimension level and a functionally dependent column
ALL_DIM_CHILD_OF	Representaion of a 1:n hierarchical relationship between a pair of levels in a dimension
ALL_DIM_HIERARCHIES	Representation of a dimension hierarchy
ALL_DIM_JOIN_KEY	Representation of a join between two dimension tables.
ALL_DIM_LEVELS	Description of dimension levels visible to DBA
ALL_DIM_LEVEL_KEY	Representations of columns of a dimension level
ALL_DIRECTORIES	Description of all directories accessible to the user
ALL_ERRORS	Current errors on stored objects that user is allowed to create
ALL_HISTOGRAMS	Synonym for ALL_TAB_HISTOGRAMS
ALL_INDEXES	Descriptions of indexes on tables accessible to the user
ALL_IND_COLUMNS	Columns comprising indexes on accessible tables
ALL_IND_EXPRESSIONS	Functional index expressions on accessible tables
ALL_IND_PARTITIONS	Index partitions on accessible tables.
ALL_IND_SUBPARTITIONS	Index subpartitions on accessible tables.
ALL_INTERNAL_TRIGGERS	Description of the internal triggers on the tables accessible to the user

TABLE_NAME	Comments
ALL_JOBS	Synonym for USER_JOBS
ALL_LIBRARIES	Description of libraries accessible to the user
ALL_LOBS	Description of LOBs contained in tables accessible to the user
ALL_LOB_PARTITIONS	LOB partitions of accessible tables.
ALL_LOB_SUBPARTITIONS	LOB subpartitions of accessible tables.
ALL_METHOD_PARAMS	Description of method parameters of types accessible to the user.
ALL_METHOD_RESULTS	Description of method results of types accessible to the user.
ALL_MVIEW_AGGREGATES	Description of the materialized view aggregates accessible to the user
ALL_MVIEW_ANALYSIS	Description of the materialized views accessible to the user
ALL_MVIEW_DETAIL_RELATIONS	Description of the materialized view detail tables accessible to the user
ALL_MVIEW_JOINS	Description of a join between two columns in the WHERE clause of a materialized view accessible to the user
ALL_MVIEW_KEYS	Description of the columns that appear in the GROUP BY list of a materialized view accessible to the user
ALL_NESTED_TABLES	Description of nested tables in tables accessible to the user
ALL_OBJECTS	Objects accessible to the user
ALL_OBJECT_TABLES	Description of all object tables accessible to the user
ALL_OUTLINES	Synonym for USER_OUTLINES
ALL_OUTLINE_HINTS	Synonym for USER_OUTLINE_HINTS
ALL_PARTIAL_DROP_TABS	All tables with partially dropped columns accessible to the user
ALL_PART_COL_STATISTICS	Column statistics for partitions
ALL_PART_HISTOGRAMS	Histogram statistics for partitions
ALL_PART_INDEXES	Indexes on accessible partitions
ALL_PART_KEY_COLUMNS	Key columns for accessible partitions
ALL_PART_LOBS	LOB columns of accessible partitions
ALL_PART_TABLES	Accessible partitioned tables
ALL_POLICIES	All policies for objects if the user has system privileges or owns the objects
ALL_QUEUES	All queues accessible to the user
ALL_QUEUE_TABLES	All queue tables accessible to the user
ALL_REFRESH	All the refresh groups that the user can touch
ALL_REFRESH_CHILDREN	All the objects in refresh groups, where the user can touch the group
ALL_REFRESH_DEPENDENCIES	Description of the detail tables that materialized views depend on for refresh
ALL_REFS	Description of REF columns contained in tables accessible to the user
ALL_REGISTERED_SNAPSHOTS	Remote snapshots of local tables that the user can see
ALL_REPAUDIT_ATTRIBUTE	Information about attributes automatically maintained for replication
ALL_REPAUDIT_COLUMN	Information about columns in all shadow tables for replicated tables which are accessible to the user
ALL_REPCAT	Replication catalog
ALL_REPCATLOG	Information about asynchronous administration requests

TABLE_NAME	Comments
ALL_REPCOLUMN	Replicated columns for a table sorted alphabetically in ascending order
ALL_REPCOLUMN_GROUP	All column groups of replicated tables which are accessible to the user
ALL_REPCONFLICT	All conflicts with available resolutions for user's replicated tables
ALL_REPDDL	Arguments that do not fit in a single repcat log record
ALL_REPFLAVORS	Flavors defined for replicated object groups
ALL_REPFLAVOR_COLUMNS	Replicated columns in flavors
ALL_REPFLAVOR_OBJECTS	Replicated objects in flavors
ALL_REPGENERATED	Objects generated to support replication
ALL_REPGENOBJECTS	Objects generated to support replication
ALL_REPGROUP	Information about replicated object groups
ALL_REPGROUPED_COLUMN	Columns in the all column groups of replicated tables which are accessible to the user
ALL_REPGROUP_PRIVILEGES	Information about users who are registered for object group privileges
ALL_REPKEY_COLUMNS	Primary columns for a table using column-level replication
ALL_REPOBJECT	Information about replicated objects
ALL_REPPARAMETER_COLUMN	All columns used for resolving conflicts in replicated tables which are accessible to the user
ALL_REPPRIORITY	Values and their corresponding priorities in all priority groups which are accessible to the user
ALL_REPPRIORITY_GROUP	Information about all priority groups which are accessible to the user
ALL_REPPROP	Propagation information about replicated objects
ALL_REPRESOLUTION	Description of all conflict resolutions for replicated tables which are accessible to the user
ALL_REPRESOLUTION_METHOD	All conflict resolution methods accessible to the user
ALL_REPRESOLUTION_STATISTICS	Statistics for conflict resolutions for replicated tables which are accessible to the user
ALL_REPRESOL_STATS_CONTROL	Information about statistics collection for conflict resolutions for replicated tables which are accessible to the user
ALL_REPSCHEMA	N-way replication information
ALL_REPSITES	N-way replication information
ALL_SEQUENCES	Description of SEQUENCEs accessible to the user
ALL_SNAPSHOTS	Snapshots the user can access
ALL_SNAPSHOT_LOGS	All snapshot logs in the database that the user can see
ALL_SNAPSHOT_REFRESH_TIMES	Snapshots and their last refresh times for each master table that the user can look at
ALL_SOURCE	Current source on stored objects that user is allowed to create
ALL_SUBPART_COL_STATISTICS	Column statistics for subpartitions
ALL_SUBPART_HISTOGRAMS	Histogram statistics for subpartitions
ALL_SUBPART_KEY_COLUMNS	Key columns of accessible subpartitions
ALL_SUMDELTA	Direct path load entries accessible to the user
ALL_SUMMARIES	Description of the summaries accessible to the user
ALL_SUMMARY_AGGREGATES	Description of the summary aggregates accessible to the user
ALL_SUMMARY_DETAIL_TABLES	Description of the summary detail tables accessible to the user

TABLE_NAME	Comments
ALL_SUMMARY_JOINS	Description of a join between two columns in the WHERE clause of a summary accessible to the user
ALL_SUMMARY_KEYS	Description of the columns that appear in the GROUP BY list of a summary accessible to the user
ALL_SYNONYMS	All synonyms accessible to the user
ALL_TABLES	Description of relational tables accessible to the user
ALL_TAB_COLUMNS	Columns of user's tables, views and clusters
ALL_TAB_COL_STATISTICS	Columns of user's tables, views and clusters
ALL_TAB_COMMENTS	Comments on tables and views accessible to the user
ALL_TAB_HISTOGRAMS	Histograms on columns of all tables visible to user
ALL_TAB_MODIFICATIONS	Information regarding modifications to tables
ALL_TAB_PARTITIONS	Partitions of accessible tables
ALL_TAB_PRIVS	Grants on objects for which the user is the grantor, grantee, owner, or an enabled role or PUBLIC is the grantee
ALL_TAB_PRIVS_MADE	User's grants and grants on user's objects
ALL_TAB_PRIVS_RECD	Grants on objects for which the user, PUBLIC or enabled role is the grantee
ALL_TAB_SUBPARTITIONS	Subpartitions of accessible tables
ALL_TRIGGERS	Triggers accessible to the current user
ALL_TRIGGER_COLS	Column usage in user's triggers or in triggers on user's tables
ALL_TYPES	Description of types accessible to the user
ALL_TYPE_ATTRS	Description of attributes of types accessible to the user
ALL_TYPE_METHODS	Description of methods of types accessible to the user
ALL_UNUSED_COL_TABS	All tables with unused columns accessible to the user
ALL_UPDATABLE_COLUMNS	Description of all updatable columns
ALL_USERS	Information about all users of the database
ALL_VARRAYS	Description of varrays in tables accessible to the user
ALL_VIEWS	Description of views accessible to the user
AUDIT_ACTIONS	Description table for audit trail action type codes. Maps action type numbers to action type names
CAT	Synonym for USER_CATALOG
CLU	Synonym for USER_CLUSTERS
COLS	Synonym for USER_TAB_COLUMNS
COLUMN_PRIVILEGES	Grants on columns for which the user is the grantor, grantee, owner, or an enabled role or PUBLIC is the grantee
DICT	Synonym for DICTIONARY
DICTIONARY	Description of data dictionary tables and views
DICT_COLUMNS	Description of columns in data dictionary tables and views
GLOBAL_NAME	Global database name
IND	Synonym for USER_INDEXES
INDEX_HISTOGRAM	statistics on keys with repeat count
INDEX_STATS	statistics on the b-tree
NLS_DATABASE_PARAMETERS	Permanent NLS parameters of the database
NLS_INSTANCE_PARAMETERS	NLS parameters of the instance
NLS_SESSION_PARAMETERS	NLS parameters of the user session
OBJ	Synonym for USER_OBJECTS
RESOURCE_COST	Cost for each resource

TABLE_NAME	Comments
ROLE_ROLE_PRIVS	Roles which are granted to roles
ROLE_SYS_PRIVS	System privileges granted to roles
ROLE_TAB_PRIVS	Table privileges granted to roles
SEQ	Synonym for USER_SEQUENCES
SESSION_PRIVS	Privileges which the user currently has set
SESSION_ROLES	Roles which the user currently has enabled.
SYN	Synonym for USER_SYNONYMS
TABLE_PRIVILEGES	Grants on objects for which the user is the grantor, grantee, owner, or an enabled role or PUBLIC is the grantee
TABS	Synonym for USER_TABLES
USER_ALL_TABLES	Description of all object and relational tables owned by the user's
USER_ARGUMENTS	Arguments in object accessible to the user
USER_AUDIT_OBJECT	Audit trail records for statements concerning objects, specifically: table, cluster, view, index, sequence, [public] database link, [public] synonym, procedure, trigger, rollback segment, tablespace, role, user
USER_AUDIT_SESSION	All audit trail records concerning CONNECT and DISCONNECT
USER_AUDIT_STATEMENT	Audit trail records concerning grant, revoke, audit, noaudit and alter system
USER_AUDIT_TRAIL	Audit trail entries relevant to the user
USER_CATALOG	Tables, Views, Synonyms and Sequences owned by the user
USER_CLUSTERS	Descriptions of user's own clusters
USER_CLUSTER_HASH_EXPRESSIONS	Hash functions for the user's hash clusters
USER_CLU_COLUMNS	Mapping of table columns to cluster columns
USER_COLL_TYPES	Description of the user's own named collection types
USER_COL_COMMENTS	Comments on columns of user's tables and views
USER_COL_PRIVS	Grants on columns for which the user is the owner, grantor or grantee
USER_COL_PRIVS_MADE	All grants on columns of objects owned by the user
USER_COL_PRIVS_RECD	Grants on columns for which the user is the grantee
USER_CONSTRAINTS	Constraint definitions on user's own tables
USER_CONS_COLUMNS	Information about accessible columns in constraint definitions
USER_DB_LINKS	Database links owned by the user
USER_DEPENDENCIES	Dependencies to and from a users objects
USER_DIMENSIONS	Description of the dimension objects accessible to the DBA
USER_DIM_ATTRIBUTES	Representation of the relationship between a dimension level and a functionally dependent column
USER_DIM_CHILD_OF	Representation of a 1:n hierarchical relationship between a pair of levels in a dimension
USER_DIM_HIERARCHIES	Representation of a dimension hierarchy
USER_DIM_JOIN_KEY	Representation of a join between two dimension tables
USER_DIM_LEVELS	Description of dimension levels visible to DBA
USER_DIM_LEVEL_KEY	Representations of columns of a dimension level
USER_ERRORS	Current errors on stored objects owned by the user
USER_EXTENTS	Extents comprising segments owned by the user

TABLE_NAME	Comments
USER_FREE_SPACE	Free extents in tablespaces accessible to the user
USER_HISTOGRAMS	Synonym for USER_TAB_HISTOGRAMS
USER_INDEXES	Description of the user's own indexes
USER_IND_COLUMNS	Columns comprising user's indexes and indexes on user's tables
USER_IND_EXPRESSIONS	Functional index expressions in user's indexes and indexes on user's tables
USER_IND_PARTITIONS	Partitions of a user's indexes
USER_IND_SUBPARTITIONS	Subpartitions of a user's indexes
USER_INTERNAL_TRIGGERS	Description of the internal triggers on the user's own tables
USER_JOBS	All jobs owned by this user
USER_LIBRARIES	Description of the user's own libraries
USER_LOBS	Description of the user's own LOBs contained in the user's own tables
USER_LOB_PARTITIONS	User's LOB partitions
USER_LOB_SUBPARTITIONS	User's LOB subpartitions
USER_METHOD_PARAMS	Description of method parameters of the user's own types
USER_METHOD_RESULTS	Description of method results of the user's own types
USER_MVIEW_AGGREGATES	Description of the materialized view aggregates created by the user
USER_MVIEW_ANALYSIS	Description of the materialized views created by the user
USER_MVIEW_DETAIL_RELATIONS	Description of the materialized view detail tables of the materialized views created by the user
USER_MVIEW_JOINS	Description of a join between two columns in the WHERE clause of a materialized view created by the user
USER_MVIEW_KEYS	Description of the columns that appear in the GROUP BY list of a materialized view created by the user
USER_NESTED_TABLES	Description of nested tables contained in the user's own tables
USER_OBJECTS	Objects owned by the user
USER_OBJECT_SIZE	Sizes, in bytes, of various pl/sql objects
USER_OBJECT_TABLES	Description of the user's own object tables
USER_OBJ_AUDIT_OPTS	Auditing options for user's own tables and views
USER_OUTLINES	Stored outlines owned by the user
USER_OUTLINE_HINTS	Hints stored in outlines owned by the user
USER_PARTIAL_DROP_TABS	User tables with unused columns
USER_PART_COL_STATISTICS	Statistics on user's partition columns
USER_PART_HISTOGRAMS	Histograms for user's partition columns
USER_PART_INDEXES	Indexes on user's partitions
USER_PART_KEY_COLUMNS	Key columns for user's partitions
USER_PART_LOBS	LOBs in user's partitions
USER_PART_TABLES	User's partition tables
USER_PASSWORD_LIMITS	Display password limits of the user
USER_POLICIES	All row level security policies for tables or views owned by the user
USER_QUEUES	All queues owned by the user
USER_QUEUE_SCHEDULES	Schedules for user queues
USER_QUEUE_TABLES	All queue tables created by the user
USER_REFRESH	All the refresh groups

TABLE_NAME	Comments
USER_REFRESH_CHILDREN	All the objects in refresh groups, where the user owns the refresh group
USER_REFS	Description of the user's own REF columns contained in the user's own tables
USER_REGISTERED_SNAPSHOTS	Remote snapshots of local tables currently using logs owned by the user
USER_REPAUDIT_ATTRIBUTE	Information about attributes automatically maintained for replication
USER_REPAUDIT_COLUMN	Information about columns in all shadow tables for user's replicated tables
USER_REPCAT	User's replication catalog
USER_REPCATLOG	Information about the current user's asynchronous administration requests
USER_REPCOLUMN	Replicated columns for the current user's table in ascending order
USER_REPCOLUMN_GROUP	All column groups of user's replicated tables
USER_REPCONFLICT	User's replication conflicts
USER_REPDDL	Arguments that do not fit in a single repcat log record
USER_REPFLAVORS	Flavors current user created for replicated object groups
USER_REPFLAVOR_COLUMNS	Replicated columns from current user's tables in flavors
USER_REPFLAVOR_OBJECTS	Replicated user objects in flavors
USER_REPGENERATED	Objects generated for the current user to support replication
USER_REPGENOBJECTS	Objects generated for the current user to support replication
USER_REPGROUP	Replication information about the current user
USER_REPGROUPED_COLUMN	Columns in the all column groups of user's replicated tables
USER_REPGROUP_PRIVILEGES	Information about users who are registered for object group privileges
USER_REPKEY_COLUMNS	Primary columns for a table using column-level replication
USER_REPOBJECT	Replication information about the current user's objects
USER_REPPARAMETER_COLUMN	All columns used for resolving conflicts in user's replicated tables
USER_REPPRIORITY	Values and their corresponding priorities in user's priority groups
USER_REPPRIORITY_GROUP	Information about user's priority groups
USER_REPPROP	Propagation information about the current user's objects
USER_REPRESOLUTION	Description of all conflict resolutions for user's replicated tables
USER_REPRESOLUTION_METHOD	All conflict resolution methods accessible to the user
USER_REPRESOLUTION_STATISTICS	Statistics for conflict resolutions for user's replicated tables
USER_REPRESOL_STATS_CONTROL	Information about statistics collection for conflict resolutions for user's replicated tables
USER_REPSCHEMA	N-way replication information about the current user
USER_REPSITES	N-way replication information about the current user
USER_RESOURCE_LIMITS	Display resource limit of the user
USER_ROLE_PRIVS	Roles granted to current user
USER_RSRC_CONSUMER_GROUP_PRIVS	Switch privileges for consumer groups for the user
USER_RSRC_MANAGER_SYSTEM_PRIVS	System privileges for the resource manager for the user
USER_RULESETS	Rulesets owned by the user

TABLE_NAME	Comments
USER_SEGMENTS	Storage allocated for all database segments
USER_SEQUENCES	Description of the user's own SEQUENCEs
USER_SNAPSHOTS	Snapshots the user can look at
USER_SNAPSHOT_LOGS	All snapshot logs owned by the user
USER_SNAPSHOT_REFRESH_TIMES	Snapshots and their last refresh times for each master table that the user can look at
USER_SOURCE	Source of stored objects accessible to the user
USER_SUBPART_COL_STATISTICS	Column statistics for user's subpartitions
USER_SUBPART_HISTOGRAMS	Histograms for user's subpartitions
USER_SUBPART_KEY_COLUMNS	Key columns for user's subpartitions
USER_SUMMARIES	Description of the summaries created by the user
USER_SUMMARY_AGGREGATES	Description of the summary aggregates created by the user
USER_SUMMARY_DETAIL_TABLES	Description of the summary detail tables of the summaries created by the user
USER_SUMMARY_JOINS	Description of a join between two columns in the WHERE clause of a summary created by the user
USER_SUMMARY_KEYS	Description of the columns that appear in the GROUP BY list of a summary created by the user
USER_SYNONYMS	The user's private synonyms
USER_SYS_PRIVS	System privileges granted to current user
USER_TABLES	Description of the user's own relational tables
USER_TABLESPACES	Description of accessible tablespaces
USER_TAB_COLUMNS	Columns of user's tables, views and clusters
USER_TAB_COL_STATISTICS	Columns of user's tables, views and clusters
USER_TAB_COMMENTS	Comments on the tables and views owned by the user
USER_TAB_HISTOGRAMS	Histograms on columns of user's tables
USER_TAB_MODIFICATIONS	Information regarding modifications to tables
USER_TAB_PARTITIONS	User's table partitions
USER_TAB_PRIVS	Grants on objects for which the user is the owner, grantor or grantee
USER_TAB_PRIVS_MADE	All grants on objects owned by the user
USER_TAB_PRIVS_RECD	Grants on objects for which the user is the grantee
USER_TAB_SUBPARTITIONS	Subpartitions of user's tables
USER_TRIGGERS	Triggers owned by the user
USER_TRIGGER_COLS	Column usage in user's triggers
USER_TS_QUOTAS	Tablespace quotas for the user
USER_TYPES	Description of the user's own types
USER_TYPE_ATTRS	Description of attributes of the user's own types
USER_TYPE_METHODS	Description of methods of the user's own types
USER_UNUSED_COL_TABS	User tables with unused columns
USER_UPDATABLE_COLUMNS	Description of updatable columns
USER_USERS	Information about the current user
USER_VARRAYS	Description of varrays contained in the user's own tables
USER_VIEWS	Description of the user's own views
V$ACTIVE_INSTANCES	Synonym for V_$ACTIVE_INSTANCES
V$BH	Synonym for V_$BH
V$LOADCSTAT	Synonym for V_$LOADCSTAT

TABLE_NAME	Comments
V$LOADPSTAT	Synonym for V_$LOADPSTAT
V$LOADTSTAT	Synonym for V_$LOADTSTAT
V$LOCK_ACTIVITY	Synonym for V_$LOCK_ACTIVITY
V$MAX_ACTIVE_SESS_TARGET_MTH	Synonym for V_$MAX_ACTIVE_SESS_TARGET_MTH
V$MLS_PARAMETERS	Synonym for V_$MLS_PARAMETERS
V$NLS_PARAMETERS	Synonym for V_$NLS_PARAMETERS
V$NLS_VALID_VALUES	Synonym for V_$NLS_VALID_VALUES
V$OPTION	Synonym for V_$OPTION
V$PARALLEL_DEGREE_LIMIT_MTH	Synonym for V_$PARALLEL_DEGREE_LIMIT_MTH
V$PQ_SESSTAT	Synonym for V_$PQ_SESSTAT
V$PQ_TQSTAT	Synonym for V_$PQ_TQSTAT
V$RSRC_CONSUMER_GROUP	Synonym for V_$RSRC_CONSUMER_GROUP
V$RSRC_CONSUMER_GROUP_CPU_MTH	Synonym for V_$RSRC_CONSUMER_GROUP_CPU_MTH
V$RSRC_PLAN	Synonym for V_$RSRC_PLAN
V$RSRC_PLAN_CPU_MTH	Synonym for V_$RSRC_PLAN_CPU_MTH
V$SESSION_LONGOPS	Synonym for V_$SESSION_LONGOPS
V$TEMPORARY_LOBS	Synonym for V_$TEMPORARY_LOBS
V$VERSION	Synonym for V_$VERSION

DATA INDEPENDENCE

Data independence is the property of well-defined tables that allows the physical and logical structure of a table to change without affecting applications that access the table.

DATA MANIPULATION LANGUAGE (DML) STATEMENTS

DML statements are one category of SQL statements. DML statements, such as **select**, **insert**, **delete**, and **update**, query and update the actual data. The other categories are data control language (DCL) and data definition language (DDL) statements.

DATA TYPES

SEE ALSO CHARACTER FUNCTIONS, CONVERSION FUNCTIONS, DATE FUNCTIONS, LIST FUNCTIONS, NUMBER FUNCTIONS, OTHER FUNCTIONS

DESCRIPTION When a table is created and the columns in it are defined, they must each have a datatype specified. Oracle's primary datatypes are VARCHAR2, CHAR, DATE, LONG, LONG RAW, NUMBER, RAW, and ROWID, but for compatibility with other SQL databases, its **create table** statements will accept several versions of these:

Datatype	Definition
CHAR(*size*)	Fixed-length character data, *size* characters long. Maximum size is 2000. Default is 1 byte. Padded on the right with blanks to full length of size.
VARCHAR2(*size*)	Variable length character string having a maximum of *size* bytes (up to 4000).
VARCHAR(*size*)	Same as VARCHAR2. Use VARCHAR2, since VARCHAR's usage may change in future versions of ORACLE.
NCHAR(*size*)	Multi-byte character set version of CHAR.
NVARCHAR2(*size*)	Multi-byte character set version of VARCHAR2.

Datatype	Definition
DATE	Valid dates range from January 1, 4712 B.C. to December 31, 4712 A.D.
BLOB	Binary large object, up to 4Gb in length.
CLOB	Character large object, up to 4Gb in length.
NCLOB	Same as CLOB, but for multi-byte character sets.
BFILE	Pointer to a binary operating system file.
LONG	Character data of variable size up to 2Gb in length. Only one LONG column may be defined per table. LONG columns may not be used in subqueries, functions, expressions, **where** clauses, or indexes. A table containing a LONG column may not be clustered.
LONG RAW	Raw binary data; otherwise the same as LONG.
LONG VARCHAR	Same as LONG.
RAW(*size*)	Raw binary data, *size* bytes long. Maximum size is 255 bytes.
NUMBER	For NUMBER column with space for 40 digits, plus space for a decimal point and sign. Numbers may be expressed in two ways: first, with the numbers 0 to 9, the signs + and -, and a decimal point (.); second, in scientific notation, such as, 1.85E3 for 1850. Valid values are 0, and positive and negative numbers with magnitude $1.0E-130$ to $9.9..E125$.
NUMBER(*size*)	For NUMBER column of specified *size*.
NUMBER(*size,d*)	For NUMBER column of specified *size* with *d* digits after the decimal point. For example, NUMBER(5,2) could contain nothing larger than 999.99 without an error.
NUMBER(*)	Same as NUMBER.
DECIMAL	Same as NUMBER. Does not accept size or decimal digits as an argument.
FLOAT	Same as NUMBER.
INTEGER	Same as NUMBER. Does not accept decimal digits as an argument.
INTEGER(*size*)	Integer of specified *size* digits wide.
MLSLABEL	4-byte representation of a secure operating system label.
SMALLINT	Same as NUMBER.
RAW MLSLABEL	Binary format for secure operating system label.
ROWID	A value that uniquely identifies a row in an Oracle database. It is returned by the pseudo-column ROWID.

DATABASE

Database can have one of two definitions:

- A set of dictionary tables and user tables that are treated as a unit.
- One or more operating system files in which Oracle stores tables, views, and other objects; also, the set of database objects used by a given application.

DATABASE ADMINISTRATOR (DBA)

A DBA is an Oracle user authorized to **grant** and **revoke** other users' access to the system, modify Oracle options that affect all users, and perform other administrative functions. *See* Chapter 38.

DATABASE LINK

A database link is an object stored in the local database that identifies a remote database, a communication path to the remote database, and, optionally, a username and password for it.

Once defined, the database link is used to perform queries on tables in the remote database. *See* Chapter 22.

DATABASE NAME

A database name is a unique identifier used to name a database. It is assigned in the **create database** command or in the init.ora file.

DATABASE OBJECT

A database object is something created and stored in a database. Tables, views, synonyms, indexes, sequences, clusters, and columns are all types of database objects.

DATABASE SYSTEM

A database system is a combination of an instance and a database. If the instance is started and connected to an open database, then the database system is available for access by users.

DATAFILE

A datafile is any file used to store data in a database. A database is made up of one or more tablespaces, which in turn are made up of one or more datafiles.

DATATYPE

See DATA TYPES.

DATE

DATE is a standard Oracle datatype to store date and time data. Standard date format is 01-NOV-99. A DATE column may contain a date and time between January 1, 4712 B.C. and December 31, 4712 A.D.

DATE FORMATS

SEE ALSO   DATE FUNCTIONS, Chapter 9

DESCRIPTION   These date formats are used with both **TO_CHAR** and **TO_DATE**:

Format	Meaning
MM	Number of month: 12
RM	Roman numeral month: XII
MON	Three-letter abbreviation of month: AUG
Mon	Same as MON, but with initial capital: Aug
mon	Same as MON, but all lowercase: aug
MONTH	Month fully spelled out: AUGUST
Month	Month with initial capital: August
month	Month all lowercase: august
DDD	Number of the day in the year, since Jan 1: 354
DD	Number of the day in the month: 23
D	Number of the day in the week: 6
DY	Three-letter abbreviation of the day of the week: FRI
Dy	Same as DY, but with initial capital: Fri

Format	Meaning
dy	Same as DY, but all lowercase: fri
DAY	Day fully spelled out: FRIDAY
Day	Day with initial capital: Friday
day	Day all lowercase: friday
YYYY	Full four-digit year: 1946
Y,YYY	Four-digit year, with comma
SYYYY	Signed year if B.C. 01000 B.C. = -1000
IYYY	ISO four-digit standard year
YYY	Last three digits of year: 946
IYY	Last three digits of ISO year
YY	Last two digits of year: 46
IY	Last two digits of ISO year
Y	Last digit of year: 6
I	Last digit of ISO year
RR	Last two digits of year, possibly in another century
RRRR	Rounded year, accepting either 2-digit or 4-digit input
YEAR	Year spelled out: NINETEEN-FORTY-SIX
Year	Year spelled with initial capitals: Nineteen-Forty-Six
year	Year in lowercase: nineteen-forty-six
SYEAR	Year, with - before BC dates
Q	Number of quarter: 3
WW	Number of week in year: 46
W	Number of week in month: 3
IW	Week of year from ISO standard
J	"Julian"-days since December 31, 4713 B.C.: 02422220
HH	Hour of day, always 1-12: 11
HH12	Same as HH
HH24	Hour of day, 24-hour clock: 17
MI	Minute of hour: 58
SS	Second of minute: 43
SSSSS	Seconds since midnight, always 0-86399: 43000
/,-:.	Punctuation to be incorporated in display for TO_CHAR or ignored in format for TO_DATE
A.M.	Displays A.M. or P.M., depending on time of day
a.m.	Same as A.M. but lowercase
P.M.	Same effect as A.M.
p.m.	Same effect as a.m.
AM or PM	Same as A.M. but without periods
am or pm	Same as a.m. but without periods
CC or SCC	Century; S prefixes BC with "-"
B.C.	Displays B.C. or A.D. depending upon date
A.D.	Same as B.C.
b.c. or a.d.	Same as B.C. but lowercase
BC or AD	Same as B.C. but without periods
bc or ad	Same as b.c. but without periods
E	Abbreviated era name, for Asian calendars
EE	Full era name, for Asian calendars

These date formats work only with **TO_CHAR**. They do not work with **TO_DATE**:

Format	Meaning
"*string*"	*string* is incorporated in display for **TO_CHAR0**.
Fm	Prefix to Month or Day: fmMONTH or fmday. Suppresses padding of Month or Day (defined earlier) under format. Without fm, all Months are displayed at same width. The same is true for days. With fm, padding is eliminated. Months and days are only as long as their count of characters.
Fx	Format Exact-specifies exact format matching for the character argument and the date format model.
TH	Suffix to a number: ddTH or DDTH produces 24th or 24TH. Capitalization comes from the case of the number-DD-not from the case of the TH. Works with any number in a date: YYYY, DD, MM, HH, MI, SS, and so on.
SP	Suffix to a number that forces number to be spelled out: DDSP, DdSP, or ddSP produces THREE, Three, or three. Capitalization comes from case of number-DD-not from the case of SP. Works with any number in a date: YYYY, DD, MM, HH, MI, SS, and so on.
SPTH	Suffix combination of TH and SP that forces number to be both spelled out and given an ordinal suffix: Mmspth produces Third. Capitalization comes from case of number-DD-not from the case of SP. Works with any number in a date: YYYY, DD, MM, HH, MI, SS, and so on.
THSP	Same as SPTH.

DATE FUNCTIONS

SEE ALSO   DATE FORMATS, Chapter 9

DESCRIPTION   This is an alphabetical list of all current date functions in Oracle's SQL. Each of these is listed elsewhere in this reference under its own name, with its proper format and use.

Function	Definition
ADD_MONTHS(*date,count*)	Adds count months to date.
GREATEST(*date1,date2,date3,. . .*)	Picks latest of list of dates.
LAST_DAY(*date*)	Gives date of last day of month that *date* is in.
MONTHS_BETWEEN(*date2*,date1)	Gives *date2-date1* in months (can be fractional months).
NEXT_DAY(*date,*'day')	Gives date of next 'day' after date.
NEW_TIME('*date*','*this*','*other*')	DATE is the date (and time) in this time zone. *this* is a three-letter abbreviation for the current time zone. *other* is a three-letter abbreviation of the other time zone for which you'd like to know the time and date. Time zones are as follows:

AST/ADT   Atlantic standard/daylight time
BST/BDT   Bering standard/daylight time
CST/CDT   Central standard/daylight time
EST/EDT   Eastern standard/daylight time
GMT   Greenwich mean time
HST/HDT   Alaska-Hawaii standard/daylight time
MST/MDT   Mountain standard/daylight time
NST   Newfoundland standard time
PST/PDT   Pacific standard/daylight time
YST/YDT   Yukon standard/daylight time

Function	Definition
ROUND(*date, 'format'*)	Rounds a date to 12 A.M. (midnight, the beginning of the day) if time of date is before noon, otherwise **rounds** up to next day, or according for format. Look up ROUND later in this reference for details of 'format'.
TO_CHAR(*date, 'format'*)	Reformats date according to format (*see* DATE FORMATS)
TO_DATE(*string, 'format'*)	Converts a string in a given format into an Oracle date. Also accepts a number instead of a string, with certain limits. 'FORMAT' is restricted.
TRUNC(*date, 'format'*)	Sets a date to 12 A.M. (midnight, the beginning of the day), or according to format. Look up **TRUNC** later in this reference for details of format.

DBA

See DATABASE ADMINISTRATOR (DBA).

DBWR PROCESS

One of the background processes used by Oracle. The **D**ata**b**ase **Wr**iter process writes new data to the database.

DCL

See DATA CONTROL LANGUAGE (DCL) STATEMENTS.

DDL

See DATA DEFINITION LANGUAGE (DDL) STATEMENTS.

DDL LOCK

When a user executes a DDL command, Oracle locks the objects referred to in the command with DDL locks. A DDL lock locks objects in the data dictionary. (Contrast this to parse locks, the other type of dictionary lock.)

DEADLOCK

A deadlock is a rare situation in which two or more user processes of a database cannot complete their transactions. This occurs because each process is holding a resource that the other process requires (such as a row in a table) in order to complete. Although these situations occur rarely, Oracle detects and resolves deadlocks by rolling back the work of one of the processes.

DECLARATIVE SQL STATEMENT

A declarative SQL statement is one that does not generate a call to the database, and is therefore not an executable SQL statement. Examples are **BEGIN DECLARE SECTION** or **DECLARE CURSOR**. Declarative statements are used primarily in precompiled and PL/SQL programs. (Compare to EXECUTABLE SQL STATEMENT.)

DECLARE

The DECLARE command allows you to declare cursors, variables, and exceptions for use within PL/SQL blocks. *See* Chapter 25.

DECLARE CURSOR (Form 1—Embedded SQL)

SEE ALSO   CLOSE, DECLARE DATABASE, DECLARE STATEMENT, FETCH, OPEN, PREPARE, **SELECT**, **SELECT** (Embedded SQL)

FORMAT

```
EXEC SQL [AT {database | :host_variable}]
DECLARE cursor CURSOR
    FOR {SELECT command | statement}
```

DESCRIPTION   The **DECLARE CURSOR** statement must appear before any SQL that references this cursor, and must be compiled in the same source as procedures that reference it. Its name must be unique to the source.

database is the name of a database already declared in a **DECLARE DATABASE** and used in a SQL CONNECT; *host_variable* is a variable with such a name as its value. *cursor* is the name you assign to this cursor. **SELECT** command is a query with no **INTO** clause. Alternatively, a SQL statement or a PL/SQL block already declared in a SQL **DECLARE STATEMENT** statement can be used.

When the **FOR UPDATE OF** clause is included in the **SELECT** statement, an **update** can reference the cursor with **where current of cursor**, although the cursor must still be open, and a row must be present from a **FETCH**.

EXAMPLE

```
exec sql at TALBOT declare FRED cursor
     for select ActionDate, Person, Item, Amount
          from LEDGER
        where Item = :Item
          and ActionDate = :ActionDate
          for update of Amount
```

DECLARE CURSOR (Form 2—PL/SQL)

SEE ALSO   CLOSE, FETCH, OPEN, SELECT...INTO, Chapter 25

FORMAT

```
DECLARE
CURSOR cursor (parameter datatype [,parameter datatype]...)
    IS select_statement
    [FOR UPDATE OF column [,column]...];
```

DESCRIPTION   A cursor is a work area that Oracle uses to control the row currently in process. **DECLARE CURSOR** names a cursor and declares that it IS (the result of) a certain *select_statement*. The *select_statement* is required, and may not contain an **INTO** clause. The cursor must be declared. It can then be **OPEN**ed, and rows can then be **FETCH**ed into it. Finally, it can be **CLOSE**d.

Variables cannot be used directly in the **where** clause of the *select_statement* unless they've first been identified as parameters, in a list that precedes the select. Note that DECLARE CURSOR does not execute the **select** statement, and the parameters have no values until they are assigned in an **OPEN** statement. Parameters have standard object names, and datatypes, including VARCHAR2, CHAR, NUMBER, DATE, and BOOLEAN, all without size or scale, however.

FOR UPDATE OF is required if you wish to affect the current row in the cursor using either **update** or **delete** commands with the **CURRENT OF** clause.

DECLARE DATABASE (Embedded SQL)

SEE ALSO   **COMMIT RELEASE** (Embedded SQL), **CONNECT** (Embedded SQL), *Programmer's Guide to the Oracle Precompilers*

FORMAT

```
EXEC SQL DECLARE database DATABASE
```

DESCRIPTION   **DECLARE DATABASE** declares the name of a remote database for use in later AT clauses of SQL statements, including **COMMIT**, **DECLARE CURSOR**, **DELETE**, **INSERT**, **ROLLBACK**, **SELECT**, and **UPDATE**.

DECLARE STATEMENT (Embedded SQL)

SEE ALSO   CLOSE, FETCH, OPEN, PREPARE

FORMAT

```
EXEC SQL [AT {database | :host_variable}]
DECLARE STATEMENT {statement | block_name} STATEMENT
```

DESCRIPTION   *statement* is the name of the statement in a **DECLARE CURSOR**, and must be identical to the statement name here. *database* is the name of a database previously declared with **DECLARE DATABASE**; *host_variable* may contain such a name as its value. This command is only needed if **DECLARE CURSOR** will come before a **PREPARE**. When it is used, it should come prior to **DECLARE**, **DESCRIBE**, **OPEN**, or **PREPARE**, and must be compiled in the same source as procedures that reference it.

DECLARE TABLE

SEE ALSO   CREATE TABLE

FORMAT

```
EXEC SQL DECLARE table TABLE
(column datatype [NULL|NOT NULL],
     ...);
```

DESCRIPTION   *table* is the name of the table being declared. *column* is a column name and *datatype* is its datatype. This structure is nearly identical to that of **create table**, including the use of **NULL** and **NOT NULL**.

You use **DECLARE TABLE** to tell precompilers to ignore actual Oracle database table definitions when running with SQLCHECK=FULL. The precompilers will regard the table description here as relevant to the program and ignore the table definitions in the database. Use this when table definitions will change, or when a table has not yet been created. If SQLCHECK is not equal to FULL (which means tables and columns will not be checked against the database anyway), this command is ignored by the precompiler and becomes simply documentation.

EXAMPLE

```
EXEC SQL DECLARE COMFORT TABLE (
            City          VARCHAR2(13) NOT NULL,
            SampleDate    DATE NOT NULL,
            Noon          NUMBER(3,1),
            Midnight      NUMBER(3,1),
            Precipitation NUMBER
            );
```

DECODE

SEE ALSO   OTHER FUNCTIONS, **TRANSLATE**, Chapter 17

FORMAT

```
DECODE(value,if1,then1[,if2,then2,]... ,else)
```

DESCRIPTION   *value* represents any column in a table, regardless of datatype, or any result of a computation, such as one date minus another, a **SUBSTR** of a character column, one number times another, and so on. For each row, *value* is tested. If it equals *if1*, then the result of the **DECODE** is *then1*; if value equals *if2*, then the result of the **DECODE** is *then2*, and so on, for virtually as many if/then pairs as you can construct. If *value* equals none of the *if*s, then the result of the **DECODE** is *else*. Each of the *if*s, *then*s, and the *else* also can be a column or the result of a function or computation. Chapter 16 is devoted entirely to **DECODE**.

EXAMPLE

```
select DISTINCT City,
       DECODE(City, 'SAN FRANCISCO', 'CITY BY THE BAY', City)
  from COMFORT;

CITY           DECODE(CITY,'SA
-------------  ---------------
KEENE          KEENE
SAN FRANCISCO  CITY BY THE BAY
```

DEFAULT

Default is a clause or option value that is used if no alternative is specified. You can specify the default value for a column in a table via a DEFAULT column constraint.

DEFAULT VALUE

The default value is a value that is used unless a different one is specified or entered.

DEFERRED ROLLBACK SEGMENT

A deferred rollback segment is one containing entries that could not be applied to the tablespace, because the given tablespace was offline. As soon as the tablespace comes back online, all the entries are applied.

DEFINE (SQL*PLUS)

See **SET**.

DEFINE PHASE

The define phase is one phase of executing a SQL query, in which the program defines buffers to hold the results of a query to be executed.

DEL

SEE ALSO   APPEND, CHANGE, EDIT, INPUT, LIST, Chapter 6

FORMAT

```
DEL
```

DESCRIPTION   **DEL** deletes the current line of the current buffer. You can delete multiple lines with a single DEL command.

EXAMPLE   List the contents of the current buffer with this:

```
list
```

```
1  select Person, Amount
2    from LEDGER
3  where Amount > 10000
4*   and Rate = 3;
```

The asterisk shows that 4 is the current line. To delete the second line, you'd first enter this:

```
list 2
```

```
2*  from LEDGER
```

which makes 2 the current line in the current buffer. Then you'd enter this:

```
del
```

and the line would be gone. The old line 3 would now be line 2; line 4 would be line 3, and so on.
    To delete a range of lines with one command, specify the line numbers of the beginning and ending of the range in the **DEL** command. The following command would delete lines 2 through 8 in the current buffer.

```
del 2 8
```

DELETE (Form I—PL/SQL)

SEE ALSO   DECLARE CURSOR, UPDATE, Chapter 25

DESCRIPTION   In PL/SQL, **DELETE** follows the normal SQL command rules, with these added features:

- A PL/SQL function and/or variable can be used in the **where** clause just as a literal could be.

- **DELETE. . .WHERE CURRENT OF cursor** can be used in conjunction with a SELECT FOR UPDATE to delete the last row **FETCH**ed. The **FETCH** can either be explicit or implicit from a FOR LOOP.

- Like **update** and **insert**, the **delete** command executes only within the SQL cursor. The SQL cursor's attributes can be checked for the success of the **delete**. SQL%ROWCOUNT will contain the number of rows deleted. If this is 0, none were **delete**d. (Also, SQL%FOUND will be FALSE if none were **delete**d.)

EXAMPLE   To eliminate all workers who are 65 or over from the worker table (an idea Talbot would have found silly), use this:

```
DECLARE
    cursor EMPLOYEE is
        select Age from WORKER
            for update of Age;

    WORKER_RECORD    EMPLOYEE%ROWTYPE;

BEGIN
    open EMPLOYEE;
    loop
        fetch EMPLOYEE into WORKER_RECORD;
        exit when EMPLOYEE%NOTFOUND;
        if WORKER_RECORD.Age >= 65
            then delete WORKER where current of EMPLOYEE;
    end loop;
    close EMPLOYEE;

END;
```

DELETE (Form 2—SQL Command)
SEE ALSO   **DROP TABLE, FROM, INSERT, SELECT, UPDATE, WHERE,** Chapter 15
SYNTAX

table_expression_clause::=

with_clause::=

table_collection_expression::=

where_clause::=

returning_clause::=

DESCRIPTION   **DELETE** deletes from *table* all rows that satisfy *condition*. The *condition* may include a correlated query and use the alias for correlation. If the table is remote, a database link has to be defined. @*link* specifies the link. If *link* is entered, but *user* is not, the query seeks a table owned by the user on the remote database.

When using the **DELETE** command, you may specify a partition or subpartition. In order to delete rows from a table, you must have SELECT and DELETE privileges on the table.

EXAMPLE   This example deletes all rows for the city of Keene from the COMFORT table:

```
delete from COMFORT
  where City = 'KEENE';
```

DELETE (Form 3—Embedded SQL)

FORMAT

```
EXEC SQL [AT {db_name | :host_variable} ] [FOR :host_integer]
  DELETE [FROM] { [user.] {table [PARTITION (partition_name)]
              | view [@dblink]}
              | ( subquery )}
          [alias]
      [WHERE {condition | CURRENT OF cursor} ]
```

DESCRIPTION   This form of the **DELETE** command allows you to delete rows (from a table, view, or index-only table) from within a precompiler program.

DEREF

The **DEREF** operator returns the value of a referenced object. *See* Chapter 31.

DESCRIBE (Form 1—SQL*PLUS Command)

SEE ALSO   **CREATE TABLE**

FORMAT

```
DESC[RIBE] [user.]table
```

DESCRIPTION   **DESCRIBE** displays a specified table's definition. If *user* is omitted, SQL*PLUS displays the table owned by you. The definition includes the table and its columns, with each column's name, **NULL** or **NOT NULL** status, datatype, and width or precision.

EXAMPLE

```
describe COMFORT

Name                              Null?     Type
--------------------------------  --------  ----
CITY                              NOT NULL  VARCHAR2(13)
SAMPLEDATE                        NOT NULL  DATE
NOON                                        NUMBER(3,1)
MIDNIGHT                                    NUMBER(3,1)
PRECIPITATION                               NUMBER
```

DESCRIBE (Form 2—Embedded SQL)

SEE ALSO   **PREPARE**

FORMAT

```
EXEC SQL DESCRIBE [ BIND VARIABLES FOR
                   | SELECT LIST FOR]
             { statement_name
             | block_name} INTO descriptor
```

DESCRIPTION   The **DESCRIBE** command initializes a descriptor to hold descriptions of host variables for a dynamic SQL statement or PL/SQL block. The **DESCRIBE** command follows the **PREPARE** command.

DESCRIBE PHASE

The describe phase is one phase of executing a SQL query, in which the program gathers information about the results of the query to be executed.

DETACHED PROCESS

See BACKGROUND PROCESS.

DICTIONARY CACHE

The dictionary cache stores data dictionary information in the SGA. Caching dictionary information improves performance because the dictionary information is used frequently. The dictionary cache is part of the Shared SQL Pool.

DICTIONARY LOCKS

A dictionary lock is a shared lock owned by users parsing DML statements, or an exclusive lock owned by users doing DDL commands, to prevent a table from being altered while the dictionaries are queried. There may be many such locks concurrently.

DIMENSION

A dimension is a named set of hierarchies among columns of tables. For example, in the geography dimension, countries are parts of continents, and states are parts of countries. When you define the dimension relationships, Oracle can use that information when evaluating optimizer choices. If there are materialized views that contain aggregated data, the optimizer can use the dimension definitions to determine if the materialized view can be accessed instead of the base table. *See* **CREATE DIMENSION**.

DIRECTORY

A logical name that points to a physical directory, used by BFILE LOBs. *See* **CREATE DIRECTORY**.

DISASSOCIATE STATISTICS

SEE ALSO   ASSOCIATE STATISTICS

SYNTAX

DESCRIPTION   **ASSOCIATE STATISTICS** associates a set of statistics functions with one or more columns, standalone functions, packages, types, or indexes. **DISASSOCIATE STATISTICS** revokes the associations. You must have ALTER privilege on the base object.

DISCONNECT

SEE ALSO   CONNECT, EXIT, QUIT

FORMAT

```
DISC[ONNECT]
```

DESCRIPTION   **DISCONNECT** commits pending changes to the database and logs you off of Oracle. Your SQL*PLUS session remains active and the features of SQL*PLUS continue to function, but without any connection to the database. You can edit buffers, use your own editor, spool and stop spooling, or connect to Oracle again, but until a connection is established, no SQL can be executed.

    EXIT or **QUIT** will return you to your host's operating system. If you are still connected when you **EXIT** or **QUIT**, you will be automatically disconnected and logged off of Oracle.

DISMOUNTED DATABASE

A dismounted database is one that is not mounted by any instance, and thus cannot be opened and is not available for use.

DISTINCT

Distinct means unique. It is used as a part of **select** statements and group functions. *See* GROUP FUNCTIONS, **SELECT**.

DISTRIBUTED DATABASE

A distributed database is a collection of databases that can be operated and managed separately and also share information.

DISTRIBUTED PROCESSING

Distributed processing is performing computation on multiple CPUs to achieve a single result.

DISTRIBUTED QUERY

A distributed query is one that selects data from databases residing at multiple nodes of a network.

DML

See DATA MANIPULATION LANGUAGE (DML) STATEMENTS.

DML LOCK

When a user executes a SQL statement, the data to which the statement refers is locked in one of several lock modes. The user can also lock data explicitly with a **LOCK** statement.

DOCUMENT

SEE ALSO   #, /* */, REMARK
FORMAT

DOC [UMENT]

DESCRIPTION   **DOCUMENT** tells SQL*PLUS that a block of documentation is beginning. The pound sign (#) on a line by itself ends the block. DOCUMENT must also be SET to ON for this to work. If **DOCUMENT** is SET to OFF, SQL*PLUS will try to execute the lines in between **DOCUMENT** and #. Thus, this could be used to execute or not execute a sequence of commands based on a prior result.

    If you are spooling an interactive session to a file, typing the word **DOCUMENT** will change the SQLPROMPT from SQL> to DOC>. Everything you type until you type # will go into the file without SQL*PLUS attempting to execute it.

SQL*PLUS will always display the lines in the DOCUMENT section unless TERMOUT is SET to OFF.

The SQL*PLUS command line editor cannot input a # directly into a buffer (in the first position on the line), so enter another character, followed by the #, and then delete the other character.

DOCUMENT is considered an obsolete command; **REMARK** is recommended for general documentation purposes instead.

EXAMPLE   The following would be executed if **DOCUMENT** were **SET** to OFF:

```
DOCUMENT
column password print

REM changes the display of the passwords
#
```

DROP CLUSTER

SEE ALSO   **CREATE CLUSTER**, **DROP TABLE**, Chapter 20
SYNTAX

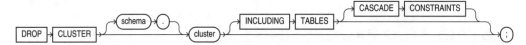

DESCRIPTION   **DROP CLUSTER** deletes a cluster from the database. You must have DROP ANY CLUSTER privilege if the cluster is not in your own schema. You cannot drop a cluster that contains tables. The tables must be dropped first. The INCLUDING TABLES clause will drop all the clustered tables automatically. The **CASCADE CONSTRAINTS** option drops all referential integrity constraints from tables outside the cluster that refer to keys in the clustered tables.

Individual tables cannot be removed from a cluster. To accomplish the same effect, copy the table under a new name (use **CREATE TABLE** with AS SELECT), drop the old one (this will remove it from the cluster), **RENAME** the copy to the name of the table you dropped, and then issue the appropriate **GRANT**S, and create the needed indexes.

DROP CONTEXT

SEE ALSO   **CREATE CONTEXT**
SYNTAX

```
DROP → CONTEXT → ( namespace ) → ( ; )
```

DESCRIPTION   **DROP CONTEXT** deletes a context namespace from the database. You must have the DROP ANY CONTEXT system privilege.

DROP DATABASE LINK

SEE ALSO   **CREATE DATABASE LINK**, Chapter 22
FORMAT

```
DROP [PUBLIC] DATABASE LINK link
```

DESCRIPTION   **DROP DATABASE LINK** drops a database link you own. For a public link, the optional **PUBLIC** keyword must be used, and you must be a DBA to use it. **PUBLIC** cannot be used when dropping a private link. *link* is the name of the link being dropped. You must have DROP PUBLIC DATABASE LINK system privilege to drop a public database link. You may drop private database links in your account.

EXAMPLE   The following will drop a database link named ADAH_AT_HOME:

```
drop database link ADAH_AT_HOME;
```

DROP DIMENSION

SEE ALSO   **CREATE DIMENSION**

SYNTAX

DESCRIPTION   **DROP DIMENSION** drops a dimension you own. You must have DROP ANY DIMENSION system privilege.

EXAMPLE   The following will drop the GEOGRAPHY dimension:

```
drop dimension GEOGRAPHY;
```

DROP DIRECTORY

SEE ALSO   **CREATE DIRECTORY**, Chapter 30

SYNTAX

```
DROP → DIRECTORY → directory_name → ;
```

DESCRIPTION   **DROP DIRECTORY** drops an existing directory (used by BFILE datatypes). You must have DROP ANY DIRECTORY privilege to drop a directory.

NOTE
Do not drop a directory while its files are in use.

EXAMPLE   The following will drop a directory called PROPOSALS:

```
drop directory PROPOSALS;
```

DROP FUNCTION

SEE ALSO   **ALTER FUNCTION, CREATE FUNCTION**, Chapter 27

SYNTAX

DESCRIPTION   **DROP FUNCTION** drops the specified function. Oracle invalidates any objects that depend on or call the function. You must have DROP ANY PROCEDURE system privilege to drop a function that you do not own.

DROP INDEX

SEE ALSO   ALTER INDEX, CREATE INDEX, CREATE TABLE, Chapter 20
SYNTAX

DESCRIPTION   DROP INDEX drops the specified index. You must either own the index or have DROP ANY INDEX system privilege.

DROP INDEXTYPE

SEE ALSO   CREATE INDEXTYPE
SYNTAX

DESCRIPTION   DROP INDEXTYPE drops the specified indextype and any association with statistics types. You must have the DROP ANY INDEXTYPE system privilege.

DROP JAVA

SEE ALSO   CREATE JAVA, Chapter 34
SYNTAX

DESCRIPTION   DROP JAVA drops the specified Java class, source, or resource. You must have the DROP PROCEDURE system privilege. If the object is in another user's schema, you must have the DROP ANY PROCEDURE system privilege.

DROP LIBRARY

SEE ALSO   CREATE LIBRARY, Chapter 27
SYNTAX

DESCRIPTION   DROP LIBRARY drops the specified library. You must have the DROP LIBRARY system privilege.

DROP MATERIALIZED VIEW/SNAPSHOT

SEE ALSO   ALTER MATERIALIZED VIEW/SNAPSHOT, CREATE MATERIALIZED VIEW/SNAPSHOT, Chapter 23

SYNTAX

DESCRIPTION DROP MATERIALIZED VIEW/SNAPSHOT drops the indicated materialized view or snapshot. You must either own the materialized view or you must have DROP ANY SNAPSHOT or DROP ANY MATERIALIZED VIEW system privilege.

DROP MATERIALIZED VIEW LOG/SNAPSHOT LOG

SEE ALSO ALTER MATERIALIZED VIEW LOG/SNAPSHOT LOG, CREATE MATERIALIZED VIEW LOG/SNAPSHOT LOG, Chapter 23

SYNTAX

DESCRIPTION DROP MATERIALIZED VIEW LOG/SNAPSHOT LOG drops the indicated log table. You must either own the materialized view or you must have DROP ANY SNAPSHOT or DROP ANY MATERIALIZED VIEW system privilege. After dropping the log, any materialized views on the master table will get complete refreshes, not fast refreshes.

DROP OPERATOR

SEE ALSO ALTER OPERATOR

SYNTAX

DESCRIPTION DROP OPERATOR drops a user-defined operator. You must either own the operator or have DROP ANY OPERATOR system privilege.

DROP OUTLINE

SEE ALSO CREATE OUTLINE

SYNTAX

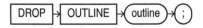

DESCRIPTION DROP OUTLINE drops a stored outline from the database. You must have the DROP ANY OUTLINE system privilege. Subsequent executions of SQL statements that used the outline will have their execution paths evaluated at runtime.

DROP PACKAGE
SEE ALSO ALTER PACKAGE, CREATE PACKAGE, Chapter 27
SYNTAX

DESCRIPTION **DROP PACKAGE** drops the specified package. Using the optional **BODY** clause drops only the body without dropping the package specification. ORACLE invalidates any objects that depend on the package if you drop the package specification but not if you just drop the body. You must either own the package or have DROP ANY PROCEDURE system privilege.

DROP PROCEDURE
SEE ALSO ALTER PROCEDURE, CREATE PROCEDURE, Chapter 27
SYNTAX

DESCRIPTION **DROP PROCEDURE** drops the specified procedure. ORACLE invalidates any objects that depend on or call the procedure. You must either own the procedure or have DROP ANY PROCEDURE system privilege.

DROP PROFILE
SEE ALSO ALTER PROFILE, CREATE PROFILE, Chapter 19
SYNTAX

DESCRIPTION **DROP PROFILE** drops the specified profile. You must have DROP PROFILE system privilege.

DROP ROLE
SEE ALSO ALTER ROLE, CREATE ROLE, Chapter 19
SYNTAX

DESCRIPTION **DROP ROLE** drops the specified role. You must have either been granted the role WITH ADMIN OPTION or you must have DROP ANY ROLE system privilege.

DROP ROLLBACK SEGMENT
SEE ALSO ALTER ROLLBACK SEGMENT, CREATE ROLLBACK SEGMENT, CREATE TABLESPACE, SHUTDOWN, STARTUP, Chapter 38

SYNTAX

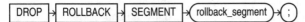

DESCRIPTION   *segment* is the name of an existing rollback segment to be dropped. The segment must not be in use when this statement is executed. **PUBLIC** is required for dropping public rollback segments.

The Status column of the data dictionary view DBA_ROLLBACK_SEGS can reveal which rollback segments are in use. If the segment is in use, you can either wait until it no longer is in use, or SHUTDOWN the database using IMMEDIATE, and then bring it up in EXCLUSIVE mode using **STARTUP**. You must have DBA privilege in order to drop a rollback segment.

DROP SEQUENCE

SEE ALSO   **ALTER SEQUENCE**, **CREATE SEQUENCE**, Chapter 20
SYNTAX

DESCRIPTION   *sequence* is the name of the sequence being dropped. To drop a sequence, you must either own the sequence or have DROP ANY SEQUENCE system privilege.

DROP SNAPSHOT

See **DROP MATERIALIZED VIEW/SNAPSHOT**

DROP SNAPSHOT LOG

See **DROP MATERIALIZED VIEW LOG/SNAPSHOT LOG**

DROP SYNONYM

SEE ALSO   **CREATE SYNONYM**, Chapter 22
SYNTAX

DESCRIPTION   **DROP SYNONYM** drops the specified synonym. To drop a public synonym, you must have DROP ANY PUBLIC SYNONYM system privilege. To drop a private synonym, you must own the synonym or have DROP ANY SYNONYM system privilege.

DROP TABLE

SEE ALSO   **ALTER TABLE**, **CREATE INDEX**, **CREATE TABLE**, **DROP CLUSTER**, Chapter 18
SYNTAX

DESCRIPTION   **DROP TABLE** drops the specified table. To drop a table, you must either own the table or have DROP ANY TABLE system privilege. Dropping a table also drops indexes and grants associated with it. Objects built on dropped tables are marked invalid and cease to work.

The **CASCADE CONSTRAINTS** option drops all referential integrity constraints referring to keys in the dropped table.

You can drop a cluster and all of its tables by using the INCLUDING TABLES clause on **DROP CLUSTER**.

DROP TABLESPACE

SEE ALSO   **ALTER TABLESPACE, CREATE DATABASE, CREATE TABLESPACE,** Chapters 20 and 38.

SYNTAX

DESCRIPTION   *tablespace* is the name of the tablespace being dropped. The **INCLUDING CONTENTS** option allows you to drop a tablespace that contains data. Without **INCLUDING CONTENTS**, only an empty tablespace can be dropped. Tablespaces should be offline (*see* **ALTER TABLESPACE**) before dropping, or the dropping will be prevented by any users accessing data, index, rollback, or temporary segments in the tablespace. You must have DROP TABLESPACE system privilege to use this command.

DROP TRIGGER

SEE ALSO   **ALTER TRIGGER, CREATE TRIGGER,** Chapters 26 and 28

SYNTAX

DESCRIPTION   **DROP TRIGGER** drops the specified trigger. You must either own the trigger or you must have DROP ANY TRIGGER system privilege.

DROP TYPE

SEE ALSO   **CREATE TYPE,** Chapter 4

SYNTAX

DESCRIPTION   **DROP TYPE** drops the specification and body of an abstract datatype. You must either own the type or have DROP ANY TYPE system privilege. You cannot drop a type if a table or other object references it.

DROP TYPE BODY

SEE ALSO   **CREATE TYPE, CREATE TYPE BODY, DROP TYPE**, Chapter 28

SYNTAX

DESCRIPTION   **DROP TYPE BODY** drops the body of the specified type. You must either own the type or have DROP ANY TYPE system privilege.

DROP USER

SEE ALSO   **ALTER USER, CREATE USER**, Chapter 19

SYNTAX

DESCRIPTION   **DROP USER** drops the specified user. You must have DROP USER system privilege. The **CASCADE** option drops all the objects in the user's schema before dropping the user, and you *must* specify **CASCADE** if the user has any objects in the schema.

DROP VIEW

SEE ALSO   **CREATE SYNONYM, CREATE TABLE, CREATE VIEW**, Chapter 18

SYNTAX

DESCRIPTION   **DROP VIEW** drops the specified view. Only DBAs can drop views created by other users. Views and synonyms built on dropped views are marked invalid and cease to work. The view must either be in your schema or you must have DROP ANY VIEW system privilege.

DROPJAVA

DROPJAVA is a utility for removing Java classes from the database. *See* LOADJAVA.

DUAL

SEE ALSO   **FROM, SELECT**, Chapter 9

DESCRIPTION   DUAL is a table with only one row and one column in it. Since Oracle's many functions work on both columns and literals, it is possible to demonstrate some of its functioning using just literals or pseudo-columns, such as SysDate. When doing this, the **select** statement doesn't care which columns are in the table, and a single row is more than sufficient to demonstrate a point.

EXAMPLE   The following shows the current User and SysDate:

```
select User, SysDate from DUAL;
```

DUMP

SEE ALSO   RAWTOHEX

FORMAT

```
DUMP( string [,format [,start [,length] ] ] )
```

DESCRIPTION   **DUMP** displays the value of *string* in internal data format, in ASCII, octal, decimal, hex, or character format. *format* defaults to ASCII or EBCDIC, depending upon your machine; 8 produces octal, 10 decimal, 16 hex, and 17 character (the same as ASCII or EBCDIC). *start* is the beginning position in the string, and *length* is the number of characters to display. *string* can be a literal or an expression.

EXAMPLE   The following shows how characters 1 through 8 are represented in hex for just the first row of the COMFORT table:

```
select City, dump(City,16,1,8) a from COMFORT where rownum < 2;

CITY            DUMP(CITY,16,1,8)
-------------   -------------------------------------
SAN FRANCISCO   Typ=1 Len= 13: 53,41,4e,20,46,52,41,4e
```

EBCDIC

EBCDIC is an acronym for **E**xtended **B**inary **C**oded **D**ecimal **I**nterchange **C**ode-the collation sequence used by IBM's mainframe computers and other computers compatible with them.

ECHO (SQL*PLUS)

See **SET**.

EDIT

SEE ALSO   DEFINE, SET, Chapter 6

FORMAT

```
EDIT [file[.ext]]
```

DESCRIPTION   **EDIT** calls an external standard text editor and passes to it the name of the file. If *.ext* is omitted, the extension SQL is appended. If *file* and *ext* are both omitted, the editor is called and passed the name of a file (invented by SQLPLUS) that contains the contents of the current buffer. The local user variable _EDITOR determines which text editor is used by **EDIT**. _EDITOR can be changed with **DEFINE**, and this is usually best done in the LOGIN.SQL file, which is read whenever SQL*PLUS is invoked.

   EDIT will fail if the current buffer is empty and **EDIT** is called without a file name. You can use the **SET EDITFILE** command to set the default name of the file created by the **EDIT** command.

EMBEDDED (SQL*PLUS)

See **SET**.

END

SEE ALSO   BEGIN, BLOCK STRUCTURE, Chapter 25

FORMAT

```
END [block] ;
```

DESCRIPTION   END is unrelated to the END IF and END LOOP statements. *See* IF and LOOP for details on either of them.

END is the closing statement of a PL/SQL block's executable section (and the entire block). If the block is named at the **BEGIN**, the name must also follow the word **END**. At least one executable statement is required between **BEGIN** and **END**. *See* BLOCK STRUCTURE and Chapter 22 for more details.

ENQUEUE

Enqueue is the lock on a given resource. Those waiting for a given resource have not yet gotten the enqueue. Enqueues exist for many database resources.

ENTITY

An entity is a person, place, or thing represented by a table. In a table, each row represents an occurrence of that entity.

ENTITY-RELATIONSHIP MODEL

An entity-relationship model is a framework used to model systems for a database. It divides all elements of a system into two categories: entities or relationships.

EQUI-JOIN

An equi-join is a join in which the join comparison operator is an equality, such as

```
where WORKER.Name = WORKERSKILL.Name
```

ESCAPE (SQL*PLUS)

See **SET**.

EXCEPTION

SEE ALSO   BLOCK STRUCTURE, **DECLARE EXCEPTION**, **RAISE**, Chapter 25

FORMAT

```
EXCEPTION
   {WHEN {OTHERS | exception [OR exception]...}
       THEN statement; [statement;]...}
 [ WHEN {OTHER | exception [OR exception]...}
       THEN statement; [statement;]...]...
```

DESCRIPTION   The EXCEPTION section of a PL/SQL block is where program control is transferred whenever an exception flag is raised. Exception flags are either user-defined or system exceptions raised automatically by PL/SQL. *See* **RAISE** for details on user-defined exception flags. The system exception flags are all, in effect, BOOLEAN variables that are either TRUE or FALSE. The **WHEN** clause is used to test these. For example, the NOT_LOGGED_ON flag is raised if you attempt to issue a command to Oracle without being logged on. You do not need to have **DECLARE**d an exception, or **RAISE**d this flag yourself. PL/SQL will do it for you.

When any exception flag is raised, the program immediately halts whatever it was doing and jumps to the EXCEPTION section of the current block. This section, however, doesn't know automatically which exception flag was raised, nor what to do. Therefore, you must code the EXCEPTION section first to check all of the exception flags that are likely to have occurred, and then give action instructions for each. This is what the **WHEN...THEN** logic does. You can use WHEN OTHERS as a catch-all to handle unanticipated errors for which you have not declared exceptions.

EXAMPLE   Here one exception flag is tested in the EXCEPTION section. The ZERO_DIVIDE flag is raised when any calculation attempts to divide by zero.

```
declare
  pi      constant NUMBER(9,7) := 3.1415926;
  radius INTEGER(5);
  area   NUMBER(14,2);
  some_variable   NUMBER(14,2);
begin
  radius := 3;
  loop
    some_variable := 1/(radius-4);
    area := pi*power(radius,2);
      insert into AREAS values (radius, area);
    radius := radius+1;
    exit when area >100;
  end loop;
exception
  when ZERO_DIVIDE
   then insert into AREAS values (0,0);
end;
.
/
```

The system-raised exception flags are:

- ACCESS_INTO_NULL is raised if your program attempts to assign values to the attributes of an uninitialized object (error is ORA-06530).

- COLLECTION_IS_NULL is raised when your program attempts to apply collection methods other than EXISTS to an uninitialized nested table or varray (error is ORA-06531).

- CURSOR_ALREADY_OPEN is raised if an **OPEN** statement tries to open a cursor that is already open. SQLCODE is set to -6511 (error is ORA-06511).

- DUP_VAL_ON_INDEX is raised if an **insert** or **update** would have caused a duplicate value in a unique index. SQLCODE is set to -1 (error is ORA-00001).

- INVALID_CURSOR is raised if you attempted to **OPEN** an undeclared cursor, **CLOSE** one that was already closed, or **FETCH** from one that wasn't open, and so on. SQLCODE is set to -1001 (error is ORA-01001).

- INVALID_NUMBER is raised on a conversion error from a character string to a number when the character string doesn't contain a legitimate number. SQLCODE is set to -1722 (error is ORA-01722).

- LOGIN_DENIED is raised if Oracle rejects the user/password in the attempt to log on. SQLCODE is set to -1017 (error is ORA-01017).

- NO_DATA_FOUND is raised if a **select** statement returns zero rows. (This is not the same as a **FETCH** returning no rows. NO_DATA_FOUND means the **select** returned nothing.)

SQLCODE is set to +100 (error code is ORA-01403). The error numbers differ here because the +100 is now the ANSI standard code for no data found. Oracle's 1403 predates the standard. Note that this error number is positive, which generally indicates a recoverable, nonfatal error. Your EXCEPTION section logic may want to branch and attempt something other than an **EXIT**.

- NOT_LOGGED_ON is raised if you attempt any sort of database call without being logged on. SQLCODE is set to -1012 (error is ORA-01012).

- PROGRAM_ERROR is raised if PL/SQL itself has a problem executing code. SQLCODE is set to -6501 (error is ORA-06501).

- ROWTYPE_MISMATCH is raised if a host cursor variable and PL/SQL cursor variable involved in an assignment have incompatible return types (error is ORA-06504).

- SELF_IS_NULL occurs when your program attempts to call a MEMBER method on a null instance (error is ORA-30625).

- STORAGE_ERROR is raised if PL/SQL needs more memory than is available, or if it detects corruption of memory. SQLCODE is set to -6500 (error is ORA-06500).

- SUBSCRIPT_BEYOND_COUNT occurs when your program references a nested table or varray element using an index number larger than the number of elements in the collection (error is ORA-06533).

- SUBSCRIPT_OUTSIDE_LIMIT occurs if your program references a nested table or varray element using an index number outside the legal range (error is ORA-06532).

- SYS_INVALID_ROWID occurs if the conversion of a character string into a rowid fails because the character string does not represent a valid rowid (error is ORA-01410).

- TIMEOUT_ON_RESOURCE is raised when a resource Oracle is waiting for isn't available when it should be. This usually means an instance has had an abnormal termination. SQLCODE is set to -51 (error is ORA-00051).

- TOO_MANY_ROWS is raised when a **select** statement that is supposed to return just one row returns more than one (this is also raised by a subquery that is only supposed to return one row). SQLCODE is -1427 (error is ORA-01427).

- TRANSACTION_BACKED_OUT is raised when the remote part of a transaction is rolled back. SQLCODE is -61 (error is ORA-00061).

- VALUE_ERROR is raised when the value of a column or PS/SQL variable is damaged, such as by truncation. This kind of problem usually occurs during a conversion of one datatype to another, the copying of a value from one data field to another, or a numeric calculation that violates the precision of the variable. This flag is not raised when a string is truncated while being copied into a host variable (such as by a **FETCH**). In this case the host variable indicator (if one is used) is set to the number that is the correct length of the string (before it was truncated). If the copy is successful the indicator variable is 0. *See* INDICATOR VARIABLE. VALUE_ERROR sets SQLCODE to -6502 (error is ORA-01476).

- ZERO_DIVIDE is raised when a statement tries to divide a number by zero. SQLCODE is -1476 (error is ORA-01476).

- OTHERS is the catch-all for any exception flags you did not check for in your EXCEPTION section. It must always be the last WHEN statement, and must stand alone. It cannot be included with any other exceptions.

Exception handling, particularly as it relates to exceptions you declare, should really be reserved for errors that are fatal-that means normal processing should stop.

If an exception flag is raised that is not tested for in the current block, the program will branch to the EXCEPTION block in the enclosing block, and so on, until either the exception raised is found, or control falls through to the host program.

EXCEPTION sections can reference variables in the same manner that the execution block can. That is, they can reference local variables directly, or variables from other blocks by prefixing them with the other block's name.

Use caution in testing for certain kinds of exceptions. For instance, if the EXCEPTION section takes the error message and inserts it into a database table, a NOT_LOGGED_ON exception would put the EXCEPTION section into an infinite loop. Design the statements that follow THEN not to duplicate the error that got the program there in the first place. You also may use **RAISE** without an exception name. This will automatically pass control to the next outer exception block, or the main program. *See* **RAISE** for further details.

EXCEPTION_INIT

SEE ALSO   DECLARE EXCEPTION, EXCEPTION, SQLCODE

FORMAT

```
PRAGMA EXCEPTION_INIT(exception,integer);
```

DESCRIPTION   The standard system exceptions, such as ZERO_DIVIDE, which are referenced by name, are actually no more than the association of a name with the internal Oracle error number. There are hundreds of these error numbers, and only the most common dozen have been given names. Any that are not named will still raise an exception flag and transfer control to the EXCEPTION block, but they will all be caught by OTHERS, rather than by name.

You can change this by assigning your own names to other Oracle error numbers. EXCEPTION_INIT allows you to do this. *exception* is the one-word name you assign to the integer error number (*see* Oracle's *Error Messages and Codes Manual* for a complete list). *integer* should be negative if the error code is negative (true for fatal errors), and *exception* must follow normal object naming rules.

Note that the format of this command requires the word PRAGMA before EXCEPTION_INIT. A pragma is an instruction to the PL/SQL compiler, rather than executable code. The pragma must be in the DECLARE section of a PL/SQL block, and must be preceded by an exception declaration.

EXAMPLE

```
DECLARE
    some_bad_error          exception;
    pragma                  exception_init(some_bad_error, -666);
BEGIN
    ...
    EXCEPTION
        when some_bad_error
            then ...
END;
```

EXCLUSIVE LOCK

An exclusive lock is one that permits other users to query data, but not change it. It differs from a SHARE lock because it does not permit another user to place any type of lock on the same data; several users may place SHARE locks on the same data at the same time.

EXECUTABLE SQL STATEMENT

An executable SQL statement is one that generates a call to the database. It includes almost all queries, DML, DDL, and DCL statements. (Compare to DECLARATIVE SQL STATEMENT.)

EXECUTE

SEE ALSO **CALL, CREATE PROCEDURE, CREATE FUNCTION, CREATE PACKAGE, CREATE PACKAGE BODY, GRANT** (Form 2—Object Privileges), Chapters 27 and 28

FORMAT

```
execute procedural_object_name [arguments];
```

DESCRIPTION **EXECUTE** executes a procedure, package, or function. To execute a procedure within a package, specify both the package name and the procedure name in the execute command, as shown in the following example. This example executes a procedure named NEW_WORKER, in a package named LEDGER_PACKAGE; the value ADAH TALBOT is passed as input to the procedure.

```
execute LEDGER_PACKAGE.NEW_WORKER('ADAH TALBOT');
```

To execute a procedural object, you must have been granted EXECUTE privilege on that object. *See* **GRANT** (Form 2—Object Privileges).

EXECUTE (Dynamic Embedded SQL)

SEE ALSO **EXECUTE IMMEDIATE, PREPARE**

FORMAT

```
EXEC SQL [FOR :integer]
EXECUTE {statement_name | block_name}
  [USING :variable[:indicator][,:variable[:indicator]...]
```

DESCRIPTION *database* is the name of a database connection other than the default. *:integer* is a host variable used to limit the number of iterations when the **where** clause uses arrays. *statement_name* is the name of a prepared **insert**, **delete**, or **update** statement to be executed (**select** is not allowed). *block_name* is the name of a prepared PL/SQL block. **USING** introduces a list of substitutions into the host variables of the previously prepared statement.

EXAMPLE

```
work_string : string(1..200);
worker_name : string(1..25);
get(work_string);
exec sql at TALBOT prepare ADAH from :work_string;
exec sql execute ADAH using :worker_name;
```

EXECUTE IMMEDIATE (Dynamic Embedded SQL)

SEE ALSO **EXECUTE, PREPARE**

FORMAT

```
EXEC SQL [AT {database | :host_variable]
EXECUTE IMMEDIATE {:string | literal}
```

DESCRIPTION *database* is the name of a database connection other than the default; *host_variable* may contain such a name as its value. *:string* is a host variable string containing a SQL statement. *literal* is a character string containing a SQL statement. The **EXECUTE IMMEDIATE** statement cannot contain host variable references other than an executable SQL statement in *:string*. The SQL statement is parsed, put into executable form, executed, and the executable form is destroyed. It is intended only for statements to be executed just once. Statements that require multiple executions should use **PREPARE** and **EXECUTE**, as this eliminates the overhead of parsing for each execution.

EXAMPLE

```
get(work_string);
exec sql execute immediate :work_string;
exec sql execute immediate
  "delete from SKILL where Skill = 'Grave Digger'";
```

EXECUTE PHASE

The execute phase of SQL statement execution is when all the information necessary for execution is obtained and the statement is executed.

EXISTS

SEE ALSO ANY, ALL, IN, NOT EXISTS, Chapter 12

FORMAT

```
select ...
 where EXISTS (select...)
```

DESCRIPTION **EXISTS** returns *true* in a **where** clause if the subquery that follows it returns at least one row. The **select** clause in the subquery can be a column, a literal, or an asterisk—it doesn't matter. (Convention suggests an asterisk or an 'x'.)

Many people prefer **EXISTS** over **ANY** and **ALL** because it is easier to remember and understand, and most formulations of **ANY** and **ALL** can be reconstructed using **EXISTS**.

EXAMPLE The query shown in the following example uses EXISTS to list from the SKILL table all those records that have matching Skills in the WORKERSKILL table. The result of this query will be the list of all skills that the current workers possess.

```
select SKILL.Skill
   from SKILL
 where EXISTS
       (select 'x' from WORKERSKILL
        where WORKERSKILL.Skill = SKILL.Skill);
```

EXIT (Form I—PL/SQL)

SEE ALSO END, LOOP, Chapter 25

FORMAT

```
EXIT [loop] [WHEN condition];
```

DESCRIPTION Without any of its options, **EXIT** simply takes you out of the current loop, and branches control to the next statement following the loop. If you are in a nested loop, you can exit from any enclosing loop simply by specifying the loop name. If you specify a condition, you will exit when the condition evaluates to TRUE. Any cursor within a loop is automatically closed when you **EXIT**.

EXAMPLE

```
<<adah>>
for i in 1..100 loop
    ...
    <<george>>
    for k in 1..100 loop
      ...
      exit when...
      delete...
      exit adah when...;
    end loop george;
    ...
end loop adah;
```

EXIT (Form 2—SQL*PLUS)

SEE ALSO   COMMIT, DISCONNECT, QUIT, START

FORMAT

```
{EXIT | QUIT} [SUCCESS|FAILURE|WARNING|integer|variable]
```

DESCRIPTION   **EXIT** ends a SQL*PLUS session and returns user to the operating system, calling program, or menu. **EXIT** commits pending changes to the database. A return code is also returned. SUCCESS, FAILURE, and WARNING have values that are operating-system specific; FAILURE and WARNING may be the same on some operating systems.

integer is a value you can pass back explicitly as the return code; *variable* allows you to set this value dynamically. This can be a user-defined variable, or a system variable, such as sql.sqlcode, which always contains the sqlcode of the last SQL statement executed, either in SQL*PLUS or an embedded PL/SQL block.

EXP

SEE ALSO   LN, NUMBER FUNCTIONS, Chapter 8

FORMAT

```
EXP(n)
```

DESCRIPTION   **EXP** returns *e* raised to the *n*th power; e = 2.718281828....

EXPLAIN PLAN

SEE ALSO   Chapter 36

SYNTAX

DESCRIPTION   *name* identifies this plan explanation for this *sql_statement* when it appears in the output table, and follows normal object naming conventions. If *name* is not specified, the STATEMENT_ID column in the table will be NULL. *table* is the name of the output table into which the plan explanation will go. It must be previously created before this procedure can be executed. The start file UTLXPLAN.SQL contains the format and can be used to create the default table, named PLAN_TABLE. If *table* is not specified, EXPLAIN PLAN will use PLAN_TABLE. *sql_statement* is the simple text of any **select**, **insert**, **update**, or **delete** statement you wish to have analyzed for Oracle's execution plan for it.

EXPORT

Export can have either of two definitions:

- Export is the Oracle utility used to store Oracle database data in export format files for later retrieval into an Oracle database via Import.

- To export is to use the Export utility to write selected table data to an export file.

For information on the Export utility, *see* the *Oracle Server Utilities User's Guide* and Chapter 38.

EXPRESSION

An expression is any form of a column. This could be a literal, a variable, a mathematical computation, a function, or virtually any combination of functions and columns whose final result is a single value, such as a string, a number, or a date.

FEEDBACK (SQL*PLUS)

See **SET**.

FETCH

One phase of query execution is the fetch phase, where actual rows of data meeting all search criteria are retrieved from the database.

FETCH (Form I—Embedded SQL)

SEE ALSO   **CLOSE, DECLARE CURSOR, DESCRIBE,** INDICATOR VARIABLE, **OPEN, PREPARE**

FORMAT

```
EXEC SQL [FOR :integer] FETCH cursor
INTO :variable[[ INDICATOR ]:indicator]
    [,:variable[[ INDICATOR ]:indicator] ]...
EXEC SQL [FOR :integer] FETCH cursor
    USING DESCRIPTOR descriptor
```

DESCRIPTION   *integer* is a host variable that sets the maximum number of rows to fetch into the output variables. *cursor* is the name of a cursor previously set up by **DECLARE CURSOR**. *:variable[:indicator]* is one or more host variables into which fetched data will be placed. If any of the host variables is an array, then all of them (in the **INTO** list) must be arrays. The **INDICATOR** keyword is optional.

descriptor is a descriptor from a previous **DESCRIBE** statement.

EXAMPLE

```
exec sql fetch CURSOR1 into :Name, :Skill;
```

FETCH (Form 2—PL/SQL)

SEE ALSO   %FOUND, %ROWTYPE, CLOSE, DECLARE CURSOR, LOOP, OPEN,
SELECT. . .INTO, Chapter 25
FORMAT

```
FETCH cursor INTO {record | variable [,variable]...};
```

DESCRIPTION   FETCH gets a row of data. The named cursor's select statement determines which columns are retrieved, and its **where** statement determines which (and how many) rows can be retrieved. This is called the "active set," but it is not available to you for processing until you fetch it, row by row, using the **FETCH** statement. The **FETCH** gets a row from the active set and drops the row's values into the record (or string of variables), which has been defined in the **DECLARE.**

If you use the variable list method, each column in the select list of the cursor must have a corresponding variable, and each of them must have been declared in the **DECLARE** section. The datatypes must be the same or compatible.

If you use the record method, the record is **DECLARE**d using the %ROWTYPE attribute, which declares the structure of the record to be the same (with the same datatypes) as the column list in the select. Each variable within this record can then be accessed individually using the record name as a prefix, and a variable name that is the same as the column name.

EXAMPLE

```
declare
    pi      constant NUMBER(9,7) := 3.1415926;
    area    NUMBER(14,2);
    cursor rad_cursor is
            select * from RADIUS_VALS;
        rad_val rad_cursor%ROWTYPE;
begin
    open rad_cursor;
      loop
        fetch rad_cursor into rad_val;
        exit when rad_cursor%NOTFOUND;
          area := pi*power(rad_val.radius,2);
          insert into AREAS values (rad_val.radius, area);
      end loop;
    close rad_cursor;
end;
.
/
```

FIELD

In a table, a field is the information stored at the intersection of a row and a column. Field is generally synonymous with a column, but also can mean an actual column value.

FILE TYPES

Files usually have a name and an extension, for example **comfort.tab** where **comfort** is the file name, and **tab** is the extension, or file "type." In SQL*PLUS, **start** files that are created using **EDIT** are given the default extension SQL if no extension is specified. In other words, this:

```
edit misty
```

will create or edit a file named **misty.sql**, while this:

```
start misty
```

will attempt to start a file named **misty.sql** because no extension was specified. Similarly, this:

```
spool bellwood
```

will create an output file named **bellwood.lst**, because **lst** is the default extension for spooled files. Of course, if either **edit** or **spool** is followed by both a file name and extension, the given extension will be used, not the default.

filespec

SEE ALSO   ALTER TABLESPACE, CREATE CONTROLFILE, CREATE DATABASE, CREATE LIBRARY, CREATE TABLESPACE

SYNTAX

filespec_datafiles & filespec_tempfiles::=

filespec_redo_log_file_groups::=

DESCRIPTION   *filespec* defines the name, location, and size of a file used by the database. For example, when you create a tablespace you must specify at least one datafile for the tablespace to use. *filespec* provides the format for the datafile portion of the **CREATE TABLESPACE** command.

FLOOR

SEE ALSO   CEIL, NUMBER FUNCTIONS, Chapter 8

FORMAT

```
FLOOR(value)
```

DESCRIPTION   **FLOOR** is the largest integer smaller than or equal to *value*.

EXAMPLE

```
FLOOR(2)    =   2
FLOOR(1.3)  =   1
FLOOR(-2)   =  -2
FLOOR(-2.3) =  -3
```

FLUSH (SQL*PLUS)

See **SET**.

FOR

See **LOOP** and CURSOR FOR LOOP.

FOREIGN KEY

A foreign key is one or more columns whose values are based on the primary or candidate key values from another table.

FORMAT

See **BTITLE**, CHAR FORMAT, **COLUMN**, DATE FORMAT, **TO_CHAR**, **TO_DATE**, **TTITLE**.

FORMAT MODEL

A format model is a clause that controls the appearance of numbers, dates, and character strings. Format models for DATE columns are used in date conversion functions such as **TO_CHAR** and **TO_DATE**.

FRAGMENTED DATABASE

A fragmented database is one that has been used for a while so that data belonging to various tables is spread all over the database and free space may be in many small pieces rather than fewer large pieces, due to much database activity or use. Fragmentation makes space usage less efficient and can be remedied by exporting and importing some or all data.

FREE EXTENTS

Free extents are extents of database blocks that have not been allocated to any table or index segment. *Free extents* is another term for free space.

FROM

SEE ALSO   **DELETE**, **SELECT**, Chapter 3

FORMAT

```
DELETE FROM [user.]table[@link] [alias]
  WHERE condition

SELECT... FROM [user.]table[@link] [, [user.]table[@link] ]...
```

DESCRIPTION   *table* is the name of the table used by **delete** or **select**. *link* is the link to a remote database. Both **delete** and **select** commands require a **from** clause to define the tables from which rows will be deleted or selected. If the table is owned by another user, its name must be prefixed by the owner's user name.

If the table is remote, a database link has to be defined. *@link* specifies the link. If *link* is entered, but *user* is not, the query seeks a table owned by the user on the remote database. The *condition* may include a correlated query and use the *alias* for correlation.

FULL TABLE SCAN

A full table scan is a method of data retrieval in which Oracle directly searches in a sequential manner all the database blocks for a table (rather than using an index), when looking for the specified data. *See* Chapter 36.

FUNCTION

A function is a predefined operation, such as "convert to uppercase," which may be performed by placing the function's name and arguments in a SQL statement. *See* CHARACTER FUNCTIONS, CONVERSION FUNCTIONS, DATE FUNCTIONS, GROUP FUNCTIONS, LIST FUNCTIONS, NUMBER FUNCTIONS, and individual functions.

FUZZY MATCH

A fuzzy match is a type of text search that allows for misspellings or variant spellings. *See* TEXT SEARCH OPERATORS and Chapter 24.

GET

SEE ALSO   EDIT, SAVE

FORMAT

```
GET file [LIST | NOLIST]
```

DESCRIPTION   **GET** loads a host system file named *file* into the current buffer (whether the SQL buffer or a named buffer). If the file type is not included, **GET** assumes a file type of SQL. **LIST** makes SQL*PLUS list the lines being loaded into the buffer. This is the default. **NOLIST** gets the file without listing its contents.

EXAMPLE   This example gets a file called **work.sql**:

```
get work
```

GIST

A gist is a summarized version of a longer text entry, as processed by ConText (interMedia). *See* Chapter 24.

GLB

SEE ALSO   DATA TYPES, GROUP FUNCTIONS

FORMAT

```
GLB(label)
```

DESCRIPTION   The GLB group function returns the greatest lower bound of a secure operating system label. The label must be either an expression evaluating to an MLSLABEL value or a quoted text literal in the standard MLS label format. This function is available only in Trusted Oracle; *see* the *Trusted Oracle Server Administrator's Guide* for more information.

GLOBAL INDEX

When a table is partitioned, its data is stored in separate tables. When an index is created on the partitioned table, the index can be partitioned so that each of the table partitions has a matching index partition. If the index partitions do not match the table partitions, then the index is a global index. *See* Chapter 18.

GOTO

SEE ALSO   BLOCK STRUCTURE, Chapter 25
FORMAT

```
GOTO label;
```

DESCRIPTION   **GOTO** transfers control to a section of code preceded by the named *label*. Such a label can be used to precede any legitimate statement within an execution block, or within an EXCEPTION section. There are certain restrictions:

- A **GOTO** cannot transfer control to a block enclosed in the current block, or inside of a FOR LOOP or an IF statement.

- A **GOTO** cannot transfer to a label outside of its own block unless it is to a block that encloses its block.

EXAMPLE   Here's an informal loop built from a **GOTO** that, without actually knowing ahead of time what the top number will be, **insert**s a geometric progression from 1 to about 10,000 into a table:

```
DECLARE
   ...
BEGIN
   x := 0;
   y := 1;
   <<alpha>>
   x := x + 1;
   y := x*y;
   insert ...
   if y > 10000
      then goto beta;
   goto alpha;
<<beta>>
   exit;
```

GRANT (Form 1—System Privileges and Roles)

SEE ALSO   ALTER USER, **CREATE USER**, PRIVILEGE, **REVOKE**, ROLE, Chapter 19
SYNTAX

DESCRIPTION   **GRANT** extends one or more system privileges to users and roles. A system privilege is an authorization to perform one of the various data definition or control commands, such as **ALTER SYSTEM**, **CREATE ROLE**, or **GRANT** itself. *See* PRIVILEGE for details of these privileges. A user is created by **CREATE USER** and is then granted system privileges to enable logging into the database and other operations. A user without grants is unable to do anything at all in Oracle. A *role* is a collection of privileges created by **CREATE ROLE**. As with a user, a role has no privileges when created, but gets them through one or more **GRANT**s. One can grant one role to another role to create a nested network of roles, which gives the database administrator a great deal of flexibility in managing the security of the system.

The **WITH ADMIN OPTION** option lets the granted user or role (the grantee) grant the system privilege or role to other grantees. The grantee can also alter or drop a role granted **WITH ADMIN OPTION**.

EXAMPLE   The following grants the role BASIC permission to log into Oracle, to change session parameters, and to create tables, views, and synonyms. It also lets a user granted the BASIC role grant these permissions to other users or roles.

```
grant CREATE SESSION, ALTER SESSION, CREATE TABLE,
      CREATE VIEW, CREATE SYNONYM
   to BASIC
 with admin option;
```

GRANT (Form 2—Object Privileges)

SEE ALSO   **GRANT** (Form 1), PRIVILEGE, ROLE, Chapter 19

SYNTAX

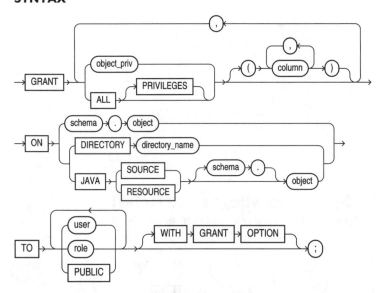

DESCRIPTION   The second form of the **GRANT** command grants object privileges, privileges that affect specific kinds of objects in Oracle databases, to any user or role. *object* can be a table, view, sequence, procedure, function, package, snapshot, or a synonym for one of these objects. **GRANT**s on a synonym actually become grants on the underlying object that the synonym references. *See* PRIVILEGE for a complete list of object privileges and a discussion of which can be granted for the various objects.

If you are granting INSERT, REFERENCES, or UPDATE privileges on a table or view, **GRANT** can also specify a list of columns of the table or view to which the **GRANT** applies. The **GRANT** applies only to those columns. If **GRANT** has no list of columns, the **GRANT** applies to all columns in the table or view.

PUBLIC grants the privileges to all users present and future.

The **WITH GRANT OPTION** passes along the right to grant the granted privileges to another user or role.

GREATEST

SEE ALSO   COLLATION, **LEAST**, **MAX**, OTHER FUNCTIONS, Chapters 8 and 9
FORMAT

```
GREATEST(value1, value2, ...)
```

DESCRIPTION   **GREATEST** chooses the greatest of a list of values. These can be columns, literals, or expressions, and CHAR, VARCHAR2, NUMBER, or DATE datatypes. A number with a larger value is considered greater than a smaller one. All negative numbers are smaller than all positive numbers. Thus, -10 is smaller than 10; -100 is smaller than -10.

A later date is considered greater than an earlier date.

Character strings are compared position by position, starting at the leftmost end of the string, up to the first character that is different. Whichever string has the greater character in that position is considered the greater string. One character is considered greater than another if it appears after the other in the computer's collation sequence. Usually this means that a B is greater than an A, but the value of A compared to a, or compared to the number 1, will differ by computer.

If two strings are identical through to the end of the shorter one, the longer string is considered greater. If two strings are identical and the same length, they are considered equal. In SQL, it is important that literal numbers be typed without enclosing single quotes, as '10' would be considered smaller than '6', since the quotes will cause these to be regarded as character strings rather than numbers, and the '6' will be seen as greater than the 1 in the first position of '10'.

Unlike many other Oracle functions and logical operators, the **GREATEST** and **LEAST** functions will not evaluate literal strings that are in date format as dates. In order for **LEAST** and **GREATEST** to work properly, the **TO_DATE** function must be applied to the literal strings.

GREATEST_LB

SEE ALSO   **LEAST_UB**, LIST FUNCTIONS
FORMAT

```
GREATEST_LB(label[,label]...)
```

DESCRIPTION   **GREATEST_LB** returns the greatest lower bound of a list of labels in Trusted Oracle.

GROUP BY

SEE ALSO   **HAVING**, **ORDER BY**, **WHERE**, Chapter 11

FORMAT

```
SELECT expression [,expression]...
 GROUP BY expression [,expression]...
HAVING condition
   ...
```

DESCRIPTION   **GROUP BY** causes a **select** to produce one summary row for all selected rows that have identical values in one or more specified columns or expressions. Each expression in the **select** clause must be one of these things:

- A constant
- A function without parameters (SysDate, User)
- A group function like **SUM**, **AVG**, **MIN**, **MAX**, **COUNT**
- Matched identically to an expression in the **GROUP BY** clause

Columns referenced in the **GROUP BY** clause need not be in the **select** clause, though they must be in the table.

You use **HAVING** to determine which groups the **GROUP BY** is to include. A **where** clause, on the other hand, determines which rows are to be included in groups.

GROUP BY and **HAVING** follow **WHERE**, **CONNECT BY**, and **START WITH**. The **ORDER BY** clause is executed after the **WHERE**, **GROUP BY**, and **HAVING** clauses (which execute in that order). It can employ group functions, or columns from the **GROUP BY**, or a combination. If it uses a group function, that function operates on the groups, then the **ORDER BY** sorts the *results* of the function in order. If the **ORDER BY** uses a column from the **GROUP BY**, it sorts the rows that are returned based on that column. Group functions and single columns can be combined in the **ORDER BY** (so long as the column is in the **GROUP BY**).

In the **ORDER BY** clause you can specify a group function and the column it affects even though they have nothing at all to do with the group functions or columns in the **SELECT**, **GROUP BY**, or **HAVING** clause. On the other hand, if you specify a column in the **ORDER BY** that is not part of a group function, it must be in the **GROUP BY** clause.

EXAMPLE

```
select Person, COUNT(Item), SUM(Amount) Total
   from LEDGER
 where Action = 'PAID'
 group by Person
having COUNT(Item) > 1
 order by AVG(Amount);
```

GROUP FUNCTIONS

SEE ALSO   AVG, **COUNT**, GLB, LUB, **MAX**, **MIN**, NUMBER FUNCTIONS, **STDDEV**, SUM, VARIANCE, Chapter 8

DESCRIPTION   A GROUP FUNCTION computes a single summary value (such as sum or average) from the individual number values in a group of values. This is an alphabetical list of all current group functions in Oracle's SQL. Each of these is listed elsewhere in this reference under its own name, with its proper format and use. Group functions are useful only in queries and subqueries. **DISTINCT** makes a group function summarize only distinct (unique) values.

FUNCTION NAME AND USE   AVG([DISTINCT | ALL] *value*) gives the average of the values for group of rows.

COUNT([DISTINCT | ALL] *value* /*) gives the count of rows for a column, or for a table (with *).
GLB(*label*) gives the greatest lower bound of a secure operating system *label.*
LUB(*label*) gives the least upper bound of a secure operating system *label.*
MAX([DISTINCT | ALL] *value*) gives the maximum of all values for a group of rows.
MIN([DISTINCT | ALL] *value*) gives the minimum of all values for a group of rows.
STDDEV([DISTINCT | ALL] *value*) gives the standard deviation of all values for a group of rows.
SUM([DISTINCT | ALL] *value*) gives the sum of all values for a group of rows.
VARIANCE([DISTINCT | ALL] *value*) gives the variance of all values for a group of rows.

GROUPING

GROUPING is a function used in conjunction with **ROLLUP** and **CUBE** functions to detect **NULL**s.
See **ROLLUP**.

HASH CLUSTER

A hash cluster is a cluster stored by a hash key instead of by an index key. A hash key is a value computed from the key values that represents the location on disk. An index key requires Oracle to look up the location in the index, while a hash key lets Oracle calculate the location.

HASH JOIN

A hash join is a method of performing a join of two tables. A hash join uses hash algorithms (similar to those used for hash clusters) to evaluate rows that meet the join criteria. Although they use similar algorithms, there is no direct relation between hash joins and hash clusters.

HASH PARTITION

In a hash partition, data to be partitioned is processed by a hash algorithm rather than simply being partitioned by range. Hash partitioning will therefore spread small sets of sequential data over more partitions than range partitioning. *See* **CREATE TABLE**.

HAVING

See GROUP BY.

HEADING (SQL*PLUS)

See **SET**.

HEADSEP (SQL*PLUS)

See **SET**.

HEXADECIMAL NOTATION

Hexadecimal notation is a numbering system with a base of 16 instead of the decimal base of 10. The numbers 10 through 15 are represented by the letters A through F. This system is often used to display the internal data stored in a computer.

HEXTORAW

SEE ALSO   RAWTOHEX

FORMAT

HEXTORAW(*hex_string*)

DESCRIPTION   HEXadecimal **TO RAW**, **HEXTORAW** changes a character string of hex numbers into binary.

HINT

Within a query, you can specify hints that direct the cost-based optimizer in its processing of the query. To specify a hint, use the following syntax. Immediately after the **select** keyword, enter the string:

/*+

Next, add the hint, such as

FULL(worker)

Close the hint with the following string:

*/

   See Chapter 36 for a description of the available hints, and their impact on query processing.

HISTOGRAM

A histogram shows the distribution of data values for a column. The Oracle optimizer can use histograms to determine the efficiency of indexes for specific data value ranges. *See* **ANALYZE**.

HOST (SQL*PLUS)

SEE ALSO $, @, @, START

FORMAT

HO[ST] host command

DESCRIPTION   A host is a computer on which the Oracle RDBMS is running. The **HOST** command in SQL*PLUS passes any host command back to the operating system for execution without exiting SQL*PLUS. SQL*PLUS permits embedding local or PL/SQL variables in the host command string. This doesn't work on all hardware or operating systems.

IF

SEE ALSO   LOOP, Chapter 25

FORMAT

```
IF condition
    THEN statement; [statement;]...
 [ELSIF condition THEN statement; [statement;]...
 [ELSIF condition THEN statement; [statement;]...]... ]
[ELSE statement; [statement;]...]
END IF;
```

DESCRIPTION   The IF statement will execute one or more *statements* if *condition* evaluates to TRUE, after which the program branches to END IF. If the *condition* is FALSE, then any number of a series of optional ELSIF conditions are tested. If any one is TRUE, the associated *statements* (following THEN) are executed, and then the program branches to END IF. If none of the ELSIF conditions are TRUE (and the original IF condition was not TRUE), then the statements following the optional ELSE are executed. Note that the final ELSE does not have a condition.

EXAMPLE

```
declare
   pi      constant NUMBER(9,7) := 3.1415926;
   area    NUMBER(14,2);
   cursor rad_cursor is
     select * from RADIUS_VALS;
   rad_val rad_cursor%ROWTYPE;
begin
   open rad_cursor;
   fetch rad_cursor into rad_val;
   area := pi*power(rad_val.radius,2);
     if  area >30
       then
          insert into AREAS values (rad_val.radius, area);
     end if;
   close rad_cursor;
end;
.
/
```

IMPORT

Import is the Oracle utility used to retrieve Oracle database data found in export format files into an Oracle database. To import is to use the Import utility to move data from an export file into database table(s). *See* EXPORT. For details on using Import, *see* the *Oracle Server Utilities Users Guide* and Chapter 38.

IN

SEE ALSO   ALL, **ANY**, LOGICAL OPERATORS, Chapter 3

FORMAT

```
where expression IN ({'string' [,'string']... | select...})
```

DESCRIPTION   IN is equivalent to **=ANY**. In the first option, **IN** means the expression is equal to any member of the following list of literal *strings*. In the second option, it means the expression is equal to any value in any row selected from the subquery. The two are logically equivalent, with the first giving a list made of literal strings, and the second building a list from a query. **IN** works with VARCHAR2, CHAR, DATE, and NUMBER datatypes, as well as RowID.

INDEX

Index is a general term for an Oracle/SQL feature used primarily to speed execution and impose uniqueness upon certain data. Indexes provide a faster access method to table data than doing a full table scan. There are several types of indexes; *see* CONCATENATED INDEX, COMPRESSED INDEX, and UNIQUE INDEX. An index has an entry for each value found in the table's indexed field(s) (except those with a **NULL** value) and pointer(s) to the row(s) having that value.

INDEX SEGMENT

The index segment is the storage that is allocated for an index, as compared to storage allocated to the data in a table.

INDEX-ORGANIZED TABLE

An *index-organized table* keeps its data sorted according to the primary key column values for the table. An index-organized table allows you to store the entire table's data in an index. A normal index only stores the indexed columns in the index; an index-organized table stores all of the table's columns in the index.

Because the table's data is stored in an index, the rows of the table do not have RowIDs. Therefore, you cannot select the RowID pseudo-column values from an index-organized table.

To create an index-organized table, use the **organization index** clause of the **create table** command, as shown in the following example:

```
create table TROUBLE (
City            VARCHAR2(13),
SampleDate      DATE,
Noon            NUMBER(4,1),
Midnight        NUMBER(4,1),
Precipitation NUMBER,
constraint TROUBLE_PK PRIMARY KEY (City, SampleDate))
organization index;
```

In order to create TROUBLE as an index-organized table, you must create a PRIMARY KEY constraint on it.

In general, index-organized tables are appropriate for associative tables in many-to-many relationships. Ideally, an index-organized table will have few (or no) columns that are not part of its primary key.

See Chapter 18 and **CREATE TABLE**.

INDICATOR VARIABLE

SEE ALSO   : (colon, the host variable prefix)

FORMAT

```
:name[INDICATOR]:indicator
```

DESCRIPTION   An indicator variable—used when both name and indicator are host language variable names—is a data field whose value indicates whether a host variable should be regarded as **NULL**. (The INDICATOR keyword is for readability and has no effect.)

name may be any legitimate host variable data name used in the host program and included in the precompiler's DECLARE SECTION. *indicator* is defined in the precompiler's DECLARE SECTION as a two-byte integer.

Few procedural languages directly support the idea of a variable with a **NULL** or unknown value, although Oracle and SQL do so easily. In order to extend languages for which Oracle has developed precompilers to support the **NULL** concept, an indicator variable is associated with the host variable, almost like a flag, to indicate whether it is **NULL**. The host variable and its indicator variable may be referenced and set separately in the host language code, but are always concatenated in SQL or PL/SQL.

EXAMPLE

```
BEGIN
    select Name, Skill into :Worker, :JobSkill:JobSkillInd
      from WORKERSKILL
      where Name = :First||' '||:Last;

   IF :JobSkill:JobSkillInd IS NULL
     THEN :JobSkill:JobSkillInd := 'No Skills'
   END IF;
END;
```

Note that the test to see if the variable is **NULL**, and the assignment of 'No Skills' to it if it is, are both done with the concatenated variable name. PL/SQL knows enough to check the indicator in the first case, and set the variable value in the second case. The two variables together are treated just like a single Oracle column. These important points must be noted:

■ Within any single PL/SQL block, a host variable must either always stand alone, or always be concatenated with its indicator variable.

■ An indicator variable cannot be referenced alone within PL/SQL, although it can be in the host program.

When setting host variables within the host program, but outside of PL/SQL, note these points:

■ Setting the indicator variable equal to -1 will force the concatenated variable to be regarded within PL/SQL as **NULL**, both in logic tests and for **insert**s or **update**s.

■ Setting the indicator variable greater than or equal to 0 will force the concatenated variable to be regarded as equal to the value in the host variable, and **NOT NULL**.

■ PL/SQL tests the value of all indicator variables on entering a block, and sets them on exiting the block.

When loading concatenated host variables within PL/SQL, via a SQL statement with an INTO clause, the following rules apply when checking the indicator variable within the host program, but outside of PL/SQL:

■ The indicator variable will be equal to -1 if the value loaded from the database was **NULL**. The value of the host variable is uncertain, and should be treated as such.

■ The indicator variable will be equal to 0 if the value from the database is loaded completely and correctly into the host variable.

■ The indicator variable will be greater than 0 and equal to the actual length of the data in the database column if only a portion of it could fit in the host variable. The host variable will contain a truncated version of what was in the database column.

init.ora

init.ora is a database system parameter file that contains settings and file names used when a system is started using the **CREATE DATABASE**, **STARTUP**, or **SHUTDOWN** command. *See* Chapter 38.

INITCAP

SEE ALSO   CHARACTER FUNCTIONS, **LOWER**, **UPPER**, Chapter 7

FORMAT

```
INITCAP(string)
```

DESCRIPTION **INIT**ial **CAP**ital changes the first letter of a word or series of words into uppercase. It also notes the presence of symbols, and will **INITCAP** any letter that follows a space or a symbol, such as a comma, period, colon, semicolon, !, @, #, $, and so on.

EXAMPLE

```
INITCAP('this.is,an-example of!how@initcap#works')
```

produces this:

```
This.Is,An-Example Of!How@Initcap#Works
```

INPUT

SEE ALSO　　APPEND, **CHANGE**, **DEL**, **EDIT**, Chapter 6

FORMAT

```
I[NPUT] [text]
```

DESCRIPTION　　**INPUT** adds a new line of text after the current line in the current buffer. Using **INPUT** by itself allows multiple lines to be keyed in after the current line, which stops when the system encounters ENTER with nothing else on the line. The space between **INPUT** and *text* will not be added to the line but any additional spaces will be. *See* **DEL** for a discussion of current line.

INSERT (Form 1—Embedded SQL)

SEE ALSO　　EXECUTE, FOR

FORMAT

```
EXEC SQL [AT{database|:host_variable] [FOR :integer]
INSERT INTO [user.]table[@db_link] [ (column [,column]...)]
            { VALUES (expression[,expression]...) | query }
```

DESCRIPTION　　*database* is a database other than the user's default, and *host_variable* contains the name of the database. *:integer* is a host value that limits the number of times the **INSERT** will be processed (*see* **FOR**). *table* is any existing table, view, or synonym, and *db_link* is the name of a remote database where the table is stored. (*See* the **INSERT** Form 3 definition for a discussion of the **VALUES** clause, columns, and query.) *expression* here can be an expression or a host variable in the form *:variable*[*:indicator*].

INSERT (Form 2—PL/SQL)

SEE ALSO　　SQL CURSOR, Chapter 25

FORMAT

```
INSERT INTO [user.]table[@db_link] [(column [,column]...)]
    VALUES (expression [,expression]...) | query...);
```

DESCRIPTION　　PL/SQL's use of **INSERT** is identical to its general form (Form 3 in the following section), with these exceptions:

■　　You may use a PL/SQL variable in an expression for the value in the VALUES list.

■ Each variable will be treated in the same way that a constant, with the value of the variable, would be treated.

■ If you use the *query. . .* version of the **INSERT**, you cannot use the **INTO** clause of the **select**.

INSERT (Form 3—SQL Command)

SEE ALSO   **CREATE TABLE**, Chapters 4, 15, 28, and 29

SYNTAX

table_expression_clause::=

with_clause::=

table_collection_expression::=

values_clause::=

returning_clause::=

DESCRIPTION INSERT adds one or more new rows to the table or view. The optional *user* must be a user to whose table you have been granted insert authority. *table* is the table into which rows are to be inserted. If a list of columns is given, an expression (SQL expression) must be matched for each of those columns. Any columns not in the list receive the value **NULL**, and none of them can be defined **NOT NULL** or the **INSERT** will fail. If a list of columns is not given, values must be given for all columns in the table.

INSERT with a subquery adds as many rows as the query returns, with each query column being matched, position for position, with columns in the column list. If no column list is given, the tables must have the same number and type of columns. The USER_TAB_COLUMNS data dictionary view shows these, as does DESCRIBE in SQL*PLUS.

EXAMPLE The following inserts a row into the COMFORT table:

```
insert into COMFORT values ('KEENE','23-SEP-99',99.8,82.6,NULL);
```

The following inserts City, SampleDate (both NOT NULL columns), and Precipitation into COMFORT:

```
insert into COMFORT (City, SampleDate, Precipitation) values
                    ('KEENE','22-DEC-99',3.9);
```

To copy just the data for the city of KEENE into a new table named NEW_HAMPSHIRE, use this:

```
insert into NEW_HAMPSHIRE
select * from COMFORT
 where City = 'KEENE';
```

See Chapters 4 and 28 for information on inserting rows into tables that use abstract datatypes. *See* Chapter 29 for details on inserting rows into nested tables and varying arrays.

INSTANCE

An instance is everything required for Oracle to run: background processes (programs), memory, and so on. An instance is the means of accessing a database.

INSTANCE IDENTIFIER

An instance identifier is a means of distinguishing one instance from another when multiple instances exist on one host.

INSTANCE RECOVERY

Instance recovery is recovery in the event of software or hardware failure. This occurs if the software aborted abnormally due to a severe bug, deadlock, or destructive interaction between programs. *See also* MEDIA RECOVERY.

INSTEAD OF TRIGGER

An INSTEAD OF trigger executes a block of PL/SQL code in place of the transaction that causes the trigger to be executed. INSTEAD OF triggers are commonly used to redirect transactions against views. *See* **CREATE TRIGGER** and Chapters 26 and 28.

INSTR

SEE ALSO   CHARACTER FUNCTIONS, **SUBSTR**, Chapter 7

FORMAT

```
INSTR(string,set[,start[,occurrence]])
```

DESCRIPTION   **INSTR** finds the location of a *set* of characters in a *string*, starting at position *start* in the string, and looking for the first, second, third, and so on, *occurrence* of the *set*. This function will also work with NUMBER and DATE datatypes. *start* also can be negative, meaning the search begins with the characters at the end of the string and searches backward.

EXAMPLE   To find the third occurrence of PI in this string, use this:

```
INSTR('PETER PIPER PICKED A PECK OF PICKLED PEPPERS','PI',1,3)
```

The result of this function is 30, the location of the third occurrence of PI.

INSTRB

SEE ALSO   CHARACTER FUNCTIONS, **INSTR**, Chapter 7

FORMAT

```
INSTRB(string,set[,start[,occurrence]])
```

DESCRIPTION   **INSTRB** finds the location of a *set* of characters in a *string*, starting at the byte position *start* in the string, and looking for the first, second, third, and so on, *occurrence* of the set. This function also works with NUMBER and DATE datatypes. *start* also can be negative, which means the search begins with the characters at the end of the string and searches backward.

This function is the same as **INSTR** for single-byte character sets.

INTEGRITY CONSTRAINT

An integrity constraint is a rule that restricts the range of valid values for a column. It is placed on a column when the table is created. For the syntax, see the ***constraint_clause*** entry in the Alphabetical Reference.

If you do not name a constraint, Oracle assigns a name in the form SYS_C*n*, where *n* is an integer. An Oracle-assigned name will usually change during an import, while a user-assigned name will not change.

NULL permits **NULL** values. **NOT NULL** specifies that every row must have a non-**NULL** value for this column.

UNIQUE forces column values to be unique. There can be only one PRIMARY KEY constraint on a table. If a column is UNIQUE it cannot also be declared the PRIMARY KEY (PRIMARY KEY also enforces uniqueness). An index enforces the unique or primary key, and the USING INDEX clause and its options specify the storage characteristics of that index. *See* **CREATE INDEX** for more information on the options.

REFERENCES identifies this column as a foreign key from [*user.*]*table* [*(column)*]. Omitting *column* implies that the name in the *user.table* is the same as the name in this table. Note that when REFERENCES is used in a *table_constraint* (described shortly) it must be preceded by FOREIGN KEY. This is not used here, as only this column is referenced; *table_constraint* can reference several columns for FOREIGN KEY. ON DELETE CASCADE instructs ORACLE to maintain referential integrity automatically by removing foreign key rows in the dependent tables if you remove the primary key row in this table.

CHECK assures that the value for this column pass a condition such as this:

```
Amount number(12,2) CHECK (Amount >= 0)
```

condition may be any valid expression that tests TRUE or FALSE. It can contain functions, any columns from this table, and literals.

The **EXCEPTIONS INTO** clause specifies a table into which Oracle puts information about rows that violate an enabled integrity constraint. This table must be local.

The **DISABLE** option lets you disable the integrity constraint when you create it. When the constraint is disabled, ORACLE does not automatically enforce it. You can later enable the constraint with the **ENABLE** clause in **ALTER TABLE**.

You can also create constraints at the table level. Table constraints are identical to column constraints except that a single constraint can reference multiple columns-for example in declaring a set of three columns as a primary or foreign key.

INTERSECT

SEE ALSO   MINUS, QUERY OPERATORS, **UNION**, Chapter 12
FORMAT

```
select...
INTERSECT
select...
```

DESCRIPTION   **INTERSECT** combines two queries and returns only those rows from the first **select** statement that are identical to at least one row from the second **select** statement. The number of columns and datatypes must be identical between **select** statements, although the names of the columns do not need to be. The data, however, must be identical in the rows produced for the **INTERSECT**ion to pass them.

IS NULL

SEE ALSO   LOGICAL OPERATORS, Chapters 3 and 8
FORMAT

```
WHERE column IS [NOT] NULL
```

DESCRIPTION   **IS NULL** tests column (or an expression) for the absence of any data. A **NULL** test is distinctly different from a test for equality, because **NULL** means that the value is unknown or irrelevant, and it therefore cannot be said to be equal to anything, including another **NULL**.

Java

Java is a programming language originally developed by Sun Microsystems. As of Oracle8i, you can write stored procedural objects in either PL/SQL or Java. See Chapter 32.

JDBC

JDBC is an acronym for Java Database Connectivity, an industry standard application programming interface to databases. Oracle supports JDBC connections. See Chapter 33.

JOIN

SEE ALSO   **SELECT**, Chapter 3

FORMAT

```
WHERE {table.column = table.column}
```

DESCRIPTION   A join combines columns and data from two or more tables (and in rare cases, of one table with itself). The tables are all listed in the **from** clause of the **select** statement, and the relationship between the two tables is specified in the **where** clause, usually by a simple equality, such as this:

```
where WORKER.Lodging = LODGING.Lodging
```

This is often called an *equi-join* because it uses the equal sign in the **where** clause. You could join tables using other forms of equality, such as >=, <, and so on, but the results are seldom meaningful. There also are cases in which one or both sides of the equal sign contain an expression, perhaps a **SUBSTR** or a combination of columns, which is used for equality with the other side. This is a fairly common usage.

Joining two tables together without a **where** clause produces a Cartesian product, which combines every row in one table with every row in the other table. An 80-row table combined with a 100-row table would produce an 8000-row result (which is usually quite meaningless).

An *outer join* is a method for intentionally retrieving selected rows from one table that don't match rows in the other table. A classic example of this is Talbot's workers and their skills. Suppose you combined the WORKER table and the SKILL table with an equi-join, like this:

```
select WORKER.Name, Skill
  from WORKER, WORKERSKILL
 where WORKER.Name = WORKERSKILL.Name
```

Unfortunately, you would get only those workers who have skills, and therefore have rows in the WORKERSKILL table. But what if you want to list *all* workers and skills, including those who have none? An outer join, accomplished with a + sign, will allow you to do it:

```
select WORKER.Name, Skill
  from WORKER, WORKERSKILL
 where WORKER.Name = WORKERSKILL.Name(+);
```

The plus says, effectively, "if a row exists in the WORKER table that doesn't correspond to a row in the WORKERSKILL table, add one to make the match." It's like adding a **NULL** row, but it allows rows from the WORKER table to be in the result, even if there is no match for them in the WORKERSKILL table. *See* Chapter 12 for a full discussion.

JOIN COLUMN

A join column is a column used to join one table to another. You identify a join column by using it in a **where** clause that specifies the relationship between the two tables.

JULIAN DATE

Julian dates are a means of converting date data so that every date can be expressed as a unique integer. Julian dates can be obtained by using the format mask 'J' with functions on date data. *See* DATE FORMATS.

KERNEL

Kernel is the base Oracle RDBMS program code (a collection of many modules) that can be called by the background processes.

KEY

A key is a column or columns used to identify rows; it is not the same as an index, although indexes are often used with such columns. *See* FOREIGN KEY, PRIMARY KEY, and UNIQUE KEY.

LABEL (PL/SQL)

A label is a word associated with an executable statement, usually for the purpose of being the target of a GOTO statement.

LAST_DAY

SEE ALSO   ADD_MONTHS, DATE FUNCTIONS, **NEXT_DAY**, Chapter 9
FORMAT

```
LAST_DAY (date)
```

DESCRIPTION   **LAST_DAY** gives the date of the last day of the month that *date* is in.
EXAMPLE   This:

```
LAST_DAY ('05-NOV-99')
```

produces a result of 30-NOV-99.

LEAF

In a tree-structured table, a leaf is a row that has no child row.

LEAST

SEE ALSO   GREATEST, LIST FUNCTIONS, Chapter 9
FORMAT

```
LEAST(value1, value2, ...)
```

DESCRIPTION   **LEAST** is the value of a list of columns, expressions, or values. Values may be VARCHAR2, CHAR, DATE, or NUMBER datatypes, although **LEAST** will not properly evaluate literal dates (such as '20-MAY-49') without the **TO_DATE** function. *See* **GREATEST** for a discussion of evaluating relative values.

LEAST_UB

SEE ALSO   GREATEST_LB, LIST FUNCTIONS

FORMAT

```
LEAST_UB(label[,label]...)
```

DESCRIPTION   **LEAST_UB** returns the least upper bound of a list of labels in Trusted Oracle. A label is used in Trusted Oracle to assign a security level to a record. For further information, *see* the *Trusted Oracle Server Administrator's Guide.*

LENGTH

SEE ALSO   CHARACTER FUNCTIONS, **VSIZE**, Chapter 7

FORMAT

```
LENGTH(string)
```

DESCRIPTION   **LENGTH** tells the length of a string, a number, date, or expression.

LENGTHB

SEE ALSO   CHARACTER FUNCTIONS, **LENGTH**, **VSIZE**, Chapter 7

FORMAT

```
LENGTHB(string)
```

DESCRIPTION   **LENGTHB** tells the length of a string, a number, date, or expression, in bytes (a series of eight bits) rather than in characters. This gives the number of bytes in multi-byte character strings, while **LENGTH** gives you the length in terms of number of characters.

LEVEL

SEE ALSO   **CONNECT BY**, PSEUDO-COLUMNS, Chapter 13

FORMAT

```
LEVEL
```

DESCRIPTION   Level is a pseudo-column, used with **CONNECT BY**, that is equal to 1 for a root node, 2 for a child of a root, 3 for a child of a child of a root, and so on. Level tells basically how far down a tree you've traveled.

LGWR

LGWR (**L**o**G W**riter process) writes redo log entries from the System Global Area to the online redo logs. *See* BACKGROUND PROCESS.

LIBRARY

PL/SQL blocks can reference external subprograms, stored in libraries. *See* **CREATE LIBRARY**.

LIKE

SEE ALSO   LOGICAL OPERATORS, Chapter 3

FORMAT

```
WHERE string LIKE string
```

DESCRIPTION **LIKE** performs pattern matching. An underline represents exactly one space. A percent sign represents any number of spaces or characters. If **LIKE** uses either the _ or % in the first position of a comparison (as in the second and third examples following), any index on the column is ignored.

EXAMPLES

```
Feature LIKE 'MO%'   "Feature begins with the letters MO."
Feature LIKE '_ _I%'  "Feature has an I in the third position."
Feature LIKE '%0%0%'  "Feature has two 0's in it."
```

LINESIZE (SQL*PLUS)

See **SET**.

LIST

SEE ALSO APPEND, CHANGE, EDIT, INPUT, RUN, Chapter 6

FORMAT

```
L[IST] [ {start/*} [end/*] ]
```

DESCRIPTION **LIST** lists lines of the current buffer starting at *start* and ending at *end*, both of which are integers. The end line becomes the current line of the buffer, and is flagged with an asterisk. **LIST** without *start* or *end* lists all lines. An asterisk in either place will set it to the current line. **LIST** with a single number will display just that line, and **LIST** with just an asterisk will display just the current line. The space between **LIST** and *start* is not necessary but it does help readability.

EXAMPLE Use this to list the current SQL buffer:

```
list
```

```
1   select Person, Amount
2      from LEDGER
3    where Amount > 10000
4*      and Rate = 3;
```

The asterisk shows that 4 is the current line. To list just the second line, use this:

```
LIST 2
```

```
2*   from LEDGER
```

This also makes 2 the current line in the current buffer.

LIST FUNCTIONS

SEE ALSO All other function lists, Chapter 9

DESCRIPTION The following is an alphabetical list of all current list functions in Oracle's SQL. Each of these is listed elsewhere in this reference under its own name, with its proper format and use.

This gives the greatest value of a list:

```
GREATEST(value1, value2, ...)
```

This gives the least value of a list:

```
LEAST(value1, value2, ...)
```

LN
SEE ALSO   NUMBER FUNCTIONS, Chapter 8
FORMAT

```
LN(number)
```

DESCRIPTION   LN is the "natural", or base *e*, logarithm of a **number**.

LOADJAVA
LOADJAVA is a utility for loading Java classes, resources, and sources into the database. You must load your Java classes into the database if you plan to use them in stored procedures. To remove the Java classes from the database, use the DROPJAVA utility. *See* Chapter 34.

LOB
A LOB is a large object. Oracle supports several large object datatypes, including BLOB (binary large object), CLOB (character large object), and BFILE (binary file, stored outside the database). *See* Chapter 30 and the **LOB** clause of **CREATE TABLE**.

LOCAL DATABASE
The local database is usually a database on your host computer. *See* REMOTE DATABASE.

LOCAL INDEX
When a table is partitioned, its data is stored in separate tables. When an index is created on the partitioned table, the index can be partitioned so that each of the table partitions has a matching index partition. The matching index partitions are called local indexes. *See* Chapter 18.

LOCALLY MANAGED TABLESPACE
A locally managed tablespace maintains its extent usage information in bitmaps with the tablespace's datafiles. By default, tablespaces store their extent usage information in the data dictionary (and are referred to as "dictionary-managed"). See **CREATE TABLESPACE**.

LOCK
To lock is to temporarily restrict other users' access to data. The restriction that is placed on such data is called "a lock." Lock modes are SHARE, SHARE UPDATE, EXCLUSIVE, SHARE EXCLUSIVE, ROW SHARE, and ROW EXCLUSIVE. Not all locks can be acquired in all modes.

LOCK TABLE
SEE ALSO   COMMIT, DELETE, INSERT, ROLLBACK, SAVEPOINT, UPDATE

SYNTAX

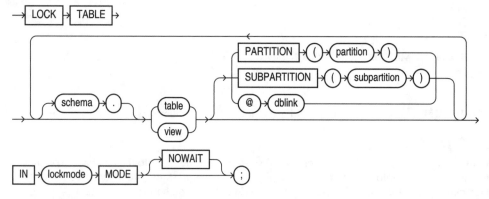

DESCRIPTION   **LOCK TABLE** locks a table in one of several specified modes, allowing it to be shared, but without loss of data integrity. Using **LOCK TABLE** allows you to give other users continued but restricted access to the table. Regardless of which option you choose, the table will remain in that lock mode until you **commit** or **rollback** your transactions.

Lock modes include ROW SHARE, ROW EXCLUSIVE, SHARE UPDATE, SHARE, SHARE ROW EXCLUSIVE, and EXCLUSIVE.

EXCLUSIVE locks permit users to query the locked table but not to do anything else. No other user may lock the table. SHARED locks permit concurrent queries but no updates to the locked table.

With a ROW SHARE or SHARE UPDATE lock, no user can lock the whole table for exclusive access, allowing concurrent access for all users to the table. The two types of lock are synonymous, and SHARE UPDATE exists for compatibility with previous versions of Oracle.

ROW EXCLUSIVE locks are similar to ROW SHARE but they prohibit shared locking, so only one user may access the table at a time.

If a **LOCK TABLE** command cannot be completed (usually because someone else has executed a prior and competing **LOCK TABLE** of some sort) then your **LOCK TABLE** will wait until it can complete. If you wish to avoid this, and simply have control returned to you, use the **NOWAIT** option. Note that you can lock specific partitions and subpartitions.

LOG

SEE ALSO   NUMBER FUNCTIONS, Chapter 8

FORMAT

```
LOG(base, number)
```

DESCRIPTION   **LOG** gives the *base*10 logarithm of a number.

EXAMPLE

```
LOG(base, value)
LOG(EXP(1),3) = 1.098612   -- log(e) of 3
LOG(10,100)   = 2          -- log(10) of 100
```

LOG WRITER PROCESS (LGWR)

See **LGWR**.

LOGICAL EXPRESSION

A logical expression is one whose value evaluates to either TRUE or FALSE. It is a synonym for CONDITION.

LOGICAL OPERATORS

SEE ALSO   PRECEDENCE

FORMAT   The following lists all current logical operators in Oracle's SQL. Most of these are listed elsewhere in this reference under their own names with their proper format and use. All of these operators work with columns or literals.

Logical Operators that Test a Single Value

```
=    expression    is equal to expression
>    expression    is greater than expression
>=   expression    is greater than or equal to expression
<    expression    is less than expression
<=   expression    is less than or equal to expression
!=   expression    is not equal to expression
^=   expression    is not equal to expression
<>   expression    is not equal to expression

EXISTS (query)
NOT EXISTS (query)

LIKE expression
NOT LIKE expression

expression IS NULL
expression IS NOT NULL
```

Logical Operators that Test More than a Single Value

```
ANY (expression [,expression]... | query)
ALL (expression [,expression]... | query)
```

ANY and **ALL** require an equality operator as a prefix, such as **>ANY**, **=ALL**, and so on.

```
IN (expression [,expression]... | query)
NOT IN (expression [,expression]... | query)

BETWEEN expression AND expression
NOT BETWEEN expression AND expression
```

Other Logical Operators

```
()          Overrides normal precedence rules, or encloses a
            subquery
NOT         Reverses logical expression
AND         Combines logical expressions
OR          Combines logical expressions
UNION       Combines results of queries
INTERSECT   Combines results of queries
MINUS       Combines results of queries
```

LOGICAL UNIT OF WORK

See TRANSACTION.

LOGIN ACCOUNT

A login account is a username and password that allows people to use the Oracle RDBMS. This account is usually separate from your operating system account.

LONG (SQL*PLUS)

See **SET**.

LONG DATATYPE

See DATA TYPES.

LONG RAW DATATYPE

A LONG RAW column contains raw binary data, but is otherwise the same as a LONG column. Values entered into LONG RAW columns must be in hex notation.

LOOP

You can use loops to process multiple records within a single PL/SQL block. PL/SQL supports three types of loops:

Simple Loops	A loop that keeps repeating until an **exit** or **exit when** statement is reached within the loop
FOR Loops	A loop that repeats a specified number of times
WHILE Loops	A loop that repeats until a condition is met

You can use loops to process multiple records from a cursor. The most common cursor loop is a cursor FOR loop. *See* CURSOR FOR LOOP and Chapter 25 for details on using loops for both simple and cursor-based processing logic.

LOWER

SEE ALSO   CHARACTER FUNCTIONS, **INITCAP**, **UPPER**, Chapter 7

FORMAT

```
LOWER(string)
```

DESCRIPTION   **LOWER** converts every letter in a string to lowercase.

EXAMPLE

```
LOWER('PENINSULA') = peninsula
```

LPAD

SEE ALSO   CHARACTER FUNCTIONS, **LTRIM**, **RPAD**, **RTRIM**, Chapter 7

FORMAT

```
LPAD(string,length [,'set'])
```

DESCRIPTION   Left **pad** makes a *string* a certain *length* by adding a certain *set* of characters to the left of the string. If *set* is not specified, the default pad character is a space.

EXAMPLE

```
LPAD('>',11,'- ')
```

produces

```
- - - - - >
```

LTRIM

SEE ALSO   CHARACTER FUNCTIONS, **LPAD**, **RPAD**, **RTRIM**, Chapter 7

FORMAT

```
LTRIM(string [,'set'])
```

DESCRIPTION   Left **TRIM** trims all the occurrences of any one of a *set* of characters off of the left side of a *string*.

EXAMPLE

```
LTRIM('NANCY','AN')
```

produces this:

```
CY
```

LUB

SEE ALSO   COMPUTE, **GLB**, GROUP FUNCTIONS

FORMAT

```
LUB(label)
```

DESCRIPTION   LUB gives the least upper bound of a secure operating system label. The label expression must have datatype MLSLABEL or be a quoted text literal in the standard label format. The resulting value is datatype RAW MLSLABEL. This function is available only with Trusted Oracle. *See* the *Trusted Oracle Administrator's Guide* for more information.

MAKE_REF

The **MAKE_REF** function constructs a REF (reference) from the foreign key of a table that references the base table of an object view. **MAKE_REF** allows you to construct references superimposed on existing foreign key relationships. *See* Chapter 31.

MAIN QUERY

A main query is the outermost or top query in a query containing a subquery. It's the query whose columns produce a result.

MAINTENANCE RELEASE

The maintenance release is the second number in Oracle software version numbering. In Oracle version 8.1.5, the maintenance release is 1.

MATERIALIZED VIEW

You can use materialized views to aggregate data and improve query performance. A materialized view is structurally the same as snapshots in earlier versions of Oracle. When you create a materialized view, Oracle creates a physical table to hold data that would usually be read via a view. When you create a materialized view, you specify the view's base query as well as a schedule for the refreshes of its data. You can then index the materialized view to enhance the performance of queries against it. As a result, you can provide data to your users in the format they need, indexed appropriately. *See* **CREATE MATERIALIZED VIEW/SNAPSHOT**.

MATERIALIZED VIEW LOG

When you refresh a materialized view, you can perform a full or incremental refresh. An incremental refresh, called a "fast" refresh, sends only the DML changes from the master table to the materialized view. To track changes to the master table for the materialized view, you must create a materialized view log. The materialized view log must be in the same schema as the master table for the materialized view. Fast refreshes are not available for complex materialized views. *See* **CREATE MATERIALIZED VIEW LOG/SNAPSHOT LOG**.

MAX

SEE ALSO   **COMPUTE**, GROUP FUNCTIONS, **MIN**, Chapter 8
FORMAT

```
MAX([DISTINCT | ALL] value)
```

DESCRIPTION   **MAX** is the maximum of all *values* for a group of rows. **MAX** ignores **NULL** values. The **DISTINCT** option is not meaningful, since the maximum of all values is identical to the maximum of the distinct values.

MAXDATA (SQL*PLUS)

See **SET**.

MEDIA RECOVERY

Media recovery is recovery in the event of hardware failure, which would prevent reading or writing of data and thus operation of the database. *See also* INSTANCE RECOVERY.

METHOD

A method is a block of code. In reference to abstract datatypes, a method is a block of PL/SQL code used to encapsulate the data access method for an object. Methods are specified as part of the abstract datatype specification (*see* CREATE TYPE) and their body is specified as part of the CREATE TYPE BODY command. Users can execute methods on the datatypes for which the methods are defined. The constructor method created for each abstract datatype is an example of a method. *See* Chapter 28 for examples of methods.

In Java, a method is a member of a class. You can call a class method and pass parameters to it for it to use when executing its commands. See Chapter 32 for an example.

MIN

SEE ALSO   **COMPUTE**, GROUP FUNCTIONS, **MAX**, Chapter 8

FORMAT

MIN([DISTINCT | ALL] *value*)

DESCRIPTION   **MIN** is the minimum of all *values* for a group of rows. **MIN** ignores **NULL** values. The **DISTINCT** option is not meaningful, since the minimum of all values is identical to the minimum of the distinct values.

MINUS

SEE ALSO   **INTERSECT**, QUERY OPERATORS, **UNION**, TEXT SEARCH OPERATORS, Chapters 12 and 24

FORMAT

```
select
MINUS
select
```

within ConText and IMT queries:

```
select column
  from TABLE
 where CONTAINS(Text,'text MINUS text') >0;
```

DESCRIPTION   **MINUS** combines two queries. It returns only those rows from the first **select** statement that are not produced by the second **select** statement (the first **select MINUS** the second **select**). The number of columns and datatypes must be identical between **select** statements, although the names of the columns do not need to be. The data, however, must be identical in the rows produced for the **MINUS** to reject them. *See* Chapter 12 for a discussion of the important differences and effects of **INTERSECT**, **MINUS**, and **UNION**.

Within ConText and IMT, **MINUS** tells the text search of two terms to subtract the score of the second term's search from the score of the first term's search before comparing the result to the threshold score.

MOD

SEE ALSO   NUMBER FUNCTIONS, Chapter 8

FORMAT

MOD(*value*, *divisor*)

DESCRIPTION   **MOD** divides a *value* by a *divisor*, and gives the remainder. **MOD**(23,6) = 5 means divide 23 by 6. The answer is 3 with 5 left over, so 5 is the result of the modulus. *value* and *divisor* can both be any real number, except that *divisor* cannot be 0.

EXAMPLES

```
MOD(100,10)    =   0
MOD(22,23)     =  22
MOD(10,3)      =   1
MOD(-30.23,7)  =  -2.23
MOD(4.1,.3)    =    .2
```

The second example shows what **MOD** does whenever the divisor is larger than the dividend (the number being divided). It produces the dividend as a result. Also note this important case:

```
MOD(value,1)   = 0
```

if *value* is an integer. This is a good test to see if a number is an integer.

MONTHS_BETWEEN

SEE ALSO   ADD_MONTHS, DATE FUNCTIONS, Chapter 9

FORMAT

```
MONTHS_BETWEEN(date2,date1)
```

DESCRIPTION   MONTHS_BETWEEN gives *date2 - date1* in months. The result is usually not an integer.

MOUNT A DATABASE

To mount a database is to make it available to the database administrator.

MOUNT AND OPEN A DATABASE

To mount and open a database is to make it available to users.

MULTI-THREADED SERVER

The multi-threaded server (MTS) supports connections to Oracle via dispatcher processes and shared server processes. Dispatcher processes accept connection requests from users, and shared server processes communicate with the database. MTS allows many users to share a small number of shared server processes, potentially reducing the amount of memory required to support the database's users. MTS is most effective when there are many users initiating connections, and when the application users frequently interrupt their data input activity.

NAMES

See OBJECT NAMES.

NEAR

SEE ALSO   CONTAINS, TEXT SEARCH OPERATORS, Chapter 24

DESCRIPTION   Within ConText and IMT, **NEAR** indicates that a proximity search should be executed for the specified text strings. If the search terms are "summer" and "lease," then a proximity search for the two terms could be

```
select Text
  from SONNET
 where CONTAINS(Text,'summer NEAR lease') >0;
```

When evaluating the text search results, text with the words "summer" and "lease" near each other in the text will have higher scores than text with the words "summer" and "lease" farther apart.

NESTED TABLE

Nested tables are collectors available as of Oracle8. A nested table is, as its name implies, a table within a table. In this case, it is a table that is represented as a column within another table. You can have multiple rows in the nested table for each row in the main table. There is no limit to the number of entries per row. *See* Chapter 29 for details on creating, using, and querying nested tables.

NESTING

Nesting is the practice of placing a statement, clause, query, and so on, within another statement, clause, query, and so on.

Net8

Net8 is an optional product that works with the Oracle RDBMS to enable two or more computers running Oracle to exchange data through a network. Earlier versions were called SQL*Net.

NETWORK

A network is a connection among two or more different computers that enables them to exchange information directly.

NEWPAGE (SQL*PLUS)

See **SET**.

NEW_TIME

See DATE FUNCTIONS.

NEXT_DAY

See DATE FUNCTIONS.

NEXTVAL

See PSEUDO-COLUMNS.

NLSSORT

SEE ALSO   *Oracle Server Administrator's Guide,* Chapter 35

FORMAT

```
NLSSORT(character)
```

DESCRIPTION   National Language Support **SORT** gives the collating sequence value (an integer) of the given *character* based on the National Language Support option chosen for the site.

NLS_INITCAP

SEE ALSO   CHARACTER FUNCTIONS, **INITCAP**, Chapter 8

FORMAT

```
NLS_INITCAP(number[, nls_parameters])
```

DESCRIPTION NLS_INITCAP is like the **INITCAP** function except with the addition of a parameter string. The *NLS parameters* string, enclosed in single quotation marks, gives a sort sequence for capitalizing special linguistic sequences. You would usually use **INITCAP** with the default sort sequence for the session, but this function lets you specify the exact sort sequence to use.

NLS_LOWER

SEE ALSO CHARACTER FUNCTIONS, **LOWER**, Chapter 8

FORMAT

```
NLS_LOWER(number[, nls_parameters])
```

DESCRIPTION NLS_LOWER is like the **LOWER** function except with the addition of a parameter string. The *NLS parameters* string, enclosed in single quotation marks, gives a sort sequence for lowercasing special linguistic sequences. You would usually use **LOWER** with the default sort sequence for the session, but this function lets you specify the exact sort sequence to use.

NLS_UPPER

SEE ALSO CHARACTER FUNCTIONS, **UPPER**, Chapter 8

FORMAT

```
NLS_UPPER(number[, nls_parameters])
```

DESCRIPTION NLS_UPPER is like the **UPPER** function except with the addition of a parameter string. The *NLS parameters* string, enclosed in single quotation marks, gives a sort sequence for capitalizing special linguistic sequences. You would usually use **UPPER** with the default sort sequence for the session, but this function lets you specify the exact sort sequence to use.

NOAUDIT (Form 1—SQL Statements)

SEE ALSO AUDIT, **NOAUDIT** (Form 1), PRIVILEGE

SYNTAX

DESCRIPTION   **NOAUDIT** stops auditing of SQL statements being audited as a result of the **AUDIT** command (Form 2). It stops auditing either a statement (*see* **AUDIT**) or a statement authorized by a system privilege (*see* PRIVILEGE). If there is a BY clause with a list of users, the command stops the auditing of statements issued by these users. If there is no BY clause, Oracle stops auditing the statements for all users. The **WHENEVER SUCCESSFUL** option stops auditing only for those statements that successfully complete; **WHENEVER NOT SUCCESSFUL** stops only for those statements that result in an error.

NOAUDIT (Form 2—Schema Objects)

SEE ALSO   **AUDIT**, **CREATE DATABASE LINK**, DATA DICTIONARY VIEWS, Chapter 35
SYNTAX

DESCRIPTION   This form of **NOAUDIT** stops the audit for an option of the use of a table, view, or synonym. To stop the audit of any table, view, or synonym, you must either own them or have DBA authority. *option* refers to the options described shortly. *user* is the username of the object owner. *object* is a table, view, or synonym. *option* specifies what commands the audit should be stopped for. For a table, options are **ALTER, AUDIT, COMMENT, DELETE, GRANT, INDEX, INSERT, LOCK, RENAME, SELECT**, and **UPDATE**. For procedures, functions, types, libraries, and packages, **EXECUTE** commands can be audited. For snapshots, **SELECT**s can be audited. For directories, **READ** can be audited. **GRANT** audits both **GRANT** and **REVOKE** commands. **NOAUDIT GRANT** stops both of them. **ALL** stops the audits of all of these.

ON *object* names the object being audited, and includes a table, view, or a synonym of a table, view or sequence.

For views, **ALTER** and **INDEX** cannot be used. The default options of a view are created by the union of the options of each of the underlying tables plus the DEFAULT options.

For synonyms, the options are the same as tables.

For sequences, the options are **ALTER, AUDIT, GRANT**, and **SELECT**.

WHENEVER SUCCESSFUL turns off auditing for successful writes to the table. **WHENEVER NOT SUCCESSFUL** turns auditing off for unsuccessful writes to the table. Omitting this optional clause turns off both kinds of auditing.

Both formats commit any pending changes to the database. If remote tables are accessed through a database link, any auditing on the remote system is based on options set there. Auditing information is written to a table named SYS.AUD$. *See* Chapter 35 for details on the auditing views.

EXAMPLES The following stops auditing of all attempts at **update** or **delete** on the WORKER table:

```
noaudit update, delete on WORKER;
```

This stops auditing of all unsuccessful access to WORKER:

```
noaudit all on WORKER whenever not successful;
```

NODE

Node can be either of two definitions:

- In a tree-structured table, a node is one row.
- In a network, a node is the location in the network where a computer is attached.

NOLOGGING

The **NOLOGGING** clause for object creation (tables, LOBs, indexes, partitions, etc.) specifies that the creation of the object will not be logged in the online redo log files, and thus will not be recoverable following a media failure. The object creation is not logged, and neither are certain types of transactions against the object. **NOLOGGING** takes the place of the **UNRECOVERABLE** keyword introduced in Oracle7.2. See Chapters 21 and 38.

NON-EQUI-JOIN

A non-equi-join is a join condition other than "equals" (=). *See* EQUI-JOIN.

NOT

SEE ALSO LOGICAL OPERATORS, Chapter 3

DESCRIPTION **NOT** comes before and reverses the effect of any of these logical operators: **BETWEEN**, **IN**, **LIKE**, and **EXISTS**. **NOT** can also come before **NULL**, as in **IS NOT NULL**.

NOT EXISTS

SEE ALSO ANY, ALL, EXISTS, IN, Chapter 12

FORMAT

```
select ...
where NOT EXISTS (select...);
```

DESCRIPTION **NOT EXISTS** returns false in a **where** clause if the subquery that follows it returns one or more rows. The **select** clause in the subquery can be a column, a literal, or an asterisk—it doesn't matter. The only part that matters is whether the **where** clause in the subquery will return a row.

EXAMPLE **NOT EXISTS** is frequently used to determine which records in one table do not have matching records in another table. The query shown in the following example uses **NOT EXISTS** to exclude from the SKILL table all those records that have matching Skills in the WORKERSKILL table. The result of this query will be the list of all skills that no workers possess.

```
select SKILL.Skill
  from SKILL
 where NOT EXISTS
       (select 'x' from WORKERSKILL
         where WORKERSKILL.Skill = SKILL.Skill);


SKILL
----------------
GRAVE DIGGER
```

NULL (Form 1—PL/SQL)

SEE ALSO   BLOCK STRUCTURE

FORMAT

```
NULL;
```

DESCRIPTION   The **NULL** statement has nothing to do with **NULL** values. Its main purpose is to make a section of code more readable by saying, in effect, "do nothing." It also provides a means of having a null block (since PL/SQL requires at least one executable statement between **BEGIN** and **END**). It is usually used as the statement following one (usually the last) of a series of condition tests.

EXAMPLE

```
IF Age > 65 THEN
   ...
ELSEIF AGE BETWEEN 21 and 65 THEN
   ...
ELSE
  NULL;
ENDIF;
```

NULL (Form 2—SQL Column Value)

SEE ALSO   **CREATE TABLE**, GROUP FUNCTIONS, INDICATOR VARIABLE, **NVL**, Chapter 3

DESCRIPTION   A **NULL** value is one that is unknown, irrelevant, or not meaningful. Any Oracle datatype can be **NULL**. That is, any Oracle column in a given row can be without a value (unless the table was created with **NOT NULL** for that column). **NULL** in a NUMBER datatype is not the same as zero.

Few procedural languages directly support the idea of a variable with a **NULL** or unknown value, although Oracle and SQL do so easily. In order to extend languages for which Oracle has developed precompilers to support the **NULL** concept, an INDICATOR VARIABLE is associated with the host variable, almost like a flag, to indicate whether it is **NULL**. The host variable and its indicator variable may be referenced and set separately in the host language code, but are always concatenated in SQL or PL/SQL.

You use the **NVL** function to detect the absence of a value for a column, and convert the **NULL** value into a real value of the datatype of the column. For instance, **NVL**(Name,'NOT KNOWN') converts a **NULL** value in the column Name into the words NOT KNOWN. For a non-**NULL** value (that is, where a name is present), the **NVL** function simply returns the name. **NVL** works similarly with NUMBERs and DATEs.

Except for **COUNT**(*) and **COMPUTE NUMBER**, group functions ignore null values. Other functions return a null value when a **NULL** is present in the value or values they are evaluating. Thus, the following example:

```
NULL + 1066 is NULL.
LEAST(NULL,'A','Z') is NULL.
```

Since **NULL** represents an unknown value, two columns that are each **NULL** are not equal to each other. Therefore, the equal sign and other logical operators (except for **IS NULL** and **IS NOT NULL**) do not work with **NULL**. For example, this:

```
where Name = NULL
```

is not a valid **where** clause. **NULL** requires the word **IS**:

```
where Name IS NULL
```

During **order by** sorts, **NULL** values always come first when the order is ascending, and last when it is descending.

When **NULL** values are stored in the database, they are represented with a single byte if they fall between two columns that have real values, and no bytes if they fall at the end of the row (last in the column definition in the **create table**). If some of the columns in a table are likely to often contain **NULL** values, those columns can be usefully grouped near the end of the **create table** column list; this will save disk space.

NULL values do not appear in indexes, except in the single case where all the values in a cluster key are **NULL**.

NUMBER DATATYPE

A NUMBER datatype is a standard Oracle datatype that may contain a number, with or without a decimal point and a sign. Valid values are 0, and positive and negative numbers with magnitude 1.0E-130 to 9.99.. E125.

NUMBER FORMATS

SEE ALSO   **COLUMN**, Chapter 14

DESCRIPTION   These options work with both **set numformat** and the **column format** command.

Format	Definition
9999990	Count of nines or zeroes determines maximum digits that can be displayed.
999,999,999.99	Commas and decimals will be placed in the pattern shown. Display will be blank if the value is zero.
999990	Displays a zero if the value is zero.
099999	Displays numbers with leading zeros.
$99999	Dollar sign placed in front of every number.
B99999	Display will be blank if value is zero. This is the default.

Format	Definition
99999MI	If number is negative, minus sign follows the number. Default is negative sign on left.
99999S	Same as 99999MI.
S99999	If number is negative, minus sign precedes the number; if number is positive, plus sign precedes the number.
99D99	Displays a decimal character in this position.
C99999	Displays the ISO currency character in this position.
L99999	Displays the local currency character in this position.
RN	Displays the number as a roman numeral.
99999PR	Negative numbers displayed surrounded by < and >.
9.999EEEE	Display will be in scientific notation (must be exactly four Es).
999V99	Multiplies number by 10n where n is number of digits to right of V. 999V99 turns 1234 into 123400.

NUMBER FUNCTIONS

This is an ordered list of all current number functions in Oracle's SQL. Each of these is listed elsewhere in this reference under its own name, with its proper format and use. Each can be used as a regular SQL as well as a PL/SQL function, except for **VSIZE**, which is not available in PL/SQL.

Function	Meaning
value1 + value2	Addition
value1 - value2	Subtraction
value1 * value2	Multiplication
value1 / value2	Division
ABS(value)	Absolute Value of value
ACOS(value)	Arc cosine of value
ASIN(value)	Arc sin of value
ATAN(value)	Arc tangent of value
CEIL(value)	Smallest integer larger than or equal to value
COS(value)	Cosine of the value
COSH(value)	Hyperbolic cosine of the value
EXP(value)	e raised to the valueth power
FLOOR(value)	Largest integer smaller than or equal to value
LN(value)	Natural (base e) logarithm of value
LOG(base, value)	Base logarithm of value
MOD(value,divisor)	Modulus of value divided by divisor
NVL(value,substitute)	Substitute for value if value is NULL
POWER(value,exponent)	Value raised to an exponent
ROUND(value,precision)	Rounding of value to precision
SIGN(value)	1 if value is positive, -1 if negative, if zero
SIN(value)	Sine of value
SINH(value)	Hyperbolic sine of value
SQRT(value)	Square root of value
TAN(value)	Tangent of value
TANH(value)	Hyperbolic tangent of value
TRUNC(value,precision)	Value truncated to precision
VSIZE(value)	Storage size of value in Oracle

NUMWIDTH (SQL*PLUS)

See **SET**.

NVL

SEE ALSO GROUP FUNCTIONS, NULL, OTHER FUNCTIONS, Chapter 8

FORMAT

NVL(*value, substitute*)

DESCRIPTION If *value* is **NULL**, this function is equal to *substitute*. If *value* is not **NULL**, this function is equal to *value*. *value* can be any Oracle datatype. *Substitute* can be a literal, another column, or an expression, but must be the same datatype as *value*.

OBJECT

An object is a named element in the Oracle database, such as a table, index, synonym, procedure, or trigger.

OBJECT NAMES

These database objects may be given names: tables, views, synonyms, aliases, columns, indexes, users, sequences, tablespaces, and so on. The following rules govern naming objects.

- The name of an object can be from 1 to 30 characters long, except for database names, which are up to eight characters, and host file names, whose length is operating system dependent. Snapshot names may not exceed 19 characters in length, and the name of the base table for a snapshot log should not exceed 19 characters in length.

- A name may not contain a quotation mark.

- A name must:
  Begin with a letter
  Contain only the characters A-Z, 0-9, $, #, and _
  Not be an Oracle reserved word (*see* RESERVED WORDS)
  Not duplicate the name of another database object owned by the same user

Object names are not case sensitive. Object names should follow a sensible naming convention, such as is discussed in Chapter 2.

OBJECT TABLE

An object table is a table in which each of its rows is a row object. *See* Chapter 31 and the CREATE TABLE command entry.

OBJECT VIEW

An object view superimposes abstract datatypes on existing relational tables. Object views allow you to access the relational table's data either via normal SQL commands or via its abstract datatype structures. Object views provide a technological bridge between relational and object-relational databases. *See* Chapters 28 and 31 for examples of object views.

OBJECT-RELATIONAL DATABASE MANAGEMENT SYSTEM

An object-relational database management system (ORDBMS) supports both relational database features (such as primary keys and foreign keys) and object-oriented features (such as inheritance and encapsulation). *See* Chapter 4 for a description of Oracle's implementation of an ORDBMS.

OEM

See ORACLE ENTERPRISE MANAGER

OID

An OID is an object identifier, assigned by Oracle to each object in a database. For example, each row object within an object table has an OID value assigned to it; the OID is used to resolve references to the row objects. Oracle does not reuse OID values after an object is dropped. *See* Chapter 31.

ONLINE BACKUP

Online backup is the ability of Oracle to archive data while the database is still running. The DBA does not need to shut down the database to archive data. Even data currently being accessed can be archived.

ONLINE REDO LOG

Online redo logs are redo log files that are not yet archived. They may be available to the instance for recording activity, or have previously been written but are awaiting archiving.

OPEN

SEE ALSO　　CLOSE, DECLARE CURSOR, FETCH, LOOP, Chapter 25

FORMAT

```
OPEN cursor [(parameter[,parameter]...]
```

DESCRIPTION　　**OPEN** works in conjunction with **DECLARE** cursor and **FETCH**. The **DECLARE** cursor sets up a **SELECT** statement to be executed, and establishes a list of parameters (PL/SQL variables) that are to be used in its **where** clause, but it does not execute the query.

　　OPEN *cursor*, in effect, executes the query in the named cursor and keeps its results in a staging area, where they can be called in, a row at a time, with **FETCH**, and their column values put into local variables with the INTO clause of the **FETCH**. If the cursor **SELECT** statement used parameters, then their actual values are passed to the **SELECT** statement in the parameter list of the **OPEN**. They must match in number and position and have compatible datatypes.

　　There is also an alternative method of associating the values in the **OPEN** with those in the **SELECT** list:

```
DECLARE
    cursor talbot(Moniker, Age) is select ...
BEGIN
    open talbot(new_employee => Moniker, 50 => Age);
```

Here, new_employee, a PL/SQL variable, loaded perhaps from a data entry screen, is pointed to Moniker, and therefore loads it with whatever is currently in the variable new_employee. Age is loaded with the value 50, and these then become the parameters of the cursor talbot. (*See* **DECLARE CURSOR** for more details on parameters in cursors.)

You also may combine pointed associations with positional ones, but the positional ones must appear first in the **OPEN**'s list.

You cannot reopen an open cursor, though you can **CLOSE** it and re**OPEN** it, and you cannot use a cursor for which you have a current **OPEN** statement in a cursor FOR LOOP.

OPEN CURSOR (Embedded SQL)

SEE ALSO   CLOSE, DECLARE CURSOR, FETCH, PREPARE

FORMAT

```
EXEC SQL OPEN cursor
  [USING {:variable[ INDICATOR ]:indicator_variable
  [,:variable[ INDICATOR ]:indicator_variable]... |
DESCRIPTOR descriptor}]
```

DESCRIPTION   *cursor* is the name of a cursor previously named in a **DECLARE CURSOR** statement. The optional USING references either the host variable list of variables that are to be substituted in the statement in the **DECLARE CURSOR**, based on position (the number and type of variables must be the same), or a descriptor name that references the result of a previous DESCRIBE.

OPEN cursor allocates a cursor, defines the active set of rows (the host variables are substituted when the cursor is opened), and positions the cursor just before the first row of the set. No rows are retrieved until a **FETCH** is executed. Host variables do not change once they've been substituted. To change them, you must reopen the cursor (you don't have to **CLOSE** it first).

EXAMPLE   This example **DECLARE**s a cursor, **OPEN**s it, **FETCH**es rows, and after no more are found, **CLOSE**s the cursor as shown in the following:

```
EXEC SQL at TALBOT declare FRED cursor
      for select ActionDate, Person, Item, Amount
            from LEDGER
          where Item = :Item
            and ActionDate = :ActionDate
            for update of Amount;

EXEC SQL open FRED;

ledger: loop

  EXEC SQL fetch FRED into :Check_Date, :Buyer, :Choice, :Value;

  if sqlca.sqlcode = oracle.error.not_found
    then exit loop ledger;
  end if;

end loop ledger;

EXEC SQL close FRED;
```

OPEN DATABASE

An open database is a database available for access by users.

OPERATING SYSTEM

An operating system is a computer program that manages the computer's resources and mediates between the computer hardware and programs.

OPERATOR

An operator is a character or reserved word used in an expression to perform an operation, such as addition or comparison, on the elements of the expression. Some examples of operators are * (multiplication), > (greater than comparison), and **ANY** (compares a value to each value returned by a subquery).

OPS$ LOGINS

OPS$ LOGINS are a type of Oracle username in which OPS$ is prefixed to the user's operating system account ID, to simplify logging into Oracle from that ID.

OPTIMIZER

An optimizer is the part of an Oracle kernel that chooses the best way to use the tables and indexes to complete the request made by a SQL statement. *See* Chapter 36.

OR

SEE ALSO   **AND**, TEXT SEARCH OPERATORS, Chapters 3 and 24

DESCRIPTION   **OR** combines logical expressions so that the result is true if either logical expression is true.

EXAMPLE   The following will produce data for both KEENE and SAN FRANCISCO:

```
select * from COMFORT
  where City = 'KEENE' OR City = 'SAN FRANCISCO'
```

Within ConText and IMT, an **OR** operator can be used for searches involving multiple search terms. If either of the search terms is found, and its search score exceeds the specified threshold value, the text will be returned by the search. *See* Chapter 24.

ORACLE APPLICATION SERVER

Oracle Application Server (OAS) allows developers to access Oracle databases from Web-based applications. The developers call procedures from within the database. The procedures, in turn, retrieve or manipulate data, and return results to the developers.

ORACLE ENTERPRISE MANAGER

Oracle Enterprise Manager (OEM) is a product from Oracle Corporation. OEM provides a graphical interface for common DBA tasks, and has add-on features for extended performance tuning and data management capabilities.

ORACLE PARALLEL SERVER

In an Oracle Parallel Server (OPS) environment, multiple instances (usually on a cluster of servers) access a single set of datafiles. OPS provides server failover capability in a high-availability environment, since users can be directed to multiple servers to access the same data.

ORDBMS

See OBJECT-RELATIONAL DATABASE MANAGEMENT SYSTEM.

ORDER BY

SEE ALSO   COLLATION, FROM, GROUP BY, HAVING, SELECT, WHERE
FORMAT

```
ORDER BY { expression [,expression]... |
           position [,position]... }
           alias [,alias]... }
[ ASC | DESC ]
```

DESCRIPTION   The **ORDER BY** clause causes Oracle to sort the results of a query before they are displayed. This can be done either by *expression*, which can be a simple column name or a complex set of functions, an *alias* (*see* Note below), or a column *position* in the **select** clause (*see* Note below). Rows are ordered first by the first expression or position, then by the second, and so on, based on the collating sequence of the host. If **ORDER BY** is not specified, the order in which rows are selected from a table is indeterminate, and may change from one query to the next.

NOTE
Oracle still supports the use of column positions in ORDER BY clauses, but this feature is no longer part of the SQL standard and is not guaranteed to be supported in future releases. Use column aliases instead.

ASC or **DESC** specifies ascending or descending order, and may follow each expression, position, or alias in the **ORDER BY**. **NULL** values precede ascending and follow descending rows in Oracle.

ORDER BY follows any other clauses except FOR UPDATE OF.

If **ORDER BY** and **DISTINCT** are both specified, the **ORDER BY** clause may only refer to columns or expressions that are in the **SELECT** clause.

When the **UNION, INTERSECT,** or **MINUS** operator is used, the names of the columns in the first **select** may differ from the names in subsequent **selects**. **ORDER BY** must use the column name from the first **select**.

Only CHAR, VARCHAR2, NUMBER, and DATE datatypes—and the special datatype RowID—can appear in an **ORDER BY**.

EXAMPLE

```
select Name, Age from WORKER
  order by Age;
```

OTHER FUNCTIONS

This is an alphabetical list of all current functions in Oracle's SQL that do not readily fall into any other function category. Each of these is listed elsewhere in this reference under its own name, with its proper format and use.

DUMP(*string* [,*format* [,*start* [,*length*]]])

DUMP displays the value of *string* in internal data format, in ASCII, octal, decimal, hex, or character format.

NVL(*value*, *substitute*)

If *value* is **NULL**, the **NVL** function is equal to *substitute*. **NVL** also can be used as a PL/SQL function.

VSIZE(*expression*)

VSIZE tells how many bytes Oracle needs in order to store the *expression* in its database.

OUTER JOIN

See JOIN for a detailed explanation.

PACKAGE

A package is a PL/SQL object that groups PL/SQL types, variables, SQL cursors, exceptions, procedures, and functions. Each package has a specification and a body. The specification shows the objects you can access when you use the package. The body fully defines all the objects and can contain additional objects used only for the internal workings. You can change the body (for example, by adding procedures to the package) without invalidating any object that uses the package.

See **CREATE PACKAGE, CREATE PACKAGE BODY**, CURSOR, EXCEPTION, FUNCTION, TABLE (PL/SQL), RECORD (PL/SQL), PROCEDURE, and Chapter 27.

PAGESIZE (SQL*PLUS)

See **SET**.

PARAMETER

A parameter is a value, a column name, or an expression, usually following a function or module name, specifying additional functions or controls that should be observed by the function or module. *See* PARAMETERS for an example.

PARAMETERS

SEE ALSO   &, &&, **ACCEPT, DEFINE**, Chapter 16

DESCRIPTION   Parameters allow the execution of a start file with values passed on the command line. These are simply spaced apart following the name of the start file. Within the file they are referenced by the order in which they appeared on the command line. &1 is the first, &2 the second, and so on. Aside from this, the rules for use are the same as for variables loaded using **DEFINE** or **ACCEPT**, and they may be used in SQL statements in the same way.

There is one limitation, however. There is no way to pass a multiple word argument to a single variable. Each variable can take only one word, date, or number. Attempting to solve this by putting the parameters in quotes on the command line results in the words being concatenated.

EXAMPLE   Suppose you have a start file named **fred.sql** that contains this SQL:

```
select Name, Age
  from WORKER
 where Age > &1;
```

Starting it with this command line:

```
start fred.sql 21
```

produces a report of all workers who are older than 21 years of age.

PARENT

In tree-structured data, a parent is a node that has another node as a descendent, or child.

PARENT QUERY

The parent query is the outermost query (the one that displays a result) in a main query containing a subquery. *See* MAIN QUERY.

PARENTHESES

See LOGICAL OPERATORS and PL/SQL KEY WORDS AND SYMBOLS.

PARSE

Parsing is the mapping of a SQL statement to a cursor. At parse time, several validation checks are made, such as, do all referenced objects exist, are grants proper, and is statement syntax correct? Also, decisions regarding execution and optimization are made, such as which indexes will be used.

PASSWORD

A password is a set of characters that you must enter when you connect to the host computer's operating system or to an Oracle database. Passwords should be kept confidential.

PASSWORD (SQL*PLUS Command)

SEE ALSO   ALTER USER, Chapter 19

DESCRIPTION   You can use the **password** command in SQL*Plus to change your password. If you use the **password** command, your new password will not be displayed on the screen as you type. Users with dba authority can change any user's password via the **password** command; other users can change only their own password.

When you enter the **password** command, you will be prompted for the old and new passwords.

EXAMPLE

```
password
Changing password for dora
Old password:
New password:
Retype new password:
```

When the password has been successfully changed, you will receive the feedback:

```
Password changed
```

PARALLEL QUERY OPTION

The Parallel Query Option (PQO) splits a single database task into multiple coordinated tasks, enabling the task to use multiple processors. For example, a full table scan or a large sort may be parallelized, enabling multiple processors to take part in the completion of the operation. If there are adequate resources available on the server, then the parallelized operation may complete faster than if it ran as a single task.

The number of parallel query server processes used to execute an operation is called the *degree of parallelism*, and is set via the **DEGREE** parameter of hints. See Chapter 36.

PARTITION

To partition a table is to systematically divide its rows among multiple tables, each with the same structure. You can direct the database to automatically partition a table and its indexes. *See* Chapter 18.

PARTITIONED TABLE

A partitioned table is a table whose rows have been partitioned across multiple smaller tables.

PAUSE (Form 1—SQL*PLUS)

See **SET**.

PAUSE (Form 2—SQL*PLUS)

SEE ALSO   **ACCEPT**, **PROMPT**, Chapter 6

FORMAT

```
PAU[SE] [text];
```

DESCRIPTION   **PAUSE** is similar to **PROMPT**, except **PAUSE** first displays an empty line, then a line containing *text*, then waits for the user to press RETURN. If *text* is not entered, **PAUSE** displays two empty lines, then waits for user to press RETURN.

NOTE

PAUSE waits for a RETURN *from the terminal even if the source of command input has been redirected to be from a file, which means a start file with SET TERMOUT OFF could hang, waiting for a* RETURN, *with no message as to why it was waiting (or that it was waiting). Use* **PAUSE** *with caution.*

EXAMPLE

```
prompt Report Complete.
pause Press RETURN to continue.
```

PCTFREE

PCTFREE is a portion of the data block that is not filled by rows as they are inserted into a table, but is reserved for later updates made to the rows in that block.

PCTUSED

PCTUSED is the percentage of space in a data block which Oracle attempts keep filled. If the percent used falls below PCTUSED, then block is added to the list of free blocks in the segment. PCTUSED may be set on a table-by-table basis.

PERSONALITY

ConText servers are configured to support different categories of commands. The collection of categories supported by a ConText server (see Category) defines the server's personality. IMT only requires one personality for its servers. *See* Chapter 24.

PL/SQL Key Words and Symbols

See RESERVED WORDS.

PMON PROCESS

The **P**rocess **MON**itor is a background process used for recovery when a process accessing a database fails. *See* BACKGROUND PROCESS.

POWER

SEE ALSO **SQRT**, Chapter 8

FORMAT

```
POWER(value, exponent)
```

DESCRIPTION **POWER** is *value* raised to an *exponent*.

EXAMPLE

```
POWER(2,4) = 16
```

PRAGMA

A pragma statement is a directive to the compiler, rather than a piece of executable code. Even though a pragma statement looks like executable code, and appears in a program (such as a PL/SQL block), it is not actually executable and doesn't appear as a part of the execution code of that block. Rather, it gives instructions to the compiler. *See* **EXCEPTION_INIT** and Chapter 28.

PRECEDENCE

SEE ALSO LOGICAL OPERATORS, QUERY OPERATORS, Chapter 12

DESCRIPTION The following operators are listed in descending order of precedence. Operators with equal precedence are on the same line. Operators of equal precedence are evaluated in succession from left to right. All **AND**s are evaluated before any **OR**. Each of these is listed and described separately under its own symbol or name in this Alphabetical Reference.

Operator	Function
-	SQL*PLUS command continuation. Continues a command on the following line.
&	Prefix for parameters in a SQL*PLUS start file. Words are substituted for &1, &2, and so on. *See* START.
& &&	Prefix for a substitution in a SQL command in SQL*PLUS. SQL*PLUS will prompt for a value if an undefined & or && variable is found. && also defines the variable and saves the value; '&' does not. *See* & and &&, DEFINE, and ACCEPT.
:	Prefix for a host variable in PL/SQL.
.	Variable separator, used in SQL*PLUS to separate the variable name from a suffix, so that the suffix is not considered a part of the variable name.
( )	Surrounds subqueries or lists of columns.
'	Surrounds a literal, such as a character string or date constant. To use a ' in a string constant, use two ' marks (not a double quotation mark).
"	Surrounds a table or column alias that contains special characters or a space.
"	Surrounds literal text in a date format clause of **TO_CHAR**.
@	Precedes a database name in a COPY, or a link name in a **from** clause.
( )	Overrides normal operator precedence.
+ -	Prefix sign (positive or negative) for a number or number expression.
* /	Multiplication and division.
+ -	Addition and subtraction.
||	Char value concatenation.
NOT	Reverses result of an expression.
AND	True if both conditions are true.
OR	True if either condition is true.
UNION	Returns all distinct rows from both of two queries.
INTERSECT	Returns all matching distinct rows from two queries.
MINUS	Returns all distinct rows in first query that are not in the second.

PRECOMPILER

A precompiler program reads specially structured source code, and writes a modified (precompiled) source program file that a normal compiler can read.

PREDICATE

The predicate is the **where** clause and, more explicitly, a selection criteria clause based on one of the operators (=, !=, IS, IS NOT, >, >=) and containing no **AND**, **OR**, or **NOT**.

PREPARE (Embedded SQL)

SEE ALSO   CLOSE, DECLARE, CURSOR, FETCH, OPEN

FORMAT

```
EXEC SQL PREPARE statement_name FROM {:string | text}
```

DESCRIPTION   **PREPARE** parses SQL in the host variable *:string* or the literal *text*. It assigns a *statement_name* as a reference to the SQL. If the *statement_name* has been used previously, this reference replaces it. The SQL is a select statement, and may include a **for update of** clause. *:string* is not the actual name of the host variable used, but a placeholder. **OPEN CURSOR** assigns input host variables in its **using** clause, and **FETCH** assigns output host variables in its **into** clause, based on position. A statement only needs to be **PREPARE**d once. It can then be executed multiple times.

EXAMPLE

```
query_string : string(1..100)
get(query_string);
EXEC SQL prepare FRED from :query_string;
EXEC SQL execute FRED;
```

PRIMARY KEY

The primary key is the column(s) used to uniquely identify each row of a table.

PRINT

SEE ALSO   BIND VARIABLE, **VARIABLE**

FORMAT

```
PRINT variable1 variable2
```

DESCRIPTION   Displays the current value of the specified variable (which is created via the **VARIABLE** command). You can **print** the current values of multiple variables in a single command.

PRIOR

See **CONNECT BY**.

PRIVILEGE

A privilege is a permission granted to an Oracle user to execute some action. In Oracle, no user can execute any action without having the privilege to do so.

There are two kinds of privileges: system privileges and object privileges. System privileges extend permission to execute various data definition and data control commands such as **CREATE TABLE** or **ALTER USER**, or even to log onto the database. Object privileges extend permission to operate on a particular named database object.

System privileges in Oracle include CREATE, ALTER, and DROP privileges for the various **CREATE**, **ALTER**, and **DROP** commands. Privileges with the keyword **ANY** in them mean that the user can exercise the privilege on any schema for which the privilege has been granted, not just his or her own schema. The standard privileges in the list following just give permission to execute the indicated command, and don't require further explanation. Some of the privileges aren't intuitively clear; these are explained here.

Privilege	Permission to
ADMINISTER DATABASE TRIGGER	CREATE TRIGGER
ALTER ANY CLUSTER	ALTER CLUSTER
ALTER ANY DIMENSION	ALTER DIMENSION
ALTER ANY INDEX	ALTER INDEX
ALTER ANY MATERIALIZED VIEW	ALTER MATERIALIZED VIEW
ALTER ANY OUTLINE	ALTER OUTLINE
ALTER ANY PROCEDURE	ALTER PROCEDURE, ALTER FUNCTION, ALTER PACKAGE
ALTER ANY ROLE	ALTER ROLE
ALTER ANY SEQUENCE	ALTER SEQUENCE

Privilege	Permission to
ALTER ANY SNAPSHOT	ALTER SNAPSHOT
ALTER ANY TABLE	ALTER TABLE
ALTER ANY TRIGGER	ALTER TRIGGER
ALTER ANY TYPE	ALTER TYPE
ALTER DATABASE	ALTER DATABASE
ALTER PROFILE	ALTER PROFILE
ALTER RESOURCE COST	ALTER RESOURCE COST
ALTER ROLLBACK SEGMENT	ALTER ROLLBACK SEGMENT
ALTER SESSION	ALTER SESSION
ALTER SYSTEM	ALTER SYSTEM
ALTER TABLESPACE	ALTER TABLESPACE
ALTER USER	ALTER USER
ANALYZE ANY	ANALYZE
AUDIT ANY	AUDIT (FORM 1)
AUDIT SYSTEM	AUDIT (FORM 2)
BACKUP ANY TABLE	Allows export of objects from any schema
BECOME USER	Allows import of objects from any schema
COMMENT ANY TABLE	COMMENT
CREATE ANY CLUSTER	CREATE CLUSTER
CREATE ANY CONTEXT	CREATE CONTEXT
CREATE ANY DIMENSION	CREATE DIMENSION
CREATE ANY DIRECTORY	CREATE DIRECTORY
CREATE ANY INDEX	CREATE INDEX
CREATE ANY INDEXTYPE	CREATE INDEXTYPE
CREATE ANY LIBRARY	CREATE LIBRARY
CREATE ANY MATERIALIZED VIEW	CREATE MATERIALIZED VIEW
CREATE ANY OPERATOR	CREATE OPERATOR
CREATE ANY OUTLINE	CREATE OUTLINE
CREATE ANY PROCEDURE	CREATE PROCEDURE
CREATE ANY SEQUENCE	CREATE SEQUENCE
CREATE ANY SNAPSHOT	CREATE SNAPSHOT
CREATE ANY SYNONYM	CREATE SYNONYM
CREATE ANY TABLE	CREATE TABLE
CREATE ANY TRIGGER	CREATE TRIGGER
CREATE ANY TYPE	CREATE TYPE, CREATE TYPE BODY
CREATE ANY VIEW	CREATE VIEW
CREATE CLUSTER	CREATE CLUSTER
CREATE DATABASE LINK	CREATE DATABASE LINK
CREATE DIMENSION	CREATE DIMENSION
CREATE DIRECTORY	CREATE DIRECTORY
CREATE INDEXTYPE	CREATE INDEXTYPE
CREATE LIBRARY	CREATE LIBRARY
CREATE MATERIALIZED VIEW	CREATE MATERIALIZED VIEW
CREATE OPERATOR	CREATE OPERATOR
CREATE PROCEDURE	CREATE PROCEDURE, CREATE FUNCTION, CREATE PACKAGE

Privilege	Permission to
CREATE PROFILE	CREATE PROFILE
CREATE PUBLIC DATABASE LINK	CREATE PUBLIC DATABASE LINK
CREATE PUBLIC SYNONYM	CREATE PUBLIC SYNONYM
CREATE ROLE	CREATE ROLE
CREATE ROLLBACK SEGMENT	CREATE ROLLBACK SEGMENT
CREATE SESSION	CREATE SESSION (log onto database)
CREATE SEQUENCE	CREATE SEQUENCE
CREATE SNAPSHOT	CREATE SNAPSHOT
CREATE SYNONYM	CREATE SYNONYM
CREATE TABLE	CREATE TABLE
CREATE TABLESPACE	CREATE TABLESPACE
CREATE TRIGGER	CREATE TRIGGER
CREATE TYPE	CREATE TYPE, CREATE TYPE BODY
CREATE USER	CREATE USER
CREATE VIEW	CREATE VIEW
DELETE ANY TABLE	DELETE (from tables or views)
DROP ANY CLUSTER	DROP CLUSTER
DROP ANY CONTEXT	DROP CONTEXT
DROP ANY DIMENSION	DROP DIMENSION
DROP ANY DIRECTORY	DROP DIRECTORY
DROP ANY INDEX	DROP INDEX
DROP ANY INDEXTYPE	DROP INDEXTYPE
DROP ANY LIBRARY	DROP LIBRARY
DROP ANY MATERIALIZED VIEW	DROP MATERIALIZED VIEW
DROP ANY OUTLINE	DROP OUTLINE
DROP ANY OPERATOR	DROP ANY OPERATOR
DROP ANY PROCEDURE	DROP PROCEDURE, DROP FUNCTION, DROP PACKAGE
DROP ANY ROLE	DROP ROLE
DROP ANY SEQUENCE	DROP SEQUENCE
DROP ANY SNAPSHOT	DROP SNAPSHOT
DROP ANY SYNONYM	DROP SYNONYM
DROP ANY TABLE	DROP TABLE
DROP ANY TRIGGER	DROP TRIGGER
DROP ANY TYPE	DROP TYPE
DROP ANY VIEW	DROP VIEW
DROP LIBRARY	DROP LIBRARY
DROP PROFILE	DROP PROFILE
DROP PUBLIC DATABASE LINK	DROP PUBLIC DATABASE LINK
DROP PUBLIC SYNONYM	DROP PUBLIC SYNONYM
DROP ROLLBACK SEGMENT	DROP ROLLBACK SEGMENT
DROP TABLESPACE	DROP TABLESPACE
DROP USER	DROP USER
EXECUTE ANY INDEXTYPE	Reference an indextype
EXECUTE ANY OPERATOR	Reference any operator
EXECUTE ANY PROCEDURE	Allows execution of any function or procedure or reference to any public package variable

Privilege	Permission to
EXECUTE ANY TYPE	Allows use of any abstract datatype and its methods
FORCE ANY TRANSACTION	Allows forcing of commit or rollback of any in-doubt transaction (*see* TWO-PHASE COMMIT*)*
FORCE TRANSACTION	Allows forcing of commit or rollback of user's own in-doubt transactions
GLOBAL QUERY REWRITE	Enable rewrite using materialized views based on objects in other schemas
GRANT ANY PRIVILEGE	GRANT system privilege
GRANT ANY ROLE	GRANT a role
INSERT ANY TABLE	INSERT
LOCK ANY TABLE	LOCK TABLE
MANAGE TABLESPACE	Allows taking tablespaces on and off line and tablespace backups
QUERY REWRITE	Enable rewrite using materialized views
READUP	Allows query of data with a higher access class than the current session possesses (Trusted Oracle)
RESTRICTED SESSION	Allows logon after instance startup in restricted access mode by Server Manager
SELECT ANY SEQUENCE	SELECT from sequences
SELECT ANY TABLE	SELECT
UNLIMITED TABLESPACE	Allows overriding of assigned quotas
UPDATE ANY TABLE	UPDATE
WRITEDOWN	Allows CREATE, ALTER, DROP, INSERT, UPDATE, or DELETE of objects with access classes lower than the current session's (Trusted Oracle)
WRITEUP	Allows CREATE, ALTER, DROP, INSERT, UPDATE, or DELETE of objects with access classes higher than the current session's (Trusted Oracle)

Object privileges apply only to certain kinds of objects. The following table shows the relationships. The REFERENCES privilege allows a user to create a constraint that refers to the base table.

Object Privilege	Table	View	Sequence	Procedures, Functions, Packages	Materialized View/ Snapshot	Directory	Library	User-defined Type	Operator	Indextype
ALTER	X		X							
DELETE	X	X			X					
EXECUTE				X			X	X	X	X
INDEX	X									
INSERT	X	X			X					
READ						X				
REFERENCES	X									
SELECT	X	X	X		X					
UPDATE	X	X			X					

As shown in this table, you can select from tables, views, sequences, or materialized views.

PRO*C

PRO*C is an extension to C that lets you develop user exits and other programs that access the Oracle database. A precompiler converts PRO*C code into normal C code, which can then be compiled.

PROCEDURE

A procedure is a set of instructions (usually combining SQL and PL/SQL commands) saved for calling and repeated execution. *See* **CREATE PROCEDURE**.

PRODUCT_USER_PROFILE

A PRODUCT_USER_PROFILE is a SYSTEM table in Oracle used to restrict use of individual Oracle products, by disabling one or more commands available in the product. *See SQL*Plus User's Guide and Reference.*

PROFILE

A profile is a collection of settings in Oracle that limit database resources. *See* **CREATE PROFILE** and Chapter 19.

PROMPT

SEE ALSO   ACCEPT

FORMAT

```
PROMPT [text]
```

DESCRIPTION   Displays the *text* to the user's screen. If no *text* is specified, then a blank line will be displayed. To display a variable, *see* **PRINT**.

PSEUDO-COLUMNS

DESCRIPTION   A pseudo-column is a "column" that yields a value when selected, but which is not an actual column of the table. An example is RowID or SysDate. Here are the current Oracle pseudo-columns:

Pseudo-column	Value Returned
sequence.CurrVal	Current value for this sequence name.
Level	Equal to 1 for a root node, 2 for a child of a root, and so on. Tells basically how far down a tree you've traveled.
sequence.NextVal	Next value for this sequence name. Also increments the sequence.
NULL	A null value.
RowID	Returns the row identifier for a row. Use the RowID in the UPDATE ... WHERE and SELECT ... FOR UPDATE. This guarantees that only a certain row is updated, and no others.
RowNum	Returns the sequence number in which a row was returned when selected from a table. The first row RowNum is 1, the second is 2, and so on. An **order by** will affect the sequence of the ROWNUMs. *See* RowNum in this Alphabetical Reference and Chapter 16 for a discussion.
SysDate	The current date and time.
UID	User ID. A unique number assigned to each user.
User	Name by which the current user is known.

PUBLIC

Public can have either of two definitions:

- Something public can be visible or available to all users. Synonyms and database links can be public. In Oracle, a user must have CREATE PUBLIC SYNONYM or CREATE PUBLIC DATABASE LINK privilege. Users may GRANT PUBLIC access to their own objects.
- A group to which every database user belongs—the name of that group.

PUBLIC SYNONYM

A public synonym is a synonym for a database object that a user with CREATE PUBLIC SYNONYM privilege has created for use by all Oracle users.

QUERY

A query is a SQL instruction to retrieve data from one or more tables or views. Queries begin with the SQL keyword **select**.

QUERY OPERATORS

The following is an alphabetical list of all current query operators in Oracle's SQL. Each of these is listed elsewhere in this reference under its own name, with its proper format and use. *See also* Chapter 12.

Operator	Purpose
UNION	Returns all distinct rows from both of two queries
UNION ALL	Returns all rows from both of two queries
INTERSECT	Returns all matching distinct rows from two queries
MINUS	Returns all distinct rows in first query that are not in the second

QUIT

SEE ALSO   **COMMIT, DISCONNECT, EXIT, SET AUTOCOMMIT, START**

FORMAT

```
QUIT
```

DESCRIPTION   QUIT ends a SQL*PLUS session and returns the user to an operating system, calling program, or menu.

QUOTA

A quota is a resource limit. Quotas can limit the amount of storage used by each user of the database. *See* **CREATE USER** and **ALTER USER**.

RAISE

SEE ALSO   **DECLARE EXCEPTION, EXCEPTION, EXCEPTION_INIT**

FORMAT

```
RAISE [exception]
```

DESCRIPTION   **RAISE** names the exception flag you want to raise, based on a condition that is being tested. The exception must either be one you've explicitly **DECLARE**d, or an internal system exception such as DIVIDE_BY_ZERO (*see* EXCEPTION for a complete list).

A **RAISE** statement causes control to be transferred to the EXCEPTION section of the current block, where you must test to see which exception was raised. If no EXCEPTION section is present, control is passed to the nearest EXCEPTION section of an enclosing block (basically backward through the nesting of the blocks). If no logic is found to handle the exception, control is passed from the PL/SQL to the calling program or environment with an unhandled exception error. (The use of OTHERS can avoid this. *See* EXCEPTION.)

RAISE without an explicitly named exception can only be used in one circumstance: within an EXCEPTION section, in order to force the current exception to be handled by an enclosing block's EXCEPTION section, rather than the current one. If, for instance, a NOT_LOGGED_ON error had occurred, and your local EXCEPTION section says this:

```
when not_logged_on
    then raise;
```

it would pass control back to the EXCEPTION section of the next enclosing block that had one, or to the program if none were found. That EXCEPTION block could also test for NOT_LOGGED_ON. The benefit here is that for a certain class of errors, particularly where the recovery, tracing, or error-logging steps you want to take may be extensive, you can set every nested block's EXCEPTION section to simply hand the EXCEPTION backward to a single spot for disposition.

RAW DATATYPE

A RAW column contains binary data in whatever form the host computer stores it. Raw columns are useful for storing binary (non-character) data.

RAWTOHEX

SEE ALSO   HEXTORAW

FORMAT

```
RAWTOHEX(binary_string)
```

DESCRIPTION   RAW TO HEXadecimal changes a string of binary numbers to a character string of hex numbers.

RDBMS

See RELATIONAL DATABASE MANAGEMENT SYSTEM.

READ CONSISTENCY

Read consistency is a state that guarantees that all data encountered by a statement/transaction is a consistent set throughout the duration of the statement/transaction. *See* **SET TRANSACTION**.

RECORD

Record is a synonym for row.

RECORD (PL/SQL)

SEE ALSO   TABLE (PL/SQL), DATA TYPES

FORMAT

```
TYPE new_type IS RECORD
  (field {type | table.column%TYPE}[NOT NULL]
  [,field {type | table.column%TYPE}[NOT NULL]...]);
```

DESCRIPTION   A RECORD declaration declares a new type that can then be used to declare variables of that type. The individual components of the record are fields, and each has its own datatype. That datatype can either be one of the standard PL/SQL datatypes (including another RECORD but not a TABLE), or it can be a reference to the type of a particular column in a specific table. Each field also may have a NOT NULL qualifier that specifies that the field must always have a non-null value.

You can refer to the individual fields in a record using dot notation.

EXAMPLE

```
type SkillRecord is record(
  name char(25),
  skill WORKERSKILL.Skill%TYPE);
SkillRecord MySkill;
MySkill.Name = 'DICK JONES';
MySkill.Skill = 'SMITHY';
```

RECORD LOCKING

Record locking protects two users from updating the same row of data at the same time.

RECOVER

See **ALTER DATABASE** for the complete syntax for the **RECOVER** clause.

The **RECOVER** clause of the **ALTER DATABASE** command recovers a database using various options. **AUTOMATIC** recovery generates the redo log file names automatically during recovery. The **FROM** clause specifies the location of the archived redo log file group and must be a fully qualified filename. The default is set by the initialization parameter LOG_ARCHIVE_DEST.

The **DATABASE** option recovers the entire database and is the default. The **UNTIL CANCEL** alternative recovers the database until you cancel the recovery with the **CANCEL** option. The **UNTIL TIME** alternative recovers up to a specified date and time. The **UNTIL CHANGE** alternative recovers up to a *system change number* (a unique number assigned to each transaction) specified by an integer. The **USING BACKUP CONTROLFILE** alternative recovers by applying the redo log in a backup control file.

RECOVERY MANAGER

Recovery Manager (RMAN) is a product from Oracle Corporation. RMAN is used by DBAs to perform database backups. The information about the backups is stored either in an RMAN repository database or in the control files of the databases being backed up.

RECSEP (SQL*PLUS)

See **SET**.

RECSEPCHAR (SQL*PLUS)

See **SET**.

RECURSIVE CALLS

A recursive call is a nested invocation of the RDBMS; for example, auditing information is recorded in system tables using a recursive call. That is, during a normal database operation, such as an **update**, another database operation is executed to write log, auditing, or other vital information *about* the normal database operation underway. *See* CALL, RECURSIVE.

REDO LOG

A redo log is a sequential log of actions in the database. The log always consists of at least two files; one is optionally being archived while the other is being written. When the one currently being written fills, the next one is reused.

REDO LOG SEQUENCE NUMBER

The redo log sequence number is a number used to identify a redo log, used when applying the log file for recovery.

REF

A reference datatype used with object tables. *See* Chapter 31.

REFERENTIAL INTEGRITY

Referential integrity is the property that guarantees that values from one column depend on values from another column. This property is enforced through integrity constraints. *See* INTEGRITY CONSTRAINT.

REFERENTIAL INTEGRITY RULE

A referential integrity rule is an integrity constraint that enforces referential integrity.

RELATION

See TABLE and Chapter 1.

RELATIONAL DATABASE MANAGEMENT SYSTEM

An RDBMS is a computer program for general-purpose data storage and retrieval that organizes data into tables consisting of one or more units of information (rows), each containing the same set of data items (columns). Oracle is a relational database management system.

RELATIONAL OPERATOR

A relational operator is a symbol used in search criteria to indicate a comparison between two values, such as the equal sign in "where Amount = .10". Only those rows are returned (fetched) for which the comparison results in TRUE.

REMARK

SEE ALSO /* */, - -, DOCUMENT, Chapter 6
FORMAT

```
REM[ARK] text
```

DESCRIPTION **REMARK** begins a single line of remarks, usually documentation, in a start file. It is not interpreted as a command. **REMARK** cannot appear within a SQL statement.
EXAMPLE

```
REM Reduce the default column width for this data field:
column ActionDate format a6 trunc
```

REMOTE COMPUTER

A remote computer refers to any computer in a network other than one's own host computer.

REMOTE DATABASE

A remote database is one that resides on a remote computer, in particular, one that you use through a database link.

RENAME

SEE ALSO COPY, CREATE SYNONYM, CREATE TABLE, CREATE VIEW
SYNTAX

```
RENAME ─▶(old)─▶ TO ─▶(new)─▶( ; )
```

DESCRIPTION **RENAME** changes the name of a table, view, or synonym from its old name to a new one. No quotes are used around the names, and the new name must be neither a reserved word nor the name of an existing object for the user.
EXAMPLE The following changes the WORKER table to the EMPLOYEE table:

```
rename WORKER to EMPLOYEE;
```

REPEATABLE READ

Repeatable read is a feature in which multiple subsequent queries return a consistent set of results, as though changes to the data were suspended until all the queries finished.

REPFOOTER

SEE ALSO ACCEPT, BTITLE, DEFINE, PARAMETERS, **REPHEADER**, Chapter 14
FORMAT

```
REPF[OOTER] [option [text|variable]... | OFF|ON]
```

DESCRIPTION **REPFOOTER** (**REP**ort **FOOTER**) puts a footer (may be multi-line) on the last page of a report. OFF and ON suppress and restore the display of the text without changing its contents. **REPFOOTER** by itself displays the current **REPFOOTER** options and *text* or *variable*.

text is a footer you wish to give this report, and *variable* is a user-defined variable or a system-maintained variable, including SQL.LNO, the current line number; SQL.PNO, the current page number; SQL.RELEASE, the current Oracle release number; SQL.SQLCODE, the current error code; and SQL.USER, the username.

Valid values for option are

- **PAGE** prints the report footer on the last page of the report, following the last page of the body of the report.

- **COL[UMN]** *n* skips directly to position *n* from the left margin of the current line.

- **S[KIP]** *n* prints *n* blank lines. If no *n* is specified, one blank line is printed. If *n* is 0, no blank lines are printed and the current position for printing becomes position 1 of the current line (leftmost on the page).

- **TAB** *n* skips forward *n* positions (backward if *n* is negative).

- **LE[FT]**, **CE[NTER]**, and **R[IGHT]** left-justify, center, and right-justify data on the current line. Any text or variables following these commands are justified as a group, up to the end of the command, or a LEFT, CENTER, RIGHT, or COLUMN. CENTER and RIGHT use the value set by the **SET LINESIZE** command to determine where to place the text or variable.

- **FORMAT** string specifies the format model that will control the format of subsequent text or variables, and follows the same syntax as FORMAT in a **COLUMN** command, such as FORMAT A12 or FORMAT $999,990.99. Each time a FORMAT appears, it supersedes the previous one that was in effect. If no FORMAT model has been specified, the one set by **SET NUMFORMAT** is used. If NUMFORMAT has not been set, the default for SQL*PLUS is used.

Date values are printed according to the default format unless a variable has been loaded with a date reformatted by **TO_CHAR**.

REPHEADER

SEE ALSO   ACCEPT, **BTITLE**, **DEFINE**, PARAMETERS, **REPFOOTER**, Chapter 14
FORMAT

```
REPH[EADER] [option [text|variable]... | OFF|ON]
```

DESCRIPTION   **REPHEADER** (**REP**ort **HEADER**) puts a header (may be multi-line) on the first page of a report. OFF and ON suppress and restore the display of the text without changing its contents. **REPHEADER** by itself displays the current **REPHEADER** options and *text* or *variable*.

text is a header you wish to give this report, and *variable* is a user-defined variable or a system-maintained variable, including SQL.LNO, the current line number; SQL.PNO, the current page number; SQL.RELEASE, the current Oracle release number; SQL.SQLCODE, the current error code; and SQL.USER, the username.

Valid values for option are

- **PAGE** prints the report header on the first page of the report, and prints the body of the report starting on the second page.

- **COL[UMN]** *n* skips directly to position *n* from the left margin of the current line.

- **S[KIP]** *n* prints *n* blank lines. If no *n* is specified, one blank line is printed. If *n* is 0, no blank lines are printed and the current position for printing becomes position 1 of the current line (leftmost on the page).

- **TAB** *n* skips forward *n* positions (backward if *n* is negative).
- **LE[FT]**, **CE[NTER]**, and **R[IGHT]** left-justify, center, and right-justify data on the current line. Any text or variables following these commands are justified as a group, up to the end of the command, or a LEFT, CENTER, RIGHT, or COLUMN. CENTER and RIGHT use the value set by the **SET LINESIZE** command to determine where to place the text or variable.
- **FORMAT** string specifies the format model that will control the format of subsequent text or variables, and follows the same syntax as FORMAT in a **COLUMN** command, such as FORMAT A12 or FORMAT $999,990.99. Each time a FORMAT appears, it supersedes the previous one that was in effect. If no FORMAT model has been specified, the one set by **SET NUMFORMAT** is used. If NUMFORMAT has not been set, the default for SQL*PLUS is used.

Date values are printed according to the default format unless a variable has been loaded with a date reformatted by **TO_CHAR**.

REPLACE

SEE ALSO   CHARACTER FUNCTIONS, **TRANSLATE**
FORMAT

```
REPLACE(string,if,then)
```

DESCRIPTION   **REPLACE** replaces a character or characters in a string with 0 or more characters. *if* is a character or characters. Every time it appears in *string*, it is replaced by the contents of *then*.

EXAMPLE

```
REPLACE('ADAH','A','BLAH') = BLAHDBLAHH
REPLACE('GEORGE','GE',null) = OR
REPLACE('BOB','BO','TA') = TAB
```

REPLICATION

Replication is the process of copying data from one database to another. The target to which the replicated data is copied is called the replica. To manage replication, you will need to determine:

- The location, structure, and ownership of the source data
- The update frequency of the source data
- The timeliness requirements for the replica data
- The volatility of the source data
- The intended uses of the replica

If the replica will also be able to make changes, and those changes must be propagated back to the original source database, then you have a *multi-master* configuration, and you will have to manage conflict resolution and error handling for the environment. In general, single-site ownership of data with multiple read-only replicas will be simpler to manage than a multi-master configuration.

See **CREATE MATERIALIZED VIEW**, **CREATE DATABASE LINK**.

RESERVED WORDS

SEE ALSO   OBJECT NAMES

DESCRIPTION   A reserved word is one that has a special meaning to SQL, and therefore may not be used as the name of an object. Contrast this to keyword, which may be used as an object name, but may become a reserved word in the future. Not every word is reserved in all products, so this list is structured to show which products reserve which words. In the following table, the entries with *s are reserved in SQL and in PL/SQL. The entries without *s are reserved only in PL/SQL.

ALL*	ALTER*	AND*	ANY*	ARRAY
AS*	ASC*	AUTHID	AVG	BEGIN
BETWEEN*	BINARY_INTEGER	BODY	BOOLEAN	BULK
BY*	CHAR*	CHAR_BASE	CHECK*	CLOSE
CLUSTER*	COLLECT	COMMENT*	COMMIT	COMPRESS*
CONNECT*	CONSTANT	CREATE*	CURRENT*	CURRVAL
CURSOR	DATE*	DAY	DECLARE	DECIMAL*
DEFAULT*	DELETE*	DESC*	DISTINCT*	DO
DROP*	ELSE*	ELSIF	END	EXCEPTION
EXCLUSIVE*	EXECUTE	EXISTS*	EXIT	EXTENDS
FALSE	FETCH	FLOAT*	FOR*	FORALL
FROM*	FUNCTION	GOTO	GROUP*	HAVING*
HEAP	HOUR	IF	IMMEDIATE*	IN*
INDEX*	INDICATOR	INSERT*	INTEGER*	INTERFACE
INTERSECT*	INTERVAL	INTO*	IS*	ISOLATION
JAVA	LEVEL*	LIKE*	LIMITED	LOCK*
LONG*	LOOP	MAX	MIN	MINUS*
MINUTE	MLSLABEL*	MOD	MODE*	MONTH
NATURAL	NATURALN	NEW	NEXTVAL	NOCOPY
NOT*	NOWAIT*	NULL*	NUMBER*	NUMBER_BASE
OCIROWID	OF*	ON*	OPAQUE	OPEN
OPERATOR	OPTION*	OR*	ORDER*	ORGANIZATION
OTHERS	OUT	PACKAGE	PARTITION	PCTFREE*
PLS_INTEGER	POSITIVE	POSITIVEN	PRAGMA	PRIOR*
PRIVATE	PROCEDURE	PUBLIC*	RAISE	RANGE
RAW*	REAL	RECORD	REF	RELEASE
RETURN	REVERSE	ROLLBACK	ROW*	ROWID*
ROWLABEL	ROWNUM*	ROWTYPE	SAVEPOINT	SECOND
SELECT*	SEPARATE	SET*	SHARE*	SMALLINT*
SPACE	SQL	SQLCODE	SQLERRM	START*
STDDEV	SUBTYPE	SUCCESSFUL*	SUM	SYNONYM*
SYSDATE*	TABLE*	THEN*	TIME	TIMESTAMP
TO*	TRIGGER*	TRUE	TYPE	UID*
UNION*	UNIQUE*	UPDATE*	USE	USER*
VALIDATE*	VALUES*	VARCHAR*	VARCHAR2*	VARIANCE
VIEW*	WHEN	WHENEVER*	WHERE*	WHILE
WITH*	WORK	WRITE	YEAR	ZONE

RESOURCE

Resource is a general term for a logical database object or physical structure that may be locked. Resources that users can directly lock are rows and tables; resources that the RDBMS can lock are numerous and include data dictionary tables, caches, and files.

RESOURCE is also the name of a standard role in Oracle. *See* ROLE.

REVERSE-KEY INDEX

In a reverse-key index, the bytes of the indexed value are reversed prior to being stored in the index. Thus, values 1234 and 1235 are indexed as if they were 4321 and 5321. As a result of this reversal, those two values will be stored farther apart. If you are frequently querying the column for an exact match (*column=1234*) then a reverse-key index may reduce block contention within your index. If you are frequently performing range queries (*column>1234* or *column like 123%*) then traditional indexes should be more appropriate for your needs. *See* **CREATE INDEX**.

REVOKE (Form 1—System Privileges and Roles)

SEE ALSO　　DISABLE, ENABLE, **GRANT**, **REVOKE** (Form 2), PRIVILEGE, Chapter 19
SYNTAX

DESCRIPTION　　The **REVOKE** command takes privileges and roles away from users or privileges away from roles. Any system privilege may be revoked; *see* PRIVILEGE.

If you revoke a privilege from a user, the user can no longer execute the operations allowed by the privilege. If you revoke a privilege from a role, no user granted the role can execute the allowed operations, unless they are permitted by another role or directly as a user. If you revoke a privilege from **PUBLIC**, no user granted the privilege through **PUBLIC** can execute the operations allowed by the privilege.

If you revoke a role from a user, the user can no longer enable the role (*see* **ENABLE**) but may continue exercising the privilege in a current session. If you revoke a role from a role, users granted the role can no longer enable the role but may continue using the privilege during the current session. If you revoke a role from **PUBLIC**, users granted the role through **PUBLIC** can no longer enable the role.

REVOKE (Form 2—Object Privileges)

SEE ALSO　　**GRANT**, **REVOKE** (Form 1), PRIVILEGE, Chapter 19

**SYNTAX
DESCRIPTION**

The **REVOKE** command takes object privileges on a specific object away from a user or role. If a user's privileges are revoked, the user may not execute the operations allowed by the privilege on the object. If a role's privileges are revoked, no user granted the role may execute those operations unless they are granted through another role or directly to the user. If the PUBLIC's privileges are revoked, no user granted the privilege through **PUBLIC** may execute those operations.

The **CASCADE CONSTRAINTS** clause drops any referential integrity constraints defined by the user or by users granted the role. This applies to a REFERENCES privilege.

ROLE

A role is a set of privileges that a user can grant to another user. Oracle has many system- supplied roles, as listed in the following table. The first three are the most commonly used.

These default roles have the following granted roles and privileges (*see* PRIVILEGE):

Role	Privileges
CONNECT	ALTER SESSION, CREATE CLUSTER, CREATE DATABASE LINK, CREATE SEQUENCE, CREATE SESSION, CREATE SYNONYM, CREATE TABLE, CREATE VIEW
RESOURCE	CREATE CLUSTER, CREATE INDEXTYPE CREATE OPERATOR, CREATE PROCEDURE, CREATE SEQUENCE, CREATE TABLE, CREATE TRIGGER, CREATE TYPE UNLIMITED TABLESPACE
DBA	All system privileges WITH ADMIN OPTION, EXP_FULL_DATABASE role, IMP_FULL_DATABASE role
EXP_FULL_DATABASE	SELECT ANY TABLE, BACKUP ANY TABLE, INSERT, UPDATE, DELETE ON SYS.INCEXP, SYS.INCVID, SYS.INCFIL
IMP_FULL_DATABASE	BECOME USER
DELETE_CATALOG_ROLE	DELETE on SYS.AUD$
EXECUTE_CATALOG_ROLE	EXECUTE on data dictionary packages
SELECT_CATALOG_ROLE	SELECT on data dictionary views
SNMPAGENT	SELECT on a variety of data dictionary views, for use by the DBSNMP account for the Intelligent Agent

Role	Privileges
AQ_ADMINISTRATOR_ROLE	Administrative privileges for the advanced queueing option
AQ_USER_ROLE	User privileges for the advanced queueing option
HS_ADMIN	Administrative privileges for the heterogeneous services
RECOVERY_CATALOG_OWNER	Ownership of the recovery catalog used by Recovery Manager

See Chapter 19 for examples of creating and using roles.

ROLL FORWARD

Roll forward is the reapplying of changes to the database. You sometimes need it for media recovery and sometimes for instance recovery. The **REDO LOG** contains the redo entries used for roll forward.

ROLLBACK

A rollback discards part or all of the work you have done in the current transaction, since the last **COMMIT** or **SAVEPOINT**.

ROLLBACK (Form I—SQL)

SEE ALSO   **COMMIT**, **SET AUTOCOMMIT**, Chapter 15

SYNTAX

DESCRIPTION   **ROLLBACK** reverses all changes made to tables in the database since changes were last committed or rolled back and releases any locks on the tables. An automatic rollback occurs whenever a transaction is interrupted, such as by an execution error, a power failure, and so on. **ROLLBACK** affects not just the last **insert**, **update**, or **delete** statement but any that have occurred since the last **COMMIT**. This allows you to treat blocks of work as a whole and only **COMMIT** when all of the changes you want are completed.

With **SAVEPOINT**, **ROLLBACK** goes to a specific, named place in the sequence of transactions being processed, the **SAVEPOINT**. It erases any interim **SAVEPOINT**s and releases any table or row locks that occurred after the **SAVEPOINT** was made.

With **FORCE**, **ROLLBACK** manually rolls back an in-doubt transaction identified by the literal text, which is a local or global transaction ID from the data dictionary view DBA_2PC_PENDING.

Note that if **SET AUTOCOMMIT** is ON, every **insert**, **update**, or **delete** will immediately and automatically commit the changes to the database. Typing the word **ROLLBACK** will produce this message:

```
ROLLBACK COMPLETE
```

but it won't mean anything. The changes will stay, because **ROLLBACK** only rolls back to the last COMMIT, and that happened automatically after your last change.

ALTER, **AUDIT**, **CONNECT**, **CREATE**, **DISCONNECT**, **DROP**, **EXIT**, **GRANT**, **NOAUDIT**, **QUIT**, **REVOKE**, and **SAVE** all cause a **COMMIT**.

ROLLBACK (Form 2—Embedded SQL)

SEE ALSO   COMMIT, SAVEPOINT, SET TRANSACTION
FORMAT

```
EXEC SQL [AT database | :variable]
ROLLBACK [WORK]
{[TO [SAVEPOINT] savepoint] [RELEASE] |
 [FORCE text]}
```

DESCRIPTION   **ROLLBACK** ends the current transaction, reverses any changes resulting from the current transaction, and releases any locks being held, but does not affect host variables or program flow. *database* indicates the name of the database where the **ROLLBACK** should take effect. Its absence indicates the default database for the user. **SAVEPOINT** allows a rollback to a named **SAVEPOINT** that has been previously declared. (*See* **SAVEPOINT**.)

FORCE manually rolls back an in-doubt transaction specified by a literal text containing the transaction ID from the DBA_2PC_PENDING data dictionary view. WORK is entirely optional and is for readability only.

Both **ROLLBACK** and **COMMIT** have **RELEASE** options. **RELEASE** should be specified by one of them after the last transaction, otherwise locks put on during the program will block other users. **ROLLBACK** occurs automatically (with a **RELEASE**) if the program abnormally terminates.

ROLLBACK SEGMENT

A rollback segment is a storage space within a tablespace that holds transaction information that is used to guarantee data integrity during a rollback and to provide read consistency across multiple transactions. See Chapter 38.

ROLLUP

SEE ALSO   GROUPING, CUBE, Chapter 13
FORMAT

```
GROUP BY ROLLUP(column1, column2)
```

DESCRIPTION   ROLLUP generates subtotals for groups of rows within a query. See Chapter 13.

ROOT

In a table with tree-structured data, the root is the origin of the tree, a row that has no parent, and whose children, grandchildren, and so on, constitute the entire tree. In a tree-structured query, the root is the row specified by the **START WITH** clause.

ROUND (Form 1—for Dates)

SEE ALSO   DATE FUNCTIONS, **ROUND** (NUMBER), **TRUNC**, Chapter 9
FORMAT

```
ROUND (date, 'format')
```

DESCRIPTION   **ROUND** is the rounding of date according to format. Without a format, date is rounded to 12 A.M. of the next date as of 12:00:00 P.M. (exactly noon) today, or to today's date if before noon. The resulting date has its time set to 12 A.M., the very first instant of the day.

FORMATS AVAILABLE FOR ROUNDING

Format	Meaning
cc,scc	century (rounds up to January 1st of next century, as of midnight exactly on the morning of January 1st of 1950, 2050, and so on).
syear,syyy,y,yy,yyy,yyyy and year	year (rounds up to January 1st of the next year as of midnight exactly on the morning of July 1st).
q	quarter (rounds up in the 2nd month of the quarter as of midnight exactly on the morning of the 16th, regardless of the number of days in the month).
month,mon,mm	month (rounds up as of midnight exactly on the morning of the 16th regardless of the number of days in the month).
ww	rounds to closest Monday (see text following list).
w	rounds to closest day which is the same day as the first day of the month (see text following list).
ddd,dd,j	rounds up to the next day as of noon exactly. This is the same as ROUND with no format.
day,dy,d	rounds up to next Sunday (first day of the week) as of noon exactly on Wednesday.
hh,hh12,hh24	rounds up to the next whole hour as of 30 minutes and 30 seconds after the hour.
mi	rounds up to the next whole minute as of 30 seconds of this minute.

ww produces the date of the nearest Monday with the time set at 12 A.M. Since a week is seven days long, this means any date and time up to three and one-half days after a Monday (the next Thursday at 11:59:59 A.M.), or three and one-half days before (the previous Thursday at noon exactly), will be rounded to Monday at 12 A.M. (midnight) in the morning.

w works similarly, except that instead of producing the date of the nearest Monday at 12 A.M., it produces the date of the nearest day that is the same day as the first day of the month. If the first day of a month was Friday, for instance, then, since a week is seven days long, this means any date and time up to three and one-half days after a Friday (the next Monday at 11:59:59 A.M.), or three and one-half days before (the previous Monday at noon exactly), will be rounded to the Friday at 12 A.M. (midnight) in the morning.

When **ww** and **w** round, the time of the date being rounded is compared to a date (either Monday or the day of the first day of the month) which is set to 12 A.M., the very beginning of the day. The result of **ROUND** is a new date, which is also set to 12 A.M.

ROUND (Form 2—for Numbers)
SEE ALSO   CEIL, **FLOOR**, NUMBER FUNCTIONS, **ROUND** (DATE), **TRUNC**, Chapter 8
FORMAT

ROUND(*value*,*precision*)

DESCRIPTION   ROUND rounds *value* to *precision*. *precision* is an integer and may be positive, negative, or zero. A negative integer rounds to the given number of places to the left of the decimal point, a positive integer rounds to the given number of places to the right of the decimal point.

EXAMPLE

```
ROUND(123.456,2) = 123.46
ROUND(123.456,0) = 123
ROUND(123.456,-2) = 100
ROUND(-123.456,2) = -123.46
```

ROW

Row can have either of two definitions:

- One set of fields in a table; for example, the fields representing one worker in the table WORKER.
- One set of fields in the output of a query. RECORD is a synonym.

ROW HEADER

A row header is the portion of each row that contains information about the row other than row data, such as the number of row pieces, columns, and so on.

ROW-LEVEL LOCKING

Row-level locking is a type of locking in which **update**s to data occur through locking rows in a table and not the entire page.

ROW SEQUENCE NUMBER

A row sequence number is a number assigned to a row as it is inserted into a data block for a table. This number is also stored as row overhead and forms a part of the ROWID.

ROWID

SEE ALSO   **CHARTOROWID**, PSEUDO-COLUMNS, **ROWIDTOCHAR**, Chapter 10
FORMAT   AAAAsYABQAAAAGzAAA
DESCRIPTION   ROWID is the logical address of a row, and it is unique within the database. ROWID can be **select**ed, or used in a **where** clause, but cannot be changed by an **insert**, **update**, or **delete**. It is not actually a data column, but merely a logical address, made of the database address information. ROWID is useful when used in a **where** clause for rapid **update**s or **delete**s of rows. However, it can change if the table it is in is exported and imported.

ROWIDTOCHAR

SEE ALSO   **CHARTOROWID**, CONVERSION FUNCTIONS
FORMAT

```
ROWIDTOCHAR(RowId)
```

DESCRIPTION   **Row Id**entifier **TO CHAR**acter changes an internal Oracle row identifier, or RowId, to act like a character string. However, Oracle will do this kind of conversion automatically, so this function isn't really needed. It seems to be a debugging tool that has made its way into general availability.

ROWNUM

SEE ALSO PSEUDO-COLUMNS, Chapter 16

FORMAT

ROWNUM

DESCRIPTION ROWNUM returns the sequence number in which a row was returned when first selected from a table. The first row has a ROWNUM of 1, the second is 2, and so on. Note, however, that even a simple **order by** in the **select** statement will *disorder* the ROWNUMs, which are assigned to the rows before any ordering takes place. *See* Chapter 16 for a discussion of this.

RPAD

SEE ALSO CHARACTER FUNCTIONS, **LPAD**, **LTRIM**, **RTRIM**, Chapter 7

FORMAT

RPAD(*string*,*length* [,'*set*'])

DESCRIPTION **R**ight **PAD** makes a string a certain length by adding a certain *set* of characters to the right. If *set* is not specified, the default pad character is a space.

EXAMPLE

select RPAD('HELLO ',24,'WORLD') from DUAL;

produces this:

HELLO WORLDWORLDWORLDWOR

and this:

select RPAD('CAROLYN',15,'-') from DUAL;

produces this:

CAROLYN--------

RTRIM

SEE ALSO CHARACTER FUNCTIONS, **LPAD**, **LTRIM**, **RPAD**, Chapter 7

FORMAT

RTRIM(*string* [,'*set*'])

DESCRIPTION **R**ight **TRIM** trims all the occurrences of any one of a *set* of characters off of the right side of a string.

EXAMPLE

RTRIM('GEORGE','OGRE')

produces *nothing*, a **NULL**, empty string with zero length! On the other hand, this:

RTRIM('EDYTHE','HET')

produces this:

EDY

RUN

SEE ALSO   /, @, @@, **EDIT**, **START**

FORMAT

R[UN]

DESCRIPTION   **RUN** displays the SQL command in the SQL buffer, and then executes it. **RUN** is similar to the **/** command, except that the **/** doesn't display the SQL first.

SAVE

PRODUCT   SQL*PLUS

SEE ALSO   **EDIT**, **GET**, Chapter 6

FORMAT

SAV[E] *file*[.ext] [CRE[ATE] | REP[LACE] | APP[END]]

DESCRIPTION   **SAVE** saves the contents of the current buffer into a host file with the name *file*. If no file type (extension) is specified, the file type SQL is added to the file name. This default extension can be changed with **SET SUFFIX**. **SAVE** commits pending work to the database.

If the file already exists, the **CREATE** option will force **SAVE** to abort and will produce an error message. The **REPLACE** option will replace any existing file, or create a new one if none exists.

The **APPEND** option adds this file to the end of any existing file, or creates a new one if none exists.

EXAMPLE   The following saves the contents of the current buffer into a file named lowcost.sql:

save lowcost

SAVEPOINT

SEE ALSO   **COMMIT**, **ROLLBACK**, **SET TRANSACTION**

SYNTAX

SAVEPOINT →(savepoint)→(;)

DESCRIPTION   **SAVEPOINT** is a point within a transaction to which you may rollback. Savepoints allow you to **ROLLBACK** portions of your current transaction. *See* **ROLLBACK**.

The first version here is typical of SQL*PLUS. The purpose of **SAVEPOINT** is to be able to assign a name to the beginning of a group of SQL statements and later, if necessary, **ROLLBACK** to that name, thus undoing the results of *just that group*. These can be nested or sequenced, allowing great control over recovery from errors. The idea here is to collect together a series of SQL statements that make up one logical transaction, and hold the **COMMIT** until all the steps within it have been completed successfully. It may be that an attempted step will fail, but you'll want to be able to try it again without having to undo everything else prior to it. Here is a possible structure, shown logically in pseudo-code:

start of logical transaction

```
   savepoint ALPHA
   SQL statement 1
```

```
function a
function b

if (condition) then rollback to savepoint ALPHA

  savepoint BETA
  function c
  SQL statement 2
  SQL statement 3

  if (condition) then rollback to savepoint BETA

if (condition) then rollback to savepoint ALPHA

    savepoint GAMMA
    SQL statement 4

    if (condition) then rollback to savepoint GAMMA

  if (condition) then rollback to savepoint BETA

 if (condition) then rollback to savepoint ALPHA

if (condition) then either commit or rollback
```

This shows that SQL statements, or groups of them, can be collected together and undone in sets or singly. In a host program, or using PL/SQL or SQL*PLUS, you may want to set up SAVEPOINTs that you can **ROLLBACK** to, based on the results of your most recent SQL statement or condition test. **ROLLBACK** allows you to return to a specific step where you named a SAVEPOINT.

If a function, a section of logic, or an attempted SQL statement fails, you can return the data in the database back to the state it was in before the local step began. You can then try it again.

SAVEPOINT names must be unique to a transaction (defined by where it ends, with either a **COMMIT** or unconditional **ROLLBACK**) but do not have to be unique to all of your database objects. You can give a **SAVEPOINT** the same name as a table, for instance (this might even result in more understandable code if the **SAVEPOINT** had the name of the table being updated). Names for **SAVEPOINT**s follow object-naming conventions.

If you give a new **SAVEPOINT** the same name as a previous one, the new one replaces the earlier one. The earlier one is lost, and you can no longer roll back to it.

Once a **COMMIT** or an unconditional **ROLLBACK** (not to a SAVEPOINT) is issued, all previous **SAVEPOINT**s are erased. Recall that all DDL statements (such as **DISCONNECT**, **CREATE TABLE**, **CREATE INDEX**, and so on) automatically issue an implicit **COMMIT**, and any severe failure (if the program terminates abnormally or the computer goes down), will result in an automatic **ROLLBACK**.

SCAN (SQL*PLUS)

See **SET**.

SCORE

The **SCORE** function is used by ConText and IMT to evaluate how well a text string met the specified search criteria. You can display the score of an individual search; more often, the score is compared to a threshold value. *See* Chapter 24.

SEGMENT

A segment is the physical storage for the space allocated to a table, index, or cluster. A table has one segment that consists of all of its extents. Every index has one segment similarly defined. A cluster has at least two segments, one for its data and one for its cluster key index.

SEGMENT HEADER BLOCK

The segment header block is the first block in the first extent of a segment.

SELECT (Form 1—SQL)

SEE ALSO   COLLATION, **CONNECT BY, DELETE, DUAL, FROM, GROUP BY, HAVING, INSERT, JOIN**, LOGICAL OPERATORS, **ORDER BY**, QUERY OPERATORS, SUBQUERY, SYNTAX OPERATORS, **UPDATE, WHERE**

SYNTAX

subquery::=

table_expression_clause::=

sample_clause::=

with_clause::=

table_collection_expression::=

where_clause::=

outer_join::=

hierarchical_query_clause::=

group_by_clause::=

order_by_clause::=

for_update_clause::=

DESCRIPTION   **SELECT** retrieves rows from one or more tables (or views or snapshots), either as a command, or as a subquery in another SQL command (within limitations), including **select**, **insert**, **update**, and **delete**. **ALL** means that all rows satisfying the conditions will be returned (this is the default). **DISTINCT** means that only rows that are unique will be returned; any duplicates will be weeded out first.

An * (asterisk) by itself results in all columns from all tables in the **from** clause being displayed. *table*.* means that all columns from this table will be displayed. An asterisk by itself cannot be combined with any other columns, but a *table*.* can be followed by column names and expressions, including ROWID.

expression means any form of a column. This could be a column name, a literal, a mathematical computation, a function, or several functions combined. The most common version is a simple column name, or a column name prefixed by a table name or table alias. *Column alias* is a renaming of the column or expression. The column alias can be preceded by the word AS. The column alias will become the column heading in the display, and may be referenced by the **column**, **ttitle**, and **btitle** commands in SQL*PLUS. The column alias may be used in the **order by** clause. If it is more than one word, or will contain characters that are neither numbers nor letters, it must be enclosed in double quotation marks.

user, *table*, and *dblink* denote the table or view from which the rows will be drawn. *user* and *dblink* are optional, and their absence makes Oracle default to the current user. However, specifying the user in a query may reduce Oracle's overhead and make the query run more quickly. A subquery can be specified in the FROM clause. Oracle will execute the subquery and the resulting rows will be treated as if they came from a view.

A table *alias* here will rename the table for this query. This alias, unlike the expression alias, can be referenced elsewhere within the **select** statement itself, for instance as a prefix to any column name coming from that table. In fact, if a table has an alias, the alias *must* be used whenever a column from that table has a table name prefix. Tables are typically aliased when two tables with long names are joined in a query, and many of their columns have the same name, requiring them to be unambiguously named in the **select** clause. Aliases are also commonly used in correlated subqueries, and when a table is being joined to itself.

condition may be any valid expression that tests true or false. It can contain functions, columns (from these tables), and literals. *position* allows the **order by** to identify the expressions based on their relative position in the **select** clause, rather than on their names. This is valuable for complicated expressions. You should discontinue the use of ordinal positions in **order by** clauses; column aliases may be used in their place. The current SQL standard does not include support for ordinal positions in **order by** clauses, and Oracle may not support them in the future. **ASC** and **DESC** specify whether it is an ascending or descending sequence for each expression in the **order by**. *See* COLLATION for a discussion of what these sequences are.

column is a column in a table listed in the **from** clause. This cannot be an expression, but must be a real column name. **NOWAIT** means that a **select for update** attempt that encounters a locked row will terminate and return immediately to the user, rather than wait and attempt to update the row again in a few moments.

The **for update of** clause puts locks on the rows that have been selected. **select . . . for update of** should be followed immediately by an **update. . .where** command, or, if you decide not to update anything, by a **COMMIT** or **ROLLBACK**. The **for update of** also includes the actions of **insert** and **delete**. Once you have locked a row, other users cannot update it until you free it with a **COMMIT** command (or **AUTOCOMMIT**) or **ROLLBACK**. **select . . . for update of** cannot include **DISTINCT**, **GROUP BY**, **UNION**, **INTERSECT**, **MINUS**, or any group function, such **MIN**, **MAX**, **AVG**, or **COUNT**. The columns named have no effect and are present for compatibility with other dialects of SQL. Oracle will lock only the tables that appear in the **for update** clause. If you don't have an **of** clause listing any tables, Oracle will lock all the tables in the **from** clause for update. All the tables must be on the same database, and if there are references to a LONG column or a sequence in the **select**, the tables must be on the same database as the LONG or the sequence.

If you are querying from a partitioned table, you can list the name of the partition you are querying as part of the **from** clause of the query. *See* Chapter 18.

The other individual clauses in the **select** statement are all described under their own names elsewhere in this reference.

OTHER NOTES   Clauses must be placed in the order shown, except for these:

- **connect by**, **start with**, **group by**, and **having**, which may be in any order in relation to each other.

- **order by** and **for update of**, which may be in any order in relation to each other.

SELECT (Form 2—Embedded SQL)

SEE ALSO   CONNECT, DECLARE CURSOR, DECLARE DATABASE, EXECUTE, FETCH, FOR, PREPARE, UPDATE (Form 2), WHENEVER

FORMAT

```
EXEC SQL [AT {database|:variable}]
SELECT select_list
INTO :variable [,:variable]...
FROM table_list
 [ WHERE condition ]
 [ CONNECT BY condition [START WITH condition] ]
 [ GROUP BY expression [,expression]... ] [HAVING condition]
 [ { UNION [ALL] | INTERSECT | MINUS } SELECT ... ]
 [ ORDER BY {expression | position} [ASC|DESC] ...
 [ ,expression | position} [ASC|DESC] ]...
 [ FOR UPDATE [OF column_list] [NOWAIT] ]
```

DESCRIPTION   See the description of the various clauses in **SELECT** (Form 1). The following are the elements unique to embedded SQL:

- **AT** database, which optionally names a database from a previous **CONNECT** statement, for a database name from a previous **DECLARE DATABASE** statement.

- **INTO** :*variable* [,:*variable*] is the list of host variables into which the results of the **select** statement will be loaded. If any variable in this list is an array, all of the variables in the list must be arrays, though they need not all be the same size arrays.

- The **where** clause may reference non-array host variables.

- The **select** clause may reference host variables anywhere a constant would have been used.

You can use the embedded **SQL SELECT** with variable arrays to return multiple rows with a single **FETCH**. You also can use it to either **DECLARE CURSOR** or **PREPARE** statements for use with a later **FETCH**, and may include the **for update of** clause. The later **update** statement can then reference the columns named in the **for update of** using its own **current of** clause. See **DECLARE CURSOR** and **UPDATE** (Form 2).

If the embedded **select** returns no rows, SQLCODE is set to +100, and the host variables are left unchanged. In that case, **WHENEVER** lets you change the program flow.

All rows that meet the **select** criteria are locked at the **OPEN**. **COMMIT** releases the locks, and no further **FETCH**ing is permitted. This means you must **FETCH** and process all of the rows you wish to update before you issue a **COMMIT**.

EXAMPLE

```
exec sql select Name, Age, Lodging, Age - :Retirement
into :Employee, :Age, :Domicile, :Over_Limit
from WORKER
where Age >= :Retirement;
```

SELECT...INTO

SEE ALSO   %ROWTYPE, %TYPE, DECLARE VARIABLE, FETCH

FORMAT

```
SELECT expression [,expression]...
   INTO {variable [,variable]... | record}
   FROM [user.]table [,[user.]table]...
 [where...][group by... [having...]] [order by...];
```

DESCRIPTION   This is not the form of the **select** statement used in **DECLARE CURSOR**.
This form utilizes the implicit cursor named SQL, executes within an execution section of a block
(between **BEGIN** and **END**), and copies the values from a single row being returned into either a
string of named variables, or a record whose structure is declared by **%ROWTYPE** to be just like
the columns being selected. If the form that uses variables is used, they must each be **DECLARE**d
and have compatible datatypes with those being retrieved. The order in which they appear in the
into clause must correspond to the order of the associated columns in the **select** clause.

This **select** may be used in a loop with PL/SQL variables appearing in the **where** clause (or even
acting like constants in the **select** clause), but each time the **select** executes it must return only one
row. If it produces more than one row, the TOO_MANY_ROWS exception will be **RAISE**d, and
SQL%ROWCOUNT will be set to 2 (*see* EXCEPTION for details). SQL%FOUND will be TRUE.

If it produces no rows, the NO_DATA_FOUND exception is **RAISE**d, and SQL%ROWCOUNT
will be set to 0. SQL%FOUND will be FALSE.

EXAMPLE

```
DECLARE
EMPLOYEE          WORKER%ROWTYPE;
  ...
BEGIN
 select Name, Age, Lodging into EMPLOYEE
    from WORKER
where Worker = 'BART SARJEANT';
```

or alternatively,

```
DECLARE
    Who       VARCHAR2(25);
    How_Old   NUMBER;
    Home      VARCHAR2(25);
    ...
BEGIN
    select Name, Age, Lodging into Who, How_Old, Home
      from WORKER
      where Worker = 'BART SARJEANT';
```

SEQUENCE

A sequence is a database object used to generate unique integers for use as primary keys. *See* **CREATE SEQUENCE**.

SERVER MANAGER

Server Manager is an Oracle utility used by DBAs to help perform database maintenance and monitoring. See Chapter 38.

SERVER PROCESS

Server processes work on behalf of user processes. *See* BACKGROUND PROCESS.

SERVICE NAME

A service name, found in the tnsnames.ora file, is an alias for a database accessed by Net8. Within the tnsnames.ora file, the service name is mapped to a host, port, and instance. You can therefore change the service name for a database without changing the database name, and you can move a database to a different host without changing its service name. You can use Oracle Names instead of tnsnames.ora to map service names to instances.

SESSION

The session is the series of events that happens between the time a user connects to SQL and the time he or she disconnects.

SET

SEE ALSO **SET TRANSACTION, SHOW**, Chapter 6
FORMAT

```
SET feature value
```

where feature and value are from the following list. The default value is underlined.

```
APPI[NFO]{ON|OFF|text}
ARRAY[SIZE] {15|n}
AUTO[COMMIT] {OFF|ON|IMM[EDIATE]|n}
AUTOP[RINT] {OFF|ON}
AUTORECOVERY {ON|OFF}
AUTOT[RACE] {OFF|ON|TRACE[ONLY]} [EXP[LAIN]] [STAT[ISTICS]]
BLO[CKTERMINATOR] {.|c}
CMDS[EP] {;|c|OFF|ON}
COLSEP {_|text}
COM[PATIBILITY] {V7|V8|NATIVE}
CON[CAT] {.|c|OFF|ON}
COPYC[OMMIT] {0|n}
COPYTYPECHECK {OFF|ON}
DEF[INE] {'&'|c|OFF|ON}
DESCRIBE [DEPTH {1|n|ALL}][LINENUM {ON|OFF}][INDENT {ON|OFF}]
ECHO {OFF|ON}
EDITF[ILE] file_name[.ext]
EMB[EDDED] {OFF|ON}
ESC[APE] {\|c|OFF|ON}
```

```
FEED[BACK] {6|n|OFF|ON}
FLAGGER {OFF|ENTRY|INTERMED[IATE]|FULL}
FLU[SH] {OFF|ON}
HEA[DING] {OFF|ON}
HEADS[EP] {|||c|OFF|ON}
INSTANCE [instance_path|LOCAL]
LIN[ESIZE] {80|n}
LOBOF[FSET] {n|1}
LOGSOURCE [pathname]
LONG {80|n}
LONGC[HUNKSIZE] {80|n}
NEWP[AGE] {1|n|NONE}
NULL text
NUMF[ORMAT] format
NUM[WIDTH] {10|n}
PAGES[IZE] {24|n}
PAU[SE] {OFF|ON|text}
RECSEP {WR[APPED]|EA[CH]|OFF}
RECSEPCHAR {_|c}
SCAN {ON|OFF}
SERVEROUT[PUT] {OFF|ON} [SIZE n] [FOR[MAT] {WRA[PPED]|
    WOR[D_WRAPPED]|TRU[NCATED]}]
SHIFT[INOUT] {VIS[IBLE]|INV[ISIBLE]}}
SHOW[MODE] {OFF|ON}
SQLBL[ANKLINES] {ON|OFF}
SQLC[ASE] {MIX[ED]|LO[WER]|UP[PER]}
SQLCO[NTINUE] {>|text}
SQLN[UMBER] {OFF|ON}
SQLPRE[FIX] {#|c}
SQLP[ROMPT] {SQL>|text}
SQLT[ERMINATOR] {;|c|OFF|ON}
SUF[FIX] {SQL|text}
TAB {OFF|ON}
TERM[OUT] {OFF|ON}
TI[ME] {OFF|ON}
TIMI[NG] {OFF|ON}
TRIM[OUT] {OFF|ON}
TRIMS[POOL] {ON|OFF}
UND[ERLINE] {-|c|ON|OFF}
VER[IFY] {OFF|ON}
WRA[P] {OFF|ON}
```

DESCRIPTION   **SET** turns a SQL*PLUS feature ON or OFF or to a certain value. All of these features are changed with the **SET** command and displayed with the **SHOW** command. **SHOW** will display a particular command if its name follows the word **SHOW**, or all commands if **SHOW** is entered by itself. In the features below, the default value is always the first in the list.

APPI[NFO] enables the registering of command files via the DBMS_APPLICATION_INFO package. The registered name appears in the Module column of the V$SESSION dynamic performance table.

ARRAY[SIZE] will set the size of the batch of rows that SQL*PLUS will fetch at one time. The range is 1 to 5000. Larger values improve the efficiency of queries and subqueries where many rows will be fetched, but use more memory. Values above 100 generally do not produce much improvement. ARRAYSIZE has no other effect on the workings of SQL*PLUS.

AUTO[COMMIT] ON or OFF makes SQL immediately commit any pending changes to the database upon the completion of every SQL command. *n* allows you to specify the number of commands after which a commit will occur. OFF stops automatic committing, and you must instead commit changes intentionally with the **COMMIT** command. Many commands, such as **QUIT, EXIT, CONNECT**, and all DDL commands will cause a **COMMIT** of any pending changes.

AUTOP[RINT] sets whether SQL*Plus automatically displays bind variables used in a PL/SQL block or EXECUTEd procedure.

AUTOT[RACE] allows you to see the execution path for a query after the query has completed. To see the execution path, you first must have the PLAN_TABLE table created in your schema (it can be created by running the UTLXPLAN.SQL file in the /rdbms/admin directory under your Oracle software directory

BLOCKTERMINATOR sets the symbol used to denote the end of a PL/SQL block. This cannot be a letter or a number. To execute the block, use **RUN** or **/** (slash).

CMDS[EP] sets the character used to separate multiple SQL*PLUS commands entered on a line. ON or OFF controls whether multiple commands may be entered on a line.

COLSEP sets a value to be printed between columns. *See* SET RECSEP.

COM[PATIBILITY] specifies the version of Oracle to which you are connected. If NATIVE is chosen, the database determines which version of Oracle you are connected to.

CONCAT sets a symbol that may be used to terminate or delimit a user variable that is followed by a symbol, character, or word that would otherwise be interpreted as a part of the user variable name. Setting CONCAT ON resets its value to '.'.

COPYCOMMIT The **COPY** command will commit rows to the destination database on a cycle of *n* batches of rows (the number of rows in a batch is **SET** by ARRAYSIZE). Valid values are 0 to 5000. If value is 0, a **COMMIT** will occur only at the end of a copy operation.

COPYTYPECHECK enables the suppression of datatype checks when using the COPY command.

DEF[INE] Here, *symbol* defines the character used to prefix and denote a substitution variable.

DEF[INE] determines whether SQL*PLUS will look for and substitute commands for substitution variables and load them with their DEFINEd values.

ECHO ON makes SQL*PLUS echo (display) commands to the screen as they execute from a start file. OFF makes SQL*PLUS execute them without displaying them. The results of the commands, on the other hand, are controlled by **TERMOUT**.

EDITF[ILE] sets the default filename created by the EDIT command.

EMBEDDED ON allows a new report in a series of reports to begin anywhere on a page, just after the previous one ended. OFF forces the new report to start at the top of a new page.

ESCAPE *symbol* defines an ESCAPE character that can be used to prefix the DEFINE symbol so that it can be displayed, rather than interpreted as the beginning of a variable.

ESCAPE OFF disables the ESCAPE character so that it no longer has any effect. ON always defines the ESCAPE character to be \ (backslash). For example, if the ESCAPE character were defined as \, then this:

```
ACCEPT Report prompt 'Please Enter P\&L Report Name:'
```

would display this:

```
Please Enter P&L Report Name:
```

and &L would not be treated as a variable.

FEED[BACK] makes SQL*PLUS show "records selected" after a query if at least *n* records are selected. ON or OFF turns this display on or off. **SET FEEDBACK** to 0 is the same as OFF.

FLAGGER sets the FIPS level for SQL92 compliance.

FLUSH OFF is used when a start file can be run without needing any display or interaction until it has completed. The OFF lets the operating system avoid sending output to the display. ON restores output to the user's display. OFF may improve performance.

HEA[DING] OFF suppresses the headings, both text and underlines, that normally appear above columns. ON allows them to be displayed.

In HEADS[EP] *symbol* is the heading separator character. The default is the broken vertical bar (a solid vertical bar on some computers). Wherever it appears, SQL*PLUS will break the title or heading down on to a new line. This works both in the **column** command, and in the old method of using **btitle** and **ttitle**.

HEADS[EP] ON or OFF turns it on or off. If it is off, the heading separator symbol is printed like any other character.

LIN[ESIZE] sets the line width, the total number of characters on a line that can be displayed before wrapping down to the next line. This number is also used when SQL*PLUS calculates the proper position for centered or right-aligned titles. The maximum value of *n* is 999.

LONG is the maximum width for displaying or copying (spooling) LONG values. *n* may range from 1 to 32767, but must be less than the value of **MAXDATA**.

LONGC[HUNKSIZE] sets the size, in characters, of the increments in which SQL*Plus retrieves a LONG value.

MAXD[ATA] *n* sets the maximum total row width (including a row folded onto many lines) that SQL*PLUS is able to handle. The default and maximum values for **MAXDATA** are different for different host operating systems. *See* the *Oracle Installation and User's Guide* for further details.

NEWP[AGE] sets the number of blank lines to be printed between the bottom of one page and the top title of the next. A 0 (zero) sends a form feed at the top of each page. If the output is being displayed, this will usually clear the screen.

NULL text sets the text that will be substituted when SQL*PLUS discovers null value. NULL without text displays blanks.

NUMF[ORMAT] format sets the default number format for displaying number data items. *See* NUMBER FORMATS for details.

NUM[WIDTH] sets the default width for number displays.

PAGES[IZE] sets the number of lines per page. *See* Chapter 4 for use of **pagesize** and **newpage**.

PAU[SE] ON makes SQL*PLUS wait for you to press RETURN after it displays each page of output. OFF means no pause between pages of display. *text* is the message SQL*PLUS will display at the bottom of the screen as it waits for you to hit the RETURN key. Pause will wait before the very first page is displayed; you'll have to hit RETURN to see it.

RECSEP: Each row SQL*PLUS brings back can be separated from other rows by a character, defined by RECSEPCHAR (*see also* **SET**). By default, the character is a space, and this only happens for records (and therefore columns) that wrap. For example, here the eight rows of the City column are queried, but the format is too narrow for one of the cities, so it wraps just for that city:

```
column City format a9

select City from COMFORT;

CITY
---------
SAN FRANC
ISCO

SAN FRANC
```

```
ISCO

SAN FRANC
ISCO

SAN FRANC
ISCO

KEENE
KEENE
KEENE
KEENE
```

However, when RECSEP is OFF, the effect is this:

```
set recsep off

select City from COMFORT;
CITY
---------
SAN FRANC
ISCO
SAN FRANC
ISCO
SAN FRANC
ISCO
SAN FRANC
ISCO
KEENE
KEENE
KEENE
KEENE
```

RECSEPCHAR works with RECSEP. The default is a space, but you can set it to another symbol if you wish.

SCAN : Variable substitution normally occurs because SQL*PLUS scans SQL statements for the substitution symbol. If SCAN is set OFF, it won't scan and the substitution of variables will be suppressed.

SERVEROUT[PUT] allows you to display the output of PL/SQL procedures (from the DBMS_OUTPUT package—*see* the *Application Developer's Guide*). WRAPPED, WORD_WRAPPED, TRUNCATED, and FORMAT determine the formatting of the output text.

SHOW[MODE] ON makes SQL*PLUS display the old and new settings of a SET feature and its value when it is changed. OFF stops the display of both of these.

SPA[CE] sets the number of spaces between columns in a row in the output. The maximum value is 10.

SQLC[ASE] converts all the text, including literals and identifiers, in either SQL or PL/SQL blocks, before it is executed by Oracle. **MIXED** leaves case just as it is typed. **LOWER** converts everything to lowercase; **UPPER** converts it all to uppercase.

SQLC[ONTINUE] sets the character sequence to be displayed as a prompt for a long line that must continue on the next line. When you enter a - (hyphen) at the end of a SQL*PLUS command line, the SQLCONTINUE symbols or text will prompt you from the left of the next screen line.

SQLN[UMBER] If this is ON, then lines of SQL beyond the first one you enter will have line numbers as prompts. If this is OFF, the SQLPROMPT will appear only on additional lines.

SQLPRE[FIX] sets the SQL prefix character, which can be used to cause immediate execution of a SQL*PLUS command (such as **COLUMN**), even when entering SQL or PL/SQL commands. The SQL*PLUS command will go into effect immediately. Using this with a SQL statement will cause any preceding SQL keyed in thus far to be replaced completely by the text following the #.

SQLP[ROMPT] sets the SQL prompt that is displayed if SQLNUMBER is OFF.

SQLT[ERMINATOR] sets the symbol used to end SQL commands, and start immediate execution of the SQL. OFF means that no SQL symbol will be recognized as a terminator, and the user must instead terminate the command by entering an empty line after the last line of SQL.

SQLT[ERMINATOR] ON always resets the terminator to the default (';'), regardless of what else has been set.

SUFFIX sets the default file name extension (also called the file type) that SQL*PLUS appends to files you **SAVE**. *See* **SAVE**.

TAB OFF makes SQL use spaces in formatting columns and text on reports. The default value for TAB is system-dependent. **SHOW TAB** will display it. ON sets SQL*PLUS to use tabs instead of spaces.

TERM[OUT] ON displays regular SQL*PLUS output from a start file. OFF suppresses the display, and is valuable when the output is being spooled to a file, but you don't want to see it displayed on the screen as well. OFF will also improve performance.

TI[ME] ON displays the current time (from the system clock) before each command prompt. OFF suppresses the display of the current time.

TIMI[NG] ON has SQL*PLUS show timing statistics for each SQL command that is executed. OFF suppresses the display of the timing of each command. (*See* **TIMING** for another command by the same name that operates completely differently.)

TRIM[OUT] : SET TAB ON must be in effect for this to operate. When ON, it trims blanks at the end of each displayed line rather than displaying them, which often results in significant performance gains, especially over dial-up lines. OFF allows trailing blanks to be displayed. TRIMOUT ON does not change spooled output.

TRIMS[POOL] ON removes blanks at the end of each spooled line. OFF allows SQL*Plus to include trailing blanks at the end of each spooled line.

UND[ERLINE] sets the character used as the underline for column headings. The default is - (hyphen).

UND[ERLINE] turns underlining on or off without changing the character.

VER[IFY] ON makes SQL*PLUS show the old and new values of variables before executing the SQL in which they are embedded. OFF suppresses the display.

WRAP ON wraps a row to the next line if it exceeds the width set in **COLUMN**. OFF truncates (clips) the right-hand side of a column display if it is too long to fit the current line width. Use the **COLUMN** command's **wrapped** clauses to override WRAP for specific columns.

SET CONDITION

Set condition is a logical expression containing a query, for example "Name IN (select. . .)". The name derives from the idea that the query condition will produce a set of records.

SET CONSTRAINTS

SEE ALSO   INTEGRITY CONSTRAINT

SYNTAX

DESCRIPTION **SET CONSTRAINTS DEFERRED** tells Oracle not to check the validity of a constraint until the transaction is committed. This allows you to temporarily defer integrity checking of data. Deferred constraints are usually used when performing DML against multiple related tables when you cannot guarantee the order of the transactions. You must either own the table modified by the constraint or you must have SELECT privilege on the table.

The default setting is **SET CONSTRAINTS IMMEDIATE**, in which case the constraints are checked as soon as a record is inserted into the table.

SET OPERATOR

The set operator is always either **UNION**, **INTERSECT**, or **MINUS**. *See also* QUERY OPERATORS.

SET ROLE

SEE ALSO **ALTER USER, CREATE ROLE**, Chapter 19
SYNTAX

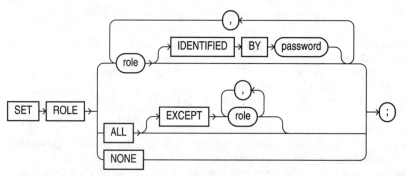

DESCRIPTION **SET ROLE** enables or disables roles granted to a user for the current SQL session. The first option lets the user enable specific roles, optionally giving a password if the role has one (*see* **CREATE ROLE**). The second option lets the user enable **ALL** roles **EXCEPT** for specific ones; these roles must be directly granted to the user, not roles granted through other roles. The **ALL** option does not enable roles with passwords. The third option, **NONE**, disables all roles for the current session.

SET TRANSACTION

SEE ALSO **COMMIT, ROLLBACK, SAVEPOINT, TRANSACTION**, Chapter 38

SYNTAX

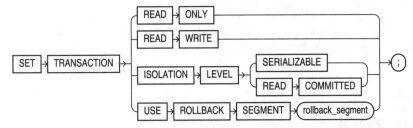

DESCRIPTION   **SET TRANSACTION** starts a transaction. The standard SQL transaction guarantees statement level read consistency, making sure that the data from a query is consistent while the statement is executing. But some transactions need a stronger guarantee that a series of **select** statements, accessing one or more tables, will see a consistent snapshot of all of the data in one instant in time. **SET TRANSACTION READ ONLY** specifies this stronger read consistency. No changes to the queried data by other users will affect the transaction's view of the data. In a read-only transaction, you can use only the **select**, **lock table**, **set role**, **alter session**, and **alter system** commands.

For transactions that include **insert**, **update**, or **delete** commands, Oracle assigns a rollback segment to the transaction. **SET TRANSACTION USE ROLLBACK SEGMENT** specifies that the current transaction will use a specific rollback segment.

```
select Name, Manager
  from WORKER, LODGING
 where WORKER.Lodging = LODGING.Lodging;
```

Changes that occur to a Manager after the query is executed, but before all the rows have been fetched, will not appear in the result. However, if the two tables were queried sequentially, as follows:

```
select Name, Lodging from WORKER;

select Manager, Lodging from LODGING;
```

the Manager in LODGING could well change while the first **select** was still executing, and the Lodging in WORKER could change while the second **select** was executing. Attempting to then join the results of these two separate **select**s using program logic (rather than the table join in the first example) would produce inconsistent results. This gives the solution:

```
commit;
set transaction read only;
select Name, Lodging from WORKER;

select Manager, Lodging from LODGING;
commit;
```

This freezes the data (for this user) in both tables before either **select** retrieves any rows. It will be as consistent as the data in the first example with the table join. The data is held constant until a **COMMIT** or **ROLLBACK** is issued.

The use of the two **commit**s (one before and one after) is important. **SET TRANSACTION** must be the first SQL statement in a transaction. The **COMMIT** just before it assures that this is true. The

COMMIT at the end releases the snapshot of the data. This is important because Oracle needs to recapture the resources it has set aside to hold the data constant.

If the data you are freezing is from tables with high update volume, or your transaction is lengthy and will take a good deal of time, the DBA may need to **CREATE** additional **ROLLBACK SEGMENT**s to provide the storage space for the frozen data.

SGA

See System Global Area.

SHARED SQL POOL

An area in the Oracle SGA that contains both the dictionary cache and a shared area for the parsed versions of all SQL commands within the database. The Shared SQL Pool is also referred to as the Shared SQL Area; its size is determined by the SHARED_POOL_SIZE parameter in the database's init.ora file.

SHOW

SEE ALSO   SET

FORMAT

```
SHO[W] { option }
```

option may be:

```
ALL
BTI[TLE]
ERR[ORS] [{FUNCTION|PROCEDURE|PACKAGE|PACKAGE BODY|
    TRIGGER|VIEW|TYPE|TYPE BODY} [schema.]name]
LNO
PARAMETERS [parameter_name]
PNO
REL[EASE]
REPF[OOTER]
REPH[EADER]
SGA
SPOO[L]
SQLCODE
TTI[TLE]
USER
```

DESCRIPTION   SHOW displays the value of a feature of SET, or **ALL** features of SET, or of the other SQL*PLUS items. More than one of these (including more than one SET feature) can follow the word SHOW, and each will be displayed on a separate line. The rows returned will be ordered alphabetically.

BTI[TLE] displays the current **btitle** definition.
ERR[ORS] shows the latest errors encountered with the compilation of a stored object.
LNO shows the current line number (the line in the current page being displayed).
PARAMETERS shows the setting of a specific parameter, or all if none is specified.
PNO displays the page number.
REL[EASE] gives the release number of this version of Oracle.
REPF[OOTER] shows the report footer.

REPH[EADER] shows the report header.

SGA shows the current memory allocations for the SGA.

SPOO[L] tells whether output is being spooled (ON or OFF). *See* **SPOOL**.

SQLCODE shows the error message number of the most recent Oracle error.

TTI[TLE] displays the current **ttitle** definition.

USER shows the user's ID.

SHOWMODE (SQL*PLUS)

See **SET**.

SHUTDOWN

To shut down is to disconnect an instance from the database and terminate the instance. *See* (and contrast with) STARTUP. As a Server Manager command, **SHUTDOWN**'s options are **NORMAL**, **IMMEDIATE**, and **ABORT**. See Chapter 38.

SIGN

SEE ALSO   +, **PRECEDENCE**, Chapter 8

FORMAT

```
SIGN(value)
```

DESCRIPTION   It equals 1 if *value* is positive, -1 if negative, 0 if zero.

EXAMPLE

```
SIGN(33)  =  1
SIGN(-.6) = -1
SIGN(0)   =  0
```

SIN

SEE ALSO   ACOS, ASIN, ATAN, ATAN2, COS, **COSH**, NUMBER FUNCTIONS, **SINH**, TAN, Chapter 8

FORMAT

```
SIN(value)
```

DESCRIPTION   **SIN** returns the sine of an angle *value* expressed in radians.

EXAMPLE

```
select SIN(30*3.141593/180) Sine -- sine of 30 degrees in radians
from DUAL;

     SINE
----------
.50000005
```

SINH

SEE ALSO   ACOS, ASIN, ATAN, ATAN2, COS, NUMBER FUNCTIONS, **SIN**, **TAN**, Chapter 8

FORMAT

```
SINH(value)
```

DESCRIPTION   **SINH** returns the hyperbolic sine of an angle *value*.

SMON

The **S**ystem **Mon**itor Process is one of the Oracle background processes used to perform recovery and clean up unused temporary segments. *See* BACKGROUND PROCESS.

SNAPSHOT

"Snapshot" is an old name for a materialized view. *See* Chapter 23, **CREATE MATERIALIZED VIEW/SNAPSHOT, CREATE MATERIALIZED VIEW LOG/SNAPSHOT LOG**.

SNAPSHOT REFRESH GROUP

A snapshot refresh group is a set of local materialized views that are all refreshed as a group. Snapshot refresh groups allow data consistency to be enforced between materialized views. *See* Chapter 23.

SOUNDEX

SEE ALSO   **LIKE**, Chapters 7 and 24

FORMAT

```
SOUNDEX(string)
```

DESCRIPTION   **SOUNDEX** finds words that **SOUND** like an **EX**ample *string*. **SOUNDEX** makes certain assumptions about how letters and combinations of letters are usually pronounced. The two words being compared must begin with the same letter. You can perform **SOUNDEX** searches of individual words within text strings.

EXAMPLE

```
select LastName
from ADDRESS
where SOUNDEX(LastName) = SOUNDEX('SEPP');
```

```
LASTNAME                  FIRSTNAME                  PHONE
------------------------  ------------------------  ------------
SZEP                      FELICIA                    214-522-8383
SEP                       FELICIA                    214-522-8383
```

SPACE (SQL*PLUS)

See **SET**.

SPOOL

SEE ALSO   **SET**, Chapter 6

FORMAT

```
SPO[OL] [file|OFF|OUT];
```

DESCRIPTION   **SPOOL** starts or stops spooling (copying) of SQL*PLUS output to a host system file or the system printer. **SPOOL** *file* makes SQL*PLUS spool all output to the named file. If the file type is not specified, **SPOOL** adds a default, similar to what **SAVE** does, usually .LST, but with some variation by host. OFF stops spooling. OUT stops spooling and sends the file to the printer. To spool output to a file without displaying it, **SET TERMOUT OFF** in the start file prior to the SQL statement, but before the **SPOOL** command. **SPOOL** by itself shows the name of the current (or most recent) spool file.

SQL

SQL is the ANSI industry-standard language, used to manipulate information in a relational database and used in Oracle and IBM DB2 relational database management systems. SQL is formally pronounced "sequel," although common usage also pronounces it "S-Q-L."

SQL CURSOR

SEE ALSO   %FOUND, %ISOPEN, %NOTFOUND, %ROWCOUNT, Chapter 25

DESCRIPTION   *SQL* is the name of the cursor opened implicitly any time the SQL statement being processed is not part of an explicitly named and opened cursor (*see* **DECLARE**). There is only one of these at any time. The cursor attributes **%FOUND** and **%NOTFOUND** can be tested by checking SQL%FOUND and SQL%NOTFOUND before or after an **insert**, **update**, or **delete** (which are never associated with an explicit cursor) or a single-row **select** that happened to be executed without an explicit cursor.

See **%FOUND** for details on these tests. See **%ROWCOUNT** for details on the values this attribute has under different conditions. SQL%ISOPEN always evaluates FALSE because Oracle closes the SQL cursor automatically after executing the SQL statement.

SQL*LOADER

SQL*LOADER is a utility for loading data into an Oracle database. *See* **SQLLDR** and Chapter 21.

SQL*PLUS

See **SQLPLUS**.

SQLCASE (SQL*PLUS)

See **SET**.

SQLCODE

SEE ALSO   EXCEPTION, SQLERRM

FORMAT

```
variable := SQLCODE
```

DESCRIPTION   SQLCODE is an error function that returns the latest error number, but outside of an exception handler (*see* EXCEPTION WHEN) always returns 0. This is because the occurrence of an exception (that is, when SQLCODE would be nonzero) is expected to immediately transfer control to the EXCEPTION part of the PL/SQL block. Once there, SQLCODE can be tested for its value, or used to assign a value to a variable.

SQLCODE cannot be used as a part of a SQL statement (such as to insert the value of the error code into a error table). However, you can set a variable equal to SQLCODE, and then use the variable in a SQL statement:

```
sql_error := sqlcode;
insert into PROBLEMLOG values (sql_error);
```

SQLCONTINUE (SQL*PLUS)

See **SET**.

SQLERRM

SEE ALSO   EXCEPTION, EXCEPTION_INIT, PRAGMA, SQLCODE

FORMAT

```
SQLERRM[(integer)]
```

DESCRIPTION   Without *integer* supplied, SQLERRM returns the error message related to the current SQLCODE. With an integer supplied, it returns the error message related to that integer value. Like SQLCODE, this function cannot be used directly in a SQL statement, but can be used in an assignment:

```
error_message := sqlerrm;
```

or, to retrieve the error message associated with the error code 1403:

```
error_message := sqlerrm(1403);
```

Outside of an exception handler (*see* SQLCODE), this function without an integer argument will always return "normal, successful completion." In an exception handler, you will get one of these messages:

- The message associated with an Oracle error.
- The words "User-defined exception" for an explicitly raised user-exception where you did not assign a message text.
- A user-defined message text, loaded using the PRAGMA EXCEPTION_INIT.

SQLJ

SQLJ is a pre-processor that generates JDBC-compatible code. In general, SQLJ code is simpler to write and debug than JDBC code. *See* Chapter 34.

SQLLDR

SEE ALSO   Chapter 21

FORMAT   Parameters for the SQLLDR command:

Userid	Username and password for the load, separated by a slash.
Control	Name of the control file.
Log	Name of the log file.
Bad	Name of the bad file.
Discard	Name of the discard file.
Discardmax	Maximum number of rows to discard prior to stopping the load. Default is to allow all discards.
Skip	Number of logical rows in the input file to skip prior to starting to load data. Usually used during re-loads from the same input file following a partial load. Default is 0.
Load	Number of logical rows to load. Default is all.
Errors	Number of errors to allow. Default is 50.

Rows	Number of rows to commit at a time. Use this parameter to break up the transaction size during the load. Default for conventional path loads is 64, for Direct Path loads is all rows.
Bindsize	Size of conventional path bind array in bytes. Default is operating system-dependent.
Silent	Suppress messages during the load.
Direct	Use Direct Path loading. Default is FALSE.
Parfile	Name of the parameter file that contains additional load parameter specifications.
Parallel	Perform parallel loading. Default is FALSE.
File	File to allocate extents from (for parallel loading).
Skip_Unusable_ Indexes	Allows loads into tables that have indexes in unusable states. Default is FALSE.
Skip_Index_ Maintenance	Stops index maintenance for Direct Path loads, leaving them in unusable states. Default is FALSE.

DESCRIPTION   SQL*LOADER loads data from external files into tables in the Oracle database. See Chapter 22 for examples. The syntax for the control file is:

Options clause

Load statement

infile_clause

on_file_proc_clause

concatenate_clause

into_table_clause

cond_spec

delim_spec

full_fieldname

termination_spec

enclosure_spec

OID_spec

SID_spec

field_list

d_gen_fld_spec

REF_spec

init_spec

BFILE_spec

filler_fld_spec

scalar_fld_spec

LOBFILE_spec

pos_spec

datatype_spec

col_obj_fld_spec

collection_fld_spec

nested_table_spec

VARRAY_spec

SDF_spec

count_spec

SQLNUMBER (SQL*PLUS)

See **SET**.

SQLPLUS

SEE ALSO   Chapters 6, 14

FORMAT

```
SQLPLUS [user[/password][@database] [@file] ] [-SILENT] |
   [/NOLOG] [-SILENT] | [-?]
```

DESCRIPTION   SQLPLUS starts up SQL*PLUS. Entering both username and password will log you onto your default database. Entering just your username will cause SQL*PLUS to prompt you for your password, which will not be displayed as you enter it. Entering @*database* will connect you to the named database instead of your default. The @*database* can be anywhere, so long as the computer you are logging onto is connected to it through Net8. There must be no space between *password* and @*database*. For more information about Net8, see Chapter 22. @*file* will run the start file immediately after SQL*PLUS is loaded. There must be a space before @*file*. If the username and password are not entered on the command line with SQLPLUS, they must be the first line in the file. If they are in the file, and you enter them on the command line, you'll get an error message but the start file will run correctly anyway. To put user and password at the top of the file, separate them with a slash (/):

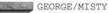

```
GEORGE/MISTY
```

/NOLOG makes SQL*PLUS start, but does not log you onto the Oracle database. You must then use **CONNECT** to attach to Oracle. (*See* **CONNECT**).

-SILENT suppresses all of SQL*PLUS's screen displays, including the command prompts and even the SQL*PLUS logon and copyright information. It makes the use of SQL*PLUS by another program invisible to the program's user.

-? displays the current version and level number for SQL*PLUS without actually starting it up.

EXAMPLE Normal startup of SQL*PLUS follows:

```
sqlplus george/misty
```

To start up on the database EDMESTON, use this:

```
sqlplus george/misty@EDMESTON
```

To start the report file REPORT6, which includes the name and password as its first line, use this:

```
sqlplus @report6
```

To start the report file REPORT6, which includes the name and password as its first line, on the database EDMESTON, use this:

```
sqlplus george/misty@EDMESTON @report6
```

SQLPREFIX (SQL*PLUS)
See **SET**.

SQLPROMPT (SQL*PLUS)
See **SET**.

SQLTERMINATOR (SQL*PLUS)
See **SET**.

SQRT
SEE ALSO POWER
FORMAT

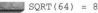

```
SQRT(value)
```

DESCRIPTION **SQRT** finds the square root of value.
EXAMPLES

```
SQRT(64) = 8
```

The square root of negative numbers is not available in Oracle (mathematically, it's an imaginary number, which isn't supported).

START

SEE ALSO **@@, ACCEPT, DEFINE, SPOOL**, Chapter 6
FORMAT

```
STA[RT] file [parameter] [parameter]...
```

DESCRIPTION START executes the contents of the specified start file (so called because it is started by this command). The file may contain any SQL*PLUS commands. If no file type is specified, START assumes it is **.sql**. Any parameters following the file name are substituted into variables in the start file; the variables must be named &1, &2, &3, and so on, and will receive the parameters in order, from left to right. Every occurrence in the start file of &1 will get the first parameter. Parameters consisting of more than one word may be enclosed in single quotes (''); otherwise, parameters are limited to a single word or number each.

EXAMPLE

```
start skill HELEN
```

where the file **skill.sql** contains the following:

```
select * from WORKERSKILL
  where Name LIKE '&1%';
```

   This will produce the following:

```
NAME                      SKILL                     ABILITY
------------------------- ------------------------- -------------
HELEN BRANDT              COMBINE DRIVER            VERY FAST
```

STARTUP

Starting up is the process of starting an instance, presumably with the intent of mounting and opening a database in order to make a database system available for use. See Chapter 38.

STATEMENT

A statement is a SQL instruction to Oracle.

STDDEV

SEE ALSO GROUP FUNCTIONS, VARIANCE, Chapter 8
FORMAT

```
STDDEV(value)
```

DESCRIPTION STDDEV gives the standard deviation from the norm of values in a group of rows. It ignores **NULL** values in its calculation.

STORAGE

SEE ALSO **BLOCK, CREATE CLUSTER, CREATE INDEX, CREATE ROLLBACK SEGMENT, CREATE MATERIALIZED VIEW/SNAPSHOT, CREATE MATERIALIZED VIEW LOG/SNAPSHOT LOG, CREATE TABLE, CREATE TABLESPACE**, as well as the **ALTER** statement for each of these.

SYNTAX

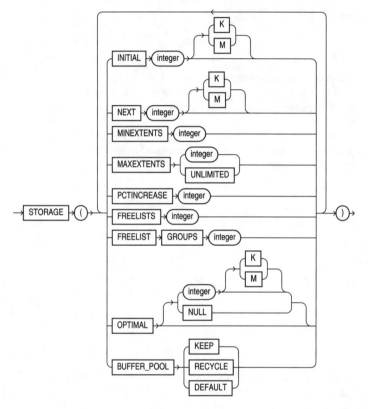

DESCRIPTION The **STORAGE** clause is optional in any of the **CREATE** and **ALTER** statements listed under the "See also" section. It is not a SQL statement, and cannot stand alone. In the following paragraphs, a block is a database block (*see* **BLOCK**) with a size depending on the operating system.

   INITIAL allocates the first extent of space to the object. If **INITIAL** is not specified, it defaults to five data blocks. The smallest initial extent you can allocate is two data blocks, and the largest depends on your operating system. You can express these numbers either as a simple integer or as an integer followed by K or M to indicate kilobytes or megabytes, respectively.

   NEXT is the size of the extent allocated after the initial extent has been filled. If not specified, it defaults to five data blocks. The smallest next extent you can allocate is one data block, and the largest depends on the operating system. You can use K and M for kilobytes and megabytes.

   PCTINCREASE controls the rate of growth of extents beyond the second. If set to 0, every additional extent will be the same size as the second extent, specified by **NEXT**. If **PCTINCREASE** is a positive integer, each succeeding extent will be that percentage larger than the previous one. For example, if **PCTINCREASE** was 50 (the default, if it is not specified), each additional extent would be 50 percent larger than the previous one. **PCTINCREASE** cannot be negative. The minimum **PCTINCREASE** is 0, and the maximum depends on the operating system. Oracle rounds the extent size up to the next multiple of the operating system block size.

MINEXTENTS defaults to 1 (or 2 for a rollback segment) if it is not specified, meaning that when the object is created, only the initial extent is allocated. A number larger than 1 will create that many total extents (which don't need to be contiguous on disk, as each extent itself does), and the size of each of them will be determined by the values set with **INITIAL**, **NEXT**, and **PCTINCREASE**. All of these will be allocated when the object is created.

MAXEXTENTS sets the limit on the total number of extents that can be allocated. The minimum limit is 1, with the default and maximum depending on the operating system. You can specify a **MAXEXTENTS** value of **UNLIMITED**.

OPTIMAL sets an optimal size in bytes for a rollback segment. You can use K and M for kilobytes and megabytes. Oracle will dynamically deallocate extents in the rollback segment to maintain the optimal size. **NULL** means that Oracle never deallocates the rollback segment extents, and this is the default behavior. You must supply a size greater than or equal to the initial space allocated for the rollback segment by the **MINEXTENTS**, **INITIAL**, **NEXT**, and **PCTINCREASE** parameters.

FREELIST GROUPS gives the number of groups of free lists, with a default value of 1. This setting applies to the Parallel Server option of Oracle for tables, clusters, or indexes.

FREELISTS sets the number of free lists for each free list group.

BUFFER_POOL sets the buffer pool into which the table's blocks will be read. By default, all blocks are read into the **DEFAULT** pool. You can create separate pools for blocks you want to keep in memory longer (the **KEEP** pool) or for those you wish to age out of memory quickly (**RECYCLE**). *See* the *Oracle8i DBA Handbook* for details.

STORE

PRODUCT　　SQL*PLUS
SEE ALSO　　**SAVE**, **START**, Chapter 14
FORMAT

```
STORE SET file[.ext] [ CRE[ATE] | REP[LACE] | APP[END] ]
```

DESCRIPTION　　**STORE** saves all of your SQLPLUS environment settings to a file.

EXAMPLE　　The following command saves the current SQLPLUS environment settings to a file named SETTINGS.SQL.

```
store settings.sql
```

STRUCTURED QUERY LANGUAGE

See **SQL**.

SUBPARTITION

A subpartition is a partition of a partition. Typically, a range partition is hash partitioned, creating multiple hash subpartitions for each of the range partitions. *See* Chapter 18.

SUBQUERY

A query (that is, a **select** statement) may be used as a part of another SQL statement (called the parent, or outer statement), including **CREATE TABLE**, **delete**, **insert**, **select**, and **update**, or in the SQL*PLUS **COPY** command, in order to define the rows or columns that the parent will use in its execution. The results of the child query (also called a subquery) are not themselves displayed, but are passed to the parent SQL statement for its use. The following rules apply:

- In an **update** or **CREATE TABLE** command, the subquery must return one value for each column to be inserted or updated. The value or values are then used by the parent SQL statement to **insert** or **update** the rows.

- A subquery cannot contain **order by** and **for update of** clauses.

- A "correlated" subquery is used in the **where** clause of a **select** statement, and references an alias for the table used by the parent select command. It is tested once for each row evaluated for selection by the parent select statement (a standard subquery evaluated just once for the parent query). *See* Chapter 12 for further details.

Other than these restrictions, normal rules for a **select** statement apply.

SUBSTITUTION
See **&, &&, ACCEPT, DEFINE**

SUBSTR
SEE ALSO ||, CHARACTER FUNCTIONS, **INSTR**, Chapter 7
FORMAT

```
SUBSTR(string, start [,count])
```

DESCRIPTION   **SUBSTR**ing clips out a piece of a string beginning at *start* and going for *count* characters. If *count* is not specified, the string is clipped from *start* and goes to the end of the string.
EXAMPLE

```
SUBSTR('NEWSPAPER',5)
```

produces this:

```
PAPER
```

SUBSTRB
SEE ALSO ||, CHARACTER FUNCTIONS, **INSTRB**, **SUBSTR**, Chapter 7
FORMAT

```
SUBSTRB(string, start [,count])
```

DESCRIPTION   **SUB STR**ing **B**yte clips out a piece of a string beginning at a *start* byte and going for *count* bytes. If *count* is not specified, the string is clipped from *start* and goes to the end of the string. This function lets you clip multi-byte character strings byte by byte instead of character by character, as **SUBSTR** does.

SUFFIX (SQL*PLUS)
See **SET**.

SUM
SEE ALSO   **COMPUTE**, GROUP FUNCTIONS, Chapter 8

FORMAT

```
SUM([DISTINCT] value)
```

DESCRIPTION   **SUM** is the sum of all *values* for a group of rows. **DISTINCT** makes SUM add each unique value to the total only once; this is usually not very meaningful.

SVRMGRL

SVRMGRL invokes Server Manager in line mode. Server Manager is used by DBAs while performing database maintenance and monitoring. See Chapter 38.

SYNONYM

A synonym is a name assigned to a table, view, or sequence that may thereafter be used to refer to it. If you have access to another user's table, you may create a synonym for it and refer to it by the synonym alone, without entering the user's name as a qualifier. *See* Chapter 22 and Chapter 35.

SYNTAX

Syntax is a set of rules that determine how to construct a valid statement in a computer language such as SQL.

SYNTAX OPERATORS

SEE ALSO   LOGICAL OPERATORS, PRECEDENCE

DESCRIPTION   Syntax operators have the highest precedence of all operators, and may appear anywhere in a SQL statement. Here they are listed in descending order of precedence. Operators of equal precedence are evaluated from left to right. Most of these are listed and described separately under their own symbols.

Operator	Function
-	SQL*PLUS command continuation. Continues a command on the following line.
&	Prefix for parameters in a SQL*PLUS start file. Words are substituted for &1, &2, and so on. *See* START.
& &&	Prefix for a substitution variable in a SQL command in SQL*PLUS. SQL*PLUS will prompt for a value if an undefined & or && variable is found. && also defines the variable and saves the value; '&' does not. *See* **& and &&**, **DEFINE**, and **ACCEPT**.
:	Prefix for a variable in SQL*FORMS and for a host variable in PL/SQL.
.	Variable separator, used in SQL*PLUS to separate the variable name from a suffix, so that the suffix is not considered a part of the variable name, and in SQL between user, table, and column names.
( )	Surrounds subqueries, lists of columns, or controls precedence.
'	Surrounds a literal, such as a character string or date constant. To use a ' in a string constant, use two ' marks (not a double quotation mark).
"	Surrounds a table or column alias that contains special character or a space.
"	Surrounds literal text in a date format clause of **TO_CHAR**.
@	Precedes a database name in a COPY, or a link name in a **from** clause.

SYS (ORACLE USER)

SYS is one of the DBA users that is created when a database system is installed and initialized (the other is SYSTEM). SYS owns most of the data dictionary tables, while SYSTEM owns the views created on those base tables.

SYSDATE

SEE ALSO   PSEUDO-COLUMNS

FORMAT

```
SYSDATE
```

DESCRIPTION   SYSDATE contains the current date and time. SYSDATE acts like a DATE datatype.

SYSTEM (ORACLE TABLESPACE)

SYSTEM is the name given to the first tablespace in a database. It contains the data dictionary and a rollback segment.

SYSTEM (ORACLE USER)

SYSTEM is one of the DBA users that is created when database system is installed and initialized (the other is SYS). While SYS owns most of the data dictionary tables, SYSTEM owns the views created on those base tables.

SYSTEM GLOBAL AREA (SGA)

SGA is a shared storage area in memory that is the center of Oracle activity while the database is running. The size of the SGA (and performance of the system) depends on the values of the variable init.ora parameters. The SGA provides communication between the user and the background processes.

SYSTEM PRIVILEGED COMMANDS

The system privileged commands are a subset of the SQL commands that require not only access to the DBA utilities, but a special operating system account. These commands require the highest level of security.

TABLE

A table is the basic data storage structure in a relational database management system. A table consists of one or more units of information (rows), each of which contains the same kinds of values (columns). *See* **CREATE TABLE**.

TABLE—PL/SQL

SEE ALSO   DATA TYPES, **RECORD** (PL/SQL)

FORMAT

```
TYPE new_type IS TABLE OF
{type | table.column%TYPE}[NOT NULL]
INDEX BY BINARY_INTEGER;
```

DESCRIPTION   A TABLE declaration declares a new type that can then be used to declare variables of that type. A PL/SQL table has one column and an integer key and can have any number of rows. The datatype of the column can either be one of the standard PL/SQL datatypes (including another RECORD but not a TABLE), or it can be a reference to the type of a particular column in a specific database table. Each field may also have a NOT NULL qualifier that specifies that the field must always have a non-null value.

The **index by binary integer** clause is required and reminds you that the index is an integer. You can refer to any row of the table with the index in parentheses.

If you refer to an index to which you have not assigned any data, PL/SQL raises the NO_DATA_FOUND exception.

EXAMPLE

```
type SkillTable is table(skill WORKERSKILL.Skill%TYPE);
SkillRecord MySkill;
MySkill(1) := 'GRAVEDIGGER';
MySkill(5) := 'SMITHY';
```

TABLE ALIAS

A table alias is a temporary substitute for a table name, defined in the **from** clause of a **select** statement. *See* **AS** and Chapter 11.

TABLE CONSTRAINT

A table constraint is an integrity constraint that applies to multiple columns of the same table. *See* INTEGRITY CONSTRAINT.

TABLESPACE

A tablespace is a file or set of files that is used to store Oracle data. An Oracle database is composed of the SYSTEM tablespace and possibly other tablespaces. *See* Chapters 20 and 38.

TAN

SEE ALSO   ACOS, ASIN, ATAN, ATAN2, COS, COSH, NUMBER FUNCTIONS, **SIN**, **TANH**, Chapter 8

FORMAT

```
TAN(value)
```

DESCRIPTION   **TAN** returns the tangent of an angle *value* expressed in radians.

EXAMPLE

```
select TAN(135*3.141593/180) Tan -- tangent of 135 degrees in radians
from DUAL;

       TAN
----------
        -1
```

TANH

SEE ALSO   ACOS, ASIN, ATAN, ATAN2, COS, COSH, NUMBER FUNCTIONS, **SIN**, **TAN**, Chapter 8

FORMAT

```
TANH(value)
```

DESCRIPTION   **TANH** returns the hyperbolic tangent of an angle *value*.

TEMPORARY SEGMENT

A temporary segment is a storage space within a tablespace used to hold intermediate results of a SQL statement. For example, temporary segments are used when sorting large tables. Temporary segments are usually stored in tablespaces dedicated to them; *see* **CREATE TABLESPACE**.

TERMINAL NODE

In a tree-structured table, a terminal node is a row that has no child row. It's the same as LEAF.

TERMINATOR

PL/SQL can be embedded in a host language using an Oracle precompiler. When it is, the entire section of PL/SQL blocks is treated as a single SQL statement. Thus, it is framed by the precompiler commands EXEC SQL EXECUTE and ENDEXEC. The character that follows ENDEXEC tells the precompiler that this is the end of the PL/SQL code. In C, this character is the semicolon (;). In COBOL it is a period (.), and in FORTRAN an end-of-line character.

TERMOUT (SQL*PLUS)

See **SET**.

TEXT INDEX

A text index is a set of tables and indexes used by text search programs. Like the index in a book, a text index contains tables of text entries and their locations.

TEXT SEARCH OPERATORS

The following operators are used within the **CONTAINS** function during ConText and interMediaText (IMT) searches. *See* Chapter 24 for examples and usage.

Operator	Description
OR	Returns a record if either search term has a score that exceeds the threshold.
|	Same as OR.
AND	Returns a record if both search terms have a score that exceeds the threshold.
&	Same as AND.
ACCUMUL	Returns a record if the sum of the search terms' scores exceeds the threshold.
,	Same as ACCUMUL.
MINUS	Returns a record if the score of the first search minus the score of the second search exceeds the threshold.
-	Same as MINUS.
*	Assigns different weights to the score of the searches.
NEAR	The score will be based on how near the search terms are to each other in the searched text.
;	Same as NEAR.
{}	Encloses reserved words such as AND if they are part of the search term.
%	Multiple-character wildcard.
_	Single-character wildcard.
$	Performs stem expansion of the search term prior to performing the search.
?	Performs a fuzzy match (allowing for misspellings) of the search term prior to performing the search.
!	Performs a SOUNDEX (phonetic) search.
()	Specifies the order in which search criteria are evaluated.

THEME

A theme is a category of a text document. Text entries may contain themes that do not appear as words within the document. For example, a document about mortgages could have "banking" as one of its themes even if the word "banking" did not appear in the document.

THROW

In Java, programs throw exceptions via the **try** clause, and process exceptions via the **catch** and **finally** clauses. See Chapter 32.

TIME (SQL*PLUS)

See **SET**.

TIMING (Form 1—SQL*PLUS)

See **SET**.

TIMING (Form 2—SQL*PLUS)

SEE ALSO   CLEAR, SET
FORMAT

```
TIMI[NG] [ START area | STOP | SHOW ];
```

DESCRIPTION   **TIMING** keeps track of elapsed time from START to STOP by area name. **START** opens a timing area and makes *area* its title. *area* must be a single word. Several areas may exist at once. The most recently created one is the current timing area until it is deleted, when the previously created one becomes current. Timing areas are, in effect, nested. The most recently created will always show the least amount of time, because the elapsed time of those before it will be, by definition, longer. Total time for any timing area is its own net time plus those of all the timing areas that followed it.

SHOW gives the current timing area's name and elapsed time.

STOP gives the current timing area's name and elapsed time, deletes the area, and makes the one previous to it (if there was one) the current timing area. *See* the *SQL*Plus User's Guide and Reference* for your host operating system for details on the precise meaning of time on your machine.

EXAMPLE   To create a timing area named 1, you enter this:

```
timing start 1
```

To see the current area name and time, but allow it to continue running, enter the following:

```
timing show
```

To see the current timing area's name and accumulated time, stop it, and make the previous one current, use this:

```
timing stop
```

TO_BINARY_INTEGER

SEE ALSO   TABLE—PL/SQL

FORMAT

```
TO_BINARY_INTEGER(string)
TO_BINARY_INTEGER(number)
```

DESCRIPTION **TO_BINARY_INTEGER** converts a CHAR or VARCHAR2 string or a NUMBER number into a binary integer. You can use this as an index into a PL/SQL table. The *string* must be a valid number.

TO_CHAR (Form 1—Date and Number Conversion)

SEE ALSO DATE FORMATS, DATE FUNCTIONS, NUMBER FORMATS, **TO_DATE**, Chapter 9

FORMAT

```
TO_CHAR(date,'format')
TO_CHAR(number, 'format')
```

DESCRIPTION **TO_CHAR** reformats number or date according to *format*. *date* must be a column defined as an Oracle DATE datatype. It cannot be a string even if it is in the default date format of DD-MON-YY. The only way to use a string in which *date* appears in the **TO_CHAR** function is to enclose it within a **TO_DATE** function. The formats possible for this function are numerous. They are listed under NUMBER FORMATS and DATE FORMATS.

EXAMPLE Note the format in the following example. This is necessary in SQL*PLUS to avoid the current default date width produced by **TO_CHAR**, which is about 100 characters wide:

```
column Formatted format a30 word_wrapped heading 'Formatted'

select BirthDate, TO_CHAR(BirthDate,MM/DD/YY) Formatted
  from BIRTHDAY
 where FirstName = 'VICTORIA';

BIRTHDATE Formatted
--------- ------------------------------
20-MAY-49 05/20/49
```

TO_CHAR (Form 2—Label Conversion)

SEE ALSO TO_CHAR (Form 1), TO_LABEL

FORMAT

```
TO_CHAR(label,'format')
```

DESCRIPTION For users of Trusted Oracle, the **TO_CHAR** function can be used to convert *labels* of the MLSLABEL datatype to VARCHAR2 datatypes, using an optional *format*. If the format is omitted, then the label is converted to a VARCHAR2 value in the default label format. *See* the *Trusted Oracle Server Administrator's Guide*.

TO_DATE

SEE ALSO DATE FORMATS, DATE FUNCTIONS, **TO_CHAR**, Chapter 8

FORMAT

```
TO_DATE(string,'format')
```

DESCRIPTION   **TO_DATE** converts a *string* in a given format into an Oracle date. It also will accept a number instead of a string, with certain limits. *string* is a literal string, a literal number, or a database column containing a string or a number. In every case but one, the format must correspond to that which is described by the *format*. Only if a string is in the format 'DD-MON-YY' can the format be omitted. Note that *format* is restricted. *See* DATE FORMATS for a list of acceptable formats for **TO_DATE**.

EXAMPLE

```
select TO_DATE('02/22/90','MM/DD/YY') from DUAL;

TO_DATE('
---------
22-FEB-90
```

TO_LABEL

SEE ALSO   DATA TYPES, **TO_CHAR** (Form 2)

FORMAT

```
TO_LABEL(string, format)
```

DESCRIPTION   **TO_LABEL** converts a CHAR or VARCHAR2 *string* into a secure operating system label of type RAW MLSLABEL using a label *format*.

TO_LOB

SEE ALSO   INSERT, Chapter 30

FORMAT

```
TO_LOB(long_column)
```

DESCRIPTION   **TO_LOB** converts LONG values in *long_column* to LOB values. You can apply this function only to a LONG column, and only in the **select** list of a subquery in an **insert** command.

TO_MULTI_BYTE

SEE ALSO   CONVERSION FUNCTIONS, Chapter 10

FORMAT

```
TO_MULTI_BYTE(string)
```

DESCRIPTION   **TO_MULTI_BYTE** converts the single-byte characters in a character *string* to their multi-byte equivalents. If a character has no multi-byte equivalent, the function returns the character unconverted.

TO_NUMBER

SEE ALSO   CONVERSION FUNCTIONS, Chapter 10

FORMAT

```
TO_NUMBER(string)
```

DESCRIPTION   **TO_NUMBER** converts a character *string* to a number datatype. It requires that the characters in the string be a properly formatted number with only the characters 0-9, -, +, and .

included. This function is largely unnecessary due to automatic data conversion done by Oracle, except when used for a character column containing numbers in an **order by** or a comparison.

EXAMPLE

```
TO_NUMBER('333.46')
```

TO_SINGLE_BYTE

SEE ALSO   CONVERSION FUNCTIONS, Chapter 10

FORMAT

```
TO_SINGLE_BYTE(string)
```

DESCRIPTION   **TO_SINGLE_BYTE** converts the multi-byte characters in a character *string* to their single-byte equivalents. If a multi-byte character has no single-byte equivalent, the function returns the character unconverted.

TRANSACTION

A transaction is a sequence of SQL statements that Oracle treats as a single unit. The set of changes is made permanent with the **COMMIT** statement. Part or all of a transaction can be undone with the **ROLLBACK** statement.

Oracle manages transactions both with locking (*see* LOCK) and a *multiversion consistency model,* which essentially behaves as though each transaction had its own copy of the database—that is, that there are multiple, overlapping versions of the database in existence at any given time. A transaction starts with the execution of the first SQL statement in the transaction and ends with either the **COMMIT** or **ROLLBACK** statement. By default, Oracle guarantees that a transaction has *statement-level read consistency,* which means that when you execute a query, the data stays the same while Oracle is gathering and returning it. But if a transaction has multiple queries, each query is consistent but not with each other. If you want to be able to maintain a consistent view of the data throughout such a transaction, the transaction needs to have *transaction- level read consistency,* which guarantees that the transaction will not see the effects of the committing of other transactions. This read-only transaction, started with **SET TRANSACTION READ ONLY**, can only execute queries and certain control commands (*see* **SET TRANSACTION**).

TRANSACTION PROCESSING

Transaction processing is a form of processing oriented toward logical units of work, rather than separate and individual changes, in order to keep the database consistent.

TRANSLATE

SEE ALSO   REPLACE, Chapter 10

FORMAT

```
TRANSLATE(string,if,then)
```

DESCRIPTION   **TRANSLATE** looks at each character in *string*, and then checks *if* to see if that character is there. If it is, **TRANSLATE** notes the position in *if* where it found the character, and then looks at the same position in *then*. Whatever character it finds there, it substitutes for the character in *string*.

EXAMPLE

```
select TRANSLATE('I LOVE MY OLD THESAURUS','AEIOUY','123456')
from DUAL;

TRANSLATE('ILOVEMYOLDTH
----------------------
3 L4V2 M6 4LD TH2S15R5S
```

TRANSPORTABLE TABLESPACE

A transportable tablespace is a tablespace that can be "unplugged" from one database and "plugged into" another. To be transportable, a tablespace—or a set of tablespaces—must be self-contained. That is, the tablespace cannot contain any objects that refer to objects in other tablespaces. Thus, if you transport a tablespace containing indexes, you must move the tablespace containing the indexes' base tables as part of the same transportable tablespace set. To transport tablespaces, you need to generate a tablespace set, move that tablespace set to the new database, and plug the set into the new database. The databases must be on the same operating system, with the same version of Oracle, database block size, and character set.

GENERATING A TRANSPORTABLE TABLESPACE SET
A transportable tablespace set contains all of the datafiles for the tablespaces being moved, along with an export of the metadata for those tablespaces. The tablespaces being transported should be self-contained—they should not contain any objects that are dependent on objects outside of the tablespaces. The better you have organized and distributed your objects among tablespaces, the easier it is to generate a self-contained set of tablespaces to transport.

You can optionally choose whether to include referential integrity constraints as part of the transportable tablespace set. If you choose to use referential integrity constraints, the transportable tablespace set will increase to include the tables required to maintain the key relationships. Referential integrity is optional because you may have the same codes tables in multiple databases. For example, you may be planning to move a tablespace from your test database to your production database. If you have a COUNTRY table in the test database, then you may already have an identical COUNTRY table in the production database. Since the codes tables are identical in the two databases, you do not need to transport that portion of the referential integrity constraints. You could transport the tablespace and then re-enable the referential integrity in the target database once the tablespace has been moved, simplifying the creation of the transportable tablespace set.

To determine if a tablespace set is self-contained, execute the TRANSPORT_SET_CHECK procedure of the DBMS_TTS package. This procedure takes two input parameters: the set of tablespaces and a Boolean flag set to TRUE if you want referential integrity constraints to be considered. In the following example, referential integrity constraints are not considered for the combination of the AGG_DATA and AGG_INDEXES tablespaces:

```
execute DBMS_TTS.TRANSPORT_SET_CHECK('AGG_DATA,AGG_INDEXES','FALSE');
```

If there are any self-containment violations in the specified set, Oracle will populate the TRANSPORT_SET_VIOLATIONS data dictionary view. If there are no violations, the view will be empty.

Once you have selected a self-contained set of tablespaces, make the tablespaces read only, as shown here:

```
alter tablespace AGG_DATA read only;
alter tablespace AGG_INDEXES read only;
```

Next, export the metadata for the tablespaces, using the TRANSPORT_TABLESPACES and TABLESPACES Export parameters:

```
exp TRANSPORT_TABLESPACE=Y TABLESPACES=(AGG_DATA,AGG_INDEXES) CONSTRAINTS=N  GRANTS=Y TRIGGERS=N
```

As shown in the example, you can specify whether triggers, constraints, and grants are exported along with the tablespace metadata. You should also note the names of the accounts that own objects in the transportable tablespace set. You can now copy the tablespaces' datafiles to a separate area. If needed, you can put the tablespaces back into read-write mode in their current database. After you have generated the transportable tablespace set, you can move its files (including the export) to an area that the target database can access.

PLUGGING IN THE TRANSPORTABLE TABLESPACE SET   Once the transportable tablespace set has been moved to an area accessible to the target database, you can plug the set into the target database. First, use Import to import the exported metadata:

```
imp TRANSPORT_TABLESPACE=Y DATAFILES=(agg_data.dbf, agg_indexes.dbf)
```

In the import, you specify the datafiles that are part of the transportable tablespace set. You can optionally specify the tablespaces (via the TABLESPACES parameter) and the object owners (via the OWNERS parameter).

After the import completes, all tablespaces in the transportable tablespace set are left in read-only mode. You can issue the **alter tablespace read write** command in the target database to place the new tablespaces in read-write mode.

```
alter tablespace AGG_DATA read write;
alter tablespace AGG_INDEXES read write;
```

Note that you cannot change the ownership of the objects being transported.

Transportable tablespaces support very fast movement of large datasets. In a data warehouse, you could use transportable tablespaces to publish aggregations from core warehouse to data mart, or from the data marts to a global data warehouse. Any read-only data can be quickly distributed to multiple databases—instead of sending SQL scripts, you can send datafiles and exported metadata. This modified data movement process may greatly simplify your procedures for managing remote databases, remote data marts, and large data movement operations.

TREE-STRUCTURED QUERY

A tree-structured query is one whose result shows hierarchical relationships among rows in a table. *See* **CONNECT BY**.

TRIGGER

A database trigger is a stored procedure associated with a table that Oracle automatically executes on one or more specified events (**BEFORE**, **AFTER**, or **INSTEAD OF** an **insert**, **update**, or **delete**) affecting the table. Triggers can execute for the table as a whole or for each affected row in the table. *See* Chapters 23 and 25 for a full discussion of triggers and examples, and **CREATE TRIGGER** in this Alphabetical Reference for syntax.

TRIMOUT (SQL*PLUS)

See **SET**.

TRUNC (Form I—for Dates)

SEE ALSO   COLUMN, DATE FUNCTIONS, **TRUNC** (Form 2—for Numbers), Chapter 9

FORMAT

TRUNC(date,'format')

DESCRIPTION   **TRUNC** is the truncating of *date* according to *format*. Without a *format*, *date* is truncated to 12 A.M. (midnight) in the morning, with the first moment of the new day, today's date, for any time up to and including 11:59:59 P.M. (just before midnight). These are the formats available for truncating:

Format	Meaning
cc, scc	century (truncates up to January 1st of this century, for any date and time up to December 31st, 1999 at 11:59:59 P.M.).
syear,syyy,y,yy,yyy,yyyy	year (truncates up to January 1st of this year for any date up to December 31st at 11:59:59 P.M.).
q	quarter (truncates to the first day of the current quarter for any date in this quarter, up to 11:59:59 P.M. of the last day of the quarter).
month,mon,mm	month (truncates to the first date of the current month for any date up to 11:59:59 P.M. on the last day of the month).
ww	same day of the week as the first day of the year.
w	truncates to the last day that is the same day of the week as the first day of the month (*see* text following list).
ddd,dd,j	truncates to 12 A.M. of current day, up to 11:59:59 P.M. This is the same as **TRUNC** with no format.
day,dy,d	truncates back to Sunday (first day of week) for any date up to 11:59:59 P.M. on Saturday.
hh,hh12,hh24	truncates to the last whole hour, up to 59 minutes and 59 seconds after the hour.
mi	truncates to the last whole minute as of 59 seconds of the current minute.

ww produces the date of the current week's Monday with the time set at 12 A.M., for any day in the week up to Sunday night at 11:59:59 P.M. Any time on Monday is truncated to the same Monday at 12 A.M.

w works similarly, except that instead of producing the date of the current week's Monday at 12 A.M., it produces the date of the current week's day that is the same day of the week as the first day of the month. If the first day of a month was Friday, for instance, since a week is seven days long, this means any date and time up to seven days after a Friday (the next Thursday at 11:59:59 P.M.), will be truncated to the last Friday at 12 A.M. (midnight) in the morning (the first moment of the day on Friday). Any time on Friday is truncated to the same Friday at 12 A.M.

The result of **TRUNC** is always a date with its time set to 12 A.M., the first moment of the day.

TRUNC (Form 2—for Numbers)

SEE ALSO   COLUMN, NUMBER FUNCTIONS, **TRUNC** (Form 1—for Dates), Chapter 8

FORMAT

TRUNC(value,precision)

DESCRIPTION   TRUNC is value truncated to precision.

EXAMPLES

```
TRUNC(123.45,1) = 123.4
TRUNC(123.45,0) = 123
TRUNC(123.45,-1) = 120
TRUNC(123.45,-2) = 100
```

TRUNCATE

SEE ALSO   **CREATE CLUSTER, DELETE, DROP TABLE**, TRIGGER, Chapter 18

SYNTAX

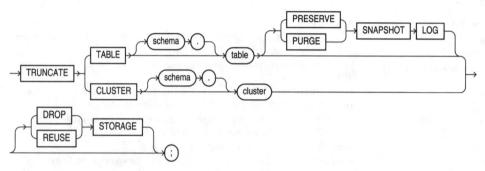

DESCRIPTION   **TRUNCATE** removes all the rows from a table or cluster. You can only truncate an indexed cluster, not a hash cluster (*see* **CREATE CLUSTER**). If you add the **DROP STORAGE** option, **TRUNCATE** will deallocate the space from the deleted rows; if you add the **REUSE STORAGE** option, **TRUNCATE** will leave the space allocated for new rows in the table. **DROP STORAGE** is the default.

The **TRUNCATE** command is faster than a **DELETE** command because it generates no rollback information, does not fire any **DELETE** triggers (and therefore must be used with caution), and does not record any information in a snapshot log. In addition, using **TRUNCATE** does not invalidate the objects depending on the deleted rows or the privileges on the table.

NOTE
*You cannot roll back a **TRUNCATE** statement.*

TTITLE

SEE ALSO   ACCEPT, **BTITLE**, DEFINE, PARAMETERS, **REPFOOTER, REPHEADER**, Chapter 14

FORMAT

```
TTI[TLE] [option [text|variable]... | OFF | ON]
```

DESCRIPTION   **TTITLE** (Top **TITLE**) puts a title (may be multi-line) at the top of each page of a report. OFF and ON suppress and restore the display of the text without changing its contents. **TTITLE** by itself displays the current **TTITLE** options and *text* or *variable*.

text is a title you wish to give this report, and *variable* is a user-defined variable or a system-maintained variable, including SQL.LNO, the current line number; SQL.PNO, the current page number; SQL.RELEASE, the current Oracle release number; SQL.SQLCODE, the current error code; and SQL.USER, the username.

SQL*PLUS uses **ttitle** in the new form if the first word after **ttitle** is a valid option. The valid options are

COL[UMN] *n* skips directly to position *n* from the left margin of the current line.

S[KIP] *n* prints *n* blank lines. If no *n* is specified, one blank line is printed. If *n* is 0, no blank lines are printed and the current position for printing becomes position 1 of the current line (leftmost on the page).

TAB *n* skips forward *n* positions (backward if *n* is negative).

LE[FT], **CE[NTER]**, and **R[IGHT]** left-justify, center, and right-justify data on the current line. Any text or variables following these commands are justified as a group, up to the end of the command, or a LEFT, CENTER, RIGHT, or COLUMN. CENTER and RIGHT use the value set by the **SET LINESIZE** command to determine where to place the text or variable.

FORMAT string specifies the format model that will control the format of subsequent text or variables, and follows the same syntax as FORMAT in a **COLUMN** command, such as FORMAT A12 or FORMAT $999,990.99. Each time a FORMAT appears, it supersedes the previous one that was in effect. If no FORMAT model has been specified, the one set by **SET NUMFORMAT** is used. If NUMFORMAT has not been set, the default for SQL*PLUS is used.

Date values are printed according to the default format unless a variable has been loaded with a date reformatted by **TO_CHAR**.

Any number of options, pieces of text, and variables may be used in a single **ttitle**. Each is printed in the order specified, and each is positioned and formatted as specified by the clauses that precede it.

TUPLE

TUPLE is a synonym for row. It rhymes with "couple."

TWO-PHASE COMMIT

Oracle manages distributed transactions with a special feature called *two-phase commit.* Two-phase commit guarantees that a transaction is valid at all sites by the time it commits or rolls back. All sites either commit or roll back together, no matter what errors occur in the network or on the machines tied together by the network. You don't need to do anything special to have your applications use a two-phase commit.

TYPE

See ABSTRACT DATATYPE and **CREATE TYPE**.

TYPE (Embedded SQL)
FORMAT

```
EXEC SQL TYPE type IS datatype
```

DESCRIPTION　　PL/SQL lets you to assign an Oracle external datatype to a user-defined datatype. The datatype may include a length, precision, or scale. This external datatype is equivalenced to the user-defined type and assigned to all host variables assigned to the type. For a list of external datatypes, see *Programmer's Guide to the Oracle Precompilers*.

TYPE BODY

See ABSTRACT DATATYPE, **CREATE TYPE**, and METHOD.

UID

SEE ALSO   PSEUDO-COLUMNS

FORMAT

```
UID
```

DESCRIPTION   The User **ID** is a number assigned by Oracle to each user, and is unique on the current database. It may be used in a **select** statement, but is not a real column and cannot be updated by the user.

UNDEFINE

SEE ALSO   **ACCEPT**, **DEFINE**, PARAMETERS, Chapters 14 and 16

FORMAT

```
UNDEF[INE] variable
```

DESCRIPTION   **UNDEFINE** deletes the definition of a user variable that has been defined by **ACCEPT**, **DEFINE**, or as a parameter to the **START** command. You can **undefine** the current values of multiple variables in a single command. The format is shown in the following listing:

```
undefine variable1 variable2 ...
```

EXAMPLE   To undefine a variable named Total, use this:

```
undefine Total
```

UNDERLINE (SQL*PLUS)

See **SET**.

UNION

SEE ALSO   **INTERSECT**, **MINUS**, QUERY OPERATORS, Chapter 12

FORMAT

```
select...
  UNION [ALL]
select...
```

DESCRIPTION   **UNION** combines two queries. It returns all distinct rows for both **select** statements, or, when **ALL** is specified, all rows regardless of duplication. The number of columns and datatypes must be identical between **select** statements, although the names of the columns do not need to be. *See* Chapter 12 for a discussion of the important differences and effects of **INTERSECT**, **UNION**, and **MINUS**, and the role that precedence plays in the results.

UNIQUE INDEX

A unique index is an index that imposes uniqueness on each value it indexes. The index may be one single column or concatenated (multiple columns). *See* INTEGRITY CONSTRAINT.

UNIQUE KEY

A unique key is one or more columns that must be unique for each row of the table. *See* KEY, PRIMARY KEY, and INTEGRITY CONSTRAINT.

UNIT OF WORK

In Oracle, a transaction is equivalent to a logical unit of work, which includes all SQL statements since you either logged on, last committed, or last rolled back your work. Thus, a transaction can encompass numerous SQL statements, or only one.

UNRECOVERABLE

In prior versions of Oracle (Oracle7.2 and upward), the **UNRECOVERABLE** keyword was used to disable the writing of online redo log entries for the duration of a **CREATE TABLE AS SELECT** or **CREATE INDEX** command. As of Oracle8, it has been superseded by the **NOLOGGING** clause, which disables the writing of online redo log entries for an object even after its creation. *See* **CREATE TABLE** and **CREATE INDEX**. **UNRECOVERABLE** is still used in SQL*Loader—see Chapter 21.

UPDATE (Form 1—Embedded SQL)

SEE ALSO   EXECUTE IMMEDIATE, FOR, PREPARE, SELECT (Form 2)

FORMAT

```
EXEC SQL [AT database | :variable] [FOR :integer]
UPDATE [user.]table[@dblink] [alias]
SET { column = expression [,column = expression]... |
 (column [,column]... ) = (subquery) }
[ WHERE condition | CURRENT OF cursor];
```

DESCRIPTION   *See* the description of the various clauses in **UPDATE** (Form 3). The elements unique to Embedded SQL follow:

- **AT database**, which optionally names a database from a previous **CONNECT** statement for a database name from a previous **DECLARE DATABASE** statement.

- **FOR** *:integer*, which sets the maximum number of rows that can be fetched. *integer* is a named host variable.

- *expression* may include a host :*variable*[:*indicator*].

- The **where** clause may include host variables or arrays.

- **CURRENT OF** updates the last row fetched for the named **cursor**. However, the cursor must be open and positioned on the row. If it isn't, the **CURRENT OF**, which is a part of the **where** clause, causes the **where** to find no rows, and none will be updated. The cursor must have previously been named in a **DECLARE CURSOR** statement with a **select. . .for update of**.

   If any host variable in either the **set** or **where** is an array, then all host variables in both must be arrays, though they do not all need to be the same size arrays. If they are arrays, **update** is executed once for each set of components in the array, and may update zero or more rows. The maximum number depends on either the size of the smallest array, or the integer value in the **for** clause, if one is specified. *See* **FOR** for additional details.

UPDATE (Form 2—PL/SQL)

SEE ALSO   DECLARE CURSOR, SUBQUERY

FORMAT

```
UPDATE [user.]table[@dblink]
SET { column = expression | column = (select expression...)
 [ [,column = expression]... |
 [,column = (select
expression...)]... ] |
 (column [,column]...) = (subquery)}
 [WHERE {condition | CURRENT OF cursor}];
```

DESCRIPTION   **UPDATE** in PL/SQL works identically to the normal SQL UPDATE statement, with the exception of the alternative **where** clause **WHERE CURRENT OF** cursor. In this instance, the **update** statement affects just the single row currently in the cursor as a result of the last **FETCH**. The cursor **select** statement must have included the words FOR UPDATE.

Like **insert**, **delete**, and **select. . .into**, the **update** statement always uses the implicit cursor named SQL. This is never declared (although the **select. . .for update** statement must be **DECLARE**d in a cursor for **WHERE CURRENT OF cursor** to be used). Its attributes are set as follows:

- SQL%ISOPEN is irrelevant.

- SQL%FOUND is TRUE if one or more rows is updated, FALSE if no rows are updated. SQL%NOTFOUND is the opposite of SQL%FOUND.

- SQL%ROWCOUNT is the number of rows updated.

EXAMPLE

```
<<overage>>
DECLARE
    cursor EMPLOYEE is
        select Age from WORKER
            for update of Lodging;
    WORKER_RECORD    EMPLOYEE%rowtype;
BEGIN
    open EMPLOYEE;
    loop
        fetch EMPLOYEE into WORKER_RECORD;
        exit when EMPLOYEE%notfound;
            if WORKER_RECORD.Age >= 65
                then update WORKER
                        set Lodging = 'YOUTH HOSTEL'
                    where current of EMPLOYEE;
    end loop;
    commit;
    close EMPLOYEE;
END overage;
```

UPDATE (Form 3—SQL Command)
SEE ALSO   **DELETE**, **INSERT**, **SELECT**, SUBQUERY, **WHERE**, Chapter 14
SYNTAX

table_expression_clause::=

with_clause::=

table_collection_expression::=

set_clause::=

where_clause::=

returning_clause::=

DESCRIPTION   **UPDATE** updates (changes) the values in the listed columns in the specified table. The **where** clause may contain a correlated subquery. A subquery may select from the table that is being updated, although it must return just one row. Without a **where** clause, all rows will be updated. With a **where** clause, only those rows it selects will be updated. The expressions are evaluated as the command is executed, and their results replace the current values for the columns in the row(s).

A subquery must select the same number of columns (with compatible datatypes) as are in parentheses on the left side of the **set** clause. Columns set to equal expression may precede columns in parentheses set equal to a subquery, all within a single **update** statement.

EXAMPLE   To set **NULL** ages for all workers over the age of 65, use this:

```
update WORKER set Age = NULL where Age > 65;
```

The following will update the city of Walpole in the COMFORT table, setting the precipitation for all Walpole rows to **NULL**, the noon temperature equal to that in Manchester, and the midnight temperature equal to the noon temperature minus 10 degrees.

```
update COMFORT set Precipitation = NULL,
              (Noon, Midnight) =
       (select Temperature, Temperature - 10
          from WEATHER
         where City = 'MANCHESTER')
 where City = 'WALPOLE';
```

UPPER

SEE ALSO   **LOWER**, Chapter 7

FORMAT

```
UPPER(string)
```

DESCRIPTION   **UPPER** converts every letter in a *string* into uppercase.

EXAMPLE   upper('Look what you''ve done, Lauren!')
produces this:

```
LOOK WHAT YOU'VE DONE, LAUREN!
```

USED EXTENTS

Used extents are those that either have been allocated to a data (table) segment—and thus have data in them—or have been reserved for data.

USER

SEE ALSO   PSEUDO-COLUMNS, UID

FORMAT

USER

DESCRIPTION   *User* is the name by which the current user is known to Oracle. *User* is a pseudo-column, and as such can be queried in any **select** statement, but because it is not a real column, it cannot be updated.

USER VARIABLES

See **ACCEPT**, **DEFINE**, PARAMETERS

USERENV

SEE ALSO   CHARACTER FUNCTIONS

FORMAT

USERENV(*option*)

DESCRIPTION   *UserEnv* returns information about the user environment, usually for an audit trail. Options include ' ENTRYID', ' SESSIONID', and ' TERMINAL'.

USERNAME

Username is a word that identifies you as an authorized user of your host computer's operating system or of Oracle. Associated with each username is a password.

VAR (Embedded SQL)

SEE ALSO   *See* **SELECT (Form 2)**, VARIABLE DECLARATION.

FORMAT

EXEC SQL VAR *host_variable* IS *datatype*

DESCRIPTION   PL/SQL lets you override the default datatype assignment of a variable via the **VAR** command. Once a variable has been declared, its uses the datatype assigned to it in the **declare** command. **VAR** allows you to change the datatype of a declared variable within a PL/SQL block.

VARCHAR

See DATA TYPES.

VARCHAR2

See DATA TYPES.

VARIABLE

SEE ALSO   PRINT

FORMAT

VAR[IABLE] [*variable_name* {NUMBER|CHAR|CHAR (*n*)}]

DESCRIPTION   **VARIABLE** declares a bind variable which can be referenced in PL/SQL. Each variable is assigned a *variable_name* and a type (NUMBER or CHAR). For CHAR variables, a maximum length (*n*) can be specified.

EXAMPLES   In the following example, a variable named *bal* is created and is set equal to the result of a function.

```
variable bal NUMBER
begin
   :bal := BALANCE_CHECK('ADAH TALBOT');
end;
```

VARIABLE DECLARATION (PL/SQL)
FORMAT

```
variable [CONSTANT]
{type | identifier%TYPE | [user.]table%ROWTYPE}
 [NOT NULL]
 [{DEFAULT | :=} expression];
```

DESCRIPTION   PL/SQL lets you declare variables in a PL/SQL block. If you declare the variable to be CONSTANT, you must initialize the variable with a value in the declaration and you cannot assign a new value to the variable.

The type of the variable can be a PL/SQL type (*see* DATA TYPES), the type of another PL/SQL variable or database column given by an identifier, or a ROWTYPE (*see* **%ROWTYPE**) that lets you refer to a record corresponding to a database table.

If you add **NOT NULL** to the declaration, you cannot assign a NULL to the variable and you must initialize the variable. The initialization (following a DEFAULT or assignment :=) expression is any valid PL/SQL expression that results in a value of the type declared.

VARIANCE
SEE ALSO   **ACCEPT**, **COMPUTE**, **DEFINE**, GROUP FUNCTIONS, **PARAMETERS**, **STDDEV**, Chapter 8
FORMAT

```
VARIANCE([DISTINCT] value)
```

DESCRIPTION   **VARIANCE** gives the variance of all *values* for a group of rows. Like other group functions, **VARIANCE** ignores NULL values.

VARRAY
VARRAY is a clause within the CREATE TYPE command that tells the database the limit to the number of entries within the varying array. *See* Chapter 29 for detailed examples of varying arrays. *See* CREATE TYPE for syntax information.

VARYING ARRAY
A varying array is a collector—for a single row in a table, it can contain multiple entries. The maximum number of varying array entries per row is set when the varying array is created (via **CREATE TYPE**). *See* Chapter 29.

VERIFY (SQL*PLUS)
See **SET**.

VERSION NUMBER
The version number is the primary identifying number of Oracle software. In V8.1.5.1, 8 is the version number.

VIEW
A view is a database object that is a logical representation of a table. It is derived from a table but has no storage of its own and often may be used in the same manner as a table. *See* **CREATE VIEW** and Chapter 18.

VIRTUAL COLUMN
A virtual column is a column in a query result whose value is calculated from the value(s) of other column(s).

VSIZE
SEE ALSO   CHARACTER FUNCTIONS, **LENGTH**, NUMBER FUNCTIONS, Chapter 8

FORMAT

```
VSIZE(value)
```

DESCRIPTION   VSIZE is the storage size of value in Oracle. For character columns, **VSIZE** is the same as LENGTH. For numbers it is usually smaller than the apparent length, because less space is required to store numbers in the database.

EXAMPLES

```
VSIZE('VICTORIA') = 8
VSIZE(12.345) = 4
```

WALKING A TREE
Walking a tree is the process of visiting each node of a tree in turn. *See* **CONNECT BY**.

WebDB
Oracle's WebDB product is a development tool that also supports database administration activities. Chapter 37 provides a high-level overview of its capabilities.

WHENEVER (Form 1—Embedded SQL)
SEE ALSO   EXECUTE, FETCH

FORMAT

```
EXEC SQL WHENEVER {NOT FOUND | SQLERROR | SQL WARNING}
    {CONTINUE |
     GOTO label |
     STOP |
     DO routine}
```

DESCRIPTION   **WHENEVER** is not an executable SQL statement, but rather an instruction to the Oracle language processor to embed an "IF *condition* THEN GOTO *label* " statement after every SQL statement to follow. As each SQL statement executes, its results are tested to see if they meet the *condition*. If they do, the program branches to the *label*.

WHENEVER may be used with **CONTINUE** or a different label for each of the three possible conditions. Each of these will be in effect for all subsequent SQL statements. A new **WHENEVER** with one of these conditions will completely replace its predecessor for all subsequent SQL statements.

NOT FOUND condition is raised any time SQLCODE is 100, meaning, for instance, that a **FETCH** failed to return any rows (this includes subqueries in **insert** statements).

SQLERROR occurs whenever SQLCODE is less than 0. These are typically fatal errors and require serious error handling.

SQLWARNING occurs when a nonfatal "error" occurs. These include truncation of character strings being loaded into host variables, a select list of columns that doesn't match the INTO list of host variables, and **delete** or **update** statements without **where** clauses.

Usually initial branching, continuation, stopping, or routine execution is set up at the very beginning of a program, before any executable SQL statements, something like this:

```
exec sql whenever not found  goto close_down;
exec sql whenever sqlwarning continue;
exec sql whenever sqlerror   goto fatal_error;
```

However, within particular blocks of logic in the body of the program, any or all of these could be replaced depending upon local needs. Note that **WHENEVER** knows nothing about the host languages scoping rules, calls, or branching. From the moment a **WHENEVER** is asserted, its rules remain in effect until another **WHENEVER** (with the same condition) replaces it. On the other hand, your program must obey language scoping rules with regard to the **GOTO** and label.

The **STOP** option stops program execution; the **DO** option calls a host language routine of some kind, the syntax of which depends on your host language.

Lastly, in an error-handling routine, particularly one that may contain SQL statements, WHENEVER SQLERROR should probably contain **CONTINUE** or **STOP** or should call an exit routine in order to avoid an infinite loop back into the same error-handling routine.

WHENEVER SQLERROR (Form 2—SQL*PLUS)

SEE ALSO   EXIT, **WHENEVER** (Form 1)

FORMAT

```
WHENEVER SQLERROR {EXIT
 [SUCCESS|FAILURE|WARNING|integer|variable] |
 CONTINUE}
```

DESCRIPTION   With **EXIT**, WHENEVER SQLERROR ends a SQL*PLUS session and returns user to the operating system or calling program or menu if a fatal error is detected (sqlcode < 0). This does not include warning sqlcodes, such as "no rows selected" or "update without a where clause." It does include "table or view does not exist." It commits pending changes to the database. A return code is also returned. SUCCESS, FAILURE, and WARNING have values that are operating system specific; FAILURE and WARNING may be the same on some operating systems.

With **CONTINUE** (instead of **EXIT**), SQL errors are ignored and succeeding statements continue to be executed. This might be used with a series of start files, where some reports, for instance, were not dependent on the success of earlier SQL statements, and you wanted to avoid leaving SQL*PLUS until they were all completed.

You may place WHENEVER SQLERROR in a start file in front of as many SQL statements as you wish. Each WHENEVER SQLERROR will supersede the one before, and will remain in effect until it is itself superseded.

integer is a value you can pass back explicitly as the return code; *variable* allows you to set this value dynamically. This can be a user-defined variable, or a system variable, such as **sql.sqlcode**, which always contains the sqlcode of the last SQL statement executed, either in SQL*PLUS or an embedded PL/SQL block.

EXAMPLE When the **create table** in the following example fails because the literal KEENE is not enclosed in single quotation marks, the subsequent **update** and **select** will never even execute. The WHENEVER SQLERROR will exit SQL*PLUS immediately, and pass the **sql.sqlcode** back to the host:

```
whenever sqlerror exit sql.sqlcode;

create table KEENE as
select * from COMFORT
 where City = KEENE;

update KEENE set Noon = 75;

select * from KEENE;
```

WHERE

SEE ALSO DELETE, LOGICAL OPERATORS, PRECEDENCE, **SELECT**, SYNTAX OPERATORS, UPDATE

FORMAT

```
DELETE FROM [user.]table ...
   [ WHERE condition ]
SELECT ...
   [ WHERE condition ]
UPDATE [user.]table [alias] ...
   [WHERE condition ]
```

DESCRIPTION **WHERE** defines those logical conditions that will control which rows a **select** statement will return, a **delete** statement will delete, or an **update** statement will update.

A condition may be defined in one of several ways:

- ■ A comparison between expressions (=, >, !=, and so on).
- ■ A comparison between an expression and a query.
- ■ A comparison between a list of expressions and a list of expressions from a query.
- ■ A comparison between an expression and **ANY** or **ALL** members of a list or between an expression and the values brought back from a query.
- ■ A test to see if an expression is **IN** or **NOT IN** a list, or the results of a query.
- ■ A test for being **BETWEEN** or **NOT BETWEEN** one value and another.
- ■ A test to see if an expression **IS NULL** or **IS NOT NULL**.
- ■ A test to see there **EXISTS** (or **NOT EXISTS**) any results for a query.
- ■ A combination of any of the above, using the conjunctions **AND** and **OR**.

EXAMPLES

```
where Amount >= Rate * Quantity;
where Item = 'MEDISON';
where ('GEORGE','VICTORIA') = (select Husband, Wife from COUPLES);
where Section >ANY ('A','C','D');
where City !=ALL (select City from LOCATION);
where Section IN ('A','C','D');
where City NOT IN (select City from LOCATION);
where Page BETWEEN 4 and 7;
where Skill IS NULL;
where EXISTS (select * from WORKER where Age > 90);
where Section = 'A' or Section = 'B' and Page = 1;
```

WHILE (PL/SQL)

See **LOOP**, Chapter 25.

WRAP (SQL*PLUS)

See **SET**.

WRAPPING

Wrapping is moving the end of a heading or title, or the contents of a column, down to a new line when it is too long to fit on one line. (Contrast with **TRUNCATE**.) *See* **COLUMN**.

PART
IX

Appendix

APPENDIX
A

Tables Used in this Book

his appendix contains the complete listings of all the tables used in the examples throughout this book. They can be keyed in to a start file "as is" to load into a database using SQLPLUS. If these tables are a part of your Oracle database, you can easily work your way through the examples in this book and experiment with the many techniques that are illustrated.

For ease of use, set up a user named **practice**, with a password of **practice**. Give this user CONNECT and RESOURCE authority so that new users can access it to learn Oracle. If you are a new user on an existing Oracle installation, check with your DBA to see if this has already been done. If not, you might request it, or at least request that the tables and start files be available to you through public synonyms. Whatever "damage" is done on the **practice** id can always be repaired simply by reloading the tables from their start files.

Using the Tables in this Book

The tables in this appendix are on the CD that comes bundled with this book, so you can access these tables without retyping. You can use these tables to easily work your way through the examples and experiment with the many techniques that are illustrated in the book.

The activity.sql Start File

```
rem          Name: activity.sql    Type: start file report
rem    Written by: G. Koch
rem
rem    Description: Report on G. B. Talbot sales by product
rem                 during second half of 1901.
set headsep !


ttitle 'Sales by Product During 1901!Second Six Months (Jul-Dec)'

btitle 'from G. B. Talbot"s Ledger'

column Item heading 'What Was!Sold'
column Item format a18
column Item truncated

column Person heading 'To Whom Sold' format a18 word_wrapped
column Rate format 90.99
column ActionDate heading 'Date'
column QuantityType heading 'Type' format a8 truncated
```

```
column Quantity heading 'Quan' format 9990
column Ext format 990.99


break on Item skip 2
compute sum of Ext on Item


set linesize 79
set pagesize 50 set
newpage 0

spool activity.lst

select ActionDate, Person, Item, Quantity, QuantityType,
       Rate, Quantity * Rate AS Ext
  from Ledger
 where Action = 'SOLD'                /* last 6 months only */
       and ActionDate BETWEEN
           TO_DATE('01-JUL-1901','DD-MON-YYYY') AND
           TO_DATE('31-DEC-1901','DD-MON-YYYY')
 order by Item, ActionDate;

spool off
```

The math.sql Start File

```
rem         Name: math.sql       Type: start file report
rem     Written by: G. Koch
rem
rem   Description: Illustrates ORACLE math functions. Produces
rem                an output file named MATH.LST
set echo off
set pagesize 32000
set linesize 132
column Plus format 99.999
column Minus format 999.999
column Times format 9999.999999
column Divided format .999999
column VSIZE(Above) heading 'VSIZE|(Above)'
column VSIZE(Below) heading 'VSIZE|(Below)'
column VSIZE(Empty) heading 'VSIZE|(Empty)'
column NVL(Above,11) heading 'NVL|(Above,11)'
column NVL(Below,11) heading 'NVL|(Below,11)'
column NVL(Empty,11) heading 'NVL|(Empty,11)'
column ROUND(Above,2) heading 'ROUND|(Above,2)'
```

```
column ROUND(Below,2) heading 'ROUND|(Below,2)'
column TRUNC(Above,2) heading 'TRUNC|(Above,2)'
column TRUNC(Below,2) heading 'TRUNC|(Below,2)'
column ROUND(Above,0) heading 'ROUND|(Above,0)'
column ROUND(Below,0) heading 'ROUND|(Below,0)'
column TRUNC(Above,0) heading 'TRUNC|(Above,0)'
column TRUNC(Below,0) heading 'TRUNC|(Below,0)'
column ROUND(Above,-1) heading 'ROUND|(Above,-1)'
column ROUND(Below,-1) heading 'ROUND|(Below,-1)'
column TRUNC(Above,-1) heading 'TRUNC|(Above,-1)'
column TRUNC(Below,-1) heading 'TRUNC|(Below,-1)'
set echo on
set numwidth 7
set numformat ""
spool math.lst
select Name, Above, Below, Empty from MATH;

select Name, Above, Below, Empty,
       Above + Below "Plus",
       Above - Below "Minus",
       Above * Below "Times",
       Above / Below "Divided"
  from MATH where Name = 'HIGH DECIMAL';

select Name, Above, Below, Empty,
       Above + Empty "Plus",
       Above - Empty "Minus",
       Above * Empty "Times",
       Above / Empty "Divided"
  from MATH where Name = 'HIGH DECIMAL';

select Name, Above, Below, Empty,
       ABS(Above),
       ABS(Below),
       ABS(Empty)
  from MATH where Name = 'HIGH DECIMAL';

select Name, Above, Below, Empty,
       VSIZE(Above),
       VSIZE(Below),
       VSIZE(Empty)

  from MATH;

select Name, Above, Below, Empty,
       NVL(Above,11),
       NVL(Below,11),
       NVL(Empty,11)
```

```
      from MATH where Name = 'HIGH DECIMAL';

select Name, Above, Below,
       CEIL(Above),
       CEIL(Below)
  from MATH;

select Name, Above, Below,
       FLOOR(Above),
       FLOOR(Below)
  from MATH;

select Name, Above, Below,
       MOD(Above,11),
       MOD(Below,11)
  from MATH where Name = 'HIGH DECIMAL';

set numformat 9999.999999
select Name, Above, Below,
       POWER(Above,2),
       POWER(Below,2)
  from MATH where Name = 'HIGH DECIMAL';

select Name, Above, Below,
       POWER(Above,2.9),
       POWER(Below,2.9)
  from MATH;

set numformat ""
select Name, Above, Below,
       SQRT(Above),
       SQRT(Below)
  from MATH where Name = 'HIGH DECIMAL';

select Name, Above, Below,
       ROUND(Above,2),
       ROUND(Below,2),
       TRUNC(Above,2),
       TRUNC(Below,2)
  from MATH;

select Name, Above, Below,
       ROUND(Above,0),
       ROUND(Below,0),
       TRUNC(Above,0),
       TRUNC(Below,0)
  from MATH;
```

```
select Name, Above, Below,
       ROUND(Above,-1),
       ROUND(Below,-1),
       TRUNC(Above,-1),
       TRUNC(Below,-1)
  from MATH;


select Name, Above, Below,
       SIGN(Above),
       SIGN(Below)
  from MATH where Name = 'HIGH DECIMAL';

spool off
```

The ADDRESS_TY Type

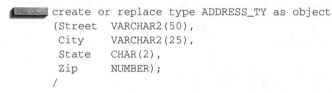

```
create or replace type ADDRESS_TY as object
(Street  VARCHAR2(50),
 City    VARCHAR2(25),
 State   CHAR(2),
 Zip     NUMBER);
/
```

The ANIMAL_TY Type

```
create or replace type ANIMAL_TY as object
(Breed      VARCHAR2(25),
 Name       VARCHAR2(25),
 BirthDate  DATE,
member function AGE (BirthDate IN DATE) return NUMBER,
PRAGMA RESTRICT_REFERENCES(AGE, WNDS));
/

create or replace type body ANIMAL_TY as
member function Age (BirthDate DATE) return NUMBER is
begin
  RETURN ROUND(SysDate - BirthDate);
end;
end;
/

rem  For the Nested Table examples:
create type ANIMALS_NT as table of ANIMAL_TY;
/
```

The PERSON_TY Type

rem   Requires that the ADDRESS_TY type already exist.

```
create type PERSON_TY as object
(Name       VARCHAR2(25),
 Address    ADDRESS_TY);
/
```

The TOOLS_VA Type

rem   Creates a varying array datatype.

```
create or replace type TOOLS_VA as varray(5) of VARCHAR2(25);
/
```

The ADDRESS Table

```
drop table ADDRESS;
create table ADDRESS (
LastName    VARCHAR2(25),
FirstName   VARCHAR2(25),
Street      VARCHAR2(50),
City        VARCHAR2(25),
State       CHAR(2),
Zip         NUMBER,
Phone       VARCHAR2(12),
Ext         VARCHAR2(5)
);

insert into ADDRESS values ('BAILEY', 'WILLIAM',
    null,null,null,null,'213-293-0223',null);
insert into ADDRESS values ('ADAMS', 'JACK',
    null,null,null,null,'415-453-7530',null);
insert into ADDRESS values ('SEP', 'FELICIA',
    null,null,null,null,'214-522-8383',null);
insert into ADDRESS values ('DE MEDICI', 'LEFTY',
    null,null,null,null,'312-736-1166',null);
insert into ADDRESS values ('DEMIURGE', 'FRANK',
    null,null,null,null,'707-767-8900',null);
insert into ADDRESS values ('CASEY', 'WILLIS',
    null,null,null,null,'312-684-1414',null);
insert into ADDRESS values ('ZACK', 'JACK',
    null,null,null,null,'415-620-6842',null);
```

```
insert into ADDRESS values ('YARROW', 'MARY',
    null,null,null,949414302,'415-787-2178',null);
insert into ADDRESS values ('WERSCHKY', 'ARNY',
    null,null,null,null,'415-235-7387',null);
insert into ADDRESS values ('BRANT', 'GLEN',
    null,null,null,null,'415-526-7512',null);
insert into ADDRESS values ('EDGAR', 'THEODORE',
    null,null,null,null,'415-525-6252',null);
insert into ADDRESS values ('HARDIN', 'HUGGY',
    null,null,null,null,'617-566-0125',null);
insert into ADDRESS values ('HILD', 'PHIL',
    null,null,null,null,'603-934-2242',null);
insert into ADDRESS values ('LOEBEL', 'FRANK',
    null,null,null,null,'202-456-1414',null);
insert into ADDRESS values ('MOORE', 'MARY',
    null,null,null,601262460,'718-857-1638',null);
insert into ADDRESS values ('SZEP', 'FELICIA',
    null,null,null,null,'214-522-8383',null);
insert into ADDRESS values ('ZIMMERMAN', 'FRED',
    null,null,null,null,'503-234-7491',null);
```

The AREAS Table

```
drop table AREAS;
create table AREAS
(Radius        NUMBER(5),
 Area          NUMBER(14,2)
);
```

```
REMARK No inserts. This table is empty.
```

The ASOF Table

```
drop table ASOF;
create table ASOF (
AsOf          DATE
);
```

```
insert into ASOF values (TO_DATE('15-DEC-1901','DD-MON-YYYY'));
```

The BIRTHDAY Table

```
drop table BIRTHDAY;
create table BIRTHDAY (
```

```
FirstName       VARCHAR2(15),
LastName        VARCHAR2(15),
BirthDate       DATE,
Age             NUMBER
);

insert into BIRTHDAY values ('GEORGE','SAND',
        TO_DATE('12-MAY-1946','DD-MON-YYYY'),42);
insert into BIRTHDAY values ('ROBERT','JAMES',
        TO_DATE('23-AUG-1937','DD-MON-YYYY'),52);
insert into BIRTHDAY values ('NANCY','LEE',
        TO_DATE('02-FEB-1947','DD-MON-YYYY'),42);
insert into BIRTHDAY values ('VICTORIA','LYNN',
        TO_DATE('20-MAY-1949 3:27','DD-MON-YYYY HH24:MI'),42);
insert into BIRTHDAY values ('FRANK','PILOT',
        TO_DATE('11-NOV-1942','DD-MON-YYYY'),42);
```

The BORROWER Table

rem   Requires that the TOOLS_VA datatype be created first.

```
create table BORROWER
(Name           VARCHAR2(25),
 Tools          TOOLS_VA,
constraint BORROWER_PK primary key (Name));

insert into BORROWER values
('JED HOPKINS',
  TOOLS_VA('HAMMER','SLEDGE','AX'));
```

The BREEDER Table

rem   Requires that the ANIMAL_TY and ANIMALS_NT types
rem   already exist.

```
create table BREEDER (
BreederName       VARCHAR2(25),
Animals           ANIMALS_NT)
nested table ANIMALS store as ANIMALS_NT_TAB;
```

The BREEDING Table

drop table BREEDING;
create table BREEDING (

```
Offspring    VARCHAR2(10),
Sex          CHAR(1),
Cow          VARCHAR2(10),
Bull         VARCHAR2(10),
Birthdate    DATE
);

insert into BREEDING values ('EVE','F',null,null,null);
insert into BREEDING values ('ADAM','M',null,null,null);
insert into BREEDING values ('BANDIT','M',null,null,null);
insert into BREEDING values ('BETSY','F','EVE','ADAM',
    TO_DATE('02-JAN-1900','DD-MON-YYYY'));
insert into BREEDING values ('POCO','M','EVE','ADAM',
    TO_DATE('15-JUL-1900','DD-MON-YYYY'));
insert into BREEDING values ('GRETA','F','EVE','BANDIT',
    TO_DATE('12-MAR-1901','DD-MON-YYYY'));
insert into BREEDING values ('MANDY','F','EVE','POCO',
    TO_DATE('22-AUG-1902','DD-MON-YYYY'));
insert into BREEDING values ('NOVI','F','BETSY','ADAM',
    TO_DATE('30-MAR-1903','DD-MON-YYYY'));
insert into BREEDING values ('GINNY','F','BETSY','BANDIT',
    TO_DATE('04-DEC-1903','DD-MON-YYYY'));
insert into BREEDING values ('CINDY','F','EVE','POCO',
    TO_DATE('09-FEB-1903','DD-MON-YYYY'));
insert into BREEDING values ('DUKE','M','MANDY','BANDIT',
    TO_DATE('24-JUL-1904','DD-MON-YYYY'));
insert into BREEDING values ('TEDDI','F','BETSY','BANDIT',
    TO_DATE('12-AUG-1905','DD-MON-YYYY'));
insert into BREEDING values ('SUZY','F','GINNY','DUKE',
    TO_DATE('03-APR-1906','DD-MON-YYYY'));
insert into BREEDING values ('RUTH','F','GINNY','DUKE',
    TO_DATE('25-DEC-1906','DD-MON-YYYY'));
insert into BREEDING values ('PAULA','F','MANDY','POCO',
    TO_DATE('21-DEC-1906','DD-MON-YYYY'));
insert into BREEDING values ('DELLA','F','SUZY','BANDIT',
    TO_DATE('11-OCT-1908','DD-MON-YYYY'));
```

The CD Table

```
drop table CD;
create table CD (
Account      NUMBER not null,
Amount       NUMBER not null,
MaturityDate DATE not null
);

insert into CD values (573334, 10000,
```

```
    TO_DATE('15-JAN-2009','DD-MON-YYYY'));
insert into CD values (677654, 25000,
    TO_DATE('15-JAN-2001','DD-MON-YYYY'));
insert into CD values (976032, 10000,
    TO_DATE('15-JAN-1995','DD-MON-YYYY'));
insert into CD values (275031, 10000,
    TO_DATE('15-JAN-1997','DD-MON-YYYY'));
insert into CD values (274598, 20000,
    TO_DATE('15-JAN-1999','DD-MON-YYYY'));
insert into CD values (538365, 45000,
    TO_DATE('15-JAN-2001','DD-MON-YYYY'));
insert into CD values (267432, 16500,
    TO_DATE('15-JAN-2004','DD-MON-YYYY'));
```

The COMFORT Table

```
drop table COMFORT;
create table COMFORT (
City          VARCHAR2(13) NOT NULL,
SampleDate    DATE NOT NULL,
Noon          NUMBER(3,1),
Midnight      NUMBER(3,1),
Precipitation NUMBER
);

insert into COMFORT values ('SAN FRANCISCO',
    TO_DATE('21-MAR-1999','DD-MON-YYYY'),62.5,42.3,.5);
insert into COMFORT values ('SAN FRANCISCO',
    TO_DATE('22-JUN-1999','DD-MON-YYYY'),51.1,71.9,.1);
insert into COMFORT values ('SAN FRANCISCO',
    TO_DATE('23-SEP-1999','DD-MON-YYYY'),NULL,61.5,.1);
insert into COMFORT values ('SAN FRANCISCO',
    TO_DATE('22-DEC-1999','DD-MON-YYYY'),52.6,39.8,2.3);
insert into COMFORT values ('KEENE',
    TO_DATE('21-MAR-1999','DD-MON-YYYY'),39.9,-1.2,4.4);
insert into COMFORT values ('KEENE',
    TO_DATE('22-JUN-1999','DD-MON-YYYY'),85.1,66.7,1.3);
insert into COMFORT values ('KEENE',
    TO_DATE('23-SEP-1999','DD-MON-YYYY'),99.8,82.6,NULL);
insert into COMFORT values ('KEENE',
    TO_DATE('22-DEC-1999','DD-MON-YYYY'),-7.2,-1.2,3.9);
```

The COMMA Table

```
drop table COMMA;
create table COMMA (
```

```
Amount        NUMBER,
AmountChar    VARCHAR2(20)
);

insert into COMMA values (0,'0');
insert into COMMA values (0.25,'0.25');
insert into COMMA values (1.25,'1.25');
insert into COMMA values (12.25,'12.25');
insert into COMMA values (123.25,'123.25');
insert into COMMA values (1234.25,'1,234.25');
insert into COMMA values (12345.25,'12,345.25');
insert into COMMA values (123456.25,'123,456.25');
insert into COMMA values (1234567.25,'1,234,567.25');
insert into COMMA values (12345678.25,'12,345,678.25');
insert into COMMA values (123456789.25,'123,456,789.25');
REM insert into COMMA values (1234567890.25,'1,234,567,890.25');
REM insert into COMMA values (12345678901.25,'12,345,678,901.25');
```

The CUSTOMER Table

```
rem   Requires that the ADDRESS_TY and PERSON_TY types already
rem   exist.

create table CUSTOMER (
Customer_ID    NUMBER,
Person         PERSON_TY
);

insert into CUSTOMER
(1,
 PERSON_TY('NEIL MULLANE',
          ADDRESS_TY('57 MT PLEASANT ST',
                     'FINN', 'NH', 11111)));
insert into CUSTOMER
(2,
 PERSON_TY('SEYMOUR HESTER',
          ADDRESS_TY('1 STEPAHEAD RD',
                     'BRIANT', 'NH', 11111)));
```

The EMPTY Table

```
drop table EMPTY;
create table EMPTY (
```

```
Nothing        VARCHAR2(25),
Less           NUMBER
);
```

REMARK No inserts. This table is empty.

The **HOLIDAY** Table

```
drop table HOLIDAY;
create table HOLIDAY (
Holiday         VARCHAR2(25),
ActualDate      DATE,
CelebratedDate DATE
);

insert into HOLIDAY values ('NEW YEAR DAY',
    TO_DATE('01-JAN-2000','DD-MON-YYYY'),
    TO_DATE('01-JAN-2000','DD-MON-YYYY'));
insert into HOLIDAY values ('MARTIN LUTHER KING, JR.',
    TO_DATE('15-JAN-2000','DD-MON-YYYY'),
    TO_DATE('17-JAN-2000','DD-MON-YYYY'));
insert into HOLIDAY values ('LINCOLNS BIRTHDAY',
    TO_DATE('12-FEB-2000','DD-MON-YYYY'),
    TO_DATE('21-FEB-2000','DD-MON-YYYY'));
insert into HOLIDAY values ('WASHINGTONS BIRTHDAY',
    TO_DATE('22-FEB-2000','DD-MON-YYYY'),
    TO_DATE('21-FEB-2000','DD-MON-YYYY'));
insert into HOLIDAY values ('FAST DAY, NEW HAMPSHIRE',
    TO_DATE('22-FEB-2000','DD-MON-YYYY'),
    TO_DATE('22-FEB-2000','DD-MON-YYYY'));
insert into HOLIDAY values ('MEMORIAL DAY',
    TO_DATE('30-MAY-2000','DD-MON-YYYY'),
    TO_DATE('29-MAY-2000','DD-MON-YYYY'));
insert into HOLIDAY values ('INDEPENDENCE DAY',
    TO_DATE('04-JUL-2000','DD-MON-YYYY'),
    TO_DATE('04-JUL-2000','DD-MON-YYYY'));
insert into HOLIDAY values ('LABOR DAY',
    TO_DATE('04-SEP-2000','DD-MON-YYYY'),
    TO_DATE('04-SEP-2000','DD-MON-YYYY'));
insert into HOLIDAY values ('COLUMBUS DAY',
    TO_DATE('08-OCT-2000','DD-MON-YYYY'),
    TO_DATE('09-OCT-2000','DD-MON-YYYY'));
insert into HOLIDAY values ('THANKSGIVING',
    TO_DATE('23-NOV-2000','DD-MON-YYYY'),
    TO_DATE('23-NOV-2000','DD-MON-YYYY'));
```

The INVOICE Table

```
drop table INVOICE;
create table INVOICE
(ClientName   VARCHAR2(25),
InvoiceDate   DATE,
Amount        NUMBER(9,2)
);

insert into INVOICE values (
   'ELBERT TALBOT',    TO_DATE('23-OCT-1901','DD-MON-YYYY'),5.03);
insert into INVOICE values (
   'JOHN PEARSON',     TO_DATE('09-NOV-1901','DD-MON-YYYY'),2.02);
insert into INVOICE values (
   'DICK JONES',       TO_DATE('12-SEP-1901','DD-MON-YYYY'),11.12);
insert into INVOICE values (
   'GENERAL STORE', TO_DATE('09-NOV-1901','DD-MON-YYYY'),22.10);
insert into INVOICE values (
   'ADAH TALBOT', TO_DATE('17-NOV-1901','DD-MON-YYYY'),8.29);
insert into INVOICE values (
   'GENERAL STORE', TO_DATE('01-SEP-1901','DD-MON-YYYY'),21.32);
insert into INVOICE values (
   'ADAH TALBOT', TO_DATE('15-NOV-1901','DD-MON-YYYY'),7.33);
insert into INVOICE values (
   'GENERAL STORE', TO_DATE('04-OCT-1901','DD-MON-YYYY'),8.42);
insert into INVOICE values (
   'KAY WALLBOM', TO_DATE('04-OCT-1901','DD-MON-YYYY'),1.43);
insert into INVOICE values (
   'JOHN PEARSON', TO_DATE('13-OCT-1901','DD-MON-YYYY'),12.41);
insert into INVOICE values (
   'DICK JONES', TO_DATE('23-OCT-1901','DD-MON-YYYY'),4.49);
insert into INVOICE values (
   'GENERAL STORE', TO_DATE('23-NOV-1901','DD-MON-YYYY'),40.36);
insert into INVOICE values (
   'GENERAL STORE', TO_DATE('30-OCT-1901','DD-MON-YYYY'),7.47);
insert into INVOICE values (
   'MORRIS ARNOLD', TO_DATE('03-OCT-1901','DD-MON-YYYY'),3.55);
insert into INVOICE values (
   'ROLAND BRANDT', TO_DATE('22-OCT-1901','DD-MON-YYYY'),13.65);
insert into INVOICE values (
   'MORRIS ARNOLD', TO_DATE('21-SEP-1901','DD-MON-YYYY'),9.87);
insert into INVOICE values (
   'VICTORIA LYNN', TO_DATE('09-OCT-1901','DD-MON-YYYY'),8.98);
insert into INVOICE values (
   'GENERAL STORE', TO_DATE('22-OCT-1901','DD-MON-YYYY'),17.58);
```

The **LEDGER** Table

```
drop table LEDGER;
create table LEDGER (
ActionDate      DATE,
Action          VARCHAR2(8),
Item            VARCHAR2(30),
Quantity        NUMBER,
QuantityType    VARCHAR2(10),
Rate            NUMBER,
Amount          NUMBER(9,2),
Person          VARCHAR2(25)
);

insert into ledger values (
  TO_DATE('01-APR-1901','DD-MON-YYYY'),
  'PAID','PLOWING',1,'DAY',3,3,'RICHARD KOCH AND BROTHERS');
insert into ledger values (
  TO_DATE('02-MAY-1901','DD-MON-YYYY'),
  'PAID','WORK',1,'DAY',1,1,'DICK JONES');
insert into ledger values (
  TO_DATE('03-JUN-1901','DD-MON-YYYY'),
  'PAID','WORK',1,'DAY',1,1,'ELBERT TALBOT');
insert into ledger values (
  TO_DATE('04-JAN-1901','DD-MON-YYYY'),
  'PAID','WORK',1,'DAY',1,1,'GERHARDT KENTGEN');
insert into ledger values (
  TO_DATE('04-FEB-1901','DD-MON-YYYY'),
  'PAID','WORK',.5,'DAY',1,.5,'ELBERT TALBOT');
insert into ledger values (
  TO_DATE('05-APR-1901','DD-MON-YYYY'),
  'PAID','WORK',1,'DAY',1,1,'DICK JONES');
insert into ledger values (
  TO_DATE('06-AUG-1901','DD-MON-YYYY'),
  'PAID','PLOWING',1,'DAY',1.8,1.8,'VICTORIA LYNN');
insert into ledger values (
  TO_DATE('07-OCT-1901','DD-MON-YYYY'),
  'PAID','PLOWING',.5,'DAY',3,1.5,'RICHARD KOCH AND BROTHERS');
prompt Going into silent mode.
set termout off
insert into ledger values (
  TO_DATE('09-SEP-1901','DD-MON-YYYY'),
  'PAID','WORK',1,'DAY',1,1,'ADAH TALBOT');
insert into ledger values (
  TO_DATE('09-OCT-1901','DD-MON-YYYY'),
  'PAID','WORK',.5,'DAY',1.25,.63,'DONALD ROLLO');
```

```
insert into ledger values (
  TO_DATE('10-NOV-1901','DD-MON-YYYY'),
  'PAID','WORK',1,'DAY',1.25,1.25,'JOHN PEARSON');
insert into ledger values (
  TO_DATE('10-AUG-1901','DD-MON-YYYY'),
  'PAID','WORK',1,'DAY',1,1,'HELEN BRANDT');
insert into ledger values (
  TO_DATE('11-AUG-1901','DD-MON-YYYY'),
  'PAID','WORK',1,'DAY',2,2,'HELEN BRANDT');
insert into ledger values (
  TO_DATE('11-SEP-1901','DD-MON-YYYY'),
  'PAID','WORK',1,'DAY',.75,.75,'ROLAND BRANDT');
insert into ledger values (
  TO_DATE('12-DEC-1901','DD-MON-YYYY'),
  'PAID','WORK',1,'DAY',1,1,'BART SARJEANT');
insert into ledger values (
  TO_DATE('12-JAN-1901','DD-MON-YYYY'),
  'PAID','WORK',1,'DAY',1,1,'GEORGE OSCAR');
insert into ledger values (
  TO_DATE('13-JUN-1901','DD-MON-YYYY'),
  'PAID','WORK',1,'DAY',1,1,'PETER LAWSON');
insert into ledger values (
  TO_DATE('14-JUL-1901','DD-MON-YYYY'),
  PAID','WORK',1,'DAY',1.2,1.2,'WILFRED LOWELL');
insert into ledger values (
  TO_DATE('15-JUL-1901','DD-MON-YYYY'),
  'PAID','WORK',1,'DAY',2.25,2.25,'KAY AND PALMER WALLBOM');
insert into ledger values (
  TO_DATE('03-OCT-1901','DD-MON-YYYY'),
  'SOLD','BOOT BETWEEN HORSES',1,'EACH',12.5,12.5,'GARY KENTGEN');
insert into ledger values (
  TO_DATE('01-NOV-1901','DD-MON-YYYY'),
  'BOUGHT','CALF',2,'EACH',2,4,'GARY KENTGEN');
insert into ledger values (
  TO_DATE('02-NOV-1901','DD-MON-YYYY'),
  'BOUGHT','MARE',1,'EACH',5,5,'JAMES COLE');
insert into ledger values (
  TO_DATE('03-NOV-1901','DD-MON-YYYY'),
  'BOUGHT','PIG',1,'EACH',2,2,'ANDREW DYE');
insert into ledger values (
  TO_DATE('04-NOV-1901','DD-MON-YYYY'),
  'BOUGHT','HAY',1,'WAGON',5,5,'ANDREW DYE');
insert into ledger values (
  TO_DATE('05-NOV-1901','DD-MON-YYYY'),
  'BOUGHT','HAY',4,'WAGON',5,20,'ANDREW DYE');
insert into ledger values (
  TO_DATE('05-NOV-1901','DD-MON-YYYY'),
  'BOUGHT','LINE',1,'SET',.75,.75,'ANDREW DYE');
```

```
insert into ledger values (
   TO_DATE('06-NOV-1901','DD-MON-YYYY'),
   'BOUGHT','COLT',2,'COLT',4.5,9,'ANDREW DYE');
insert into ledger values (
   TO_DATE('06-AUG-1901','DD-MON-YYYY'),
   'PAID','PLOWING',2,'DAY',2,4,'ANDREW DYE');
insert into ledger values (
   TO_DATE('07-NOV-1901','DD-MON-YYYY'),
   'PAID','SAWED WOOD',1,'DAY',.5,.5,'ANDREW DYE');
insert into ledger values (
   TO_DATE('09-NOV-1901','DD-MON-YYYY'),
   'BOUGHT','COLT',1,'EACH',10,10,'ANDREW DYE');
insert into ledger values (
   TO_DATE('10-NOV-1901','DD-MON-YYYY'),
   'SOLD','HEFER',1,'EACH',28,28,'PAT LAVAY');
insert into ledger values (
   TO_DATE('11-NOV-1901','DD-MON-YYYY'),
   'SOLD','BOOT BETWEEN HORSES',1,'EACH',6,6,'PAT LAVAY');
insert into ledger values (
   TO_DATE('11-NOV-1901','DD-MON-YYYY'),
   'SOLD','BUTTER',1,'LB',.15,.15,'PAT LAVAY');
insert into ledger values (
   TO_DATE('12-NOV-1901','DD-MON-YYYY'),
   'PAID','WORK',2,'DAY',.75,1.5,'PAT LAVAY');
insert into ledger values (
   TO_DATE('13-NOV-1901','DD-MON-YYYY'),
   'PAID','CUT LOGS',.5,'DAY',.5,.25,'PAT LAVAY');
insert into ledger values (
   TO_DATE('13-NOV-1901','DD-MON-YYYY'),
   'PAID','DRAWED LOGS',1.5,'DAY',.5,.75,'PAT LAVAY');
insert into ledger values (
   TO_DATE('13-DEC-1901','DD-MON-YYYY'),
   'PAID','SAWED WOOD',1,'DAY',.5,.5,'PAT LAVAY');
insert into ledger values (
   TO_DATE('14-NOV-1901','DD-MON-YYYY'),
   'SOLD','HEFER',1,'EACH',35,35,'MORRIS ARNOLD');
insert into ledger values (
   TO_DATE('15-NOV-1901','DD-MON-YYYY'),
   'SOLD','BEEF',37,'LB',.04,1.48,'FRED FULLER');
insert into ledger values (
   TO_DATE('16-NOV-1901','DD-MON-YYYY'),
   'SOLD','BUTTER',5,'LB',.16,.8,'VICTORIA LYNN');
insert into ledger values (
   TO_DATE('18-NOV-1901','DD-MON-YYYY'),
   'SOLD','BUTTER',6,'LB',.16,.96,'JOHN PEARSON');
insert into ledger values (
   TO_DATE('20-NOV-1901','DD-MON-YYYY'),
   'SOLD','HEFER',1,'EACH',30,30,'PALMER WALLBOM');
```

```
insert into ledger values (
  TO_DATE('21-NOV-1901','DD-MON-YYYY'),
  'SOLD','BEEF',116,'LB',.06,6.96,'ROLAND BRANDT');
insert into ledger values (
  TO_DATE('22-NOV-1901','DD-MON-YYYY'),
  'SOLD','BEEF',118,'LB',.06,7.08,'GERHARDT KENTGEN');
insert into ledger values (
  TO_DATE('01-DEC-1901','DD-MON-YYYY'),
  'BOUGHT','BEEF',138,'LB',.05,6.9,'VICTORIA LYNN');
insert into ledger values (
  TO_DATE('01-DEC-1901','DD-MON-YYYY'),
  'BOUGHT','BEEF',130,'LB',.06,7.8,'GEORGE B. MCCORMICK');
insert into ledger values (
  TO_DATE('03-DEC-1901','DD-MON-YYYY'),
  'BOUGHT','BEEF',130,'LB',.05,6.5,'PETER LAWSON');
insert into ledger values (
  TO_DATE('03-DEC-1901','DD-MON-YYYY'),
  'BOUGHT','BEEF',125,'LB',.06,7.5,'HELEN BRANDT');
insert into ledger values (
  TO_DATE('05-DEC-1901','DD-MON-YYYY'),
  'BOUGHT','BEEF',140,'LB',.05,7,'ROBERT JAMES');
insert into ledger values (
  TO_DATE('05-DEC-1901','DD-MON-YYYY'),
  'BOUGHT','BEEF',145,'LB',.05,7.25,'ISAIAH JAMES');
insert into ledger values (
  TO_DATE('07-DEC-1901','DD-MON-YYYY'),
  'BOUGHT','HORSE',1,'EACH',30,30,'GEORGE AUGUST');
insert into ledger values (
  TO_DATE('07-DEC-1901','DD-MON-YYYY'),
  'BOUGHT','REAPER/BINDER',1,'EACH',47.5,47.5,'JANICE TALBOT');
insert into ledger values (
  TO_DATE('03-JAN-1901','DD-MON-YYYY'),
  'BOUGHT','HOMINY',1,'BUSHEL',1.25,1.25,'GENERAL STORE');
insert into ledger values (
  TO_DATE('09-JAN-1901','DD-MON-YYYY'),
  'BOUGHT','LICE KILLER',1,'BOX',.5,.5,'GENERAL STORE');
insert into ledger values (
  TO_DATE('11-JAN-1901','DD-MON-YYYY'),
  'BOUGHT','MENDING BRACE',1,'EACH',.15,.15,'GENERAL STORE');
insert into ledger values (
  TO_DATE('11-JAN-1901','DD-MON-YYYY'
  'BOUGHT','STOVE BLACKING',1,'BOX',.05,.05,'GENERAL STORE');
insert into ledger values (
  TO_DATE('13-JAN-1901','DD-MON-YYYY'),
  'BOUGHT','GRINDING BAT',10,'EACH',.03,.3,'GENERAL STORE');
insert into ledger values (
  TO_DATE('14-JAN-1901','DD-MON-YYYY'),
  'SOLD','BEEF HIDE',1,'EACH',5.46,5.46,'GENERAL STORE');
```

```
insert into ledger values (
   TO_DATE('14-JAN-1901','DD-MON-YYYY'),
   'SOLD','CHEESE FLAT',13,'EACH',3.15,40.95,'GENERAL STORE');
insert into ledger values (
   TO_DATE('14-JAN-1901','DD-MON-YYYY'),
   'BOUGHT','LANTERN GLOBE',1,'EACH',.1,.1,'GENERAL STORE');
insert into ledger values (
   TO_DATE('15-JAN-1901','DD-MON-YYYY'),
   'BOUGHT','STAMP FOR LETTER',1,'EACH',.02,.02,'POST OFFICE');
insert into ledger values (
   TO_DATE('15-JAN-1901','DD-MON-YYYY'),
   'BOUGHT','STOCKING',2,'PAIR',.15,.3,'GENERAL STORE');
insert into ledger values (
   TO_DATE('16-JAN-1901','DD-MON-YYYY'),
   'BOUGHT','OIL',4,'GALLON',.1,.4,'GENERAL STORE');
insert into ledger values (
   TO_DATE('16-JAN-1901','DD-MON-YYYY'),
   'BOUGHT','SUGAR',25,'LB',.07,1.75,'GENERAL STORE');
insert into ledger values (
   TO_DATE('16-JAN-1901','DD-MON-YYYY'),
   'BOUGHT','MOLASSES',1,'GALLON',.6,.6,'GENERAL STORE');
insert into ledger values (
   TO_DATE('16-JAN-1901','DD-MON-YYYY'),
   'BOUGHT','CARD OF THANKS',1,'EACH',.3,.3,'GENERAL STORE');
insert into ledger values (
   TO_DATE('17-JAN-1901','DD-MON-YYYY'),
   'BOUGHT','HORSE SHODDING',1,'EACH',.85,.85,'LIVERY');
insert into ledger values (
   TO_DATE('17-JAN-1901','DD-MON-YYYY'),
   'BOUGHT','CORN',230,'LB',.01,2.3,'FEED STORE');
insert into ledger values (
   TO_DATE('18-JAN-1901','DD-MON-YYYY'),
   'BOUGHT','CORN MEAL',213,'LB',.01,2.13,'FEED STORE');
insert into ledger values (
   TO_DATE('18-JAN-1901','DD-MON-YYYY'),
   'BOUGHT','PAPER',50,'SHEETS',.01,.5,'GENERAL STORE');
insert into ledger values (
   TO_DATE('18-JAN-1901','DD-MON-YYYY'),
   'BOUGHT','COFFEE',1,'LB',.3,.3,'GENERAL STORE');
insert into ledger values (
   TO_DATE('18-JAN-1901','DD-MON-YYYY'),
   'BOUGHT','SEEDED RAISINS',1,'LB',.12,.12,'GENERAL STORE');
insert into ledger values (
   TO_DATE('18-JAN-1901','DD-MON-YYYY'),
   'BOUGHT','COTTON STOCKING',3,'PAIR',.08,.24,'GENERAL STORE');
insert into ledger values (
   TO_DATE('19-JAN-1901','DD-MON-YYYY'),
   'BOUGHT','COTTON STOCKING',3,'PAIR',.08,.24,'GENERAL STORE');
```

```
insert into ledger values (
   TO_DATE('19-JAN-1901','DD-MON-YYYY'),
   'BOUGHT','GRINDING BAT',24,'EACH',.03,.72,'GENERAL STORE');
insert into ledger values (
   TO_DATE('19-JAN-1901','DD-MON-YYYY'),
   'BOUGHT','TELEPHONE CALL',1,'EACH',.15,.15,'PHONE COMPANY');
insert into ledger values (
   TO_DATE('19-JAN-1901','DD-MON-YYYY'),
   'BOUGHT','TEA',.5,'LB',.5,.25,'GENERAL STORE');
insert into ledger values (
   TO_DATE('19-JAN-1901','DD-MON-YYYY'),
   'BOUGHT','HAT',1,'EACH',.1,.1,'GENERAL STORE');
insert into ledger values (
   TO_DATE('19-JAN-1901','DD-MON-YYYY'),
   'BOUGHT','SALT PETER',1,'TABLET',.08,.08,'GENERAL STORE');
insert into ledger values (
   TO_DATE('19-JAN-1901','DD-MON-YYYY'),
   'BOUGHT','ENVELOPES',6,'EACH',.02,.12,'GENERAL STORE');
insert into ledger values (
   TO_DATE('19-JAN-1901','DD-MON-YYYY'),
   'BOUGHT','CREOAL',2,'QUART',.37,.74,'GENERAL STORE');
insert into ledger values (
   TO_DATE('23-JAN-1901','DD-MON-YYYY'),
   'SOLD','WOOD',1,'CORD',2,2,'METHODIST CHURCH');
insert into ledger values (
   TO_DATE('24-JAN-1901','DD-MON-YYYY'),
   'BOUGHT','SCHOOLING',1,'TERM',1,1,'SCHOOL');
insert into ledger values (
   TO_DATE('24-JAN-1901','DD-MON-YYYY'),
   'BOUGHT','HOMINY',186,'TERM',.01,1.86,'GENERAL STORE');
insert into ledger values (
   TO_DATE('28-JAN-1901','DD-MON-YYYY'),
   'BOUGHT','GRINDING',1,'EACH',.9,.9,'MILL');
insert into ledger values (
   TO_DATE('28-JAN-1901','DD-MON-YYYY'),
   'BOUGHT','POPCORN',5,'LB',.04,.2,'GENERAL STORE');
insert into ledger values (
   TO_DATE('02-FEB-1901','DD-MON-YYYY'),
   'BOUGHT','SULPHER',5,'LB',.25,1.25,'GENERAL STORE');
insert into ledger values (
   TO_DATE('03-FEB-1901','DD-MON-YYYY'),
   'BOUGHT','OIL',4,'GALLON',.13,.52,'GENERAL STORE');
insert into ledger values (
   TO_DATE('03-FEB-1901','DD-MON-YYYY'),
   'BOUGHT','SWAMP ROOT',1,'BOTTLE',.75,.75,'GENERAL STORE');
insert into ledger values (
   TO_DATE('04-FEB-1901','DD-MON-YYYY'),
   'BOUGHT','SHOEING NED',1,'EACH',.5,.5,'BLACKSMITH');
insert into ledger values (
```

```
    TO_DATE('04-FEB-1901','DD-MON-YYYY'),
    'BOUGHT','GRINDING',1,'EACH',.47,.47,'MILL');
insert into ledger values (
    TO_DATE('05-FEB-1901','DD-MON-YYYY'),
    'BOUGHT','PILLS',1,'BOX',.25,.25,'GENERAL STORE');
insert into ledger values (
    TO_DATE('07-FEB-1901','DD-MON-YYYY'),
    'BOUGHT','THREAD',2,'SPOOLS',.05,.1,'GENERAL STORE');
insert into ledger values (
    TO_DATE('08-FEB-1901','DD-MON-YYYY'),
    'BOUGHT','SHIRTS',2,'EACH',.5,1,'GENERAL STORE');
insert into ledger values (
    TO_DATE('10-FEB-1901','DD-MON-YYYY'),
    'SOLD','BUTTER',9,'LB',.25,2.25,'GENERAL STORE');
insert into ledger values (
    TO_DATE('18-FEB-1901','DD-MON-YYYY'),
    'BOUGHT','HORSE MEDISON',1,'ENVELOPE',.13,.13,'GENERAL STORE');
insert into ledger values (
    TO_DATE('18-FEB-1901','DD-MON-YYYY'),
    'BOUGHT','ELBO STOVE PIPE',1,'EACH',.15,.15,'GENERAL STORE');
insert into ledger values (
    TO_DATE('18-FEB-1901','DD-MON-YYYY'),
    'SOLD','CALF',1,'EACH',4,4,'LILY CARLSTROM');
insert into ledger values (
    TO_DATE('25-FEB-1901','DD-MON-YYYY'),
    'SOLD','BUTTER',21,'LB',.25,5.25,'GENERAL STORE');
insert into ledger values (
    TO_DATE('28-FEB-1901','DD-MON-YYYY'),
    'BOUGHT','SWAMP ROOT',1,'BOTTLE',.75,.75,'GENERAL STORE');
insert into ledger values (
    TO_DATE('28-FEB-1901','DD-MON-YYYY'),
    'BOUGHT','LIVER PILLS',1,'BOX',.2,.2,'GENERAL STORE');
insert into ledger values (
    TO_DATE('28-FEB-1901','DD-MON-YYYY'),
    'SOLD','BUTTER',3,'LB',.25,.75,'HELEN BRANDT');
insert into ledger values (
    TO_DATE('01-APR-1901','DD-MON-YYYY'),
    'BOUGHT','GRINDING',1,'EACH',.45,.45,'MILL');
insert into ledger values (
    TO_DATE('06-MAR-1901','DD-MON-YYYY'),
    'BOUGHT','MEDISON FOR INDIGESTION',1,'BOTTLE',.4,.4,
'DR. CARLSTROM');
insert into ledger values (
    TO_DATE('06-JUN-1901','DD-MON-YYYY'),
    'BOUGHT','BREADING POWDER',1,'BOX',.9,.9,'MILL');
insert into ledger values (
    TO_DATE('06-MAR-1901','DD-MON-YYYY'),
    'BOUGHT','PANTS',1,'PAIR',.75,.75,'GENERAL STORE');
```

```
insert into ledger values (
  TO_DATE('07-APR-1901','DD-MON-YYYY'),
  'BOUGHT','HOMINY',200,'LB',.01,2,'MILL');
insert into ledger values (
  TO_DATE('08-MAR-1901','DD-MON-YYYY'),
  'BOUGHT','TOBACCO FOR LICE',1,'BOX',.25,.25,'MILL');
insert into ledger values (
  TO_DATE('07-MAR-1901','DD-MON-YYYY'),
  'BOUGHT','SHOEING',1,'EACH',.35,.35,'BLACKSMITH');
insert into ledger values (
  TO_DATE('07-APR-1901','DD-MON-YYYY'),
  'BOUGHT','PINS',1,'BOX',.05,.05,'GENERAL STORE');
insert into ledger values (
  TO_DATE('07-MAR-1901','DD-MON-YYYY'),
  'BOUGHT','MAIL BOX',1,'EACH',1,1,'POST OFFICE');
insert into ledger values (
  TO_DATE('10-MAR-1901','DD-MON-YYYY'),
  'BOUGHT','STOVE PIPE THIMBLES',2,'EACH',.5,1,'VERNA HARDWARE');
insert into ledger values (
  TO_DATE('13-MAR-1901','DD-MON-YYYY'),
  'BOUGHT','THERMOMETER',1,'EACH',.15,.15,'GENERAL STORE');
insert into ledger values (
  TO_DATE('14-MAR-1901','DD-MON-YYYY'),
  'BOUGHT','LOT IN CEMETERY NO. 80',1,'EACH',25,25,'METHODIST CHURCH');
insert into ledger values (
  TO_DATE('14-MAR-1901','DD-MON-YYYY'),
  'PAID','DIGGING OF GRAVE',1,'EACH',3,3,'JED HOPKINS');
insert into ledger values (
  TO_DATE('16-APR-1901','DD-MON-YYYY'),
  'BOUGHT','GRINDING',1,'EACH',.16,.16,'MILL');
insert into ledger values (
  TO_DATE('16-MAR-1901','DD-MON-YYYY'),
  'BOUGHT','GRINDING',1,'EACH',.16,.16,'MILL');
insert into ledger values (
  TO_DATE('23-MAR-1901','DD-MON-YYYY'),
  'BOUGHT','CLOTH FOR DRESS LINING',2,'YARD',.27,.54,'GENERAL STORE');
insert into ledger values (
  TO_DATE('18-AUG-1901','DD-MON-YYYY'),
  'BOUGHT','SYRUP THERMOMETER',1,'EACH',1,1,'GENERAL STORE');
insert into ledger values (
  TO_DATE('25-MAR-1901','DD-MON-YYYY'),
  'BOUGHT','BOOTS FOR SHIRLEY',1,'PAIR',2.5,2.5,'GENERAL STORE');
insert into ledger values (
  TO_DATE('27-APR-1901','DD-MON-YYYY'),
  'BOUGHT','SYRUP CANS',2,'DOZEN',1.07,2.14,'VERNA HARDWARE');
insert into ledger values (
  TO_DATE('22-MAR-1901','DD-MON-YYYY'),
  'BOUGHT','MILK CANS',2,'EACH',2.5,5,'VERNA HARDWARE');
```

```
insert into ledger values (
  TO_DATE('23-APR-1901','DD-MON-YYYY'),
  'BOUGHT','DUBBLE STRAINER',1,'EACH',.95,.95,'VERNA HARDWARE');
insert into ledger values (
  TO_DATE('25-JUN-1901','DD-MON-YYYY'),
  'BOUGHT','MILK STIRRER',1,'EACH',.25,.25,'VERNA HARDWARE');
insert into ledger values (
  TO_DATE('27-MAR-1901','DD-MON-YYYY'),
  'BOUGHT','HOMINY',77,'LB',.01,.77,'MILL');
insert into ledger values (
  TO_DATE('28-APR-1901','DD-MON-YYYY'),
  'BOUGHT','CORN',104,'LB',.01,1.04,'MILL');
insert into ledger values (
  TO_DATE('06-APR-1901','DD-MON-YYYY'),
  'BOUGHT','FUNERAL',1,'EACH',3.19,3.19,'UNDERWOOD BROS');
insert into ledger values (
  TO_DATE('30-APR-1901','DD-MON-YYYY'),
  'BOUGHT','BRUSH',1,'EACH',.05,.05,'GENERAL STORE');
insert into ledger values (
  TO_DATE('30-APR-1901','DD-MON-YYYY'),
  'BOUGHT','SAND',5,'BUSHEL',.03,.15,'QUARRY');
insert into ledger values (
  TO_DATE('31-MAR-1901','DD-MON-YYYY'),
  'SOLD','MOLASSES',3,'GALLON',1,3,'HAROLD SCHOLE');
insert into ledger values (
  TO_DATE('28-MAR-1901','DD-MON-YYYY'),
  'SOLD','MOLASSES',1,'GALLON',1,1,'GERHARDT KENTGEN');
insert into ledger values (
  TO_DATE('30-MAR-1901','DD-MON-YYYY'),
  'BOUGHT','FIXING SHIRLEYS WATCH',1,'EACH',.25,.25,'MANNER JEWELERS');
insert into ledger values (
  TO_DATE('04-APR-1901','DD-MON-YYYY'),
  'SOLD','BUTTER',9,'LB',.23,2.07,'HAROLD SCHOLE');
insert into ledger values (
  TO_DATE('05-APR-1901','DD-MON-YYYY'),
  'BOUGHT','SODA',1,'BOTTLE',.05,.05,'GENERAL STORE');
insert into ledger values (
  TO_DATE('05-MAR-1901','DD-MON-YYYY'),
  'BOUGHT','TELEPHONE CALL',1,'EACH',.2,.2,'PHONE COMPANY');
insert into ledger values (
  TO_DATE('06-APR-1901','DD-MON-YYYY'),
  'BOUGHT','GLOVES',1,'PAIR',.25,.25,'GENERAL STORE');
insert into ledger values (
  TO_DATE('06-APR-1901','DD-MON-YYYY'),
  'BOUGHT','SHOES FOR SHIRLEY',1,'PAIR',2,2,'GENERAL STORE');
insert into ledger values (
  TO_DATE('09-APR-1901','DD-MON-YYYY'),
  'BOUGHT','PEANUTS',1,'BAG',.05,.05,'GENERAL STORE');
```

```
insert into ledger values (
  TO_DATE('11-APR-1901','DD-MON-YYYY'),
  'BOUGHT','BRAN',300,'LB',.01,3,'GENERAL STORE');
insert into ledger values (
  TO_DATE('15-APR-1901','DD-MON-YYYY'),
  'BOUGHT','SHOEING',2,'EACH',.3,.6,'BLACKSMITH');
insert into ledger values (
  TO_DATE('17-APR-1901'','DD-MON-YYYY'),
  'BOUGHT','HOMINY',173,'LB',.01,1.73,'GENERAL STORE');
insert into ledger values (
  TO_DATE('17-APR-1901','DD-MON-YYYY'),
  'BOUGHT','BRAN',450,'LB',.01,4.5,'GENERAL STORE');
insert into ledger values (
  TO_DATE('17-APR-1901','DD-MON-YYYY'),
  'BOUGHT','CALF MEAL',110,'LB',.01,1.1,'GENERAL STORE');
insert into ledger values (
  TO_DATE('22-APR-1901','DD-MON-YYYY'),
  'BOUGHT','HOMINY',454,'LB',.01,4.54,'GENERAL STORE');
insert into ledger values (
  TO_DATE('22-APR-1901','DD-MON-YYYY'),
  'BOUGHT','BRAN',300,'LB',.01,3,'GENERAL STORE');
insert into ledger values (
  TO_DATE('22-APR-1901','DD-MON-YYYY'),
  'SOLD','CALF',1,'EACH',1,1,'PAT LAVAY');
insert into ledger values (
  TO_DATE('25-APR-1901','DD-MON-YYYY'),
  'BOUGHT','CALF MEAL',100,'EACH',.01,1,'GENERAL STORE');
insert into ledger values (
  TO_DATE('27-APR-1901','DD-MON-YYYY'),
  'BOUGHT','SHOEING NED',1,'EACH',.5,.5,'BLACKSMITH');
insert into ledger values (
  TO_DATE('07-JUN-1901','DD-MON-YYYY'),
  'RECEIVED','BREAKING COLT',1,'EACH',5,5,'SAM DYE');
insert into ledger values (
  TO_DATE('07-JUN-1901','DD-MON-YYYY'),
  'RECEIVED','KEEPING COLT',1,'EACH',4,4,'SAM DYE');
insert into ledger values (
  TO_DATE('17-JUN-1901','DD-MON-YYYY'),
  'BOUGHT','SCHOOL TAX',1,'EACH',6.56,6.56,'SCHOOL');
insert into ledger values (
  TO_DATE('17-JUN-1901','DD-MON-YYYY'),
  'RECEIVED','THRESHING',2,'DAY',1,2,'HENRY CHASE');
insert into ledger values (
  TO_DATE('18-JUN-1901','DD-MON-YYYY'),
  'PAID','THRESHING',.5,'DAY',1,.5,'WILLIAM SWING');
insert into ledger values (
  TO_DATE('18-JUN-1901','DD-MON-YYYY'),
  'BOUGHT','SHEEP',22,'EACH',.87,19.14,'BOOLE AND JONES');
```

```
insert into ledger values (
   TO_DATE('15-MAR-1901','DD-MON-YYYY'),
   'SOLD','POTATOES',5,'BUSHEL',.25,1.25,'GENERAL STORE');
insert into ledger values (
   TO_DATE('15-MAR-1901','DD-MON-YYYY'),
   'SOLD','COW',2,'EACH',33,66,'SAM DYE');
insert into ledger values (
   TO_DATE('15-MAR-1901','DD-MON-YYYY'),
'RECEIVED','BOOT BETWEEN HORSES',1,'EACH',10,10,'ADAH TALBOT');
insert into ledger values (
   TO_DATE('18-MAR-1901','DD-MON-YYYY'),
SOLD','WAGON',1,'EACH',5,5,'ADAH TALBOT');
insert into ledger values (
   TO_DATE('04-APR-1901','DD-MON-YYYY'),
   'SOLD','HARNES',1,'EACH',2,2,'ADAH TALBOT');
insert into ledger values (
   TO_DATE('16-APR-1901','DD-MON-YYYY'),
   'SOLD','COW',3,'EACH',30,90,'GEORGE B. MCCORMICK');
insert into ledger values (
   TO_DATE('09-JUN-1901','DD-MON-YYYY'),
   'BOUGHT','USE OF PASTURE',1,'EACH',10,10,'GEORGE B. MCCORMICK');
insert into ledger values (
   TO_DATE('28-JUN-1901','DD-MON-YYYY'),
   'BOUGHT','SHEEP AND BULL',1,'LOT',97.88,97.88,'EDWARD JOHNSON');
insert into ledger values (
   TO_DATE('03-JUL-1901','DD-MON-YYYY'),
   'SOLD','HEIFER',1,'EACH',35,35,'SAM DYE');
insert into ledger values (
   TO_DATE('18-MAY-1901','DD-MON-YYYY'),
   'BOUGHT','MIDDLINGS',180,'LB',.01,1.8,'DEAN FOREMAN');
insert into ledger values (
   TO_DATE('20-MAY-1901','DD-MON-YYYY'),
   'BOUGHT','MIDDLINGS',450,'LB',.01,4.5,'GEORGE OSCAR');
insert into ledger values (
   TO_DATE('22-MAY-1901','DD-MON-YYYY'),
   'BOUGHT','MIDDLINGS',640,'LB',.01,6.4,'EDYTHE GAMMIERE');
insert into ledger values (
   TO_DATE('23-MAY-1901','DD-MON-YYYY'),
   'BOUGHT','MIDDLINGS',110,'LB',.01,1.1,'JOHN AUSTIN');
insert into ledger values (
   TO_DATE('28-MAY-1901','DD-MON-YYYY'),
   'BOUGHT','COMB',1,'EACH',.07,.07,'GENERAL STORE');
insert into ledger values (
   TO_DATE('29-MAY-1901','DD-MON-YYYY'),
   'BOUGHT','BUTTONS',1,'BOX',.1,.1,'GENERAL STORE');
insert into ledger values (
   TO_DATE('05-JUL-1901','DD-MON-YYYY'),
   'BOUGHT','BEANS',6,'LB',.03,.18,'GENERAL STORE');
```

```
insert into ledger values (
  TO_DATE('29-MAY-1901','DD-MON-YYYY'),
  'BOUGHT','RAISONS',3,'LB',.08,.24,'GENERAL STORE');
insert into ledger values (
  TO_DATE('29-MAY-1901','DD-MON-YYYY'),
  'BOUGHT','CHEESE',3,'LB',.09,.27,'GENERAL STORE');
insert into ledger values (
  TO_DATE('04-JUN-1901','DD-MON-YYYY'),
  'BOUGHT','BEER',1,'BOTTLE',.2,.2,'GENERAL STORE');
insert into ledger values (
  TO_DATE('04-JUN-1901','DD-MON-YYYY'),
  'BOUGHT','COUGH SYRUP',1,'BOTTLE',.25,.25,'GENERAL STORE');
insert into ledger values (
  TO_DATE('26-JUN-1901','DD-MON-YYYY'),
  'BOUGHT','SHOE STRING',2,'PAIR',.04,.08,'GENERAL STORE');
insert into ledger values (
  TO_DATE('26-JUN-1901','DD-MON-YYYY'),
  'BOUGHT','CLOSE PINS',1,'BOX',.05,.05,'GENERAL STORE');
insert into ledger values (
  TO_DATE('26-JUN-1901','DD-MON-YYYY'),
  'BOUGHT','CLOSE BRUSH',1,'BOX',.1,.1,'GENERAL STORE');
insert into ledger values (
  TO_DATE('06-MAR-1901','DD-MON-YYYY'),
  'SOLD','EGGS',14,'DOZEN',.12,1.68,'GENERAL STORE');
insert into ledger values (
  TO_DATE('06-MAR-1901','DD-MON-YYYY'),
  'SOLD','HENS',12,'EACH',.5,6,'GENERAL STORE');
insert into ledger values (
  TO_DATE('15-APR-1901','DD-MON-YYYY'),
  'SOLD','EGGS',13,'DOZEN',.1,1.3,'GENERAL STORE');
insert into ledger values (
  TO_DATE('27-APR-1901','DD-MON-YYYY'),
  'PAID','PLOWING',1,'DAY',3,3,'RICHARD KOCH AND BROTHERS');
insert into ledger values (
  TO_DATE('16-APR-1901','DD-MON-YYYY'),
  'PAID','PLOWING',1,'DAY',3,3,'RICHARD KOCH AND BROTHERS');
insert into ledger values (
  TO_DATE('17-DEC-1901','DD-MON-YYYY'),
  'PAID','SAWING',1,'DAY',.75,.75,'DICK JONES');
insert into ledger values (
  TO_DATE('28-JUL-1901','DD-MON-YYYY'),
  'PAID','SAWING',1,'DAY',.75,.75,'DICK JONES');
insert into ledger values (
  TO_DATE('18-AUG-1901','DD-MON-YYYY'),
  'PAID','WEEDING',1,'DAY',.9,.9,'ELBERT TALBOT');
insert into ledger values (
  TO_DATE('29-SEP-1901','DD-MON-YYYY'),
  'PAID','WORK',1,'DAY',1,1,'GERHARDT KENTGEN');
```

```
insert into ledger values (
  TO_DATE('19-JAN-1901','DD-MON-YYYY'),
  'PAID','WORK',1,'DAY',1,1,'GERHARDT KENTGEN');
insert into ledger values (
  TO_DATE('30-JAN-1901','DD-MON-YYYY'),
  'PAID','WORK',.5,'DAY',1,.5,'ELBERT TALBOT');
insert into ledger values (
  TO_DATE('28-FEB-1901','DD-MON-YYYY'),
  'PAID','WORK',1,'DAY',1,1,'ELBERT TALBOT');
insert into ledger values (
  TO_DATE('20-MAR-1901','DD-MON-YYYY'),
  'PAID','WORK',1,'DAY',1,1,'DICK JONES');
insert into ledger values (
  TO_DATE('21-JUL-1901','DD-MON-YYYY'),
  'PAID','WORK',1,'DAY',1,1,'VICTORIA LYNN');
insert into ledger values (
  TO_DATE('22-OCT-1901','DD-MON-YYYY'),
  'PAID','PLOWING',1,'DAY',1.8,1.8,'DICK JONES');
insert into ledger values (
  TO_DATE('23-SEP-1901','DD-MON-YYYY'),
  'PAID','DISCUS',.5,'DAY',3,1.5,'RICHARD KOCH AND BROTHERS');
insert into ledger values (
  TO_DATE('22-AUG-1901','DD-MON-YYYY'),
  'PAID','SAWING',1,'DAY',1,1,'PETER LAWSON');
insert into ledger values (
  TO_DATE('23-AUG-1901','DD-MON-YYYY'),
  'PAID','SAWING',1,'DAY',1,1,'PETER LAWSON');
insert into ledger values (
  TO_DATE('24-MAY-1901','DD-MON-YYYY'),
  'PAID','WORK',1,'DAY',1.2,1.2,'WILFRED LOWELL');
insert into ledger values (
  TO_DATE('11-MAY-1901','DD-MON-YYYY'),
  'PAID','WORK',1,'DAY',1.2,1.2,'WILFRED LOWELL');
insert into ledger values (
  TO_DATE('26-JUN-1901','DD-MON-YYYY'),
  'PAID','PAINTING',1,'DAY',1.75,1.75,'KAY AND PALMER WALLBOM');
insert into ledger values (
  TO_DATE('02-JUL-1901','DD-MON-YYYY'),
  'BOUGHT','MIDDLINGS',220,'LB',.01,2.2,'EDYTHE GAMMIERE');
insert into ledger values (
  TO_DATE('03-JUL-1901','DD-MON-YYYY'),
  'BOUGHT','PIG',1,'EACH',3,3,'JOHN AUSTIN');
insert into ledger values (
  TO_DATE('08-JUL-1901','DD-MON-YYYY'),
  'BOUGHT','CHEESE',1,'LB',.09,.09,'GENERAL STORE');
insert into ledger values (
  TO_DATE('09-JUL-1901','DD-MON-YYYY'),
```

```
       'BOUGHT','BEER',1,'BOTTLE',.2,.2,'GENERAL STORE');
insert into ledger values (
   TO_DATE('02-AUG-1901','DD-MON-YYYY'),
   'BOUGHT','MILK CANS',3,'EACH',2.5,7.5,'GENERAL STORE');
insert into ledger values (
   TO_DATE('05-AUG-1901','DD-MON-YYYY'),
   'BOUGHT','HOMINY',120,'LB',.01,1.2,'GENERAL STORE');
insert into ledger values (
   TO_DATE('08-AUG-1901','DD-MON-YYYY'),
   'BOUGHT','BRUSH',1,'EACH',.06,.06,'GENERAL STORE');
insert into ledger values (
   TO_DATE('12-AUG-1901','DD-MON-YYYY'),
   'BOUGHT','CORN',90,'LB',.01,.9,'GENERAL STORE');
insert into ledger values (
   TO_DATE('25-MAR-1901','DD-MON-YYYY'),
   'SOLD','MOLASSES',5,'GALLON',1,5,'SAM DYE');
insert into ledger values (
   TO_DATE('29-AUG-1901','DD-MON-YYYY'),
   'SOLD','BUTTER',5,'LB',.23,1.15,'GERHARDT KENTGEN');
insert into ledger values (
   TO_DATE('06-SEP-1901','DD-MON-YYYY'),
   'BOUGHT','TELEPHONE CALL',1,'EACH',.2,.2,'PHONE COMPANY');
insert into ledger values (
   TO_DATE('09-SEP-1901','DD-MON-YYYY'),
   'BOUGHT','PEANUTS',1,'BAG',.05,.05,'GENERAL STORE');
insert into ledger values (
   TO_DATE('12-SEP-1901','DD-MON-YYYY'),
   'BOUGHT','BRAN',170,'LB',.01,1.7,'GENERAL STORE');
insert into ledger values (
   TO_DATE('13-SEP-1901','DD-MON-YYYY'),
   'BOUGHT','SHOEING',4,'EACH',.3,1.2,'BLACKSMITH');
insert into ledger values (
   TO_DATE('15-SEP-1901','DD-MON-YYYY'),
   'BOUGHT','HOMINY',144,'LB',.01,1.44,'GENERAL STORE');
insert into ledger values (
   TO_DATE('20-APR-1901','DD-MON-YYYY'),
   'BOUGHT','BRAN',370,'LB',.01,3.7,'GENERAL STORE');
insert into ledger values (
   TO_DATE('17-JUL-1901','DD-MON-YYYY'),
   'BOUGHT','CALF MEAL',90,'LB',.01,.9,'GENERAL STORE');
insert into ledger values (
   TO_DATE('20-JUL-1901','DD-MON-YYYY'),
   'BOUGHT','HOMINY',300,'LB',.01,3,'GENERAL STORE');
insert into ledger values (
   TO_DATE('25-JUL-1901','DD-MON-YYYY'),
   'SOLD','CALF',1,'EACH',1,1,'SAM DYE');
insert into ledger values (
   TO_DATE('19-SEP-1901','DD-MON-YYYY'),
```

```
  'BOUGHT','BRAN',100,'LB',.01,1,'GENERAL STORE');
insert into ledger values (
  TO_DATE('23-SEP-1901','DD-MON-YYYY'),
  'BOUGHT','CALF MEAL',110,'LB',.01,1.1,'GENERAL STORE');
insert into ledger values (
  TO_DATE('25-SEP-1901','DD-MON-YYYY'),
  'BOUGHT','HOMINY',80,'LB',.01,.8,'GENERAL STORE');
insert into ledger values (
  TO_DATE('07-OCT-1901','DD-MON-YYYY'),
  'PAID','WORK',1,'DAY',1,1,'JED HOPKINS');
set termout on
prompt Waking up again.
insert into ledger values (
  TO_DATE('12-OCT-1901','DD-MON-YYYY'),
  'BOUGHT','SHEEP',12,'EACH',.9,10.8,'BOOLE AND JONES');
insert into ledger values (
  TO_DATE('15-OCT-1901','DD-MON-YYYY'),
  'SOLD','BEEF',935,'LB',.03,28.05,'GENERAL STORE');
insert into ledger values (
  TO_DATE('18-OCT-1901','DD-MON-YYYY'),
  'RECEIVED','BOOT BETWEEN HORSES',1,'EACH',10,10,'ADAH TALBOT');
insert into ledger values (
  TO_DATE('12-OCT-1901','DD-MON-YYYY'),
  'SOLD','HEFER',1,'EACH',35,35,'GEORGE B. MCCORMICK');
```

The LOCATION Table

```
drop table LOCATION;
create table LOCATION (
City       VARCHAR2(25),
Country    VARCHAR2(25),
Continent  VARCHAR2(25),
Latitude   NUMBER,
NorthSouth CHAR(1),
Longitude  NUMBER,
EastWest   CHAR(1)
);

insert into LOCATION values (
  'ATHENS','GREECE','EUROPE',37.58,'N',23.43,'E');
insert into LOCATION values (
  'CHICAGO','UNITED STATES','NORTH AMERICA',41.53,'N',87.38,'W');
insert into LOCATION values (
  'CONAKRY','GUINEA','AFRICA',9.31,'N',13.43,'W');
insert into LOCATION values (
  'LIMA','PERU','SOUTH AMERICA',12.03,'S',77.03,'W');
```

```
insert into LOCATION values (
   'MADRAS','INDIA','INDIA',13.05,'N',80.17,'E');
insert into LOCATION values (
   'MANCHESTER','ENGLAND','EUROPE',53.30,'N',2.15,'W');
insert into LOCATION values (
   'MOSCOW','RUSSIA','EUROPE',55.45,'N',37.35,'E');
insert into LOCATION values (
   'PARIS','FRANCE','EUROPE',48.52,'N',2.20,'E');
insert into LOCATION values (
   'SHENYANG','CHINA','CHINA',41.48,'N',123.27,'E');
insert into LOCATION values (
   'ROME','ITALY','EUROPE',41.54,'N',12.29,'E');
insert into LOCATION values (
   'TOKYO','JAPAN','ASIA',35.42,'N',139.46,'E');
insert into LOCATION values (
   'SYDNEY','AUSTRALIA','AUSTRALIA',33.52,'S',151.13,'E');
insert into LOCATION values (
   'SPARTA','GREECE','EUROPE',37.05,'N',22.27,'E');
insert into LOCATION values (
   'MADRID','SPAIN','EUROPE',40.24,'N',3.41,'W');
```

The LODGING Table

```
drop table LODGING;
create table LODGING (
Lodging        VARCHAR2(15) not null,
LongName       VARCHAR2(40),
Manager        VARCHAR2(25),
Address        VARCHAR2(30)
);

insert into LODGING values (
   'CRANMER','CRANMER RETREAT HOUSE','THOM CRANMER','HILL ST, BERKELEY');
insert into LODGING values (
   'MATTS','MATTS LONG BUNK HOUSE','ROLAND BRANDT','3 MILE RD, KEENE');
insert into LODGING values (
   'MULLERS','MULLERS COED LODGING','KEN MULLER','120 MAIN, EDMESTON');
insert into LODGING values (
   'PAPA KING','PAPA KING ROOMING','WILLIAM KING','127 MAIN, EDMESTON');
insert into LODGING values (
   'ROSE HILL','ROSE HILL FOR MEN','JOHN PELETIER','RFD 3, N. EDMESTON');
insert into LODGING values (
   'WEITBROCHT','WEITBROCHT ROOMING','EUNICE BENSON','320 GENEVA,
   KEENE');
```

The LONGTIME Table

```
drop table LONGTIME;
create table LONGTIME(
Name            VARCHAR2(25) not null,
Lodging         VARCHAR2(15),
Age             NUMBER
);

insert into LONGTIME values ('ADAH TALBOT', 'PAPA KING', 23);
insert into LONGTIME values ('DICK JONES', 'ROSE HILL', 18);
insert into LONGTIME values ('DONALD ROLLO', 'MATTS', 16);
insert into LONGTIME values ('ELBERT TALBOT', 'WEITBROCHT', 43);
insert into LONGTIME values ('GEORGE OSCAR', 'ROSE HILL', 41);
insert into LONGTIME values ('PAT LAVAY', 'ROSE HILL', 21);
insert into LONGTIME values ('PETER LAWSON', 'CRANMER', 25);
insert into LONGTIME values ('WILFRED LOWELL', null, 67);
```

The MAGAZINE Table

```
drop table magazine;
create table magazine (
Name            VARCHAR2(16),
Title           VARCHAR2(37),
Author          VARCHAR2(25),
IssueDate       DATE,
Page            NUMBER
);

insert into MAGAZINE values (
  'BERTRAND MONTHLY','THE BARBERS WHO SHAVE THEMSELVES.',
  'BONHOEFFER, DIETRICH',
  TO_DATE('23-MAY-1988','DD-MON-YYYY'),70);
insert into MAGAZINE values (
  'LIVE FREE OR DIE','"HUNTING THOREAU IN NEW HAMPSHIRE"',
  'CHESTERTON, G.K.',
  TO_DATE('26-AUG-1981','DD-MON-YYYY'),320);
insert into MAGAZINE values (
  'PSYCHOLOGICA','THE ETHNIC NEIGHBORHOOD',
  'RUTH, GEORGE HERMAN',
  TO_DATE('18-SEP-1919','DD-MON-YYYY'),246);
insert into MAGAZINE values (
  'FADED ISSUES','RELATIONAL DESIGN AND ENTHALPY',
  'WHITEHEAD, ALFRED',
  TO_DATE('20-JUN-1926','DD-MON-YYYY'),279);
```

```
insert into MAGAZINE values (
  'ENTROPY WIT','"INTERCONTINENTAL RELATIONS."',
  'CROOKES, WILLIAM',
  TO_DATE('20-SEP-1950','DD-MON-YYYY'),20);
```

The MATH Table

```
drop table MATH;
create table MATH (
Name          VARCHAR2(12),
Above         NUMBER,
Below         NUMBER,
Empty         NUMBER
);

insert into MATH values ('WHOLE NUMBER',11,-22,null);
insert into MATH values ('LOW DECIMAL',33.33,-44.44,null);
insert into MATH values ('MID DECIMAL',55.5,-55.5,null);
insert into MATH values ('HIGH DECIMAL',66.666,-77.777,null);
```

The NAME Table

```
drop table NAME;
create table NAME (
Name          VARCHAR2(25)
);

insert into NAME values ('HORATIO NELSON');
insert into NAME values ('VALDO');
insert into NAME values ('MARIE DE MEDICIS');
insert into NAME values ('FLAVIUS JOSEPHUS');
insert into NAME values ('EDYTHE P. M. GAMMIERE');
```

The NEWSPAPER Table

```
drop table NEWSPAPER;
create table NEWSPAPER (
Feature       VARCHAR2(15) not null,
Section       CHAR(1),
Page          NUMBER
);

insert into NEWSPAPER values ('National News', 'A', 1);
insert into NEWSPAPER values ('Sports', 'D', 1);
```

```
insert into NEWSPAPER values ('Editorials', 'A', 12);
insert into NEWSPAPER values ('Business', 'E', 1);
insert into NEWSPAPER values ('Weather', 'C', 2);
insert into NEWSPAPER values ('Television', 'B', 7);
insert into NEWSPAPER values ('Births', 'F', 7);
insert into NEWSPAPER values ('Classified', 'F', 8);
insert into NEWSPAPER values ('Modern Life', 'B', 1);
insert into NEWSPAPER values ('Comics', 'C', 4);
insert into NEWSPAPER values ('Movies', 'B', 4);
insert into NEWSPAPER values ('Bridge', 'B', 2);
insert into NEWSPAPER values ('Obituaries', 'F', 6);
insert into NEWSPAPER values ('Doctor Is In', 'F', 6);
```

The NUMBERTEST Table

```
drop table NUMBERTEST;
create table NUMBERTEST (
Value1          NUMBER,
Value2          NUMBER,
Value3          NUMBER(10,2)
);

insert into NUMBERTEST values (0,0,0);
insert into NUMBERTEST values (.0001,.0001,.0001);
insert into NUMBERTEST values (1234,1234,1234);
insert into NUMBERTEST values (1234.5,1234.5,1234.5);
insert into NUMBERTEST values (null,null,null);
insert into NUMBERTEST values (1234.56,1234.56,1234.56);
insert into NUMBERTEST values (1234.567,1234.567,1234.567);
insert into NUMBERTEST values
     (98761234.567,98761234.567,98761234.567);
```

The PAY Table

```
drop table PAY;
create table PAY (
Name            VARCHAR2(25) not null,
DailyRate       NUMBER
);

insert into PAY values ('ADAH TALBOT',1);
insert into PAY values ('ANDREW DYE',.75);
insert into PAY values ('BART SARJEANT',.75);
insert into PAY values ('DICK JONES',1);
insert into PAY values ('GEORGE OSCAR',1.25);
insert into PAY values ('PAT LAVAY',1.25);
```

The PAYDAY Table

```
drop table PAYDAY;
create table PAYDAY (
CycleDate        DATE
);

insert into PAYDAY values (TO_DATE('15-JAN-2000','DD-MON-YYYY'));
insert into PAYDAY values (TO_DATE('15-FEB-2000','DD-MON-YYYY'));
insert into PAYDAY values (TO_DATE('15-MAR-2000','DD-MON-YYYY'));
insert into PAYDAY values (TO_DATE('15-APR-2000','DD-MON-YYYY'));
insert into PAYDAY values (TO_DATE('15-MAY-2000','DD-MON-YYYY'));
insert into PAYDAY values (TO_DATE('15-JUN-2000','DD-MON-YYYY'));
insert into PAYDAY values (TO_DATE('15-JUL-2000','DD-MON-YYYY'));
insert into PAYDAY values (TO_DATE('15-AUG-2000','DD-MON-YYYY'));
insert into PAYDAY values (TO_DATE('15-SEP-2000','DD-MON-YYYY'));
insert into PAYDAY values (TO_DATE('15-OCT-2000','DD-MON-YYYY'));
insert into PAYDAY values (TO_DATE('15-NOV-2000','DD-MON-YYYY'));
insert into PAYDAY values (TO_DATE('15-DEC-2000','DD-MON-YYYY'));
```

The PROPOSAL Table

```
drop table PROPOSAL;
create table PROPOSAL
(Proposal_ID         NUMBER(10) primary key,
 Recipient_Name      VARCHAR2(25),
 Proposal_Name       VARCHAR2(25),
 Short_Description    VARCHAR2(1000),
 Proposal_Text       CLOB,
 Budget              BLOB,
 Cover_Letter        BFILE);
```

The PROSPECT Table

```
drop table PROSPECT;
create table PROSPECT (
Name            VARCHAR2(25) not null,
Address         VARCHAR2(35)
);

insert into PROSPECT values ('ADAH TALBOT','23 ZWING, EDMESTON');
insert into PROSPECT values ('DORY KENSON','GEN. DEL., BAYBAC');
insert into PROSPECT values ('ELBERT TALBOT','3 MILE ROAD, WALPOLE');
insert into PROSPECT values ('GEORGE PHEPPS','206 POLE, KINGSLEY');
```

```
insert into PROSPECT values ('PAT LAVAY','1 EASY ST, JACKSON');
insert into PROSPECT values ('TED BUTCHER','RFD 1, BRIGHTON');
insert into PROSPECT values ('JED HOPKINS','GEN. DEL., TURBOW');
insert into PROSPECT values ('WILFRED LOWELL',NULL);
```

The RADIUS_VALS Table

```
drop table RADIUS_VALS;
create table RADIUS_VALS
(Radius      NUMBER(5));
```

The ROSE Table

```
drop table ROSE;
create table ROSE (
Lodging      VARCHAR2(12)
);

insert into ROSE values ('ROSELYN');
insert into ROSE values ('ROSE HILL');
insert into ROSE values ('ROSE GARDEN');
insert into ROSE values ('ROSE');
```

The SHIPPING Table

```
drop table SHIPPING;
create table SHIPPING (
Client       VARCHAR2(13),
Weight       NUMBER
);

insert into SHIPPING values ('JOHNSON TOOL',59);
insert into SHIPPING values ('DAGG SOFTWARE',27);
insert into SHIPPING values ('TULLY ANDOVER',NULL);
```

The SKILL Table

```
drop table SKILL;
create table SKILL (
Skill        VARCHAR2(25) not null,
Description  VARCHAR2(80)
);
```

```
insert into SKILL values (
   'WOODCUTTER','MARK AND FELL TREES, SPLIT, STACK, HAUL');
insert into SKILL values (
   'COMBINE DRIVER','HARNESS, DRIVE, GROOM HORSES, ADJUST BLADES');
insert into SKILL values (
   'SMITHY','STACK FOR FIRE, RUN BELLOWS, CUT, SHOE HORSES');
insert into SKILL values (
   'GRAVE DIGGER','MARK AND CUT SOD, DIG, SHORE, FILL, RESOD');
insert into SKILL values (
   'DISCUS','HARNESS, DRIVE, GROOM HORSES, BLADE DEPTH');
insert into SKILL values (
   'WORK','GENERAL UNSKILLED LABOR');
```

The STOCK Table

```
drop table STOCK;
create table STOCK (
Company        VARCHAR2(20),
Symbol         VARCHAR2(6),
Industry       VARCHAR2(15),
CloseYesterday NUMBER(6,2),
CloseToday     NUMBER(6,2),
Volume         NUMBER
);

insert into STOCK values (
   'AD SPECIALTY', 'ADSP', 'ADVERTISING',  31.75, 31.75,
   18333876);
insert into STOCK values (
   'APPLE CANNERY', 'APCN', 'AGRICULTURE',  33.75, 36.50,
   25787229);
insert into STOCK values (
   'AT SPACE', 'ATR' , 'MEDICAL', 46.75, 48.00,
   11398323);
insert into STOCK values (
   'AUGUST ENTERPRISES', 'AGE', 'MEDICAL', 15.00, 15.00,
   12221711);
insert into STOCK values (
   'BRANDON ELLIPSIS', 'BELP', 'SPACE', 32.75, 33.50,
   25789769);
insert into STOCK values (
   'GENERAL ENTROPY','GENT', 'SPACE', 64.25, 66.00,
   7598562);
insert into STOCK values (
   'GENEVA ROCKETRY', 'GENR', 'SPACE', 22.75, 27.25,
   22533944);
```

```
insert into STOCK values (
  'HAYWARD ANTISEPTIC',  'HAYW', 'MEDICAL', 104.25,  106.00,
  3358561);
insert into STOCK values (
  'IDK', 'IDK', 'ELECTRONICS',  95.00, 95.25,
  9443523);
insert into STOCK values (
  'INDIA COSMETICS','INDI', 'COSMETICS', 30.75, 30.75,
  8134878);
insert into STOCK values (
  'ISAIAH JAMES STORAGE', 'IJS', 'TRANSPORTATION', 13.25, 13.75,
  22112171);
insert into STOCK values (
  'KDK AIRLINES',  'KDK', 'TRANSPORTATION', 85.00, 85.25,
  7481566);
insert into STOCK values (
  'KENTGEN BIOPHYSICS',  'KENT', 'MEDICAL', 18.25, 19.50,
  6636863);
insert into STOCK values (
  'LAVAY COSMETICS', 'LAVA', 'COSMETICS', 21.50, 22.00,
  3341542);
insert into STOCK values (
  'LOCAL DEVELOPMENT',  'LOCD', 'AGRICULTURE',  26.75, 27.25,
  2596934);
insert into STOCK values (
  'MAXTIDE'   , 'MAXT', 'TRANSPORTATION', 8.25, 8.00,
  2836893);
insert into STOCK values (
  'MBK COMMUNICATIONS', 'MBK', 'ADVERTISING',  43.25, 41.00,
  10022980);
insert into STOCK values (
  'MEMORY GRAPHICS', 'MEMG', 'ELECTRONICS',  15.50, 14.25,
  4557992);
insert into STOCK values (
'MICRO TOKEN', 'MICT', 'ELECTRONICS',  77.00, 76.50,
  25205667);
insert into STOCK values (
  'NANCY LEE FEATURES', 'NLF', 'ADVERTISING',  13.50, 14.25,
  14222692);
insert into STOCK values (
  'NORTHERN BOREAL', 'NBOR', 'SPACE', 26.75, 28.00,
  1348323);
insert into STOCK values (
  'OCKHAM SYSTEMS', 'OCKS', 'SPACE', 21.50, 22.00,
  7052990);
insert into STOCK values (
  'OSCAR COAL DRAYAGE', 'OCD', 'TRANSPORTATION', 87.00, 88.50,
```

```
    25798992);
insert into STOCK values (
  'ROBERT JAMES APPAREL', 'RJAP', 'GARMENT', 23.25, 24.00,
  19032481);
insert into STOCK values (
  'SOUP SENSATIONS','SOUP', 'AGRICULTURE',  16.25, 16.75,
  22574879);
insert into STOCK values (
  'WONDER LABS', 'WOND', 'SPACE', 5.00, 5.00,
  2553712);
```

The TROUBLE Table

```
drop table TROUBLE;
create table TROUBLE (
City          VARCHAR2(13) NOT NULL,
SampleDate    DATE NOT NULL,
Noon          NUMBER(4,1),
Midnight      NUMBER(4,1),
Precipitation NUMBER
);

insert into TROUBLE values ('PLEASANT LAKE',
  TO_DATE('21-MAR-1999','DD-MON-YYYY'), 39.99, -1.31, 3.6);
insert into TROUBLE values ('PLEASANT LAKE',
  TO_DATE('22-JUN-1999','DD-MON-YYYY'), 101.44, 86.2, 1.63);
insert into TROUBLE values ('PLEASANT LAKE',
  TO_DATE('23-SEP-1999','DD-MON-YYYY'), 92.85, 79.6, 1.00003);
insert into TROUBLE values ('PLEASANT LAKE',
  TO_DATE('22-DEC-1999','DD-MON-YYYY'), -17.445, -10.4, 2.4);
```

The TWONAME Table

```
drop table TWONAME;
create table TWONAME (
FirstName    VARCHAR2(25),
LastName     VARCHAR2(25)
);
```

The WEATHER Table

```
drop table WEATHER;
create table WEATHER (
```

```
City            VARCHAR2(11),
Temperature     NUMBER,
Humidity        NUMBER,
Condition       VARCHAR2(9)
);

insert into WEATHER values ('LIMA',45,79,'RAIN');
insert into WEATHER values ('PARIS',81,62,'CLOUDY');
insert into WEATHER values ('MANCHESTER',66,98,'FOG');
insert into WEATHER values ('ATHENS',97,89,'SUNNY');
insert into WEATHER values ('CHICAGO',66,88,'RAIN');
insert into WEATHER values ('SYDNEY',29,12,'SNOW');
insert into WEATHER values ('SPARTA',74,63,'CLOUDY');
```

The WORKER Table

```
drop table WORKER;
create table WORKER (
Name            VARCHAR2(25) not null,
Age             NUMBER,
Lodging         VARCHAR2(15)
);

insert into WORKER values ('BART SARJEANT',22,'CRANMER');
insert into WORKER values ('ELBERT TALBOT',43,'WEITBROCHT');
insert into WORKER values ('DONALD ROLLO',16,'MATTS');
insert into WORKER values ('JED HOPKINS',33,'MATTS');
insert into WORKER values ('WILLIAM SWING',15,'CRANMER');
insert into WORKER values ('JOHN PEARSON',27,'ROSE HILL');
insert into WORKER values ('GEORGE OSCAR',41,'ROSE HILL');
insert into WORKER values ('KAY AND PALMER WALLBOM',
  null,'ROSE HILL');
insert into WORKER values ('PAT LAVAY',21,'ROSE HILL');
insert into WORKER values ('RICHARD KOCH AND BROTHERS',
  null,'WEITBROCHT');
insert into WORKER values ('DICK JONES',18,'ROSE HILL');
insert into WORKER values ('ADAH TALBOT',23,'PAPA KING');
insert into WORKER values ('ROLAND BRANDT',35,'MATTS');
insert into WORKER values ('PETER LAWSON',25,'CRANMER');
insert into WORKER values ('VICTORIA LYNN',32,'MULLERS');
insert into WORKER values ('WILFRED LOWELL',67,null);
insert into WORKER values ('HELEN BRANDT',15,null);
insert into WORKER values ('GERHARDT KENTGEN',55,'PAPA KING');
insert into WORKER values ('ANDREW DYE',29,'ROSE HILL');
```

The **WORKERSKILL** Table

```
drop table WORKERSKILL;
create table WORKERSKILL (
Name          VARCHAR2(25) not null,
Skill         VARCHAR2(25) not null,
Ability       VARCHAR2(15)
);

insert into WORKERSKILL values ('DICK JONES','SMITHY','EXCELLENT');
insert into WORKERSKILL values ('JOHN PEARSON','COMBINE DRIVER',null);
insert into WORKERSKILL values ('JOHN PEARSON','SMITHY','AVERAGE');
insert into WORKERSKILL values ('HELEN BRANDT','COMBINE DRIVER','VERY
                                FAST');
insert into WORKERSKILL values ('JOHN PEARSON','WOODCUTTER','GOOD');
insert into WORKERSKILL values ('VICTORIA LYNN','SMITHY','PRECISE');
insert into WORKERSKILL values ('ADAH TALBOT','WORK','GOOD');
insert into WORKERSKILL values ('WILFRED LOWELL','WORK','AVERAGE');
insert into WORKERSKILL values ('ELBERT TALBOT','DISCUS','SLOW');
insert into WORKERSKILL values ('WILFRED LOWELL','DISCUS','AVERAGE');
```

Index

NOTE: Page numbers in *italics* refer to illustrations or charts.

E

G

Q

R

S

V

Get Your FREE Subscription
to *Oracle Magazine*

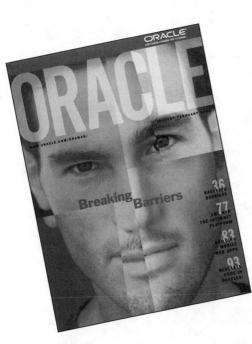

Oracle Magazine is essential gear for today's information technology professionals. Stay informed and increase your productivity with every issue of *Oracle Magazine*. Inside each **FREE,** bimonthly issue you'll get:

- Up-to-date information on Oracle Database Server, Oracle Applications, Internet Computing, and tools
- Third-party news and announcements
- Technical articles on Oracle products and operating environments
- Development and administration tips
- Real-world customer stories

Three easy ways to subscribe:

1. Web
Visit our Web site at www.oracle.com/oramag/. You'll find a subscription form there, plus much more!

2. Fax
Complete the questionnaire on the back of this card and fax the questionnaire side only to **+1.847.647.9735.**

3. Mail
Complete the questionnaire on the back of this card and mail it to P.O. Box 1263, Skokie, IL 60076-8263.

If there are other Oracle users at your location who would like to receive their own subscription to *Oracle Magazine*, please photocopy this form and pass it along.

☐ YES! Please send me a FREE subscription to *Oracle Magazine*.   ☐ NO

To receive a free bimonthly subscription to *Oracle Magazine*, you must fill out the entire card, sign it, and date it (incomplete cards cannot be processed or acknowledged). You can also fax your application to +1.847.647.9735. Or subscribe at our Web site at www.oracle.com/oramag/

SIGNATURE (REQUIRED) X _____   **DATE** _____

NAME _____   TITLE _____

COMPANY _____   TELEPHONE _____

ADDRESS _____   FAX NUMBER _____

CITY _____   STATE _____   POSTAL CODE/ZIP CODE _____

COUNTRY _____   E-MAIL ADDRESS _____

☐ From time to time, Oracle Publishing allows our partners exclusive access to our e-mail addresses for special promotions and announcements. To be included in this program, please check this box.

You must answer all eight questions below.

1 What is the primary business activity of your firm at this location? *(check only one)*
- ☐ 03 Communications
- ☐ 04 Consulting, Training
- ☐ 06 Data Processing
- ☐ 07 Education
- ☐ 08 Engineering
- ☐ 09 Financial Services
- ☐ 10 Government—Federal, Local, State, Other
- ☐ 11 Government—Military
- ☐ 12 Health Care
- ☐ 13 Manufacturing—Aerospace, Defense
- ☐ 14 Manufacturing—Computer Hardware
- ☐ 15 Manufacturing—Noncomputer Products
- ☐ 17 Research & Development
- ☐ 19 Retailing, Wholesaling, Distribution
- ☐ 20 Software Development
- ☐ 21 Systems Integration, VAR, VAD, OEM
- ☐ 22 Transportation
- ☐ 23 Utilities (Electric, Gas, Sanitation)
- ☐ 98 Other Business and Services
_____

2 Which of the following best describes your job function? *(check only one)*

CORPORATE MANAGEMENT/STAFF
- ☐ 01 Executive Management (President, Chair, CEO, CFO, Owner, Partner, Principal)
- ☐ 02 Finance/Administrative Management (VP/Director/ Manager/Controller, Purchasing, Administration)
- ☐ 03 Sales/Marketing Management (VP/Director/Manager)
- ☐ 04 Computer Systems/Operations Management (CIO/VP/Director/ Manager MIS, Operations)

IS/IT STAFF
- ☐ 07 Systems Development/ Programming Management
- ☐ 08 Systems Development/ Programming Staff
- ☐ 09 Consulting
- ☐ 10 DBA/Systems Administrator
- ☐ 11 Education/Training
- ☐ 14 Technical Support Director/ Manager
- ☐ 16 Other Technical Management/Staff
- ☐ 98 Other _____

3 What is your current primary operating platform? *(check all that apply)*
- ☐ 01 DEC UNIX
- ☐ 02 DEC VAX VMS
- ☐ 03 Java
- ☐ 04 HP UNIX
- ☐ 05 IBM AIX
- ☐ 06 IBM UNIX
- ☐ 07 Macintosh
- ☐ 09 MS-DOS
- ☐ 10 MVS
- ☐ 11 NetWare
- ☐ 12 Network Computing
- ☐ 13 OpenVMS
- ☐ 14 SCO UNIX
- ☐ 24 Sequent DYNIX/ptx
- ☐ 15 Sun Solaris/SunOS
- ☐ 16 SVR4
- ☐ 18 UnixWare
- ☐ 20 Windows
- ☐ 21 Windows NT
- ☐ 23 Other UNIX _____
- 99 ☐ **None of the above**

4 Do you evaluate, specify, recommend, or authorize the purchase of any of the following? *(check all that apply)*
- ☐ 01 Hardware
- ☐ 02 Software
- ☐ 03 Application Development Tools
- ☐ 04 Database Products
- ☐ 05 Internet or Intranet Products
- 99 ☐ **None of the above**

5 In your job, do you use or plan to purchase any of the following products or services? *(check all that apply)*

SOFTWARE
- ☐ 01 Business Graphics
- ☐ 02 CAD/CAE/CAM
- ☐ 03 CASE
- ☐ 05 Communications
- ☐ 06 Database Management
- ☐ 07 File Management
- ☐ 08 Finance
- ☐ 09 Java
- ☐ 10 Materials Resource Planning
- ☐ 11 Multimedia Authoring
- ☐ 12 Networking
- ☐ 13 Office Automation
- ☐ 14 Order Entry/Inventory Control
- ☐ 15 Programming
- ☐ 16 Project Management
- ☐ 17 Scientific and Engineering
- ☐ 18 Spreadsheets
- ☐ 19 Systems Management
- ☐ 20 Workflow

HARDWARE
- ☐ 21 Macintosh
- ☐ 22 Mainframe
- ☐ 23 Massively Parallel Processing
- ☐ 24 Minicomputer
- ☐ 25 PC
- ☐ 26 Network Computer
- ☐ 28 Symmetric Multiprocessing
- ☐ 29 Workstation

PERIPHERALS
- ☐ 30 Bridges/Routers/Hubs/Gateways
- ☐ 31 CD-ROM Drives
- ☐ 32 Disk Drives/Subsystems
- ☐ 33 Modems
- ☐ 34 Tape Drives/Subsystems
- ☐ 35 Video Boards/Multimedia

SERVICES
- ☐ 37 Consulting
- ☐ 38 Education/Training
- ☐ 39 Maintenance
- ☐ 40 Online Database Services
- ☐ 41 Support
- ☐ 36 Technology-Based Training
- ☐ 98 Other _____
- 99 ☐ **None of the above**

6 What Oracle products are in use at your site? *(check all that apply)*

SERVER/SOFTWARE
- ☐ 01 Oracle8
- ☐ 30 Oracle8*i*
- ☐ 31 Oracle8*i* Lite
- ☐ 02 Oracle7
- ☐ 03 Oracle Application Server
- ☐ 04 Oracle Data Mart Suites
- ☐ 05 Oracle Internet Commerce Server
- ☐ 32 Oracle *inter*Media
- ☐ 33 Oracle JServer
- ☐ 07 Oracle Lite
- ☐ 08 Oracle Payment Server
- ☐ 11 Oracle Video Server

TOOLS
- ☐ 13 Oracle Designer
- ☐ 14 Oracle Developer
- ☐ 54 Oracle Discoverer
- ☐ 53 Oracle Express
- ☐ 51 Oracle JDeveloper
- ☐ 52 Oracle Reports
- ☐ 50 Oracle WebDB
- ☐ 55 Oracle Workflow

ORACLE APPLICATIONS
- ☐ 17 Oracle Automotive
- ☐ 35 Oracle Business Intelligence System
- ☐ 19 Oracle Consumer Packaged Goods
- ☐ 39 Oracle E-Commerce
- ☐ 18 Oracle Energy
- ☐ 20 Oracle Financials
- ☐ 28 Oracle Front Office
- ☐ 21 Oracle Human Resources
- ☐ 37 Oracle Internet Procurement
- ☐ 22 Oracle Manufacturing
- ☐ 40 Oracle Process Manufacturing
- ☐ 23 Oracle Projects
- ☐ 34 Oracle Retail
- ☐ 29 Oracle Self-Service Web Applications
- ☐ 38 Oracle Strategic Enterprise Management
- ☐ 25 Oracle Supply Chain Management
- ☐ 36 Oracle Tutor
- ☐ 41 Oracle Travel Management

ORACLE SERVICES
- ☐ 61 Oracle Consulting
- ☐ 62 Oracle Education
- ☐ 60 Oracle Support
- ☐ 98 Other _____
- 99 ☐ **None of the above**

7 What other database products are in use at your site? *(check all that apply)*
- ☐ 01 Access
- ☐ 02 Baan
- ☐ 03 dbase
- ☐ 04 Gupta
- ☐ 05 IBM DB2
- ☐ 06 Informix
- ☐ 07 Ingres
- ☐ 08 Microsoft Access
- ☐ 09 Microsoft SQL Server
- ☐ 10 PeopleSoft
- ☐ 11 Progress
- ☐ 12 SAP
- ☐ 13 Sybase
- ☐ 14 VSAM
- ☐ 98 Other _____
- 99 ☐ **None of the above**

8 During the next 12 months, how much do you anticipate your organization will spend on computer hardware, software, peripherals, and services for your location? *(check only one)*
- ☐ 01 Less than $10,000
- ☐ 02 $10,000 to $49,999
- ☐ 03 $50,000 to $99,999
- ☐ 04 $100,000 to $499,999
- ☐ 05 $500,000 to $999,999
- ☐ 06 $1,000,000 and over

If there are other Oracle users at your location who would like to receive a free subscription to *Oracle Magazine*, please photocopy this form and pass it along, or contact Customer Service at +1.847.647.9630

Form 5   OPRESS

Knowledge is power. To which we say,

crank up the power.

Are you ready for a power surge?

Accelerate your career—become an **Oracle Certified Professional (OCP)**. With Oracle's cutting-edge *Instructor-Led Training*, *Technology-Based Training*, and this *guide*, you can prepare for certification faster than ever. Set your own trajectory by logging your personal training plan with us. Go to **http://education.oracle.com/tpb**, where we'll help you pick a training path, select your courses, and track your progress. We'll even send you an email when your courses are offered in your area. If you don't have access to the Web, call us at 1-800-441-3541 (Outside the U.S. call +1-310-335-2403).

Power learning has never been easier.

ABOUT THE CD

HOW TO USE THE *ORACLE8i: THE COMPLETE REFERENCE* CD-ROM The CD that accompanies this book contains a special electronic Adobe Acrobat pdf-format edition of *Oracle8i: The Complete Reference*. With this electronic version, you can easily transport all of the valuable information contained in the book on your PC while the printed version of the book remains in your office or home.

Note: *To view the electronic edition of the book, you will need to install the Adobe Acrobat Reader program included on the CD-ROM if you do not already have it pre-installed on your system. Please make sure you are using Acrobat Reader Search version 3.01.*

INSTALLING ACROBAT READER 3.01 SEARCH For optimal performance, you must use Acrobat Reader 3.01 Search to view the electronic edition of this book.

1. Insert the CD-ROM into the CD drive of your computer.
2. Locate and launch the file **rs32e301.exe** from your CD drive. It will display: "This will install Adobe Acrobat Reader 3.01. Do you wish to continue?"
3. Click Yes. This initiates the installation setup process and displays the Adobe Acrobat 3.01 setup screen.
4. Read the welcome message and click Next.
5. Read the license agreement and accept by clicking Yes.
6. Choose a destination directory by clicking Browse, or click Next to accept the default directory location.
7. Click Finish to complete installation. This displays a Readme file detailing product specifications and support.

VIEWING AND NAVIGATING You can easily view and navigate specific areas of interest within the book using the hyperlinked Table of Contents provided.

Viewing
1. Insert the CD-ROM into the CD drive of your computer (if you have not already done so).
2. Locate and launch the file **Book.pdf** from your CD drive. This displays the book's Table of Contents at left of the screen and the actual book pages at right.

Navigating
1. To view a chapter, click the triangle to the left of the Part in which the chapter resides. This displays all chapters in selected Part.
2. Click the name of the chapter you want to view (displays the first page of chapter at right).
3. To view a section within a chapter, click the triangle to the left of the chapter name (displays sections of chapter below chapter name), and click the name of the section you want to view.

Searching
1. Choose the Search | Query option from the Tools menu.
2. In the Adobe Acrobat Search dialog box, click Indexes.
3. In the Index Selection dialog box, make sure the box next to "Oracle8i: The Complete Reference" is checked. Click Add.
4. In the Add Index dialog box, highlight "Index for Oracle8i The Complete Reference.pdx." Click Open.
5. In the Index Selection dialog box, click OK.
6. In the Adobe Acrobat Search dialog box, type in the text for which you want to search.
7. Click Search to initiate the search.
8. In the Search Results dialog box, click View. This takes you to the first instance of found text matching search criteria. Alternatively, you can double-click each occurrence of found text in the Results field to be taken to a specific match.

USING THE CODE The tables provided in Appendix A, "Tables Used in This Book" have not been copy-protected so that you have access to all of the tables used in the print edition—without retyping! You can use these to easily work your way through the examples and to experiment with the many techniques illustrated in this book.

1. Insert the CD-ROM into the CD drive of your computer (if you have not already done so).
2. Locate and launch the file **Appendix A–Tables.pdf** from your CD drive. (Alternatively if you are already viewing chapters, you can scroll to the bottom of the Table of Contents and click "Appendix A, Tables Used in This Book.")
3. Navigate to the text you want to copy (see "Navigating" instructions above).
4. Choose the Text Selection tool from the toolbar. The tool has image of "abc" in a dashed-line box.
5. Highlight the text you want to use.
6. Copy the text by pressing CTRL-C.
7. Position the mouse cursor in the area of the application you would like it to appear and press CTRL-V.

NO TECHNICAL SUPPORT IS PROVIDED WITH THIS CD-ROM.